The New York
Botanical Garden
Illustrated Encyclopedia
of Horticulture

The New York Botanical Garden Illustrated Encyclopedia of Horticulture

Thomas H. Everett

Volume 6
Id-Ma

GP

Garland Publishing, Inc.
New York & London

15 14 13 12 11 10 9 8 7 6 5 4 3 2 1

Library of Congress Cataloging in Publication Data

Everett, Thomas H
    The New York Botanical Garden illustrated encyclopedia of horticulture.

    1. Horticulture—Dictionaries. 2. Gardening—Dictionaries. 3. Plants, Ornamental—Dictionaries. 4. Plants, Cultivated—Dictionaries. I. New York (City). Botanical Garden. II. Title.
SB317.58.E94   635.9′03′21   80-65941
ISBN 0-8240-7236-7

PHOTO CREDITS

Black and White

W. Atlee Burpee Co.: *Linum perenne* (flowers), p. 2033. Bodger Seeds Ltd.: Forced lily-of-the-valley in decorative containers, p. 2024. Brooklyn Botanic Garden: Japanese garden at the Brooklyn Botanic Garden, Brooklyn, New York (parts a & b), p. 1842; A knot garden of herbs at the Brooklyn Botanic Garden, p. 1899. Peter Henderson Company: *Linanthus androsaceus*, p. 2029. Missouri Botanical Garden: Japanese garden, with pine and flowering cherries, Missouri Botanical Garden, St. Louis, Missouri, p. 1843. Morris Arboretum Library: *Juglans nigra*, in summer, p. 1856. Netherlands Flower Institute: *Iris reticulata*, p. 1818; *Iris danfordiae*, p. 1818; *Leucojum aestivum* (flowers), p. 1989. The New York Botanical Garden: *Ilex opaca*, p. 1778; *Impatiens balsamina*, p. 1788; *Ipomopsis rubra*, p. 1806; Japanese iris (flowers), p. 1810; *Iris germanica florentina*, p. 1811; *Iris pallida*, p. 1811; *Iris giganticaerulea*, p. 1812; *Iris histrio*, p. 1818; Dividing bearded irises (part b), p. 1819; *Isotria verticillata*, p. 1826; *Ixia polystachya*, p. 1828; *Ixia micrandra*, p. 1829; *Ixia viridiflora*, p. 1829; *Jeffersonia diphylla*, p. 1853; *Juglans nigra* (fruit), p. 1857; *Juncus effusus*, p. 1865; Cultivate between growing crops to control weeds and promote growth, p. 1868; *Juniperus horizontalis*, p. 1876; *Kalanchoe daigremontiana*, showing plantlets on edges of leaves, p. 1884; *Kalanchoe tubiflora*, p. 1885; *Kalanchoe tubiflora* (flowers and leaves with plantlets), p. 1885; *Kalanchoe marmorata*, p. 1887; Kale in a vegetable garden, p. 1889; *Kalmia angustifolia*, p. 1890; *Krigia montana*, p. 1906; *Lemaireocereus*, undetermined species, p. 1972; *Leucojum vernum*, p. 1990; *Leucothoe racemosa*, p. 1994; *Lilium michauxii*, p. 2010; Many lilies like this *Lilium henryi* root from the bottom of the stem above the bulb as well as the base of the bulb, p. 2020; *Linaria vulgaris*, p. 2029; *Linnaea borealis americana*, p. 2033; *Liriodendron tulipifera* (fruits), p. 2037; *Listera cordata*, p. 2039; *Listera australis*, p. 2039; *Lophocereus schottii*, p. 2062; *Lycopodium selago*, p. 2078; *Lygodium palmatum*, p. 2081; A natural stand of *Lythrum salicaria*, p. 2087; *Magnolia soulangiana* (flowers), p. 2097; *Maianthemum canadense*, p. 2106; *Maianthemum canadense* (fruits), p. 2106; *Malaxis spicata*, p. 2108; *Malphigia glabra*, p. 2111. Oregon Bulb Farms: *Lilium martagon album*, p. 2013; *Lilium auratum platyphyllum*, p. 2014; *Lilium concolor coridion*, p. 2014; *Lilium hansonii* (flowers), p. 2014; *Lilium lankongense*, p. 2016; *Lilium nepalense robustum*, p. 2017; A selection of modern hybrid lilies (4 photographs in 3rd column), p. 2018; Bulblets (part a), p. 2021; Scales for propagation (part a), p. 2021; A pot of lily seedlings, p. 2022. O. M. Scott & Sons Co.: Well-maintained lawns are a treasured feature of many American communities, p. 1942; Regular fertilizing is needed to maintain good lawns, p. 1946; Good lawns can be had in (part a), p. 1949. Whitney Seed Co., Inc.: Turn the soil to a minimum depth of 6 inches, if the topsoil is deep enough more is better, with (part d), p. 1951. Other photographs by Thomas H. Everett.

Color

Harold Frisch: *Lilium auratum*. The New York Botanical Garden: *Ipomoea pes-caprae*, *Kalmia angustifolia*, *Kalmia latifolia fuscata*, *Lewisia brachycalyx*, *Lloydia serotina*, *Lupinus polyphyllus*, *Maianthemum canadense*. Oregon Bulb Farm: *Lilium* hybrid 'Imperial Silver'. Other photographs by Thomas H. Everett.

Published by Garland Publishing, Inc.
136 Madison Avenue, New York, New York 10016

Printed in the United States of America

This work is dedicated to the honored memory of the distinguished horticulturists and botanists who most profoundly influenced my professional career: Allan Falconer of Cheadle Royal Gardens, Cheshire, England; William Jackson Bean, William Dallimore, and John Coutts of the Royal Botanic Gardens, Kew, England; and Dr. Elmer D. Merrill and Dr. Henry A. Gleason of The New York Botanical Garden.

Foreword

According to Webster, an encyclopedia is a book or set of books giving information on all or many branches of knowledge generally in articles alphabetically arranged. To the horticulturist or grower of plants, such a work is indispensable and one to be kept close at hand for frequent reference.

The appearance of *The New York Botanical Garden Illustrated Encyclopedia of Horticulture* by Thomas H. Everett is therefore welcomed as an important addition to the library of horticultural literature. Since horticulture is a living, growing subject, these volumes contain an immense amount of information not heretofore readily available. In addition to detailed descriptions of many thousands of plants given under their generic names and brief description of the characteristics of the more important plant families, together with lists of their genera known to be in cultivation, this Encyclopedia is replete with well-founded advice on how to use plants effectively in gardens and, where appropriate, indoors. Thoroughly practical directions and suggestions for growing plants are given in considerable detail and in easily understood language. Recommendations about what to do in the garden for all months of the year and in different geographical regions will be helpful to beginners and will serve as reminders to others.

The useful category of special subject entries (as distinct from the taxonomic presentations) consists of a wide variety of topics. It is safe to predict that one of the most popular will be Rock and Alpine Gardens. In this entry the author deals helpfully and adequately with a phase of horticulture that appeals to a growing group of devotees, and in doing so presents a distinctly fresh point of view. Many other examples could be cited.

The author's many years as a horticulturist and teacher well qualify him for the task of preparing this Encyclopedia. Because he has, over a period of more than a dozen years, written the entire text (submitting certain critical sections to specialists for review and suggestions) instead of farming out sections to a score or more specialists to write, the result is remarkably homogeneous and cohesive. The Encyclopedia is fully cross referenced so that one may locate a plant by either its scientific or common name.

If, as has been said, an encyclopedia should be all things to all people, then the present volumes richly deserve that accolade. Among the many who call it "friend" will be not only horticulturists ("gardeners," as our author likes to refer to them), but growers, breeders, writers, lecturers, arborists, ecologists, and professional botanists who are frequently called upon to answer questions to which only such a work can provide answers. It seems safe to predict that it will be many years before lovers and growers of plants will have at their command another reference work as authoritative and comprehensive as T. H. Everett's Encyclopedia.

John M. Fogg, Jr.
Director Emeritus, Arboretum of the Barnes Foundation
Emeritus Professor of Botany, University of Pennsylvania

Preface

The primary objective of *The New York Botanical Garden Illustrated Encyclopedia of Horticulture* is a comprehensive description and evaluation of horticulture as it is known and practiced in the United States and Canada by amateurs and by professionals, including those responsible for botanical gardens, public parks, and industrial landscapes. Although large-scale commercial methods of cultivating plants are not stressed, much of the content of the Encyclopedia is as basic to such operations as it is to other horticultural enterprises. Similarly, although landscape design is not treated on a professional level, landscape architects will find in the Encyclopedia a great deal of importance and interest to them. Emphasis throughout is placed on the appropriate employment of plants both outdoors and indoors, and particular attention is given to explaining in considerable detail the how- and when-to-do-it aspects of plant growing.

It may be useful to assess the meanings of two words I have used. Horticulture is simply gardening. It derives from the Latin *hortus,* garden, and *cultura,* culture, and alludes to the intensive cultivation in gardens and nurseries of flowers, fruits, vegetables, shrubs, trees, and other plants. The term is not applicable to the extensive field practices that characterize agriculture and forestry. Amateur, as employed by me, retains its classic meaning of a lover from the Latin *amator*; it refers to those who garden for pleasure rather than for financial gain or professional status. It carries no implication of lack of knowledge or skills and is not to be equated with novice, tyro, or dabbler. In truth, amateurs provide the solid basis upon which American horticulture rests; without them the importance of professionals would diminish. Numbered in millions, amateur gardeners are devotees of the most widespread avocation in the United States. This avocation is serviced by a great complex of nurseries, garden centers, and other suppliers; by landscape architects and landscape contractors; and by garden writers, garden lecturers, Cooperative Extension Agents, librarians, and others who dispense horticultural information. Numerous horticultural societies, garden clubs, and botanical gardens inspire and promote interest in America's greatest hobby and stand ready to help its enthusiasts.

Horticulture as a vocation presents a wide range of opportunities which appeal equally to women and men. It is a field in which excellent prospects still exist for capable entrepreneurs. Opportunities at professional levels occur too in nurseries and greenhouses, in the management of landscaped grounds of many types, and in teaching horticulture.

Some people confuse horticulture with botany. They are not the same. The distinction becomes more apparent if the word gardening is substituted for horticulture. Botany is the science that encompasses all systematized factual knowledge about plants, both wild and cultivated. It is only one of the several disciplines upon which horticulture is based. To become a capable gardener or a knowledgeable plantsman or plantswoman (I like these designations for gardeners who have a wide, intimate, and discerning knowledge of plants in addition to skill in growing them) it is not necessary to study botany formally, although such study is likely to add greatly to one's pleasure. In the practice of gardening many botanical truths are learned from experience. I have known highly competent gardeners without formal training in botany and able and indeed distinguished botanists possessed of minimal horticultural knowledge and skills.

Horticulture is primarily an art and a craft, based upon science, and at some levels perhaps justly regarded as a science in its own right. As an art it calls for an appreciation of beauty and form as expressed in three-dimensional spatial relationships and an ability to translate aesthetic concepts into reality. The chief materials used to create gardens are living plants, most of which change in size and form with the passing of time and often show differences in color and texture and in other ways from season to season. Thus it is important that designers of gardens have a wide familiarity with the sorts of plants that lend themselves to their purposes and with plants' adaptability to the regions and to the sites where it is proposed to plant them.

As a craft, horticulture involves special skills often derived from ancient practices passed from generation to generation by word of mouth and apprenticeship-like contacts. As a technology it relies on this backlog of empirical knowledge supplemented by that acquired by scientific experiment and investigation, the results of which often serve to explain rather than supplant old beliefs and practices but sometimes point the way to more expeditious methods of attaining similar results. And from time to time new techniques are developed that add dimensions to horticultural practice; among such of fairly recent years that come to mind are the manipulation of blooming season by artificial day-length, the propagation of orchids and some other plants by meristem tissue culture, and the development of soilless growing mixes as substitutes for soil.

One of the most significant developments in American horticulture in recent decades is the tremendous increase in the number of different kinds of plants that are cultivated by many more people than formerly. This is particularly true of indoor plants or house-plants, the sorts grown in homes, offices, and other interiors, but is by no means confined to that group. The relative affluence of our society and the freedom and frequency of travel both at home and abroad has contributed to this expansion, a phenomenon that will surely continue as avid collectors of the unusual bring into cultivation new plants from the wild and promote wider interest in sorts presently rare. Our garden flora is also constantly and beneficially expanded as a result of the work of both amateur and professional plant breeders.

It is impracticable in even the most comprehensive encyclopedia to describe or even list all plants that somewhere within a territory as large as the United States and Canada are grown in gardens. In this Encyclopedia the majority of genera known to be in cultivation are described, and descriptions and often other pertinent information about a complete or substantial number of their species and lesser categories are given. Sorts likely to be found only in collections of botanical gardens or in those of specialists may be omitted.

The vexing matter of plant nomenclature inevitably presents itself when an encyclopedia of horticulture is contemplated. Conflicts arise chiefly between the very understandable desire of gardeners and others who deal with cultivated plants to retain long-familiar names and the need to reflect up-to-date botanical interpretations. These points of view are basically irreconcilable and so accommodations must be reached.

As has been well demonstrated in the past, it is unrealistic to attempt to standardize the horticultural usage of plant names by decree or edict. To do so would negate scientific progress. But it is just as impracticable to expect gardeners, nurserymen, arborists, seedsmen, dealers in bulbs, and other amateur and professional horticulturists to keep current with the interpretations and recommendations of plant taxonomists; particularly as these sometimes fail to gain the acceptance even of other botanists and it is not unusual for scientists of equal stature and competence to prefer different names for the same plant.

In practice time is the great leveler. Newly proposed plant names accepted in botanical literature are likely to filter gradually into horticultural usage and eventually gain currency value, but this sometimes takes several years. The complete up-to-dateness and niceties of botanical naming are less likely to bedevil horticulturists than uncertainties concerned with correct plant identification. This is of prime importance. Whether a tree is labeled *Pseudotsuga douglasii*, *P. taxifolia*, or *P. menziesii* is of less concern than that the specimen so identified is indeed a Douglas-fir and not some other conifer.

After reflection I decided that the most sensible course to follow in *The New York Botanical Garden Illustrated Encyclopedia of Horticulture* was to accept almost in its entirety the nomenclature adopted in *Hortus Third* published in 1976. By doing so, much of the confusion that would result from two major comprehensive horticultural works of the late twentieth century using different names for the same plant is avoided, and it is hoped that for a period of years a degree of stability will be attained. Always those deeply concerned with critical groups of plants can adopt the recommendations of the latest monographers. Exceptions to the parallelism in nomenclature in this Encyclopedia and *Hortus Third* are to be found in the Cactaceae for which, with certain reservations but for practical purposes, as explained in the Encyclopedia entry Cactuses, the nomenclature of Curt Backeburg's *Die Cactaceae*, published in 1958–62, is followed; and the ferns, where I mostly accepted the guidance of Dr. John T. Mickel of The New York Botanical Garden. The common or colloquial names employed are those deemed to have general acceptance. Cross references and synonomy are freely provided.

The convention of indicating typographically whether or not plants of status lesser than species represent entities that propagate and persist in the wild or are sorts that persist only in cultivation is not followed. Instead, as explained in the Encyclopedia entry Plant Names, the word variety is employed for all entities below specific rank and if in Latin form the name is written in italic, if in English or other modern language, in Roman type, with initial capital letter, and enclosed in single quotation marks.

Thomas H. Everett
Senior Horticulture Specialist
The New York Botanical Garden

Acknowledgments

I am indebted to many people for help and support generously given over the period of more than twelve years it has taken to bring this Encyclopedia to fruition. Chief credit belongs to four ladies. They are Lillian M. Weber and Nancy Callaghan, who besides accepting responsibility for the formidable task of filing and retrieving information, typing manuscript, proofreading, and the management of a vast collection of photographs, provided much wise council; Elizabeth C. Hall, librarian extraordinary, whose superb knowledge of horticultural and botanical literature was freely at my disposal; and Ellen, my wife, who displayed a deep understanding of the demands on time called for by an undertaking of this magnitude, and with rare patience accepted inevitable inconvenience. I am also obliged to my sister, Hette Everett, for the valuable help she freely gave on many occasions.

Of the botanists I repeatedly called upon for opinions and advice and from whom I sought elucidation of many details of their science abstruse to me, the most heavily burdened have been my friends and colleagues at The New York Botanical Garden, Dr. Rupert C. Barneby, Dr. Arthur Cronquist, and Dr. John T. Mickel. Other botanists and horticulturists with whom I held discussions or corresponded about matters pertinent to my text include Dr. Theodore M. Barkley, Dr. Lyman Benson, Dr. Ben Blackburn, Professor Harold Davidson, Dr. Otto Degener, Harold Epstein, Dr. John M. Fogg, Jr., Dr. Alwyn H. Gentry, Dr. Alfred B. Graf, Brian Halliwell, Dr. David R. Hunt, Dr. John P. Jessop, Dr. Tetsuo Koyama, Dr. Bassett Maguire, Dr. Roy A. Mecklenberg, Everitt L. Miller, Dr. Harold N. Moldenke, Dr. Dan H. Nicolson, Dr. Pascal P. Pirone, Dr. Ghillean Prance, Don Richardson, Stanley J. Smith, Ralph L. Snodsmith, Marco Polo Stufano, Dr. Bernard Verdcourt, Dr. Edgar T. Wherry, Dr. Trevor Whiffin, Dr. Richard P. Wunderlin, Dr. John J. Wurdack, Yuji Yoshimura, and Rudolf Ziesenhenne.

Without either exception or stint these conferees and correspondents shared with me their knowledge, thoughts, and judgments. Much of the bounty so gleaned is reflected in the text of the Encyclopedia but none other than I am responsible for interpretations and opinions that appear there. To all who have helped, my special thanks are due and are gratefully proffered.

I acknowledge with much pleasure the excellent cooperation I have received from the Garland Publishing Company and most particularly from its President, Gavin Borden. To Ruth Adams, Nancy Isaac, Carol Miller, and Melinda Wirkus, I say thank you for working so understandingly and effectively with me and for shepherding my raw typescript through the necessary stages.

How to Use This Encyclopedia

A vast amount of information about how to use, propagate, and care for plants both indoors and outdoors is contained in the thousands of entries that compose *The New York Botanical Garden Illustrated Encyclopedia of Horticulture*. Some understanding of the Encyclopedia's organization is necessary in order to find what you want to know.

Arrangement of the Entries

Genera

The entries are arranged in alphabetical order. Most numerous are those that deal with taxonomic groups of plants. Here belong approximately 3,500 items entered under the genus name, such as ABIES, DIEFFENBACHIA, and JUGLANS. If instead of referring to these names you consult their common name equivalents of FIR, DUMB CANE, and WALNUT, you will find cross references to the genus names.

Bigeneric Hybrids & Chimeras

Hybrids between genera that have names equivalent to genus names—most of these belonging in the orchid family—are accorded separate entries. The same is true for the few chimeras or graft hybrids with names of similar status. Because bigeneric hybrids frequently have characteristics similar to those of their parents and require similar care, the entries for them are often briefer than the regular genus entries.

Families

Plant families are described under their botanical names, with their common name equivalents also given. Each description is followed by a list of the genera accorded separate entries in this Encyclopedia.

Vegetables, Fruits, Herbs, & Ornamentals

Vegetables and fruits that are commonly cultivated, such as broccoli, cabbage, potato, tomato, apple, peach, and raspberry; most culinary herbs, including basil, chives, parsley, sage, and tarragon; and a few popular ornamentals, such as azaleas, carnations, pansies, and poinsettias, are treated under their familiar names, with cross references to their genera. Discussions of a few herbs and some lesser known vegetables and fruits are given under their Latin scientific names with cross references to the common names.

Other Entries

The remaining entries in the Encyclopedia are cross references, definitions, and more substantial discussions of many subjects of interest to gardeners and others concerned with plants. For example, a calendar of gardening activity, by geographical area, is given under the names of the months and a glossary of frequently applied species names (technically, specific epithets) is provided in the entry Plant Names. A list of these general topics, which may provide additional information about a particular plant, is provided at the beginning of each volume of the Encyclopedia (see pp. xvii–xx).

Cross References & Definitions

The cross references are of two chief types: those that give specific information, which may be all you wish to know at the moment:
Boojam Tree is *Idria columnaris*.
Cobra plant is *Darlingtonia californica*.
and those that refer to entries where fuller explanations are to be found:
Adhatoda. See Justicia.
Clubmoss. See Lycopodium and Selaginella.

Additional information about entries of the former type can, of course, be found by looking up the genus to which the plant belongs—*Idria* in the case of the boojam tree and *Darlingtonia* for the cobra plant.

ORGANIZATION OF THE GENUS ENTRIES

Pronunciation

Each genus name is followed by its pronunciation in parentheses. The stressed syllable is indicated by the diacritical mark ´ if the vowel sound is short as in man, pet, pink, hot, and up; or by ` if the vowel sound is long as in mane, pete, pine, home, and fluke.

Genus Common Names
Family Common Names
General Characteristics

Following the pronunciation, there may be one or more common names applicable to the genus as a whole or to certain of its kinds. Other names may be introduced later with the descriptions of the species or kinds. Early in the entry you will find the common and botanical names of the plant family to which the genus belongs, the number of species the genus contains, its natural geographical distribution, and the derivation of its name. A description that stresses the general characteristics of the genus follows, and this may be supplemented by historical data, uses of some or all of its members, and other pertinent information.

Identification of Plants

Descriptions of species, hybrids, and varieties appear next. The identification of unrecognized plants is a fairly common objective of gardeners; accordingly, in this Encyclopedia various species have been grouped within entries in ways that make their identification easier. The groupings may bring into proximity sorts that can be adapted for similar landscape uses or that require the same cultural care, or they may emphasize geographical origins of species or such categories as evergreen and deciduous or tall and low members of the same genus. Where the description of a species occurs, its name is designated in *bold italic.* Under this plan, the description of a particular species can be found by referring to the group to which it belongs, scanning the entry for the species name in bold italic, or referring to the opening sentences of paragraphs which have been designed to serve as lead-ins to descriptive groupings.

Gardening & Landscape Uses
Cultivation
Pests & Diseases

At the end of genus entries, subentries giving information on garden and landscape uses, cultivation, and pests or diseases or both are included, or else reference is made to other genera or groupings for which these are similar.

xvi

General Subject Listings

The lists below organize some of the encyclopedia entries into topics which may be of particular interest to the reader. They are also an aid in finding information other than Latin or common names of plants.

PLANT ANATOMY AND TERMS USED IN PLANT DESCRIPTIONS

All-America Selections
Alternate
Annual Rings
Anther
Apex
Ascending
Awl-shaped
Axil, Axillary
Berry
Bloom
Bracts
Bud
Bulb
Bulbils
Bulblet
Bur
Burl
Calyx
Cambium Layer
Capsule
Carpel
Catkin
Centrals
Ciliate
Climber
Corm
Cormel
Cotyledon
Crown
Deciduous
Disk or Disc
Double Flowers
Drupe
Florets
Flower
Follicle
Frond
Fruit
Glaucous
Gymnosperms
Head
Hips
Hose-in-Hose

Inflorescence
Lanceolate
Leader
Leaf
Leggy
Linear
Lobe
Midrib
Mycelium
Node
Nut and Nutlet
Oblanceolate
Oblong
Obovate
Offset
Ovate
Palmate
Panicle
Pedate
Peltate
Perianth
Petal
Pinnate
Pip
Pistil
Pit
Pod
Pollen
Pompon
Pseudobulb
Radials
Ray Floret
Rhizome
Runners
Samara
Scion or Cion
Seeds
Sepal
Set
Shoot
Spore
Sprigs
Spur
Stamen
Stigma
Stipule

Stolon
Stool
Style
Subshrub
Taproot
Tepal
Terminal
Whorl

GARDENING TERMS AND INFORMATION

Acid and Alkaline Soils
Adobe
Aeration of the Soil
Air and Air Pollution
Air Drainage
Air Layering
Alpine Greenhouse or Alpine House
Amateur Gardener
April, Gardening Reminders For
Aquarium
Arbor
Arboretum
Arch
Asexual or Vegetative Propagation
Atmosphere
August, Gardening Reminders For
Balled and Burlapped
Banks and Steep Slopes
Bare-Root
Bark Ringing
Baskets, Hanging
Bed
Bedding and Bedding Plants
Bell Jar
Bench, Greenhouse
Blanching
Bleeding
Bog
Bolting
Border
Bottom Heat
Break, Breaking
Broadcast
Budding
Bulbs or Bulb Plants

Gardening Terms and Information (Continued)

State Agricultural Experimental Stations
Stock or Understock
Straightedge
Strawberry Jars
Strike
Stunt
Succession Cropping
Sundials
Syringing
Thinning or Thinning Out
Tillage
Tilth
Tools
Top-Dressing
Topiary Work
Training Plants
Tree Surgery
Tree Wrapping
Trenching
Trowels
Tubs
Watering
Weeds and Their Control
Window Boxes

FERTILIZERS AND OTHER SUBSTANCES RELATED TO GARDENING

Algicide
Aluminum Sulfate
Ammonium Nitrate
Ammonium Sulfate
Antibiotics
Ashes
Auxins
Basic Slag
Blood Meal
Bonemeal
Bordeaux Mixture
Calcium Carbonate
Calcium Chloride
Calcium Metaphosphate
Calcium Nitrate
Calcium Sulfate
Carbon Disulfide
Chalk
Charcoal
Coal Cinders
Cork Bark
Complete Fertilizer
Compost and Composting
Cottonseed Meal
Creosote
DDT
Dormant Sprays
Dried Blood
Fermate or Ferbam
Fertilizers
Fishmeal
Formaldehyde
Fungicides
Gibberellic Acid
Green Manuring
Growth Retardants
Guano
Herbicides or Weed-Killers
Hoof and Horn Meal

Hormones
Humus
Insecticide
John Innes Composts
Lime and Liming
Liquid Fertilizer
Liquid Manure
Manures
Mulching and Mulches
Muriate of Potash
Nitrate of Ammonia
Nitrate of Lime
Nitrate of Potash
Nitrate of Soda
Nitrogen
Orchid Peat
Organic Matter
Osmunda Fiber or Osmundine
Oyster Shells
Peat
Peat Moss
Permagnate of Potash
Potassium
Potassium Chloride
Potassium-Magnesium Sulfate
Potassium Nitrate
Potassium Permagnate
Potassium Sulfate
Pyrethrum
Rock Phosphate
Rotenone
Salt Hay or Salt Marsh Hay
Sand
Sawdust
Sodium Chloride
Sprays and Spraying
Sulfate
Superphosphate
Trace Elements
Urea
Urea-Form Fertilizers
Vermiculite
Wood Ashes

TECHNICAL TERMS

Acre
Alternate Host
Annuals
Antidessicant or Antitranspirant
Biennals
Binomial
Botany
Chromosome
Climate
Clone
Composite
Conservation
Cross or Crossbred
Cross Fertilization
Cross Pollination
Cultivar
Decumbent
Dicotyledon
Division
Dormant
Endemic
Environment
Family

Fasciation
Fertility
Fertilization
Flocculate
Floriculture
Genus
Germinate
Habitat
Half-Hardy
Half-Ripe
Hardy Annual
Hardy Perennial
Heredity
Hybrid
Indigenous
Juvenile Forms
Juvenility
Legume
Monocotyledon
Monoecious
Mutant or Sport
Mycorrhiza or Mycorhiza
Nitrification
Perennials
pH
Plant Families
Photoperiodism
Photosynthesis
Pollination
Pubescent
Saprophyte
Self-Fertile
Self-Sterile
Species
Standard
Sterile
Strain
Terrestrial
Tetraploid
Transpiration
Variety

TYPES OF GARDENS AND GARDENING

Alpine Garden
Artificial Light Gardening
Backyard Gardens
Biodynamic Gardening
Bog Gardens
Botanic Gardens and Arboretums
Bottle Garden
City Gardening
Colonial Gardens
Conservatory
Container Gardening
Cutting Garden
Desert Gardens
Dish Gardens
Flower Garden
Fluorescent Light Gardening
Formal and Semiformal Gardens
Greenhouses and Conservatories
Heath or Heather Garden
Herb Gardens
Hydroponics or Nutriculture
Indoor Lighting Gardening
Japanese Gardens
Kitchen Garden
Knot Gardens

Types of Gardens and Gardening (Continued)

Miniature Gardens
Native Plant Gardens
Naturalistic Gardens
Nutriculture
Organic Gardening
Rock and Alpine Gardens
Roof and Terrace Gardening
Salads or Salad Plants
Seaside Gardens
Shady Gardens
Sink Gardening
Terrariums
Vegetable Gardens
Water and Waterside Gardens
Wild Gardens

PESTS, DISEASES, AND OTHER TROUBLES

Ants
Aphids
Armyworms
Bagworms
Bees
Beetles
Billbugs
Biological Control of Pests
Birds
Blight
Blindness
Blotch
Borers
Budworms and Bud Moths
Bugs
Butterflies
Canker
Cankerworms or Inchworms
Casebearers
Caterpillars
Cats
Centipede, Garden
Chinch Bugs
Chipmunks
Club Root
Corn Earworm
Crickets
Cutworms
Damping Off
Deer
Die Back
Diseases of Plants
Downy Mildew
Earthworms
Earwigs
Edema
Fairy Rings
Fire Blight
Flies
Fungi or Funguses
Galls
Gas Injury

Gophers
Grasshoppers
Grubs
Gummosis
Hornworms
Inchworms
Insects
Iron Chelates
Iron Deficiency
Lace Bugs
Lantana Bug
Lantern-Flies
Larva
Leaf Blight
Leaf Blister
Leaf Blotch
Leaf Curl
Leaf Cutters
Leaf Hoppers
Leaf Miners
Leaf Mold
Leaf Rollers
Leaf Scorch
Leaf Skeletonizer
Leaf Spot Disease
Leaf Tiers
Lightening Injury
Maggots
Mantis or Mantid
Mealybugs
Mice
Midges
Milky Disease
Millipedes
Mites
Mold
Moles
Mosaic Diseases
Moths
Muskrats
Needle Cast
Nematodes or Nemas
Parasite
Pests of Plants
Plant Hoppers
Plant Lice
Praying Mantis
Psyllids
Rabbits
Red Spider Mite
Rootworms
Rots
Rust
Sawflies
Scab Diseases
Scale Insects
Scorch or Sunscorch
Scurf
Slugs and Snails
Smut and White Smut Diseases
Sowbugs or Pillbugs
Spanworms

Spittlebugs
Springtails
Squirrels
Stunt
Suckers
Sun Scald
Thrips
Tree Hoppers
Virus
Walking-Stick Insects
Wasps
Webworms
Weevils
Wilts
Witches' Brooms
Woodchucks

GROUPINGS OF PLANTS

Accent Plants
Aquatics
Aromatic Plants
Bedding and Bedding Plants
Berried Trees and Shrubs
Bible Plants
Broad-Leaved and Narrow-Leaved Trees
    and Shrubs
Bulbs or Bulb Plants
Bush Fruits
Carnivorous or Insectivorous Plants
Dried Flowers, Foliage, and Fruits
Edging Plants
Epiphyte or Air Plant
Evergreens
Everlastings
Fern Allies
Filmy Ferns
Florists' Flowers
Foliage Plants
Fragrant Plants and Flowers
Gift Plants
Graft Hybrids
Grasses, Ornamental
Hard-Wooded Plants
Houseplants or Indoor Plants
Japanese Dwarfed Trees
Medicinal or Drug Plants
Night-Blooming Plants
Ornamental-Fruited Plants
Pitcher Plants
Poisonous Plants
Shrubs
State Flowers
State Trees
Stone Fruits
Stone or Pebble Plants
Stove Plants
Succulents
Tender Plants
Trees
Windowed Plants

The New York
Botanical Garden
Illustrated Encyclopedia
of Horticulture

IDRIA (Íd-ria)—Boojum Tree or Cirio. By some authorities *Idria*, of the fouquieria family FOUQUIERIACEAE, is included in *Fouquieria*. Treated separately, it comprises one species. The meaning of its name is unstated by its author.

The boojum tree or cirio (**I. columnaris** syn. *Fouquieria columnaris*) is a native of the deserts of Baja California and one tiny sta-

Idria columnaris in Baja California

Trunk of *Idria columnaris* in Baja California

tion on the opposite mainland. It develops one or few fat, erect trunks, shaped like thin, upside-down carrots and fringed toward their tops or in younger specimens throughout their lengths, with spirals of

In Baja California, a fence of trunks of *Idria columnaris*

Idria columnaris in Huntington Botanical Garden, San Marino, California

short, slender, spiny, horizontal branches, leafless for most of the year. It has the bizarre, out-of-the-world appearance associated with the baobab (*Adansonia*), the ghost men (*Pachypodium*), and a few other strange inhabitants of the world's deserts, but the boojum tree is related to none of these. Its stout, green, spongy trunks, 10 to 76 feet tall, contain much water-holding tissue that provides a reservoir of moisture to support the plant through long droughts. The average annual precipitation in its native range is 3 to 5 inches. Often many years pass without substantial rainfall. The stalks of the alternate, lobeless leaves of the boojum tree, after the blades have fallen, develop into spines, in the axils of which short shoots bearing secondary leaves later develop. The creamy-yellow flowers are in thick-stalked panicles, 10 inches to 1½ feet long, usually

Idria columnaris, young specimen

from the tops of the main trunks. They have five persistent sepals and tubular, lobed corollas. The blooms, ¼ inch long or a little longer, have ten protruding stamens and a short, three-lobed style. The fruits contain seeds with long hairs.

Garden Uses and Cultivation. This rare and choice species is a treasure for inclusion in collections of succulents. In warm desert and semidesert regions such as southern California, it may be grown outdoors, elsewhere it is grown in greenhouses suitable for succulents needing warm conditions. Seeds afford the most convenient means of propagation.

IEIE is *Freycinetia arborea*.

IFAFA-LILY is *Cyrtanthus mackenii*.

ILAMA. See Annona.

ILEX (Ì-lex)—Holly, Yaupon, Dahoon, Inkberry, Winterberry. Because of their popularity as Christmas decorations most people are familiar with one or more kinds of holly. The sorts chiefly used as holiday greens, English and American, represent a genus abundant as natives of North and South America and indigenous in Europe, Asia, Africa, and Australia. Its approximately 400 species constitute *Ilex*, of the holly family AQUIFOLIACEAE. The family contains just two other genera of which only one, *Nemopanthus*, is cultivated. That has a single species from which *Ilex* differs in its flowers having persistent sepals and broader petals separate to their bases instead of united there. The name *Ilex* is an ancient Latin one for the holm oak (*Quer-*

cus ilex), the foliage of which that of English and American hollies somewhat resemble.

Use of holly at Christmas traces to the Roman Saturnalia. During that December festivity it was the custom to send gifts accompanied by branches of the evergreen to friends and others held in esteem. Much religious significance and folklore associated with holly stem from the beliefs of the ancient Britons whose Druids or priests more than 2000 years ago held the tree sacred and decorated habitations with it. Some believe the word itself to be a form of "holy," but this is not certain.

Besides supplying Christmas decorations, Ilex serves mankind in other ways, most importantly as maté, a stimulating tea prepared from the leaves of yerba maté (I. paraguariensis) and other species widely used and greatly esteemed throughout much of South America. In various parts of the world the leaves of fifty or more species of holly are or have been used to make beverages. American Indians employed those of the yaupon in their black drink or cassena ceremony. To participate they journeyed sometimes hundreds of miles in spring to coastal areas where the tree grew plentifully. The brew, made by parching and boiling the leaves, was drunk in quantities sufficient to induce heavy sweating and sometimes vomiting. Only braves participated. Should any woman approach while the tea was being prepared or drunk it was at once thrown away and the offending female, her presence believed to impart evil to the drink, severely punished. The beautiful hard white wood of English and American hollies is used as inlays and for other purposes. In the past, birdlime, a sticky material spread on tree branches to entrap small birds that lighted on them, was prepared from the bark of English holly.

In America, as abroad, hollies have been appreciated as ornamentals since the beginning of decorative gardening and landscaping. But for long little thought was given to selecting superior horticultural varieties, especially of native American kinds. Some of English holly were introduced to the United States. These found favor in the Pacific Northwest, but were not hardy enough to be much grown in the north, and southward the native species sufficed. But change came. By the end of World War II concern had developed about the destructive exploitation of natural stands of native Ilex opaca for Christmas greens and far-sighted nurserymen and others became increasingly aware of the possibilities of selecting and breeding superior varieties for orchard cultivation as greens and as landscape furnishings. Sensible furtherance was given to this movement in 1947 by the organization of the Holly Society of America, Inc. This group has been very active in investigation relating to hollies, in the publication of information about them and their cultivation, and in the promotion of interest in the uses of these excellent trees and shrubs.

Hardy and nonhardy, deciduous and evergreen trees and shrubs, individually unisexual, or very rarely female trees producing a few male blooms, the sorts of Ilex have alternate, stalked, often lustrous, toothless, toothed, or spiny, undivided leaves. Small and making no appreciable display, the whitish blooms are in few- to fairly many-flowered clusters or sometimes are solitary from the leaf axils. They generally have a four-lobed calyx, four petals, and four or sometimes more stamens. The fruits, technically drupes, are

Ilex opaca

Ilex opaca (fruits)

globose and berry-like. They contain two to eight seedlike stones.

American holly (I. opaca) much resembles English holly, but because of its duller foliage and more scattered berries is less handsome. There are, however, numerous named horticultural varieties, many of them selections made from the wild, that are especially fine. As a native this evergreen species ranges from Massachusetts to Florida, Missouri, and Texas, most abundantly and most satisfactorily in deep fertile soil. At its best a narrowly-pyramidal to broad-round-headed tree 50 feet or sometimes more in height, it at times develops more than one trunk. The branches spread nearly horizontally. Broadly-elliptic to elliptic-lanceolate, 2 to 4 inches in length, flat or wavy-edged, the leathery leaves generally terminate in a sharp spine and have

Ilex opaca 'Croonenburg', the original tree, Norfolk, Virginia

rather distantly placed spines along the margins. Rarely they are spineless. Their upper surfaces are usually dull, their undersides yellowish-green. The flowers are borne on shoots of the current season's growth. The females are usually solitary, the males in clusters of up to nine. The former, if pollinated, are succeeded by lusterless, red berries about ¼ inch in diameter. In I. o. xanthocarpa the fruits are yellow. Numerous horticultural varieties of Americal holly are in cultivation. Among the most popular female (berry-bearing) ones are 'Bountiful', 'Canary', 'Croonenburg', 'Lake City', 'Merry Christmas', 'Mrs. Santa', 'Old Heavy Berry', and 'Taber 3'. Male varieties (that do not berry, but produce pollen necessary to induce females to berry) include 'Albert Price', 'Jersey Knight', 'Kentucky Gentlemen', 'McDonald', 'Santa Claus', and 'Warrior'.

English holly (I. aquifolium) is native from Europe to China. An evergreen tree with a pyramidal to oblong head up to 40

Ilex aquifolium (fruits)

Ilex aquifolium bacciflava

feet high or sometimes higher, or a tall shrub, this is evergreen and highly variable. Its beautiful, glossy, leathery leaves are typically ovate to oblong-ovate, wavy, conspicuously spine-tipped and spine-edged, and 1½ to 3 inches long. In contrast to those of American holly, the flowers are on shoots of the previous season's growth. They are in several- to many-flowered clusters. The berries, glossy and usually red and a little over ¼ inch in diameter, are in dense clusters.

Cultivated varieties grouped as English hollies include straight derivatives of *I. aquifolium* and kinds that have resulted from matings of *I. aquifolium* and nearly related *I. perado* or its variety *I. p. platyphylla*. The hybrids are correctly identified as *I. altaclarensis*. Now a group designation for all of this parentage, this name was first applied in 1838 to one such presumed hybrid later described as being a male plant scarcely distinguishable from *I. altaclarensis hodginsii*. It is not always clear whether a particular variety of English holly is pure *I. aquifolium* or of hybrid origin. The disposition of those listed here is in accordance with current beliefs.

Varieties of *I. aquifolium* include these: *I. a. argenteo-marginata*, a female with green young shoots and silver-edged, dark green leaves includes the variants 'Silver Queen', 'Silver Princess', 'Silvary', and 'Teufel's Silver Variegated'. *I. a. argentea mediopicta* has green young shoots, leaves wavy-margined and strongly-toothed and dark green with a creamy-white blotch sometimes only at the base of the blade. Females of this are grown under the name 'Silver Milkmaid', males as 'Silver Milkboy'. *I. a. aurea-marginata* is a name applied to a number of varieties with green leaves edged with yellow. Most have large leaves, some often completely yellow. *I. a. aurea medio-picta* is a name originally given to a holly with small, spiny leaves blotched at their centers

Ilex aquifolium, two undetermined variegated-leaved varieties

with yellow. It is now applied to more than one variant with this type of coloring and known as golden milkmaid hollies. *I. a. bacciflava* (syn. *I. a. fructu-luteo*) has yellow berries. *I. a. balearica*, of the Balearic Islands, differs from *I. aquifolium* in its leaves being flat and sparsely-toothed or toothless (the varietal name *balearica* has been misapplied to varieties of *I. altaclarensis*). 'Barnes' and 'Big Bull' are male varieties of *I. aquifolium* used as pollinators. 'Boulder Creek' has large, glossy leaves, brilliant red berries. 'Dr. Huckleberry', one of the best English hollies, has red berries. *I. a. ferox*, the hedgehog or green porcupine holly, is a male with small leaves spiny on the surfaces as well as margins. In *I. a. ferox-argentea* the leaf margins and spines are white, those of *I. a. ferox-aurea* are yellow. *I. a. flavescens*, the moonlight holly, has leaves suffused, especially when young, with yellow. 'Golden King' (syn. 'Golden Queen') is a male of stately habit. 'Handsworth New Silver' (syn. 'Silver Plane'), one of

the best hollies, has leaves with white margins. *I. a. hastata* is a low-growing male with small leaves of extraordinarily long basal spines. 'J. C. Van Thol' is dull-leaved, with large red fruits. 'Madame Briot', with purple young shoots, has narrow-ovate, strongly-spined leaves with mottled yellow and green centers and yellow margins. *I. a. myrtifolia* is a neat grower with small leaves. 'Oregon Select', an early-fruiting holly has bright red berries. *I. a. pendula* has drooping branches. It makes a large specimen. 'Yellow Beam' is a good yellow-berried variety.

English hollies of the *I. altaclarensis* group include these: *I. a. belgica* is a fine female with strongly-spined foliage. *I. a. camelliaefolia*, one of the finest of the group, has purple young shoots, glossy, large, spineless or nearly spineless leaves. *I. a. donningtonensis*, a male with dullish, purplish-green, sometimes sickle-shaped leaves, is often spineless or nearly so. 'Eldridge' is a very free-fruiting kind with large, red berries. *I. a. hodginsii* has purplish young shoots with large leaves distantly-spaced. It is a male. 'James G.

Ilex altaclarensis: (a) Male flowers

Ilex altaclarensis 'Eldridge' (fruits)

Ilex cornuta (fruits)

(b) Female flowers

Ilex altaclarensis camelliaefolia

Ilex altaclarensis 'James G. Esson' at The
New York Botanical Garden

Ilex cornuta burfordii

Ilex cornuta burfordii (flowers)

Ilex altaclarensis 'Eldridge', the original
specimen, Great Neck, New York

Ilex altaclarensis 'James G. Esson' (fruits)

Esson' is a very hardy and handsome, red-berried seedling of 'Eldridge'. *I. a. laurifolia* is a male with mostly spineless, flat or nearly flat leaves. *I. a. mundyi* is a male

with dullish, evenly-spined leaves. *I. a. wilsonii*, a very good, large-leaved female, has leaves with conspicuous pale veins.

Chinese holly (*I. cornuta*) is a beautiful, rounded glossy-foliaged shrub of dense habit, a native of China, and hardy in southern New England. Up to about 10 feet

tall, and generally wider than high, it has distinctively quadrangular, oblong or squarish leaves 1½ to 5 inches in length. Their broad apexes are furnished with three stout spines, the middle one strongly re-curved. There are one or two stout spines on each side near the base except that on older specimens these may be wanting. Borne on shoots of the previous year's growth, the flowers are in clusters. The stalked, lustrous, scarlet fruits, which are produced even without the flowers being pollinated, are ¼ to nearly ½ inch in diameter, those of some of the varieties larger. Distinctive *I. c. burfordii* has leaves with usually only one terminal spine, rarely more, sometimes none. Several other horticultural varieties of Chinese holly are in cultivation. Here is a selection: 'Avery Island' has light yellow fruits. 'D'Or' has both spiny and spineless leaves and large yellow fruits. 'Jungle Gardens' is a male variety useful as a pollinator. 'Lehigh Valley' has very abundant red fruits. 'Shangri-La', a fast grower, has bright red fruits.

Japanese holly (**I. crenata**), endemic to Japan and cultivated in many varieties, is much esteemed for landscaping. Densely branched and sometimes 20 feet tall, this

Ilex crenata, a sheared specimen

Ilex crenata, a low, spreading variety, flanks this entrance path

twiggy evergreen is often no more than of a shrub's dimensions and form. Its lustrous, leathery leaves, ½ inch to 1¼ inches long, are elliptic to obovate, nearly round or oblong-lanceolate. Usually sharp pointed, they have slightly scalloped or round-toothed margins. Female flowers, usually solitary on shoots of the current

Ilex crenata (fruits)

Ilex crenata helleri, 8 feet tall, at The New York Botanical Garden

year's development, after pollination produce black fruits up to ⅓ inch in diameter. These have little display value. When grown from seeds Japanese holly gives progeny showing considerable variation. American nurserymen have raised and named many such variants, some with characteristics that make them especially desirable for particular plantings. Among the oldest of these are *I. c. convexa* (sometimes misidentified as *I. c. bullata*), *I. c. helleri*, and *I. c. microphylla*. The first, distinct by reason of its leaves being strongly convex, cupped beneath and with their upper surfaces rounded or humped, is one of the hardiest kinds. In more than one-half a century following its introduction in 1919, only once, in Boston, Massachusetts and elsewhere in the northeast where it has previously flourished, did it suffer severe winter injury. This variety, bushy and wider than high, may after three or four decades attain a height of 8 or 9 feet and a spread of over 20 feet. Originated in 1926 and described as dwarf and compact, *I. c.*

Ilex crenata mariesii

helleri does indeed fill the latter part of the description and is an exceedingly slow grower. But 1-foot-tall specimens planted at The New York Botanical Garden in 1934 had, forty years later, attained heights of 7 to 8 feet. A low, bushy variety distinguished by its small foliage, *I. c. microphylla* has leaves ⅜ to ¾ inch long. Vigorous and sometimes 20 feet tall, *I. c. latifolia* (syns. *I. c. fortunei*, *I. c. major*, *I. c. rotundifolia*) has leaves up to 1½ inches long by ½ inch wide or a little wider. One of the most remarkable varieties, a collector's item rare in cultivation, is *I. c. mariesii* (syn *I. c. nummularia*). This diminutive, stiff-branched kind, is probably never more than a few inches high. Vigorous, young specimens make not more than 1 inch of growth yearly, older ones much less. This would seem to be ideal for patient developers of bonsai.

Many other varieties, probably too many, of Japanese holly selected from batches of seedlings, which normally exhibit much variation, have been named in recent years. The names 'Green Island', 'Kingsville Dwarf', 'Longfellow' and 'Stokes' refer to some of these. They are described in nursery catalogs.

Inkberry (*I. glabra*), hardiest by far of evergreen hollies, is a native chiefly of swampy soils (in cultivation it adapts well to drier ones) from Nova Scotia to Missouri and Florida. An admirable shrub that suckers from the roots, this is deserving of wider use for landscaping. It attains heights of up to about 10 feet, but frequently is lower. Its leaves are lustrous, but not holly-like in the conventional sense. They no more suggest those of Christmas holly than its black berries do the red ones of the more familiar kind. Obovate to oblanceolate, spineless and toothless or sometimes with a few obscure, blunt teeth near their apexes, they are short-stalked and ¾ inch to 2 inches long. Male flowers are in slender-stalked clusters. Females are usually solitary. The berries, not of great ornamental worth, are

Ilex glabra

Ilex glabra (flowers)

¼ inch across. Variants with white berries, one named 'Ivory Queen', are known. A dwarf female variety that can only be multiplied vegetatively, *I. g. compacta* is low and compact and fruits heavily. Much like inkberry, but much less desirable as an ornamental, the gallberry (*I. coriacea*) is a coastal plain native from Virginia to Florida and Louisiana.

The yaupon (*I. vomitoria*) is an excellent and popular evergreen for regions of mild winters, though unfortunately not hardy in the north. Native from Virginia to Arkansas, Florida, and Texas, this is a large shrub or evergreen tree up to about 25 feet tall. It succeeds in fairly dry soils better than most hollies. It has short-stalked, bluntish, elliptic to ovate-oblong, glossy leaves mostly less than but sometimes exceeding 1½ inches in length. They have round-toothed margins. Borne on shoots of the previous year, mostly in clusters of threes, but sometimes solitary, the showy, red fruits, up to ¼ inch in diameter, develop in great profusion. There are several excellent varieties including *I. v. nana*, a

compact, small-leaved form that does not fruit and *I. v. pendula*, with strongly pendulous branches. Others are 'DeWerth', 'Folsom Weeping', 'Huber's Compact', 'Otis Miley' (with yellow fruits), 'Pride of Houston', and 'Stoke's Dwarf'.

Dahoon or cassine (*I. cassine* syn. *I. dahoon*), of acid wet soils and swamps from North Carolina to Florida and Louisiana, is an extremely variable evergreen shrub or sometimes tree up to 35 feet high. It has spineless, pointed or blunt, lanceolate to elliptic or obovate leaves 1½ to 4 inches long, with often somewhat rolled-under edges. Mostly in threes, the female flowers, which if pollinated give rise to bright red or rarely yellow berries ¼ inch in diameter, are on the current season's shoots. The berries form large clusters. Variety *I. c. angustifolia* has linear to narrowly-oblong leaves. Hybrids between *I. cassine* and *I. opaca* are known as Foster holly. Growing in similar habitats to *I. cassine* and often associated with it, *I. c. myrtifolia* is native from North Carolina to Florida. It differs from *I. cassine* in having leaves usually up to 1 inch long by ⅜ to ¾ inch wide and in its female flowers and hence its berries being generally solitary.

Ilex cassine

Other evergreen hollies are cultivated less extensively than the major sorts already discussed. Many are not hardy in the north or have not been tested sufficiently to determine their tolerance of cold. Among lesser known kinds are these: *I. buergeri,* of Japan, Taiwan, the Philippine Islands, and China, is a tree up to 50 feet tall. It has ovate-elliptic to oblong leaves up to 2½ inches long by nearly as wide. Its pea-sized berries are in small clusters in the leaf axils. *I. centrochinensis* is a Chinese shrub up to 10 feet tall. It has glossy, spiny, oblong-lanceolate leaves ½ to 1 inch long. The short-stalked, pea-sized, red berries con-

tain four stones. This has been confused with *I. ciliospinosa*. Variety 'Brooklyn Queen' has downy shoots and fruits with five stones. *I. chinensis,* up to 50 feet in height, is native to China. It has shiny, toothed, oblong-elliptic leaves up to 4 inches long by 1½ inches wide. The scarlet, ¼-inch-long, ellipsoid fruits are in loose clusters of seven or fewer. *I. ciliospinosa* is a compact, western Chinese shrub or tree up to 20 feet in height. It has ovate to elliptic, leathery, dullish leaves 1 inch to 2 inches long by one-half as wide, with forward-pointing spines. Solitary or clustered, the egg-shaped, short-stalked, red berries, each containing two stones, are ¼ inch in diameter. *I. cinerea* is a shrub or tree 20 feet or less tall, a native of dry soils in Hong Kong. Its oblong leaves, 4 to 5½ inches long by 1 inch to 1½ inches wide, are toothed. The very short-stalked fruits, in large clusters in the leaf axils, are under ¼ inch in diameter. *I. corallina* is a tree 30 feet or less in height of western and southwestern China. It has leathery, ovate-lanceolate to elliptic leaves 2 to 6 inches long by ½ inch to 2 inches wide, spiny on young plants, blunt-toothed on older ones. Both male and female flowers are in crowded axillary clusters. The red fruits, in clusters of many, are ⅛ inch wide. They contain four stones. *I. cyrtura,* of Burma and southern China, becomes 50 feet high. This has toothed, oblong-elliptic to elliptic-lanceolate or oblanceolate, leathery leaves 2½ to 6 inches long by 1 inch to 2¼ inches wide. Their apexes extend as long, often sickle-shaped, tails. Both male and female flowers are clustered. The short-stalked, red, pea-sized fruits are in threes or fours in the leaf axils. They contain four stones. *I. delavayi,* a shrub or tree up to 25 feet in height, is a native of western China. It has toothed, pointed-elliptic-lanceolate leaves up to 2¾ inches long by ¾ inch wide. The red, pea-sized fruits are in clusters of three to five. *I. dipyrena,* native from the Himalayas to China, attains an ultimate height of 40 feet or sometimes more. It has very short-stalked, slender-pointed, spine-tipped, ob-

Ilex dipyrena at the National Botanic Garden, Dublin, Ireland

long to narrowly-oval, dull, leathery leaves 2 to 5 inches long by ⅝ inch to 1½ inches wide. Those of young trees are very spiny, those of old specimens much less so. The flowers are numerous, in rounded clusters in the leaf axils. The big, red, oval berries, usually with two seeds, are in crowded, globose clusters. An intermediate hybrid named *I. beanii* has *I. dipyrena* and the English holly (*I. aquifolium*) as its parents. *I. excelsa* is a Himalayan tree about 20 feet tall. It has pointed-broad-elliptic, smooth-edged leaves 2 to 4 inches long by up to 1½ inches wide. Its spherical fruits, up to ¼ inch in diameter, are in umbel-like clusters. *I. fargesii* is 15 to 20 feet tall. Native to China, this has lusterless, narrowly-oblong to narrowly-oblanceolate leaves 2 to 5 inches long by ⅜ inch to 1¼ inches wide or perhaps sometimes wider, with a few teeth near their tips. The pea-sized, red fruits are mostly in threes or fours in the leaf axils. *I. ficoidea*, a native of subtropical China and about 25 feet tall, has shiny, pointed-oblong-elliptic leaves up to 3½ inches long by one-half as wide. Its clustered, ¼-inch-wide fruits are red. *I. forrestii* is a Chinese tree about 20 feet tall. It has pointed, oblong to oblanceolate leaves, toothless, or toothed toward their tips, 2 to 3½ inches long and about 1 inch in breadth. Under ¼ inch wide, the clustered fruits each contain five to seven stones. *I. franchetiana* is a Chinese shrub or small tree. This has oblanceolate leaves 1 inch to 4½ inches long by up to 1½ inches wide, toothed toward the apex. The stalked ¼-inch-wide, red fruits are in clusters. *I. f. parvifolia* has obovate to elliptic leaves 1 inch to 2 inches in length by 1 inch wide or considerably narrower. *I. georgei*, a handsome, compact Chinese shrub, is up to 18 feet tall. It has shiny, ovate-lanceolate leaves up to 1½ inches long and ½ inch wide. They have a short terminal spine. The ellipsoid fruits, plentifully borne in clusters, are ¼ inch long. *I. graciliflora*, a native of Hong Kong and up to 30 feet tall, is a tree with glossy, leathery, blunt-obovate-elliptic, slightly round-toothed leaves ¾ inch to 2¾ inches long by up to 1 inch across. The abundant, long-stalked fruits, about ¼ inch in diameter, are in clusters. *I. hanceana* has small, ovate, smooth-edged, boxwood-like leaves much like those of better-known *I. crenata*. From *I. crenata* this differs in its fruits being red. Of compact habit, it is native of Hong Kong. *I. integra*, a decorative native of Japan, Korea, and perhaps Taiwan, in the wild is 30 to 40 feet tall, in cultivation usually less than one-half that maximum. Its completely spineless leaves are obovate to broad-elliptic, with a short-pointed or blunt apex. They are 1 inch to 3 inches long by up to 1¼ inches wide. The clustered, long-stalked, red fruits are ½ inch long. A yellow-fruited variety is known. *I. intricata*, low and often prostrate, is native from the Himalayas to China. This has small, very

short-stalked, round-toothed, obovate to round or sometimes broader-than-long leaves generally up to ½ inch long and about one-half as wide. The bright red fruits, less than ¼ inch in diameter, are solitary, in twos, or sometimes in threes. *I. latifolia* is a splendid tree 50 to 60 feet tall. Described as the handsomest broad-leaved evergreen native of Japan, this kind also occurs in China. It has stout, angular shoots and thick, lustrous, oblong leaves tapered to both ends, shallowly-toothed,

Ilex latifolia

but not spiny, and 4 to 8 inches long by 1½ to 5 inches wide. About ⅓ inch in diameter, the globose, red fruits are in crowded racemes or clusters from the leaf axils. The foliage of *I. l. variegata* is decorated with yellow. An intermediate hybrid between *I. latifolia* and *I. aquifolium* named *I. koehneana* has foliage more spiny than that of the first named. *I. memecylifolia*, a shrub up to 6 feet tall, is native to Hong Kong. It has thick, ovate to short-pointed, obovate leaves up to 3 inches long by a little over one-half as wide. The longish-stalked, red berries, ¼ inch in diameter and containing four or five stones, are in clusters of four or five. *I. meserveae* is the name of a group of excellent, hardy, intermediate hybrids between *I. aquifolium* and *I. rugosa*. *I. paraguayensis*, the yerba maté of Brazil, is a warm-climate evergreen shrub or tree up to 20 feet tall. Obovate to obovate-oblong and round-toothed, its leaves are 3 to 5 inches long or sometimes considerably longer. It is from these that the popular South American beverage maté is made. The berries, up to ¼ inch in diameter, are red or reddish-brown. *I. pedunculosa* is a very fine holly, one of the hardiest evergreen sorts. Native to Japan and China, this is a shrub or pyramidal tree up to 30 feet

Ilex pedunculosa (fruits)

tall. Its spineless, toothless, glossy, ovate to elliptic, slender-pointed leaves are 1½ to 3 inches long by approximately one-half as broad. Borne on shoots of the current season's growth, male flowers are in clusters, females solitary. A striking characteristic of this species is that the bright red, ¼-inch-wide fruits are on stalks 1 inch to 1½ inches long. *I. perado*, the Madeira holly, is not hardy in the north. Native to Madeira, and represented by varieties in the Canary Islands and the Azores, the chief renown of this species relates to the part it has played as a parent of the *I. altaclarensis* complex of English hollies. The Madeira holly is an evergreen tree with broad-elliptic to obovate or rounded leaves up to 4 inches long by 2¼ inches wide, commonly without teeth or spines, sometimes with a few teeth toward the tip, and occasionally spiny along the whole length of margin. The leaf-stalks are distinctly winged. The flowers and berries are borne like those of English holly on shoots of the previous year. The berries are red and ⅜ inch in diameter. Variety *I. p. aurantiaca* has leaves variegated with yellow. Those of *I. p. variegata* have white variegation. Native of the Azores, *I. p. azorica* has leaves 1 inch to 2½ inches long, sometimes with a few spines. Indigenous to the Canary Islands and also occurring in Madeira, where it intergrades with the typical species, *I. p. platyphylla* has larger leaves than that kind, up to 6 or even 8 inches long by 2½ to 4½ inches wide, and occasionally with a few spines. *I. pernyi* is a shrub or tree up to 25 feet tall, a native of China. Hardy at Boston, Massachusetts, this is a desirable evergreen. It has nearly stalkless, ovate leaves ½ to 1 inch long by approximately one-half as wide, with on each side one or two strong spines and a spiny apex. In pairs, the red fruits are about ½ inch in diameter. They usually contain four stones. Variety *I. p. veitchii* has leaves approximately 1½ inches long and fruits with generally only two stones. Attractive *I. aquipernyi*, its parents *I. pernyi* and *I. aquifolium*, is a very good intermediate hybrid. *I. rotunda*, an evergreen native of Ja-

Ilex pernyi

Ilex rugosa (fruits)

pan, Taiwan, Korea, and China, is adapted for cultivation in mild climates only. This has elliptic to broadly-elliptic leaves 2 to 3½ inches in length by up to 1½ inches broad. They are without teeth or spines. *I. rugosa*, of Japan, Sakhalin Island, and the Kurile Islands, is a beautiful, low, spreading evergreen with somewhat lustrous, dark green, lanceolate to oblong-ovate, toothed leaves ¾ inch to 1½ inches long. Its ¼- to ⅜-inch wide, red berries are solitary or in clusters of few on shoots of the previous year's growth. *I. wilsonii*, distinct from *I. altaclarensis wilsonii*, is a Chinese evergreen tree about 30 feet in height and very attractive. It has shiny, toothless, spineless, pointed, ovate to obovate-oblong leaves 1¾ to 2½ inches long by ½ to 1 inch wide. The fruits, under ¼ inch in diameter and with stalks about as long, each contain four stones. This is not hardy in the north. *I. yunnanensis*, an ornamental evergreen shrub and native to China, is hardy in southern New England. Its young shoots are densely-hairy. Ovate to ovate-lanceo-

late, with a tiny point at their apexes, the round-toothed leaves are ¾ inch to 1½ inches long by ¾ inch wide. Female flowers are solitary. The nodding, red berries on stalks ½ inch long are ¼ inch in diameter. They contain four stones. Blunt, ovate, round-toothed leaves are characteristic of *I. y. gentilis*.

Leaf-losing (deciduous) hollies, native to North America and mostly hardy in southern New England, and *I. laevigata* and *I. verticillata*, in considerably colder climates, include several worthy of note. Possumhaw (*I. decidua*), a native chiefly of bottom lands and low woodlands from Virginia to Florida and Texas, is a shrub or sometimes a tree up to 30 feet high, of distinctive aspect because of the short spurs crowded with leaves and flowers that develop along its branches. Its obovate to obovate-oblong, more or less clustered, slightly lustrous, thickish leaves, bluntish and round-toothed, are 1½ to 3 inches long. Male flowers are usually solitary on long stalks, females are short-stalked, usually clustered, and sometimes solitary, on short spurs. Bright orange-red and ⅜ inch in diameter, the fruits remain attractive for a very long period, sometimes until spring. Because of this, possum-haw is rated one of the best deciduous hollies. The berries differ from those of *I. verticillata* and *I. laevigata* in their stones being many-ribbed instead of smooth. Variety *I. d. longipes* has fruits with stalks distinctly longer than those of the typical species. There are a number of horticultural varieties including 'Byer's Golden', 'Fraser's Improved', 'Oklahoma', and 'Warren's Red'.

The black-alder or common winterberry (*I. verticillata*) in the wild favors swampy soils from Canada to Wisconsin, Florida, and Missouri. Variable, it is distinguishable from the smooth winterberry by its dull leaves being hairy at least on the veins beneath and by its male as well as female flowers having short stalks. Up to 10 feet tall, it has spreading branches and

Ilex verticillata

elliptic to obovate or oblanceolate, toothed or double-toothed leaves 1½ to 3 inches long. The berries, ¼ inch in diameter and often in pairs, are bright red, those of *I. v. chrysocarpa* are yellow. The smooth winterberry (*I. laevigata*), rarely exceeding 6 feet in height, has mostly slightly smaller leaves than the black-alder. Bright green and lustrous, they have never more than a suggestion of pubescence on the veins beneath. The berries about ⅓ inch in diameter and solitary, are orange-red. Variety 'Hervey Robinson' has yellow berries. The smooth winterberry is native from Maine to Georgia.

Native from North Carolina to Florida and Alabama and not reliably hardy north of Philadelphia, *I. ambigua* is a shrub or a small tree with hairless to densely-hairy shoots and dull, pointed, lanceolate, elliptic, or ovate leaves up to about 3 inches long and finely to coarsely toothed. The flowers are four-petaled, the males clustered and mostly on short spurs, the females solitary from the leaf axils. The berries are spherical, translucent, red, and about ¼ inch in diameter. Variety *I. a. montana* (syn. *I. montana*), native from Massachusetts to Georgia and Alabama, has sharply-toothed leaves 2½ to 7 inches long usually clustered on short spurs and orange-red berries ⅜ inch or slightly more in diameter.

Deciduous hollies of eastern Asia cultivated in North America include *I. geniculata* and *I. serrata*. An attractive native of Japan, hardy in southern New England, *I. geniculata* is slender-branched and 5 to 10 feet tall. It has long-pointed, ovate-oblong, sharply-toothed leaves 1½ to 3 inches long by ¾ inch to 2 inches wide. In fall they turn yellow before they drop. Occasionally in threes, the pendulous, ¼-inch-wide, red fruits, are more usually solitary. They have slender stalks ¾ inch to 2 inches long. Japanese *I. serrata* is very similar to American *I. verticillata*. It differs chiefly in all its parts being smaller. It is a shrub up to 15 feet tall with elliptic to ovate, toothed leaves not over and often under 2 inches long. Its red fruits, ⅕ inch in diameter, drop earlier than those of its American counterpart. The berries of *I. s. leucocarpa* are white, those of *I. s. xanthocarpa* are yellow. Hairy leaves characterize *I. s. sieboldii*.

Garden and Landscape Uses. Hollies include some of the most satisfactory ornamental evergreens, magnificent as single specimens, in groups, for use as backgrounds to other plantings, and as screens. They serve well as hedges, sheared or less formal, and may be trained as espaliers and as standards (tree-form specimens with a clear branchless trunk surmounted by a globular or conical head), and small-leaved ones, such as the Japanese holly, as bonsai. Additionally, those with red, or less commonly yellow or white fruits supply delightful and appropriate material for Christ-

A hedge of English holly

Ilex crenata, sheared

Ilex crenata, espaliered

mas decorations, and even berryless sprays are useful for this purpose.

Leaf-losing or deciduous hollies are most appreciated for their great wealths of brilliant berries. In fall, early winter, and sometimes well into spring these bring welcome relief from the drabber hues that prevail then. They contrast starkly with snow-covered ground.

In selecting hollies for particular sites give attention to the known preferences of various kinds. Hardiness to cold is a factor to consider in many areas as well as quality and character of the soil. All prosper in well-drained, but not dry, fertile, slightly acid to neutral soil. Acceptable variations from this type of soil are indicated with the descriptions of the various kinds presented earlier. Hollies develop best in sunny locations if there is sufficient moisture for their needs, but they accommodate to a little part-day or dappled shade. Although a few female hollies produce berries without their flowers being pollinated, most do not and even those that do are likely to perform better if a male is growing nearby. Therefore if berries are desired, be sure to plant about one compatible male for about every ten or twelve females or plant a female on which a male branch has been grafted. The first procedure is to be preferred.

Hollies have a scarcely deserved reputation for being difficult to transplant. This belief is probably based on unsuccessful attempts to grub native species from woodlands and other natural sites for transference to gardens. If transplanting from the wild is done carelessly, without great pains being exercised that an unbroken ball of roots proportionate to and adequate for the size of the plant is taken, disaster will surely follow. Other frequent causes of failure are transplanting to unacceptable sites and soils, moving at the wrong season, exposing specimens while out of the ground to drying sun and wind, and failure to prune sufficiently to compensate for the inevitable loss of roots. Well-grown nursery-raised hollies move

very much more successfully than those collected from natural stands. When large specimens are to be moved it pays to root-prune them a full year in advance, and advantage is likely to be had by removing about one-fourth of the foliage by pruning or by picking off older leaves or, alternatively, by spraying the foliage with an anti-desiccant. Mulch the ground immediately after planting and during the first summer be sure to drench it at about weekly intervals if there is insufficient rain to keep the roots moist.

Cultivation. Spring is the preferred time to plant hollies, but, especially in regions of mild winters, this can also be done successfully in early fall. When preparing the ground do an excellent job. If the natural earth is clayey or impervious to moisture do not just dig a hole a little larger than the root ball, plunk the plant in, fill in soil, and complete the planting. Instead, make a hole at least twice as broad as the ball of roots, wider is better, and of suitable depth. Break up the bottom with a spading fork and mix in generous amounts of compost, leaf mold, manure, or similar organic additive as well as some longer-lasting conditioner such as coarse sand, grit, coarse coal cinders, or brick rubble to promote drainage and aeration. While in a dryish condition or at least not so wet that it is sticky, tramp the newly loosened soil to make it firm before positioning the holly. This will prevent the ball sinking later. Set the plant scarcely deeper than it has been previously. Fill agreeable soil around it (if the natural earth does not meet this specification improve it by mixing in compost, leaf mold, peat moss, well-rotted manure, or other acceptable organic amendment and possibly coarse sand or grit), and make it firm. Complete the planting by staking or guying if needed, and by mulching. If the transplanted specimen has not been pruned prior to digging, the preferred procedure, attend to this immediately after planting. Take care to retain the desired shape of the plant. With this in view, the cutting may involve thinning out

branches that can be best spared, merely shortening shoots, or in the case of formal specimens, shearing. Up to one-fourth or sometimes even more of the total growth can with advantage be removed. The fewer the roots in comparison to the size of the top the more necessary is severe pruning to bring about a suitable balance.

Care of established hollies is not demanding. As a group they are heavy feeders appreciative of fairly generous fertilization. This is especially true of evergreen kinds expected to produce supplies of cut greens each year. Each early spring apply a complete fertilizer of relatively high nitrogen content, such as a 10-6-4, or, instead, a liberal surface dressing of half-rotted manure. In any case it is beneficial to keep hollies mulched. They are surface rooters and a covering of compost or similar material promotes the cool, evenly moist conditions favorable to root growth.

Pruning in their early stages is often needed to induce hollies to adopt forms considered desirable, later to retain these and contain the plants to size. Except with hedges and strictly formally trained specimens, pruning should never distort the natural habit or grace of the plant. Instead, use it to emphasize such characteristics. Pruning formal specimens and hedges may consist of shearing done once or sometimes twice a year. Pruning during the training period of tree-type hollies is done to develop a distinctive leader and well-disposed side branches. American holly particularly, when young is likely to assume a sprawling, shrubby habit without any dominant leading shoot. To overcome this, drive a stake into the ground, select the most promising branch, and tie it to the stake; then cut back the tips of all other branches. Sometimes hollies develop two or even three leaders so that the plant eventually develops as a multitrunked tree. If this is not wanted remove or cut back all except the best leader early. Later in life, Japanese hollies and other vigorous kinds may develop long, rangy shoots that detract from the beauty of the specimens. Cut these out promptly. Maintenance pruning may be done in early spring or with evergreen hollies before Christmas so that the parts removed can be had for seasonal decorations.

Propagation is by seed, cuttings, layering, budding, and grafting. Because seeds produce approximately equal numbers of female and male plants, where berrying specimens are the objective it is less appropriate than other methods. It is useful for raising plants to be used in formal, clipped hedges and with kinds such as Japanese holly that have berries of but slight ornamental merit. The seeds of some hollies, including American holly, English holly, Chinese holly, and certain others, normally do not germinate until the second spring after sowing. Those of others, notably those of Japanese holly, yaupon, cassine, and inkberry, are much more prompt. Collect the berries after they mature in fall. Crush them in a sieve and wash all pulp from the seeds. Discard as being not viable any seeds that float. Sow in flats or cold frames in a sandy, peaty soil mix.

An alternative method, handy with slow-to-germinate kinds, is to stratify the seeds before sowing. To do this, as before, free the seeds from surrounding pulp. Then mix them with about three times their bulk of slightly moist sand and put the mixture in a polyethylene plastic bag and store it in a refrigerator at 35 to 40°F for fourteen or fifteen months, or fill a porous container with the seed-sand mix and bury it by the north side of a building for the same period. If this last plan is followed cover the container of seeds with fine wire mesh to deny access to rodents. At the beginning of the second spring sow the stratified seeds in the normal way in flats in a cold frame or greenhouse or in a bed outdoors.

Summer cuttings, those of deciduous hollies made as soon as the new shoots become firm, but not hard, and those of evergreen sorts made in late summer or

American holly rooted in a cold frame from cuttings

fall, may be rooted in a greenhouse or cold frame propagating bed or under mist. Any of several standard rooting mixtures may be used. One consisting of equal parts coarse sand or perlite and acid peat moss is very good. Cuttings of most hollies root quite readily, those of a few a little more reluctantly. It is helpful, but not necessary, to treat the cuttings with a root-inducing hormone before planting them. Cuttings from some individual trees of English holly make roots more readily than those taken from other trees and this may be true of other kinds. Roots develop more quickly if bottom heat of 70 to 75°F is supplied to the propagating bed.

Grafting and budding may be done if understocks of the same general types as the scions are selected. (Do not attempt, for example, to implant scions of evergreens onto deciduous kinds or vice versa.) Seedling understocks are to be preferred to those raised from cuttings. Grafting is done in spring in greenhouses, budding outdoors in summer. The last is useful for establishing a male on an isolated female so that pollen is available to fertilize the female flowers so that they will produce berries. If branches are low enough to be bent to the ground, layering in fall is a slow, but very sure method of increasing hollies. Some success has been had with air-layering.

Pests and Diseases. Hollies are subject to a fairly long catalog of pests and diseases, but few are likely to be bothersome in any one place. If unduly troubled consult your Cooperative Extension Agent or your State Agricultural Experiment Station. Sprays and other recommended control treatments differ from area to area and time to time. The most aggravating pests are leaf miners that tunnel through the inner tissues and seriously disfigure the leaves with their crooked tracks. The holly midge, the larvae of which live inside fruits, cause failure of the berries of American holly to ripen and to be smaller than normal. Other pests include aphids, black vine weevil, mealybugs, scale insects, red spider mites, and root nematodes. Diseases of hollies include several leaf spots, serious only occasionally, and various conditions mostly associated with poorly selected locations or poor cultural care. In wind-swept places a speckled puncturing of the leaves of English and American hollies is likely to develop as a result of the spiny older leaves being whipped against tender, young developing ones.

ILIAMNA (Il-iámna). From closely related *Sphaeralcea* with which it was earlier combined, *Iliamna* differs in the carpels of its flowers and fruits not being of two distinct parts. It consists of seven species, mostly natives of moist soils on mountain hillsides and in open woodlands in western North America, and belongs to the mallow family MALVACEAE. The name, of Greek derivation, is of uncertain significance.

Iliamnas are herbaceous plants sparsely clothed with stellate (star-shaped) hairs. They have alternate, thin, large, three- to seven-lobed, maple-like leaves. The flowers, in erect spirelike panicles, are white, pink, or rose-purple. They have five sepals united at their bases, five petals, many stamens with the lower parts hairy and joined into a column, and a pistil of several united carpels that become the podlike fruits. The styles are tipped with knoblike stigmas.

Native from the Rocky Mountains to British Columbia and Oregon, *I. rivularis* (syn. *Sphaeralcea acerifolia*) is a handsome perennial 4 to 6 feet tall. Its leaves, heart- to kidney-shaped in outline and deeply five- or seven-lobed, are 2 to 6 inches long and wide, green on their upper surfaces and somewhat paler beneath. The mallow-like flowers, crowded in spires, are rose to lavender with purple bases to their wide-spreading petals. The latter are ¾ to 1 inch long. The bracts below the blooms are not over one-half as long as the calyx.

The largest flowered kind, *I. grandiflora,* of the mountains of Colorado, Utah, and New Mexico, is 3 to 6 feet tall. It has blooms with pink petals up to 1¼ inches in length. A distinguishing characteristic is that the bracts below the flowers are two-thirds as long as the calyx. From the last, *I. latibracteata* differs in the undersides of its leaves being decidedly paler than the upper surfaces and the bracts below the flowers being as long or longer than the calyx. This inhabits moist ground in Oregon and California.

One of the rarest native American plants, *I. remota* (syn. *Sphaeralcea remota*, *Phymosia remota*) has been found in only two very limited localities, a gravelly island in the Kankakee River, Illinois, where it was first discovered in 1872, and on Peters Mountain, Virginia, where it was found in 1927. It seems to have disappeared from the island. An attractive species, 4 to 6 feet tall, it has maple-like, five- to seven-lobed leaves up to 6 inches wide or sometimes wider. The flowers are in erect spikes. They are 2 to 2½ inches in diameter and apple-blossom to bluish-pink fading to white toward their centers.

Garden and Landscape Uses and Cultivation. Iliamnas are much better adapted to humid conditions and partial shade than sphaeralceas, and generally are considerably hardier to cold. The species described are attractive for flower beds and naturalizing and succeed in ordinary, moderately fertile soils. They are increased by seed, although those of some kinds do not germinate readily, and by division.

ILLICIACEAE—Illicium Family. Formerly included in the *Magnoliaceae*, the dicotyledonous illicium family consists of the genus *Illicium* only. Its characteristics are discussed in this Encyclopedia under Illicium.

ILLICIUM (Ill-ícium)—Star-Anise. Mostly aromatic, evergreen trees and shrubs to the number of forty-two species compose this genus of the illicium family ILLICIACEAE, which by some authorities is included in the magnolia family MAGNOLIACEAE. Its members are natives of the southeastern United States, the West Indies, eastern and southern Asia, and Malaysia. Their name, from the Latin *illicium*, allurement, alludes to their aromatic fragrance.

Illiciums have alternate, leathery, undivided, toothless, glandular-dotted leaves, and solitary, white, yellowish, or purplish flowers from the leaf axils. The blooms have three or six petal-like sepals, many petals, the outer broader than the inner, numerous stamens, and a recurved style. The leathery to woody, star-shaped fruits consist of a wheel of several to many one-seeded, podlike follicles.

Native of wet soils and woodlands from Florida to Louisiana, *Illicium floridanum* is a shrub up to 10 feet high, with stalked, pointed-elliptic to elliptic-lanceolate leaves 2¼ to 6 inches long, each with a conspicuous mid-vein. The nodding purple blooms, 2 to 2¼ inches in diameter, on stalks 1½ to 2 inches in length, have twenty to thirty narrow petals. The fruits are 1 inch wide or a little wider.

Star-anise (*I. verum*) is a native of China. A shrub or tree up to 60 feet tall, but often lower, it has lustrous, pointed-elliptic to pointed-oblanceolate leaves 3½ to 6 inches long, with prominent mid-veins, and narrow rolled-under margins. Its flowers, at first whitish or yellow, at maturity are deep pink to purple red. Their sepals do not spread, but curve inward to form a bloom only slightly over ½ inch wide. The fruits of star-anise are used as a condiment, and they and their leaves yield oils used for flavoring anisette and absinthe, as condiments, and in medicine. For these

Illicium anisatum

purposes it is extensively cultivated in China.

A tree, usually not exeeding 25 feet in height, *I. anisatum* (syns. *I. religiosum, I. japonicum*) inhabits woodlands and thickets in China, Taiwan, Japan, and the Ryukyu Islands. It is much favored for planting in Buddhist cemeteries and near temples, and its wood is used in incense. This species has lustrous, narrowly-obovate to oblong leaves up to 4 inches long. The yellowish blooms, 1 inch to 1½ inches in diameter and with spreading petals, are on ¾-inch-long stalks furnished with bracts that soon fall. This species contains a poisonous alkaloid. Plants cultivated under its name sometimes are *I. verum*. In *I. a. variegatum* the foliage is variegated.

Native to China, *I. henryi* is a shrub or tree up to 20 feet tall. Its stalked leaves are lanceolate to obovate-elliptic, and up to 6 inches in length, the largest usually not over 2 inches wide. The long-stalked flowers are under 1 inch wide.

Garden and Landscape Uses and Cultivation. Illiciums are attractive foliage evergreens for mild-climate use as ornamentals and screens. About as hardy as camellias, they succeed in ordinary soils, preferring those containing a fair amount of organic matter, which are not excessively dry. They prosper in sun or in light or part-dry shade. Propagation is by seed and by cuttings under mist or in a greenhouse propagating bench.

ILYSANTHES is *Lindernia grandiflora*.

IMANTOPHYLLUM. See Clivia.

IMBU is *Spondias tuberosa*.

IMITARIA (Imit-ària). One close relative of *Gibbaeum*, of the carpetweed family AIZOACEAE, is the only representative of the genus *Imitaria*. The name, from the Latin *imito*, to imitate, was applied because of the close resemblance of this to *Lithops* and *Conophytum*, as well as to the stones among which in the wild it grows.

A typical stone or pebble plant of South Africa, *I. muirii* (syn. *Gibbaeum neobrownii*) has been thought to be a hybrid between *Conophytum* and *Gibbaeum*, and certainly it is intermediate in appearance. From *Conophytum* it is distinct in having flowers with unequally six-lobed calyxes. Individual plants are stemless and consist of one to few soft, pubescent plant bodies each consisting of two fleshy leaves united except for a shallow cleft or fissure between them at the apex. The plant bodies are egg-shaped, globular, or obconic and somewhat translucent on top. They are up to ¾ inch in diameter and slightly taller than wide. The solitary, terminal, stalkless flowers, daisy-like in appearance, but not in structure, are rose-pink to deep red and

are about ¾ inch across. They have three or four rows of petals. There are many staminodes (nonfunctional stamens), two rows of stamens, and an elongated style. The fruits are capsules.

Garden Uses and Cultivation. This succulent gem is of much interest to collectors of desert plants. It requires the same conditions and care as *Lithops* and other pebble plants of South Africa.

IMMORTELLES. See Everlastings.

IMPALA-LILY is *Adenium obesum multiflorum*.

IMPATIENS (Im-pàtiens)—Patience Plant or Sultana, Garden Balsam, Jewel Weed or Touch-Me-Not. Few of the 600 or more species of *Impatiens*, of the balsam family BALSAMINACEAE, are cultivated, but they include some popular garden and greenhouse plants and houseplants. The vast majority are natives of Europe, temperate and tropical Asia, Indonesia, Africa, and Madagascar. About six species, including the jewel weed (*I. capensis* syn. *I. biflora*), which like its European and temperate Asian counterpart *I. noli-tangere* is often called touch-me-not (because of the manner in which the seeds are discharged), are indigenous in moist woodlands and thickets in North and Central America. These, the only kinds native to the New World, are not of horticultural interest.

Plants of this genus are more or less succulent-stemmed annuals and herbaceous perennials with opposite or whorled (in circles of three or more), undivided, usually toothed leaves. The asymmetrical flowers are solitary or in small clusters or racemes from the leaf axils. Because they are turned on their stems through an angle of 180 degrees, what appear to be the bottom sepals and petals are morphologically the upper ones and vise versa, but to avoid confusion we shall refer to them positioned as the flowers are displayed. The blooms have three or rarely five sepals, one of which is represented by an open-mouthed, backward-projecting spur of petal-like character and is much bigger than the others. This is sometimes referred to as the lip. There are five petals, but two pairs are united to give the effect of there being only three. The upper petal is called the standard or banner, the others, the wings. The latter are usually two-lobed with their lower lobes hiding the mouth of the spurred sepal. There are five flat-stalked stamens and a short style ending in a five-lobed stigma. The fruits are slender capsules so constructed that when the seeds are ripe the slightest touch causes them to split and explosively discharge their contents in all directions for considerable distances. The name, the Latin word for impatient, alludes to this characteristic.

Impatiens balsamina

Impatiens glandulifera (flowers)

Impatiens wallerana, a variegated-leaved variety

Impatiens wallerana, a double-flowered variety

The garden balsam (**I. balsamina**) is an annual with thick, erect, branched stems 1 foot to 2½ feet tall, leafy above as well as along the flowering portions. Alternate, the leaves have narrow- to broad-lanceolate, prominently-toothed blades, and stalks with glands. Short-stalked, the blooms come from the axils of the plentiful leaves of the main stem and its erect branches and are partially hidden by the foliage. They come in a wide range of colors from white through creamy-yellow and pink to lilac, bright scarlet, and deep crimson. Sometimes they are parti-colored. The spurs of the flowers are hooked at their ends. The petals are broad, the upper one notched at its apex. Because their blooms are showier and last longer, double-flowered varieties are preferred to those with single blooms. This species is native of warm parts of Asia.

An annual, and a native of the Himalayas naturalized in northeastern North America as far north as Canada, **I. glan-** *dulifera* (syn. *I. roylei*) is rather coarse, much-branched, hollow-stemmed, and 1 foot to 3 feet tall. It has ovate to ovate-lanceolate, toothed leaves 2 to 6 inches in length, the upper ones in whorls of three, the lower opposite. The lavender to rosy-purple flowers are three or more together in long-stalked clusters from the axils of the upper leaves. They are so plentiful that they almost may be described as constituting leafy panicles. The blooms have very short spurs, a two-lobed standard or banner petal, the other petals broad. The seed capsules are hairless and pendent.

Patience plant or sultana (**I. wallerana** syn. *I. holstii*) includes varieties usually listed in catalogs and garden books as *I. sultanii* and *I. petersiana*. A nonhardy perennial native of East Africa, as known in cultivation this species is highly variable in size, flower color, and other characteristics. From 6 inches to about 2 feet tall, and with erect or spreading, somewhat watery, branching stems, *I. wallerana* has mostly alternate, longish-stalked, ovate to ovate-lanceolate, toothed leaves with blades 1 inch to 3 inches long. There is a bristle at the bottom of the indentations between the marginal teeth. The foliage toward the tops of the stems forms leafy

rosettes. Singly or in twos or threes, mostly from near the ends of the branches, the flowers are produced with great freedom and practically continuously. They are 1 inch to almost 2 inches in diameter and have long, slender spurs; they range in color from brilliant scarlet to crimson, brick-red, orange, pink, white, and parti-colored according to variety. There are kinds with double flowers, one

Impatiens glandulifera

Impatiens wallerana

Impatiens pseudoviola

with foliage variegated with white, and *I. w. petersiana* with bronzy-red stems and foliage. The seed pods are hairless. Another East African, subshrubby, much-branched *I. pseudoviola* is a semitrailer with ovate, toothed leaves about ¾ inch long and very asymmetrical white flowers slightly tinged with rose-pink, and with a rosy-violet stripe down the center of each of the four lower petals. From the patience plant, *I. hawkeri,* a native of the Sunda Is-

Impatiens hawkeri

lands, differs in having leaves opposite or in whorls of three. Its showy, rich brownish-red blooms, 2½ to 3 inches wide, solitary or in clusters from the leaf axils, have white claws or shafts with bluish markings. The spurs are red and very long. Pretty *I. auricoma* of the Comoro Islands was first cultivated in France toward the end of the nineteenth century. It had been accidentally introduced there on imported tree fern trunks. Somewhat succulent, hairless, and up to 2 feet tall, this sort has alternate, lanceolate, round-toothed leaves 3 to 6 inches long with a short bristle between each pair of teeth. Bright green above and with a pale red midrib, they are

paler beneath. The long-stalked, 1-inch-long, minutely-spurred flowers, are golden yellow streaked with red.

An assortment of handsome, free-flowering kinds brought from New Guinea in 1970 occasioned considerable interest in America and Europe. Whether they represent several species, hybrids between a few, or are variants of one is not adequately determined. Certainly *I. schlechteri,* native of New Guinea, is one kind involved and until further botanical studies are made it is probably best to refer all of this New Guinea group to that species.

Typically *I. schlechteri* is a hairless, fleshy-stemmed, bushy perennial up to 3 feet tall, but usually much lower. Its ovate to ovate-oblanceolate, toothed leaves in whorls of three to seven are green or reddish, sometimes with a central band of yellowish-green. Usually solitary, the salmon-pink to orange, vermillion, or blood-red flowers have flat faces about 1¾ inches across and long, slender, curved spurs. The petals are shallowly notched at their apexes. The lateral pairs are united.

Impatiens schlechteri

Horticultural varieties of the New Guinea introductions have green, bronze, or red leaves that vary greatly in shape. Frequently they are variegated, most often with a yellowish band running lengthwise through their centers. Their brilliantly colored flowers are scarlet, red, deep purple, orange, many shades of pink, or glistening white.

Other beautiful upright, nonhardy perennials are cultivated, among them *I. balfouri* of the Himalayas. This is up to 3 feet in height and hairless. Its long-pointed,

Impatiens balfouri

ovate leaves, 3 to 5 inches long, have short, recurved teeth. The slender-stalked blooms in very short terminal racemes are rose-red with the bases of the side petals yellowish, and the standard or banner petal white suffused with rose-pink. They have a curved, horn-shaped spur. The seed capsules are hairless and 1 inch to 1½ inches long. Indian *I. campanularia,* 2 to 3 feet tall, has stalked, strongly-veined, toothed, broad-elliptic leaves, and on long-

Impatiens auricoma

Impatiens, New Guinea hybrid

Impatiens campanularia

Impatiens oliveri

Impatiens niamniamensis

Impatiens niamniamensis 'Congo Cockatoo'

ish stalks, few-flowered clusters of short-spurred, 1-inch-long white flowers heavily spotted with red in the throat and on the lower petal. A vigorous, hairless perennial 4 to 8 feet tall, *I. oliveri* of East Africa, has stout, erect, pale green stems and branches, and whorls (circles of more than two) of narrow-oblanceolate olive-green leaves 5 to 8 inches long. They have bristly-toothed edges and conspicuous light-colored midribs. The solitary, soft pink or lilac-pink blooms strangely resemble in aspect those of miltonia orchids. From 2 to 2½ inches in diameter, they are on longish stalks with a pair of small bracts above their middles. They have ovate lips, deeply two-lobed wing petals, very long, slender, curved spurs, and whitish undersides to their petals. Pink or purplish-red flowers about 1½ inches

Impatiens tinctoria

wide, with very slender, curved spurs, are borne by *I. platypetala* of Java. The sharply-toothed, oblong-lanceolate leaves, hairy on their undersides, are opposite or in whorls. In *I. p. aurantiaca* the leaves have pink midribs and the orange-yellow blooms a red eye. This variety is from the Celebes Islands. A native of high altitudes in tropical Africa, *I. tinctoria* is a bushy plant 4 to 5 feet tall. It has succulent stems and pointed-elliptic, toothed leaves 5 to 7 inches long. The deliciously scented flowers are in loose, long-stalked groups of few from the leaf axils. About 2½ inches across and each with a slender spur, they are white with purple stripes. This species has proved hardy in sheltered gardens in mild parts of Scotland.

Very different from other kinds discussed here, *I. niamniamensis*, native to tropical Africa, has flowers that often arise in groups on the main stems below the leaves. They have laterally compressed,

much-longer-than-broad faces, and large, inflated, strongly-hooked, bright crimson spurs about 2 inches in length that form showy contrasts to the comparatively small, white petals. This species grows up to 3 feet tall and has ovate, toothed leaves up to 6 inches long. As the name of the variety now to be described suggests, the blooms have somewhat the appearance of tiny colorful parrots on dangling perches. Variety *I. n.* 'Congo Cockatoo' has especially brilliantly colored blooms. They are pale green with the upper parts of the spurs golden-yellow and the lower portions bright crimson.

Extraordinary *I. mirabilis* of the Langkawi Islands develops a softish, stout trunk up to 4 feet high and 9 inches in diameter and branched above. The fleshy, stalked, round-toothed, ovate to broad-elliptic leaves form tufts at the tops of the stems and branches. The curiously inflated flowers, 1½ inches long and about 1 inch across the mouth, pale lilac-pink with deeper pink dots and a yellow blotch in the throat, have strongly-curved spurs. This sort is best adapted for growing in dry climates and in

Impatiens platypetala

Impatiens mirabilis

greenhouses conditioned for the needs of cactuses and other succulents.

Trailing, creeping kinds in cultivation are *I. repens,* of Ceylon, and *I. marianae,* of Assam. A charming perennial with rooting, freely-branching stems and numerous broadly-ovate to kidney-shaped, usually bronzy-green leaves up to 1 inch long, **I. repens** has solitary, bright yellow flowers

Impatiens repens

Impatiens marianae

with hairy, pouched spurs. Entirely different, creeping **I. marianae,** which may sometimes behave as an annual, has hairy stems. Its oblong-wedge-shaped, round-toothed leaves are dark green strongly variegated between the veins with white markings in patterns very like those of the aluminum plant (*Pilea cadierei*). The fairly large, pale purple flowers are in branched clusters. They have long, hooked spurs.

Garden and Landscape Uses. By far the most commonly cultivated impatiens are the garden balsam and the many varieties of sultana or patience plant. The first is an annual excellent for gardens or greenhouses, the other a nonhardy perennial often grown as an annual and, in the deep south, in greenhouses, and windows, as a more permanent resident. Both have the welcome ability to stand more shade than most other garden annuals and plants grown as such for summer display. This is especially true of the patience plant. Because of this, its practically continuous flowering, and the ease with which it is grown, it is a great favorite for flower beds, borders, window boxes, porch boxes, and for pot cultivation indoors. The other nonhardy perennials are chiefly grown in greenhouses and sometimes windows, and outdoors in warm frostless climates. Some of the lower, prostrate-branched varieties of the patience plant are well adapted for hanging baskets, and *I. repens* is particularly fine for this use.

Cultivation. The garden balsam is very easily grown from seeds sown outdoors in spring or started indoors about six weeks before planting out time, which is as soon as the weather is settled, warm, and danger of frost is well past. Grow the young plants individually in pots in a sunny place in a temperature of 55°F at night and

Garden balsam as a pot plant

up to fifteen degrees higher by day. For the best results garden balsams must have rich, well-drained soil that does not lack for moisture, but is not wet. At no stage should the plants suffer a check to growth. Never permit them to want for root room. If necessary repot into larger-sized pots while they are still indoors. They must not be crowded. Allow about 1½ feet between individuals. To encourage bushiness, when the plants are 3 or 4 inches tall pinch out the tips of their stems. Thin out plants raised from seeds sown outdoors to appropriate distances before they begin to crowd. Under no circumstances allow weeds to develop. As greenhouse pot plants garden balsams are very effective in 5- to 7-inch pots. To have such specimens, sow seeds in fall or in January under conditions such as are described above, and keep the plants, before they become excessively pot bound, successively repotted into larger containers until those in which they are to bloom are attained. Water to keep the soil always moist, and after the final pots are filled with roots give weekly applications of dilute liquid fertilizer. Airy conditions in a sunny greenhouse where the night temperature is 50 to 55°F and that by day is five to fifteen degrees higher suits these plants. The finest blooms are had by restricting each plant to a single stem. To do this, remove all side shoots while yet quite small, and also the first flower buds. If this is done and the plants are grown vigorously, quite superb, tall spikes of bloom result. Annual *I. glandulifera* can be grown by sowing seeds outdoors in spring and thinning the seedlings to 1½ to 2 feet apart, or by starting the seeds earlier indoors and setting out the young plants later.

The patience plant can be grown from seeds sown in late spring outdoors where the plants are to remain and the seedlings thinned to prevent undue crowding, but it is more usual, more economical of seeds, and productive of earlier blooming specimens of good size to start the seeds indoors and transplant outdoors later. Do this as recommended above for garden balsams, but sow the seeds eight to twelve weeks before transplanting outdoors and grow the plants in temperatures about five degrees higher than those suggested for garden balsams. Pinch the tips out of the stems once or twice to encourage bushiness. Instead of sowing seeds, patience plants can be raised from cuttings. These root at any time with great facility in sand, vermiculite, or perlite in a humid atmosphere, in a temperature of 60 to 70°F. The rooted cuttings are treated like seedlings. Patience plants for pot cultivation are handled throughout in the same manner as those raised for planting outside. They succeed in greenhouses or windows in sun or part-day shade, need good drainage, fertile soil kept always moist, and fer-

IMPATIENS

1792

tilizing generously after their containers are filled with roots.

The New Guinea impatiens are generally responsive to conditions that suit patience plant or sultana varieties except they respond better to exposure to full sun than partial shade. Free air circulation is also needed.

The other kinds of impatiens discussed require essentially the same care as the patience plant, but do not pinch the shoots of such strong growers as *I. oliveri* and *I. niamniamensis* too frequently otherwise a multitude of weak, poor-flowering shoots rather than fewer, stronger, abundantly blooming ones will result. Aphids, red spider mites, and white flies are the most common pests of *Impatiens*. Unfortunately the New Guinea varieties are especially susceptible to attacks from the last two of these.

INARCHING and APPROACH GRAFTING. Some authorities use the terms inarching and approach grafting interchangeably for two somewhat different modes of grafting that others identify separately. Both methods differ from other grafting techniques in that a portion of the scion (the shoot implanted on the understock) below the point of operation is retained. This scion, like the understock, usually includes the roots; but in a specialized varient of approach grafting, called bottle grafting, the scion is a rootless portion of stem standing with its base in a bottle of water.

Inarching is a repair technique employed to improve the health of trees with damaged or weak root systems by providing them with additional roots, to insure a supply of sap to an area above a large wound near the base of a tree trunk, and to strengthen crotches likely to be subject to breakage by establishing a living brace between the branches that form the crotch. To serve the first two objectives one or more young vigorous plants of the same or a very closely related kind as the tree to be improved is planted close to the tree's base. A notch is then cut in an upward direction low in the trunk or immediately above the wound. After the top of the young plant to be implanted has been cut off slantwise, its cut end is wedged into the notch and the operational area is sealed with grafting wax. Bracing by inarching is accomplished by selecting a suitable shoot from one branch of a crotch, positioning it across to the other branch, and after slicing off its end, wedging it into a notch cut into the second branch, if necessary securing it by tying, and covering the union with grafting wax.

Approach grafting is one of the oldest methods of plant propagation. It was developed by ancient man undoubtedly as a result of observing natural grafts, which occur not infrequently between branches of trees growing closely together and be-

Inarching: (a) After its top is cut off, the stem of a strong-rooted sapling is sliced obliquely to fit into a notch cut into the trunk of the tree to be strengthened

(b) A notch is cut in an upward direction into the trunk

(c) The sapling is then planted near the trunk and its cut end is inserted into the notch and is covered with grafting wax

(d) A young apple tree (lower left with light-colored bark) supplies the older tree into which it was inarched with moisture and nutrients

Approach grafting: (a) A young variegated English holly approach grafted onto a green-leaved seedling

(b) After the tissues have united, the top of the understock and the lower part of the scion are cut off, leaving the new young grafted plant

tween those of the same tree in contact with each other. As a horticultural technique approach grafting is employed to propagate plants, especially trees and shrubs, that are difficult to increase in other ways and also to change the varieties of established fruit-bearing trees and vines such as citrus fruits, figs, and grapes, and sometimes ornamental sorts. It differs from inarching in that the top of the young plant used as the scion is not cut off until after the scion and stock have grown together and the union is complete. In approach grafting both the plant that serves as scion and the understock are usually potted specimens. Putting the scion in a small pot makes it easy to position it relative to the plant with which it is to be united. At the time the operation is carried out both plants should be in the same stage of growth. To assure this, grow them in the same or in similar environments. The best season for approach grafting is spring when the sap is flowing freely, about the time the new shoots have four or five leaves.

To perform the operation, bring the shoots of understock and scion together and at the point of meeting remove corresponding strips of bark about 2 inches long from both. A tongue (as in whip and tongue grafting) may be cut in each, but this is rarely necessary. Fit the exposed surfaces together snugly and secure them with a rubber grafting strip or a tie of soft string. If the latter, watch it closely afterward to see that it does not cut into the stem as it swells. If there is indication of this, cut the string and retie it. Under favorable conditions union soon takes place and in some cases within about two weeks the tie can be taken off.

Sever the scion from its rooted part gradually, beginning when the part to be retained is growing vigorously. First remove a ring of bark from the scion below the point of union. A week or so later cut it halfway through. After the lapse of another week or two sever it completely. Meanwhile restrict the growth of the understock above the union by pinching out its growing tips, but leave a few leaves. At the time the scion is cut free from its roots, cut off all of the understock shoots above the union. You will now have what in effect is a grafted plant with roots of the understock kind and a top of the scion sort.

INBREEDING. The production of seeds by pollinating the pistils of the flowers of a plant with pollen of the same plant and continuing this for successive generations without ever using pollen from another source is called inbreeding. In some instances inbred plants are weaker than crossbreds. In others this is not so. Inbreeding is used to stabilize the progeny of first- and second-generation hybrids and so produce strains of seeds that breed true to type or nearly so.

INCARVILLEA (Incar-víllea). Plants previously known as *Amphicome* are now included in *Incarvillea*, an Asian genus of about fourteen species of the bignonia family BIGNONIACEAE. The name *Incarvillea*

commemorates Pierre Nicholas Le Cheron, or d'Incarville as he called himself, a French Jesuit missionary to China, who died in 1757.

Incarvilleas are stemless or stemmed annuals and herbaceous perennials, some with woody rootstocks. Usually alternate, rarely opposite, their leaves are generally pinnate, with a terminal as well as lateral leaflets, or pinately-lobed, less often twice-pinnately-lobed or undivided and lobeless. The leaf margins are commonly toothed. The flowers are solitary or in racemes or panicles. They have five-toothed calyxes, and a two-lipped, tubular, bell-shaped corolla with fine rounded or notched, flaring lobes. There are two pairs of nonprotruding stamens and sometimes one staminode (nonfunctional stamen). The style is slender. The fruits are capsules containing seeds that may or may not have a tuft of hairs at each end.

One of the most frequently cultivated kinds is *I. delavayi*. Stemless or with an

Incarvillea delavayi

exceedingly brief stem, this has rather few leaves up to 1 foot long or sometimes longer. They are pinnate with six to eleven pairs of toothed, lateral leaflets, the upper ones of which are sometimes somewhat united with, and might be considered part of, a deeply-lobed terminal leaflet, and which have a secondary main vein paralleling the midrib. The terminal leaflet is not as broad as the lateral leaflets are long. The two to ten trumpet-shaped flowers are in racemes with stalks 6 inches to 1 foot long. They are rose-purple with yellow corolla tubes and 2 to 2½ inches long and wide. The two upper petals are smaller than the others.

From the species just described, stemless *I. mairei* differs in its leaves having two to seven pairs of toothed lateral leaflets, the upper ones usually quite separate from the terminal one and without a secondary main vein paralleling the midrib. Also, the teeth of the calyxes of *I. mairei* are broader at their bases than they are long rather than the reverse. Variety *I. m. grandiflora* (syn. *I. grandiflora*), the dwarfer form most common in gardens, is distinguished by its flower stalks being branched below instead of above their middles. Its leaves have no more than four pairs of lateral leaflets, or these may be poorly developed or absent. The flowers of *I. m. grandiflora* are usually larger than those of *I. mairei*, sometimes 4 inches in diameter. As its name suggests, *I. compacta* is smaller and denser than the kinds described above. It sometimes develops a short stem. In bloom not over about 6 inches high, this has basal leaves only. They are up to 5 inches long and have four to nine pairs of toothless lateral leaflets up to 1½ inches long. The short racemes are of up to ten rosy-purple or rarely white

Incarvillea delavayi (flowers)

blooms 2 to 2½ inches or more long and wide. Their calyxes are thickly sprinkled with black spots. This species has the reputation of not blooming freely.

Most common in cultivation and attaining a height of about 3 feet, *I. arguta* (syns. *Amphicome arguta, A. diffusa*) has leaves of seven to nine short-stalked, coarsely-toothed, lanceolate leaflets. Its more or less drooping flowers, in terminal and axillary racemes, are rosy-red and about 1½ inches long. The corolla tube narrows at its base. From 1 foot to 1½ feet tall and having usually upturned rose-pink and orange blooms, *I. emodii* (syn. *Amphicome emodii*) has leaves with up to fifteen mostly broad-ovate, coarsely-toothed leaflets. The flowers, in axillary racemes, are 1½ to 2 inches long and are more broadly bell-shaped than those of *I. arguta*.

Other incarvilleas that may be cultivated include *I. olgae* and *I. sinensis*. These have leafy stems and, at flowering time, little basal foliage. Easily distinguished from the other, 2- to 4-foot tall *I. olgae* has its leaves all opposite and only once-pinnate, whereas those of *I. sinensis* are twice-pinnate, and on the upper parts of the stems alternate. This is the only incarvillea with twice-pinnate foliage. The leaves of *I. olgae* are up to 6 inches long. They have three or four pairs of narrow-elliptic lateral leaflets, toothless or with one or two pairs of teeth toward their apexes. The flowers are in panicles, three to ten on each branch. From 1 inch to 1½ inches long and up to 1 inch wide, they are rosy-purple to light pink. Typical *I. sinensis* is an annual, perhaps not in cultivation. Its more familiar variety, perennial *I. s. variabilis* (syn. *I. variabilis*) is grown. This variable kind generally has pink or rosy-pink blooms. The yellow-flowered plant that has been called *I. farreri* is a yellow-flowered phase of *I. s. variabilis*.

Garden and Landscape Uses. Incarvilleas are worthwhile additions to perennial beds, and *I. emodii* is easily grown as an attractive spring-blooming greenhouse plant. With the exception of *I. sinensis* and relatively tender *I. s. variabilis*, the kinds discussed here are perennial and reasonably hardy, although in regions of hard winter freezing they are more in need than many perennials of winter covering with branches of evergreens, salt hay, or other loose material that admits air.

Cultivation. A porous, well-drained, nourishing soil that does not dry excessively suits incarvilleas. A warm, sheltered, sunny location, with just a little shade from the fiercest sun, is ideal. Planting is best done in early spring, but in mild regions fall planting is satisfactory. Propagation is by division in spring and by seed. Seedlings usually first flower when about three years old.

As a greenhouse plant *I. emodii* does well potted in fertile, porous soil that contains an abundance of peat and is watered often

enough to keep it always moderately moist, but not constantly saturated. A winter night temperature of 45 to 50°F is appropriate, with a rise of five or ten degrees during the day. In winter full sun is needed. Good specimens may be grown in 6- or 7-inch pots. When these are filled with roots regular applications of dilute liquid fertilizer should be given. During the summer, pot-grown specimens may be kept in cold frames or plunged to the rims of their containers in sand or ashes in a lightly shaded place outdoors. Propagation is by seeds sown in sandy peaty soil in spring and by removing side shoots from mature plants and using them as cuttings.

INCENSE-CEDAR is *Calocedrus decurrens*.

INCENSE PLANT is *Humea elegans*.

INCHWORM PLANT is *Senecio pendulus*.

INCHWORMS. See Cankerworms or Inchworms.

INCIENSO is *Encelia farinosa*.

INDIA and INDIAN. These words appear as parts of the common names of many plants including these: India-hawthorn (*Rhaphiolepis indica*), India-wheat (*Fagopyrum tataricum*), Indian-bean (*Catalpa bignonioides* and *C. speciosa*), Indian breadroot (*Psoralea esculenta*), Indian-cherry (*Rhamnus caroliniana*), Indian-cress (*Tropaeolum majus*), Indian cucumber-root (*Medeola virginiana*), Indian-currant (*Symphoricarpos orbiculatus*), Indian-fig (*Opuntia ficus-indica*), Indian-hemp (*Apocynum cannabinum*), Indian jujube (*Ziziphus mauritiana*), Indian-laburnum (*Cassia fistula*), Indian-lilac (*Melia azedarach*), Indian-millet (*Pennisetum americanum*), Indian-mulberry (*Morinda citrifolia*), Indian paint brush (*Castilleja affinis*), Indian physic (*Gillenia*), Indian-pink (*Dianthus chinensis, Lobelia cardinalis, Silene californica*), Indian pipe (*Monotropa uniflora*), Indian-rhododendron (*Melastoma malabathricum*), Indian shot (*Canna indica*), Indian-strawberry (*Duchesnea indica*), Indian-tobacco (*Nicotiana bigelovii, Lobelia inflata*), Indian tree spurge (*Euphorbia tirucalli*), Indian-turnip (*Arisaema triphyllum*), and Indian warrior (*Pedicularis densiflora*).

INDIGENOUS. An indigenous plant (an indigene or indigin) is a kind native to a particular region or country, but not necessarily to the exclusion of it being native elsewhere. Compare Endemic and Exotic.

INDIGO. See Indigofera. The word indigo also appears in these common names: bastard-indigo (*Amorpha fruticosa*), false-indigo (*Amorpha* and *Baptisia*), Indigo bush (*Dalea*), and wild-indigo (*Baptisia*).

INDIGOFERA (Indig-ófera) — Indigo. The species of shrubs and herbaceous peren-

nials of the pea family LEGUMINOSAE that constitute *Indigofera* number 700. Indigenous chiefly in the tropics and subtropics, they are respresented to a lesser degree in the floras of temperate regions, including the United States. From some species the dye indigo, the natural product now of very much less importance than it was before synthetic substitutes were developed, is obtained. The name comes from indigo and the Latin *fero*, bearing.

Indigoferas have alternate, toothless, generally pinnate leaves with a terminal as well as side leaflets. More rarely they have leaves with leaflets that spread in finger-fashion from the end of the leafstalk or have one undivided blade. Usually the stems and foliage are more or less silky with chiefly two-branched hairs. The prevailingly small, pea-like flowers, in racemes or spikes from the leaf axils, are purple, pink, or white. The keel is dilated or spurred on each side. There are ten stamens, nine of which are united and one free, and a single style. The fruits are cylindrical or angled pods. All kinds dealt with here are shrubs.

Hardy shrub indigoferas are not numerous. The most tolerant of cold, *I. kirilowii* of China and Korea, successfully braves winters throughout most of New England. Up to about 3 feet tall, this makes a dense growth of erect stems and spreads by sucker shoots. Its leaves, 4 to 6 inches long, are generally of seven to eleven, bristle-tipped, broadly-elliptic to obovate or somewhat lozenge-shaped leaflets ½ inch to 1¼ inches long and hairy on both surfaces. The rose-pink flowers are in erect, crowded racemes that with their stalks are 4 or 5 inches long. About as tall as the last, and hardy in southern New England, *I. potaninii,* of China, is esteemed particularly for its substantial display of lilac-pink flowers over a period of many weeks from early summer on, when few other hardy shrubs bloom. From 3 to 4½ feet tall, this upright species has leaves, hairy on both surfaces, of five to nine elliptic-oblong to obovate-oblong leaflets from ½ inch to a little over 1 inch long, and with a tiny point at the rounded apex. The flowers, ⅓ inch long, are in racemes 2 to 4½ inches in length, the stalks of which are as long as the leafstalks.

Long-blooming *I. amblyantha* is hardy in southern New England and is esteemed for the generous display of bloom it supplies from midsummer until fall. This attractive native of China is about 6 feet tall and bushy. Its leaves, hairy on both surfaces, are of seven to eleven elliptic to oblong-elliptic leaflets ½ inch to 1¼ inches long, rounded at their apexes and tipped with a brief, sharp point. The ¼-inch-long pale lilac to rosy-purple or nearly pink flowers are in crowded racemes 2½ to 4 inches long, the stalks of which are much shorter than those of the leaves. Variety *I. a. purdomii* has slightly larger blooms. The

Indigofera amblyantha

Indigofera incarnata

Indigofera incarnata alba

beautiful pure-white-flowered variety of *I. incarnata* (syn. *I. decora*) named *I. i. alba* is hardy in southern New England, although there its tops may be winter-killed. Both it and typical Chinese *I. incarnata*, which differs in the color of its flowers and in being less hardy than *I. i. alba*, are suckering shrubs about 1½ feet tall. Their leaves, hairless on their upper sides, sparsely-hairy beneath, are of seven to thirteen ovate-lanceolate leaflets 1 inch to 2½ inches long. The flowers, almost or quite ¾ inch in length, are in slender ra-

cemes 5 to 10 inches long, with stalks very much longer than those of the leaves. Those of *I. incarnata* are pink, with the standard or banner petal white except for its crimson-stained base.

Less hardy than the kinds, except pink-flowered *I. incarnata*, discussed above, those now to be considered do not usually persist in the north, although *I. gerardiana* may survive in climates not harsher than that of Philadelphia. That Himalayan species, sometimes misidentified in gardens as *I. dosua*, which name belongs to another Himalayan kind, is much branched and 3 feet high or higher. Its leaves, hairy on both surfaces, are of thirteen to twenty-one broad-elliptic to obovate leaflets ½ to ¾ inch long. Rosy-purple, the flowers, under ½ inch long, are in fairly dense, upright racemes 3 to 6 inches long. Larger leaves and rosy-purple flowers slightly over ½ inch long, and in pendulous racemes up to over 1½ feet in length, are characteristic of *I. pendula*, a 3-foot-tall or somewhat taller native of western China. Its leaves, of twenty-one to twenty-seven leaflets, are hairy on their undersides, less so above. Himalayan *I. hebepetala*, 3 feet tall or taller, has leaves with hairless upper surfaces and sparingly-hairy undersides. They have seven, nine, or rarely five or eleven broad-ovate to oblong leaflets 1 inch to 2¼ inches long. A little under to a little over ½ inch in length, the flowers have rose-pink wing petals and a crimson standard or banner one. They are in dense racemes 3½ to 8 inches long, the stalks of which equal the leafstalks in length.

The sources of commercial indigo are *I. tinctoria*, of tropical Asia, and *I. suffruticosa* (syn. *I. anil*), of the West Indies. The latter is naturalized in the southern United States and Hawaii. Neither are of decorative merit, but these kinds may occasionally be cultivated in collections of plants useful to man.

Garden and Landscape Uses. Chiefly of modest rather than striking decorative

Indigofera suffruticosa

merit, the cultivated indigoferas are esteemed for their habits of growth and because they bloom later than most shrubs and continue to do so over long periods. They are without colorful fall foliage. Except for *I. incarnata alba* their flowers run mainly to not especially inspiring rose-purples. White-flowered *I. incarnata alba* and *I kirilowii* are very satisfactory groundcovers, the latter too tall for small areas but excellent for expansive ones. Even though in cold climates the branches may be killed to the ground, the roots are likely to live. If they do, new shoots come in spring, grow quickly, and bloom the first year.

Cultivation. Indigoferas are for sunny locations and well-drained soils. Their demands on the gardener are few. Branches or parts of branches killed in winter should be removed or cut back in spring. At that time, too, any pruning needed to restrain the plants to size or to shape is done. Because indigoferas bloom on current season's shoots they can with impunity be pruned severely. Propagation is easy. Rooted suckers of some kinds may be dug up and transplanted in spring or early fall. Summer cuttings made of firm, short side shoots, preferably with a heel (sliver of the wood of the shoot on which the sideshoot grew) attached, may be rooted in a greenhouse propagating bench or in a cold frame, or root cuttings may be used. Seeds, prepared by pouring nearly boiling water over them and leaving them to soak overnight immediately prior to sowing, also give satisfactory results.

INDOOR LIGHT GARDENING. Chlorophyll-containing plants, which for practical purposes include all ordinarily cultivated plants except mushrooms, use the energy of light to synthesize the foods they need to live and grow. Denied light they die. If the available light is of too low intensity they become excessively lanky or sicken.

Under natural conditions the sun is the source of this needed energy, but artificial light can be and for long has been used to supplement sunlight and in more recent times to completely substitute for it. These procedures are the basic ones of the hobby called indoor light gardening.

The first recorded experiments with the use of artificial light for growing plants were conducted by the distinguished American horticulturist L. H. Bailey, in 1893. Dr. Bailey used carbon arc lamps to supplement daylight and concluded that light from them, if the arcs were enclosed in glass globes to filter out harmful ultraviolet rays, was effective in improving plant growth. Later experiments by the same and other investigators confirmed this finding and proved that light from incandescent bulbs, which is free of harmful rays, gives similar results. Cost, and the impossibility of supplying sufficiently intense illumination for worthwhile results without the heat from incandescent lamps harming the plants precluded the adoption of artificial light from these sources as a practical aid to plant growing.

The discovery of photoperiodism, the often critical effects of the relationship between day and night lengths on the blooming of many sorts of plants, in 1920, stimulated the employment of light from incandescent bulbs in both experimental and commercial horticulture. This was practicable because low light intensities affect photoperiodism and heat generated by the bulbs posed no problem.

Introduction of fluorescent lighting made possible from about 1940 on the use of intensities adequate alone and without daylight for the growth of many kinds of plants, and without troublesome heat. This giant step forward made indoor light gardening practicable.

The light sources now employed are fluorescent tubes and incandescent bulbs of the kind used for lighting homes. For scientific experiment other types are sometimes used. Incandescent lights as previously indicated have two disadvantages. They produce much less illumination per unit of electricity used than fluorescents and so are relatively costly to operate, and they give off so much heat that the tissues of plants kept too close to them are damaged and the relative humidity of the air is seriously lowered. They do have the advantage of supplying rays from the red end of the spectrum that many plants need to induce blooming. Fluorescent lamps are much cooler than incandescents and because they much more efficiently transform electric energy into light are less expensive to operate. But the light they emit is deficient in red rays, consisting largely of those of the blue-violet end of the spectrum. Although it is possible to greatly improve the growth of plants that receive some daylight by the use of either type of lamp alone where growing is done under artificial light only it is generally believed advantageous to achieve a balance by using fluorescent bulbs for the chief illumination and supplementing it with a comparatively small amount of light from incandescent bulbs.

Lighting set-ups for indoors vary greatly. Prefabricated units, often in the form of mobile carts with one to three shelves lighted, and fitted with casters, are sold, but most indoor light gardeners design and put together their own installations. They may be as simple as a purchased reflector unit fitted with a couple of 2-foot-long fluorescent tubes hung over a tray standing on a shelf or table or as elaborate as an entire closet or a small room completely fitted to give high intensity throughout. They may be purely utilitarian cellar- or attic-type installations, with sturdy benches to support the plant trays, and no-nonsense, comparatively massive frameworks of two by fours or other strong construction

An indoor light garden with facility for raising and lowering the fluorescent lights

A terrarium illuminated with fluorescent lights

A plant cabinet illuminated with fluorescent lights

to carry the lighting units, with perhaps exposed pulleys, chains, and counterweights to make raising and lowering them easy. Or they may be ornamental installations so well designed and executed that they add beauty and added elegance to living quarters and may indeed be their chief decorative features.

African-violets and other plants prospering in an indoor light garden

Begonias, African-violets, and other plants in a terrarium illuminated with fluorescent lights

Succulents and other plants thriving in a cabinet illuminated with fluorescent lights

Lighted areas are of two types, unenclosed in which the plants except for increased light live in environments essentially those of the rooms in which they are growing, and enclosed areas such as terrariums, cabinet-type light gardens, and wholly lighted growing rooms in which humidity and sometimes temperatures are maintained at different levels to those outside. A further division can be based on lighted areas that receive some natural light during the day and those dependent entirely on artificial illumination.

Plants in open areas may suffer from such local environmental disadvantages as drafts, insufficient humidity, and too-low temperatures for which increased light cannot compensate. But if such factors are reasonably favorable, additional light supplied where illumination, natural or artificial, is deficient will improve their health and growth. Even locating plants under ordinary room lamps, so long as they are not so close to incandescent bulbs that they are harmed by heat, helps growth. In large areas such as hotel lobbies spot lights trained on plants are of some benefit in prolonging ornamental usefulness, but are inadequate to ensure their permanent well-being.

Enclosed indoor light gardens have the great advantage of making possible higher levels of humidity around the plants than are usual in open rooms and of affording shelter from drafts. To avoid undesirable build-up of heat inside, it is advisable if practicable to have the lights, or with fluorescent tubes at least their ballasts, outside the enclosure. Otherwise it may be necessary to exhaust the heated air with a fan. Have the interiors, except the viewing sides, of terrarium and cabinet-type indoor light gardens coated with flat white paint so that as much light as possible is reflected on the plants.

Light intensity is obviously important. In even the most brilliantly lit indoor light gardens it cannot approach the approximately 10,000 foot candles that a summer day may afford outdoors. Fortunately all plants grow and most flourish with very much less intense illumination and may get along well and bloom freely with less than one-tenth that of a sunny day outdoors.

It is important to remember that the intensity of artificial light drops rapidly as distance from its source increases, with incandescent bulbs in direct proportion to that measurement but with fluorescent bulbs proportionate to the square of the distance. Thus 1 foot away from an incandescent bulb each square inch of surface receives half as much light as at 6 inches, but from a fluorescent tube only one-quarter as much. Much less light is radiated from the end 3 inches or so of fluorescent tubes than from their central parts. Because of this it is most efficient to use as long tubes as practicable. Light intensity also drops rapidly as one moves laterally away from the tubes. For practical purposes it is generally desirable to have plants 6 inches below two-tube reflectors occupy a strip not more than 1 foot wide and those 1 foot beneath the lights a band 1½ feet wide.

Measurement of the foot-candles of light received at a particular spot is most easily made with a foot-candle meter. These are not expensive and can be useful and instructive for an indoor light gardener to have. To read foot-candles with an ordinary photographer's light meter calls for complicated conversions.

Fluorescent tubes of many types are available, some especially designed for indoor light gardening, but many experienced growers are of the opinion that they give little or no advantages over standard commercial tubes of which the kind identified as cool white is one of the best. Others that are popular are those known as daylight, warm white, and natural light. Excellent results are had by having one daylight and one natural light tube in the same fixture. Standard commercial lamps are readily available in 2 and 4 feet lengths.

There are fluorescent lights that emit more light per unit of tube length than standard commercial types, but these necessitate the use of special fixtures. When incandescent bulbs are used to supplement fluorescent light, it is usual to employ them in a proportion by wattage of one to three or higher of that of the fluorescents.

Plants satisfied with low light intensities, such as many foliage types, get along with 300 foot-candles or even less. Flowering plants generally require a minimum of 400 or more foot-candles to bloom. With 1,000 foot-candles a very considerable range of plants can be grown and flowered satisfactorily.

As a guide to foot-candles delivered at different distances from various numbers of cool-white fluorescent tubes spaced not more than 3 inches apart the following table, based on information supplied by the United States Department of Agriculture, is helpful. As it indicates, light output falls off as the tubes age. The drop is normally from 5 to 12 percent after the first 2,000 hours of operation, and from 10 to 45 percent, with an average of 25 percent, at the end of their rated lives of 9,000 to 12,000 hours (which not all attain).

FOOTCANDLE ILLUMINATIONS
OF COOL WHITE FLUORESCENT LAMPS
AT DIFFERENT DISTANCES

Distance from lamps (inches)	After 200 hours use		4 lamps (new)
	2 lamps	4 lamps	
1	1100	1600	1800
2	860	1400	1600
3	680	1300	1400
4	570	1100	1260
5	500	940	1150
6	420	820	1000
7	360	720	900
8	330	660	830
9	300	600	780
10	280	560	720
11	260	510	660
12	240	480	600
18	130	320	420
24	100	190	260

Note: The figures given in this table are for spots centered below the lamps.

Lamp replacement is necessary from time to time and because of the reduced efficiency of aging fluorescents indoor light gardeners usually do this before the rated life of the bulb is reached. This is especially important if when the tubes are new the total illumination is but little more than the plants' minimum needs. Ratings for standard commercial tubes are 9,000 hours of operation, those for some other types longer. But these are averages rather than certain lives of individual tubes. If the tubes are lighted for sixteen hours a day 9,000 hours approximates one and one-half years of use. Instead of reaching for the maximum it is usually better to change tubes after six to nine months operation on a sixteen-hour daily basis.

Duration of lighting during each twenty-four-hour period has important effects on some plants. There are short-day sorts that to bloom must have fourteen hours of uninterrupted darkness each twenty-four hours, others that will not bloom unless they are lighted for at least that length of time each day, and there are many that are unaffected by the precise lengths of days and nights. Most plants favored by indoor light gardeners belong to the last two categories and with them exposure to lights for fourteen to sixteen hours a day seems to consistently produce the best results. But there is room for gardeners to experiment. Excellent results are had with marigolds, petunias, and some other plants under continuous twenty-four-hour-a-day illumination.

General management of indoor light gardens, apart from details connected with the lighting apparatus, is not basically different from that of growing plants in other indoor environments. Consideration must be given to temperatures, humidity, soils or soil substitutes, watering, misting foliage with water, fertilizing, sanitation, and sometimes alas, pest and disease control. Practically all plants do better if temperatures during the hours of darkness are lower by five to ten degrees than when they are lighted. Also, if light tends to be minimal for the needs of particular plants, it is better that temperatures be on the low side rather than excessive. Remember when measuring temperatures that it is those where the plants are that matter and under lights, these will almost surely be higher than in other parts of the room. The fertilizer needs of plants grown under lights are likely to be less than for the same sorts grown in greenhouses or elsewhere where they receive high natural light intensities. A good general rule is to use dilutions not more than one-quarter as concentrated as those suggested by the manufacturers, that is to dilute them with four times the amount of water recommended.

INDUSIUM. This is the name (plural indusia) of a small flap of membranous tissue that in most ferns covers or partly covers a collection of spore capsules.

INFLORESCENCE. The flowers of plants may be solitary or variously arranged in groupings or clusters called inflorescences. No satisfactory classification of the many types of inflorescences has been devised by botanists, and by gardeners, terms describing them are usually loosely applied. They include head, panicle, raceme, spike, and others mostly less familiar. In this Encyclopedia very specialized terms for particular types of inflorescences are avoided and those more commonly used by gardeners substituted, often with some flexibility of application.

INGA (Ín-ga) — Guama, Guaba. Differing from nearly all other members of the subfamily *Mimosoideae* of the pea family Leguminosae, in that its leaves are only once-pinnate (true also of a few species of *Pithecellobium*), the genus *Inga* consists of about 200 species of tropical trees and shrubs, natives of the Americas. Its name is a native West Indian one.

Ingas have opposite, two-ranked leaves with usually winged stalks and several medium-sized to large leaflets in pairs without a terminal one. The white or whitish flowers, solitary, in clustered heads or spikes from the leaf axils, or in panicles, have small tubular or bell-shaped, five- or six-lobed calyxes, funnel-shaped corollas of five petals joined up to or above their middles, numerous long-projecting stamens, and an awl-shaped style. The fruits are pods 3 to 8 inches long, often, but not in all species, with their seeds surrounded by sweet, edible pulp. In the American tropics the first two species described are the most important trees planted to shade coffee.

The guama (*I. laurina*), of Central America and the West Indies, is a round-headed, 50- to 70-foot-tall tree. It has hairless leaves, their brief stalks and midribs without wings. Each leaf has one to three, usually two, pairs of dark green, elliptic to ovate leaflets up to 4½ inches long by about one-half as wide. When there is more than one pair the basal leaflets are smaller than those above. The slightly fragrant, white flowers are in terminal and lateral, solitary or paired, bottle-brush-like spikes 2 to 6 inches long and 1 inch in diameter. The flat, blunt seed pods are 2 to 5 inches long.

The guaba (*I. vera* syn. *I. edulis*) is native to the West Indies, and from Mexico to Brazil. Variable, broad-headed, and up to 50 or 60 feet tall, it has slightly-hairy leaves 4 inches to 1 foot long, with three to six pairs of ovate to elliptic leaflets that increase in size from base to apex. The leafstalks, and midribs between the pairs of leaflets, are broadly-winged. White, and in short spikes, the pompon-like flowers of each spike open in daily succession,

but last for only a few hours. The individual blooms are up to 3 inches long by 3½ inches in diameter.

Native to Mexico and Costa Rica and cultivated in Hawaii and southern Florida, *I. paterno* is a tree of medium to large size that under favorable conditions grows rapidly, develops a good canopy, and begins to flower when five or six years old. Its blooms are white, in globose heads, and quite showy. This species has a general resemblance to the guama, but its leaves have six to eight leaflets. Its globose seed pods are up to 5 inches long by 2 inches wide.

Garden and Landscape Uses and Cultivation. Ingas are planted to some extent for shade and ornament in southern Florida, southern California, and Hawaii. They succeed under ordinary conditions in a variety of soils including those of limestone derivation. Propagation is by seed.

INGENHOUZIA (Ingen-hoùzia). One of a few species of *Ingenhouzia*, of the mallow family Malvaceae, is planted for ornament in California and other warm parts. The genus is related to cotton and by some botanists is included in the genus *Gossypium* to which cotton belongs. It consists of shrubs and subshrubs native of Mexico. The name commemorates the Dutch botanist Dr. Jan Ingen-Housz, who died in 1799.

A partly deciduous subshrub 4 to 10 feet tall, *I. triloba* has black-dotted stems and foliage. The leaves are alternate and long-stalked. The lower ones are three- or five-cleft nearly to their bases, in palmate-(handlike) fashion into lanceolate lobes. The upper ones are lanceolate or occasionally mitten-shaped. White, becoming pink as they age, with dark dots, the flowers have 1-inch-long, spreading petals. The fruits are spherical capsules.

Garden and Landscape Uses and Cultivation. A quite attractive ornamental that prospers without special care and gets along satisfactorily in poor soils, the species described above grows well in sunny locations. It is suitable for including in informal landscapes. Propagation is by seed and by cuttings.

INKBERRY is *Ilex glabra*.

INNOCENCE is *Collinsia heterophylla*.

INSECTICIDE. Substances used to kill insects are insecticides. In common usage, but not always not quite accurately, miticides (substances that kill mites), nematicides (substances that kill nematodes), and arachnicides (substances that kill spiders) are included. There are many insecticides, some mildly, some extremely effective, some harmless to man and other warm-blooded creatures, some deadly. Treat potentially harmful ones with great respect. Store them in safe containers under lock

and key. Handle them with care, taking appropriate precautions against harm. Essentially harmless to warm-blooded creatures are certain plant products, some now made synthetically. These include pyrethrum, rotenone, and ryania. Oil emulsions hold no threat, and malathion and Sevin are of very low toxicity to man and other warm-blooded animals.

Insecticides are employed as sprays, dusts, fumigants (substances used to produce killing vapors), and baits. Chiefly they are grouped as contact insecticides, those that kill upon contact, and stomach poisons, those that must be eaten by the insect to be effective. The former are chiefly used against sucking, the latter against biting or chewing insects.

Read labels on insecticides carefully, follow manufacturer's directions implicitly. Do not mix different sorts or mix them with fungicides or other materials before making quite sure they are compatible. Practical information on insecticides and their uses is available from Cooperative Extension Agents, and State Agricultural Extension Stations.

INSECTIVOROUS PLANTS. See Carnivorous or Insectivorous Plants.

INSECTS. Properly, insects include only animals classified by entomologists as belonging to the class *Insecta*, which is by far the most numerous class as to species of the larger group or phylum called the *Arthropoda*. This last includes at least three-quarters of all known kinds of living creatures that comprise the animal world. Here belong in addition to insects, mites, spiders, and ticks, which have eight legs, crabs, crayfish, lobsters, and sowbugs, with ten to fourteen legs, centipedes with numerous legs, one pair to each body segment, symphilids or garden centipedes with twenty-four legs, and millipedes with two pairs of legs on each segment of the body. Mites, sowbugs, spider mites, spiders, ticks, and a goodly number of other small creatures often loosely grouped by gardeners and others unschooled in entomology as insects are not. It is important to make the distinction because control measures effective with insects often fail with other creatures.

Insects, without backbones, have six jointed legs. They have an outer skeleton of a usually strong, plastic-like substance called chitin that surrounds and protects the softer internal parts. The life fluid or blood does not flow in veins, but freely through the body of the creature. The eyes are compound, consisting of many lenses.

Bodies of insects are divided into three parts, head, thorax, and abdomen. Openings along the body, called spiracles, terminate air tubes used for breathing. The majority of insects at maturity have one or two pairs of wings and a pair of antennae.

Feeding is done in one of three ways, and methods of controlling and killing insects are often tailored to the one employed. Sucking insects pierce the skin with a hollow beak and suck liquid nourishment. Rasping insects accomplish the same purpose by scarifying the skin and lapping the sap that exudes. Chewing or biting insects masticate solid food.

Insects have complex life histories. Familiarity with the particular patterns of specific kinds is frequently important to destroying or controlling them, the principle being that measures taken at stages in the life cycle when the creatures are particularly vulnerable are most likely to succeed. Eggs are the most common and usual method of insect multiplication. A few kinds, among those troublesome in gardens, notably aphids, produce without sexual process generations of living young between generations that come from eggs. This they do especially in summer. From the eggs hatch young nymphs that generally resemble the adult insects, or larvae, which are totally unlike the adult phase. Of familiar garden insects aphids and scales produce nymphs; flies, moths, and butterflies, larvae. The larvae are known as caterpillars, grubs, or worms. The last is rather unfortunate terminology because insects are not related to true worms.

Growth, that is, increase in size, of insects is accomplished by molting or shedding the skin and its replacement by one of larger size. This is done several times in the nymphal and larval stages before final assumption of the adult form. The last molt of nymphs is accompanied by a certain change of form called partial metamorphosis. Larvae undergo complete metamorphosis. This they do by pupating, surrounding themselves with protective cocoons or chrysalids from which, after a period of rest and change of form, adult, sexually mature insects emerge. In this last stage some insects, butterflies and moths, for example, feed little or not at all.

In their choice of foods some insects are highly selective. Many of importance to gardeners concentrate on one or few closely related kinds of plants. Others have much more catholic appetites and feed as opportunity affords on a wide selection. Yet a third group obtain sustenance from one sort of plant at one season or stage of development and from another at other times.

Sucking insects, infestations of which typically cause deformation, stunting, and sometimes wilting, especially of young parts of plants, include aphids, bugs, hoppers of various kinds, mealybugs, and scale insects. Rasping insects, such as thrips and the larval stages (grubs or maggots) of some flies, cause as a result of their scraping of surface tissues a scarring and color change, usually a more or less whitening of the affected parts. Chewing insects bite holes in leaves, flowers, and other plant parts or bore into tissues. Examples of these are beetles, borers, caterpillars, cutworms, and grasshoppers.

Methods of controlling harmful insects are very varied. Frequently they are related to feeding habits, contact insecticides for chewers, stomach poisons for suckers, for example. Chiefly, but not exclusively, controls involve the use of chemicals and these often have the disadvantage of eliminating beneficial as well as harmful insects and other small creatures. Aside from not employing chemicals when other effective methods are available, and never using them more often, in greater amounts, or at times other than those recommended by competent authorities, there is not much to be done about this. Nonchemical methods of reducing or eliminating insect pests include selection of resistant varieties, sanitary measures such as the elimination of weeds and cleaning up of plant debris, trapping, hand-picking, and encouraging predators.

Only a small proportion of the vast number of insect species are garden pests. Most are benign, some beneficial. Among insect friends bees are the most important. They pollinate flowers and so effect fruit and seed production. Other beneficial garden insects are aphid-lions, assassin bugs, ground beetles, lady beetles, praying mantids, syrphid flies, and some wasps. It is important to become acquainted with these insect friends.

Every gardener should learn to recognize the more common insects apt to be troublesome in his area, and the best available control methods. Cooperative Extension Agents and State Agricultural Experiment Stations are convenient and reliable sources of free information on these matters.

Some common insects, including other small or minute creatures that damage plants are discussed in this Encyclopedia under the entries Ants, Aphids, Armyworms, Bagworms, Bees, Beetles, Billbugs, Borers, Budworms and Budmoths, Bugs, Butterflies, Cankerworms or Inchworms, Casebearers, Caterpillars, Centipede (Garden), Chinch Bugs, Corn Earworms, Crickets, Curculios, Cutworms, Earwigs, Earthworms, Flies, Galls, Grasshoppers, Greenhouse Orthezia, Hornworms, Lace Bugs, Leaf Cutters, Leaf Hoppers, Leaf Miners, Leaf Rollers, Leaf Skeletonizers, Leaf Tiers, Mealybugs, Midges, Millipedes, Mites, Moths, Nematodes or Nemas, Plant Hoppers, Psyllids, Rootworms, Sawflies, Scale Insects, Slugs and Snails, Sowbugs and Pillbugs, Spanworms, Spittlebugs, Springtails, Termites, Thrips, Tree Hoppers, Walking Stick Insects, Wasps, Webworms, and Weevils.

INTERCROPPING or COMPANION CROPPING. The practice of growing two or more crops on the same land at the same time is called intercropping or companion cropping. It is most commonly done in intensively cultivated vegetable gardens. Properly managed it makes possible the harvesting of quite astonishing amounts of produce from limited areas. Most often crops interplanted are kinds that, when sown or planted about the same time, mature at different times. Radishes or spinach may be sown between rows of peas, and lettuce between those of cabbages or tomatoes. Radishes and carrots make good companion crops. Nearly always intercropping consists of pairing a crop that will occupy the ground for a fairly long season with one that matures quickly. The latter (often called a catch crop) is harvested before the later-maturing kind needs additional space. Many combinations other than those suggested can be worked out. Successful intercropping in vegetable gardens calls for adequate soil preparation, plentiful supplies of nutrients, and abundant water. Intercropping vegetables between rows of trees in newly planted orchards is also a common practice.

INULA (Ín-ula) — Elecampane. Restricted as natives to Europe, Asia, and Africa, with some kinds naturalized in North America, *Inula*, of the daisy family COMPOSITAE, comprises 200 species. Most are herbaceous perennials of temperate regions, the cultivated kinds hardy in the north. The name is their ancient Latin one.

Often more or less glandular, inulas have undivided, toothed or toothless, all basal or alternate stem leaves. Often they are large, sometimes rather coarse. Solitary or clustered, the flower heads are commonly yellow, and usually, like daisies, have both disk and ray florets. Rarely the rays (the petal-like florets encircling the central disk or eye) are white. The disk florets are bisexual. The rays are female and are three-toothed at their apexes. The involucre (collar at the back of the flower head) consists of several rows of bracts. The fruits are seedlike achenes.

Elecampane (*I. helenium*) a native of dampish soils in Europe and Asia, is nat-

Inula helenium

Inula helenium (flowers)

Inula magnifica

uralized from Nova Scotia to Missouri and North Carolina. Formerly it was employed medicinally. Its thick roots are candied and used for flavoring sweetmeats as well as absinthe and other liqueurs. Robust, thick-rooted, stout-stemmed, and coarse-foliaged, this kind is up to 6 feet tall, and has branched stems. Its leaves are bristly-hairy above, soft-velvety-hairy on their under surfaces, and toothed. Elliptic-oblong, the basal leaves, up to 2 feet long, narrow to their stalks. The stem leaves are pointed-oblong-ovate, heart-shaped at their bases, and stalkless. Sometimes solitary, more commonly in loose clusters, the flower heads are long-stalked, bright yellow, and 2 to 4 inches wide. The outer bracts of their involucres are leafy. Himalayan *I. racemosa* differs from elecampane in having short-stalked or practically stalkless flower heads in racemes. They are 2 to 3 inches in diameter and yellow, with very narrow ray florets. This is 2 to 5 feet high. Its leaves have white-hairy undersides and are rough-hairy above. The basal ones are stalked and up to 1½ feet long. Those on the stems are stalkless. Also very robust and up to 6 feet tall or taller, *I. magnifica* of the Caucasus, has the stems and undersides of its elliptic-ovate to ovate leaves hairy. The largest lower leaves may be 1 foot long. The flower heads, large and clustered, are yellow.

Solitary, orange-yellow flower heads 3 to 4 inches wide or sometimes wider, with slender, hairy involucral bracts, are borne by *I. grandiflora,* of the Caucasus and Himalayas. One of the earliest inulas to bloom, this opens its first flowers in June. It is 2 to 4 feet tall, and has branchless, hairy stems and hairy foliage. The stems

Inula orientalis

are leafy throughout. The leaves are heavily glandular. They are stalkless, distinctly toothed, and elliptic-oblong. From the last, *I. orientalis* (syn. *I. glandulosa*) of the Caucasus, differs in its leaves at most being very slightly toothed and with distantly spaced glands along their margins. The basal ones are oblong-spatula-shaped, narrowed at their bases, the upper ones have somewhat heart-shaped bases. The rather shaggy, yellow flower heads are 3 inches wide or wider. In *I. o. laciniata* the golden-yellow ray florets are fringed and tend to be semipendulous. The flower heads of *I. o. superba* are larger than those of the typical species.

Others with usually solitary flower heads are *I. royleana* and closely related *I. macrocephala.* The first, one of the most handsome, is a native of the Himalayas, the

Inula hookeri

other of the Caucasus. Up to 2 feet in height, *I. royleana* has branchless stems and hairy, slightly toothed leaves narrowed to winged stalks. The basal ones are ovate to oblong and up to nearly 1 foot long. The upper leaves are eared or heart-shaped at their bases. The orange-yellow flower heads, 3 to 4 inches across, are on thick, hairy stalks. In the bud stage they are black. From the last, *I. macrocephala,* of the Caucasus, differs in being taller, coarser, and having its upper leaves narrowed at their bases. Native of the Himalayas, *I. hookeri* has sparingly-branched stems 1 foot to 2 feet tall, and minutely-toothed, stalkless or short-stalked, oblong-lanceolate leaves up to about 4 inches long.

One of the more attractive kinds, *I. ensifolia* is 1 foot to 2 feet tall. Its stems are erect and not branched. Slender, pointed, and linear-lanceolate, the stalkless leaves

Inula ensifolia

of this European and Asian species have several nearly parallel veins. Except at their margins they are hairless. The flower heads are yellow, and 1 inch to 2 inches wide. The lanceolate bracts of their involucres are cobwebby-hairy. Usually somewhat taller than *I. ensifolia* and with the upper parts of its erect stems mostly branched, *I. salicifolia* has oblong-lanceolate, stem-clasping, net-veined leaves with heart-shaped bases. Except along their margins and on the veins of their undersides they are hairless. The golden-yellow flower heads are 1 inch to 1½ inches across. This is a native of Europe and Asia.

Unfortunately not known in cultivation, *I. rhizocephaloides* would make a delightful addition to rock gardens. This Himalayan species forms a ground-hugging rosette of foliage 3 or 4 inches wide with at the center several stalkless, 1-inch-wide flower heads with short ray florets.

Garden and Landscape Uses and Cultivation. Tall inulas are generally too coarse and robust to fit graciously into flower beds, but the lower kinds can be used effectively in such places. The higher ones are better reserved for colonizing in semi-wild and naturalistic areas. Elecampane may be allotted a place in herb gardens and collections of medicinal plants. All kinds are of the easiest cultivation in any ordinary, not excessively dry soil. They do best in full sun and are readily increased by division and seeds. Elecampane can also be propagated by root cuttings. Plants raised from seeds usually bloom in their second year. If sown early, those of *I. ensifolia* may flower the first year.

INVOLUCRE. This is a whorl or collar of bracts or small leaves positioned immediately below (behind) a flower or cluster or head of flowers. Involucres are easily recognizable in the flower heads of the daisy family COMPOSITAE, which includes such familiar garden plants as asters, chrysanthemums, dahlias, daisies, marigolds, and zinnias.

IOCHROMA (Io-chròma). The genus *Iochroma*, of the nightshade family SOLANACEAE, numbers twenty-five species of nonhardy shrubs and small trees of Central and South America. A few are cultivated as ornamentals, and in South America the fruits of at least one, *I. cornifolium*, are eaten. The name, alluding to the flower color of some kinds, comes from the Greek *ion*, violet, and *chroma*, color.

Iochromas have shoots and foliage thickly or sparsely furnished with stellate (star-shaped) hairs, or hairless. Their leaves, alternate or grouped, are undivided and without lobes or teeth. The flowers, in pairs or clusters, have five-lobed calyxes and tubular or slender trumpet-shaped corollas with narrow or flaring faces with five short lobes (petals), and with folds or appendages partially closing their throats. There are five stamens and one style. The blooms are blue, purple, red, yellow, or white. The fruits are spherical to more or less egg-shaped berries.

Beautiful *I. cyaneum* of Ecuador, has long been cultivated under the unacceptable names of *I. tubulosum* and *I. lanceolatum*. This softly grayish-downy shrub is 4 to 6 feet or somewhat more in height and has pointed-elliptic to oblong-lanceolate or ovate leaves 2 to 6 inches long and up to one-third as broad. In clusters from near the branch ends the blue-lavender to purple flowers droop. They are 1½ to 2½ inches long by 1 inch or more across their faces.

Iochroma cyaneum

Native of Central America, *I. coccineum* has pubescent shoots and sharp-pointed, ovate to oblong leaves 3 to 5 inches long, hairy along the veins on their undersides. The yellow-throated, scarlet blooms, 1½ to 2 inches long and nearly or quite ¾ inch across their faces hang in clusters.

From those described above *I. fuchsioides*, of Peru, differs in being almost or quite hairless. It has blunt, ovate to obovate leaves 2 to 4 inches in length, and orange-scarlet to coral-red blooms with yel-

Iochroma coccineum

Iochroma coccineum (flowers)

low throats, 1½ to 2 inches long and more than ½ inch across the shallowly-five-lobed face of the bloom.

Garden and Landscape Uses and Cultivation. The cultivated iochromas are charming garden shrubs in climates where little or no frost is experienced and where warm, sunny weather prevails for most of the year, as in California. They are also attractive for growing in conservatories and greenhouses either in ground beds or pots or tubs. They need little attention. Moderately fertile, well-drained soil that does not dry excessively suits them, and sunny locations. They root readily from cuttings and can be raised from seeds. Pruning to shape and to control size, when needed, may be done after flowering. In greenhouses spring is the best time to attend to this, then too, repotting may be given attention. Indoors, winter night temperatures of 50 to 55°F are satisfactory, with daytime increases of five to fifteen degrees depending upon the brightness of the day. Watering should be generous from spring to fall, more restrained in winter. Plants that have filled their containers with roots benefit from applications of dilute liquid fertilizer from spring to fall.

IONE (I-ò-ne). The about seven species of *Ione*, of the orchid family ORCHIDACEAE, are natives from Thailand to Burma and the Himalayas. The name is derived from that of one of the Nereides (sea nymphs) of Greek mythology.

Tree-perching (epiphytic) orchids, iones are rare in cultivation. From *Bulbophyllum*, which they much resemble, they differ in the lip of the flower not being movable and in other technical floral details. Their clustered pseudobulbs have each one leaf. The flowers, small and in spikes of often many, are of muted colors and have petals smaller than the sepals, the lateral ones usually united. The lip is comparatively large.

From a short creeping rootstock *I. paleacea,* of Assam, develops pseudobulbs 1 inch to 1½ inches long. The scarcely stalked, broad-linear leaves are 6 to 8 inches long. Exceeding them in length, the erect flowering stalks terminate in a spike of many pendulous, 1-inch-long blooms with red-striped, pale green sepals and small, round, yellow-green petals. As long as the sepals, the trowel-shaped lip is red-brown.

Garden Uses and Cultivation. These are as for *Bulbophyllum*. For additional information see Orchids.

IONETTIA. This is the name of orchid hybrids the parents of which are *Comparettia* and *Ionopsis.*

IONIDIUM. See Hybanthus.

IONOCIDIUM. This is the name of orchid hybrids the parents of which are *Ionopsis* and *Oncidium.*

IONOPSIDIUM (Ionopsíd-ium) — Diamond Flower. One not too-well-known member of the mustard family CRUCIFERAE is the only species of *Ionopsidium*. It is the violet-cress or diamond flower, a charming little native of Portugal and North Africa. Its name comes from the Greek *ion*, violet, *opsis*, appearance, and *eidos*, form, and literally means a plant resembling a violet in form. The application is not especially apt.

The violet-cress (*I. acaule*) is very low and nearly stemless. It sends out slender, leafy runners. Its glabrous, long-stalked, toothless, almost round leaves are under ½ inch across, and its flowers, violet, lilac, or white, are fragrant and about ⅜ inch in diameter. They are solitary on long slender stalks and have four sepals, four spreading petals, six stamens, and one style. The fuits are capsules. Although perennial, the violet-cress is most often grown as an annual.

Garden Uses. This diminutive plant is useful in rock gardens and for crevices in flagstone paths and terraces and is also at-

Ionopsidium acaule

tractive in pans (shallow pots) in cool greenhouses. It does not withstand high temperatures well, nor is it winter hardy where severe freezing is experienced.

Cultivation. Any well-drained, fairly fertile, moist garden soil is suitable for *Ionopsidium*. Seeds sown thinly outdoors in early spring where the plants are to bloom give satisfactory results. For winter and spring blooming in greenhouses, where a minimum winter night temperature of 50°F is maintained, sow seed in September in pans. Scatter them thinly and allow the plants to develop without transplanting. When flower buds develop the pans may be transferred to a temperature of 55 to 60°F. Plants grown in this way need full sun throughout the winter, but outdoors the violet-cress needs shade from strong sun in late spring and summer.

IONOPSIS (Ion-ópsis)—Violet Orchid. Orchids to the number of about ten species belong in *Ionopsis*, of the orchid family ORCHIDACEAE. They are indigenous from southern Florida to Mexico, Bolivia, Paraguay, and the Galapagos Islands. The name is from the Greek *ion*, a violet, and *opsis*, like. Both its scientific and colloquial names refer to the form rather than color of the flowers.

This genus is epiphytic. This means its members perch on trees, but do not take nourishment from them. Mostly small and of neat habit, violet orchids have very small pseudobulbs. Their leaves are usually stiff and narrow. The flowers are in loose panicles terminating stems that come from the bases of the pseudobulbs. The two lateral sepals are united behind the bottom of the lip to form a small pouch. The upper sepal and two petals are free. Comparatively large, the lip has a pair of small protrusions at its base. The short column has the anther at its apex.

The only species native to the United States, *I. utricularioides* is wild from southern Florida to Central America, the West Indies, and tropical South America. It has short fans of flat, spreading leaves up to 7 inches long by ¾ inch wide. The

pseudobulbs are scarcely large enough to be recognized as such. The slender-stalked panicles, up to 10 inches long, are of from few to as many as seventy dainty blooms, white to pink, often veined or marked with purple. The most prominent feature of the flower is a two-lobed, obovate lip much narrowed to its base and almost or quite ½ inch wide. Native to the West Indies and Trinidad, *I. satyrioides* is nearly or quite without pseudobulbs. Its pointed-cylindrical leaves are 2 to 5 inches long. The flowering stalks, sometimes branched, are up to 6 inches long. The usually few flowers, about ¼ inch long, scarcely open. They are creamy-white sometimes veined with pale lilac. The lobeless lip is scarcely longer than the sepals.

Garden Uses and Cultivation. These orchids are delightful for collections. In warm, humid climates they may be grown on trees outdoors. The Florida species seems to do especially well attached to even quite small branches of citrus trees. They may also be accommodated on slabs of tree fern fiber and in very well-drained pans (shallow pots) containing chopped tree fern or osmunda fiber. They need good light, and watering throughout the year, more copiously when they are growing freely than in winter. Because they are very intolerant of root disturbance, potting should not be done oftener than necessary and then with great care. In intervening years at about the time new growth begins, as much of the old, exhausted rooting medium as can be removed without injuring the roots should be teased away and replaced with new. It has been suggested that these orchids are naturally rather short-lived. Be that as it may, they rarely persist for more than a few years in cultivation. For additional information see Orchids.

IPECAC is *Cephaelis ipecacuanha*. False-ipecac is *Psychotria emetica*, American-ipecac *Gillenia stipulata*.

IPHEION (Íph-eion)—Spring Starflower. The only cultivated species of this genus of the lily family LILIACEAE has suffered under the burden of a number of names. At various times it has been *Brodiaea uniflora*, *Triteleia uniflora*, *Milla uniflora*, and now *Ipheion uniflorum*. Its common name is spring starflower, an appropriate enough designation, because it produces a profusion of quite exquisite starry blooms well before summer comes. The meaning of the name *Ipheion* is unexplained.

The genus that concerns us consists of twenty-five species and is indigenous from Mexico to South America. The cultivated kind has a wide range in Argentina and Uruguay.

The spring starflower (*I. uniflorum*) is a charming, low bulb plant with all basal foliage and usually solitary, rarely paired, blooms atop leafless stalks. Mostly there is

A border of a double-flowered variety of
Impatiens wallerana

Ilex cassine

Impatiens New Guinea hybrid

Impatiens niamniamensis 'Congo Cockatoo'

Incarvillea delavayi

Single-flowered variety of *Impatiens wallerana*

Ipheion uniflorum

Inula ensifolia

Ipomoea purpurea

Ipomopsis rubra

Ipomoea pes-caprae

Ipheion uniflorum

Ipheion uniflorum (flowers)

only one flower stalk from each bulb, occasionally two. They are 6 to 9 inches tall. The blooms face upward and have tubular perianths with six spreading, pointed-elliptic to lanceolate-ovate lobes (petals, or more truly, tepals). The strongly marked green and purple mid-veins of the petals are continued down the perianth tubes. There are six fertile stamens in two circles. They do not protrude. The short style has three dark green veins and is capped by a knoblike stigma. Most characteristically the body color of the flowers is some shade of pale lavender-blue, but there is considerable variation and plants with white flowers occur. Also reported is a variation with flowers with more than the usual six petals that are white with pink midribs.

Garden Uses. The spring starflower is one of extremely few plants native to the southern hemisphere that is reliably hardy as far north as New York City. In well-drained soil in a fairly sheltered location outdoors it has persisted for more than two decades at The New York Botanical Garden and slowly increased. It is delightful for rock gardens, the fronts of flower borders and shrub borders, and other intimate sites. It is also excellent for growing in pots for the decoration of greenhouses,

and success may even be had in windows in cool rooms.

Cultivation. Exposure to full sun, and sharply-drained, nourishing earth of a somewhat sandy character are best for this plant. The bulbs are planted outdoors, 3 inches apart, in late summer or early fall, with their tops 3 inches beneath the surface. Once planted they may remain undisturbed for several years, until their flower production shows signs of deteriorating. Then, they are dug up, sorted to size, and replanted, preferably in a new location. An application of a complete fertilizer of a type suitable for bulbs, given each early spring, encourages vigor. The foliage dies after flowering, but reappears in fall. In cold climates the provision of a light winter covering of pine branches or those of other evergreens is recommended.

Greenhouse cultivation is simple. The bulbs are planted several together, with the distance between individuals about equaling the diameter of the bulbs, in pots or pans (shallow pots) in late summer or early fall. The soil must be fertile and porous, the containers well drained. The tips of the bulbs are covered to a depth of about ½ inch. After planting, the containers are buried to their rims in sand, peat moss, or other suitable material outdoors or in a cold frame. They are brought indoors before the ground freezes solidly and are accommodated where the night temperature is 40 to 45°F and the day temperature is not more than a few degrees higher. Watering is done to keep the soil evenly moist, but not constantly wet. From February onward the night temperature may be as high as 50°F, although this is not necessary, and day temperatures correspondingly higher. Occasional applications of dilute liquid fertilizer stimulate strong growth. After blooming, when the foliage begins to die naturally, watering is gradually reduced and, finally, the soil is dried completely and the bulbs are rested, in the pots, in an airy, shaded place. In August the bulbs are shaken free of old soil and repotted in new.

IPOMOEA (Ip-omoèa)—Ipomea, Morning Glory, Moonflower, Sweet-Potato, Cypress-Vine, Cardinal Climber. Modern botanists combine the moonflowers (previously *Calonyction*) with the morning glories in the one genus *Ipomoea*. Also included are the plants previously named *Quamoclit* and *Pharbitis*. Under this arrangement *Ipomoea* comprises about 500 species, chiefly of the tropics and subtropics of the Americas and the Old World. The group is closely related to *Convolvulus*, and some of its members at times have been so named. It is included in the morning glory family CONVOLVULACEAE. The name *Ipomoea* comes from the Greek *ips*, a worm, a word later used by Linnaeus for

the bindweed (*Convolvulus*), and *homoios*, resembling. The plant sometimes named *I. microdactyla* is *Exogonium microdactylum*.

Other plants sometimes treated as *Ipomoea* are the woodrose (*Merremia tuberosa* syn. *Ipomoea tuberosa*), some other species of *Merremia*, and the plant treated in this Encyclopedia as *Mina lobata* (syn. *Ipomoea lobata*).

Despite the very different growth habits found in *Ipomoea*, which includes twining vines, bushy herbaceous plants, shrubs, and trees, the flowers of all are remarkably similar in structure. They are solitary or in clusters in the leaf axils and are funnel- or bell-shaped or, in the species previously included in *Quamoclit* and *Calonyction*, salverform (with slender corolla tubes and a widely spreading limb or face). The calyx is five-lobed and persistent, the corolla usually five-angled or five-lobed. There are five stamens and one style. The stigmas are more or less spherical. The fruits are capsules.

Ipomeas include annuals and deciduous evergreen perennials. Their leaves are alternate and may be undivided or divided into separate leaflets, and be with or without lobes. Some kinds contain milky sap, others watery sap.

Undoubtedly the most important species is the sweet-potato (*I. batatas*), one of the basic food plants of the world. For it see Sweet-Potato. Another that provides food for man in the warm parts of eastern Asia is *I. aquatica* (syn. *I. reptans*). This native of swamps and marshy places is grown as a vegetable. The purging drug jalap is a product of *I. purga*, a woodland native of Mexico. The seeds of *I. tricolor* contain small amounts of the drug LSD.

The annuals and kinds commonly grown as annuals include a number of popular garden plants. Here belongs the common morning glory (*I. purpurea*), a tall, hairy-stemmed, tropical American vine with heart-shaped or three-lobed leaves up to 5 inches long and pale-tubed, funnel-shaped,

Ipomoea purpurea

Ipomoea purpurea (flowers)

Ipomoea tricolor

purple and pale reddish flowers 2 to 2½ inches long, solitary or few together. An identifying feature is that the ½-inch-long sepals are conspicuously bristly toward their bases. White-flowered and double-flowered varieties of this species occur, as well as one, *I. p. huberi*, with variegated foliage. A favorite morning glory, actually a tender perennial, but often grown as an annual, is *I. tricolor* (syn. *I. rubro-caerulea*), a tropical American species commonly represented in cultivation by its variety 'Heavenly Blue'. Stems and foliage of these plants, which are fast-growing vines up to a height of 20 feet, are without hairs. The heart-shaped leaves have hollow stalks. They are 3 to 5 inches long and of thin texture. The funnel-shaped blooms, 3 to 4 inches long and wide, in clusters of three or four, have white corolla tubes, are reddish in bud, but open to a fine purple or glorious azure-blue. A characteristic feature of this species is that the linear sepals are only about ¼ inch long. Some varieties of it have blooms blotched with white. Drawn-out sepals, 1 inch long or longer, and not spreading, as well as other characteristics, distinguish *I. nil* from the two previous species.

Its sepals are bristly-hairy at their bases. A native of the Old World tropics and occurring spontaneously in those of the New World, although probably as an introduction, this species is a strong-growing, smooth-stemmed vine of annual or perennial duration. Its basically heart-shaped leaves, up to 6 inches across, may be shallowly-three-lobed. The white-tubed, pale to bright blue, purple or red, funnel-shaped flowers are solitary or in clusters of up to three. They are 2 to 2½ inches long. Many highly developed horticultural varieties, some with double flowers, some with fluted and frilled blooms of various colors and combinations, some with variegated foliage, are grown. Here belongs popular 'Scarlet O'Hara', and the Imperial Japanese morning glories. The annual *I. hederacea* is a tropical American kind very similar to *I. nil*, but differing in being less robust, having smaller leaves, and flowers only 1 inch to 2 inches long with spreading or recurved sepals. This species is naturalized in North America. Varieties *I. h. grandiflora* and *I. h. superba* have bigger flowers.

Annual kinds, with flowers not funnel shaped and with protruding stamens and styles, that were previously named *Quamoclit*, include two species and one hybrid that enjoy considerable popularity. The cypress-vine (*I. quamoclit* syn. *Quamoclit pennata*) is 10 to 20 feet tall. A nonhairy, slender, graceful vine, a native of South America and naturalized in warmer parts of North America, it has short-stalked leaves 2 to 7 inches in length, pinnately-divided into eight to eighteen pairs of slender, almost hairlike segments. The flowers, up to ¾ inch across, are one to few together on long stalks. Brilliant red or more rarely white, they have corolla tubes slender below and broadening above, ¾ inch to 1½ inches long, and five wide-spreading, short corolla lobes (petals). The sepals are not tipped with bristles. The star ipomea (*I. coccinea* syn. *Quamoclit coccinea*) is a hairless vine up to 10 feet tall. Its slender-stalked, angular or toothed, ovate leaves are 2 to 6 inches long. The flowers, two to several on stalks that are as long as or longer than the leaves, have corollas with slender tubes ¾ inch to 1½ inches long, and an obscurely lobed, cup-shaped limb (face) ½ inch or rather more across. The sepals are pressed against the corollas and end in bristles. The seed capsules of this species turn downward, a feature that distinguishes it from the next. Very similar to the last, but with erect seed capsules is *I. hederifolia* (syn. *Quamoclit coccinea hederifolia*), native to tropical America. The leaves of this are three- to five-lobed, and its brilliant red or orange flowers are often somewhat larger than those of the star ipomea. The cardinal climber (*I. multifida* syns. *I. sloteri*, *Quamoclit sloteri*) is a hybrid between *I. coccinea* and *I. quamoclit*. A tall, hairless, free-flowering, annual vine, it has broadly triangular-heart-shaped leaves deeply-fingered into seven

to fifteen long-pointed lobes from ⅛ to ½ inch wide. The leaves are 2 to 4½ inches across. The bright red blooms have white eyes. Their corolla tubes, 1½ to 2 inches long, end in a limb (face) ½ to ⅔ inch in diameter. The tips of the outer, and sometimes the inner, sepals have short bristles.

Moonflower is the common name of species of *Ipomoea* that bloom at night and have big white or purple blooms with long corolla tubes that expand abruptly into a large, flat limb or face from which the stamens and style protrude. Tender perennials, these kinds were previously separated as the genus *Calonyction*. Some are commonly cultivated as annuals. The most popular, *I. alba* (syns. *I. bona-nox*, *Calonyction aculeatum*) is a milky-juiced, nearly or quite hairless vine 10 to 20 feet tall or taller. Native of the tropics, it occurs spontaneously in southern Florida. Its heart-shaped, angular or three-lobed, long-stalked, pointed leaves are 3 to 8 inches across. The fragrant, white or slightly greenish-white flowers, one to seven on stalks 2 to 6 inches long, pop open in the evening and usually close by morning, but sometimes remain open until noon. They have sepals about ½ inch long, corolla tubes 3 to 6 inches long, and across the face of the bloom measure 3 to 6 inches. Native chiefly of coastal areas in the tropics and occurring in Florida, *I. tuba* (syns. *I. grandiflora*, *Calonyction tuba*) differs from the last chiefly in having thicker, lobeless leaves and broad, blunt, rather than narrow and pointed sepals. Purple or purplish flowers up to 3 inches across distinguish *I. muricata* from the other kinds of moonflowers here discussed.

Vining morning glories grown as perennials in warm climates and in greenhouses are fairly numerous. The blue dawn flower (*I. acuminata*) is commonly cultivated. A vigorous, free-flowering species with stems up to 40 feet long, it has heart-shaped, sometimes three-lobed leaves and funnel-shaped blue or purplish blooms that exhibit a tinge of red. They are 2 to 3½ inches long and mostly three to five on a stalk. Sometimes confused with *I. purpurea*, this kind can be distinguished by its narrow sepals being finely-hairy, but not bristly. It is a native of South America. Except for its silvery, softly-hairy leaves *I. mutabilis* is scarcely distinguishable from the last and should probably be regarded as a variety of it and named *I. acuminata leari*. It also is called blue dawn flower. Very showy because of its profusion of deep pink to bright red, bell-shaped blooms, *I. horsfalliae* has somewhat woody stems up to 30 feet in length. Native to the West Indies, it has hairless, thickish, roundish leaves, deeply-cleft or completely divided into five or seven lobes or fingers. The flowers, several together on the stalks, are about 2½ inches long. They have broad sepals about ½ inch long. Variety *I. h. briggsii* has bright magenta-crimson blooms. Closely related to *I. horsfalliae*, which should perhaps be regarded as a variety of it, is white-flowered *I. ternata*. This has white, trumpet-shaped blooms 2 inches in diameter, and leaves of three leaflets.

The Brazilian morning glory (*I. setosa* syn. *I. melanotricha*) is distinguished by its robust stems, like its leafstalks and flower stalks, clothed with stiff, purplish hairs. Its roundish-toothed leaves, 5 to 10 inches in diameter and conspicuously heart-shaped at their bases, are mostly deeply-three-lobed with the center lobe markedly narrowed at the bottom. The fleshy flower stalks carry three to nine rose-purple flowers with narrow tubes and spreading, flattish faces. They are 2 to 3 inches long by 2 to 4 inches wide.

A tuberous-rooted, vining morning glory of vigorous, rapid growth and native of the American and Old World tropics, *I. mauritiana* (syn. *I. paniculata*) has long been misidentified as *I. digitata*. The latter name correctly belongs to a rare species endemic to

Ipomoea mauritiana

Haiti. The more widely distributed plant is hairless and has rounded to somewhat kidney-shaped leaves up to 7 inches across and commonly cut into three to nine narrow lobes. The reddish-purple, lilac, or pinkish funnel- to bell-shaped flowers 2 to 2½ inches long have broad sepals ⅓ inch long that hug the base of the corolla tube. The flower stalks carry two to several blooms. Another tuberous-rooted vine, sometimes known as railroad creeper, is *I. cairica*, a native of the Old World tropics now naturalized in other warm regions. A rampant grower, it has warty older stems and is hairless. Its leaves are very deeply cut into five or seven elliptic lobes and 2 inches in length. From one to several on a stalk, the reddish-purple to purple flowers, deepening in color toward their centers, are up to 2½ inches long and broad.

A shrub rather straggly and with a decided tendency to climb, *I. fistulosa* contains milky sap and has heart-shaped leaves softly-hairy on their undersides and stalks. The flowers, up to 3 inches long and as wide, are solitary or two or more on a stalk. They are purplish and have rounded sepals.

One of the most rampant morning glories, a prominent inhabitant of beaches in many parts of the tropics and subtropics, including the Gulf Coast of the United States, is *I. pes-caprae*. This produces usually nontwining stems that snake over the ground sometimes to a length of 60 feet and roots that reach several feet into the ground. Its thick leaves, elliptic to nearly round, are notched or lobed at their ends. The funnel-shaped, pink to reddish-purple blooms deepen in color toward their centers and are about 2 inches long. Except as a sand binder this species has no horticultural importance.

A hardy herbaceous perennial, the wild-sweet-potato vine (*I. pandurata*) is a trailing or twining native from Connecticut to Florida and Texas. It has large, deep-seated, tuberous roots and can become a weed difficult to eradicate. Its leaves, up to 6 inches across, are broadly-heart-shaped, fiddle-shaped, or three-lobed. The blooms are white with purple throats, broadly-funnel-shaped, and one to five on a stalk. They are about 4 inches wide.

The bush morning glory (*I. leptophylla*) is a perennial, non-vining native of dry soils from Nebraska and Wyoming to Texas and New Mexico. It has huge tuberous roots and branching stems that form a bush 2 to 4 feet in height. The linear, undivided leaves are up to 5 inches long. Rose-pink deepening to purple in their throats, the abundant funnel-shaped flowers make a fine display over a long summer period. They are 3 inches in diameter and one to a stalk.

Garden and Landscape Uses. The principal uses of morning glories, moonflowers, and other cultivated members of the genus *Ipomoea* are as twining, quick-growing,

Ipomoea leptophylla

flowering vines for the adornment of pergolas, arches, porches, fences, trellises, walls, and other supports. A few make attractive greenhouse pot plants. Most reward the cultivator generously and even magnificently. None is difficult to grow. They adapt to a wide variety of sites and soils. In general they prefer well-drained, loamy soil of at least moderate fertility and with ample moisture, but some, such as the hardy bush morning glory (*I. leptophylla*) and the tropical *I. pes-caprae*, flourish in dry soils and dry climates. Practically all are sun-lovers. Even those that will grow in some shade usually do not bloom well under such conditions. Most of the perennial species are not hardy in the north, the bush morning glory and the wild-sweet-potato vine are. The former has been successfully cultivated outdoors at The New York Botanical Garden, but for its best response it needs drier conditions than the climate New York provides. In suitable climates the bush morning glory is attractive for borders and naturalistic plantings.

Cultivation. Ipomeas of kinds commonly grown as perennials are usually raised from division of the roots, cuttings of firm, well-ripened shoots, by layering, and occasionally by grafting onto the roots of their own kind or other species. The last technique is often employed with *I. horsfalliae*, cuttings of which do not root readily and which is shy about producing seeds. Annual ipomeas and those most frequently cultivated as such, and perennials at times, are raised from seeds. To facilitate germination it is advisable to cut a little notch in each with a file or to soak the seeds for several hours in tepid water before sowing. They may be sown outdoors in spring where the plants are to remain, but in the north it is advantageous to start them earlier (six to eight weeks before the plants are to be set in the garden) indoors and to plant them out after the weather is warm and settled. By allowing the roots to become somewhat crowded in the pots before planting out it is thought that the vines are induced to come into bloom somewhat earlier.

Tender perennial kinds in the south are often wintered by cutting off their tops in fall and covering the roots with a heavy mulch. In the north the roots may be taken up and stored dry until spring, like those of dahlias.

As greenhouse plants, tender perennial morning glories are satisfactory in sunny locations and can be trained up pillars and other supports that permit them to be displayed advantageously. They thrive in ground beds, large pots, or tubs and revel in coarse, fertile, well-drained soil, with ample moisture and stimulating regular applications of dilute liquid fertilizer during their season of active growth. During the winter they are kept drier or, in the case of deciduous tuberous kinds such as

I. mauritiana, entirely without water. Pruning, consisting of cutting back or removing completely shoots of the previous year and thinning out any of those that remain that are crowded, is done in late winter or spring. Any needed potting or top dressing is also done then. Tropical morning glories succeed in greenhouses and conservatories where a minimum night temperature of 55 to 65°F is maintained with day temperatures a few degrees higher. They enjoy fairly high humidity.

Annual morning glories can be grown in pots or tubs as greenhouse and patio ornamentals. Seeds are sown in spring in a temperature of 60 to 70°F. The seedlings are potted individually in 3- or 4-inch pots. When well rooted in these they are planted, five to seven together, in 8- to 12-inch, well-drained containers nearly filled with coarse, rich soil. Canes, wires, trellis, or brushwood must be provided for the stems to entwine and clothe. Watering is at first moderate, more generous when the pots or tubs are filled with roots. When this is achieved regular applications of dilute liquid fertilizer are helpful.

IPOMOPSIS (Ipom-ópsis)—Skyrocket or Scarlet-Gilia. This group of about twenty-four species of New World herbaceous perennials, biennials, annuals, and one shrub was previously included in *Gilia,* and under that name cultivated kinds of *Ipomopsis* are often grown. This genus belongs in the phlox family POLEMONIACEAE. Its generic name is from the Greek *ipo,* to strike, and *opsis,* appearance. It alludes to the showy blooms.

From *Gilia,* plants of this genus differ in having well-developed leaves on the upper parts of the stems, short, horny, pointed tips to the lobes of the leaves, bracts at the bases of individual flowers instead of beneath groups of blooms, and long, slender, usually curved, straw-colored to pale brown seeds. The natural distribution of *Ipomopsis* is mostly western North American with one species native to the southeastern United States, westward to Texas, and occasionally naturalized elsewhere, and one South American. The flowers of *Ipomopsis* are tubular. They have five sepals, five usually spreading petals, five stamens attached in the throats of the flowers or between the petals, and a three-branched style. The fruits are capsules. The blooms are white, yellow, pink, red, or violet. The leaves are deeply-pinnately-lobed and in many kinds develop in well-marked basal rosettes as well as along the stems.

The skyrocket or scarlet-gilia (*I. aggregata*), a native of dryish soils and rocky places throughout much of the western United States, is most frequently cultivated. A variable plant, several of its variants are recognized as varieties or subspecies. The skyrocket is usually a biennial, 1 foot to 3 feet tall, with an erect stem sometimes branched from its base, and glandular to hairy, finely-dissected leaves up to 2 inches long. Its slender, funnel-shaped blooms with reflexed corolla lobes (petals) are in narrow, columnar panicles. They are typically bright red mottled with yellow or more rarely plain yellow. In *G. a. attenuata* they are pink, white, or tinged yellow, in *G. a. bridgesii,* a low, more or less perennial kind with lax stems woody at their bases, they vary from deep-magenta to salmon-magenta. Similar to the skyrocket, but coarser, more vigorous, usually branchless, and with flowers with broader, spreading but not reflexed petals is the standing-cypress (*I. rubra* syns. *Gilia rubra, G. coronopifolia*). This biennial, native to the southeastern United States, 3 or 6 feet tall, has leaves divided into needle-like segments and scarlet- to yellow-dotted red blooms in long, slender panicles. Very much resembling a phlox, *I. longiflora,* indigenous from Nebraska and Utah to Arizona and Texas, has

Ipomopsis rubra (flowers)

pale blue to white flowers with wide-spreading petals, in flattish-topped clusters. It attains a height of 1½ feet or slightly more.

Garden Uses. The species discussed here are best grown as biennials, but because they are not winter hardy in cold regions their cultivation in this way in the north is restricted to greenhouses. They can be treated as annuals by starting seeds early indoors, but plants grown in this way are smaller and usually less satisfactory than those that grow for two seasons. In the warmer parts of the United States, they are satisfactory outdoors and are welcome additions to the available summer flowers for beds and borders and for planting for naturalistic effects. In appropriate regions they may be included among collections of native plants. These plants need well-drained sandy soil and full sun. They can be used as cut flowers.

Cultivation. When grown as biennials, seeds are sown in May or June in a cold frame, cool greenhouse, or appropriate spot outdoors. The seedlings are transplanted carefully, in mild climates, to outdoor nursery beds where they are spaced 6 to 8 inches apart in rows 1 foot apart, and from which they are moved to their flowering location in fall or the following spring, in colder regions individually in small pots. From the latter they are repotted into larger containers as growth demands and by fall will occupy 5-inch pots. In these they are wintered in a sunny, airy greenhouse where a night temperature of 45 to 50°F is maintained, and day temperatures are not more than five to ten degrees higher. The objective is to protect the plants from frost, but keep them dormant until late winter or spring. Watering should be done cautiously. Constantly

Ipomopsis rubra

saturated soil is likely to cause the roots to rot. In spring the plants may be transferred to pots of 6-inch diameter or, at the time it is safe to plant tomatoes, be transplanted outdoors, spacing them about 1 foot apart. They may be had in bloom earlier and are then attractive pot plants for greenhouse decoration, by growing them from February onward in temperatures about five degrees higher than those recommended above. Such plants should be given weekly applications of dilute liquid fertilizer after they have filled their pots with roots. When grown as annuals the seeds are sown in a greenhouse in a temperature of 60 to 65°F in January or February, and the seedlings are transplanted individually to 2½-inch pots and, if growth necessitates, later to 4-inch ones. Until they are to be hardened for planting out (by standing them in a cold frame or sheltered place outdoors for a week or two), they are grown in a sunny greenhouse with a night temperature of 50 to 55°F, increased by five to ten degrees during the day. Watering must be done in moderation. Excessive applications can be fatal. The plants can be transplanted outdoors, 9 inches to 1 foot apart, as soon as it is safe to set out tomatoes.

IRESINE (Iresìn-e)—Blood Leaf. To the amaranth family AMARANTHACEAE belongs this group of eighty species of tropical and subtropical herbaceous plants and subshrubs, the cultivated ones of which are esteemed for their attractive habits and colorful foliage. In gardens they are often improperly called *Achyranthes*. The name is from the Greek *eiros*, wool, and alludes to the woolly flowers and seeds. From somewhat similar *Alternanthera* iresines differ in having their insignificant blooms in loose, usually large panicles of small spikes or clusters instead of in stalkless axillary heads. Flowers are rarely borne in cultivation.

Two species of *Iresine* are commonly grown. They are *I. herbstii* (*Achyranthes verschaffeltii*), which has nearly rounded leaves distinctly notched at their ends, and *I. lindenii* (syns. *I. acuminata*, *Achyranthes acuminata*), with pointed, lanceolate-ovate leaves. Both are natives of South America.

As grown in North America these are commonly low plants usually not more, and often less than a foot or so high. In the tropics they are bigger, *I. herbstii* attaining a height of 5 or 6 feet. Iresines have opposite, undivided, stalked leaves, and bisexual or unisexual, white or yellowish tiny flowers of no decorative significance. Usually there are three bracts to each flower. The latter have five-parted perianths, mostly five stamens with their stalks joined at their bases, and two or three stigmas. The fruits are tiny bladders containing a single seed.

Typical *I. herbstii* has purplish-red or green often somewhat puckered leaves up

Iresine herbstii

to 2½ inches long, with yellowish midribs and veins, the latter curving outward and upward from the mid-vein. The leaves of *I. h. aureo-reticulata* are similar but are bright green with yellow veining, and have stalks, like the stems, bright red.

The narrow, sharp-pointed leaves of *I. lindenii* are very dark red. The broader, pointed ones of *I. l. formosa* are green with yellow veining. The leafstalks and the stems are red.

Iresine lindenii

Iresine lindenii formosa

Garden and Landscape Uses. Among the easiest to grow of tropical plants, and so readily raised from cuttings planted in a humid atmosphere that gardeners sometimes say that they root like weeds, iresines are colorful foliage plants for permanent outdoor cultivation in the tropics and for summer use in gardens elsewhere. Because they lend themselves well to shearing they are favorites for formal bedding and edgings and are popular for furnishing urns, vases, porch and window boxes, and hanging baskets. They also make good indoor window plants.

Cultivation. Iresines are not frost hardy. In cold climates they are brought indoors before winter, or more commonly, cuttings are rooted in August or September to give young plants to be wintered indoors. They thrive in ordinary well-drained soil kept moist, but not constantly saturated. Full sun is desirable as is a night temperature of 55 to 60°F with warmer conditions by day. Through the winter the soil should be kept a little drier than at other seasons. Propagation can be carried out more or less continuously as fast as new shoots become long enough to serve as cuttings. If not needed to produce cuttings, the young plants should have the tips of their shoots pinched out occasionally to induce bushiness. For planting outdoors, which must not be done until the weather is warm and settled, say one week or ten days after it is safe to plant tomatoes in the garden, plants from 3- or 4-inch pots are usually preferred. These grow rapidly during the summer and need little attention other than shearing to shape and limit them to size.

IRIARTEA (Iri-àrtea). Extremely rare in cultivation the South American genus *Iriartea* of the palm family PALMAE comprises seven species. Its name honors Bernardo de Iriarte, a Spanish diplomat, who died in 1814.

Iriartea exorrhiza in the botanic garden at Rio de Janeiro

The sorts of *Iriartea* are pinnate-leaved palms, of striking appearance, whose unusual characteristic is that the erect trunk arises from the apex of a pyramid of above-ground, stilt-like roots.

From 50 to 60 feet tall, *I. exorrhiza*, native to Amazonian South America, has a trunk supported by three or more stilt roots so tall that a person can, without stooping, stand beneath the base of the trunk. Young specimens, miniature editions of mature ones, seldom have more than three stilt roots. The gracefully curved leaves have deeply-notched leaflets that spread in various directions.

Garden and Landscape Uses and Cultivation. The species described is appropriate in collections of palms and other rare plants. It prospers in humid tropical environments and is propagated by seed.

IRIDACEAE—Iris Family. From a horticultural point of view one of the most important families of monocotyledons, the iris family consists of sixty genera totaling some 800 species. Natives of temperate, subtropical, and tropical regions in many parts of the world, they are especially numerous as to sorts in South Africa and tropical America. Among the most familiar are freesias, crocuses, gladioluses, iris, and tigridias.

Irids (the embracing name for all members of the family) are chiefly herbaceous perennials with bulbs, corms, rhizomes, or other thick rootstocks and generally branched or branchless stems. They have mostly basal, parallel-veined, linear to sword-shaped, or sometimes cylindrical or quadrangular, deciduous or evergreen leaves and prevailingly showy blooms. The latter sprout, usually several but sometimes singly, from spathes of one, two, or more bracts and are sometimes, as in *Gladiolus*, arranged in spikes. They have perianths of six segments, the inner three petals, the outer ones petal-like and commonly called petals. There are three stamens and a usually three-branched style that, as is very obvious in *Iris*, is often petal-like. The fruits are capsules.

Cultivated genera include: *Acidanthera, Alophia, Anapalina, Antholyza, Aristea, Babiana, Belamcanda, Chasmanthe, Cipura, Crocosmia, Crocus, Curtonus, Cypella, Dierama, Dietes, Diplarrhena, Eleutherine, Eustylis, Ferraria, Freesia, Geissorhiza, Gladiolus, Gynandriris, Hermodactylus, Hesperantha, Hexaglottis, Homeria, Homoglossum, Iris, Ixia, Lapeirousia, Libertia, Melasphaerula, Moraea, Nemastylis, Neomarica, Nivenia, Orthrosanthus, Pardanthopsis, Petersonia, Rigidella, Romulea, Salpingostylis, Schizostylis, Sisyrinchium, Sparaxis, Sphenostigma, Sternbergia, Streptanthera, Synnotia, Tigridia, Trimezia, Tritonia,* and *Watsonia.*

IRIS. In addition to being the name of the genus dealt with in the next entry, the word iris is part of the common names of these plants: peacock-iris (*Moraea villosa*) and snake's-head-iris (*Hermodactylus tuberosus*).

IRIS (Ì-ris)—Fleur-de-Lis, Flags. It is hard to imagine any gardener unfamiliar with one or more representatives of the genus *Iris* of the iris family IRIDACEAE. At least that is true of North America and other temperate and warm-temperate regions. In the tropics irises are less ubiquitous. But comparatively few gardeners are acquainted with the extraordinary broad spectrum and full variety the genus affords. It comprises some 300 species plus untold thousands of varieties and hybrids of the most popular. Consideration of this vast assortment and the immense color variation its blooms exhibit inevitably leads to the conclusion that its name is well chosen. It is an ancient Greek one, given according to Dioscorides, because of the resemblance of its flowers to the "rainbow in heaven."

As natives, irises are found in most parts of the northern hemisphere. None is indigenous south of the equator. There they are replaced by *Moraea* and *Neomarica*. The sorts of *Iris* range from the practically indestructable to species so shy of domestication that the most skillful gardeners are likely to be baffled in attempting to tame them. There are hardy and nonhardy kinds. All are herbaceous perennials.

Interest in irises goes back beyond recorded history. Four millennia ago kings and priests of Crete acknowledged its flowers as their own, and the "lilies" of certain biblical references were irises. The ninth-century German monk and writer on theology Walafrid Strabo, in his poem "Hortulus," tells of growing *I. germanica* in the little garden he carefully tended. This kind was cultivated in many other monastery gardens then and later because its rhizomes as orris root were esteemed as medicines. They were employed to induce sleep, cure ulcers, and alleviate the sad affliction of a "pimpled or saucie face."

Dioscorides extolled the virtues of the rhizomes of *I. germanica* for curing many ills such as "thick humors and choler," "torments of the belly," "bites of venemous beasts," "convulsion fitts," "sciatica," "hollow sores," and "sun burning." He also points out that they "doe mollify the struma and the old Scirrhus," and further that the "roots" are "exceeding well scenting." For this last virtue they are still esteemed as sources of ingredients used to impart the odor of violets to cosmetics.

About 1147, Louis VII of France, following his excommunication from the Church, engaged in a crusade against the Saracens. As the story goes, he chose as his emblem an iris, which became known as the fleur de Louis, later corrupted through fleur de luce and fleur de lys to fleur de lis, the heraldic emblem of France. His choice was inspired, it is said, by the legend that 600 years earlier Clovis, king of the Franks, had adopted as his device *I. pseudacorus*. This, some say, because his observance of its yellow blooms far out in a river revealed the waters were shallow enough to ford and so permit him and his men escape annihilation by a superior army of pursuing Goths. Others attribute his choice to, being faced with defeat in battle, he a pagan, prayed to the God of his Christian wife, defeated his enemy, and in gratitude replaced the three toads of his banner with three iris blooms, flowers dedicated to the Virgin.

Irises, with one rare exception, have rhizomes or bulbs, the latter with or without perennial roots. The branchless or branched stems are erect, the foliage chiefly, but usually not exclusively basal. The longitudinally-parallel-veined leaves are sword-shaped, two-ranked, and overlapping at their bases or are slender and more or less grasslike or reedlike. The showy flowers are borne solitary or more often a few together that open in succession from the axils of spathelike bracts terminating the stems and branches. As is characteristic of the family, the perianth parts and stamens are above the ovary. In botanical parlance the ovary is inferior. The perianth parts are generally united at their bases into a short tube. They consist of three petal-like sepals called falls, spreading, reflexed, or pendulous, and three usually erect and often arched banner petals known as standards. Sepals and petals are narrowed below into a narrow shaft or claw. There are three stamens each covered by a style branch of petal-like texture, coloring, and appearance, that has on its underside a stigmatic surface and beyond which the style branch extends into its two-lobed or crested apex. The fruits are many-seeded, three- or six-angled, oblong capsules.

Classification of irises is based on sorting the various kinds into four subgenera some further divided into lesser groups. The subgenera are (I) *Nepalensis*, consisting of only *I. decora*, a curious species with neither bulbs nor rhizomes; (II) *Xiphium*, which includes Dutch, Spanish, and English irises and all other kinds with bulbs with slender roots that die annually at the end of the growing season; (III) *Scorpiris*, known as Juno irises, which comprises the kinds with bulbs to the bases of which are attached persistent, long, thick, brittle roots; and (IV) *Iris*, which includes all kinds with rhizomes.

Further splintering involves recognition within the subgenus *Xiphium* of two sections, one named *Xiphium*, which includes Dutch, Spanish, English, and other irises in which the bulbs have smooth skins, the other, *Reticulata*, in which the bulbs are covered with coarse-netted (reticulate) skins like those of *I. reticulata*.

More complicated subdivision is accorded the subgenus *Iris*. Its major splits are section *Iris*, in which are accommodated all irises with flowers that have falls and sometimes standard petals with usually conspicuous beards of hairs, and section *Spathulata*, in which the flowers are without such beards, but may have a crest of petal-like textured parts. Section *Iris* consists of four subsections identified as *Iris*, *Hexopogon*, *Onococyclus*, and *Pseudoregelia*. The first, its members also called true bearded or eupogon irises, is distinguished by the hairs of the beards being shaped like slender clubs, and consisting of many cells, and by the seeds being without arils (small, light-colored collars at one end of the seed). The other three subsections, conveniently grouped as aril irises, have flowers with unicellular hairs and seeds with arils.

The beardless and crested irises both belong in the *Spathulata* section of the genus. Subsection *Apogon* accounts for the former. Subsection *Evansia* accommodates those with flowers with cockscomb-like crests on their falls. In addition, *I. foetidissima* constitutes subsection *Foetidissima* and *I. dichotoma* subsection *Pardanthopsis*. The plant previously named *I. sisyrinchium* is *Gynandriris sisyrinchium*.

In the discussion that follows the various groups of cultivated irises are not presented in botanical sequence, but instead with some regard to their horticultural importance. Certain hybrid groups are treated first, followed by species and hybrid sorts of lesser consequence.

Horticultural varieties and hybrids of bearded irises are among the most familiar and popular garden plants. A large proportion of gardeners first become acquainted with the genus through these. They exist in immense variety, those classed as tall beardeds being perhaps the most magnificent. But smaller kinds are rapidly gaining popularity and for many purposes are as well or better suited than their taller kin, especially than those bred primarily for exhibition. Many of these last have immense

Tall bearded iris variety

and wondrously spectacular blooms that unfortunately do not stand up well to inclement weather. They are less satisfactory for garden embellishment than kinds with smaller, less fragile flowers on stalks that withstand wind and rainstorms better. Among bearded irises gardeners can choose from miniature dwarfs of the *I. pumila* group (4 to 10 inches tall and with flowers not over 3 inches across, held above the foliage), standard dwarfs (10 inches to 1¼ feet in height, leaves as tall as the flowering stalks, their blooms 3 to 4 inches wide), intermediate, median bearded, or border irises (from 1¼ to 2⅓ feet tall and with flowers 4 to 6 inches wide), and tall beardeds (which have stouter stalks than the last and are 2⅓ feet or more tall). Bearded irises in each of these subordinate classes are listed, described, and often splendidly illustrated in color in vast and bewildering array in the catalogs of specialist dealers, of which America has many. It is to such catalogs that interested gardeners must turn for descriptions of varieties from which to make selections. One great advantage these irises have, they ship well. Because of this, orders can be placed with distant nurseries in full expectation that the plants will arrive in good condition. And that is not by any means true of all herbaceous perennials.

Siberian irises are among the most reliable of garden perennials and delightful as cut blooms. These hardy, disease-resistant, beardless sorts succeed with minimum attention practically anywhere irises will grow. They average 2 to 3 feet in height and are chiefly of hybrid origin, *I. sibirica* and *I. sanguinea* being the parental stocks. Siberian irises are without the thick, fleshy rhizomes of the bearded varieties and have much narrower, grassy leaves. From crowded clumps of strong, tough, growth buds sprout dense sheaves of foliage 2 feet or so tall. Above these are displayed in abundance and with airy grace slender-stalked, purple, blue, or white blooms with erect, narrow standards and drooping falls. Recently, breeders have added considerably to the formerly quite limited number of Siberian irises. The color range and duration of the flowering season has been extended, and so too have the forms of the flowers. Lower varieties are also to be expected. Catalogs of iris specialists list available kinds.

Siberian iris

Japanese iris

Japanese irises, although by no means rare, are not grown as frequently by American gardeners as their patent merits suggest they should be. To many, their exquisite forms and colorings are more familiar in Japanese art than American earth. Yet they

Border of tall bearded irises

Iris pumila

Japanese iris (flowers)

are among the most showy and easiest irises to grow and are the largest flowered. Ancestral stocks of these beardless beauties are Manchurian *I. kaempferi,* and less importantly, Japanese *I. laevigata.* Both are close relatives of American *I. versicolor* and *I. virginica* and of the yellow flag (*I. pseudacorus*), of Europe, North Africa, and western Asia. The development of the many splendid varieties of Japanese irises is a tribute to the skill and patience Japanese gardeners exercised over centuries. In recent years American breeders have been active in raising varieties with more rigid flowering stems and superior branching that produce blooms over a longer period. In Europe efforts have been made to raise sorts suitable for soils containing limestone, a diet fatal to most Japanese irises.

Moist-soil and waterside plants, these are without the heavy rhizomes of bearded irises. Instead, they form dense clumps of growth buds and roots and sheaves of erect leaves. The flowers, those of some varieties as big as small plates, and because of their wide-spreading petals rather platelike in form, have much more limited color range than bearded irises. There are pure whites, lavender-blues, blues, orchid-pinks, purples, and violets. Often they are stippled, mottled, splashed, or veined with hues different from the base ones, and they may be flared with yellow. The forms of the flowers vary greatly according to variety. For Western eyes the simple six-petaled, single blooms often hold most appeal, but there are doubles with many more petals.

Louisiana irises is the name of a complex of three beardless species and natural hybrids between them that inhabit the bayou country of Louisiana and of numerous artificial hybrids that have been raised from them. Although a few had been cultivated earlier, these irises first came into prominence in the 1920s when Dr. John Kunkel Small became interested in the group. He studied them intensively in their native swamps and in plantings he made at The New York Botanical Garden, but failed to recognize that the majority were hybrids. In a wave of taxonomic enthusiasm and to the confusion of botanists and gardeners, he described and named more than seventy species.

The species involved in the hybrid complex are *I. fulva, I. brevicaulis,* and *I. giganticaerulea.* A fourth species, *I. virginica,* which grows in Louisiana, belongs to a separate botanical series and has not participated in the sexual shenanigans responsible for the astonishing array of beautiful crossbreds.

Louisiana irises vary much in size and habit from *I. brevicaulis,* sometimes under 1 foot tall to *I. giganticaerulea,* which may exceed 5 feet. Some develop long, wide-spreading rhizomes and excessive amounts of foliage, but careful breeding and selection has done much to minimize these detractions as well as to produce varieties with flowers of firmer substance. Numerous splendid varieties in an extraordinary wide range of flower colors, including white, creamy-white, yellow, bronze and coppery tones, blues, and purples are

available. Among the finest are those showing a strong influence of *I. giganticaerulea.* These are excellent in the deep south, but are less suitable for cold climates than some others.

Spuria irises are favorites in California and other Western states blessed with mild climates. They are less well known elsewhere, although certainly some, including *I. crocea, I. orientalis,* and certain hybrids, give good accounts of themselves in parts of the Northeast. Others, quite hardy, tend in cold climates to produce ample foliage, but few blooms. The beardless blooms of spurias, which open at about the same time as those of tall bearded irises, have more the aspect of Spanish, English, or Dutch irises, but unlike these, spuria irises are not bulb plants, their leaves are much wider and the flowering stalks carry several blooms. About a dozen species and hybrids between some of them comprise the spuria group. The basic species are natives of Europe, the Near East, and Middle East. Marked characteristics of spurias are their long, creeping rhizomes and plentiful, good-looking foliage. Species belonging to the spuria group include *I. spuria,* which some regard as an assembly of closely related kinds rather than a discrete species, *I. crocea, I. graminea, I. orientalis, I. sintenisii,* and *I. urumovii.* American breeders recently directed their talents to raising new and improved varieties of spurias with very satisfying results. Many lovely kinds are listed for sale by specialists. Their flower colors include white, yellow, white and yellow, bronze, blue, purple, violet, and various blends.

Spanish, English, and Dutch irises, among the most beautiful and easily cultivatable sorts, belong with the most desirable of bulb plants. Because they lend themselves so well to harvesting in summer and marketing as dormant bulbs in fall these are grown in great numbers in Holland and are listed in catalogs that offer such other Dutch bulbs as daffodils, hyacinths, and tulips. Why they are not more often grown by American gardeners is something of a mystery. They are as easy to manage as tulips, indeed their needs are much the same, except that they are slightly less hardy and in the north require some winter protection. They are as useful as tulips for garden embellishment and cut flowers.

Modern varieties of Spanish irises have been bred over a long period of years from *I. xiphium* of Spain and North Africa. Smaller-flowered than Dutch irises, they have erect, wiry stems, slender foliage, and long-lasting, shapely blooms of white, white and yellow, white and lilac, blue, yellow, and other hues including arty, smoky ones. Some are fragrant. Despite their name, English irises are descendants of Spanish *I. xiphioides,* a species introduced to England probably in the six-

Spanish iris

Dutch iris

teenth century and from thence to Holland. English irises, better suited for the Pacific Northwest than most other parts of North America, have much bigger bulbs than Spanish irises, and their period of dormancy is shorter. Their flowers come in pure white and tones of lilac-blue, blue, rosy-purple, and in mottled patterns. Dutch irises, most popular of bulbous kinds, are hybrids between *I. xiphium* and two North African species, *I. tingitana* and *I. fontanesii*. They much resemble Spanish irises, but are taller and have more massive blooms. Their flower colors include a good selection of handsome yellows, blues, and purples.

Aril irises, which include regelias (hexapogons), pseudoregelias, and oncocyclus species and hybrids between them, are generally less adaptive to climate and cultural conditions than true bearded irises. In the main they succeed better in the Pacific states than elsewhere, but some are by no means impossible in the east if given understanding care. Being natives of a region extending from the eastern Mediterranean and Asia Minor to the Himalayas and adjacent lands to China, the majority are accustomed to dry summers. In addition to the hybrids within the groups there are others between regelia and oncocyclus irises, classed as regeliocyclus hybrids, some between oncocyclus and true bearded irises, known as oncobreds, and hybrids between regelias (hexapogons) and true bearded, called regeliabreds. The aril irises and their hybrids include some of the most unusual-looking and loveliest members of the genus. The possibility of growing a few should be considered by every keen grower of irises. Among the easiest are the regeliabreds and oncobreds. These inherit much of the adaptability to climate and conditions characteristic of their true bearded parents.

Species of bearded irises include these: *I. aphylla,* its range extending from eastern Europe to the Caucasus, is up to 1 foot tall and has deciduous, sword-shaped to sickle-shaped leaves 9 inches to 1 foot long by ¼ to ¾ inch wide. Predominantly purple, the large blooms have yellow bases to their falls and blue-tipped, white beards. *I. chamaeiris,* 3 to 10 inches tall and a native of southern Europe, has, in tufts of four to six, leaves about ½ inch wide. The blooms, solitary or two to a stalk, are purple, blue, yellow, or brownish with darker veins. The beard is usually orange-yellow. *I. germanica,* probably a natural hybrid, but of uncertain origin and 2 to 3 feet tall, has few sword-shaped leaves and, in its best known form, large, fragrant blooms on stalks that branch below their middles.

The falls are purple with brown veins, white bases, and yellow beards. The standard petals are lilac. Variations in flower color are common. *I. g. florentina,* lower, has blue standards. *I. mellita* is a close relative of better known *I. pumila* from which it differs in having more pronounced stems. A native of southeast Europe, and 3 to 5 inches in height, it has narrow leaves and dusky-brownish blooms suffused and veined with reddish-purple and blue. The beard is white tipped with blue. *I. pallida* resembles *I. germanica,* but has lighter-colored foliage, and the spathes accompanying its shorter-tubed flowers are silvery throughout instead of suffused with purple. The fragrant, blue flowers are on stalks 1½ to 2½ feet tall. This kind is European. Variety *I. p. dalmatica* has broader, very glaucous leaves and larger, lavender flowers. *I. pumila,* a native of Asia Minor as well as Europe, is nearly stemless. It has sword-shaped leaves 3 to 5 inches long in tufts of usually four. The rather small flowers, of various colors, in-

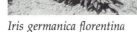

Iris germanica florentina   *Iris pallida*

cluding blue, purple, yellow, and white, are displayed in early spring. *I. variegata,* of southeast Europe, has sword-shaped leaves up to 1½ feet long by about 1 inch wide. Its branched flowering stalks are about 1½ feet tall. The medium-sized blooms are yellow conspicuously veined or the falls are brown and with yellow beards.

Native American species of beardless irises without crests include these: *I. bracteata* inhabits a very restricted region in California and Oregon. One of the most beautiful West Coast species, it occurs in dryish, open woodlands. Up to a little over 1½ feet long, the few thick, rigid leaves are about ½ inch wide. Their upper surfaces are lustrous green. Beneath they are paler and glaucous. The blooms, on stalks up to 1 foot tall, are golden-yellow with rich brown to maroon veining. Their oblanceolate falls are about 1½ inches in length, the narrowly-lanceolate standards ½ inch longer. This is said to be difficult to transplant. *I. brevicaulis* (syn. *I. foliosa*) much resembles *I. hexagona,* differing chiefly in its stalks rarely exceeding 1 foot in length and being decumbent. It is native in wet soils from Ohio to Louisiana. In *I. b. boonensis* the flowers are white. *I. chrysophylla,* in bloom not over 1 foot tall, is a native of California and Oregon. It has linear leaves up to 1½ feet long by ¼ inch wide. Mostly two together on stalks shorter than the leaves, the flowers are light yellow to white, suffused, veined, or margined with pink to reddish-purple. They have oblanceolate falls about 2 inches long and shorter standards. *I. douglasiana* is a popular, variable native of a narrow coastal strip of California and Oregon. In height it ranges from 1 foot to 3 feet. It makes a dense growth of evergreen leaves taller than the branched or branchless flower stalks. The flowers, dark purple, mauve, light blue, lavender, creamy-yellow, or white, have oblanceolate falls about 2 inches long, standards oblanceolate and somewhat shorter. *I. fulva,* one of the showiest of the Louisiana iris species, inhabits usually partly-shaded swamps in the lower Mississippi Valley region. Lifted above the abundant, arching, narrowly-sword-shaped leaves up to 3½ feet in length, the flower stalks carry coppery-red flowers with broadly-obovate-lanceolate, drooping falls up to 2¼ inches and standards about 1½ inches long. Early hybrids between *I. fulva* and *I. brevicaulis* were named *I. fulvala* and 'Dorothea K. Williamson'. These have reddish-purple to deeper purple blooms. The group known as Abbeville irises are native near Abbeville, Louisiana. They much resemble *I. fulva,* but are more robust and have bigger blooms ranging in color from coppery-red to yellow. As ornamentals they are superior. *I. giganticaerulea,* one of the parents of the Louisiana hybrids, occurs as a native along the coast of Louisiana. Its flow-

Iris giganticaerulea

ering stalks 3 to 5 feet tall or sometimes taller, this has large, blue, purple, or white blooms. *I. hexagona* inhabits wet soils in the southeastern United States. Attaining a height of up to 3 feet, it has sword-shaped leaves 2 to 3 feet long by up to 1½ inches wide. The flowers, several on each stalk, are 3 to 3½ inches deep and lilac. Their standards are about two-thirds as long as the falls. *I. innominata,* of mountains in California and Oregon, is a charming species with yellow to orange or sometimes lavender to purple blooms. From 4 to 10 inches tall, this has grassy, evergreen leaves up to 1¼ feet long by up to ⅕ inch broad, paler beneath than on their upper sides. The flowers, on branchless stalks, have usually purple-veined, broadly-oblanceolate falls almost 2 inches long and shorter, narrower standards. *I. longipetala,* a native of coastal California, is much like *I. missouriensis.* From that it differs chiefly in being bigger and in its somewhat broader foliage being evergreen and

Iris innominata (flowers)

exceeding the flower stalks in length. Also, the stalks carry up to eight blooms. *I. macrosiphon,* of California, is similar to *I. innominata.* The chief difference is that its flowers have shorter perianth tubes. *I. missouriensis,* a deciduous native mostly at high altitudes from the Rocky Mountains to California and British Columbia, in aspect resembles *I. longipetala.* It has leaves up to 1½ feet long by usually under ⅓ inch wide and slender, usually branched stalks up to 2½ feet tall with generally two or three blooms. The falls are obovate, mostly a little over 2 inches long, chiefly pale lilac to whitish with darker veins. The standards are shorter and narrower. *I. munzii* is one of the largest and least hardy of western North American irises. A native of lightly wooded, dryish slopes at low altitudes in the Sierra Nevada, it has glaucous, bluish-grayish leaves up to 1½ feet long by ¾ inch wide. Its branchless stalks, up to 2½ feet tall or taller, carry two to four light lavender to blue or blue-violet flowers with oblong-ovate to broadly-oblanceolate falls 2¼ to 3½ inches long and oblanceolate to spatula-shaped standards of approximately the same lengths. *I. prismatica,* an inhabitant of swamps in coastal

Iris innominata

Iris prismatica

eastern North America, attains heights of 1 foot to 2 feet and has slender, solid, sometimes once-branched stems and glaucous, linear leaves 1 foot to 2 feet long by ⅛ to ½ inch wide. The darker-veined, bluish-purple flowers have a whitish blotch on the base of each ovate, up to 2-inch-long fall petal. The standards, paler than the falls, are about 1¾ inches long. *I. purdyi* is a Californian much like *I. douglasiana*, but with less crowded foliage and branchless stems. Its leaves are lustrous green above, glaucous on their undersides. The blooms, usually paired, are creamy-yellow or whitish veined with brown-purple or tinged with pale lavender. This inhabits woodlands. *I. setosa*, a

Iris setosa

native of Alaska and northeastern Asia, is respresented by its dwarfer variety *I. s. canadensis* from Newfoundland to Labrador, Quebec, and Maine. Its sword-shaped leaves, up to 2 feet long by 1 inch wide, are generally overtopped by the branchless or sparsely-branched stalks with two or three lilac or pale lavender to reddish-purple blooms with falls up to 2 inches long and standards not over ¾ inch in length. *I. tenax,* native in sunny or slightly shaded places from California to Washington, has crowded clumps of leaves 1 foot to 1½ feet long by under ¼ inch wide. From 6 inches to 1 foot tall, the one- or two-flowered flower stalks carry blooms most commonly lavender or purple with white or yellow markings on the falls but pinkish-, yellow-, and almost orange-flowered variants are known. This is one of the most amenable to cultivation of West Coast irises. Natural hybrids between *I. tenax* and *I. chrysophylla* occur. *I. verna*, a delightful native of sandy soils in open woodlands from Pennsylvania to Kentucky, Georgia, and Mississippi, is up to 6 inches tall. It has bright green linear leaves less than ½ inch wide and glaucous on one side. At flowering time they are 4 to 6 inches long; later they lengthen. The violet-scented flowers, 2 inches or a little

more wide, have spreading or recurved, violet-blue or rarely paler or white falls with pubescent, yellow to orange claws, and erect, obovate, slender-clawed violet petals. *I. versicolor,* of swamps and moist soils from Newfoundland to Manitoba, Virginia, and Minnesota, is very like *I. virginica*, from which it differs in the standards not being more than two-thirds as long as the falls and in technical details. *I. virginica* has broadly-sword-shaped leaves up to 3 feet long by ¾ inch broad. Its little-branched stalks up to 3½ feet tall have blue to violet blooms with 3-inch-long, obovate-wedge-shaped falls marked with a bright yellow blotch. The standards are somewhat shorter than the falls.

Iris versicolor

European and Asian beardless species include a fairly large selection more or less commonly cultivated. Belonging are these: *I. bulleyana,* of western China, or possibly of hybrid derivation, is of the *I. sibirica* relationship. It has linear-sword-shaped leaves 1½ to 2 feet long by ½ inch wide, glaucous on their undersides. One or two blooms top each branchless, hollow flower stalk. They have ovate-oblong falls about 2 inches long, cream-colored flecked with purple, and somewhat shorter, light blue-purple, spreading standards. *I. chrysographes,* of China, is related to *I. sanguinea.* It has linear-sword-shaped leaves up to about 1½ feet long by ½ inch wide and bright violet-purple blooms with the lower parts of their 2¼-inch-long falls netted with golden-yellow. They are on thick-walled, hollow, usually branchless stalks approximately 1½ feet tall. The standards are spreading. *I. clarkei* is another close ally of *I. sanguinea.* It differs from that more familiar kind in having solid flower stalks. A high altitude Himalayan, this kind has foliage lustrous above, glaucous on its undersides. Its flower stalks are generally branched. *I. crocea* (syn. *I. aurea*) is an especially fine species of the *I. spuria* relationship. Native of the western Himalayas, it has sword-shaped leaves about 2 feet long and golden-yellow flowers in two clusters on stalks 3 to 4 feet tall. The

blooms are distinguished by the falls and standards being crisped or wavy at their edges. The former are 3 to 3½ inches long by about 1 inch wide. The standards are shorter and narrower. *I. delavayi* is Chinese, a moist-soil species related to *I. sibirica.* It has glaucous leaves up to 2½ feet long by 1 inch wide and hollow flower stalks 3 to 4 feet tall or sometimes taller. Usually in twos, the flowers have falls 2½ inches wide, red-purple with an irregular white blotch on each of the falls. The standards are spreading and much smaller than the falls. *I. ensata* is a moist-soil species native from the Caucasus to Japan. It has leaves 10 inches to 2 feet long by up to ½ inch wide, with prominent midribs. The branchless solid flower stalks have red-purple blooms about 4 inches wide. The elliptic falls are yellow toward their bases. The standards are smaller and erect. From *I. laevigata* this differs in its six-angled seed capsules containing glossy seeds. *I. forrestii,* a Chinese *I. sibirica* relative, has narrowly-linear leaves up to 1½ feet long, lustrous above, glaucous on their undersides. Its branched or branchless, hollow flower stalks, 1 foot to 1½ feet in height, have golden-yellow blooms, often veined with purple. Their falls are 2

Iris forrestii

Iris graminea

to 2½ inches long, the nearly erect standards shorter. *I. graminea,* native from central Europe to the Caucasus, belongs with the *I. spuria* group. It has an abundance of grassy leaves 1 foot to 3 feet long by ¾ to 1 inch wide. The distinctly two-edged, solid flower stalks are 8 inches to 1 foot tall. The plum-scented blooms, solitary or in pairs and hidden among the foliage, are yellowish-white conspicuously veined with blue- and reddish-purple, or are mauve to reddish-purple throughout. Their falls are 1½ to 2 inches long, the standards up to 1½ inches long. *I. kaempferi,* the Japanese iris, is a native not only of Japan, but also of China and Korea. The ancestral stock of numerous horticultural varieties of Japanese irises, this has sword-shaped leaves 2 to 2½ feet long, with distinctly evident, raised midribs. The flower stalks, 1½ to 2½ feet tall and commonly with one branch, have flat blooms, usually in twos, 3½ to 6 inches across. Their standards are about two-thirds as long as the wide-spreading about 3-inch-long falls. The blooms of the natural species are usually reddish-purple, but in horticultural varieties much variation occurs in size, form, and color of the flowers. This species is not a swamp plant. *I. laevigata,* a swamp species of Japan, has been much confused with the last and like it is called Japanese iris. From *I. kaempferi* it differs most obviously in its leaves being without distinct midribs and in its clear blue or white flowers having falls and styles of about equal (2½-inch-long) lengths. *I. minutaurea* (syn. *I. minuta*), also probably Japanese, as its names suggest is a miniature. It has linear leaves about 4 inches long by ¼ to ½ inch wide and solitary, brown-flushed, yellow flowers on stalks 1 foot long or somewhat longer. *I. monnieri,* mistakenly reported to be endemic to Crete, is apparently of garden origin and is probably only a variant of *I. spuria*. It has lemon-yellow flowers not crisped at edges of the falls. The seeds have loose-fitting coats. *I. ochroleuca* much resembles the last and it has very loose-coated seeds.

Iris pseudacorus

Iris pseudacorus (flowers)

Iris pseudacorus variegata

Probably a native of Asia Minor, and a very close relative or perhaps only a variant of *I. spuria*, this has white or very pale yellow blooms with the falls decorated with a rich yellow blotch. *I. pseudacorus,* the yellow flag of Europe, North Africa, and Asia Minor, is naturalized in eastern North America. A waterside species, it has more or less glaucous, broadly-sword-shaped leaves 2 to 3 feet long. The branched flower stalks equal or exceed the foliage in height. Each has several bright yellow blooms with falls about 2 inches long, sometimes with violet veins, and nearly erect, much shorter, narrow standards. In *I. p. manschurica* the blooms are pale yellow. The foliage of *I. p. variegata* is striped with creamy-white. *I. ruthenica,* native from eastern Europe to Korea, has rhizomes with comparatively few roots and grassy leaves, at blooming time about 6 inches in length, later becoming twice as long. Their upper surfaces are lustrous. Beneath, they are glaucous. Its flower stalks, up to 8 inches tall, carry blooms shaded and veined with bluish-purple over an almost white base. The falls spread widely. About 2 inches in length, they are longer than the semierect standards. *I. sanguinea* (syn. *I. orientalis*) of Japan, Korea, and Manchuria, is closely al-

lied to *I. sibirica,* but its leaves are broader and exceed the hollow flower stalks in length. In *I. s. alba* the blooms are white. *I. sibirica,* native not of Siberia as its name suggests, but of central Europe to Russia, is highly variable. It has given rise to many horticultural varieties, most of which are hybrids between it and *I. sanguinea*. From the last, *I. sibirica* differs in carrying its blooms on hollow, branched or branchless stalks 1½ to 3 feet tall well above the foliage and in its leaves and falls of the flowers being narrower. The leaves are linear. The blue-lilac to blue-purple flowers have roundish falls 1 inch to 1½ inches wide and shorter standards. Variety *I. s. alba* has white flowers. *I. sintenisii,* of southeastern Europe and Asia Minor, is an *I. spuria* relative with, in aspect, leanings toward *I. spuria*. It has linear leaves up to ½ inch wide, and on stalks up to 1 foot long purple blooms with spreading, narrow falls, blue-purple on a whitish base color, and erect, purple standards. *I. spuria* is a very variable species or perhaps complex of closely related species that inhabits Europe to Algeria and Iran. Shorter than the 1- to 2-foot-tall flowering stalks, the somewhat glaucous ½-inch-wide leaves are broadly-linear. On sparsely-branched or branchless stalks, the bluish-purple blooms have roundish falls about ½ inch wide and somewhat shorter and narrower standards. Many variants of this species have been given names. The one named *I. s. halophila* is shorter and has smaller blooms with narrower parts, white with yellow veins, dull yellow, or grayish-purple. *I. unguicularis* (syn. *I. stylosa*), of Algeria, blooms in fall, winter, or early spring. It has linear leaves, eventually but not at blooming time 1 foot to 2 feet long by up to ½ inch wide. The fragrant, long-tubed, lilac- to purple or white blooms, nearly stalkless or with very short, solid stalks, are well down among the foliage. The falls, 3 inches long, have a center patch of deeper lilac. *I. wilsonii* is a Chinese species of the *I. sibirica* group. With the general aspect of

Iris wilsonii

I. chrysographes, it differs from that species in its blooms being yellow with purple-brown or red veinings and in technical details.

Crested irises, those of the botanical subsection *Evansia*, are characterized by the falls of their flowers having a prominent center ridge of cockscomb-like serrations. Unlike the bearded and beardless irises, these have not produced many hybrids. As wildlings they are restricted to two species native to North America and several Asians. The Americans are *I. cristata* and *I. lacustris*. A dwarf crested iris, **I. cristata** is native in rich woodlands and on cliffs and banks where the soil is acid from Maryland to Oklahoma and Georgia. It has leaves under ½ inch wide, 4 to 8 inches long at flow-

A border of *Iris tectorum*

Iris tectorum

Iris cristata

fers in the stalks of the individual blooms being about as long instead of much shorter than the spathe (bract) in the axil of which the bloom is borne. Evergreen **I. japonica** is not hardy in the north. Native to Japan and China, it has loosely-branched flower stalks approximately or slightly exceeding in length the leaves, which are sword-shaped, 1 foot to 2 feet long by ½ to 1 inch wide or sometimes wider. Their upper surfaces are dark green, their undersides more or less glaucous. Rather flimsy, the short-lived, lilac blooms have obovate, irregularly-toothed and crisped falls, spotted with yellow and white toward their bases, 1 inch to 1½ inches long, with crisped margins. The semierect standards are smaller than the falls. Taller than *I. japonica*, which it resembles, and even less hardy, **I. wattii** is a native of Assam and western China. Up to 3 feet high, its branched flower stalks bear

Iris wattii

ering time and lengthening somewhat later. Just topping the foliage and stalkless or very short-stalked, the lilac to light purple or pale violet blooms have perianth tubes 1½ to 2 inches long, and obovate falls about 1½ inches long by approximately two-thirds as wide. The crests are whitish to yellow bordered by a white band outlined with purple or violet. The flowers of *I. c. alba* are white. Called the dwarf lake iris, **I. lacustris** suggests a miniature, more compact version of the last. Morphologically it differs in having perianth tubes only ½ to 1 inch long and in the falls of the flowers being more wedge-shaped. Its broadly-linear leaves, up to 2½ inches long at flowering time, later lengthen to up to 6 inches. The flowers are about one-half as big as those of *I. cristata*. The dwarf lake iris inhabits beaches, cliffs, sandy woods, and bogs near Lakes Superior, Huron, and Michigan.

The roof iris of Japan (**I. tectorum**) is a crested species not native of Japan, but of China. Its colloquial name alludes to it being frequently grown in Japan on the roofs of straw-thatched houses. Deciduous and of great charm, this has sword-shaped leaves 1 foot to 1½ feet long or sometimes

longer by 1 inch to 1½ inches wide. Its branched flower stalks equal or nearly equal the leaves in length. Bright lilac, the blooms have obovate falls about 2 inches long, streaked with violet in their lower parts. The crest is white and lilac. The lilac standards, nearly as big as the falls, spread widely. Variety *I. t. alba* has beautiful white blooms. Very similar to *I. tectorum*, but less attractive, **I. milesii**, of the Himalayas, dif-

Iris milesii

forty to fifty light lavender blooms. Their falls, about 2 inches long by 1¼ inches broad, spotted toward their bases with violet-blue, have yellow to orange crests. The standards, smaller than the falls, spread horizontally. Endemic to Japan, **I. gracilipes** is delightful. Its sword-shaped leaves, shorter at blooming time, later become 1 foot long to somewhat longer. They are ¼ to ½ inch wide. The sparsely-branched flowering stalks carry usually two or three pale purple to pinkish-lilac, rather short-lived blooms. The obovate falls, about 1 inch long, are notched at their apexes. The orange crest is yellowish-white below. The oblanceolate standards are a little shorter than the falls. Variants with white flowers are known horticulturally as *I. g. alba*.

Iris gracilipes

The stinking iris, gladdon or gladwin (*I. foetidissima*) is, curiously for an iris, admired more for its seed pods, which display to advantage beautiful vermilion seeds, than for its blooms. Its vernacular and botanical names allude to its usually evergreen foliage being malodorous when crushed. This, the only species of the subsection *Foetidissima* of the beardless irises, is a native of Europe and North Africa. It has sword-shaped leaves 1½ to 2 feet or more long by ¾ inch wide. The flower stalks, angled on one side and 1½ to 2½ feet tall, carry darker-veined dull, purplish or sometimes yellowish blooms 3 to 3½ inches across, with yellowish standards shorter than the falls. The club-shaped pods split into three spreading sections decorated with bright orange-red seeds. This sort is poisonous to livestock.

The vesper iris (*I. dichotoma* syn. *Pardanthopsis dichotomus*), the only member of subsection *Pardanthopsis* of the subgenus *Iris*, enjoys a wide natural distribution in temperate Asia. A short-lived, easily satisfied species, this has thin rhizomes and erect, slender, forking stems 2 to 3½ feet tall ending in racemes of pretty flowers that open in the afternoon and close the next morning. They have greenish-white outer petals flaked or spotted with lilac-purple, whitish and pale purple inner ones. A succession of blooms unfolds over a long summer season. The white-edged, bluish-green leaves 8 inches to somewhat over 1 foot long are in fanlike basal clusters. Approximately 2 inches in diameter, the flowers are without perianth tubes and have falls that toward their bases narrow to a distinct shaft or claw, three shorter standards, and a style with three branches divided with two crests on the upper side of each branch. The stamens sit firmly against the undersides of the style branches. When the blooms wither they twist into tight spirals. Variety *I. d. alba* has white flowers. Although there are no known hybrids between the vesper iris and other irises, it has been crossed with *Belamcanda* to produce *Pardancanda*.

Regelia irises, those belonging to the botanical subsection *Hexopogon* of bearded irises that have seeds with arils, are distinguished from other aril irises by having beards of unicellular hairs on both falls and standards. Except *I. arenaria* and *I. flavissima*, they are natives of hot dry regions. They have been much used, especially *I. hoogiana, I. korolkowii*, and *I. stolonifera*, by hybridizers. Regelia species cultivated include: *I. arenaria*, native of the Balkans. This, like very similar *I. flavissima* and by some authorities treated as a variety of that species, inhabits more northern and more humid lands than other regelia species. *I. bloudowii* is another *I. flavissima* relative. Native from Turkestan to China, it has leaves up to 8 inches long by ½ inch broad, yellow flowers with the lower parts of the falls brownish. *I. darwasica*, of Iran and Afghanistan, up to approximately 1 foot tall, has glaucous, linear leaves about 1 foot long by ¼ inch broad. Its blooms have narrow, pointed, greenish-yellow petals. The falls, about 2¼ inches long, are veined with brownish-purple. The beards are white tipped with blue. *I. flavissima*, native from central Europe to Mongolia, has very slender leaves 3 to 8 inches long and flower stalks 2 to 6 inches tall. The blooms are yellow more or less veined with brownish-purple. The beards are orange. *I. hoogiana*, one of the loveliest, is a native of Turkestan. This has reddish rhizomes and slightly glaucous leaves up to 1½ feet long and ¾ inch wide. The flower stalks are 1½ to 2½ feet tall. The gray-blue to blue-purple blooms have 3-inch-long falls. The beards are golden- to orange- yellow. *I. korolkowii*, of Turkestan, has glaucous, linear, approximately 1-foot-long leaves. Prevailingly creamy- or greenish-white, its flowers, on stems as tall as the foliage, are suffused and veined with brown. *I. stolonifera*, of Turkestan, has dark bluish-green, sword-shaped leaves up to 1½ feet long. Its blooms, on stalks 1 foot to 2 feet tall, are pale to deep blue with the petals faintly to conspicuously margined with purplish-brown. The wavy-edged falls up to 3 inches long are approximated in length by the erect standards. The beards are yellow or blue. In *I. s. leichtlinii* the blooms are browner, marked with violet.

Pseudoregelia species, few in number and little known in cultivation, are natives of the Himalayas, Tibet, and China. They are distinguished by having gnarled, compact rhizomes without stolons and by the arils of their seeds being small. Their flowers have falls mottled with two shades of purple, purplish-pink, or lilac, and beards of unicellular hairs. Occasionally cultivated, *I. kamaonensis*, of the Himalayas, has linear leaves about 6 inches in length at blooming time later extending to about 1½ feet. The blooms, on stalks up to about 6 inches long, have purple, oblong-ovate falls mottled with lilac and a beard of white hairs or yellow-tipped white hairs. The lighter-colored standards are erect.

Oncocyclus species include some of the most beautiful irises. Best known is the mourning iris (*I. susiana*). These kinds inhabit regions of dry summers from Egypt, Israel and adjacent lands to Turkey, the Caucasus, Iraq, and Iran. They are especially suited for growing in places with approximately similar climates in the western and southwestern United States. Many have been successfully grown in other parts. From regelia irises oncocyclus species differ in having usually strongly-sickle-shaped outer leaves, flowering stalks with one bloom, and in the beards of unicellular hairs on the falls being widespread instead

Oncocyclus irises: (a) Rare *Iris antilibanotica*

(b) Undetermined species

of restricted to a narrow central band. Here are some species of oncocyclus irises: *I. atrofusca,* of Israel, has broad leaves up to about 1 foot in length, flower stalks concealed by the sheathing bases of the leaves about as long. The blooms, thickly dotted with reddish-black against a gray background, have falls with a circular patch of black and a beard of red-tipped, dull yellow hairs. *I. atropurpurea,* of Syria, has slightly glaucous, linear leaves 6 to 9 inches in length. Its blooms top stalks about as long as the leaves. They have 2-inch-long, purplish-black falls with a patch of greenish-yellow and a beard of black-tipped, yellowish hairs. The standards are erect and reddish-purple. *I. auranitica,* a native of Syria and up to 2 feet high, has erect, narrow leaves 6 inches to 1 foot long. Its flowers are orange- or bronzy-yellow veined and dotted with brown. Their 3-inch-long falls have a purplish-brown patch and yellow beard. *I. barnumiae* (syn. *I. polakii barnumiae*), of Turkey and Iran, has narrow-linear leaves, at flowering time about 6 inches long. On stalks about 1 foot long, the flowers are purple-violet with darker veins and on the 2-inch-long falls a darker patch and a dense velvety beard of purple-tipped yellow hairs. The rich red-purple standards are up to 3¼ inches long by 2¼ inches wide. *I. gatesii,* of Asia Minor, has the largest blooms of all *Iris* species. With much the aspect of *I. susiana,* it has glaucous leaves up to 1 foot long by ¾ inch wide. Its flowers, on stalks up to 1½ feet tall, are grayish-blue or sometimes brighter blue. The grayish effect derives from a fine veining of purple against a background of grayish- or greenish-white. *I. helenae* (syn. *I. mariae*), of southern Israel, is closely related to *I. urmiensis.* It has narrow-linear leaves and medium-sized flowers on slender stalks about 1 foot long. The deep purple spreading falls are obovate. The standards, obovate and bigger than the falls, are lilac-pink lined with deeper pink. *I. lortetii* is indige-

nous to Lebanon. This has glaucous, sword-shaped leaves, at flowering time under 1 foot long, flower stalks about 1 foot tall. The large and very lovely blooms, creamy-white or pale grayish-lilac, are dotted and veined with reddish-brown or crimson. The obovate falls have a dark crimson patch and yellow beard. The standards are erect, 3 to 4 inches long and broad. *I. nigricans* is similar to and perhaps only a variety of *I. atropurpurea.* Native to Israel, its flowers have white falls dotted and veined with dark purplish-brown, white standards with purple-lilac veining. *I. samariae,* one of the largest-flowered and most beautiful oncocyclus irises, is nearly like *I. lortetii,* differing chiefly in the falls of its paler flowers being less reflexed. Native to Israel, and up to 1½ feet tall, this has erect leaves ½ to ¾ inch wide. Its flowers, sometimes 5 inches wide, have light pinkish-purple falls sprinkled with small dots of a deeper hue. The standards are nearly white. *I. susiana,* the mourning iris, has been cultivated in Eu-

Iris susiana

rope for several centuries. Probably a native of Lebanon, this has linear-sword-shaped leaves about 1 foot long by ¾ to 1 inch wide and flower stalks 1 foot to 1¼ feet tall. The blooms are pale gray heavily penciled and dotted with blackish-purple. The ovate falls, 3 to 4 inches in length, have a nearly black velvety patch and a brownish-purple beard. The broad standards are shaped like the falls, but are somewhat lighter in color. *I. urmiensis* (syn. *I. polakii urmiensis*), of Iran, has linear leaves up to 1 foot long by ¼ to ½ inch wide and flower stalks approximately as long. The lemon-yellow blooms, about 2 inches wide, have falls with fluffy, yellowish-orange beards. This species is rare in cultivation.

Juno irises, bulbous kinds belonging to the subgenus *Scorpiris,* differ markedly in aspect from other members of the genus. With those that have evident stems the chief reason for this is that their leaves alternate along erect stems and spread in opposite directions more or less in one plane. The effect has been described, not inaptly,

as that of a miniature corn plant. There are other important differences. They have bulbs with thick, fleshy, persistent roots and flowers with small or minute, often spreading or reflexed standards. Their falls are crested. Commonly the lobes of the stigma are petal-like. There are a few hybrids of Juno irises. One of the best known, *I. sindpers,* the result of mating *I. aucheri* and *I. persica,* is 4 inches tall with beautiful ruffled blooms of clear blue. Another, *I.* 'Warlsind', is a hybrid of *I. warleyensis* and *I. aucheri.* Species of juno irises include: *I. aucheri* (syn. *I. sindjarensis*), native to Iraq, which has stems about 9 inches tall with channeled leaves 8 to 10 inches long by approximately 2 inches wide. Each bears usually three, sometimes more, bluish-white to pale blue blooms with falls 2 inches long marked with deeper lilac lines and with a small yellow crest. The hafts or claws (lower parts) of the falls have large wings that curve around the style branches. *I. bucharica,* of Bokhara, one of the loveliest of the group, has stems 1 foot to 1½ feet tall, with channeled, lanceolate, horny-margined leaves up to 1 foot long by 2 inches wide or sometimes rather wider. The five to seven flowers, from the upper leaf axils, have yellow, roundish falls 1 inch or more across, with white claws and yellow crests. The small, pure white standards spread horizontally. *I. graeberiana,* of Turkestan, has stems 4 to 10 inches tall crowded with lanceolate leaves that at blooming time are up to 5½ inches long, but later extend to up to 7 inches. Their undersides are slightly glaucous. The flowers, somewhat variable in color, generally have whitish falls veined with blue and with bright blue apexes. *I. magnifica,* a native of central Asia, carries on stems 1½ to 2 feet tall up to seven large blooms with on the pale violet falls a white crest flanked with yellow. The standards are pale lilac. There is a white-flowered variant. *I. orchioides,* of Asia Minor to Afghanistan, has jointed stems up to 1¼ feet tall and 9-inch-long, 2-inch-wide leaves. The three to six usually pale to golden-yellow flowers, 2 to 3 inches across, have a green patch on the lower parts of the falls on either side of the crest. The standards, usually deflexed, sometimes spreading, are yellow. Variants with spotted and with white flowers are known. *I. persica,* native from Asia Minor to Iran, is essentially stemless. It has linear leaves, at flowering time up to 3 inches long, but lengthening considerably later. Its blooms, fragrant of violets, are typically pale sea-green to greenish-blue with a purplish patch on the 2½-inch-long, ruffled falls, but several other color forms are known. The spoon-shaped standards are about ¾ inch long and twisted or turned downward.

Bulbous iris of the subgenus *Xiphion* are without perennial roots. Although the number of species is not large the group includes some of the loveliest and best esteemed cultivated irises. Beside the garden varieties and hybrids designated Spanish, English, and Dutch and the species from which they are derived, there are some delightful dwarf species. Kinds with smooth-skinned bulbs include these: *I. tingitana,* a native of North Africa, sometimes called Tangerian iris, has pointed-ovate bulbs about 1 inch in diameter. Its stems, 1½ to 2 feet tall or taller, are clothed with glaucous, grayish-green leaves 1 foot to 1½ feet long that have silvery undersides. Their bases clasp the stems. The flowers, one to three on a stem, have perianth tubes 1 inch to 2 inches long. They are about 3 inches wide, bright purplish-blue and blue with a patch of yellow on the falls. The linear-lanceolate standards are erect and 3 to 4 inches long. *I. xiphioides,* the English iris, is a native of damp meadows in the Pyrenees. From *I. xiphium* it differs in there being no sharp constriction between the blade and the haft or claw of the falls of the blooms. Also, each stem normally carries two or three flowers. It also blooms somewhat later. This has ovoid bulbs 1 inch or a little more in diameter, stems 1½ to 2 feet tall. Its leaves, which unlike those of the other kinds of this group do not appear until spring, are deeply-channeled and 1 foot to 1½ feet long. Dark violet-purple, the blooms, occasionally as much as 5 inches in diameter, have very short perianth tubes and falls with a yellow blotch. *I. xiphium,* the Spanish iris, differs from *I. tingitana* in its blooms being without perianth tubes. A native of southwest Europe and North Africa, it has ovate bulbs approximately 1 inch in diameter. From 1½ to 2 feet tall, it has deeply-channeled, linear leaves up to 1 foot long. The usually solitary flowers are light to deeper violet-purple. They have yellow-striped falls with nearly round blades much shorter than their hafts or claws. The Spanish iris has been cultivated in Europe since 1563.

Irises with bulbs covered with a fibrous, netted coat include, as undoubtedly the best known of the group, *I. reticulata,* of the region of the Caucasus and Iran. Blooming in early spring and 4 to 6 inches high or sometimes higher, this has slender, erect, four-sided leaves that overtop the blooms and continue to lengthen after the latter fade. It varies considerably in flower color. The blooms of the form in cultivation regarded as typical, although this may not be strictly botanically true, are violet with a ridge of orange along each fall. Variety 'Cantab' blooms ever so slightly later than the violet form and has light blue flowers, and 'J. S. Digit' delays showing much foliage until the flower buds are well advanced. Its flowers are red-purple.

Iris reticulata 'Cantab'

Earlier flowering than *I. reticulata* and its varieties and in bloom often slightly taller, lovely *I. histrioides,* of Asia Minor, has blooms of royal blue with the falls marked with white and crested with golden-yellow. This is the hardiest of reticulata irises. Even finer is *I. h. major,* which has bigger flowers of more lively hue. Good intermediate hybrids between *I. histrioides* and *I. reticulata* are richly blue-flowered 'Harmony' and 'Joyce' and purple-blue-flowered 'Royal Blue' and 'Wentworth'. Other precocious bloomers among bulbous irises are variable *I. histrio* of Syria and *I. vartanii.* The hardiest form of the first is somewhat later-flowering *I. h. aintabensis,* distinguished by its pale blue blooms, or-ange-striped on their falls. The species *I. histrio,* 4 to 6 inches tall, has a purplish-violet to lilac-blue bloom 2½ to 3 inches across with a white stripe on the falls. Beautiful, solitary, bright yellow flowers 1 inch to 2 inches wide with erect standards are borne by tiny *I. danfordiae,* native to Asia Minor. This has a pair of four-angled leaves at blooming time about 4 inches long, elongating to about 1 foot later. Not hardy, dwarf *I. vartanii* is nearly stemless. Native to Israel, it has four-angled leaves, at blooming time about 4 inches long later elongating to 1 foot or more. The fragrant, slaty-blue to white flowers have falls with darker veins and a yellow crest.

Iris danfordiae

Differing from all other irises in having instead of rhizomes or bulbs a bristly-fibrous bud and a dahlia-like cluster of flattened, fleshy tubers, *I. decora* (syn. *I. nepalensis*) is the only species of the subgenus *Nepalensis.* A native of central Asia, it has linear-sword-shaped leaves about 1 foot long. The flowers are pale lilac with yellow on the haft (shank) of the falls. The standards are shorter than the 1½- to 2-inch-long falls.

Garden and Landscape Uses. Irises are garden staples. Except in the tropics, some kinds are growable wherever gardens are made. In most parts of the United States a very considerable selection of types and varieties can be cultivated with great success. Chiefly they are outdoor plants, but some bulbous sorts are excellent for forcing in greenhouses for cut flowers, and a number of choice dwarfs are well suited for alpine greenhouses.

With the exception of the few kinds of so-called remontant or reblooming varieties of bearded irises, which in favored climates make some show of flowers in fall as well as more abundant ones in spring, irises have short seasons of bloom. But then, so do many other garden favorites, daffodils, lilacs, peonies, and tulips, for example. It is arguable that a once-a-year, comparatively brief, magnificent feast of bloom is preferable to more prolonged displays. Now that chrysanthemums are available every day of the year some dim-

Iris reticulata

Iris histrio

ming of the wonder that formerly accompanied their fall debut has taken place. Modern transportation and deep freezing have removed strawberries from the list of brief-season luxuries with the consequent loss of the joys of anticipation and realization of the "strawberry season." But although individual sorts of irises bloom for comparatively short periods, by planting a suitable selection one can have flowers from earliest spring, or in mild climates midwinter, to well after midsummer, and that without counting a second blooming of the remontants, which is not at all bad, and keeps iris fans happy.

As garden and landscape plants the great uses of irises are in beds and borders, either alone or in combination with other herbaceous perennials and annuals, and, especially beardless and crested sorts, for planting informally in more naturalistic surroundings. Those crested are admirable for lightly shaded woodland gardens, and similar sites, and for rock gardens. Many other dwarf irises including kinds with reticulate (netted) bulbs are appropriate for rock gardens and some of the choicest for alpine greenhouses.

Japanese and Louisiana irises can be used in much the same ways in landscapes and are suitable for similar sites. Japanese sorts are not bog plants, and in the north the Louisianas are better not treated as such. Both need fertile, humus-rich, acid soil and are splendid for planting by watersides. Only in the south where the growing season is very long will they endure wet roots throughout the year. Elsewhere they need generous supplies of water and will even stand flooding from spring to late summer, but during the dormant season they should be much drier, without ever drying out. They are grand for ground a few inches to a foot or so above water level bordering pools and streams and are especially effective placed so that they are reflected in the water.

Irises that endure and flourish in consistently wet soils and are particularly suitable for watersides and bog gardens in full sun or where they receive perhaps a little shade for part of each day are *I. laevigata*, *I. pseudacorus*, *I. versicolor*, and *I. virginica*.

Spanish and Dutch irises are excellent for grouping in flower beds and forcing in greenhouses. Less hardy *I. tingitana* is similarly adapted for greenhouses and in mild climates outdoors. All need a warm, sheltered location and fertile, well-drained, preferably somewhat sandy soil. English irises are less suitable for greenhouse cultivation. Outdoors they appreciate moister soils than Spanish and Dutch. But the site must not be wet. They are thoroughly comfortable only in humid, fairly cool climates such as that of the Pacific Northwest. As garden plants and cut flowers they have the same uses as Spanish and Dutch irises.

Aril irises, those of the regelia, pseudoregelia, and onocyclus groups, except in favored climates, are mainly for iris collectors and fanciers, to be placed in the garden in situations good judgment suggests will be to their individual liking. Strange *I. foetidissima*, not an aril, is worth planting in a dryish location for its decorative seed pods.

Cultivation. Garden irises are species and descendents of species that grow natively in many and various climates and soils. As a consequence their needs under cultivation vary considerably according to kind. It is convenient to treat this phase of our discussion with special reference to the groups into which irises are classified, always remembering that within the groups individual sorts may have particular needs.

Bearded irises respond to full sun and dryish, well-drained, but not arid, slightly acid, neutral, or somewhat alkaline soils. They abhor shade and "wet feet." Excellent subsurface drainage is imperative to success. Any fertile soil capable of producing satisfactory cabbages, corn, potatoes, and a general run of common garden flowers satisfies bearded irises. In preparation for planting, spade and fertilize the ground. Do not use fresh manure or an over-abundance of nitrogenous fertilizer. If you do, you are likely to encourage lush, soft growth especially susceptible to disease. If the soil is deficient in organic matter work in moderate amounts of compost, very well-rotted manure, humus, leaf mold, or peat moss, or turn under a cover crop. If manure is used bury it so that it will not be in contact with the rhizomes. Mix in also a dressing of superphosphate or bonemeal and a light one of a complete garden fertilizer of comparatively low nitrogen content. Should the soil be acid, lime it as part of the preplanting preparation, but the need for this is often over-emphasized.

For their well-being, dig up, divide, and replant irises of this bearded group every third or fourth year. In the north do this shortly after blooming is through, just as

new rhizome growth and roots begin to develop. In the south and elsewhere where summer heat or dryness is great it is better to wait until the end of August or early September. Irises of this group survive if transplanted at other times, but the next season's blooming is likely to be disappointing. Even when reset at the most fa-

(b) Cut the rhizomes into pieces, each with a single fan of leaves

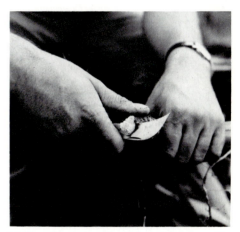

(c) Pare the cut ends of the rhizomes with a sharp knife

Dividing bearded irises: (a) Dig up the clumps after flowering is through

(d) Cut back the foliage

(e) Shorten the roots

Planting bearded irises: (a) Divisions ready for planting

(f) Dip the cut ends in, or dust them with, a fungicide

(b) Making a planting hole with a trowel

(d) A newly planted group of divisions

(c) Firming the soil about the roots with the fingers

Cutting off flowering stalks after the blooms have faded

vorable season some varieties fail to bloom the following year. Late-set irises may be heaved out of the ground by freezing.

After digging, cut back the foliage to from one-half to one-third its length. Then wash all soil from the roots with a hose and inspect the rhizomes closely for disease and borers. If enough healthy stock is available select and divide for replanting disease- and pest-free rhizomes only. If affected rhizomes must be salvaged cut away all parts made spongy or soft by rot disease, extract any larvae of the iris borer, and cut away parts tunneled through by that "beast." Also, examine the soil in the holes left when digging the clumps for the presence of any larvae that may be pupating there. Destroy any you find. With a sharp knife cut the rhizomes into sections, each consisting of a terminal healthy piece with a fan of leaves. As a precaution soak the divisions for half an hour or so in a fungicide-insecticide mixture or in a solution of Clorox, and dust all cut surfaces with sulfur or the fungicide ferbam.

When planting, allow sufficient space between the divisions for adequate normal growth. Depending upon variety this is likely to be for those set in groups 8 to 9 inches, less for dwarfs, and somewhat closer perhaps for those in more widely spaced nursery rows. Dig a deep hole for each division. Hill soil in its center so that the top of the mound is level with the surface. Position the rhizome on top with its roots hanging down the sides of the mound so that when the job is finished the top of the rhizome will be just above the soil. Fill in soil, pack it firmly, and water thoroughly. Unless a long dry spell follows, no further watering is needed. If drought comes, water thoroughly every ten days or so.

Routine maintenance of bearded irises calls for clean cultivation, keeping the beds free of weeds. This is better done by cultivating and hand weeding than by mulching. Light applications of a low-nitrogen complete fertilizer made in early spring and toward the end of summer, applied around the clumps rather than on or among the rhizomes, are conducive to good growth. In dry climates, and elsewhere in times of drought, deep irrigations at intervals of ten days or so are necessary or at least are highly beneficial, but ordinarily except on thirsty, sandy, or gravelly soils, bearded irises get along well without watering. After flowering is through cut off the flowering stalks without removing any foliage.

Siberian irises require care somewhat different from that recommended for tall bearded sorts. To begin with, they prefer ground richer in organic matter and slightly acid. Do not lime the soil for these. Rather heavy soils are preferred to sandy ones, but good results can be had on the latter if fertilizing and watering receive adequate attention. Like their meadow plant ancestors, Siberian varieties are best satisfied with moderate moisture at all times. Neither excessively wet nor dry earth are to their liking. These irises can with advantage remain undisturbed longer than bearded kinds. So long as they are flourishing it is unnecessary to lift and divide them every third or fourth year. When this becomes desirable or necessary make the planting sites ready by spading deeply and working into the soil liberal amounts of compost, rotted manure, humus, or peat moss, and a dressing of complete garden fertilizer.

Transplant in early spring or early fall, not in summer. Dig the clumps with good balls of roots, cut the foliage back about halfway, and with a sharp, heavy knife, machete, or cleaver, separate them into divisions each of four to six fans of leaves with as many roots attached as possible. Do not allow the roots to dry. Plant the division 9 inches or so apart with the tops of the thin rhizomes an inch or two below the surface. Pack the soil carefully to eliminate air pockets and drench with water.

Siberians bloom sparsely the summer after transplanting, but in favorable sites settle down and make grand displays afterward. To encourage healthy, robust, rich green foliage that will support such annual showings apply a dressing of a complete garden fertilizer in early spring and as flowering wanes. Maintaining an organic mulch and watering regularly in dry weather do much to maintain vigor.

Japanese and Louisiana irises have much the same cultural needs. Both abhor lime. For them a deep, rich soil fat with decayed organic matter and at least slightly acid is best. Lots of moisture from spring to fall is essential for fine results, but only in the deep south and elsewhere where the growing season is nearly continuous throughout the year will they tolerate constant bog conditions. Deep spading and mixing in really great amounts of compost, decayed manure, or other suitable organic material and a dressing of a complete fertilizer prepares the ground for the reception of Japanese and Louisiana irises.

Plant in early fall or early spring, the latter for preference in regions of severe winters. Lift and divide Japanese varieties every third or fourth year, Louisianas every two or three years. Divide the Japanese into pieces each of three or four leaf fans, the Louisianas into conveniently sized pieces according to kind. Do not permit the roots to dry while out of the ground. Set the divisions with their rhizomes an inch or two below the surface, those of Japanese varieties about 9 inches apart, Louisianas at that or somewhat greater distances depending upon vigor of the species or variety.

Following planting, mulch with compost, leaf mold, peat moss, decayed sawdust, bagasse, or other suitable organic material. Routine care of these irises consists of fertilizing in spring, maintaining a continuous mulch, and watering generously in dry weather, except Louisianas during their July and August period of summer dormancy. It is important to keep them well mulched at that time to prevent the rhizomes being heat-scorched. If mulch is not available a two-inch layer of sandy soil (to be removed at the end of the dormant period) may be substituted. Some southern gardeners lay boards over the plants in place of mulch.

Spuria irises are generally easy to satisfy in ordinary garden soils, somewhat acid, neutral, or slightly alkaline. They appreciate fairly high levels of fertility, and so long as they are doing well are best left undisturbed for a few years. In general they show their displeasure of transplanting by not flowering satisfactorily for a year or two afterward. Prepare the ground as you would for Siberians or indeed for a wide variety of common hardy herbaceous perennials. Fall seems to be the best time to divide and transplant spuria irises, but it can be accomplished in spring. Planting technique and aftercare are as for Siberians.

Crested irises for the most part respond best to slightly acid soils of woodland flavor. True, *I. lacustris* is reported to be a calciphile, a lover of limestone, but in its native region where limestone prevails as bedrock it occurs in organic deposits well above that and with such acid-soil companions as *Linnaea borealis*, species of *Goodyera*, and *Cornus canadensis*. In any case in gardens it grows happily in somewhat acid soils of distinctly sandy nature. This, and the beardless American, *I. verna*, often prove difficult to transplant successfully at any time other than earliest spring. In preparing for these irises make the earth agreeable by mixing in abundant decayed organic matter. Set small divisions a few inches apart, the distance depending upon the vigor of the kind, with the rhizomes just showing above the surface. Except for watering in dry weather and perhaps a spring application of a complete fertilizer, aftercare is minimal.

The vesper iris (*I. dichotoma*) often renews by self-sowing and is very easily raised from seeds sown as soon as they are ripe in a cold frame or protected place outdoors or in pots or flats indoors. Seedlings bloom when about one year old. The vesper iris is an interesting and elegant addition to flower beds and for use in less formal surroundings. It succeeds in ordinary well-drained soil in sunny locations.

Spanish and Dutch irises and *I. tingitana* and related sorts that have smooth bulbs are among the easiest to grow of bulb plants. Except that they are less hardy, their needs are essentially those of tulips, and like tulips they are commonly increased by offsets. Where winters are at all cold select sheltered sites, such as at the foot of a south- or west-facing wall for these.

Plant the bulbs 3 to 5 inches apart and at a depth of 3 to 4 inches in early fall in fertile, fairly loose, porous, sharply-drained soil. In cold climates cover them over winter with salt hay, branches of evergreens, or other material that will afford protection. Alternatively, for cut flowers plant them in cold frames and cover these as may be needed during the winter to afford additional protection from cold.

The forcing procedure to bloom Spanish and Dutch irises early in greenhouses is the same as for tulips, except that they will not stand as high temperatures. A night level of about 50°F with a daytime increase of five to ten degrees gives the best results. Bulbs that have produced flowers cut with long stems and foliage are of little further use. For forcing it is best to purchase and plant new bulbs each fall.

Outdoors, bulbs to be held over from year to year may be left in the ground, or be dug after the foliage dies and then dried on the ground surface for a few hours and stored in shallow boxes or suspended in net bags or old stockings from the roof in a dry cellar, garage, or other convenient place. English irises in regions adapted to their cultivation are more persistent in gardens than Spanish and Dutch. Their requirements are the same except that they need a cool, moist soil and are better left in the ground through the summer.

Irises with netted bulbs, such as *I. reticulata* and associated sorts, are generally easy to manage. They prosper in gritty, reasonably nourishing soil under much the same conditions as crocuses. As with crocuses, it is important that they fully develop and ripen their foliage after flowering. To encourage this, give them a light dressing of a complete fertilizer about the time blooming is through and do not permit them to lack for moisture until the leaves have died naturally. Shallow-rooted, small annuals may be sown among groups of these winter- and spring-bloomers so that what otherwise would be bare patches in the garden later are furnished. Propagation is usually by offsets.

Oncocyclus and pseudoregelia irises need different conditions and care than are satisfactory for most other kinds. They are natives of places where great drought characterizes hot summers, but even in regions where similar conditions prevail they are not always easy to tame and grow successfully. Elsewhere they may prove completely intractable. A chief requirement is that they be kept absolutely dry from when their foliage ripens until fall. This may be achieved by digging them after the leaves die and storing them in dry sand in a warm place indoors or by covering the beds or cold frames in which they are accommodated to ward off all rain.

The most satisfactory procedure with oncocyclus and pseudoregelia irises is to plant the bulblike rhizomes in thoroughly well-drained beds raised a few inches to a foot above the ground and located in a warm, sheltered place, such as at the foot of a south-facing wall. See that the soil is loose and porous, yet satisfyingly nutritious. Good loam freely lightened with brick or lime rubble and sand, sweetened by the application of ground dolomitic limestone, and fertilized with bonemeal is likely to afford the best chances of success. Do not plant before late September or early October, this as a precaution against the too-early production of foliage.

When planting, set the rhizomes with their tips 2 inches beneath the surface and with their roots angled downward. Water thoroughly immediately after planting and keep the soil moderately moist thereafter. Keep the beds covered through the winter with salt hay, straw, or excelsior to protect foliage of such kinds as *I. atropurpurea, I. burnumiae, I. helenae, I. lortetii,* and *I. susiana,* which has a tendency to soon appear. Remove the covering early in spring.

Hybrids between oncocyclus and regelia irises, called regeliocyclus hybrids, respond to the treatment suggested for oncocyclus kinds. Oncobred irises, hybrids between oncocyclus kinds, and bearded irises, are generally very much easier to grow, although they too must have very good drainage. To protect against excessive winter rains the beds may be covered with polyethylene plastic film. Covering is less necessary for sorts such as *I. gatesii,* which show no foliage until spring, but if applied it does no harm.

Regelia irises are less exacting than oncocyclus sorts, nevertheless they need some special attention especially in the matter of keeping them dry in summer. Their general needs are those of oncocyclus kinds with somewhat less strict emphasis on the need for perfect drainage. They will not prosper in soils wet in summer. In favored localities regelia irises thrive under conditions that suit bearded kinds.

Seed propagation of irises is pretty much confined to the efforts of plant breeders concerned with developing new varieties and to the multiplication of species of which inadequate stocks are available to allow for other means of increase. Seeds resulting from uncontrolled pollinations of hybrid irises are likely to produce a wide variety of mostly inferior offspring. Iris seed germinates erratically, usually over periods of from a few months to a year or more after sowing. It may be sown in fall outdoors or in cold frames.

Diseases and Pests. The most serious disease of irises is the incurable, foul-smelling bacterial soft rot that softens and destroys the rhizomes, causing the leaves to topple. This disease gains entry through wounds, most often those made by borers. A prime requisite for controlling soft rot is to eliminate borers. Other diseases include less serious bacterial leaf spot, fungus rhizome rot and other rots, rust, virus mosaic, and blue mold and ink spot diseases of bulbous irises. Sanitary measures including the prompt removal and destruction of affected parts and the cleaning up of dead foliage are helpful in limiting the spread of diseases among irises. Avoiding bruising or wounding rhizomes, bulbs, and foliage is also important. Cut surfaces may be treated with Clorox diluted in equal amounts of water and by dusting with sulfur or ferbam. As a help in disease control it is important to keep in check aphids, thrips, and other animal pests.

Iris borer is the most troublesome insect pest of bearded, Japanese, and some few other irises. The destructive phase is the brownish-black-headed, whitish larvae of a moth, which in late summer lays its eggs on old iris leaves and debris. In spring the eggs hatch and the young crawl up the leaves and tunnel into them a few inches above the ground and work their way to the rhizomes where they continue to feed. Control consists of clearing away all old leaves and debris in fall and of spraying with an insecticide about the time the eggs hatch and before the young grubs enter the leaves. Other animal pests that may infest irises include aphids, bulb mites, iris weevil (which feeds on the seeds), Japanese beetle grubs, nematodes, thrips, and yellow-striped, black zebra caterpillars.

IRISH. This word is part of the common names of these plants: Irish-heath (*Daboecia cantabrica*), Irish ivy (*Hedera helix hibernica*), and Irish-moss (*Arenaria verna caespitosa* and *Sagina subulata*).

IRISHMAN or WILD IRISHMAN is *Discaria toumatou.*

IRON CHELATES. For their satisfactory growth plants need minute amounts of iron. If they are unable to obtain this, chlorophyll development is impaired and the characteristic yellowing of the foliage called chlorosis results. This is especially likely to happen to such acid-soil plants such as rhododendrons and other member of the heath family ERICACEAE if the soil in which they grow or water they receive is alkaline or if subsurface soil drainage is inadequate.

The inability of plants to obtain iron does not necessarily indicate lack of iron in the soil. It may be present in adequate amounts, but chemically tied up in ways not available to plants. An easy and effective corrective for this condition is to use chelated iron either by applying it to the ground or as a spray to the foliage. Chelated iron, obtainable under various trade names from dealers in garden supplies, should always be used strictly according to the directions on the label, otherwise damage to foliage may result.

IRON DEFICIENCY. Iron is one of the trace elements essential in minute quantities for plant growth. Without it chlorophyll is not produced. If the supply is deficient, chlorosis (yellowing of the foliage) occurs and production of food by the leaves is seriously hampered or stopped.

Foliage of plants affected by iron chlorosis characteristically shows a pattern of green veins against a yellow background. The trouble is rarely lack of iron in the soil. Much more commonly it occurs because that element is tied up chemically in such forms that it is unavailable to the roots. In a soil at all alkaline, such acid-soil plants as azaleas and rhododendrons are especially susceptible to iron chlorosis. Planted near foundations of buildings, they sometimes suffer in this way because lime is released from the concrete or mortar. In poorly drained ground they may behave similarly.

Iron deficiency in plants is corrected by supplying minute amounts in a form available to them. The most rapid results are obtained by the convenient method of applying chelated iron as a foliage spray or to the ground. Iron chelates are marketed under various trade names. Use them strictly according to the manufacturer's directions. Too strong an application may damage foliage.

IRON TREE is *Parrotia persica.*

IRONBARK. See Eucalyptus.

IRONWEED. See Vernonia.

IRONWOOD. This word is a common name of these plants: *Carpinus caroliniana, Metrosideros, Ostrya virginiana.* It is also used as part of the common names of these: black ironwood (*Olea laurifolia* and *Krugiodendron*), Catalina ironwood (*Lyono-*

thamnus floribundus), Ceylon-ironwood (*Mesua ferrea*), desert-ironwood (*Olneya tesota*), and Santa Cruz Island ironwood (*Lyonothamnus floribundus asplenifolius*).

IRRIGATION. Agriculturists and commercial horticulturists employ irrigation as a standard, and in many parts of North America, necessary technique of crop production. In desert and semidesert regions home gardeners are largely dependent upon it and even in humid areas it is becoming more common, especially for the maintenance of lawns. As the word is employed here, although it need not be restricted to such employment, irrigation refers to the automatic application of water, usually to fairly large areas, by devices other than watering cans, hoses, and single sprinklers commonly used for watering. Actually there is no sharp distinction between watering and irrigation.

Open-ditch irrigation, a fairly common commercial method, is not often practiced in gardens, although under favorable circumstances there is no reason other than perhaps aesthetics why it should not be. This system employs shallow trenches, sometimes lined with tiles, bricks, cement, or polyethylene plastic film, to carry water by gravity from a higher source to places where it is needed to refresh plants. Wherever needed, run-off points from the main streams are installed. These can be simple devices such as suitably shaped pieces of sheet metal or pipe that can be opened or closed as needed. Portable systems of coupled, light-weight metal pipes carrying water under pressure are much used in commercial operations and occasionally in gardens.

More popular among home gardeners, and certainly work-reducing, are permanently installed underground irrigation systems. The availability of plastic pipe for this purpose has made unnecessary the cumbersome metal pipe previously used that generally needed a plumber to install. Plastic pipe systems can often be put in by a homeowner or handyman. Pipes, sprinkler heads, and control valves are sold in kits and separately.

Under lawns bury the pipes 5 or 6 inches deep and have the sprinkler heads flush with or slightly below the surface. Beneath shrubs and other deep-rooted plants set the pipes deeper. Locate them, so far as possible, at the edges of beds and borders and fit them with half head sprinklers so that the water is directed inward. Should the bed be too wide to be covered in this way, run one or more pipes through it with sprinkler heads raised on standards high enough so they will not be disturbed by cultivating operations and will distribute the water without interference by low branches. Standards that can be raised as the plants grow are available. Where the ground freezes deeply in winter, if possible lay the

pipes so that in fall they can be drained by gravity. If this cannot be done it may be necessary to blow them out by air pressure and then close them tightly to prevent water from seeping in.

In planning a subterranean irrigation system take care that the sprinkler heads are sufficiently close to ensure complete coverage. Because in still air the water dispensed from each full head is spread over a circle, it is obvious that to achieve full coverage there must be some overlapping. This is preferable to leaving spots uncovered. At the margins of the irrigated area half heads or quarter heads (heads designed to spread water over one-half or one-quarter of a full circle) can be employed. By their use water is saved and that dispensed is concentrated on the places you want irrigated. For satisfactory results water pressure of not less than 30 pounds is generally needed. Take care not to have too many sprinkler heads on any one line. If in doubt about this consult an irrigation expert or a plumber. With large installations, and where pressure is only moderate, arrange for shut-off valves so that part of the system can be operated while the remainder is closed. This can be done manually or by use of a time-switch mechanism that allows the entire area to be watered piece by piece in succession.

The amount of water to be applied at one time and the frequency of irrigation is related to the kinds of plants, type of soil, climatic conditions, and weather. Always, penetration to the depth of the roots is desirable. In a coarse, sandy soil, water equal to ¾ inch of rain, about 125 gallons to each 100 square feet, wets the ground to a depth of about 1 foot. Approximately three times as much may be required to achieve the same result in a fine-grained clay soil. On loamy soils intermediate amounts will do as much. Often it is desirable to soak the soil to a depth of 2 feet for which it will be necessary to use twice the amount of water needed to achieve a 1-foot drenching. Care must be taken, and this is especially important with clayey soils and on slopes, not to apply it faster than it can be absorbed by the ground. Surface run-off erodes soil and wastes water.

ISATIS (Í-satis)—Woad. Here belongs the plant used by the ancient Britons to stain their bodies blue, as well as a few other species sometimes grown for ornament. The genus *Isatis*, of the mustard family CRUCIFERAE, includes about forty-five species of annuals, biennials, and herbaceous perennials. It inhabits Europe and western Asia and bears as its botanical name its classical Greek one. Mostly tall, branching, leafy-stemmed, and with abundant small yellow blooms, woads have undivided, often stem-clasping leaves. Like most of their family, their flowers, in racemes, have four sepals, four petals that spread to form

a cross, two shorter and four longer stamens, and one style. The winged, broad-elliptic to oblong or paddle-shaped seed pods are pendulous and ribbed along their sides. Each has one seed. Botanically this is a difficult genus, several of its species being very similar and with or without branchless hairs.

Dyer's woad (*I. tinctoria*) is a hardy biennial indigenous to Europe and southwest Asia and naturalized in parts of North America. Julius Caesar described finding the natives of Britain with their bodies stained with the juice of this plant, and for many centuries it was cultivated extensively as the source of the most important blue dye available to Europeans until the coming of indigo from the Orient. Even after the introduction of that famous dye, woad was grown to mix with indigo to fix it and also as a mordant for a black dye. Analine dyes practically superseded indigo and woad. Woad was also used medicinally by the ancient Greeks, Romans, and others.

Isatis tinctoria

The herbalist Gerard well described dyer's woad. He said "Woad is about three feet high, with long, bluish-green leaves growing round and out of the stalk, growing smaller as they reach the top, when they branch out with small yellow flowers, which in turn produce small seedlike little black tongues. The root is white and single." The "black tongues" are of course the seed pods. To Gerard's description may be added that the plant may be hairless or finely-hairy, that its stem-clasping upper leaves are arrow-shaped with pointed basal ears, and its lower ones stalked and lanceolate, that its flowers are in large clusters and are about ¼ inch wide, and that its drooping, paddle-shaped seed pods are ½ to 1 inch long. Dyer's woad blooms in late spring and early summer.

Native to the Alps and Apennines of Europe, *I. allionii* (syn. *I. alpina*) is a hardy herbaceous perennial up to 1 foot tall, with a branching rhizome and blunt ears to its stem-clasping, arrow-shaped upper leaves. The blooms are similar to those of dyer's wood. Perennial *I. glauca,* of Turkey, 2 to 3 feet tall and hairless, has blunt, oblong, toothless, very glaucous leaves up to 10 inches long and not stem-clasping. The small, mustard-yellow flowers are in big panicles.

Garden Uses. In addition to its obvious suitability for inclusion in collections of dye and medicinal plants, dyer's wood is sufficiently attractive to be grown for variety in perennial beds and naturalistic settings. True, though it cannot be rated equal to such sophisticated garden plants as iris, phlox, and chrysanthemum, it is worth a place. The perennial kinds are appropriate for flower beds and *I. allionii* for rock gardens.

Cultivation. Woads are easily raised from seed, and the perennials, by division. They need sunny sites and well-drained, reasonably fertile soils. The biennials are sown the summer before they are to bloom, either where they are to remain and the seedlings thinned, so the plants do not crowd, or in a seed bed from which the seedlings are transplanted to nursery beds, and, in fall or early spring, are again transplanted to their flowering quarters.

ISERTIA (Isért-ia). To the madder family Ru-BIACEAE belongs *Isertia,* a genus of twenty-five species. Native of tropical America, it consists of large-leaved trees and shrubs. The name commemorates Paul Erdmann Isert, a German botanist and surgeon employed by Denmark. He died in 1789.

Isertias have opposite or less often whorled (in circles of three or more), undivided, thick, leathery, slender-pointed leaves. The stalkless or short-stalked flowers, many together in terminal clusters or panicles, are red, less often yellow or white. They have persistent, four- to six-lobed or lobeless calyxes, and tubular, funnel-shaped, fleshy, six-lobed corollas. There are four to six stamens and a style ending in a two- to six-lobed stigma. The fruits are berries.

A shrub or tree up to 50 feet high, but usually much lower, *I. parviflora,* a common native of woodlands in Trinidad and northern South America, has strongly-pinnately-veined, pointed-oblong-elliptic, short-stalked leaves. They are up to 1 foot long by one-half as wide, but are often slenderer in proportion to their lengths. Their undersides are sparsely-hairy, their upper surfaces hairless. The briefly-stalked, pink, rose-pink, or white flowers are in panicles about 6 inches long by 4 to 5 inches wide. They are about ½ inch in length. The black fruits are up to ⅕ inch in diameter.

Strikingly beautiful *I. coccinea,* of northern South America, is a large shrub or small tree. This has pointed, ovate-oblong to oblanceolate, leathery leaves up to 1 foot long or longer by one-half as broad,

hairless on their upper surfaces and rusty-hairy beneath. The flowers, red, orange, or white, the corollas hairy on their outsides, are 2 to 2½ inches long.

Garden and Landscape Uses and Cultivation. Only in the humid tropics and warm subtropics are insertias useful as outdoor ornaments. They may be rarely cultivated in large, tropical conservatories. They thrive in ordinary fertile soils and are generally increased by seed.

ISLAY is *Prunus ilicifolia.*

ISLAYA (Is-láya). Nine Chilean and Peruvian species are accounted for in this genus of the cactus family CACTACEAE. Related to *Parodia,* they differ from that genus in technical characteristics of their fruits. Their name is derived from that of the Peruvian province of Islay. Some authorities include *Islaya* in *Neoporteria.* The species seem to intergrade and are not clearly defined.

Mostly rare in cultivation, islayas are globular or shortly-cylindrical, formidably spiny plants. The plant bodies of *I. islayensis* (syns. *Parodia islayensis, Malacocarpus islayensis, Echinocactus islayensis*) have many low, somewhat spiraled, lumpy ribs and are 6 to 8 inches tall. Each lump or tubercle has an areole (the area from which spines develop) bearing a cluster of as many as fifteen to twenty radial spines and four to seven longer, straight centrals. The latter may be ¾ inch in length and are brownish-yellow to gray. The yellow flowers, about ¾ inch long, have reddish bristles on their scaly, woolly perianth tubes. A smaller, globular species with plant bodies with about seventeen sharp ribs, *I. minor* (syn. *Parodia minor*) has spine clusters of four spreading centrals and about twenty smaller radials. All are at first black, but later become gray. The yellow blooms are about ¾ inch long.

Garden Uses and Cultivation. These are the same as for *Parodia, Copiapoa,* and most other small desert cactuses. General requirements are discussed under Cactuses.

ISMENE. See Hymenocallis.

ISOCHILUS (Iso-chìlus). Native from Mexico to Argentina and the West Indies, *Isochilus,* of the orchid family ORCHIDACEAE, consists of four variable species. Its name, from the Greek *isos,* equal, and *cheilos,* a lip, alludes to the form of the lip of the flower.

These orchids in the wild grow mainly on trees as epiphytes, on rocks, or rarely in the ground. They form dense clumps of slender, erect, reedy stems 2 to 2½ feet tall furnished with grassy foliage. The leaves, in two ranks, clasp the stems with their bases. Borne at the apexes of the stems, the bright pink to magenta or more rarely white blooms are solitary or in short,

dense racemes. Individual blooms are small, do not open fully, and have similar sepals and petals that form a tube enclosing the other floral parts. The lip is small, three-lobed, and often has two prominent dark purple spots.

Native from Mexico to Panama, *I. major* has lanceolate leaves about 2½ inches long and one-sided racemes of nearly ½-inch long magenta, pink, or white flowers with the uppermost leaves, which usually partly hide half of them, commonly more or less strongly toned with the same color as the flowers. From the last, *I. linearis,* of from Mexico to Argentina and Cuba, differs in having narrowly-linear leaves not over ⅛ inch wide and magenta, pink, or white blooms solitary or comparatively loose racemes. The upper leaves are also green.

Isochilus linearis

Garden Uses and Cultivation. These are easy to manage. Accommodated in pots, hanging baskets, or on rafts, they succeed in most types of rooting materials suitable for orchids, such as bark chips, osmunda, and tree fern fiber. It is important that drainage be good and repotting receive attention before the medium becomes sour. In greenhouses winter night temperatures of 55 to 60°F are satisfactory with an increase of a few degrees by day. The atmosphere should be fairly humid and watering is necessary throughout the year. Mild applications of fertilizer from spring to fall are highly beneficial. Moderate shade from strong sun is needed. Propagation is by division. In the humid tropics these orchids prosper attached to the trunks and branches of living trees. For more information see Orchids.

ISOLATOCEREUS (Isolato-cèreus). One handsome species constitutes *Isolatocereus,* of the cactus family CACTACEAE. Its generic name, derived from the Latin *isolatus,* detached, and the name of the related genus *Cereus,* alludes to the plants in nature occurring as widely separated specimens on rocky hillsides. The genus *Isolatocereus* is by some botanists included in *Lemaireocereus.*

One of the tallest cactuses, *I. dumortieri* (syns. *Lemaireocereus dumortieri, Cereus dumortieri*), a native of Mexico, is a short-trunked, candelabrum-branched tree up to 45 feet high with a spread about equal to one-half its height. Its bright green to bluish-green branches are constricted into joints and have five to seven sharply-triangular ribs with spine clusters of nine to eleven slender, spreading, yellowish-white radials about ½ inch long and one to four 1½-inch-long centrals of the same color. One of the centrals points downward. The 2-inch-long, somewhat less wide flowers come from the sides of the stems, open at night, and have wide-spreading, white petals and brownish-red outer perianth segments. Their corolla tubes and ovaries are, like the fruits, naked of scales and hairs. The egg-shaped fruits, about 1½ inches long, contain red flesh.

Garden and Landscape Uses and Cultivation. This is an impressive cactus for outdoor landscaping in warm dry climates and for inclusion in greenhouse collections. It thrives in full sun in well-drained soil and is easily propagated by cuttings and seed. For more information see Cactuses.

ISOLEPIS. See Scirpus.

ISOLOMA. See Kohleria.

ISOMERIS. See Cleome.

ISOPLEXIS (Isopléx-is). Botanists recognize three species of *Isoplexis,* of the figwort family SCROPHULARIACEAE, inhabitants of the Canary Islands and Madeira. They are closely related to foxgloves (*Digitalis*) from which they differ in having the upper lip of the corolla as long or longer than the lower lip. The name, from the Greek *isos,* equal, and *pleko,* to plait, refers to this feature.

Members of this genus are evergreen, shrubby or subshrubby plants with alternate leaves and dense terminal racemes of five-petaled, tubular, two-lipped flowers with four stamens and a two-lobed style. The fruits are capsules.

Attaining a height of 4 to 6 feet, *I. canariensis* (syn. *Digitalis canariensis*), of the Canary Islands, is stiffly-branched and has thick, glossy green, sharply-toothed, lanceolate leaves, downy beneath and up to 6 inches long by 1 inch to 2 inches wide. The strongly two-lipped, yellow-brown flowers are in racemes up to 1 foot long. A native of Madeira, *I. sceptrum* (syn. *Digitalis sceptrum*) has larger leaves, toothed and downy on their undersides, and narrower, less obviously two-lipped, tawny-yellow flowers in broad racemes 4 to 5 inches long.

Isoplexis canariensis

Garden and Landscape Uses and Cultivation. These plants are suitable for outdoor beds and borders in warm, dry climates and may be grown in greenhouses. They succeed in ordinary, freely drained garden soil in full sun. The only pruning needed is any necessary to keep them shapely. Indoors in pots or tubs top-dress them each late winter or early spring, just before new growth begins, with rich soil. Ordinarily, repotting large specimens is done only at intervals of three or four years. Well-rooted examples are improved by regular applications of dilute liquid fertilizer from spring to fall. Greenhouse specimens benefit from being plunged (buried almost to the rims of their containers) in a bed of sand, ashes, or sawdust outdoors in a sunny place during summer. Bring them indoors before fall frost. From fall through spring keep the greenhouse night temperature 40 to 50°F and the day temperature a few degrees higher. Whenever weather permits ventilate the greenhouse freely. Never let the soil become really dry, but in winter permit it to become drier than at other times before water is given. Propagation is easily effected by cuttings taken in late sumer and planted in a greenhouse propagating bench and by seed sown in sandy soil in spring.

ISOPOGON (Iso-pògon). The Australian genus *Isopogon* consists of evergreen shrubs, chiefly inhabitants of the western part of the continent. They number thirty species and are included in the protea family PROTEACEAE. The name, from the Greek *isos,* equal, and *pogon,* a beard, alludes to the tufts of hairs at the ends of the perianth segments.

Isopogons have rigid, undivided or pinnately-divided leaves and flowers in very dense spikelike or conelike heads. Each stalkless bloom is in the axil of a deciduous bract or scale. The blooms have slender perianth tubes, split above into four petal-like lobes. The lobes are deciduous, but the lower parts of the perianths persist with the fruits. There are four stamens and an undivided style. The fruits are small nuts.

The shoots of *I. anemonifolius,* a 4- to 6-foot-tall species of New South Wales, are downy. Its twice- or thrice-narrowly-pinnately-lobed or divided, long-stalked leaves, 1½ to 4 inches long, are of slender, pointed lobes or segments. The yellow, densely crowded flowers are in spherical, solitary heads about 1½ inches in diameter, or the heads are two or three together and smaller.

Western Australia is home to *I. roseus* (syn. *I. dubius*) which has pink flowers. They are in spherical heads, usually solitary and 1 inch to 1½ inches across, but sometimes smaller and up to five or six together. The leaves, once- or twice-divided into three, or sometimes pinnate, including their stalks, are 1 inch to 3 inches long. The lobes or segments are pointed and slender. Another Western Australian, *I. sphaerocephalus* is an erect shrub about 5 feet tall, with downy shoots and young foliage. It has undivided, pale green, lobeless leaves 2 to 4 inches long, up to ½ inch wide, and with a minute sharp point at the apex. The creamy-yellow flowers, usually from a few of the uppermost leaf axils, but sometimes solitary, are crowded in spherical heads ¾ inch to 1½ inches across.

Other kinds that may be cultivated include highly decorative, rose-pink-flowered *I. cuneatus,* of Western Australia. This is 3 to 6 feet tall. About 3 inches in length, its thick, somewhat variable leaves are oblong-elliptic. Resembling the last, but with larger, purple-pink flower heads, *I. latifolius* attains heights of up to 10 feet. Its 3- to 4-inch-long, blunt leaves have tiny red apexes.

Garden and Landscape Uses and Cultivation. These unusual shrubs are very worthwhile where they do well. Conditions similar to those they know in the wild can be duplicated in California and elsewhere where a warm, dry, Mediterranean climate prevails. Not a great deal of experience in growing these plants in North America is recorded, but it is known that they need thoroughly well-drained soil that contains a reasonable amount of organic matter. Light overhead shade is seemingly beneficial for many kinds, but is not essential. It is helpful to keep the ground around the plants mulched. Water must be given with caution, too frequent applications are likely to result in trouble. Seed afford the most satisfactory means of increase.

ISOPYRUM (Iso-pỳrum). Slightly modified, the name *isopyron,* used by the ancient Greeks for a species of *Fumaria,* is the botanical name of a group of thirty species of the buttercup family RANUNCULACEAE. The sorts of *Isopyrum* inhabit north temperate regions of the Old World and the New World and are herbaceous perennials. They have basal and stem leaves, one- to three-times-palmately- (in hand-fashion) divided. The stem leaves are alternate. The flowers are without petals, but have white or sometimes pink-tinged petal-like sepals, usually five in number, many stamens, and few pistils with slender styles. The fruits are composed of two to twenty free follicles (podlike structures).

Native of moist woodlands from Ontario to Minnesota, Florida, and Arkansas, *I. biternatum* has roots with many small tubers and erect stems up to 1 foot tall or a little taller. Its ferny foliage consists of long-stalked basal leaves, twice- or thrice-divided, and stem leaves that are short-stalked or stalkless, and once- or twice-divided, or, the upper ones, only three-lobed. The anemone-like flowers, ½ to ¾ inch in width and white, are succeeded by fruits of four spreading parts.

The European and western Asian *I. thalictroides* has creeping rhizomes from which arise slender stems that branch above and are 4 inches to 1 foot tall. Its dainty, ferny foliage consists of long-stalked, three-times-divided basal leaves with three-lobed, ovate leaflets and stem leaves that resemble the basal ones, but are without stalks. The flowers, up to ⅔ inch in diameter, white or flushed pink, and suggestive of anemones, are succeeded by fruits of usually two parts. For *I. fumarioides* see *Leptopyrum fumarioides*.

Garden Uses and Cultivation. Isopyrums are plants for rock and woodland gardens and, the North American species, for native plant gardens. They need shade and a soil fat with leaf mold or other well-decayed organic matter and never excessively dry, but certainly not constantly saturated. Propagation is by careful division in early spring and by seed sown in soil similar to that recommended above, but made fine at the surface.

ISOTOMA. See Laurentia and Hippobroma.

ISOTRIA (Isòt-ria)—Five Leaves, Whorled-Pogonia. The rarest native orchid of northeastern North America is one of the only two species of this genus. It is *Isotria medeoloides*. Belonging to the orchid family ORCHIDACEAE, it has a name of uncertain reference that perhaps alludes to the sepals. It derives from the Greek *isos*, equal, and *treis*, three. From closely related *Pogonia* it differs in its leaves being in a single whorl (circle).

Unlike many orchids, isotrias do not grow perched on trees as epiphytes, but in the ground as terrestrials. From clusters of thick roots they develop slender, erect stems that near their summits have a whorl of usually five, more rarely six ovate-lanceolate leaves, and above these one, or rarely two, terminal blooms. The flowers have three linear sepals, two shorter and proportionately wider lateral petals, and a third petal, the lip, that has a conspicuous center ridge running from its bottom to or beyond its middle. The lip is not declined. It is three-lobed, with the center lobe broad and stubby, and the others at least two-thirds as long as the entire lip. The column comes forward over the lip.

Five leaves (*I. verticillata* syn. *Pogonia verticillata*) inhabits dry and moist, acid woodlands from Maine to Wisconsin, Florida, and Texas, and blooms in late spring. From 8 inches to twice that height, it has leaves that at blooming time are 1½ to 2

Isotria verticillata

inches long, but enlarge considerably later. The slender, greenish-brown to purplish-brown sepals up to 2 inches or a little more in length, are more than twice as long as the yellowish-green lateral petals. The lip is greenish-yellow, parti-colored, or veined with purple. It is slightly over ½ inch long. Extremely rare, little five leaves (*I. medeoloides*) is 6 to 10 inches tall and differs from the preceding in its flowers having sepals not over 1½ times as long as the narrowly-obovate, yellowish-green lateral petals, which are from a little under to a little over ½ inch in length. The yellowish-green lip is not quite ½ inch long. This orchid inhabits acid soils in dry woodlands from Maine to Virginia.

Garden Uses and Cultivation. Little experience is recorded on the cultivation of these orchids. Certainly they should not be taken from the wild unless in imminent danger of being destroyed as a result of building operations or other cause. Then, an attempt may be made to relocate them where soil, shade, moisture, and other environmental conditions are as similar as possible to those under which they grew before. Increase is by careful division in early spring.

ITEA (Í-tea) — Virginia-Willow or Sweet Spire. Consisting of about a dozen species, all but one native of eastern Asia, the exception North American, this genus belongs in the saxifrage family SAXIFRAGACEAE. Its name is the ancient Greek one for willow (*Salix*) and alludes to the willow-like appearance of the leaves of the American species. No near botanical relationship exists between *Itea* and *Salix*.

The genus *Itea* consists of evergreen and deciduous shrubs and trees of warm-temperate to tropical climes; few are cultivated. They have alternate leaves and branchless terminal or axillary racemes of small bisexual white flowers, each with a five-toothed calyx, five narrow petals, five stamens, and united styles. The fruits are capsules.

The Virginia-willow or sweet spire (*I. virginica*) is a native of wet woods and swamps chiefly in the coastal plain from New Jersey to Florida and Louisiana, and up the valley of the Mississippi to Illinois. A much-branched, deciduous shrub, up to 9 feet in height, but often not over one-third as tall, it has numerous slender, wandlike, pubescent stems and elliptic to oblong-lanceolate leaves up to 3½ inches long, almost or quite hairless and with sharply- or minutely-toothed margins. In late spring and early summer the flowers are borne in considerable profusion. They are in dense, fuzzy-looking, erect, terminal racemes, 2 to 6 inches long, which, because of the color of the stamens and pistils, have a slightly greenish appearance. They are delightfully fragrant. In fall the foliage turns beautiful shades of bronze and red. The Virginia-willow is hardy in sheltered places at least as far north as Boston, Massachusetts, but north of Philadelphia, Pennsylvania, it may suffer from some winter-killing of the branch ends.

Japanese *I. japonica,* a large, deciduous shrub probably hardy in sheltered locations in the vicinity of New York City, has long-pointed, oblongish, ovate, or ovate-oblong, toothed, bright green leaves 3 to 4½ inches long by 1½ to 2¼ inches wide, with short hairs along the veins and hairs often also on the paler undersides. The many tiny flowers, with petals, stamens, and style much shorter than in *I. virginica*, are crowded together in slender, more or less drooping, racemes 3 to 8 inches long.

Not hardy in the north beyond about Washington, D.C., the central Chinese *I. ilicifolia* is a handsome evergreen with

Itea virginica

Itea ilicifolia

Itea japonica

holly-like, spiny-toothed, broadly-elliptic to ovate leaves, 2 to 4 inches long by about two-thirds as wide, that are rich glossy-green above, paler beneath. The arching or pendulous, slender, tail-like racemes of slightly greenish-white flowers, 6 inches to 1 foot in length, are produced in July and August. Reported to attain a height of 18 feet in its homeland, in cultivation it is more often 6 to 9 feet tall.

Garden and Landscape Uses. The Virginia-willow is certainly worthy of more favorable attention from gardeners than it presently receives. It is a good shrub, handsome in flower, and in foliage most conspicuously so when its leaves color in fall. It is useful in shrub borders and beds, in foundation plantings, and at watersides, and can be employed effectively as an interesting informal hedge. It is a good example of a plant that succeeds in gar-

dens under conditions very different from those it knows in its natural habitat. As a wild plant it favors decidedly wet soils and often partial shade. It grows well in such environments under cultivation, but it is just as content under very much drier conditions. At The New York Botanical Garden a group in full sun on the south side of the Conservatory prospered for over thirty years in dryish soil of rather indifferent quality; under these conditions the shrub tends to be more compact and to develop even more brilliant foliage color than in shadier, moister places. The evergreen *I. ilicifolia*, in regions mild enough to make its cultivation possible, can be used in much the same manner as hollies, in groups, interplanted with other shrubs, as single specimens, or even as hedges. It prospers in any fairly good, not too dry, garden soil in sun or part-day shade.

Cultivation. Increase of iteas is easily secured either from seeds sown in sandy peaty soil kept uniformly moist or by summer cuttings; the Virginia-willow is also susceptible to division of old plants in spring or about the time the leaves drop in fall. Their routine care makes no special demands. The Virginia-willow may be pruned rather severely in late winter or spring by removing all very weak shoots and old, worn-out branches. At that time, too, any winter-killed shoot tips are removed. When pruning this kind, it must be remembered that each season the shrub sends up slender branchless shoots that in their second season develop branches that flower; therefore as many as possible of the stronger branchless stems should be retained when thinning is done to relieve crowding. The evergreen *I. ilicifolia* re-

sponds less well to drastic pruning and little is ordinarily necessary. Such as is needed may be done in spring.

ITHURIEL'S SPEAR is *Triteleia laxa*.

IVESIA (Iv-èsia). Distinguished from closely related *Horkelia* by having narrow or threadlike instead of dilated stalks to its stamens, this close relative of *Potentilla* comprises twenty-two species of western North American herbaceous perennials of the rose family ROSACEAE. Its name commemorates Lt. E. Ives, who led a Pacific Railroad Survey.

Ivesias have woody rootstocks and mostly basal, pinnate leaves commonly divided into many overlapping lobes. The upper leaflets are more or less joined. The yellow, purple, or white flowers are generally in crowded clusters. They have usually five each sepals and petals, five, ten, fifteen, or twenty stamens, and rarely more than fifteen pistils. The seedlike fuits are achenes.

Occurring in dry, rocky places at high elevations from California to Washington, Montana, and Colorado, *Ivesia gordonii* (syns. *Horkelia gordonii*, *Potentilla gordonii*) is tufted and up to 10 inches tall. It has very thick rootstocks. More or less glandular-short-hairy, its leaves, up to about 6 inches in length, but often shorter, have ten to twenty-five pairs of deeply-forked or divided leaflets up to ⅓ inch long. The flowers, many together in one or more headlike clusters ¾ inch across, at the tops of long stems that usually bear a few very small bracts, are yellow.

Garden Uses and Cultivation. Little known outside its native territory, this species suggests itself as a possibility for planting in rock gardens and on slopes, in full sun, where soil drainage is sharp. The extent of its hardiness is not reported, but it probably will survive considerable cold in climates not excessively wet. Propagation is by seed.

IVORY-NUT PALM. See Phytelephas.

IVY. This is the common name of the genus *Hedera*. Belonging here are Algerian ivy (*H. canariensis*), Baltic ivy (*H. helix baltica*), English ivy (*H. helix*), Irish ivy (*H. h. hibernica*), and Italian ivy (*H. h. poetica*).

For other plants with common names that include the word ivy see the generic entries indicated in the parentheses that here follow their names. Boston-ivy (*Parthenocissus*), Cape-ivy (*Senecio*), Devil's-ivy (*Epipremnum*), German-ivy (*Senecio*), grape-ivy (*Cissus*), ground-ivy (*Glechoma*), ivy-arum (*Epipremnum*), ivy-gourd (*Coccinea*), ivy-leaved geranium (*Pelargonium*), Japanese-ivy (*Parthenocissus*), Kenilworth-ivy (*Cymbalaria*), marine-ivy (*Cissus*), Natal-ivy (*Senecio*), parlor-ivy (*Senecio*), poison-ivy (*Rhus*), redwood-ivy (*Vancouveria*), and Swedish-ivy (*Plectranthus*).

IWANAGARA. This is the name of multigeneric orchid hybrids the parents of which include *Cattleya, Caularthron, Laelia,* and *Ryncholaelia*.

IXIA (Íx-ia) — Corn-Lily. This genus of beautiful plants is confined in the wild to the southernmost, particularly to the southwestern, part of the Cape Province of South Africa. It has forty-four species and several natural varieties. Hybrids are frequent in the wild and in cultivation, which tends to complicate identification. The genus belongs to the iris family IRIDACEAE and, as now interpreted, includes the plants previously referred to the subgenus *Dichone* of *Tritonia*. Its name, appropriately applied, is derived from an ancient Greek one for some plant notable for the variability of its flower colors.

Ixias, like their relatives freesias and tritonias, have bulblike organs called corms. These differ from bulbs in being solid rather than constructed of concentric layers as are onions, or of overlapping scales like the bulbs of lilies. The corms of ixias are ovoid to spherical and usually under ¾ inch in diameter. The branched or branchless stems are typically slender, wiry, and sinuous and have soft or firm, slender to sword-shaped, prominently longitudinally-veined leaves in two ranks. The nearly always symmetrical flowers are rarely solitary, usually in few- to many-flowered spikes occasionally crowded and headlike, more commonly rather loose and graceful, with the blooms arranged along one side or spiraled. In size the flowers of cultivated species are mostly 1¼

to 1½ inches across, but sometimes somewhat smaller or larger. They have six perianth parts, commonly called petals but more properly tepals, three nearly always evenly spaced stamens, and a style with three short branches. The fruits are capsules. This genus is not to be confused with Bartram's Ixea (*Sphenostigma*).

Brilliant orange or yellow-orange flowers, with at their centers a circular patch of brown on purple nearly always relieved by a starlike pattern of yellow, and with the three outer petals reddish on their outsides, are characteristic of *I. maculata.* Other distinguishing features are the comparatively large, rusty-reddish, papery bracts and bractlets associated with the

Ixia maculata

blooms, which become torn at their ends and shrivel early, and the stalks of the stamens being nearly always united at their bases. This species has branchless stems 9 inches to 1½ feet tall, and five to eight linear to lanceolate leaves from 4 inches to 1 foot long, and mostly under ⅓ inch wide. The flower spikes are short. The corolla tubes are cylindrical. Variety *I. m. intermedia* has smaller floral bracts, blooms with broader, more concave petals, and stamen stalks joined at least to their middles and sometimes to their tops. Variety *I. m. fusco-citrina* is distinguished by its broader leaves up to ¾ inch wide, and primrose-yellow flowers with dark centers without yellow stars. Often confused with *I. maculata*, chiefly because of its similarity in flower color, *I. dubia* differs in having smaller, firmer, colorless or pinkish floral bracts that do not wither, but persist unchanged into the fruiting stage.

The most variable species, running into many flower color forms, is *I. monadelpha.* This has firm, often fairly thickish stems 6 inches to 1¼ feet tall, usually with one or two branches. The short, crowded flower spikes have up to a dozen blooms, pale to dark blue, mauve, purple, violet, pink, or white, commonly with a green, brown, or

reddish-brown center generally outlined with a band of another color. The corolla tube is slender and cylindrical. A give-away feature of this species is that the stamens, their stalks nearly always united to their middles or above, form an erect column with the anthers more or less touching and the short style branches projecting between them. The plant formerly called *I. columellaris*, belongs with *I. monadelpha.*

Another variable species, *I. polystachya,* in some of its forms closely approximates *I. flexuosa.* Commonly of more delicate appearance, *I. flexuosa* has slenderer, sometimes almost hairlike stems, narrower leaves, and more compact spikes of small, faintly scented, pale pink, mauve, white, or pink- or purplish-streaked white flowers. The flowers of *I. polystachya,* on slender, branched or branchless stems 1 foot

Ixia polystachya

to 3 feet tall, vary much in color and size and are slightly scented. Few to many in loose or dense spikes, they have slender cylindrical perianth tubes and are white, pale to deep mauve, pinkish mauve, or bluish, often tinged with blue or green on the outsides of the outer petals. They are with or without a small center stain of yellow, green, blue, mauve, or purple. The five to eight leaves, arranged in fan-fashion and usually reaching halfway up the stems, are generally up to ⅓ inch wide and linear or lanceolate. Variety *I. p. lutea* has golden- or orange-yellow blooms, with the outsides of the outer petals sometimes reddish or purplish, and rarely with a dark blotch in the middle of the bloom.

Variety *I. p. crassifolia* is distinguished by its firmer foliage and more compact flower spikes. The plant formerly known as *I. leucantha* is referable to *I. polystachya*.

With flowers ranging from pale mauve through pink to magenta, and usually greenish inside their throats, **I. latifolia** (syn. *I. scariosa*) has stems 6 inches to 1½ feet tall, usually with three or fewer branches, and three leaves, the longest one on the stem, the others basal and reaching to the middle of the stem or above. The flower spikes have three to seven loosely arranged or rather crowded blooms. In *I. l. angustifolia* the leaves are narrower than those of the typical species. Variety *T. l. curviramosa* is distinguished by its short, curved branches.

Ixia micrandra

White, pink, mauve-pink, or mauve flowers are borne on branchless stems 9 inches to 2 feet long by **I. micrandra.** The leaves usually number two, rarely three. They are narrow, up to 1 foot long, and usually cylindrical below. The two- to six-flowered flower spikes are short.

One of the most striking and distinctive ixias, with flowers of a color extremely rare if not unique in the plant world, is *I. viridiflora*. It is with sorrow that gardeners have learned that this beautiful species is

Ixia viridiflora

in grave danger of being exterminated in the wild. Its stems rarely branched and 1½ to 3 feet tall, **I. viridiflora** has five to seven erect leaves up to 1½ feet long and up to ⅙ inch wide. Usually loose, the flower spikes have several of their dozen or more blooms open at one time. They are beautiful, almost metallic-green with prominent, circular, purple, purplish-black, or reddish-violet centers. The stamens have purple stalks and purple or yellow anthers. Individual blooms remain in good condition for several days.

Rich crimson to pure white is the range of flower color of **I. campanulata** (syns. *I. crateroides, I. speciosa*), with intermediates such as white flushed with red, and white with the outsides of the petals red with a white stripe, common. The very rarely branched stems are 4 inches to a little over 1 foot tall. There are five to ten linear to awl-shaped leaves up to 8 inches long by up to ⅕ inch wide and never much more than one-half as long as the flower stems. The racemes of very short-tubed blooms are short, crowded, and have up to nine flowers.

The cream- to biscuit-colored flowers of **I. paniculata** have slender perianth tubes 1½ to 2½ inches long that expand slightly from base to top, and petals under one-half the length of the tube, often tinged pink on their undersides. The usually purplish anthers may protrude or not from the throat of the bloom. The stems, 1 foot to 3 feet tall, have usually one or two branches. The leaves are erect or nearly so, linear to lanceolate, and 6 inches to 2 feet long. Five to eighteen blooms compose each loose to fairly compact flower spike. This quite variable species in the wild is partial to marshy ground. Similar, quite attractive **I. splen-**

dida has rose-pink flowers. It differs from *I. paniculata* in its stems being branchless and in having shorter perianth tubes from which the anthers do not protrude.

Horticultural varieties, hybrids, and selected forms of wild species are popular and are listed in considerable variety in the catalogs of specialist dealers in bulbs. Among these are 'Afterglow', with orange-buff blooms with dark red centers, and petals shaded pink on their outsides; 'Blue Bird', with blue-centered white flowers, pinkish on their outsides; 'Bridesmaid', the white flowers of which have a carmine center; 'Hogarth', with creamy-yellow blooms with purple centers; 'Rose Queen', the flowers of which are soft pink; 'Uranus', with lemon-yellow flowers with

Ixia 'Bridesmaid'

Ixia 'Rose Queen'

red centers; and 'Vulcan', which has scarlet blooms suffused with orange.

Garden and Landscape Uses. Ixias are among the most beautiful and useful of the several genera of South African irids cultivated in North America. Their colorful blooms bring gaiety to gardens and greenhouses and are delightful and long-lasting when cut. Only in regions where frost does not penetrate the ground deeply are they likely to survive outdoors, although under heavy mulch at the base of a south-facing wall they have been grown at The New York Botanical Garden. In California, in the south, and in other regions kindly to plants of southernmost Africa they are excellent for flower beds. Blooming in spring, they need for the best results well-drained, porous soil of agreeable fertility and full sun. In many places they reseed freely.

Cultivation. Planting is done in California in early fall, in late fall in mild parts the state of Washington and in the south. Set the corms 3 to 4 inches deep and as far apart, or for cut flowers closer together in rows 1 foot to 1½ feet apart. If there is danger of frost penetrating to the corms or developing shoots protect them with a loose mulch, which must be removed gradually in spring. Each fall apply a complete fertilizer to established plantings. Keep the beds free of weeds, and do not cut the foliage down until it dies naturally after flowering. Lifting and replanting is necessary at intervals of a few years, as soon as overcrowding with attendant reduction of blooms becomes evident. The best time to do this is as soon as the foliage dies. Before replanting sort the corms to size and revitalize the soil by spading in compost, peat moss, or other suitable organic conditioner and a slow-acting complete fertilizer.

Greenhouse cultivation in pots or pans (shallow pots) calls for planting in August or September. The corms are spaced so that the distance between individuals is about one-half the width of a corm. Five to eight corms are accommodated in a container 5 or 6 inches in diameter. Make sure the pots or pans are well drained, and use fertile, porous soil packed moderately firmly. Set the corms with their tops 1 inch below the surface. After planting water thoroughly and stand in a shaded cold frame or other cool place. It is a good plan to cover the soil surface with a layer of moss, peat moss, or similar material to prevent rapid drying. Watering at this stage must be done with caution, but the earth must never be allowed to become completely dry.

Before there is any danger of the plants freezing they are transferred to a sunny greenhouse where the night temperature is 45 to 50°F, and there they are grown until they bloom and afterward until their tops die, and they begin their season of dormancy. Day temperatures must not be more than five to ten degrees above those maintained at night, and on all favorable days the greenhouse must be ventilated freely. As roots permeate the soil the frequency of watering is increased, and after the containers are filled with roots weekly applications of dilute liquid fertilizer are given. Discreet staking with wires or thin bamboo canes is likely to be needed.

After blooming, watering is continued until, in anticipation of dormancy, the foliage begins to die naturally, then intervals between applications are successively increased until, finally, water is withheld entirely. Then the corms are stored dry, either in the soil in which they grew, or they are removed from the soil and kept in bags or shallow boxes in a dry, shaded, cool place, such as a cellar, until replanting time in early fall. Propagation is by natural multiplication of the corms and by seed.

IXIOLIRION (Ixio-lírion). Although less familiar to most gardeners than many bulb plants, ixiolirions are well worth having. The commonly available *Ixiolirion tataricum* (syns. *I. ledebouri, I. pallasii, I. montanum*) is variable. Some botanists describe its major elements as separate species, others as varieties. Because of this, the number of species recognized differs according to the authority accepted; three to five is approximately correct. The genus belongs in the amaryllis family AMARYLLIDACEAE. Its name comes from that of another genus, *Ixia*, and the Greek *leirion*, a lily, and alludes to the blooms.

Ixiolirions, natives to central Asia, have small bulbs, very long, slender, mostly basal leaves, and thin, stiff flower stalks about 1 foot or so tall ending in umbels of star-shaped blue or violet, or rarely white, flowers. The six perianth segments, commonly called petals, separate to their bases, form shallowly-funnel-shaped blooms.

There are six stamens shorter than the petals and a slender style tipped with a three-lobed stigma. The fruits are capsules.

Widespread in the wild, *I. tataricum* has long-necked bulbs about 1 inch thick and three or four bright green, linear basal leaves up to 1 foot long or longer. Shorter

Ixiolirion tataricum

leaves furnish the lower parts of the 1- to 1½-foot-tall flower stems. The latter terminate in umbels of four to eight lavender or darker blue blooms that, because of the unequal lengths of their individual stalks, appear to be in racemes. The stalks of the stamens, like the style and stigma, are violet and tipped with white anthers. The flowers come in spring, those of some variants appearing a little later than those of others. Earlier blooming than *I. tataricum*, and a native of Turkestan, *I. kolpakowskianum* (syn. *Kolpakowskia ixiolirioides*) has smaller bulbs, tufts of erect, grassy leaves 1 foot long or sometimes longer, and pale blue or white flowers in umbels of four or less.

Garden and Landscape Uses. Except in warm, sheltered locations ixiolirions are not satisfactorily hardy in climates appreciably harsher than that of Washington, D.C. At The New York Botanical Garden, *I. tataricum* lived in the rock garden for several years, but gradually deteriorated. Ixiolirions are delightful for beds and rock gardens, and their blooms are pleasing and last well as cut flowers. They are also charming for growing in pots in cool greenhouses.

Cultivation. Ixiolirions will not tolerate "wet feet." Their planting site must be well-drained, and the soil porous and satisfyingly nutritious. Full sun is needed. The bulbs are planted in fall at a depth of about 4 inches and 3 to 4 inches apart. Where winters are cold it is advisable to mulch the ground, before it freezes, to a depth of more than an inch or two, with material that will check deep penetration of frost. This is removed in spring. Where they thrive the bulbs may be left undisturbed until they show signs of becoming overcrowded. This is indicated by less vigorous growth and fewer blooms. Then, they should be lifted, separated, and replanted. This is best done in spring as soon as the foliage has died. During the period when they are in leaf water during dry periods.

In greenhouses bulbs are planted in early fall 2 inches or so apart in 5- or 6-inch pots of well-drained, fertile, porous soil. After planting, the containers are watered thoroughly and stood in a cold frame, root cellar, or other place where they can be kept evenly moist and at about 35 to 45°F. In January or February they are moved to a sunny greenhouse where the night temperature is about 50°F and is by day five to ten degrees higher, and are watered regularly. When the foliage is about one-half grown a program of supplying dilute liquid fertilizer about once a week is initiated. After blooming watering is continued for as long as the foliage remains green, but when the leaves begin to die naturally the amount of water given is gradually reduced. Finally it is withheld, and the dry bulbs are stored for their period of dormancy in the soil in which they grew. In late summer or early fall they are shaken from their old soil, sorted to size, and repotted.

IXORA (Ix-òra) — Flame-of-the-Woods. Many fine ornamentals are among the 400 species of *Ixora*, of the madder family RUBIACEAE. The group consists of evergreen shrubs and small to large trees, natives of the Old World and New World tropics. Its name is a Portuguese rendering of the Sanskrit name of the god Siva.

Ixoras have undivided leaves, opposite or less commonly in whorls (circles) of three. In terminal or axillary, usually crowded, showy clusters, the smallish flowers are scarlet, crimson, pink, yellow, orange, or white. They have long, slender, tubular corollas with usually four, less often five, wide-spreading lobes (petals). There are four or five short-stalked or stalkless stamens and a slightly protruding, slender, two-branched style. The fruits are two-seeded, hard or fleshy berries. In addition to the natural species there are numerous horticultural hybrids and varieties, their precise botanical origins often not known.

Flame-of-the-woods (*I. coccinea*), of India, is a variable, bushy shrub about 4 feet tall. It has lustrous, broad-elliptic to heart-shaped, stalkless leaves 1 inch to 4 inches long. Its terminal or axillary clusters of flowers are 2 to 5 inches across. They are typically bright red, but varieties with pink, yellow, and orange-yellow blooms occur. Almost 2 inches long, the flowers

Ixora chinensis

have pointed petals. From the last, generally similar *I. chinensis* may be distinguished by its flowers having blunt instead of pointed petals. Up to about 3 feet tall and native of China and Malaya, this is a shrub with pointed-elliptic-lanceolate to obovate, scarcely stalked leaves 2 to 3 inches in length. The flowers, in dense, red-stalked clusters 2 to 4 inches in diameter, are typically yellow to light orange changing to brick-red as they age, but there are many color variants including white-, pink-, and red-flowered varieties of this species. These are often identified by varietal names, such as *I. c. rosea*, for a form with pink blooms, and *I. c. aurantiaca*, for one with flowers that change from red to orange.

Ixora chinensis rosea

Popular *I. duffii* (syn. *I. macrothyrsa*), of the Celebes Islands, is a shrub 3 to 10 feet tall with pointed, lanceolate to oblong, rather leathery leaves 6 inches to 1 foot long by up to 2½ inches wide. The deep red flowers, verging to crimson with age, are

Ixora javanica

very many together in loose clusters 6 to 8 inches across. Native of Java, *I. javanica* is a shrub or tree up to 25 feet in height with slender, forked, red branches and short-stalked, leathery, pointed-elliptic to ovate-oblong leaves up to 10 inches long by 3½ inches wide. Its light salmon-red to light orange, 1- to 1½-inch-long flowers are in terminal clusters 2 to 4 inches across. Variety *I. j. flava* (syn. 'Apricot Gold') has large clusters of apricot-tinted blooms.

Fragrant flowers are borne by several species, among them *I. acuminata*, of India. A shrub 5 to 7 feet tall, this has pointed, linear-oblong to elliptic leaves 5 inches to 1 foot long, up to 3½ inches wide. Its 1- to 1½-inch-long, ⅔-inch-wide, four- or five-petaled flowers are in clusters 3 to 5 inches across. They have red calyxes, white corollas. Probably native of Thailand, *I. finlaysoniana* is a compact shrub or tree up to 18 feet in height with lanceolate-elliptic to elliptic or slightly obovate leaves 3 to 7 inches in length. The fragrant flowers, 1 inch to 1¼ inches across and white, are in dense terminal clusters approximately 1 inch long. As known in cultivation this is perhaps identical with *I. thwaitesii*.

A shrub or small tree, of Polynesia, *I. fragrans* has hairless, elliptic to ovate or obovate leaves 2 to 5 inches long, and sweetly scented, red flowers the corollas of which are about ½ inch long, their lobes (petals) somewhat shorter. Western tropical America is the homeland of *I. laxiflora*. A shrub or tree up to about 12 feet tall, this has pointed, oblong-lanceolate leaves 6 to 8 inches long and big, three-forked panicles of fragrant, 1¼-inch-long white flowers blushed with pink. Native to Malagasy (Madagascar), *I. odorata* is a small shrub with ovate to slightly obovate leaves up to 1 foot long, and, in large, purple-stalked panicles up to 1 foot wide or wider, fragrant, white, pink-tinged, or yellowish, slender-tubed blooms 3 to 5 inches long. Indian *I. parviflora* is a small tree with oblong to

Ixora parviflora

Ixora 'Superking'

Ixora chinensis variety, as a pot plant

elliptic leaves up to 6 inches long. Its fragrant, white or sometimes pink flowers have corollas with tubes about ⅓ inch long. A large shrub or small tree, **I. thwaitesii** has oblong to broadly lanceolate leaves up to 5 or 6 inches in length. Its fragrant white blooms, in compact clusters, have corolla tubes 1¼ inches long. This is a native of Ceylon.

Other species cultivated include these: **I. barbata,** of India, a somewhat straggly shrub up to about 6 feet high, has lustrous pointed-elliptic to elliptic-oblong leaves up to 9 inches long and almost one-half as wide. The flowers, in panicles 6 inches to 1 foot across and approximately 1½ inches long, have greenish-white corolla tubes and spreading or backward-slanting petals, pure white on their upper sides. At the mouth of the tube is a fringe of hairs. **I. congesta,** of Malaya and Burma, is a tree with oblong-elliptic to elliptic or lanceolate leaves up to 1 foot long and one-third to one-half as wide. The flowers, many together in large trusses, red, and ½ to ⅝ inch in diameter, have corolla tubes 1 inch to 1¼ inches long. **I. fulgens,** of unknown provenance, about 4 feet tall, has narrow to broad oblong to obovate leaves up to 10 inches long and 3¼ inches wide. The orange-red or orange flowers, which become scarlet as they age, are 1 inch long or a little longer. **I. griffithii,** of southeast Asia and Indonesia, is a shrub 8 or 9 feet tall with oblong to oblong-elliptic leaves up to 9 inches long by 3¼ inches wide. In big, showy, flattish panicles, the 1¾-inch-long flowers are 1¼ to 1½ inches across. They have slender, red corolla tubes and four red-orange petals. **I. longifolia,** of the Molucca Islands, is a shrub with slender-pointed, lanceolate-oblong to lanceolate leaves up to 10 inches long and loose clusters of deep red flowers.

Attractive foliage is the chief merit of **I. borbonica,** a native of Réunion Island in the Indian Ocean. A tall shrub, it has lustrous olive-green, pointed-lanceolate leaves up to 10 inches in length. They are netted with rose-carmine veins. The coloring is most distinct on the young foliage of young plants.

Horticultural hybrids and varieties of ixoras include the following. 'Angela Busman', compact, with large clusters of shrimp-pink blooms; 'Frances Perry', with medium to large clusters of rich yellow flowers; 'Gillette's Yellow', which has large clusters of light yellow blooms; 'Helen Dunaway', a tall, profuse bloomer with large clusters of deep orange flowers; 'Henry Morat', a good pink-flowered kind, its flowers fragrant; 'Herrera's White', white-flowered; 'Superking', a hybrid of I. duffii and much like that species, but distinguished by its compact growth and freedom with which it bears its handsome clusters of deep red flowers; and **I. williamsii** (syn. 'Trinidad Red') with long-stemmed clusters of deep red flowers.

Garden and Landscape Uses. In the tropics and warm, humid subtropics ixoras are among the most satisfactory and showy flowering shrubs. They also do well in pots and tubs in tropical greenhouses. Most kinds bloom profusely over a long season, some almost continuously. They are suitable for general landscaping and are effective as single specimens or in groups. They may be used as informal and sheared hedges. They do best in light or part-day shade in ordinary, well-drained, fertile garden soil, preferably slightly acid and kept reasonably moist.

Cultivation. Ixoras can be increased by seeds, cuttings, and grafting. Horticultural varieties, which do not come true from seeds, are mostly raised commercially by grafting, because this produces salable

In Key West, Florida: (a) A hedge of *Ixora coccinea*   (b) An archway of *Ixora coccinea*

plants more quickly than cuttings. The understocks used are vigorous species raised from seeds or cuttings. If cuttings are used to increase ixoras make them from vigorous shoots. They will make better plants more quickly than cuttings of weak shoots. However propagated, the young plants are transferred as soon as they have a fair amount of roots individually in small pots. Later they are repotted into 4-inch pots and successively to bigger ones. As soon as they are well established in their first pots, pinch the tips out of their shoots. This induces branching. A second pinching is desirable when the branches are 6 inches or so long. Flowering-size specimens are pruned, after blooming, by cutting back the shoots of the current year,

leaving only one node or joint unless it is desired to improve symmetry or grow the plants on to larger sizes. These objectives may be achieved by cutting back less severely. Hedges of ixoras are kept shapely and neat by shearing after flowering is over and more often if a strictly formal effect is desired.

Routine care of ixoras in containers consists of keeping them indoors, or in summer outdoors in a sunny location with their pots buried to their rims in a bed of sand, sandy soil, or similar material. Indoors they need light shade from strong sun. From spring through fall water copiously, less freely in winter. Plants that have filled their pots or tubs with roots benefit from weekly or biweekly applica-

tions of dilute liquid fertilizer from spring to fall. A humid atmosphere, but not a heavy, dank one with little air circulation, is favorable. So long as the air is humid ixoras revel in heat. A minimum winter night temperature of 60°F should be maintained, but somewhat higher is appreciated. By day the temperature may exceed the night level by five to fifteen degrees, depending upon the brightness of the weather. Summer temperatures may considerably exceed winter ones. Specimens in large pots or tubs need repotting at intervals of several years only. In intervening years in spring remove as much of the surface soil as possible without unduly damaging the roots and replace it with new.

J

JABOROSA (Jabo-ròsa). Native to Mexico and from Bolivia to Patagonia, *Jaborosa*, of the nightshade family SOLANACEAE, contains twenty species. Its name is derived from the Arabic one for a related plant, the mandrake (*Mandragora*).

Herbaceous perennials not hardy in the north, jaborosas have pinnately-lobed or toothed leaves and white to yellowish, tubular or bell-shaped flowers with a five-lobed calyx, a five-lobed corolla, five stamens, and one style. The fruits are berries.

Native to Argentina, *J. integrifolia* succeeds outdoors in sheltered places in southern England. From 6 to 9 inches tall, it has long, creeping rhizomes and long-

Jaborosa integrifolia

stalked, elliptic to obovate leaves remotely small-toothed along their margins, with blades 4 to 6½ inches long by 1½ to 2¼ inches wide. Suggestive of out-size nicotianas, the fragrant, creamy-white flowers approximately 2½ inches long by 2 to 3 inches across face upward.

Garden and Landscape Uses and Cultivation. The species described is attractive as a groundcover, but because of its invasive, spreading habit it should not be planted where it is not contained or can be controlled. It succeeds in ordinary soil in sun or part-day shade and is easily increased by division, cuttings, and seed.

JABOTICABA. This is the name of a fruit, very popular in Brazil, which is occasionally planted in southern Florida and other warm regions. The evergreen tree that bears it is described under its botanical name, *Myrciaria cauliflora*. Wine-flavored and slightly acid, the grapelike fruits are eaten out of hand and made into jelly and wine. They freeze well.

Jaboticabas succeed in deep, fertile soils, of either a limestone or non-limy nature. Under favorable conditions they yield several crops each year. The trees are easy to raise from seeds, which germinate in about a month. In Brazil superior varieties are inarched onto seedling understocks. Side grafting is also practiced. In trials in Florida young plants grew very slowly in ordinary soils and were chlorotic (yellow-foliaged because of inadequate development of chlorophyll). Better results were had by planting in peat or other soil-less mixes treated with iron frit (to compensate for insufficient iron, which results in chlorosis) and fertilizing regularly with complete liquid fertilizer.

JABURAN is *Ophiopogon jaburan*.

JACARANDA (Jaca-ránda). Blue-flowered trees are sufficiently unusual to attract attention even though they lack other merit, but the cultivated jacarandas have, in addition to their marvelously showy blooms, pleasing habits of growth and remarkably elegant foliage. In warm climates in many parts of the world *Jacaranda mimosifolia* is a favorite. Thousands of miles from its native South America it is so freely planted in Pretoria, South Africa, that Pretoria is called the jacaranda city.

Native to the American tropics, including the West Indies, *Jacaranda* belongs in the bignonia family BIGNONIACEAE. There are fifty species. The name comes from a Brazilian Indian one. In English-speaking countries its initial letter is pronounced as "j." In Spanish-speaking countries it takes the sound of "h" in English, and in Brazil it has the sound of "z" in azure. The pink-jacaranda is *Stereospermum kunthianum*.

Jacarandas are lacy-foliaged, deciduous and evergreen trees and shrubs with opposite, twice- or rarely once-pinnate leaves with numerous toothed or smooth-edged, small leaflets. Mostly in terminal or axillary panicles, the blue to violet-blue or rarely pinkish or whitish flowers have small toothless or five-toothed calyxes, corollas with a straight or curved tube and five roundish, spreading lobes (petals) that form a two-lipped face to the bloom. There are four stamens in two pairs and one club-shaped staminode (nonfunctional stamen), often hairy at its apex. The fruits, oblong to ovate capsules, contain many winged seeds.

Jacaranda mimosifolia in South Africa

Most frequent in cultivation, *J. mimosifolia* (syn. *J. ovalifolia*), of Brazil, is a deciduous tree 25 to 40 feet tall. Its ferny, pubescent leaves, ovate in outline and 9 inches up to 1½ feet long by 5 to 9 inches wide, have ten to twenty pairs of primary divisions each with fourteen to twenty-four pairs of bristle-tipped, oblong-elliptic leaflets up to ½ inch long and a larger ter-

Spanish iris variety

Iris cristata

Iris pallida variegata

Siberian iris variety

Iris pseudacorus

A variety of tall-bearded iris

A variety of tall-bearded iris

Iris pallida dalmatica

Jasminum nudiflorum

Jasione perennis

Jacaranda mimosifolia, young seedling

Jacaranda acutifolia (flowers)

minal one. From 1¼ to 2 inches in length and 1 inch to 1½ inches across their mouths, the blue to blue-purple blooms, in much-branched, terminal panicles that may be 1 foot in length by 8 inches in width, have five-toothed calyxes, a bent corolla tube swollen on one side above the bend, and wavy-edged petals. The flattened-egg-shaped, narrowly-winged seed pods are about 2 inches long.

The plant called *J. chelonia* is probably not specifically distinct from *J. mimosifolia*. It is described as a native of Argentina with smaller blue flowers that open earlier in the season than those of the last, and is said to bloom when quite young.

Jacaranda acutifolia

Garden and Landscape Uses. In the warm subtropics and parts of the tropics jacarandas are held in high esteem as street and avenue trees, lawn specimens, and for general landscaping. In bloom they become hazes of blue. As the flowers fall they besprinkle the ground, forming pools of the same hue, that seemingly reflect the blooms still on the branches. In temperate climes young specimens are sometimes grown as foliage pot plants for decorating greenhouses and windows and for planting temporarily outdoors as dot plants in summer flower beds.

Cultivation. Jacarandas are very easily raised from seeds and can be increased by cuttings. They grow quickly and succeed in any fairly good, well-drained soil, in sunny locations. Pruning is not necessary, but may be done to control the sizes and shapes of the trees. Even large limbs cut back develop new growth freely from below the cuts. To have pot plants with foliage suitable for the embellishment of greenhouses, windows, and summer flower beds, seeds are sown in a temperature of 60 to 70°F in January, the young plants are set individually in small pots and later are transferred to those 4 or 5 inches in diameter. Until the weather is warm enough to plant out tomatoes and geraniums, they are grown indoors in full sun in a night temperature of 55 to 60°F, and by day five to ten degrees higher. Pot specimens a year or more old are refurbished each late winter or early spring by pruning them back fairly severely (this is usually desirable to check their tendency to become too tall and skinny), taking them from their containers, removing some of the old soil, and repotting them into pots of the size they previously occupied or larger ones. The soil should be porous and fertile. After it is filled with roots regular applications of dilute liquid fertilizer are helpful. At no time must the soil be allowed to become really dry. If it does, leaf dropping is likely to occur.

JACK-BEAN is *Canavalia ensiformis*.

JACK-IN-THE-PULPIT is *Arisaema triphyllum*.

JACKFRUIT is *Artocarpus heterophyllus*.

JACOBAEA. See Senecio.

JACOBEAN-LILY is *Sprekelia formosissima*.

JACOBINIA. See Justicia.

JACOB'S LADDER is *Polemonium caeruleum*.

JACOB'S ROD. See Asphodeline.

JACOBSENIA (Jacob-sénia). Endemic to South Africa, *Jacobensia* consists of one or perhaps two species of the *Mesembryanthemum* relationship of the carpetweed family AIZOACEAE. The name honors one of the foremost students of the group to which they belong, Dr. Hermann Jacobsen, curator of the botanic garden, Kiel, Germany.

An evergreen, succulent subshrub up to 1 foot high, *J. kolbei* has erect branches with widely-spaced pairs or abbreviated shoots each with four up-pointing fleshy, approximately cylindrical leaves, flattened slightly on their upper sides, united at their bases, and one of each pair slightly longer than the other. From ¾ inch to 1½ inches long and about ⅓ inch wide, they are green, roughened with numerous tiny protrusions. The white or pale yellow flowers, solitary, terminal, and up to about 3½ inches in diameter, have many slender petals. At a glance they suggest a daisy relationship. Structurally they are completely different from daisies. Each is a single bloom instead of a head of many florets. They have five sepals, numerous slender petals in three or four rows, and five stigmas. The fruits are capsules.

Garden Uses and Cultivation. These are as for *Mitrophyllum*. For further information see Succulents.

JACQUEMONTIA (Jacque-móntia). Chiefly New World in its nativity, *Jacquemontia* is a member of the morning glory family CONVOLVULACEAE. It comprises more than 100 species of trailing or twining vines and upright shrubs. None is hardy. The name commemorates the French naturalist Victor Jacquemont, who died in 1832.

Jacquemontias have alternate leaves with usually smooth-edged, rarely lobed or toothed margins. Their morning-glory-like, blue, violet or white flowers are in loose clusters or less often are solitary. They have five-angled or obscurely five-lobed corollas, five stamens, and a style with two stigmas. The fruits are capsules. From *Ipomoea* these plants differ chiefly in their flowers having more than one stigma, from *Convolvulus* in the stigmas being ovate to oblong instead of slender-linear to awl-shaped.

Native to southern Florida, the Florida Keys, the West Indies, and South America, *J. pentantha* (syn. *J. violacea*) is a perennial vine. It has hairy to nearly hairless, slender, twining stems 6 to 8 feet long and leaves with ovate to ovate-lanceolate blades ¾ inch to 2 inches in length. The somewhat bell-shaped, white-centered, violet-blue flowers are 1 inch to 1¼ inches across in clusters of up to a dozen. They are produced in abundance over a long season. Like those of morning glories the flowers close in mid-afternoon and are followed by another crop of open flowers the following morning, and on many succeeding mornings. Native to Hawaii, *J. sandwicensis* inhabits beaches. It is a vine with thickish, obovate leaves about 1 inch in length and in clusters of up to seven or solitary, bell-shaped, blue flowers up to 1 inch in diameter.

Garden Uses and Cultivation. Scarcely as attractive as morning glories, jacquemontias are less often grown. In warm climates the Hawaiian species discussed can be used in seashore areas. The Florida kind is interesting for outdoors in warm, humid climates. It has been grown in greenhouses. Indoors it succeeds without difficulty under conditions that suit begonias, but needs more light. Jacquemontias may be propagated by seed and by cuttings.

JACQUINIA (Jac-quínia). Named after Nicholas Joseph de Jacquin, collector and painter of West Indian plants, who died in 1817, *Jacquinia* consists of fifty species of tropical and subtropical American trees and shrubs of the theophrasta family THEOPHRASTACEAE.

Jacquinias have opposite or more or less whorled (in circles of more than two) stiff, undivided, toothless leaves, and white, purple, or orange flowers in umbels or racemes or solitary. The blooms have five sepals, tubular corollas with five spreading lobes (petals), five short stamens, and the same number of aborted stamens (staminodes) that appear as rounded appendages at the throats of the corollas. The fruits are leathery berries.

Jacquinia arborea, Fairchild Tropical Garden, Miami, Florida

Most frequent in cultivation, *J. arborea* (syn. *J. armillaris*) is a very good-looking, dense evergreen shrub or small tree with grayish, oblanceolate, broad to rather narrow leaves 2 to 3 inches long or a little longer, and sometimes notched at their apexes. The panicles of fragrant white flowers are succeeded by red berries about

⅓ inch in diameter. This species often grows in limestone areas.

Native to southern Florida and the Bahamas, *J. keyensis*, an evergreen, brittle-twigged shrub or tree up to 15 feet tall, but often not more than one-half this maximum, has lustrous, blunt, thick, obovate to spatula-shaped, evergreen leaves, up to 2 inches long, usually in whorls, and with rolled-under margins. The honey-scented, approximately ⅓-inch-wide, straw-colored or pinkish flowers, displayed in small racemes or panicles in winter, are followed by little dull yellow or greenish-yellow, globular fruits.

Native to Mexico and tropical America, *J. pungens* is a dense evergreen shrub or tree up to 15 feet tall, but commonly lower. It has rigid, very obviously sharply spine-tipped, linear-lanceolate, elliptic, or linear-oblong leaves 1½ to 2¼ inches long. The reddish-orange flowers, about ¼ inch long, are in short racemes. They are succeeded by yellow or orange calamondin-like fruits, about ¾ inch in diameter, that contain a substance called barbasco, which is used as a fish poison. When green, the fruits are eaten by Indians. They are also used as ornaments and as the source of a yellow dye. Also with spine-tipped leaves, *J. aurantiaca*, of Mexico, Central America, and the West Indies, is a shrub or tree up to 25 feet tall. It has pubescent branchlets and oblong to elliptic, evergreen leaves, 1½ to a little more than 2 inches long. The orange flowers are ⅓ inch wide and are in short panicles. The fruits are globose and ¾ inch in diameter. They also are used in Mexico to stupify fish.

Garden and Landscape Uses and Cultivation. Jacquinias are hardy only in warm climates where there is little or no frost. The kinds described here are pleasing for general landscaping and, because they are salt-tolerant and survive exposure to strong winds, are especially esteemed for planting near the sea. They grow well in full sun in ordinary garden environments, and are usually propagated by seed.

JACQUINPARIS. This is the name of orchid hybrids the parents of which are *Jacquiniella* and *Liparis*.

JADE PLANT is *Crassula argentea*.

JADE VINE is *Strongylodon macrobotrys*.

JAGUA is *Genipa americana*.

JAGUEY BLANCO is *Ficus citrifolia*.

JAKFRUIT is *Artocarpus heterophyllus*.

JAM FRUIT. See Muntingia.

JAMAICA. This name forms part of the common names of these plants: Jamaica-honeysuckle (*Passiflora laurifolia*), Jamaica-

privet (*Lawsonia inermis*), and Jamaica-sorrel (*Hibiscus sabdariffa*).

JAMBOLAN or JAMBOLAN-PLUM is *Syzygium cuminii*.

JAMBOS. See Syzygium.

JAMESIA (Jamès-ia). One species constitutes *Jamesia*, of the saxifrage family SAXIFRAGACEAE. Native from Nevada and Utah to California, it was named for Dr. Edwin James, a botanist who accompanied Major Long's exploratory expedition to the Rocky Mountains in 1820.

Attractive but not showy, *J. americana* is a deciduous shrub of upright growth. Ordinarily 3 to 4 feet tall, exceptionally it may be twice as tall. Usually it is wider than high. Its stems have solid pith and peeling bark. The short-stalked leaves are ovate to elliptic, toothed, and ¾ inch to 2½ inches long. They are wrinkled, dull green, with a few flattened hairs above, and on their lower sides are covered with almost a felt of whitish or grayish hairs. In fall, in sunny locations, they become orange and red. The faintly fragrant, white or pinkish flowers are many together in erect, terminal panicles 1 inch to 2½ inches long and about as broad. The blooms are ½ inch or slightly more across and have five woolly sepals, five petals hairy on their insides, ten stamens, and three to five persistent styles that remain as beaks on the fruits. The fruits are capsules with many seeds. Variety *J. a. rosea* has pink blooms. Variety *J. a. californica* is comparatively low, from 1 foot to 3½ feet tall. Jamesias are hardy in New England.

Garden and Landscape Uses and Cultivation. This quite pretty species and its varieties are usable at the fronts of shrub plantings and as single specimens in rock gardens and other such places. It needs a sunny location and well-drained, not overfertile, soil. It is easily multiplied by cuttings and by seed.

JAMESTOWN WEED is *Datura stramonium*.

JANKAEA (Ján-kaea). Not many genera of the gesneria family GESNERIACEAE are hardy. The few that are include *Jankaea*. Unfortunately, its only species, *J. heldreichii*, is notoriously difficult to satisfy, and only skilled and painstaking gardeners are likely to persuade it to stay and bloom. Native of Greece, *J. heldreichii* (syn. *Ramonda heldreichii*) differs from *Ramonda* in having short bell- or funnel-shaped flowers with five very short stamens, and from *Haberlea* in its flowers being four-lobed and not two-lipped, and its four straight-stalked stamens not being in pairs. The name honors a student of the flora of the Danube region, Victor de Janka, who died in 1890.

An evergreen perennial herbaceous plant with somewhat the aspect of an African-

Jankaea heldreichii in a rock crevice

Remove heavy accumulations of snow from evergreens: (a) With a rake, teeth side up

(b) With a broom

violet (*Saintpaulia*), *J. heldreichii* has 1-inch-long, blunt-ovate leaves in solitary rosettes. Thickish, they have their upper sides covered with white hairs that lay flat against the leaf surface and their undersides rusty-hairy. The flowers are about ¾ inch long with the corollas lobed to about their middles and the lobes of almost equal size. They are blue-violet and nod in twos or threes atop stems 2 or 3 inches tall. The fruits are many-seeded capsules. At home *Jankaea* lives in the crevices of vertical rocks in gorges on Mount Olympus.

Garden Uses and Cultivation. This choice alpine needs gritty, peaty soil and a shaded location beneath an overhanging ledge so that rain does not wet its foliage. Moisture is obtained from that which seeps through the soil. This plant is perhaps best accommodated in pans (shallow pots) in alpine greenhouses. Propagation is by seed, treated like those of *Ramonda*, and by leaf cuttings placed in a greenhouse propagating bed in summer.

JANUARY, GARDENING REMINDERS FOR. Not a great deal needs to be or can be done outdoors in northern gardens in January. Be alert for possible damage to evergreens from heavy accumulations of snow. Before they become wet and soggy or freeze solidly shake or brush them off with a wooden rake or a broom. Protective winter coverings of salt hay, leaves, and similar materials spread around shrubs and over perennials, if not weighted down by cut branches or chicken wire laid over them, may be blown by winds and the ground bared and exposed to deep frost penetration. After wind storms check for disturbances of this kind and rake the mulches back over bared patches.

New seed and nursery catalogs now begin to become available. Send for any you particularly want. For the more elaborate a small fee, usually fully justified, may be charged. Others are free. Study the catalogs carefully and after suitable delibera-

tion, but without undue delay, send orders for the seeds and bulbs you want. In making selections rely largely upon varieties well tested and known to be satisfactory in your area, but try some items new or less well known to you. Include a few of the seedsmen's "novelties," but do not go overboard with these. The newcomers are not always as good as their glowing catalog descriptions may lead you to believe, nor are they by any means always superior to older sorts. If you kept a garden notebook last year it should be helpful in making this year's selections. One word of caution, do not fall for sensationally advertized, apparently low-priced offerings of less reputable mail order firms. Stick with reliable seedsmen of recognized reputation and expect to pay fair prices. The original price of seeds, bulbs, or plants is but a small part of the total cost of planting and raising flowers, vegetables, trees, and shrubs. Keen disappointment can result from starting with inferior stock. Order not only seeds and plants, but also supplies you are in need of, such as pots, flats, labels, fertilizers, pesticides, and such as you will need for greenhouse and outdoor use later. Of course if you are near a good garden center you may prefer

to pick these up as you need them, but if such facilities are remote and you must order by mail do so early.

In greenhouses as days lengthen and the sun becomes stronger many plants, especially annuals, will make greatly improved growth. There is less tendency for stems to lengthen unduly and become weak. Foliage is likely to be firmer and more richly colored. Still, one must watch temperatures carefully, taking care that at night they do not vary more than two or three degrees from the ideals set for whatever plants are being grown. In really cold weather it is better that temperatures drop a little below the ideal than that so much heat be used to maintain the greenhouse that the pipes or other heating elements become hot enough to parch the atmosphere.

Faster growth may necessitate spacing pot plants more widely. Calceolarias, cinerarias, Paris-daisies, primulas, and others will make weak growth and become drawn and unshapely unless well lighted from all sides. Increased growth also signals the need for repotting some plants becoming pot-bound. This is especially true of kinds grown as annuals and biennials. Do not permit annuals sown last fall for late winter and spring display to become pot-bound until they are in their final containers. Potting permanent plants is mostly best left until later.

Fertilize sparingly, after the middle of the month, annuals and biennials in final pots that have become filled with roots. Pot-bound permanent plants of many kinds, including ferns, palms, and most other foliage plants, will likewise benefit from sparing applications of fertilizer. It is important not to fertilize more often than about every two weeks and to use decidedly small amounts or weak dilutions.

Watering must still be done with considerable care to minimize the serious dangers of overwetness. In dull, damp weather it is better for the earth to be a little dryish than saturated for long periods. Keep stock

After poinsettias are through flowering, cut them partly back

In greenhouses these bulb plants need cool growing conditions:
(a) Babianas

(b) Freesias

(c) 'Paper White' narcissuses

(e) Lachenalias

(d) Nerines

(f) Ornithogalums

plants of chrysanthemums, winter-flowering buddleias, and other kinds that are semidormant, but retain some foliage "on the dry side." Cut back lightly poinsettias that are through flowering and lay the pots on their sides under a bench in a greenhouse or in a cellar or similar place where the temperature is 55 to 60°F; they can be kept quite dry until May.

Bulbs to flower in winter and spring must be afforded appropriate attention according to kind. Such nonhardy sorts as babianas, baby gladioluses, freesias, lachenalies, 'Paper White', 'Soleil d'Or', and Chinese sacred-lily narcissuses, nerines, ornithogalums, and tritonias must be "grown cool" and in full sun at all times. High temperatures, high humidity, and poor light can only result in miserable specimens. Guard, too, against overwatering bulbs of this type. Examine amaryllis (*Hippeastrum*) bulbs at about two-week intervals and treat any that show signs of growth as suggested in the Encyclopedia entry December, Gardening Reminders For.

Hardy bulbs as pot plants or for cut flowers need quite different treatment. Once they have filled their containers with roots they may be brought from the outdoor plunge bed or cellar where they have been cool and moist since they were planted in fall and introduced to the greenhouse. To ensure a long season of bloom bring in batches in succession. Most recommendations are to begin forcing in comparatively cool conditions and to raise the temperatures after growth indoors has well started, but this is not essential with all kinds. Hyacinths, lily-of-the-valleys,

Bulbs to force for early bloom include:
(a) Hyacinths

(b) Lily-of-the-valleys

(c) Narcissuses

(d) Tulips

Annuals to sow now for early bloom
indoors include: (a) African marigolds

(b) Clarkias

(c) Nemesias

(d) Salpiglossis

(e) Stocks

narcissuses, and tulips respond to temperatures of 60 to 70°F from the beginning
and of course come into bloom more
quickly when afforded them.

Fast-growing annuals sown this month
and grown in a night temperature of 45 to
50°F will give good bloom well before any
from the same kinds become available outdoors. Sorts suitable include African marigolds, baby's breath (*Gypsophila*), chrysanthemums, clarkias, larkspurs, leptosynes
(*Coreopsis*), nemesias, salpiglossis, and
stocks.

Sow seeds now of: (a) Gloxinias (*Sinningia*)

(b) Tuberous begonias

Other seeds to sow indoors in January include gloxinias and tuberous begonias. A few, very few, annuals for later planting outdoors may also now be sown. For most sorts it is yet far too early. Kinds to sow now or next month for summer display are annual carnations, lobelias, verbenas, and Madagascar-periwinkle (*Catharanthus rosea*). Seeds of pansies and sweet peas sown now in a cool greenhouse will give plants for setting out early that will bloom for extended periods. Certain herbaceous perennials can be had in bloom the first year from seeds sown indoors now. Most important of these are delphiniums. Care of cold frames in January is as for December.

Houseplants in January face the same difficult conditions, perhaps in some ways

Seeds sown in a greenhouse now give plants to set outdoors later: (a) Pansies

(b) Sweet peas

From seeds sown in a greenhouse in January, delphiniums will bloom in July

Branches of flowering shrubs and trees to force into early bloom: (a) Pussy willow

(b) Forsythia

intensified, that are theirs in December. Read about these in the entry in this Encyclopedia titled December, Gardening Reminders For and be guided accordingly. One encouraging factor is that days are lengthening and light is strengthening. All

(c) Bush honeysuckle

(d) Flowering dogwood

(b) Evergreens, water, and a bridge are featured here

plants can still take maximum sunshine, none need shade yet. Now you can force into bloom in containers of water indoors cut branches of early flowering hardy shrubs such as bush honeysuckles, dogwoods, forsythias, pussy willows, and winter jasmine. These provide a pleasant foretaste of spring.

In the south, locality to a large extent determines outdoor garden tasks that may be done in January. In northern and mountain parts of that region the practicabilities are about the same as for gardens in the north except that weather conditions are more likely to make preparing ground in readiness for spring sowing and planting feasible and to permit construction work.

Planting deciduous and evergreen trees and shrubs, including fruit trees and roses, is an important task in the middle and lower south. Finish pruning grape vines without delay and the pruning of fruit trees well before they start into new growth. Where needed, dormant sprays must be applied to fruit and other trees and shrubs before that time too, but only when there is not danger of freezing occurring during the following night.

Seed sowing now calls for attention. In the upper and middle south this will be confined to the hardiest kinds of annuals and vegetables, such as cornflowers, larkspurs, poppies, scabious, sweet peas, carrots, peas, radishes, and spinach. Plant onion sets and cabbage plants and asparagus, horseradish, and rhubarb. Sowings throughout the month of a much wider selection of annuals and vegetables are in order in the lower south.

On the West Coast pruning is an important task in January, but in northern reaches that of roses is best delayed until February. Finish all needed pruning of deciduous trees and shrubs before new growth starts. Before then, too, complete any dormant spraying that is to be done.

Planting deciduous and evergreen trees and shrubs, grape vines, roses, herbaceous

perennials and annuals following rains will now occupy gardeners in southern California. Seeds of baby's breath, gaillardias, larkspurs, poppies, sweet peas, and other quick-growing annuals may be sown. In northern California toward the end of the month make first plantings of tuberous begonias, cannas, calla-lilies, gladioluses, tigridias, and tuberoses.

JAPAN or JAPANESE. These words form part of the common names of these plants: Japan wood oil tree (*Aleurites cordata*), Japanese-andromeda (*Pieris japonica*), Japanese-cedar (*Cryptomeria japonica*), Japanese-ivy (*Parthenocissus tricuspidata*), Japanese lawn grass (*Zoysia japonica*), Japanese pagoda tree (*Sophora japonica*), Japanese-quince (*Chaenomeles speciosa*), Japanese raisin tree (*Hovenia dulcis*), Japanese-spurge (*Pachysandra terminalis*), and Japanese varnish tree (*Firmiana simplex*).

JAPANESE DWARFED TREES. See Bonsai.

JAPANESE GARDENS. The popularity of gardens in the Japanese style reflects increased interest in the unique horticultural arts of Japan. This interest is especially

(c) A willow tree and a wisteria-clothed bamboo pergola are dominant here

(d) A small garden with stone lanterns

Gardens in Japan: (a) View in a stroll garden

manifest on the West Coast, but it is gaining everywhere. The best American Japanese gardens are satisfying creations that interpret a great Oriental art in terms understandable to Occidentals. They are not merely imitative, but are selective and adaptive. Far too many of our Japanese gardens have been poorly conceived and as a result are travesties of the landscape art developed in Japan. They appear to be

(c) Arched bridge links island to mainland

Japanese garden at the Brooklyn Botanic Garden, Brooklyn, New York: (a) Pleasant view of a pond with stepping stones, torii (decorative portal or gateway), sheared evergreens, and a willow tree

(b) A well-placed low bridge, sheared evergreens, and a stone lantern are seen in this view

Japanese garden with waterfall and "cloud-pruned" evergreen, Longwood Gardens, Kennett Square, Pennsylvania

designed on the assumption that all that is necessary are pagodas, stone lanterns, bamboo screens and fences, arched bridges, a pool containing goldfish, and curiously shaped rocks, placed in an area that includes pines and other trees and shrubs contorted by pruning.

The first requirement of a Japanese garden is that it should closely integrate nature and the house. It must serve as a link between the natural and the man-made. Emphasis is placed on simplicity.

A whole philosophy is involved in the planning of Japanese gardens. They are intended for contemplation and meditation, as places where one may quietly appreciate and enjoy, without distraction,

beauties of line, mass and texture in perfect relationship to each other.

Japanese gardens do not contain great collections of different kinds of plants or emphasize masses of color as do English gardens, or stress symmetry, lavishness and architectural qualities as do Italian gardens. Unlike gardens in America, Japanese gardens reflect few seasonal changes. Evergreens dominate the scene. Deciduous maples and azaleas may add touches of foliage color in fall. Flowering cherries, Japanese iris and tree peonies, discreetly used, afford some spring bloom, but there is little else. Asymmetric balance, rather than symmetry, characterizes these gardens. There is no attempt to gain effects

by repetition. Plants are not used in matched pairs, in rows, or in formal beds; rocks are grouped purposefully with no bilateral symmetry. An important point to remember about Japanese gardens is that they attempt to epitomize nature. Each represents in miniature an expanse of natural scenery, somewhat stylized and formalized and often with details suggested, rather than copied.

The mountains, hills, lakes, streams, waterfalls, and seashores of Japan have inspired its traditional gardens. Scale and proportion are very important. Most Japanese gardens are created on comparatively small areas, and every effort is made to establish the illusion of space and distance. To help this, false perspectives may be realized by planting gradually smaller trees as the distance from the house or other viewing point increases. Larger rock groups may occupy the foreground, smaller ones farther from the viewer. The nearer island in a lake may be larger than one slightly more distant and its vegetation taller. Paths and bridges are scaled to minimum usable dimensions, and such features as lanterns and pagodas are never out of proportion to their surroundings.

Japanese garden, with pine and flowering cherries, Missouri Botanical Garden, St. Louis, Missouri

A Japanese style wooden lantern

Japanese garden, the Botanical Garden, Durban, South Africa

Similarly, the garden is made to appear vaster by the clever use of trees and shrubs that give an appearance of maturity and age, even though they are of moderate size. Such trees and shrubs are kinds that grow naturally this way or can be induced to do so by pruning. By locating brighter-colored plants toward the foreground and those of less insistence farther away, the feeling of distance is enhanced. This is true too when large, bold-leaved plants are restricted to near-to-the-viewer locations and the background planting is of finer-textured foliage. Spaciousness is further suggested by employing the horizontal lines of lakeshores, low roofs, and surfaces of still water and of stretches of carefully tended sand or gravel.

Japanese gardens may be "stroll" gardens or "viewing" gardens. Through the former, one walks along a path and enjoys a series of carefully planned landscape pictures from various points of vantage. The viewing garden is designed to be seen from one place only, perhaps through a window, and is often quite small.

A stroll garden may include one or more hills to represent mountains. Usually associated with the hills will be a stream or miniature lake or both and perhaps a waterfall. A rocky island, planted with a low juniper or picturesque pine, may occupy an off-center position in the lake; sometimes two islands of varying size are used. From the chief viewing point, the hills are background to the water features. The path is contrived to lead the stroller naturally from vantage point to vantage point. Or the garden may be without hills or even water. Representations of these may

be achieved by the skillful use of bold rocks and stretches of mowed turf, fine gravel, coarse sand or, possibly, "pools" or "streams" of flat, waterworn, oval or circular black stones. When gravel or sand is used, it is often raked to produce patterns—straight and placid, or swirling to suggest flowing water.

Viewing gardens are often gems. They are, in fact, three-dimensional pictures achieved with living plants and rocks and, sometimes, water, with perhaps a lantern or other artifact added. Every line, every mass, each particular texture is carefully studied and related to the whole. They are sculptured gardens, showing minimum change from season to season and with plant growth carefully controlled. The smaller the garden, the more important becomes the detail. To a perfect viewing garden nothing can be added, nor can anything be taken from it, without diminishing its effect.

Japanese gardens are enclosed, screened from the outside by plantings, fences or hills, but never so that these are obtrusive.

It is too much to expect that a Japanese garden designed by a Westerner, installed in North America and built of plants and materials available here, will have the same meaning and emotional significance, the same historical and religious associations for a Japanese as the gardens of his homeland. In North America, however, gardens can be based on the principles of design that the Japanese employ so effectively so that they are congruous with their surroundings and satisfying in their appeal, and not merely quaint or unusual. Japanese gardens here need not be copies of gardens in Japan; they should be Western expressions of a Japanese art.

Before beginning a Japanese garden, it is wise to read carefully one or more of the excellent books devoted to this subject and especially to study pictures of well-designed Japanese examples. So far as possible, the plants used should be native Japanese kinds, and the soil should be acid—at least slightly so. Few Japanese plants grow satisfactorily in alkaline soil. When selecting trees for the garden, remember that the Japanese like to see the trunks and branches. Careful pruning may improve a tree that is too symmetrical or too well clothed. Often more formal pruning or shearing tends to stylize azaleas and other shrubs.

Although rocks are conspicuous in Japanese gardens, their use is quite different from that in Western rock gardens, where the aim is to duplicate natural rock formations as closely as possible. The rocks in a Japanese garden are considered individually as sculptural pieces, and either stand alone or are grouped for strong accents. The more rugged rocks symbolize mountains and cliffs, the rounded, water-worn boulders suggest riverbeds.

Sculptured rocks and water-worn pebbles are featured in many Japanese gardens

Stepping-stones arranged in a variety of interesting patterns provide charming paths that sometimes lead a stroller across water. Natural stone steps are often found on slopes. Bridges of many styles, of wood or stone, are installed only where they serve the purpose of spanning water or simulated water.

Maintenance of a Japanese garden is largely a matter of housekeeping. It involves weeding, clearing away dead leaves, raking sand and gravel areas and keeping paths and lakes clean. There is little or no seasonal replanting. Pruning must be precise and frequent. Trees and shrubs must never be permitted to grow out of bounds or out of character. Watering and disease and pest control are, of course, just as necessary in a Japanese garden as in any other.

Among plants best suited for Japanese gardens in North America are the following. Not all are hardy in all sections.

Evergreen trees: *Abies koreana*, Atlas cedar (*Cedrus atlantica*), *Cryptomeria*, Cun-

Evergreen trees for Japanese gardens:
(a) Deodar cedar

(b) Hinoki false-cypress

(c) Japanese white pine

ninghamia lanceolata, deodar (*Cedrus deodara*), Hinoki false-cypress (*Chamaecyparis obtusa*), Japanese black pine (*Pinus thunbergii*), Japanese red pine (*Pinus densiflora*), Japanese white pine (*Pinus parviflora*), jun-

(d) Sawara false-cypress

Evergreen shrubs for Japanese gardens:
(a) *Aucuba japonica*

(b) Bamboo (*Arundinaria vagans*)

ipers (*Juniperus*) (several kinds), mugo pine (*Pinus mugo mugo*), Nikko fir (*Abies homolepis*), sawara false-cypress (*Chamaecyparis pisifera*), and umbrella-pine (*Sciadopitys verticillata*).

Evergreen shrubs: *Ardisia crenata*, *Aucuba japonica* and varieties, azaleas (*Rhododendron*) (Japanese sorts), bamboos (various sorts), butcher's-broom (*Ruscus aculea-*

(c) *Camellia japonica*

(f) Japanese-andromeda

Deciduous trees for Japanese gardens:
(a) Japanese cherry

(d) *Fatsia japonica*

(g) Juniper

(b) Japanese maple

(c) Japanese pagoda tree (fruits)

(h) *Podocarpus macrophyllus maki*

(e) Heavenly-bamboo

tus,) *Camellia japonica* and *C. sasanqua* varieties, *Daphne odora, Euonymus japonicus,* evergreen privets (*Ligustrum japonicum, L. lucidum*), *Fatsia japonica,* heavenly-bamboo (*Nandina domestica*), Japanese-andromeda (*Pieris japonica*), Japanese holly (*Ilex crenata*), Japanese pittosporum (*Pittosporum tobira*), junipers (*Juniperus*) (several kinds), *Mahonia bealii, Osmanthus* (Asian kinds), plum-yew (*Cephalotaxus harringtonia* and varieties), *Podocarpus* (Asian sorts), sweet bay (*Laurus nobilis*), and Yeddo-hawthorn (*Raphiolepis umbellata*).

Deciduous trees: Amur maple (*Acer ginnala*), crab apple (*Malus*) (various kinds), Japanese cherry (*Prunus*) (various kinds), Japanese maples (*Acer japonicum*) (many varieties), Japanese pagoda tree (*Sophora japonica*), katsura tree (*Cercidiphyllum japonicum*), kousa dogwood (*Cornus kousa*), magnolias (Asian sorts), maidenhair tree

(d) Kousa dogwood

(e) *Magnolia soulangeana*

Deciduous shrubs for Japanese gardens:
(a) Azalea (*Rhododendron kaempferi*)

(b) *Enkianthus campanulatus*

(c) Firethorn

(d) Glossy abelia

(e) Japanese barberry

(f) Japanese witch-hazel

(g) Tree peony

(*Ginkgo biloba*), pomegranate (*Punica granatum*), and *Zelkova serrata*.

Deciduous shrubs: azaleas (*Rhododendron*) (Japanese kinds), Chinese redbud (*Cercis chinensis*), *Cotoneaster apiculata* and *C. horizontalis*, dwarf cork-winged euonymus (*Euonymus alatus compactus*), *Enkianthus campanulatus* and *E. perulatus*, firethorn (*Pyracantha*), five-leaf-aralia (*Acanthopanax sieboldianus*), glossy abelia (*Abelia grandiflora*), *Hydrangea macrophylla*, Japanese barberry (*Berberis thunbergii*), Jap-

Vines for Japanese gardens: (a) Boston-ivy

(d) Wisteria

(b) *Clematis montana rubens*

Herbaceous perennials for Japanese gardens: (a) Japanese iris

(c) *Akebia quinata*

(b) Japanese primrose

anese quince and dwarf Japanese quince (*Chaenomeles speciosa* and *C. japonica*), Japanese witch-hazel (*Hamamelis japonica*), Korean barberry (*Berberis koreana*), *Rosa rugosa*, and tree peonies (*Paeonia suffruticosa*).

Vines: Boston-ivy (*Parthenocissus tricuspidata*), bower actinidia (*Actinidia arguta*), *Clematis montana rubens*, English ivy (*Hedera helix*), five-leaf akebia (*Akebia quinata*), and wisterias.

Groundcovers and herbaceous perennials: English ivy (*Hedera helix*), *Gaultheria*

miqueliana, Japanese iris (*Iris kaempferi*), Japanese primrose (*Primula japonica*), Japanese-spurge (*Pachysandra terminalis*), and sand-myrtle (*Leiophyllum buxifolium*).

JAPONICA. This word forms part of the botanical names of many plants, commonly indicating they are natives of Japan.

It is also used as a common name of flowering-quinces (*Chaenomeles*) and in the British Isles sometimes for *Aucuba japonica*.

JARRAH is *Eucalyptus marginata*.

JASIONE (Jasiòn-e)—Sheep's-Bit-Scabious or Shepherd's Scabious. Annual, biennial, and perennial herbaceous plants to the number of about twenty species compose *Jasione*, of the bellflower family CAMPANULACEAE. They are natives of Europe, the Mediterranean region, and Asia Minor. The name is one used by Theophrastus for the convolvulus.

Jasiones have much the appearance of globularias and phyteumas and some resemblance to scabiosas. They have alternate, undivided, toothless or toothed, narrow leaves, the basal ones usually in rosettes, and blue or rarely white flowers in terminal heads with involucres (collars of bracts). The flowers have calyxes and corollas deeply divided into five narrow lobes, five stamens, and one style. The fruits are capsules.

The sheep's-bit-scabious or shepherds-scabious (*J. perennis* syn. *J. laevis*), of southern Europe, is a more or less hairy

Jasione perennis

Jasione perennis (flowers)

perennial 9 inches to 1½ feet tall. It has sterile as well as flowering stems, the latter leafless in their upper parts. The leaves are linear-oblong to linear-lanceolate, and up to 4 inches long, the upper ones much shorter than those below. Up to 2 inches in diameter, the spherical heads of blue flowers terminate long, erect stalks. Called by the same vernacular names as the last, biennial or annual *J. montana* (syn. *J. jankae*) occurs throughout most of Europe including the British Isles. Very variable, 1 foot to 1½ feet tall, and more or less hairy, this branches from the base or is branchless. It has linear to lanceolate, toothless or distantly-toothed leaves, up to nearly 2 inches long, and long-stalked, spherical flower heads ¾ to 1 inch wide or sometimes wider. The flowers are blue, rarely pink or white.

Also sometimes cultivated, *J. bulgarica*, of the Balkan Peninsula, is similar to *J. perennis* except that its stems and foliage are hairless and its flower heads are not over 1 inch wide. Native to the Pyrenees, perennial *J. humilis* (syn. *J. crispa*) is densely-tufted, with linear-oblong to linear-lanceolate leaves less than ½ inch long. Its branchless stems 2 to 4 inches tall terminate in short-stalked heads up to ½ inch wide of blue flowers.

Garden and Landscape Uses and Cultivation. Although they make no great shows of bloom these easily grown, hardy plants are pleasant adornments for rock gardens and the fronts of flower borders. They need sunny sites and well-drained, preferably sandy soil. All are easily raised from seeds, the perennials also by division in spring or early fall. Seeds of *J. montana* are sown in spring where the plants are to remain, and the seedlings thinned to stand about 4 inches apart.

JASMINE and JESSAMINE. These are common names of *Jasminum*, the last also of *Cestrum*. Other plants with common names that include one of these words are Cape-jasmine (*Gardenia jasminoides*), Carolina yellow-jasmine (*Gelseminum sempervirens*), Chilean-jasmine (*Mandevilla laxa*), Confederate- or star-jasmine (*Trachelospermum jasminoides*), crape-jasmine (*Tabernaemontana divaricata*), Madagascar-jasmine (*Stephanotis floribunda*), Night-jasmine (*Nyctanthes arbortristis*), orange-jessamine (*Murraya paniculata*), and rock-jasmine (*Androsace*).

JASMINUM (Jás-minum)—Jasmine, Jessamine. The approximately 200 species of *Jasminum*, of the olive family OLEACEAE, are natives of the Old World, mostly of warm-temperate, subtropical, and tropical regions. The name is a Latin rendition of the Persian one *yasmin* for plants of this genus. Oil of jasmine extensively employed in perfumery is a product of *J. grandiflorum*. For it this species is much cultivated in the south of France, especially in the vicinity of Grasse. In Hawaii the flowers of *J. sambac* are used in leis, and perfume for local sale is made from them. The Chinese employ unopened flower buds of the same species to perfume jasmine tea, and the open blooms as a source of perfume. For plants other than *Jasminum* that have jasmine or jessamine as parts of their colloquial names see Jasmine and Jessamine.

Jasmines are deciduous and evergreen vines or lax-branched to erect shrubs or small trees. They have usually alternate, more rarely opposite leaves with three to eleven, or sometimes only one leaflet. When there is only one leaflet, the leaf to the casual observer appears to be undivided rather than pinnate. The flowers are generally in branchless or forking terminal clusters. Less commonly they are solitary. Often they are fragrant. They have a four- to nine-toothed, tubular or bell-shaped calyx and a corolla with a slender tube and normally four to eleven wide-spreading petals. There are two short-stalked, non-protruding stamens and a short style with a club-shaped or two-lobed stigma. The fruits are normally two-lobed berries containing two to four seeds, but often one lobe fails to develop.

The winter jasmine (*J. nudiflorum*) is one of the only two species with opposite

leaves and yellow flowers. It is also the hardiest member of the genus. A native of China, it survives outdoors in sheltered places as far north as Boston, Massachusetts. In mild climates it blooms throughout much of the winter, in harsher ones in late winter usually a little ahead of forsythias, and before its leaves expand. From 3 feet to, when grown against a wall or other support, nearly 15 feet tall, this attractive deciduous shrub has numerous long, slender branches and rigid, hairless, four-angled branchlets. Its leaves are of three ovate leaflets, ½ to 1 inch long, with tiny points at their apexes. The solitary, scentless blooms, ¾ to 1 inch in diameter, have calyxes with spreading, leafy lobes, and five or six obovate, often wavy petals about one-half as long as the corolla tube. The foliage of *J. n. aureum* is blotched with yellow.

The other yellow-flowered species with opposite leaves is the primrose jasmine (*J. mesnyi* syn. *J. primulinum*). From the winter jasmine, this differs in being evergreen, later-flowering, in having larger blooms and foliage, and in not being hardy in the north. A native of China, primrose jasmine is a lax-stemmed shrub, when supported up to 10 feet tall. It has hairless, four-angled branch-

Jasminum nudiflorum cascading down a bank

Jasminum mesnyi

Jasminum nudiflorum (flowers)

Jasminum mesnyi (flowers)

lets, leaves of three oblong-lanceolate leaflets up to 3 inches long, and solitary, often semidouble blooms 1½ to nearly 2 inches in diameter, with a calyx of leafy sepals, and six to ten petals.

Yellow-flowered jasmines with alternate leaves include *J. humile,* a widely variable species with a natural range from Afghanistan to western China. An erect or sometimes scrambling, hairless to pubescent, evergreen shrub or small tree up to 20 feet tall, this has leaves of mostly five, sometimes seven, pinnately-arranged leaflets, but those near the bottoms of the shoots may have only three or one leaflet. The leaflets, their margins more or less recurved, are narrowly-lanceolate to elliptic or ovate, the terminal ones ¾ inch to nearly 2 inches long, the lateral leaflets smaller. Scented or scentless, the flowers, ½ to ¾ inch wide, are in clusters of two to ten. The Italian jasmine (*J. h. revolutum* syn. *J. revolutum*) is somewhat less hardy than the typical kind and is hairless. This, the best variety, has leaves with three to seven leaflets, the terminal ones 1½ to 2½ inches long, the lateral ones smaller. The fragrant blooms are in clusters of six to twelve or more. They are ¾ to 1 inch wide. From the typical species *J. h. wallichianum* (syn. *J. h. glabrum*) differs in its leaves having more numerous leaflets, seven to eleven, the terminal one long and pointed, and in its clusters of fewer flowers being more or less pendulous. Variety *J. h. farreri* (syn. *J. farreri*) is a broad, slightly-hairy shrub 6 to 8 feet tall with leaves of three to five leaflets, the terminal ones 1¼ to 3½ inches long, the lateral ones smaller. The scentless flowers are in clusters of seven to twelve.

Less hardy than *J. humile* to which it is closely related, subtropical *J. subhumile* (syn. *J. diversifolium*) is grown outdoors in Florida and California. Probably the biggest alternate-leaved jasmine, this is a hairless to pubescent large shrub or small tree up to about 12 feet tall and broader than tall. Native from the eastern Himalayas to western China at lower altitudes than *J. humile,* it differs from that species in having leaves of one to three leaflets with the terminal ones mostly exceeding 2 inches and sometimes being as much as 5 inches long, and in the flower clusters being generally of twenty to 120 or rarely fewer, fragrant, yellow blooms ½ to ¾ inch wide.

Other close relatives of *J. humile* are *J. floridum,* of China, *J. odoratissimum,* of the Canary Islands and Madeira, and its variety *J. o. goetzeanum,* of East Africa. A scrambling, hairless, evergreen or semievergreen shrub, **J. floridum** differs from *J. humile* in that the calyx lobes of its yellow blooms, which are in terminal clusters, are more slender and longer, about ⅛ inch long. The leaves have sometimes five, more usually three, elliptic, ovate, or obovate, pointed leaflets ½ inch to 1½ inches long. Chiefly **J. odoratissimum** differs from *J. humile* in having leafier flower clusters and flowers with shorter stalks. Also, the leaves are more often of only three leaflets. Its blooms are yellow.

In habit and foliage **J. bignoniaceum** (syn. *J. revolutum peninsulare*), of the mountains of southern India and Ceylon, much resembles *J. humile.* It differs most obviously in its yellow blooms being fewer and nodding and in having corolla tubes much broader at their tops and petals proportionately much shorter than those of *J.*

humile. A shrub or small tree 3 to 4½ feet tall, hairless *J. bignoniaceum* has leaves mostly with five to nine, rarely eleven, narrow to broad, elliptic to obovate leaflets, but the leaves toward the bases of the shoots have three or one leaflet. The flowers, in clusters of up to six at the ends of side shoots, are not fragrant. Their petals are not more than one-third as long as the corolla tube and are as wide as long.

Others with yellow flowers and alternate leaves are *J. fruticans* and *J. parkeri.* The only native European jasmine, *J. fruticans's* natural range extends from Portugal and Morocco to western Asia. Semievergreen or evergreen, hairless, and 2 to 5 feet tall, or much taller when planted against a support, this sort forms dense growths of erect, slender stems. Its leaves are of three or one narrowly-oblong to linear-ovate leaflets ⅓ to ¾ inch long by about one-third as wide. The flowers, a little over ½ inch wide, are in clusters of three to five at the ends of short branchlets. The fruits are spherical and glossy-black. A remarkable low, prostrate kind, **J. parkeri,** of the Himalayas, is 6 inches to 1 foot tall. Its leaves, ½ to 1 inch long, have three or five leaflets ⅛ to ⅜ inch in length. Solitary or in pairs from the leaf axils, the flowers, about ½ inch in diameter, are succeeded by spherical, translucent, greenish-white fruits about ⅙ inch in diameter.

White flowers and opposite leaves that have more than three leaflets are characteristic of *J. officinale, J. grandiflorum,* and *J. polyanthum.* In addition *J. dispermum* in large part meets these specifications. Common jasmine or poet's Jasmine (**J. officinale**) is a deciduous or nearly deciduous, vigorous hairless or nearly hairless vine

Jasminum odoratissimum

Jasminum polyanthum

that may eventually attain a height of 40 feet. Native from the Caucasus to China, it has slender shoots and leaves of five to nine leaflets ½ inch to 2½ inches long by less than ¼ to 1 inch wide. The terminal leaflet is stalked and much bigger than the stalkless lateral ones. In abundant, terminal clusters of three to five, the deliciously fragrant, approximately ¾-inch-wide, starry blooms on 1-inch-long stalks, have four or five petals. The black fruits are about ⅓ inch in length. Variety *J. o. affine* has somewhat bigger blooms with broader calyx lobes than those of the nearly threadlike ones of the typical species, and corollas pink on their outsides. The foliage of *J. o. aureo-variegatum* is blotched with yellow.

Spanish jasmine, Catalonian jasmine, or royal jasmine (***J. grandiflorum*** syn. *J. officinale grandiflorum*) differs only slightly from common jasmine (*J. officinale*). It is notably less hardy and has larger, fragrant flowers, with five or six petals, pink-tinged on their undersides. Those in the same umbel have stalks of different lengths, which is not true of common jasmine. Also, the leaflets of *J. grandiflorum* tend to be proportionately shorter and blunter than those of *J. officinale*, and the lower ones are often more or less united. The native origin of *J. grandiflorum* is not known; it is perhaps Arabia.

Broad, almost winged bases to the leafstalks, and flowers with calyxes with decidedly shorter teeth (less than 1/12 inch long) distinguish ***J. polyanthum*** from the common and Spanish jasmines. A native of China and rather more tender to cold than the common jasmine, this evergreen or deciduous vine has leaves of five or seven lanceolate leaflets, the terminal one much the biggest. The fragrant, white flowers, ¾ inch wide, have five petals, suffused on their outsides with purplish-red or pink. Smaller-flowered than the last and deciduous, ***J. dispermum*** also differs in having leaves with three leaflets and leaves with more on the same shoots. Also, the terminal leaflets have five veins pinnately arranged, whereas those of *J. polyanthum* have three that come from the base. Native of the Himalayan region, *J. dispermum* is appropriate for outdoor cultivation in mild climates only. Its profusely borne flowers are white, tinged with pink on their outsides.

White flowers and opposite leaves of three leaflets typify a number of jasmines; among them is ***J. fluminense,*** of tropical Africa, a species now naturalized in Florida and the West Indies. Widely cultivated in warm lands, especially the Caribbean region, it is frequently misidentified as *J. azoricum*. A vigorous, more or less hairy, scrambling vine or shrub, this has long branches and usually densely-pubescent leaves with ovate leaflets, the middle one nearly 2 inches long, the others smaller. The flower clusters, terminal and from the upper leaf axils, have densely-hairy branches. The fragrant blooms have a calyx not more than 1/16 inch long, with five or six tiny teeth, and a corolla with a tube up to 1 inch long and five or six petals about ½ inch long by ¼ inch wide. The fruits are shiny, brown or black, spherical, and nearly ⅓ inch in diameter.

South African ***J. angulare*** is a variable, scrambling or climbing shrub up to 20 feet tall characterized by its branchlets being angled. Most of its leaves have three leaflets up to ¾ inch long and one-half as wide or wider. Greenish or pinkish on their outsides, the flowers are in rather compact clusters. They have five petals from a little under to a little over ½ inch long by ¼ inch wide. Another South African twining or scrambling vine, ***J. tortuosum*** differs from the last two in having linear-lanceolate to linear-oblong leaves of three leaflets less than one-half as wide as long. Its clusters of white flowers are at the ends of the stems and side branches. Each flower has usually six petals ½ inch long by ⅕ inch wide.

Jasminum angulare in a greenhouse

Jasminum angulare (flowers)

A rare endemic of Madeira misleadingly named ***J. azoricum*** (meaning a native of the Azores) was cultivated in Europe as early as the end of the seventeenth century. Similar, except for shape and size of blooms to *J. fluminense,* this has leaves with ovate, wavy leaflets with somewhat heart-shaped bases. The flowers have corollas with five petals as long as their tubes.

White-flowered jasmines with leaves of one leaflet, opposite or sometimes in threes, include a number of popular kinds. Here belongs everygreen ***J. rex,*** with the largest flowers of all cultivated sorts. This splendid species delights with beautiful, pristine, eight- or nine-petaled blooms 2 inches wide and of good texture. A hairless vine, *J. rex* has broad-oblong leaves 4 to 8 inches long, paler on their undersides than above. Its flowers, in terminal panicles of groups of two or three, are scentless.

Jasminum rex

Jasminum rex (flowers)

Arabian jasmine or pikake (***J. sambac***) is even more widely cultivated than the last. Its leaves are opposite or sometimes in pairs. Probably native of southeast Asia and old in cultivation, this is an evergreen, more or less climbing shrub up to about 5 feet tall. It has downy branches and broad-elliptic to ovate or nearly round, nearly stalkless leaves 1½ to 3 inches long. The white, fragrant flowers, mostly in three-branched clusters, are about 1 inch in diameter, have four to nine or in some varieties more, oblong to rounded, blunt petals. Variety *J. s. multiplex* (syn. 'Maid of Orleans') has semidouble flowers. The blooms of *J. s. flore-pleno* (syns. 'Grand Duke', 'Grand Duke of Tuscany') are extremely double and button-like. They somewhat resemble small roses.

Jasminum sambac flore-pleno

Pinwheel jasmine (*J. multiflorum* syns. *J. gracillimum, J. pubescens*) is sometimes called, as is completely different *Trachelospermum jasminoides*, star jasmine. The name *J. multiflorum* is that of a complex of several slightly different varieties or perhaps species indigenous to southeast Asia and Indonesia and widely cultivated throughout the tropics and subtropics. Pinwheel jasmine is a clambering evergreen with hairless or pubescent shoots and slender, usually more or less pendulous branches. Its pointed-elliptic to heart-shaped leaves 1 inch to 3 inches long are in pairs. The few to numerous fragrant or odorless white blooms, mostly about 1 inch in diameter and with four to nine pointed petals, are generally in short clusters forming many-flowered panicles.

Starry-flowered *J. nitidum* (syn. *J. amplexicaule*) is commonly cultivated in warm-temperate, subtropical, and tropical regions, not uncommonly under the names of other kinds. There is little excuse for this, since it is one of the most easily recognized jasmines. Tell-tale features are the awl-shaped, downy calyx lobes spreading at right angles from the corolla tube, the open flower clusters, the fragrant blooms, which are ½ to nearly ¾ inch in diameter with narrow, pointed petals often tinged on their outsides with purplish-red, and the more or less glossy fo-

Jasminum nitidum

liage. This charming species is a native of the Admiralty Islands near New Guinea.

Other white-flowered species with leaves of one leaflet in pairs or threes include *J. dichotomum*. A tropical African, this nearly continuous-blooming evergreen vine is naturalized in Florida. It has thick, lustrous leaves about 3 inches long. Sweetly fragrant and opening at night, the starry blooms are wine-red on their outsides. They are 1 inch or a little more in length and have six to eight oval petals ⅓ inch long.

Red- or pink-flowered jasmines are *J. beesianum* and its hybrid *J. stephanense*. The only red- or pink-flowered species, *J. beesianum* is more remarkable for the color of its blooms than for any considerable show they make. Native to China, this is a deciduous or partially evergreen vine or shrub that forms tangles of slightly-downy stems. Its opposite, ovate-lanceolate to lanceolate leaves, each of a single leaflet, are slightly-downy on both surfaces. They are 1¼ to 2 inches long by up to ¾ inch wide. The usually six-petaled, fragrant flowers, ½ to ¾ inch wide and solitary, or in twos or threes, are succeeded, if more than one clone is grown in proximity, by long-lasting, attractive glossy, black fruits. Hybrid *J. stephanense*, its parents *J. beesianum* and *J. officinale* or *J. o. grandiflorum*, favors the latter in having a large proportion of pinnate leaves of rarely if ever more than five leaflets, the former with its blooms pale pink and ½ inch wide. This, the only hybrid jasmine, survives at least as a groundcover outdoors in the vicinity of New York City. In milder climates it attains a height of 15 to 20 feet. Raised in France with reportedly *J. officinale grandiflorum* one parent and first exhibited there in 1920, this hybrid occurs spontaneously in China between straight *J. officinale* and

J. beesianum. The vining species generally cultivated as *J. simplicifolium* is *J. volubile*, an attractive Australian species sometimes called wax jasmine. This has opposite leaves of one oblong leaflet. Its delightfully fragrant, smallish, starry, white flowers are rather sparsely produced.

Garden and Landscape Uses. The vining jasmines are among the most satisfactory climbers for clothing trellises, arbors, posts, and similar supports. Some such as *J. beesianum* and *J. stephanense* can be employed to good purpose as groundcovers. The great majority of jasmines are not hardy in the north. An outstanding exception is the winter jasmine. In sheltered locations *J. stephanense* is moderately hardy. Winter jasmine (*J. nudiflorum*) and related *J. mesnyi* are not climbers, but if treated in espalier fashion and tied to trellises or wires they can be used effectively to clothe walls. Winter jasmine is also good for covering and stabilizing steep banks. The other is attractive when trained as a standard with a single, branchless trunk 5 to 6 feet tall and a well-furnished head of branches. In greenhouses and conservatories jasmines are charming for training up walls and pillars or under the roof glass. They can be accommodated in ground beds or containers.

Cultivation. Jasmines are easy to grow outdoors in climates suitable to the needs of particular kinds, and in greenhouses. They adapt to any fertile, well-drained soil. In the main they prefer sun, but tropical kinds succeed with part-day shade. No systematic annual pruning is required, but thinning out older, crowded stems should be given attention from time to time. Standard specimens of *J. mesnyi* grown in containers for blooming indoors in late winter benefit from being stood outdoors in full sun in summer. Propagation is simple by cuttings of moderately firm shoots, by layering, and by seed.

JASONIA (Ja-sònia). Six species constitute this Mediterranean region and Canary Island genus of the daisy family COMPOSITAE. None is well known in cultivation. The name presumably is based on that of the mythological hero Jason.

Jasonias differ from closely related *Inula* in details of their fruits. They are glandular, herbaceous perennials with woody rootstocks, erect stems, alternate leaves, and yellow, daisy-like flower heads with a center of disk florets encircled by petal-like ray florets. The seedlike fruits are achenes.

Occasionally cultivated, **Jasonia tuberosa,** of southern Europe, is 1 foot to 1½ feet tall. It has erect stems, branched above, pointed-linear leaves up to about 3 inches in length, and loosely arranged flower heads 1 inch or so in diameter.

Garden Uses and Cultivation. To provide variety the kind described above may be included in beds of herbaceous perennials. It thrives in ordinary soil in sun and is easily increased by division and by seed. Its degree of hardiness is not fully established. In all probability it will survive in climates not more severe than that of New York City.

JATROPHA (Ját-ropha)—Tartogo or Gout Plant, Barbados Nut or Physic Nut, or Coral Plant, Peregrina, Jicamilla. The spurge family EUPHORBIACEAE includes an amazing variety of plants of highly diverse appearance, from the familiar poinsettia to that commonest source of natural rubber, *Hevea brasiliensis*, from lowly garden weeds to grotesque cactus-like giants of the deserts of Africa. To it belongs *Jatropha*, a pantropical genus of 175 species, most abundant in the Americas and Africa. Its name, alluding to medicinal qualities, is from the Greek *iatros*, a physician, and *trophe*, food.

Jatrophas contain pale to colored milky latex, and are trees, shrubs, and herbaceous perennials, some with stinging hairs. None is hardy in the north. They have alternate, lobed or lobeless, smooth-edged or toothed leaves, those of some kinds divided into separate leaflets that radiate from the ends of the leafstalks. The flowers are unisexual and are in terminal or axillary clusters, with one or both sexes on the same plant. They have five sepals and usually five petals, or more rarely, are without petals. Male blooms have usually eight to twelve stamens. Females have three, less often two, four, or five carpels with their styles, sometimes forked, joined or not below. The fruits are capsules.

The poisonous fruits of *J. curcas, J. multifida*, and other species are powerful purgatives that are or have been, as the name physic nut applied to some species indicates, used medicinally. The poison they contain is inactivated by high temperatures, and in some regions the seeds are baked and eaten. Abundant oil is contained in the chestnut-like seeds of *J. curcas* and this has been used for illuminating, lubricating, soap-making, and other purposes. In Mexico and elsewhere living

Jatropha podagrica

fences or hedges of *J. curcas* that have the advantage of not being eaten by livestock are started by planting large branches, which soon root and become established.

The tartogo or gout plant (*J. podagrica*), 1 foot to 5 feet high, has a short, thick, little-branched stem or trunk of gouty appearance. Its leaf blades, whitish on their undersides, are rounded-ovate, and have three to five deep, round lobes. They are up to 10 inches in diameter and peltate, which means that the stalks are attached to them some distance in from the leaf margin. Coral-red, the smallish flowers are in long-stalked clusters. This species is a native of Central America.

The Barbados nut or physic nut (*J. curcas*), native from Mexico to South America, is an essentially hairless shrub or tree 6 to 18 feet tall. Its leaves, with stalks 4 to 6 inches long, have ovate to round-ovate blades up to about 1 foot long by two-thirds as wide, and usually shallowly three-, five-, or seven-lobed. The greenish-yellow to yellowish-white flowers are in clusters at the branch ends. The more or less fleshy capsules are a little over 1 inch long by ¾ inch wide.

Also called physic nut, the coral plant (*J. multifida*), of tropical America, is a shrub or tree up to 20 feet tall that has leaves with slender stalks that equal in length the diameter of the nearly round blades. The latter are up to 1 foot across and have whitish undersides. They are cleft almost to their bases into many lobes that may or may not be again lobed. The scarlet flowers are in terminal, red-stemmed, stiffly-branched clusters about 2 inches wide. Each cluster is of one or two

Jatropha curcas (flowers)

Jatropha curcas (fruits)

Jatropha integerrima, two different leaf forms

4 to 8 inches high in bloom, taller later. They have palmately (spreading like the fingers of a hand) -veined, or lobed basal leaves and leafless, slender flower stems each carrying a solitary bloom with usually four sepals and eight petals. The stamens equal the petals in number. The fruits are dry, more or less pear-shaped capsules, containing numerous seeds and opening with a lid formed by a horizontal split that extends halfway around the capsule.

The rheumatism root (*J. diphylla*) is a native of rich woods, especially in limy soils, from Ontario to New York to Wisconsin, Iowa, Maryland, and Alabama. The leaves, only partially developed when the plant is in bloom, may eventually be 1 foot to 1½ feet tall. They are shield-shaped and divided into two obliquely half-ovate

female blooms surrounded by several males. The females are succeeded by 1-inch-long, egg-shaped fruits with up to three seeds.

The peregrina (*J. integerrima* syns. *J. pandurifolia, J. hastata*), of Cuba, is an attractive hairless or shortly-hairy, slender shrub 3 to 5 feet tall, with long-stalked, short-pointed, obovate to fiddle-shaped leaves, the stalked end of the 3- to 6-inch-long blade forming the neck of the fiddle. The rose-red to bright red blooms, 1 inch in diameter, are in terminal, long-stalked, branched clusters.

The jicamilla (*J. cathartica* syns. *J. berlandieri, Adenoropium berlandieri*) inhabits arid soils along the Rio Grande river in Texas and Mexico. It has subterranean, turnip-shaped roots 2 to 4 inches in diameter from the tops of which sprout one or more stems to heights of 6 inches to 1 foot. The lower leaves are long-stalked, those above have shorter stalks. Glaucous, hairless, rounded in outline, 2 to 5 inches across, the leaf blades are split almost to where they join the stalk into five or seven broad-elliptic to obovate lobes, which are again lobed or irregularly toothed. In terminal, long-stalked, erect clusters, the starry, red or purple-red flowers are ½ to ¾ inch wide.

Jatropha nudicaulis

Rare in cultivation, *J. nudicaulis* of Ecuador and Colombia has thick, fleshy stems and twice-deeply-palmately-lobed leaves. The ³⁄₈-inch-wide, deep apple-blossom-pink flowers each with five petals, at first spreading, later reflexed, and ten cream stamens, are in loose clusters with bright rose-pink branches.

Garden and Landscape Uses. Jatrophas are grown outdoors in the tropics and subtropics for interest and ornament, and in warm greenhouses, *J. cathartica,* usually in association with such succulent plants as euphorbias and cactuses. In Mexico and other warm, dry places *J. curcas* is often used for hedges.

Cultivation. Little difficulty attends the cultivation of these plants. They do best in well-drained, porous, sandy earth in full sun, but will stand part-day shade. High temperatures are to their liking. In greenhouses on winter nights 55 to 60°F suits, with a five to fifteen degree rise by day permitted. Pot specimens are likely to need repotting at intervals of two to three years. Late winter or spring are the best times to do this. Watering is done to keep the soil moderately moist without being for long periods wet. New plants are raised from seeds, and from cuttings planted in a greenhouse propagating bench, preferably with mild bottom heat. To encourage their cut ends to dry and begin healing, the cuttings are left in a shady place for a day or two before they are planted.

JAVA-PLUM is *Syzygium cuminii.*

JEFFERSONIA (Jeffer-sònia)—Rheumatism Root, Twin-Leaf. Named after Thomas Jefferson, third President of the United States, *Jeffersonia* comprises one species native to eastern North America and one of eastern Asia. It belongs in the barberry family BERBERIDACEAE and is remindful of *Epimedium.*

Jeffersonias are deciduous, spring-blooming, hairless, herbaceous perennials,

Jeffersonia diphylla

parts. The flowers are white and ¾ inch to 1¼ inches wide. Asian *J. dubia* has heart-shaped, glaucous, metallic-violet-tinted leaves with irregularly scalloped margins. Its flowers, about 1½ inches in diameter and a beautiful pale blue, somewhat resemble those of a beautiful *Hepatica.* This is a choice and precious contribution to Western gardens.

Garden Uses. Jeffersonias are delightful for rock and woodland gardens and, the American one, for inclusion in collections of native plants. They are cultivated with comparative ease in any moderately good garden soil in part-shade, preferring earth that contains a generous proportion of leaf mold, peat moss, or other decayed organic matter. The American benefits from the addition of lime if the earth is at all acid.

Cultivation. Fresh seeds sown in the protection of a cold frame or cool greenhouse afford a satisfactory means of increasing jeffersonias. They may also be divided successfully if the operation is carefully done in early spring. Routine care is not demanding. The maintenance of an organic mulch around them is beneficial and watering is needed in dry weather.

JERUSALEM. The word Jerusalem appears as part of the common names of these plants: false-Jerusalem-cherry (*Solanum* capsicastrum), Jerusalem artichoke (*Helianthus tuberosus*), Jerusalem-cherry (*Solanum pseudocapsicum*), Jerusalem-date (*Bauhinia monandra*), Jerusalem-oak (*Chenopodium botrys*), Jerusalem-sage (*Phlomis fruticosa* and *Pulmonaria officinalis*), and Jerusalem-thorn (*Paliurus spina-christi* and *Parkinsonia aculeata*).

JESSAMINE and JASMINE. These are common names of *Jasminum*, the first also of *Cestrum*. Orange-Jessamine is *Murraya paniculata*. For other plants with common names including the word jasmine see the entry Jasmine and Jessamine.

JESUITS' BARK. See Cinchona.

JESUITS' NUT is *Trapa natans*.

JETBEAD is *Rhodotypos scandens*.

JEW and JEWS'. One or other of these words forms part of the common names of these plants: jew bush (*Pedilanthus carinatus*), jews'-mallow (*Corchorus olitorius*), and wandering jew (*Tradescantia fluminensis* and *Zebrina pendula*).

JEWEL and JEWELS. One or other of these words is employed as part of the common names of the following plants: Christmas jewels (*Aechmea racinae*), jewel orchid (*Anoectochilus, Dossinia marmorata, Haemaria discolor,* and *Macodes petola*), jewels-of-Ophir (*Talinum paniculatum*), jewel weed (*Impatiens capensis*), Malay jewel vine (*Derris scandens*), and tower-of-jewels (*Echium*).

JICAMA is *Pachyrhizus tuberosus*.

JICAMILLA is *Jatropha cathartica*.

JIM BRUSH is *Ceanothus sorediatus*.

JIMSON WEED is *Datura stramonium*.

JOB'S TEARS is *Coix lacryma-jobi*.

JOE PYE WEED. See Eupatorium.

JOHN INNES COMPOSTS. Frequent reference to these is made in British horticultural literature. They are not employed to any appreciable extent in North America. Briefly, they are a few approximately standardized mixes for seed sowing and potting soils devised at the John Innes Horticultural Institution in England. The standardization is only approximate because the mixes consist very largely of such variable ingredients as loam (topsoil), leaf mold or peat, and sand. To these are added measured amounts of ground limestone and superphosphate, horn and hoof fertilizer, and sulfate of potash. The loam and leaf mold are sterilized before use.

JOHNNY-JUMP-UP is *Viola tricolor*.

JOHNSON GRASS is *Sorghum halepense*.

JOINT-FIR. See Ephedra.

JOINTWOOD is *Cassia nodosa*.

JOJOBA is *Simmondsia chinensis*.

JONQUIL. Most appropriately jonquil is restricted as a vernacular name to slender, rush-leaved *Narcissus jonquilla* and its hybrids, but in parts of the United States, including New York City and its environs, other narcissuses, especially large-trumpet daffodils, are known as jonquils.

Jonquil (*Narcissus jonquilla*)

JOPOY is *Esenbeckia runyonii*.

JOSEPHINE'S-LILY is *Brunsvigia josephinae*.

JOSEPH'S COAT. This is a common name applied to *Amaranthus tricolor splendens* and varieties of *Acalypha wilkesiana*.

JOSHUA TREE is *Yucca brevifolia*. The name miniature Joshua tree is sometimes applied to *Sedum multiceps*.

JOVELLANA (Jovel-làna). The half-dozen or so species of *Jovellana* are sometimes included in nearly related, and to gardeners more familiar, *Calceolaria*. From it they differ in having flowers slashed horizontally into two almost similarly sized parts that are not shoe-shaped or baglike. Herbaceous or subshrubby, they are natives of the cool parts of South America and New Zealand. Jovellanas belong in the figwort family SCROPHULARIACEAE. Their name commemorates D. Caspari Melchiori de Jovellanus, a botanist interested in the flora of Peru.

These plants have opposite, undivided, usually toothed leaves. Their flowers are rarely solitary, more commonly in panicles, usually at the branch ends, occasion-

ally from the leaf axils. The blooms have a four-lobed calyx, a two-lipped corolla, the lips concave, two stamens, a short style, and a headlike stigma. The fruits are capsules.

Three species are rarely cultivated in mild climates where hot summers are not prevalent. The hardiest, Chilean *J. violacea* attains 6 feet in height and has densely-hairy, brown stems and 1-inch-long, broad-ovate, sparsely-hairy leaves with wedge-shaped bases that are evergreen or deciduous according to climate. The yellowish or pale violet, purple-spotted flowers, about ½ inch in diameter and downy on their outsides, are in terminal panicles. Another Chilean, *J. punctata*, is a shrub up to 4 feet in height with younger shoots finely-downy. This has oblong to oblong-ovate pointed leaves, 3 to 4 inches in length, with double-toothed margins and stalks about ½ inch long. The blooms, pale violet with purple spots, are in many-flowered panicles. From New Zealand comes *J. sinclairi*, a subshrub with erect, hairy shoots and 3-inch-long, ovate-ob-

Jovellana sinclairi

long, coarsely-double-toothed leaves, sparsely-hairy on their upper surfaces and paler and hairless below, their leaf stalks about 2 inches long. This species has loose panicles of bell-shaped, whitish to pale lilac, red-spotted flowers about ⅓ inch across.

Garden Uses and Cultivation. But little is known about the cultivation of these plants in North America. They may be expected to grow under conditions suitable for calceolarias.

JOVIBARBA. See Sempervivum.

JUANIA (Juàn-ia). The one species of this genus has the distinction of being the only palm native to Juan Fernandez, that lonely island 365 miles off the coast of Chile where, in 1704, Alexander Selkirk was marooned and spent a solitary five years and whose experiences later became the basis for Daniel Defoe's *Robinson Crusoe*. The name of the island inspired that of the palm *Juania*, of the palm family PALMAE.

A graceful, slender-trunked, unisexual, feather palm, *J. australis*, about 30 feet in height, has an erect, strongly-ringed trunk and a rather untidy head of foliage without a crownshaft. Its leaves, with many narrow leaflets cleft at their apexes, are 4 to 6 feet in length, green above, grayish beneath. The branched flower clusters develop among the leaves and are about 1 foot long. Male and female blooms are in separate clusters. The males have six stamens. The fruits, about as big as cherries, are orange-red. Technical characteristics separate *Juania* from closely related *Ceroxylon*.

Garden and Landscape Uses and Cultivation. Although attempts have been made to grow this palm in the United States, they have not been successful. From the climate of its native island one might expect that it would be adaptable to southern California and parts of Florida and Hawaii. Factors other than climatic ones may have been responsible for the disappointing results so far reported. This is a challenge for collectors of palms and keen horticulturists. It would certainly be a welcome and attractive addition to palm collections. For additional information see Palms.

JUANULLOA (Juan-ullòa). The name *Juanulloa* was applied to this genus of the nightshade family SOLANACEAE in tribute to the eighteenth-century Spaniards Don George Juan and Don Antonio Ulloa, travelers in Chile and Peru. The group consists of a dozen species native from Mexico to South America.

Juanulloas are shrubs, some epiphytes (plants that perch on other plants without taking nourishment from them). They have undivided, leathery leaves, and yellow, orange, or red blooms, solitary or in clusters of few. The flowers have showy, colored calyxes and a tubular corolla often narrowed at its throat and with five small lobes (petals). There are five stamens and one style. The fruits are fleshy or dry berries.

In its native Peru an epiphyte, *J. mexicana* (syn. *J. aurantiaca*) is an attractive ornamental 3 to 6 feet tall. It has alternate, elliptic to oblongish, felty stems and leaves 3 to 5 inches in length. In forked racemes, its pendulous, bright orange, long-urn-shaped blooms have fleshy, angled calyxes and large corollas.

Garden and Landscape Uses and Cultivation. The species described may be grown outdoors in warm, frostless climates, in greenhouses, and in window gardens. It thrives in porous, nourishing soil in sunny locations and is propagated

Juanulloa mexicana

by cuttings and seed. Indoors, it is satisfied with a winter night temperature of about 55°F and is appropriate for growing along with cactuses and other succulents.

JUBAEA (Jubaè-a)—Coquito Palm or Wine Palm or Chilean Syrup Palm. The name of the only species of *Jubaea*, of the palm family PALMAE, commemorates Juba, King of Numidia. It is a native of Chile.

One of the hardiest palms, the coquito or wine palm (*J. chilensis*) occurs as a native farther south than any other New World palm. It has a trunk up to 6 feet in diameter that towers to a height of 80 feet and terminates in a heavy crown of pinnate leaves 6 to 12 feet long. Each leaf has many narrow leaflets 1 foot to 2 feet in length, notched at their tips, and with comparatively short stalks margined with stiff filaments. The branched flower clusters have long, persistent spathes. The male flowers are on the upper parts of the clusters and have fifteen to thirty stamens.

Jubaea chilensis, Huntington Botanic Garden, San Marino, California

The yellow one-seeded, globose-ovoid fruits are about 1½ inches in diameter. They look somewhat like miniature coconuts.

This palm is exploited for the sugary sap of its trunk, which is extracted after felling the tree and converted by boiling into palm honey. The seeds, called coquitos, are eaten fresh and candied and from them an edible oil is obtained. The leaves are used for basketmaking and other handicrafts. The largest palm in the greenhouses of the Royal Botanic Gardens, Kew, England, in 1968 was a specimen of *J. chilensis* 55 feet high with a trunk 34 feet tall and more than 8 feet in girth. It is believed that this specimen was raised from seeds sown in 1843.

Garden and Landscape Uses. This impressive palm thrives outdoors in southern California and in similar Mediterranean climates, but fails to prosper in hot, humid ones, such as that of Florida. Outdoors it is effective as a single specimen and in groups, and can be used for lining driveways and avenues. It may be grown in greenhouses and is worthy of inclusion in conservatory collections of plants useful to man.

Cultivation. The coquito palm is not difficult to grow. Outdoors it thrives in full sun in ordinary garden soil. It may be raised from fresh seeds sown in sandy peaty soil in a temperature of 70 to 75°F. In greenhouses the minimum winter night temperature should be about 50°F, with a five to ten degree rise permitted in the day. At other seasons a night temperature of about 60°F, with an increase in the day of five or ten degrees is satisfactory. A moderately humid atmosphere and some shade from strong summer sun is necessary, and watering should be done freely from spring through fall, more moderately in winter. The containers or ground beds in which this palm is planted must be well drained and the soil coarse, porous, and fertile. For more information see Palms.

JUBAEOPSIS (Jubaeóp-sis). The only species of *Jubaeopsis* is a close relative of the Chilean wine palm *Jubaea*, as its name, derived from *Jubaea* and the Greek *opsis*, similar to, indicates. It belongs in the palm family PALMAE.

A rare native of South Africa, *J. caffra*, 20 feet tall, has multiple trunks and gracefully recurved pinnate leaves 12 to 15 feet long. Male and female flowers are in the same branched clusters, the males in the upper parts, the females below. The former have eight to sixteen stamens. The nearly globular fruits about the size of walnuts have a fibrous covering, yellow at maturity, and edible kernals. In general appearance this palm resembles *Phoenix reclinata*.

Garden and Landscape Uses and Cultivation. Because of its scarcity this attractive palm is primarily a collectors' item. It has been successfully cultivated in southern California and probably can be grown outdoors wherever it is not subjected to hard freezes, as well as in greenhouses. Fresh seeds sown in sandy, peaty soil germinate in a temperature of 75 to 85°F. Because of their peculiar habit of development they must be sown in containers at least 2 feet deep. Upended drain-pipes suggest themselves as suitable. When the seed begins to grow it sends down a hypocotyl or primary rootlike structure from which, at considerable depth below the surface, the new palm, consisting of roots, stem, and leaves, develops. If the seeds are sown in ordinary pots or other shallow containers the descent of the hypocotyl is interfered with and the young plant cannot develop. It is also possible to increase this palm after it has more than one trunk, by dividing it very carefully. For further information see Palms.

JUDAS TREE is *Cercis siliquastrum,* so called because according to legend Judas Iscariot was hanged on a tree of this species. In the United States the native *C. canadensis* is sometimes, inappropriately, called Judas tree.

JUGLANDACEAE — Walnut Family. Fifty species of deciduous trees or rarely shrubs accommodated in seven genera constitute this family of dicotyledons, native of the northern hemisphere, Central America, and the Andes of South America. Many are sources of excellent lumber. Sorts esteemed for their edible fruits (nuts) include butternuts, hickories, pecans, and walnuts.

The kinds of this family have alternate or much less commonly opposite, pinnate leaves, usually with resin dots on their undersides. The flowers are unisexual with both sexes on the same plant. The males, with or without perianths and with three to many stamens, are in drooping catkins. The females, solitary or in spikes of few to several, usually have a three- to five-lobed calyx and a short style with two stigmas. The fruits are nuts, winged nutlets, or drupes. Cultivated genera are *Carya, Juglans, Platycarya,* and *Pterocarya.*

JUGLANS (Júg-lans)—Walnut, Butternut, Heartnut. This important group of hardy and nonhardy, deciduous, nut-bearing trees is represented in the native floras of North America, Central America, South America, the West Indies, Europe, and Asia. There are fifteen species. They belong in the walnut family JUGLANDACEAE. The generic name *Juglans* is derived from *Jovis glans* (Jupiter's acorn), the ancient Latin name for the Persian walnut.

These are quite handsome trees although mostly less ornamental than their close relatives the hickories (*Carya*). They have large, pinnate leaves, aromatic when bruised, each with an odd number of leaflets. The inconspicuous male and female flowers are borne separately, the male in slender, drooping catkins from toward the ends of the previous year's shoots, the female in spikes terminating the shoots of the current season's growth. The fruits are familiar walnuts and butternuts, hardshelled and enclosed in more or less fleshy husks or rinds. Members of this genus are easily distinguished from hickories by slicing a branchlet longitudinally and examining the pith. That of hickories is solid, that of walnuts and butternuts is in thin, transverse layers with spaces between. It is what botanists term lamellate or chambered pith. The pith of the nearly related wingnuts (*Pterocarya*) is also lamellate, but members of that genus have small, conspicuously winged nuts, very different from walnuts and butternuts, in long, pendulous racemes.

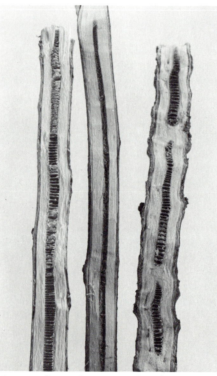

Twigs split to show, at right, chambered pith of walnut; center, solid pith of hickory; and left, chambered pith of wingnut

These trees are of commercial importance as sources of lumber and edible nuts. Selected varieties of some species are cultivated for the latter. The lumbers of the Persian walnut and the black walnut are especially esteemed. They are considered the finest of all woods for gun stocks. Walnut lumber is much used for furniture, paneling, veneers, and other purposes where beautiful grain and high polish are virtues. Especially handsomely figured wood is obtained from old stumps and burls of mature black walnut trees. Such wood is very valuable. The lumber of the butternut, although of less value than that

of the walnuts discussed above, is used for furniture and also for interior trim and general carpentry. The bark of walnuts is used for tanning and from the husks of their fruits yellow and brown dyes are obtainable.

The Persian walnut or English walnut (***J. regia***), native from the Balkan Peninsula to Kashmir and beyond, at its best is 100 feet tall. It can be distinguished from other walnuts considered here by its leaflets being scarcely or not toothed and by its nuts having thin partitions and splitting open naturally. This is a broad-crowned tree with silvery bark. Its leaves have usually five to nine (occasionally more) leaflets. Typically they are 8 inches to 1 foot long, or on young, vigorous shoots longer. The terminal leaflet is the largest. The Persian walnut has been cultivated for centuries and has given rise to many varieties including some horticultural kinds of special merit as nut producers. Other distinct varieties include *J. r. laciniata,* which has deeply-dissected leaflets and is one of the most ornamental walnuts; *J. r. monophylla,* with leaves of one large leaflet and sometimes two smaller ones; *J. r. pendula,* with stiffly pendulous branches; and *J. r. praeparturiens,* a low, bushy tree that fruits when young. The Persian walnut is hardy in southern New England, but does not fruit satisfactorily there. For its best development it needs a warmer climate. It is much planted in California and in the south.

The black walnut (***J. nigra***) is one of North America's finest trees. It ranges from Massachusetts to Florida and Texas, has a wide-spreading crown, and is sometimes 150 feet in height, with a trunk up to 6 feet in diameter. A more beautiful ornamental than the Persian walnut, it is readily distinguished

Juglans nigra, in summer

Juglans nigra, in winter

Juglans nigra (fruit)

from that species by its toothed leaflets, which are pubescent on their undersides, and by its nuts, which do not split open naturally. The nuts are edible and horticultural varieties that bear superior ones have been developed and are cultivated. For more about these see Walnut. The black walnut has deeply-furrowed bark, leaves with fifteen to twenty-three, irregularly-toothed leaflets, and deeply furrowed nuts with thick, very hard shells enclosing their richly flavored meats.

The butternut (*J. cinerea*) is native from New Brunswick to Georgia, the Dakotas, and Arkansas. Less ornamental than the black walnut, under favorable conditions it attains a height of 100 feet and has a wide-spreading crown. From the Persian and black walnuts it is distinguishable by

the prominent fringe of hairs that adorns the upper edge of each leaf scar (mark on the branchlets that remains after a leaf falls) and by its fruits being covered with sticky hairs. These latter characteristics are shared with some Asian species, but the butternut differs from those in having red or purplish-brown mature branches and in the teeth of its leaflets spreading outward rather than pointing forward. The fruits of the butternut have eight or ten conspicuous ridges. They do not split open naturally.

Hind's black walnut (*J. hindsii*) is a native of central California that is much used in that state as a street tree and as an understock upon which to graft Persian walnuts. It is much more sensitive to winter cold than the species already discussed and cannot be expected to thrive north of Virginia in the eastern United States. Hind's black walnut is a round-headed tree up to 75 feet in height, with shoots densely-pubescent when young. Its leaves have fifteen to nineteen coarsely-toothed leaflets and hairy stalks. The nuts are scarcely or not grooved. A variety, *J. h. quercinifolia,* has leaves of usually three leaflets, rarely only one.

Other native Americans include *J. californica* and *J. microcarpa.* Native to southern California and hardy in mild climates only, *J. californica* is a shrub or small tree closely related to *J. hindsii,* with hairless leaves with eleven to fifteen leaflets. Its softly-hairy, thick-shelled, spherical fruits are about ¾ inch in diameter. Usually under 30 feet tall, *J. microcarpa* (syn. *J. rupestris*) is a graceful shrub or tree with branches, that when young are pubescent, and leaves of fifteen to twenty-three finely-toothed or sometimes nearly toothless, narrow leaflets. Its hard shelled, almost hairless spherical nuts ¾ inch in diameter do not split open naturally. This native from Texas to New Mexico is hardy in southern New England.

The heartnut (*J. ailanthifolia cordiformis*) is, based on the eating quality of its nuts, the most meritorious eastern Asian walnut. In this it is superior to, and in other respects it equals, the Japanese walnut, the Chinese walnut, and the Manchurian walnut. The heartnut is a stout-branched tree up to 60 feet in height with a big, rounded crown and leaves of nine to seventeen toothed leaflets. It has large, thin-shelled, much-flattened heart-shaped nuts.

The Japanese, Chinese, and Manchurian walnuts are all trees up to 60 feet in height hardy in southern New England. They are broad-topped and like the American butternut have fruits covered with sticky hairs and leaf scars with a prominent band of hairs along their upper edge. The Japanese species (*J. ailanthifolia* syn. *J. sieboldiana*) has its fruits in long, drooping racemes and its nuts, wrinkled or nearly smooth, are not strongly ridged. The Chinese and

Japanese walnuts have yellowish-brown or grayish mature branches and leaflets with teeth that point forward. Those of the Chinese species (*J. cathayensis*) are densely-hairy on the veins beneath, those of the Manchurian kind (*J. mandshurica*) are often nearly hairless. These walnuts also differ in their fruits, those of the Chinese being in 6- to 10-inch-long hanging racemes, those of the Manchurian species in much shorter racemes.

There are several hybrid walnuts, none of special value for their nuts. Those between the Persian walnut and the black walnut are grouped as *J. intermedia.* Hybrids between the Persian walnut and the butternut are called *J. quadrangulata.* The progeny of the Persian walnut and the Manchurian walnut is named *J. chinensis.* Plants resulting from hybridizing the Persian walnut with the Japanese walnut are known as *J. notha.* A hybrid between the Persian walnut and *J. hindsii* is named 'Paradox' and one between *J. hindsii* and the black walnut 'Royal'. These last were raised by Luther Burbank.

Garden and Landscape Uses. Walnuts include species of noble aspect especially well adapted for use in parks and similar spacious areas. Their special decorative appeal is their handsome foliage. A peculiarity of the black walnut is that its roots modify the soil in which they grow, perhaps by producing a substance toxic to certain other plants, to the extent that sensitive species are seriously harmed or killed. Notable among kinds to which black walnut is antagonistic are members of the heath family ERICACEAE. Here belong rhododendrons, mountain laurels, blueberries, and many other garden plants. But many plants are adversely affected by contact with the roots of black walnut, including apples, white pines, and the shrubby cinquefoil (*Potentilla fruticosa*). Strangely enough, clovers and many grasses, including Kentucky bluegrass, find areas beneath black walnuts highly to their liking and make superior growth there.

Cultivation. Walnuts thrive best in deep, well-drained, moderately moist, fertile soil. Perfect drainage is especially important for the Persian walnut. The butternut appreciates somewhat moister conditions. Large specimens do not recover from transplanting well so the best procedure is to plant two- or three-year-old trees in their final locations. Whenever practical, walnuts should be raised from seeds, which must not be allowed to dry, but must be sown as soon as ripe or be stratified as soon as they are gathered and sown the following spring. Use a seed bed of sandy, peaty soil. Protect it from rodents. Keep it uniformly moist. As soon as the young plants are big enough, plant them in a nursery in sandy soil that contains a reasonable amount of organic matter. Under these conditions the young trees develop superior fibrous roots that enable them to recover more surely from later transplanting. Horticultural varieties and hybrid walnuts do not reproduce true to type from seeds. To secure increase of these, grafting in winter in greenhouses is done on understocks of seedling *Juglans*. Alternatively, budding is performed in summer on understocks growing in a nursery.

Diseases and Pests. Walnuts are affected by a number of fungus diseases including brown leaf spot, yellow leaf blotch, canker, die-back, and trunk decay. A bacterial blight of the leaves and fruit occurs, and a canker of the bark caused by a bacterium affects the Persian walnut. A witches' broom condition caused by a virus results in the well-known proliferation of twigs and bunching of branchlets that is responsible for the common name of this effect. Insect and other small creatures that are harmful to walnuts include aphids, caterpillars, lace bugs, scale insects, and mites.

JUJUBE. See Ziziphus.

JULY, GARDENING REMINDERS FOR. In the north as elsewhere in North America, the full heat of summer, often accompanied by dry periods and sometimes droughts, characterizes July. Then and in August garden tasks are much the same throughout the land. First and foremost are those designed to alleviate the harm caused by lack of moisture. These consist of supplying water by watering cans, hoses, sprinklers, and irrigation and of conserving water in the ground.

When needed apply water in copious quantities, but not at such rates that the ground cannot absorb it fast enough so that loss by run-off occurs. Be especially sensitive to the particular need for periodic deep soakings during their first summer of recently transplanted deciduous and evergreen trees and shrubs that have not yet had time to reestablish the extensive root systems they had prior to moving. It takes a surprisingly large amount of water to

(b) With an automatic oscillating sprinkler

(c) With underground sprinklers

drench the soil to a depth of 8 inches to 1 foot, generally the minimum required for a worthwhile job.

Conservation of water in the soil is achieved by mulching with some material, such as hay, crushed corncobs, or peat moss, or alternatively by frequent shallow stirring of the 1-inch surface of soil with a hoe or cultivator to maintain a dust mulch. If the last plan is adopted cultivating should follow within a few hours of the finish of each rain or watering.

Early in the month, if not done in June, plant caladiums, elephant's ears, ismenes, tigridias, tuberoses, and tuberous begonias in deeply spaded and fertilized soil. Until the end of the month continue planting gladioluses and montbretias.

Before midmonth make successional sowings of beans, carrots, corn, leaf lettuce, and radishes, somewhat later those of Chinese cabbage, endive, and rutabagas. Toward the end of July is the ideal time to sow, in a shaded place outdoors or in a cold frame, seeds of pansies and violas. Earlier sowing is likely to give plants too big to winter well, later seeding, plants smaller than desirable. For the best results with Russell lupines treat them as biennials or short-lived perennials. Sow their seeds in July in a sunny place where the

Partially rotted wood chips: (a) Being loaded to use as a mulch

(b) Being spread around recently planted shrubs

A started plant of *Caladium* ready for planting outdoors in July

plants are to remain and, before the seedlings begin to crowd, thin them enough to allow for adequate development. It is still not too late to sow seeds of hardy perennials, although the resulting plants will be smaller than if this had been done earlier.

Watering is likely to need attention now: (a) With a hand-held hose

Make successional sowings of a selection of vegetables in July

Bearded irises can be: (a) Divided in July

If necessary divide, after their foliage has died, old clumps of: (a) Bleeding hearts

A cold frame in a shady location is right for sowing seeds of pansies

(b) Transplanted in July

(b) Oriental poppies

For blooming next year, sow seeds of Russell lupines now

Consult June, Gardening Reminders For for suggestions.

Lawn seeding is best done in early September, but July is none too early to begin developing the fertile, practically weed-free seed bed so essential to best success.

Grading may first need attention. It may be necesssary to bring in additional topsoil. Almost certainly the topsoil, existing or imported, will be benefited by mixing with it such additional organic material as compost, peat moss, or humus or by sowing buckwheat or rye grass in early July and turning this under five or six weeks later. Perhaps the soil needs liming (a simple pH test will indicate this). Aim to have a minimum of 6 inches, better 8 inches, of soil thoroughly agreeable to the roots of grasses. If the surface is left fallow after final grading cultivate it shallowly at intervals to destroy weeds while they are yet in seedling stage.

Divide and replant bearded irises anytime in July. Cut away diseased parts of the rhizomes and dust cut surfaces with sulfur or fermate. Delay until the end of the month or early August the same operation for Siberian and Japanese irises. Incidentally, these last two may go for longer periods than the beardeds without lifting and dividing. Late in July or early in August, when their foliage has practically died, is the time to divide and transplant bleeding hearts and Oriental poppies in need of this attention. If Madonna lilies are to be transplanted do this in July, but only if you must. If agreeably located and prospering these lilies are best left undisturbed. Re-

member when replanting that the bulbs should be set with their tips not more than 2 inches below the surface. If you intend to buy new bulbs of Madonna lilies arrange for delivery as early as possible and plant immediately upon arrival.

Prune rambler roses of kinds that produce an abundance of new, strong, cane-like shoots from their bases by cutting out

Prune rambler roses that: (a) Make an abundance of strong young shoots from the base by

(b) Cutting out old canes after flowering is through

Summer prune: (a) Espaliered apples and pears

(b) Wisterias as needed

as low as possible as many old flowering stems as can be spared. Tie the new ones to the supports. Cut blind shoots (those that do not end in a flower bud) of bush roses back to a strong leaf bud. Shorten others, as their flowers fade, to about one-half their lengths. Attend to the summer pruning of espaliered fruit trees and shrubs and ornamentals including wisterias. This consists of cutting back part way

all shoots except leading ones (those that terminate main branches).

Other growth-limiting practices are shearing and pinching. Many annuals that tend to become straggly will remain compact and bloom more freely if sheared lightly after their first flush of bloom has passed. Such sorts as annual phloxes, lobelias, and sweet alyssum respond to this. By nipping out the extreme tips of the shoots of geraniums at one or two leaves above each truss of bloom while it is still in the bud stage the plants can be kept from becoming leggy. As soon as dahlias are tall enough pinch out the tip of the main shoot and select, according to variety and method of growth adopted, secondary shoots for retention. Remove all others while quite small. Give hardy chrysanthemums their last pinch not later than mid-July.

Propagation of many kinds of hardy deciduous shrubs by cuttings is easy this month. It can be done successfully in a greenhouse, cold frame, or even under a Mason jar or little tent made by stretching polyethylene plastic over a wire or

Cuttings of many deciduous shrubs may be rooted under mist or in a greenhouse or cold frame

Cuttings of many shrubs root readily in June: (a) *Potentilla fruticosa*

(b) Buddleias

(c) Hydrangeas

(d) Kerrias

wooden framework. A greenhouse or outdoor mist system makes rooting cuttings especially easy. Among kinds that root readily are buddleias, deutzias, forsythias, hydrangeas, kerrias, mock-oranges, roses, and viburnums. There are many others. Anchusas, bleeding hearts, Oriental poppies and some other plants with thick roots can be increased by cutting these into pieces 2 to 3 inches long and planting them in a well-drained bed or pot of sandy soil.

Greenhouse work in July is chiefly routine. It consists mainly of watering and

(e) Mock-oranges

Oriental poppies and bleeding hearts are among several plants to propagate now by root cuttings

(f) Roses

fertilizing and, when needed, of staking and tying plants needing support and of spraying or employing other methods of combating pests. If the greenhouse is empty or relatively empty this is a good time to thoroughly clean its interior, to wash down the glass and the wooden or metal structural parts, or to repaint the latter if needed. Choose dull weather for this and be sure to get rid of weeds and to wash or replace with new, gravel or similar materials on and under the benches. If the greenhouse stands free of a dwelling, and it can be cleared of plants, fumigating may be part of this annual cleaning, but even if this is not practicable the scrubbing, washing, and other cleaning done will do much to destroy lurking pests.

Plants that prefer cool temperatures, such as calceolarias, cinerarias, cyclamens, cymbidiums, and primulas, have a somewhat difficult time during July and August. Keep them shaded and the gravel or other loose material on which they stand constantly moist, and of course do not allow them to suffer from lack of moisture. Misting their foliage with water in bright

weather helps greatly. Ventilate greenhouses containing tropical plants more freely than earlier and spray or mist with water the foliage of all sorts except hairy-leaved kinds twice or more often on bright days.

Encourage roses that have been in benches or beds a year or more and have been pruned back to make strong new growth by applying a dressing of fertilizer and by watering to keep the soil moist. Stir the soil shallowly and frequently between newly planted roses. This promotes growth. In bright weather and when the humidity tends to be low moisten the air by wetting down floors and other interior surfaces at intervals during the day. Encourage buds to swell and new shoots to grow by spraying the plants lightly several times on clear days with water.

Carnations grown in outdoor beds for later transfer to greenhouses should be lifted and planted in benches or beds toward the month's end or during the first week of August. Be careful not to plant too deeply. Shade very lightly for the first few days after moving, and maintain a humid atmosphere by wetting floors and other surfaces. On sunny days spray the plants lightly with water. Keep the surface of the soil loose by shallow cultivation.

Potting in July should be done on a selective basis. Among permanent plants move only those that can be expected to fill larger containers with roots before the advent of winter. Rely upon fertilizing to keep others growing. Chrysanthemums for fall blooming may now be put in their final pots or planted in benches or beds.

Do not water plants that rest during the summer and make sure that they are kept where their soil is not accidentally wetted. The best plan is to store them with their pots lying on their sides beneath a greenhouse bench, in a cold frame, or other suitable place. But do not forget them when the time for new growth arrives. Sorts that rest in summer include many South African bulb plants, such as calla-lilies, ixias, lachenalias, and nerines. Keep Martha Washington geraniums dry from early July to mid-August.

Propagate indoor azaleas and poinsettias by cuttings, and also abutilons, fuchsias, geraniums, heliotropes, and lantanas that you intend to train as standards (tree-form specimens with a bare stem or trunk topped by a head of leafy branches and blooms).

Sow, to give early crops of bloom in greenhouses, seeds of annual chrysanthemums, browallias, cinerarias, clarkias, leptosynes (Coreopsis), nemesias, salpiglossises, schizanthuses, stocks, and wallflowers.

Cold frames now require the same attention as in June. Care must be taken that temperatures inside those covered with sash do not rise too high. To guard against this keep them shaded and ventilated. Frames sheltering rooted plants may be ventilated freely, those containing cuttings in the process of rooting much more cautiously.

As soon as seedlings of biennials and perennials to be wintered in frames are big enough to handle with ease transplant them to beds of fertile soil inside the

Plants to be rested now by turning their pots on the sides and keeping the soil dry include: (a) Calla-lilies

(b) Freesias and lachenalias

To bloom early in greenhouses sow seeds in July of: (a) Browallias

(b) Nemesias

(c) English wallflowers

frames. Such sorts may include English daisies, forget-me-nots, sweet williams, and wallflowers that were sown in a frame or outdoor bed, as well as young plants of polyanthus primroses sown earlier indoors and afterward transplanted to flats.

Houseplant care in July does not materially differ from that detailed in the Encyclopedia entry June, Gardening Reminders For. Now as then most kinds should be making good growth and prospering under the influence of long hours of daylight and the absence of air-drying artificial heating. Some few kinds that are resting or partially resting will need greatly reduced supplies of water or none at all. Included here are many succulents and bulb plants that are natives of South Africa as well as Martha Washington geraniums.

Normal watering to keep the soil evenly moist is, however, requisite for most houseplants and those that have filled their containers with roots will benefit from regular mild applications of fertilizer. All except those such as African-violets and some other hairy-leaved sorts and certain waxy-coated succulents appreciate having their foliage sprayed or misted with water on bright days.

Take care that houseplants put outdoors for the summer are not permitted to root through the drainage holes of their pots into the ground. Once in a while lift them and break off any roots that may be coming through. The summer vacationing outdoors of houseplants affords splendid opportunity to free them of pests by spraying as needed with insecticides and miticides.

Achimenes, caladiums, gloxinias, and tuberous begonias should be making nice growth in July. With the coming of settled warm weather they appreciate more airy conditions than before. A shaded porch or similar place is excellent for all except the caladiums, which are best in full sun or at most very light shade.

July is an excellent time to increase by cuttings and other means a great variety of houseplants. African-violets, gloxinias, and other gesneriads and many succulents, such as cotyledons, echeverias, and

Many houseplants may be rooted in July from cuttings: (a) Begonias

(b) Fuchsias

(c) Hoyas

kalanchoes, come readily from leaf cuttings made now.

In the south permit roses to partially rest by watering not at all or only when the soil becomes really dry and by refraining from fertilizing. Do not neglect to spray or dust them regularly. Mulch azaleas, camellias, and other shrubs that have many near-the-surface roots and enjoy cool, moist conditions with 4 to 6 inches of bagasse, peat moss, pine straw (fallen needles), or other suitable organic material.

As camellias begin to make a second growth fertilize them lightly. Do not allow them to suffer for lack of moisture. Azaleas benefit from these same considerations. Also, fertilize chrysanthemums, dahlias, and other plants that need to be kept growing uninterruptedly.

Seeds to sow include those of such quick-growing annuals as African and French marigolds, ageratums, annual phloxes, balsams, calendulas, celosias,

Many houseplants may be rooted in July from leaf cuttings: (a) Cotyledons

(b) Echeverias

nicotianas, and zinnias. In addition, in the lower south, sow those of annual coreopsises, coleuses, cosmos, gaillardias, Madagascar-periwinkle (*Catharanthus roseus,*) moonflowers, morning glories, salvias, sunflowers, and tithonias. Vegetable garden crops to sow include beans, beets, broccoli, cabbage, carrots, collards, lettuce, and rutabagas. Irish potatoes may be planted. In the lower south, sow beans, cow-peas, New Zealand spinach, peppers, pumpkins, and rutabagas. It is not too late

Annuals to sow now in the south in July include: (a) Ageratums

to seed new Bermuda grass lawns. Use hulled seed for this to ensure quick germination.

Cuttings of azaleas, camellias, and hydrangeas planted now in a shaded cold frame or under mist root readily as do those of many other evergreen and deciduous shrubs.

Remove faded blooms from crape-myrtle and other plants to prolong the season of

(b) Celosias

(c) Cosmos

(d) French marigolds

(e) Tithonias

(f) Zinnias

bloom as well as in the interest of neatness and possibly pest and disease control.

In West Coast gardens attend as needed and as promptly as possible to routine weeding, watering, fertilizing, spraying, staking and tying, and such housekeeping as removing faded blooms. But do not water indiscriminately. Bougainvilleas for instance seem to respond best if kept somewhat on the dryish side when in bloom.

After it has died remove the foliage of narcissuses and other spring-flowering bulbs. If these are in beds by themselves instead of intermixed with plants that retain their foliage through the summer refrain from watering them. A season of complete dryness is of much help in ripening the bulbs and encouraging prolific bloom the next spring. Many gardeners find that they are most successful if they lift the bulbs from areas that must be watered and store them until fall planting time in a cool, airy place indoors.

Give chrysanthemums their last pinch from the middle to end of the month. Disbranch dahlias being grown for big blooms.

Increase of spring- and early-summer-blooming rock garden plants can be had by dividing such kinds as arabises, armerias, aubretias, creeping phloxes, and others that lend themselves to this simple means of propagation. Keep newly planted divisions shaded for a while and watered.

Seeds to sow in mild regions in late July or early August to give plants for late winter and spring blooming include many annuals and biennials, among them calendulas, cornflowers, forget-me-nots, Iceland poppies, linarias, pansies, snapdragons, and stocks.

Pinch the tips out of the shoots of chrysanthemums for the last time in July

JUMELLEA (Ju-méllea). Closely related to *Angraecum*, with which by some botanists it is united, *Jumellea*, of the orchid family ORCHIDACEAE, comprises a few more than fifty species, mostly natives of Malagasy (Madagascar), but some of tropical Africa, the Comoro Islands, and the Mascarine Islands. The name honors Henry Jumelle, a French botanist who studied the flora of Madagascar in the late nineteenth century and early twentieth century.

Chiefly epiphytes (plants that perch on other plants without taking nourishment from them), jumelleas differ from angraecums in technical differences of the flowers. Unlike those of most angraecums, the blooms are solitary. According to species, they vary considerably in appearance; many are handsome. Jumelleas are rare in cultivation.

Native to the Mascarine Islands, *J. fragrans* (syn. *Angraecum fragrans*) has stems up to about 1 foot long with, in their upper

Jumellea papangensis

parts, narrow-oblong leaves grooved along their centers, notched at their apexes, and 3 to 4 inches long. The fragrant flowers, about 2 inches across, have pure white sepals, petals, and lip, the last with a greenish spur 1¼ to 3 inches long. The fragrant, dried foliage of this species was imported into England in the Victorian era and used to prepare a pleasantly flavored tea. Rarer in cultivation, *J. papangensis*, of Malagasy, has pure white blooms about 3 inches in diameter with a lip considerably wider than the sepals and petals and with a longer, drooping, very slender spur.

Garden Uses and Cultivation. Of particular interest to collectors of orchids, these plants respond to conditions and care appropriate for angraecums.

JUMPING-BEAN. See Mexican Jumping-Bean.

JUNCACEAE—Rush Family. Widely distributed through most parts of the world, but rare or absent in the tropics, the rush family consists of more than 300 species of monocotyledons contained in eight genera of which six are restricted to the southern hemisphere. Mostly denizens of moist soils, its members are rushlike or grasslike annuals and herbaceous perennials, frequently with rhizomes and hairy roots, or very less commonly are shrubs. Their generally cylindrical or flat leaves are linear to threadlike, with sheathing bases. Mostly greenish, the small bisexual or unisexual flowers are solitary or in heads, clusters, or panicles. They have perianths of three or six segments, six or three stamens, one or three styles. The fruits are capsules. Genera cultivated are *Juncus* and *Luzula*.

JUNCUS (Jún-cus) — Rush. True rushes (other plants are sometimes referred to by this name) are members of the genus *Juncus*, a group of nearly cosmopolitan distribution in the wild and numbering about 225 species. They belong in the rush family JUNCACEAE. Their name is an ancient Latin one for these or similar plants.

Rushes are wet-land and shallow water herbaceous perennials and annuals with smooth, round, usually branchless stems that have a few undivided flat or triangular leaves (sometimes represented by leafstalks only). The minute flowers, in terminal, loose or compact branched clusters, have little decorative merit. The fruits are capsules. In Japan the tatami mats used as floor coverings are woven from stems of *J. effusus*.

The soft rush (*J. effusus*) is a native of all continents of the northern hemisphere as well as Australia, New Zealand, and Africa. A hardy herbacious perennial 1 foot to 6 feet tall, this forms clumps of erect or arching stems that develop in their upper parts loose clusters of yellowish-green to pale brownish flowers. Horticultural varieties

are *J. e. spiralis*, the corkscrew rush, which is about 2 feet tall and has curious spiraled stems intriguing to admirers of the grotesque, and *J. e. vittatus*, about 2½ feet tall, with stems striped longitudinally with yellow.

Garden and Landscape Uses and Cultivation. Except for horticultural varieties of *J. effusus*, the rushes are scarcely to be considered garden plants. Where conditions are favorable they are likely to be aggressively invasive and not easy to control or eliminate once they have taken over an area. Because of this, it is usually advisable to grow them in tubs or other containers rather than plant them in ground beds. The soil surface may be at, just above, or slightly below the level of water. These rushes are suitable for ponds and watersides, where they provide needed height. They do best in sunny sites. Cultivated varieties of rushes are propagated very easily by division in spring. Sometimes they develop tufts of stems typical of the species. These should be promptly pulled out, otherwise, being more vigorous than the horticulturally superior varietal forms, they are likely to outgrow them to the extent that the clump reverts to type.

JUNE BERRY. See Amelanchier.

JUNE, GARDENING REMINDERS FOR. In northern gardens June is a pretty month. Everywhere warm, settled weather has arrived and the results of work done earlier are apparent. Now even the tenderest plants can be set out without fear of harm from cold. Cut flower and vegetable gardens are producing abundantly. This is the month of roses, hollyhocks, irises, peas, peonies, strawberries, and many other pleasant fruits of the earth. Now *Cornus kousa* delights with its long display of exquisite blooms, and so does beauty bush (*Kolkwitzia*) and mountain laurel.

But gardeners must not idle. Much besides enjoying floral displays and harvesting needs doing. Early in the month, if it were not attended to in late May, as in

(b) Geraniums

(c) Lantanas

(d) Tuberous begonias

warmer sections may have been done, plant out such nonhardy ornamentals as caladiums, cannas, elephant's ears, fuchsias, geraniums, heliotropes, iresines, lantanas, plumbagos, and tuberous begonias, as well as warm-weather annuals raised in flats, pots, or cold frames, such as marigolds, nierembergias, petunias, torenias, verbenas, wax begonias, and zinnias. Early June is the best time to plant dahlias, both tubers and green plants raised from cuttings.

Juncus effusus

Plant now: (a) Cannas

Annuals to plant out now include:
(a) Petunias

(d) Nierembergias

Biennials to sow in June include:
(a) Canterbury bells

(b) Verbenas

Dahlias: (a) Started into growth indoors

(b) English daisies

(c) Wax begonias

(b) Ready now for planting outdoors

(c) Foxgloves

Seed sowing is important in June. In the vegetable garden fertilize and spade or rototill areas from which early crops have been harvested and resow with such as beans, beets, carrots, lettuce, New Zealand spinach, parsnips, and sweet corn. Toward the end of the month sow for fall harvesting kohlrabi and turnips. Sow in seed beds for transplanting later broccoli, cabbage, and cauliflower. Good results are had from early-in-the month sowings of such fast-growing annuals as cosmos, globe-amaranths, marigolds, sunflowers, sweet alyssum, tithonias, and zinnias.

Biennials and perennials should be sown now. Pansies are a notable exception. Do not plant seeds of them until late July. Biennials to sow in early June include Canterbury bells, English daisies, forget-me-nots, foxgloves, honesty, sweet williams, verbascums, and wallflowers. Plants you may wish to treat as biennials (that is raise from seeds and discard the following year after they are through blooming) are *Arabis caucasica*, aubretias, columbines, and hollyhocks. Sow these before mid-June. Not all perennials are satisfactory from seeds.

Perennials to sow now to treat as biennials include: (a) Aubrietas

Perennials to sow now include: (a) Delphiniums

(d) Liatrises

(b) Columbines

(b) Gaillardias

(c) Hollyhocks

(c) Geums

Many improved garden varieties do not come true to type. Among kinds likely to give satisfaction are coreopsises, delphiniums, gaillardias, geums, liatrises, and pyrethrums. The method to follow with biennials and perennials is to sow in a cold frame or well-prepared outdoor bed. Sprinkle the seeds in drills spaced about 4 inches apart and cover them to two to three times their diameter with soil. Keep the seed bed evenly moist. When the seedlings have made their second pair of leaves transplant them at spacings appropriate for their kind to nursery beds or cold frames. Aftercare consists of promoting growth by watering and keeping the surface soil cultivated. The plants will be ready for transfer to their flowering quarters in early fall or spring.

Early-flowering rock garden plants that tend to become too loose and rampant unless their growth is checked are improved by shearing back at the beginning of June.

Among sorts that benefit from this attention are arabises, arenarias, creeping phloxes, and evergreen candytufts (*Iberis*). Some June-flowering sorts, such as vigorous-growing campanulas and dianthuses, may with advantage be treated similarly as soon as they are through flowering.

Spring-flowering bulb plants have now finished blooming and the leaves of most have either yellowed or died or are in process of doing so. Even though the foliage remains green longer than you would wish, as it is likely to do if rainfall is plentiful and in well-watered areas, do not remove it until it is completely brown. Then pull or rake and dispose of it on the compost pile. To remove foliage from such plants before it is dead reduces the amount of foodstuffs the plants can store in readiness for next season's blooming. As soon as their leaves have died is the best time to lift, separate, and replant or transplant Dutch and Spanish irises and narcissuses. There is no advantage in storing them out of the ground until fall. This last is often the favored and most convenient way, however, with tulips and is advisable with brodiaeas and calochortuses.

Lawns may still be mown to a height of 1½ to 2 inches, but with the advent of really hot weather raise the cutting blades ½ inch higher. If crab grass was troublesome last year and you failed to use a preemergent herbicide, use a postemergent herbicide when seedlings become visible.

Prune May- and June-flowering shrubs in need of this attention as soon as they are through blooming. Not all kinds are benefited by this. Rhododendrons, including azaleas, and lilacs, for example, normally need no annual pruning. Sorts that do are those that bloom on shoots of the previous year's development and make abundant new growth each season. They

Needed pruning of birch trees may be done now

Cover pruning cuts with tree wound paint

Trim hedges now

include deutzias, enkianthuses, mock-oranges (*Philadelphus*), spireas, and weigelas. If shade trees need pruning, June is an appropriate time for the operation. Birches and maples, which lose excessive amounts of sap if pruned before they are in full leaf, do not do so if pruned now and pruning cuts made on them and other trees have ample time to heal substantially before fall. Cover all cuts over 1 inch in diameter with tree wound paint. Most formally trimmed hedges will need shearing

this month. Trim so that they narrow inward slightly from bottom to top. This ensures better light to prevent the base of the hedge becoming thin or bare of foliage.

Pick faded blooms from lilacs, mountain-laurels, pierises, and rhododendrons, including azaleas, promptly. Do not wait until the incipient seed pods have swollen and the developing seeds have drained the plant of energy it could more profitably expend upon making flowering shoots for next season. Be careful in breaking off the blooms not to injure the developing buds just below the trusses. These are the sources of next year's flowers.

Promote as long flowering as possible by keeping spent blooms of sweet peas picked and those of delphiniums also, unless you intend to save seeds. When cutting delphiniums do not take more foliage than quite necessary to give stems as long as you must have. As soon as the main flush of bloom is over, fertilize and two or three times at weekly or ten-day intervals spray with a miticide and if needed an insecticide. Keep the soil well watered. All this will go far to encourage a fine second crop of flowers.

Weed control is important. It is far easier to destroy most weeds when young than later. Between growing crops frequent shallow use of the scuffle hoe, or somewhat less effectively of a cultivator with tines, is highly effective and especially beneficial early in the season because it does not interfere with the sun warming the soil as does mulching and by aerating the soil promotes growth. But when the ground has warmed sufficiently, and hot weather comes, mulching can prove of great advantage and be a big labor-saver even with plants that enjoy warm weather most.

Cultivate between growing crops to control weeds and promote growth

Stake and tie or otherwise support plants likely to be disturbed and damaged by wind and rain before harm occurs. There are few tasks more discouraging to

face than that of attempting to restore and reshape storm-ruined flower beds.

Greenhouses mainly used for raising plants for outdoors will be pretty empty now and attention can be given to cleaning them, as described in July, Gardening Reminders For. If soil in beds or benches is to be changed this is a good time to do it.

Plant carnations from 4-inch pots into benches or beds. Take care to keep the tops of the root balls slightly above soil level to minimize danger of rotting. After planting water with considerable discretion. New roses may be planted now in greenhouses and old ones pruned and partially rested by keeping them almost dry.

Chrysanthemums for fall blooming may be potted this month or early next into the containers in which they are to flower. Vigorous young foliage plants of many kinds are likely to benefit from shifting to pots a size larger than those they occupy. Older specimens and kinds known to prosper with their roots crowded can be kept growing satisfactorily by fertilizing. See they do not suffer from lack of water but make sure that the soil is not constantly mudlike as it may be if the drainage of the pots is inadequate or becomes clogged.

More airy conditions achieved by freer ventilation of the greenhouse are in order for achimenes, gloxinias, hippeastrums, and many other plants that earlier needed less ventilation and a warm, humid environment to encourage growth.

Root cuttings of *Buddleia asiatica*, *B. farquhari*, and *Iboza riparia* to have plants to bloom in a cool greenhouse in late fall and winter. Make the first batch of cuttings of poinsettias. These will produce tall plants. For lower ones root cuttings in July and August. Cuttings of many permanent indoor foliage and flowering plants root with facility now.

Seeds to sow in June for plants to bloom in winter include those of snapdragons and stocks. For plants to flower in spring sow seeds of tuberous anemones. Well managed, plants raised in this way give superior results to those from tubers purchased and planted in fall.

Transplant seedlings of calceolarias, cinerarias, and primulas to well-drained flats of soil containing an abundance of organic matter. These plants, cyclamens, and other lovers of cool growing conditions have trying days ahead. A cold frame faced more or less to the north and shaded from direct sun, except possibly that of earliest mornings or latest afternoons, affords the best environment other than that of an air-cooled greenhouse.

Christmas cherries and Christmas peppers set out as small plants in an outdoor nursery bed in June will make good specimens for lifting, potting, and bringing indoors before frost. Choose a sunny location, take care not to have the soil too fertile (too much nitrogen induces exces-

Take cuttings now of: (a) *Buddleia asiatica*

For plants to bloom later in the greenhouse sow in June: (a) Tuberous anemones

A lath house provides an ideal summer environment for such plants as: (a) Clivias

(b) *B. farquhari*

(b) Stocks

(b) Cymbidiums

(c) *Iboza riparia*

(c) Snapdragons

edly mild climates for their year-around accommodation) than a cold frame. Such a structure is ideal for begonias, clivias, cymbidiums, and a host of other kinds that benefit from filtered sunlight and a cooler, more humid environment than an unsheltered location outdoors supplies.

There are other uses for cold frames in June. In them may be sown seeds of biennials and perennials. Cuttings, including those of many rock garden plants, root readily in June in a frame located on the north side of a wall or building and given no ventilation at first and only very little until they have rooted.

Houseplants should now be prospering. Long days and adequate temperatures without a need for artificial heat are to their liking. In dull and humid weather many may need less frequent watering than when the heating plant was operating. Those the containers of which are filled with roots will benefit from fertilizing on a regular schedule.

Repotting of big specimens in need of shifting to a larger container may still be done, but do not delay this longer than you must. Smaller plants of fairly fast-growing sorts, such as begonias, fuchsias, and geraniums, may be moved to pots a size or two larger as their growth makes necessary.

sively lush growth), and make the soil reasonably firm by treading it before you plant.

Care of Christmas cherries and Christmas peppers after planting, and of other plants such as carnations, foxgloves, hydrangeas, and rambler roses that are to be dug up later and brought into the greenhouse for flowering, consists of watering and fertilizing as needed and keeping them free of weeds, diseases, and pests, all of which calls for vigilance and suitable relief measures promptly given.

Cold frames can be very useful at this season. Reasonably deep ones afford excellent summer accommodations for a wide variety of greenhouse plants especially those such as fuchsias, that prefer a relatively cool and humid environment. For most, shade is necessary. This can be supplied by wood slat shades, Saran cloth, or by applying a painted-on or sprayed-on coating to the glass.

A walk-in lath house of wood or aluminum affords more versatile accommodation for summering plants (and in decid-

Summering outdoors is a useful management procedure with many houseplants. Do not put them out until the weather is warm and settled and there is no danger of too-cool nights having harmful effects. Select sunny or partially shaded sites according to the needs of the various kinds and attend to any needed pruning, potting, top dressing, and staking and tying before you set them outdoors. Choose dull, humid weather for the move.

By plunging the pots (that is sinking or burying them) to one-half their depths or more in a bed of sand, sawdust, peat moss or some similar material you will greatly reduce the need for frequent watering. When you do this place under the drainage hole or holes in each pot or tub a piece of slate, tile, or flat stone to check roots growing outward and earthworms entering.

Forcibly spraying with water at weekly intervals in summer benefits all plants except those few (mostly hairy-leaved kinds) known to resent having their foliage wetted. A great virtue of this is that it does much to free plants of pests, especially aphids, red spider mites, and mealybugs. When spraying be sure to reach the undersides as well as the upper surfaces of the foliage. Plants kept indoors may be moved outside for their weekly shower. It may be desirable to supplement the water sprayings with one or more of an insecticide, especially if scale insects are present. In any case use the summer months to good advantage to assure having pest-free, healthy plants by fall.

In the south many of the same tasks that occupy gardeners in the north keep their southern counterparts busy in June. Lawn grasses that delight in warm weather will now make substantial growth and winter rye sown to give winter greenness will die out. Keep lawns of Bermuda grass mown at least at weekly intervals, otherwise they will become brownish. If not done earlier apply crab grass controls where this pestiferous weed is troublesome. It is still not too late to make new lawns by planting sprigs or plugs of Bermuda, centipede, St. Augustine, and zoysia grasses.

Fertilizing to encourage and maintain the growth of many plants is desirable now, but in the northernmost parts of the south it is better to rest roses partially by withholding such stimulus until fall.

To maintain successional harvesting over as long a period as practicable make sowings of beans and other vegetables that come into bearing fairly quickly. In the flower garden sow cosmos, cypress vine, dwarf dahlias, love-lies-bleeding, marigolds, morning glories, tithonias, torenias, zinnias, and other quick growers that thrive in hot weather.

Many shrubs, including azaleas and camellias, can be propagated at this season from greenwood cuttings, cuttings made of what gardeners call half-ripened shoots,

Cuttings of many shrubs can be rooted now: (a) Azaleas

(b) In a polyethylene-covered flat

which means those of the current season that have become firm, but not hard. Plant the cuttings in a shaded cold frame or even under a little tent made by covering a wire or wooden framework with polyethylene plastic film or under a Mason jar. If you have a mist propagating system operating there is no need for covering or for shade.

Plants that benefit from June fertilizing, done judiciously with attention to the particular needs of different kinds, include dahlias, gladioluses, and many vegetables. Give azaleas and camellias one last application of fertilizer.

Plant cannas, dahlias, elephant's ears, gladioluses, gloriosas, hedychiums, and tuberoses early in the month as well as such summer bedding plants as begonias, fuchsias, geraniums, heliotropes, and lantanas. In the upper south set out nonhardy aquatics including tropical waterlilies. Plant young chrysanthemums for fall flowering. After blooming is over divide and replant bearded iris in need of this attention, but wait until later with Japanese and Louisiana varieties. In subtropical Florida set out container-grown palms and other tropical trees and shrubs.

In West Coast gardens watch for infections of mildew encouraged by warm, humid nights, and spray begonias, roses, and other plants susceptible to this before the disease becomes well established. Other disease and pest control measures are likely to be needed, depending upon where you garden and what you grow. Vigilance, early detection, and prompt action are necessary.

Other housekeeping tasks include picking faded blooms from azaleas and other rhododendrons and tree peonies before seed pods have the opportunity to develop and from other plants too, except those grown for their ornamental fruits and unless it is intended to save seeds. Seed production takes much out of plants and if heavy not infrequently results in a poorer display of blooms the following year. Keep clematises, dahlias, and other plants subject to storm damage neatly staked and tied, and dahlias other than dwarf bedding sorts, disbranched.

Weeding by cultivating and hand pulling are likely now to call for much attention. The need for such work can be reduced by mulching. Do not fail to keep growing plants, including lawn grasses, adequately watered, and kinds in active growth, such as bird-of-paradise (Strelitzia), and chrysanthemums fertilized. But remember that many native plants of California are conditioned to dry summers and can be harmed by watering or fertilizing to excess.

In the northwest sow seeds of vegetables to give crops in fall. Such sorts include beets, broccoli, cauliflower, kohlrabi, lettuce, and rutabagas. Dig spring-flowering bulbs to be stored indoors until the fall planting season. Make successional plantings of gladioluses and tuberoses and plant colchicums, fall-flowering crocuses, and sternbergias as soon as you can obtain them from the dealer. If not available now, place orders for their earliest possible delivery. Lift, divide, and replant polyanthus primroses.

JUNIPER. See Juniperus.

JUNIPERUS (Juníp-erus)—Juniper. The genus *Juniperus*, of the cypress family CUPRESSACEAE, of about seventy species, is almost restricted in the wild to the northern hemisphere. Only in the mountains of East Africa does it occur south of the Equator. It is represented in the native floras of North America, Europe, Africa, and Asia and ranges from the Arctic Circle to Mexico, Abyssinia, East Africa, the Himalayas, and China, as well as to various outlying islands including the West Indies, Azores, Canary Islands, and Taiwan. The name is the ancient Latin one.

Several junipers are valued for their commercial products. Their lumber is mostly a beautiful reddish or reddish-brown or is handsomely variegated. That of many kinds is used in the home territories of the species but often is not available in sufficient amount to justify its wider exploitation.

In North America the fragrant wood of the red-cedar or pencil-cedar (*J. virginiana*) is used for lining clothes closets. The outstanding commercial importance of juniper wood is for the manufacture of lead pencils, for which purpose the red-cedar and Southern red-cedar (*J. silicicola*), of the eastern United States, and the West Indian *J. lucayana* are employed, as well as that of East African *J. procera*. The wood of the Himalayan pencil-cedar (*J. macropoda*) is also suitable for pencils and is used in India for beams, wall plates, and incense. In Burma the wood of *J. recurva*, sometimes called the coffin juniper, is greatly esteemed for coffins and it, as well as the wood of *J. thurifera*, are used for incense. The red-cedar and some other kinds are of considerable importance as sources of poles, posts, and stakes, for fencing, rustic garden construction, supporting plants, and similar purposes. From the woods of the prickly juniper (*J. oxycedrus*) and *J. phoenicea* fragrant oils are distilled, that of the former known as oil of cade. Other sources of useful oils are the common juniper (*J. communis*), the Greek juniper (*J. excelsa*), and the red-cedar (*J. virginiana*). The oil of the last is called red-cedar wood oil and is used as an insect repellent and in perfumery, and from it is refined an immersion oil used in microscopy. The poisonous oil of savin, from the savin juniper (*J. sabina*), is used similarly to red-cedar wood oil. Both have been used to induce abortion, not infrequently with fatal results. As a flavoring for gin and certain liqueurs and cordials the berries of the common juniper (*J. communis*) are important, although perhaps less used now than formerly. The berries of certain other kinds were eaten by the Indians of North America.

Junipers are evergreen trees and shrubs mostly with thin, shreddy bark. As with other members of the cypress family, they usually have two distinct types of leaves,

Juniper, showing both adult and juvenile leaves

thin, needle-like ones that are always borne by seedlings in their younger stages and that constitute the juvenile foliage, and shorter, stubbier, scale-like ones called adult foliage. The application of these terms to junipers is a little misleading because, whereas some kinds when raised from seeds make an orderly transition from all-juvenile foliage when young to all-adult foliage when mature, as do the wild forms of arbor-vitaes, cypresses, and false-cypresses, others retain the juvenile foliage throughout their lives, and some produce both types on plants of mature age. It is of interest to note that some horticultural varieties of arbor-vitaes and cypresses behave in this way, but they have to be propagated and maintained artificially. With certain junipers the phenomenon is natural. The primitive flowers of junipers are unisexual with the sexes on the same or different individuals, or rarely are bisexual. Male flowers consist of numerous stamens arranged in catkin-like cones. Female cones are soft and berry-like. They have three to eight succulent scales some or all of which bear one or two ovules that, after fertilization, become seeds that mature in from one to three years according to kind.

In its family *Juniperus* is unique in the character of its fruits. Technically they are cones with soft, fleshy scales. Nevertheless, they are distinctly berry-like and so completely unlike the dry cones of their nearest relatives, the arbor-vitaes, cypresses, and false-cypresses, that they could never be confused. Junipers in fruit are easily recognized as such. This helps the would-be identifier to a degree only, because most kinds have the sexes on separate plants and the males never fruit. But even with females in fruit the identification of specimens as to species, and more especially as to variety, is often complicated by natural variation within species and by the great number of varieties.

In the treatment that follows those of tree size are dealt with first, then sorts of shrub dimensions, and finally, low, prostrate, and trailing kinds. Under this arrangement varieties of the same species may be found in more than one of these categories.

The red-cedar (**J. virginiana**), one of the tallest of the genus, is occasionally 100 feet high. Native to eastern North America, it has a broadly-pyramidal or slender-columnar, erect head. The broad-headed type is confined in the wild from Virginia southward, the narrow-headed phase, more northern in its distribution, is distinguished as *J. v. crebra*. The red-cedar is common in fields and pastures from Canada to Florida east of the Rocky Mountains and flourishes especially in dry, limestone soils. Its trunk, often fluted and buttressed at its base, is covered with reddish, shredding bark. Its branches, erect or spread-

Juniperus virginiana crebra

Juniperus virginiana (foliage and fruits)

ing, have very slender branchlets with mostly scalelike leaves, although juvenile-type needle leaves usually appear together with the adult foliage of mature trees. The needle leaves are mostly in twos, but on vigorous shoots and young specimens are often in threes. The scale leaves are sharp-pointed and often have a small gland on their backs. The dark bluish, glaucous fruits ripen in their first season. In winter this species normally becomes yellowish-brown or purplish. It has given rise to many erect varieties, some of the best of which are *J. v. albospica*, with white tips to the branchlets; *J. v.* 'Boskoop Purple', which resembles *J. v. hillii*, of which it is a faster growing mutant; *J. v. burkii*, narrowly-pyramidal with steel-blue foliage that becomes bronzed or purplish in winter; *J. v. canaertii*, which has bright green leaves and decorative, bluish fruits and which originated in Belgium prior to 1868; *J. v.* 'DeForest Green', similar to *J. v. canaertii*, but darker green and faster growing; *J. v. elegantissima*, with golden-tipped

Juniperus virginiana canaertii

Juniperus virginiana hillii

Juniperus virginiana glauca: (a) Young specimen

(b) Mature specimen

round-topped. The branchlets are slender and have glaucous, bluish or yellowish-green leaves similar to those of *J. virginiana* and with an obscure gland on the back of each. Ripening in their second year, the fruits are bright blue and glaucous.

When raised from seeds the progeny of *J. scopulorum* is extremely variable and includes both slender and broad individuals as well as plants differing greatly in color and other foliage characteristics. Many of these have been selected and given varietal names and undoubtedly others will be in the future. Unfortunately nurserymen have been over-enthusiastic in selecting and naming variants of the Rocky Mountain juniper and too many selections not sufficiently distinct from each other or of doubtful superiority have been given varietal designations. Among tall, upright varieties are *J. s.* 'Blue Heaven', a fine blue-foliaged variety that fruits heavily; *J. s.* 'Chandler's Silver', loosely pyramidal, with leaves glaucous above and green beneath; *J. s.* 'Cologreen', one of the better kinds, with light green foliage; *J. s. columnaris*, of columnar habit; *J. s.* 'Hill's Silver', broadly-pyramidal, with frosty bluish foliage; *J. s. horizontalis*, an upright variety with horizontal branches and bluish-white foliage; *J. s.* 'North Star', pyramidal, compact, with bright green foliage; *J. s. pendula*, with pendulous branchlets and very resistant to drought; *J. s.* 'Platinum', with bright silvery foliage, which retains its color well throughout the year; and *J. s.* 'Silver Glow', silvery-glaucous-

wide-spreading branches and drooping branchlets, and looser and more open-topped than most columnar varieties; *J. v. pyramidalis*, columnar and dense; *J. v. pyramidiformis*, narrowly-pyramidal with bright green foliage that turns purplish in winter; and *J. v. schottii*, a small narrowly-columnar variety with scalelike leaves, which tends to discolor in winter.

The Southern red-cedar (*J. silicicola*), native from North Carolina to Florida and Louisiana, is up to 50 feet in height. Not hardy in the north, it differs from *J. virginiana* chiefly in its twigs being more slender, its male cones larger, and its fruits smaller. In cultivation this species is sometimes misidentified as *J. barbadensis* and *J. lucayana*.

The Rocky Mountain juniper or Colorado red-cedar (**J. scopulorum**), native from British Columbia to Alberta, Texas, and Arizona, is better suited for gardens in the drier western states than is the red-cedar (*J. virginiana*), but is less well adapted to conditions in the east. Variable, it is represented by a number of interesting varieties. This species grows up to 40 feet tall and has reddish-brown bark and quite commonly a trunk that divides low down into several secondary trunks. Its branches spread so that usually it is irregularly-

Juniperus scopulorum

Juniperus scopulorum pendula

blue and slender-pyramidal. Other varieties of the Rocky Mountain juniper are described in nursery catalogs.

The Western red-cedar (*J. occidentalis*) is adaptable for planting only in mild climates such as those of the Pacific Coast and the south. This species, up to 60 or rarely 80 feet in height and with spreading branches, occurs on mountain slopes from southern California to British Columbia and may have a single straight, massive trunk or be shrublike with several trunks.

branchlets, and good, bronzy coloring in fall; *J. v. glauca*, with glaucous blue-green foliage; *J. v. hillii* (syn. *J. pyramidiformis hillii*), dense, columnar, and up to 12 feet tall, with spreading branches and greenish-blue foliage that turns pinkish-plum in winter; *J. v.* 'Hillspire', often grown as *J. v. cupressifolia* 'Green', a symmetrical female sort with bright green foliage; *J. v.* 'Manhattan Blue', a compact, pyramidal female variety with blue-green foliage; *J. v. pendula*, the weeping red-cedar, with

Its scaly bark is bright cinnamon-red, its branchlets much stouter than those of *J. virginiana*. From the latter species it differs, too, in having its gray-green, scale-like leaves usually in threes, with those of alternate triads arranged so that each branchlet has six rows of leaves. The backs of the leaves have conspicuous glands. The fruits of the Western red-cedar are glaucous-bluish-black. This juniper often attains great age and trunks of impressive size. A specimen estimated to be at least 3,000 years old had a trunk diameter at breast height of 14 feet, but this is exceptional.

One of the most beautiful North American native kinds is the alligator juniper (*J. deppeana pachyphlaea* syn. *J. pachyphlaea*), indigenous to Texas, Arizona, and Mexico. This is a variety of a Mexican species. The alligator juniper is broadly-pyramidal or round-topped, up to 60 feet in height, with a short trunk and spreading branches. Its common name refers to its distinctly scaly and checkered bark. On older trees most of the foliage is of the adult type, glaucous blue-green, and with a gland on the back of each leaf. The juvenile leaves, in twos or threes, are spiny-pointed and usually bluish-green or, on young specimens, often an extremely attractive, almost silvery-white. The glaucous, reddish-brown fruits ripen in their second year.

The common juniper (*J. communis*), native to all three northern hemisphere continents, is a shrub or tree up to 45 feet in height, with reddish-brown, peeling bark. Its leaves are all needle-like, linear to awl-shaped, and taper to fine points. Their concave upper sides are marked with a broad white band. Rarely the flowers are bisexual. The slightly glaucous, black or bluish fruits usually contain two or three seeds and ripen in their second or third year. This, the hardiest juniper, succeeds about as far north as trees grow. It is very variable and exists in many varieties, some natural ones of particular geographic regions, others of horticultural origin. The typical wild upright form is a common na-

Juniperus communis suecica

tive of Europe and occurs less abundantly in eastern North America. A broadly-columnar small tree or shrub of distinctive appearance *J. c. oblonga-pendula*, one of the most graceful of all junipers, has drooping branchlets up to 2 inches long. It forms a denser and more shapely specimen than *J. formosana* or *J. rigida*, both of which it somewhat resembles in gross appearance. *J. c. suecica*, the Swedish juniper, forms a dense column of short, upright branches and short, bluish-green leaves. Its fruits are oblong. This suffers winter damage to its foliage in the vicinity of Boston, Massachusetts. *J. c. hibernica* (syn. *J. c. stricta*), the Irish juniper, is more compact and slightly hardier than the somewhat similar Swedish juniper. Forming a dense, dark green column, it originally was brought to America from Ireland in 1836.

Juniperus communis hibernica

Juniperus chinensis, varieties

The Chinese juniper (*J. chinensis*) is a most useful kind. In addition to shrubby and prostrate varieties dealt with later, it is represented by a number of upright ones. Up to 60 feet in height and pyramidal or columnar, mature trees usually have some juvenile leaves among the more plentiful adult foliage, but even in the wild some trees when mature bear only juvenile leaves. The latter, spiny-pointed and

Juniperus chinensis 'Ames', young specimen

needle-like, are usually in threes and have two white lines on the upper surface. The blunt, adult, scalelike leaves are in pairs and form four rows along the branchlets. On the back of each is a depressed gland. The brown fruits, conspicuously glaucous, mature in their second year. In aspect the Chinese juniper differs from the red-cedar of eastern North America in being less dense-foliaged and of a lighter, less somber green. Its chief upright varieties are *J. c.* 'Ames', with needle leaves that first are bluish-green but become green when mature; *J. c. arbuscula*, bushy and pyramidal, with many erect major branches, mostly scalelike leaves, and the ends of its fruits bilobed; *J. c. aurea*, with scalelike leaves and young shoots golden-yellow; *J. c. columnaris*, a narrowly-columnar, green-leaved kind with sharp-pointed, awl-shaped leaves, introduced from China in 1905; *J. c. c. glauca*, introduced at the same time, and similar except that its foliage is silvery-gray; *J. c. foemina*, a female and therefore fruit-bearing form of the typical species; *J. c.* 'Iowa', similar to *J. c.* 'Ames', but less compact and more spreading; *J. c. keteleeri*, broadly-pyramidal, with bright green foliage that even in exposed locations changes color but little throughout the year, and one of the best varieties; *J. c. mas*, dense, col-

Juniperus chinensis columnaris

Juniperus chinensis keteleeri

umnar, with only male flowers and mostly juvenile foliage, also an excellent variety; *J. c.* 'Mountbatten', dense and slender, with grayish, mostly needle-like leaves and attractive fruits, and so formal in outline that it almost appears to be sheared; *J. c. pyramidalis*, of rigid habit, dense and narrowly-pyramidal, with upright branches, and bluish-green, mostly juvenile foliage, often misnamed *J. excelsa stricta* (true *J. chinensis stricta* is not hardy in the north), *J. c.* 'Story', a male variety, very slender and dark green,

with horizontal branches and a dominant central leader; *J. c. sylvestris*, grayish-green foliage and very broadly pyramidal; *J. c. torulosa* (syn. *J. c.* 'Kaizuka'), the Hollywood juniper, an irregularly-shaped, dark green tree with peculiar twisted clusters of whip-like branchlets, and suitable for mild climates only; and *J. c. torulosa variegata* (syn. 'Variegated Kaizuka'), with foliage attractively variegated with yellow.

The needle juniper (*J. rigida*), a native of Japan, Korea, and China, is akin to the common juniper (*J. communis*), but is more open-headed, elegant, and looser in appearance. It has longer, more slender leaves with the central white stripe on each narrower than the green that margins it. This pyramidal tree has ascending branches and decidedly pendulous branchlets. It attains a maximum height of 35 feet or slightly more. The fruits, about ¼ inch in diameter and brownish-black and glaucous, become glossy at maturity and ripen in their second year. It is similar to *J. formosana* and is hardy at the Arnold Arboretum, near Boston, Massachusetts.

Native to Taiwan and China, *J. formosana*, which attains heights up to 45 feet, has drooping branchlets and spiny-pointed, spreading leaves each with two broad, white bands on its upper surface. The fe-

male cones are orange-brown. The two white bands on the leaves and the color of the female cones distinguish this species from similar *J. communis oblonga-pendula*.

Two tree species of juniper indigenous to southern Europe and Asia Minor of horticultural significance are the Syrian juniper (*J. drupacea*) and the Greek juniper (*J. excelsa*). Neither is hardy in the north. Attaining a height of 60 feet, *J. drupacea* is very distinct. It has only juvenile-type foliage. Its sharp-pointed, linear-lanceolate leaves are in whorls of three. They are ½ to ⅞ inch long and on their concave upper surfaces have two white lines separated by a broad band of green. Their lower portions are adherent to the shoots. The glaucous, brown or bluish fruits, the largest of any juniper, are ¾ to 1 inch in diameter and ripen in their second year. In cultivation this handsome juniper is usually columnar, but in the wild is often pyramidal. The Syrian juniper grows well in limestone soils. The Greek juniper (*J. excelsa*) is sometimes 100 feet tall and has a narrow-pyramidal head of erect or spreading branches and slender branchlets. Its leaves are usually scalelike and in opposite pairs that form four rows, closely pressed against the shoots. Those on the leading shoots are commonly in threes. Each leaf has a gland

Juniperus chinensis pyramidalis, young plant

Juniperus rigida

Juniperus excelsa

Juniperus chinensis torulosa

Juniperus rigida (foliage)

on its back. Only rarely do mature plants of this species exhibit some juvenile foliage. The juvenile leaves are spreading, about ¼ inch long, and in opposite pairs. The trees may be unisexual or bisexual. The fruits, up to ½ inch in diameter, ripen in their second year and are dark purplish-brown and glaucous. The variety *J. e. stricta* is very handsome, narrowly-pyramidal and has only juvenile foliage. Its leaves are glaucous and have a white band on their upper surface and a minute gland near the base beneath. This kind is sometimes called the spiny Greek juniper. Like *J. excelsa* itself, it is not hardy in the north, but a kind that is hardy, *J. chinensis pyramidalis*, is sometimes mistakenly grown under the name of *J. excelsa stricta*.

Juniperus chinensis pfitzerana

Juniperus chinensis variegata

Juniperus sabina 'Von Ehren'

Shrubby junipers, those that neither attain tree size nor are so low and prostrate that they rank only as groundcovers, are among the most useful of garden evergreens, especially for regions where cold winters prevail. Some are species normally low, others varieties of kinds typically tall and treelike. The best known of the latter is Pfitzer's juniper (***J. chinensis pfitzerana***), undoubtedly one of the best evergreen shrubs cultivated in North America. Pfitzer's juniper originated in Germany in 1899; it attains an eventual height of 10 feet and spreads widely to form a flat-topped shrub. If staked when young it develops a more pyramidal shape. A more compact form is called *J. c. p. compacta*, a form with especially glaucous foliage, *J. c. p. glauca*, and one with golden leaves, *J. c. p. aureo-pfitzerana*. Typical *J. c. pfitzerana* is much branched and full-foliaged. Its branches are long and its branchlets droop slightly. Its leaves are slightly glaucous and awl-shaped. Another variety of the Chinese juniper that somewhat resembles Pfitzer's juniper in appearance is *J. c. p. armstrongii*, which has light green foliage. The leaves toward the center of this shrub are mostly of the needle type, those of the terminal branchlets, scalelike. The variety *J. c. hetzii* is somewhat similar to Pfitzer's juniper, but taller and more vigorous. It has pale bluish foliage. Attaining a height of 3 to 4½ feet, *J. c.* 'Blaauw' has spreading branches and branchlets and mostly densely-arranged, scalelike, grayish-blue leaves, which, except those in the interior of the bush, are needle-like. This variety is much like *J. c. plumosa*. Dwarf, *J. c. globosa* is a female variety, loosely-spherical, with crowded branchlets and mostly scalelike, green leaves. Variety *J. c. japonica* at most attains a height of 4½ feet. It has dense, very prickly foliage that includes both scalelike and needle leaves. A male variety, *J. c. plumosa* has spreading branches, nodding at their tips. The leaves are mostly scalelike. With attractive variegated foliage, *J. c. variegata* is a low shrub with distinctly glaucous foliage. Its terminal

Juniperus chinensis variegata (foliage)

shoots are sometimes entirely, often partly, creamy-white. Other shrubby varieties of Chinese juniper are described in nursery catalogs.

The savin juniper (***J. sabina*** syn. *J. lusitanica*) is less pleasing than some kinds, but prospers on limestone soils. It sometimes attains a height of 10 to 15 feet but is often much lower and spreading. It has slender branches and foliage that emits a strong, unpleasant odor when bruised. Usually both juvenile and adult leaves are present, the former slightly spreading, concave, and glaucous, with a prominent midrib above. The adult scalelike leaves are dark green and usually have a resin gland on their backs. The glaucous, brownish-blue fruits are pendulous and ripen in the fall of their first season or the following spring. There are several varieties of the savin juniper, some of which are discussed below under kinds suitable for groundcovers. Variety *J. s.* 'Von Ehren', said to be resistant to juniper blight disease, is a slow-growing shrub broader than high, and eventually attaining 10 to 15 feet in height. An erect, columnar variety, *J. s. fastigiata*, has dark green, mostly adult foliage. A dwarf kind with scalelike leaves and the tips of some of its branchlets white is *J. s. variegata*. Variety *J. s. cu-*

pressifolia is a low, spreading bush with glaucous-green, mostly scalelike leaves. It is female and bears fruits.

Among shrubby varieties of the common juniper (*J. communis*), which is native of the northern hemisphere around the globe, *J. c. depressa* is endemic to eastern North America. Often not over 3 feet in height, it sometimes reaches twice that and with age forms broad patches many feet through. Its leaves are shorter and broader than those of typical *J. communis*. In its dwarfer forms this variety can be used effectively as a large-scale groundcover. Much smaller and less vigorous are *J. c. compressa*, a narrow-columnar variety with strongly-ascending branches and crowded, short leaves, usually not more than 1 foot tall, and *J. c. echiniformis*, which becomes a dense, upright, rounded bush 1 foot to 2 feet tall, and has small, deep green, prickly leaves.

There are shrub forms of typically prostrate *J. squamata*. Of these the best known is the remarkably distinct and handsome *J. s. meyeri*, which has many erect branches furnished with short, straight branchlets and straight leaves that on their back sides are very glaucous blue. Inasmuch as this variety can under favorable conditions attain a height of 20 feet one might question including it among shrub junipers, but it is a slow grower and in gardens usually has the dimensions of a shrub rather than a tree. Another variety, *J. s. wilsonii*, grows to 6 feet in height and has short, crowded branches that recurve at their tips, and leaves shorter than those of typical *J. squamata*. It is slightly less hardy than *J. s. meyeri*, but will live outdoors in southern New England. The eastern American red-cedar (*J. virginiana*) has produced some shrubby varieties. Among them is *J. v. chamberlaynii*, a female form with spreading and reflexed branches, drooping branchlets, and mostly needle-like, grayish-green leaves. *J. v. globosa* is slow-growing, densely-branched, and rounded. It eventually, after perhaps half a century, becomes 15 feet tall. *J. v. tripartita*, sometimes called the fountain

Juniperus horizontalis

red-cedar, forms a shallow, vase-shaped shrub up to 5 feet tall, of irregular habit. It branches from the base. *J. v. kosteri*, with a maximum height of about 2 feet, is an excellent variety that originated in a nursery in Holland about 1880.

Low, prostrate, and trailing junipers useful as groundcovers are numerous. The creeping juniper (*J. horizontalis*) is a native North American with needle-like leaves, chiefly opposite, but on the terminal shoots in threes. Its scale leaves are sharp-pointed. Handsome and vigorous, this has long trailing branches and many short branchlets. Its foliage ranges from bluish-green to steel-blue and its light blue fruits are only slightly glaucous. There are several excellent varieties of the creeping juniper. One of the best is the Waukegan juniper (*J. h. douglasii*), which has fine steel-blue foliage that changes to a beautiful lavender-pink to plum-purple in winter. It is a vigorous spreader. The Bar Harbor juniper (*J. h.* 'Bar Harbor') is a splendid, compact, low-growing, spreading variety with steel-blue foliage. The Andorra juniper (*J. h. plumosa*), named after the eastern American nursery where it was discovered, is a very beautiful, widespreading kind, normally up to 1½ feet in height. Its grayish-green summer foliage changes to pinkish-purple in winter. The leaves are longer and more pointed than those of typical *J. horizontalis*. A compact form of the Andorra juniper is known as *J. h. plumosa* 'Youngstown' and *J. h. plumosa compacta*. A pleasing variety with creamy-white-tipped branchlets is *J. h. variegata*. A more recent addition to the several splendid varieties of the creeping juniper is one discovered on Vinalhaven Island, Maine, and called blue rug juniper (*J. h. wiltonii*). Its special merit lies in the lovely soft blue-gray and more frondlike effect of its foliage than that of the Bar Harbor and Andorra junipers. Growing rather more slowly than them, it is one of the finest of goundcover junipers. Yet another excellent variety of this species is *J. h. glauca*, which was selected by the Ar-

nold Arboretum, Jamaica Plain, Massachusetts, as a variety with especially fine colored foliage. It is prostrate and has slender branches and steel-blue leaves.

The common juniper (*J. communis*) is represented by a few dwarf, spreading varieties. Discovered in Ireland, *J. c. hornibrookii* is a prostrate, spreading shrub with comparatively broad leaves about ¼ inch long, incurved, forward-pointing, and marked with a clear white band. Another variety, *J. c. nana* (syn. *J. c. minima*), occurs naturally in Europe. It rarely exceeds 1 foot in height and has crowded leaves less spreading than those of typical *J. communis*. Found in Oregon and California, *J. c. jackii* has mostly branchless, trailing, whiplike branches and linear-lanceolate, incurved leaves.

The shore juniper, *J. conferta*, is a Japanese native, related to *J. rigida*, but prostrate and with crowded, overlapping, awl-shaped leaves and black, decidedly glaucous, abundantly produced fruits. Its glaucous green leaves, about ½ inch long, taper to sharp points. Above, they are deeply grooved and marked with a white band. This vigorous spreader is hardy in southern New England.

Juniperus conferta

The Chinese juniper (*J. chinensis*) has two low natural varieties that have produced variations to which horticultural names are applied. Native to Japan, *J. c. procumbens* (syn. *J. procumbens*), 2 feet or often less high, has prostrate lower branches and sinuous or twisted and more or less upcurved others. Its branchlets are glaucous. The leaves, up to ½ inch long, have white-spotted, glaucous under surfaces. Variants of this variety include sorts identified horticulturally as *J. c. procumbens albovariegata*, its foliage variegated with white; *J. c. p. aureo-variegata*, with yellowish-variegated foliage; *J. c. p. glauca*, which is very blue-glaucous; and *J. c. p. nana*, dwarfer than the typical variety.

The other low natural variety of the Chinese juniper is *J. c. sargentii* (syn. *J. sargentii*). Native of the Kurile Islands and

Juniperus chinensis sargentii

northern Japan, this much-admired sort attains 8 to 10 feet in diameter and typically 2 feet or somewhat more in height. It forms dense mounds or mats of short, erect stems that arise from prostrate branches. The leaves are green with glaucous undersides, those of young specimens needle-like and mostly under ¼ inch long, those of older plants scalelike. Horticultural variants of *J. c. sargentii* include sorts known in cultivation as *J. sargentii glauca*, with young foliage that is decidedly blue-green; *J. s. viridis*, the young leaves of which are grass-green; and *J. s.* 'Manay', which is up to 4 feet tall with blue-green foliage. One of the handsomest and most distinct junipers suitable for use as a groundcover is *J. sabina tamariscifolia*. This has procumbent or mostly horizontal-spreading branches and bright green, chiefly needle-type leaves, which are mostly in twos, but on older branches are sometimes in threes. It has been cultivated for centuries. Especially lovely *J. s. prostrata* is a slow-growing sort that makes a carpet of ground-hugging stems from which sprout a thick pile of very short branchlets with narrow, awl-shaped green leaves with narrow white bands. Very dwarf and compact *J. squamata prostrata* has long,

Juniperus squamata prostrata

ground-hugging main stems and branches that closely follow the contours of the ground or rocks over which they trail, and from which sprout short, leafy branchlets that form a beautiful carpet of greenery.

Garden and Landscape Uses. Because of their great diversity in form and foliage junipers are among the most useful evergreens for landscape effects and lend themselves for use for many purposes. The tree kinds, attractive as single specimens or in groups, form effective screens, backgrounds, and windbreaks and associate well with other trees and shrubs in mixed plantings. The narrow-pyramidal and strictly columnar kinds, such as certain varieties of red-cedar (*J. virginiana*),

These tall junipers form an effective screen

A bed of low junipers forms an important part of this front garden planting

Colorado red-cedar (*J. scopulorum*), Chinese juniper (*J. chinensis*), and common juniper (*J. communis*) are splendid accent plants that can be used in much the same way as the Italian cypress to produce very formal effects. Lower and bushier junipers, such as Pfitzer's juniper (*J. chinensis pfitzeriana*), are admirable shrubs for borders, foundation plantings, groups, and single specimens; some are well adapted for rock gardens. For rock gardens, too, and as

Trailing junipers clothe this rock outcrop

groundcovers on banks, slopes, and similar places the creeping, prostrate kinds, including selected varieties of the common juniper, Chinese juniper, and savin juniper (*J. sabina*), as well as *J. squamata* and *J. horizontalis*, are superb. Junipers need full sun and grow best in well-drained, moderately moist, somewhat sandy soil, but will succeed even in dryish, rocky or gravelly earth. They withstand wind and seashore conditions.

Cultivation. Juniper species can be raised from seeds sown in a cold frame in fall or early spring. The seeds do not germinate until the second or sometimes third spring after sowing. Horticultural varieties must be, and natural species can be, increased by cuttings taken in summer or early fall and inserted under mist or in a propagating bench in a humid greenhouse. These plants transplant readily provided a good ball of soil is kept intact about their roots; it is advisable to mulch newly transplanted specimens with wood chips or other suitable material and to water them thoroughly and periodically if long spells of dry weather follow planting. Junipers stand pruning and shearing well, but cuts should not be made so far back on the branches that no leafy side branches remain. The best time to prune or shear is just before new growth begins in spring.

Diseases and Pests. Cedar-apple rust disease affects the red-cedar (*J. virginiana*), but only if certain alternate hosts of the disease, apples, crabapples, and hawthorns, are growing nearby. Infection, which ordinarily does no serious harm to the red-cedars, manifests itself on them by producing galls on the foliage that in spring develop many long horns or tongues and are 1 inch or more in diameter. Control is had by eliminating alternate hosts from the proximity of red-cedars. Another rust fungus produces larger galls on trunks and branches, but does no serious harm. Insect pests of junipers are more numerous and include aphids, bagworms, webworms, scales, red spider mites, and juniper midge

(which causes blisters at the bases of the needles and dying of the leaf tips).

JUPITER'S BEARD. This common name is applied to *Anthyllis barba-jovis* and *Centranthus ruber*.

JURINEA (Jur-inea). About 100 species of biennials, herbaceous perennials, and subshrubs, of the daisy family COMPOSITAE, belong here. Native from southern Europe to central Asia, this quite variable genus has a name that commemorates a professor of medicine, Louis Jurine, who died in 1819.

Jurineas are tall or dwarf plants with nonspiny leaves covered beneath or on both sides with white hairs, and long-stalked, thistle-like, purple flower heads, each consisting of many florets, in clusters. The seedlike fruits are four- or five-sided and are furnished with tufts of rough hairs of unequal lengths. They technically are achenes.

Native of the Caucasus, **Jurinea alata** is a perennial or biennial 3 to 4 feet tall. It has lobed, oblong-fiddle-shaped basal leaves up to 6 inches long and lanceolate, toothed stem ones with stalks continued as wings down the stems. The leaves are slightly hairy on their upper surfaces, more densely so beneath. About 1 inch in diameter, the flower heads are purple. From the last, **J. anatolica** (syn. *J. mollis*), a native of southeast Europe and Asia Minor, differs in its stalks being only slightly or not at all winged. This variable kind has erect, branchless or sparsely branched, few-leaved stems. Its lower leaves are pinnately-lobed, the upper ones more often without lobes. The upper sides of the leaves are green and have a cobweb of white hairs; beneath the leaves are white-hairy. The rose-purple flower heads are 1¼ to 2½ inches in diameter.

Garden and Landscape Uses and Cultivation. The cultivated jurineas are best adapted to informal, semiwild areas where they may be grouped for ornamental effects in sunny locations. They do well in ordinary soils, including dryish ones, and are easily raised from seed. They can also be increased by division in spring. Their hardiness is not fully known. They are worth trying as far north as southern New England.

JUSSIAEA. See Ludwigia.

JUSTICIA (Jus-tícia)—Shrimp Plant, Chuparosa. As here understood, this genus of the acanthus family ACANTHACEAE includes plants by some authorities identified as *Adhatoda*, *Beloperone*, *Drejerella*, *Jacobinia*, *Libonia*, and *Nicoteba*. So accepted, *Justicia* comprises approximately 300 species, is represented in the native floras of the tropics and subtropics of the western and eastern hemispheres and in temperate parts of North America. Its name commemorates a Scottish gardener, James Justice, who died in 1754.

Justicias are nonhardy herbaceous perennials, subshrubs, and shrubs, with opposite, undivided leaves and, in racemes or spikes sometimes with conspicuous overlapping bracts, flowers with deeply-five-parted or rarely four-parted calyxes and small to large, red, purple, yellow, or white, two-lipped corollas with straight or curved tubes. Frequently the corolla tube is expanded in its upper part. The upper lip is erect and two-toothed or toothless, the lower three-lobed and spreading. There are two stamens and one style tipped with a headlike stigma. The fruits are capsules.

The common shrimp plant (*J. brandegeana* syns. *Beloperone guttata, Drejerella guttata*), native to Mexico and naturalized in Florida, is popular as a houseplant and greenhouse plant and in warm climates as an outdoor ornamental. Its vernacular name alludes to the curious appearance and color of its conspicuously bracted spikes of bloom. A loosely branched subshrub 1 foot to 3 feet tall, this has rather weak stems and short-pointed, ovate, stalked, hairy leaves 1 inch to 3 inches in

Justicia brandegeana

length. The flowers, borne almost continuously, are crowded in curved spikes 3 to 6 inches long or somewhat longer that are attractive and conspicuous because of their many broad-ovate, shrimp-pink to reddish-brown bracts ½ inch to almost 1 inch in length that overlap like slates or shingles on a roof. The corollas of the 1¼-inch-long flowers protrude from between the bracts. They are white, pubescent, and deeply-cleft, with the lower lip shallowly-three-lobed and spotted with purple. The upper lip is scarcely lobed. In *J. b.* 'Yellow Queen' the floral bracts are soft yellow. The leaves of *J. b. variegata* are conspicuously blotched with cream. Much like the shrimp plant, Mexican *J. fulvicoma* (syns. *Beloperone comosa, Justicia comosa*) has less showy, copper-bracted spikes shorter than those of the shrimp plant and erect rather than arching or somewhat drooping.

Justicia brandegeana variegata

Justicia fulvicoma

The white shrimp plant (*J. betonica* syn. *Nicoteba betonica*), a native of warm parts of Asia and Africa and naturalized in Hawaii, has much the aspect of the common shrimp plant. A weak-stemmed shrub up to about 4 feet tall, it has short-stalked, narrow to broad, pointed-elliptic leaves, finely-hairy on their undersides and 2 to 5 inches long. From the branch ends spikes about 4 inches long of white and lilac blooms in association with prominent, overlapping, pointed, ovate or heart-shaped, green-veined, white bracts develop.

Handsome and showy *J. carnea* (syns. *Jacobinia carnea, J. magnifica, J. obtusior, J. pohliana, J. velutina*) is a somewhat variable, bushy subshrub or shrub up to 6 feet tall and native to northern South America. Long popular for greenhouses and for outdoor cultivation in the tropics and warm subtropics, this has angled or grooved stems and almost hairless to velvety-hairy, lanceolate-ovate to oblong-ovate, conspicuously-veined leaves 5 to 10 inches long. Its clear pink to purplish-pink or nearly crimson, arching, hooded, about 2-inch-long flowers are in dense, erect, showy, terminal and axillary headlike spikes 4 to 5 inches in length and furnished with prominent blunt or pointed, green bracts about ¾ inch long.

Justicia carnea

Red justicia (*J. secunda*), a much-branched shrub, is up to about 8 feet tall. Native to northern South America, it has long-pointed, ovate-oblong to lanceolate-ovate, slightly-toothed or toothless leaves up to 6 inches long. The slender, bright red blooms, in fairly wide, loose to quite massive, elongating panicles with bracts smaller than the sharp calyx lobes, and 1½ inches long, have corollas with lips longer than their tubes. A slender-stemmed, bushy shrub up to 2 feet tall, *J. rizzinii* (syns. *J. pauciflora, Jacobinia pauciflora, Libonia floribunda*) is a native of Brazil. It has downy stems and very short-stalked leaves, not over and often under 2 inches long. They are toothless and broad-elliptic to oblong or obovate. The solitary, short-stalked, drooping to nearly horizontal flowers are from the leaf axils. From ¾ to 1 inch long and cleft for not more than ¼ inch, they are scarlet, tipped with yellow.

The species previously named *Beloperone amherstiae* is now correctly identified as *J. brasiliana*. A shrub 3 or 4 feet tall with

Justicia brasiliana

graceful, wandlike stems, it has short-stalked, hairless or lightly-hairy, pointed-ovate to pointed-lanceolate leaves 3 to 6 inches long. The 1½-inch-long, rose-red flowers, in crowded, erect, short spikes, without conspicuous bracts, come from the leaf axils. They have a straight upper lip and a reflexed, three-lobed lower one.

Rare in cultivation, *J. angustifolia* of Brazil is an attractive bushy plant with linear-lanceolate, dark green leaves with a pale mid-vein, and abundant rosy-lavender flowers veined with white in their throats.

Justicia angustifolia

Golden-yellow to orange-yellow, 2-inch-long flowers in dense terminal spikes up to 4 inches long are borne by Mexican *J. chrysostephana.* This hairless or nearly hairless subshrub, 1 foot to 2 feet tall, has four-angled stems and pointed, ovate to ovate-lanceolate leaves 5 to 6 inches long with reddish veins. The flowers are slightly curved and have an arched upper lip and a down-pointing, three-lobed lower one. Tropical African *J. flava* is an erect, semierect, or straggling, loosely branched herbaceous perennial or subshrub 1 foot to 4 feet tall. It has grooved stems and ovate-lanceolate to pointed-el-liptic leaves 1 inch to 4 inches long. The yellow, often dark-streaked, approximately ½-inch-long flowers have a prominent three-lobed lip and are in slender, erect, terminal, pubescent spikes 3 to 8 inches in length. Yellow to reddish-yellow, 2-inch-long blooms in spikes up to 1 foot long are borne by *J. aurea* (syn. *J. umbrosa*), a shrub 4 to 15 feet tall and native to Mexico and Central America. This has angled stems and lanceolate-ovate to ovate leaves 4 inches to 1 foot long, sometimes with wavy margins. The flowers, from the axils of narrow, pointed bracts, have hairy corollas cleft to their middles.

A hairless to sparsely-hairy, much-branched shrub up to 6 feet tall, *J. spicigera* (syn. *Jacobinia spicigera*) is native from Mexico to South America. It has four-angled stems and arching, oblong-lanceolate, short-stalked leaves 3 to 7 inches long. In forking terminal and axillary, one-sided racemes, the orange to crimson blooms are 1¼ inches long or longer. They are cleft to about one-third of their length and have a down-pointing lower lip. Sometimes misidentified as *Anisacanthus thurberi*, Mexican *J. leonardii* (syns. *Justicia incana, Jacobinia incana*) is a densely-gray-hairy shrub up to 2 to 3 feet tall with oblongish to ovate leaves up to 6 inches long. Few together in branched terminal and axillary clusters, the red, hairless flowers, 1½ to 1¾ inches long, have a coiled lower lip. A solution made by steeping the leaves of this species in water is used in Mexico and Central America as bluing for whitening laundry. It is the plant frequently cultivated as *J. ghiesbreghtiana.* The species correctly so identified is Mexican. Similar to *J. spicigera*, it has slightly larger flowers in panicles and is perhaps not in cultivation. A hybrid between *J. ghiesbreghtiana* and *J. pauciflora*, named *J. penrhoziensis*, much resembles its first-named parent except that its leaves are usually larger and those of each pair are about equal in size. Also, its flowers are yellow. A shrub 3 to 5 feet tall, *J. can-*

dicans, of Mexico, has pointed, ovate to broad-ovate, stalked, pubescent to nearly hairless leaves 1 inch to 3 inches long. In small, few-flowered, stalkless or nearly stalkless clusters, its red flowers are up to 1½ inches long. Very similar to and by some botanists included in the last is *J. ovata,* of Arizona and Mexico.

A more or less vining or sprawling shrub up to 10 feet tall, *J. cydoniaefolia* (syns. *Adhatoda cydoniaefolia, Jacobinia cydoniaefolia*), of Brazil, slightly to more obviously downy, has short-stalked pointed-elliptic to ovate leaves 2 to 3 inches long and about one-half as wide. Its short-stalked flowers intermingled with leafy bracts are borne freely in small clusters from the leaf axils. They are 1¼ inches long and have an arched upper lip, white, tipped with violet, and a broad, three-lobed lower lip that is violet with a white center line on the upper surface of its bottom half, and white beneath. The anthers are lemon-yellow. In Florida, *Megaskepasma erythrochlamys* has been mistakenly named *Adhatoda cydoniaefolia.* Native of India, Ceylon, and China, *J. adhatoda* (syn. *Adhatoda vasica*) is an evergreen shrub up to 10 feet tall. It has pointed, elliptic to

Justicia adhatoda

oval, short-stalked leaves up to 8 inches long, and terminal and axillary, conspicuously-bracted spikes of white flowers about 1¼ inches long and ½ inch across, with the lower lip netted with pink or purple-pink. A west African, sometimes vining herbaceous perennial or subshrub up to 10 feet tall, *J. extensa* has densely-hairy young stems and ovate leaves often attractively blotched with silvery markings. Its tiny, pink-spotted, green flowers are in short-branched, terminal panicles up to 10 inches long.

Justicia flava

Justicia candicans

Justicia californica

The chuparosa (*J. californica*) is a decorative flowering shrub 3 to 6 feet tall that occurs along watercourses in the deserts of Arizona, California, and adjacent Mexico. Its blooms attract hummingbirds. Of dense habit, this has greenish, often sparsely-foliaged or leafless, slender branches. The leaves are ovate or sometimes ovate-lanceolate, short-stalked, and approximately ¾ inch long by about ½ inch wide. They are thickly clothed with fine hairs. Brilliant red, the tubular blooms are in terminal, bractless racemes. From slender corollas ¾ inch to nearly 1½ inches long the stamens protrude slightly. The blooming period is spring and early summer. Chuparosa is also a name of *Anisacanthus thurberi*.

Garden and Landscape Uses. Justicias are suitable for outdoor beds, borders, and other ornamental plantings in the tropics and warm subtropics and for growing in pots and ground beds in greenhouses. A few, notably the shrimp plant, succeed as window plants. Not infrequently the shrimp plant becomes straggly and unshapely. To avoid this, pinch out the tips of the shoots of young specimens fairly frequently to encourage bushiness. Crowding among other plants and too much shade are other factors that result in leggy specimens. Shrimp plants bloom continuously even when very small, and then the production of flowers interferes with growth. To prevent this it is desirable to remove all flower buds while they are yet small until the plants have attained a respectable size.

Cultivation. The cultural needs of justicias differ somewhat according to kind. Among the least demanding are the shrimp plant and *J. fulvicoma*. In pots these succeed in porous, loamy earth, such as is appropriate for geraniums and chrysanthemums. Outdoors in warm climates almost any well-drained garden soil satisfies. A little part-day shade is acceptable, too much is

detrimental. Exposure to full sun promotes flowering. Too-high indoor temperatures from fall through spring, especially if accompanied by insufficient light, are a frequent cause of weak, straggly growth. During the winter season 55°F at night is adequate, with an increase of five to fifteen degrees by day appropriate. The shrimp plant and *J. fulvicoma* need free circulation of air, but not exposure to cold drafts. Stagnant, dank conditions are not to their liking. Moderate humidity is needed. Water by soaking the soil thoroughly then allowing it to become dryish, but not to the extent that the foliage wilts before drenching it again. Avoid constant saturation. Well-rooted specimens benefit from biweekly applications of dilute liquid fertilizer from spring through fall. Rarely cultivated except in southern California and other desert or semidesert regions, the chuperosa needs a sunny, well-drained site.

The other justicias dealt with here for their best development require nourishing soil that contains rather generous amounts of leaf mold, compost, peat moss, or other suitable decayed organic material, and that drains freely. A coarse earth instead of one consisting of mostly too-fine particles is to their liking. Keep it moderately moist.

Winter night temperatures indoors of about 60°F give the best results. By day, increases of five to fifteen degrees are in order. Propagation is generally by cuttings, which root very readily in a greenhouse propagating bench or under similar conditions. Seeds may also be used. The young plants grow rapidly and bloom well during their second or in some cases their first year. Those of kinds that do not have large, spikelike heads of bloom should, while small, have the tips of their stems pinched out to induce branching. It is better not to pinch kinds with large flower heads. Left to develop one stem only, within a few months they produce a beautiful head of bloom. Such specimens in 4- or 5-inch pots are highly decorative.

Pruning second-year and older plants to shape and size is done as soon as flowering is through, or indoors in late winter or early spring. Then, too, repotting is given attention. Container specimens that have been cut back may have much of the soil about their roots teased away before they are planted in their new pots. Later in the season a second potting is likely to be needed. During the summer such plants are better kept in cold frames or even with their pots buried nearly to their rims in a bed of sand outdoors, than in a greenhouse. They must, of course, be brought inside before frost. Specimens that have filled their containers with roots benefit from regular applications of dilute, liquid fertilizer. The chief pests of justicias are scale insects and mealybugs.

JUTE is *Corchorus capsularis*.

JUTTADINTERIA (Jutta-dintèria). Native only to a very limited area of South African desert, this group consists of eleven species of low, cushion-forming and subshrubby, nonhardy, succulent perennials. It belongs in the *Mesembryanthemum* complex of the carpetweed family AIZOACEAE. Its name honors a Mrs. Jutta Dinter.

Juttadinterias have very thick, fleshy leaves in opposite pairs set closely together. Alternate pairs are at right angles to each other. The upper parts of the leaf margins and the keels of the undersurfaces are often bluntly-toothed. Borne in summer, the red-violet to violet flowers suggest those of daisies, but unlike daisies each is a single bloom, not a head of many florets. A distinguishing feature is the four-lobed calyxes of the flowers. In closely related *Dracophilus*, to which some species of *Juttadinteria* have previously been referred, the calyxes have five lobes. The fruits are capsules.

A subshrub with short, erect branches, *J. albata* has crowded, somewhat spreading, whitish gray-green leaves besprinkled with translucent dots and finely margined and keeled with red. The leaves are ¾ to 1 inch long or longer. At their bases a little more than ⅓ inch wide, they broaden somewhat above and become keeled toward their triangular apexes. The flowers are white and 1½ inches wide or wider. Of unusual appearance, *J. simpsonii* is a cushiony subshrub with many erect branches thickly clothed with triangular-pointed leaves 1 inch to 1½ inches in length that narrow to their bases where they are somewhat under ½ inch wide. Toward their ends they have keels that, like the leaf margins, are furnished with short, backward-pointing teeth. The leaf surfaces toward the apexes are also toothed. Terminal, and with short stalks, the white flowers are almost 1½ inches across.

Reported to be the easiest to grow, *J. deserticola* does not form colonies. It has short, upright, very leafy stems and thick, blunt, nearly egg-shaped, scarcely-keeled, smooth, whitish or gray-green leaves with translucent dots along their margins. The leaves are ¾ to 1 inch long and ⅓ to nearly ½ inch wide. The white blooms are ¾ inch in diameter.

Garden Uses and Cultivation. Strictly for specialists and skilled growers of dwarf, nonhardy succulents, juttadinterias have not, as a group, proven easy to cultivate. Conditions that suit *Lithops* and other small members of the *Mesembryanthemum* complex are most likely to favor their well-being. They rest in winter and then should be kept dry or nearly so. For further information see Succulents.

JUVENILE FORMS. Some kinds of plants when immature bear foliage so markedly different from that of normally flowering and fruiting samples of the same kinds

English ivy: (a) Juvenile form

(b) Adult form

JUVENILITY. The physiology of young seedlings differs from that of older plants. This manifests itself chiefly in their growth being vegetative, characterized by the elongation of stems and production of foliage associated with increase in size, and by the nondevelopment of flowers and fruits. This condition, termed juvenility, contrasts with maturity, when growth normally slows and flowers and fruits are borne.

With some plants transition from the juvenile to mature state, which may be fairly rapid or may extend over several years, is accompanied by such marked morphological changes as reduction in thorniness or change of leaf shape. Striking examples of the latter are found among some vining plants, English ivy and *Monstera deliciosa*, for example, in which the foliage of mature growth differs so much from that of the juvenile stage that it could easily be mistaken for that of an entirely different species.

Plants raised from cuttings and by other vegetative procedures may also go through an initial phase of juvenility, but this is usually considerably shorter than with seedlings. Recognition of the juvenile stage of growth is often of importance to plant propagators. Cuttings taken from such growth often root much more readily than those made from mature shoots.

that to be uninitiated they may appear to be different species. English ivy in its familiar, non-flowering vining form, usually with markedly angled leaves, is juvenile. When it matures, as it eventually does if allowed to climb high, it produces erect, nonvining, flowering and fruiting branches without aerial roots and with ovate to heart-shaped leaves without angles. Plants rooted from cuttings of such growth retain the mature, bushlike characteristics.

Many other woody plants, mostly evergreens and including acacias, arbor-vitaes (*Thuja*), eucalyptuses, false-cypresses (*Chamaecyparis*), and junipers (*Juniperus*), exhibit similar differences at separate stages of their development. With some, either or both forms may be perpetuated by propagating from appropriate shoots, and such forms are sometimes given identifying names.

Juvenility may last for a short time or persist for many years. It is not unusual for branches with juvenile foliage and those with mature foliage to be present at the same time.

K

KADSURA (Kad-sùra). This is not to be confused with the katsura tree (*Cercidiphyllum*). The genus *Kadsura* comprises about ten, or according to some authorities, as many as twenty-two species of twining, evergreen, woody vines of warm and temperate eastern Asia. They belong in the magnolia family MAGNOLIACEAE, or, according to some authorities, to the segregate schisandra family SCHISANDRACEAE. The name is a Japanese one.

Kadsuras have alternate, stalked, undivided, toothed leaves and usually solitary, whitish to pinkish, unisexual flowers from the leaf axils. The blooms have nine to fifteen perianth segments or tepals, the inner ones petal-like, the outer smaller and more like sepals; there is no sharp distinction between the two. The male blooms have numerous stamens. The berry-like fruits, attached to a fleshy axis or receptacle, are in globose heads.

The kind ordinarily cultivated, **K. japonica,** a slim-stemmed native of Japan, China, and Taiwan, is about 12 feet tall. Its dark green, lustrous leaves, paler and often purplish on their undersides, are 2 to 4 inches long by 1¼ to 1¾ inches wide. They are oblong to ovate, slender-pointed, distantly-toothed, and without hairs. On stalks 1 inch to 1½ inches long, the ¾-inch-wide, pendulous yellowish-white flowers are borne in summer from the leaf axils of the current season's shoots. They have nine fleshy perianth segments and are succeeded by red berries in showy, 1-inch-wide spherical clusters. The leaves of *K. j. variegata* are irregularly edged with creamy-white.

Garden and Landscape Uses and Cultivation. The hardiest species *K. japonica* succeeds only in mild climates; it will not withstand winters in the north, but it is hardy in sheltered locations in southern England and presumably would be in places as mild elsewhere. It grows without difficulty in moderately fertile soil in sunny locations or in part-day shade. It is attractive for pergolas, arches, and similar uses and for growing on trellis or other supports against walls. The only pruning needed, any deemed desirable to thin out crowded branches, is done in spring or summer. Propagation is by seed, by summer cuttings inserted in a greenhouse or cold frame propagating bed, preferably with a little bottom heat, and by layering.

KAEMPFERIA (Kaemp-fèria). Belonging in the ginger family ZINGIBERACEAE, the about seventy species of *Kaempferia* are natives of eastern tropical Asia and Africa. The name commemorates Engelbert Kaempfer, a German physician and botanist, who died in 1716.

These are herbaceous perennials with fleshy, aromatic rhizomes and roots sometimes irregularly thickened or with small tubers. Apparently stemless or with short, erect stems, kaempferias have leaves all basal or two-ranked on the stems. Their few to many flowers are spirally arranged in bracted spikes terminating leafy stems or are on separate stalks in evidence when foliage is absent. The blooms, one in the axil of each bract, have a usually short, unequally toothed calyx split part way down one side, a long corolla tube with nearly equal spreading or reflexed lobes (petals), two staminodes (petal-like, infertile stamens), and a broad flat lip with two long lobes usually similar in appearance to the staminodes. The solitary stamen is very short. The fruits are capsules. Throughout southeastern Asia *K. galanga* and *K. rotunda* are widely cultivated for medicinal purposes and to flavor foods. Variegated-leaved kinds are attractive ornamentals.

Native to Borneo, **K. atrovirens** is a beautiful sort about 6 inches tall. Ovate and up to 6 inches long by one-half as wide, its leaves, the lower ones stalkless, are deep iridescent green. The flowers are white with a pink, lavender, or violet lip spotted with yellow at its base. A native of tropical Asia, and commonly low, **K. elegans** is somewhat variable in stature and in the width of its quite plentiful, more or less spreading, broad-elliptic, green leaves. Its flowers, pinkish-lavender to blue, with

Kaempferia elegans

Kaempferia grandiflora

a small yellow eye, have four spreading, equal-sized, obovate petals. The erect shoots of **K. grandiflora** are of shining, fresh green, lanceolate leaves with depressed veins and overlapping stalks. About 2¼ inches in diameter, the clear lavender to light blue flowers have a white throat with a yellow blotch. This is native to Kenya.

Sometimes called peacock plant, **K. roscoeana,** of Burma, is one of the handsomest. It has usually two, sometimes one

Kaempferia roscoeana

or three, very broad-ovate, fleshy, stalkless leaves 4 to 5½ inches wide that spread close to the ground. They are beautifully marked on their upper sides with iridescent, light green veinings and peacock-tail-like zonings. Their purplish undersides are glossy. The white-eyed, lilac flowers open in succession over a long summer period. Belying its name, if that alludes to its foliage, **K. rotunda,** has pairs of short-stalked, erect, elliptic leaves 6 inches to 1 foot or sometimes more in length and one-third as broad as long. Usually they are variegated above in a feathered pattern of dark and pale green and have purplish, finely-hairy undersides. Produced before the leaves, the fragrant, 2-inch-long blooms, in spikes of up to six, are white with a violet lip. The original home of this species is not definitely known; it may have been Indochina.

Clear milky-white marginal bands decorate the leaves of **K. gilbertii,** a Burmese species that has tufts of three or four elliptic to pointed-oblong, bright green leaves about 4 inches long and with gray undersides. The 1-inch-long white flowers have violet-striped lips 1 inch or slightly more in length.

Kaempferia gilbertii

With plain green leaves, **K. galanga** is a tuberous, stemless kind with spreading, short-stalked leaves in twos. They are roundish to pointed-ovate and 3 to 6 inches long. In spikes of six to twelve, the predominantly white flowers, about 1 inch long and with lips about as wide, have violet-spotted, white or pink lips. This species is believed to be a native of India. The pale green leaves of eastern Asian, tuberous **K. ovalifolia** are in groups of three or four and have stalks 2½ to 5 inches in length. Their slender-pointed, oblongish blades are 6 to 8 inches long and approximately one-half as wide. The 1-inch-long white flowers have violet lips.

Kaempferia galanga

Garden and Landscape Uses and Cultivation. Only in the humid tropics and warm subtropics are kaempferias suitable for outdoor cultivation. There, in rich, fertile soil, that does not lack for moisture while foliage is in evidence, and where they are shaded from strong sun, these attractive plants are appropriate for rock gardens, underplantings, and edgings. They succeed with minimum care. A mulch of compost, leaf mold, or peat moss

is advantageous. The best time for planting is at the beginning of a new cycle of growth. In greenhouses devoted to the cultivation of tropical, shade-loving ornamentals they well deserve places. For their best comfort a minimum winter night temperature of 60°F is required. By day an increase of five to fifteen degrees is in order. During the summer temperatures may rise above 90°F with advantage. At all times a humid atmosphere is desirable. Ample supplies of water should be given during the season of active growth, less or none, depending upon the amount of foliage, when the plants are dormant or semidormant. Repotting, in well-drained pots or pans (shallow pots), in coarse, fertile soil well provided with organic matter, should be given attention in spring. Propagation is commonly by division and by tubers. Seeds are also satisfactory.

KAFIR. As part of their common names the word Kafir is associated with these plants: Kafir-corn (*Sorghum bicolor*), Kafir-lily (*Clivia* and *Schizostylis*), and Kafir-plum (*Harpephyllum caffrum*).

KAGAWARA. This is the name of orchid hybrids the parents of which include *Ascocentrum, Renanthera,* and *Vanda.*

KAGENECKIA (Kagen-éckia). A Netherlands ambassador to Spain, Frederick de Kageneck, is honored by the name *Kageneckia* for three species of the rose family ROSACEAE. He lived in the eighteenth century.

Native to southern Chile and Argentina, kageneckias are evergreen shrubs or small trees under 25 feet tall. They have alternate, leathery, more or less glutinous, sharply-toothed leaves and, from the ends of the shoots and from the leaf axils, white, five-petaled, unisexual flowers, the females solitary, the males in racemes or clusters. The blooms are ¾ inch across. They have persistent calyxes and broad, rounded petals. The females have five downy carpels, the males ten to twenty stamens. The star-shaped fruits are of five downy podlike structures.

The species cultivated, **K. oblonga** has hairless shoots and foliage and is 10 to 30 feet tall. Its leaves, edged with small, sharp, gland-tipped teeth, are elliptic-lanceolate to obovate, 1 inch to 2½ inches long by ⅓ to 1 inch wide, with prominent midribs. Its male flowers are in clusters of six to nine. Very much narrower leaves distinguish **K. lanceolata,** the leaves of which in its homeland are used as a source of a black dye, and medicinally.

Garden and Landscape Uses and Cultivation. These little-known plants are suitable for trial in California and other warm-temperate regions where summer humidity is not unduly high. Little experience is recorded about their cultivation.

They are thought to prosper in ordinary well-drained soils. Propagation is by seed and by summer cuttings.

KAHIKATEA is *Podocarpus dacrydioides*.

KAI-WETA is *Carpodetus serratus*.

KAKI is *Diospyros kaki*.

KALANCHOE (Kalán-cho-e)—Air Plant or Life Plant or Floppers, Panda Plant. This genus (the name is pronounced in four syllables and with a "k" sound given to the "ch") belongs in the orpine family CRASSULACEAE and includes plants sometimes segregated as the separate genera *Bryophyllum* and *Kitchingia*. It contains more than 200 species, the majority African or Madagascan, but some Asian and one a native of South America. The name is an adaptation of the Chinese name for one kind.

Kalanchoes are nonhardy, succulent, herbaceous or sometimes slightly woody-stemmed herbaceous perennials, erect and branching or less commonly prostrate and trailing. Their thick, fleshy, generally opposite leaves are most often undivided, but sometimes are pinnately-lobed or pinnate. Often they are toothed. Those of some kinds produce new plantlets spontaneously at their margins. The flowers, solitary or in panicles or other assemblages, are nodding or up-facing. They have four-cleft calyxes and corollas, the latter often with inflated tubes and wide-spreading lobes (petals). There are usually eight stamens attached at about the middle of the corolla tube and four separate or somewhat united pistils. The fruits are podlike follicles. Here, the kinds belonging to the group once segregated as *Bryophyllum* are presented first, then kinds that represent *Kalanchoe* as once restricted, and one, *K. peltata* that if segregation of the genera is followed belongs in *Kitchingia*.

Air plant, life plant, or floppers (**K. pinnata** syns. *Bryophyllum pinnatum, B. calycinum*) is so proliferous that visitors to Florida take home leaves that have such urge to regenerate that, even when pinned to a window curtain in a city apartment, develop plantlets along their margins (actually they do much better if the leaf is pinned or weighted down on the surface of slightly moist sand or sandy soil). This ubiquitous species, probably a native of the East Indies or perhaps Madagascar, is freely naturalized in many tropical and subtropical parts of the globe. Under good conditions, *K. pinnata* is 6 feet in height. Its stout, fleshy stem has leaves of mostly three to five ovate or oblong, toothed, fleshy leaflets up to 5 inches long, but the lower leaves may be undivided. The flowers have red-brown corollas up to 3 inches long. These protrude for about one-third of their length from the showy, inflated calyxes, which are pale green or yellowish

tinged with purple or purple-red. They remain attractive over a long period. This, an old plant in cultivation, was known to Europeans in the very first years of the seventeenth century. Natives of Madagascar brewed from its leaves a kind of tea and used the leaves for dressing sores.

More prolific of plantlets on its leaves than the air plant is **K. daigremontiana,** of Madagascar. This vigorous grower is a handsome ornamental up to 3 feet in height. It has a branchless, erect stem and thick, long-triangular leaves with neat fringes of plantlets along their crenated margins that, if the atmosphere is somewhat moist, trail hairlike roots downward and may even develop tiny plantlets along the edges of their own small leaves before the original plantlets drop from the mother plant. The leaves are rich green marbled with red-brown. The flowers, in compact clusters, are about 1 inch long. They have gray-violet corollas enclosed only at their bases by the calyxes.

Kalanchoe daigremontiana

Kalanchoe daigremontiana, showing plantlets on edges of leaves

Another Madagascan species, *K. fedtschenkoi,* is a beautiful plant, more productive of foliage than most kinds and forming bushy, branched specimens up to 1 foot in height. The lower parts of its stems

Kalanchoe fedtschenkoi

Kalanchoe fedtschenkoi marginata

often lie on the ground surface. The leaves, in four longitudinal rows, are obovate or roundish, short-stalked, round-toothed, and glaucous-bluish or purplish-blue often faintly tinged with red at the margins. The flowering stems with along their lengths pairs of bractlike leaves of diminishing size from below upward are terminated by loose clusters of coral-pink or brown-pink flowers ¾ inch long, with slightly inflated calyxes. Especially beautiful is *K. f. marginata*, which has pale bluish-gray leaves delightfully edged with creamy-white; it often produces shoots with all creamy-white foliage. The kind cultivated as *K. f.* 'Giant' is similar to the typical plant, but much larger. Its leaves, up to 4½ inches long, are scalloped at their margins and glaucous-bluish to purplish with orange-red edges. This may be a tetraploid or, possibly, it is the species *K. waldheimii*. Endemic to Madagascar, **K. laxiflora** (syn. *Bryophyllum crenatum*) must not be confused with West African *K. integra crenata*. The Madagascan plant is 2 to 3 feet tall and has oblong or ovate, round-toothed, glaucous-gray-green leaves up to 3 inches in length and branched panicles of hanging, brownish-orange or yellowish-brown flowers on opalescent stalks. Plantlets frequently develop along the leaf edges. A distinguishing feature is the pair of ear-like lobes at the base of the leaf blade.

Nearly as common in cultivation as the air plant, **K. tubiflora** (syn. *Bryophyllum tubiflorum*), a native of Madagascar, has erect stems up to 3 feet tall, sparsely or not branched, and four longitudinal rows of semicylindrical leaves up to 6 inches long and up to ¼ inch wide and thick, grooved along their upper surfaces. The leaves develop many plantlets from near their tips

Kalanchoe tubiflora

Kalanchoe tubiflora (flowers and leaves with plantlets)

and are whitish-green with many reddish-brown spots. The about 1-inch-long flowers, in compact, flat-topped clusters, are bright reddish. Distinct **K. beauverdii**, of Madagascar, has slender, climbing stems up to 10 feet long and narrow-linear-lanceolate, stalkless, stem-clasping leaves up to 4 inches long that spread horizontally from the stems and are purplish or dark green. Their ends are deflexed and somewhat hooklike, which aids the plant in climbing. In loose clusters, the flowers are dull gray-violet with bluish, glaucous calyxes. Variety *K. b. parviflora* (syn. *K. scandens*) differs in having somewhat smaller blooms. Also Madagascan, **K. pubescens** (syn. *K. aliciae*), 3 feet tall, is glandular-white-hairy. Rather sparingly branched, it has nearly round, toothed leaves up to 4 inches long, the lowermost stalkless, those above with distinct stalks. This species generates plantlets not from the leaf margins, but abundantly in the flower clusters after the blooms fade. The drooping flowers, about 1 inch long, have corolla tubes not much inflated and spreading petals notched at their ends. They are in candelabrum-like panicles and are red-orange or red-brown with darker lines inside the throat.

Kalanchoe pubescens

A delightful little trailer, **K. uniflora** (syns. *Bryophyllum uniflorum, Kitchingia uniflora*) inhabits humid woods in Madagascar, often as an epiphyte (a plant that grows on another plant but does not take nourishment from its host). Its slender stems have pairs of well-spaced small leaves strung like rosary beads. They are very thick, almost or quite without stalks, broad-ovate to nearly round and with crenated margins. Up to 1 inch long, they are usually smaller. The drooping blooms are in groups of two to five, but occasionally solitary. They are distinctly urn-shaped, clear soft salmon-pink or lavender-pink with a pearl-like luster and with four short, spreading orange petals. The stems produce aerial roots readily. Another Madagascan, **K. manginii**, has lax branches

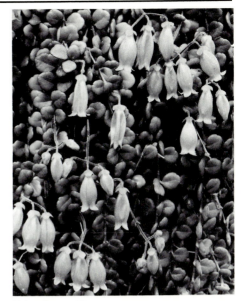

Kalanchoe uniflora

Kalanchoe manginii

and succulent, ovate-spatula-shaped leaves up to 1¼ inches long. Its flowers, few together in terminal clusters, are 1 inch long, deep coral-red outside, and with yellow with coral striping inside the throat of the corolla.

Commonly known simply as kalanchoe and grown in several varieties and perhaps some hybrids by florists and amateur gardeners chiefly for winter flowers, **K. blossfeldiana**, of Madagascar, is characteristically a compact, free-branching, billowy

Kalanchoe blossfeldiana

plant with bright, glossy-green, toothed or smooth-edged, obovate leaves up to 1 inch long by three-quarters as wide and concave above, and an abundance of bright red flowers that face upward. It attains a height of 6 to 8 inches. The flowers are about ⅜ inch across. Horticultural varieties vary in compactness, size, shade of red of the flowers, and other details. One, 'Yellow Darling', possibly a hybrid between *K. blossfeldiana* and *K. schumacheri*, has clear yellow blooms. Somewhat like *K. blossfeldiana*, but taller, less bushy, and much larger in its parts is **K. flammea,** of tropical Africa. This splendid species attains a height of 2 feet or more, is sparsely-branched and has dull green or grayish-green, but not glaucous, ovate-oblong leaves, concave above, with obscurely round-toothed margins. The flower clusters sometimes 1 foot across terminate long, erect stalks furnished with two or three pairs of small leaves and consist of many upturned, bright red or orange-red flowers usually with yellow corolla tubes. The individual blooms, about 1 inch across, are mildly fragrant. This blooms in spring. A variety or perhaps hybrid of it with coppery-tinted foliage and canary-yellow flowers is cultivated as *K. f.* 'Yellow'.

Kalanchoe flammea (flowers)

Kalanchoe thyrsiflora (flowers)

An attractive hybrid between *K. flammea* and white-flowered *K. teretifolia*, of Arabia, **K. kewensis** has clear yellow, sweetly-scented flowers. It is 2 to 3 feet tall. Native to Africa, tropical Asia, Java, China, and Brazil, **K. laciniata** is a winter-bloomer with ½ inch wide, upturned flowers of yellow, orange, pink, or red. From 2 to 4 feet tall, it has oblong or lanceolate leaves up to 5 inches long with the margins toward their apexes scalloped, and the uppermost often deeply-lobed. South African **K. thyrsiflora** is of distinct appearance. It has densely-leafy stems up to 2 feet tall and yellow flowers. Its broad-oblong to spatula-shaped leaves are up to 6 inches long by somewhat under one-half as broad. They diminish gradually in size from the lower part of the stem upward and, like leaves and calyxes, are covered conspicuously with white meal. The sweetly-fragrant blooms are in dense, cylindrical, spikelike clusters. The petals, yellow suffused with green, are reflexed. A delightful low species, **K. pumila** has stems and toothed, obovate leaves covered with whitish meal. The leaves are up to 1½ inches long. The flowers, pink with yellow anthers and very pretty, are in clusters about 1½ inches across.

Kalanchoe pumila

The panda plant (**K. tomentosa**), is a popular and pleasing succulent that has all its parts covered with light gray or silvery-white, velvety hairs. Rarely does it grow as tall as 3 feet. It branches freely. This is distinct in that its leaves are alternate, whereas those of other cultivated kalanchoes are opposite. They are oblanceolate and coarsely-toothed above their middles, and each tooth is spotted with a showy dark brown blotch that contrasts pleas-

Kalanchoe blossfeldiana 'Yellow Darling'

Kalanchoe flammea

Kalanchoe thyrsiflora

Kalanchoe tomentosa

ingly with the remainder of the leaf. The flowers, of little decorative value, are carried on long, branched stalks. Another sort of interest because of its decorative foliage, irregularly mottled on both upper and lower surfaces with maroon or brownish-purple spots and blotches, is **K. marmorata,** of Ethiopia. This has erect stems and obovate, coarsely-toothed leaves up to 8 inches long. The flowers, about 1½ inches across and borne in fall and early winter, are upturned, white, yellowish, or red-tinged and have very long, slender corolla tubes.

Kalanchoe marmorata

Very distinct **K. beharensis** is shrubby. Under exceptionally favorable conditions it may become 20 feet tall, but usually it is very much lower. It has stout, stiff, woody stems and branches and probably the largest leaves of any *Kalanchoe.* They are in great rosettes at the ends of the stems and, broadly-triangular to arrow-shaped, are up to 1¼ feet long and wide. Like the younger parts of the stems, the leaves are thickly clothed with three-branched, short hairs, more or less rusty-brown on the upper surfaces and silvery-gray beneath. On older leaves the hairs shed in patches. The flowers, white or yellowish-green with violet stripes inside, are more or less drooping. This kalanchoe is a native of Madagascar.

Kalanchoe beharensis

Another very unusual kind, **K. synsepala** is a native of Madagascar. It has a short stem that increases in length, but slowly, and spreading or drooping lanceolate to ovate-lanceolate leaves up to 10 inches long. From the upper leaf axils are developed long, slender, stolon-like stems, the lowermost of which bear small clusters of dingy white or pinkish flowers and the uppermost young plantlets. The plant-bearing stems gradually bend downward until they touch the ground. This allows the plantlets to root and become established as separate individuals. Formerly named *Kitchingia peltata,* and a native of Madagascar, **K. peltata** is 1 foot to 2 feet tall, subshrubby, and sparsely-branched. A vigorous grower, this has coarsely-toothed, elliptic to ovate, bright green leaves and purplish stems. Its tubular-bell-shaped flowers are in terminal panicles. The corolla tube is greenish and at maturity becomes four-angled because of interior pressure from the divergent ovaries. The spreading corolla lobes (petals) are light pink.

Other kinds sometimes cultivated are these: **K. eriophylla,** of Madagascar, is a white-woolly-hairy subshrub with spreading branches up to 1 foot long and thick and broad-ovate to nearly cylindrical leaves up to ¾ inch long that are tipped with reddish-brown. Its 3- to 6-inch-long flowering stalks display to good advantage from two to seven up-facing, yellow-stamened, pink

Kalanchoe eriophylla

to blue-violet blooms ½ inch wide or slightly wider. **K. hildebrandtii** is shrubby and has gray-green, pubescent, ovate leaves. Its small flowers are pale greenish-yellow. This is a native of Madagascar. **K. integra** (syn. *K. coccinea*), native to Arabia and East Africa, is 1 foot to 6 feet tall and glandular-pubescent. It has ovate to oblong, round-toothed, stalked leaves 2 to 6 inches long or sometimes longer and red to orange-red flowers with corollas swollen on their undersides. They are nearly or quite ½ inch long and from a little more than ¼ to ½ inch wide. Variety *K. i. crenata*

(syns. *K. crenata, K. schumacheri*), of East Africa and the Malay Archipelago, is hairless and has yellow flowers. Variety *K. i. crenata-rubra,* of East Africa to South Africa, is hairless and has red flowers. Variety *K. i. subsessilis,* of Mozambique, has nearly stalkless, hairy leaves and red flowers. Variety *K. i. verea* (syn. *K. brasiliensis*), of Central Africa, the Malay Archipelago, and coastal Brazil, the only *Kalanchoe* native in the New World, is pubescent and has ovate-lanceolate, toothed lower leaves and linear upper ones and yellowish flowers in dense clusters. This is naturalized in the West Indies. **K. longiflora,** of South Africa, 2 to 3 feet tall, has squarish stems, broad-ovate

Kalanchoe marnierana

to nearly round, coarsely-toothed, gray-green leaves, and panicles of bright yellow blooms. **K. marnierana,** of Madagascar, is 1 foot high, has slender stems and somewhat overlapping, short-stalked, obovate to broad-elliptic, up-pointing leaves about 1 inch long. They are blue-green with a distinct red edging and are slightly-toothed near their apexes. The many rose-pink flowers are about ¾ inch wide. **K. millotii,** of Madagascar, is a low, softly-pubescent shrub with short-stalked leaves the opposite pairs of which spread at right angles to the pairs next below and above them. They are triangular-ovate, coarsely-toothed and up to 3 inches long by 2½ inches wide. In rather crowded, roundish clusters lifted

Kalanchoe millotii

Kalanchoe mortagei

Kalanchoe quartiniana

Kalanchoe serrata

well clear of the foliage, the up-facing, cream-colored flowers, ⅓ inch wide, have lemon-yellow anthers. *K. mortagei,* of Madagascar, has an erect stem 1 foot to 2 feet tall and branchless. Its opposite, stalked leaves are narrowly-ovate to elliptic and toothed. Up to 4½ inches long by about one-half as wide as their lengths, the older ones develop plantlets from their tips. The drooping, tubular flowers are 1¼ inches long and purplish-red with orange lobes (petals) about ½ inch long. *K. orgyalis,* of Madagascar, is up to 5 feet tall, branched,

Kalanchoe scapigera

Kalanchoe suarezensis

Kalanchoe orgyalis

and with its younger leaves covered with silver-bronze or rusty-bronze, scalelike hairs. Its oblong-spatula-shaped leaves are very thick and brittle. The small flowers are greenish-yellow. *K. quartiniana,* a white-flowered native of tropical Africa, is up to 2½ feet in height and somewhat glaucous. It has broad-elliptic, stalked leaves. The flowers are about 2 inches across. *K. rotundifolia* is about 1½ feet in height. Native to South Africa and the island of Socotra, it is erect and glabrous and has oblong or oblong-lanceolate, toothless leaves up to about 1 inch long. The blooms are cinnabarred. *K. scapigera,* with obovate leaves about 2 inches long covered with white scurf, has tight clusters of cherry-red flowers. It is a

native of the island of Socotra. *K. serrata* of Madagascar is a hairless subshrub 1 foot to 2 feet tall with short-stalked, toothed, slightly waxy, elliptic leaves 1¼ to 2¼ inches long, the alternate pairs of which spread at right angles to the pairs above and below. In terminal clusters, the tubular, red-orange flowers are 1 inch to 1¼ inches long. *K. suarezensis* of Madagascar is a shrub 1½ to 2 feet tall. It has irregularly-toothed, pointed-elliptic, light green leaves, glaucous toward their bases and 4½ to 6 inches long. Adventitious buds capable of developing as plantlets are borne near the apexes of mature leaves. The flowers have reddish-violet calyxes, corollas with a cylindrical tube a little more than ½ inch long, and spreading or recurved lobes (petals). *K. velutina* of tropical Africa and Zanzibar has a thick, fleshy rootstock and creeping stems. A hairy species, its lower leaves are ovate, round-toothed, and up to 4 inches long. Those above are smaller and narrower. The up-facing flowers, in headlike clusters, are yellow to salmon or tangerine.

Garden and Landscape Uses. In warm, dryish, and semidesert climates kalanchoes are agreeable plants for outdoor gardens; they associate pleasingly with other succulents. They are not generally suitable for gardens in humid climates, although *K.*

Kalanchoe velutina

beharensis and a few others are sometimes grown in Hawaii. Some, such as *K. blossfeldiana* and *K. flammea* and their varieties and hybrids, are splendid decorative pot plants. Varieties of the former are popular florists' plants. Yet others are worth growing in greenhouses for their flowers or foliage or both, and several including the air plant, panda plant (*K. tomentosa*), *K. marmorata,* *K. pumila,* trailing *K. uniflora,* and lax-stemmed *K. manginii* are good window plants. All interest fanciers of succulents.

Cultivation. The chief need of kalanchoes is a porous, loose, fertile soil, one that is nourishing yet permits water to drain through quickly. If the basic loam in the planting or potting mixture is heavy and likely to compact, the addition of generous amounts of broken brick, broken crock, crushed sandstone, grit, perlite, or other material that increases porosity and does not decay, as well as of coarse sand, is needed. Good specimens cannot be had in soils lacking in fertility, therefore the addition of dried cow manure, bonemeal, or other organic fertilizers is desirable. Specimens in pots should be repotted fairly frequently, usually once a year at the beginning of the growing season with permanent specimens, more often in the case of such kinds as *K. blossfeldiana* and *K. flammea*, which are usually raised anew each year and discarded after blooming. It is important, however, especially with such kinds as *K. blossfeldiana* that have rather meager root systems, not to put them in too large containers. Specimens that have filled their pots with roots benefit from weekly or biweekly applications of dilute liquid fertilizer in summer and fall.

In summer kalanchoes may be set to the rims of their containers in a bed of sand or ashes outdoors. Although they may be wintered in a greenhouse with a night temperature of 50°F, they grow and retain their foliage better in a 55°F minimum and for *K. blossfeldiana* and *K. flammea* 60°F is desirable. Day temperatures may be five to ten degrees higher than night temperatures. Watering practice must vary somewhat according to kind. Very thick-leaved and hairy-leaved species, such as *K. beharensis* and *K. tomentosa*, may be permitted to become drier before water is given than thin-leaved kinds. All need watering more copiously when in active growth than when partially resting and all need full sun. Propagation is very easy by seed, stem cuttings, leaf cuttings with a small piece of stem attached, of some kinds by plantlets, and the trailers, by division. The seeds are exceedingly small and should be pressed into the surface of the soil or other sowing medium, but not covered with it. For florists' pot plants sow seeds of *K. blossfeldiana* from January to July to produce plants to bloom the following winter and spring. This kind, and perhaps other kinds, is very responsive in its time of flowering to the day length. Normally a spring-bloomer, it can be flowered any time of the year by manipulating the day length so that for a period of about three months the plants are in total darkness for sixteen hours of each twenty-four. In winter this kind can be prevented from blooming by giving additional illumination to extend the normal day length to thirteen hours or by interrupting darkness by having lights on for one hour in the night.

Diseases and Pests. Crown rot is likely to affect plants grown in excessively wet soil especially under cool conditions. Powdery mildew may infect plants in excessively humid atmospheres. Pests include scales, mealybugs, and mites. For more information see Succulents.

KALE or BORECOLE. There are several kinds of kale or borecole of which the one called collard is commonly grown in the south. In addition to vegetable garden kales there are those with brightly colored foliage esteemed as garden ornamentals delightful for flower beds, window boxes, and pots. All are of the brassica tribe of plants to which cabbage and cauliflower belong. Botanically kales are identified by the names *Brassica oleracea acephala*, *B. napus*, and others. With the exception of collards, which stand heat well and can be grown where summers are too hot for other brassicas, kales are cool-season crops harvested from spring to fall. The chief kinds are common kale, Scotch or curley kale, and blue Siberian kale. For ruvo kale see Broccoli Raab or Turnip Broccoli.

Kale in a vegetable garden

Soils for kales and their preparation for planting are as for cabbage. Plants are raised from seeds sown in late spring for fall and winter harvesting, in late summer or early fall to give crops to harvest in spring. The plants are sometimes left to mature where the seeds are sown, but far better results are had if like cabbages they are transplanted when young and spaced to allow ample room for their development. Depending upon variety this may mean in rows 1½ to 2½ feet or more apart, with 1 foot to 2 feet allowed between plants in the rows. Routine care is as for cabbages. Harvesting may be done by cutting entire heads or by taking off individual leaves as needed over a long period.

Ornamental kale, the centers of its loose, flattish heads of more or less frilled leaves creamy-white, pink, bright crimson-red, or purple, are raised from seeds started indoors early or sown directly outdoors in spring. They need rich, well-drained, evenly moist soil and a sunny lo-

Ornamental kale: (a) With pink center leaves

(b) With white center leaves

cation, and for the best results must be kept growing without check. Be sure they do not suffer from dryness and supply well-rooted container specimens with dilute liquid fertilizer at weekly intervals. Ornamental kale, although edible, is not recommended for eating.

Pests and Diseases. Kales are subjects to the same pests and diseases as cabbage.

KALMIA (Kál-mia)—Mountain-Laurel or Calico Bush, Lambkill or Sheep-Laurel, Bog-Laurel or Bog Kalmia. The plants of this attractive genus are not botanically related to true laurel (*Laurus*), but belong with rhododendrons, heathers, and barberries in the heath family ERICACEAE. There are seven or eight species of *Kalmia* confined in the wild to North America and Cuba. This genus consists of evergreen or rarely deciduous shrubs. Its name honors the Swedish botanist Pehr Kalm, who collected plants in North America. He died in 1779.

Kalmias have alternate, opposite, or whorled (in circles or more than two), smooth-edged leaves. Their cup- or saucer-shaped, shallowly-five-lobed flowers, usually in terminal or lateral showy clusters, more rarely are solitary and axillary.

The calyx is five-parted. There are small pouches or depressions midway between the base and margin of the corolla. Into these, during the bud stage and early development of the blooms the anthers of the ten stamens fit. The filaments (stalks) of the stamens bend outward like arched, pulled-down springs. When the pollen is ripe the outer ends of the springs are released by the slightest touch or disturbance, such as that made by a bee alighting, and the stamens jerk upward and shake loose and distribute the pollen. The wood of the mountain-laurel is heavy, hard, strong and brittle. It is used to some extent for fuel, tool handles, and turnery. The roots are made into tobacco pipes and are an excellent substitute for *Erica arborea* from which brier pipes are fashioned. The kinds discussed below are evergreens.

The mountain-laurel or calico bush (*K. latifolia*) is one of America's finest flowering shrubs and hardiest of broad-leaved (as distinct from coniferous) tall-shrub evergreens. It is native to woods, both dry and moist, from New Brunswick to Ontario, Indiana, Florida, and Louisiana. A handsome shrub or tree up to 30 feet tall under favorable conditions, it often grows natively in dense thickets and in bloom is one of the glories of the countryside as any who have traveled New England

roads, where it is abundant, at flowering time can testify. Its leathery, glossy green, hairless leaves, all or mostly alternate, are elliptic to lanceolate-elliptic and 2 to 3½ inches long. Usually they are pointed at both ends and have stalks up to ¾ inch in length. The flowers are many together in large terminal clusters. They vary from white to deep rose-pink with purple markings and vary considerably in size. Ordinarily they are about ¾ inch in diameter, but individuals with considerably larger flowers occur. Varieties are *K. l. alba*, with white or nearly white blooms; *K. l. angustata*, which has leaves much narrower than those of the typical species; *K. l. fuscata*, its flowers with a broad, purple-brown zone on their insides; *K. l. myrtifolia*, dwarf, slow-growing, and with dark green leaves 1 inch to 2 inches long; *K. l. obtusata*, a compact, slow-growing kind with blunt leaves 2 to 3 inches long; *K. l. polypetala*, which has its flowers divided into narrow, petal-like segments; and *K. l. rubra*, with deep pink flowers.

Lambkill or sheep-laurel (*K. angustifolia*) has foliage poisonous to livestock if eaten in large amounts. As a wildling it occurs from Newfoundland and Hudson Bay to Michigan and Georgia. Usually not over 3 feet tall, but sometimes taller, it has nearly opposite, short-stalked, oblong to

The bog-laurel or bog kalmia (*K. polifolia*) is a rather straggling shrub up to 2 feet in height. It is native from Labrador and Hudson Bay to Pennsylvania and Minnesota, from Washington to Alaska. Its almost stalkless leaves, opposite or in whorls of three, are lanceolate to linear and up to 1½ inches long. They have rolled-back margins and white-glaucous undersides. In terminal clusters of several, the flowers are ⅓ to slightly over ½ inch in diameter and rose-purple. The blooms of *K. p. leucantha* are white. From the typical species, *K. p. rosmarinifolia* is distinguished by having linear-oblong leaves with markedly rolled back margins.

Kalmia polifolia

The Western mountain-laurel (*K. microphylla* syns. *K. polifolia microphylla*, *K. p. nana*), a native of boggy and wet places from the Rocky Mountains to California and Alaska, is characteristically somewhat straggling and not over about 8 inches high. It has opposite, nearly-stalkless, ovate to elliptic or obovate leaves ¼ to ¾ inch long, with margins usually flat, at most slightly rolled back. The flowers, not over ½ inch across, are rose-purple. More robust *K. m. occidentalis*, up to 2 feet high, has linear leaves 1 inch to 1½ inches long.

Endemic to the southeastern United States and not reliably hardy in the north, *K. cuneata* and *K. hirsuta* are low shrubs. Deciduous or semievergreen, *K. cuneata* is up to 2½ feet in height, has alternate, obovate leaves up to 2 inches long, and pale pinkish flowers in clusters from the leaf axils. Not over 2 feet tall, *K. hirsuta* has elliptic to lanceolate, hairy leaves less than ½ inch long and from the leaf axils solitary pink to rose-purple flowers.

Garden and Landscape Uses. Except for rhododendrons the mountain-laurel is without doubt the most ornamental flowering evergreen that survives in climates too cold for camellias. It is hardier than nearly all rhododendrons. Truly magnificent, it can be used with gorgeous effects in masses to clothe banks, form borders and beds, contain driveways, provide back-

Kalmia latifolia

Kalmia latifolia (flowers)

Kalmia angustifolia

lanceolate leaves up to 2½ inches in length. Their upper sides are bright green, beneath they are paler. The flowers are in axillary clusters along the upper parts of the branches below the terminal cluster of foliage. They are under ½ inch in diameter and normally pinkish-purple to crimson. In *K. a. candida* the blooms are white. Those of *K. a. rubra* are dark purple. Ovate to elliptic leaves distinguish *K. a. ovata*. Small leaves with gray-hairy undersides characterize *K. a. carolina*.

grounds for lower plantings, and as informal hedges, as well as to add winter greenery and summer bloom to open woodlands and other lightly shaded places. It is appropriate in rock gardens and wild gardens, in foundation plantings and on lawns. Surely, this splendid native is rarely equaled and not surpassed in usefulness. Both its foliage and flowers are splendid for cutting for indoor decoration, but in many places commendable conservation laws prohibit taking mountain-laurel from the wild. It is permissible to cut from garden plants. Potted or tubbed specimens force readily in greenhouses and may easily be had in early bloom for indoor and conservatory decoration and for display at spring flower shows. Although of less general usefulness, partly because they do not grow as tall and partly because their flower clusters and flowers are smaller, the other species, though not as showy in bloom as the mountain-laurel, are worthwhile plants for those interested in American natives or in adding variety to shrub plantings. For bog gardens and wet places in rock gardens and wild gardens, the bog-laurel is well adapted. Kalmias do not take kindly to alkaline soils. They need at least mildly acid conditions. Preferably, a somewhat sandy peaty or loamy earth, not excessively dry, should be provided, they will, however, stand considerable dryness, but not grow as luxuriantly, if the ground is kept mulched with peat moss, pine needles, or compost. Heavy clay soils are not to their liking. They stand considerable moisture, indeed almost bog conditions, but such an extreme is by no means necessary except for *K. polifolia* and its varieties, which are definitely wet-soil plants. Magnificent specimens of mountain-laurel are often seen at the water's edge where the bank stands a foot or two above the surface and the roots can reach into an always moist substratum. Light shade is desirable for all except the bog-laurel or bog kalmia, which prefers full sun, but even kinds that benefit from light shade succeed in sun if the ground is never excessively dry.

Cultivation. Kalmias even when large transplant without difficulty provided good, unbroken balls of roots are dug and they are not allowed to dry out. Their reestablishment is favored and hastened if they are set in well-prepared sites. Preparation should consist of excavating pits for their reception considerably larger than the root balls, breaking up the subsoil and mixing in liberal amounts of compost, peat moss, or other decayed organic matter, and having available suitable soil fortified with peat moss or other suitable organic material and possibly sand, for packing around the roots and back-filling the holes. Early spring and late summer or early fall are the most favorable times for transplanting. Following this operation the ground should be mulched and care taken that adequate

water is supplied during dry weather for at least a year after transplanting. The maintenance of an organic mulch around kalmias is always helpful. Good displays of flowers every year are promoted by removing faded flower clusters promptly. If seed pods are allowed to develop, the following season's bloom may be less profuse because much of the energy of the plant has gone into seed production rather than into the production of flower buds. These plants need no regular systematic pruning, but they respond well to cutting back when this is desirable or necessary and such treatment can be severe, especially if the objective is to restore old, straggly specimens. Even if cut down to within a foot or two of the ground, old kalmias will renew themselves from the base. This process is helped considerably if following spring pruning the plants are fertilized with an acid fertilizer and if they are mulched and kept well watered during dry spells throughout the summer. Propagation is most commonly effected by seeds sown in sandy peaty soil or milled sphagnum moss kept moist. The seeds are very fine and should be scarcely or not covered with the sowing medium, but shaded glass should be placed over the pot, flat, or seed bed to assure a humid atmosphere. Other methods of propagation are by layering (a very slow, but reasonably sure way), grafting (usually adopted only for particularly desirable varieties), and cuttings. The latter do not root readily. Greater success is had if they are taken from plants that have been forced into growth in a greenhouse rather than from outdoor plants. The shoots from which the cuttings are made should be moderately firm, but not woody, in a condition gardeners term half-ripe.

Diseases and Pests. Fungus leaf spot diseases are likely to infect kalmias, and heavy attacks can cause the dropping of foliage. A leaf blight that looks much like sunscald or winter injury also affects these plants. Fortunately, both leaf spots and blight are controllable by spraying with a fungicide when new growth starts in spring and twice more at two-week intervals. A flower blight, the same as that which attacks azaleas, sometimes infects kalmias. Insects that infest these plants are lace bugs, stem borers, and the mulberry whitefly.

KALMIOPSIS (Kalmi-ópsis). First discovered in 1930 in the mountains of southern Oregon, *Kalmiopsis leachiana* was described, the following year, as *Rhododendron leachianum*. The correction to *Kalmiopsis* was made in 1932. A later, but not valid name is *Rhodothamnus leachianus*. The genus *Kalmiopsis*, which consists of one species, belongs in the heath family ERICACEAE, and as it name implies, is closely related to mountain-laurel (*Kalmia*). The designation is derived from *Kalmia*, and the Greek *opsis*, resembling.

One of the rarest native American plants, *Kalmiopsis* is restricted in the wild to very limited areas in Oregon. It is a freely-branched evergreen shrub usually not over 1 foot in height, occasionally attaining 1½ feet. One specimen 3½ feet tall is reported. The shoots are covered with short, fine hairs. The alternate, lustrous, dark green, lobeless, toothless leaves are very shortly stalked. Their blades are elliptic-oblong to obovate, ⅜ to ¾ inch long, and on their undersides have numerous tiny glandular dots that can be seen clearly with a hand lens. On slender stalks up to ¾ inch long are borne the widely-bell-shaped blooms. They are pale to deep pink and arise singly from the axils of thin bracts in terminal racemes of three to ten. The blooms are approximately ½ inch across. They have a persistent, five-parted calyx, and broad-ovate corolla lobes about as long as the corolla tube. There are ten stamens, hairy at the bases of their filaments (stalks), and a straight style tipped with a slightly-lobed stigma. The fruits are many-seeded small capsules.

Garden Uses and Cultivation. A choice and rare plant for collectors of alpines and rock garden enthusiasts, *Kalmiopsis* is challenging to grow. Unfortunately it does not take kindly to cultivation and many failures are reported by even experienced gardeners. Apparently well-established specimens die unaccountably. It may be that health is dependent upon some soil microorganism with which the plant has a symbiotic relationship and which does not survive under garden conditions. Be that as it may, about all that can be suggested is that an acid soil containing an abundance of decayed organic matter be provided, and that it be kept evenly moist, but not sodden. A little light shade from scorching sun is undoubtedly beneficial. Propagation is not simple. Seeds may be sown under conditions appropriate for rhododendrons and other members of the heath family. The seeds are not covered with soil, but simply sprinkled on the surface and pressed in. It is possible that they would succeed on milled sphagnum moss. Plants from seed take four to six years to bloom. Cuttings taken in early fall, treated with a root-inducing hormone, and planted in a mixture of peat moss and coarse sand in a propagating bed in a cold frame or cool greenhouse root fairly surely with a "take" of up to about fifty percent. They bloom in about two years. The hardiness of this species is not exactly determined; it has lived outdoors about as far north as New York City, but is, there, surer when accommodated in a cold frame.

KALOPANAX (Kalópan-ax). Easily distinguished from closely related *Acanthopanax* by the fact that its leaves are lobed, but not divided into separate leaflets, the only species of *Kalopanax* is a native of northeastern

Asia. It belongs in the aralia family ARAL-IACEAE. The name derives from the Greek *kalos,* handsome, and *Panax,* a related genus of plants. The lumber of *Kalopanax,* which has a disagreeable odor, is used in the Orient for construction, furniture, drums, and railroad ties. It is compact, straight-grained and fairly hard. The young leaves of *Kalopanax* are eaten in Japan.

Attaining its greatest size in the forests of northern Japan and Manchuria, **K. pictus** (syn. *Acanthopanax ricinifolius*) there not uncommonly is 100 feet tall and has a trunk 5 feet or so in diameter. The bark is dark gray and furrowed. A few massive branches form an open, rounded crown. The long-stalked leaves more closely resemble those of the sweet gum than of any other hardy, deciduous tree, but are considerably bigger, being 6 to 12 inches across. Five- to seven-lobed, they have toothed margins, and are slightly hairy beneath when young. In a general way they are remindful of the foliage of the castor oil plant (*Ricinus*). Sometimes trunk and branches are furnished with stout, short, sharp spines, but often these develop only on vigorous young shoots. In late July the flowers open. They are tiny, whitish, and in globular clusters about 1 inch across arranged in umbels 6 to 8 inches in diame-

Kalopanax pictus

Kalopanax pictus (foliage)

Kalopanax pictus (flowers)

ter. The tiny bluish-black fruits are esteemed by birds. Variety *K. p. magnificus* is spineless or nearly so. Its leaves are pubescent beneath. Variety *K. p. maximowiczii* is smaller than the typical species and has deeper-lobed leaves, silky-gray-hairy beneath.

Garden and Landscape Uses and Cultivation. A handsome tree of impressive stature that succeeds well throughout most of the northern United States and parts of southern Canada, *Kalopanax* should be more generally planted for ornament and shade. It gives the impression of being subtropical and is probably the most exotic-looking tree hardy in the north. It thrives without special care in deep, fairly rich soil that does not lack moisture, and is extremely resistant to pests and diseases. None of serious import are reported as attacking it. Seeds afford a ready means of propagation, but do not germinate until the second spring from the time of sowing. After their early years young trees grow quite rapidly.

KALOROCHEA (Kalo-ròchea). This name has been applied to hybrids between *Rochea coccinea* (syn. *Kalosanthes coccinea*) and *Crassula falcata,* of the orpine family CRASSU-LACEAE. One, *Kalorochea* 'Capitola', raised in California, is intermediate between its parents. It is almost 2 feet tall, and has gray-green foliage, and carmine flowers. It is reported to thrive better in southern California than *Rochea coccinea.* The name is derived from *Kalosanthes* and *Rochea.*

KALOSANTHES. See Rochea.

KAMANI is *Calophyllum inophyllum.*

KAMEMOTOARA. This is the name of orchid hybrids the parents of which include *Aerides, Euanthe, Rhynchostylis,* and *Vanda.*

KANGAROO. The word kangaroo is part of the common names of these plants: kangaroo-apple (*Solanum aviculare*), kangaroo paws (*Anigozanthos*), kangaroo-thorn (*Acacia armata*), and kangaroo vine (*Cissus antarctica*).

KAPOK TREE is *Ceiba pentandra.*

KARAKA is *Corynocarpus laevigata.*

KARANDA. See Carissa.

KARO is *Pittosporum crassifolium.*

KASSOD TREE is *Cassia siamea.*

KATSURA TREE is *Cercidiphyllum japonicum.*

KAULFUSSIA. See Charieis.

KAURI-PINE See Agathis.

KAWAKA is *Libocedrus plumosa.*

KEDROSTIS (Ked-róstis). The genus *Kedrostis,* of the gourd family CUCURBITACEAE, comprises thirty-five species of African, Madagascan, and tropical Asian, sometimes prostrate, perennial herbaceous plants. The name is the ancient Greek one for the related bryony (*Bryonia*).

Kedrostises are tuberous-rooted vines. They have alternate, undivided, deeply-cleft, lobed, or toothed leaves and branchless or rarely two-branched tendrils. The flowers are small, the males in racemes or stalked clusters, the females solitary or clustered. Usually both sexes are on the same plant. Males have five short sepals, a wheel-shaped, five-parted corolla, and three or rarely five short-stalked stamens. Female flowers have three short staminodes (nonfunctional stamens), or none, and two or three broad stigmas. The fruits are often few-seeded berries.

The only kind known to be cultivated, **K. africana** has short-stalked, triangular leaves deeply cleft into usually three lanceolate or linear-lanceolate, pinnately-lobed or toothed lobes, the center one 1½ to 2 inches long, the lateral ones smaller. The upper leaves are much smaller than these dimensions indicate. The flowers are tiny. The roundish, short-beaked, scarlet fruits are about ⅓ inch long.

Garden and Landscape Uses and Cultivation. The species described succeeds outdoors in frostless or nearly frostless climates and is occasionally grown in greenhouses, usually in collections of succulent plants. It needs well-drained, porous soil, kept dry during the plant's dormant period, but moist at other times. Propagation is by seed.

KEI-APPLE is *Dovyalis caffra.*

KELSEYA (Kélsey-a). The only species of *Kelseya,* of the rose family ROSACEAE, is closely related to *Petrophytum,* from which it differs in its flowers being solitary instead of in clusters and in having only ten or fewer stamens. Native at high elevations in Wyoming, Montana, and Idaho, this species grows in vertical crevices in limestone cliffs. Contrary to statements sometimes made, *Kelseya* was not named to honor an American nurseryman named Kelsey, but to commemorate its discoverer, the Reverend Francis Duncan Kelsey, who found it on the 4th of July, 1888 at Gate of the Mountains in Montana.

In aspect *K. uniflora* is reminiscent of certain curious raoulias and azorellas of New Zealand and South America. In form all of these plants are admirably adapted to their native environments. They are shrubs so intricately branched and unbelievably compact that their above-ground parts are unattractive to browsing animals and they are protected against excess water loss resulting from exposure to strong sun and high winds and are so constructed that their dead foliage remains to decay and nourish the roots instead of being blown or washed away. This is of no small importance to plants that grow where organic matter in the soil is almost nonexistent.

Kelseya uniflora at the Royal Horticultural Society's Gardens, Wisley, England

Kelseya uniflora, at home on Pikes Peak, Colorado

The evergreen leaves of *K. uniflora* are so densely crowded that they form unbroken surfaces to the broad, hummocky, firm, blue-green cushions, a few inches high, that are the plant bodies. Individual leaves are about ⅛ inch long and are at the ends

of the twigs. About ¼ inch across, the flowers, hugged by the rosettes of leaves, are pink. Each has a five-parted calyx, five petals, seven to ten stamens, and usually four to six pistils. The fruits are follicles.

Garden Uses and Cultivation. There appear to be no records of this exceedingly rare and choice plant having been successfully cultivated outdoors, but it is grown successfully in pots in alpine greenhouses in Great Britain. At The New York Botanical Garden it survived in pots in a cool greenhouse in winter and in a cold frame in summer for a few years. Soil containing abundant limestone is apparently necessary for its survival. Of plants grown at The New York Botanical Garden under otherwise identical conditions, those in limestone soils survived, others died. The soil must be exceedingly sharply drained and watering must be done with great care so that no suspicion of stagnation or of excessively wet conditions exists. So far as is known *Kelseya* has not been successfully propagated except by seed. It is a plant for skilled and optimistic alpine gardeners, undoubtedly hardy to much cold, but absolutely intolerant of wetness.

KENAF is *Hibiscus cannabinus.*

KENILWORTH-IVY is *Cymbalaria muralis.*

KENNEDIA (Ken-nédia). About fifteen species of Australia and Tasmania constitute *Kennedia,* of the pea family LEGUMINOSAE. Named to commemorate Lewis Kennedy, a London, England, nurseryman who died in 1818 and was an early cultivator of Australian plants, these vining or prostrate, evergreen, herbaceous or somewhat woody plants are adaptable for outdoor cultivation in southern California and similar mild regions. They are closely related to *Hardenbergia,* from which they differ in having larger flowers, solitary, or in pairs, clusters, or racemes, with their upper calyx lobes slightly united and the keel petals of the corolla not shorter than the lateral ones.

Kennedias have alternate leaves mostly with three, but in some kinds varying to one or five, egg-shaped to nearly round leaflets, and red, purplish-red, pink, or yellow-and-black flowers structured like those of a pea bloom. The keel and wing petals are long, the standard or upper one strongly curved backward over the five-pointed calyx. There are nine stamens joined together and one separate, and a slender style. The fruits are long, flat pods.

Three vigorous climbers are *K. coccinea, K. nigricans,* and *K. rubicunda.* In Australia the first is known as coral vine, a name applied elsewhere to *Antigonon leptopus.* Less hardy than the other kinds discussed, *K. coccinea* has good-looking foliage, and long-stalked, tight clusters of three to twelve red and orange blooms on stalks 2

to 6 inches long. The flowers are ½ inch long. Its leaves, usually with three, but occasionally five, leaflets are 1 inch to 2 inches long, and when young are silvery-hairy on their undersides. Dark violet-purple flowers 1½ inches long and with yellow centers are borne in one-sided racemes 3 to 4 inches long by *K. nigricans.* This species in Australia is called blackbean because of the appearance of its seed pods. A very strong grower, it is more or less hairy, with leaves with one broadovate leaflet 2 to 3 inches long, or three smaller ones. The red-bean of Australia, *K. rubicunda,* has downy shoots and yellowish-green leaves with ovate to ovate-lanceolate leaflets 2 to 3 inches long. Its flowers are dull red with a paler blotch at the base of the upper petal. They are 1 inch to 1¾ inches long and usually in short-stalked pairs from the leaf axils.

Kennedia rubicunda

Running postman and scarlet coral-pea are names given to *K. prostrata,* a vigorous, downy trailer that under favorable circumstances covers several square feet. Its bluish-green leaves have broad-ovate leaflets that may be over 1 inch long, but are often smaller. Its flowers, solitary or paired in the leaf axils, are scarlet with a yellow blotch at the base of the upper petal. They are under ¾ inch long. Variety *K. p. major* has larger leaves and flowers.

Garden and Landscape Uses. In warm-temperate and subtropical, nearly frost-free climates the climbing kinds of *Kennedia* are useful for growing on fences, wires, or other supports around which their slender stems can twine; and running postman is useful as a groundcover for banks and similar places and for rock gardens where there is no danger of it overgrowing its neighbors. As a rule these plants are best in full sun, but they will stand part-day shade. They do well in average soils, mostly favoring those of a clayish character, but running postman prefers those that are somewhat sandy and fairly moist. As greenhouse plants Kennedias may be grown in ground beds, pots, and hanging baskets.

Kennedia rubicunda, staked

Kennedia rubicunda, as a groundcover in southern California

Cultivation. Propagation is by seed, which germinate more readily if they are treated before sowing by pouring boiling water over them and allowing them to stand in the water for twelve to twenty-four hours, or by filing a nick in the coat of each seed. The seeds are sown in sandy peaty soil in a temperature of 60 to 70°F. As soon as the seedlings have formed a second pair of leaves they are potted individually in small pots and later into the 4-inch size. It is a mistake to plant them in the ground until they are quite well rooted in these pots. Porous soil and good drainage are important.

Specimens to be kept permanently indoors grow well in a greenhouse with a minimum winter night temperature of about 50°F, raised five or ten degrees by day. Whenever weather is favorable the greenhouse should be ventilated freely. Repotting, topdressing, and any needed pruning to shape is done in late winter. Water rather cautiously during winter, freely from spring through fall. Well-established specimens benefit from occasional applications of dilute liquid fertilizer from spring to fall.

KENSITIA (Ken-sítia). The only species of *Kensitia,* of the carpetweed family AIZO-

ACEAE, is endemic to South Africa. The name honors Edward George Kensit, a botanical collector in South Africa, who died in 1916.

A nonhardy, shrubby, succulent perennial 1 foot to 2 feet tall, **K. pillansii** (syn. *Piquetia pillansii*) has branched stems with opposite, pointed, three-angled, boat-shaped, fleshy, spreading, glaucous leaves up to 1¼ inches long, ¼ inch wide, and ⅜ inch deep or thick. Those of each pair are only slightly joined at their bases. The 2-inch-wide flowers, solitary at the shoot ends, have a five-lobed calyx, spreading, rose-purple petals united at their bases, many staminodes (nonfunctional stamens) and stamens, and radiating stigmas. The fruits are capsules.

Kensitia pillansii

Garden and Landscape Uses and Cultivation. These are as for *Lampranthus.*

KENTIA. The palms commonly cultivated under this name belong in *Howea* and *Chambeyronia.* The one formerly named *Kentia canterburyana* is *Hedyscepe canterburyana.*

KENTIOPSIS (Kentióp-sis). A solitary species native of New Caledonia, *Kentiopsis olivaeformis,* is the only member of this genus of the palm family PALMAE. It is a tall, graceful feather-leaved kind, reported to be the most plentiful palm in its native land, but scarcely known in cultivation. The name *Kentiopsis* is from *Kentia,* another genus of palms and the Greek, *opsis,* similar to. The plant formerly called *K. macrocarpa* is *Chambeyronia macrocarpa.* It is to be expected that *Kentiopsis* will respond to the same cultural conditions and care as *Howea.* For more information see Palms.

KENTRANTHUS. See Centranthus.

KENTROPHYLLUM. See Carthamus.

KENTUCKY BLUE GRASS is *Poa pratensis.*

KENTUCKY-COFFEE TREE is *Gymnocladus dioica.*

KERNERA (Kern-èra). Very closely related to *Cochlearia,* from which it is distinguished by its sharply curved rather than straight stamens, *Kernera* consists of one variable, or according to some botanists three or four more discretely defined species of the mustard family CRUCIFERAE. Native to the mountains of central and southern Europe, this genus was named in honor of Johann Simon von Kerner, Professor of Botany at Stuttgart, Germany, who died in 1830.

Kerneras are hardy herbaceous perennials with stalked basal leaves, short-stalked or stalkless stem leaves, and racemes of small flowers with four sepals, four petals that spread to form a cross, four long and two shorter stamens, and a short style with two stigmas. The fruits are small, plump pods containing two rows of seeds in each compartment.

From 4 inches to 1 foot tall, **K. saxatilis** is usually branched and has ovate-lanceolate to spatula-shaped, stalked basal leaves and alternate, lanceolate to ovate, more or less stalkless stem ones. The many-flowered racemes are borne in summer. Individual blooms are tiny and white-petaled. Kinds distinguished as *K. boissieri, K. decipiens,* and *K. auriculata* differ in minor detail and tend to intergrade with the species described.

Garden Uses and Cultivation. Although not of prime ornamental value, *K. saxatilis* and its variants may be worth modest accommodations in rock gardens. They respond to porous, not too dry soils in sunny places, and are easy to raise from seed.

KERRIA (Kér-ria). The only species of *Kerria* is not, as its specific name suggests, a native of Japan, although it is cultivated freely there. The true home of *K. japonica* is China. Europeans knew of the existence in Japan of the double-flowered variety as early as 1700, but it was more than a hundred years later before living specimens were brought to England. When botanists examined them, because the double blooms lacked the reproductive parts necessary to make an accurate diagnosis, they misinterpreted the affinities of the newcomer and, thinking it was allied to the lindens, named it *Corchorus japonicus.* Not until the single-flowered type bloomed two or three years after its introduction to Europe in 1834 was the error discovered. It was then realized that *Kerria* belonged in the rose family ROSACEAE, and it was properly described and named *K. japonica.* The generic name honors William Kerr, the English plant collector who first sent home the double-flowered variety. He died in 1814.

A deciduous shrub 5 to 6 feet in height, **K. japonica** has numerous slender green branches and pointed, ovate-lanceolate to oblong-ovate, double-toothed leaves 1½ to 4 inches long with parallel veins angled from the mid-veins. They are bright green

Kerria japonica

Kerria japonica aureo-variegata

and smooth above, hairy beneath, especially on the veins. The leaves on non-flowering shoots are conspicuously bigger than on those that bear blooms. The flowers are solitary and develop on short shoots that come from shoots of the previous year. Clear golden-yellow, they are 1¼ to 1¾ inches across and have usually five petals. The stamens are numerous, yellow, and about one-half as long as the petals. The fruits are small, brownish-black nutlike bodies. The most common variety is K. j. pleniflora, which has deep orange-yellow double flowers. The branchlets of K. j. aureo-vittata are attractively striped green and yellow, K. j. picta has leaves edged with white, and the leaves of K. j. aureo-variegata are margined with yellow.

Kerria japonica pleniflora

Garden and Landscape Uses. Kerrias are easy-to-grow, satisfactory general purpose shrubs for beds, foundation plantings, and lightly shaded places on the fringes of woodlands. The hardiest is the double-flowered variety, which survives New England winters, the others are slightly more tender to cold. All stand some shade and the single-flowered type and the variegated varieties are better for it. The double-flowered kind provides a display of flower color for a longer period than the others. All have

attractive green stems that add color to the winter landscape.

Cultivation. These are among the easiest of shrubs to grow. They thrive in any reasonably good, not excessively dry garden soil. Pruning to thin out over-crowded shoots should receive attention every two or three years after flowering, and old and much overcrowded specimens may be pruned back and thinned out severely in late winter. This procedure results in loss of some or all of the current season's bloom, but stimulates strong growth that blooms the next season. Following drastic pruning, fertilizing is advisable, and if long spells of dry weather prevail, generous watering is needed to encourage and sustain vigorous new growth.

KETELEERIA (Keteleèr-ia). Four to eight species of evergreen trees of eastern Asia belonging in the pine family PINACEAE are included in the genus *Keteleeria*. The exact number recognized depends upon interpretations of individual botanists. Two or three kinds only are known to have been cultivated. The name commemorates the Belgian-born French nurseryman Jean Baptiste Keteleer, who died in 1903.

Keteleerias are closely related to firs (*Abies*) and in gross appearance resemble that more familiar genus. They differ in having leaves that are flat or have a longitudinal ridge on their never grooved or channeled upper sides and in the scales of their cones being persistent and not breaking away. The undersides of the leaves of *Keteleeria* are paler than their upper surfaces and are never marked with distinct longitudinal lines of white.

Keteleerias are pyramidal when young, but tend to be flat-topped when old. Their branches are in whorls (tiers) and spread horizontally. The buds, not resinous, have many overlapping scales persistent at the bases of the new branchlets as sheaths. The linear leaves are glossy, on young trees usually sharp-pointed, but blunter on older ones. They are spirally arranged on the shoots, but are twisted at their

bases so that on all except leading shoots they appear to be in two ranks. As with firs their leaves when they fall leave smooth circular scars and not short, peg-like stumps as do leaves of spruces (*Picea*). Male cones are in terminal or lateral clusters, the females, borne on the same trees, are erect and ripen and bear seeds the first season. There are two seeds to each cone scale. The cone scales bend slightly inward at their tips.

The hardiest kind is **K. davidiana,** but even this cannot be expected to survive in climates sensibly more severe than that of coastal Virginia. A native of central and western China and Taiwan, its eventual height under favorable circumstances is about 100 feet, and it may develop a trunk 7½ feet in diameter. It has massive, wide-spreading branches and leaves about ⅙ inch wide up to 2½ inches long on young trees, not over 1½ inches long on more mature specimens. They are keeled on both surfaces. The fruiting cones are approximately cylindrical and 3 to 8 inches long. The phase of this species endemic to Taiwan is sometimes distinguished as K. d. formosana. Both it and the mainland trees are reported to be quite rare in their homelands. Eastern Chinese **K. fortunei** attains a height of 80 feet. It differs from K. davidiana in having young shoots that are orange-red rather than yellowish-gray and cone scales that bend outward at their tips.

Garden and Landscape Uses and Cultivation. In regions of comparatively mild winters these trees serve the same purposes and produce essentially the same effects as firs (*Abies*), which they closely resemble, except that in advanced age their tops broaden and flatten and assume more the form of cedars of Lebanon (*Cedrus libanii*). They have the advantage of withstanding drier soil and atmospheric conditions than firs, and also warmer summers. Otherwise their cultural needs are the same and they are propagated in the same manner. For more information see Conifers.

KEURTJIE is *Podalyria calyptrata.*

KHAT is *Catha edulis.*

KIBUSHI is *Stachyurus praecox.*

KICKXIA (Kíckx-ia)—Fluellen, Cancerwort. A group of thirty species closely allied to *Linaria*, and often included in it, composes the temperate Old World genus *Kickxia*, of the figwort family SCROPHULARIACEAE. The name commemorates Jean Kickx, a Belgian botanist, who died in 1831.

This genus consists of prostrate annuals with alternate, stalked, pinnately-veined leaves and, solitary, asymmetrical, tubular, spurred flowers from the axils of leaf-like bracts. The blooms are two-lipped and have a palate-like elevation closing their throats. They are not showy. The fruits are spherical or egg-shaped capsules. The kinds described here are naturalized in North America.

Densely-glandular-hairy and with ovate leaves ¾ inch to 1¼ inches across, *K. spuria*, of Europe, North Africa, and southwest Asia, has yellow blooms ⅓ to ½ inch long. They have ovate sepals and corollas with curved spurs, brownish-purple upper lips, and hairy stalks. Similar, but with its upper leaves with arrowhead-like spreading basal lobes, and differing in other details, *K. elatine*, of Europe and Asia, has blooms with pointed-lanceolate sepals and usually hairless stalks. Its flowers, approximately ⅓ inch long, are pale yellow with the throat and upper lip violet-purple. The spur formed by the base of the corolla tube is straight.

Garden Uses and Cultivation. Although without showy blooms, the neat and pleasing appearance of these plants suggests their use as temporary groundcovers for bare places in rock gardens and similar places. They can be used to cover areas where spring bulbs have died down. Both kinds described are satisfactory in sun or part-day shade. They are raised from seeds sown in spring where the plants are to remain. The seedlings should be thinned so that they stand about 6 inches apart.

KIDNEY-VETCH is *Anthyllis vulneraria*.

KIGELIA (Kigèl-ia)—Sausage Tree. This extraordinary genus of the bignonia family BIGNONIACEAE consists of one evergreen species, a native of tropical West Africa. Its name is an adaptation of its native one.

The sausage tree (*Kigelia pinnata*) is found in grassy plains and open country rather than forested areas and often is not more than 15 to 25 feet in height, although it sometimes attains twice the latter dimension. The leaves are of seven, nine, or eleven, oblong or obovate, leathery leaflets 3 to 6 inches long, and toothed or smooth-margined. Hairless above, they are sometimes slightly pubescent on their undersides. The flowers, which open at night, are bell-shaped, dull red, 3 to 4 inches long by 4 or 5 inches across, and rather unpleasantly scented. They are in long-stalked, pendulous, loose clusters. Each has a leathery, irregularly-lobed calyx, a two-lipped corolla with the lower lip down-turned, four three-lobed stamens in pairs, and a slender style terminated with a two-lobed stigma. The most striking feature is the fruits, which hang on cordlike stems up to several feet long. As the common name suggests, each looks like a giant sausage, or perhaps more closely resembles a cylindrical, blunt-ended gourd. They are hard-shelled, 1 foot to 1½ feet long, about one-quarter as wide, and contain a hard pulp and numerous seeds. The fruits, which remain dangling on the trees

Kigelia pinnata in Jamaica, West Indies

Kigelia pinnata (fruit)

Kigelia pinnata, fruits in greenhouses at the University of Michigan Botanic Garden, Ann Arbor, Michigan

for many months, are not edible, but are used in native medicines, and, it is said, for dyeing.

Garden and Landscape Uses. Only in humid tropical and near-tropical climates will this species thrive outdoors. Good examples grow near Miami, Florida and in Hawaii. It is also sometimes cultivated in tropical greenhouses. Its chief use is as a curiosity and to illustrate botanical instruction.

Cultivation. Given suitably warm and humid conditions no difficulties attend the cultivation of the sausage tree. In greenhouses a minimum night temperature of 60 to 70°F is satisfactory, and a rich, well-drained soil kept always evenly moist is appropriate. Some shade from direct summer sun should be provided. The plant stands pruning well and is easy to keep within reasonable bounds. It may be grown in large tubs, but is better planted out in the greenhouse in a ground bed. To ensure fruiting the flowers should be hand pollinated. Regular applications of dilute liquid fertilizer during the season of active growth are beneficial. Propagation is easy by seed sown in a temperature of 70 to 75°F.

KING-WILLIAM-PINE is *Athrotaxis selaginoides*.

KINGNUT is *Carya laciniosa*.

KINNIKINNICK is *Arctostaphylos uva-ursi*.

KIRCHARA. This is the name of multigeneric orchid hybrids the parents of which include *Cattleya*, *Epidendrum*, *Laelia*, and *Sophronitis*.

KIRENGESHOMA (Kireng-eshòma). The genus *Kirengeshoma*, of the saxifrage family SAXIFRAGACEAE, consists of one or possibly two species and is a rare native of mountain woods in Japan and Korea. The genus name is the same as its Japanese colloquial name, which means yellow *Anemonopsis macrophylla*, and alludes to *Kirengeshoma* looking something like *Anemonopsis*.

A deciduous herbaceous perennial, not reliably hardy in the vicinity of New York City, but surviving in slightly milder climates, *K. palmata* is vigorous, beautiful, and 3 to 4 feet tall. It has short, thick rhizomes and erect, smooth, purple stems. Its opposite, palmately-lobed and toothed, thin leaves, shaped much like those of the sycamore maple (*Acer pseudoplatanus*) and 4 to 8 inches in diameter, are slightly hairy. The lower ones are long-stalked,

Kirengeshoma palmata

but upward, the length of the stalks of successive leaves gradually diminishes until the topmost are stalkless. The stems end in open clusters of showy, waxy, bright yellow flowers, more or less nodding, bell-shaped, and about 1¾ inches across the mouth. There are usually three blooms on each pedicel (flower stalk), each with five petals, about fifteen stamens, and three or sometimes four styles.

Garden Uses. Best adapted for partially shaded locations in soil that contains abundant organic matter and never dries for long periods, this attractive Japanese is a choice item for flower borders, woodland gardens, and large rock gardens. It must have good light, but not strong unfiltered sun. It blooms late, in September and October and is a fitting companion for Japanese anemones.

Cultivation. Given suitable soil and location, no particular difficulties attend the growing of *Kirengeshoma*. Although not quite as hardy as Japanese anemones it responds to essentially the same culture as they. Planting should be done in spring, allowing about 2 feet between individuals. Propagation is by division in spring and by seed sown in sandy soil containing an abundance of leaf mold or peat moss and kept evenly moist.

KIRKOPHYTUM. See Stilbocarpa.

KITAIBELIA (Kitai-bèlia). There is only one species of *Kitaibelia*, of the mallow family MALVACEAE, native to damp thickets and meadows in southeastern Europe. The name commemorates Paul Kitaibel, who died in 1817; he was associated with the botanic garden at Pesth (Budapest).

A hardy herbaceous perennial, *K. viti-folia* is a vigorous species with sparingly-branched, roughly-white-hairy stems up to 9 feet tall. Its long-stalked, roundish, heart-shaped leaves have five or seven triangular, toothed lobes. Their grape-leaf-like blades, up to 7 inches in diameter, are slightly hairy, their stalks much more so. Borne in axillary clusters of up to four, or occasionally solitary, the flowers have false calyxes of six to nine bracts slightly joined at their bases, five-parted true calyxes, five white petals, obovate to triangular with their broad ends outward. The numerous stamens are joined into a column frayed at its top into many anther-tipped filaments. The style branches are threadlike. The blooms are about 4 inches in diameter.

Garden and Landscape Uses and Cultivation. Of somewhat coarse appearance, this plant is better suited for naturalistic effects in semiwild areas than for beds or borders in refined, sophisticated landscapes. It grows well in moistish, well-drained soil, and is increased by seed and by division.

KITAMBILLA is *Dovyalis hebecarpa*.

KITCHEN GARDEN. Less used than formerly, the term kitchen garden, as the name implies, alludes to an area of ground set aside to supply the needs of the kitchen. The chief crops grown in such a place are vegetables and salad crops, but herbs, small fruits, and sometimes even a few fruit trees may be included. See Vegetable Gardens.

KITCHINGIA. See Kalanchoe.

KIWI BERRY is *Actinidia chinensis.*

KLEINIA. See Senecio.

KLUGIA. See Rhynchoglossum.

KNAUTIA (Knaù-tia)—Field-Scabious or Blue Buttons. Closely allied to *Scabiosa*, from which it differs in the receptacles of its flowers being without bracts, but densely-hairy, *Knautia*, of the teasel family DIPSACACEAE, is little known to gardeners. It comprises fifty species of annuals and herbaceous perennials of Europe and temperate Asia. The name commemorates a German physician, Christoph Knaut, who died in 1716.

Knautias have opposite leaves. Their flowers are in dense, long-stalked heads dotted in pincushion fashion with projecting stamens. At the bottom of each head is an involucre (collar) of leafy bracts. The blooms that compose the heads are small. They have short-toothed calyxes, four-lobed, more or less asymmetrical, tubular corollas, four stamens, and one style. The fruits are achenes.

Field-scabious or blue buttons (*K. arvensis* syn. *Scabiosa arvensis*), a native of Europe and adjoining Asia, is naturalized in fields, roadsides, and waste places in northeastern North America. From 1½ to 3 feet tall or sometimes taller, it is a little-branched perennial with lanceolate leaves, the basal ones often without lobes, those above pinnately-lobed. The upper pairs of leaves are gradually reduced in size. The slightly domed, lilac-blue to sky-blue, scabious-like, delicately fragrant flower heads are ¾ inch to 1½ inches wide. Their outer flowers are distinctly bigger than the inner ones. This is a variable species of which European botanists recognize many varieties.

Garden and Landscape Uses and Cultivation. Although by no means without decorative appeal, the species above described is infrequently included in garden plantings. It is hardy and may be colonized in semiwild areas in sunny places in any ordinary well-drained soil. It is easily raised from seed.

KNAWEL. See Scleranthus.

KNIGHTIA (Knìght-ia)—Rewarewa. One species of *Knightia* endemic to the warmer

parts of New Zealand is planted in California and other mild regions, the other two, not known to be in cultivation, are indigenous to New Caledonia. The group belongs in the protea family PROTEACEAE. Its name honors an English horticulturist, Thomas A. Knight, who died in 1838. The wood of *K. excelsa* is esteemed for cabinet work.

Knightias are closely allied to *Persoonia*, but differ in their fruits. They are evergreen trees or shrubs with alternate leaves and unisexual, symmetrical, small flowers with cylindrical perianths of four segments that separate and become spirally twisted. The styles are persistent. The blooms, on paired stalks, are in racemes. Contained in leathery, podlike follicles, the seeds are winged.

A tree sometimes exceeding 90 feet in height, **K. excelsa** is called rewarewa and sometimes New-Zealand-honeysuckle. It has upright branches and in outline strongly suggests a Lombardy poplar. Its shoots are angled and clothed with rusty down. As is true of many New Zealanders, its leaves vary at different stages of the plants' development. Those of juvenile trees are much thinner than adult-type foliage. They are linear-lanceolate, sharply-toothed, up to 1 foot long, and occasionally forked. Adult foliage is rigid, thick, and leathery. At this stage the leaves are 4 to 6, rarely 8, inches long and 1 inch to 1½ inches wide. They are stalked, oblong to ovate-oblong, and occasionally forked. Their margins are round-toothed. The stout, cone-shaped or cylindrical racemes, 2 to 4 inches long, have rusty, hairy stalks and are crowded with red flowers 1 inch to 1½ inches long. In the bud stage the flower clusters resemble velvety bottle brushes. They open by splitting into four parts from the top down, very gradually at first, then explosively, with the segments rolling backward and becoming coiled. The hairy, narrow seed pods are 1¼ to 1½ inches long and contain four seeds.

Garden and Landscape Uses and Cultivation. Like other tall trees of slender outline and exclamation-point slimness, the rewarewa is excellent for emphasizing vertical lines. It can be used to good effect near tall buildings and in avenues. In suitable surroundings it is also effective planted rather closely together in groups of several. It is adapted to frostless and nearly frostless, subtropical climates and is responsive to ordinary locations and soils. Propagation is by seed and by cuttings.

KNIPHOFIA (Knip-hòfia)—Poker Plant, Red Hot Poker, Torch-Lily. A German professor of medicine much interested in botany, who died in 1763, Johannes Hieronymus Kniphof, is commemorated by the name of this genus of seventy species of the lily family LILIACEAE. Except for one species in Madagascar and one in Arabia, *Kniphofia*, which was at one time named *Tritoma*, is restricted in the wild to eastern and southern Africa. The species discussed here are natives of those regions.

From closely related *Aloe* kniphofias are readily distinguished by their foliage not being fleshy. They are stout, herbaceous perennials with thick rhizomes, cordlike, fleshy roots, and deciduous or evergreen, prevailingly grasslike to sword-shaped leaves. A few kinds develop aerial stems, most do not. The majority are clump-forming, others have more or less solitary leaf clusters. The leaves are long, tapering, and generally narrow. Those of most kinds are keeled and have their upper surfaces channeled. Commonly they bend sharply downward at or below their middles, rarely they are erect. The spreading to pendulous, tubular flowers are in dense or rather loose spikelike racemes atop stout, erect, usually branchless stalks naked of leaves except for a few bracts. The blooms are cylindrical to narrowly-funnel-shaped. They have six-lobed perianths with the lobes (petals) much shorter than the tubes. The six stamens, three of which are shorter than the others, are as long or longer than the perianths. The style is slender. The blooms are generally yellow to brownish or red, more rarely white. Commonly, but not invariably, the buds and younger flowers at the tops of the racemes are more richly colored than those below, which gives reason for the names poker plant, red hot poker, and torch-lily. The fruits are ovoid, often three-angled capsules. Both in the wild and in cultivation hybrids are of frequent occurrence, and some of these are among the most splendid of flower garden ornamentals.

Variable **K. uvaria** forms crowded clumps of deciduous, tough, fibrous leaves 2 to 3½ feet long by up to 1 inch wide. The showy, typical red-hot-poker-like cylindrical to somewhat globose racemes are on stalks 1½ to 4 feet tall. The flowers are 1 inch to 2 inches long, their stamens not or only slightly protruding. The buds and younger flowers are brilliant

Kniphofia uvaria

Kniphofia uvaria, garden variety

Kniphofia uvaria nobilis

scarlet to greenish suffused with red. The older blooms are orange-yellow to greenish-yellow. Stouter and taller than the typical species, *K. u. maxima* (syn. *K. u. grandis*) has longer spikes of larger blooms. Variety *K. u. nobilis*, up to 6 feet tall, has leaves up to 3 feet long and red flowers that gradually change to orange.

Closely allied to *K. uvaria* but more robust, **K. linearifolia** has softer, deciduous foliage, and on stalks 2½ to 5 feet tall, larger racemes of bloom. Another close ally, also with comparatively soft, deciduous leaves is robust **K. rooperi**. This has flowers with individual shorter stalks, in more globular racemes than those of either *K. uvaria* or *K. linearifolia*. Another ally of *K. uvaria* much like *K. linearifolia* is **K. tysonii**. The most obvious differences are its proportionately longer racemes of shorter-stalked, shorter flowers that usually are orange-red, opening to yellow. A fourth species related to *K. uvaria*, that in the wild blends with it, is much smaller **K. citrina**. Its flowers, in bud red or yellow tipped with red, when older are yellow or greenish-yellow. They are from a little under to a little over 1 inch long and in racemes 2 inches or so long on stalks up to 2 feet tall. The stamens protrude slightly. Sometimes confused with *K. uvaria* and *K. linearifolia*, and like them with large, showy, red-hot-poker-type racemes, robust

K. praecox differs chiefly in the stalks of its individual blooms being longer, and in the tiny bracts in the axils of which the flowers come being long and pointed instead of oblong with rounded or blunt ends.

Robust and with glaucous, sword-shaped, usually toothed leaves 1½ to 4 feet long by ¾ inch to nearly 1½ inches wide and flower stalks 2 to 4 feet tall, **K. ensifolia** has very dense, slightly tapering, cylindrical racemes, 4 to 8 inches in length, of pendulous, narrowly-funnel-shaped flowers up to ¾ inch long that are greenish-white to yellowish when open, reddish in bud. The name *K. tuckii* applies to a richly colored variant of *K. ensifolia* not considered sufficiently distinct to warrant ranking it as a separate species. Related **K. splendida** differs from *K. ensifolia* in having leaves no more and often less than ¾ inch wide and flowers more highly colored, and in blooming later.

With distinctly glaucous, soft foliage, **K. sarmentosa** grows in its homeland beside mountain streams. First discovered and sent to Europe in 1789, it was not again found wild for almost 140 years. Its toothless leaves are 1 foot to 2 feet long and up to a little over 1 inch wide. The flower spikes, ovoid, conical, or subcylindrical, are at first very dense, but loosen as they age. They are up to 1 foot long. The flower buds, coral to coral-scarlet, open into pendulous to salmon-buff blooms ¾ to 1 inch in length. The stamens protrude sightly. Closely related **K. coralligemma**, an inhabitant of marshy places and moist soils, differs in having longer, less glaucous leaves toothed toward their apexes. Its flowers are coral-pink in bud and creamy-white when open, orange-scarlet in bud opening to orange-yellow, or orange-yellow in bud and pale yellow later. Grayish-green leaves 1 foot to 1½ feet long, and about ½ inch wide, and with rough margins are characteristic of **K. pumila**. Its crowded spikes of flowers, 3 to 6 inches long, are on stalks that lift them to heights of 2 to 3

Kniphofia pumila

Justicia candicans, orange-red-flowered form

Juniperus scopulorum 'Gray Gleam'

Kerria japonica pleniflora

Kalanchoe pumila

Kalmia angustifolia

Ornamental kale

Kolkwitzia amabilis

Kniphofia uvaria variety

Kochia scoparia trichophylla

Koelreuteria paniculata (flowers)

Kalmia latifolia fuscata

feet. The lower blooms of each spike are yellow, the immature upper ones coral-red. Their stamens protrude.

Narrow, grasslike leaves are characteristic of K. macowanii (syns. K. triangularis, K. nelsonii), K. rufa, and K. galpinii. Variable, graceful K. macowanii has solitary or small groups of clusters of leaves 1 foot to 2 feet long, triangular in cross section or flatter, up to 1/3 inch broad, and sometimes with toothed margins. The drooping flowers, 1 inch to 1¼ inches long, topping stalks approximately as long as the leaves, are crowded in cylindrical to egg-shaped racemes 2 to 3½ inches in length. They are of nearly uniform color, from coral-red to orange-yellow. The lobes of the perianths are usually somewhat spreading. The stamens and styles protrude. From this K. rufa differs in its very much looser racemes, 4 to 10 inches long, of drooping flowers that overtop the foliage. The blooms, ¾ inch to 1¼ inches long, are cream-colored, yellow, or coral-red and have included or sightly protruding stamens. Differing from K. macowanii in its flowers changing markedly from flame-red in bud to orange-yellow as they open, K. galpinii has flowers with nonspreading perianth lobes.

Kniphofia macowanii

Two of the few species that as they age develop aboveground trunklike stems are K. caulescens and K. northiae. The stems of K. caulescens become 1 foot to 2 feet tall, those of K. northiae may attain an impressive 3 feet or more. The biggest leaves of the evergreen rosettes of K. caulescens, a high mountain plant that favors marshy, peaty soils, 1½ to 2½ feet long by 1 inch to 2 inches wide, are V-shaped in cross section, and tapering. Those of K. northiae, an inhabitant of drier mountain sites, form a handsome, evergreen, aloe-like rosette. They are tapered, recurved, broadly U-shaped to V-shaped in section, and up to 4½ feet long by 2½ to 4½ inches broad. The stout flower stalks of K. caulescens are 1 foot to 2 feet long. The dense racemes,

up to 1 foot long, are of flowers pink to flame-colored in bud, greenish or creamy-yellow when expanded. They are slightly under 1 inch long and have long-protruding stamens. The flower stalks of K. northiae are up to 1 foot in length. The very dense racemes that terminate them are nearly as long and resemble those of K. caulescens. The flowers, from a little under to somewhat over 1 inch in length, may be pinkish in bud and open almost white, or orange-red in the bud stage and yellow when expanded. The stamens protrude conspicuously.

Garden and Landscape Uses. Poker plants are striking and handsome summer- and fall-flowering garden ornamentals, especially well suited for perennial borders and similar places. They associate pleasingly with such architectural features as steps, terraces, and buildings, and revel in full sun. The flowers are excellent for cutting. These plants appreciate deep, fertile, well-drained soil, preferably of a sandy character, that does not dry excessively from spring to fall. Unfortunately poker plants are not as hardy as might be wished, and north of New York City even the hardiest cannot be depended upon to survive outdoors. Where winters are severe it is important to select sheltered locations for them and to protect the plants over winter with a substantial covering of cut branches of evergreens, salt hay, or other suitable material. Some gardeners dig the plants up in fall and store them with moist soil packed about their roots in a cool cellar or similar place, and replant them in spring, but because poker plants are rather intolerant of root disturbance this has disadvantages.

Cultivation. Given suitable locations and soils, little difficulty attends the cultivation of poker plants. As it is unwise to disturb their roots, they should not be transplanted more often than necessary. Spring is the best time to do this, and at that season, too, the plants may be divided. It is important not to allow the roots to dry while they are out of the ground. An annual spring application of a complete fertilizer is beneficial. Seed affords an alternative to division as a means of securing increase.

KNOB CELERY. See Celeriac, Knob Celery, or Turnip-Rooted Celery.

KNOCKAWAY is *Ehretia anacua*.

KNOT GARDENS. Once popular, especially in medieval and Renaissance Europe, but no longer seen except in gardens of historical interest and sometimes as features in herb gardens, knot gardens are geometrically arranged small beds separated by edgings of low, shrubby plants such as dwarf boxwood, lavender-cotton, and germander, often intricately crossed

A knot garden of herbs at the Brooklyn Botanic Garden

and intertwined to form a dominant pattern. The edgings are kept formally clipped and are higher than the low plants set in the beds. Sometimes instead of being planted, the beds are surfaced with different colored stones or pebbles.

KNOTROOT. This is a name for the Chinese artichoke. See Artichoke, Chinese or Japanese.

KNOTWEED. See Polygonum.

KOA is *Acacia koa*.

KOCHIA (Kòch-ia) — Summer-Cypress, Belvedere, Burning Bush. The genus *Kochia* consists of about ninety species of annual and perennial herbaceous plants and low shrubs, chiefly natives of the Old World, but represented in the natural flora of western North America. It belongs in the goosefoot family CHENOPODIACEAE. Its name commemorates the German botanist Wilhelm Daniel Josef Koch, who died in 1849.

Kochias have slender, opposite or alternate, undivided leaves and inconspicuous small flowers, solitary or clustered in the leaf axils, each with a five-lobed calyx, five stamens, and two stigmas. The fruits are utricles.

The only sort cultivated at all widely is the annual summer-cypress, belvedere, or burning bush (K. scoparia trichophylla syn. K. s. culta). The last of these common names, which is applied also to *Dictamnus fraxinella* and sometimes to *Euonymus alatus*, alludes to the brilliant color assumed by the foliage in late summer and fall. The species K. scoparia, much less commonly grown than its variety, attains a height of 5 feet and is much branched. It has leaves up to 2 inches long. Variety K. s. trichophylla is dense and egg-shaped, with a decidedly formal outline. About 2 feet in height, it forms a mass of fine, soft green foliage that in late summer becomes first purplish and finally brilliant crimson and remains attractive for a long time. A native of Europe and Asia, K. scoparia is naturalized in some parts of North America. Less

Kochia scoparia trichophylla

Kochia scoparia trichophylla with an underplanting of lantanas

ornamental **K. hyssopifolia** is an annual 1½ feet tall, with oblong-linear leaves up to 4 inches long. This is native to southern Europe and western Asia.

Garden Uses. Kochias are cultivated for their foliage effects. Especially appreciated for its very formal aspect, *K. s. trichophylla* is grown in flower gardens largely because of this. Often it is employed in ribbon beds or rows edging paths or other garden features. It is also a good plant for window boxes and porch boxes and for use in urns, tubs, and other decorative containers.

Cultivation. No annuals are easier to grow than these. They may be raised from seeds sown outdoors as soon as the ground is warm in spring and the seedlings transplanted to where they are to remain or, and this is the more usual procedure, seeds may be sown indoors early and the seedlings transplanted to flats or individually to small pots and set in their flower garden quarters after the weather is warm and settled, at about the time that tomatoes and peppers are planted out. They may be spaced 8 inches to 2 feet apart, the former if a continuous hedgelike effect is desired, the wider spacing if the plants are to stand as separate individuals. When seeding is done early indoors the seeds should be sown about eight weeks before the young plants

are to be set outdoors. Kochias prefer light, fertile, well-drained soil. Usually they stand without support, but in exposed locations a single light cane stake to each plant may be helpful. When grown in containers an occasional application of dilute liquid fertilizer during the summer promotes good growth.

KOELERIA (Koel-èria)—Crested Hair Grass. Between twenty and thirty species of annual and perennial grasses that inhabit temperate parts of North America, Europe, Asia, and mountains in tropical Africa belong in *Koeleria*, of the grass family GRAMINEAE. A few are cultivated as ornamentals. The name commemorates the German botanist G. L. Koeler, who died in 1807.

Koelerias are tufted and have slim, erect stems and usually very slender leaf blades. The flowers are in dense, lustrous, spikelike, lobed or interrupted panicles. The short-stalked, flattened spikelets have two to eight flowers and are sometimes bristletipped.

Crested hair grass (**K. cristata**) occurs as a native in North America, Europe, and Asia. Up to 2 feet in height, it has leaf blades that may attain 1 foot in length by up to ¼ inch in width. The erect, silvery flower panicles are up to 6 inches in length. This is perennial and hardy. Other perennial sorts include *K. glauca*, native from central Europe to Siberia, and *K. reuteri*, of France. With stems up to 2 feet tall, **K. glauca** has swollen bases, and short, flat or inrolled leaf blades, glaucous on their upper surfaces, hairy below. The spikelets are up to ¼ inch long. Up to 1 foot tall, **K. reuteri** (syn. *K. brevifolia*) has leaf blades up to 1¼ inches long, rolled lengthwise and very slender. The whitish-green to purplish flower panicles are up to 1½ inches long.

Annual **K. pheloides**, of the Mediterranean region, is naturalized in California. In loose tufts or solitary, its stems are 1 foot to 1½ feet tall. The flat, usually hairy leaf blades are up to 6 inches long and not over ¼ inch wide. The very dense flower panicles, cylindrical or lobed, are up to 4 inches in length.

Garden Uses and Cultivation. Adaptable for the fronts of flower borders and for fresh and dry arrangements, these grasses are of the easiest culture. They thrive in ordinary well-drained ground in sunny locations and do especially well in limestone soils. The annual kind is propagated by sowing seeds in spring where the plants are to remain and thinning the seedlings sufficiently to prevent overcrowding. The perennials are easily increased by division in spring or early fall and by seed.

KOELLIKERIA (Koellik-èria). Named after Rudolf Albrecht von Koelliker, botanist and professor of anatomy in Bavaria, who died in 1905, this genus of three species

belongs in the gesneria family GESNERIACEAE. Confined in the wild to northern South America, it has the distinction among those members of its family that have scaly rhizomes of having flowers in raceme-type clusters with markedly-two-lobed corollas. The genus is related to *Kohleria* and has been hybridized with it to produce *Koellikohleria*.

The only species cultivated, **Koellikeria erinoides** is a low herbaceous plant with rosettes of African-violet-like, broad-elliptic to ovate, dark green leaves flecked with white, and with reddish veins and pink under surfaces. They are 1 inch to 2½ inches long by two-thirds as broad. From the axils of the upper leaves or terminal on the stems are produced racemes of flowers to a height of about 1 foot. The blooms are about ½ inch long and have the upper sides of the corolla tubes deep pink or red and the undersides white. The upper corolla lobes (petals) form a small lip, the lower lobe a larger, fringed one that juts forward. There are four united stamens. The fruits are capsules.

Koellikeria erinoides

Garden Uses and Cultivation. A quite pretty little plant for inclusion in collections of gesneriads, *K. erinoides* grows well in a humid atmosphere where the minimum night temperature is 60°F and daytime levels are ten to fifteen degrees higher. Shade from strong sun is needed and a coarse, fertile, freely drained soil that contains abundant organic matter. Except when the plants are resting the soil must be alway fairly moist, and even when dormant the small rhizomes must not be allowed to dry completely. Then it is expedient to store them in a polyethylene plastic bag or mixed with peat moss, in a temperature of 55 to 60°F. Propagation is easy by seed, tubers, and leaf cuttings. For further information see Gesneriads.

KOELLIKOHLERIA (Koelli-kohlèria). The name of this hybrid genus of the gesneria family GESNERIACEAE is constructed from parts of those of its parent genera. The first such hybrid *Koellikohleria rosea*, raised at Cornell University, was described in 1968. Its parents were *Koellikeria erinoides* and *Kohleria spicata*.

This hybrid (*K. rosea*), which more closely resembles *Koellikeria* than its other parent, differs from *Koellikeria erinoides* in having much larger flowers with usually more than one from each bract of the flower spike. It has scaly, white rhizomes and is a softly-hairy, short-stemmed plant with crowded, opposite, broadly-ovate to obovate leaves 1½ to 5 inches long, with round-toothed margins. The upper leaf surfaces are dark green without the white spots characteristic of those of *Koellikeria erinoides*. The undersides are pale green to purplish. The narrow, panicle-like clusters, about 4 inches long, are carried on erect stems to a height of about 1 foot. The short-stalked, tubular flowers, intermediate between those of the parents, are about ½ inch long. The upper sides of their corolla tubes are deep red, beneath they are whitish. There are five spreading lobes (petals), the lowermost is jagged-toothed and forward-pointing. Across their faces the flowers measure rather less than ½ inch. There are four stamens and a slender style with glandular hairs.

Garden Uses and Cultivation. This hybrid has promise as an interesting addition to the many members of the gesneria family that find favor with cultivators of greenhouse and house plants. It grows without any dormant period and responds to conditions that suit *Koellikeria*. Propagation is by rhizomes, division, and leaf cuttings. For additional information see Gesneriads.

KOELREUTERIA (Koelreutèr-ia) — Golden-Rain Tree. Three species of deciduous trees constitute *Koelreuteria*, of the soapberry family SAPINDACEAE. Native to China, Taiwan, and Fiji, this genus has a name that commemorates Joseph Gottlieb Koelreuter, Professor of Natural History at Karlsruhe, who died in 1806.

Koelreuterias are round-headed trees with sometimes more than one trunk and alternate, stalked, pinnate or bipinnate leaves with toothed or rarely toothless leaflets. Their small, yellow, asymmetrical flowers in large, pyramidal, terminal panicles have unequally-five-lobed calyxes and four, five, or occasionally six petals with two upturned appendages at the base of each. The usually eight, sometimes fewer stamens have long stalks, hairy especially in their lower halves. The style is three-cleft. There are three stigmas. The fruits, conspicuous in late summer and fall, are large papery, bladder-like capsules each containing three or four black seeds. In China the seeds of the golden-rain tree are used for necklaces and its flowers are employed medicinally and as a source of a yellow dye. In Fiji the leaves of *K. elegans*

are boiled to produce a black hair dye. The golden-rain tree is prominently featured in public and private plantings in New Harmony, Indiana, where each summer, when the trees are in bloom, the Raintree Festival is held.

Golden-rain tree (*K. paniculata*) is best known. A native of China and naturalized in Korea and Japan, it is up to 40 feet tall and in cultivation it is generally much lower and often broader than high. The hardiest species, it lives outdoors as far north as Massachusetts, but there it is sometimes injured in severe winters. It thrives in the Ohio valley and other parts of the Middle West where hot dry summers prevail. Pinnate or sometimes partly bipinnate, the leaves of the golden-rain tree, up to 1½ feet long, consist of seven to fifteen leaflets coarsely-irregularly-toothed and at their bases often lobed. Both surfaces are hairless or are minutely-hairy along the veins. The slightly fragrant flowers, about ⅓ inch wide and with tiny red-orange centers, are in loose, broad panicles up to 1¼ feet long. At their best in June and July, they are succeeded by quite decorative nodding fruits. More or less ovoid and three-angled, these have three heart-shaped sides and gradually narrow to a short-pointed apex. They

Koelreuteria paniculata

Koelreuteria paniculata (bark)

Koelreuteria paniculata (flowers)

Koelreuteria paniculata (fruits)

are 1½ to 2 inches long and at first pale green, but as they ripen they gradually change to pinkish-tan and finally to light brown. Blooming four or five weeks later than the typical species, *K. p.* 'September' is otherwise identical. Variety *K. p. fastigiata*, narrowly-columnar, has erect branches.

Not hardy in the North, **K. bipinnata** (syn. *K. integrifolia*), a native of China, is reported to attain a maximum height of about 65 feet, but more usually to be about 45 feet tall. Its always bipinnate leaves, up to about 1 foot long, have toothless or shallowly-toothed leaflets pubescent on the veins and midribs beneath. The flowers, similar in aspect to those of the golden-rain tree have usually only four petals. The fruits are like those of the golden-rain tree.

An endemic at low altitudes in Taiwan, **K. elegans formosana** (syn. *K. formosana*) is a variant of a species native in Java and attains a height of about 50 feet. Its bipinnate leaves 1 foot to 2 feet long each have nine to eleven subdivisions of five to fifteen long-pointed, toothed leaflets hairless on both surfaces. The small yellow flowers in hairless panicles up to 10 inches long are followed by pinkish or orange-pinkish capsules nearly 2 inches long. This is planted in Hawaii.

Koelreuteria elegans formosana, Fairchild Tropical Garden, Miami, Florida

Garden and Landscape Uses. If for no other reason, the golden-rain tree would be well worth growing as the only yellow-flowered tree excepting *Laburnum* hardy in the northeastern United States. The fact that it blooms in high summer when so few trees are in flower adds to its charm. Well adapted for small- and medium-sized properties, it is tolerant of city conditions and poor and dry soils, which should commend it to those faced with such conditions. Although it has been much employed in some parts of the United States as a street tree, its weak branches and comparatively short life limit its usefulness.

Cultivation. The golden-rain tree revels in hot, sunny locations and is not particular as to soil provided it is well drained. It transplants without difficulty, requires no regular pruning, and is rather intolerant of any severe cutting back. When raised from seed differences in growth habit may be noticeable. Some seedlings seem not to respond well to having their lower limbs removed to produce clear, high trunks, advantageous with street trees, whereas others can be trained in this way with conspicuous success. Propagation is very easy by seed sown in fall or stratified and sown in spring. Self-sown seedlings are likely to spring up around older trees. The golden-rain tree is also easily increased by root cuttings, and this method should be followed when especially desirable forms are to be multiplied.

Diseases. These trees are occasionally affected by a leaf spot disease, a wilt disease, a root rot, and a canker. They are remarkably free of pests.

KOHEKOHE is *Dysoxylum spectabile*.

KOHLERIA (Koh-lèria). This is the correct name of a group of fifty species of the gesneria family GESNERIACEAE, natives from Mexico to northern South America and Trinidad. The designation commemorates Michael Kohler, a nineteenth-century instructor in natural history at Zurich, Swit-

zerland. The names *Isoloma* and *Tydaea* sometimes applied to species and hybrids of *Kohleria* are obsolete.

Kohlerias are nonhardy herbaceous perennials and subshrubs with hairy, sometimes branched stems from about 9 inches to 4 feet tall or taller. They have scaly, more or less caterpillar-like rhizomes. Their undivided leaves, generally hairy, are in opposite or in whorls (circles) of three or four. Their blades are from 2 to 5 inches long. The blooms are solitary in the leaf axils or are in terminal clusters or raceme- or panicle-like arrangements. The corollas are tubular, generally contracted at the base and top of the tube. They are hairy and have five lobes (petals), unequal or spreading to form a somewhat two-lipped, small to quite large face to the bloom. The upper two petals are smaller than the others and may be reflexed. Corolla colors range from orange to rose-pink and red to lavender and white and various mixtures of these. There are four stamens, their anthers united to form a square, and one style with a two-lobed or mouth-shaped stigma. The fruits are capsules.

Species kohlerias are less commonly cultivated than the numerous splendid horticultural varieties and hybrids derived from them. Here are descriptions of those sometimes grown or that have played parental roles in the development of hybrid kohlerias: *K. allenii* is a hairy species with stout stems and large lanceolate leaves. Its flowers have a hairy, inflated, red corolla tube 1½ inches long and small, spreading, red-spotted, yellow corolla lobes (petals).

Kohleria allenii

K. amabilis (syns. *Isoloma amabile, Tydaea amabilis*) is a handsome native of Colombia. It has been misnamed *K. seemannii*. This has weak stems up to 2 feet long, beautiful scalloped-margined, ovate, hairy, dark green leaves, along the veins patterned with purplish-brown and sometimes silvery markings. From ¾ to 1 inch long, the long-stalked, bright pink flowers, abundantly spotted with red or purple, are solitary or few together from the leaf axils.

Kohleria amabilis

They are white-hairy on their outsides. Their tubes are swollen toward their tops along their undersides. The stigma is two-lobed. *K. bogotensis* is sometimes misnamed *K. picta* (syn. *Isoloma pictum*). These names are not synonyms of *K. bogotensis*, but identify a species perhaps not in cultivation, *K. rubiflora*. Native to Colombia, *K. bogotensis* is erect and up to 2 feet tall. Its stems are stiffer than those of *K. amabilis*. Sometimes they branch above. Velvety and with ovate blades, the softly-hairy leaves have toothed margins. They are green, or sometimes the older ones brownish, with paler green or whitish featherings along the veins. They do not have a conspicuous fringe of hairs. The 1-inch-long, solitary or paired, slightly two-lipped, somewhat nodding blooms have 2-inch-long stalks. Their corolla tubes are red above merging to yellow on their undersides. The upper petals are red with darker markings, the lower ones, like the insides of the tubes, are yellow dotted and penciled with red. The stigma is two-lobed. *K. digitaliflora* is robust and up to 2 feet tall or taller. This has softly-hairy, elliptic-lanceolate to elliptic-ovate, plain green leaves. Its flowers, of unusual color for the genus, are in clusters of up to six or sometimes are solitary from the axils of the upper leaves. They have woolly calyxes with backward-reaching lobes. The corolla tube, slightly swollen at the base and along the lower side, expands upward. It is 1 inch to 1¼ inches long, on the outside woolly-white-hairy flushed with pink. The tiny petals are green, finely spotted with purple. The stigma is mouth-shaped. *K. eriantha* (syn. *Isoloma erianthum*), of Colombia, has been wrongly identified in gardens as *K. hirsutum* (syn. *Isoloma hirsutum*), which names belong to another species. Attaining heights up to 4 feet and in the wild often shrubby, *K. eriantha* has stout, densely-hairy stems and softly-hairy, scalloped-margined, thickish, elliptic leaves conspicuously fringed with red hairs. The woolly-hairy, nodding, brick-red flowers, their lower petals spotted with yellow, are soli-

Kohleria digitaliflora

Kohleria eriantha

Kohleria eriantha (flowers)

tary or more usually in threes or fours on red, 4-inch-long stalks. From 1½ to 2 inches long, they have tubes that expand nearly evenly from bottom to top. The petals are small. The stigma is two-lobed. **K. lindeniana** somewhat resembles *K. amabilis,* but differs in having stems usually not over 1 foot long and green leaves with brown

margins and pale or silvery veins, and also in the flowers being white with a blotch of lavender-violet at the throat and on the bottoms of the two lower petals and a band of the same color across the upper petals. **K. ocellata,** of Colombia, is distinguishable by its lustrous, sharply-toothed, ovate leaves having notably wrinkled upper surfaces with short, stiff hairs lying parallel to them. The somewhat woody, up to 2-foot-tall stems are similarly hairy. The hairy flowers, ¾ inch long, are solitary or few together from the leaf axils. Bright red, they have tiny petals with black, red, yellow, and white spots and markings. **K. spicata,** native from Mexico to northern South America, differs from other species discussed here in having its blooms, solitary in twos or threes, on stalks not more than twice the length of the corolla, arising from the axils of much reduced leaves or bracts and crowded in terminal racemes. They are

Kohleria spicata

brick-red, ¾ inch long, and spotted on the lower petals with orange-yellow. The stigma is two-lobed. This kohleria has been confused with *K. strigosa,* a kind perhaps not in cultivation. *K. spicata* has stout stems up to 4½ feet tall, and pointed, elliptic to elliptic-lanceolate leaves, opposite or in circles of three. **K. tubiflora,** of Colombia, is 1 foot to 2 feet tall and densely-hairy. Opposite or in whorls of three, its pointed, elliptic to ovate leaves are green with the veins on their undersides reddish. Crowded near the tops of the stems, the yellow-tipped, scarlet flowers have a pubescent corolla strongly constricted at the mouth and with a row of purplish-red dots outlining the tiny, spreading lobes.

Hybrids and horticultural varieties are more plentiful in gardens than natural species. Often their parentage is not fully known, but not infrequently the identity of one parent is or can be deduced. Hybrids that show a strong influence of *K. amabilis* are grouped as "Amabilis Hybrids." In general they resemble *K. amabilis,* but have less strongly patterned foliage and blooms with

Kohleria tubiflora

an infusion of white, yellow, or deep red. The "Bogotensis Hybrids" closely resemble their one known parent, *K. bogotensis.* They differ chiefly in their more slender leaves not having pale veins and often assuming brown tones and in the red and yellow zones of their flowers being less clearly defined. The term "Sciadotydaea Hybrids" is applied to kinds in which the *K. digitaliflora* or *K. warszewiczii* influence is most strongly marked. They share with those species a vigorous growth. The usually numerous flowers have rose-pink, red, or violet corolla tubes and petals maroon, rose-pink with blackish or maroon dots, or green spotted with purple. The "Eriantha Hybrids" are kohlerias with elements of *K. eriantha* strongly evident in their appearance. From that species they differ most particularly in the swelling of the corolla tube of their flowers being more exaggerated and in having larger, varicolored, spreading petals. Attractive *K.* 'Longwood' was introduced to the United States by Longwood Gardens, Kennett Square, Pennsylvania from the University Botanical Gardens, Coimbra, Portugal. Of unknown provenance, this vigorous sort is up to 3 feet tall. It has broad-ovate to broad-elliptic leaves and large, bright red flowers with prominent, spreading, densely-red-spotted, white petals.

Kohleria 'Longwood'

Garden and Landscape Uses. Among kohleria species and hybrids are some of the most attractive cultivated gesneriads adaptable for outdoor cultivation in reasonably humid tropical and subtropical climates and for greenhouses. Some amateur gardeners attain tolerable success with them as houseplants, especially under artificial light. Those with weak stems are highly satisfactory in hanging baskets, the others in pots.

Cultivation. Kohlerias are easy to satisfy. They respond well to environments that suit the florists' gloxinia and *Achimenes*. Like the latter their scaly rhizomes afford ready means of increase. They may be multiplied also by cuttings and seed. Unlike achimenes, which in growth habit they otherwise resemble, kohlerias do not die down entirely during their winter season of rest; therefore the soil should not be permitted to dry completely then. Instead, watering should be greatly reduced, only enough water being given to prevent desiccation. At that time, too, provide cooler conditions than when the plants are growing. A temperature of 55°F is adequate. Rhizomes are normally started into growth in late winter or spring. To do this shake them free of all old soil and plant them in fresh earth. Use a mix containing an abundance of organic matter, such as leaf mold or coarse peat moss, and be sure it is coarse-textured so that water drains through it freely and air is admitted. In addition to the organic matter, use some fertile top soil, coarse sand, grit, or perlite, a generous dash of dried cow manure, and perhaps some crushed charcoal. Start the rhizomes in flats or small pots. Later transplant them to 4-inch pots and successively to larger ones as growth makes necessary. Throughout the growing season kohlerias appreciate a humid atmosphere, a minimum night temperature of 70°F rising five to fifteen degrees or more by day, and just sufficient shade to prevent the foliage from becoming yellowed or scorched. Water sufficiently to keep the soil always moderately moist, not constantly saturated. When the final pots are filled with roots apply dilute liquid fertilizer at weekly or biweekly intervals. When flowering is over gradually reduce the water supply by increasing the periods between applications until the rest period procedure is established. For further information see Gesneriads.

KOHLRABI. Kohlrabi looks much like and has similar uses to ordinary turnips and is grown in about the same way. Unlike turnips it grows satisfactorily in hot as well as cool weather and so can be harvested in summer in regions where it is too hot for turnips. Botanically *Brassica caulorapa*, of the mustard family CRUCIFERAE, the precise nativity of its ancestral stock is not known, but undoubtedly is Old World.

Kohlrabi

The edible, nearly globular, tuberous stems, produced a little above ground level, have leaves sprouting from their sides as well as tops. Good varieties are "Prague Special', 'Purple Vienna', 'Triumph of Prague', and 'White Vienna'.

Soil preparation is as for cabbage. Sow seeds thinly outdoors in rows 1¼ to 1½ feet apart as early in spring as the ground can be gotten into condition. To provide succession, follow this first sowing with others at intervals of two to three weeks. Make the last sowing eight to ten weeks before the expected date of the first fall frost. Cover the seeds to a depth of about ½ inch. Thin the seedlings so the plants left stand 4 to 6 inches apart. If the young thinnings are transplanted they will mature about a week later than those left undisturbed. A light application of nitrate of soda, urea, or other quickly available nitrogenous fertilizer made about a week after thinning promotes desirable rapid growth. Shallow cultivation between the rows and hand pulling along them keeps weeds in check and aerates the soil. Water thoroughly at weekly intervals in dry weather.

Harvest by pulling up the entire plant and trimming off the roots and leaves while the stem tubers are still crisp, tender, and sweet (1½ to 2 inches in diameter). Larger ones and those that have developed slowly become tough, stringy, and bitter. Diseases and pests are those common to cabbage and other brassica crops.

KOKIA (Kò-kia). Endemic to the Hawaiian Islands, the genus *Kokia*, of the mallow family MALVACEAE, is related to *Hibiscus*. The name is a corruption of *kokio*, its native Hawaiian name.

Four species are known to have existed. One is extinct, two no longer occur in the wild, but persist to a limited extent in cultivation, and the other *K. dryarioides* (syn. *K. rockii*) exists as a native in one isolated valley.

Kokias are trees about 25 feet tall, with alternate leaves divided in handlike fash-ion. From the axils of the uppermost leaves solitary, showy, large red or brick-red flowers develop. They exhibit characteristics of *Hibiscus* and of cotton (*Gossypium*). Below or behind each bloom are three large, persistent, spreading bracts. The flowers have a five-lobed calyx the top half of which soon drops off. There are five petals, many stamens joined in a column, and a branched style. The fruits are very ornamental woody capsules with three spreading wings and contain brown-hairy seeds.

Garden Uses and Cultivation. Suitable for cultivation only in the tropics, warm subtropics, and in tropical greenhouses, kokias respond to environments and care that suit tropical hibiscuses.

KOLA. See Cola.

KOLKWITZIA (Kolk-wítzia)—Beauty Bush. One handsome, hardy, deciduous, Chinese shrub is the only species of *Kolkwitzia*, of the honeysuckle family CAPRIFOLIACEAE. Its name commemorates Richard Kolkwitz, a German professor of botany, who died in 1956. From nearly related *Weigela* and *Diervilla* this genus is distinguished by its flowers having four instead of five stamens and by the bark of its older stems hanging in big loose shreds.

The beauty bush (*K. amabilis*) is an erect shrub, up to 10 feet tall, with opposite, short-stalked, dull, ovate, slightly-toothed leaves 1½ to 3 inches long. They have hairy stalks, sparingly-hairy upper surfaces, and hairs on the veins on their undersides. The abundant flowers, ⅝ inch long and about as wide across the mouth, are in pairs grouped in showy clusters that terminate short branchlets. They have five or six narrow, spreading, hairy sepals that persist and remain with the fruits. The bell-shaped corollas have five rounded, spreading lobes (petals). They are pink with yellow throats. The four stamens are about as long as the corolla tube. There is one style. Dry and bristly, the brown, egg-shaped fruits are about ¼ inch long.

Kolkwitzia amabilis

Kolkwitzia amabilis, shredding bark on main stems

Kolkwitzia amabilis (foliage and flowers)

Garden and Landscape Uses. The beauty bush is an easy-to-grow shrub of no particular attraction when out of bloom. It grows vigorously, flowers profusely in May, then lapses into a mass of stems and foliage of undistinguished appearance. It is without attractive autumn color. For massing in large landscapes and for screening it can be used effectively, and single plants can be attractive in mixed shrub borders and as lawn specimens. They need adequate room for their best display; an area 10 or 12 feet across is not too much. One important point to remember is that when raised from seeds the plants exhibit great variation in color, and to some extent in quality and size, of their flowers. They range from insipid, washy, lavender pinks to really good clear pinks. Only the best should be chosen for planting. These are easily propagated by cuttings. The beauty bush thrives in ordinary soil in full sun.

Cultivation. Established plants require little regular attention other than the cutting out of old crowded branches and stems immediately blooming is over. A mulch of compost or other organic material is helpful and in dry periods deep watering at intervals of about a week promotes vigor. Specimens that have de-

pleted their soil of nutrients benefit from a spring application of a complete garden fertilizer. Old overgrown plants can be rejuvenated by thinning out their branches and cutting them back quite severely in late winter. This drastic treatment, which involves the sacrifice of a season's bloom, should be followed by fertilizing, thinning out any excessive new shoots that appear, and watering freely in dry weather. Propagation is easy by leafy summer cuttings and by hardwood cuttings in fall. Seeds germinate very readily, but, as already indicated, are likely to give rise to a large proportion of inferior plants.

KOPSIA (Kóp-sia). Approximately twenty-five species of the dogbane family APOCYNACEAE constitute *Kopsia*, a genus of southeastern Asia, western Malaysia, and the Caroline Islands. The name commemorates the Dutch botanist Jan Kops, who died in 1849.

Kopsias are evergreen shrubs and trees with some resemblance to oleanders. They have short-stalked, rather leathery, opposite leaves. The clustered white, pink, or red flowers have deeply-five-cleft calyxes, corollas with long slender tubes, five wide-spreading petals, and hairy throats. There are five stamens and one style. The fruits are fleshy or leathery.

Native of Malaya, Java, and Borneo, *K. fruticosa* is 5 feet or so tall and has pointed-elliptic to pointed-ovate leaves 4 to 8 inches long. The clusters of *Vinca*-like flowers 1¼ to 2 inches across are white or pink with a crimson or purple central eye. A very ornamental, medium-sized tree, *K. flavida*, of Java, has leaves with broad-elliptic blades 4 to 8 inches long. Its white flowers are 2 inches in diameter.

Kopsia fruticosa

Garden and Landscape Uses and Cultivation. The species described are suitable for outdoors in southern Florida, Hawaii, and other warm humid climates. Satisfied with ordinary garden soils in sun or part-day shade, they stand seaside environments well. Propagation is by cuttings and by seed.

KOREAN BRIDAL WREATH is *Spiraea trichocarpa*.

KORTHALSIA (Korthál-sia). Thirty-five species, of Indomalaysia, belong in *Korthalsia*, of the palm family PALMAE. The name commemorates Peter Willem Korthals, a Dutch botanist, who died in 1892.

Korthalsias are related to *Calamus* and like members of that genus have thin, usually spiny stems and alternate, pinnate leaves commonly with tail-like extensions of their midribs fiercely armed with short backward-pointing spines. The flowers are bisexual and are in crowded, catkin-like spikes arranged in loosely-branched clusters that develop from the axils of the leaves. The fruits are globular to ovoid each with a solitary seed. The stems of some kinds are employed in the same ways as those of *Calamus*, for basketwork and wickerwork.

Native to Burma and Indonesia, *K. laciniosa* has stems about ½ inch thick and up to 50 feet long. Its 2- to 4-foot long leaves have a thorny, whiplike extension of the midrib and short-stalked, rhomboidal leaflets 6 to 9 inches long and about one-half as wide. From their middles they taper to the base and apex. The margins above their middles are coarsely and irregularly toothed.

Garden and Landscape Uses and Cultivation. These palms are not likely to be grown except in collections of fanciers. They require the same culture as *Calamus*. For additional information see Palms.

KOSTELETZKYA (Kostel-étzkya). Related to *Hibiscus* and belonging in the mallow family MALVACEAE, this genus of perhaps thirty species is little known horticulturally. It is native in the Americas, Europe, Asia, Africa, and Madagascar, mostly in the subtropics and tropics. Its name commemorates the Bohemian medical botanist V. K. Kosteletzky, who died in 1887.

Kosteletzkyas are herbaceous plants and shrubs with somewhat arrow-shaped leaves, and pink, purple, yellow, or white flowers with false calyxes of many narrow bracts. The true calyx is five-lobed. There are five spreading or erect petals and many stamens joined into a tube that surrounds the pistil. The fruits are five-compartmented capsules with one seed in each section.

An inhabitant of brackish and salt marshes from southern New York to Florida, Texas, Bermuda, and the West Indies, *K. virginica* is a perennial herbaceous plant up to 3 feet in height. Its branching stems and foliage are rough-hairy. The leaves are triangular-ovate, mostly with two lateral lobes, and are toothed. In terminal panicles and in the leaf axils, the pink blooms, with stalked, spreading, obovate-wedge-shaped petals, are 2 to 3½ inches wide. The seed capsules, less than

½ inch across, are much flattened spheres with five sharp ridges or angles.

Native from the West Indies and Mexico to northern South America, **K. pentasperma** (syn. *K. hastata*) is an erect, more or less hairy subshrub up to 10 feet tall. Its lower leaves, up to 6 inches long, are frequently of three to seven leaflets or are lobed. The mostly lobeless upper leaves are somewhat arrow-shaped. From 1 inch to 2 inches in diameter and generally in panicles, the flowers are white to yellowish or purplish.

Garden and Landscape Uses and Cultivation. The first species described above is suitable for sunny locations in moist and wet soils in native plant gardens and other naturalistic areas and may be included in flower borders. It is hardy and easily raised from seed. The other, adaptable to the same purposes, is hardy only in the tropics and subtropics.

KOWHAI. The red kowhai is *Clianthus puniceus*, the yellow kowhai *Sophora tetraptera*.

KRAINZIA (Krain-zia). Two species many botanists include in *Mammillaria* are by those who favor splitting genera finely segregated as *Krainzia*, of the cactus family CACTACEAE. Natives of Mexico, these are choice plants. The name commemorates the twentieth-century Swiss botanist Hans Krainz.

Krainzias, small and spiny, have clusters of spherical plant bodies similar to those of *Mammillaria*, but with blooms with a long, narrow perianth tube and large black seeds.

Beautiful **K. guelzowiana** (syn. *Mammillaria guelzowiana*) much resembles *Mammillaria bocasana*. Its plant bodies, 1½ to a little over 2 inches across are clothed with a halo of hairlike white spines in clusters of sixty to eighty radials ½ inch long and one yellow to reddish-brown central about the same length. Some 2½ inches in diameter, the flowers are brilliant purple-red. From the last, **K. longiflora** (syn. *Mammillaria longiflora*) differs in its spine clusters consisting of about thirty ½-inch-long, white radials and four needle-like, yellow to brown centrals 1 inch long, one of which is hooked. The flowers are pink and 1½ inches across.

Garden Uses and Cultivation. These are as for *Mammillaria*, but krainzias often prove difficult to satisfy and are best left to the ministrations of experienced cultivators of cactuses. For more information see Cactuses.

KRAMERIA (Kra-mèria). Consisting of twenty-five species, *Krameria* occurs natively from the southern United States to Chile. Its name commemorates the eighteenth-century Austrian botanist and military doctor Johann Georg Heinrich Kramer. Usually allotted to the pea family LEGUMINOSAE, this genus has by some botanists been placed in the milkwort family POLYGALACEAE, and by others is segregated as the only genus of the krameria family KRAMERIACEAE.

Of minor horticultural importance, this genus includes some kinds that are sources of rhatany root, used medicinally and for tanning. Kramerias include spiny shrubs and herbaceous perennials, generally silky-hairy. They have alternate leaves, undivided or of three leaflets, and blooms, frequently fragrant, solitary or in terminal racemes. The flowers are not pea-like. They have four or five more or less unequal sepals and five petals, the three upper tapering at their bases to long shafts or claws and usually connected, the others much shorter and more nearly round. There are four or less commonly three stamens, joined below, and one style. The fruits are one-seeded, spiny pods.

Native from Florida to Mexico, **K. secundiflora** (syn. *K. spathulata*) is a herbaceous perennial with prostrate, shaggy-hairy stems up to about 1½ feet long. The three partly joined purple petals of its blooms have a common shaft longer than their blades so that together they resemble a three-lobed lip. The fruits are globular and spiny.

Garden Uses and Cultivation. The kind described inhabits sandy soils. It is occasionally cultivated in collections of plants native to the southeastern United States. Propagation is by seed. This is not hardy in the north.

KRAUSSIA (Kraùs-sia). To the madder family RUBIACEAE belong the three or four species of *Kraussia*, a genus of shrubs or small trees native in Africa. The name commemorates Dr. Christian Ferdinand Friedrich von Krauss, a German zoologist and botanist who collected plants in South Africa. He died in 1890.

Kraussias have opposite leaves, and few- to many-flowered clusters of little flowers from the leaf axils. The blooms have five-lobed or five-toothed calyxes, a top- to bell-shaped corolla, four to eight stamens, and a slender style with two stigmas. The fruits are two-seeded berries.

Native to South Africa, **K. floribunda** is a shrub or rarely a tree up to 20 feet tall. It has pointed, obovate-oblong to lanceolate leaves up to 3 inches long and with well-defined midribs. The white flowers ¼ inch or a little more across are in stalked clusters. The spherical, black fruits are ¼ inch in diameter. This species has been cultivated as *Tricalysia floribunda*.

Garden and Landscape Uses and Cultivation. Cultivated to some extent as an ornamental in California and other places with Mediterranean-type climates, the species described is a general-purpose ornamental that succeeds under ordinary garden conditions. It may be increased by seed and by cuttings.

KRIGIA (Kríg-ia)—Dwarf-Dandelion. Annuals and hardy herbaceous perennials numbering seven or eight species comprise North American *Krigia*, of the daisy family COMPOSITAE. Because they look much like dandelions they are called dwarf-dandelions. Their name commemorates the late seventeenth- and early eighteenth-century German physician David Krig, who collected plants in North America.

Like their namesakes, dwarf-dandelions contain milky juice. They have all-basal, or alternate or nearly opposite, undivided, pinnately-lobed or lobeless leaves. The flower heads, solitary or more than one to a stem, are of all strap-shaped, yellow or orange florets. The seedlike fruits are achenes. From dandelions members of this genus differ in the pappus of the flower head being of chaffy scales and bristles, instead of only bristles.

A slender annual, **K. virginica** inhabits dry, sandy soils from Maine to Michigan, Missouri, Florida, and Texas. Up to 1 foot tall or a little taller, it has all basal or nearly basal foliage. The linear to oblanceolate leaves, up to 4½ inches long or sometimes longer, are coarsely-jagged-toothed to toothless. The orange- to reddish-orange-flower heads are about ½ inch wide.

Perennial **K. montana** occurs in North Carolina, South Carolina, and Georgia. Up to about 1 foot tall, it has oblong to linear leaves, toothed or not, and solitary flower heads 1 inch wide. A larger perennial, up to 1½ feet tall, and with solitary flower heads 1 inch across, **K. dandelion** occurs commonly in sandy places from New Jersey to Missouri, Kansas, Florida, and Texas. It is easily recognizable because its roots have tubers. Its finely- to coarsely-toothed leaves are lanceolate to nearly linear.

Krigia montana

Garden and Landscape Uses and Cultivation. Unlike dandelions krigias are not likely to become pestiferous weeds. They are suitable for native plant gardens, naturalistic areas, and rock gardens. They are satisfied with ordinary, even poorish soil and need full sun. All are easily raised from seed and the perennials by division.

KRUBI is *Amorphophallus titanum.*

KRUGIODENDRON (Krugio-dèndron)— Black Ironwood. The only species of *Krugiodendron,* of the buckthorn family RHAMNACEAE, is a native of the West Indies and southern Florida. Its name is a personal commemorative one.

Black ironwood (*K. ferreum*) is an evergreen shrub or tree 25 to 35 feet tall with broad-elliptic leaves up to a little over 2 inches long. Of no decorative value, the green flowers, without petals, have five crested sepals and five stamens. The subspherical fruits are black drupes, up to ⅓ inch long. The heartwood of this tree is the heaviest of any hardwood tree native in the United States. It sinks in water.

Garden and Landscape Uses and Cultivation. This is interesting as a foliage shrub for use in southern Florida and regions with similar climates. It succeeds in ordinary soils and may be propagated by seed and cuttings.

KUDZU VINE is *Pueraria lobata.*

KUHNIA (Kùhn-ia). One of the many genera of the daisy family COMPOSITAE that inhabit North America, *Kuhnia* is of minor horticultural importance. It comprises about six species and was named to commemorate Dr. Adam Kuhn, of Philadelphia, who was responsible for directing the attention of Linnaeus to these plants. He died in 1817.

Kuhnias are tap-rooted, herbaceous perennials with opposite to alternate leaves, and bell-shaped to nearly cylindrical small flower heads in terminal clusters. The flower heads are without ray florets. They are composed of all tubular disk (like those of the eye of a daisy) ones, all of which are bisexual. The flowers are creamy-white, dull yellow, or purplish. From *Eupatorium* the genus *Kuhnia* is segregated because of technical differences in the achenes (seeds).

A variable native of dry, sunny locations from New Jersey to Montana, Florida, Arizona, and Texas, *K. eupatorioides* has, as its name implies, much the appearance of *Eupatorium.* From 1 foot to 4 feet tall, it is almost hairless to densely-clothed with short hairs. Its leaves, dotted with glands on their lower surfaces, are narrowly- to broadly-lanceolate, and sometimes toothed. They have short stalks or none, and are 1 inch to 4 inches long. About ½ inch long, the flower heads, in smallish clusters, are creamy-white.

Garden Uses and Cultivation. Sometimes planted in flower borders, and suitable for native plant gardens and naturalizing, the species described grows with great ease under conditions that approximate those it favors in the wild, and is especially well adapted for dryish, sandy soils. Propagation is easy by seed and by division.

KULUI is *Nototrichium sandwicense.*

KUMQUAT. Kumquats, the name is a modification of a Chinese one meaning gold orange, belong to the genus *Fortunella,* and their kinds are described under that name. They are beautiful, densely-branched, evergreen trees and shrubs suitable for planting as outdoor ornamentals where climate permits, and attractive in pots and tubs in greenhouses and as window plants. Cut branches with ripe fruits are beautiful in containers of water as indoor decorations. The lustrous green foliage is satisfyingly abundant, the white flowers pleasing, and the small, long-lasting, bright golden-yellow to orange-yellow fruits very ornamental. In addition, the fruits make delightful preserves and can be candied or eaten out of hand. The skins as well as the pulp are edible.

Kumquats

Kumquats are hardier than the orange, except the Satsuma orange and its close relatives and the trifoliate-orange (*Poncirus trifoliata*). Their resistance to cold is increased by grafting them on trifoliate-orange understocks. Nevertheless, they will not stand hard freezing and are not hardy under conditions very much harsher than oranges survive. They succeed best in fertile, well-drained soil, in sunny locations, and require about the same management as oranges. The most common method of propagation is by grafting onto trifoliate-orange. Seed can also be used.

As pot or tub plants kumquats are very satisfactory. See that their containers are well drained and the soil is porous, but nourishing. Earth suitable for geraniums, chrysanthemums, and similar "ordinary soil" type plants suits. Established specimens in fairly large receptacles need repotting at intervals of several years only, but in late winter or spring prick away some of the surface soil and replace it with a rich, loamy mixture. Small specimens are likely to require moving into slightly larger pots every year or two. Repot in spring. Then, too, trim both young and older specimens to shape and cut out any too-crowded branches. More severe pruning may be needed to rejuvenate old, neglected, unshapely plants. Water to keep the soil always fairly moist, but not constantly soaked. Less frequent applications are needed in winter than from spring to fall. Give well-rooted specimens, but not recently planted ones, monthly or twice-monthly applications of dilute liquid fertilizer from spring to early fall.

In summer, kumquats in containers benefit from being outdoors in a sunny location. They make handsome ornaments for patios, terraces, and steps. In winter, temperatures at night of about 50°F, with a five to ten degree increase by day, are adequate. Too much warmth and excessively low humidity are detrimental. Watch carefully for infestation by scale insects and mealybugs and take prompt steps to eliminate any such either by sponging the leaves or spraying them with a contact insecticide. For the plant called Australian desert-kumquat see Eremocitrus.

KUNZEA (Kún-zea). Kunzeas are beautiful, nonhardy, evergreen shrubs or rarely small trees, and natives of Australia. They belong to the myrtle family MYRTACEAE and are kin to *Leptospermum* and *Metrosideros.* From *Leptospermum* they are readily distinguished by their numerous, very long, protruding stamens, the most conspicuous parts of the blooms, from *Metrosideros* by their flowers, rarely in spikes, having persistent sepals, and the fruits not being hard and woody. There are thirty species. The name commemorates Gustav Kunze, a German botanist, who died in 1851. The plant previously named *K. ericoides* is *Leptospermum ericoides.*

The leaves of *Kunzea* are prevailingly alternate. Very rarely a few may be opposite. They are small, undivided, lobeless, and toothless and are largely responsible for the heathlike appearance of the plants. The flowers sometimes come from the upper leaf axils and are stalkless or, less commonly, stalked. More frequently they are in heads or short spikes, generally at the ends of branchlets, but sometimes from below the extremities of the shoots. Each small bloom has a five-lobed calyx with a spherical or ovoid tube partly joined to the ovary, five rounded, spreading petals, many long, protruding, separate stamens, and a slender style. The fruits are capsules crowned with the persistent calyx.

Having edible fruits in Australia called muntries, *K. pomifera* is nearly hairless. It has prostrate, sometimes rooting stems and ovate to nearly circular, bristle-pointed leaves about ⅕ inch long. In crowded, terminal heads of few, the white-petaled blooms have white stamens nearly 1 inch long. The pleasant tasting, purplish fruits, ⅓ inch in diameter, are in clusters of up to eight. With white or whitish flowers, **K. peduncularis** is a tall, erect shrub or rarely a small tree. It has wandlike branches, and pointed, linear to linear-lanceolate leaves mostly about ½ inch long, but sometimes smaller or bigger. The stalked flowers are in short, terminal, leafy clusters or in long, interrupted leafy racemes. The more than thirty stamens are one-and-a-half times to twice as long as the petals. From this sort, **K. ambigua** (syn. *K. corifolia*) differs chiefly in its flowers being stalkless.

Pink-flowered **K. recurva** is a shrub up to about 7 feet tall. Its blooms are in dense, spherical heads, approximately ½ inch in diameter, at the ends of the branchlets. About ¼ inch long, obovate to spatula-shaped, and with minute, recurved tips, the leaves sit close to the stems. Variety *K. r. montana* has yellow blooms. Excellent **K. capitata** is a twiggy shrub with erect leaves, recurved in their upper parts, ovate-lanceolate to linear-oblong, and about ⅓ inch long. The stalkless flowers, in roundish, terminal heads about ½ inch in diameter, are pink to purple-mauve.

Brilliant red blooms, their stamens tipped with yellow anthers, are borne by **K. sericea** (syn. *K. pulchella*). Up to 12 feet tall, this splendid kind has its flowers concentrated in bottle-brush-like spikes at or near the branchlet ends. The blooms have silky-hairy calyxes and 1-inch-long stamens. The leaves are obovate, up to ½ inch long, and silky-hairy. Also with bright red blooms in bottle-brush-like spikes at or near the shoot ends, **K. baxteri** is a broad shrub up to 6 feet in height. It has narrow-lanceolate to elliptic leaves ½ to ¾ inch in length.

Yellow-flowered **K. ericifolia** has blooms in tight, globular heads ½ to ¾ inch in diameter at the ends of short branchlets from longer shoots. Up to 15 feet tall, this has long, wandlike branches, that in its homeland are cut and used as stakes for young tomato plants. The narrow, heath-like leaves are ¼ to ½ inch long.

Garden and Landscape Uses and Cultivation. These are essentially the same as for *Callistemon* and *Leptospermum*.

KURRAJONG is *Brachychiton populneum*.

L

LABELS. To keep track of and be able to readily identify plants in gardens it is often necessary to label them. In public places labels serve additionally to inform and educate visitors. Numerous sorts of plant labels have been devised. None is ideal. Probably none ever will be, for to meet that requirement, the device would need to be inexpensive, long-lasting or even permanent, easily read from some distance without being obtrusive or detracting from the beauty of the plants. Compromise then is necessary when selecting labels for various purposes.

For short-time use, as with seed pots for annuals and flats of bedding and vegetable plants soon to be set in the garden, standard commercial wooden pot labels, available in lengths of from 4 inches to 1 foot are satisfactory. These may be obtained painted or unpainted and are easily written upon with an ordinary lead pencil. Such labels have the virtue of being inexpensive, but do not ordinarily last more than one season. Similar labels of thin plastic are also commercially available. These can be written upon with pencil or indelible waterproof ink. Unlike wooden labels they do not rot, but with age become brittle and liable to breakage.

Much longer-lasting wooden labels, their life-spans three years, or considerably longer depending upon the conditions under which they are exposed, can be made of good quality pine lumber about ¼ inch thick. If to be stuck into the ground treat their lower parts with cuprinol or other wood preservative and paint their above-ground portions with one or two coats of good white paint. Labels to be displayed above ground on trees, shrubs, or stakes should be painted all over.

Writing on wooden labels, the commercially available sorts prepainted or not, as well as the longer-lasting ones just described, will be very much more permanent if done in the manner now to be described; in fact, it is likely to be legible as long as the label lasts. Smear a little paint (preferably one of white lead, linseed oil,

To have writing last well on wooden labels: (a) Put a little white paint on the label

(b) Smear it over the surface with a rag and wipe off as much as possible

(c) Inscribe immediately with an ordinary pencil

and a slight amount of driers) of a somewhat thicker consistency than normally used for painting on the surface to be written upon and with a cotton rag wipe it nearly dry. Then *immediately*, do not wait even five minutes, make the inscription with a soft lead pencil. For even longer life some authorities recommend applying a coat of varnish after the paint has dried, but this is not necessary.

Long-lasting but difficult to read except on close scrutiny are tag labels of strips of very thin copper upon which the message is impressed with a stylus. These, attached by copper wire or nylon thread to wire stakes thrust into the ground, or directly to the branches or trunks of trees and shrubs, are among the least obtrusive of labels. Easier to read, but more visible are aluminum strip labels upon which block letters are impressed by a special hand-held or larger machine. These are attached in the same ways as copper tag labels. Great permanence, but with the passage of time not very easy readability is had with labels made of strips of zinc burnished with emery paper and written upon with special metallic ink. Absolutely permanent results are had with an ink made by dissolving one gram of platinum chloride in 1½ ounces of distilled water. Writing must be done with a pen fitted with a gold-plated point.

Labels of laminated plastic upon which lettering is embossed with a machine that cuts through the outer skin to reveal a different colored layer beneath are much in vogue in botanical gardens and other public places where clear visibility and easy readability are of first importance. Attractive in appearance and highly resistant to weathering, these have the disadvantages that the embossing machine needed is rather costly (those who prefer not to buy a machine can have the labels made commercially) and the labels, which break with sharp impact, are easily damaged by vandals and sometimes accidentally by careless workmen.

Other labels among the many that have

been tried include those made of small pieces of terra-cotta set in metal holders. These are attractive and, written on with black indelible ink, very durable. A variation sometimes employed for collections of little succulents and alpine gardens is to write on pebbles or stones partly buried in the soil, but these have the serious disadvantage of being easily moved accidentally.

LABIATAE—Mint Family. This horticulturally important family of dicotyledons numbers among its 180 genera some 3,500 species of chiefly annuals and herbaceous perennials, some subshrubs and shrubs, and a few trees. Rarely its members have vining stems. Of cosmopolitan natural distribution, this family is especially prolific as to sorts in the Mediterranean region. Among its best known kinds are the herbs, basil, horehound, hyssop, lavender, marjoram, mint, pennyroyal, rosemary, savory, and thyme.

Labiates, to employ the accepted embracing name for plants of this family, are mostly hairy and usually secrete volatile oils responsible for the characteristic scents or odors of many. They mostly have square stems. Their leaves are opposite with each pair positioned at right angles to those immediately above and below, or sometimes are in whorls (circles of more than two). They are undivided, pinnately-lobed, or pinnate. The markedly asymmetrical or occasionally nearly symmetrical flowers are most often in clusters from the axils of leaves or bracts, the clusters often forming spikelike inflorescences. Sometimes they are solitary from the leaf or bract axils. The blooms, tubular, bell- or funnel-shaped, frequently two-lipped, most usually have five-toothed or five-lobed calyxes and corollas. There are two or four stamens, if four, in pairs of different lengths or nearly equal, and one style. The fruits are generally of four nutlets. Cultivated genera are *Acinos, Agastache, Ajuga, Amethystea, Ballota, Blephilia, Calamintha, Cedronella, Clinopodium, Coleus, Collinsonia, Colquhounia, Conradina, Cunila, Dracocephalum, Ereomostachys, Glechoma, Hedeoma, Hemiandra, Horminum, Hyssopus, Iboza, Lallemantia, Lamiastrum, Lamium, Lavandula, Leonotis, Leonurus, Lepechinia, Leucosceptrum, Lycopus, Marrubium, Melissa, Melittis, Mentha, Micromeria, Molucella, Monarda, Monardella, Nepeta, Ocimum, Origanum, Perilla, Perovskia, Phlomis, Physostegia, Plectranthus, Pogostemon, Prostanthera, Prunella, Pycnanthemum, Pycnostachys, Rosmarinus, Salvia, Satureja, Scutellaria, Sideritis, Stachys, Teucrium, Thymus, Tinnea, Trichostema,* and *Westringia.*

LABLAB is *Dolichos lablab.*

LABRADOR-TEA is *Ledum groenlandicum.*

LABURNOCYTISUS (Laburno-cýtisus). This is the name of a so-called graft-hybrid (chimera) between *Laburnum* and *Cytisus,* of the pea family LEGUMINOSAE. Chimeras differ from true hybrids in not being the result of sexual mating and so not having cells containing genes derived from two parents. Instead, they are composed of separate pure cells of two species living in intimate association within one plant body. In *Laburnocytisus adamii* the interior of the plant is of all *Cytisus purpureus* cells. These are overlaid or surrounded by a layer of cells of *Laburnum anagyroides.* The name of the chimera is formed of those of the two genera.

Remarkable and interesting rather than beautiful, **Laburnocytisus adamii** is a deciduous tree of irregular outline 15 to 25 feet tall. In general appearance it resembles *Laburnum anagyroides,* but is hairless, and smaller in its parts than that species. Its flowers, in pendulous racemes, are mostly purplish-pink. Occasionally it develops branches from its outer layer of laburnum cells that have the characteristic foliage and yellow flowers of that kind, and sometimes from the interior, branches of pure *Cytisus purpureus* push out and carry typical foliage and flowers of that species. And so *Laburnocytisus* displays on the same individual three types of foliage and flowers. The laburnum flowers it bears produce seeds that develop into typical *Laburnum anagyroides,* the cytisus flowers, seeds that develop into typical *Cytisus purpureus.* Rarely produced, seeds from intermediate-type blooms are reported to produce plants of true *Laburnum anagyroides.*

This unusual tree originated in France in 1825. A nurseryman named Jean Louis Adam had grafted *Cytisus purpureus* onto *Laburnum anagyroides.* By accident all except a small portion of the *Cytisus* scion was broken off, but the part lived and grew along with the *Laburnum* tissues of the understock and gave rise to the new chimera. At first this was thought to be a true hybrid, and was named *Laburnum adamii* and *Cytisus adamii.* Not until very much later was its true nature discovered.

Garden Uses and Cultivation. Often included as a curiosity in botanical collections, but rarely seen elsewhere, this chimera thrives under conditions suitable for *Laburnum.* It is increased by grafting onto understocks of *Laburnum.*

LABURNUM (Lab-úrnum)—Golden Chain. Spring visitors to Great Britain and some other parts of Europe are likely to be thrilled with the grand displays made by laburnums, so popular there for planting in front yards, gardens, and parks, often in association with white- and pink-flowered hawthorns. Well-flowered specimens, and they are common, simply drip with a profusion of panicles of golden-yellow, wisteria-like blooms. Laburnums are less common in America; they should be planted more freely. A possible disadvantage is that, in the rather unlikely event that they are eaten, their seeds and other parts, especially the young fruits, are poisonous. This does not seem to cause significant trouble in Europe, and there is small reason to suppose that it would here. There are three or four species of the Mediterranean region and adjacent Asia. They belong in the pea family LEGUMINOSAE. The name is an ancient Latin one. The tree sometimes called *Laburnum adamii* is *Laburnocytisus adamii.* Indian-laburnum is *Cassia fistula.*

Laburnums are deciduous small trees or tall shrubs closely related to *Cytisus.* They have alternate, stalked leaves with three leaflets, and slender-stalked, pea-like flowers in pendulous racemes. The two-lipped calyx has five short teeth. The corolla is yellow and has wing petals longer than the keels. There are nine stamens joined, and one separate. The fruits are flat, linear, several-seeded pods.

Common golden chain (**L. anagyroides** syn. *L. vulgare*) is a tall shrub or tree up to 25 feet or a little more in height. Native to southern Europe, it has grayish-green twigs, pubescent when young, and leaves with stalks 2 to 3 inches long, and elliptic to elliptic-ovate leaflets 1½ to 3 inches long that are downy on their undersides. The silky-hairy racemes of bloom, up to 1 foot in length, are of many ¾-inch-long, golden-yellow blooms. The seed pods, 1½ to 2½ inches long, are pubescent and without wings. Variety *L. a. aureum* has yellowish foliage. Variety *L. a. autumnale* often blooms in fall as well as spring. With pendulous branches, *L. a. pendulum* is a graceful weeping tree. Very erect is *L. a. pyramidalis.*

Laburnum anagyroides

Scotch laburnum (*L. alpinum*) belies its vernacular name because in the wild it is confined to southcentral and southern Europe. From common golden chain it differs in its young shoots being very slightly hairy and greener, and in its seed pods being hairless or almost so, and winged. It is more erect and rigid than common laburnum, often vase-shaped, and the undersides of its leaves are less densely-hairy. Additionally, its panicles of blooms are considerably longer and more densely flowered. Scotch laburnum is much more cold-resistant than common laburnum and, from a landscape point of view, superior. It is hardy throughout much of New England.

Laburnum alpinum

The laburnum finest as an ornamental is a hybrid between the two species described above, *L. watereri.* This is somewhat more tender to cold than the Scotch laburnum, but survives outdoors in southern New England. It is denser and has larger, deeper-colored blooms than *L. alpinum* and is much superior to *L. anagyroides.* The plant known as *L. vossii* is a minor variant of *L. watereri;* it should be called *L. w. vossii.*

Laburnum watereri

Laburnum watereri vossii

Garden and Landscape Uses. Laburnums provide no colorful displays of fall foliage or fruits; their summer garb is unexciting. Their only decorative appeal lies in their glorious displays of sunny blooms. For two weeks well-flowered specimens are among the most gorgeous sights of the garden world. They are effective as single lawn specimens and may be used to good purpose in plantings of mixed shrubbery. An especially pleasing way to exhibit them is behind walls so that their lower parts are hidden and their branches overhang. Grown in large tubs or other containers, they can be gently forced into bloom in greenhouses and similar places. Laburnums are not fussy about soil; they adapt to most types that are well drained and moderately fertile. They prosper in full sun but do well also in light shade or part-day shade.

Cultivation. Once established, laburnums call for little care. Except to remove sucker shoots that sometimes arise or to take off occasional unwanted, crowded shoots, no pruning is needed. Propagation is easy by seeds sown as soon as they are ripe in a cold frame, cool greenhouse, or sheltered spot outdoors. The hybrid kinds and varieties of the species are multiplied by grafting onto seedlings, either in a greenhouse in winter or outdoors in spring.

For forcing in greenhouses shapely trees should be established in their containers, for at least a year, in fertile, loamy, porous soil. They may be brought indoors from February onward, at first into a greenhouse maintained at 45 to 50°F at night and five to ten degrees higher by day. When growth has well begun the temperatures may be raised five to ten degrees, and dropped again after the flowers open. Full sun is required, and until the leaf buds have well started into growth the branches should be sprayed with water several times a day to soften the buds and encourage them to sprout. After flowering, the plants are kept in a cool greenhouse until all danger of frost is passed and then are stood outdoors in a sunny place. Individual specimens should be forced only every other year. Where severe freezing is experienced container specimens may be wintered in a cool shed or elsewhere where their soil does not freeze solidly or have their containers packed around with sand, peat moss, or other insulating material.

LACE. The word lace forms part of the common names of these plants: blue lace flower (*Trachymene caerulea*), lace cactus (*Echinocereus caespitosus*), lace fern (*Cheilanthes gracillima* and *Sphenomeris chusana*), lace leaf (*Aponogeton fenestralis*), St. Catherine's lace (*Eriogonum giganteum*), and silver lace vine (*Polygonum aubertii*).

LACE BUGS. Several species of lace bugs, each usually restricted to one kind of plant, are serious pests. They commonly infest azaleas and rhododendrons, chrysanthemums, photinias, and a wide variety of trees. True bugs, these insects have dark-veined, transparent front wings and peculiar projections covering the thorax and back of the head. They creep over the undersides of the leaves, sucking juices and bespeckling the surfaces with tiny spots of dark excreta. They are weak flyers. Migration from plant to plant generally takes place in the evening. Lace bugs cause mottling of foliage and general debilitation of the host plant. They are controlled by spraying with contact insecticides. Take particular care to reach the undersides of the leaves.

LACEBARK TREE is *Brachychiton acerifolium.* For the lacebarks or lacebark trees of New Zealand see Hoheria.

LACHENALIA (Lachen-àlia)—Cape-Cowslip. The last part of the vernacular name Cape-cowslip is singularly inappropriate. Lachenalias have neither resemblance nor relationship to cowslips (*Primula veris*) nor to *Caltha palustris* or *Mertensia virginica*, which are also called cowslips. They have more the aspect of veltheimias or English or Spanish bluebells (*Endymion*), with which they share relationship in the lily family LILIACEAE. The name *Lachenalia* commemorates Professor Werner de la Chenal, of Basel, Switzerland, who died in 1800.

Lachenalias are deciduous bulb plants endemic to South Africa. There are sixty-five species, none hardy in the north. Outdoors, their cultivation is restricted to such regions as California that have Mediterranean-type climates that encourage growth from early fall through spring, and dormancy in summer. Lachenalias are excellent for cool greenhouses. Their longitudinally-parallel-veined, slender to broad, all basal leaves are more or less fleshy. Usually two, less commonly one or several, come from each bulb. In late winter or spring the one to three erect flower stalks, naked of foliage, appear. Each terminates in a spike or raceme of nodding, horizontal, or ascending blooms. Cylindrical to bell-shaped, stalked or not, the flowers have six perianth segments (usually called petals, but more correctly tepals), their lower parts more or less united into a tube. Most commonly they are in tones of cream, yellow, orange, or red, but some kinds have purple to blue, and some white, flowers. Generally the outer three petals are shorter than the others and swollen at their tips. There are six slender-stalked stamens and one style with a headlike stigma at its summit. The fruits are three-angled capsules containing glossy, black seeds.

Two of the most popular species, to satisfy the botanical rule of priority, have had their names changed. Instead of long familiar *L. pendula* we must use *L. bulbifera,* and *L. tricolor* becomes *L. aloides.* These are both up to 1 foot high and have usually two, occasionally one, thin, strap-shaped to lanceolate leaves, those of **L. aloides** spotted with dull reddish-purple, those of **L. bulbifera** usually plain green. Both have cylindrical, few to many, stalked, pendulous flowers. The blooms of *L. bulbifera,* 1 inch to 1½ inches in length, have inner segments pale yellow with a center stripe of red, and green and purple apexes. The outer petals, only slightly shorter than the inner, are vermilion or coral-red except for a green swelling at the apex. The flowers of *L. aloides* are ¾ to 1 inch long. Their outer segments are much shorter than the inner. The latter are green with yellow bases and reddish-purple tips. The outer petals are bright red suffusing to yellow above and with a green swelling at their

ends. Popular varieties of *L. aloides* that by some authorities have been regarded as separate species are *L. a. aurea,* with quite massive spikes of beautiful bright golden-yellow to nearly orange-yellow flowers; *L. a. luteola,* the flowers of which are lemon-yellow; and *L. a. nelsonii,* which has slightly green-tinged, orange-yellow blooms. The only other commonly cultivated kind with one or two leaves and stalked flowers is **L. mediana.** From the kinds previously discussed this differs in having flowers rather less than ½ inch long, the inner segments of which are white with a green center vein and purplish tips. The outer ones, slightly shorter, are light yellow with purplish bases and a purplish swelling at their ends. This attains a height of 1¼ feet and has lanceolate to strap-shaped leaves up to 1 foot long, their bases usually tinged or spotted purple.

Lachenalia aloides nelsonii

Lachenalia bachmannii

Lachenalia aloides aurea

A first-prize winning pan of *Lachenalia aloides aurea* at a New York flower show

White-flowered lachenalias include several attractive species. The blooms of some are tinged with red. Here belongs **L. bachmannii,** free-flowering and up to 10 inches tall, with usually two linear leaves 4 to 8 inches long, and bell-shaped, nearly stalkless white flowers with a central red ridge to the petals. The outer petals are a little

Lachenalia aloides

Lachenalia bachmannii (flowers)

shorter than the inner ones. The flowers, with stamens about as long as the corollas, are crowded in racemes shorter than the leaves. The latter are deeply channeled and have margins folded toward each other. From this, **L. juncifolia** differs in having subcylindrical leaves, channeled on their upper sides, and flowers with conspicuously protruding stamens. Blister-like processes on the foliage characterize *L. liliflora* and *L. pallida,* both of which have white blooms. Attaining heights up to 1¼ feet, **L. liliflora** has flowers ¾ inch long and practically without individual stalks. The blooms of **L. pallida,** with individual stalks about ¼ inch long, are in racemes that with their stalks are up to 10 inches tall. Differing from other white-flowered species in cultivation in having four to ten leaves are *L. contaminata* and *L. orthopetala.* The flowers of both are small, those of **L. contaminata** ⅕ inch long, those of **L. orthopetala** ⅓ to ½ inch in length. Other differences are that the corolla segments of *L. contaminata* are spreading, whereas those of *L. orthopetala* are erect; also the former has cylindrical leaves, the latter flatter linear ones. The blooms of *L. contaminata* are fragrant.

Lachenalia contaminata

Lachenalias other than popular *L. bulbifera* and *L. aloides* that have colored flowers are cultivated and are very handsome. One of the best is **L. orchioides,** a variable kind that has flowers that may be creamy-white, yellow, pink, or blue-green. In dense spikes and numerous, they are fragrant and ⅓ inch long or longer. Their corolla segments are longer than the stamens. Very similar **L. mutabilis** differs chiefly in the upper flowers of the spike being aborted and having much longer stalks than the lower ones. Like the upper part of the flower stalk that bears them, these improperly developed blooms are pale blue. The normal flowers are sky-blue to gray-green and have yellow-green inner segments marked with a purple-brown blotch that changes to crimson. The inner and outer segments are the same length.

Lachenalia orchioides

Lachenalia mutabilis

Pustulated (blistered), lanceolate leaves, 6 to 8 inches long, about ½ wide, and two or rarely three from each bulb, are characteristic of **L. purpureo-caerulea.** The bell-shaped blooms, in racemes of thirty to forty, are purplish-blue or are lavender with red-purple-tipped petals.

Lachenalia purpureo-caerulea

Other species sometimes cultivated are *L. glaucina, L. reflexa,* and *L. roodeae.* From 4 to 6 inches to sometimes over 1 foot tall, **L. glaucina** has one or two slightly glaucous leaves, strap-shaped, up to nearly 1 foot in length, and sometimes rather indefinitely-spotted with brown. Its many fragrant, iridescent flowers, essentially without individual stalks, are in fairly dense spikes with sometimes spotted stalks. They are up-facing, about ¾ inch long, and whitish more or less suffused with yellow, green, pink, lilac-blue, or blue. Considerably longer than the three outer petals, the inner three petals have wavy margins and markedly recurved apexes. The stamens and style are about as long as the inner petals. Usually not more than 6 inches in height, but up to twice that, **L. reflexa** has a pair of spreading, finally reflexed, lanceolate leaves 4 to 6 inches long, with wavy margins. The thick flowering stalks carry racemes of few yellowish-green blooms, the outer petals of which are slightly shorter than the inner. The stamens do not protrude. Very lovely **L. roodeae** is undoubtedly one of the finest species. It has two ovate-lanceolate leaves up to about 1 foot in length, the lower longer than the other, and many-flowered, short-stalked flower spikes 4 to 6 inches tall. The nearly stalkless, bell-shaped, richly colored blooms are rosy-purple to blue-purple and ⅓ inch long or a little longer. Their inner petals are longer than the outer. The stamens protrude.

Lachenalia roodeae

Garden and Landscape Uses. Where they can be grown outdoors, which means where freesias and babianas can be so grown, lachenalias are charming in rock gardens and similar intimate surroundings. They are also delightful for blooming in late winter and spring in pots, pans (shallow pots), and hanging baskets in greenhouses and are worth trying in cool sun-rooms and similar sunny places where temperatures can be kept within the range the plants will accept. Their flowers are delightful for cutting for use in small arrangements.

Cultivation. Lachenalias prosper in any ordinary porous soil that is fairly nourishing. Plant or pot the bulbs in August or September, in mild climates outdoors about 3 inches deep and approximately the same distance apart, for blooming indoors in containers, 1½ to 2 inches apart, with the tips of the bulbs just covered with soil. Be sure the pots, pans, or baskets are well drained. As soon as potting is completed drench the soil with water, and stand the containers in a shaded cold frame or cool spot in a greenhouse. It is a good plan to cover the soil with a layer of sphagnum moss or peat moss to keep it from drying too rapidly. Excessively high temperatures must at all costs be guarded against. The nearer the night temperature can be to 45°F, and that by day to not more than about ten degrees higher, the better. It is unlikely that you will be able to attain these ideals at first, but as fall advances and winter comes they should be realizable. Too much warmth is fatal. When growth breaks through the surface soil, remove the moss or peat moss and after a few days of very light shade expose the plants to full sun in a frostproof cold frame or cool greenhouse. Whenever the weather is favorable, ventilate the structure freely. Water moderately at first, with increasing frequency as roots occupy the available soil. From February on, lachenalias that have filled their containers with roots benefit greatly from weekly applications of dilute liquid fertilizer. Never allow the soil to dry really out during the growing season, but do not keep it constantly sodden. Either extreme is very damaging. After flowering is through, unless seeds are to be collected, remove the old flower stalks. Keep the plants growing in the same cool conditions and continue weekly fertilizing until the foliage begins to die naturally. Then cease fertilizing, and gradually dry the bulbs off by increasing the periods between waterings. Do not withhold water suddenly or altogether until the leaves have completely dried. Then stop watering and store the bulbs in the soil in which they grew in a cool, dry, shaded place until late summer. Just before they begin to make new roots sift them from the soil, sort the bulbs to size, repot them, and begin the growth cycle over again. Lachenalias increase fairly rapidly by offset bulblets and are easily grown from seeds, although horticultural varieties do not, of course, reproduce themselves truly when raised in that way. Other practicable means of propagation are by leaf cuttings and bulb cuttings.

LACHNANTHES (Lach-nánthes)—Redroot. The only species of this genus inhabits swamps and bogs from Nova Scotia to Florida and Cuba. It belongs in the bloodwort family HAEMODORACEAE. Its name, from the Greek *lachne*, wool, and *anthos*, a flower, alludes to a characteristic of the blooms.

Redroot (**Lachnanthes caroliana** syn. *L. tinctoria*) is a stout, hardy herbaceous perennial. Its roots are fibrous and red, its pubescent stems 1 foot to 2½ feet tall. The leaves are linear and erect, the lower up to 1¼ feet long by under ½ inch wide, those above gradually reduced in size until the top ones are represented by bracts. The densely-woolly-hairy, branched flower clusters terminate the stems and are 1½ to 3½ inches across. Dull yellow, the narrowly-bell-shaped blooms are erect, densely-hairy, about ⅓ inch long, and have six perianth lobes (petals, or more correctly, tepals) of which the outer three are shorter than the others, and three protruding stamens. The fruits are capsules.

Garden and Landscape Uses and Cultivation. Not exciting as an ornamental, this species is occasionally planted in bog gardens and wet places. It needs acid soil and is increased by division and by seeds sown, before they have a chance to become dry, in boggy soil.

LACTUCA (Lac-tùca)—Lettuce. Except for lettuce and more rarely celtuce, which are known only in cultivation, *Lactuca* is scarcely represented in American horticulture. It belongs in the daisy family COMPOSITAE and comprises perhaps 100 species chiefly of Europe and temperate Asia, but represented also in Africa. Some kinds are naturalized in North America. The name comes from the Latin *lac*, milk, and alludes to the character of the sap.

Lactucas are annuals, biennials, and herbaceous perennials mostly too weedy to be garden plants. They have basal or alternate, often pinnately-lobed leaves. Their erect stems bear usually large clusters of blue, violet, pink, white, or yellow flower heads with all strap-shaped florets. The fruits are achenes.

Lettuce is too well known to warrant description. It is *L. sativa* and comes in many varieties. One unusual variant is the vegetable called celtuce. For the cultivation of these edible kinds of *Lactuca*, see Lettuce and Celtuce. Perennial *L. perennis* of southern Europe may occasionally be cultivated as an ornamental. The limits of its hardiness are not recorded. It is an erect, hairless perennial 8 inches to 2 feet in height, with glaucous, deeply-pinnately-lobed leaves and long-stalked blue or violet flower heads, 1¼ to 1½ inches wide, in loose clusters.

Mountain- or blue-sow-thistle (**L. alpina** syns. *Cicerbita alpina*, *Mulgedium alpinum*) inhabits alpine and arctic parts of Europe and Asia. A hardy perennial 2 or 3 to 6 feet tall, this, except for the upper parts of its stems, which are furnished with reddish, glandular hairs, is practically hairless. The leaves are up to 8 inches or more long and slashed deeply into triangular lobes of which the terminal one is the biggest. The short-stalked flower heads, ¾ inch across and somewhat resembling those of chicory and dandelions, are pale blue to blue-violet and in cylindrical clusters at the tops of wandlike stems. Similar **L. plumieri**, of the mountains of central Europe, has hairless, not glandular stems, deeply-pinnately-lobed leaves, and long-stalked blue or violet flower heads, 1¼ to 1½ inches wide, in loose clusters. Native to Asia Minor, **L. bourgaei** (syn. *Mulgedium bourgaei*) is a thick-stemmed perennial, 4 to 6 feet tall, with bristly-hairy, oblong-lanceolate to fiddle-shaped, lobed leaves and loose, terminal panicles of upfacing, starry, lavender to pink flowers.

Garden Uses and Cultivation. The sorts described are appropriate for perennial beds and borders. They adapt well to ordinary well-drained soils and are grateful for a little light shade from the brightest, middle-of-the-day sun. Propagation is easy by seed and by division in early spring.

Lactuca bourgaei

LAD'S LOVE is *Artemisia abrotanum*.

LADY, LADY'S, or LADIES. These words appear as parts of the common names of various plants including these: lady fern (*Athyrium filix-femina*), lady-of-the-night (*Brunfelsia americana*), lady palms (*Rhapis*), lady slipper (*Cypripedium, Paphiopedilum,* and *Phragmipedilum*), lady's bedstraw (*Galium verum*), lady's mantle (*Alchemilla*), lady's smock (*Cardamine pratensis*), ladies'-tobacco (*Antennaria plantaginifolia*), ladies' tresses (*Spiranthes*), lords-and-ladies (*Arum maculatum*), Our-Lady's-thistle (*Cnicus benedictus*), and Quaker ladies (*Houstonia caerulea*).

LADYBELL. See Adenophora.

LADYBUG and LADYBIRD. These are names sometimes used for the lady beetle. See Beetles.

LAELIA (Làe-lia). One of the best known components of the orchid family ORCHI-DACEAE, this genus is a close relative of *Cattleya*, with which it hybridizes freely to produce plants identified as *Laeliocattleya*. The only constant difference between *Laelia* and *Cattleya* is that the flowers of the former have eight, and those of the latter have four pollinia (pollen masses). In *Laeliocattleya* the number is irregular. Some authorities include *Schomburgkia* in *Laelia*. In this Encyclopedia it is treated separately. The name is that of Laelia, a vestal virgin. Native in Mexico and Guatemala and in tropical and subtropical South America, *Laelia* contains about thirty species.

Laelias are evergreen epiphytes (tree-perchers that do not take nourishment from their hosts) or lithophytes (plants that grow on rocks). They have clustered pseudobulbs generally, but not always, shorter and squatter than those of cattleyas. The flowering stalks come from the tops of the pseudobulbs. They are commonly long and slender with the blooms clustered near their apexes, but some species have solitary flowers.

Winter-blooming **L. anceps,** of Mexico, has flattened, longitudinally-ribbed, ovate-oblong pseudobulbs 2 to 4 inches tall generally more or less widely spaced along thickish, creeping rhizomes. Each has usually a solitary, stiff, leathery, somewhat pointed, oblong-lanceolate leaf 6 to 8 inches

Laelia anceps

Laelia anceps (flowers)

long. The erect or arching, jointed flowering stalks 2 to 4 feet in length have near their ends two to five, or rarely more, fragrant or scentless blooms 2½ to 4 inches in diameter with very pale pink or rose-purple sepals and somewhat broader and darker-colored petals. The three-lobed lip, pale rose-pink edged with purple, has a forward-extended, magenta-red or purple-crimson middle lobe with a white-bordered, yellow disk and side lobes that form a tube enclosing the column. The slender, stalklike ovaries are decidedly sticky. There are many varieties, including *L. a. alba*, with

Laelia anceps alba

flowers pure white except for a light yellow spot in the throat; *L. a. grandiflora*, with flowers twice as big as those of the typical species; *L. a. percivaliana*, which has narrower leaves and blush-pink flowers with the tip of the lip purple-magenta and its base white; *L. a. rosea*, with pale pink flowers with a large, unlined, rosy-magenta lip and pale yellow throat; *L. a. scottiana*, with dark violet-purple flowers 5 inches in diameter and with an orange-throat; and *L. a. williamsii*, the white flowers of which have a lip with a yellow disk and a crimson-purple-striped, yellow throat.

Laelia anceps williamsii

Fall- and winter-blooming **L. autumnalis** is a Mexican with clustered or only slightly separated pseudobulbs that are approximately conical, 4 to 6 inches long, the older ones ridged lengthwise. The pseudobulbs have two or three blunt, lanceolate, stiffish leaves 5 to 7 inches long. Thickish and dull red, the 2- to 3-foot-long flowering stalks terminate in loose racemes of up to nine long-lasting, fragrant blooms. From 3 to 4 inches wide and varying considerably in intensity of color, these typically have bright rose-purple to magenta sepals and petals and a three-lobed lip with the lateral lobes partially surrounding the column. The center lobe is rose-purple with yellow at its base. Varieties include *L. a. alba*, with pure white blooms; *L. a. atrorubens*, the flowers of which are deep rose-pink to magenta; and *L. a. venusta*, which has large, rosy-mauve blooms.

Laelia autumnalis

Robust and handsome, **L. purpurata,** highly variable in the wild, is cultivated in numerous horticultural varieties. The national flower of Brazil, of which country it is native, this blooms in late spring and summer. Its pseudobulbs are elliptic to slender-club-shaped. Each has a solitary, rigid, oblong-lanceolate leaf approximately 1 foot in length. The stout flowering stalks have three to seven or more long-lasting, scented blooms 6 to 8 inches in diameter. Most usually the sepals and petals are white or white suffused and veined with purple, sometimes they are light amethyst-purple with darker veins. The petals, ovate and wavy-edged, are generally twice as broad as the linear-oblong sepals. Rather bell-shaped, the slightly three-lobed lip, whitish on its outside, its inside yellow lined with purple, forms a tube around the column. Its spreading center lobe, rich purple with darker veins, has a yellow throat and is crisped at its edges. Among the many varieties are *L. p. alba*, with flowers pure white except for the pink-veined lip; *L. p. atropurpurea*, which has blooms with deep rose-pink sepals and petals, a large purple-magenta lip, and a purple-veined, yellow throat; *L. p. carnea*, with white flowers marked on the lip with rose-pink; *L. p. purpurea*, with red-purple blooms; *L. p. rosea*, which has flowers with white sepals and petals tinted pink along their centers and a rose-pink lip; and *L. p. russelliana*, the comparatively large flowers of which have lilac-tinged sepals, lilac petals, a rosy-lilac lip, and a pink-veined, yellow throat.

Brazilian **L. grandis** has fragrant blooms up to 6 inches or sometimes more across. They have tawny-yellow, wavy sepals and petals. The lower portion of the lip is tubular and white, veined with rose-purple. Variety *L. g. tenebrosa* (syn. *L. tenebrosa*) has citron-yellow sepals and petals. The trumpet-shaped lip is purple, edged with white veined with purple.

Laelia grandis tenebrosa

Graceful and distinctive, **L. rubescens** is native from Mexico to Panama. It has strongly-flattened, egg-shaped, roundish, or oblongish pseudobulbs a little over 2 inches tall, about one-half as broad as their height, each with usually one, occasionally two lustrous leaves. The latter are oblong-elliptic, 6 to 8 inches long by 1½

Laelia rubescens

inches wide. From 1 foot to 2 or occasionally 3 feet tall, the flowering stalks end in short racemes of few to several rather short-lived blooms that frequently do not open fully. They are of various shades of pink with the lip generally darker than the sepals and petals or are white or white with the tube formed of the side lobes of the three-lobed lip pink or red. The side lobes of the lip surround the column.

Other species include these: **L. albida**, of Mexico and Guatemala, has pseudobulbs about 2 inches long with a pair of narrow leaves 6 or 7 inches in length. Its wiry-stalked, loose racemes, up to about 1½ feet long and appearing in winter,

Laelia albida

Laelia albida (flowers)

Laelia albida, yellowish flowered variety with a pink-striped lip

Laelia cinnabarina

carry several 2-inch-wide, fragrant, white or yellowish blooms often suffused with pink and with the lip pink or white lined at its center with yellow. **L. cinnabarina** is a spring-blooming Brazilian with usually single-leaved pseudobulbs 5 to 10 inches long. The flowering stalks, 1 foot to 2 feet long, carry up to fifteen bright orange-red, 2- to 3-inch-wide blooms. **L. crispa** blooms in summer. Brazilian, it has one-leaved, club-shaped pseudobulbs up to 10 inches long and very beautiful, fragrant blooms, 4 to 6 inches in diameter, in 1-foot-long racemes of usually four to seven. The very conspicuously crisped sepals and petals are pure white. The similarly crisped, yellow-throated, purple lip has a white margin. **L. crispilabia**, of Brazil, has cylindrical pseudobulbs that widen at their bases, with a single fleshy leaf. Up to 1 foot long or a little longer, the flowering stalks display in loose arrangement 2-inch-wide, amethyst-purple blooms that have a three-lobed lip with a white center lobe. **L. dormaniana** is a Brazilian with thin, stemlike pseudobulbs, up to 1¼ feet tall, with two to three short leaves. The flowering stalks carry up to four 3-inch-wide blooms with darker-veined, olive-brown sepals and petals and a lip with a crimson-purple center lobe and purple-veined, rose-pink side ones. **L. flava** is a winter- and spring-blooming native of Brazil, with slender pseudobulbs up to 8 inches tall each with a solitary 6-inch-long leaf. The 2½-inch-wide, golden-yellow blooms are from five to fifteen on stalks about 1½ feet long. **L. harpophylla**, of Brazil, is a natural hybrid that blooms in winter and spring. It has stemlike pseudobulbs 1 foot to 1½ feet tall topped by a single 8-inch-long leaf. The flowers, in racemes of up to about seven, are 2 to 3 inches across. They have orange-red sepals and petals and a lip similarly colored except that the middle lobe is yellow, edged with white. **L. jongheana** is a spring-blooming Brazilian. This has ovoid pseudobulbs about 2½ inches tall each with one or sometimes two leaves up to 5 inches in length. Shorter than the leaves,

Laelia harpophylla

Laelia jongheana

the flowering stalks carry one or two blooms, 4 to 5 inches wide, with rose-purple sepals, petals, and lip, the last with a yellow center and at its edges crisped. **L. pumila** is a low native of Brazil with, on creeping rhizomes, little, rather widely-spaced pseudobulbs each with one leaf 2 to 5 inches long. The short-stalked, solitary flowers are fragrant, 3 to 4 inches in diameter, and somewhat variable in coloring. They have usually rose-purple to

Laelia pumila

lavender-rose sepals and petals and a yellow-throated, maroon-purple, three-lobed lip, the side lobes embracing the column. **L. rupestris** is a Brazilian with pseudobulbs 1½ to 4 inches long, each with one strap-shaped leaf 2 to 6 inches in length. The violet flowers, two to four on slender stalks, are approximately 1½ inches wide. They have a nearly circular lip with a crisped-margined center lobe. Variety **L. r. nana** has pseudobulbs and leaves together only 1½ inches in length and flowers about 1 inch in diameter.

Laelia rupestris

A presumed natural hybrid between *L. anceps* and *L. albida*, originally from Mexico, **L. finckeniana** has two-leaved pseudobulbs and flowers 3½ to 4 inches wide with pure white sepals and petals and a large lip with purple-lined side lobes.

Laelia finckeniana

Garden Uses and Cultivation. These are as for cattleyas. A few species that in the wild grow at high altitudes perhaps prefer slightly cooler conditions. All, to bloom well, must be exposed to as intense light as they can take without the foliage being scorched. For further information see Orchids.

LAELIOCATONIA. This is the name of orchid hybrids the parents of which include *Broughtonia, Cattleya,* and *Laelia*.

LAELIOCATTKERIA. This is the name of trigeneric orchid hybrids the parents of which are *Laelia, Cattleya,* and *Barkeria*.

LAELIOCATTLEYA. This is the name of orchid hybrids between the genera *Laelia* and *Cattleya*.

Laeliocattleya variety

LAELIOPLEYA. This is the name of orchid hybrids the parents of which are *Cattleya* and *Laeliopsis*.

LAELIOPSIS (Laeli-ópsis). Two West Indian species constitute *Laeliopsis*, of the orchid family ORCHIDACEAE. From closely related *Broughtonia* they differ in minor floral details and in their stiff, fleshy leaves being sharply-toothed. The name, from that of the related genus *Laelia* and the Greek *opsis*, resembling, alludes to similarities in appearance.

Native of Hispaniola, **L. domingensis** (syn. *Broughtonia domingensis*) finds favor with orchid fanciers. It is an evergreen with clusters of slightly-flattened, longitudinally ridged, egg-shaped to more cylindrical pseudobulbs up to 3 inches long, with from their tops usually two blunt, fleshy, oblong leaves up to 5 inches in length. Generally branched above, the flower stem, which originates from the top of the pseudobulb, is slender and up to 2 feet long. It bears few to many cattleya-like blooms 2 to 2½ inches wide that open in succession over a long time. The linear-oblong sepals and broader, sometimes toothed petals are rosy-mauve with darker veinings. The lip is long, and at its mouth broad. Below it is tubular and whitish or yellowish, but the flaring part of its apex is rose-purple with darker veins. A rare white-flowered variant occurs.

Garden Uses and Cultivation. These are as for *Broughtonia*. For more information see Orchids.

LAELONIA. This is the name of orchid hybrids between the genera *Broughtonia* and *Laelia*.

LAEOPSIS. This is the name of orchid hybrids between the genera *Laelia* and *Laeliopsis*.

LAGAROSIPHON (Lagaro-sìphon). The genus *Lagarosiphon* belongs in the frog's bit family HYDROCHARITACEAE and includes fifteen species of alternate-leaved aquatics. The group is indigenous in Africa, Madagascar, and India. Its name comes from the Greek *lagaros*, hollow, and *siphon*, a tube. A variety of the South African *L. muscoides* named *L. m. major* is sometimes grown in aquariums under its synonym of *Elodea crispa*, which, in turn, is a synonym of *Anacharis crispa*. It has been confused with *Hydrilla verticillata crispa*.

A submersed aquatic with long, stout stems closely and evenly furnished with narrowly strap-shaped leaves, up to ¾ inch long, *L. m. major* resembles *Elodea densa* except that its leaves are strongly and gracefully recurved. From *Hydrilla* it is readily distinguished by its leaves not being in whorls (circles of more than two). Also, in *Hydrilla*, the midrib is often reddish. The female flowers float on the surface without detaching themselves; the males break away from the spathes in the leaf axils, rise to the surface, and float free. The flowers are minute and have three small white petals and, the males, three fertile and usually three sterile stamens. The species *L. muscoides* has smaller, less markedly recurved leaves and is of less robust appearance than variety *L. m. major*.

Garden Uses and Cultivation. Attractive plants for well-lighted aquariums, *L. muscoides* and its variety grow well in river sand containing some clay and organic matter. The water should be neutral or slightly alkaline and contain available calcium and potassium. Water temperatures of 55 to 65°F are satisfactory. Propagation is easily achieved by cuttings.

LAGENANDRA (Lagen-ándra). Belonging to the arum family ARACEAE, the genus *Lagenandra*, of India and Ceylon, consists of about six species. In allusion to the prolongation of the peculiar anther cells, which suggest the neck of a flask or a penis, the name is derived from the Greek *lagenos*, a flask, and *aner*, man.

Related to *Cryptocoryne*, lagenandras are perennial, herbaceous aquatic or bog plants with elongating stems and generally long-stalked, undivided leaves. The flowers, as is usual in the family, are small and clustered on a spikelike spadix shorter than the usually purple spathe that envelops it. Male and female flowers are separated by a short piece of spadix without flowers. The fruits are technically berries.

The species now to be described are all natives of Ceylon: *L. lancifolia* has leaves with elliptic to lanceolate blades 2 to 4 inches long, green above, beneath paler and spotted with white. *L. ovata* has leaves with pointed-elliptic to ovate blades up to 1½ feet long and nearly 5 inches wide. *L. thwaitesii* has leaves with oblong-lanceolate, wavy-margined blades up to 6 inches in length and 1½ inches wide.

Lagenandra ovata

Lagenandra thwaitesii

Garden Uses and Cultivation. These plants are sometimes grown in aquariums. They may also be cultivated in pots or pans kept with their bottoms standing in water. They need fertile soil, a humid atmosphere, and tropical temperatures. Propagation is by division and by cuttings.

LAGENARIA (Lagenàr-ia) — White-Flowered Gourd. Six species constitute *Lagenaria*, a native of Africa, Madagascar, and South America, now widely naturalized in many parts of the tropics, and a member of the gourd family CUCURBITACEAE. Its name is derived from the Greek *lagenos*, a flask, in allusion to the shapes of the fruits.

An interesting problem concerns the wide natural distribution of *Lagenaria*. Although its origin is regarded as definitely Old World, it is certain that these plants were growing in South America long before Europeans discovered that continent. Artifacts made from the shells of their fruits, excavated in northern Peru and carbondated, are 3,000 to 5,000 years old. They predate the use of silver and copper in Peru. Many theories have been advanced, but there is no agreement among botanists who have studied the problem as to how this plant traveled so long ago from tropical Asia or tropical Africa to the New World. Were the fruits transported across vast distances by ocean currents or brought by primitive man on rafts or other craft across the Bering Strait when a land bridge connected Asia with North America? No one knows. The land bridge theory seems unlikely, for the men who traversed that were hunters not agriculturists. Nor does it seem probable that the white-flowered gourd reached America by island-hopping across the wide stretches of the Pacific against prevailing winds and currents even with the help of man. Immigration to South America from Africa across the Atlantic involves about 1,700 miles of ocean travel, and the fruits of *Lagenaria* can float for months and their seeds still retain their ability to germinate, so perhaps this is the way these gourds came to the Americas.

The white-flowered gourd (*L. siceraria* syn. *L. vulgaris*) is the only species cultivated. It is a rapid-growing, cucumber-like, annual vine with grooved stems that attain a length of up to 30 feet or more in a single season. It has softly-hairy, round-heart-shaped leaves, usually without lobes, but

Lagenaria siceraria (foliage and flower)

sometimes angled, and forked tendrils. Its stems and foliage are covered with slightly sticky hairs and are musk-scented. Male and female flowers are usually on the same plant. Of flimsy texture, white, solitary, and funnel-shaped, they open at night and close in strong light. The males are on long, slender stalks, the females, usually on shorter stalks, have three bilobed stigmas. The fruits, smooth, or those of some sorts longitudinally-ridged or conspicuously-warted, are green, mottled, longitudinally-striped, or white, and at maturity are hard-shelled. They vary tremendously in shape and size and are known by such names as bottle gourd, calabash gourd, dipper gourd, Hercules' club gourd, siphon gourd, snake gourd, and sugar-trough gourd, according to kind.

Because they are of many shapes and sizes the shells of the fruits of this species lend themselves to a great many uses as utensils, musical instruments, toys, and ornaments and were, and to a considerable extent are, still employed for such purposes by the natives of many lands, although tinware, plastics, and other products of industry are reducing the need for gourd vessels and utensils. From a pear-shaped small-fruited variety people in Paraguay and other parts of South America drink maté (tea made from the holly, *Ilex paraguariensis*). In parts of Asia and other places the young fruits are eaten, but are usually considered to be less satisfactory for this purpose than their relatives, the squashes, pumpkins, cucumbers, and melons.

A selection of fruits of *Lagenaria siceraria*

A selection of fruits of *Lagenaria siceraria*

Garden and Landscape Uses. White-flowered gourds are useful for covering fences and other supports as temporary screens and are cultivated for their unusual fruits, which excite curiosity and interest and are decidedly decorative on the vines and can be picked, preserved, and used for indoor decoration and other purposes. It is best if the fruits are not picked until they have turned brown and dry and have thoroughly ripened on the vine, but where frost is likely to occur before this happens, they may be picked when fully grown, but still green and be "finished" indoors. A generous length of stalk should be taken with each gourd, and the fruits should be spread out in a dry, airy place where the temperature is about 70°F until they become a pleasing light brown or straw-yellow. This airing process may take several weeks. Handle uncured specimens gently to avoid damage. If, after they are cured, the thin, soft, outer skin has not completely disintegrated dip the gourds in boiling water and rub off any remaining skin, then lay the fruits out to dry again slowly and naturally. Any rough spots on their surfaces may be smoothed with fine sandpaper. It is not necessary to remove the insides of this species of gourd, but if you want to extract the seeds it can be done either by sawing off the top of the fruit with a fine-toothed saw, or if the fruit is not too big, by drilling a hole in an in-

conspicuous place. The outer surface can be left as is or be waxed and polished or shellacked. Yet another treatment consists of rubbing with oil or fat and then baking in an oven at 100°F for ten minutes or so and cooling slowly and repeating this process several times, gradually increasing the temperature following successive oilings until a maximum of 200°F is reached. The secret lies in doing this slowly. Fast baking and excessive temperatures are disastrous.

For Arts and Crafts. Besides being decorative without any preparation other than curing, the ripened fruits of these gourds are excellent for arts and crafts. Many methods of treating them and uses will suggest themselves to clever and inventive artists and handicrafters. Among their many uses are bases for table lamps, nesting boxes for wrens and other small birds, decorative boxes and vases, ash trays, maracas (rattles), novelty items of many kinds, and toys. The outsides of the dried gourds can be decorated by painting, carving, burning with hot irons, and other techniques.

Cultivation. Lagenarias need essentially the same cultivation as squashes and cucumbers. Where the season is long enough for the fruits to mature from seeds sown outside, sow, where the plants are to remain, in fertile, well-drained soil in a sunny location as soon as the ground is warm and all danger of cold nights has passed. Where the growing season is too short to permit fruits to ripen on vines from outdoor-sown seed, sow indoors in pots about a month before it is safe to set the resulting plants in the garden (about the same time that it is safe to plant tomatoes, peppers, and egg plants).

LAGENIFERA (Lagen-ífera). Consisting of herbaceous perennial plants resembling English daisies, *Lagenifera* differs from the genus *Bellis*, to which English daisies belong, by its fruits being beaked at their tips. It belongs in the daisy family COMPOSITAE and has a name, sometimes spelled *Lagenophora*, derived from the Latin *lagena*, a flask, and *fero*, to carry, that alludes to the shape of the involucre (collar of bracts at the rear of the flower head). Containing thirty species, *Lagenifera* is native from Japan and the Ryukyu Islands to Borneo, New Caledonia, New Zealand, islands of the Pacific, and Central and South America. It is not hardy in the north.

Lageniferas have lanceolate to spatula-shaped, undivided, toothed or toothless leaves, and solitary, slender-stalked, daisy-like flower heads with central eyes composed of numerous tubular, yellow disk florets surrounded by many spreading, white or light blue, petal-like ray florets. The seedlike fruits are achenes.

New Zealand **L. pumila** (syn. *L. forsteri*) has slender, branching rhizomes and basal rosettes of leaves with rough-hairy blades about ½ inch long by three-quarters as wide, and toothed or nearly toothless. The flower heads, ⅓ to ½ inch wide, are on stalks 3 to 6 inches long. Native of Malaysia, **L. billardieri** is pubescent and has obovate to oblong leaves, sinuately-toothed at their margins, and up to 2 inches long. The flower heads, with white or blue rays, top stalks 2 inches to 1 foot in length. Wild from Japan, Taiwan, and southern China to Australia, **L. stipitata** has basal rosettes of coarsely-toothed, obovate to spatula-shaped, hairy leaves ½ inch to 1¼ inches long. Its ½-inch-wide flower heads on stalks 1½ to 4½ inches long are white.

Lagenifera stipitata

Garden Uses and Cultivation. In regions of mild winters lageniferas may be grown in rock gardens and other places where small plants can be appropriately accommodated. They prefer sandy, peaty, well-drained soil of reasonable fertility and are raised from seed or increased by division in spring.

LAGENOPHORA. See Lagenifera.

LAGERSTROEMIA (Lager-stròemia)—Crape-Myrtle. Favorite shrubs and trees for use in warm climates, crape-myrtles are of the genus *Lagerstroemia*, of the loosestrife family LYTHRACEAE. Their name commemorates Magnus von Lagerstroem, naturalist friend of the great Swedish botanist Carolus Linnaeus, and Director of the Swedish East Indies Company. He died in 1759.

There are approximately fifty species, deciduous and evergreen, of *Lagerstroemia*. All are natives of the Old World tropics. They have undivided leaves, mostly opposite or whorled (in circles of more than two), but the upper ones sometimes alternate. The symmetrical flowers, in often showy, terminal or axillary panicles or clusters, are white, pink, lavender-pink, red, or purple. They have top-shaped to hemispherical, often ribbed or winged calyxes with six to nine segments (sepals).

The petals, commonly six, have broad, fringed or crinkled blades. Their lower portions are narrowed into long, slender shafts or claws. There are many long-stalked stamens and a long style tipped with a headlike stigma. The fruits are capsules containing seeds winged at their tops.

The crape-myrtle (**L. indica**), a native of China, is naturalized to some extent in the southern United States. Typically a multi-trunked shrub or tree usually not over 30 feet in height, but occasionally nearly twice as tall, it has smooth, fluted, pale pinkish-brown trunks with peeling bark. The mostly opposite, deciduous, privet-like leaves are stalkless or very short-stalked and have generally pointed, elliptic to oblongish blades 1 inch to 3 inches long. Before they drop in fall they change from dark green to yellow, orange, and red. The large, loose, sometimes minutely-downy panicles, 6 inches to 1½ feet long, are of bright to pale pink, lavender-pink, purplish, or white blooms 1 inch to 2 inches wide. The flowers have ribless, nearly or quite hairless calyxes, usually six petals, and about forty stamens. The fruits are ½ inch in diameter.

Lagerstroemia indica in Virginia

Lagerstroemia indica (flowers)

In recent years plant breeders have given much attention to the common crape-myrtle, seeking to raise not only dwarf varieties

and kinds with desirable flower colors, but also varieties less susceptible to mildew disease and more cold resistant. With these objectives in view hybridization between *L. indica*, *L. fauriei*, and *L. subcostata* was initiated. The common crape-myrtle is reliably hardy about as far north as Baltimore, Maryland, and specimens sometimes survive in very protected locations even in the vicinity of New York City. Named varieties including dwarfs about 3 feet tall, medium-sized kinds 6 to 12 feet tall, and tall varieties that exceed this last dimension are available from nurseries in a wide selection of flower colors.

Lagerstroemia indica, in a sheltered location outdoors at The New York Botanical Garden

Lagerstroemia speciosa

Queen or giant crape-myrtle (**L. speciosa** syn. *L. flos-reginae*), in effect a larger edition of the common crape-myrtle, is popular in southern Florida, southern California, and Hawaii. Where native, this may be 60 to 100 feet tall, but in cultivation is much less lofty, in Florida ordinarily 20 to 30 feet in height. Indigenous from India to Australia, this has light, scaling bark, and short-stalked, pointed-elliptic to ovate leaves 3 inches to 1 foot long and 1 inch to 5½ inches wide. The 2- to 3-inch-wide flowers, in loose panicles 1½ to 2½ feet

Lagerstroemia speciosa (flowers)

Lagerstroemia indica, as a hedge in Jamaica, West Indies

long, have twelve-ribbed, bell-shaped calyxes with six or occasionally seven lobes or teeth, and corollas of six crinkled, crapelike, pink to mauve petals. Their centers are crowded with many more than 100 yellow stamens. The fruits are 1 inch in diameter. The queen crape-myrtle is much less hardy than common crape-myrtle. It is suitable only for the warmest parts of the United States.

Other species cultivated include *L. fauriei*, of Japan and the Ryukyu Islands, and *L. subcostata*, of China, Japan, the Ryukyu Islands, and Taiwan. A deciduous tree with beautifully colored bark and hairless shoots, *L. fauriei* has oblong to ovate, leathery leaves 3 to 4 inches long by approximately 2 inches wide with eight to thirteen pairs of lateral veins. Their under surfaces have tufts of hair in the axils of the veins. The flowers, in rather dense terminal panicles 2 to 4 inches long, have thirty to thirty-six stamens. Differing from the last in its shoots and branches of its panicles of bloom being short-hairy, *L. subcostata* is a deciduous tree with ovate, elliptic, or obovate leaves 1½ to 3½ inches long with two to five pairs of lateral veins and tufts of hair in the axils of the veins beneath. The white to pink flowers, each with fifteen to thirty stamens, are crowded in panicles 2 to 4 inches long. An intermediate hybrid between *L. fauriei* and *L. subcostata* is named *L. amabilis*.

Garden and Landscape Uses. With much justification the common crape-myrtle has been called lilac of the south. There, it is used even more freely than are lilacs in the north around homes and in many other landscape plantings. If kept pruned it makes a good flowering screen or hedge. It is an especial favorite for avenues. Not only are its uses similar to those of lilac, but the appearance of its foliage and trusses of bloom suggest that popular shrub or small tree, even though the flowers come in different colors and lack fragrance. One advantage crape-myrtle has over lilac is that its blooms are borne on shoots of the current year's growth. Because of this, it flow-

ers freely even when pruned back each year. Of noble aspect, the queen crape-myrtle serves similar purposes, as do the other sorts described.

Cultivation. Crape-myrtles are very responsive to the gardener's art. They succeed in a wide variety of well-drained, not excessively dry soils, blooming most profusely in those rather low in nutrients. Too much nitrogen results in extravagant shoot and foliage growth at the expense of bloom. For best results, full sun and a free circulation of air about them are essential. Because crape-myrtles are sensitive to root disturbance it is important when transplanting them to take a sizable, unbroken ball of earth. Late spring, before new growth begins, is the best time to undertake this task.

The forms assumed by crape-myrtles are largely determined by pruning. Normally several trunks or branches grow from near the ground, but single-trunked, tree-form specimens can be had by, from the beginning, cutting out all unwanted shoots. Normal pruning consists of thinning out thin, twiggy, and crowded shoots so that those that remain receive abundant light and air. Pollard pruning, the severe heading back of large trunks and branches is sometimes practiced. Specimens so treated renew themselves by broomlike clumps of new shoots from below the cuts, but such severe cutting is likely to result in graceless, ungainly specimens. The propagation of crape-myrtles is best accomplished by cuttings made from leafy summer shoots, and by leafless hardwood cuttings. Seeds germinate readily, but may give rise to a large proportion of plants with flowers of inferior colors.

In addition to their usefulness for open-ground planting, crape-myrtles are excellent in large tubs and other containers for decorating patios, steps, terraces, and suchlike places. In cold climates they can be wintered in light locations indoors where the temperature ranges between 35 and 50°F. During that period they are kept

nearly, but not absolutely, dry. In late winter or early spring all weak and crowded shoots are cut out, and others are shortened as much as seems desirable. If the plants are not to grow bigger, the shoots retained are cut back to within 3 or 4 inches of their bases. At the time of pruning, specimens in need of repotting or retubbing are given those attentions. This is needed only at intervals of several years. In intervening years as much as possible of the old surface soil is pricked away with a fork or pointed stick and is replaced with a top dressing of new rich earth. Following potting or top dressing, tubs are moved to a sunny, warmer place. A night temperature of about 55°F and day temperatures some five to fifteen degrees higher suit. Normal watering is then resumed. Specimens not repotted in spring benefit from regular applications of dilute liquid fertilizer given at about two-week intervals from spring to fall.

LAGOTIS (Lag-òtis). Here belongs a group of twenty species of perennial herbaceous plants of the figwort family SCROPHULARIACEAE. Natives of arctic and subarctic regions, including Alaska and other parts of North America, they are related to *Castilleja* and *Pedicularis*. The name is from the Greek *lagos*, a hare, and *otos*, an ear.

Lagotises have stout, creeping rootstocks, and alternate, usually undivided, toothed or toothless leaves, but those of *Lagotis globosa* are pinnately-lobed, the basal ones clustered, the stem ones well spaced and becoming progressively smaller, and finally bractlike, upward. The small, usually asymmetrical, bluish or lavender, tubular blooms, each from the axil of a conspicuous bract, are in congested cylindrical, or rarely nearly globular, terminal spikes. Each flower has a two-lobed calyx, and a two-lipped corolla, with the lower lip two-lobed and the upper toothed or toothless. There are two stamens, and one style. The fruits consist of two seedlike nutlets, one of which often fails to develop.

Occurring on tundra, talus slopes, and sandy river banks, *L. glauca* is up to 1 foot tall. Its basal leaves, ovate to lanceolate, stalked, and more or less scallop-toothed, have blades approximately 1 inch long. The flower spike is 1 inch to 4 inches long and up to ¾ inch in diameter. A minor variant is named *L. g. stelleri*.

Garden Uses and Cultivation. This is a plant for dedicated alpine gardeners to attempt. It cannot be expected to survive hot, dry summers. Cool, moist conditions are to its liking, as is soil that is porous and freely drained, but not dry. Increase is had by seed and by division in early spring.

LAGUNA. See Abelmoschus.

LAGUNARIA (Lagunàr-ia) — Queensland Pyramid Tree or Whitewood, Cowitch

Tree. This genus, which inhabits New South Wales, Queensland, Norfolk Island, and Lord Howe Island, is variously regarded by botanists as consisting of one species and of being represented by three, one in Australia and one in each of the islands. Be that as it may, these geographical populations are much alike, and plants of the Australian type are the most likely to be found in cultivation. In Australia the tree is known as Queensland pyramid tree and whitewood, in Norfolk Island as cowitch tree. The name *Lagunaria* honors Andrea Laguna, who died in 1560. He was a Spanish botanist and physician to Pope Julius III.

Probably the largest species in the mallow family MALVACEAE, the Queensland pyramid tree (*L. patersonii*) is an ornamental evergreen, the source of a close-grained, easily worked, white lumber used for building. It attains a height of 60 feet and has alternate, oblong-ovate, toothless, thick leaves 3 to 4 inches long that are pale beneath and scurfy-pubescent when young. The flowers, axillary and solitary, have very short stalks and five spreading petals 1½ inches long or longer, and slightly tomentose on their outsides. They are pale lavender-rose. The center of the bloom is occupied by a column of fused stamens and a five-lobed stigma. The fruits are capsules.

Lagunaria patersonii

Garden and Landscape Uses. The Queensland pyramid tree is an attractive outdoor garden and park plant for frost-free or nearly frost-free climates, such as are characteristic of parts of California, Florida, and Hawaii. It grows without difficulty in any well-drained soil in full sun. It flowers when quite small and is easy to grow in conservatories and large greenhouses.

Cultivation. Lagunarias transplant without difficulty and outdoors need no particular care beyond that afforded the general run of evergreens. In greenhouses they may be accommodated in large well-drained pots or tubs or in beds of fertile, porous, peaty, potting soil kept uniformly moist

from spring through fall, and a little drier in winter. Full sun, a winter night temperature of 45 to 50°F, with a daytime increase of five or ten degrees, and free ventilation whenever outside conditions permit, provide suitable growing conditions.

In summer the pots or tubs may be plunged to their rims in a bed of sand, ashes, sawdust, or other suitable material outdoors. If their containers are well filled with healthy roots, the plants will benefit from weekly applications of dilute liquid fertilizer from spring through late summer. Any pruning necessary to shape them or curtail their growth should be done immediately after they are through blooming. Needed repotting may receive attention in early spring before new growth begins. Propagation is by seed and by cuttings of young, half-ripened shoots in summer.

LAGURUS (Lag-ùrus)—Hare's Tail Grass. The only species of *Lagurus* is the hare's tail grass, a native of western Europe including the British Isles, and the Mediterranean region, and naturalized to some extent in California. It belongs in the grass family GRAMINEAE. Its generic name is derived from the Greek *lagos*, a hare, and *oura*, a tail, and refers to the appearance of the flower panicles.

Hare's tail grass (**L. ovatus**) is an attractive erect biennial or annual, 1 foot to 2 feet tall. It has softly-hairy leaves usually much shorter than the stems and about ⅛ inch broad. The flowers are in terminal, egg-shaped, plumy, spikelike, whitish-woolly panicles 1 inch to 2 inches long. The spikelets are single-flowered. This grass is also known as rabbit's tail grass.

Lagurus ovatus

Garden Uses. Hare's tail grass is suitable for the fronts of flower borders and for using as a cut flower. It may be dried as an everlasting. To do this pull or cut the plants just before the flower heads mature, tie them in small bundles, and hang them upside down in a dry, airy, shaded

place until they are quite dry. Hare's tail grass needs well-drained soil and a sunny location.

Cultivation. Seeds are sown outdoors in spring or, in mild climates, in late summer or fall, and the seedlings thinned to about 1 foot apart. Gardeners sometimes sow seed in pots in early fall, winter the plants in cold frames, and set them out in the garden in spring. This grass needs no staking.

LAKE-CRESS is *Armoracia aquatica*.

LALLEMANTIA (Lallemánt-ia). Belonging in the mint family LABIATAE, the Asian genus *Lallemantia* consists of five species of annuals and biennials closely related to *Dracocephalum*. Its name honors Julius Leopold Ave-Lallement, a German botanist associated with the botanic garden of St. Petersburg (Leningrad), Russia, who died in 1867. These plants have opposite, toothed leaves and small two-lipped flowers, grouped in tiers, with four stamens. Their fruits are seedlike nutlets.

About 1½ feet in height, *L. canescens* is softly-hairy and has oblong-lanceolate

Lallemantia canescens

leaves. Its flowers, bright blue and 1¼ to 1½ inches long, have corolla tubes much longer than the calyxes. Its variety *L. c. albiflora* has pretty white flowers. Although a biennial, this species is usually grown as an annual and gives good results the first year from seed. Similar, but not hairy, *L. iberica* has smaller blue flowers and leaves scarcely toothed. The corolla tubes of its blooms are included in the calyxes. It is an annual. Another annual, *L. peltata* rarely exceeds 1 foot in height; it may be hairless or slightly pubescent and has more or less oval to oblong leaves and small blue flowers with corolla tubes scarcely longer than the calyxes. All the above are native to western Asia.

Garden Uses and Cultivation. These are attractive for flower beds and borders and rock gardens, but their blooms are not suitable for cutting. They are at their best in light, well-drained soils and sunny locations and need little care beyond the usual control of weeds and occasional watering in very dry weather. Sow seeds in early spring where the plants are to bloom and thin the seedlings to about 6 inches apart. Staking is not ordinarily needed.

LAMA is *Maba sandwicensis*.

LAMARCKIA (Lamárck-ia)—Golden Top. One annual species of the grass family GRAMINEAE constitutes *Lamarckia*. A native of the Mediterranean region, it is naturalized as a common weed in California. Its name commemorates the French naturalist J. B. Lamarck, who died in 1829.

Golden top (*L. aurea*) grows in tufts up to 1 foot tall or slightly taller. It has numerous soft, flat, hairless leaves, up to 6 inches long and ¼ inch wide, with expanded basal sheaths. Its flowers are in fairly dense, one-sided, panicles 1 inch to 3 inches long and ⅓ to ⅔ inch wide. When mature the panicles are shining golden-yellow sometimes tinged with purple.

Garden Uses and Cultivation. The most appropriate uses for this unpretentious annual are in small groups at the fronts of flower borders and in rock gardens and for cutting and drying as an everlasting for use in flower arrangements. Its culture is simple. Seeds are sown in well-drained soil in sunny locations in spring. The resulting plants are thinned to 6 inches apart. Intruding weeds are eliminated.

LAMB or LAMB'S. These words are employed as part of the common names of several plants: lamb's ears (*Stachys byzantina*), lamb's-lettuce (*Valerianella locusta*), lamb's quarters (*Chenopodium album*), lamb's tails (*Eurotia lanata*), and Scythian lamb or tartarian (*Cibotium barometz*).

LAMBERTIA (Lam-bértia). Restricted in the wild to Australia where its members are called honeysuckles, *Lambertia* belongs to the protea family PROTEACEAE. It has eight species. Its name commemorates Aylmer Bourke Lambert, an English botanist, who died in 1842.

Lambertias are evergreen shrubs with several stems coming from the ground. Their toothless or spine-toothed leaves are mostly in whorls (circles) of three or sometimes four. Occasionally toward the bases of luxuriant shoots they are alternate. The red, yellow, or greenish flowers are solitary or in terminal or axillary clusters of normally seven, with two or three such clusters sometimes grouped to give the effect of a much larger assemblage. At the base of each cluster is an involucre (collar) of colored bracts. The blooms have four petal-like perianth segments joined for much of their lengths into a narrow tube, with their free ends coiled backward.

These are morphologically sepals. There are no petals. There are four stamens and a slender, protruding style. The fruits are woody, podlike follicles.

Erect, 3 to 5 feet tall, with rigid, stalkless, linear leaves 1 inch to 2 inches long, *L. multiflora* has flowers at first golden-yellow that become orange as they age. They are about 1½ inches long, in clusters of normally seven, sometimes two or three together. A chief difference between this and red- and pink-flowered *L. formosa* is that the inner bracts of its involucres are as long instead of only one-half as long as the blooms. From 6 to 12 feet tall, bushy *L. ericifolia* has blunt, linear leaves ½ to ¾ inch long, with rolled-under margins. Its terminal umbels, solitary or in twos or threes, are of seven flowers 1½ inches in length. The inner bracts of the involucre are about ½ inch long.

Garden and Landscape Uses and Cultivation. Lambertias are unusual flowering shrubs for California and elsewhere with dry, warm, essentially frostless climates. Very little is recorded about their needs. It is to be expected that these are similar to the quite specialized ones of proteas. Propagation is by seed.

LAMBKILL is *Kalmia angustifolia*.

LAMIASTRUM (Lami-ástrum) — Yellow Archangel. A variegated-leaved form of the only species of this genus of the mint family LABIATAE has become popular in American gardens in recent years. It and the less frequently cultivated plain green-leaved species are often known by their older name of *Lamium*. From *Lamium*, as now understood, *Lamiastrum* (syn. *Galeobdolon*) differs in having the lower tip of the corolla with three lobes of approximately equal size instead of having a comparatively large central lobe and two toothlike lateral ones. Also, the anthers are hairless, whereas those of *Lamium* are usually hairy. The name, composed of *Lamium* and the Latin termination *astrum*, somewhat resembling, is self-explanatory.

Yellow archangel (*L. galeobdolon* syns. *L. luteum*, *Lamium galeobdolon*, *Galeobdolon luteum*) is native to woodlands, thickets, hedges, and similar partly shaded locations where the soil is fertile, throughout much of Europe. A hardy herbaceous perennial, 1 foot to 2 feet tall, of vigorous, even rampant, growth, it develops long, above-ground, creeping runners that root into the soil and sprawling or erect slender, square, hollow stems with rather distant, opposite, stalked, heart-shaped leaves, 1½ to 3 inches long, and round-toothed. The bright yellow flowers, with brownish markings, clustered in the upper leaf axils, are in tiers that form loose, lax, leafy spikes. They are hairy on their outsides, about ¾ inch long, tubular, and very asymmetrical. The bell-shaped calyx

Lamiastrum galeobdolon variegatum

Lamiastrum galeobdolon variegatum (flowers)

has five pointed teeth. The corolla has a strongly arched upper lip under which lie the four stamens, two long and two short, and a style with two stigmas. The lower lip of the corolla droops. The fruits are tiny nutlets. Variety *L. g. variegatum* has leaves conspicuously brushed with aluminum-silver. It is an attractive foliage plant.

Garden and Landscape Uses and Cultivation. Although it lacks the virtue of being evergreen, as a vigorous groundcover for lightly shaded places, or for sunny ones where the soil is not excessively dry, the yellow archangel, and especially its variegated variety, is extremely useful. The latter is also cultivated in pots, hanging baskets, decorative urns, and the like and serves much the same purpose as *Vinca major variegata* and *Glechoma hederacea variegata*. The yellow archangel flourishes without appreciable care and is easily increased by division, cuttings, and seed. Most usually the kind with leaves variegated with silver is chosen for planting. Sometimes this reverts to the plain green-leaved kind. Possibly this is the result of self-sown seedlings. To retain the silvery-leaved effect all plain green shoots that appear should be pulled out.

LAMIUM (Là-mium)—Dead-Nettle. A few worthwhile garden plants of simple culture are among the forty species of *Lamium*, of the mint family LABIATAE. The name is one used by Pliny and is derived from the Greek *laimos* or *lamos*, a throat. It alludes to the corolla. The group consists of annuals and perennials. Only the latter are cultivated. In the wild the dead-nettles are confined to the Old World, but several species are naturalized in North America and persist more or less as weeds.

Lamiums are mostly low, spreading, hairy plants with square stems and opposite, stalked, usually broad, round-toothed leaves. Their asymmetrical, tubular flowers are in leafy, short and crowded spikes or are in whorls (tiers) more distantly spaced. The corolla tube is broad above, slender toward its base. The upper lobe of the corolla, almost as long to slightly longer than the tube, is erect and curved, the lower one is slightly three-lobed. There are four stamens located under the upper corolla tip. Two are longer than the others. There is one style. The fruits are seedlike nutlets. The yellow-flowered plant previously named *L. galeobdolon* is *Lamiastrum galeobdolon*.

An old-fashioned garden plant, **L. album** has escaped from cultivation and in the United States and Canada has established itself along roadsides and waste places. From prostrate bases its stems ascend to a height of 8 inches to 1½ feet and may be branched or not. Ovate to triangular-ovate, the leaves are coarsely-crenately-toothed and 1½ to 4 inches long. The flowers are white and 1 inch long or slightly longer. Differing from *L. album* in having leaves with a conspicuous central stripe of white and a blunt rather than a sharp-pointed terminal tooth, **L. maculatum**, of Europe and temperate Asia, is naturalized in North America. Its 1-inch-long

Lamium maculatum

flowers are purplish-red. Varieties are *L. m. album*, with creamy-white blooms; *L. m.* 'Chequers', with leaves, except for a nar-

Lamium maculatum 'Chequers'

Lamium garganicum

row margin of green, silvery-white; and *L. m. variegatum*, with leaves mottled with green and white. About 1 foot tall, **L. garganicum,** of southern Europe, differs from *L. album* and *L. maculatum* in its red-purple, 1- to 1¼-inch-long flowers having a two-lobed upper lip and in its toothed leaves being somewhat smaller.

Garden Uses. As garden plants dead-nettles are usually not over 1 foot tall. Although by no means indispensable, they serve usefully as easy-to-grow fillers for the fronts of flower borders, rock gardens, and other places where a clump of something attractive, but not too showy will do. They prosper in full sun or part-shade. If in sun, a moistish soil is advantageous. The sorts described above are hardy perennials.

Cultivation. Among the easiest of hardy herbaceous perennials to grow, dead-nettles thrive in ordinary soil and are very easily propagated by division and by cuttings. They may be raised from seeds, but the variegated-foliaged kinds are not likely to come true when so increased; neither is the white-flowered form of *L. maculatum*. Planting may be done in spring or early fall, preferably the former. To keep the plants compact they should be sheared about midsummer. No other particular care is needed.

LAMPRANTHUS (Lamprán-thus). None of the many genera once included in *Mesembryanthemum*, of the carpetweed family AIZOACEAE, is more rewarding to the admirer of magnificent floral displays than *Lampranthus*. Its name, from the Greek *lampros*, bright, and *anthos*, a flower, is richly deserved. Lampranthuses are endemic to South Africa. There are about 100 species. From closely related *Mesembryanthemum* they differ in their seed capsules having marginal wings and in more recondite botanical details.

Shrubby plants of vigorous growth, these have much-branched, spreading or prostrate stems and often more or less curved, opposite leaves, the pairs generally united at their bases. The leaves are cylindrical or three-angled in section, and have blunt or tapered apexes. The flowers, solitary or clustered, from the leaf axils or terminal, are white, pink, purple-pink, red, yellow, or orange. They are daisy-like in appearance, but in structure very different. Each is a single bloom, instead of a head of many florets. The fruits are capsules. Kinds additional to those described below may be in cultivation.

A purple-flowered unidentified variety of *Lampranthus*

One of the most popular kinds, **L. aurantiacus** is 1 foot tall or a little taller and has erect or spreading stems. Its slender, taper-tipped leaves, with three blunt angles, are approximately 1 inch long. They are green, roughened with tiny translucent dots. Solitary, orange, and on stalks nearly or quite 2 inches long, the many blooms are about 2 inches wide. From the last, **L. aureus** differs in having smooth rather than roughened leaves, up to 2 inches long and with somewhat convex sides. Its brilliant orange blooms slightly exceed 2 inches in diameter. Yellow-flowered **L. reptans** has creeping, slender, branched stems up to 1 foot long or sometimes longer along which are spaced tufts of gray-green leaves covered with translucent dots. The leaves are triangular in section, incurved, and ½ to 1 inch long.

Lampranthus aurantiacus

Lampranthus amoenus

covered with small translucent dots. Usually in groups of three, its light rose-pink flowers are about 2 inches wide.

White, creamy-white, or pink-tinged flowers with rosy-purple centers are borne by **L. comptonii** (syn. *Mesembryanthemum comptonii*). From 6 to 10 inches tall, this has spreading to erect, slightly sickle-shaped, apple-green to bluish-glaucous leaves up to 1½ inches long. They have flat upper surfaces, more or less rounded undersides, thickened toward their apexes. The flowers, mostly in threes, are 1 inch wide or slightly wider.

Brilliant scarlet blooms are borne by 2- to 3-foot-tall **L. coccineus.** About 1½ inches wide, they are solitary or in twos or threes. Crowded on short shoots with the bases of each pair only shortly united, the slender, conspicuously-dotted, gray-green, bluntish, three-angled leaves, are ½ to 1 inch long.

Glowing purple-red flowers 2 inches wide and solitary or two or three together are plentifully borne by **L. conspicuus.** This attains 1 foot to 1½ feet in height and has mostly crowded toward the branch ends,

Conspicuous light purple blooms about 2¾ inches across are carried in large numbers by **L. haworthii** (syn. *Erepsia haworthii*). From 1 foot to 2 feet tall and freely-branched, the stems of this are more or less erect. Its leaves are slender, gray-green, smooth, and 1 inch to 1½ inches long. They are semicylindrical, their upper sides flattened, their undersides rounded. The bases of each pair are slightly joined. The flowers, on 1½-inch-long stems, open about midday.

Pink to purplish-pink or rarely white flowers are borne by **L. multiradiatus** (syn. *L. roseus*). Up to 2 feet tall and

Lampranthus comptonii

Garden and Landscape Uses and Cultivation. Among the finest garden plants of the *Mesembryanthemum* complex, lampranthuses are easy to grow outdoors in warm, dry, essentially frost-free climates and in greenhouses. They are splendid for edgings, banks, rock gardens, other rocky areas, and the fronts of flower beds, Their needs are simple: sharply-drained, ordinary soil, dryish rather than moist, and full sun. In greenhouses they may be accommodated in ground beds, pots, or large pans (shallow pots). Indoors in winter a night temperature of 50°F is satisfactory, with a rise of a few degrees during the day. In summer, high temperatures and low humidity, are appreciated. On all favorable occasions the greenhouse must be ventilated freely. Moderate watering, allowing the soil to nearly dry between applications, is required from spring to fall. Drier conditions are preferred in winter. Increase is easy by cuttings, seed, and in some cases by the removal of rooted portions of established plants. For additional information see Succulents.

LAMPWICK PLANT is *Phlomis lychnitis.*

LANCEOLATE. Shaped like a lance or spear head. Considerably longer than broad, widest just above the base and tapering gradually from there to the apex.

LANCEPOD. See Lonchocarpus.

Lampranthus conspicuus

spreading, erect or incurved, slender leaves 2 to 3 inches in length, with the bases of the pairs briefly united. They taper to small red apical points and are semicylindrical or sometimes three-angled in section. Much like the last, but with shorter branches, **L. amoenus** has cylindrical to three-angled, slightly-spreading, slender leaves up to 2 inches long, and usually in threes, bright purple flowers about 1½ inches in diameter. Its stems prostrate, **L. spectabilis** has tufted, three-angled leaves 2 to 3¼ inches in length, ending in a short, reddish point. Its purple blooms, on stalks up to 6 inches long are 2 to 2¾ inches wide. This is especially beautiful. Variants with pink and white flowers are known.

Lamranthus multiradiatus

spreading, this has three-angled, compressed, incurved, spine-tipped leaves 1 inch to 1½ inches long, with conspicuous translucent dots. The flowers have 2-inch-long stalks, are 1 inch to 1½ inches across. Erect **L. emarginatus**, about 1 foot tall, has crowded, curved, gray-green semicylindrical leaves about ½ inch long, thickened toward their bluntish tips and with many translucent dots. The violet-pink blooms are in twos or threes, or are solitary. Variety *L. e. puniceus* is more robust and has brilliant violet blooms. Its stems erect and red, **L. blandus** is about 1½ feet tall. This has pale gray-green, three-angled leaves

LANCEWOOD is *Pseudopanax crassifolius*.

LANDSCAPE ARCHITECTURE. The art of designing with professional competence for human use and enjoyment outdoor areas in which plants are to be featured prominently is called landscape architecture. Akin to architecture in its spatial implications, it differs in its emphasis on the employment of living elements. Because of this, the compositions or creations of landscape architects, unlike those of architects, are not static. The plants they use grow and otherwise change with the passing of time, and allowances must be made for this in the original planning.

As an organized profession landscape architecture developed chiefly during the twentieth century from the much older art of landscape design usually designated landscape gardening, the outstanding practitioners of which were responsible for the magnificent gardens and park landscapes, many extant, developed in Europe and the United States in earlier centuries.

Modern landscape architecture, in response to the needs of changing society and technologies, has altered considerably in scope and emphasis. The impracticability of establishing and maintaining large private estates has resulted in much less emphasis on designing gardens and private pleasure grounds. The chief employment now of landscape architects is concerned with planning and developing public and commercial properties such as college campuses, civic centers, housing developments, parks and recreation areas, parkways, freeways, shopping centers, cemeteries, and industrial sites and complexes.

Modern landscape architects are likely to be involved with land and master planning to encourage the conservation or best environmental use and development of considerable areas, land subdivision, urban design, site planning, and a variety of other projects designed to improve the visual landscape and protect the environment.

The qualifications of a competent landscape architect obviously include a well-developed appreciation of the aesthetic and the ability to design pleasing landscapes by appropriate contouring and the employment of living and nonliving elements in a variety of forms, colors, and textures. As a basis a grounding study in the history of landscape gardening and its development in different countries through the centuries is important. To function effectively the landscape architect must be well versed in the characteristics, practicabilities, and appropriate uses of available materials and with plants, especially, with their suitability for particular climates, soils, and sites. His, or her, work is likely to include making feasibility studies as well as preparing complete and detailed drawings and specifications. Selection of landscape contractors and supervision of their work is often normally the responsibility of landscape architects.

In preparation for a career in landscape architecture it is desirable and indeed almost essential that studies leading to a college degree in the subject be completed. Supplementation of these by practical work under the direction of a practicing landscape architect of excellent capability is necessary, travel that permits studying outstanding examples of gardens and other landscaped areas, highly desirable. A comparative weakness of many modern landscape architects, as compared with those of earlier years, is their comparative unfamiliarity with a wide range of plants. In some states a license is necessary to legally practice as a landscape architect.

LANDSCAPE GARDENER. This is the name for gardeners whose chief or only horticultural employments are the installation and establishment of gardens and similar landscape plantings. Usually they are not landscape architects and, except sometimes for small projects, they do not design gardens. Their qualifications are most commonly based on practical experience with grading, soil preparation, transplanting and planting, lawn making, and associated tasks and with the installation of drains and the construction of driveways, paths, steps, terraces, retaining walls, pools, and other features appropriate to gardens.

Often the business of landscape gardening is combined with that of nurseryman and sometimes with that of garden or landscape maintenance. The latter is distinct from landscape gardening proper in that its primary concern is with the continuing care of established landscapes rather than with their initial installation.

Landscape gardeners usually are employed on a contract basis and are sometimes called landscape contractors, although the latter designation is more commonly applied to those who specialize in comparatively large landscape projects of a more or less public nature. Landscape gardeners or landscape contractors are usually employed to install gardens and other landscapes designed by landscape architects.

LANGLOISIA (Langlòis-ia). Named after Father Langlois, of Louisiana, this genus of six species consists of plants of the deserts of western North America. It belongs in the phlox family POLEMONIACEAE. Langloisias are diffuse, rigid, low annuals with alternate, pinnately-toothed, linear or wedge-shaped leaves, with the teeth ending in bristles and the lower ones often consisting only of bristles. The flowers are few together and are in leafy, bracted heads. They are slightly or evidently two-lipped with the upper lip three-lobed.

The kind most likely to be cultivated is *Langloisia setosissima*, a tufted plant 2 to 3 inches in height or with prostrate branches up to 4 inches in length. It may be hairless or slightly-hairy. The leaves are ½ to ¾ inch long and wedge-shaped and have five conspicuous teeth. The flowers are scarcely two-lipped and are pale lavender-blue or light violet. They are on short, wiry stems and are borne in profusion. The fruits are capsules.

Garden Uses and Cultivation. This quite charming plant is suitable for sunny rock gardens where it can be afforded a well-drained soil rather poor in fertility. Seeds sown in early spring where the plants are to bloom are raked shallowly into the soil surface, and the young plants are thinned to about 3 inches apart. The plants bloom freely through the summer.

LANKESTERIA (Lan-kestèria). The tropical African genus *Lankesteria*, of the acanthus family ACANTHACEAE, comprises four species. Its name commemorates the British botanist Dr. H. Lankester, who died in 1874.

Lankesterias are shrubs with undivided, opposite leaves and flowers in conspicuously bracted spikes or panicles. The blooms have a calyx of five nearly equal linear lobes, a slender-tubular corolla with five nearly equal lobes (petals), two each stamens and staminodes (nonfunctional stamens), and a slender style. The fruits are two-seeded capsules.

Sorts cultivated are *L. barteri* and *L. elegans* (syn. *Eranthemum elegans*). The first has elliptic leaves nearly white on their undersides and, in terminal spikes, buff-yellow flowers ⅝ to ¾ inch in diameter and with an orange eye. The bracts are green. The leaves of *L. elegans* are elliptic, short-stalked, and 5 to 9 inches long. In terminal spikes, the nearly 1-inch-wide flowers are orange, fading to dull reddish.

Lankesteria barteri

Lankesteria barteri (flowers)

Garden Uses and Cultivation. These are as for *Eranthemum*.

LANTANA (Lan-tàna). As presently understood, *Lantana*, of the vervain family VERBENACEAE, consists of more than 150 species of shrubs and herbaceous perennials, mostly natives of the tropics and subtropics of the Americas, but some natives of warm parts of the Old World. Their name is an ancient one used for the quite unrelated genus *Viburnum* and still as part of the specific name of the wayfaring tree (*V. lantana*).

Lantanas are hairy, mostly roughly so, and often prickly-stemmed. Their leaves, which if bruised usually have a disagreeable odor, are opposite, toothed, and usually wrinkled. Their verbena-like flowers, in crowded, stalked clusters or spikes from the leaf axils or at the ends of branches, are small. They have tiny calyxes and slender, tubular corollas with four or five spreading lobes (petals) of nearly equal size. There are four stamens in pairs and one style. The juicy, berry-like fruits contain two nutlets, often called seeds. From verbenas, lantanas differ in their flowers having very short calyxes and their fruits being berry-like.

The popular lantanas that gardeners cultivate in summer beds, window and porch boxes, hanging baskets, and other ways are botanically puzzling. They, or at least their progenitors, have been cultivated for so long that no one really knows precisely the species from which they originated. No doubt they are complex hybrids most probably of South American, Mexican, and West Indian species. Before 1700 over fifty kinds of *Lantana* had been named as growing in the West Indies, and at least one was in cultivation at Leiden, Holland, and two at the Royal Garden at Hampton Court, England.

It is probable that European interest in New World lantanas was first excited by their reputed medicinal virtues. Spanish colonists used the camaras, as they called them, to make infusions to be taken as

medicine and used in baths. In some places such infusions are still used medicinally. Later, botanists named one species *Lantana camara* and this name has since been applied rather indiscriminatingly in gardens and garden books to include many plants of hybrid origin that should correctly be referred to *L. hybrida*. More recently the name *L. collowiana* has been used for plants said to be hybrids between *L. camara* and *L. montevidensis*. It is possible that the actual parentage of these is *L. hybrida* and *L. montevidensis*. But even if that were true, it would seem that they properly belong within the concept of *L. hybrida*.

In Hawaii and some other tropical and subtropical regions lantanas are troublesome weeds, chiefly spread by birds that are very fond of their juicy fruits, and agriculturists have been much concerned with controlling them effectively. These spontaneous types are often very rank, sometimes attaining a height of 20 feet, and usually are more prickly than cultivated varieties.

The species **L. camara,** which occurs in the wild from the southern United States to tropical America, is a robust more or less prickly shrub, 6 feet or considerably more in height, with ovate to ovate-oblong, short-pointed, toothed and wrinkled leaves 1 inch to 5 inches in length. Like the stems, the foliage is covered with short hairs. The flat flower clusters, 1 inch to 2 inches in diameter, terminate stout stalks often longer than the leaves. Most commonly the flowers are yellow or orange, changing to red as they age. Somewhat similar, and often cultivated as *L. camara*, is **L. tiliaefolia.** The most obvious difference is that its stems and foliage have longer, coarser, and harsher spreading hairs. Also, it has hemispherical flower clusters on stalks as long as the leaves. It is a native of Brazil.

Garden hybrids, here referred to *L. hybrida*, exhibit characteristics of the above species, but are mostly much more compact and less ungainly. Many do not exceed 1 foot in height, at least in their first

Lantana hybrida

Lantana hybrida (flowers)

season. Commonly, their leaves are closer together and their clusters of flowers more numerous and less given to dropping under the influence of rain than those of the species, so that their display value is superior. These horticultural varieties are available in many colors from white through lemon-yellow, golden-yellow, and orange, to deep red. Often the older outer flowers of each cluster are of a different hue to the younger, inner ones. These dwarf varieties, which were first developed in France, are offered in nurserymen's catalogs under horticultural varietal names. The hybrids offered as *L. callowiana* are described as having the finer qualities of *L. camara* (perhaps *L. hybrida*) and the trailing lantana (*L. montevidensis*).

The trailing or weeping lantana (**L. montevidensis** syns. *L. sellowiana*, *L. delicatissima*) is quite distinct from other cultivated kinds. It has slender trailing or pendulous, hairy stems up to 3 feet long or longer and ovate leaves approximately 1 inch in length, coarsely-toothed, and stalked. Its long-stalked clusters of rosy-lilac flowers are 1 inch or more across.

Lantana montevidensis growing in a dry wall in California

Garden and Landscape Uses. In warm climates lantanas are attractive outdoor shrubs and can be used effectively as hedges. Even if damaged by light freezing they soon recover, but they will not live through a hard freeze. In the continental United States only in the very south of Florida are they likely to live without occasionally suffering to some extent from this cause. The most common use of lantanas is as bedding plants to provide summer color in flower gardens, window and porch boxes, and hanging baskets. For the last purpose *L. montevidensis* is especially suitable. The other kinds commonly used are varieties of *L. hybrida*. Basically, these are all sun-lovers; they will stand a little shade, but are only at their best in full sun.

Cultivation. Except when grown in pots, lantanas are best in poor, well-drained soil. Earth too fertile, too rich in nitrogen, encourages rank growth at the expense of bloom. When used to fill summer beds in which the soil is rich it is well to plant them without taking them out of their pots. They then root through the drainage holes and from the surface of their root balls, but the restriction imposed on the roots by the container results in more compact growth and handsomer displays of bloom. It also makes it easier to lift the plants in fall before bringing them indoors. For bedding, a planting distance of 8 or 10 inches apart is about right. Little summer care is required. Except for a short time after they are planted, until they establish new roots, even in dry weather little or no watering is needed.

In fall, just before or immediately after the first frost, planted-out lantanas are dug up and the stems pruned back so that they are about 1 foot long. If they were planted in pots, roots made outside their containers are cut off, if they were planted out of pots, the roots are trimmed and the plants potted in 4- or 5-inch pots in sandy soil. Then they are watered and kept in a warm, humid atmosphere for three or four weeks to induce root growth. After that, like plants lifted in their pots, they are kept in a greenhouse or other light place where the night temperature is 40 to 45°F and the day temperature not more than a few degrees higher. At this season they are kept nearly dry. In late January those that are to supply cuttings are brought into a humid, sunny greenhouse with a night temperature of 55 to 60°F and a day temperature five to ten degrees higher, and are watered more freely; those not needed for propagation are treated in the same way one month to six weeks later and, at the same time are pruned back so that the stems are 4 to 6 inches long, and are repotted in fertile soil.

Tree lantanas, plants trained as standards as gardeners term specimens so developed, are very attractive. They are useful as accent plants in flower beds and borders

A standard-trained lantana with ageratums and other annuals beneath

Propagating lantanas: (a) Taking cuttings from a stock plant

and for ornamenting terraces, patios, and other places where summer-flowering plants in this form are attractive. It takes about two years to develop a good standard, but once attained they remain attractive indefinitely if cared for properly. A standard has a single, branchless trunk, 3 or 3½ feet tall and topped by a more or less rounded head of branches, foliage, and flowers. To obtain such plants strong rooted cuttings are grown without pinching their tips until they reach a height at which branches are required to form their heads. In the meantime, all side shoots are pinched out as soon as they appear, and the main stem is tied neatly to a stake. The leaves are not picked off the main stem. When the stem has attained the desired height its tip is pinched out and about six side branches allowed to grow. As soon as these are 5 or 6 inches long their tips are pinched out, and this is repeated every time subsidiary shoots are about 5 inches long. This results in a well-branched head. During the winter the plants are rested by being kept in a cool greenhouse with the soil drier than in summer. In February or March they are started into growth again as recommended previously for bush-type bedding lantanas. At that time they will probably need repotting into larger containers. Older standards may remain in pots or tubs 9 to 12 inches in diameter for many years. When used in outdoor beds they should be sunk in the ground in their containers rather than removed from them. In fall they are taken indoors and are wintered as previously recommended for bush plants. Needed pruning to shape the heads is done in late winter or spring. From spring to fall well-established specimens should be given frequent applications of dilute liquid fertilizer and be watered so that their soil is always fairly moist.

Propagation of lantanas is almost entirely by cuttings. Seeds germinate readily, but usually seedlings are a mish-mash of coarse, ungainly plants with inferior flower colors. Cuttings of young shoots root read-

(b) The cuttings with a basal heel of old wood

ily either in late summer or in February or March. If a warm, humid propagating greenhouse is available, the latter period is usually preferred because it avoids the necessity of growing the young plants through most of the winter which, if done, requires that they be kept in a minimum temperature of 55 to 60°F, with sunny and humid conditions. Plants raised from February cuttings by planting out time will occupy 3½- or 4-inch pots and be almost or quite as large as those from late summer propagations. If the shoots used for cuttings are weak, as they may be in late winter if the plants are not exposed to full sun, it is advisable to retain at their bases a heel (sliver) of older wood of the branch from which the cutting was taken. Cuttings root readily in sand, perlite, or vermiculite, in a humid atmosphere where the temperature is about 70°F. It is helpful if the rooting medium is supplied with bottom heat to keep it about five degrees warmer than the air temperature. As soon as the cuttings have made roots ½ to 1 inch long they are potted individually in sandy soil in small pots. Unless they are to be grown as standards (in tree form) their tips are pinched out when the young plants are 3 or 4 inches high, and this is repeated two or three times. They are kept growing in a humid, sunny greenhouse in a night temperature of 60°F, and day temperatures five to fifteen degrees higher, until ten days or two weeks before they are planted outdoors, which should not be done until the weather is really settled and warm, a couple of weeks after it is safe to plant out the first tomatoes. In preparation for planting out, lantanas are hardened by standing them in a cold frame or sheltered sunny place outdoors. Whitefly and mealybugs are the chief pests of lantanas, especially when they are grown in greenhouses.

LANTANA BUG. See Greenhouse Orthezia.

LANTERN-FLIES. See Plant Hoppers.

LAPAGERIA (Lapag-èria)—Chilean-Bell-flower or Chile Bells. The only species of *Lapageria*, of the lily family LILIACEAE, is endemic to Chile and is the national flower of that country. Its name honors a keen gardener and amateur botanist, Marie Josephine Rose Tascher de la Pagerie, Napoleon's Empress Josephine.

A slender-stemmed, twining vine, the Chilean-bellflower (**L. rosea**) has alternate, leathery, long-pointed, ovate leaves 3 to 5 inches long. Its blooms, which hang like waxen bells, are deep pink to nearly red.

Lapageria rosea

About 3 inches long by 2 inches wide, they are borne singly or two or three together from the upper leaf axils or at the ends of branches. Each has six fleshy petals, or more correctly, tepals, the three inner larger than the outer ones, six stamens, and one style. The fruits are oblong-ovate, many-seeded berries. White flowers are borne by *L. r. alba*. Variety *L. r. ilsemannii* blooms more freely and has brighter colored, larger blooms than *L. rosea*. Variety *L. r. superba* has crimson flowers, larger than the typical species. The bigeneric hybrid *Philageria* resulted from crossing *Lapageria* with *Philesia*.

Lapageria rosea alba

Garden Uses. These choice vines are best accommodated in cool greenhouses. Even in their native Chile they are considered difficult to accommodate outdoors. Certainly they can be expected to adapt themselves to garden conditions only where little or no frost is experienced and summers are fairly cool and humid, in parts of California, for instance. They need very well-drained, nourishing peaty soil and shade from sun.

Cultivation. For good results lapagerias must be supplied with liberal amounts of water, especially from spring to fall, but at no time must the soil be waterlogged so that the roots are deprived of air. The atmosphere must be constantly humid. High temperatures are to be avoided, a condition difficult to achieve in summer in most parts of North America. Nevertheless every effort should be made to locate the plants in as cool a part of the greenhouse as possible. In winter a night temperature of 40 to 45°F, with a daytime rise of five to ten degrees, is adequate. Although it is possible to achieve good specimens in pots, lapagerias usually respond better and are more easily cared for when planted in a ground bed with plenty of root room. They are propagated by seed sown in sandy, peaty soil, or more usually by layering. Increase is also easily had by coiling one of the long slender shoots, removed from the parent plant, on the surface of a pan (shallow pot) or flat containing a mixture of sand and peat moss with which a little soil has been mixed, and pegging the shoot in place with wire "hairpins." If kept in a temperature of 55 to 60°F, shaded, and in a humid atmosphere, young plants develop from the leaf axils of the shoot so treated. When they have made good root growth the stems that connect them are severed and they are potted individually. It is usually wiser to keep the plants in pots until they are two years old; small specimens set in ground beds often fail to prosper because the soil sours before the roots are vigorous enough to explore it thoroughly. Early spring is the favored time for planting and at that season, too, pot-grown specimens should receive what attention they need in the matter of repotting. Each spring established specimens in beds should have an inch or two of the surface soil removed and replaced by fresh earth containing a goodly amount of peat moss and coarse sand and some slow-acting complete fertilizer. Lapagerias naturally produce new shoots from just below ground level. These keep the plants well furnished so that little pruning is needed; all that is necessary is to cut out old, weak shoots in spring so that newer, stronger ones are not crowded. Wires or other supports around which the stems may twine must be provided.

LAPEIROUSIA (Lapeir-oùsia). The sixty species of *Lapeirousia* belong in the iris family IRIDACEAE.* Nearly all, including those discussed here, with the exception of *L. compressa*, are natives of Africa, chiefly of the southern reaches of that continent. They are corm plants, which means that they have underground, bulblike food-storage parts that differ from true bulbs in being solid instead of constructed of superimposed layers like onions, or of overlapping scales like lily bulbs. The name, sometimes spelled *Lapeyrousia*, commemorates the distinguished French naturalist Baron Philippe Picot de la Peirouse, who died in 1818. The botanically illegitimate name *Anomatheca* has been applied to some species of *Lapeirousia*.

Lapeirousias have one or two basal, often more or less spreading, usually linear to sickle-shaped leaves and one or more smaller ones on the generally short, usually branched stem. The flowers, few together in spikes terminating the stems, have straight or nearly straight, tubular corollas slightly expanded toward their throats and decidedly longer than the six spreading, nearly equal petals (more correctly, tepals). There are three stamens and a slender style with three short, forked branches. The fruits are capsules.

Commonest in cultivation and one of the best, **L. laxa** (syns. *L. cruenta*, *Anomatheca cruenta*) has about six tapered leaves, approximately 8 inches long by ½ inch wide, and slender stems 1 foot or less in height. The bright carmine-red blooms, in spikes of up to a dozen, have a blackish-red patch at the base of each of the three lower petals. Their perianth tubes are about 1½ inches long, the petals one-half as long. A pure white-flowered variety that comes true from seeds is recorded, but is rare in cultivation.

Differing from *L. laxa* in its blooms having perianth tubes under ¾ inch long, **L. juncea** (syn. *Anomatheca juncea*) has four to eight broad-linear leaves, stems 1 foot to 1½ feet tall, and loose spikes of up to nine rose-pink blooms with dark red basal blotches on the lower petals. Also with

Lapeirousia laxa

four to nine blooms with perianth tubes less than ¾ inch long and stamens only one-half as long as the petals, but with only one basal leaf, *L. divaricata* has whitish flowers in panicles.

Confusion has existed over the application of the name *L. anceps*. The species to which this rightly belongs has commonly two basal leaves and spikes of white-marked, dark purple to magenta blooms with perianth tubes under ½ inch long. A species that has been incorrectly named *L. anceps* is *L. denticulata*. This has only one basal leaf, crisped or wavy at its edges. Its flowers, in panicles on stems up to 1 foot high, have stamens with yellow anthers. They have perianth tubes ¾ inch to 2 inches long or longer. It is probable that plants cultivated as *L. compressa* are really *L. anceps*. True *L. compressa,* of Mauritius, is described as having pale blue flowers striped with darker blue that does not reach the edges of the petals. Its flowers with perianth tubes about 2 inches long, *L. fissifolia* has purple-anthered, pink or white blooms in spikes. Its stems are up to 6 inches tall, its solitary basal leaf flat rather than crisped or wavy-edged.

Purple-blue flowers decorated with a large white star outlined in dark purple at their middles are typical of *L. corymbosa.* This has much-branched, flattened stems with leaflike, wavy margins. The blooms are crowded into headlike clusters of few, and have perianth tubes rarely ¾ inch, more often about one-third of that, long. The one, prominently three-veined basal leaf is sickle-shaped and about 4½ inches long, the other two are shorter. From 1 foot to 1½ feet or a little more in height, *L. sandersonii* differs from *L. corymbosa* in having two erect, linear basal leaves and sharp-angled flower-bearing branches.

Garden and Landscape Uses and Cultivation. Although they are commonly less showy than ixias, the uses and cultivation of lapeirousias are essentially similar to those appropriate for ixias.

LAPIDARIA (Lapid-ària). One species constitutes this genus. A *Mesembryanthemum* relative much like *Dinteranthus* and somewhat resembling *Lithops,* and native of South Africa, it is *Lapidaria margaretiae* (syns. *Dinteranthus margaretiae, Argyroderma margaretiae*). The name is from the Latin *lapis,* stone, and alludes to the appearance of the plants. The species belongs in the carpetweed family, AIZOACEAE.

One of the stone plants, so called because they closely mimic pebbles and broken rock that commonly strew the ground, *L. margaretiae* is a charming succulent. Its plant bodies consist of two to four pairs of opposite leaves, joined at their bases and attached to a scarcely apparent stem. The alternate pairs of leaves are at right angles to each other. The leaves are very thick, ½ inch long or a little longer and nearly as broad. They are flat on their upper sides, rounded beneath except for a keel near their tips, and are whitish with reddish angles, or sometimes are reddish all over. The flowers, 1¼ to 2 inches across, and daisy-like in aspect, but not in structure (each is a single bloom, not a composite head of many florets as in daisies), are golden-yellow with whitish-yellow undersides to the petals. They have six or seven stigmas. The fruits are capsules.

Garden Uses and Cultivation. This species is chiefly adapted for growing in greenhouses devoted to succulent plants. With care it may also be cultivated in windows. Its chief requirements are full sun, a dry atmosphere, moderate warmth, and exceedingly well-drained, never too wet soil. In winter a night temperature of 50 to 55°F is suitable. By day five or ten degrees more is appropriate. During the summer growing period water is given sparingly, care always being taken to permit the soil to become nearly dry before soaking it. In winter water less frequently, often enough only to prevent drastic shriveling of the leaves. Seed affords a ready and easy means of propagation.

LAPORTEA (Lapòrt-ea)—Nettle-Tree. Laporteas are plants of which to beware. Most have stinging hairs, and the results of brushing against virulent kinds can cause excruciating pain lasting for several days and diminishing only slowly. Despite this, some kinds are occasionally cultivated in greenhouses as ornamentals and botanical curiosities. The genus belongs in the nettle family URTICACEAE and has twenty-three species. It is represented in many parts of the tropics and subtropics, in temperate eastern Asia, and by one species in eastern North America. Its name commemorates the French entomologist François L. de Laporte, who died in 1880.

Herbaceous plants, shrubs, and trees constitute *Laportea.* Some, including the giant nettle-tree or touch-me-not tree (*L.*

gigas), of Australia, attain heights of up to 100 feet. The fibers of the inner barks and roots of some species are used for native cordage. Laporteas have opposite, often large, generally toothed, leaves. Their tiny petal-less flowers, in clusters, panicles, or racemes, are unisexual with the sexes on the same or separate plants. Male flowers have perianths of four or five lobes or sepals and as many stamens. Female blooms have four lobes or sepals and a functional ovary. The fruits are achenes. The hairs of laporteas are single cells, hollow like surgical needles, and with silicified tips that, after puncturing the skin, break off and permit the irritating, blistering fluid contained within the hairs to enter the flesh.

A shrub or tree up to 20 feet tall, but bearing showy fruits and attractive even as a small pot-grown specimen, *L. moroides* has long-stalked, prominently toothed, very broad-ovate leaves, that like other parts are furnished with painfully stinging hairs. The seedlike fruits are surrounded by enlarged fleshy perianth segments so that groups of them look like reddish-purple mulberries. They are displayed in considerable clusters below the crown of foliage, are highly decorative, and remain so for many months.

The chief attraction of *L. schomburgkii versicolor* is its handsomely colored foliage. A native of Polynesia, this has large, deep green leaves with purplish midribs and veins mottled or patched with creamy-white.

Garden Uses and Cultivation. Horticultural uses of these plants is explained at the beginning of the entry. Laporteas are easily grown under conditions of warmth, shade from strong sun, and high humidity. A minimum night temperature in winter of 60°F is best. During the day, and at other seasons, temperatures may be higher. Coarse, well-drained, fertile soil is to their liking. It should be kept evenly and moderately moist. Regular applications of dilute liquid fertilizer benefit specimens that have filled their containers with roots. Heavy gloves should be worn when handling these plants. Propagation is easy by seed and by cuttings planted in a greenhouse propagating bench where there is mild bottom heat.

LAPPULA. See Hackelia.

LARCH. See Larix. Golden-larch is *Pseudolarix kaempferi.*

LARDIZABALA (Lardizabà-la). Two woody vines of Chile constitute *Lardizabala,* of the lardizabala family LARDIZABALACEAE, which is closely related to the barberry family BERBERIDACEAE. The name commemorates the eighteenth-century Spanish naturalist Miguel de Lardizabel y Uribe.

Lardizabalas have leaves with leaflets in threes or multiples of groups of three. The

Lantana hybrida variety

Lagerstroemia indica (flowers)

Lampranthus amoenus variety

Lachenalia aloides aurea

Lathyrus vernus

Lampranthus, undetermined species

Lapeirousia laxa

Lavatera, garden variety

Lasthenia glabrata

unisexual, purple-brown flowers are without petals. They have six petal-like sepals and six petal-like nectaries. The males, in drooping racemes, have six united stamens. Female flowers are solitary and have six staminodes (sterile stamens) and three ovaries. The fruits are many-seeded berries.

Only *L. biternata* is cultivated. This closely resembles its relative *Akebia quinata*, but is less hardy. It has short-stalked, leathery, ovate leaves that are ternate (composed of three leaflets) or biternate (each leaf consisting of three sets of three leaflets). The leaflets, 2 to 4 inches long, are sometimes toothed. The flowers are borne in late summer. The males are about 1 inch across, the females slightly larger. They have very dark purple-brown sepals and white, petal-like nectaries. The fruits, sausage-shaped and 2 to 3 inches long, are an article of diet in Chile. The stems are macerated and made into cordage.

Lardizabala biternata

Garden Uses and Cultivation. This is an unusual, interesting, and vigorous twining vine for pergolas, pillars, and other supports. It is hardy in mild climates, such as that of California, but will not stand much frost. It is adaptable to ordinary garden soils and is propagated by cuttings in summer, by layering, and by seed.

LARDIZABALACEAE—Lardizabala Family. There are thirty-five species distributed among seven genera in the lardizabala family, a group of dicotyledons native in Chile and from Japan to the Himalayas. They are woody vines or much less commonly erect shrubs with alternate leaves of several leaflets that spread in finger fashion from the tops of the leafstalks. The small, symmetrical flowers are in racemes or are solitary from the axils of reduced or scalelike leaves near the bottoms of the branches.

The majority of kinds have unisexual blooms with one or both sexes on the same plant. Male flowers have three or six often petal-like sepals, no corolla or one of six petals smaller than the sepals, six stamens, and usually a rudimentary pistil. Female flowers have three to fifteen separate pistils and usually vestigial, nonfunctional stamens. The fruits are berries. Cultivated genera are *Akebia*, *Decaisnea*, *Holboellia*, *Lardizabala*, and *Stauntonia*.

LARIX (Là-rix)—Larch, Tamarack. Trees native of northern and cool parts of North America, Europe, and Asia, larches are the best known and most abundant deciduous (leaf-losing) conifers. They constitute the genus *Larix*. The only other genera of deciduous conifers are *Glyptostrobus*, *Metasequoia*, *Pseudolarix*, and *Taxodium* (some species). There are ten to twelve species of *Larix* and a number of interesting varieties. They belong in the pine family PINACEAE. As such they are without showy blooms. The primitive unisexual flowers are in male and female cones, the latter, after fertilization by pollen from males, develop seeds. The name is an ancient Latin one.

Larches are readily distinguished from most conifers by the loss of their leaves in winter, from other deciduous kinds by their male cones being solitary, and from all deciduous conifers except *Pseudolarix*, by the arrangement of the leaves, which do not form fernlike sprays on short lateral branchlets that drop with the leaves attached. From golden-larch (*Pseudolarix*), the genus with which larches are most likely to be confused, larches are distinguished by their blunt, rather than pointed bud scales and by the scales of their cones being persistent rather than deciduous. Larches are closely related to cedars (*Cedrus*). Their appearance does not suggest this, but the manner in which the leaves are arranged is the same. Male flowers of *Cedrus*, like those of larches, are solitary, but their female cones do not ripen until the second or third year. Those of larches mature in their first season. Cedars are evergreen.

Larches are beautiful at all seasons, but never more so than in early spring. Then, in a brief period the naked branches and branchlets are transformed into clouds of fresh young foliage, first noticeable as a delicate green haze. This gradually becomes denser and deepens to the light green that remains all summer. Then, too, the twigs are spangled with small, attractive, bright red or purple-red female cones. If one looks closely, less conspicuous silvery-red male cones can also be seen. When fall comes summer's verdure slowly changes to lemon-yellow or gold, and finally the leaves are shed to reveal again the stark pattern of trunk, branches, and branchlets. Of all larches, the Japanese *L. kaempferi* assumes the most brilliant fall garb.

Until they reach old age, when if not crowded they become somewhat irregular in outline, larches are symmetrical, pyramidal trees of refined, delicate aspect. They suggest the femininity of birches rather than the masculinity of oaks. Their trunks are tall and straight and taper gradually from base to top. Their branches, usually in whorls (tiers), spread horizontally or are slightly pendulous. The younger ones are furnished with rather regularly spaced short spurs, really miniature branches that elongate but a fraction of an inch each year. Most of the slender, needle-like leaves are in crowded clusters at the ends of these spurs, but other leaves are scattered spirally along the slender terminal shoots of the branches, which may make a foot or more new growth each season. In the arrangement of their branches and leaves larches are very much like *Ginkgo*, cedars (*Cedrus*), and golden-larch (*Pseudolarix*).

The economic uses of larches are important. As sources of lumber they rate highly. The wood is hard, heavy, strong and durable, and lasts well in contact with moist soil. It is employed extensively for fence posts, telegraph and telephone poles, piles, props in mines, railroad ties, scaffolding, building and ship building, flooring, garden furniture, and other purposes, and is excellent fuel. Larch bark contains much tannin and is used to some extent for processing leather. From the European larch (*L. decidua*) an oleo-resin similar to Canada balsam is obtained and used in veterinary medicine. By distillation ethyl alcohol is recovered from the wood of this species.

For landscape decoration the most ornamental species is the Japanese larch (**L. kaempferi** syn. *L. leptolepis*); it is also one of the fastest growers. At home this tree is sometimes 100 feet tall and has a trunk diameter of 4 feet. Its older branches are orange and the bark of young trees reddish. With ample room to develop it is fairly broad and pyramidal. Distinguishing characteristics are its waxy twigs, two clearly defined longitudinal white bands on the undersides of its leaves, and the strongly reflexed tips of the scales of its spherical cones, which are up to 1½ inches long. The cone bracts are shorter than the scales and usually hidden by them. The glaucous-green leaves of the spurs are up to 1½ inches long, those of the terminal shoots are up to 1¼ inches long. Very dwarfed specimens of the Japanese larch clothe the high slopes of Mount Fuji, and at one time it was thought that these represented a genetically distinct variety or race. Investigations have proved that suppression and restriction of their trunks and branches is the result of adverse environmental conditions and that plants raised from their seeds and grown under favorable conditions become normal, full-sized trees. At the highest altitudes, these high mountain specimens have gnarled and twisted branches that hug the inhospitable, cindery ground. The name *L. k. minor* has been applied to these low plants, but under the circumstances the name seems to describe no distinct variety.

The larch most commonly planted for ornament in North America and Europe is the European larch (**L. decidua**). It differs from the Japanese larch in having non-waxy twigs, leaves without highly contrasting white lines on their under surfaces, and cones up to 1½ inches long with thirty to fifty straight scales that hide bracts one-half as long as the scales. At its

Larix decidua

Larix decidua (cone and foliage)

best it is 140 feet in height and may have a trunk diameter of 5 feet. Characteristically, its yellowish-gray branches and branchlets tend to be pendulous. Variety *L. d. fastigiata*, probably synonymous with *L. d. pyramidalis*, is slender, has spreading or upright branches and drooping branchlets. Similar in its branching, but much broader is *L. d. pendula*. Variety *L. d. repens* is distinguished by its lower branches elongating along the ground. A variety native of Russia and Poland with smaller cones is *L. d. polonica*. A hybrid between the European larch and the Japanese larch, the Dunkeld larch (**L. eurolepis**) is intermediate between its parents.

Native American larches are less planted as ornamentals than European and Japanese kinds, although the noblest of the entire genus is the Western larch (**L. occidentalis**). At its finest this slender-pyramidal inhabitant of a region ranging from Montana to Oregon and British Columbia exceeds 200 feet in height and has a trunk diameter up to 8 feet. Its bark is deeply furrowed and on old trees is bright cinnamon-red. The leaves, triangular and pale green, are 1 inch to 1¾ inches long. From

Larix occidentalis

the 1- to 1½-inch-long ovoid cones the bracts protrude well beyond the cone scales. The Western larch can be distinguished from closely similar *L. lyallii*, a high mountain kind from the same general region, by its shoots being hairy only when young. Those of **L. lyallii** are covered with a dense felt of persistent hairs. Also, the leaves of the last are quadrangular and its cones are 1¼ to 2 inches long. It is possible that intermediates between these species occur. In cultivation *L. lyallii* has not proven satisfactory.

The tamarack, hackmatack, or American larch (**L. laricina**) is the only other species native to North America, where it grows as far north as trees survive, in Alaska to latitude 67° north. Most abundant in swampy soils, it is distributed from Labrador to Alaska and southward to Pennsylvania, Illinois, and Minnesota. The maximum height attained by the tamarack is about 75 feet and its trunk may reach 2 feet in diameter; very commonly its dimensions are much more modest. It is a slender tree with short, horizontal branches and reddish-brown bark. Its twigs are usually waxy and its light, bluish-green leaves 1 inch to 1½ inches long. The cones are slightly ovoid, about ¾ inches long, and have twelve to eighteen scales and bracts shorter than and completely hidden by the cone scales. The Alaskan trees are sometimes distinguished as *L. l. alaskensis*, but this does not seem to be a well-marked va-

riety. A presumed hybrid between the tamarack and the European larch, named **L. pendula,** becomes 90 feet tall. It is quite variable, but in general is intermediate between its supposed parents, its cones, for instance, are 1 inch long.

Other larches sometimes cultivated include these: *L. gmelinii,* the Dahurian larch, of eastern Siberia, may become 100 feet tall, but under difficult conditions in the wild it is sometimes only a few feet in height. It has leaves 1½ inches long and cones up to 1½ inches long with enclosed bracts that differ from those of *L. laricina* in having twenty to forty instead of twelve to eighteen scales. Its young shoots are usually pubescent. *L. g. japonica* is more densely branched and has bluish-red young branchlets. It is a native of Saghalin Island, the Kurile Islands, and northeast Asia. *L. g. olgensis*, of eastern Manchuria, has young shoots densely covered with reddish-brown hairs, and larger cones than the typical species. *L. g. principis-ruprechtii* is a vigorous variety with cones up to 1¾ inches long. **L. griffithiana** (syn. *L. griffithii*) may be recognized by its cones, which are 2 to 4 inches long and have exerted bracts, and its long, pendulous branchlets. A native of the Himalayas and China, it is not hardy in the north. **L. mastersiana,** of western China, is closely related to *L. griffithiana*, but its cones are only 1¼ inches long and it is less tender. **L. potaninii,** the Chinese larch, is up to 100 feet tall and has cones up to 1¾ inches long with protruding purple bracts. Its leaves, like those of *L. lyallii* are quadrangular, its branchlets slender and pendulous. It is native to western China. **L. sibirica** (syn. *L. russica*), the Siberian larch, of Siberia and Russia, attains 100 feet in height and from quite similar *L. decidua* differs in having narrower leaves, cones with slightly incurved tips, and bracts decidedly less than one-half the length of the scales.

Garden and Landscape Uses. As ornamentals larches have the disadvantage of being subject to attack by several disfiguring pests and diseases of which the larch casebearer is one of the most serious. Except for this, they are eminently suitable for decorating parks and large spaces, but are not well adapted for small gardens. With the exception of *L. griffithiana*, all are hardy, most kinds extremely so. Despite this they are not, as might be thought, good windbreak trees, but in the wild grow closely together in forest communities where they protect each other. In man-made landscapes they should be afforded similar shelter by planting them in groups or where they receive some protection from nearby evergreens. But they must not be crowded against other trees. Above all they are lovers of sunshine and need free air circulation. They are likely to grow well on north-facing slopes. As for soil, they show no great preference, growing as well in those of a limestone character as in neutral or acid earth if the subsoil is porous. With the exception of the American larch (*L. laricina*), which grows in muskeg and swampy locations, they will not tolerate waterlogged or very wet soils, but they prosper on banks of lakes, ponds, and streams that are a couple of feet or more above water level and in such locations are usually displayed to fine advantage.

Cultivation. Larches transplant easily and, apart from measures necessary to control any diseases and pests, need no special care. No pruning is ordinarily needed. Propagation is by seeds sown outdoors or in a cold frame with shade provided for the seedlings during their early stages. They may also be increased by veneer grafting onto seedling understocks in a greenhouse in winter and by cuttings inserted under mist or in a humid greenhouse or cold frame propagating bench in summer.

Diseases and Pests. Among diseases that affect these trees are canker (serious on American and European larches, much less so on the Japanese larch); leaf-cast, which causes a yellowing and browning of the foliage and finally the death of the spur shoots and for which gathering and burning all fallen leaves in fall is the recommended preventative, needle rusts, which have as alternate hosts willows, poplars, and birches on which the causative funguses must live for part of each year; and wood decay funguses, the control of which consists of the prompt treatment of all wounds of appreciable size and attention to fertilizing, watering during dry periods, and other vigor encouraging practices. The chief insect pests are woolly aphids, sawflies, caterpillars of the tussock moth and gypsy moth, and the larch casebearer. The larvae of the latter tunnel within the tissues of the leaves causing extensive browning in spring and early summer. From pieces of the leaves the creatures form small cigar-shaped cases, which remain attached to the branchlets and in which the insects winter. The adult moths emerge in late June or July. Control is by spraying with dormant strength limesulfur or miscible oil before the leaves expand or with malathion when the needles are about half-grown and before the young worms have entered them.

LARKSPUR. See Consolida and Delphinium.

LARREA (Lár-rea)—Creosote Bush. Strongly balsam-scented, evergreen, resinous shrubs compose *Larrea*, of the caltrop family ZYGOPHYLLACEAE. Its three or four species are natives of warm, arid regions of the Americas. The name commemorates Don Anthony Hernandez deLarrea, an eighteenth century Spaniard who was Dean of Sargossa and a patron of science.

Larreas have opposite, olive-green leaves, each usually with a pair of stalkless, asymmetrical leaflets. The solitary flowers, borne in spring at the ends of the shoots, are yellow. They have five each sepals and petals, ten stamens, and a slender style with five stigmas. The spherical, hairy fruits are capsules that at maturity split into five one-seeded nutlets.

A common and widely dispersed native of dry parts of the western United States, Mexico, and South America, the creosote bush (*L. divaricata*) was used by Indians for fuel and medicinally as an antiseptic. From 3 to 10 feet tall or occasionally taller, it is much branched and has its leaves concentrated chiefly near the ends of the branches. The leaves have lanceolate-ovate, toothless leaflets ¼ to nearly ½ inch long. The flowers have twisted petals up to ⅓ inch in length. The fruits, about ⅕ inch long, are clothed with reddish-brown or whitish hairs.

Garden and Landscape Uses and Cultivation. Horticulturally creosote bush has slight importance. Native stands may be preserved as parts of developed landscapes, and in desert and semidesert regions it may occasionally be planted for ornament and in gardens of native plants. For these purposes small young plants should be chosen, large ones do not transplant readily. Propagation is by seed.

LARVA, LARVAE. The adults of many insects differ totally in appearance and often life-style from their young. From egg to maturity such sorts undergo a complete metamorphosis. The eggs hatch into larvae, which may experience several molts involving increases in size until the last, when they change into pupae (singular pupa), a resting stage. From the pupa eventually emerges the adult insect, which does not increase in size afterward. Larvae, usually more or less wormlike, feed voraciously. Those of butterflies and moths are caterpillars, those of beetles grubs, those of flies maggots. Destruction of larvae is most commonly by poison baits or stomach poison sprays or dusts, or by hand picking.

LASERPITIUM (Laser-pítium). This genus of the carrot family UMBELLIFERAE, inhabits the Mediterranean region, southwest Asia, and the Canary Islands. It consists of thirty-five species. The name comes from an ancient Latin one.

Laserpitiums are mostly tall, herbaceous perennials, with leaves two- or more-times-pinnately-divided. Their little white, pinkish, yellowish, or greenish flowers, each with a five-toothed calyx and five petals and in large umbels, are succeeded by rounded or slightly flattened, ellipsoid, ovoid or cylindrical, winged fruits.

From 1 foot to 3 feet tall or sometimes taller, *Laserpitium siler*, of Europe, is nearly hairless, sometimes slightly glaucous, and

has stout stems that may or may not branch above. The largest leaves are up to 3 feet long and two- to four-times-divided, with the ultimate divisions narrow and toothless. The flowers are white and in umbels with twenty to fifty rays. The fruits are ¼ to nearly ½ inch long. Variety *L. s. garganicum* (syn. *L. garganicum*), of Italy and the Balkan Peninsula, differs in having wider leaf lobes than the typical species. A usually taller kind, 2 to 5 feet in height, *L. latifolium* differs from *L. siler* and its variety in the very broad ultimate divisions of its twice-pinnate leaves being toothed. It is a native of Europe and western Asia.

Garden and Landscape Uses and Cultivation. Chiefly of use for grouping to give bold effects in semiwild, informal areas and in perennial borders, these plants are successfully grown in well-drained, ordinary soil in sun or part-day shade. They are raised from seed or by division in spring or early fall. The kinds discussed are hardy.

LASTHENIA (Lasthèn-ia)—Goldfields. The genus *Lasthenia*, of the daisy family COMPOSITAE, includes sixteen species and has a natural range extending from western North America to Chile. Its name is that of a lady pupil of Plato, who, wearing men's clothes, attended the master's lectures.

Lasthenias are hairy or hairless annuals, biennials, or short-lived perennials with opposite, undivided to pinnately-lobed leaves and, terminal on the shoots, stalked, daisy-type flower heads, with yellow centers and yellow, greenish, or white, petal-like ray florets. The fruits are seedlike achenes.

Goldfields (*L. chrysostoma* syn. *Baeria chrysostoma*) is a slender, branching, hairy annual up to 1 foot tall. Its linear or threadlike leaves are 1¼ to 4 inches long, its flower heads about 1 inch across and bright yellow. This kind is native from Oregon to Arizona and Baja California. From the last, *L. coronaria* (syns. *Baeria californica*, *B. coronaria*), of southern California

Lasthenia coronaria

and Baja California, differs in being glandular- or sticky-hairy. A branched or branchless annual 6 inches to 1¼ feet tall, it has linear leaves up to 2¼ inches long and yellow flower heads ½ to ¾ inch across.

Other species cultivated include *L. glabrata* and *L. macrantha*. An annual indigenous to northern California, **L. glabrata** is slightly fleshy and 1 foot to 2 feet tall. It has narrow, glossy green leaves up to 6 inches long and long-stalked, yellow flower heads ¾ to 1 inch across. Beneath each is a cuplike collar of green bracts. In its native range of Oregon to California, **L. macrantha** (syn. *Baeria macrantha*) is an annual, biennial, or short-lived perennial. Rather sparsely-branched, it has thick, horizontal roots and attains a height of 1 foot to 2 feet. It has erect, more or less hairy stems, and narrowly-linear or threadlike leaves up to 8 inches long. Its flower heads are yellow and about 1 inch wide.

Lasthenia glabrata

Garden Uses and Cultivation. These plants are grown as annuals. They are attractive in flower gardens and rock gardens and can be used effectively as edgings. They are also pretty in pots in cool greenhouses. They flourish in rather poor soils, thoroughly well-drained and porous, in full sun. Their needs are simple. Seeds are sown in early spring where the plants are to bloom and are raked into the surface soil. The young plants are thinned to 4 or 5 inches apart. Except in exposed locations lasthenias normally require no staking. Their need for watering is minimal. When they show signs of failing to bloom freely, as they do after a month to six weeks, the stems should be cut low down to stimulate new growth and renewed flowering. In regions of mild winters seeds sown outdoors in fall result in comparatively early blooming plants.

To have pot plants for blooming in a greenhouse in late winter or spring, sow seeds in September or January and transplant the seedlings three to five together in 5- or 6-inch pots. Grow them in full sun in a night temperature of 50°F and daytime temperatures five or ten degrees higher. Stake the plants neatly, and water to keep the soil fairly moist. After the containers are well filled with roots give weekly applications of dilute liquid fertilizer.

LATANIA (Latàn-ia)—Latan Palm. Consisting of three species of beautiful palms of the Mascarene Islands, *Latania* is of considerable horticultural interest because of the noble appearance of its massive fan-shaped leaves, which are attractively displayed. The name of the genus, which belongs in the palm family PALMAE, is a modification of its native one, *latanier*.

Latanias are stout, slow-growing, single-trunked trees up to about 40 feet in height with leaves that fall cleanly from the trunks and leave prominent, rough scars. The leaf blades are 5 to 8 feet across, their stalks 3 to 6 feet long. The latter, especially those of young specimens, and sometimes the leaf margins of young plants, are finely-toothed or spined. The blades are very stiff, almost as rigid as thin sheet metal, and are divided about halfway to their bases into many long-pointed segments. Male and female flowers are on separate trees. The males, each with fifteen to thirty stamens, are in clusters several feet long of numerous handlike groups of spikes that radiate like fingers. The female blooms are in much looser-branched clusters. The fruits, spherical, pear-shaped, or ovoid, and often angled, contain one to three seeds.

Latan palms are easily distinguished as to kind by the colors of their foliage, especially the young foliage. There are also clear differences in their seeds. The blue latan (**L. loddigesii**) has glaucous-blue leaves thickly covered on their undersides and on the sheath at the base of the stalk with fluffy, whitish scurf. Its fruits 2 to 2½ inches long are often three-angled. The seeds, about 2 inches long and under one-half as wide are ridged along their tops and backs. The other kinds have predominantly green leaves, scarcely if at all glaucous, and with distinguishing color chiefly at the leaf margins, on the leafstalks, or in young leaves, suffusing the entire blade. The red latan (**L. lontaroides** syn. *L. borbonica*) has reddish or purplish young foliage and leafstalks, and pear-shaped to globose fruits rather longer than broad. The seeds are under 2 inches long with curved low ridges on the convex side. The yellow latan (**L. verschaffeltii,** often called *L. aurea* in gardens) is characterized by the light yellowish-green or yellow that suffuses its young leaves and the yellow to orange-yellow of its leafstalks. Its obovoid to globose, blunt-angled fruits, about 2 inches long, contain seeds almost as big that are bristly on their concave sides and beaked at their tips.

Latania lontaroides, young specimen, Fairchild Tropical Garden, Miami, Florida

Latania lontaroides, Hope Gardens, Jamaica, West Indies

Garden and Landscape Uses. Latans are among the most handsome of the fan-leaved palms. They are spectacular and can be used with dramatic effects in tropical landscapes as single specimens, in groups, or in rows for lining driveways and avenues. They grow slowly so that for many years their lowermost leaves may touch or almost touch the ground. Nevertheless, even when low, they are arresting objects that give a feeling of strength and permanence to the landscape. It is important that latans are not crowded among other plants, otherwise much of their beauty is lost. They are excellent when used in association with buildings and other bold architectural features and for growing in large tubs to decorate terraces, steps, and large conservatories. Outdoors they grow in full sun or part-day shade and revel in deep, fertile soil.

Cultivation. No particular difficulties attend the cultivation of latans. They are among the easiest of palms to grow. They are tolerant of a wide variety of soils so long as they are well drained and not excessively dry. They are gross feeders and respond to generous fertilizing. Propagation is by fresh seed sown in sandy, fertile soil in a temperature of 75 to 85°F. In greenhouses they need a minimum night temperature of 55 to 60°F in winter and warmer conditions from spring through fall. At all seasons day temperatures should be five to ten degrees higher than those maintained at night. Watering should be done copiously from spring through fall, more moderately in winter. Biweekly applications of dilute liquid fertilizer to well-rooted specimens may be made with advantage from spring through fall. For more information see Palms.

LATH HOUSE. Walk-in-size structures of wood or metal slats built to improve the environments of plants grown in them by affording shade, moderating wind, and providing humidity, are called lath houses. They are extremely useful in warm climates where they can be put to effective use throughout the year, and for summer use in regions of harsher winters. Garden centers and retail nurseries frequently employ lath houses, often open to the north, for the display and temporary storage of plants in selling areas. The plants may be in containers or be dug, balled, and burlapped, and have their root balls buried in peat moss, sawdust, or similar material.

Besides such temporary uses, lath houses are employed as long-term growing environments for plants, especially sorts that need or benefit from some shade. Here belong such kinds as camellias and rhododendrons, as well as ferns, palms and other foliage plants, and orchids.

Lath houses are of many designs and usually are homemade. The supporting framework may be of rustic or squared lumber or metal pipes. The lathwork covering may be permanent or removable. Sometimes snow fencing is used. The distance between the laths must be accommodated to the amount of shade desired. Usually it is equal to from one-half to the full width of the laths themselves. Structures similar to lath houses and serving similar purposes are sometimes covered with Saran cloth instead of laths or in the

A lath house sheltering cymbidiums:
(a) Exterior

(b) Interior

Interior of a large lath house in California sheltering mahonias

tropics and subtropics with palm leaves or with Florida-moss (Spanish-moss) draped from overhead wires.

LATHYRUS (Láthy-rus)—Sweet-Pea, Everlasting-Pea, Grass-Pea, Beach-Pea, Pride-of-California, Vetchling. This is a genus of 130 species of the pea family LEGUMINOSAE. By far the best known ornamentals among its members are the sweet-pea and everlasting- or perennial-pea. Others are less frequently grown. From related *Vicia* and *Pisum*, this last the genus to which edible garden peas belong, *Lathyrus* is distinguished by its flowers having wing petals practically separate from, instead of joined for one-half their lengths to, the keels. Native chiefly of temperate parts of the northern hemisphere and of South America, *Lathyrus* has a name derived from the Greek *lathyros*, a pea or some other legume. The grass-pea (*L. sativus*), a native of southeast Europe and Asia, and some other species are grown for forage and in some countries for food.

Lathyruses include annuals and chiefly herbaceous perennials. Most are tendril-climbing vines. A few are erect. The stems are prominently angled or winged. Their alternate, pinnate leaves have an even

number of leaflets and often a terminal one represented by a tendril, but some species are without tendrils. Often showy, the pea-like blooms, usually in racemes, come from the leaf axils. They have five sepals and the same number of petals, the upper one the banner or standard, the two side ones the wings. The lower pair are joined to form the keel. There are ten stamens, nine joined and one free, and a single flattened style with a beard of hairs down its face. This contrasts with the slender, not flattened style of *Vicia*, which has a tuft or circle of hairs only at its top. The fruits are pea-like pods. In addition to the kinds described below other native species are likely to be brought into gardens from time to time.

The sweet-pea (*L. odoratus*) is scarcely known to gardeners in its original form, but is widely appreciated and cultivated in its vastly superior garden varieties. These represent late nineteenth- and twentieth-century triumphs of the plant breeders' art and science. In its wild state, in its native southern Italy and Sicily, the sweet-pea is a slightly hairy, weak-stemmed, annual vine that attains a height of several feet. Its stems are winged. Its leaves have one pair of broad leaflets up to 2 inches long and a terminal, branched tendril. The very fragrant blooms, usually purple with paler wing petals, are small in comparison with those of most horticultural varieties of sweet-pea, and the margins of their petals are not wavy or frilled. There are up to four blooms in each longish-stalked raceme. The seed pods, about 2 inches long, are pubescent. The dwarf sweet-pea, *L. o. nanellus*, is low, compact, and not climbing. Horticultural varieties are discussed under Sweet-Pea. In parts of California the sweet-pea has become naturalized.

Lathyrus odoratus, garden variety

Everlasting- or perennial-pea (*L. latifolius*) is a popular, easily cultivated, hardy herbaceous perennial that has much the aspect of the sweet-pea. This several-foot-high native of Europe is a climber, with

Lathyrus latifolius

Lathyrus niger

strongly-winged stems, and leaves with a single pair of conspicuously three- or five-veined, ovate-lanceolate leaflets 2 to 4 inches in length, broad stipules, and a terminal, branched tendril. Several to many on stalks much longer than the leaves, the flowers much resemble those of sweet-peas, but unfortunately are not fragrant. Bright purplish-rose-pink, they have standard or banner petals 1 inch wide or wider. The flattish seed pods are 3 to 5 inches long. The blooms of *L. l. splendens* are purple-red. Those of *L. l. albus* and of 'Snow Queen' are pure white. The two-flowered-pea (*L. grandiflorus*) is a less rampant hardy perennial. It has leaves with small, narrow stipules and rose-purple flowers with dark purple wings, in racemes of two or three. Its leaves have a pair of large, ovate leaflets and a short, branched tendril. This is a native of southern Europe. It stands partial shade. Native to western Asia, *L. rotundifolius* is a hairless, perennial climber with winged stems, leaves of one pair of roundish-ovate leaflets, and narrow stipules. The racemes, longer than the leaves, have large, rose-pink flowers. This stands partial shade.

Tangier-pea (*L. tingitanus*) is a hairless annual somewhat resembling the sweet-pea, but its flowers are not fragrant and its leaves have one pair of linear-lanceolate leaflets up to about 2 inches long and a terminal tendril. From the grass-pea (*L. sativus*) this differs in its brilliantly colored flowers having calyxes with teeth shorter rather than much longer than the tube, and in its flat, 3- to 5-inch-long, hairless seed pods not being winged along their upper margins. The blooms, in long-stalked racemes of two or three, have scarlet wings and keels, and a much larger, about 1-inch-wide purple banner or standard petal. This native of the western Mediterranean region is naturalized in California.

Beach-pea (*L. maritimus*) is a variable, sprawling to more or less erect, hardy perennial that inhabits beaches and shores of lakes and seas in North America, Europe, and Asia. It has wingless, angled stems 1 foot to 5 feet long and leaves with three to six pairs of oblong to blunt-ovate leaflets 1 inch to 2 inches in length, each with a brief point at the apex and a branched, terminal tendril. The broad-ovate stipules are about as long as the leaves. Terminating stalks about as long as the leaves, the racemes are of five to ten flowers ¾ to 1 inch long, with purple banner or standard petals and paler wings and keels. The linear-oblong seed pods are up to 2 inches long.

Marsh-pea (*L. palustris*) is a hardy perennial, a native of moist and wet soils in North America, Europe, and Asia. This has slender, more or less erect or trailing stems, up to 3 feet long and often winged. The leaves, with two to four pairs of pointed, oblong-lanceolate leaflets up to 2 inches in length, have small stipules and end in branched tendrils. The ½-inch-long purplish flowers are succeeded by seed pods 2 inches long. The showy wild-pea (*L. venosus*) is native in woodlands and along streams from Canada to Georgia. Finely-hairy, it has prominently four-angled stems and leaves of four to six pairs of blunt, oblong-ovate leaflets about 2 inches long. The stipules are short and slender. The purple flowers are crowded in racemes of eight to sixteen, with stalks shorter than the leaves. They are ¼ to ⅓ inch long.

Lord Anson's blue-pea (*L. magellanicus*) carries an intriguing, but rather misleading vernacular name. Its blooms are bluish-purple, not blue. A vigorous, nearly evergreen, woody perennial climber 4 to 6 feet tall, not hardy in the north, this is adapted for regions with mild winters and fairly cool summers. It has sometimes branched, angled stems, and leaves with a solitary pair of ovate to oblong-linear leaflets, a branched tendril, and large arrow- to heart-shaped stipules, broader than the leaves. The flowers are in long-stalked racemes of three to four. This is native to the southern tip of South America.

Vetchling is a name used for nonclimbing species of *Lathyrus*, some kinds without tendrils. To the casual observer they resemble vetches (*Vicia*). In the past these were segregated as *Orobus* and are still sometimes known as such by gardeners. One of the best, the spring vetchling (*L. vernus* syn. *Orobus vernus*) is a pretty, spring-blooming, hardy perennial, 6 inches to 2 feet in height, with many crowded, branchless or sparsely-branched, erect stems. Its leaves, without tendrils, have two or three pairs of pointed-ovate leaflets, 1½ to 3 inches long, each with two prominent veins running upward from their bases. In stalked, loose racemes of four to eight, the nodding, short-stalked, ¾-inch-long flowers are borne and are succeeded by slender, hairless seed pods about 1½ inches long. Black vetchling (*L. niger* syn. *Orobus niger*) earned its common name because, in contrast to those of the last, when dried its leaves, without tendrils, turn black. Native to Europe, this differs from the spring vetchling in having rhizome-like instead of fibrous roots and in its leaves having five to eight pairs of broad-elliptic, blunt leaflets with a tiny point at the tip. The short-stalked, purple flowers, ½ inch long, are in long-stalked, crowded racemes of six to twelve. The blooms are held horizontally. The pods, linear-oblong, are about 1½ inches long. European *L. luteus* (syn. *Orobus luteus*) is a perennial 1 foot to 2 feet tall with branchless stems and leaves 3 to 4½ inches long of three to five pairs of broad-elliptic leaflets, glaucous on their under-sides. It is without tendrils. Its yellow flowers are in long-stalked racemes, longer than the leaves, from the leaf axils. They are up to 1 inch long. Variety *L. l. aureus* (syn. *Orobus aureus*) has branched stems and erect racemes of brownish-yellow to fawn or tangerine flowers.

Lathyrus luteus aureus

Pride-of-California (*L. splendens*), a beautiful native of southern California and Baja California, is a hairless or pubescent sub-shrubby perennial 1½ to 10 feet tall, with wingless stems. The leaves, ending with a tendril, have three to five pairs of usually few-toothed, linear to ovate-oblong leaflets ¾ inch to 2½ inches long. The rich red to crimson blooms, about ¾ inch long, are in racemes of four to twelve. They have a backward-pointing standard or banner petal. The slender, hairless pods are 2 to 3½ inches long. This inhabitant of dry hills is hardy in mild climates only.

Garden and Landscape Uses. For the sweet-pea these are explained under Sweet-Peas. The Tangier-pea has similar uses. The other kinds here considered are easy to grow, and except for a few indicated in the above treatment as being unsuitable for regions of hard winters, are hardy in the north. The taller vining kinds, such as the everlasting-pea, are excellent for trellises and other supports their tendrils can grasp. So supported, they make effective summer screens. They may also be allowed to sprawl over rocks, tree stumps, low walls, and similar rough supports. Pride-of-California is for regions with climates similar to that of the southern part of its native state. Lord Anson's blue-pea is only likely to be attempted by lovers of the unusual who garden in mild regions where cool summers prevail.

Vetchlings are splendid for planting at the fronts of flower beds, in semiformal areas, and in rock gardens. The showy wild-pea, the two-flowered-pea, and *L. rotundifolius* do well in light shade, the everlasting-pea and the vetchlings tolerate part-day shade. Generally the others prefer full sun. All except the marsh-pea must have well-drained soil. As is to be expected, the beach-pea adapts well to sandy places near the sea and elsewhere, and the marsh-pea to bog gardens and other wet-soil areas.

Cultivation. Few difficulties attend the cultivation of lathyruses. The vining ones transplant poorly, and it is usually better to set out young specimens from pots than to move old ones. Vetchlings transplant much more successfully. Planting may be done in fall or spring. In cold climates spring is preferable. Spacing should depend largely on the vigor of the species and the size the plants are expected to attain. Established plants need no special care. If they lack vigor a spring application of a complete fertilizer is helpful. Old stems and foliage are cut off and removed after they die in fall. Propagation is chiefly by seed, but cuttings of some kinds can be rooted, and the vetchlings lend themselves to increase by division in early fall or spring. For the cultivation of sweet-pea see Sweet-Pea.

LATTICE LEAF is *Aponogeton madagascariensis*.

LAURACEAE—Laurel Family. Thirty-two genera comprising from 2,000 to 2,500 species of aromatic trees and shrubs or rarely parasitic, almost leafless, herbaceous vines constitute this family of dicotyledons. Predominantly inhabitants of the tropics and subtropics, they are most abundantly represented in Brazil and southeastern Asia. Among the best known products of this family are avocados, camphor, and cinnamon. Several of its sorts are exploited commercially for their lumbers and fragrant oils.

Members of the laurel family have alternate or much less frequently opposite, undivided, lobeless and generally toothless, leaves, those of warm climate kinds characteristically leathery and evergreen, those of the much fewer natives of temperate climates much thinner and deciduous. The flowers, small and variously clustered or in racemes, usually from the leaf axils, are sometimes subterminal. Typically they have a perianth of six similar sepal-like parts, twelve stamens or stamens and staminodes (aborted, nonfunctional stamens), and one style terminated by a sometimes lobed stigma. The fruits are drupes or berries. Cultivated genera include *Beilschmiedia, Cinnamomum, Cryptocarya, Laurus, Lindera, Litsea, Neolitsea, Parabenzoin, Persea, Phoebe, Sassafras,* and *Umbellularia.*

LAUREL. See Laurus. The name Alexandrian-laurel is applied to *Calophyllum inophyllum* and *Danae racemosa.* Other plants that have the word laurel as part of their common names are bog-laurel (*Kalmia polifolia*), California-laurel (*Umbellularia californica*), cherry-laurel (*Prunus*), great-laurel (*Rhododendron maximum*), mountain-laurel (*Kalmia latifolia*), New-Zealand-laurel (*Corynocarpus laevigata*), Portugal-laurel (*Prunus lusitanica*), sheep-laurel (*Kalmia angustifolia*), spotted-laurel (*Aucuba japonica variegata*), spurge-laurel (*Daphne laureola*), and Texas-mountain-laurel (*Sophora secundiflora*).

LAURELIA (Laurèl-ia)—Pukatea. The similarity of the pungent aroma of the crushed foliage and other parts of the two or three species of *Laurelia* to that of laurel (*Laurus*), suggested its name. There is no close botanical relationship between the two genera. Native to New Zealand and Chile, *Laurelia* belongs in the monimia family MONIMIACEAE.

Laurelias are tall evergreen trees with opposite, stalked, leathery, undivided, toothed leaves and, on the same plant, unisexual and bisexual tubular blooms of no appreciable ornamental merit. They are tiny and in racemes or clusters from the leaf axils. The bell-shaped males have five- to twelve-lobed calyxes and six to twelve stamens. The female and the bisexual flowers have tubular calyxes that elongate as fruits develop and become three- to five-lobed. All stamens in the females and some in bisexual flowers are reduced to nonfunctional scales. The styles are plume-like. The fruits are achenes with the styles attached. The fruits of the Chilean species are used as substitutes for nutmegs and its leaves for flavoring.

In New Zealand, exceeding 100 feet in height, the pukatea (*L. novae-zealandiae*) favors moist and wet soils. Its nearly white trunks develop large planklike buttresses. Its twigs are four-angled and sparsely-hairy. Dark green above and paler on their undersides, the elliptic to elliptic-obovate leaves are 1½ to 3½ inches long by 1 inch to 2 inches wide. On softly-hairy stalks the ¼-inch-wide flowers are in axillary racemes up to 1½ inches long.

The Chilean *L. aromatica* (syn. *L. serrata*) usually attains a height of 40 to 50 feet and has downy shoots. Its leaves, one-half as wide as their 2- to 5-inch lengths, are elliptic and hairless. A little over ¼ inch wide, the yellowish-green flowers are in short clusters of three to nine.

Garden and Landscape Uses and Cultivation. No particular difficulties accompany the cultivation of these good-looking trees. They are not hardy in the north, but are suited for planting in California, the Pacific Northwest, and other regions where New Zealand and Chilean plants are known to succeed. Propagation is by seed and by cuttings of firm shoots taken in summer and planted under mist or in a propagating bed in a greenhouse or cold frame. Layering has also been successfully employed to increase these trees.

LAURENTIA (Laurént-ia). The genus *Laurentia*, of the bellflower family CAMPANULACEAE, includes sorts previously named *Isotoma.* There are twenty-five species, natives of the Americas, the Mediterranean region, Africa, and Australia. Its name honors the seventeenth-century Italian botanist M. A. Laurent. The plant sometimes named *L. longiflora* is *Hippobroma longiflora.*

Laurentias are annuals and herbaceous perennials that differ from *Lobelia* in their flowers having a corolla tube not slit along one side. Their leaves are alternate or less often whorled (in circles of more than two). Solitary or in racemes, the flowers have five sepals and a two-lipped to nearly symmetrical, five-lobed corolla. There are five stamens, one style, and a two-lobed stigma. The fruits are capsules. Some species, possibly all, are poisonous.

An erect, hairless perennial up to 1½ feet tall, Australian *L. petraea* (syn. *Isotoma petraea*) has jagged-toothed, ovate-lanceolate leaves, tapered toward their tips and bases and 1 inch to 2½ inches long. The solitary white to lilac blooms, very long-stalked, have corollas 1½ to 1¾ inches long. The two lower stamens end in solitary long bristles. Stemless and forming loose rosettes of spatula-shaped to oblong leaves, *L. minuta* (syn. *L. tenella*), of the Mediterranean region and South Africa, has light violet flowers, white or spotted

Laurentia petraea

Laurentia fluviatilis

Laurus nobilis in Ireland

with yellow on their insides. They are borne on erect, bracted stalks up to 4 inches long. This kind is perennial.

Annual **L. axillaris** (syn. *Isotoma axillaris*), of Australia, is 1 foot to 2 feet tall and loosely-branched. Its practically stalkless leaves are 2 to 3 inches long and deeply-pinnately-lobed. Clear lavenderblue often with a darker mid-vein to each petal, the solitary, almost symmetrical flowers on stalks from the leaf axils about three times as long as the leaves, are approximately 1 inch long and wide. They have narrow, spreading petals.

Laurentia axillaris

A delightful carpeter, perennial **L. fluviatilis** (syn. *Isotoma fluviatilis*), of Australia, Tasmania, and New Zealand, is hairless or nearly so. Less than 1 inch high, it has slender, prostrate, branched stems that root from the nodes and leaves generally not over and often considerably under ½ inch long. The lower ones are ovate to nearly circular, those above linear. The starry flowers, slightly longer than the leaves, light blue to white, have nearly equal, pointed-oblong petals.

Garden and Landscape Uses and Cultivation. The sorts described here are suitable for outdoor cultivation in mild, dry

climates such as that of California. They may be used in flower beds and rock gardens, and *L. fluviatilis* is a neat groundcover. For this last purpose plants may be spaced 6 inches apart. All succeed in sunny locations in well-drained soil. Propagation is by division, cuttings, and seed.

LAURESTINUS is *Viburnum tinus*.

LAURUS (Laùr-us)—Laurel or Sweet Bay. This is the genus to which the name laurel, unmodified by adjectival prefix such as mountain-, sheep-, cherry-, Portugal-, or California- belongs. From leafy shoots of *Laurus nobilis*, the ancient name of which was *laurus*, the Romans fashioned wreaths to crown victors. Doctors upon passing final examinations were similarly decorated with berried branches of the same species. From this ancient custom derives our word baccalaureate (from *bacca*, a berry, and *laureus*, of laurel) as well as the English poet-laureate, and, by modification the word bachelor. By the ancients *L. nobilis* was held sacred to Apollo and was favored for planting near temples. Now, as in the past, leaves of *L. nobilis* have been esteemed for more prosaic use. They are the bay leaves of the cook.

The genus *Laurus* belongs in the laurel family LAURACEAE and consists of two species, the one already mentioned, which inhabits the Mediterranean region, and *L. canariensis* of the Canary Islands and Madeira. They are evergreen trees not hardy in the north, that under favorable conditions attain heights of 50 or 60 feet, but are often lower. They have alternate, lobeless, leathery leaves and unisexual or more rarely bisexual, little yellowish flowers of no display value, in small umbels from the leaf axils. The blooms have four-lobed calyxes, no petals, and, the males, usually a dozen or more stamens; the females have four aborted stamens or staminodes, and one style. The fruits, cherry-like in appearance, are technically berries.

Laurel or sweet bay (**L. nobilis**) has hairless, lanceolate to oblong, dull green, short-

stalked leaves 1½ to 3½ inches long by ½ inch to 1½ inches broad. When crushed they are strongly and pleasantly aromatic. The flowers, with the sexes usually on separate trees, are produced in spring. The spherical to slightly egg-shaped, shining black fruits are ½ inch long. There are few varieties, of which the most distinctive is *L. n. angustifolia* (syn. *L. n. salicifolia*), which has much narrower leaves than those of the typical species. Another, *L. n. undulata*, has wavy leaves. The species **L. canariensis** differs from *L. nobilis* in having downy twigs and larger leaves, 2½ to 5 inches long by 2 to 3 inches broad. The kind is much more tender to cold than *L. nobilis*.

Laurus canariensis in California

Garden and Landscape Uses. In California and elsewhere in Mediterranean-type climates, where mild winters and warm summers prevail, the sweet bay is a fine ornamental evergreen for general landscaping, screening, hedges, backgrounds, and suchlike uses. It withstands considerable frost and can be sheared to almost any desired size and shape. Because of this adaptability it has long been favored for growing in large tubs and other containers for decorating steps, terraces, patios, and

Laurus nobilis, in a large tub

similar areas. Usually such specimens are trained and sheared as globes, cones, spheres atop short trunks, and other formal shapes. In mild climates such specimens can remain outdoors all year, but where harsher winters are the rule they must be stored inside. Except that it is less hardy, *L. canariensis* can be used similarly.

Cultivation. Laurels prosper in sun or part-day shade in any reasonably good garden soil that is neither excessively wet nor parched. Specimens in containers appreciate fertile, loamy soil and adequate drainage. They are watered very freely from spring to fall, less generously in winter, but their roots must never be permitted to dry completely. Laurels are gross feeders and it is important to satisfy their needs by soaking the soil of specimens that have filled their containers with roots at weekly to biweekly intervals in spring and summer with dilute liquid fertilizer. To keep trained specimens shapely they are sheared annually after the new growth of the season is well matured. Repotting and retubbing are done in spring. With large specimens this attention is needed only at intervals of several years. Propagation is most commonly done by cuttings 4 or 5 inches long from pieces of fairly mature current season's shoots in summer and inserted under mist, or in a cold frame or greenhouse propagating bench. Seed can also be used as a means of increase. The winter storage of container specimens may be in any fairly light, cool, airy place. Temperatures over 50°F at night are detrimental; they may drop to 35°F with impunity. Day temperatures should not be greatly higher.

LAVANDULA (Laván-dula)—Lavender. Even as today, the ancients and people of later centuries employed fragrant products of this genus in toiletries, which was recognized by Linnaeus when he bestowed the name, derived from the Latin *lavo*, to wash. But the lavender that delighted citizens of the Roman Empire is distinct from the kinds most esteemed at the time of Linnaeus and now. Our plants are *Lavandula angustifolia*, *L. latifolia*, and hybrids between them, and the species favored by the Romans was *L. stoechas*.

Belonging to the mint family LABIATAE, the genus *Lavandula* comprises twenty-eight species of herbaceous perennials, subshrubs, and low shrubs, prevailingly aromatic. The Mediterranean region is the chief center of their natural occurrence, but the group is also represented in the native floras of the Canary Islands, Arabia, and India. It has opposite, smooth-edged, toothed, or pinnately-lobed, more or less hairy and generally glandular leaves. At the ends of branched or branchless stems, the asymmetrical flowers, associated with well-developed bracts, are displayed in cylindrical, spikelike racemes. They are lavender, purple-blue, blue, or dingy white. From the more or less two-lipped, five-toothed calyx the five-lobed corolla protrudes. The upper lip is two-, the lower three-lobed. There are four stamens in two pairs and a shortly two-cleft style. The fruits consist of four seedlike nutlets.

Besides the commercial employment of oils obtained from some of these plants in perfumery and in the manufacture of soap and related products, the dried flowers are favorites for sachets and potpourris. Lavenders are good bee plants.

English or common lavender (**L. angustifolia** syns. *L. delphinensis*, *L. officinalis*, *L. spica*, *L. vera*) has for centuries been highly esteemed for garden adornment and for sachets and other delights and conceits of herb fanciers. Its varieties and perhaps hybrids are sources of oil of lavender. A much-branched Mediterranean region shrub or subshrub up to 3 feet tall, this has hoary-gray, lobeless and toothless, oblong-linear to narrowly-lanceolate leaves up to 2 inches long, with turned-under margins. Often they have tufts of smaller leaves clustered in their axils. The spikes of lavender-purple blooms, each flower with a woolly calyx having thirteen ribs, are composed of tiers of ten or fewer, so spaced that short lengths of stem show between. The stalks of the flower spikes are 6 to 8 inches long. The floral bracts are ovate, papery, brown, and conspicuously-veined. Floral bracts as long as the calyxes, and considerably longer than those of the typical species distinguish *L. a. pyrenaica*, of Spain and the Pyrenees. Among the many fine varieties of English lavender, some perhaps hybrids between it and *L. latifolia*, are these: *L. a. alba* has white flowers; *L. a. atropurpurea* has dark purple blooms; *L. a. compacta* is comparatively low and compact; *L. a.* 'Dutch' blooms late, has deep blue flowers; *L. a.* 'Hidcote' blooms early, has dark purple flowers and grows slowly; *L. a.* 'Munstead' blooms early and has lavender-blue blooms; *L. a. nana* is dwarf and compact; *L. a. praecox* blooms early and has flower spikes with

Lavandula angustifolia

Lavandula angustifolia (flowers)

A bed of *Lavandula angustifolia*

stalks not over 3½ inches long; *L. a. rosea* has pink flowers; *L. a.* 'Twickel Purple' has fanlike clusters of long spikes of purple blooms; and *L. a.* 'Waltham' has dark purple flowers. Presumably a variety of *L. angustifolia*, the plant sometimes cultivated as *L. a. triphylla* is distinguished by most of its leaves having two tiny leaflets at their bases.

Spike lavender (**L. latifolia**), of the Mediterranean region and Portugal, is distinguishable from English lavender by the

Lavandula angustifolia alba

Lavandula stoechas

Lavandula multifida canariensis

bracts at the bases of its flowers being linear or narrowly-lanceolate instead of ovate to rhombic-lanceolate, and green with only the center vein conspicuous. Also, its leaves, more densely-hairy, are without recurved margins and are broader than those of L. angustifolia. Oil of spike, less choice than oil of lavender and differing in chemical composition, is a product of L. latifolia. It is used to scent soaps and for other purposes. When crushed, the calyxes of spike lavender have the odor of English lavender together with a suggestion of camphor.

Distinct because of its very gray-woolly foliage and the calyxes of its flowers having eight each ribs and teeth, Spanish L. lanata is an attractive close relative of L. angustifolia. A shrub 1 foot to 2 feet tall, it has linear to oblanceolate leaves and tiny bright violet blooms in long-stalked spikes up to 3 inches long.

Lavandula angustifolia triphylla

The flower spikes of the kinds now to be considered are crowned with a tuft of colorful, usually blue, lavender, or purple, petal-like bracts without flowers in their axils, that flare like the flames of a torch. A shrub 3 feet tall, **L. stoechas,** sometimes called Spanish or French lavender, inhabits

the Mediterranean region, Canary Islands, and Madeira. It is the source of stoechas oil. Its young shoots like its foliage are thickly clothed with hairs. The leaves, ½ to 1 inch long, have somewhat revolute margins and are linear. On stalks usually from under to slightly over ½ inch long are borne broad, compact flower spikes crowned with several flaring, purple-veined and tinted bracts up to 1½ inches long. The blooms are dark purple, their exposed part about ⅛ inch long. Very similar to L. stoechas, but differing in the stalks of the flower spikes being 4 to 10 inches long, **L. pedunculata** inhabits the western Mediterranean region, Canary Islands, and Madeira. Like L. stoechas, called French lavender, quite different **L. dentata** is a native of the western Mediterranean region. It has linear leaves 1 inch to 1½ inches long, clearly toothed in comblike fashion along both margins, green, and with hairy undersides. Its deep purple blooms, ⅛ inch or slightly more wide, are in dense spikes 1½ to 2 inches long carried on long stalks. A crown of lavender-blue bracts tips each spike. This lavender is not infrequently misnamed L. delphinensis, which name is properly a synonym of L. angustifolia.

Lavenders with dissected, somewhat ferny foliage include L. multifida and L. pinnata. Native of the western Mediterranean region and Portugal, **L. multifida** up to 2 feet tall, has ovate leaves, about 1½ inches long by one-half as wide, usually twice pinnately-divided into narrow segments and gray-hairy. The ½-inch-long, blue-violet flowers are in dense spikes, solitary or in threes and 1 inch to 2½ inches long, atop stems 6 inches to 1½ feet long. Variety L. m. canariensis (syns. L. canariensis, L. abrotanoides), of the Canary Islands, has less dissected leaves. This is sometimes misnamed L. pinnata buchii. Native of the Canary Islands and Madeira, **L. pinnata** (syn. L. buchii), up to 3 feet tall, differs from L. multifida in having coarser, usually once-pinnate, white-hairy leaves. They are up to 3 inches long by one-half as broad. The crowded, branched or branchless flower

spikes, 2 to 3 inches long, top stalks 8 inches to over 1 foot long.

Garden and Landscape Uses. Except for a few dwarf forms of the English lavender these plants are not reliably hardy north of Philadelphia, and even there only L. angustifolia and its varieties and L. latifolia can be expected to survive. The others need climates with winters less severe. Lavenders with petal-like bracts crowning their racemes of bloom and those with finely-divided leaves are sometimes grown as pot plants in greenhouses and windows and like all nonhardy kinds may be wintered in such environments and planted outdoors for summer display. All lavenders are appropriate for herb gardens and make pleasant borders, edgings to paths, and low hedges. They revel in full sun and a free circulation of air. Most do best in soil not very fertile, well drained, and dryish rather than wet. They especially appreciate soils of a limestone character. One kind, L. multifida, responds to somewhat moister soil that contains abundant peat or other decayed organic matter.

Cultivation. Old-established lavender plants do not transplant readily. It is usually best to start with young, sturdy stock. Planting is done in spring or early fall, the former being best in regions where the plants are near the borderline of hardiness. Planting distances are governed by the size the plants are expected to attain and may be in the order of 9 inches to 3 feet between individuals, according to variety and purpose for which they are being grown. Routine care is minimal. If the plants lack vigor a spring application of a complete fertilizer is likely to help. If the flowers are not harvested and seeds are not wanted, all flower spikes should be cut off as soon as they fade. In the north lavenders appreciate the winter protection afforded by a covering of branches of evergreens or salt hay or by being shielded from sun and wind by screens of burlap. Any shearing or pruning needed to shape the plants may be done as soon as flowering is through or in early spring. Lavenders can be raised from seeds, but horticultural varieties will not breed true and other kinds may not. Cuttings are generally preferred as a means of increase. These are taken in summer after the shoots have become firm, but not hard. They are made from side shoots 2 or 3 inches long, each with or without a sliver of older wood attached at the base. Cuttings root with little difficulty in a shaded cold frame or under mist. Careful division in early fall or spring, especially of dwarf varieties, is also sometimes practicable.

To propagate *Lavandula:* (a) Make cuttings in late summer

(b) The cuttings ready for insertion

(c) Plant the cuttings in sand or sandy soil in a cold frame

(d) Water immediately afterward, cover with a frame sash, and shade from direct sun

As pot plants in greenhouses or windows, lavenders need no special attention. They thrive in any coarse, porous, moderately fertile soil, which must not be kept too wet. The temperature on winter nights should range between 40 and 50°F and should not be increased by more than five to ten degrees or so by day. In summer the plants can with advantage be put outdoors. At all seasons they need full sun.

LAVANGA. See Luvunga.

LAVATERA (Laváter-a)—Rose-Mallow, Tree-Mallow. This genus comprises twenty-five species of annuals, biennials, and shrubs and has a wide geographical range, being native in California, Baja California, Australia, the Canary Islands, and from the Mediterranean region to the northwestern Himalayas. Several attractive garden plants are included in *Lavatera*, a member of the mallow family MALVACEAE. Its name honors J. R. Lavater, a sixteenth-century physician and naturalist of Zurich, Switzerland.

Lavateras are mostly hairy plants with lobed or angled leaves, those of some kinds distinctly maple-like in shape. The flowers, in terminal racemes or from the leaf axils, resemble the blooms of mallows and hibiscuses and are mostly white, pink, lavender, or red, but rarely are yellow. They have five spreading petals that reflex as the bloom fades. The column formed by the fused stalks of the stamens frays at the top into numerous ends each tipped with an anther. Behind each bloom is a collar or involucre formed of three, six, or nine leafy bracts that are united. This distinguishes *Lavatera* from the true mallows (*Malva*), which have one to three separate bracts. The fruits are one-seeded, kidney-shaped capsules.

The rose-mallow (**L. trimestris**), native to the Mediterranean region, is a very attractive annual available in several varieties including *L. t. rosea,* with deep rose-pink blooms; *L. t. alba,* with white flowers;

and *L. t. splendens,* with larger flowers than the typical species. The plant known as *L. t. grandiflora* is similar to and perhaps identical with *L. t. splendens.* There are several color forms of *L. t. splendens* to which English varietal names are applied. One of the finest is 'Loveliness', which has large, clear pink flowers with carmine veins and quite free of any suspicion of magenta. The rose-mallow attains a height of 3 to 5 feet and grows and branches vigorously. Its lower leaves are rounded with little or no evidence of lobing, those above are angled. All are irregularly-toothed and may be hairy or almost hairless. The flowers, solitary in the leaf axils, are 3 to 4 inches in diameter. They are numerous and produce a colorful display over a period of many weeks.

Lavatera trimestris

The common tree-mallow (**L. arborea**) is a hardy biennial, a native of southern Europe that grows 3 to 10 feet in height and has stout, erect stems and velvety-hairy, five- to nine-lobed, long-stalked leaves up to 9 inches long and broad. The almost stemless flowers, about 2 inches in diameter, are in short, leafy racemes and axillary clusters. They are abundant and make a good display. A variegated-leaved variety, *L. a. variegata,* has mottled foliage.

The most important shrubby lavatera, an evergreen native of islands off the coast of southern California, is **L. assurgentiflora.** Under good conditions it may become 15 feet tall, but often is considerably lower. It has leaves up to 6 inches across that are five- to seven-lobed and glabrous or finely-pubescent. The blooms, on stalks 3 to 6 inches long, are in groups of up to four or sometimes are solitary in the leaf axils. They are 2 to 3 inches in diameter, light purple-red with darker veins. A distinguishing feature is the two dense tufts of hairs at the base of the petals. This is hardy in mild climates only.

Other sorts include these: **L. bicolor,** a shrub about 3 feet high from southern Europe, has rounded, five-lobed, gray-hairy leaves and flowers, about 3 inches across,

Lavatera assurgentiflora

Lavatera olbia

Lavatera bicolor

that are white or pale pink with purple veinings and a purple center. **L. davaei** is a showy annual from Portugal with deeply-lobed leaves. It grows up to 3 feet tall and has rose-violet flowers in groups of two to five. **L. insularis** is an evergreen shrub with grayish, seven-lobed leaves and solitary, stalked, yellowish-white flowers striped and tipped with purple. It is a native of the Coronado Islands off the coast of California. **L. mauritanica,** of North Africa, is a pleasing annual rarely more than 1½ feet in height with densely-woolly, five- to seven-lobed leaves and pale violet flowers deeper colored toward their centers. **L. olbia** is a southern European evergreen shrub up to 6 feet in height that has solitary reddish-purple flowers 1½ to 2 inches across with very short stalks or none. The leaves are softly-hairy, the lower ones five-lobed, those above three-lobed. **L. thuringiaca** is a herbaceous perennial native of southern Europe, with rose-pink flowers up to 2½ inches across and ovate-lanceolate, three-lobed, bluntly-toothed leaves.

Garden and Landscape Uses. Annual *L. trimestris* and its varieties are beautiful flower garden ornamentals and, unlike many members of the mallow family, the flowers last well when cut. Even uno-

pened buds expand on cut stems standing indoors in water. This sort is well worth growing in greenhouses as a winter- and spring-blooming pot plant and for cutting. The common tree-mallow is usually cultivated in its variegated-leaved variety. It is best suited for less formal areas. Much used as a windbreak in California, *L. assurgentiflora* withstands seaside conditions well and is very drought resistant.

Cultivation. None of the cultivated kinds of this genus are difficult to grow. Seeds of *L. trimestris* are sown outdoors directly where the plants are to bloom as soon as it is possible to work the ground in spring. The seeds are large, and since the seedlings must be thinned to 1 foot to 1½ feet apart, it is a mistake to sow too thickly. Do not have the ground excessively rich, otherwise foliage growth is likely to be too lush and flower production diminished. A sunny location is desirable. Cover the seeds to a depth of about ¼ inch. Routine care consists of cultivating the surface soil shallowly to keep down weeds, staking if there is any tendency for the stems to fall over, and removing faded blooms to prevent seed production. This last does much to prolong the blooming season.

To have plants for late winter and spring blooming in the greenhouse sow seeds from September to January in light porous soil and as soon as the seedlings are big enough to handle transplant them about 2½ inches apart in flats, or individually to small pots. Keep them growing in full sun where the night temperature is 50°F and that by day is five to ten degrees higher. As soon as the young plants begin to crowd, plant them in benches 8 or 9 inches apart or repot them into larger containers. Eventually those from early fall sowings may be in 8- or 9-inch pots and those from January sowings in containers 6 inches in diameter. When the available soil is filled with roots and spring is approaching, applications of dilute liquid fertilizer made with discretion will retain good foliage color and promote the well-being of the plants. At all times an airy, buoyant atmosphere should be maintained.

Plants of biennial *L. arborea* are raised from seeds sown directly outdoors or in a cold frame in May. The young seedlings are transplanted to nursery beds or cold frames in fertile soil and full sun as soon as they are large enough to handle, spacing them outdoors 6 to 8 inches apart in rows 1 foot to 1½ feet apart, and in frames about 6 to 8 inches each way. Throughout the summer cultivation is practiced to keep down weeds and in fall or early the following spring the plants are transferred to their flowering quarters, spacing them about 1½ feet apart. Shrubby kinds may be raised from seeds or cuttings. Herbaceous perennial kinds are increased by seed and by division. They need no particular care and grow without difficulty in any ordinary garden soil in full sun.

LAVENDER. See Lavandula. Lavender-cotton is *Santolina chamaecyparissus*. For sea-lavender see Limonium.

LAWN-LEAF. See Dichondra.

LAWN MAINTENANCE. To keep a lawn in good condition calls for intelligent care. Without that it will deteriorate, and to bring it back to acceptable condition will necessitate major renovation or remaking. The major elements of lawn maintenance are widely known, but less commonly well carried out. They involve mowing, fertilizing, watering, and controlling pests and diseases, and sometimes other attentions.

Mowing is an important part of lawn management. Among amateurs it is poorly understood, a chore to be done periodically and perhaps protestingly. Yet bad mowing can quickly ruin good turf; intelligent cutting encourages a perfect sward.

Well-maintained lawns are a treasured feature of many American communities

The principal purpose of mowing a lawn is to maintain it as such. Unless cropped regularly, grassed areas soon develop into something akin to hayfields; the plants become loose and spindly as they reach upward; tall-growing weeds that cannot persist under frequent cutting come into the picture. The result may be pastoral and charming, but it is not a lawn. Another objective is to encourage the grasses to tiller (form side shoots freely from their bases), and spread and develop laterally into a tight sod. Proper mowing does this, but never forget that basically it is a weakening process; only when accompanied by intelligent watering and fertilizing can it be expected to produce fine results.

Lawn mowers: (a) For small home grounds

(b) For out-of-the-way corners of larger areas, hand mowers are often most suitable

(c) Power mowers are usually needed for large lawns

You will not get the best results if you mow on a strict schedule, the same day every week for example, nor if you leave the matter to a young son or some equally busy (and be it confessed unenthusiastic) person to do at their convenience. Weather and speed of growth make modifications of fixed schedules necessary.

Do not mow too early in spring. Let the grass make obvious growth first. This encourages new roots, which feed the grass through the season. Before the first cutting sweep the area to remove sticks, stones, or other debris and if the turf seems loose and springy and a medium-weight roller is available, on a day when the lawn is fairly dry roll it slowly to compress the surface.

Turf that is springy underfoot may benefit from rolling in spring

Once started, mow whenever growth necessitates. With most grasses as soon as they are ½ to ¾ inch to 1 inch higher than established cutting height. This may mean once a week at times, but in periods of rapid growth twice-a-week attention is necessary, and when growth is slow more time may elapse between mowings. It pays to mow frequently and to take a little each time rather than a lot. Do not let the grass get so high before mowing that after cutting it looks yellowish or brownish. This is an invitation to weeds, diseases, and pests. If bad weather prevents mowing before the grass is conspicuously longer than proper, raise the cutting height a little at the first mowing and gradually bring it to normal at subsequent cuttings.

Northern lawns in sunny locations, except those of creeping bent, are best cut to a height of 1¼ to 1½ inches. In really hot weather raise the cutting height an extra ½ inch. Avoid mowing grass in shaded areas too closely. The leaves of the grass are factories that convert simple elements absorbed by the roots from the soil and by the leaves from the air into complex tissue-building foods. These foods strengthen the grass plants. Because the foods are less abundant when the leaves are closely cut,

this practice weakens the grass. During hot summer weather a cutting height of 2 to 2½ inches is best for shaded lawns; in fall this may be reduced to 1½ inches. Give the last mowing of the season so that the grass goes into winter 2 to 3 inches long. Lawns of creeping bent may be cut to a height of from 1 inch to under ½ inch.

Southern lawns of subtropical grasses are generally mowed to a height of 1 inch. Temporary winter lawns of rye grass are cut at 1¼ inches.

Mowing machines should be used when the grass is dry, scythes and sickles when it is slightly moist.

If the "cut" of grass is heavy: (a) Do not leave the clippings on the lawn

(b) Instead use a mower fitted with a grass catcher or rake them up

(c) Remove them from the lawn

If the "cut" is short and light and the weather dry, the clippings may be left on the lawn surface to dry and sift downward to form a slight mulch and provide organic matter. This may be done, but it is better to pick up clippings, put them on the compost pile, and return them to the soil in the form of a topdressing of sifted compost each fall or spring. Clippings left sometimes encourage disease. They should certainly be removed if so thick that they keep light and air from the grass and tend to smother it. Do not allow fallen leaves to accumulate on the lawn. These cause additional shade and so further reduce root growth, thus weakening the grass. If allowed to mat down, they encourage disease and dying of the grass in a pockmarked pattern.

Rake up fallen leaves: (a) Promptly

(b) Remove them from the lawn

Patterns of mowing may vary according to contours, plantings, and machine used. Always cut first turning spaces across the ends of the runs. Usually it is convenient to leave mowing close-in around trees, bushes, and the like, to the last. Overlap the mowed strips slightly so that no ridges of uncut grass are left. Best results with a hand mower are usually had by crossing the lawn alternately in opposite directions,

each strip mowed being adjacent to the last one cut. With power mowers sharp turns can be avoided by mowing down one side of a rectangle, crossing the turning space at the far end and mowing back down the opposite side of the rectangle, then crossing the turning space at the beginning end and mowing along beside the first cut and so on until the center strip of the rectangle is reached and cut. A variant is to start on the outside of a rectangle and keep mowing around and around it, each time decreasing both its length and breadth until the center is reached.

Mow up and down steep slopes. Cutting crosswise scalps the ridge and the weight of the mower bearing on its low side is likely to scar the lawn surface.

Untidy margins to a lawn and untrimmed strips around trees, beds, seats, and at the bottoms of fences, hedges, and walls detract from even the best cultivated lawn. Sharp lines of demarcation between the turf and adjacent areas are usually desirable. This gives snap to the picture. It is good housekeeping. An exception is where formal lawns gradually merge into

Neatly trimmed edges to lawn areas add much to the appearance of a garden: (a) Defining a flower border

(b) Around a tree

naturalistic or wild garden plantings. There, a less manicured effect is more convincing and preferable. Even so the grass should not be left to grow at will. The objective is controlled wildness and that calls for intelligent trimming from time to time, trimming done so cleverly that it can scarcely be detected, trimming that does not emphasize geometric lines nor produce a freshly shaved appearance.

Edges look best when the lawn is an inch or two higher than the paths or beds it borders.

Commercially available edgings of: (a) Steel

(b) Corrugated aluminum or plastic can be installed to support the edges of lawns

To keep these lawn margins neat and intact poses problems. It can be done with or without artificial supports. Without supports it is necessary to trim the edges vertically with an edging tool about once a year and to cut the grass that grows out and overhangs more frequently. The latter can be done with edging machines, long-handled edging shears, or even sheep shears.

Lawn edges that have become overgrown and untidy can be reestablished by:
(a) Setting a taut garden line along them

(b) Slicing along the line with a special edging tool

(c) Or a spade

(d) Then lifting away the surplus fringe of grass with a spade

Treat unsupported lawn edges with special respect. Do not break them down when stepping on or off the lawn. Do not drag mowers, wheelbarrows, carts, spray equipment, and the like across them without using a portable ramp. Take care not to run automobiles over them. Be careful when backing your car.

Trim lawn edges regularly to preserve a manicured appearance

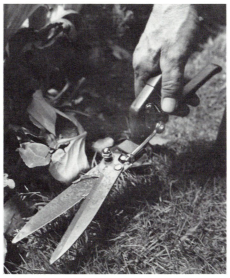

Trimming with: (a) Short-handled grass shears

(b) Sheep shear type grass shears

(c) Long-handled border or edging shears

If the edge of the turf is hurt, repair it by cutting out one or more rectangles of sod containing the damaged part and reversing them—damaged edges inward, newly cut edges forming a new margin to the lawn.

To repair a break in the edge of a lawn:
(a) Cut out a rectangle of the damaged turf

(b) Remove it with a spade

(c) Reverse so that the injured edge is turned inward

(d) Fill good soil into the crevice between the new patch and the lawn

(h) Finish by brushing it lightly with a broom

(c) Periodic adjusting and sharpening the blades; a piece of paper is inserted and the blades revolved to test for adjustment and sharpness

(e) Press it firm

Care of mowers during the operating season, and especially before winter storage, is of great importance. Keep the mower clean. After each use free it of grass clippings, wipe its blades with an oily rag, and if it is wet, put it where it will dry quickly. Be sure it is oiled occasionally.

Winterize your mower at the end of the season by having it sharpened and, if necessary, repaired. Clean it by scraping, brushing and washing and then coat all unpainted metal, such as knives, with heavy oil. Oil all bearings and moving parts; revolve or move them to spread the oil.

Drain old oil out of power mowers, flush with gasoline, then fill with regular oil (not the thin winter type). Drain the gas tank and rinse it with clean gas. Do the same with the sediment bowl if the engine has one. Remove the spark plug, squirt a little motor oil into the head of the cylinder, and give the engine a few turns to cover the cylinder walls and moving parts with it.

Store mowers in a dry place. Take care that oil is not spilled on rubber tires or on floors tires touch.

Fertilizing calls for regular attention. Nutrients leached or lost from the soil in other ways, as for instance in the substance of removed clippings, must be replaced. To maintain a lawn in fertile condition and accomplish this economically demands knowledge and judgment. Beguiling advertisements do not always tell the whole story. It may be amazing to see your name appear in lush green on a weary-looking patch of turf within a few days of sprinkling fertilizer in the required pattern, but it's no proof that the fertilizer used is best for your lawn. It does indicate that it contains generous amounts of ready available nitrogen. Lawns need nitrogen, some readily, some more slowly available, but they need other nutrients too. Bal-

(f) Tap the turf inward to align it with the lawn edge

Care of mowers includes: (a) Brushing and wiping the blades with an oily rag after each use

(g) Pat it down firmly with the back of a spade

(b) Occasional oiling of the moving parts

Regular fertilizing is needed to maintain good lawns

anced fertilization is the idea. Too much nitrogen induces soft growth, attractive to insects and susceptible to diseases.

When to feed is as important as how and with what. Do not fertilize blue grasses or fescues in summer. They are partially dormant then and added nutrients stimulate crab grass and other weeds. Creeping bent and subtropical grasses, including zoysia, benefit from summer feeding. Provide stimulants when the grasses are waking into new growth or are active, not when they are sleeping or about to sleep.

The most important nutrients provided by fertilizers are nitrogen, phosphoric acid, and potash. The percentages contained are indicated on the bag or package by a series of three numbers such as 5-10-5 and 4-8-4. The first refers to nitrogen, the second phosphoric acid, the third potash. Some fertilizers supply only one or two of these nutrients; others, called complete, supply all three, and are often sold under trade names.

It is not enough to know the proportions of the nutrients. The availability of the nitrogen must be considered. Formerly all synthetic carriers of nitrogen, such as nitrate of soda, sulfate of ammonia, and urea acted quickly. Because the nitrogen they contain is highly soluble it is readily available to plants, and by the same token is soon lost from the soil by leaching. Thus, their effects do not last long. They provide shot-in-the-arm treatments for pepping up growth.

In the past reliance was placed upon such organic fertilizers as tankage, dried blood, sheep manure, and fish meal to provide slowly available nitrogen. These were, and still are, mighty good. They release nitrogen slowly over a period of several weeks or months.

The introduction in the 1950s of ureaform fertilizers, synthetics that imitate natural organics in releasing their nitrogen slowly over a long time, provided acceptable alternates to natural fertilizers. Before choosing between the two types compare prices. Do not do this on the basis of the cost per pound of the fertilizer you buy, but on that of the actual amounts of nitrogen, phosphoric acid, and potassium you are getting for your money. This can be determined from the analysis. Its three figures tell, in pounds, the amounts of nitrogen, phosphoric acid, and potash contained in 100 pounds.

Dress your lawn in early spring and again in early fall with a fertilizer or combination of fertilizers that supply 1 pound of actual nitrogen to each 1,000 square feet. To find how much is needed to do this, divide 100 by the first figure of the analysis. For example, with a 10-6-4 fertilizer divide 100 by 10; the answer, 10, is the number of pounds of fertilizer you must apply to each 1,000 square feet.

Amounts of phosphoric acid and potash are less critical. Excessive applications do no harm, but, as grass needs lesser amounts of these than of nitrogen, it is economical to use a fertilizer in which the first figure of the analysis (the nitrogen figure) is highest, 10-6-4 or 10-5-5, for example.

Subtropical grasses and zoysia and creeping bent in the north benefit from fertilizing every four weeks through the growing season, with ½ pound of actual nitrogen to each 1,000 square feet.

When grass is in active growth, particularly in warm weather, dry, quick-acting synthetic fertilizers such as urea, nitrate of soda, and sulfate of ammonia (these are contained in many name-brand mixtures) are likely to burn it unless special care is taken. At such times it is best to use organics, the new slow-acting ureaform synthetics or quick-acting synthetics in water. The latter give quickest results.

Apply dry fertilizers when the grass is dry, the soil moist. Spread them evenly, by hand or with a spreader. If there is any danger of burning, drag a doormat over the lawn to brush fertilizer off the blades. With summer and fall applications, carefully water in dry fertilizer as soon as it is spread. This is not necessary in early spring.

Periodic applications of lime are needed in some regions to maintain a satisfactory pH for some grasses but many amateurs lime unnecessarily and sometimes to the detriment of achieving a really good lawn. Even on soils that are benefited from the addition of lime, applications are unlikely to be needed more often than every two or three years. A simple test, which can be made with a kit obtainable from a dealer in garden supplies, or which your Cooperative Extension Agent can arrange, will determine the pH of the soil. If this is too low apply sufficient ground limestone or hydrated lime to raise it to the desired pH level. See the Encyclopedia entry Lime and Liming.

Lime lawns only when needed, preferably as indicated by a simple soil test

Watering is part of the required maintenance with nearly all lawns. The regularity with which it must or should be done depends largely on climate. In semi-desert and desert parts of the west, it is needed throughout much or all of the year, in many other regions only during dry spells in summer. As with all lawn maintenance this calls for some thought. Watering too frequently, shallowly, or at wrong times is likely to promote the growth of crab grass, encourage disease, or work other damage. Intelligent watering brings greenness, healthy growth, turf that repels weed development and, to some extent at least, pests and diseases. Know-how is needed to water well. Good practices must be based on sound principles. Let us examine these.

First, do not water early in the season unless there is evident need. Grass stands considerable dryness without harm.

The second rule: when you water soak to a depth of at least 6 inches, provide no more water until there is obvious need. Usually this will not be sooner than five to seven days even in dry weather. Avoid frequent, shallow sprinklings that cause roots to be largely confined to the surface couple of inches where they are most likely to suffer from heat and drying conditions. Exceptions are newly planted lawns. Sprinkle them every two or three days if the weather is dry.

The amount of water necessary to soak in six inches varies with the type of soil; more is needed on fine clays than coarse sands. Soils containing much organic matter take more than those with little. Usually an amount equal to 1 inch or 1½ inches over the whole surface will do the job. An inch of water is equivalent to 600 gallons to each 1,000 square feet.

Do not water faster than the soil can absorb water. Run-off causes erosion and is wasteful. The speed at which water is absorbed can be determined by observation. It differs with the character of the soil, its dryness, the slope of the land, and other factors. Sandy and gravelly earth absorbs moisture faster than clayey types. On sloping ground slower application over a longer period may be necessary.

The spray should be coarse enough not to be blown away, but not so coarse that it causes erosion. It should be put down evenly. To test for this, and also how much water is laid down in a given period, stand jars or cans at various distances from the sprinklers and note the amounts of water they collect. Poorly designed sprinklers often fail miserably at delivering water evenly over the area of coverage; even the best do not do a perfect job. For that reason, when moving sprinklers some overlapping of the coverage areas is usually desirable.

To test whether or not water is needed remove a few 6-inch-deep plugs of turf from different locations and examine the under soil. If it seems dry and a handful when squeezed crumbles rather than sticks together when the hand is opened, water. Other indications of dryness are (1) the grass remains pressed down and footmarks show clearly when walked across, and (2) the grass wilts slightly and assumes a slight bluish color.

The time of day when watering is done is not important except that it is better not to have the foliage of bent grass wet for long periods; it should dry before nightfall, otherwise disease may be encouraged. Watering in bright sunshine does no harm unless the ground is so compact that shallow pools of water lie on the surface for considerable periods; then heat scald may kill the grass. More water is lost by evaporation when watering is done in sun, but this is scarcely significant.

Sprinklers of many different sorts are available for watering lawns, but hand-held ones such as are often used for flower beds and plants in containers have little merit for the purpose. Even the most patient gardener tires of holding them long enough to do a satisfactory job and, although in an emergency it is possible to improvise by fixing a sprinkler head attached to a hose temporarily to the handle of a spading fork stuck into the ground or to some other suitable support, such makeshift arrangements are not for general use.

The chief equipment used for watering lawns are movable rotary and oscillating sprinklers, and permanently installed underground spinkler systems with pop-up heads. For special locations, such as banks and around trees, perforated hoses and soil-soaker types are effective. Rotary sprinklers dispense water in circular patterns and, to cover areas, make necessary considerable overlapping. The areas covered by oscillating sprinklers are rectangular, thus much reducing the need for overlapping. Perforated and soil-soaker hoses can be laid in any way that best suits.

Watering lawns with: (a) A rotary sprinkler

(b) An oscillating sprinkler

(c) An underground system with pop-up heads

Underground systems, when properly installed, make watering a lawn a matter of simply turning a valve. More important, however, they ensure complete lawn coverage. At one time all underground systems made use of metal pipes. Now flexible and semiflexible plastic are used almost exclusively. These are much less expensive than copper or galvanized iron and are not injured by freezing, an important consideration especially in northern areas. Sprinkler heads generally cover a circle of 20 feet in diameter when operating under adequate pressure. If pressure is over 30 pounds, an underground system is worth installing; 40 to 60 pounds (delivering about 18 gallons of water per minute) is ideal for up to eight heads. When carefully planned in accordance with manufacturer's instructions, a lawn of any area can be adapted for underground sprinklers. Systems having five to twenty heads are common for most home lawns. For larger areas they may have up to 300 heads.

Plan the system on paper first. Sprinkler heads should generally be 10 to 14 feet apart, somewhat more, perhaps, if the land slopes. Arrange the pipes with as few turns as possible; each turn reduces pressure. Employ sprinkler heads that give full-circle, half-circle, or quarter-circle cov-

erage as their location makes most desirable. The number of separate lines of sprinklers depends upon the size of the lawn and the pressure and amount of water delivered by the supply line. Each group of heads should have a separate control valve. Close to the supply bib, an anti-syphon valve should be installed to prevent surface water syphoning back into the service supply line. This is a legal requirement in many communities.

Keeping lawns weed-free demands understanding and effort. The surest discouragement to weeds is to grow good grass that, in turn, depends upon an adequate depth of fertile soil and proper fertilizing, watering, mowing, and other attentions. The ploy is to create a total environment more favorable to the growth of grass than to the pesky intruders. Killing weeds without correcting the basic faults of the soil, location, or management of the turf does little more than create openings inviting to other weeds and soon filled by them. The primary question to ask is not "How can I kill the weeds?" although this of course needs some consideration, but "How can I encourage a dense growth of turf grasses?" But even in well-managed lawns some weeds are likely to gain foothold. The appearance of certain sorts clearly indicate the conditions adverse to lawn grasses that trigger their development. Eliminating them depends upon correcting the basic fault. Sheep sorrel, a sure indicator of too-acid soil, is eliminated by liming sufficiently. Clover flourishes in neutral or alkaline soil. Do not lime if it is abundant and you want to discourage it. Chickweed, mouse-eared chickweed, speedwell, self-heal, ground ivy, sedge, and lawn pennywort invade lawns where the soil is too moist and the grass weak. Attention to drainage and fertilization must be given. Spotted spurge surely indicates lack of fertility and excessive dryness; annual blue grass favors soils compacted by heavy use when wet, as well as areas damaged by diseases, fertilizer burn, or other cause. Corrective measures are obvious.

Apart from encouraging a heavy growth of grass, which discourages weeds, but does not necessarily eliminate them, there are several active modes of attack that can be employed. Chiefly they are hand weeding and chemical controls. Do not recoil from mention of hand weeding; it is effective indeed if the lawn is not overrun with weeds. The most weed-free lawns are those gotten into that condition and then maintained so by good cultural practices (fertilizing, watering, aerating, and so forth) and hand weeding. With a vigorous lawn, a little hand weeding each year will keep it clean. But you must start early. Grub them out or kill them while they are tiny. Do not let weeds get to the seeding stage. Then you have raised a crop of headaches for the following season.

To hand weed well you must keep at it. Inspect the lawn fairly frequently. Do not just look at it as a whole. Walk back and forth across it with head bent, really seeing each square yard of sod. At the first sign of invasion by an unwanted plant take action. Get rid of it. If it is a kind that indicates soil conditions unfavorable for turf, take steps to correct that. Unfavorable conditions often get worse with neglect.

Hand weeding is easiest when the soil is moist. Some weeds you can pull with your fingers without difficulty. For certain surface-rooting kinds, such as chickweed, you will find a thin-bladed knife of great help. For deep-rooted weeds, such as dandelions and docks, a deep-reaching tool, such as an asparagus knife or one of the weeding tools especially made for the purpose, is splendid. With these you can cut the tap roots deep under the surface, after which the plants can be pulled with relative ease. Sometimes, with dense matting weeds, it is simplest to cut out sods containing them and replace with good turf, or fill with soil and sow grass seed over the patches.

Eliminating dandelions: (a) By cutting them out with an asparagus knife

(b) By placing a teaspoonful of sulfate of ammonia in the center of each

A simple, old-fashioned method of killing deep-rooted dandelions and plantains is to place in the center of each a small teaspoonful of sulfate of ammonia, nitrate of soda, or urea. These fertilizers applied in strong concentrations kill plants instead of stimulating their growth. That is exactly what the teaspoonful placed in the center of each weed does. Then, as the fertilizer is diluted by rain or watering, it spreads laterally as well as downward and fertilizes the adjacent grass. To repair the small "bald" spot left by the death of the weed scratch it over with a cultivator or hand fork and sow a little new grass seed.

Controlling: (a) Crab grass

(b) Spray with a selective herbicide

LAWNS, THEIR MAKING and RENOVATION. A good lawn represents an ideal for which most American homeowners and gardeners strive. In fact with some its attainment becomes almost an obsession. There are communities where achievement of this horticultural perfection gives distinct status, and scarcely anyone denies that a stretch of fine greensward adds immensely to the appearance and amenity of a home. It suggests tranquility and affords a perfect setting for trees, shrubs, flowering plants, and other garden features. The lawns considered here are composed of grasses. Other plants are sometimes employed, notably dichondra (*Dichondra micrantha*) and, more rarely, yarrow (*Achillea millefolium*). For discussion of the uses of these as lawn plants see the Encyclopedia entries Dichondra, and Yarrow.

Good lawns can be had in: (a) Full sun

(b) Partial shade, if given intelligent care

In North America there are many regions where grasses were not originally dominant or even plentiful, vast areas in the east for example that were once forested, and desert and semidesert parts of the west where rainfall alone is too scanty to support permanent grasslands. In such regions desirable grasses are indeed cultivated plants, and lawns composed of them need regular attention to maintain them in an acceptable condition and to protect them from invasion by weeds and from animal (chiefly insect) pests as well as fungus and other diseases.

But unless one is a perfectionist who simply *must* achieve the finest of lawns it really is not necessary to go absolutely overboard in one's efforts for a respectable lawn. Attractive swards can be had with much less cost and anguish, and surely a lawn that approaches 90 percent perfection will satisfy most of us.

The installation of a new lawn calls for careful consideration of the site and soil and of what may be needed to bring the latter into satisfactory condition for supporting good greensward. Effort and money invested intelligently at this time may save much in future expenditures and tribulations.

Site evaluation should take into account the contours of the ground and possible desirability of modifying them to achieve more pleasing effects or improve surface drainage, whether or not an installed sub-surface drainage system is needed and if so how best to satisfy the need, the amount of shade and if too much the practicability of improving matters by pruning or perhaps removing sparable trees and shrubs, and of course the soil.

In considering the soil remember that adequate depth and porosity are important. It is quite possible to achieve very good turf on as little as 4 inches of topsoil overlying porous subsoil, but to do so calls for skilled and constant maintenance, a chore too demanding for the majority of people. Better by far to arrange for a minimum of 6 inches and better still 8 inches or even more topsoil from the start. And these figures refer not to loose, freshly spaded earth or soil as it is dumped from a truck but to a layer that has been firmed in readiness for seed sowing, sprigging, plugging, or sod laying.

If the site for a new lawn has (a) Been stripped of topsoil or the depth of topsoil is inadequate

(b) It may be necessary to bring in more soil

The quality of the topsoil is obviously important. Besides being porous enough to permit easy passage of water and air it should be fertile or capable of being made so. Freedom from large stones, tree roots, builders' debris, and other trash is important. In the main, soils capable of producing satisfactory crops of vegetables are best for lawns. Medium loams are easier

Add to the soil such bulk organic materials as: (a) Compost

(b) Peat moss

(c) Manure

(d) Commercial humus

(e) One or more green cover crops, turned under

to bring into receptive condition than adobe, stiff clay, or sand, but all can be made suitable. Frequent needs are to raise the organic content by mixing in compost, peat moss, manure, or other materials that will form humus or to achieve the same result by a preparatory program of green manuring, to increase available nutrients by applying fertilizer, and if a soil test indicates the need, liming. But the most important factor is the structure and texture of the soil. No matter how fertile it is, or how rich it is in organic matter, or that its pH be exactly right for the grasses to be grown, if it is compact to the extent that it

If the soil is acid: (a) As indicated by a soil test

(b) Raise the pH of the soil by spreading lime by hand

(c) With a mechanical spreader

Turn the soil to a minimum depth of 6 inches, if the topsoil is deep enough more is better, with: (a) A spade

(d) On large areas with a power-drawn spreader

(b) A spading fork

(c) A rotary tiller

(d) Spread fertilizer and mix it thoroughly with the top 3 inches of soil

strongly resists the admittance of air and passage through it of water it is hostile to the growth of grass roots.

If you must purchase topsoil be very sure of its source and quality. That stripped from abandoned fields may bring with it roots and seeds of weeds that will prove troublesome later. And do not be misled into believing that because it is dark in color it is necessarily satisfactorily structured or fertile. It is not unusual for unscrupulous suppliers to palm off on unsuspecting buyers subsoil for topsoil. Rather than this, it may be less expensive to improve your own poor soil or subsoil by adding adequate amounts of organic material and by fertilizing.

If severe grade changes are involved in contouring the area to be made into lawn do not make the mistake of burying acceptable existing topsoil at considerable depths. Instead, have it pushed aside and stockpiled with a bulldozer or by other means, to be spread over the inferior fill after that is within about 8 inches of the finish grade and properly compacted.

It is quite possible to make a lawn of one kind of grass. You will find that some people advocate lawns made exclusively of creeping bent, of 'Merion' blue grass, and of other special types. When perfectly kept, such greenswards can be magnificent, but they need considerable upkeep and demand special knowledge on the part of their caretakers. In a one-grass

lawn any other grass is a weed and must be eliminated (not always an easy task). Should a disease or insect to which the particular grass is especially susceptible gain a hold, you have real trouble on your hands. The whole lawn is likely to be affected quickly, perhaps with disastrous results. In a lawn composed of several kinds of grasses the less susceptible make a brave stand against the enemy and hold out; their weaker relatives succumb.

Except for very special purposes (making a putting green, for example), it is always better to sow a grass seed mixture than just one kind. In a way it is insurance. Different grasses, even different varieties of the same kind, prefer different soil conditions, and often these preferences are for minor variations not easy to recognize by simple soil tests. If you sow several kinds in mixture, those best adapted to your soil flourish; the others expire or become minor elements in the turf. It often happens that soil and other environmental conditions, such as shade and moisture, vary from place to place in the same lawn. By sowing a mixture of grasses, you provide for the varying needs of these different situations.

There are other advantages. In most cases a mixture gives more uniform greenery throughout the season than a single type of grass. Because of seasonal growth and temperature preferences, blue grasses thrive in the cool weather of spring and fall and go partially dormant during hot weather. Bent grasses generally make their best growth in hot weather. In dry weather, fescues prosper better than other grasses. There are grasses more resistant to being walked upon than others. There are grasses valuable because they germinate and grow quickly, act as "nurses" to the slower-to-get-going kinds and then gradually die out. In the meantime they prevent erosion and help to keep weeds out.

It is unusual and unnecessary for homeowners to buy different sorts of grass seeds separately and mix them. Commercial mixtures, if wisely selected, are perfectly satisfactory. In all regions such mixtures, compounded with special thought given to local soils and climates, are available. All that is really necessary is to choose one best adapted to your own garden—for sun or shade, for example, or for particularly dry soils.

The most important point to remember is to avoid cheap mixtures. The cost of the seed is but a small proportion of the cost of making a new lawn. It is much better to sow a high-priced mixture thinly than a cheap mixture too thickly (as most beginners do). As a matter of fact, because cheaper mixtures contain larger proportions of grasses with large seeds, you will probably get as many potential grass plants in a dollar's worth of an expensive mixture as in a dollar's worth of a cheap one.

Cheap mixtures are largely composed of the less permanent grasses, the kinds least costly for the seedsmen or packager to buy. It has to be that way. Good seeds of desirable varieties are comparatively expensive. They cannot be sold to compete with cheaper types. Percentages count, and even cheap seed mixtures usually contain some blue grass and perhaps some bents and fescues. The point is, how many good seeds are present in proportion to rye grass, timothy, and other quick growers? A total of more than 30 percent of temporary grasses is usually the maximum permissible in satisfactory lawn seed mixtures, although the distinguished turf specialist Dr. Howard B. Sprague recommended a "standard mixture for soils of average to good fertility and sunny exposure" that includes 40 percent temporary grasses. This mixture consists of 45 percent Kentucky blue grass, 10 percent colonial bent grass, 25 percent redtop, 5 percent white clover, and 15 percent perennial rye grass.

In many states the law requires that lawn seed mixtures be labeled with the names and percentages of the grasses they contain and also the percentages of germination that may be expected. These are protections for the buyer. Study the labels carefully when comparing prices.

In most parts of the country, except the subtropical south, Kentucky blue grass or selected varieties of it should be the foundation of mixed-seed lawns in sunny or predominantly sunny locations. It is generally the most satisfactory and permanent of general purpose lawn grass for everywhere except where considerable shade exists. For shaded lawns, Chewings fescue and Illahee fescue are real standbys. Mixtures should contain adequate amounts of these basic grasses to ensure good stands. Beware especially of mixtures that are advertised and offered on the basis of "quick" results. They usually contain much too high proportions of rye grass, timothy, and other quick growers of a temporary nature.

The best time to sow a new lawn is early fall. Then the soil is still warm enough to stimulate growth, and the grasses make good roots before called upon to face the rigors of winter. A great advantage of fall sowing is that the young plants do not have to compete with as many different kinds of seedling weeds. Warm-weather weeds, such as crab grass, do not germinate then. Another great advantage is that the grasses are established and ready to grow in earliest spring. They have a great start on spring-sown grasses and, incidentally, on weeds that begin their natural period of growth in spring. And, of course, there is usually ample time to prepare the ground for a fall-sown lawn, whereas in spring the season is so rushed that all too often preparatory work must be skimped.

But it is quite possible to get a good lawn from a spring sowing, although it requires more care and attention than a fall sowing. Two special problems that must be faced are the rapid growth of weeds and the need for more abundant watering during dry periods throughout the first summer, this latter because the roots have not penetrated as deeply as those of grasses sown the previous fall. Weeds are likely to be especially abundant if such plants flourished in the topsoil the previous year, and there is really no practical way of getting rid of them in spring before the lawn grass is sown. In preparation for fall sowing, a few weeks' repeated shallow cultivation before the grass seed is sown will clear the surface soil of most weeds.

Assume that the site for your new lawn does not need draining, that it has a satisfactory grade, and that you do not plan to bring in additional soil. What needs to be done before seed is sown or turf is planted? This will depend upon the kind of soil and its condition. Unless you are familiar with your soil and its capabilities,

As final preparation rake the surface to a fine even surface: (a) With an iron rake

(b) More easily, with a wooden rake

almost surely a soil test will provide helpful information to guide you as to procedures. Your Cooperative Extension Agent can make this for you or advise you where you can have it made.

Nearly all soils, except peaty ones and mucks, benefit from having added to them liberal amounts of decayed organic matter. Because this will be your last chance to incorporate such materials beneath the surface take advantage of it. If you can obtain rotted manure, compost, sedge peat (commercial humus), leaf mold, or peat moss in quantities sufficient to spread a 3-inch layer over the whole surface, do so. Unless your soil is humus-rich, and especially if it is sandy, try not to settle for less than 2 inches. Well in advance of sowing, turn the organic matter under with a rotary tiller, spade, or spading fork, mixing it thoroughly with the upper 6 inches of soil. If you can provide organic matter in greater amounts than those suggested, mix it with the upper 8 inches of soil.

Should your soil be very clayey, add also coarse sand, grit, or gritty coal cinders sifted free of fine ash. If the soil is very sandy, mix in, if obtainable, a 3- or 4-inch layer of clayey soil in addition to organic matter. If you can get only a limited amount of clayey soil, incorporate it with the top 2 inches of garden soil.

If lime, as indicated by the soil test, is needed, spread ground limestone or hydrated lime in amounts necessary to bring the pH of the soil to between 6.0 and 7.0, and mix it thoroughly with the upper 3 to 4 inches of soil. Do not feel that this second mixing is a waste of labor. Working and reworking, provided it is always done when the soil is reasonably dry, in preparation for lawn-making, is highly beneficial. It brings the zone in which most roots will be into a fine uniform condition conducive to even growth. Nothing is more likely to result in spotty development of grass than lack of uniformity of the soil. Clods or patches of clayey soil, wads or masses of nearly pure organic matter, areas of unmixed sand or subsoil, and large stones, rocks, and builder's debris within a few inches of the surface are all inimicable to the attainment of a good lawn.

Fertilizer will be needed. The results of the soil test or practical empirical experience can guide you in this. Nitrogen, phosphorus, and potash are the elements usually most essential, and it is important that at least one-half of the nitrogen be in an organic or slow-release nonorganic form so that it becomes available over a fairly long period. Some nitrogen may, often with advantage, be in a more quickly available form, although excellent results can be had from organics alone.

If you favor organics, a good treatment is 200 pounds of pulverized sheep manure and 100 pounds of bonemeal to each 1,000 square feet. If, in addition, you can spread unleached wood ashes at the rate of 35 to 50 pounds to each 1,000 square feet, this is all to the good. For each 100 pounds of bonemeal you may substitute, at a considerable saving, 50 pounds of 48 percent superphosphate, or proportionately greater amounts of superphosphate containing less phosphorus.

If you favor mixed commercial fertilizers, and most are excellent, for each 1,000 square feet use 40 to 60 pounds of one with a 4-8-4 analysis, or 30 to 50 pounds of a 5-10-4, or 20 to 30 pounds of a 10-6-4, or proportionate amounts of those having other analyses, basing the amounts used on the amount of nitrogen (indicated by the first figure of the analysis) they contain. Apply the fertilizer a week or two before sowing or planting, and rake it into the top 2 or 3 inches. Be sure to spread it evenly.

You may feel that the above recommendations involve a lot of work. They do, but no less thorough a procedure will provide a foundation for a really good lawn. Preparation need not be as arduous as it sounds in the telling. If you get an early start and proceed methodically, if you have the supplies at hand, and if you take every advantage the weather offers, you will be surprised at your progress.

Scheduling operations for readying the soil for sowing or planting, calls for thought. Here are the considerations. Early fall is by far the best time to sow seeds. Turf may be laid at any time when the ground is not frozen, preferably in early spring or in fall; plugs and sprigs are best set in spring. If a green manure cover crop is to be turned under, do it not later than six weeks before sowing or planting. Rotted manure, compost, humus, peat moss, and other decomposed organic matter may be incorporated any time in advance of sowing or planting. Lime may be added any time before sowing or planting, but not at the same time as manure or fertilizer. Add fertilizer one to four weeks before sowing or planting. If you prepare the soil, except for spreading and incorporating fertilizer, a month or more in advance of the fall sowing date, weed seeds will have an opportunity to germinate and you can destroy the seedlings by shallow cultivation or by a chemical spray. This assures a clean seed bed.

A good timetable for fall lawn-making in many parts of North America (adjustments are likely to be desirable in some regions) is, in early August, mix in organic matter, sand, and clay according to the needs of the soil. One week later, incorporate lime if needed. In late August or early September, mix in fertilizer. Sow the grass seed in mid-September or lay sods then or later, but before the ground freezes. If the lawn is to be sown or planted in spring, mix in organic matter, sand, and clay, according to needs, as early as possible, preferably the fall before, and lime, if needed, a week later. Fertilize in spring a week or more before sowing or planting.

If your soil is deep enough to carry a lawn, but is of such poor quality that the addition of decayed organic matter, in amounts available or in amounts you can afford, and of fertilizer and lime, will not make it suitable for growing turf, you can

remedy the situation without bringing in additional topsoil. This takes time, but it can be done. Even subsoil can be converted into excellent topsoil within a year or two. And subsoil, or subsoil covered with a thin layer of passibly good topsoil, is what many homeowners acquire from builders. It is not uncommon for builders to strip good topsoil, sell most of it or use it elsewhere, and then spread a thin layer back on the original site. Others carelessly bury topsoil or hopelessly mix it with poor undersoil. On other sites, little or no good topsoil may be there when the builder begins. Whatever the cause, if your topsoil is thin or nonexistent, the condition must be corrected.

To improve a soil seriously lacking in organic matter without adding considerable amounts of decayed or partly decayed organic materials of the sorts already mentioned, you must rely heavily on green manuring. Green manuring means growing cover crops especially for the purpose of turning them under and converting them into humus. The humus is formed by the decay of the extensive root systems as well as the tops. To induce maximum growth in cover crops, add fertilizer before each crop, and lime if a soil test indicates its need.

You may begin this type of soil improvement at any time. If in late summer or fall, sow as a cover crop winter rye (2 quarts per 1,000 square feet). If in spring, sow rye grass (2 quarts per 1,000 square feet) or Canada field peas (2 quarts per 1,000 square feet). If you begin in summer, sow soy beans (2 quarts per 1,000 square feet), crimson clover (1 pound per 1,000 square feet), or buckwheat (2 quarts per 1,000 square feet).

It is not necessary to rake the surface perfectly smooth before or after sowing any of these crops, but rake the seeds in so that most are covered. When top growth is 6 inches to 1 foot tall, spade the cover crop under or bury it with a rotary tiller and immediately refertilize and sow another cover crop. Do not turn the last cover crop under later than six weeks before sowing the permanent grass seed.

If you begin in late summer or early fall, you should be able to grow and turn under three or four cover crops by the following August. Each will add a great quantity of humus to the soil and improve its texture and granulation tremendously. Most poor soils will be sufficiently improved after one full year of green manuring to be in condition for sowing permanent lawn grass on them, but if yours is not, you can, with advantage, continue the green manuring program for a second year.

An alternative procedure, if the soil does not seem in suitable condition to support a permanent turf at the end of the year and you do not feel you can wait longer before having a respectable-looking lawn, is to sow in early spring a crop of Italian or domestic rye grass. These grasses are inexpen-

sive and quickly produce a beautiful temporary lawn you can mow and use just like any other lawn. In early August turn it under (it too will add considerably to the humus content of the soil), and you are then ready to sow your permanent lawn.

If you cannot tolerate even one summer with a coarse cover crop occupying the land, follow this two-year plan of improvement. Grow alternate crops of winter rye, sown in fall and turned under in spring when 6 to 8 inches tall, and crops of Italian rye grass or domestic rye grass, sown in spring, kept neatly mowed all summer, and turned under in fall. Give the rye grass two or three light applications of fertilizer during the summer. If you begin this schedule in the fall, you will turn under two crops of winter rye and two of rye grass before you sow your permanent lawn two years later. If you begin in spring, you will turn under one crop of winter rye and two of rye grass before you sow your permanent lawn about a year and one-half later.

Final preparation for sowing involves making sure the soil is reasonably compact and bringing its surface to a fine and even state. If satisfactory compactness has not come about as a result of the soil lying undisturbed for a few weeks, firm it with a roller or by treading (tramping across it). It should be firm enough so that walking across it does not leave appreciably indented footmarks, but not so firm that it approaches the compactness of a path or a road. Then rake the surface to as fine a condition as possible. For this task, because of its longer head, a wooden rake is easier to use than an iron one, although the latter serves well on small areas.

Let us suppose that your seed bed is in perfect condition and the seed is at hand. Now comes the business of sowing. Choose a calm day. It is impossible to sow evenly if it is breezy. Divide the seed to be sown in half; then, walking in parallel paths in one direction (say, north and south), sow one-half the seed as evenly as you possibly can over the whole area. When this has been accomplished, sow the remaining seed over the same area, walking in parallel paths at right angles to the original direction. In this way you will get the most even distribution. The sowing may be done by hand or with a mechanical seeder adjusted to let the seed fall at the density required.

If you sow by hand, use this technique. Bend your back. Take a handful of seeds. Hold them with the fingers somewhat cupped and very slightly separated. Then with your hand moving parallel with the ground and about 1½ feet above it, swing your arm freely in a semicircular motion and allow the seeds to scatter in an even, fine cloud from the upper part of the hand. Do not close your fist so tightly that the seed leaves your hand in a heavy stream from between forefinger and thumb. To se-

On a still day distribute the seed evenly:
(a) By hand

Rake the seed into the surface; this is most conveniently done with a wooden rake

(b) With a spreader

Roll the newly-sown lawn to firm its surface

(c) On large areas with a tractor-drawn spreader

cure even distribution, you may find it advantageous to stretch parallel strings, 6 to 10 feet apart (to suit your convenience) across the ground surface and to walk slowly down the center of each marked-off strip as you sow, scattering the seeds from string to string. With practice you will have no difficulty in perfecting this technique so that you sow evenly.

After the seeds have been scattered, rake them into the surface so that they are covered to a depth of one-half an inch or

so. When the whole area is sown, roll it slowly with a medium-weight roller or pat the surface firm with the back of a spade or light wooden tamper.

Within a reasonable period, longer or shorter according to the temperature, but usually in ten days to three weeks, the young grass will appear above the ground. Do not make the mistake of sprinkling it daily; but if the upper inch or so of soil becomes obviously dry, then water it freely with a fine sprinkler adjusted so that it will not wash the surface soil away. Once the seed has started to germinate, the young plants must not be permitted to suffer from lack of water. In the very young stages of the grass, the surface soil must never be allowed to get really dry, but as the grass gets taller and stronger and as its roots strike deeper, watering can be less frequent, but more water should be given at each application. Watering is only needed, of course, during dry periods.

When the grass is 2 inches tall or very slightly more, cut it with a very sharp mower with the blades set at a height of 1¾ inches. A mower with dull cutting knives will pull the plants out of the ground and cause much damage. Even with the best care there may be some bare spots in a lawn sown with seeds (particularly if sowing is done in the spring).

These should be reseeded as soon as they become apparent.

Of the thousands of kinds of grass known, very few are useful for lawns. Of those that are, some are suitable for the northern United States and Canada, others for the south. In each of these divisions are kinds more adaptable than others for shade or sun, close cropping and higher mowing, drier soils or moister ones and so on.

Kinds of grasses best suited for lawns in the north fall into five groups: blue grasses, fescues, bents, *Zoysia japonica*, and a mixed group of nonpermanent grasses. We shall consider these and various mixtures of them. In addition, clover is sometimes used.

Kentucky blue grass (*Poa pratensis*) is the most important lawn grass in cooler, humid regions. Where summers are not excessively long and hot, it forms a dense turf of high quality and pleasing green. It spreads by short, creeping, underground stems and stands wear well. Injury to its surface heals quickly. A fertile, reasonably moist, slightly acid or neutral soil is needed. It will not stand shade.

Kentucky blue grass is raised from seeds. These germinate much better in fall than in spring. A fair sowing rate is 2 to 4 pounds to 1,000 square feet. The seedlings are rather slow starting. It takes a year or more before a really good sod is established. Best growth is made in spring and fall. In hot weather this grass goes partly dormant, an unfortunate feature that, if the sod is at all sparse, gives crab grass a great opportunity to become established. Kentucky blue grass grows well in mixture with other grasses. Mowing height should be not less than 1¼ to 1½ inches.

Selected varieties of Kentucky blue grass in some places have distinct advantages over regular Kentucky blue grass. One of the best known of these, 'Merion', which is more resistant to leaf spot disease, may be cut closer—to a height of 1 inch if desired—without weakening it, is more resistant to crab grass invasion, and stands drought better. It needs the same growing conditions as the Kentucky type. Seed is comparatively expensive. Do not waste it on ill-prepared soil and do not expect good results unless 'Merion' forms the greatest proportion of a seed mixture; small percentages are of no value. This is also true of other choice blue grass varieties.

Rough-stalked blue grass (*Poa trivialis*) is a creeping kind of special value for shaded places. South of New England, summer sun kills it. It bears a general resemblance to Kentucky blue grass, but is lighter green. It requires the same soil conditions as Kentucky blue grass, but is less tolerant of dryness. It is also less tolerant of high summer temperatures. Seeding rate is 2 to 2½ pounds to 1,000 square feet.

Chewings fescue (*Festuca rubra commutata*) does not spread by creeping and has little ability to heal if the surface of the turf is scarred. It has slender, wiry leaves of fine green color and grows well on either poor or fertile soils in shade or sun, and best during cool weather. It withstands dry conditions well and hence is a good grass for planting on banks. It will not tolerate wet soil. Unlike most fescues, it has no objectionable blue-green color. It forms a good, hard-wearing, close turf on reasonably fertile soil; if the soil is very poor, it tends to grow in separate tufts. Two to 4 pounds of seed to each 1,000 square feet is satisfactory. Chewings fescue stands close mowing and needs cutting frequently.

'Illahee' and 'Trinity' fescues are similar to Chewings, but of more creeping habit and so tend to spread and heal over injured turf. They require the same conditions and care. 'Illahee' or 'Trinity' and Chewings are good in mixture.

Creeping bent (*Agrostis stolonifera*) forms a magnificent turf, but needs a great deal of care and attention, including frequent topdressing. It is subject to diseases and pests. This is a specialist's grass, splendid for putting greens, but usually too much trouble for the amateur. The plants are low and spread by runners. They thrive in rich, moist, slightly acid soil and grow well throughout the summer. Creeping bent will not grow in shade. It is propagated by stolons (except the seaside strain mentioned below). Various named varieties are available. Two of the best are 'Washington' and 'Metropolitan'.

Seaside bent is a type of creeping bent that can be raised from seeds (sowing rate 4 to 8 ounces to 1,000 square feet) and produces a good turf almost as uniform as 'Metropolitan' and 'Washington' creeping bents. Its leaves are bluish-green, and it forms a tight turf. It is strongly creeping.

Velvet bent (*Agrostis canina*) is the very dwarfest of lawn grasses and produces a sod of beautiful bright green velvet. It spreads by short creeping stems and is tolerant of high temperatures and cold and is quite drought resistant. It grows well in either sun or partial shade. This kind is useful for ordinary lawns and may be included in mixtures. It will not grow on poorly drained soils. It stands close mowing. Superior strains are 'Raritan' and 'Emerald'. Velvet bent is raised from seeds. The sowing rate is 4 to 8 ounces to 1,000 square feet.

Rhode Island or colonial bent (*Agrostis tenuis*) is also known as 'Astoria' bent, 'Highland' bent, New Zealand bent, browntop bent, and Prince Edward Island bent. This is a good grass to use in mixture with other grasses for lawns in full sun, and it may be used alone for putting greens and other special purposes where a fine sod is required, although it does not produce as excellent an appearance as either creeping bent or velvet bent. Rhode

Island bent thrives under the same soil conditions as creeping bent. If it is used alone, mow it to a height of ¾ inch. If it is used in mixture with Kentucky blue grass or fescues, mow it to 1¼ to 1½ inches high. This grass is impatient of dry conditions, but stands less fertile soil than creeping bent and does not need the frequent topdressing that the latter does. Because it does not make creeping stems, turf of this grass does not heal well if its surface is injured. Like other bents, it grows well in summer, but less rapidly in the cool weather of spring and fall than Kentucky blue grass. Seeding rate should be 4 to 8 ounces to 1,000 square feet.

'Meyer' zoysia is a variety of the Japanese lawn grass (*Zoysia japonica*), publicized as suitable for northern as well as southern lawns. It has a lot to recommend it and some serious disadvantages. It grows well on a wide variety of soils, provided they are not really wet, and resists drought. It keeps out crab grass and other summer weeds to a remarkable degree and is little affected by pests and diseases. It grows in sun or partial shade. It forms a beautiful, thick, hard-wearing, resilient turf that can be mowed at any height from 1 inch to 3 inches without weakening the grass. It thrives in summer heat. 'Meyer' zoysia has proved hardy in recent winters as far north as Massachusetts and Michigan and may be expected to survive permanently in climates as severe as that of New York City. The chief disadvantage is that it goes completely dormant in winter. It becomes a whitish thatch in mid-fall and remains that way until late spring. It can even be a fire hazard. Cool-season weeds, such as chickweed, annual blue grass, and ground ivy, invade zoysia.

'Meyer' zoysia is propagated by plugs or sprigs, preferably the former. It is most useful in the south and in the more southerly parts of the north and is excellent for summer homes where absence of greenery early and late is unimportant.

The following quick-growing kinds are "nurse" grasses to be sown in mixtures with more permanent grasses, and rye grass for temporary winter lawns in the south and, occasionally, temporary summer lawns in the north. When added to seed mixtures, they help to prevent erosion before the slower growing permanent grasses are big enough to do so, and they tend to crowd out weeds.

Redtop (*Agrostis gigantea*) succeeds on infertile soil both dry and moist and will stand slight shade. It has creeping stems and, during its first year, fine-textured foliage. When cut at regular lawn height, it gradually disappears after the first season and has normally gone completely by the end of the second or third year. Seeding rate is 2 to 4 pounds to 1,000 square feet.

Meadow (*Festuca pratensis*) fescue is a rather coarse grass that makes quick

growth and is shade tolerant. It is a good nurse grass for use under trees. It will grow on poorish soils, but does better on fertile ones and is especially adapted for clayey ground. It does not creep or form a dense sod. Alta fescue is a deep-rooting variety of meadow fescue adaptable on a wide variety of soils, but thrives best on heavy soils well supplied with organic matter. Sow at 2 to 4 pounds to 1,000 square feet.

Perennial rye grass (*Lolium perenne*), not to be confused with rye, the grain, is used chiefly as a "nurse." It holds the soil and forms good-looking turf for two to three years. The leaves are rich green. Well-drained, moderately moist soil and full sun suit this grass. Sowing rate is 2 to 4 pounds for 1,000 square feet. Variety *L. p. paceyi*, called English rye grass, has smaller seeds.

Italian rye grass (*Lolium multiflorum*) is coarser than perennial rye grass and lives but one season. It forms good sod in three or four weeks. Conditions and sowing rate are the same as for perennial rye grass.

Domestic rye grass, a hybrid between perennial and Italian rye grass, is much used for temporary winter lawns in the south and the northwest.

Most northern lawns consist of mixtures of two or more of the grasses discussed above with sometimes the addition of white clover. Whether or not this last should be included is a matter of individual preference. It withstands drought better than grass, but does not stand wear well. It should never be used in turf on which games are played. Five percent clover seed is ample in any mixture.

If you buy mixtures, study their analysis before purchasing and when comparing prices. Avoid those containing excessive amounts of temporary grasses and "inert" matter (usually mostly chaff).

In general avoid "cheap" mixtures and all sold under such names as "fast grow," "quick green," "rapid lawn," and the like.

If you make up your own mixtures—it is an easy and often wise procedure—buy ingredients from a seedsman of repute. The following are good mixtures that have been recommended by the New Jersey Agricultural Experiment Station.

For sunny lawns: Kentucky blue grass 45 percent, redtop 25 percent, Rhode Island bent 10 percent, perennial rye grass 15 percent, white clover 5 percent. The clover may be omitted and an extra 5 percent of Kentucky blue grass substituted if desired.

For fine turf: redtop 15 percent, Rhode Island bent 15 percent, Kentucky blue grass 35 percent, Chewings fescue 35 percent.

For partial shade: rough-stalked blue grass 10 percent, Chewings fescue 50 percent, velvet bent 5 percent. Rhode Island bent 5 percent, redtop 10 percent, Kentucky blue grass ('Merion' could be substituted) 10 percent, meadow fescue 10 percent.

For poor and sandy soils and banks: redtop 20 percent, Chewings fescue 40 percent, Kentucky blue grass or one of its named varieties, 10 percent, Rhode Island bent 10 percent, perennial rye grass 15 percent, white clover 5 percent.

Sow the above mixtures, except the one for banks, at 2 to 4 pounds per 1,000 square feet. Sow the bank mixture, if the slope is steep, at 6 to 8 pounds per 1,000 square feet.

For lawns in the south that are neither poorly drained, acid, or shaded, Bermuda grass (*Cynodon dactylon*) makes the best permanent turf. This spreads rapidly by stolons and needs well-limed, fertile soil. Sow seed (that called hulled seed germinates fastest) at the rate of 2 pounds to 1,000 square feet or propagate by sprigs planted 2 to 3 feet apart. In southern Florida Bermuda grass is permanently green, but in cooler regions it turns brown in winter. To have a green lawn in winter where this happens, rake, top-dress, and oversow the Bermuda grass with domestic rye grass each fall. Rake and topdress again when rye grass is killed with the coming of hot spring weather. Mow to a height of 1¾ inches. 'Tifton 57' is an improved strain of Bermuda. It must be planted from sprigs.

Carpet grass (*Axonopus affinis*) grows on moist, sandy, and poor soils, and has some tolerance for shade. It is coarse and winter-kills north of Augusta, Georgia, and Birmingham, Alabama. Sow 2 pounds to 1,000 square feet. It needs little care, but in winter it turns brown.

Centipede grass (*Eremochloa ophiuroides*) is suited for south of Tennessee. It grows on poor, moist or wet soils and stands some shade. It needs minimum care. Sow 2 pounds to 1,000 square feet. In winter it turns brown. Mow to a height of ½ inch.

St. Augustine grass (*Stenotaphrum secundatum*) is for south of Tennessee only. It stands shade well, needs highly fertile, well-drained soil, withstands dryness, is resistant to diseases and pests, forms a coarse, dark green sod, and is propagated by sprigs. In winter it turns brown. Mow it ½ to 1 inch high.

Manila grass (*Zoysia matrella*) has the texture of Kentucky blue grass; it is propagated by sprigs planted 6 inches apart and needs close mowing. It is shade tolerant, needs well-drained soil of high fertility, and is resistant to diseases and pests. It turns brown in winter. A disadvantage is that it spreads and forms a good turf slowly. It is hardy as far north as Washington, D.C.

Japanese lawn grass (*Zoysia japonica*) and its variety 'Meyer' form good fine-textured turfs. They are increased by plugs or sprigs, are shade tolerant, need well-drained soil of moderate fertility, withstand drought, and are disease and pest resistant. Mow to a height of 1 inch to 2 inches. It turns brown in winter.

Laying sod is the quickest means of establishing a new lawn, in fact instant lawns can be had in this way. The procedure consists of transplanting cultivated grass sods (turfs) from one area to another and laying them to produce a new greensward. If you must buy the sod, and in many regions there are sizable commercial sod farms that supply landscape contractors, nurseries, and individuals needing this material, sodding is the most expensive way of making a new lawn, but sometimes the sod can be taken from another part of the garden. Possibly a building, a paved terrace or a path is to be installed where lawn exists, and the grass sod can be removed and used elsewhere. New beds and borders cut in lawns also provide supplies.

Ready for sod laying: (a) A wheelbarrow with rolls of commercial sod and tools, left to right, tamper, iron rake, edger, broom, and wooden rake

(b) Laying commercial sod, which usually comes in strips 3 feet long by 1 foot wide

A lawn made of sod looks well from the beginning and is usable almost immediately. If properly installed and given adequate care, it can be put down successfully any time from spring to fall.

For clothing slopes, a lawn made of sod has the advantage of checking erosion immediately. A border of turf provides excellent well-defined margins to a lawn, the major center part of which is sown from seed after the sods are laid.

Turf is easy to cut and install once the best techniques are mastered. The sod should be at least three years old. Choose a time when the soil is moist. Mow the grass closely. Then with an edger (a tool with a long handle and a crescent-shaped blade) slice the sod into squares of appropriate size (1-foot sides are generally suitable). Use a garden line stretched tightly across the grass or the edge of a plank lying flat on the turf as a guide for cutting the lines straight. If you have no edger, you can make do with a spade for slicing the sod into squares.

For cutting beneath the sods so that each square may be lifted cleanly and intact, you may use a spade, too, but if you have any considerable amount to lift, it will pay to obtain a sod or turf cutter. This is a sort of long-handled spade with a sharp cutting blade and a shaft set at such an angle that the blade can be easily pushed horizontally beneath the sod by an operator who bends over and pushes the handle at about knee level or slightly higher. Before cutting, the thickness of the finished turfs should be decided upon. From 1½ to 2 inches is suitable. Cut the sods slightly thicker than the finished dimension.

Home-cut grass sods may be of any convenient size: (a) Cut the tuft into rectangles with an edging tool

(b) Slice beneath them with a special sod-cutting tool or with a spade

(c) Lift each sod individually

As each sod is lifted, place it grass side down in a tray as deep as the finished sod is to be thick. This tray should have three sides only, the fourth being left open to permit the sod to be slipped in and out.

Let the side of the tray opposite the open side rest against a "stop" of some kind to prevent the tray from slipping; then with an old scythe blade or a two-handled knife having a blade longer than the width of the tray, cut off all surplus soil and roots by standing in front of the closed end of the tray and drawing the blade toward you

To standardize the thickness of home-lifted sods, place each grass-side down in a shallow box with one side lacking:
(a) Cut off surplus soil with an old scythe blade or other suitable tool

(b) Up end the box to release the turf

while it rests across the tray's edges. In this way all sods are cut to a uniform thickness, and laying them evenly is greatly facilitated.

Prepare the soil on which turf is to be laid exactly as for seeding, but with its surface as much lower than the finish grade as the sods are thick. Make sure that the soil is moderately compacted and then loosened slightly on its surface by raking. This helps to assure a better bond between sods and soil.

After the soil has been moderately compacted, rake it to a fine surface

Lay the sods in rows, with the joints staggered like joints between bricks in a wall. If the sods have been well cut and carefully handled, little or no packing of soil beneath them will be needed, but should they have lost some of their soil and be thinner in spots than the required thickness, pack sufficient soil beneath them as the work proceeds to bring them perfectly level. Butt the sods closely together and set them firmly in position by giving each several blows with the back of the spade. When several square yards have been laid, give them an additional firming by beating them with a wooden tamper. Then water

Laying sods: (a) Lay sods on an even surface with the joints of adjacent rows alternating like bricks in a wall

(b) Butt the sods together by tapping them with the face of the spade

(c) Fill any crevices that exist with a little good soil

(d) Sweep this in

(e) Finish by tamping or rolling the surface

thoroughly with a sprinkler giving a fine spray. The following day, or as soon as the grass has dried, sprinkle enough sifted soil over the surface so that when brushed down it fills any crevices or openings that show between the sods. Next, spread a little grass seed along the joints and in any spots where the grass is not too thick and brush it in.

Care of a turf-laid lawn is simple. It must never be permitted to dry out during its first season. During its first month, if the weather is dry, it should be soaked every second or third day. It may need rolling once or twice in its early weeks. On heavy soil newly laid sods tend to heave out of position during winter. It is better to turf such soils in spring or late summer rather than fall. On steep slopes it is a good plan to drive pegs into some of the sods. These will hold all the sods in position until they have rooted firmly into the soil beneath them. If this is not done, they may slide down the slope under the influence of rain or frost.

Planting stolons, sprigs, and plugs are other methods of making new lawns, appropriate with grasses that spread rapidly by creeping stems (stolons). With such sorts it is entirely practicable to establish excellent turf by planting small pieces of rootless and leafless stolons or of stolons with roots and leaves or by setting pieces of turf close enough together, but still at fairly distant intervals to assure that when they begin to grow they will soon touch one another. Grasses that can be propagated in this way are chiefly subtropical sorts such as St. Augustine, Bermuda, centipede, and zoysia. Cool-climate creeping bent also lends itself to stolon planting, and some varieties of it can only be increased in this way. Many golf course putting greens are produced by planting bent grass stolons.

Creeping bent grass grows satisfactorily from stolons and forms excellent turf, but before deciding to start such a lawn in this way consider these facts. The labor cost will be much higher than that of seeding a lawn and stolons are much more expensive than seed (but possibly you can obtain them from an established lawn without cost). Lawns of creeping bent require a tremendous amount of upkeep—frequent mowing, watering, fertilizing, topdressing, and so forth. They are really for specialists.

One other point. Seaside bent is a kind that creeps and can be easily raised from seeds. It produces a turf almost as good as the 'Washington' and 'Metropolitan' strains of true creeping bent, which can only be increased by stolons.

To begin a lawn from stolons chop the stolons into pieces ½ to 1 inch long and scatter them over soil that has been prepared as thoroughly as it should be for seed sowing. Make sure it is firm and raked smooth before you distribute the stolons. Sow them as you would seed, but not as thickly. The pieces should be spaced about ½ inch apart. One and one-half bushels of chopped stolons are sufficient for 1,000 square feet. Make sure they are distributed evenly and press them into the surface by rolling. Spread a covering of fine soil, ¼ to ½ inch thick over the stolons and roll again. An easy way of doing this is to lay a flexible steel door mat over the newly distributed stolons, heap fine soil on it, then, with the back of a rake, spread it level with the tops of the treads of the mat. Remove any surplus soil, lift the mat carefully (a two-person job), and treat the adjoining area in the same way. Repeat this until the whole planted surface is covered with soil. Then roll lightly.

It is very important to water a lawn newly planted in this manner often enough to keep the soil moist.

Where a lawn of a kind exists and the soil is known to be good to a depth of 6 to 8 inches, it is possible to establish a turf of creeping bent without spading or turning it over. Simply destroy the grass already there. This you may do by skimming it off very thinly with a spade or by applying a very heavy dressing of sulfate of ammonia. Scratch the surface with a rake and then sow the stolons and treat as advised above.

Sprigs are young rooted shoots—pieces of stolon with leaves and roots attached. Lawns of subtropical grasses—Bermuda, carpet, St. Augustine, and centipede—may be established by planting such shoots at distances of 6 to 9 inches apart. This is called sprigging.

In preparation for sprigging, the soil is made ready as for sowing seed. It is then well watered, and the sprigs (each consisting of several joints and shoots) are planted with a dibber (pointed stick) and firmed in place. After planting, the area is again well watered.

Plugs are pieces of sod, 1½ to 2 inches or so in diameter, of creeping grasses. When planted, they quickly grow together and cover the ground. They differ from sprigs in that each consists of many rather than a few shoots and includes the soil in which the roots grow (sprigs carry little or no soil with them). Zoysia grasses are the ones chiefly propagated by plugs. They make good turf sooner when grown in this way rather than from sprigs. More recently success had been had in establishing good lawns by planting plugs of selected, vigorous growing varieties of Kentucky blue grass.

Make the soil ready as you would for seeding. Plant the plugs with a trowel, 6 inches to 1 foot apart, setting the surface of each level with or very slightly below the soil surface. Make the soil about the roots firm. Water thoroughly after planting. Old lawns may be plugged with zoysia, which will gradually intermingle with established grasses and eventually may take over entirely.

Lawns in shade present special problems in choosing the best grasses and caring for them afterward. Where shade is too dense or surface-rooting trees, such as maples, compete strongly with the grasses for moisture and nutrients it is often unrealistic to attempt to grow a lawn. It may be far more practical to settle for English ivy, pachysandra, *Euonymus fortunei coloratus,* or other willing groundcover, or in extreme cases to cover the area with pebbles, gravel, paving stones, or other nonliving surfacing. But do not be too easily discouraged. Many shaded locations that appear impossible to the amateur are simply a little difficult. With understanding and know-how, you can get them to support very good lawns. One advantage of shade, if it is not too heavy, is that the turf will be free of crab grass because that pestiferous weed must have plenty of direct sunlight. It's an ill wind that blows nobody any good!

Shade is usually caused by trees or buildings. Trees bring with them the problems of roots competing with the grass for moisture and food, the possibility of fallen leaves smothering the grass, and overhead drip. Buildings may pose difficulties because of drip from roofs as well as dryness near their bases caused by roof overhangs and prevailing winds tending to drive rain away. We shall consider how best to meet these difficulties.

Scientific investigation has shown that grass plants growing in shade and the adverse conditions often associated with it invariably have much more limited root systems than those growing in sun. As the root system diminishes, the entire plant is weakened; if the process is carried too far, it dies.

It clearly follows that anything that encourages the development of vigorous roots is advantageous. Of special importance are satisfactory underdrainage and favorable mechanical and chemical conditions of the soil, an adequate supply of nutrients, the provision of water during dry weather, the avoidance of too close mowing, and the removal of fallen leaves before they smother the grass. Last, but by no means least, is the selection of kinds of grass most likely to flourish in shade.

The minimum amount of direct sunlight (that is, light uninterrupted by buildings, trees, or other shade-casting objects) needed by turf is two hours each day between 8 A.M. and 6 P.M. or three or four times as long a period of dappled sunlight (light filtering through trees in such a way that patches of sun and shadow play across the grass as the sun moves).

You may have a location that receives only morning light or sun only in late afternoon. Do not be discouraged. If shade at other times is not absolutely too dense, and if other conditions are favorable or can be made so, you can have good lawn.

Many trees, such as pin oaks, elms, birches, locusts, and honey-locusts, allow considerable light to filter through their leafage; others, notably some of the maples, cast very dense shade. The Norway maple is an especially bad offender in this respect and so are its varieties, Schwedler's maple and 'Crimson King' maple.

Dense shade often can be ameliorated by cutting off some of the lower branches of offending trees. If this is intelligently done, it may improve the appearance of the landscape immensely. There are few prettier garden effects than sweeps of green lawn beneath high-branched trees, trees with their lowest branches so high that you can easily see beneath them. Remember, light from directly above is not necessary for a good lawn; that which comes from the side is equally stimulating to growth of grass.

As with lawns anywhere, the quality of the soil is of great importance in shaded areas, even more so than in sunny places. It must not pack down and become pasty and "puddled" under the influence of heavy drip from leaves and branches. If it does, air cannot enter and grass roots die.

If the soil is sandy or gravelly, packing will not occur. Heavy, clayey soils are particularly subject to packing and should be protected against it when the ground is first made ready for seeding. The upper 3 to 4 inches of earth should be mixed with very liberal amounts of coarse sand, grit, or gritty coal cinders, as well as organic matter such as peat moss, compost, or commercial humus. One-third part by bulk in the upper soil is not too much if the soil is clayey. In very heavy (clayey) soils more may be used.

Soil under trees may become excessively acid or in other ways toxic to grass as a result of substances formed in leaves that are washed into the ground, and in some instances, it is suspected, roots may give off harmful substances. Walnut trees have long been believed to bring about conditions inimical to the growth of grass and other plants. Turf cannot usually be persuaded to grow beneath well-established conifers (narrow-leaved evergreens), such as pines, firs, and spruces. If possible, it is better to leave the fallen brown needles (leaves) as groundcover in such places. These look attractive and form a natural mulch that keeps the roots cool and reasonably moist.

Toxicity (poisoning) of soil is most likely to occur where subsurface drainage is so poor that the ground lies wet for long periods. This is especially likely to happen in winter and early spring. As a result of the wetness, soil bacteria, necessary for the proper development of grasses, do not prosper and cannot play their part in creating favorable soil conditions. Spiking with an aerating tool or machine helps

drainage to some extent, but if conditions are extreme, an installed drainage system is the only answer.

If a soil test shows that the ground is excessively acid, apply lime, but do not do this as a matter of general principle without ascertaining that lime is indeed needed. Be careful not to use it around azaleas, rhododendrons, or other decidedly acid-soil plants.

Tree roots present problems in many shaded areas. They compete vigorously with the grasses for nutrients and often more importantly for water. Those near the surface are in immediate competition with turf for moisture, but even the deeper roots absorb moisture that might rise in the ground by capillarity (in the way oil travels up a lamp wick) and be useful to the grass if the tree and shrub roots did not get it first.

But that is not the whole story. Although the roots of trees and shrubs take water from the soil, the shade of their branches and leaves checks loss of water from the surface soil by evaporation. This gives the gardener something of a break early in the season, but he pays for it later.

Until the spring is well advanced and early summer is at hand, shaded areas are less likely to dry to the extent that they need watering than are sunny ones, but after that—watch out. A week or two of really dry weather, and the grass under trees will surely suffer if you fail to water it.

Choosing kinds of grasses for shaded places needs consideration. If the lawn-to-be will receive at least two hours of direct sunlight or its equivalent in dappled sunshine (very light shade with sun filtering in through for most of the day), ordinary grass mixtures intended for sunny places are satisfactory, but in places more densely or consistently shaded use blends of special grasses.

The great shady lawn grasses are Chewings fescue, 'Illahee' fescue, rough-stalked blue and velvet bent. Redtop and meadow fescue are temporary "nurse" grasses. In the south, St. Augustine grass and centipede grass are useful in shade, as is zoysia.

Where shade is so heavy that even with the best care the grass plants are weakened to the extent that many do not live more than one to three years, you may be able to maintain a fair stand of grass by lightly reseeding each fall.

Watering and fertilizing lawns in shade calls for special attention. As with all lawns, when water is needed, give enough to penetrate to a depth of at least 6 inches, then no more for several days, perhaps four or five days in hot weather in areas where tree roots abound. The water should be applied in a fine spray.

Grass growing in the shade of trees and shrubs has to compete with them for food as well as moisture. Relieve the pressure of this competition by providing for the

needs of the trees and shrubs as well as the grass. Fertilize the lawn regularly and also the trees and shrubs. So far as possible, place the fertilizer intended especially for the trees and shrubs deep in the soil so that their roots are encouraged to strike downward.

For the grass two substantial feedings a year are normally sufficient. Apply one in early spring and one in early fall, after the really hot weather of summer has passed. If the soil is known to be infertile, a third feeding in early summer is beneficial, but this is not recommended on rich soils because excessive fertilization, particularly during hot weather, is liable to harm grass by making available more nitrogen than it can use. This may make the grass more susceptible to disease.

An annual topdressing of sandy soil, organic matter, and fertilizer, applied in spring, not only provides the roots of the grass with nutrients, but, by adding humus and replacing surface soil that may have washed away, serves as a cushion to break the weight of falling drops of water that compact the soil. Should the soil have

Aerating a lawn with a garden fork

become excessively compacted as a result of being rolled, being walked upon when wet, or some other cause, it is likely to benefit from being aerated by a special spiked roller or a fork designed for that particular purpose, or even by being jabbed vigorously with an ordinary spading fork, making holes 3 to 4 inches apart, the fork being wiggled back and forth so that the prongs enlarge the holes. This treatment may be done immediately before topdressing.

Renovating instead of completely remaking old, worn, or shabby lawns is often practicable, but usually only if the soil is of sufficient depth, say at least 6 inches of topsoil, and of fair quality. Suppose your present turf is a bit thin in spots and has too many weeds, and its surface is not as even as it should be. Altogether it looks a little sad and ragged, not exactly a feature of which you are proud. Perhaps you've made attempts to improve it—a little seeding in spring, occasional fertilizing, ineffective stabs at eliminating weeds. You may even have topdressed it with humus or something that a persuasive peddler sold as humus. All with little advantage. Now you want to do a job, without excessive cost or labor.

First determine if the area can be repaired more easily than renewed. If the soil is very poor or shallow or if more than one-half the greenery is weeds, forget about renovation and decide upon remaking. It will be cheaper and better in the end. Test the depth and quality of the soil by lifting a few plugs to a depth of six inches or more and examining them carefully. Have a lime test made.

If you decide to renovate, plan to do the topdressing and reseeding involved in early spring, late summer or early fall, not in late spring or summer. Begin preliminary weed elimination any time. Make the job as thorough as possible. If the area is large, use one of the selective commercial chemical weed killers. Follow the manufacturer's directions carefully. Although, when making over a lawn, discoloration of desired grasses is of small importance, you do not want to kill any. Even with these aids some hand weeding will likely be needed.

When the time comes for the major fixing, mow at a height of 1 inch. Eliminate obvious low spots by lifting a few turfs, packing good soil beneath, and replacing them. Then, with an ordinary iron rake, scarify the soil surface, removing as much dead grass, leaves and other debris as possible. If the soil is compacted, aerify it, preferably by using a powered machine made for the purpose or a special hollow-tined aerifying fork, but if these are not available a regular spading fork jabbed in to make holes a few inches apart will produce some improvement.

Should the soil be acid, apply agricultural lime or ground limestone and in any case a fertilizer that has most of its nitrogen in an organic or slow-release form. Use sufficient fertilizer to supply 1 pound of actual nitrogen for every 1,000 square feet. Spread it when the grass is dry and work it shallowly into the surface with a rake. Then spread a ¼-inch-thick layer of a screened mixture of good topsoil, coarse sand, and some bulk organic matter, such as compost, sedge peat (humus), leaf mold, or peat moss. Smooth with the back of a rake and then sow a good-quality grass seed mixture at 2 to 4 pounds to each 1,000 square feet. Work the seed into the soil with a rake or broom and roll or pat it with the back of a spade or a wooden tamper. If you water afterward, make sure you use a very fine spray to avoid washing away the seed. Usually it is better to wait for rain.

Removing thatch by raking vigorously

A rich topdressing spread evenly over the lawn surface and worked in with a rake followed by a light sowing of grass seed is a helpful rejuvenation procedure

Following this treatment give consistent attention to eliminating weeds. Keep up a regular schedule of fertilizing, watering, and other cultural care as described in the Encyclopedia entry Lawn Maintenance, and repeat the renovation treatment described above in the following year if it seems desirable. There is no magic formula for making a poor lawn good at one fell swoop.

Renovating a lawn calls for effort and money. Before embarking on the project, be sure the measures outlined are likely to bring results. There are areas—dense shade or matted tree roots near the surface, for example—where it is better to plant groundcovers than it is to plant grass.

A condition known as thatch is likely to develop on lawns that are consistently cut too high or not mowed often enough. Thatch is a surface layer of matted, spongy vegetation that includes considerable amounts of dead grass stems and leaves through which the living blades of grass must push their way toward the light. If heavy, it may reduce the effectiveness of watering by interfering with penetration. It also is harmful in that it favors the development of fungus diseases and makes controlling them more difficult. Remove thatch by vigorous raking and brushing. Follow this by mowing closely and then by a light topdressing of sandy, fertile soil.

If the thatch is very thick it may be advisable to cut through it with a verti-cut machine (these can be rented in some places) before raking.

LAWSONIA (Law-sònia) — Henna or Mignonette Tree or Jamaica-Privet. Millenia before the advent of modern beauty parlors ladies engaged in dyeing their hair, fingernails and toenails, and in other cosmetic adornment. Egyptian mummies mutely testify that the gentle arts of the beautician were practiced at least five thousand years ago and that henna was even then important. In biblical times it was well known and is the plant referred to as camphire in the authorized King James version of the Bible. The beard and hair of the Prophet Mohammed were reddened with henna and at one time horses' manes were colored with it. It has been used to dye fabrics and leather. Henna dye is very color-fast. It is prepared from the ground leaves. The wizardry of modern chemistry largely obviated the need for henna as a beauty aid and dye, but in response to a trend toward the use of natural instead of artificial products that developed in the 1970s it once again gained favor. The plant that yields henna, the only one of its genus, is widely grown in the tropics and subtropics as an ornamental.

The genus *Lawsonia*, named to honor a Scottish friend and patron of Linnaeus, Dr. Isaac Lawson, who died about 1747, belongs in the loosestrife family LYTHRACEAE and consists of one variable species. It is native to North Africa, Asia, and Austrialia, and is freely naturalized in parts of the American tropics.

Henna, mignonette tree, or Jamaica-privet (*L. inermis*) is a rather loose-growing shrub or sometimes small tree, related to, but very different in appearance from, the crape-myrtle (*Lagerstroemia*). The name mignonette tree alludes to the sweet fragrance of its flowers. Up to about 20 feet tall, but usually much lower, it is loosely-branched, often somewhat spiny, and hairless. It has opposite, short-stalked, elliptic to elliptic-lanceolate leaves ½ inch to 2 inches long. In few- to many-flowered terminal clusters, its white, pink, or cinnabar-red flowers are up to ¼ inch across. They have four-parted calyxes, four-parted, wrinkled corollas, and usually eight, but sometimes four or twelve stamens. The style is long. The fruits are capsules partly enclosed in the calyxes.

Garden and Landscape Uses and Cultivation. Henna is adapted to warm climates only. It may be grown in Florida and southern California and succeeds in ordinary well-drained soil in sunny locations. Because of its open habit, small leaves, and inconspicuous blooms it is not insistent in the landscape and so may be placed wherever a shrub or small tree of its size and type are fitting. It stands pruning well. If it is desirable to shape it or contain it to size, do this at the beginning of a growing season. Propagation is easy by seed and by cuttings.

LAYCOCKARA. This is the name of orchid hybrids the parents of which include *Arachnis, Phalaenopsis,* and *Vandopsis.*

LAYERING. Layering or layerage is an easy and very reliable method of propagating a wide variety of plants, especially trees, shrubs, and woody vines. It is much employed in commercial nurseries in Europe, to a lesser, but still considerable extent in America. Amateurs could with much advantage make greater use of this method of increase to obtain new plants for their gardens.

The procedure consists of causing roots to develop from stems still attached to their parent plants, and after this is effected of severing the rooted portions and potting or planting them individually. There are several forms of layering, all except one involving bringing the stem into contact with the ground or with soil or other rooting medium heaped upon it. These methods may be grouped as ground layering. Air layering, Chinese layering, or marcottage differs from ground layering in root formation being induced from parts of stems not brought into contact with the ground. In temperate regions this is used chiefly for indoor plants. It is dealt with separately in this Encyclopedia under Air Layering.

With all ground layering it is desirable to have the soil into which the layered shoots are to root encouragingly porous and containing a liberal proportion of humus. To make sure of this, it is generally advisable to fork into it or otherwise mix with it generous amounts of peat moss, screened leaf mold, or commercial humus and, unless it is decidedly sandy, coarse sand or perlite. Instead of soil other rooting media may be used, such as peat moss, partly decayed sawdust, or a mixture of either of these and sand. After the

layering operation, it is important that the soil or other rooting medium be kept continually moist, but not constantly saturated until the rooted layers are ready for removal from the parent.

Simple layering gives one new plant from each layered stem. To do this, select shoots sufficiently low that by bending they can be brought into contact with the ground. Make a small hollow or slit in the soil and lay a part of the stem located some little distance, usually 6 inches to 1 foot, from its tip but sometimes more or less depending upon the shoot, into the depression. Leave the free end of the shoot sticking up into the air. Then secure the partially buried branch to prevent movement.

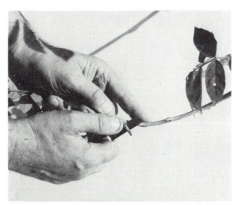

Layering: (a) Wounding the shoot of a wisteria to be layered

(b) Pegging the wounded part into a slight hollow in the ground

(c) Sometime later roots have begun to develop

Layering a *Davallia* fern onto the surface of soil in a pot

Shoots layered in spring, the usual season for this work, may be taken from the mother plant in fall or the following spring, those made in summer are usually best left attached until spring, except that tip layers are generally ready for removal the first fall after they are made. At the time of their removal prune back their tops to temporarily reduce the demands on the roots for moisture and nourishment, which, until the layers were cut free, the mother plant partially supplied.

Refinements include selecting shoots usually of the previous season's growth. Only with such plants as azaleas, other rhododendrons and camellias, and other shrubs that do not produce suitable shoots of this age, should older ones be layered. Before inserting in the ground the part of the shoot that will be buried, wound it by removing from all around it a ½-inch-wide strip of bark, or cut a notch to form a tongue of bark and wood on its underside, or with a sharp knife remove from its underside a thin slice of bark and underlying wood. When the shoot is positioned in the hollow of slit, peg it securely into place with a sturdy forked twig or a piece of wire bent like a hairpin, then pile a generous amount of soil over it, leaving the upturned end of the shoot exposed. Additional security may be had by driving a short stake into the ground and tying the exposed end to it.

Serpentine layering is a variation of simple layering adaptable to such plants as clematises, muscadine grapes, and wisterias that have long, flexible shoots. Lay these along the ground in undulating fashion with alternate portions exposed and buried. The exposed sections should each have at least one bud. Wound and peg into place each section to be buried as is done in simple layering, then cover it with soil. When the layered shoot is removed from the mother plant cut it into sections each consisting of a young new plant and pot or replant these.

Mound, or stool, layering is a favorite with European nurserymen. To accomplish this, and it is only practicable with such plants as apple understocks, currants, shrubby dogwoods, hydrangeas, and viburnums, that after severe pruning produce multitudes of new shoots, cut the mother plant to within 1 inch of the ground in late winter and after the young shoots are 3 to 5 inches high, or before in the cases of a few reluctant-to-root kinds such as certain sorts of *Prunus*, work soil between and around them to form a mound one-half their heights. As growth continues add soil once or twice more, but never to more than one-half the heights of the shoots and finally making a mound not more than 6 to 8 inches high. The rooted layers may be detached and planted in fall or spring; the latter is preferable in regions of severe winters.

Trench layering is a modification of mound layering. To accomplish it, make one or more furrows or trenches 2 to 3 inches deep radiating from the base of the mother plant. Bend down one-year shoots so that one extends along the bottom of each trench. Peg them securely into place with hairpin-like wires or forked pegs as for simple layering, and as shoots develop hill soil around them in the way recommended for mound layering. After rooting, dig up the layered stems and cut them into sections to give individual young rooted plants for potting or planting.

Tip layering, practiced with blackberries, dewberries, black and purple raspberries, and a few other plants with cane-like shoots that tend naturally to bend to the ground and take root, is done in late summer. To encourage the development of a greater number of shoots suitable for layering it is usual to pinch or cut the tips out of new shoots earlier, when they are 1½ to 2½ feet long. By layering time the side branches that result will begin to bend over and their extremities to assume a characteristic rat-tail appearance because as they elongate their new leaves are small and curled. When a portion of the tip has attained this condition, dig a hole with a trowel or spade 3 or 4 inches deep, insert the tip of the shoot, and cover with soil.

LAYIA (Lày-ia)—Tidy Tips, White-Daisy. Predominantly Californian (all fifteen species are native to California and only two as wild plants extend outside its boundaries), the genus *Layia* belongs in the daisy family COMPOSITAE. Its members are among the showiest of western American spring-blooming annuals. The name commemorates the botanist G. Tradescant Lay, who visited California in 1827.

Layias have mostly alternate, usually toothed to pinnately-lobed, but occasionally nearly smooth-edged, narrow leaves. Their solitary flower heads terminate usually naked stalks. Except in *L. discoidea*, in which ray florets are lacking, each head has eight to twenty-four strap-shaded ray florets, three-toothed or three-lobed at their tips. They are white, yellow, or yellow tipped with white. The disk is yellow, its florets, tubular and five-toothed, have black or yellow anthers. Both ray and disk florets are fertile. The fruits are achenes.

Tidy tips (*L. platyglossa*), is one of the most popular. It has more or less prostrate, succulent, branched stems 4 inches to 1 foot long, and more-or-less-toothed, softly-hairy, green leaves. The subspecies or variety *L. p. campestris* (syn. *L. elegans*) is erect, up to 1½ feet tall, and grayer. It differs in minor botanical characteristics from the species. The ray florets of both species and variety are usually bright yellow with white ends, more rarely entirely yellow. The disk florets have black anthers. The flower heads are about 1¾ inches across.

Layia platyglossa (flowers)

The white-daisy (*L. glandulosa*) is a pretty native from Washington to Idaho, Utah, New Mexico, California, and Baja California. Up to 1¼ feet tall or rarely taller, it has branched stems and rough-hairy leaves, the lower ones toothed or lobed. The flower heads are about 1½ inches across, their ray florets glistening white, commonly fading to pinkish-purple. In variety *L. g. lutea* the ray florets are golden-yellow.

The plant previously known as *L. g. heterotricha* is *L. heterotricha*. It is a stout, comparatively few-branched plant, strongly scented and more roughly hairy than *L. glandulosa*, and up to 3 feet tall. Its ray florets vary from white to pale yellow not tipped with white; they commonly fade to rose-purple.

Other kinds worthy of consideration by gardeners include *L. chrysanthemoides* (syns. *L. calliglossa, Calliglossa douglasii*), an erect, branching, aromatic species up to 1¼ feet in height, with leaves hairless except for fringes around their margins and the lower ones pinnately-lobed. The ray florets are yellow with white tips. Note-

Layia platyglossa in California

worthy because of the variability of its flower color is *L. gaillardioides*. Its ray florets range from golden-yellow to pale yellow with whitish tips. This species, up to 2 feet tall, has branched or branchless stems and pungently scented foliage. Its slightly sticky leaves are toothed or lobed.

Garden and Landscape Uses. These are admirable plants for grouping in flower borders, for furnishing gentle slopes, and for adding color to rock gardens. They need full sun and are adaptable to dryish, porous soils. Their flowers are useful for cutting; they last well in water.

Cultivation. In regions of mild winters seeds may be sown outdoors, where the plants are to bloom, in fall, or sowing may be done in early spring. The seedlings are thinned to stand from 4 to 9 inches apart, according to the vigor of the species. No other care is needed except the suppression of weeds, and watering if the weather is extremely dry. Staking is not necessary; the plants stand up well to beating rains and strong winds. Like many western American annuals they are not at their best and may fail completely in the hot, humid summers of the eastern and central United States. There, it is best to sow as early in spring as possible in the expectation of having blooms before the hottest weather arrives or to sow early indoors and grow the young plants in flats in a cool greenhouse (night temperature 50°F) until they can be planted in the garden as soon as all danger of frost is past.

LAZY-DAISY. See Aphanostephus.

LEAD PLANT is *Amorpha canescens*.

LEAD TREE is *Leucaena glauca*.

LEADER. This means the terminal or leading shoot of a trunk or branch that by its continued growth extends the length of an axis. When pruning trees and shrubs it is often important to distinguish between leaders and secondary shoots.

Leontopodium alpinum

Leptodactylon californicum glandulosum

Leptospermum scoparium, double-flowered

Leontopodium wilsonii

Leptotes unicolor

Leucodendron daphnoides

Lewisia brachycalyx

Leucojum aestivum

Leucospermum reflexum

Lewisia cotyledon

LEADWORT. See Plumbago.

LEAF. Generally easily recognizable as such, leaves (singular leaf) are characteristic of most plants that concern gardeners, those botanists call vascular plants. They are lacking in certain lower groups, such as algae, fungi, and mosses, although some of these have organs that superficially resemble leaves.

Leaves are appendages to stems, sometimes very short ones. Most are thin and flat, but others are cylindrical or approximately so, and some are of other forms. In size, shape, and other characteristics the leaves of different kinds of plants vary greatly, and sometimes there is considerable variation between those of the same species and even between those on the same plant. Most leaves are green, but some are consistently of some other color, such as yellow, bronze, or red, and some are variegated with other colors or with white. Others, those of *Pieris forrestii* for instance, and those of many tropical trees and shrubs are bronzy-red or red when young, but soon become green. Yet other plants, such as the sugar maple and many other temperate region deciduous trees and shrubs, have leaves that are green throughout most of their lives, but change to red, yellow, brown, pink, or purple before they drop.

A typical leaf consists of a broad, expanded blade and frequently a stalk (petiole) with often at the base of the stalk two small appendages called stipules. The apex of the angle formed by the upperside of the leaf or leafstalk and the stem from which the leaf sprouts is called the leaf axil. Normally in each axil there is a bud or buds capable of developing as branches or as flowers or flowering shoots.

The leaf blade may be in one piece or consist of two or more separate leaflets. If the blade is in one piece it is said to be simple, if there are separate leaflets it is compound or divided. Compound leaves are of two principal types depending upon the arrangement of the leaflets. If all arise from a common point at the apex of the leafstalk, the leaf is palmately-compound, if they are disposed along a central axis in feather-like fashion, they are pinnately-compound. The primary divisions of a pinnately-compound leaf may be further divided to give bipinnate and tripinnate leaves, which are leaves, respectively, two- and three-times-pinnately-compound. Both simple leaves and the leaflets of compound leaves may be variously lobed and toothed. Because it is not always easy to be certain whether leaves with only two or three leaflets are actually palmately-compound or pinnately-compound, they are often described, respectively, as bifoliate and trifoliate.

The arrangement of leaves on the stems is often of significance in identifying plants. Those that sprout singly from separate nodes (points of attachment to the stem) are alternate, if two come from each node they are opposite, if more than two come from a node they are whorled.

The chief function of leaves is to manufacture food for the entire plant from elements obtained from the air and the soil or other medium the roots permeate. This process, called photosynthesis, takes place only in cells containing chlorophyll under the influence of light. It is a supportive basis of all life because animals, using the term in its broad sense to include all living creatures, ultimately depend upon plants for their food and for the oxygen they require. Oxygen is released into the air in the process of photosynthesis.

Nearly all leaves have a limited life. Those of annuals and deciduous plants last for one full growing season. The leaves of some evergreens remain active much longer, sometimes for several years, but ultimately they too are shed and are replaced by new ones. Remarkable *Welwitschia mirabilis* has only two leaves, which last for the life of the plant, over one hundred years or longer.

LEAF BLIGHT. See Blight.

LEAF BLISTER. This is a name for several plant diseases that cause blister-like and sometimes other deformities of foliage, sometimes premature falling of leaves. Fungi of the genus *Taphrina* are responsible for many such diseases including maple leaf blister, leaf blister of oaks, and leaf blisters of ferns.

LEAF BLOTCH. Diseases so named are generally similar to leaf spot diseases and have similar origins, but the damage manifests itself as usually larger, irregular rather than more discrete damaged or dead areas. Such diseases include avocado blotch and sooty blotch of apples, pears, citrus, and other fruits caused by fungi. Infestations of some leaf miners produce effects somewhat similar to those of leaf blotch diseases.

LEAF CURL. This is a name for various plant diseases usually caused by fungi, bacteria, or environmental conditions, a prominent sign of which is curling, puckering, or similar distortion of the foliage. Peach leaf curl is such a disease caused by a fungus. Other leaf curls, including one of ash trees and one of plums, are caused by infestations of aphids. Similar signs may come from faulty environmental conditions and from drift onto foliage of certain herbicides (weed killers) used as sprays in nearby areas.

LEAF CUTTERS. Some caterpillars that feed by neatly cutting out parts of leaves are called leaf cutters. One of the most distressing, because it cannot be conveniently controlled as can others by spraying with a stomach poison insecticide, is the waterlily leaf cutter. Hand picking is a recommended control.

LEAF MINERS. Insects the larvae of which tunnel in leaves between the upper and lower epidermises, feeding on the soft tissues between, are called leaf miners. The adults may be beetles, flies, moths, or sawflies. Signs may be an erratic pattern of pale lines on the foliage, a blistered effect, or young foliage whitening and dying. Plants frequently attacked by leaf miners include beets, birches, chrysanthemums, columbines, hollies, and spinach. Because of the difficulty of reaching them with most sprays and dusts leaf miners are difficult to control. Hand picking is helpful. Spray applications should be timed for soon after eggs are laid on the foliage. Consult a Cooperative Extension Agent about the best spray to use.

Columbine (*Aquilegia*) leaf infested with leaf miners

LEAF MOLD. One of the most useful organic soil amendments, leaf mold is a compost made from the leaves of deciduous trees and shrubs without admixture of other materials. At its best it is dark brown, flaky, sweet-smelling, and a joy to handle.

As an ingredient of potting and seed soils leaf mold for the purposes it serves is unsurpassed. Its chief virtue is its ability to improve the physical condition of the soil by promoting a crumbly structure that favors the admission of air and free drainage of water. It also sustains bacterial action and as it slowly decays releases mild nutrients.

For outdoor gardening, leaf mold is excellent to mix with the soil when preparing seed beds especially those for shade-loving and woodland plants, such as primulas and numerous natives of the forest lands of North America. It is particularly suited to the needs of rhododendrons, including azaleas and other plants that belong to the heath family ERICACEAE. For all these leaf mold is invaluable as a mulch as well as for mixing with the soil.

To make leaf mold, collect the leaves of any and all deciduous trees when they fall and stack them in a suitable place outdoors. True, those of some sorts, beeches and oaks, for example, are better for the purpose than leaves of maples, horse-chestnuts, and other sorts that tend to pack

To make good leaf mold: (a) Rake fallen leaves of deciduous trees

(b) In an out-of-the-way corner of the garden, stack them in a neat heap

(c) As stacking proceeds, tread the heap to compact it

(d) After about two years, it will have decomposed into splendid leaf mold for use in the garden

(e) Leaf mold can be rubbed through a coarse sieve

(f) Sieved leaf mold is excellent for use in potting soil

together and become wet and rather slimy. Yet all are acceptable. Discard any branches or twigs of dimensions that will not rot evenly with the leaves and do not include leaves of evergreens except for perhaps a small proportion inadvertently raked up with the deciduous sorts.

Choose for the leaf mold pile an out-of-

the-way corner sheltered from sweeping winds and if possible shaded. Avoid low spots where water is likely to collect. If the bulk to be dealt with is comparatively small it is advantageous to define the sides of the pile-to-be by driving stakes into the ground at its corners and stretching chicken wire around them to form a bin, but this is unnecessary for large piles.

Gather the leaves as they fall and put them in the bin, compacting them by treading as the work proceeds, or with piles not surrounded by chicken wire simply dump the leaves in rough piles until all have been gathered, then after they have been well wetted by fall rains, construct the pile.

Leaf mold in small amounts can often be found in hollows in woodlands

First, outline it with shallow walls made by positioning forkfuls of sodden leaves along the four sides, making the pile of leaves 4 feet wide and of any convenient length. Then fill the interior of the rectangle so formed with leaves and tramp them firmly. As the work proceeds keep adding sizable clumps of wet leaves to the walls so that they are kept always a little higher than the inside and as each foot or so is added to the interior tread it firmly. Slope the sides slightly inward as the work proceeds. The height of the pile may be 5 to 7 feet.

To promote even and reasonably rapid decay, it is helpful, but not essential to turn the pile after six to nine months. This involves taking it down forkful by forkful and building a new heap with the same material. If you do this, place what have been the outer parts of the old pile at the interior of the new and vice versa.

Ordinarily it takes 1½ to 2 years before the leaf mold is in the most desirable condition for use, but the exact time will depend upon the kind of leaves and other circumstances.

For most uses the product is at its best when it has attained a flaky stage of decay with the structure of the leaves still clearly visible yet their tissues sufficiently rotted for them to be easily rubbed through a sieve with a ½- or ¾-inch mesh. Contrary to a rather commonly held belief oak leaf mold made in this way is not excessively acid. It is, in fact, one of the very finest leaf molds for all purposes.

LEAF ROLLERS. Caterpillars that roll the leaves of plants they infest to afford hiding and protection for themselves are called leaf rollers. There are many kinds, examples of which are the avocado leaf roller, bean leaf roller, fruit tree leaf roller, and strawberry leaf roller. Control is usually had by spraying well before the rollers become well established with a stomach poison insecticide. In some cases killing the insects by squeezing rolled leaves between finger and thumb is satisfactory.

LEAF SCORCH. This may result from actual scorching, changing of color and texture without the tissues being consumed, by exposure to excessive high temperatures in summer, by hot sun shining through a window, or as a result of high temperatures caused by a nearby radiator, fire, or other source of heat. Injury from sun heat is also called sun scald. The term leaf scorch is also used for some fungus diseases, such as black scorch of certain palms, prickly pear or opuntia leaf scorch, and narcissus leaf scorch, that produce the appearance of heat scorch.

Heat or physiogenic leaf scorch, common on horse-chestnuts, maples, and some other trees, especially those along streets and in paved areas, is likely to be particularly prevalent following a humid spring and early summer conducive to the growth of soft, succulent foliage. Similar scorching may in hot spells affect tender young shoots of hemlocks, wisterias, and other plants. The coming of high temperatures, especially if accompanied by drying wind, initiate it. Unlike leaf scorches caused by fungi, scorch from this cause most obviously and often dramatically affects the exposed side of the tree much more than the one not facing the sun. Aids in minimizing damage of this sort include encouraging the development of a more extensive root system by fertilizing, reducing the size of the head of the tree by pruning, and deep watering at intervals during dry weather. Of great importance is choice of sites for trees known to be susceptible to those not too exposed to hot sun, wind, or reflected heat from buildings and pavements. Leaf scorches caused by fungi are controlled by spraying with Bordeaux mixture or other fungicide and with palms by cutting out and destroying affected parts.

LEAF SKELETONIZER. Caterpillars that feed on the more tender tissues of leaves, leaving veins and much of the epidermis and without conspicuously rolling the leaves as

do leaf rollers, are called leaf skeletonizers. These often, like leaf tiers, link parts of leaves or more than one leaf together with silken webs. Some kinds feed only on the undersides, others on only the upper sides of the leaves. Spraying with a contact insecticide at the first evidence of infestation is the recommended control.

LEAF SPOT DISEASES. These numerous diseases are usually caused by fungi or bacteria. As the name indicates, the chief observable sign is discoloration of foliage in a pattern of spots. Similar marring can be caused by faulty environmental factors and by the improper use of sprays.

Leaf spot diseases on: (a) Hawthorn (*Crataegus*)

(b) English ivy (*Hedera*)

(c) Tulip tree (*Liriodendron*)

(d) Roses

LEAF TIERS. These caterpillars feed in much the manner of leaf skeletonizers, tying leaves together with silken webs and more or less skeletonizing the tissues. Common sorts attack beeches, hydrangeas, and a wide range of other plants. Control may be by spraying or dusting with a stomach poison insecticide before the leaves are tightly tied or, in some cases, as with hydrangeas, by opening the ties by hand and killing the insects before the flower buds are destroyed.

LEAFHOPPERS. A considerable number of related, mostly small, wedge-shaped insects that when at rest fold their wings in rooflike fashion over their bodies and when disturbed hop rapidly out of the way are called leafhoppers. They feed mostly on the undersides of the leaves of a wide variety of plants by sucking their juices. Infestations often result in marked stippling of the foliage. Leafhoppers excrete a sticky substance called honeydew on which a disfiguring sooty mold may grow. They transmit from plant to plant many virus diseases including aster yellows, peach yellows, phloem necrosis of elms, and sugar beet curly top. Control is chiefly by spraying with contact insecticides.

LEATHER. This word is employed as part of the common names of these plants: leather flower (*Clematis fremontii* and *C. ochroleuca*), leather leaf (*Chamaedaphne calyculata* and *Viburnum wrightii*), leather-leaf fern (*Rumohra adiantiformis*), and leather root (*Psoralea macrostachya*.)

LEATHERWOOD. See Dirca. Southern-leatherwood is *Cyrilla racemiflora*.

LEBBEK TREE is *Albizia lebbek*.

LECHENAULTIA. See Leschenaultia.

LECYTHIDACEAE—Lecythis Family. Tropical trees and shrubs numbering about twenty genera and perhaps 450 species of dicotyledons constitute this family. These numbers are reduced if, as is done by some botanists, certain of the group are segregated as the family BARRINGTONIACEAE. Included are the Brazil nut (*Bertholletia*), cannon ball tree (*Couroupita*), monkey pots (*Lecythis*), and *Barringtonia*.

Members of this group have alternate, undivided leaves more or less clustered at the shoot ends and symmetrical or asymmetrical flowers, solitary or in racemes. The calyx is commonly four- to six-lobed. There are four to six petals, many stamens or stamens and staminodes (nonfunctional stamens) more or less united at their bases, often in two very unequal bundles, and a usually branchless style. The woody, fibrous, or fleshy fruits, often of large size, are technically capsules or berries. Cultivated genera include *Barringtonia*, *Bertholletia*, *Couroupita*, and *Lecythis*.

LECYTHIS (Lécy-this)—Monkey Pot, Paradise Nut or Sapucaia Nut. Closely related to the Brazil nut (*Bertholletia*) and to the cannon ball tree (*Couroupita*), members of the genus *Lecythis* belong in the lecythis family LECYTHIDACEAE. The name is from the Greek *lechythos*, an oil jar, from the shape of the fruits. All fifty species are tropical American. Some are exploited for their lumber, which is used for railroad ties, construction, and cabinet work, others for their edible nuts. The inner bark of some is used for caulking and making cigarette papers and from some kinds tanning material is obtained.

A distinctive feature of monkey pots is their huge fruits, which may be as big as a good-sized melon and weigh many pounds. They are hard and woody and are fitted with a lid that covers an opening at the apex. The common name derives from a use made of the fruits by inhabitants of their native lands. Exploiting the greed and limited intelligence of the monkeys, they trap these animals by removing the lid of a monkey pot fruit, extracting the seeds, placing sugar in the pot, and securing it to a tree or other fixed object. The monkey, finding such a baited pot, inserts its hand and grasps a handful of sugar but, because the hole is too small, it cannot withdraw its clenched fist. Unwilling to relinquish the sugar, it remains until the trapper comes to collect his victim, which is likely to end up in another kind of pot or to be roasted to provide welcome meat for an Indian feast. Some confusion exists as to the identify of species of *Lecythis*, but the fruits of several are undoubtedly employed as described. Paradise or sapucaia nuts are produced by *L. zabucajo*, *L. ollaria*, and other species. They are superior to the similarly sized Brazil nuts.

Members of the genus *Lecythis* are trees or shrubs with alternate, leathery, toothed or toothless leaves, and flowers, which although much smaller, resemble those of the cannon ball tree (*Couroupita*). They differ in that the stamens at the top of the central column do not have fertile pollen. The blooms of some kinds are quite ornamental. They are in clusters and commonly have a four- to six-parted calyx, usually six, but sometimes only four nearly equal-sized petals, and stamens joined to form a curved, hood-shaped central feature with fertile anthers on its underside. The fruits, which vary in shape according to species, are more or less spherical, cup- or urn-shaped. They contain few, often large seeds.

A common source of paradise or sapucaia nuts, *L. zabucajo*, of northern South America, is a beautiful medium-sized tree with a broad crown and good-looking foliage. It has small creamy-white flowers and very large fruits. Known as the Panama monkey pot, *L. tuyrana* branches low and has large, toothless leaves and erect clusters of purplish blooms that are succeeded by fruits about 5 inches in diameter. The Brazilian monkey pot (*L. pisonis*) is a wide-headed tree 100 feet tall or taller with quite pleasing violet-tinted white flowers.

Lecythis zabucajo

Lecythis zabucajo (foliage and fruit)

Garden and Landscape Uses and Cultivation. No species of *Lecythis* is of importance as a cultivated plant in the continental United States. Excellent specimens of *L. zabucajo* are at Summit Gardens in the Panama Canal Zone, and this and other species are grown in other parts of tropical America. A hot, humid climate is necessary for best results. They are commonly propagated by seed.

LEDEBOURIA (Ledeb-oùria). Formerly included in *Scilla*, to which it is evidently related, *Ledebouria* belongs to the lily family LILIACEAE. Except for one native also in India and Ceylon, its species in the wild are restricted to Africa. Some eighty-five have been described, but critical study by botanists may reduce that number. The name commemorates the botanist Carl Friedrich von Ledebour, who died in 1851.

Ledebourias are bulb plants with all basal foliage, often mottled or spotted with purple and frequently with more or less purplish undersides. The flowers are in stalked racemes, without leaves, from the leaf axils. They have perianths of six petals (more properly, tepals), greenish-purple, purple, dull red, or pink, commonly with white margins. The stalks of the half dozen stamens are not united. There is a single style. The fruits are capsules. These plants differ from scillas in having axillary flowering stalks and in their stamens not being joined at their bases and other details.

Fairly commonly cultivated, *L. socialis* (syn. *Scilla violacea*) has bulbs that are on the surface rather than beneath the soil. They are ovoid, and in crowded clusters. Each is ½ to ¾ inch long and from the apex comes two to five more or less spreading, rather fleshy, lanceolate to oblong-lanceolate leaves 2 to 4 inches long and up to ¾ inch wide. Their lower surfaces are generally dark pink to bright purple. Above they have prominent blotches of dark green. In loose racemes of twenty-five or fewer, the flowers, erect in bud,

Ledebouria socialis

nod when open. Green with whitish margins to the petals, they have purple-stalked stamens.

Other species occasionally cultivated are *L. cooperi* (syns. *Scilla adlamii*, *S. sandersonii*, *S. saturata*), *L. revoluta* (syn. *Scilla lan-*

ceaefolia), and *L. floribunda* (syn. *Scilla mega-phylla*). The bulbs of these are subterranean. Those of variable *L. cooperi* are not always well developed, or they may be globose. There are one to five linear to ovate leaves up to 10 inches long, green above and streaked with purple and with spots of purple toward their bases on their under surfaces. The fifty or fewer flowers of each long-stalked, 2-inch-long, crowded raceme are reddish-pink to purple or sometimes green. The bulbs, 1 inch to 3 inches long, of *L. revoluta* each develop four to eight lanceolate to ovate leaves up to 6 inches long and 1¼ inches wide, often with their upper surfaces mottled with darker green. The flowers, in rather dense racemes of thirty to fifty or more rarely up to a hundred, are green, greenish-brown, or purplish. The bulbs of *L. floribunda* are 3 to 6 inches long and 4 to 6 inches in diameter. The four to eight leaves, commonly 8 inches to 1 foot long or a little longer, are often dark-spotted, and frequently have purplish, wavy, narrow cross-bands on their undersides. Long-stalked, the racemes of 100 to 150 flowers are about 6 inches in length. The blooms, grayish, greenish, or pinkish, have white-stalked stamens.

Garden and Landscape Uses and Cultivation. Ledebourias are not hardy in the north. They can be grown outdoors in regions of no or little frost and where summers are dry or dryish, and in greenhouses and sunny windows. Most experience has been had with *L. socialis,* which thrives with minimum care in well-drained pots or pans (shallow pots) of porous, fertile soil. For the best effect the bulbs should be planted closely together, but not touching. This species may be grown in full light or where it receives some shade from the strongest sun. A winter night temperature of about 55°F is suitable, with higher temperatures during the day and at other seasons appropriate. Watering is done freely when the plants are in leaf, suspended during the summer season of dormancy. Repotting is likely to be needed about every third year. Overcrowding of the bulbs due to their multiplication signals the need for this. Propagation is by offsets, seed, bulb cuttings, and leaf cuttings. Other species presumably will prosper under conditions approximating those that suit *L. socialis.*

LEDUM (Lè-dum)—Labrador-Tea, Wild-Rosemary. Depending upon the botanical authority followed, the number of species of *Ledum* varies from three to ten. The tendency is to accept the more conservative figure. Belonging in the heath family ERICACEAE, the group consists of erect or spreading, freely-branched, evergreen shrubs of cold-temperate, alpine, and arctic regions, in the northern hemisphere. The name derives from *ledon*, the ancient

Greek name for unrelated *Cistus.* The name Labrador-tea applied to one species reminds us that its leaves served as a tea substitute during the American Revolution.

Ledums have thick, leathery, alternate, undivided, toothless, stalkless or nearly stalkless leaves, and crowded, terminal clusters (racemes) of short-stalked, white flowers. The blooms have calyxes with five very short teeth, corollas of five spreading, separate petals, five to eleven slender-stalked stamens, and a slender style. The fruits are capsules that open from the base upward into five parts.

Labrador-tea (*L. groenlandicum* syn. *L. latifolium*) is native from Greenland to Alaska, New Jersey, Pennsylvania, Michigan, Wisconsin, and Minnesota. Up to 3 feet in height, it has densely-hairy shoots and younger parts often with resinous dots. The leaves are lanceolate to narrowly-elliptic or oblong, ¾ inch to 2 inches long or somewhat longer, with rolled-under margins. Their dark green upper sides at first are slightly-hairy. Their under surfaces have a dense, felty covering of persistent, rusty hairs that effectively conceals the midribs. About ½ inch wide, the flowers have five to eight stamens. Dwarf *L. g. compactum* has broader leaves and smaller clusters of blooms.

Ledum groenlandicum

Ledum groenlandicum (flowers)

Wild-rosemary (*L. palustre*), of the northern parts of Europe and Asia, differs from Labrador-tea in the midribs on the undersides of its leaves not being hidden by felt, but being more or less exposed, and in the flowers having usually ten, but varying from seven to eleven stamens. The leaves are linear, linear-oblong or sometimes oblong. A low, spreading variety is *L. p. decumbens.* Native to eastern Asia, *L. p. diversipilosum* (syns. *L. p. dilatum, L. hypoleucum*) has somewhat wider leaves than the typical species.

Ledum palustre diversipilosum

Western American *L. glandulosum* in the wild ranges from Alberta and British Columbia to Wyoming and California. Quite variable, it attains heights of up to 6 feet, and differs from the kinds discussed above in having leaves elliptic, ovate, to oblong, and ¾ inch to 2 inches long, without rolled-under margins. Also, their undersides are glaucous, scaly and usually resinous-glandular, rather than densely felted with longish hairs. The ½-inch-wide flowers have ten stamens. From the typical species *L. g. columbianum* (syn. *L. columbianum*) differs in having leaves with rolled-under margins and shoots and under leaf surfaces with very short, stiff, white hairs and fewer resinous granules.

Ledum glandulosum columbianum

Garden and Landscape Uses and Cultivation. Where summers are cool these excellent shrubs are admirable for bog gardens and other wet-soil areas. If the soil is acid they get along under somewhat drier conditions, but not where their roots become really dry. They are intolerant of high temperatures and arid air. Less hardy than the others, which may be grown far north in Canada, *L. glandulosum* is unlikely to survive climates more severe than that of southern New England. In suitable locations ledums need no special care. They can be raised from seed sown in moist acid soil and from cuttings made in late summer from firm shoots. Careful division in early spring is also satisfactory.

LEEA (Le-èa). Inhabiting the Old World tropics, *Leea* includes about seventy species. By some it is placed in the grape family VITACEAE, by others a family of its own, the leea family LEEACEAE. Its name commemorates the distinguished English nurseryman James Lee, who died in 1795.

Shrubs, small trees, or rarely herbaceous plants, unlike most of the grape family in being without tendrils, leeas have sometimes prickly stems. Their often very large leaves are alternate, one-, two-, or three-times-pinnate, or more rarely of three or of one leaflet. Usually they are toothed. The little, reddish, yellow, or greenish blooms are many together in clusters, generally erect and at the ends of the branches, more rarely pendulous or from the leaf axils. The calyx and corolla are usually five-parted, in a very few species four-parted. There are as many stamens as corolla parts. The fruits are berries.

One of the best known leeas, *L. amabilis* is a native of Borneo. This small tree has leaves with five to nine rather widely spaced, stalked, toothed, velvety, elliptic leaflets up to 6 inches long or longer, bronzy-green above, and in cultivated plants at least, with a pronounced white stripe along each side of the red mid-vein, and on the undersides claret-red with a light green center stripe. When they first

Leea amabilis

unfold the leaves are rich, bronzy-red. Variety *L. a. splendens* has leafstalks, midribs, and leaf undersides red.

Quite variable *L. sambucina*, which ranges in the wild from tropical Asia to Australia, has leaves two- or three-times, or sometimes perhaps only once-pinnately-divided. They may be 3½ to 4½ feet in length and have toothed leaflets varying considerably in size and shape. The greenish-white flowers have no display value. The fruits are about the size of peppercorns. Attractive *L. s. roehrsiana* has once-pinnate leaves, bronze-green when young, and with wavy margins. They are usually not over 1½ feet long.

A shrub, its leaves three-times-pinnately-divided, *L. coccinea* begins bearing attractive clusters of pink blooms when quite small. In bud its flowers are red. They open to display stamens tipped with yellow anthers. The leaflets, oblong-lanceolate and toothed, are loosely arranged, so that the leaves have somewhat the aspect of those of *Polyscias fruticosa*. The flowers, ½ inch in diameter, are in clusters about 3 inches wide. This is a native of Burma. A more recent introduction to horticulture, *L. rubra*, of India, Burma, and Malaya, is a small shrub or subshrub 1 foot to 2 feet tall, with twice- or thrice-pinnate, toothed, dark bronzy leaves, with elliptic ovate leaflets 3 to 4 inches long. The flowers, many together in clusters, are brick-red in bud and open with pink insides and red outsides to the petals. The berries are ¼ inch in diameter and deep red.

Leea rubra

Garden and Landscape Uses. Adaptable only to the moist tropics and warm subtropics, and for cultivation in tropical greenhouses, the leeas described are highly decorative and easy to grow. Habits of growth, foliage, and in some kinds, flowers and fruits, are attractive.

Cultivation. Where high temperatures and high humidity prevail leeas prosper in ordinary fertile soil drained sufficiently to remove surplus moisture, but never excessively dry. They do well in part-shade, but stand sun. In greenhouses the minimum temperature on winter nights should be 60°F. At other times considerably more warmth is appreciated. Shade from strong summer sun is required. Pruning, to shape or contain to size greenhouse specimens, is done in late winter or spring, and then repotting is given attention. The receptacles must be thoroughly drained. From spring to fall water leeas generously and give well-rooted specimens regular applications of dilute liquid fertilizer. It is better not to fertilize in winter, and then the soil is kept drier than at other times, even according to the advice of some growers, to the extent that some of the foliage drops. Propagation is by cuttings, air layering, and seed.

LEECHEE. See Litchi.

LEEK. Less well known in North America than their merits deserve, leeks are onion relatives that, like onions, belong to the lily family LILIACEAE. Botanically *Allium porrum*, they are of Old World ancestry, probably of Mediterranean region origin. Leeks are esteemed for their elongated, cylindrical, stemlike bulbous lower parts, scarcely wider at their bases than above. These, less strongly flavored than onions, are eaten boiled and cooked in other ways, such as in soups and stews. The bluish-green, strap-shaped leaves are in two ranks.

Soil for leeks must be deep, fertile, and fairly moist. A sunny location is needed. Prepare it by spading, rotary tilling, or plowing and incorporating liberal quantities of decayed manure, compost, or other humus-providing organic material as well as a dressing of a complete garden fertilizer.

Leeks need a long season of continuous growth. Good crops can be had from outdoor sowings, but in many sections superior results come from sowing early indoors or on a hotbed and transplanting to the garden when there is no longer danger of frost. An indoor temperature of 60 to 65°F is satisfactory for germination. When the seedlings are big enough to handle comfortably transplant them 2 inches apart in flats and grow them in a sunny greenhouse or hotbed where the temperature at night is 50 to 55°F, and that by day a few degrees higher.

Outdoor sowings are made as early in spring as the ground can be brought into suitable condition. Sow in a fertile seed bed of crumbly soil in rows 6 to 8 inches apart. If the seedlings come up too thickly, thin them to about 1 inch apart. Unlike many vegetables to be transplanted, leeks are left in the seed bed until quite big, 6 inches or so tall. Keep the seed bed free of weeds and reasonably moist. Transplant in June to where the crop is to mature.

Two chief modes of planting are advocated, both based on the desirability of securing produce with as long, white, succulent stem portions as possible. You may dig out a vertical-sided trench or ditch about 6 inches deep and as wide as the blade of a spade, spreading the excavated soil along the sides of the trench, then fork into the bottom of the trench a generous amount of manure or compost. Plant the young leeks in a single row or in two rows 6 inches apart along the bottom of the trench, allowing 8 to 9 inches between individuals in the rows. As the leeks grow and the stems elongate, gradually fill back the soil removed in digging the trench. This excludes light from

Leeks growing in trenches

the stems and blanches them. The second method consists of planting in holes punched in the soil with a dibble about as thick as a broom handle and short-pointed or rounded at its base rather than long-tapering. Let the holes be 6 to 8 inches apart in rows 1 foot to 1¼ feet apart. Make the holes 6 inches deep or, and this is particularly recommended if the soil is not a loose one, make a furrow 3 or 4 inches deep and along its bottom punch the planting holes to a depth of 3 inches. Lift the leeks (they should be 6 or 7 inches long) from the seed bed or flats and trim off the bottoms of their long roots so that they can be easily dropped into the holes and, to effect a balance between roots and tops, the upper one-third of the foliage. Drop one plant into each hole and pour in water. Do not fill back any soil. Earth will gradually wash into the holes as the season advances.

After-planting care consists chiefly of keeping down weeds by frequent shallow cultivation and supplying water in generous amounts during dry weather. A light dressing of a fertilizer that supplies readily available nitrogen, such as nitrate of soda or urea, may be given with advantage about a month after planting. To secure the maximum length of blanched stem portions as the plants grow, gradually hill soil along the rows, but not to a height that it collects in the bases of the leaves.

Young leeks planted in individual holes

Planting young leeks in holes made along the bottom of a furrow

Harvesting leeks, which are very hardy to cold, begins in early fall and continues until spring. In regions of severe winters deep freezing of the ground is likely to make winter digging difficult or impossible. This may be alleviated to some extent by mulching the rows in fall after the ground has frozen to a depth of an inch or two with straw or other suitable material held in place to prevent blowing, or the leeks may be dug with root balls attached and be stored like celery in a root cellar or

The harvest: (a) Dug for use

(b) Trimmed for the kitchen or for sale

other cool, humid place indoors or in an outdoor pit.

Varieties of leeks are not numerous. The chief ones are 'American Flag', which has comparatively slender, tall, edible parts, and thicker and squatter 'Italian Winter' and 'Musselburg'. This crop is remarkably free of diseases and pests.

LEGGY. This term is used by gardeners to describe plants that have stems unnaturally or undesirably long usually as a result of mismanagement. Often such specimens are devoid or sparse of foliage in their lower parts and the internodes (distances between the joints) of the stems are often longer than they should be. Common causes of legginess are crowding plants together, lack of adequate light, and too high temperatures. Excessive supplies of nitrogen in the form of fertilizers may also encourage legginess.

LEGOUSIA (Legoù-sia)—Venus' Looking Glass. This genus, previously known as *Specularia*, differs from the bellflowers (*Campanula*), to which it is closely related, in its flowers having long, slender ovaries. The flowers are wheel-shaped (rotate) or slightly saucer- rather than bell-shaped, as they most usually, but not always, are in *Campanula*. The name *Legousia* commemorates Bénigne Legouz de Gerland, a French botanist, who died in 1772. The genus consists of fifteen species of annuals of temperate parts of the northern hemisphere and South America. They are in the bellflower family CAMPANULACEAE.

Legousias are erect or decumbent, hairy or hairless. They have alternate leaves with toothed or toothless margins. The flowers have deeply three- to five-lobed calyxes and corollas with five deep lobes (petals). There are five stamens and a style with three stigmas. The fruits are slender capsules.

The only kind ordinarily grown in gardens is the Venus' looking glass (*L. speculum-veneris* syn. *Specularia speculum-veneris*), a pretty native of Europe, North

Africa, and western Asia. Hairless or nearly so, it is up to 1½ feet tall and has oblong to spatula-shaped, toothed leaves ½ inch to 2 inches long. Its violet-blue or white, starry flowers, solitary or in twos or threes on stalks from the upper leaf axils, are about ¾ inch in diameter. Their sepals are prominent and reflexed. Variety *L. s. grandiflora* has blooms about 1 inch wide. The flowers of *L. s. alba* are white. Double-flowered varieties are known.

Garden Uses and Cultivation. The species described is an easily grown annual suitable for flower beds. It thrives in sunny places in ordinary soil and is raised by sowing seeds outdoors in spring where the plants are to remain. The seedlings are thinned out as soon as they are big enough to handle easily, to an extent sufficient to prevent excessive crowding.

LEGUME. Plants of the pea family LEGU-MINOSAE are leguminous. Technically the fruits (seed pods) of such plants are legumes. Familiar examples are beans, clovers, lupines, and peas.

LEGUMINOSAE—Pea Family. Horticulturally and economically one of the most important plant families, this by some authorities is treated as three families, the PAPILIONACEAE, MIMOSACEAE, and CAESALPINIACEAE. In this Encyclopedia it is accepted as one, the LEGUMINOSAE, for which an alternative name is FABACEAE. The separate families are considered as subfamilies under the names *Papilionoideae*, *Mimosoideae*, and *Caesalpinioideae*.

Of practically worldwide natural distribution, the 12,000 species of this family are accommodated in 600 genera. Dicotyledons, they include trees, shrubs, vines, herbaceous perennials, biennials, and annuals of diverse habits and habitats. Among them are sorts that inhabit inhospitable deserts; others are aquatics and vast numbers are intermediate in their needs for water. Many prosper in poor and infertile soils, their success largely dependent on their ability to fix and make use of significant amounts of free atmospheric nitrogen.

Nitrogen fixation is common in nearly all leguminous plants (legumes). It is effected in peculiar small tubercles on the roots that contain bacteria that convert atmospheric nitrogen into a form usable by the plant. Because of this, such legumes as cowpeas, clovers, and soy beans are much favored as green manures. They enrich the soil with nitrogen.

Plants of the family LEGUMINOSAE have usually alternate, rarely opposite leaves, generally pinnate, much less often undivided or of leaflets arranged in palmate fashion. Sometimes they have terminal tendrils. With many acacias and some other sorts, the leaves are represented by phyllodes (expanded, leaflike leafstalks).

In *Ulex* and some other kinds they are tiny and inconspicuous, whereas in some, for example, *Carmichaelia*, the stems are much flattened, the leaves scalelike. Nearly always the leaves of legumes exhibit sleep movements by "closing" at night, moving upward, downward, or in other fashion so that their surfaces are vertical rather than horizontal. In the sensitive plants *Mimosa* and *Neptunia*, these same movements take place immediately the leaves are touched or in other ways irritated, recovery taking place after an elapse of time and slowly. The telegraph plant (*Desmodium gyrans*) has leaves with small side leaflets that so long as the temperature is sufficiently high move continuously.

The flowers of plants of this family are in terminal or axillary racemes, crowded heads, or solitary. They typically have five sepals generally more or less united, five or rarely one or no petals, few to numerous stamens, one style, and one stigma. The fruits are one-celled pods called legumes.

Pea-like flowers, markedly asymmetrical and with an upstanding standard or banner petal behind the others, two lateral wing petals, and a pair of basal petals more or less united into a keel enclosing the usually ten, but sometimes fewer stamens, separate or one free and the others joined, are characteristic of the subfamily *Papilionoideae* (examples beans, clovers, lupines, peas, wisterias). This subfamily is widely dispersed throughout temperate, subtropical, and tropical regions.

Pea-shaped flowers, like those of this sweet pea, are characteristic of the subfamily *Papilionoideae* of the family LEGUMINOSAE

Not pea-like or only slightly so, the blooms of the subfamily *Caesalpinioideae* (examples *Bauhinia*, *Caesalpinia*, *Cassia*, *Cercis*, *Gleditsia*) are asymmetrical and have the upper petal in front of the others and ten or fewer usually separate stamens. Members of this group are mostly tropical or subtropical.

This *Cassia closiana* has flowers typical of the subfamily *Caesalpinioideae* of the family LEGUMINOSAE

Small, symmetrical flowers are characteristic of the subfamily *Mimosoideae* (examples *Acacia*, *Albizia*, *Calliandra*, *Mimosa*). They have petals usually united in their lower parts and few to numerous generally separate or variously joined stamens. The majority of the species of this subfamily are tropical or subtropical.

The tiny symmetrical flowers of the subfamily *Mimosoideae* of the family LEGUMINOSAE are in crowded heads as in: (a) *Acacia baileyana*

(b) *Albizia lebbeck*

Cultivated genera of the LEGUMINOSAE include these: *Abrus, Acacia, Adenanthera, Adenocarpus, Albizia, Amburana, Amherstia, Amicia, Amorpha, Amphicarpaea, Andira, Anthyllis, Apios, Arachis, Astragalus, Baphia, Baptisia, Barklya, Bauhinia, Bolusanthus, Bossiaea, Brachysema, Brownea, Brya, Butea, Caesalpinia, Cajanus, Calicotome, Calliandra, Calophaca, Calpurnia, Camoensia, Camptosema, Campylotropis, Canavalia, Caragana, Carmichaelia, Cassia, Castanospermum, Centrosema, Ceratonia, Cercidium, Cercis, Chorizema, Cicer, Cladrastis, Clianthus, Clitoria, Colutea, Colvillea, Copaifera, Coronilla, Crotalaria, Cytisus, Dalbergia, Dalea, Daviesia, Delonix, Derris, Desmanthus, Desmodium, Detarium, Dillwynia, Dolichos, Dorycnium, Ebenus, Enterolobium, Erinacea, Erythrina, Eutaxia, Galega, Genista, Gleditsia, Gliricidia, Glycine, Glycyrrhiza, Gompholobium, Goodia, Gourliea, Gymnocladus, Haematoxylon, Halimodendron, Hardenbergia, Hedysarum, Hippocrepis, Hovea, Hymenaea, Indigofera, Inga, Kennedia, Krameria, Laburnocytisus, Laburnum, Lathyrus, Lens, Lespedeza, Leucaena, Lonchocarpus, Lotus, Lupinus, Lysidice, Lysiloma, Maackia, Maughania, Medicago, Melilotus, Millettia, Mimosa, Mucuna, Myrospermum, Myroxylon, Neptunia, Notospartium, Olneya, Onobrychis, Ononis, Ormosia, Oxylobium, Oxytropis, Pachyrhizus, Parkia, Parkinsonia, Parochetus, Peltophorum, Petalostemon, Petteria, Phaseolus, Phyllocarpus, Pickeringia, Piptadenia, Piptanthus, Pisum, Pithecellobium, Platymiscium, Podalyria, Pongamia, Prosopis, Psophocarpus, Psoralea, Pueraria, Pultenaea, Rhynchosia, Robinia, Sabinea, Samanea, Saraca, Schizolobium, Schotia, Schrankia, Scorpiurus, Securigera, Sesbania, Sophora, Spartium, Strongylodon, Strophostyles, Sutherlandia, Swainsona, Tamarindus, Templetonia, Tephrosia, Thermopsis, Tipuana, Trifolium, Trigonella, Ulex, Vicia, Vigna, Virgilia, Willardia,* and *Wisteria.*

LEHUA is *Metrosideros collinus.*

LEIOPHYLLUM (Leio-phýllum) — Sand-Myrtle. Some authorities regard the genus *Leiophyllum,* of the heath family ERICACEAE, as consisting of one species with two varieties, other accept one or both of the varieties as separate species. The first interpretation is followed here. The genus is endemic to eastern North America. It differs from closely allied *Ledum* in the manner in which its anthers open. The name derives from the Greek *leios,* smooth, and *phyllon,* a leaf, and refers to the foliage.

Sand-myrtles are low, much-branched, compact or prostrate, evergreen shrubs with small, alternate or opposite, short-stalked, undivided, leathery leaves crowded on slender stems, and many terminal, umbel-like clusters of white or pink-tinged flowers in spring. The blooms have five sepals about one-half as long as the five spreading, separate petals, ten slender stamens, and a slender style no longer than

the stamens. The fruits are small, many-seeded, egg-shaped capsules.

The box sand-myrtle (**L. buxifolium**) in its typical form is restricted as a wildling to New Jersey. About 1½ feet in height and upright, it has usually alternate, oblong to obovate-oblong leaves under ½ inch long and paler beneath than on their glossy upper surfaces. Its flowers, with stamens about twice as long as the petals, are ap-

Leiophyllum buxifolium

proximately ⅓ inch across and have short hairless stalks. Variety *L. b. hugeri* (syn. *L. hugeri*) has alternate leaves up to ½ inch long, and finely-glandular-hairy stalks to its flowers, the stamens of which are about as long as the petals. It is native from New Jersey to South Carolina and Kentucky. The Allegheny sand-myrtle (*L. b. prostratum* syn. *L. lyonii*) is much lower than the others and prostrate. It has mostly opposite, ovate to elliptic-oblong leaves, about ¼ inch long, and hairy flower stalks. This variety is endemic in the mountains of North Carolina and Tennessee.

Leiophyllum buxifolium prostratum

Garden and Landscape Uses. Although less showy than many shrubs of the heath family, sand-myrtles are pretty and pleasant additions to gardens. They are most

effective in groups, but single specimens may be adequate in small-scale rock gardens and other intimate landscapes. They associate especially well with heaths, heathers, azaleas, and suchlike plants and are are hardy in southern New England. In fall their foliage turns bronzy-green.

Cultivation. Sandy, peaty, acid soil affords suitable conditions for these plants. They prosper in full sun or part-day shade. Propagation is by seeds, which are exceedingly small and should not be more than barely covered with soil, by layering, and by cuttings taken in late summer and inserted in a mixture of peat moss and sand, under mist or in a cool greenhouse propagating bench. A mulch of peat moss or other acid organic material is beneficial to plants in the garden.

LEITNERIA (Leit-nèria)—Corkwood. The one species of *Leitneria* constitutes the corkwood family LEITNERIACEAE. It is most nearly related to bayberries, willows, and populars. Corkwood gained its common name in recognition of characteristics of its wood, which is sometimes used for floats and stoppers, and is the lightest of any North American plant. It weighs less than cork. The scientific name commemorates Dr. E. T. Leitner, a German naturalist killed in the Seminole war in 1838.

Corkwood (**L. floridana**) inhabits swampy, often tidal regions in Georgia, Florida, Missouri, Arkansas, and Texas. It varies considerably in height, leaf shape, and other details, sometimes becoming an open-headed tree up to a little more than 20 feet tall, at other times remaining shrubby. It is deciduous and spreads freely by suckers. The hairy-stalked leaves are alternate, pointed, elliptic-lanceolate to lanceolate, and without lobes or teeth. Arranged in five rows, they are bright green and 4 to 6 inches long. Their upper sides are hairy at least along the veins, their silky-hairy undersides are paler. The flowers develop before the leaves. They are in grayish, erect catkins. Those of male flowers curve outward, are ¾ inch to 1½ inches long, and have silky-hairy bracts. Female catkins are smaller and more slender than the males and are straight, rigid, and spikelike. Male flowers have three to twelve stamens, but are without sepals or petals. The females have small scales, perhaps representing petals, at the base of the ovary, and a slender style. One to four light olive-brown, erect fruits ½ to ¾ inch long develop on each female catkin. They are structured like little plums, but have leathery flesh.

Garden Uses and Cultivation. Corkwood is scarcely ornamental, but because of its interest is cultivated in botanical collections and perhaps elsewhere. It needs wet or moist soil of a peaty character and an open location. Stock obtained from the northern limits of the natural range of the species is hardy in southern New England and New York. Propagation is by suckers and by seed.

LEITNERIACEAE—Corkwood Family. The characteristics of this family of dicotyledons are those of its only genus, *Leitneria*.

LEMAIREOCEREUS (Lemaireo-cèreus). Interpreted in the narrow sense favored by those who split cactus genera finely, which is done in this Encyclopedia as a matter of practical convenience rather than conviction that it necessarily reflects the best botany, many species conservative botanists accept in *Lemaireocereus*, of the cactus family CACTACEAE, are referred by other botanists to *Heliabravoa*, *Hertrichocereus*, *Isolatocereus*, *Machaerocereus*, *Marginatocereus*, *Marshallocereus*, *Polaskia*, *Ritterocereus*, and *Stenocereus*, and in this Encyclopedia are treated under those names. When so narrowed, *Lemaireocereus* consists at most of about six species and according to some interpretations only one. The name commemorates Charles Lemaire, a French cactus fancier, who died in 1871.

Lemaireocereus, undetermined species

The type species and the one indisputably entitled to the name **L. hollianus** is Mexican. It has erect stems branched from their bases and 12 to 15 feet tall by 1½ to 2½ inches thick. They have eight to fourteen ribs and prominent clusters of spines each of eight to fourteen needle-like radials ½ inch to 1½ inches long and three to five thickish, flattened, red-based, gray centrals 1½ to 4 inches long. The bell-shaped, ivory-white flowers open at night. They are 1¼ to 1½ inches wide and have scaly, hairy perianth tubes 3 to 4 inches long. The ovaries and fruits are also scaly and hairy. The latter are egg-shaped, 2½ to 3½ inches long, and brownish-green.

Garden and Landscape Uses and Cultivation. The attractive species described is suitable for outdoor cultivation in mild desert and semidesert regions and for in-

clusion in greenhouse collections of cactuses. Prospering in sunny locations and porous soil, it is easily increased by cuttings and seed. For more information see Cactuses.

LEMANDARIN is *Citrus limonia*.

LEMMAPHYLLUM (Lemma-phýllum). Five species of creeping ferns of the polypody family POLYPODIACEAE comprise *Lemmaphyllum*. They are natives from Japan to the Himalayas. The name comes from the Greek *lemma*, a scale, and *phyllon*, a leaf. It alludes to the leaf shapes of the plants.

Lemmaphyllums are epiphytes (plants that grow on trees without taking nourishment from their hosts). They have slender rhizomes that cling tightly to trunks and branches and two distinct types of fronds (leaves). The spore-bearing (fertile) fronds are linear-elliptic. The spore-capsules form a pair of longitudinal lines on their under surfaces. The barren fronds are fleshy, mostly ovate to nearly round.

Grown in collections of choice tropical ferns, **L. microphyllum** (syns. *Drymoglossum microphyllum*, *D. carnosum*) forms a matlike growth of threadlike, rooting, creeping rhizomes and glossy, thick sterile fronds more or less overlapping in shingle fashion. They are elliptic to nearly round and ½ inch to 2 inches long. The fertile fronds, leathery, linear-spatula-shaped, narrowed to their bases, much longer than wide, are 2 to 3 inches long. The spore-clusters form a line on each side of the midrib, midway between it and the leaf margin. This charming fern is a native of Japan, Taiwan, and Korea.

Lemmaphyllum microphyllum

Garden and Landscape Uses and Cultivation. The species described is useful outdoors only in the humid tropics. It is easy to grow in tropical greenhouses where a minimum temperature of about 60°F and a humid atmosphere are maintained. Sufficient shade to offset any danger of the foliage being scorched is needed, not more.

Best results are had by attaching the plant to a slab of tree fern trunk or to a piece of cork bark. Watering should be done to keep the roots always moderately moist. Propagation is easy by division and spores. For more information see Ferns.

LEMNA (Lém-na)—Duckweed. The duckweeds are more likely to be local nuisances to gardeners than plants to be sought. Some rapidly cover the surfaces of shallow, stagnant pools with their floating flakes of greenery until considerable expanses of water look almost like solid carpets of lawn; others are underwater plants. They are sometimes grown in aquariums, in botanical gardens, and in collections of plants used for teaching. The group is cosmopolitan in its natural distribution. There are fifteen species. The name *Lemna* is perhaps from the Greek *limnos*, a lake, in allusion to the plants' habitat. Together with *Spirodela*, *Wolffiella*, and, smallest of all flowering plants, *Wolffia*, they constitute the duckweed family LEMNACEAE, which most botanists consider to be akin to the arum family ARACEAE.

Duckweeds have a simple plant body, without separate stems and leaves, called a thallus. This may be round, ovate, or obovate, and is rarely more, often less, than ⅓ inch across. Each plant has a single root, peculiar because it is weighted with a large, comparatively heavy root cap that holds it in a vertical position. The rarely borne microscopic flowers are in two pouches at the edges of the thallus. The male flowers consist of a single stamen, the females of one pistil. They occur in groups of two males and one female.

A pond with patches of *Lemna* floating on it

One of the commonest species, indigenous throughout North America as well as much of the Old World, is **L. minor,** which occurs as solitary individuals or joined in colonies of up to eight individuals. Its thallus is convex on both sides and ⅙ inch, or often less, in diameter. In regions where

Part of a colony of *Lemna minor*

the water freezes, duckweeds sink to the bottom in fall and rise to the surface in spring. They provide food for ducks, geese, and some other birds, beavers, muskrats, and a variety of other animals, and some fish.

Garden Uses and Cultivation. The garden uses are those indicated at the beginning of this discussion. The plants grow readily and multiply rapidly, especially in good light, by natural offsets, which soon float free from the parent. They grow with most abandon in still water containing nutrients, especially nitrates and lime. The only attention necessary is to skim off and remove unwanted progeny so that they do not become so numerous that they inhibit the growth of other, generally more desirable plants.

LEMNACEAE — Duckweed Family. Comprising forty species of dicotyledons distributed among four genera, the duckweed family LEMNACEAE consists of tiny to minute floating or more rarely submerged plants with leaflike organs not differentiated into stems and leaves. The unisexual flowers consist of a single stamen or carpel. Genera dealt with in this Encyclopedia are *Lemna*, *Spirodela*, *Wolffia*, and *Wolffiella*.

LEMON. The familiar fruit of this name is discussed in the next entry. Other plants of which the word lemon is part of their common names are these: garden-lemon (*Cucumis melo chito*), lemon balm (*Melissa officinalis*), lemon bee-balm or lemon-mint (*Monarda citriodora*), lemon bottle brush (*Callistemon citrinus*), lemon grass (*Cymbopogon citratus*), lemon-mint (*Mentha piperita citriodora*), lemon-verbena (*Aloysia triphylla*), lemon-vine (*Pereskia aculeata*), and water-lemon (*Passiflora laurifolia*).

LEMON. This well-known fruit is *Citrus limon*. The familiar type has not been found in the wild, but there is little doubt its ancestors were natives of the Himalayan region of India. Lemons are believed to have been cultivated in the Mediterranean

region as early as the end of the second century B.C.; they were brought to the New World by Columbus on his second voyage in 1493.

Rather open-headed trees, usually more or less spiny, lemons are of vigorous growth and have upright-spreading branches. Their fairly large flowers are tinged purple on the undersides of the petals. Tight-skinned, the fruits, characteristically have a prominent nipple at the apex and usually very acid, pale straw-colored flesh. When mature, commonly lemon-yellow, they are much esteemed for ade, for flavoring and garnishing foods and beverages, their rinds for making candied peel. Lemon juice, citric acid, and calcium citrate are important products.

The chief varieties of typical lemons include 'Eureka', of which there are several minor variants including 'Cascade' and 'Cook'. These, favored because they are practically spineless, crop while young and throughout the year. Variety 'Lisbon' is similar to 'Eureka', but has smoother, less markedly ribbed fruits. Its minor variants include 'Bradbury', 'Cavers', and 'Deaver'. In growth habit resembling 'Lisbon', but less upright and less thorny, 'Villafranca' has fruits indistinguishable from those of 'Eureka'. It is chiefly represented in cultivation by its minor variants called 'Corona Foothill' and 'Galligan Lisbon'.

Lemon (foliage and flowers)

Lemon (fruits)

The 'Rough' lemon is a vigorous tree up to 25 feet tall with many small thorns. Its very variable, more or less spherical-obovate fruits are 2¼ to 3¾ inches long and rough at their apexes. The chief use of this variety, which is naturalized in southern Florida, is as an understock upon which to bud or graft choicer citruses.

The 'Meyer' lemon, probably a hybrid between a true lemon and some other species of *Citrus*, was introduced to the United States from near Peking, China, in 1908. On its own roots it attains a height of about 12 feet and becomes wider than high, but grown on a dwarfing rootstock is only about one-half as big. Because it stands heat well, yet is a little hardier than the sweet orange, it can be grown in re-

The 'Meyer' lemon as a pot plant

Fruits of the 'Meyer' lemon

gions unsuitable for the growth of most lemons. It begins bearing while young and has small to medium-sized, acid fruits with abundant juice. Esteemed as a landscape ornamental, as a producer of fruits for home use, and for growing in pots and tubs, it has a serious disadvantage responsible for its cultivation being banned by law in some citrus-growing regions. With respect to certain virus diseases the Meyer lemon acts as a sort of Typhoid Mary, harboring the viruses without itself showing symptoms, but serving as a reservoir of infection for other citruses.

The 'Ponderosa' or 'American Wonder' lemon, esteemed as something of a novelty dooryard tree, and for cultivating in pots and tubs, is a small, thorny tree with distantly-spaced leaves and large, grapefruit-like, obovoid, agreeably flavored, seedy, acid fruits not infrequently weighing 2 pounds. It originated in Maryland about 1886. Thought to be a hybrid between a lemon and a citron (*Citrus medica*), this begins bearing at an early age.

The 'Ponderosa' lemon as a pot plant:
(a) In bloom

(b) In fruit

Fruit of the 'Ponderosa' lemon

The 'Otaheite' lemon or 'Otaheite' orange, as it is frequently called, is markedly different from other lemons; it is sometimes accorded the rank of a separate species under the name of *C. taitensis*. Commonly grown as an indoor ornamental in pots and tubs, this was offered for sale as a pot plant in the United States in 1882. It had been taken from England to France in 1813. A smallish tree, this has deep yellow, nearly spherical fruits approximately 2 inches in diameter, with juicy, orange, insipid or distasteful flesh.

The 'Otaheite' lemon as a pot plant

Garden and Landscape Uses and Cultivation. In addition to being cultivated for their fruits, lemons are planted to some extent in favorable climates as ornamentals. Although hardier than limes, regular sorts are considerably less so than oranges and grapefruits and so are suitable for outdoor planting only in limited areas of the continental United States, the chief region for their commercial production being coastal southern California. Temperatures of 30°F and below cause young fruits to drop. This can also come from a sudden onset of temperatures of 95°F or above. At 28°F or below young shoots are killed and severe damage by sun scald to fruits results. High winds can bruise these fruits.

Soils of various types produce good lemons, but poorly drained sites are to be avoided and so is soil containing alkali. Care must be taken not to unduly disturb the roots and so container or balled and burlapped trees are used for planting. It is usual to prune young trees to be transplanted back to a height of 2 to 2½ feet a few weeks before moving them. Planting distances of 25 to 30 feet between individuals are satisfactory.

Routine care involves generous fertilization with nitrogen and, in arid climates, regular irrigation. The maintenance of a mulch around the trees is advantageous. Pruning to maintain compactness of the heads of the trees so that danger from wind injury is minimized and to improve the number of fruits available for harvest-

ing in a desirable premature condition consists of thinning crowded branches and shortening laterals. Harvesting is done before the fruits attain maturity. They are stored to ripen. The cultivation of lemons in pots and tubs is as for container-grown oranges. Diseases and pests are those of oranges.

LEMONADE BERRY is *Rhus integrifolia*.

LEMONWOOD. This is a colloquial name for *Calycophyllum candidissimum* and *Pittosporum eugenioides*.

LENOPHYLLUM (Leno-phýllum). Sedum-like succulents numbering half a dozen species constitute *Lenophyllum*, of the orpine family CRASSULACEAE. They inhabit Texas and northern Mexico. The name, alluding to the form of the leaf, comes from the Greek *lenos*, a trough, and *phyllon*, a leaf.

Lenophyllums are perennials, branching freely from their bases and having along the lower parts of their stems thick, fleshy, opposite leaves with deeply-cupped upper surfaces. The flowers are in terminal racemes or interrupted spikes or are sometimes solitary. They are small and yellow and have five sepals and five petals, which because they are erect except for their recurved apexes give a tubular appearance to the bloom. There are ten stamens and five carpels.

Species cultivated include these: *L. guttatum*, of Mexico, up to 9 inches tall, has blunt, elliptic-ovate to rhomboidal leaves ¾ inch to 1½ inches long and about one-half as wide. They are gray flecked with dark purple. The about ¼-inch-long flowers have club-shaped sepals and are up to a dozen together on each branch of the inflorescence. *L. pusillum*, of uncertain provenance, but probably Mexican, 2 to 3 inches tall, has pointed leaves up to a little over ½ inch long and, at the ends of the stems, solitary flowers with pointed sepals. *L. texanum* (syns. *Sedum texanum*, *Villadia texanum*), of Texas and Mexico, 6 inches to over 1 foot tall, has pointed, elliptic-ovate to lanceolate leaves ½ inch to 1½ inches long. The flowers have lanceolate to ovate sepals and are in spikelike to somewhat paniculate racemes. *L. weinbergii*, has obovate-wedge-shaped, troughlike leaves up to a little over ½ inch long and wide. The flowers, in clusters of few, have club-shaped sepals. *L. acutifolium*, of California and Mexico, attains a height of about 4 inches. It has pointed-lanceolate leaves with slightly hollowed upper surfaces, and many small, greenish-yellow flowers.

Garden and Landscape Uses and Cultivation. The species described are suitable for collections of succulents, outdoors in warm, dry climates and in greenhouses and as window plants. They grow with

Lenophyllum acutifolium

great ease and are easily increased by cuttings, leaf cuttings, and seed. The leaves of *L. texanum* shed readily and in contact with earth soon give rise to new plants. Pans (shallow pots) are suitable containers for plants grown indoors. They must be well drained. Any porous soil suits. It should be kept dryish rather than constantly wet. Full sun is needed.

LENS (Léns)—Lentil. One of the about six species of *Lens*, of the pea family LEGUMINOSAE, the lentil has been cultivated for untold centuries as a source of nutritious food and for forage. In some parts of the world, notably in the Mediterranean region, it is a major agricultural crop. The genus name is the ancient one of the lentil. It is of interest that the lenses used in telescopes and microscopes were so named because they are shaped like lentil seeds. And red lentils were the chief ingredient of the mess of pottage for which Esau sold his birthright.

The sorts of *Lens*, native to the Mediterranean region and western Asia consist of herbaceous plants related to vetches (*Vicia*), but differing in having only one or two seeds in each pod. They have pinnate leaves with the terminal leaflet replaced by a tendril or bristle-like extension of the midrib. The small, whitish, pea-like flowers, solitary or in small clusters from the leaf axils, are followed by flattened seed pods.

The lentil (*L. culinaris* syn. *L. esculenta*) is an annual 1 foot to 1½ feet high with leaves of eight to fourteen small leaflets and usually a terminal tendril. Its bluish-white blooms are solitary or in twos or threes. The seed pods are ¾ inch long and brown.

Garden Uses and Cultivation. Rarely cultivated as a horticultural crop, the lentil is occasionally included in gardens in which food crops are displayed for educational purposes. It thrives with minimum care in porous dryish soils in warm, sunny locations. Sow seeds in early spring in rows 1½ to 2½ feet apart.

LENTEN-ROSE is *Helleborous orientalis.*

LENTIBULARIACEAE—Bladderwort Family. This family of aquatic and wet-soil carnivorous or insectivorous dicotyledons is of nearly worldwide natural distribution. It comprises four genera, about 170 species. Many of its sorts are without roots. Leaf types are very diverse. The flowers, usually in racemes or spikes, but sometimes solitary, are asymmetrical, have a two- to five-lobed calyx, a two-lipped corolla often with a spur, two stamens, generally no style, and a two-lobed stigma. The fruits are capsules. Genera cultivated are *Pinguicula* and *Utricularia.*

LENTIL is *Lens culinaris.*

LEONOTIS — Lion's Ear, Lion's Tail. One species of *Leonotis*, of the mint family LABIATAE, is a widespread native of the tropics, the other forty are restricted as wild plants to Africa. The name, from the Greek *leon*, a lion, and *ous*, an ear, alludes to the corollas of the flowers fancifuly resembling a lion's ear.

Leonotises include annuals, herbaceous perennials, and subshrubs. They have opposite, undivided, ovate to lanceolate leaves and, clustered in the axils of the upper ones, dense, mostly distantly-spaced whorls (tiers) of white to brilliant orange-red blooms that arch upward. The flowers have tubular calyxes with eight to ten ribs and the same number of teeth, and funnel-shaped, two-lipped corollas with tubes as long or longer than the calyxes. The upper lip of the corolla is densely-hairy and extends forward, the shorter, three-lobed, lower lip is deflexed. There are four arching stamens and a two-lobed style. The fruits consist of four nutlets that have much the appearance of seeds.

Most popular, the lion's ear or lion's tail (*L. leonurus*), a native of South Africa, is a showy-flowered subshrub 3 to 6 feet tall. It has hairy, four-angled, leafy stems. The leaves are short-stalked, coarsely-toothed, pubescent, lanceolate to oblanceolate, and 2 to 5 inches long. More than three times as long as the calyxes, the brilliant orange

Leonotis leonurus

or orange-red, or in variety *L. l. albiflora* white, woolly-hairy corollas of the flowers are 1½ to 2 inches long. The upper lips of the flowers are long, the lower ones much smaller. A peculiarity is that the lower lips wither within a few hours of expanding, but the upper ones remain in good condition for several days. The stamens and style do not protrude. This species has been much used in native medicine, and by the Hottentots for smoking like tobacco. It is one of the oldest cultivated South African plants. It was grown in Holland in 1663.

Also South African, *L. dysophylla* is a downy subshrub 2 to 3 feet tall, with ovate-lanceolate to lanceolate, coarsely-toothed leaves 2½ to 3½ inches long, and often broader than those of *L. leonurus*. The orange-yellow flowers, up to 1½ inches long, and in dense tiers, have spiny calyx teeth much longer than those of *L. leonurus*.

Annual *L. nepetaefolia*, 2 to 6 feet high, has four-angled stems, and long-stalked round-toothed, broad-ovate leaves up to 4 inches long by about as wide. The 1-inch-long, yellow to orange-red flowers have spiny bracts and are in very dense, distantly spaced, spherical, burrlike whorls up to about 3 inches in diameter. This inhabits the tropics of the Old and the New Worlds.

Garden and Landscape Uses. Exceedingly showy *L. leonurus* and other kinds are handsome for flower beds, the fronts of shrubberies, and similar places in warm climates, and for greenhouses. They thrive near the sea, and have blooms attractive for cutting. Ordinary well-drained soil of reasonable fertility gives good results, and a sunny location or one with a little part-day shade satisfies.

Cultivation. After flowering or at the beginning of a new season of growth, the old stems of perennial kinds are cut well back to encourage the development of new ones from the base, and at the beginning of each new growing season an application of a complete fertilizer is helpful. Staking may be needed, and during dry weather, watering.

In greenhouses new plants are raised annually. The perennials are usually started from cuttings rooted in late winter or spring, the annual from seed. The young plants are transferred successively from small to larger pots until as finals they occupy containers 6 to 9 inches in diameter. During their early lives the tips of the shoots are pinched out two or three times to encourage the development of branches. Staking receives attention. Throughout, the plants are grown in a well-ventilated greenhouse or, better still, in summer outdoors with their pots buried nearly to their rims in a bed of sand, ashes, peat moss, soil, or other medium that prevents excessive drying and keeps the roots cool. Regular watering to prevent the leaves from wilting is needed and, after the containers in which the plants are to bloom are filled with roots, dilute liquid fertilizer should be given at weekly intervals. Plants that have been outdoors during the summer are brought into a sunny greenhouse before the first frost. Indoors a night temperature of 50°F, with an increase by day of five to fifteen degrees, is satisfactory.

LEONTICE (Leoń-ti-ce). The up to ten species of *Leontice*, of the barberry family BERBERIDACEAE, inhabit southern Europe and western Asia. The name, derived from the Greek *leon*, a lion, alludes to a fanciful resemblance between the shape of the leaves and the footprint of a lion.

Spring-flowering, tuberous-rooted herbaceous perennials, these unusual plants have practically all basal, twice- or thrice-pinnate or pinnately-lobed leaves, and in racemes or panicles, small flowers with six to nine petal-like sepals, six petals much shorter than the sepals and sometimes reduced to scales or nectaries, six stamens, and one style. The fruits are bladdery capsules.

From 6 inches to 1 foot tall or somewhat taller **L. leontopetalum** has twice-three-

Leontice leontopetalum

Leontice leontopetalum (flowers)

parted leaves with ovate or obovate leaflets, and panicles of yellow flowers with showy sepals and scalelike petals.

Garden Uses and Cultivation. Not reliably hardy in the north, the sorts of *Leontice* are best adapted for rock gardens and similar plantings in mild, dry climates. They need well-drained soil, adequate moisture during their growing period, and dryness during their season of dormancy. Propagation is by seed.

LEONTOPODIUM (Leontopò-dium)—Edelweiss. Variable and taxonomically rather confusing, *Leontopodium* contains thirty species of Europe, Asia, and South America, chiefly of mountain regions. By far the most renowned is the edelweiss of the European Alps. The generic name, meaning lion's foot, is derived from the Greek *leon*, lion, and *pous*, foot. It refers to a fanciful resemblance the flannelly, starfish-like flower heads bear to the paws of the king of beasts. The genus belongs in the daisy family COMPOSITAE. It is allied to *Antennaria*, *Gnaphalium*, and *Anaphalis*. A distinguishing feature is the collar of usually white-woolly leaves or bracts that surrounds the flower heads. These, looking somewhat like petals, form the most conspicuous part of the "flowers" (really the inflorescences) of the more attractive species.

Leontopodiums are hardy herbaceous perennials. They vary in height according to kind and location where they grow from 1 inch to 1 foot and have tufts of undivided leaves, mostly basal, those on the erect or ascending stems alternate. At the tops of the stems are clusters of small heads of flowers of all disk florets that sit on collars of spreading bracts. The fruits are seedlike achenes.

Contrary to general opinion, leontopodiums are among the easiest of plants to raise and bloom. True, near cities where air pollution occurs, their floral stars are apt to be somewhat murky and less dazzlingly white than those produced in the purer atmosphere of high mountain regions. But edelweisses are by no means confined to alpine habitats. In the deserts and semi-deserts of Asia and central Europe they occur at quite low elevations. Typically they are xerophytes, plants adapted to grow where moisture is scarce and to conserve that which they obtain. This suggests to gardeners the conditions they need under cultivation. In Switzerland and adjacent mountain regions where much glamour has been generated and retailed regarding the edelweiss it is by no means uncommon. At altitudes of 5,500 to 7,000 feet it is one of the plentiful species in the mountain meadows. In Kashmir and elsewhere in the Himalayas other species ascend to 18,000 feet and possibly higher.

The edelweiss of central Europe (**L. alpinum**), usually 4 to 6 inches tall, is quite

Leontopodium alpinum

Leontopodium alpinum (flowers)

variable. Its best forms have most ample and satisfying flower heads. In poorer samples they are leaner and often bedraggled. Only the best are worth growing. Other species include **L. leontopodioides** (syn. *L. sibiricum*), which is often taller than *L. alpinum*, although at great elevations it may be quite dwarf. This has larger heads and narrower leaves than *L. alpinum*. It is a native of Russia to Korea. Noteworthy because of its intense lemon fragrance, **L. haplophylloides** (syn. *L. aloysiodorum*) is a native of China. Remarkable **L. ochroleucum**, of Turkestan, has flower heads covered with pale yellow instead of gray-white wool. The floral bracts of the solitary flower heads of **L. monocephalum,** of the Himalayas, are also pale lemon. From 9 inches to 1¼ feet tall, **L. palibinianum,** of northeastern Asia, has gray-hairy lanceolate to linear-lanceolate leaves and flower heads 2 to 2¼ inches wide with narrow bracts densely-white hairy on the upper surfaces, greenish beneath. Native to China and Japan, **L. japonicum** has rather loosely-arranged flower heads the bracts of which have rich green upper surfaces, silvery-white under ones. Western Chinese **L. wilsonii** is much like *L. japonicum* but is showier. It has narrower leaves with rolled-under margins and a star of white-hairy floral bracts up to 3½ inches

Leontopodium palibinianum

Leontopodium palibinianum (flowers)

Leontopodium wilsonii

Leontopodium stoechas

across. Another Chinese, vigorous *L. stoechas*, up to 2 feet tall, is a looser, more rangy plant than the other species described here. It has linear leaves up to 1½ inches long and abundantly produced flower heads with white, woolly bracts. Robust *L. calocephalum* (syn. *L. alpinum himalayanum*), of western China and Tibet, is up to 1¼ feet tall. Its lower lanceolate to linear-lanceolate leaves are usually withered by the time the flowers are fully developed. The upper leaves are shorter and ovate-lanceolate. Their upper surfaces are gray-silky-hairy to nearly hairless and their undersides are clothed with white to gray hairs. The flower heads are 3 to 4 inches across.

Leontopodium calocephalum

Garden Uses and Cultivation. These plants are most suitable for rock gardens, but are easy to grow in other places. Lean soil (earth not rich in nitrogen), sharply-drained and containing abundant lime, is ideal. In more nourishing mediums they become gross and unlovely, and in poorly drained places, in soil that does not permit the free passage of water and air, they soon die. Full sun is essential. Beyond these simple requirements edelweisses make no special demands. They are raised from seeds as easily as the commonest annuals. Sow them in spring, indoors or out, in well-drained pots or pans of porous sandy soil with which a sprinkling of ground limestone has been mixed. As soon as the seedlings are big enough to handle easily, transplant them to beds or flats of similar, coarser soil. Later set them in their permanent locations. Although edelweisses are true perennials the best results are often obtained by treating them as biennials and raising fresh plants every year.

LEONURUS (Leon-ùrus) — Motherwort. These plants have little claim to beauty. Their only recommendation to gardeners is based on interest they have as once-esteemed medicinal herbs. They serve no useful purpose in modern medicine. The genus *Leonurus* belongs in the mint family LABIATAE. It consists of about ten annuals, biennials, and herbaceous perennials, natives of Europe and Asia; some are naturalized in North America. They are of more or less weedy appearance, with much the aspect, when out of bloom, of ragweeds. The name is derived from the Greek *leon*, a lion, and *oura*, a tail; its implication is not clear.

The principle kind is the motherwort (*Leonurus cardiaca*), a native of central Asia, now established as a weed in waste places throughout much of eastern North America and as far west as Texas. Up to 4 or 5 feet tall, this stout perennial has erect,

Leonurus cardiaca

four-angled, branched, softly-hairy stems, and long-stalked, dull green leaves, in outline broadly-ovate to nearly round, with deep lobes that spread in handlike fashion. Their veins are strongly impressed on their upper sides. The chief leaves are five-lobed with the lobes three-toothed at their apexes. The uppermost leaves are smaller than those below and are three-lobed or sometimes only three-toothed. The tiny, washed-out-pink or lavender-pink flowers have scarcely any ornamental value. They are densely crowded in the axils of the upper leaves and bracts to form interrupted, cylindrical, terminal, leafy spikes. The outside of the upper lip of the corolla is densely-white-hairy.

Motherwort received this name because of its supposed efficacy in treating disorders of women. Particularly, it was believed to be useful in "allaying nervous irritability and inducing quiet and passivity of the whole nervous system." It was recommended for "strengthening and gladdening the heart." Of it, Culpepper says, "Venus owns this herb and it is under Leo. There is no better herb to drive melancholy vapors from the heart, to strengthen it and make the mind cheerful, blithe and merry." Culpepper lists other virtues, among them that it "killeth worms in the belly." Ladies who dosed themselves with motherwort (it was recommended that wineglassfuls of a strong infusion be taken) required fortitude, for it is one of the bitterest and most unpleasantly tasting of herbs. It is doubtful that patients felt particularly cheerful, blithe, and merry while imbibing. Less well known than *L. cardiaca* and decidedly more decorative, *L. sibiricus* is similar in its habit of growth. Its leaves are twice-lobed and its flowers, in dense axillary whorls that form interrupted, leafy, terminal spikes, are pale pink with a crimson lip.

Garden Uses and Cultivation. Only in herb and medicinal gardens is motherwort worthy of a place. It grows without difficulty in any ordinary soil, including those of a limestone character, and is completely hardy and perennial. It prospers in part-shade or sun and is easily raised from seed and by division. Single plants occupy at least a square yard of ground. The other species described here responds to similar conditions. It is suitable for naturalizing in informal areas.

LEOPARD and LEOPARD'S. These words occur as part of the common names of these plants: leopard orchid (*Ansellia*), leopard plant (*Ligularia tussilaginea*), and leopard's bane (*Doronicum* and *Senecio doronicum*).

LEPACHYS. See Ratibida.

LEPANTHES (Le-pánthes). Closely allied to *Pleurothallis*, the genus *Lepanthes* consists of approximately 100 species of the orchid family ORCHIDACEAE. It is native to the American tropics and subtropics including the West Indies. Its name, derived from the Greek *lepis*, a scale, and *anthos*, a flower, alludes to the manner in which the diminutive flowers are borne.

Lepantheses are small, tree-perching (epiphytic) plants that form tufts of erect slender stems with, at their apexes, one or rarely more fleshy or rigid leaves. The tiny, usually short-lived flowers are in spikes that originate from the bases of the leaves and are often brightly colored.

Densely-tufted *L. wageneri* is 2 to 3 inches tall. It has thick, broad-elliptic to broad-ovate or nearly circular leaves and short racemes of minute yellow flowers.

Lepanthes wageneri

Garden Uses and Cultivation. These are strictly plants for the avid collector of orchids. They respond to conditions appropriate for the sorts of *Pleurothallis* that prefer cool or intermediate greenhouse temperatures to those more tropical.

LEPECHINIA (Lepech-ínia)—Pitcher-Sage. One species previously named *Sphacele calycina*, and sometimes cultivated under that designation, is included in *Lepechinia*, a genus of forty species of the mint family LABIATAE, native from California to western South America, and in Hawaii. Its name commemorates the Russian botanist Lepechin.

Lepechinias are aromatic shrubs and subshrubs with opposite leaves, and often showy blooms in the axils of leafy bracts, forming short racemes. The flowers have bell-shaped, unequally-five-toothed calyxes that often increase in size as seeds form, and broad-tubed, five-lobed corollas, with one lobe larger than the others. There are four stamens of two lengths or nearly equal, and a slender, two-lobed style. The fruits are smooth, black nutlets (commonly called seeds).

Native to California, the pitcher-sage (*L. calycina* syn. *Sphacele calycina*) is cultivated in mild climates. From 2 to 5 feet tall, and becoming woody at the base, it is hairy or woolly, with erect stems and veiny, blunt, oblong-ovate to ovate, toothed leaves 2 to 4 inches in length, and short-stalked, except for the upper ones, which are stalkless. An inch long or a little longer, the dull white or pink blooms, veined and blotched with purple, appear in spring or early summer, usually singly in the axils of leafy bracts. Their calyxes enlarge as the fruits are formed and become quite showy.

Garden Uses and Cultivation. An open situation and ordinary soil is satisfactory for this species. Propagation is by seed and division.

LEPIDIUM (Lepíd-ium) — Pepper-Grass, Cress. The only species of horticultural interest of the 130 that constitute this group of the mustard family CRUCIFERAE, is common garden cress (*Lepidium sativum*). Its cultivation is discussed under Cress. The name *Lepidium* is from the Greek *lepidion*, a little scale, and refers to the shape of the pods.

Lepidiums are mostly weedy, annual, biennial, and perennial herbaceous or subshrubby plants with white or rarely yellowish, four-sepaled, four-petaled flowers, with normally two short and four longer stamens, but sometimes, as a result of abortion, with only two or four. The pistil has no style or only a very short one. The petals spread to form a cross. Ovate to obovate, the seed pods often are winged. The genus, widely distributed in temperate regions, includes sorts called pepper-grass.

Common garden cress is hairless and usually slightly glaucous. Its slender, erect stems are up to 1½ feet tall or taller and are branched above. The leaves are pinnately-cut into a few slender, toothed lobes, and in some cultivated varieties are curled. Tiny and white, the flowers are succeeded by ovate-elliptic pods, notched at their apexes and up to ⅓ inch long by two-thirds as broad. Somewhat naturalized in North America, this species is a native of western Asia. For cultivation see Cress.

LEPIDOZAMIA (Lepido-zàmia). Until recently commonly included in *Macrozamia*, the two species of *Lepidozamia* belong in the cycad family CYCADACEAE or, according to those who divide that into three families, in the zamia family ZAMIACEAE. Endemic to eastern Australia, the genus has a name derived from the Greek *lepis*, a scale, and the name of the related genus *Zamia*. It alludes to the scalelike frond bases that clothe the stems.

Lepidozamias are tall, evergreen, palm-like plants. They have trunks, usually branchless, clothed with the bases of fallen leaves, and a crown of many large, pinnate, not twisted, spirally-arranged fronds (leaves), interspersed with abundant rudimentary leaves called cataphylls. Each frond has numerous spreading, sickle-shaped, more or less alternate leaflets. Typical of the cycad family, lepidozamias are without recognizable flowers. Their reproductive elements are in large, almost stalkless cones, males and females separate. After fertilization by pollen from male cones the females develop large seeds. Lepidozamias grow slowly and undoubtedly attain great ages, but absurd estimates, such as 10,000 years, have been made as to how old ancient specimens may be. A more realistic figure seems to be about 500 years. A specimen of *L. peroffskyana* in the botanic garden at Sydney, Australia attained heights of 6 feet in less than a century.

Tallest of cycads, attaining a maximum height of more than 60 feet, *L. hopei* (syn. *Macrozamia hopei*) has fronds, at first erect, later spreading, 6 to 9 feet in length. They have up to eighty glossy leaflets each with seventeen or more veins. The broadest leaflets are 9 inches to over 1 foot long by from ⅝ inch to 1¼ inches wide. Female cones are up to 2 feet long or sometimes longer. Not over about 20 feet tall, *L. peroffskyana* (syns. *Macrozamia peroffskyana*, *M. denisonii*) differs in the leaflets of its fronds being narrower and in having not more than fourteen veins. The broadest measures up to 1 foot long by just in excess of ½ inch wide. This sort comes from south of the native range of *L. hopei* and so is accustomed to a cooler climate.

Garden and Landscape Uses and Cultivation. Rare in cultivation outside their native country, these handsome cycads are choice collectors' items. They are adapted to warm, essentialy frostless climates and to greenhouses, thriving in sun or part-day shade. It is reported that specimens collected from the wild are very difficult to reestablish. Seeds germinate easily, and for cycads, seedlings grow quite rapidly. Cultural needs are as for *Macrozamia*.

LEPISMIUM (Lepís-mium). As interpreted by those who separate this genus from *Rhipsalis* which not all authorities do, *Lepismium* comprises seventeen or more South American species of the cactus family CACTACEAE. Its name, from the Greek *lepis*, a scale, alludes to small scales that surround the areoles.

Lepismiums are bushy, tree-perching (epiphytic) or rock-perching plants with spineless, but sometimes bristly, flat, cylindrical, or three-winged, more or less leaflike, jointed, frequently prostrate or pendulous stems. In each areole (position from which the spines and flowers of cactuses arise) is usually a tuft of hairs. Their white or pink flowers, which open by day, are small, wheel-shaped, and in little clusters. The fruits are smooth, spherical, purple berries.

Occasionally cultivated, variable *L. cruciforme* (syn. *Rhipsalis cruciformis*), of Brazil, occurs on rocks. It has flat stems with coarsely-crenated margins, at their broadest parts 1 inch wide or a little wider. The

Lepismium cruciforme

Lepismium cruciforme (flowers)

flowers are about ½ inch across. Variety *L. c. myosurus* (syn. *Rhipsalis myosurus*) has branches that narrow at their tips to long points and pinkish-white flowers that become yellow as they age. From *L. cruciforme* and its variants, **L. paradoxum** (syn. *Rhipsalis paradoxa*) differs in its pendulous stems being triangular, without conspicuous wool at the areoles, and the white flowers being ¾ inch in diameter.

Lepismium cruciforme myosurus

Cylindrical stems are characteristic of the sorts now to be described. Those of **L. grandiflorum** (syn. *Rhipsalis grandiflora*) are slender, forked, often reddish. Very freely produced along the lengths of the branches, the ¾- to 1-inch-wide flowers have few petals, white striped with pale green, cream-colored, or slightly pinkish. Very similar to the last and sometimes cultivated under its name, **L. megalanthum** (syn. *Rhipsalis megalantha*) differs in having thicker stems and blooms up to 1½ inches across. Pendulous, cylindrical stems up to ¼ inch in diameter, branched toward their ends, are characteristic of **L. puniceo-discus** (syn. *Rhipsalis puniceo-discus*). Exceeding ½ inch in diameter, the white flowers have recurved petals and yellow stamens.

Garden Uses and Cultivation. These are as for *Rhipsalis*. For additional information see Cactuses.

LEPISORUS. See Pleopeltis.

LEPTARRHENA (Leptar-rhèna). There is only one species of this *Saxifraga* relative. It inhabits high mountains and subarctic and arctic regions from Montana to Washington and Alaska and is a member of the saxifrage family SAXIFRAGACEAE. Its name comes from the Greek *leptos*, slender, and *arrhen*, male, and alludes to the stalks of the stamens.

Streamsides, wet meadows, and similar locations are the preferred habitats of **Leptarrhena pyrolifolia.** It has horizontal rootstocks and leathery, hairless, mostly

basal, narrow-obovate to eliptic or ovate-oblong leaves 1½ to 6 inches long, roundish-toothed, and paler on their undersides than above. There are one to three distantly spaced leaves on the more or less glandular, branchless flowering stems which are up to about 1½ feet tall. These stem leaves are smaller than the basal ones, and stalkless. The tiny white flowers, in branched clusters, at first are much crowded but become less so later. They have five-lobed calyxes, five spatula-shaped to oblanceolate petals, ten stamens as long or longer than the petals, and an ovary of two carpels joined only at their bases and each with a nearly stalkless style. The fruits are paired, many-seeded, usually red follicles.

Garden Uses and Cultivation. Of easy cultivation, at least in regions with climates not too dissimilar to those under which it grows naturally, *Leptarrhena* is suitable for rock gardens. Its foliage and red fruits are attractive. It succeeds in gritty, moist, but not wet soil, in sun or with a little shade during the heat of the day, and is increased by seed and by division in spring or early fall.

LEPTINELLA. See Cotula.

LEPTOCEREUS (Lepto-cèreus). Eleven West Indian species of the cactus family CACTACEAE constitute *Leptocereus*. The name, which alludes to the thin ribs of the stems, originates from the Greek *leptos*, slender, and that of the related genus *Cereus*.

The growth habits of leptocereuses are various. Some have weak, clambering stems, those of old specimens forming considerable tangles; others have stout woody trunks. The stems have prominent ribs and clusters of needle-like spines. The flowers are small and bell-shaped.

Sorts sometimes cultivated include *L. leonii* (syn. *Cereus leonii*), of Cuba, a bushy shrub or tree up to almost 20 feet in height with stems not exceeding about 1¼ inches in diameter and having six to eight slightly-scalloped ribs with closely-set clusters of six to eight yellowish to gray spines about 1½ inches long. Puerto Rican *L. quadricostatus* (syn. *Cereus quadricostatus*), up to 12 feet in height, has numerous usually four-ribbed branches with clusters of 1½-inch-long spines. The flowers, about 1½ inches long, are white tinged with yellow or green. Native of Hispaniola, *L. weingartianus* (syn. *Cereus weingartianus*) is a trailing, clambering, or climbing sort the stems of which attain lengths or heights of up to 30 feet and have four to seven ribs. The ½-inch-long spines are in closely set clusters of ten to twelve. The flowers are about 1½ inches long.

Garden and Landscape Uses and Cultivation. Horticulturally among the less interesting of cactuses, the sorts of this genus are likely to appeal only to collectors of the group. They grow readily in environments that suit most others of the *Cereus* relationship. For additional information see Cactuses.

LEPTOCHITON (Lepto-chìton). One native of Ecuador, a beautiful bulb plant closely related to *Pamianthe*, is the only representative of *Leptochiton*, of the amaryllis family AMARYLLIDACEAE. From *Pamianthe* it differs in having eight or fewer seeds, instead of more, in each compartment of the ovary, and in the seeds being comparatively large, spherical, and thin-skinned. The name, from the Greek *leptos*, thin, and *chiton*, a covering, refers to the seeds.

Impressive in bloom, *L. quitoensis* has a bulb about 3 inches in diameter. Its erect to arching, all-basal leaves are linear and 1 foot to 2 feet long by about ¾ inch wide. Solitary atop a stalk 1 foot or so long, the fragrant flower is 6 to 8 inches across. It has a green perianth tube 3½ to 5 inches long and six narrow perianth segments (petals) 3 to 4 inches long that are white with greenish undersides. The broadly-bell-shaped staminal cup, two-thirds as long as the petals and frilled along its margin, is white and somewhat suggests the trumpet of a daffodil. The free portions of the six stamens attached to it incline inward from its edge. The style is long and green. The fruits are capsules.

Garden Uses and Cultivation. These are the same as for *Pamianthe* and temperate-region species of *Hymenocallis*.

LEPTOCHLOA (Leptó-chloa)—Spike Grass. Some twenty-seven species, natives chiefly of warm regions of the Old and New Worlds, constitute *Leptochloa*, of the grass family GRAMINEAE. The name, from the Greek *leptos*, slender, and *chloa*, grass, alludes to the flower spikes.

Leptochloas include annuals and perennials. They have flat leaf blades and flower panicles composed of few to many slender racemes of overlapping spikelets, each with three to twelve flowers, the lower one or two bisexual, the others male or sterile.

Sometimes cultivated for ornament, spike grass (**L. fascicularis**) is a widely distributed native from the United States to South America and the West Indies. It is a tufted annual 1 foot to 3 feet tall, with leafy, sparingly-branched stems. The leaf blades are up to 1¼ feet in length by ¹⁄₁₂ to ⅓ inch wide. The flower panicles, 6 inches to 1 foot long, have fourteen to thirty-five erect or ascending branches, and are up to 2 inches wide. In the wild spike grass often occurs in muddy places, sometimes where the soil is somewhat saline or alkaline.

Garden and Landscape Uses and Cultivation. The species described is suitable for flower beds and for naturalizing. Good results are had by sowing seeds outdoors in spring, where the plants are to stay,

and thinning out the seedlings to preclude harmful overcrowding. Moist, fertile soil and exposure to full sun provide suitable growing conditions.

LEPTODACTYLON (Lepto-dáctylon) — Prickly-Phlox. The western American genus *Leptodactylon*, of the phlox family POLEMONIACEAE, was previously included in *Gilia*. It consists of about a dozen species. The name, from the Greek *leptos*, narrow, and *dactylon*, a finger, alludes to the dissected leaves.

Leptodactylons are compact or loose-growing shrubs, subshrubs, and herbaceous perennials with opposite or alternate, linear-lobed, usually glandular leaves. The short-stalked to nearly stalkless blooms are commonly in crowded terminal clusters, more rarely solitary. They have a calyx with more or less spine-tipped lobes and a narrowly-funnel-shaped to more typically phloxlike, five-lobed corolla with the five stamens and the one style included. The fruits are capsules.

Prickly-phlox (*L. californicum* syn. *Gilia californica*) is a beautiful broad shrub 1 foot to 3 feet tall, with hairy, but not glandular leafy stems. The leaves are divided in handlike fashion into five to nine lobes. The pink, pinkish-lilac, or nearly white, stalkless blooms, in few-flowered, dense clusters, are ¾ to 1 inch long and about 1½ inches wide. Their corolla lobes (petals) spread widely. This is a native of dry slopes at fairly low altitudes in California. Variety *L. c. glandulosum* differs in having glandular hairs on its upper parts.

Considerably smaller, *L. pungens* (syn. *Gilia pungens*) inhabits dry, rocky, and sandy places high in the mountains from California to Oregon and Nevada. It is variable and has much the appearance of a mat-forming phlox. It is 3 inches to 1 foot tall or slightly taller and glandular-hairy. The numerous leaves are cleft into three to seven slender lobes. The funnel-shaped blooms, white tinged with pink or purple, are ¾ to 1 inch long.

Leptodactylon californicum glandulosum

Garden and Landscape Uses and Cultivation. The species described are best adapted for rock gardens, native plant gardens, and other special plantings in regions where conditions under which they grow naturally can be approximated. They are not satisfactorily hardy in the north, but are worth trying in alpine greenhouses. Excellent soil drainage is a necessity. Propagation is by seed and by cuttings.

LEPTODERMIS (Lepto-dérmis). There are about thirty species of *Leptodermis*, a genus native from Japan to the Himalayas. It consists of deciduous shrubs of the madder family RUBIACEAE. The name comes from the Greek *leptos*, thin, and *derma*, a skin or membrane, and alludes to the bractlets.

Leptodermises have opposite leaves and, in the leaf axils, crowded, headlike clusters of usually few, small flowers, with five-toothed, persistent calyxes, tubular to funnel-shaped, white or purplish corollas with five lobes (petals), four stamens, and a five-branched style. The fruits are capsules.

The hardiest and most often cultivated sort, *L. oblonga*, a native of northern China, lives outdoors at least as far north as Boston, Massachusetts. It is a pretty, late summer-blooming shrub, about 3 feet tall. Of twiggy growth, it has purplish, downy young shoots, and ovate to oblongish leaves ½ to 1 inch long, with roughish upper surfaces, and their undersides pubescent. The flowers, which somewhat resemble those of lilacs, are downy on the outsides of the corollas, violet-purple, and ½ to ¾ inch long.

Rarer in cultivation and their hardiness not determined, but considerably less tolerant of severe cold than *L. oblonga*, are *L. pilosa*, and *L. purdomii*. Chinese *L. pilosa*, 6 to 10 feet tall, has downy young shoots, and gray-green pointed-ovate leaves 1 inch to 1¼ inches long, conspicuously hairy on both sides. In dense, terminal, and toward the branch ends axillary, clusters are ½-inch-long, funnel-shaped, fragrant flowers with lavender corollas, hairy on their outsides. Also Chinese, *L. purdomii*, is a slender-stemmed, 5-foot-tall kind, with wiry shoots, downy when young. The hairless, often clustered leaves are ovate to ovate-lanceolate and less than ½ inch in length. Crowded toward the branch ends in lilac-like groups of clusters, the tubular flowers are less than ½ inch long. Japanese *L. pulchella* is a shrub with downy shoots and ill-smelling foliage, a few feet tall and having narrowly-ovate to broadly-lanceolate leaves ½ inch to 1½ inches long. The purple, funnel-shaped blooms are about ½ inch long and are shortly-hairy on their outsides.

Garden and Landscape Uses and Cultivation. Blooming much later than the vast majority of shrubs is an endearing virtue of these leptodermises. To the botanically inclined they have the added interest of being much hardier than almost all woody plants of the madder family. They are useful for shrub borders. Toward the northern limits of their hardiness, they should be afforded sheltered locations. Not fussy as to soil, so long as it is not constantly wet, they prosper with little attention. They are sun-lovers. Propagation is easy by seed and summer cuttings.

LEPTOPTERIS (Leptó-pteris). Very closely allied to *Todea*, and by some authorities united with it, *Leptopteris* differs most noticeably in its very much thinner, flimsy fronds (leaves). There are six much-alike species distributed in the wild from New Zealand to Tasmania, Samoa, and New Guinea. They belong in the osmunda family OSMUNDACEAE. The name, from the Greek *leptos*, slender, and *pteris*, a fern, is of obvious application.

Sometimes small tree ferns with erect trunklike stems, or branching and forming tufted clumps, leptopterises have large, evergreen, twice-pinnate or more finely divided fronds crowded at the ends of the stems. The clusters of spore-bearing capsules are along the veins and veinlets.

Two New Zealand species are sometimes cultivated. With a trunk up to 4 feet tall but usually lower, **L. superba** (syn. *Todea superba*) has spreading, thrice-pinnate fronds up to 2 feet long, and pointed-lanceolate. Their primary divisions are closely set; the largest are up to 6 inches long. From the middle of the leaf downward as well as toward the tip they gradually decrease in size. The final divisions are toothed and overlapping. With leaves up to 3 feet long that have more widely spaced primary divisions not becoming markedly smaller from the center of the leaf downward, and with final segments that do not overlap, **L. hymenophylloides** (syn. *Todea hymenophylloides*) has trunks up to 2 feet long. It is believed that the two species described hybridize in the wild to produce a kind that has been called *L. intermedia*.

Garden and Landscape Uses and Cultivation. Rather delicate, these ferns succeed only where the atmosphere is heavily charged with moisture and their thin fronds are shaded from sun. They are hardy in very mild climates only. They may be grown in greenhouses where the winter night temperature is 45 to 50°F, and by day at that season not more than five or ten degrees higher. Sandy peaty soil of fairly nourishing quality, and consisting largely of organic material such as leaf mold and peat moss, is proper for these plants. In warm weather the foliage should be misted with a fine spray of water on all bright days. Spores afford a ready means of propagation, but unless kept under somewhat warmer conditions than recommended above for mature

specimens, the young plants grow slowly. For more information see Ferns.

LEPTOPYRUM (Lepto-pỳrum). There is only one species in this northern Chinese and Siberian genus of the buttercup family RANUNCULACEAE. It is a woodland plant closely related to and very like *Isopyrum*. Its name is derived from the Greek *leptos*, slender, and *pyros*, wheat, and alludes to the seed pods being approximately the size and shape of grains of wheat.

An erect or spreading annual 6 to 8 inches high, with many slender stems from its base, **Leptopyrum fumarioides** (syns. *Isopyrum fumarioides*, *Neoleptopyrum fumarioides*) has finely-divided basal and stem foliage. The stem leaves are whorled (in circles of more than two). The flowers have each four or five white, petal-like sepals about ⅕ inch long, the same number of minute yellow petals, and numerous stamens. The erect seed pods, about ⅓ inch long, are in headlike clusters.

Garden Uses and Cultivation. This little plant is occasionally planted for variety in woodland and rock gardens. It thrives under conditions appropriate for *Isopyrum* and is raised from seeds sown yearly in fall or spring where the plants are to flower.

LEPTOSIPHON. See Linanthus.

LEPTOSPERMUM (Lepto-spérmum)—Tea Tree. Known in the wild from Australia, New Zealand, and Malaya, *Leptospermum*, of the myrtle family MYRTACEAE, includes fifty or fewer species. These are shrubs or occasionally small trees. The meaning of the name, from the Greek *leptos*, slender, and *sperma*, a seed, is apparent. The name tea tree was given because the English navigator Captain Cook brewed a tea from the leaves and administered it to his crew in an attempt to control scurvy.

The leaves of leptospermums are alternate, often small, rigid, and heathlike. The blooms, solitary, or in twos or threes from the leaf axils or ends of short branchlets, have a usually shallowly-bell-shaped calyx tube with five lobes, five spreading petals, many stamens approximately as long as the petals, and a single slender style. The fruits are leathery capsules.

The Manuka or New Zealand tea tree (**L. scoparium**) and its varieties are the best known and most popular. Native of New Zealand, this very variable shrub is 6 feet tall or sometimes taller. It has sharp-pointed, linear-lanceolate to elliptic or ovate leaves, silky-hairy on their undersides and under ½ inch long. The usually solitary white flowers are ¼ to ½ inch or slightly more in diameter. Variety *L. s. keatleyi* is distinguished by having pink blooms with much deeper colored centers and almost ¾ inch in diameter. They are produced in summer and winter. Double pale pink flowers are carried by compact

An unusually tall specimen of *Leptospermum scoparium* in southern California

Leptospermum scoparium (foliage and flowers)

Leptospermum scoparium keatleyi

Leptospermum scoparium flore-plenum

L. s. flore-plenum. Dwarf and compact *L. s. boscowanii* has purple-tinged foliage and white flowers tinged with pink and red.

Leptospermum scoparium flore-plenum (flowers)

Variety *L. s. chapmanii* has brownish foliage and rose-pink blooms. The bronzy leaves of *L. s. nichollsii* make a splendid foil for its carmine-red flowers. A number of highly regarded California-raised varieties came from crossing the last-named variety with double-pink-flowered 'Dwarf Double Rose'. Outstanding among this progeny are 'Ruby Glow', with dark purplish stems and foliage and fully double blooms produced over a very long season;

Leptospermum scoparium 'Ruby Glow'

'Red Damask', with red-tinged leaves and ruby-red somewhat less fully double flowers; and 'Snow Flurry', with reddish foliage and very double, greenish-centered, white blooms. Other good varieties of this relationship are 'Pompon', with dark green foliage and double pink flowers; 'Fairy Rose', with double pink flowers, and leaves that turn mostly red; 'Scarlet Carnival', with red-tinged leaves and medium-red double flowers; 'Red Sparkler', with very deep red double flowers, and brown stems; and low and compact 'Snow White', the green-centered white flowers of which are of medium size. Not exceeding 1 foot in height and forming spreading

groundcovers, *L. s. horizontalis* and *L. s. pictergillii* have pink blooms, those of the former almost ¾ inch wide and bigger than those of *L. s. pictergillii*.

The Australian tea tree (**L. laevigatum**) is a shrub or tree up to 30 feet tall. Hairless, its narrowly-oblong to ovate-oblong, sharp-pointed, three-veined leaves are ½ to 1 inch long and about one-half as wide. The flowers are white, ½ to ¾ inch in diameter. Variety *L. l. reevesii* (syn. *L. nanum*) is dwarfer and more compact.

Other species in cultivation include **L. petersonii** (syn. *L. flavescens citratum*). This native of Australia is 6 to 8 feet tall. It has loosely-arranged, pendulous branches, and light green, linear to linear-lanceolate leaves ½ inch to 2 inches long that when bruised are strongly lemon-scented. The flowers are white. Distinguishable by the downy character of its young shoots and leaf surfaces, **L. lanigerum** (syn. *L. pubescens*), of Australia, is 8 to 15 feet high. The leaves are gray-green, ½ inch long by ⅛ inch wide. The solitary, white blooms are ¾ inch across. From 4 to 8 feet tall, Australian **L. rotundifolium** has roundish-elliptic or ovate leaves about ½ inch in length. The crinkle-petaled, apple-blossom-pink blooms are 1 inch in diameter. Native to Australia and Tasmania, **L. liversidgei**, 6 to 12 feet tall, has more or less pendulous branches. Its obovate to oblong leaves, mostly not over ¼ inch long, have oil glands and when bruised give off a strong odor of lemon. Solitary from the leaf axils or at the ends of short shoots, the white flowers are a little over ¼ inch wide. The plant grown as *L. flavescens citriodorum* probably belongs here. Closely similar, **L. minutifolium** differs in having foliage without the characteristic lemon odor of *L. liversidgei*. Its tiny leaves are markedly concave above and rounded on their undersides. The flowers are white.

Leptospermum minutifolium

A shrub or tree up to about 18 feet tall, variable **L. ericoides** (syn. *Kunzea ericoides*) has branches often gracefully pendulous at their ends and leaves solitary or in small clusters. They are linear to narrowly-lan-

ceolate, but not sharp-pointed, and less than ½ inch long. The stalkless, small white or pinkish flowers, usually in clusters of two to five, face upward. Their stamens are longer than those of most leptospermums.

Garden and Landscape Uses. Leptospermums are extremely useful, decorative landscape components in regions of mild winters and warm, dry or dryish summers. Elegant and graceful, they are attractive both in and out of bloom and are charming for use in cut flower arrangements. Depending upon their height and habits of growth, the various kinds are appropriately employed in mixed shrub plantings, as free-standing specimens, as bank and groundcovers, and in rock gardens. The Australian tea tree is excellent for seaside planting and for stabilizing shifting sands. For this last use it was extensively and successfully employed in Golden Gate Park, San Francisco. It can be sheared to form a good tall hedge. Leptospermums are drought resisters, but despite their reasonable tolerance, most die if their roots become completely dry. To prevent this, plants newly set out should be watered regularly until they are well established. They flourish in open places in sun, but not where exposed to hot, dry, searing winds. They need well-drained, neutral to somewhat acid soil. In alkaline earth they develop the yellow, unhealthy condition called chlorosis. Poorly drained soil encourages root rot.

Cultivation. Leptospermums are easy to raise from cuttings and seed. Once well established they need little attention. They do not respond satisfactorily to pruning that involves cutting into leafless wood, but light annual shearing that removes not more than two-thirds of the foliage can be practiced to shape, contain, or thicken the bushes, or this may be done by pinching out the tips of the growing shoots. Pruning is best done as soon as flowering is through.

As greenhouse plants in containers or ground beds varieties of *L. scoparium* give satisfaction. They need cool, airy conditions. A winter night temperature of 40 to 50°F, with a five or ten degree increase by day, is adequate. Good drainage is essential, with watering to keep the soil, which should be a fertile, sandy, peaty loam, always fairly moist, but somewhat drier during winter than at other times. Plunging (burying the containers nearly to their rims) outdoors in a bed of sand, peat moss, or similar material in summer is helpful, but they must be transferred to the greenhouse before frost. Light pruning or trimming to shape and any needed repotting is done in spring as soon as flowering is through.

LEPTOSYNE. See Coreopsis.

LEPTOTAENIA PURPUREA is *Lomatium columbianum*.

LEPTOTES (Leptò-tes). Half a dozen Brazilian and Paraguayan species of chiefly tree-perchers (epiphytes) constitute *Leptotes*, of the orchid family ORCHIDACEAE. Only one is at all commonly grown. The name is from the Greek *leptotes*, delicateness, in reference to the blooms.

These orchids have thin, stemlike pseudobulbs, and fleshy, cylindrical leaves that give them much the aspect of brassavolas. From the bases of the pseudobulbs come the flower stems, which have short racemes of comparatively large blooms.

Blooming chiefly in winter and spring, *L. bicolor* has clustered pseudobulbs commonly under 1 foot in length, and generally erect, sharp-pointed, fleshy leaves with a longitudinal groove, up to about 5 inches in length. The quite long-lasting, scented blooms, from one to six on each stalk, are 1½ to 2 inches in diameter. They have slender, white sepals and petals and a large magenta-pink lip, whitish at its apex. Much like *L. bicolor* but usually smaller, *L. unicolor,* of Brazil, has often purplish-tinged, slender leaves, grooved longitudinally, and in clusters of two or three or sometimes solitary, pendulous, lavender-pink to violet-rose flowers that have narrow sepals and petals.

Leptotes bicolor

Garden Uses and Cultivation. Of interest for inclusion in orchid collections, the species described prospers under conditions appropriate for cattleyas and is well suited for growing on slabs of tree fern trunk. For more information see Orchids.

LESCHENAULTIA (Leschen-aùltia). The name of this genus of twenty species commemorates L. T. Leschenault de la Tour, French botanist who accompanied a voyage of exploration to Australia in 1802–03. He died in 1826. The group belongs to the goodenia family, GOODENIACEAE. Its name has been spelled *Lechenaultia*.

Leschenaultias are heathlike shrubs and herbaceous perennials endemic to Australia. Usually hairless, they have small, narrow, crowded or more distant, alternate, undivided leaves. Their showy flowers, white, greenish, yellow, red, or violet, are solitary or clustered. They have small,

five-lobed calyxes, oblique corollas usually with their tubes slit in one place to the base, and five lobes (petals) that may spread or not. There are five stamens. The fruits are capsules.

Blue leschenaultia (*Leschenaultia biloba*) is one of the most lovely flowering plants of the beauty-rich flora of western Australia. Spreading to semierect, in the wild it rarely exceeds 1½ feet in height and width, although in cultivation these dimensions may be doubled. The leaves are up to ½ inch long. Typically rich blue, but varying to purple-blue and white, the stalkless flowers, 1 inch to 1¼ inches in diameter, are in the axils of the upper leaves. Their petals are deeply-cleft into two lobes.

Yellow leschenaultia (*L. linarioides*) somewhat belies its popular name, for its multicolored blooms are chiefly white, brown, or greenish-yellow and red. The bush becomes 3 to 4 feet tall or may be more or less prostrate. It branches freely. The leaves are pointed and up to ½ inch long or a little longer. Stalkless in the axils of the upper leaves or at the ends of brief twigs, the 1½- to 2-inch-wide blooms form leafy clusters.

Red leschenaultia (*L. superba*) is a very handsome sort normally up to 1½ feet tall. Its leaves are 1 inch in length, its blooms, in twos or threes at the ends of the branchlets, bright orange-red or red. Bluish-white blooms are borne by *L. floribunda,* a shrub often not over 1 foot tall, but sometimes taller. Its leaves are not over ⅓ inch in length. The flowers have spreading petals and are clustered near the branch ends.

Garden and Landscape Uses and Cultivation. Not among the easiest plants to cultivate, leschenaultias offer challenges to gardeners in mild, dry climates that are amply rewarded if successfully met. They are suitable for rock gardens and other locations outdoors in California and prefer well-drained soil with which is mixed some peat or other decayed organic material. Light shade from the strongest sun is recommended, and a gravel, stone, or organic mulch is helpful. Great care must be taken not to water excessively. Indiscretion here can soon result in disaster. In general, fertilizing is to be avoided. Discretionary pruning after blooming is through is helpful in maintaining shapeliness and compactness, and tends to improve flowering. Plants are raised from seed and cuttings. Seedlings usually first bloom when about two years old.

LESPEDEZA (Lesped-èza) — Bush-Clover. To the pea family LEGUMINOSAE belong the 100 species of *Lespedeza*. They are natives of North America, Asia, and Australia. The name, a misspelling, honors Vincente Manuel de Cespedes, who was Spanish governor of Florida about 1790. The genus is very closely related to *Desmodium*. Some

of its members are important forage crops, some are used as green manures. The plant sometimes called *L. macrocarpa* is *Campylotropis macrocarpa*.

Lespedezas are mostly herbaceous perennials and deciduous subshrubs or shrubs. A few are annuals. Erect, they have alternate, toothless leaves, usually with three leaflets, more rarely undivided. The typically pea-shaped flowers, in racemes or heads from the leaf axils, are small, purple, pink, yellowish, or white. Often petal-less blooms that produce seeds are borne in addition to more showy, pea-like, sterile ones. The flowers have calyxes with fine, nearly equal short teeth or lobes. There are ten stamens, nine joined and one free, and an incurved, hairless style tipped with a small stigma. The fruits are short, ovate to elliptic, one-seeded pods partly enclosed by the calyx.

One of the most decorative bush-clovers, *L. bicolor* (syn. *Desmodium bicolor*), of Japan, China, and Manchuria, is a shrub up to 10 feet tall. It has slender-stalked, broad-elliptic to ovate leaves of three bristle-tipped leaflets from ¾ inch to 2 inches long and two-thirds as wide as long. The middle leaflet is the biggest. Darker green above than on their lower sides, the leaflets are sparsely clothed with hairs or may have hairless upper surfaces. The racemes, plentifully displayed from the leaf axils in terminal panicles 2 feet or so long, have slender stalks with, along their upperparts, bright rosy-purple blooms under ½ inch long. This is hardy through most of New England. Variety *L. b. alba* has white flowers. Slightly less hardy, and very variable, *L. thunbergii* (syns. *L. sieboldii,* *Desmodium penduliflorum*) is subshrubby and about 6 feet in height. It has leaves of three bluntish, elliptic to elliptic-oblong leaflets, hairy on their undersides, and 1¼ to 2 inches long, the center one the biggest. The ½-inch-long, rosy-purple blooms clothe the upper parts only of the racemes, which are stalked, 3½ to 8 inches long, and form loose, terminal panicles 2 to 3 feet long. This differs from *L. bicolor* in the calyxes of its flowers having teeth not longer than the tube. It is native to Japan and China. Variety *L. t. versicolor* has white and rose-purple blooms on the same plant. Much like *L. thunbergii,* but with broader, nearly-hairless leaves and pure white flowers, *L. japonica* (syn. *L. thunbergii japonica*) is a native of Japan.

Differing from the kinds discussed above in having slender racemes of bloom with flowers extending from their bases to their tips, *L. maximowiczii* is a native of Korea. Up to 12 feet tall, this has leaves of three pointed, elliptic-ovate to ovate leaflets 1 inch to 2 inches long, light-colored and silky-hairy on their undersides. The flowers, about ⅓ inch long and purple, are in slender racemes 1¼ to 3½ inches long. Their calyxes have lobes longer than their tubes. This is hardy in southern New England. Unusual because its racemes of rose-purple flowers are not longer than its very short-stalked leaves, **L. cyrtobotrya** attains a maximum height of about 15 feet. Its leaves have three broad-elliptic leaflets, up to 1¼ inches long, hairless above, with brief hairs on their undersides. The flowers are up to ½ inch long. They are displayed along the slender leafy shoots. Native to Japan, China, and Korea, this species is as hardy as the last.

Garden and Landscape Uses. The chief horticultural merit of bush-clovers is their late summer and fall blooming. Their displays are much later than those of most shrubs. Nevertheless they are scarcely choice enough to warrant planting on small properties. Better adapted to more expansive landscapes, they can be used in mixed shrub plantings, at the backs of perennial borders, and in other ways. Although technically shrubs, near the northern limits of their hardiness they behave like herbaceous perennials, their tops being killed to the ground each winter and vigorous shoots that attain nearly the full height common for the species and bloom the first year, coming from the base each spring. Bush-clovers are plants for open, sunny locations and well-drained soils of moderate or even low fertility.

Cultivation. Where their tops are winter-killed pruning consists of cutting them to the ground in late winter. Even where winters do not kill the tops the same method can be adopted if it is desired to keep the plants to minimum size. Alternatively, pruning is done in late winter by removing or severely shortening the oldest branches and thinning out crowded weak ones. Propagation is easy by seed sown in a cold frame or in pots in a greenhouse. Other means of increase are division in early spring and summer cuttings, of firm, semiwoody shoots inserted in a propagating bed in a greenhouse or cold frame or under mist.

LESQUERELLA (Lesquer-élla) — Bladderpod. Some species of *Lesquerella*, as well as some of closely related *Physaria*, are because of their inflated seed pods called bladderpods. Annuals, biennials, and herbaceous perennials, the about fifty species of *Lesquerella* are natives of the New World, the majority of western North America. They belong in the mustard family CRUCIFERAE. The name commemorates the American botanist Leo Lesquereux, who died in 1889.

Lesquerellas much resemble alyssums, and mostly have moderately showy blooms. Because of the presence of stellate (starry) hairs their stems and foliage are prevailingly grayish. The leaves are chiefly in basal rosettes, with smaller ones on the lower parts of the flowering stems. They are undivided, and toothed or toothless.

As is usual in the family, the flowers have four each sepals and petals, the latter spreading to form a cross. There are six stamens, of which two are shorter than the others, and one style, usually prominent. The fruits are inflated, ovoid to nearly globular pods.

Highly variable **L. alpina** (syn. *L. spathulata*), which includes as variety *L. a. condensata* previously named *L. condensata*, is a tufted perennial 2 to 4 inches tall or sometimes taller, with a branched or branchless stem. Native to the Rocky Mountains and adjacent areas, this has basal cushiony rosettes of linear to oblanceolate or obovate leaves ½ inch to 1½ inches long. The leaves of the flowering stems are similar, but often narrower. In racemes nearly concealed by the foliage or longer, are borne the yellow blooms, which are from a little under to a little over ½ inch wide. Slender-stemmed, and 2 inches to over 1 foot tall, **L. ludoviciana** is a biennial or perennial native of the north-central and Rocky Mountain states and adjacent Canada. Its basal leaves, ovate-lanceolate to narrow-oblanceolate, are 1 inch to 4 inches long. The often-branched racemes have many yellow blooms, ½ to ¾ inch wide. The seed pods are inflated. A biennial or short-lived perennial, **L. globosa** is up to 1½ feet tall. It has wavy-toothed or toothless, obovate or linear leaves 1 inch to 2 inches long. Native to Kentucky and Tennessee, often growing in limestone soils, it has usually branched stems and small, globose seed pods.

Garden Uses and Cultivation. Lesquerellas do not do well where summers are hot and humid. Under less trying conditions they are worth considering as modest additions to rock gardens and should be given sunny locations in very gritty soil or in a scree or moraine. Propagation is easy by seed.

LESSER CELANDINE is *Ranunculus ficaria*.

LESSINGIA (Les-síngia). In the wild scarcely extending beyond the boundaries of California, *Lessingia* comprises seven species of the daisy family COMPOSITAE. Its name commemorates a German family named Lessing, of which Gotthold Ephraim was an author, Karl an artist, and Christian F, who died in 1862, a botanist.

Lessingias are spreading or erect, usually glandular annuals, woolly-hairy to nearly hairless. They have alternate, lobed, toothed, or smooth-edged leaves, the lowermost stalked, those above stalkless and often represented by bracts. Arranged in panicles, spikes, or rounded clusters, the small top- or bell-shaped flower heads consist of few to many florets with the involucres (collars of bracts) consisting of several rows. Technically there are no ray florets (those that in a daisy look like petals), all are of the disk type

(like those of the eye of a daisy), but the outer florets are enlarged, and have a palmately five-parted, more or less reflexed lobe that is somewhat petal-like. They are white, lavender, pink, or yellow.

Formerly included in *L. leptoclada*, the species now named **L. hololeuca** produces from its base one or more wiry stems that branch in their upper parts, are 8 inches to 1½ feet tall, and have persistent white hairs or become nearly hairless as they age. They are without glands. The lower leaves, more or less persistent through the blooming period, and generally without lobing or teeth, are oblanceolate, up to 2 inches long, and more or less hairy. The small flower heads, of thirteen to eighteen pinkish to lavender florets, the outer ones with enlarged corollas, are nearly ½ inch long. They are in panicled clusters. Variety *L. h. arachnoidea*, 1 foot to 2½ feet tall, has foliage only slightly hairy and broadly-branching panicles of bloom. Its lower foliage usually withers (at least in the wild) before the flowers are fully open. There are eight to eighteen florets in each flower head.

In the wild inhabiting open, dry ground, **L. leptoclada**, 1 foot to 3 feet tall, has erect stems with many slender, spreading branches. Its leaves, the lower ones spatula-shaped and toothed, the upper ones bractlike and glandular-dotted, at first hairy, often become nearly hairless as they age. The heads of lavender to purple or white flowers are in panicles.

Garden Uses and Cultivation. The species described are fairly attractive summer-bloomers adapted for native plant gardens in their home territory and for flower borders. The blooms last well in water and are useful for arrangements. Like many western annuals, this sort does not respond well to extremely hot and humid weather. Sow seeds in early spring in a sunny location in well-drained soil of ordinary garden quality and thin out the seedlings to about 6 inches apart.

LETTSOMIA. See Argyreia.

LETTUCE. In addition to being the name of the familiar salad plant discussed in the next entry, the word lettuce appears as part of the names of these plants: asparagus-lettuce (discussed under Celtuce), lamb's-lettuce (*Valerianella locusta*, discussed under Corn Salad), miner's-lettuce (*Montia perfoliata*), and water-lettuce (*Pistia stratiotes*).

LETTUCE. Undoubtedly the most widely used salad vegetable in America, lettuce (varieties of *Lactuca sativa*) is easy to grow, at least during reasonably cool weather, and is worth some special effort to have. To achieve good results selection of varieties appropriate for the locality and the time of year is important.

The gardener who knows the exquisite crispness and flavor of freshly picked, home-grown lettuce can but pity urbanites and other unfortunates whose only acquaintance with the queen of salads is the monstrous, hard, cabbage-like heads of the 'Iceberg' relationship so popular commercially because they ship well. And that is the only virtue such miserable apologies for what good lettuce should be really have. Away with them—try varieties selected from the catalog of a good seedsman—heading and semiheading varieties to harvest during cooler weather, leaf sorts for summer use.

To assure excellent lettuce begin with the soil. Have it deep, fertile, and mellow, in good heart as old-time gardeners expressed it. Choose a sunny spot for early and late crops, perhaps a little shade, ideally during the middle day heat, for summer crops. A supply of water must be available to see the crop through spells of dry weather. Lettuce must never be checked in its growth from start to finish. If it is it loses much in tenderness and the plants may become balky and shoot up flowering stalks—run to seed as the saying has it.

Lettuce: (a) Several varieties growing vigorously

(b) Harvesting the crop

Begin then by spading, rotary tilling, or plowing the soil deeply and incorporating a generous amount of compost, well-rot-ted manure, or other decayed organic material. If this is not available turning under a cover crop about a month before sowing or planting the lettuce may be substituted. In addition to providing bulk organic matter, work into the upper few inches a dressing of a complete fertilizer of a kind suitable for vegetables. One more consideration; lettuce prefers soil approaching neutrality, if yours is decidedly acid fork or rake a dressing of lime into its surface two or three weeks prior to planting.

For the earliest crop outdoors, in the north sow seeds in a temperature of 60°F in a greenhouse or other suitable place indoors about eight weeks before weather will make possible setting the resulting young plants in the garden. Until they are ready for hardening in preparation for their transfer outdoors, grow the seedlings in full sun where the temperature by night is 50 to 55°F, that by day five to ten degrees higher depending upon the brightness of the weather.

As soon as the seedlings are big enough to handle comfortably transplant them 2 to 2½ inches apart in flats, individually into small peat pots, or to a hotbed. Keep them growing without check. Some two weeks before transplanting to the garden begin to condition them by ventilating the greenhouse or other location where they are more freely or by transferring them to a cold frame. For the last three or four days let them stand outdoors without the protection of glass or plastic sash.

If possible choose cloudy weather for transplanting. Set the plants in rows 1 foot to 1½ feet apart, allowing 9 inches to 1 foot between individuals or one-half those distances if you plan to harvest alternate plants when they are half-grown.

Make the first sowing outdoors as soon in spring as the soil can be gotten into workable condition, at the earliest time you can walk on the ground without it sticking to your shoes, as soon as it is dry and friable enough to manipulate easily with fork and rake.

A good plan with this first sowing is to make it as a short row in a sheltered spot and to transplant the seedlings when they have their second pair of true leaves to where they are to grow to harvesting size. By following this method only a small area need be readied at seeding time and the selection of a specially sheltered site may give the advantage of a few days earlier harvesting. Sow rather thinly so the seedlings will not crowd each other too much before you transplant. Cover the seeds shallowly. If set too deeply in cold soil they are liable to rot.

A steady supply of lettuce is assured by making successional sowings of comparatively small amounts of seeds at three-week or monthly intervals rather than fewer bigger sowings. In the north, upper south, and elsewhere where winter cold precludes the possibility of having lettuce outdoors then, make the last sowing early enough, which in many areas will be about mid-August, to allow the crop to attain harvesting size before killing frost. In the deep south and other regions where climate permits fall and winter sowings are practicable.

Sowing directly where the plants are to remain rather than in seed beds and transplanting is a technique preferred by many gardeners for all except the very earliest seeding. The mistakes so many amateurs make in doing this is sowing too thickly and failing to thin out the seedlings early enough. As a result they finish with a healthy crop of young lettuce leaves, but never a respectable lettuce.

A reasonably mature specimen needs space, a circle of from 8 to 9 inches in diameter perhaps. If in a row just one seed germinated and grew at these distances plants would touch each other at harvest time. Of course not every seed may grow, not all that do will be spaced in proper relationship to their neighbors, and some seedlings may be lost from one cause or another after they germinate. Therefore one must sow more seeds than the number of plants needed, but not vast numbers more, perhaps four or even five times as many. This means eight to ten seeds to each foot of row. Before the seedlings crowd thin them out to one-half the distances you intend to allow the plants at maturity, then when about half-grown cut out for table use every alternate plant.

A good alternative method is to sow a cluster or hill of two or three seeds ½ inch or so apart about every 4½ inches, to thin those in each hill to one as soon as they are well up, and to harvest alternate plants when part grown and before they begin to crowd those on either side, the ones to be allowed to grow to maturity.

Growing-season management of lettuce is not arduous. All that is necessary is to keep the plants moving. Rapid, uninterrupted growth makes for crops of good eating quality. Any check to continuous increase in size stunts and toughens lettuce.

Plenty of water is necessary and weeds must be rigorously kept down by frequent shallow surface cultivation or, after the ground has warmed, by mulching.

A light side dressing when the plants are about half-grown of a quickly available nitrogenous fertilizer, such as nitrate of soda, sulfate of ammonia, or urea is of great help, but do not overdo this. In home gardens the best way to apply these stimulants is to dissolve them in water to make a liquid fertilizer to be given only when the soil is moist. It is often useful to encircle the heads of cos varieties when they are about half-grown with a tie of raffia or soft string so that they remain tight rather than becoming open and loose.

In sunny greenhouses and hotbeds excellent out-of-season crops of lettuce can be had. Sowings made in greenhouses from September to January give young plants for transplanting to beds or benches of rich soil where temperatures of 40 to 50°F at night and by day five to ten degrees higher are maintained, and ventilation as full as possible is afforded on all favorable occasions. Similar results can be had from seeds sown in late winter in a hotbed and the young plants grown on under those conditions, with careful attention to ventilating, until they are big enough to harvest.

Cold frame cultivation of lettuce is a highly practicable, simple procedure. It makes possible both extra early and extra late crops. The latter are had by sowing in late summer or early fall after it is too late to reasonably expect that there will be time for the plants to reach harvestable size outdoors before frost, and to transplant to the frames in beds of rich soil. When frosty nights come the frames are protected by glass or polyethylene plastic sash and later, as the cold intensifies, perhaps additionally by mats or similar insulation. During the day ventilate the frames as liberally as weather permits. Spring crops can be had two weeks to a month earlier than outdoor-grown ones by sowing early, transplanting, and managing the frames to afford pleasant conditions conducive to the growth of the young plants during the day and to protect them from night frosts.

A head lettuce variety

Varieties of lettuce fall into three chief groups. Head lettuce, best suited for comparatively cool growing conditions include 'Iceberg' types that form very firm large heads but generally lack epicurean quality, and smaller, less firm-headed varieties such as 'Bibb', 'Buttercrunch', 'Great Lakes', and 'White Boston' that afford better eating. All have more or less rounded heads and belong to the group the British identify as cabbage varieties. Romaine or cos lettuce such as 'Paris Island Cos' and

A romaine or cos lettuce variety

'Lobjoit's Green Cos' are distinguished by tall, erect leaves that form elongated heads in the main less firm than varieties of the round-headed types. Many varieties of

Three varieties of leaf lettuces

these are of splendid quality. Romaine lettuce thrives best in cool weather. Lastly there are leaf lettuce varieties. These withstand hot weather far better than other sorts. Characteristically they form round, loose bunches of leaves without any tight head. They include such favorite varieties as 'Black Seeded Simpson', 'Grand Rapids', 'Oak Leaf', 'Ruby', and 'Salad Bowl'.

Pests and Diseases. The chief pests of lettuce are slugs and rabbits. A disease called tip burn results from unfavorable weather, especially high temperatures at night. A virus disease that causes the foliage to become yellow or mottled is spread from plant to plant by leafhoppers. To minimize danger of this destroy all nearby weeds and control the insects.

LEUCADENDRON. See Leucodendron.

LEUCAENA (Leu-caèna)—White-Popinac or Lead Tree. Of the fifty species of *Leucaena*, of the pea family LEGUMINOSAE, a genus native from Mexico to Peru and the Pacific Islands, the white-popinac or lead tree is now naturalized in many parts of the tropics and subtropics and in Florida and Texas.

Leucaenas are acacia-like, usually spineless trees and shrubs with lacy foliage. Their twice-pinnate leaves are composed of many small leaflets or fewer larger ones. The tiny blooms are crowded into tight heads. The flowers are usually bisexual. They have a five-parted calyx, five petals, ten slender, protruding stamens, and one style. The fruits are flat and broadly-linear, stalked pods. The name *Leucaena* derives from the Greek *leukos*, white, and refers to the prevailing color of the flowers.

The white-popinac or lead tree (*L. glauca*) is 15 to 25 feet in height. It has leaves 4 to 8 inches long with four, six, or eight major divisions arranged in pairs on either side of the midrib. Each division has ten to twenty pairs of stalkless, oblong or lanceolate, gray-green leaflets, slightly under to slightly over ½ inch long and under ⅛ inch wide. They are paler beneath than above. The balls of white flowers, ¾ to 1 inch across, are on stalks ¾ inch to 1¼ inches long. They are distantly spaced in terminal panicles. The pods are in drooping clusters. Dark brown at maturity, they are 4 to 6 inches long by up to ¾ inch broad and flat with thickened edges.

Some animals are harmed if they eat the young foliage or pods of the white-popinac. This is true of horses, donkeys, mules, and hogs. The effect is to cause their hair to shed as well as, it is reported, their hooves if feeding is long continued. The manes and tails of the first three animals mentioned are especially likely to be affected. Rabbits and chickens are also harmed. Curiously, cattle, sheep, and goats suffer no ill effects from browsing on this plant, and in Hawaii and elsewhere it is cultivated for cattle fodder. In parts of the tropics the white-popinac is planted to shade coffee, cacao, and other crops that need such care. The tree is used also in soil improvement programs; its young shoots and foliage are employed as green manure. This is a vigorous grower; where conditions are to its liking it becomes weedy and invasive. The seeds are used in leis and for making table mats, purses, necklaces, and other such items.

Garden and Landscape Uses and Cultivation. In addition to the economic purposes already mentioned, the white-popinac is useful as an ornamental and a shade tree. It grows well even in poor ground and with little or no care. It is propagated by seed, which should be soaked in warm water for twenty-four hours prior to sowing. Routine care is minimal. The tree may be pruned to any extent necessary to maintain a desirable size and shape.

LEUCERIA. See Leucheria.

LEUCHERIA (Leuchèr-ia). One of the sixty species of annual and perennial herbaceous plants of South America that constitute *Leucheria* is sometimes cultivated in flower gardens. The genus belongs in the daisy family COMPOSITAE and is named from the Greek *leucheres*, white, because some kinds are covered with white woolly hairs. The name is sometimes spelled *Leuceria*.

Native of Chile, *L. senecioides* is an annual that attains a height of about 1½ feet and is much branched and of spreading, diffuse habit. It has gray- or whitish-hairy, narrow leaves that are deeply-dissected or lobed and are stem-clasping at their bases, and dense sprays of flower heads with white rays and yellow centers, each ¼ to ½ inch in diameter. The fruits are achenes.

Garden Uses and Cultivation. This is a quite charming plant for adding variety and interest to flower gardens and its blooms have some modest use as cut flowers. It is useful for the fronts of borders and may be employed to provide summer bloom in rock gardens. It needs a sunny location and porous, well-drained soil. Seeds are usually sown in greenhouses in a temperature of 60 to 65°F some eight or nine weeks before the young plants are transplanted to the garden, which may be done about the time it is safe to set out tomatoes and petunias. Until then, the plants are grown, spaced about 2 inches apart, in flats. In the garden they should be set about 6 inches apart. Where the growing season is sufficiently long satisfactory results are had by sowing directly in the open garden.

LEUCHTENBERGIA (Leuchten-bérgia). One of the most distinctive cactuses, *Leuchtenbergia*, although not related to *Agave*, has much the aspect of a small member of that genus. There is only one species, a Mexican member of the cactus family CACTACEAE. Its name honors Prince Maximilian E. Y. N. von Beauharnais, Duke of Leuchtenberg, Germany, who died in 1852.

The agave cactus (*L. principis*) has a long, parsnip-like root, and a fat, erect, usually branchless, but sometimes divided, thick stem or plant body 1 foot to 2 feet tall furnished with long, narrow protrusions called tubercles that look much like leaves. As the plants age portions of the stem bearing raised scars, marking places from which old dead tubercles have fallen, become visible below. Triangular in section and up to 4½ inches long, the tubercles are grayish-green, sometimes tinged along their angles with red and are more or less spiraled around the stems. They point upward. The areoles (specialized locations from which the spines of cactuses arise) are large. There is one at the tip of each tubercle. They have gray, woolly hairs and several large, spreading, pliable, papery spines. The blooms develop from the areoles of young tubercles and so are located near the center of the plant. They are funnel-shaped, 2 to 2¼ inches across, fragrant, and have lustrous, yellow perianth lobes (petals), reddish-brown on their undersides. The stamens and style, the latter topped with a ten- to fourteen-lobed stigma, are yellow. The dry fruits contain black seeds.

Garden and Landscape Uses and Cultivation. This is a choice collectors' item suitable for cultivation outdoors only in warm desert regions and in greenhouses. Its general cultivation is that of most small desert cactuses. Deep, very porous, fertile soil and if grown in pots an especially deep container are needed because of the long stout roots. Care must be taken not to keep the soil too wet, especially in winter. Slight shade from the strongest sun is advisable. For further information see Cactuses.

LEUCOCORYNE (Leucocorỳ-ne)—Glory-of-the-Sun. Of the five species of this Chilean genus of the lily family LILIACEAE, only one is known to be cultivated. The group consists of nonhardy bulb plants related to *Brodiaea*. The name, from the Greek *leukos*, white, and *koryne*, a club, called attention to the staminodes.

Leucocorynes have narrowly-linear, channeled, all-basal leaves and branchless, leafless flower stalks topped by umbels of few to several, individually stalked, white or white-centered lavender-blue blooms each with six petals (more correctly tepals), three stamens, three staminodes (nonfunctional stamens), and a short style. The fruits are capsules. At the bases of the umbels of *Leucocoryne* are two linear bracts, as opposed to one or three or more in *Brodiaea*. Also, the underground organs of this last genus are corms rather than bulbs.

Glory-of-the-sun (*L. ixioides*) has few

Leucocoryne ixioides

leaves 1 foot or thereabouts long, and taller slender flower stalks with loose umbels of six to ten beautiful, starry, usually heliotrope-scented blooms about 1½ inches wide, in aspect reminiscent of those of a large glory-of-the-snow (*Chionodoxa*). Seedlings vary considerably in color. The name *L. i. odorata* has been applied to those with deeper-colored, fragrant flowers, and *L. i. alba* to white-flowered individuals.

Garden and Landscape Uses and Cultivation. Except that glory-of-the-sun does not multiply by offsets and so far as is recorded can only be increased by seed (although bulb cuttings would certainly be worth trying), its culture is that of *Freesia*. In water, cut flowers of glory-of-the-sun last extremely well.

LEUCOCRINUM (Leucó-crinum) — Sand-Lily or Star-Lily. The only species of *Leucocrinum*, of the lily family LILIACEAE, is a delightful small native of sandy meadows and flats from Oregon to Nebraska, California, and New Mexico. Its name is from the Greek *leucos*, white, and *krinon*, a lily.

The sand-lily or star-lily (*L. montanum*) has leaves that spread close to the ground and are 4 to 8 inches long and ¼ inch wide. They spring directly from a short rhizome buried 1½ to 3 inches deep, furnished with fleshy roots. From the center of each plant and at ground level a cluster of four to eight 2-inch-wide, often fragrant blooms develops. Each flower has a stalk 1 inch to 1½ inches long and six spreading petals (actually tepals) with their bases united to form a 2- to 3-inch-long slender tube. The ovaries are below ground and there, too, the flower stalks join a common stalk so that technically the clusters are umbels. So far as appearance goes sand-crocus would be a more descriptive name than sand-lily, but botanically *Leucocrinum* belongs with the lilies. Its possession of six rather than three stamens readily distinguishes it from *Crocus*. Its fruits are capsules.

Garden Uses and Cultivation. This is a real gem for a choice location in the rock garden where it can be isolated from plants of a more arrogant, spreading nature, and so long as it is doing well it can remain undisturbed for long periods. Transplanting is often followed by one or more years of non-blooming. An extremely well-drained slope of sandy, gritty soil that contains a little organic matter suits it well. A rock garden moraine or scree is apt to be to its liking. Full sun is needed. Plants collected from the wild are the most common source of garden stock, but they are usually slow to reestablish. Every care should be taken to prevent the roots from drying. Immediately following the natural dying of the foliage is the most auspicious time for transplanting. Seed sown in pots or flats of sandy soil in fall afford means of increase. The containers should be buried to their rims in sand, ashes, or peat moss in a cold frame over winter.

LEUCODENDRON (Leuco-déndron)—Silver Tree. The silver tree, of South Africa, is one of the most noteworthy members of the remarkable flora of that botanically rich region. It is one of more than seventy species of *Leucodendron*, of the protea family PROTEACEAE, a genus endemic to southern Africa. The name, derived from the Greek *leukos*, white, and *dendron*, a tree, alludes to the foliage of *L. argenteum*.

Leucodendrons are trees and shrubs with alternate, hairy or hairless leaves. Male and female flowers are on separate plants. The former are showy and aggregated in conical, globular, or cylindrical heads, the less conspicuous females in conelike structures. Each flower has four perianth parts (petals) that ultimately become separated to their middles or lower. In the males there is a stamen and in the females a staminode (nonfunctional stamen) in a depression in each petal. The style, functional in female flowers, conspicuous, but abortive in males, is usually slender. The flower heads of many kinds are ornamented by encircling, brightly colored bractlike leaves. After flowering, female heads develop seedlike dry fruits.

Leucodendron argenteum in South Africa

Leucodendron argenteum, young plants in southern California

Leucodendron argenteum (foliage)

The silver tree (**L. argenteum**), beautiful, but rather short-lived, attains a height of 20 to 30 feet. Its gleaming, silvery, lanceolate leaves are 2½ to 4½ inches long and up to 2 inches wide or slightly wider. Spherical and conspicuous at the branch ends, the male flower heads are of apricot blooms surrounded by a collar of handsome silver bracts. They are 1¼ to nearly 2 inches in diameter. The heads of female flowers, hidden among the foliage, are somewhat larger, and with age increase in size and become very silvery.

Other leucodendrons are worth attempting by enthusiasts for the protea family. Among them are **L. daphnoides,** a handsome, compact, shrubby kind that has flower heads surrounded by brilliant red or yellow bracts, and somewhat similar but much more robust *L. grandiflorum*. The female flower heads of **L. grandiflorum** are purplish-red encircled by red-marked, green bracts, the more showy males are yellow surrounded by yellow-marked, red bracts. Up to about 4 feet tall and said to be a slow grower, **L. venosum** has both male and female flower heads adorned with bracts of rusty-red and green. Attaining 8 feet in height, **L. plumosum** has hairy, silvery-grayish foliage, clusters of yellow male

Leucodendron daphnoides in South Africa

Leucodendron daphnoides (flowers)

Leucodendron grandiflorum

Leucodendron grandiflorum (flowers)

flower heads, and much larger brownish female ones clothed with white hairs.

Garden and Landscape Uses and Cultivation. In southern California the silver tree thrives outdoors, and other species are grown there. They require very well-drained soil and full sun. Often they are tricky at first, but once passed the seedling stage are easier to manage. In general they respond to conditions and care that suit *Protea*. The silver tree is sometimes cultivated in pots and tubs in cool greenhouses, where it usually does well under conditions that suit acacias.

LEUCOGENES (Leucógen-es)—New-Zealand-Edelweiss. Peculiar to New Zealand, *Leucogenes* consists of two species of the daisy family COMPOSITAE that bear some resemblance to the northern hemisphere edelweiss (*Leontopodium*). At one time included in *Helichrysum*, these plants are segregated because of technical characteristics of their fruits and because of marked differences between their basal and stem leaves. Their name, from the Greek *leukos*, white, and *eugenes*, noble, alludes to the appearance of the flowering parts of the plants.

Leucogenes are alpine and subalpine subshrubs with woody bases and hairy foliage. Their flower heads consist of florets all of the disk type (like those of a daisy's eye). There are no ray florets (the kind that in daisies resemble petals). Small groups of florets are assembled in dense heads that nestle above a collar of spreading raylike bracts that suggest petals and are densely clad with white hairs.

Having thick, woody stems, prostrate at their bases, and upright branches, **L. grandiceps** is tufted and 1 inch to 7 inches tall.

Leucogenes grandiceps

Its foliage is silvery-hairy on both surfaces. The obovate-wedge-shaped leaves, up to ⅓ inch long, usually are recurved at their apexes. They overlap, closely or loosely, like shingles on a roof, and are clothed with white or light buff hairs. The tight

clusters of small flower heads with an encircling collar of densely-white-woolly raylike bracts, up to fifteen in number, are about 1 inch in diameter. Handsomer than the last, **L. leontopodium** exceeds the edelweiss of the European Alps in beauty. It has the same habit of growth as *L. grandiceps* except that its basal leaves are in more definite rosettes. Also, its linear to lanceolate-oblong leaves and floral structures are about twice as large as those of *L. grandiceps*. They are clothed with lustrous white to pale buff hairs.

Garden Uses and Cultivation. In favored climates where little freezing occurs in winter, and summers are not extremely hot, New-Zealand-edelweisses are beautiful plants for well-drained, sunny rock gardens. They are increased by seed.

LEUCOJUM (Leu-còjum) — Snowflake, Snowdrop. In the northern United States and most other parts of the English-speaking world the name snowdrop is reserved for *Galanthus*, but in the southern United States it is commonly applied to *Leucojum*. This is confusing to the user of common names, but Canute trying to stem the tide with a broom faced a task no more difficult than attempting to deprive a people of a regional colloquial plant name to which they are accustomed. Undoubtedly leucojums will remain snowdrops to southerners, while northerners, other English-speaking peoples, books, and bulb catalogs will call them snowflakes. By whichever name, leucojums comprise a group of a dozen species of comely bulb plants of the amaryllis family AMARYLLIDACEAE, natives of Europe and North Africa. Their name is a modification of an old Greek one, *leukoion*, used for these plants by Hippocrates and others. It is derived from *leucos*, white, and *ion*, a violet. The latter is not at all descriptive of the form of the flowers.

Leucojums bloom in spring or fall according to species. They differ from *Galanthus* in having the segments of the perianth, correctly identified as tepals, but more familiarly known as the petals and so referred to in this treatment, all of nearly the same size and shape, whereas those of *Galanthus* are of two distinctly unequal types. Also, the flower stalks of *Leucojum* are hollow instead of, like those of *Galanthus*, solid. Leucojums have few to many, all-basal, strap-shaped or linear leaves, those of spring-flowering kinds appearing with the blooms, those of fall-bloomers shortly after the flowers. The flowers are solitary or in umbels of few atop erect stalks. They nod, and are white tinged or marked with green or red. They have six petals, six stamens, and one style. The fruits are triangular capsules containing nearly spherical seeds.

The summer snowflake (**L. aestivum**) is the sort most commonly grown in America. In parts of the south it is found in almost every yard. In catalogs it often masquerades as the spring snowflake, which name by right belongs to altogether different *L. vernum*. Both its common and botanical names (*aestivum* means summer) indicate that it is a summer-bloomer, but actually it flowers in spring (in winter in the south), later, it is true, than *L. vernum*, but nevertheless, well before the onset of summer. The summer snowflake is the most robust kind. It has an abundance of lush, strap-shaped leaves up to 1½ feet long by ½ inch wide. Its flower stalks are 1 foot tall or taller and carry two to eight blooms with white petals tipped with green and up to ¾ inch long. This species is a native of central and southern Europe.

Leucojum aestivum

Leucojum aestivum (flowers)

The spring snowflake (**L. vernum**) is extraordinarily rare in America. The bulbs sent out under this name by bulb dealers almost invariably turn out to be those of the summer snowflake. But the spring snowflake is worth diligent search even if one must send to Europe to obtain it. It has strap-shaped leaves, short when flowering first begins but becoming 6 to 9 inches long later, and up to ½ inch wide. The flower stalks are 6 inches to 1 foot in height and usually have only one, white-tipped-with-green, bloom. A variety, *L. v. carpathicum* has petals tipped with yellow.

Leucojum vernum

Variety *L. v. vagneri* is more robust and has two flowers to a stem. The spring snowflake has its home in central and southern Europe.

The autumn snowflake (*L. autumnale*) is altogether different. Native to dry hillsides in Spain, Portugal, Morocco, and the Ionian Islands, it has slender, grassy, almost threadlike, leaves that appear in fall. Before them come frail stalks, up to 6 inches tall, each carrying a few pink-flushed, dependent blooms, less showy, but not less beautiful than those of its spring-blooming kin.

Leucojum autumnale

There are other kinds worth seeking, but tracking them down is a task for the dedicated connoisseur of rare and difficult-to-acquire plants. The winter snowflake (*L. nicaeense* syn. *L. hiemale*) inhabits a limited area of sea cliffs near Nice on the French Riviera and is reported to be well on its way to oblivion in the wild as the result of building activities. The twin-flowered *L. tricophyllum,* a miniature from Spain, Portugal, and Morocco, has leaves that are triangular in section. From Corsica comes *L. roseum,* similar to *L. autumnale,* but with rose-pink blooms.

Garden and Landscape Uses. The summer snowflake and spring snowflake are abundantly hardy, the autumn snowflake and probably the others, less so. The two former, especially the first named, are as easily cultivated as daffodils and under reasonable circumstances make themselves as much at home. However, to produce a good effect they should be planted more closely than daffodils; they are effective in clumps, but not when they stand solitary or widely spaced. They are excellent for naturalizing and for planting informally as well as for setting in groups in perennial beds or at the fronts of shrub plantings and by watersides. They prefer shade from the hottest sun and do well where they receive only morning sun. The spring snowflake is appropriate in larger rock gardens; the other is too gross for that purpose. Only for rock gardens and similar intimate plantings where the tiny and the frail can receive special attention is the autumn snowflake suited, and this is true also of the rarer species.

Cultivation. The spring snowflake and the summer one have strong constitutions and flourish without worry to the gardener in any deep, porous, fertile soil, well-drained, but sufficiently moist through spring and early summer to encourage good foliage growth. The incorporation of generous amounts of good compost, leaf mold, or other humus-forming material at the time the soil is prepared for planting is greatly beneficial. The bulbs must not be set deeply; if their tops are covered to a depth of 2 inches that is enough. They may be spaced about 3 inches apart. Planting should be done in late summer or as early in fall as the bulbs can be obtained. Once established and doing well, these plants should not be disturbed unless quite necessary for purposes of propagation or other compelling reason. Following planting, a couple of years may elapse before they settle down and bloom freely. When bulbs are to be transplanted the best time to do that is in late spring as soon as the foliage has died.

Growing the autumn snowflake is a little less simple. A gritty, porous soil, well enriched with leaf mold and never too dry but well drained, suits it best and, in the north at least, a sheltered location in sun or lightest shade. It may also be handled successfully planted in pans kept plunged almost to their rims in sand in a cold frame. Propagation of snowflakes is easy by seed. Plants so raised take about four years to reach blooming size. Offsets form the most usual mode of increase. Bulb-cuttings also give good results.

LEUCOPHYLLUM (Leuco-phýllum)—Cenizo. The genus *Leucophyllum* is endemic to the southwestern United States and Mexico. It belongs in the figwort family SCROPHULARIACEAE and comprises about fourteen species. Its name, from the Greek *leucos*, white, and *phyllon*, a leaf, refers to the whitish foliage.

Leucophyllums have alternate, lobeless leaves and axillary tubular flowers with five-lobed calyxes, five-lobed corollas, four stamens arising from the base of and included in the corolla tube, and one style. The fruits are capsules.

The cenizo (*L. frutescens* syn. *L. texanum*) is a loosely-branched, white-tomentose shrub 3 to 8 feet tall, native from Texas to Mexico. It has very short-stalked, elliptic to obovate leaves ½ to 1 inch long, and solitary purplish-pink flowers about 1 inch long and wide and hairy on their insides. Horticultural selections are *L. f. compactum* and *L. f. floribundum*.

Leucophyllum frutescens

Leucophyllum frutescens (foliage)

Leucophyllum frutescens (flowers)

Garden Uses and Cultivation. The cenizo is cultivated primarily for its attractive foliage. It is not hardy in the north, but in the deep south it is esteemed as a hedge plant and as a specimen shrub on lawns, in foundation plantings, and elsewhere. It succeeds with minimum care in well-drained, dryish, even poor soil, in full sun, and stands any pruning and shearing necessary to keep it shapely. Propagation is by seed and by cuttings.

LEUCOPOGON (Leuco-pògon). Few of the approximately 130 species of shrubs and small trees that compose *Leucopogon*, of the epacris family EPACRIDACEAE, are known to gardeners in North America. Natives of Australia, New Zealand, and some other islands of the Pacific, they are hardy in mild climates only. The name, from the Greek *leukos*, white, and *pogon*, a beard, alludes to the hairs on the flowers of some sorts.

The leaves of these plants are alternate and usually stalkless. In spikes or clusters or solitary, the small flowers have five each sepals, petals, and stamens. The fruits are small, berry-like drupes.

A pretty dwarf shrub, *L. fraseri* (syn. *Cyathodes fraseri*), of Australia, Tasmania, and New Zealand, inhabits dunes, dry rocky places, and grazed fields. It forms dense, wide mats 3 to 6 inches high of prostrate stems from which rise erect, wiry branches encircled by closely overlapping, prickly-pointed, ½-inch-long, ovate to linear-oblong, shiny leaves. Solitary from the leaf axils, the sweetly fragrant, pinkish flowers are about ½ inch long. They are succeeded by oblongish, bright orange to yellow, edible, sweet fruits about ¼ inch in diameter.

Garden Uses and Cultivation. The species described is charming for rock gardens and other intimate landscaped areas. It associates well with heaths and heathers. Locations in full sun, with acid, peaty soil suit. Following flowering or fruiting it is well to shear the shoots back quite severely to encourage compact new growth, which then develops abundantly from the base of the plant and from underground stolons. A mulch of peat moss or similar material maintained about the plants is beneficial. Propagation is easy by seed, cuttings, and division.

LEUCOSCEPTRUM (Leuco-scéptrum). This genus of a few species of the mint family LABIATAE inhabits Asia from Japan to the Himalayas. Its name derives from the Greek *leukos*, white, and *skeptron*, a rod, in allusion to the hoary stems.

Leucosceptrums are subshrubs or perennial herbaceous plants with slightly woody bases. They have squarish stems, opposite, toothed leaves, and dense, terminal spikes of short-stalked, asymmetrical, two-lipped blooms with corolla tubes longer than the five-toothed, tubular calyxes. The upper corolla-lip is two-lobed, the lower three-lobed. There are four long-protruding stamens of nearly equal size. The fruits consist of four seedlike nutlets. The clasping, scalelike bracts of the flower spikes fall early.

There are two Japanese species, *Leucosceptrum stellipilum* (syn. *Comanthosphace stellipila*), a subshrub, and *L. japonicum*, a herbaceous perennial, the latter slightly woody at its base. From 1¼ to 3 feet tall, *L. stellipilum* has smooth stems, when young furnished with stellate (star-shaped) hairs. The leaves have stalks up to 2 inches long and thin, broadly-elliptic to oblong blades 3 to 6 inches long by 2 to 4½ inches wide. They are stellate-hairy on their upper sides and on the veins beneath. The rose-pink flowers, about ⅓ inch in length, are in spikes 4 to 6½ inches long. Closely allied *L. japonicum* (syns. *Comanthosphace japonica, C. sublanceolata*) has erect stems slightly stellate-hairy above. Its lanceolate to oblong leaves are about as long as those of the last, but not over 3 inches wide. Only when young are they slightly stellate-hairy. The flowers are pale yellow and about ⅓ inch long.

Garden and Landscape Uses and Cultivation. These hardy, fall-blooming woodland plants are grateful for a little shade and need soil containing a fair amount of organic matter. Suggested for flower borders and informal plantings, they need no special attention and are easily increased by seed and cuttings.

LEUCOSIDEA (Leuco-sídea). The genus *Leucosidea* consists of one species of the rose family ROSACEAE, endemic to southern Africa. Its name derives from the Greek *leucos*, white, and *eidos*, appearance.

A densely-leafy shrub about 10 feet tall and with deciduous bark, or sometimes a tree up to 30 feet tall, *L. sericea* has alternate, pinnate, aromatic leaves with three or four pairs of coarsely-toothed, elliptic, green or gray leaflets ½ inch to 1½ inches long and a similar terminal leaflet. They

Leucosidea sericea

are densely silky-hairy and glandular on their undersides, sparingly silky-hairy above. Minute leaflets alternate with the pairs of bigger ones. The small yellowish-green or yellow flowers, in hairy, terminal, short-stalked spikes, have a ten- or twelve-lobed, persistent calyx, constricted in its throat, five petals, ten or twelve stamens, and slender styles. The fruits are achenes included in the nearly bony calyx tube.

Garden Uses and Cultivation. This is an attractive general purpose shrub for regions, such as parts of California, with prevailingly warm, dry climates. Well-drained soils and sunny locations suit. Propagation is by seed and cuttings.

LEUCOSPERMUM (Leuco-spérmum)—Pincushion. As American gardeners come to understand better the needs of South African members of the protea family PROTEACEAE, these magnificent evergreen flowering shrubs are likely to become more common in parts of California and elsewhere where climates are similarly salubrious. The genus *Leucospermum* belongs to this group and contains among its approximately forty species many highly desirable ones. Its name derives from the Greek *leukos*, white, and *sperma*, a seed, and has obvious application.

A close ally of *Protea*, from which it differs in its heads of flowers having a collar of small, comparatively inconspicuous bracts rather than a cuplike formation of large, prominent ones, in the upper and lateral perianth segments of its individual blooms being fused only in their lower parts, and in having a solitary stamen with each segment, *Leucospermum* has usually crowded leaves that often are toothed at their apexes. The most conspicuous features of leucospermum flower heads are the long, protruding styles that radiate like pins from a pincushion, the stigmas representing the pin heads. The older flowers in each head are at its circumference, the younger ones toward the center. The styles of those not fully mature arch inward and are held under tension with their tips enclosed in the calyx. Finally, often in response to the visit of a pollinating bird, they spring free and spread outward and upward. The fruits, technically nuts, are hard-shelled, smooth, and whitish-gray. The leaves of leucospermums are hairy, at least when young.

One of the finest species is *L. reflexum*. The tallest kind, it attains a height of 10 to 14 feet and has long shoots with downy, gray-green, oblong to oblanceolate, 1- to 2-inch-long leaves along their lengths. The leaves do not spread widely, and may be toothed at their ends. The flower heads, suggestive of sky rockets speeding heavenward, are solitary or paired, and 2 inches wide by twice as long. They are terminal and have many 3-inch-long, bright

Leucospermum reflexum

Leucospermum nutans at San Diego, California

Leucospermum incisum

Leucospermum reflexum (flowers)

Leucospermum nutans (flowers)

red styles that look longer because the stigmas attached to them continue in the same direction. As the styles are freed from the flowers they point downward so that those forming the lower parts of the head of bloom droop while the others curve upward.

The broad-leaved pincushion (**L. nutans** syn. *L. cordifolium*) is another splendid kind. Rarely over 4 feet in height, it has minutely-downy shoots and ovate to broadly-elliptic leaves 1 inch to 3 inches

long and about one-half as wide, toothed at their apexes and, when young, slightly hairy. The normally solitary flower heads, waxy in appearance, and 3 to 4 inches in diameter, consist of brick-red to orange or pinkish-yellow flowers with hairless perianth tubes up to ⅓ inch long, and styles, up to 3 inches long, tipped with club-shaped, yellow stigmas.

The narrow-leaved pincushion (**L. lineare**), 2 to 4 feet tall, may sprawl or be upright. It has hairless shoots and almost needle-like, linear leaves 3 to 4 inches long by up to ¼ inch broad. Usually solitary, its greenish-yellow, orange-yellow, or red flower heads, up to 4 inches in diameter, are much like those of the last except that their cone-shaped stigmas appear bigger in relation to the slender styles.

A showy ornamental that attains a height of 4 to 5 feet, **L. incisum** has branches thickly clothed with oblongish leaves 2 to 2½ inches long by up to almost 1 inch wide and coarsely five- to seven-toothed at their apexes. The stalkless flower heads, up to 5 inches in diameter and yellowish-red, much resemble those of *L. nutans*.

A rounded shrub or tree 6 to 12 feet tall, **L. conocarpodendron** (syn. *L. conocarpum*) has minutely-hairy shoots practically hidden by the crowded leaves. The latter, red and toothed at their apexes, are about 3

inches long by one-half as wide. Hairy at first, they become smooth later. The flower heads, cone-shaped and pink in bud, are a beautiful bright yellow when they open and gradually change to reddish-orange. They are about 3½ inches across. With flower heads rather similar to those of the last, and either unchanging yellow with light orange styles or yellow changing to orange and finally red at the heads mature, **L. cuneiforme** (syn. *L. attenuatum*) is 3 to 6 feet tall. It has spreading branches and smaller leaves less crowded than *L. conocarpodendron*.

A low trailer capable of covering a wide area, **L. prostratum** has dull green, slightly hairy leaves, and powder-puff-like, globular flower heads, ¾ inch to 1½ inches wide, of yellow, orange, and red. The leaves are linear and 1 inch to 1½ inches long by up to ³⁄₁₆ inch wide. A trailer, often with its stems more or less covered with the sand in which it grows, **L. hypophyllocarpodendron** has more or less hairy leaves of various forms from channeled-linear to flat and oblanceolate. Its sweetly fragrant yellow flowers are in small heads.

Leucospermum hypophyllocarpodendron

Attractive **L. spathulatum** is a rare native of the Transvaal. A low shrub, it differs from most leucospermums in having

Leucospermum nutans in South Africa

Leucospermum spathulatum

Leucospermum spathulatum (flowers)

stems that spread more or less horizontally near to the ground and curve upward toward their ends to hold the pinkish-orange or flame-colored flower heads a foot or two above the surface. The upper leaves are elliptic-spatula-shaped; those lower on the stems are narrower.

Garden and Landscape Uses and Cultivation. That this magnificent genus offers tremendous possibilities to gardeners in parts of California and other warm-temperate climates with dry summers is obvious. Experimental and trial-and-error plantings need to be made to determine which species will prove most satisfactory and just where they can be grown. As garden ornamentals and cut flowers many kinds are superb. The remarks on cultivation made under *Protea* apply to *Leucospermum*, but seeds of the latter germinate more slowly.

LEUCOTHOE (Leucó-tho-e) — Fetterbush, Sweetbells. The genus *Leucothoe* consists of about fifty species of evergreen and deciduous shrubs, natives of North and South America and eastern Asia. They belong in the heath family ERICACEAE and have as a name that of a legendary princess of Babylon whom the god Apollo was believed to have changed into a shrub after she had been buried alive by her father.

Leucothoes have alternate, usually sharply-fine-toothed, undivided, lobeless leaves. Their small white blooms are in axillary or terminal racemes or panicles. They have five-parted, bell- to saucer-shaped, persistent calyxes, tubular, slender-urn-shaped corollas, constricted at their throats and with five brief lobes (petals), ten flat-stalked stamens much shorter then the corolla, and a style equaling it in length. The fruits are capsules.

Eastern North American *L. fontanesiana* (syn. *L. editorum*) and *L. axillaris* (syn. *L. catesbaei*) are excellent evergreens. Native along banks of mountain streams from Virginia to North Carolina, Tennessee, and Georgia, **L. fontanesiana** is from 3 to 6 feet tall, with erect or gracefully arching stems, reddish when young. Its short-stalked leaves are pointed, lanceolate, ob-

Leucothoe fontanesiana

longish, or oblanceolate, usually toothed, and 3½ to 6 inches long. The racemes of approximately ¼-inch-long, crowded flowers are stalkless and 1½ to 4 inches long. The flattened-spherical capsules are ⅕ inch in diameter. Two varieties with foliage, at least early in the season, variegated with pink, yellow, and coppery colors are *L. f.* 'Girard's Rainbow' and *L. f.* 'Trivar'. Variety *L. f. nana* does not exceed 2 feet in height. An inhabitant of moist and wet woodlands of the coastal plain from Virginia to Florida and Mississippi, **L. axillaris** is generally similar to *L. fontanesiana*, from which it differs in the sepals of its flowers being broadly-ovate with blunt or rounded apexes, rather than pointed-ovate-lanceolate, in its flowers being in racemes not over, and usually under, 2 inches long, and in having shorter-stalked, more abruptly pointed leaves with more distantly spaced teeth.

Western North American **L. davisiae** differs from those described above in that its flowers are in terminal panicles. Native from Oregon to California, it is 3 feet tall. It has short-stalked, ovate-oblong to broadly-elliptic, blunt or pointed leaves ¾ inch to 3 inches long, slightly toothed or

Leucothoe axillaris

Leucothoe axillaris (flowers)

Leucothoe davisiae

toothless. The nodding flowers, up to ⅓ inch long, are in panicles up to 4 inches long. Related to the last, Japanese **L. keiskei** is up to 4 feet in height. A less robust grower than *L. fontanesiana*, it has slender stems, and long-pointed, ovate to ovate-oblong leaves 1½ to 3½ inches long, indistinctly and distantly round-toothed. The racemes of comparatively large pendulous flowers, terminal and from the leaf axils at the ends of the stems, are up to 4 inches long. This species in its homeland inhabits shaded, wet cliffs in the mountains.

Sweetbells (**L. racemosa** syn. *Eubotrys racemosa*) is a deciduous, erect shrub, up to

Leucothoe racemosa

12 feet tall, with short-stalked, bright green, oblong to obovate, finely-toothed leaves up to 3 inches long that turn scarlet in fall. Its white or pinkish flowers, up to ⅓ inch long, come in spring at the ends of the leafless shoots of the previous season. They are in slender, one-sided racemes 1½ to 3 inches long. This species is indigenous from Massachusetts to Florida and Louisiana. Variety *L. r. projecta,* which occurs from Maryland southward, has racemes 3 to 6 inches long. Differing in its flowers having ovate instead of lanceolate sepals, anthers with two instead of four awns, winged seeds, and usually curving rather than mostly straight racemes of bloom, **L. recurva** (syn. *Eubotrys recurva*) inhabits moist mountain woods from Virginia to Georgia. Deciduous, it is lower and more straggling than *L. racemosa,* but otherwise much resembles it. Both species are hardy in southern New England.

Garden and Landscape Uses. The chief value of these shrubs is as furnishings for open woods and other lightly shaded areas where naturalistic effects are sought. They are plants of moist, acid soils, but in cultivation *E. racemosa* stands dryish situations remarkably well. They make few calls on the gardener's skill. Given such conditions all discussed above are hardy, at least in sheltered locations, as far north as southern New England, and *L. fontanesiana* even further north.

Cultivation. Once established in agreeable locations, leucothoes need little attention. Like most shrubs of the heath family they are benefited by mulching annually with leaf mold, peat moss, or well-decayed compost and by periodic deep waterings if the ground becomes dry. They can be raised from seeds sown in pots or pans (shallow pots) containing sandy peaty soil in a cool greenhouse or cold frame. The seeds are very fine and need only the slightest covering with finely sifted soil. The soil must not be allowed to dry. Other means of propagation are division and cuttings. Early spring and early fall are appropriate seasons to attend

to the first. Cuttings root with little difficulty if made in late summer or early fall and planted in a cold frame or cool greenhouse propagating bed in sand, a mixture of sand and peat moss, or other suitable medium. They must be kept moist, shaded from sun, and in a highly humid atmosphere while rooting takes place.

LEUZEA (Leùz-ea). Four species of the daisy family COMPOSITAE comprise *Leuzea,* a southern European and North African genus some authorities include in *Centaurea.* Its name honors Joseph Philippe François Deleuze, a friend of the distinguished botanist deCandolle. He died in 1835.

Leuzeas are herbaceous perennials with usually pinnate or pinnately-lobed or rarely undivided, lobeless leaves in rosettes or alternate on the stems. Their large, solitary flower heads consist of a conspicuous subspherical or egg-shaped, conelike involucre capped with a tuft of all tubular florets. The fruits are seedlike achenes.

Hardy and 6 inches to 1½ feet tall, **L. conifera** (syn. *Centaurea conifera*), of southern Europe and Algeria, has lanceolate, mostly pinnately-cleft leaves, the lower

Leuzea conifera

Leuzea centauroides

ones sometimes undivided and lobeless. Their undersides are clothed with a felt of white hairs. The pine-cone-like flower heads up to 2 inches long have involucres clothed with glossy, brownish, blunt, cleft scales, and not-showy, purple florets. A robust native of the Pyrenees 2 to 3½ feet tall, **L. centauroides** (syn. *Rhaptonicum cynaroides*) develops a large clump of acanthus-like, arching, deeply-pinnately-cleft and toothed basal leaves up to 1½ feet long and smaller stem leaves. All have green upper surfaces, white-hairy undersides. The spherical flower heads are 2 to 2½ inches wide, the flowers purple.

Garden and Landscape Uses and Cultivation. The species described are useful for flower beds and borders, for naturalistic plantings, and *L. conifera* for rock gardens. They need full sun and succeed in ordinary, moderately fertile, well-drained soils, even rocky and gravelly ones. They are easily increased by seed and by division.

LEVISTICUM (Lev-ísticum)—Lovage. A coarse, deciduous, aromatic, hardy herbaceous perennial called lovage is the only cultivated species of the three that constitute the Eurasian genus *Levisticum,* of the carrot family UMBELLIFERAE. The name is an old Latin one derived from the Greek *lithostikon,* used for an unidentified plant. Resembling related *Angelica,* plants of *Levisticum* have leaves characteristically twice- or thrice-pinnately-divided and compound umbels of small greenish-yellow or yellowish flowers. For Scotch-lovage or alpine-lovage see Ligusticum.

Lovage (**L. officinale**), a native of southern Europe naturalized in parts of the United States, is 3 to 6 feet tall. Its dark glossy green leaves progressively decrease in size toward the top of the plant. The uppermost ones are sometimes undivided. The leaflets are narrowly- to broadly-wedge-shaped and above their middles are sharply and conspicuously lobed or toothed. The umbels are 1½ to 4 inches

Levisticum officinale

Libertia elegans

Ligularia hessei

Lilium auratum

Liatris pycnostachya

Lilium hybrid in a mixed flower border

Lilium canadense

Lilium tigrinum

Lilium hybrid 'Imperial Silver'

Liquidambar styraciflua in fall foliage

Limnanthes douglasii

Levisticum officinale (flowers)

wide. The flowers are succeeded by slightly-flattened or boat-shaped, longitudinally-ribbed, aromatic fruits, commonly referred to as seeds, about ¼ inch long. These are used in confectionary. In the past the leafstalks of lovage were blanched and eaten. Like the roots and other parts they have a celery-like flavor.

Garden Uses. Lovage is generally restricted as a cultivated plant to herb gardens. Its fresh green leaves may be used to flavor salads or, if the gardener is so minded, the leafstalks may be blanched by heaping soil around the plants or by wrapping them with light-excluding paper collars, as is done when celery is blanched. This tenderizes the stalks and leaves, subdues their strong flavor, and makes them palatable. Although it will never come near to replacing celery in popularity, lovage has some of its qualities and is much more easily grown.

Cultivation. Lovage rejoices in deep, fertile, reasonably moist soil in a sunny location. The plants may be spaced about 3 feet apart. Unlike celery, they are perennial and may remain for many years without disturbance. Established plantings should be fertilized in spring and kept well watered in dry weather. New plants may be raised from seed sown in early fall or spring, or even more easily, by division at either season, preferably in spring.

LEWISARA. This is the name of orchid hybrids the parents of which include *Aerides, Arachnis, Ascocentrum,* and *Vanda.*

LEWISIA (Lewís-ia)—Bitter Root. Captain Meriweather Lewis, who with William Clark made a historic journey of exploration to the West Coast early in the nineteenth century, is honored by the name *Lewisia.* He died in 1809. The genus consists of possibly twenty species of the purslane family PORTULACACEAE. All are natives of western North America.

Lewisias are hardy, low, evergreen and deciduous, thick-rooted herbaceous perennials mostly with rosettes of more or less fleshy, chiefly basal foliage and handsome white, yellowish, pink, or rarely red blooms, solitary or in panicles. The flowers have two to six persistent sepals, four to eighteen petals, five or more stamens, and three to eight styles joined at their bases. The fruits are capsules containing few to many seeds.

From *Portulaca* lewisias differ in their flowers having ovaries that are completely superior (entirely above the petals) and not joined to the calyx, and in their seed capsules splitting upward to their apexes. The manner in which the seed capsules open, and the not more than three style branches, differentiate *Lewisia* from *Calandrinia.* The roots of lewisias contain considerable starch and those of some kinds were important foods of the Indians. Recognition and naming of *Lewisia* species has caused much confusion, and the situation is not eased by the tendencies of some sorts to vary considerably and to hybridize freely.

Lewisias with evergreen foliage include *L. columbiana* and *L. c. rosea,* the latter superior because of its rich pink blooms in contrast to the pale pink to pink-veined white ones of the other. These plants have rosettes of flat, narrow, spatula-shaped, dark green, toothless leaves 1 inch to 3 inches in length and, on their several slender flower stalks, a few small bractlike leaves. In few- to many-flowered, loose sprays 6 inches to 1 foot tall, the starry blooms, ½ to ¾ inch across, are held aloft on upright, rather than wide-spreading branches. They have two toothed sepals, four to seven petals, and five or six stamens. Although among the easiest to grow, *L. columbiana* and its variety are far from being the most spectacular. They are natives of the mountains of Washington and Oregon. Sometimes confused with *L. c. rosea,* although of quite different aspect, is closely related **L. rupicola.** It has many narrow, toothless, evergreen leaves up to 2 inches long, with the biggest on the outsides, and the others becoming progressively smaller toward the centers of the rosettes. Short-stalked offset rosettes are developed freely and hug the parent. From each rosette one to several stalks rise to a height of 4 or 5 inches, and end in loose clusters of 1-inch-wide, seven- to ten-petaled rose-pink blooms striped with deeper pink or red.

Similar to *L. columbiana* the rare **L. cantelowii,** first discovered in 1941, differs chiefly in its nearly stalkless evergreen leaves having sharp, almost bristly teeth. They are blunt, oblanceolate, and up to 3 inches long. The flower stalks, up to a little over 1 foot tall, have a few bracts and, loosely arranged, many ½-inch-wide blooms with creamy-white to pale pink, darker-veined petals. This species is a denizen of wet granite cliffs at from 1,500 to about 3,000 feet in California. From rocky places at considerably higher elevations in California comes the not dissimilar evergreen *L. congdonii.* Unlike the last its leaves are not toothed. From its base spread many, mostly basal, pointed-oblanceolate leaves with blades 2 to 4 inches long and stalks as long. Higher on the stalks the leaves become gradually reduced in size and finally are represented by toothed bracts. The rather few, pink blooms, a little over ½ inch wide, are in wide-branched panicles.

Slender-sausage-shaped or thick, evergreen, pointed-linear leaves are a distinguishing feature of *L. leana.* There may be forty to fifty or sometimes more of these in each basal rosette. They point in all directions, upward as well as outward. Under ⅕ inch wide, they are 1 inch to 2½ inches long and much resemble those of deciduous *L. rediviva.* The blooms are much more like those of *L. columbiana.* Each plant has up to six freely-branched panicles, 4 to 6 inches tall, with toothed bracts and numerous five- to eight-petaled flowers ⅓ to ½ inch in diameter, and pale pink with darker pink lines. Rare variations have pure white or cherry-red flowers. One gardener reported 377 flowers and flower buds on a single plant. When out of bloom *L. leana* has much the appearance of the succulent South African *Senecio scaposus.*

Favorite evergreen lewisias are *L. cotyledon* (syns. *L. finchae, L. purdyi*) and its many botanical and horticultural variants. All are beautiful, all have rosettes of comparatively broad leaves, and flowers much larger than kinds previously considered. Native from California to Oregon at elevations of 4,000 to 7,500 feet, typical *L. cotyledon* has many stalked, toothless, broadly-spatula-shaped to oblanceolate basal leaves, with sometimes undulating margins, 1 inch to 4 inches in length. Its bractlike flower stalk leaves are toothed. There are one to several rather thick, widely spreading stalks 4 inches to 1 foot tall, with many eight- to ten-petaled, stout-stalked flowers 1 inch to 1¼ inches across, and white, creamy-white, or yellowish, most

Lewisia cotyledon

commonly with red to orange-red longitudinal stripes that become paler as the blooms age. Individual plants have produced more than 500 blooms in a season. As previously indicated, *L. cotyledon* is highly variable. This is especially true of its foliage, and flower color. The fleshy leaves are brittle and in some forms have wavy or wrinkled margins. The margins may be semitransparent. From the typical species *L. c. heckneri*, which is found in California at elevations above 4,000 feet, differs in having strongly-toothed, plain-margined leaves, and flowers 1¼ to 1½ inches wide. The leaves of *L. c. howellii* are markedly crisped at their edges and sometimes toothed. The blooms are about 1¼ inches across. This occurs in California and Ore-

Lewisia cotyledon howellii

gon at 500- to 1,000-foot altitudes. Other variants of the *L. cotyledon* complex that must be considered as not more than varieties of that species include one named **L. eastwoodiana,** a native of Oregon with flat, narrow, green leaves and tight clusters of rather small, purple-veined, pink flowers. Other variants as well as hybrids of this group have been accorded horticultural names, but let the confusion not dismay, all are beautiful.

Loveliest of the evergreens, and perhaps of all lewisias, is **L. tweedyi.** This glorious species inhabits the mountains of central Washington where temperatures in summer sometimes exceed 100°F and in winter drop to −30°F, a range of more than 160 degrees. But in winter a comfortable snow blanket affords protection. This species grows on slopes of disintegrated granite with a content of decayed organic debris. It has long thick roots. Its many, leathery leaves, up to 6 inches long including their stalks, are obovate, sometimes notched at their apexes, and are paler on their undersides than above. There are a dozen or fewer flower stalks, as long or a little longer than the leaves, with small bracts and each with one to three blooms, the uppermost of which opens first and

Lewisia tweedyi at The New York Botanical Garden

the others in succession. The saucer-shaped flowers may be 3 inches or slightly more in diameter. They have two sepals, and eight to twelve spreading petals. They are creamy-colored, flushed with apricot toward the ends of the petals.

Bitter root (**L. rediviva**) rivals *L. tweedyi* in beauty. It is the handsomest deciduous species. So important was this as Indian food, and so well known to white man, that a range of mountains, a valley, and a river are endowed with its most familiar common name. It is also sometimes known as rock-rose and sand-rose. Indians ate the nutritious fresh roots raw and cooked, and dried them for winter storage. They have a slightly bitter flavor even after the very bitter, orange inner bark is removed. Bitter root has slender, cylindrical, fleshy leaves 1 inch to 2 inches long that resemble those of *L. oppositifolia* and are many together in basal rosettes. They develop in late summer or fall, persist through the winter, and die at about the time the flowers come in spring or early summer. The flowers are solitary on stalks ½ inch to 1½ inches long, with a whorl (circle) of a few bracts. They are usually pink, rarely white, and have four to eight petal-like sepals, and several petals. They are about 2 to 3 inches in diameter. Variety *L. r. minor* has smaller flowers. Bit-

Lewisia rediviva

ter root is native from the Rocky Mountains to California and British Columbia, often favoring rocky places and loose gravelly slopes. From bitter root **L. disepala,** a high alpine Californian species, differs in having smaller blooms.

Other deciduous species include *L. brachycalyx* and *L. kelloggii* (syn. *L. yosemitana*). Ranging from Utah, New Mexico, and Arizona to California, **L. brachycalyx** is found in wet meadows above 4,500 feet, and is one of the easier kinds to grow. Its spatula-shaped to oblanceolate leaves are 2 to 3 inches long. Usually its flowers are solitary on stalks 1 inch to 2 inches long. They have, in addition to two sepals, immediately beneath the sepals two bracts that look like sepals. The five to nine petals are white or sometimes flushed pink, and ½ inch to 1¼ inch long. From this **L. kelloggii** differs chiefly in having larger sepals with glandular teeth along their margins. A smaller plant, it occurs in California and Nevada.

Lewisia brachycalyx

Two rather similar deciduous kinds are **L. pygmaea** and **L. nevadensis** (syn. *L. bernardina*). Neither is outstanding, but the latter is the better. Sepals strongly glandular-toothed that with age become conspicuously veined characterize the former.

Lewisia pygmaea

The sepals of the latter have few or no glandular teeth and are not as prominently veined. Also, the flowers of *L. nevadensis* are mostly a little bigger than those of *L. pygmaea*. The few to many leaves of these kinds are basal, linear to narrowly-oblanceolate, and up to 3½ inches long. There are opposite bracts about the middles of the 1- to 2½-inch-long stalks. Each stalk carries one to three white to pink flowers ½ to ¾ inch in diameter, with two sepals and five to eight petals. In *L. p. longipetala* the flowers are larger.

Very distinctive and easily recognized is early blooming **L. oppositifolia.** It is deciduous and has few to several pointed-linear basal leaves 1 inch to 4 inches long that narrow from their middles or slightly above to both ends, and are up to one-third as broad as long. Erect or spraying outward, the slender stalks have on their lower parts one or two pairs of opposite leaves similar to the basal ones, but smaller. The stalks, up to 8 inches tall, in spring carry in umbel-like clusters two to six flowers ¾ to 1 inch in diameter, with four to seven sepals, and eight to ten white or pink petals. They look like miniature water-lilies. This lewisia inhabits moist, rocky sites from California to Oregon. Variety *L. o. richeyi* has been described as dwarfer, and a more profuse bloomer.

Very distinct in that it has no basal rosette of leaves is deciduous **L. triphylla.** A high mountain species at home from the Rocky Mountains to California and Washington, it has an underground globose tuber ¼ inch in diameter, and stems 1 inch to 2 inches long above ground, with a few linear leaves 1 inch to 2 inches in length. The umbel-like clusters of blooms consist of three to fifteen. They have five to eight white or pink petals and are about ⅓ inch in diameter. This is one of the less showy species.

Garden Uses and Cultivation. In general lewisias are for sophisticated rock gardeners only. The inexperienced are well advised to master the growing of less tricky plants before embarking on the cultivation of these gems of our western mountains. Not that they are impossible, they just demand rather special know-how and care. As a group they will not tolerate stagnant moisture about their roots and especially around the collars of the plants. Under such circumstances they quickly die. Some do need considerable moisture in spring and early summer, but it must drain freely so that abundant air as well as water enters the soil. It is common practice to plant lewisias on slopes and to surface the soil about them with an inch or two of pea-sized to larger gravel or crushed stone, to ensure acceptable conditions about their collars. The deciduous species flourish in full sun, and this is especially needed by *L. rediviva*, but the evergreen kinds are better with light shade. Vertical or nearly vertical crevices into which their roots can strike deeply are favorable locations for *L. tweedyi, L. cotyledon, L. brachycalyx,* and others that tend to collect and hold water in their rosettes. In such a place at The New York Botanical Garden *L. tweedyi* grew and bloomed well for many years. This brings up the question of hardiness. Insufficient experience is recorded to state forthrightly the hardiness of many kinds, but it may be supposed that all or most survive hard freezing and low winter temperatures, especially if protected by snow or by a layer of pine branches or other cover that admits air freely. The main villains are not cold, but prolonged wetness and alternate freezing and thawing that heaves the plants and tears their roots. In Europe lewisias are favorites for growing in pots in alpine greenhouses and in cold frames. This assures control of the moisture factor and permits the plants to be displayed to fine advantage.

In cultivation lewisias are at their best in soils richer than might be expected when those in which they grow in their mountain habitats are considered. It is true that in nutritious media they may not be as long lived as on a poorer diet, but semi-starvation produces miserable specimens compared with the husky ones that are had from more generous treatment, and as the plants are so easily propagated there is little reason for prolonging life at the expense of vigor and beauty. Neutral or slightly acid soils are most to the liking of lewisias. Those of a loamy character rather than very sandy or gritty earths are best, but they must, of course, be sufficiently porous to allow water to pass readily through them. The admixture with the earth of leaf mold or rich compost and a generous dash of bonemeal is recommended, and a moderate amount of dried cow manure does not come amiss. Always, the surface layer, that which surrounds the collar or neck of the plants, should consist of crushed rock or gravel. Seeds, provided they are fresh, afford the most satisfactory means of increase. It is best that they be sown as soon as they are ripe or in fall. They germinate freely in well-drained pots or pans (shallow pots) of gritty peaty soil in a cold frame or cool greenhouse. Not infrequently, in favorable climates, self-sown seedlings spring up in undisturbed soil in gardens. The careful separation from parent plants of offset rosettes is a practical means of multiplying some kinds. Spring and summer are the seasons for this division, and the plants-to-be are set in gritty sand in a lightly shaded cold frame until they have developed sufficient roots to be ready for potting or transplanting. Some growers report success with leaf cuttings taken with a sliver of the main rootlike stem attached to their bases and planted in coarse sand, kept barely moist, in a lightly shaded cold frame or greenhouse.

LEYCESTERIA (Leycest-èria)—Himalaya-Honeysuckle. Of the six species of *Leycesteria* only one is fairly well known to gardeners. The genus consists of deciduous shrubs, natives of the Himalayas and southwestern China, and belongs in the honeysuckle family CAPRIFOLIACEAE. Its generic name memorializes William Leycester, a judge in Bengal.

Leycesterias have hollow stems, opposite, undivided leaves, and erect or drooping spikes of flowers interspersed with leafy bracts. The persistent calyxes are unequally five-lobed. The corollas are funnel-shaped with swollen bases and have five lobes (petals) of nearly equal size. The fruits are many-seeded berries.

The Himalaya-honeysuckle (*L. formosa*) is a handsome, variable native of woodlands throughout the natural range of the genus; the other species are of more limited distribution. Ordinarily 4 to 6 feet in height, *L. formosa* has ovate leaves with heart-shaped bases. They vary from 2 to 7 inches in length, depending upon the vigor of the shoot, and are about one-half as wide as long, and taper to long points. Their margins are toothed or toothless, their stalks up to 1 inch long. The flowers, ¾ inch long and purplish, are in drooping spikes. They appear at or toward the ends of the shoots in summer. Stalkless, they are in tiers among claret-colored bracts shaped like the leaves and up to 1½ inches long. Reddish-purple and downy, the ¾-inch-long fruits ripen in fall and are great favorites of birds.

Leycesteria formosa

A much rarer kind, **L. crocothyrsos,** collected in 1928 in Assam and introduced to European and American gardens, has hollow stems and attains a height of 6 to 8 feet. It differs from *L. formosa* in having golden-yellow flowers. Its almost evergreen, slender-pointed, ovate leaves, 2 to 6 inches long, have deeply impressed veins and are glaucous beneath. Those on lateral shoots are arranged in one plane. Between the pairs of leaves there are kidney-shaped leafy outgrowths representing the fusion of opposite pairs of stipules. Borne in whorls (tiers) in arching racemes 5 to 7 inches long at the ends of current season's shoots, the attractive, fleshy blooms are ¾ to 1 inch long and are succeeded by grapelike, greenish fruits.

Garden and Landscape Uses. The Himalaya-honeysuckle is not hardy in the north, but in climates as mild as that, say, of Virginia, it is excellent for shady and windswept locations and for planting near the sea. It is effective in naturalistic and informal surroundings and for facing down tree and shrub borders. Although native to shaded places, it prospers in sun provided the soil is not too dry. It stands city conditions well. The yellow-flowered *L. crocothyrsos* is rather less hardy than *L. formosa*.

Cultivation. No special care is needed. Established specimens are kept vigorous by an annual spring application of a complete fertilizer. A mulch of compost or other suitable organic material is beneficial. Pruning is done in spring. Then, the plants may be cut back to whatever extent is necessary to keep them shapely and of desirable size. Because they bloom and fruit on shoots of the current year's growth the partial killing back of shoots in winter, which may occur in coldish climates, does not interfere with flowering and fruiting. The damaged parts are simply pruned out in spring. New plants are very easily raised from seed sown in sandy peaty soil. Cuttings are reported to be rather difficult to root.

LEYLAND-CYPRESS is *Cupressocyparis leylandii*.

LHOTSKYA (Lhóts-kya). The ten Australian species that comprise *Lhotskya* (sometimes incorrectly spelled *Lhotzkya*) belong in the myrtle family MYRTACEAE. The name honors Dr. John Lhotzky, an early nineteenth-century Viennese botanist, who collected plants in Australia.

Heathlike in aspect, these shrubs have alternate or rarely opposite, small, stiff, hairless or hairy, subcylindrical to three- or four-angled leaves. The flowers, solitary or in terminal, leafy heads, are stalked or stalkless. They have a five-lobed calyx with a long tube enveloped by two bracts, five petals, many stamens, and one style. The fruits consist of the ovary and calyx tube crowned with the calyx lobes.

Sorts cultivated include these: *L. alpestris* (syn. *L. genetylloides*), much-branched, has branchlets with short, bristly hairs, and closely-set, angled, linear to oblong, spreading leaves up to ¼ inch long, similarly hairy. The pinkish flowers, with petals up to ¼ inch long, are clustered at the ends of the branchlets. *L. brevifolia* has branchlets sparingly furnished with short hairs. Its hairless leaves are up to ½ inch

Lhotskya brevifolia

long. *L. ericoides* has sparsely-hairy to hairless branchlets and leaves. The latter up to ⅓ inch long, are erect, slender, short-linear, and three-angled. The white or whitish flowers, clustered some distance below the apexes of the leafy shoots, have petals about ¼ inch long.

Garden and Landscape Uses and Cultivation. Appropriate for outdoor landscaping in California and other places with similar mild, dry climates lhotskyas succeed in sunny locations in porous, well-drained, peaty soils. They may be propagated by seed and by cuttings of firm, but not hard young shoots planted in a mixture of coarse sand or perlite and peat moss.

LIATRIS (Liàt-ris)—Blazing Star or Gayfeather or Button Snakeroot. This genus of the daisy family COMPOSITAE is endemic to North America and occurs wild in most parts east of the Rocky Mountains from southern Canada to northern Mexico. Its name is of unknown derivation. Because of the variability of some kinds and because natural hybrids occur, botanists differ as to the number of species of *Liatris* they recognize. From thirty to forty is usual. Identification as to species is not always easy. But this is no excuse for not trying. At least it is worth while for gardeners to become acquainted with the very few kinds that are at all commonly cultivated and to be able to identify them with some degree of certainty.

The blazing stars, gayfeathers, or button snakeroots are herbaceous perennials with thick, often tuberous roots, erect stems, without branches except sometimes for a few laterals that develop from the flowering parts, and alternate, narrow, lobeless leaves. The flower heads are in wandlike spikes or racemes. An interesting and easily observable characteristic is that the racemes or spikes open from the top downward, the uppermost flower head always expanding first, followed in succession by the others until the one lowest on the stem opens. The heads are composed of all disk florets. There are no petal-like ray florets such as there are in daisies, black-eyed Su-

sans, and sunflowers. Below or behind each flower head is a collar or cuff of leafy or dryish bracts called an involucre. The character of this is often important in distinguishing species. The flowers are rose-purple, magenta-pink, or white.

The most commonly grown kind is *L. pycnostachya*, native from South Dakota to Indiana, Texas, and Louisiana. This fine plant attains a height up to 5 feet and is distinguished from the very similar *L. spicata* by its involucral bracts being pointed and recurved. A very leafy species, its lower leaves may be 1 foot long, those above gradually becoming smaller. They are up to ½ inch wide. The flower heads, individually stalkless and mostly of five to seven rosy-purple florets, are about ½ inch long; in dense, narrow spikes up to 1½ feet long, they are on pubescent stems. The quite

Liatris pycnostachya

popular *L. spicata* has usually blunt, erect, and never recurved, involucral bracts. Its flower heads, of five to fourteen florets, are also without individual stalks; they sit di-

Liatris spicata

rectly upon the main stem of the flower spike, which is not pubescent. This species is native from New York to Michigan, Florida, and Louisiana. There is a white-flowered variant, *L. s. albiflora*. Another frequently cultivated kind, **L. aspera,** is often misnamed *L. scariosa* in gardens and nurseries. From the true *L. scariosa* it differs in that its innermost and middle involucral bracts have broad, thin, dry, non-green, strongly reflexed margins. Those of **L. scariosa** are green almost or quite to their edges and are fringed with hairs. From 4 to 6 feet in height, *L. aspera* has many narrowly-linear-lanceolate leaves. The flower heads, shortly stalked and ¾ to 1 inch in diameter, are larger than those of most species, well separated rather than crowded on the stems, and rosy-purple. Each has

Liatris aspera

twenty-five to forty florets. There is a white-flowered form called *L. aspera benkii* and two excellent garden varieties, *L. a.* 'September Glory' and *L. a.* 'White Spire', which have rosy-purple and white flowers, respectively. In the wild *L. aspera* ranges from North Dakota to Ontario, Ohio, Texas, and Florida. Two other species likely to be confused with *L. scariosa* are **L. ligulistylis** and *L. novae-angliae.* The former has the terminal flower head conspicuously bigger than the others. The flower heads mostly consist of thirty to 100 florets. It is native from Wisconsin to Alberta, and New Mexico. Native of New England and New York, **L. novae-angliae** closely resembles *L. scariosa.* It has more, twenty to eighty-five, rather than up to twenty, leaves below the lowest flower heads. Decidedly handsome is **L. elegans,** indigenous from South Carolina to Florida, Arkansas, and Texas and probably less hardy to cold than the more northern species. Up to 5 feet tall, its flower stems are often branched below. The flower heads, of four or five rosy-purple florets, stalkless or very short-stalked, are about ½ inch long. They are distinguished by having inner involucral bracts much longer than the florets, with bright rosy-purple tips. The

Liatris novae-angliae

leaves are numerous and up to 6 inches long by up to ¼ inch wide.

Other kinds include these: **L. acidota,** of Louisiana and Texas, is very like *L. spicata,* but is slenderer, has shorter flower spikes, and fewer flowers in each head. **L. cylindracea** is similar to *L. squarrosa,* but has its involucral bracts pressed together, not spreading at their tips. It is native from Ontario to Missouri. **L. gracilis** differs from *L. graminifolia* and *L. helleri* in having its flower heads, each of three to five florets, on stalks as long or longer than the heads. It is a native of the southeastern United States. **L. graminifolia** occurs from New Jersey and Pennsylvania to Florida and Alabama. A variable kind, it closely resembles *L. spicata,* differing in being ordinarily smaller and more graceful and having less crowded, slightly bigger flower heads. **L. helleri** grows as a native only in the mountains of North Carolina. It is similar to *L. gracilis,* but has five to fifteen florets in each flower head. Although in the wild it often is not more than 8 inches tall, it exceeds this considerably under cultivation. **L. punctata** is similar to *L. elegans,* but its involucral bracts are green throughout. It is indigenous from Michigan to Manitoba to Mexico. **L. squarrosa** has rather loose racemes of not very numerous flower heads with recurved or spreading involucral bracts. It is indigenous from Delaware to South Dakota, Florida, and Texas.

Garden and Landscape Uses. Blazing stars are excellent for late summer and fall bloom in perennial borders and beds, wild gardens, and semiformal areas. Their strong vertical lines provide a distinctive element in the landscape and their prevailing rosy-purple colors associate well with yellow-flowering plants of which there are many in late summer and fall. For the best effects they should be planted several to many together. They are attractive as cut flowers and for this use should be taken without denuding the plants of foliage. That on the lower parts of the stems, if left, helps to develop strong tubers that are likely to flower well the following year.

Cultivation. Although blazing stars will grow in poorer and in most cases drier soils than many perennials, they respond to fertile ones by producing longer stems and becoming finer horticultural specimens. Any reasonably good garden soil suits them. Unusual among the group, *L. spicata* prefers, or at least grows well, in decidedly moist earth. These plants are lovers of sun, they are for open locations. No particular difficulties attend their cultivation. As long as they prosper they may remain undisturbed for years. Transplanting may be done in early fall or spring. Propagation is by division at transplanting time or by seed sown in a cold frame or outdoor bed in fall.

LIBERTIA (Libért-ia). The ten species of *Libertia* belong to the iris family IRIDACEAE. They are natives of Australia, New Zealand, Andean South America, and New Guinea. The New Zealanders are the only members of the iris family native there. The name honors Marie A. Libert, a Belgian botanist, who died in 1863.

Libertias are evergreen, clump-forming plants with short rhizomes, long fibrous roots, and many erect or arching, slender, linear leaves of a more or less coarse-grass-like appearance. The leafless flower stalks arise from the bases of the plants and carry many usually white flowers, each with six petals or more precisely tepals, the three outer less showy and shorter than the three inner. There are three stamens and one style. The fruits are capsules.

Native to Chile, **L. elegans,** 1 foot to 2 feet tall, has an abundance of arching narrow-linear leaves and makes a good display of its stalkless clusters of small flowers, the three inner petals of which are white, the three outer ones greenish. Also Chilean, **L. formosa,** 1½ to 3 feet tall, has stiff leaves and flowers with three white inner petals and three greenish-brown outer ones. The blooms, up to ¾ inch long, larger than those of *L. elegans,* are carried well above the foliage. The individual flowers, which lie in tightish clusters along the scapes, have stalks shorter than the bracts. In these

Libertia elegans

Libertia formosa

Libertia formosa (flowers)

respects this plant differs from 3-foot-tall **L. grandiflora,** a New Zealander, which, like the three other native kinds from that land, has loose panicles of flowers on individual stems longer than the bracts. The blooms of *L. grandiflora* are waxy-white, 1 inch or more in diameter, and are succeeded by fruits with bright orange seeds. Another New Zealander, **L. ixioides,** 1 foot to 2 feet tall, has blooms up to 1 inch in diameter. They scarcely rise above the foliage and have greenish outer petals and

Libertia grandiflora

white inner ones. The chief attraction of this species is the bright yellow or orange seeds, displayed to advantage and up to ½ inch in diameter.

Garden Uses. Libertias are interesting for flower beds and borders and for planting in informal parts of the garden, but are too tender for outdoor cultivation where much frost is experienced. They need full sun and well-drained, but fairly moist soil. They may also be grown in beds or pots in cool greenhouses. A winter minimum night temperature of 50°F is satisfactory, daytime temperatures may be a few degrees higher.

Cultivation. Propagation is by division in early spring or early fall and by fresh seed, which usually germinate well, but slowly. Sow them in sandy peaty soil. Plants established and doing well should not be disturbed (unless to secure increase). Only when they begin to deteriorate is it desirable to dig them up and divide and replant in newly spaded and fertilized soil. This will normally be at intervals of several years. Annual care consists of fertilizing with a complete garden fertilizer in spring and watering thoroughly during dry weather. Where winters are a little colder than is best for these plants it is well to mulch the ground around them in fall with compost, peat moss, leaves, or other protective material.

LIBOCEDRUS (Libocéd-rus)—Kawaka. The group of evergreen coniferous trees formerly known as *Libocedrus* is now divided into five genera. Five species remain in *Libocedrus,* one is *Austrocedrus,* three belong in *Calocedrus,* three are named *Papuacedrus,* and one constitutes the genus *Pilgerodendron.* The familiar incense-cedar, formerly *Libocedrus decurrens,* is *Calocedrus decurrens.* The tropical genus *Papuacedrus,* native to New Guinea and the Molucca Islands, is not known to be in cultivation in the United States and is not discussed in this Encyclopedia. The five species recognized as belonging in *Libocedrus* are natives of New Zealand and New Caledonia. The only ones likely to be occasionally cultivated are *L. bidwillii* and *L. plumosa,* both natives of New Zealand. The genus belongs in the cypress family CUPRESSACEAE. Its name, derived from the Greek *libos,* a tear or drop, and the name of the genus *Cedar,* presumably alludes to the drops of a gum exuded from wounds and cuts.

The kawaka (*L. plumosa* syn. *L. doniana*) is a lowland species up to 100 feet tall that has flat, fernlike sprays of branchlets with opposite pairs of tiny scalelike leaves forming four rows. Alternate pairs of juvenile leaves are very unequal in size, but those of adult shoots are more similar and hug the stems more closely. The fruiting cones are ½ inch, or slightly more or less, in length and each consists of four scales, the two fertile ones having each a solitary

seed. Attaining a maximum height of 70 feet, *L. bidwillii,* at high elevations, is often low and shrublike. It differs from the better known *L. plumosa* in being smaller and having smaller leaves and cones.

Garden and Landscape Uses and Cultivation. These trees are chiefly for botanical and other special collections. Except in particularly favored regions, such as parts of the Pacific Northwest, they are not likely to prove satisfactory in cultivation. Where they can be grown they are likely to respond to the conditions recommended for *Calocedrus.* For further information see Conifers.

LIBONIA. See Justicia.

LICORICE is *Glycyrrhiza glabra.*

LICUALA (Licuà-la). One hundred species, natives of humid, hot forests in tropical Asia, Indomalaysia, and the Bismarck and Solomon Islands, comprise *Licuala,* of the palm family PALMAE. Only a few are cultivated. The generic name is a native Moluccan one.

Licualas are handsome, low-growing palms with clustered or solitary stems. Characteristically their trunks are slender. Their leaves vary, according to species, from fan-shaped to nearly circular and are undivided or deeply- and irregularly-cleft into several or many segments. The loose flower clusters, with usually spiny stalks, develop among the foliage. They bear bisexual blooms with six stamens. The globose to ellipsoid, one-seeded fruits, ordinarily about the size of peas, are red, pink, or orange.

One of the best known horticulturally is **L. grandis,** native from New Britain Island to northern New Guinea. Having a single stem up to about 6 feet in height and nearly circular leaves somewhat broader than long, this splendid sort is an outstandingly fine ornamental. The blades of its leaves, which are not divided into segments, but have closely-toothed margins with each major tooth cleft to form two smaller teeth, are pleated and about 3 feet in diameter. Their spiny stalks are about as long. The leaves of multistemmed **L. spinosa,** of southeast Asia, which attains a height of about 10 feet, are about the same size as those of *L. grandis,* but are deeply-cut into about eighteen long-wedge-shaped segments, 2 to 5 inches broad at their tips and toothed. The leafstalks are longer than those of *L. grandis* and the flower clusters are erect and rise well above the foliage.

Garden and Landscape Uses. It is unlikely that these palms will be satisfactory outdoors in the continental United States, but in Hawaii and other humid, tropical climates they are charming for shady places, beneath other trees, or where protection from strong sun is afforded by buildings or walls and where the soil is constantly moist. They are intolerant of dry conditions. Licualas are elegant in groups or dotted among lower-growing plants. They are among the choicest of tropical greenhouse plants.

Cultivation. These palms are at their best in fertile, constantly moist soil. Exposure to strong sun is to be avoided because it reduces the intense deep green of the foliage, which is one of the chief beauties of licualas. Fresh seeds, sown in sandy, peaty soil in a temperature of 80 to 90°F afford the means of increase. In greenhouses high humidity and a minimum winter night temperature of 65 to 70°F, with a daytime rise of five to ten degrees, are necessary. At other seasons the night temperature should not fall below 70°F, and the day temperature not below 75°F. These palms need fertile, coarse soil, well drained, but watered sufficiently often to keep it always decidedly moist. Specimens that have filled their containers with healthy roots benefit from applications of dilute liquid fertilizer at biweekly intervals. Shade from strong sun is necessary. It is a good plan to keep the pots of very well-rooted licualas with their bases standing in saucers kept filled with water. This reduces the danger of the soil drying between waterings. For more information see Palms.

LIFE PLANT is *Kalanchoe pinnata*.

LIFTING. This is a gardeners' term for digging plants from the ground for storage, transplanting, or other purpose. Crops of potatoes are lifted when harvested. Bulbs of daffodils, tulips, and other plants are lifted when they become crowded and are to be separated and transplanted and when they must be taken out of flower beds to make way for succeeding displays. Most herbaceous perennials need lifting, dividing, and transplanting periodically. Trees and shrubs to be transplanted are lifted either bare-root (without a soil ball) or with an intact ball of soil around their roots. See Planting and Transplanting.

LIGHT. The vast majority of plants, all those containing chlorophyll, manufacture (photosynthesize) the foods they need from water and simple elements obtained from the soil and air. Exceptions are funguses and other lowly sorts and a few degraded higher plants that are without chlorophyll and obtain the foods they need from living or dead tissues of other organisms. If they feed on living plants or animals they are called parasites, if on dead ones, saprophytes.

Light supplies the energy needed for photosynthesis. Not necessary for growth of saprophytic and parasitic plants, it is essential for green (chlorophyll-containing) kinds. When these last are forced in darkness, as is commonly done with such sorts as lily-of-the-valley, rhubarb, and such bulb plants as hyacinths, narcissuses, and tulips, the growth they make is at the expense of foods synthesized during the previous growing season and stored in the plant parts.

In horticultural practice experience based on trial and error, either one's own or that of others as reflected in books and other recommendations, serves well as a prime guide in determining the amount of light best suited for particular plants. Some knowledge of the environments in which the various sorts grow in the wild is also very helpful. But nothing obviates the need for close observation of the plants themselves and of readiness to make adjustments that seem needed as indicated by the responses of the plants.

Lack of sufficient light is generally manifested by weak, sickly-looking growth. Stems elongate and have longer than normal distances between leaves. Foliage is pale, excessively soft, and often reduced in size. Flowers may not develop or if they do are likely to exhibit the same faults as the foliage and not to last well on the plants or when cut. One of the most damaging and frequent results of insufficient light is the spindling or excessive elongation of seedlings that are kept in the dark too long or are kept in poor light. Besides

becoming very weak, such seedlings quickly succumb to damping off disease.

Too intense light can also cause paling of foliage, but from this cause it is generally most evident on parts exposed to the sun, being less obvious or absent elsewhere. Also, the foliage tends to have firmer texture than normal. In extreme cases the cells are severely damaged or destroyed and become brown or black to produce the condition called leaf scorch or leaf burn. It is common practice to reduce light intensity by shading greenhouses, by using lath houses, and in other ways.

It is very important when plants that have been growing in comparatively low intensities are to be exposed to considerably stronger light to increase exposure gradually over a period of a week or two or longer. This gives the tissues opportunity to adjust to the new conditions without suffering harm.

Foliage damaged by exposure to too strong sunlight: (a) Orchid

(b) A clivia

If light comes strongly from one side only as with plants in windows or at the margins of shrub plantings and woodlands, the stems frequently bend toward the source of illumination. Specimens in containers may be kept symmetrical by

Lifting potatoes

Geranium grown with insufficient light

Plants bending toward light coming from one side: (a) Seedlings

(b) African-violets

(c) Geranium

turning them periodically before the bending becomes pronounced.

Sunlight, the most common source of energy for plant growth, is by gardeners sometimes supplemented with or even entirely replaced by artificial illumination. Although all green plants need light, not all respond favorably to the same intensities. Natives of woodlands and other places of low illumination are likely to be seriously injured by intensities to which meadow, alpine, and desert plants are normally exposed, and these last to pine

and eventually die unless they receive brighter illumination than is adequate for woodlanders.

The duration of the light received during each twenty-four-hour period has a pronounced influence on the behavior of certain plants. Near the equator days and nights are of equal length throughout the year. As one moves northward or southward days in summer become progressively longer, winter days shorter. This seasonal change in the relative lengths of days and nights determines the blooming time of many sorts of plants. Not all exhibit this photoperiodism as it is called. Those that do not, day-neutral plants, will flower at any time of the year if other environmental factors are favorable. Tomatoes are a familiar example.

Sorts affected by photoperiodism are divided into short-day, long-day, and intermediate-day plants. Because it actually is the duration of darkness rather than the length of the lighted period that determines the results it would be more accurate to identify them as short-night, long-night, and intermediate-night plants, but the other terminology was first used and is generally accepted.

Manipulation of day length, or rather night length, to influence the time of flowering of chrysanthemums and some other popular flowers is common practice. Adjustments of the natural day to optimums needed to induce or delay blooming are achieved by lengthening the day by using electric lights or shortening it by completely excluding light by covering the plants with black cloth shading for the necessary part of each twenty-four-hour period. Coincident with making these adjustments it is often necessary or advisable to control temperatures so that fullest advantage is taken of complex relationships that frequently exist between them and photoperiodism.

Other light factors that affect plant growth include its quality or color. Consideration of this, except to a minor extent in selecting the kind of light bulbs for use

in artificial light gardening, plays no part in practical horticulture, but are sometimes important in scientific experiments. Seeds of most plants germinate best in the dark and are inhibited by light, but the germination of some, for instance those of most epiphytes, of many grasses, and of lettuce and tobacco, is promoted by exposure to light. Because other factors including the availability of nitrates in the soil can usually substitute for light in stimulating seed germination in gardening practice most seeds are covered with soil and so begin to grow in darkness or if not covered with soil are shaded until they germinate. See also Indoor Light Gardening.

LIGHT SOIL. As applied to soils, light refers neither to color nor weight. It alludes to the work needed to manipulate them. Light soils are comparatively loose and sandy. To work them with tools and implements calls for less effort than for heavy ones. In light soils the clay content is negligible or low in comparison to the amount of sand and other coarse ingredients. Light soils are less retentive of moisture and nutrients than heavy ones, warm earlier in spring, and are often best suited for early crops.

LIGHTNING INJURY. Lightning strikes are a fairly common cause of injury to trees, especially free-standing specimens. The harm may vary from little damage to complete shattering. Often it causes a streak-like strip of bark and shallow layer of wood to be torn from the trunk. Treatment may call for no more than smoothing the edges of the wound and covering exposed tissues with tree-wound paint to pruning and bracing. Valuable trees can be protected by properly installed lightning conductors (lightning rods).

Covering chrysanthemums with black cloth to shorten natural day length

Typical injury to a tree caused by lightning

LIGULARIA (Ligu-lària)—Leopard Plant. Related to *Senecio* and sometimes included there, *Ligularia*, of the daisy family COMPOSITAE, contains among its about 150 species a number of very fine ornamentals.

They are herbaceous perennials, mostly hardy and deciduous, but the well-known, old-fashioned leopard plant and its varieties are evergreen and not hardy in the north. Except for *L. sibirica*, which is indigenous to Europe as well as Asia, the entire genus is Asian, and is especially abundant in Siberia, China, and Japan. From *Senecio* it is most easily distinguished by the stalks of all except the uppermost leaves having broad bases that completely encircle, and for a short distance hug, the stem. The name, from the Latin, *ligula*, a strap, alludes to the ray florets.

Mostly of bold and noble aspect, but sometimes verging toward coarseness, ligularias have loose rosettes of basal foliage, and usually a number of stem leaves that decrease successively and rapidly in size from below upward. The leaves are heart-shaped, kidney-shaped, ovate-oblong, or triangular. The up-facing or nodding flower heads, of medium to large size, are accommodated in usually showy, terminal racemes, panicles, or clusters. The heads are of two kinds of florets. Those at their centers are of the disk type, similar to those of the "eyes" of daisies. Encircling the centers are few to many petal-like ray florets. The fruits are cylindrical, usually hairless, seedlike achenes.

Popular *L. dentata* is better known in gardens by its botanically inadmissable names *L. clivorum* and *Senecio clivorum*. Handsome and striking in appearance, this native of China and Japan is from 3 to 5 feet tall. Its rounded-kidney-shaped, toothed but not lobed leaves, with blades up to 1 foot long and wider than their lengths, are short-hairy beneath and along the veins on their upper sides. In broad, loose clusters up to 1 foot across, the bright orange flower heads make magnificent displays. Each head is 3½ to 4½ inches in diameter, and has ray florets up to 2 inches long.

Horticultural varieties and hybrids of *L. dentata* are grown. 'Orange Queen' is a vigorous grower with especially large, brilliant orange flower heads. 'Othello' has

Ligularia dentata (flowers)

large orange flower heads and leaves purplish on their undersides. 'Desdemona' is compact, and has dark purple stems, leaf-stalks, veins, and under leaf surfaces, and reddish-orange flower heads. A beautiful hybrid between *L. dentata* and *L. japonica*, named **L. palmatiloba** (syn. *Senecio palmatilobus*), has foliage intermediate between that of its parents, and clustered yellow flower heads. It attains a height of 3½ to 4½ feet. The round leaves are shallowly but very distinctly many-lobed, and are toothed. Believed to be a hybrid between *L. dentata* and *L. wilsoniana*, and up to 6 feet in height, **L. hessei** has characteristics intermediate between those of those species. Its 3½-inch-wide orange-yellow flower heads are in shorter panicles than those of *L. wilsoniana*. A hybrid between *L. dentata* and *L. veitchiana* is *L. hessei* 'Gregynog Gold'. About 3 feet tall, it has nearly round leaves, and slender spires of orange-yellow flower heads.

Ligularia hessei

Rarely exceeding 3 feet in height, **L. hodgsonii** has orange, or perhaps sometimes yellow, flower heads not over 2¼ inches in diameter, and more densely clustered than those of *L. dentata*, which in most other respects it closely resembles.

Ligularia hessei 'Gregynog Gold'

The stalks of the individual flower heads of *L. hodgsonii* have two slender bractlets well below the collar of bracts (involucre) that is part of the flower head. These are lacking in *L. dentata*.

With similarly flattish clusters of flower heads, **L. japonica** is easily distinguished from the kinds described above by its long-stalked leaves, rounded-heart-shaped in outline, and with blades up to 1 foot long, being deeply-three-lobed, with the middle lobes pinnately-lobed and toothed and the side ones also lobed and toothed. When young, the foliage is densely-hairy. Up to 3 feet or more tall, this native of Japan, Taiwan, Korea, and China has flower heads up to 4½ inches wide or wider in clusters of up to eight. The disk florets are yellow, the rays orange.

Flower heads in elongated racemes or slender panicles rather than broad, flattish clusters distinguish all ligularias discussed below, except *L. tussilaginea* and its varieties, from those described above. An outstanding ornamental with tall spires of bloom that in effect suggest those of a yellow foxtail-lily (*Eremurus*), is Chinese **L. veitchiana**. From 5 to 7 feet tall, it has triangular-heart-shaped, toothed leaves up to 1 foot long, with blades broader than

Ligularia dentata

Ligularia veitchiana

their lengths. In contrast to those of *L. wilsoniana* the leafstalks are solid, and somewhat channeled along their upper sides. The flowering portion of the stem is without branches, 2 to 2½ feet long, and crowded all around with bright yellow flower heads about 2½ inches wide. The ray florets, about 1 inch long, are more than four times as long as broad.

From the last, handsome 3- to 6-foot-tall *L. wilsoniana* differs in its leafstalks being cylindrical and hollow and in its 1-inch-wide flower heads having ray florets not more than four times as long as broad. The flower heads are crowded in cylindrical racemes that have a few short branches near their bases.

Ligularia wilsoniana

Ligularia wilsoniana (flowers)

The most widely distributed species in the wild, **L. sibirica** is a variable kind with *L. s. speciosa* most likely to be cultivated. This native from Siberia to Japan differs from the typical species mostly in being bigger in all its parts. Exceeding 3 feet in height, it has heart-shaped leaves, hairless except at their toothed margins. The flower heads, 2 to 2½ inches wide, in short racemes, are sometimes branched at their bases.

Leopard plant is a variegated-leaved variety of evergreen **L. tussilaginea** (syns. *L.*

kaempferi, Farfugium japonicum). The green-leaved species is endemic to Japan, China, Korea, and Taiwan. It has stout rhizomes, and is woolly-haired to nearly hairless. Long-stalked and nearly round to kidney-shaped, its leaves have blades up to 6 inches long by 1 foot wide, heart-shaped at their bases, lustrous above. Their margins are angular-toothed to nearly toothless. The large, loosely-arranged clusters of yellow flower heads, each 1½ to over 2 inches across, are on stalks that overtop the foliage and are 1 foot to 2 feet tall. Coming in fall, they are very ornamental. Variety *L. t. gigantea* is larger. The leopard plant (*L. t. aureo-maculata*) has leaves unevenly, but conspicuously spotted with yellow, creamy-white, or sometimes delicate pink. Variety *L. t. argentea* has foliage beautifully blotched and segmented with creamy-white. In *L. t. crispata* (syn. *L. t. cristata*) the margins of the green leaves are much frilled and crested.

Ligularia tussilaginea aureo-maculata

Ligularia tussilaginea argentea

Hardy kinds other than those discussed above worth growing include **L. macrophylla**, of the Altai Mountains. This is 4½ to 6 feet tall and has glaucous-blue-green, toothed, elliptic to ovate-oblong leaves with winged stalks. The usually yellow flower heads, 1 inch to 2 inches across, are in

Ligularia macrophylla

crowded, conical panicles about 1 foot long. Except for its deeply-palmately-lobed leaves, **L. przewalskii** much resembles *L. stenocephala*. It is a native of northern China. Dark purple stems are characteristic of **L. stenocephala,** of China, Japan, and Taiwan. From 3 to 4½ feet tall, this has heart-shaped, kidney-shaped, to nearly triangular, coarsely-toothed leaves about 1 foot across and yellow flower heads 1½ inches wide, in long, slender racemes.

Ligularia przewalskii

Garden and Landscape Uses. Deciduous ligularias, all of which are believed to be hardy, are admirable for bold garden effects. They are sociable and are grand for colonizing in broad sweeps in informal landscapes and near watersides and for grouping in more formal flower beds. They make few demands on the skill or time of the gardener. Chiefly in late summer they present brilliant displays of bloom. Deep, rich, moistish soil, and a location in full sun or partial shade suits these plants.

The leopard plant and other varieties of *L. tussilaginea* are hardy about as far north as Washington, D.C. and are suitable for flower beds and groundcovers. Their most frequent use, however, is as greenhouse and window plants. Tolerant of rather poor environments, they respond handsomely to more favorable ones and good care. Porous, fertile, loamy soil kept moderately moist, but not wet, suits them.

Cultivation. Because ligularias are gross feeders, for the best results it is necessary to fertilize liberally. Outdoors, they are benefited by being mulched with compost or other decayed organic material and by an annual spring application of a complete garden fertilizer. In dry weather regular watering is very helpful. As soon as the plants show signs of loss of vigor as a result of crowding or soil depletion, they should be dug up and divided and replanted in deeply spaded and fertilized ground improved by incorporating with the soil generous amounts of rotted manure, compost, or peat moss. Early fall or early spring is the best time to do this. Propagation is usually by division. When procurable seed may be used.

Grown indoors, the leopard plant and other varieties of *L. tussilaginea* do well in minimum winter night temperatures of 40 to 50°F, with daytime increases of five to fifteen degrees. A moderately moist atmosphere is appreciated. On all favorable occasions the greenhouse should be ventilated freely. Pot-grown specimens are helped by occasional applications of dilute liquid fertilizer, but this should not be given too often to variegated-leaved kinds because it may encourage the development of plain green foliage. If such appears remove it promptly. A little shade from the strongest summer sun is needed. Division is the readiest means of securing increase, and spring the best season to carry this out. Spring is also most appropriate for repotting specimens crowding their pots with roots.

LIGUSTICUM (Ligúst-icum)—Scotch-Lovage, Alpine-Lovage. Members of the carrot family UMBELLIFERAE, the sixty species of *Ligusticum* are natives of North America, Europe, and Asia. Mostly they inhabit subarctic and arctic regions, rocky coasts, and mountains. The name is from *ligustikon*, a name applied by the ancient Greeks to some plant of the same family and refers to the ancient Italian province of Liuria. Ligusticums are hardy perennials with leaves two- to five-times-pinnately-lobed, or twice- or thrice-divided. The usually white or greenish-white flowers, in umbels of lesser umbels, are small and have calyxes with five tiny teeth or none, and five each petals and stamens. The egg-shaped, seedlike fruits are very slightly or not at all flattened. They have prominent, narrowly-winged, longitudinal ridges. For the plant previously named *L. latifolium* see Anisotome.

Scotch-lovage (*L. scoticum,* sometimes spelled *scothicum*) in Europe is sometimes employed as a potherb and salad. It has a strong, not very pleasant flavor. As a wild

Ligusticum scoticum

plant it inhabits shores and sea cliffs in northern Europe, Greenland, and southward from Labrador to Long Island. A hairless, leafy perennial, it has bright green foliage that when crushed has the odor of celery. Its hollow stems are ribbed, somewhat branched, and 1 foot to 3 feet tall. The thickish leaves, triangular in outline, are 4 to 8 inches long and have three primary divisions each of three broad-ovate, toothed leaflets ¾ inch to 2 inches long. The umbels of tiny greenish-white flowers are 1½ to 2½ inches wide.

Alpine-lovage (*L. mutellina*) is nearly hairless. Its rootstock has many coarse fibers. The hollow stems, usually with one or two alternate branches, are 4 inches to 1½ feet tall. Triangular in outline, the twice- or thrice-pinnate leaves have linear-lanceolate lobes mostly under ¼ inch long, but sometimes bigger. The flowers are generally red or purple. This is a native of mountains in southern Europe. Similar to the last, but with few or no fibers to the rootstocks, and with branchless, nearly solid stems up to 1 foot tall, the small-alpine-lovage (*L. mutellinoides*) has white or pink flowers. It is native to the mountains of central Europe, the Carpathians, the Urals, and to arctic Russia.

Native to mountains in southern Europe, *L. lucidum* (syn. *L. pyrenaeum*) is nearly hairless. Its rootstock has abundant fibers, and its solid stems attain heights of 4 or 5 feet and carry several leaves. They are branched, with the upper branches opposite or in whorls (circles of more than two). The leaves, triangular in outline, are three- to five-times-pinnately-divided into linear lobes up to ½ inch long. The umbels of small flowers are about 2½ inches wide.

Garden Uses and Cultivation. Ligusticums are hardy plants of small importance as ornamentals. Occasionally *L. lucidum* is planted for ornament and the other kinds to provide variety. The Scotch-lovage may be included in herb gardens. These plants thrive in ordinary well-drained soils in sunny locations. They are increased by seed and by division.

LIGUSTRINA. See Syringa.

LIGUSTRUM (Lig-ùstrum) — Privet. Although in the regard of most gardeners less noble than their close relatives lilacs, privets, a group name for the about fifty species of *Ligustrum*, their varieties, and hybrids, include many useful kinds. They belong to the olive family OLEACEAE and, except for one species native to the Mediterranean region, are restricted in the wild to Asia and Australia. Their name is an ancient Latin one.

Privets are deciduous and evergreen, much-branched shrubs or less commonly small trees. They have opposite, undivided, toothless leaves and panicles of white or whitish blooms terminating the branch ends and short branchlets. The calyxes are bell-shaped and have four minute teeth. The corollas are funnel-shaped, with four spreading lobes (petals). There are two stamens and a short style. The fruits are small, most frequently black or bluish-black berries or, those of *L. sempervirens*, fleshy at first, but becoming dry capsules.

Common privet (*L. vulgare*), native to Europe, North Africa, and western Asia, is naturalized in parts of the United States. Hardy in southern New England, it is less ornamental than most cultivated kinds. Deciduous or in mild climates semievergreen, and up to about 15 feet tall, this has oblong-ovate to lanceolate, hairless leaves 1 inch to 2½ inches long. The cream-white, peculiarly-scented, stalked flowers are in dense, pyramidal panicles up to about 2½ inches in length. The spreading petals and corolla tubes are of about equal length. The stamens do not protrude. Varieties with plain green leaves include *L. v. buxifolium*, a semievergreen with 1-inch-long leaves and large fruits; *L. v. italicum* (syn. *L. v. sempervirens*), which retains its foliage later than other deciduous privets; *L. v.* 'Lodense', dense, compact, and much dwarfer than the typical kind; *L. v. pendulum*, with drooping branches; and *L. v. densiflorum* and *L. v. pyramidale*, notable for their upright, narrow growth habits, the first more compact than the second. Varieties with fruits other than black are *L. v. chlorocarpum*, with greenish; *L. v. leucocarpum*, with white; and *L. v. xanthocarpum*, with yellow berries. Kinds with variegated foliage are *L. v. aureum*, with yellow leaves; *L. v. aureo-variegatum*, with yellow-blotched leaves; *L. v. argenteo-variegatum*, its leaves with white variegation; and *L. v. glaucum*, with bluish-green leaves narrowly edged with white.

Chinese *L. sinense* differs from common privet in its leaves being hairy along the midribs of their undersides and in the stamens protruding from its short-stalked flowers. One of the handsomest deciduous or semievergreen privets, this is hardy as far north as Washington, D.C. Up to 12 feet tall or taller, it has elliptic to oblong leaves 1 inch to 3 inches long, and loose, downy panicles 2½ to 4 inches long. Its blue-black berries remain for a long time. Variety *L. s. pendulum* has drooping branches, *L. s. stauntonii* is lower and more spreading. Also native to China, **L. quihoui** is a deciduous, rounded bush about 6 feet tall, hardy about as far north as New York City. It has spreading, stiffish branches, when young downy, and blunt, elliptic to narrow-oblong, hairless leaves up to 2 inches long. Borne in late summer or early fall, the blooms are few together in panicles up to ½ inch long. Their petals are about one-third as long as the corolla tubes. A deciduous hybrid between *L. obtusifolium* and California privet named **L. ibolium** is much like its first-named parent, but somewhat hardier. From it, it can be distinguished by its young shoots and the midribs on the undersides of the leaves being pubescent.

California privet (**L. ovalifolium**) has a somewhat misleading name. It is native to Japan. In mild climates semievergreen, in colder ones deciduous, it is reasonably hardy in southern New England, but in severe winters sheared specimens, hedges for example, may be killed to the ground there. This favorite hedge plant, of erect, stiff habit, is up to 15 feet tall. It has hair-

(c) As formally sheared specimens

less branchlets and glossy, elliptic-ovate to elliptic-oblong, pointed leaves 1 inch to 2½ inches in length, yellowish on their undersides. The very short-stalked, ill-scented flowers are in erect, hairless panicles up to 4 inches long. The petals are up to one-half as long as the corolla tube. Variety *L. o. aureo-marginatum* (syn. *L. o. aureum*) has leaves broadly margined with yellow. The leaves of *L. o. argenteum* are edged with creamy-white. Handsomest of golden-leaved privets, **L. vicaryi** is a hy-

Ligustrum vicaryi

brid between *L. ovalifolium aureum* and *L. vulgare*. Hardy in southern New England, this may attain a height of 12 feet. It is distinguished by its foliage remaining bright yellow instead of fading as the season advances as does that of most other golden-variegated privets. Its flowers are in small panicles. Its berries are blue-black.

Japanese **L. tschonoskii** (syn. *L. acuminatum*), about 6 feet tall and deciduous, is similar to, but less graceful than *L. obtusifolium*. It has pubescent shoots and pointed, ovate to lanceolate leaves up to 3 inches in length, pubescent beneath along the midribs. The flowers, in downy-stemmed panicles up to 2 inches long, are nearly stalkless and have petals about one-third as long as the corolla tubes. The anthers are conspicuously protruded. Also native of Japan, **L. ibota** is decidedly inferior. The plant commonly grown under its name is *L. obtusifolium*. True *L. ibota*, deciduous and up to 6 feet tall, may be distinguished from *L. obtusifolium* by the hairless calyxes of its flowers.

Hardiest of privets, surviving throughout most of New England and parts of Canada, are Amur privet (**L. amurense**) and *L. obtusifolium*. Native to northern China, **L. amurense** somewhat resembles Califor-

Ligustrum ovalifolium: (a) As a tall hedge

Ligustrum ovalifolium (flowers)

(b) As a low hedge in partial shade

Ligustrum ovalifolium (fruits)

Ligustrum amurense

nia privet. Of erect habit, it has elliptic to oblong leaves 1 inch to 2½ inches long, dullish or lustrous above, on their undersides hairy along the veins. In pubescent panicles 2 inches long, the flowers have slightly protruding stamens. The fruits are dull black. Japanese **L. obtusifolium** is often misidentified as *L. ibota*. Up to 10 feet tall, it has arching or spreading branches. Its elliptic to oblong-obovate leaves, hairy on their undersides at least along the veins, are ¾ inch to 2½ inches long. The flowers, in nodding panicles up to 1½ inches long, terminate short branchlets. The stamens protrude. The fruits are dull black. Regal's privet (*L. o. regelianum*) is a low, handsome variety with horizontal branches and leaves in two rows. This is hardy as far north as southern New England.

Ligustrum japonicum rotundifolium

Ligustrum lucidum (flowers)

Ligustrum obtusifolium

Evergreen privets include several beautiful species, hardy about as far north as Washington, D.C. Most frequent in cultivation are *L. japonicum* and *L. lucidum*, to both of which the name wax-leaf privet is applied. These sorts are often confused in gardens and nurseries. Native to Japan and Korea, **L. japonicum** rarely is over 10 feet tall. Its firm, dark green, glossy, hair-

less leaves are ovate to ovate-lanceolate, not over 4 inches long, and blunt or short-pointed. The flowers, in panicles up to 6 inches in length, have corolla tubes slightly longer than the petals. Variety *L. j. rotundifolium* (syn. *L. coriaceum*) has blunt, nearly round leaves 2 to 2½ inches long, sometimes notched at their apexes. The leaves of *L. j. variegatum* are margined with white. A tall shrub or tree up to 30 feet in height, **L. lucidum,** of Japan, Korea, and China, has ovate to ovate-lancelate leaves 3 to 6 inches long, lighter green and longer-pointed than those of *L. japonicum*. Another difference is that the flowers of *L. lucidum* have petals as long as the corolla tubes. Varieties in gardens attributed to *L. lucidum*, although some perhaps should be referred to *L. japonicum*, include these: *L. l. aureo-marginatum* has leaves edged with yellow; *L. l. excelsum-superbum* has leaves with creamy-white variegation; *L. l. tricolor* has leaves variegated with yellow and when young with pink; *L. l. ciliatum* has smaller leaves than the typical species; *L. l. compactum*, compact, has dark, waxy green foliage; *L. l. gracile, L. l. nobile,* and *L. l. pyramidale* are of erect outline; *L. l. macrophyllum* has leaves bigger than those of the species; and *L. l. repandum* has narrow, crisped leaves.

Ligustrum lucidum variety

Said to be a hybrid between *L. j. rotundifolium* and *l. lucidum*, the evergreen kind called 'Suwanne River' is compact and slow-growing. It grows to 4 feet tall. Its leaves are somewhat twisted. From *L. japonicum* and *L. lucidum* evergreen **L. indicum** (syn. *L. nepalense*), of the Himalayas and Indochina, is distinguishable by its pointed, ovate to ovate-lanceolate, 2- to 5-inch-long leaves being downy on their undersides, at least along the midribs. The

Ligustrum japonicum

Ligustrum lucidum

Ligustrum 'Suwanne River'

shoots are also pubescent. The panicles of bloom, up to 5 inches long, have downy stalks. The petals are as long or slightly longer than the corolla tube. Native to central China, *L. henryi* is an evergreen shrub up to about 12 feet high. It has downy shoots, and ovate to ovate-lanceolate, short-pointed, scarcely stalked, lustrous, dark green leaves ¾ inch to 2½ inches long, usually rounded at their bases. The pyramidal panicles of bloom are 2 to 5 inches in length. The flowers have petals about one-half as long as the corolla tubes. Also Chinese, evergreen *L. delavayanum* (syn. *L. ionandrum*) reaches about 6 feet, but is often lower. It has slender, spreading, twiggy branches. Its shoots are downy, as are the short-stalked leaves on their midribs above. The bases of the leaves are rounded to wedge-shaped. In narrow, cylindrical panicles, leafy at their bases, and up to 2 inches or less long, the flowers are like those of *L. henryi*.

Because its fruits at maturity are dry capsules instead of fleshy berries *L. sempervirens* is by some authorities segregated from *Ligustrum* as *Parasyringa sempervirens*. A native of China probably not hardy in climates colder than that of Washington, D.C., this is a shapely evergreen shrub up to about 6 feet tall. It has minutely-downy young shoots and opposite, stalked, hairless, lanceolate to nearly round, toothless leaves, dark green above, and paler with numerous black dots on their undersides. They are ½ inch to 2½ inches long. The fragrant, tubular flowers are creamy-white, about ¼ inch long, and as much across their faces which are of four spreading corolla lobes (petals). The little blooms are crowded in clusters 2 to 4 inches long at the ends of short shoots. They appear in late summer. The fruits are black.

Garden and Landscape Uses. The preeminent use of deciduous privets is as hedge plants. As such they make effective screens, barriers, backgrounds, dividers, and boundary markers. They can be sheared as formal, dense, even walls of greenery unequaled by most other hardy shrubs. They prosper in any ordinary soil, and stand, but do not prefer, some shade. Regal's privet and common privet withstand dryish soils and considerable shade and will often succeed, except common privet in areas where it is subject to blight, under extremely adverse conditions. With these virtues come less advantageous characteristics. To maintain privets formally and neatly involves shearing at least two or three times a year. Their "hungry" roots are invasive, and impoverish flower beds located too close to the bases of hedges. But deciduous privets have uses other than as hedges. When allowed to grow unsheared, in sunny places most develop as quite good-looking flowering shrubs, useful as single specimens and informal screens for places unsuitable for choicer shrubs. Evergreen privets,

where hardy, have the same uses as deciduous kinds. They are more often allowed to develop as unsheared bushes or small trees but are also much used for hedges. They are good container plants for use indoors and out.

Cultivation. Few woody plants are less demanding of gardeners' skills or are as tolerant of difficult soils and conditions as privets. The chief care needed is shearing those grown as hedges or in other formal ways. This may be done at any time and usually involves more than once a year attention. Specimens overgrown or shabby can be rejuvenated by pruning back to any extent, even to ground level. It is helpful to follow severe pruning by fertilizing and, if practicable, with periodic thorough waterings in dry weather. Propagation can be by seed, but is so easily accomplished by leafy summer cuttings, and with deciduous kinds by hardwood cuttings taken in fall, that these are the methods usually employed.

Pests and Diseases. Privets may become infested with aphids, thrips, mealybugs, leaf miners, whiteflies, nematodes, and the privet weevil, the last destroying the young shoots. They may be affected by root rots, powdery mildew, and anthracnose twig blight, the last highly destructive of common privet in some areas and difficult to control. It is not advisable to plant common privet where this is prevalent.

LILAC. See Syringa. Australian-lilac is *Prostanthera lasianthos*. California-lilac is *Ceanothus*. Indian-lilac is *Melia azedarach*.

LILIACEAE—Lily Family. Of cosmopolitan natural distribution and containing many beautiful ornamentals as well as such familiar edibles as asparagus, garlic, leeks, and onions, the lily family as accepted here consists of some 3,700 species of monocotyledons distributed in some 250 genera. Certain sorts are under other botanical interpretations allotted to other families, notably the ALLIACEAE and AMARYLLIDACEAE. The great majority of species are herbaceous perennials; many including colchicums, grape-hyacinths, hyacinths, lilies, scillas, and tulips, are bulb plants; a considerable number, in which belong aloes, gasterias, and haworthias, are succulents; and a few, including *Dracaena* and *Yucca*, are shrubs or trees. Other familiar members of the family are aspidistras, day-lilies, dracaenas, lily-of-the-valley, and plantain-lilies.

The lily family includes deciduous and evergreen sorts. Their habit of growth and foliage is very diverse, some such as *Gloriosa* and *Smilax* having vining stems. The flowers are in racemes, panicles, or umbels or are solitary. Symmetrical or nearly so, most usually have six-parted perianths, rarely, as in *Aspidistra*, *Paris*, and *Trillium*, fewer

segments. Most often the perianth segments are all petal-like and are commonly called petals, although a more exact name for them is tepals. There are as many stamens as perianth segments and one or three styles. The possession of a superior ovary, that is an ovary with the perianth segments originating from below rather than above it, is the most ready means of distinguishing flowers of *Liliaceae* from those of *Amaryllidaceae*, but the distinction is blurred a little in such cases as *Aletris*, in which the flowers have a partly interior ovary. The fruits are capsules or berries.

Genera in cultivation include: *Agapanthus, Albuca, Aletris, Allium, Aloe, Amianthium, Androstephium, Anemarrhena, Anthericum, Aphyllanthes, Arthropodium, Asparagus, Asphodeline, Asphodelus, Aspidistra, Astelia, Astroloba, Beaucarnea, Bellevalia, Bessera, Blandfordia, Bloomeria, Boophone, Bowiea, Brimeura, Brodiaea, Bulbine, Bulbinella, Bulbocodium, Calibanus, Calochortus, Camassia, Cardiocrinum, Chamaelirium, Chionodoxa, Chionographis, Chionoscilla, Chlorogalum, Chlorophytum, Clintonia, Colchicum, Convallaria, Cordyline, Danae, Dasylirion, Dianella, Dichelostemma, Dipcadi, Dipidax, Disporum, Dracaena, Drimia, Drimiopsis, Drymophila, Endymion, Eremurus, Erythronium, Eucomis, Eustrephus, Fritillaria, Gagea, Galtonia, Gasterhaworthia, Gasteria, Gastrolea, Geitonoplesium, Gloriosa, Haworthia, Helonias, Heloniopsis, Hemerocallis, Hesperaloe, Hesperocallis, Hosta, Hyacinthella, Hyacinthus, Ipheion, Kniphofia, Lachenalia, Lapageria, Ledebouria, Leucocoryne, Leucocrinum, Lilium, Liriope, Littonia, Lloydia, Maianthemum, Massonia, Medeola, Melanthium, Merendera, Milla, Muilla, Muscari, Narthecium, Nolina, Nomocharis, Notholirion, Nothoscordum, Ophiopogon, Ornithogalum, Paradisea, Paris, Pasithea, Philagraea, Philesia, Phormium, Pleea, Poellnitzia, Polygonatum, Puschkinia, Reineckea, Rhodocodon, Ripogonum, Rohdea, Ruscus, Samuela, Sandersonia, Sanservieria, Scilla, Semele, Smilacina, Smilax, Speirantha, Stenanthium, Streptopus, Stypandra, Theropogon, Thysanotus, Tolfieldia, Trichopetalum, Tricyrtis, Trillium, Triteleia, Tulbaghia, Tulipa, Tupistra, Urginea, Uvularia, Veltheimia, Veratrum, Whiteheadia, Xanthorrhoea, Xerophyllum, Yucca,* and *Zigadenus*.

LILIUM (Líli-um)—Lily. This, the genus to which belong all true lilies, consists of eighty species and a considerable number of varieties and hybrids. For leads to the botanical names of other plants with common names that include the word lily, such as Amazon-lily, day-lily, fawn-lily, and lily-of-the-valley see Encyclopedia entries under their vernacular names, or Lily. Here we are concerned only with true lilies. Their botanical name *Lilium* is a Latin one similar to the Greek name *leirion* for the Madonna lily. Three species of Himalayan plants with long-stalked, broadly-heart-shaped leaves that were previously included in *Lilium* have been separated as *Cardiocrinum*, some others belong in *Notholirion*.

The genus *Lilium*, confined in the wild to the northern hemisphere, with very few exceptions to temperate parts, belongs to the lily family LILIACEAE. Its members are deciduous or in rare cases in mild climates semievergreen herbaceous perennials. Except for one maverick sort all grow in the ground. The notable exception, not in cultivation, is Burmese *L. arboricola*. This perches on trees as an epiphyte.

Lilies have erect leafy stems and scaly bulbs, that is the bulbs are composed of scales that overlap like shingles on a roof in contrast to those of such bulbs as onions and tulips, in which successive layers of scales completely enclose each other and an outer thin skin envelops all. Lily bulbs are of two sorts. In those called concentric the bulb changes little except for increase in size from year to year, and new or daughter bulbs grow from within the mother clustered against its central axis. With lily bulbs that are rhizomatous or stoloniferous the mother bulb sends out slender horizontal stems (stolons or underground rhizomes) upon which develop new daughter bulbs. The leaves of lilies are undivided and either scattered singly along the stems or in whorls (circles of three or more). The flowers, up-facing, horizontal, declined, or pendulous, and solitary or clustered, are commonly large and showy. They may be white or of various shades of yellow, orange, pink, or red. Often they are spotted or striped with hues other than the base one. They have six segments or petal-like parts commonly called petals, but more correctly identified as tepals, with at the base of each a groove containing nectar, six slender-stalked stamens, and a long style with a three-lobed stigma. The ovary is behind (below) the petals. The fruits are capsules, those even of kinds with drooping flowers usually upright at maturity.

The history of lilies in cultivation is long. The Madonna lily, symbol of purity dedicated to the Virgin Mary and frequently included in early paintings and other works of art depicting her, was treasured in monastic gardens of the middle ages. A few other native sorts, including *L. pyrenaicum*, were cultivated by Europeans as early as the fifteenth and sixteenth centuries.

But long before that the Madonna lily found favor with gardeners and those concerned with medicinal qualities of plants. In Anatolia it was cultivated for a healing salve prepared from its bulbs 1,500 years before the birth of Christ. Ancient Egyptians grew its bulbs for eating, and early Greeks and Romans cultivated it for medicine and garden adornment. In the Herbal of Dioscorides it is recognizably pictured and described as having healing qualities.

From the seventeenth century on or ear-lier the regal lily found a place in Chinese gardens and the gold-banded lily in those of Japan. But much sooner, at least 1,000 years ago, Chinese, Koreans, and Japanese were growing bulbs of the tiger lily for food.

The coming of non-native lilies to European gardens began early. From eastern North America *L. canadense* arrived before 1620, possibly by 1535 or shortly thereafter. American *L. superbum* first bloomed in England in 1738. The first lily from the Far East to reach Europe was *L. pensylvanicum*, which came from Japan to England about 1743. From eastern North America *L. philadelphicum* was sent to France in 1765.

The nineteenth century saw the bringing into European and subsequently American gardens a flood of species of *Lilium*, including from Asia *L. tigrinum* in 1804, *L. concolor* in 1806, *L. pumilum* in 1810, *L. longiflorum* in 1819, *L. speciosum* and varieties of it in 1830, *L. nepalense* in 1855, *L. neilgherrense* and *L. auratum* in 1862, *L. hansonii* in 1869, *L. philippinense* in 1871, *L. henryi*, *L. leucanthum*, and *L. l. chloraster* in 1888 or the following year, *L. sulphureum* in 1889, *L. davidii willmottiae* in 1895, and *L. rubellum* in 1898.

Western American natives were chiefly introduced to gardens via England. The first to come was the leopard lily in 1848 to be followed twenty-one years later by the Washington and Humboldt lilies. In 1872 *L. parvum* arrived in England as did *L. columbianum* in 1873, *L. maritimum* two years later, and *L. parryi* in 1876.

The twentieth century brought further introductions of new species from the wild, although the time was rapidly approaching when nearly all had been at least tried in gardens. Undoubtedly the great benchmark in the new century was the 1903 discovery and introduction to cultivation of *L. regale* from the Min valley in western China by that indefatigable plant collector, "Chinese" Wilson. This gave new impetus to popular interest in lilies. Other twentieth-century introductions include from western North America *L. kelloggii* in 1901, *L. duchartrei* from China in 1903, Korean *L. amabile* in 1905, and *L. wardii* from Tibet in 1925.

Hybrid lilies are by no means all new. One of the earliest of which there is record is the Nankeen lily (*L. testaceum*). This, its parents the Madonna lily and *L. chalcedonicum*, was discovered in 1835 growing in a bed of other lilies by a nurseryman in Erfurt, Germany. English nurseryman Henry Groom, active in hybridizing in the third decade of the nineteenth century, was so far as is known the first Westerner to engage in breeding lilies. As parents he employed *L. maculatum* varieties from Japan and European *L. bulbiferum*. In 1869 Francis Parkman, of Jamaica Plain, Massachusetts, raised beautiful *L. parkmannii* by crossing *L. auratum* and *L. speciosum*. Toward the end of the nineteenth century, *L. martagon* and *L. hansonii* were hybridized in Holland to give *L.* 'Marhan', a sort with orange, reddish-spotted blooms that grows 4 to 6 feet high. About 1890 *L. dalhansonii* was produced simultaneously in Holland and England as a result of crossing *L. hansonii* with *L. martagon dalmaticum*. Before the turn of the century a group called Backhouse hybrids were raised by Mrs. R. O. Backhouse in England as a result of crossing and recrossing *L. martagon album*, *L. dalmaticum*, and *L. hansonii*. The newcomers included such notable varieties as 'Brocade', 'Golden Orb', 'Mrs. R. O. Backhouse', and 'Sceptre'.

A new era in the development of hybrid lilies was ushered in about the middle of the twentieth century, the chief center of the renascence being North America, but not confined there. With few exceptions, notably *L. hollandicum*, and *L. testaceum*, earlier hybrids were by then either completely lost to cultivation or were precariously preserved by a few enthusiastic specialists. Various reasons accounted for this, one of the most significant being that the plants, all propagated vegetatively, had become ridden with debilitating virus diseases.

The cultivation of hybrid lilies in gardens almost everywhere, which made available a great number of sorts with improved or completely new forms and colorings as well as of agreeable vigor and dispositions, depended upon a few findings. Among these were methods of storing in a viable state for weeks or even months pollen collected from early-blooming lilies and using it to cross-fertilize late-flowering sorts. Another breakthrough came with the discovery that many hybrid lilies could be crossed with one another and be backcrossed with their parent species with much greater success than was generally had with hybridizing two natural species. Quantity production from seeds of hybrid lilies under carefully controlled conditions that ensured high quality, virus-free bulbs was magnificently pioneered by Jan de Graaf of Oregon.

The botanical classification of lilies is difficult and the results are by no means satisfying to all botanists. The earliest attempt, made in 1836, relied entirely on the shapes of the flowers. Other efforts followed, all of which, until the publication of a proposed classification by Harold F. Comber in 1949, laid great stress on the forms of the blooms. From the botanists' point of view, such emphasis was unsatisfactory because it frequently brought into the same group species that quite surely were not closely related and distributed among separate groups some that were. Nevertheless, systems based on easily observable floral characteristics served moderately well as aids to recognition.

Comber's classification took into consideration the sum total of fifteen different characteristics including the manner in which the seeds germinate, leaf arrangement, whether the scales of the bulbs are jointed or not, whether the seeds are light or heavy, and the shape and habit of the bulbs. As a result he established seven sections for the genus excluding *Cardiocrinum* (as compared with the four sections previously used). Although Comber makes clear that his offering is neither perfect nor final, he believes his proposal reflects the natural affinities of the wild lilies of the world more accurately than any previous one.

Horticultural classifications, of necessity, must take into account not only species, but the numerous hybrids now available and so far as can be anticipated the many more that are sure to come. The North American Lily Society and the Royal Horticultural Society of England have been active in working out classifications for these, useful for registration of varieties, flower shows, and catalog preparation.

Because America is rich in native species, many challenging to grow, but all lovely and appropriate for wild gardens and many for other garden uses, it has been decided to group the lilies treated in this Encyclopedia on a geographical basis, first accounting among the selection to be considered American species native east of the Rocky Mountains, then natives from west of that great range. Next we shall turn to the species of Europe, a few which overlap into adjacent western Asia, and finally species of eastern Asia and adjacent islands. Finally, that is, so far as species of the genus *Lilium* go, hybrid lilies will be considered.

Native lilies of eastern North America include some that accommodate well to gardens, others that do not. Among the former the lovely and long-lived American Turk's cap ranks high. Fully as beautiful and almost as easy are the graceful meadow lily and its close relative the bell lily. The wood or orange cup lily, the Southern red lily, and *L. michauxii* are much less dependable. Not hardy in the north, the Southern red lily is unlikely to succeed even in its natural range unless afforded the acid, swampy, sandy soil and half-shady environment it knows in the wild. Also of doubtful hardiness, although in favorable locations it may succeed as far north as southern New York, *L. michauxii* is decidedly more delicate, and less accommodating than its more splendid and agreeable relative the American Turk's cap lily. We shall now consider individually these lilies of eastern North America.

The meadow lily (**L. canadense**), of eastern North America, inhabits moist or wet meadows from Quebec to Maine, Minnesota, Alabama, Ohio, and Indiana. A graceful sort, it has white, stoloniferous

Lilium canadense

Lilium canadense (flowers)

bulbs that renew themselves annually and stems 2 to 5 feet tall not rooting from their bases. Mostly in whorls of four to twelve, but with the lower ones and sometimes a few of the uppermost scattered, the leaves are linear-elliptic, 3 to 6 inches long by ⅓ to ¾ inch broad. Occasionally solitary, more often with up to fifteen blooms in umbels of two to five or in an umbel with a few blooms forming a short raceme above it, the bell-shaped flowers with spreading, but not strongly-recurved petals nod from the ends of long, erect, individual stalks. From 2 to 3½ inches long, their petals range from yellow to orange-yellow or almost red, are greenish at their bases, and within are spotted with purple. The stamens do not protrude. Yellow flowers are borne by *L. c. flavum*, red ones by *L. c. rubrum*.

The Southern red lily (**L. catesbaei**) shares with *L. philadelphicum* the distinction of being the only eastern American lily with up-faced blooms. From that species it differs in the uppermost leaves not being in whorls. Native of the southeastern United States, this inhabitant of acid-soil swamps, 1 foot to 2 feet tall, has white bulbs 1 inch to 2 inches long of loosely-arranged, fragile scales with prolonged, leaflike tips. The numerous scattered, grasslike leaves are 1 inch to 3 inches long by up to ½ inch wide. The yellow and red, brown- to purple-spot-

ted blooms, solitary or up to three on a stem, are 3 to 4 inches wide. The bulbs of *L. c. longii* lack prolonged leaflike apexes.

The bell lily (**L. grayi**) is a native of rich moist woodlands in the mountains of Virginia, North Carolina, and Tennessee. A close relative of the meadow lily, the bell lily differs from that sort chiefly in its less vigorous growth and its pendulous to horizontal flowers having petals with tips that spread but slightly and are deep red on their outsides. The stamens do not protrude. This slender-stemmed lily is 2 to 3 feet tall.

Similar to *L. superbum*, but less exciting and less satisfactory as a garden plant, **L. michauxii** (syn. *L. carolinianum*) in the wild favors partially to more heavily shaded places with dampish, acid, loamy, organic soils along the coastal plain from Virginia to Louisiana and in the mountains from Virginia and West Virginia southward. This differs from *L. superbum* chiefly in being of lower stature, in having leaves that are broader distinctly above instead of at or below their middles, in having fewer blooms, in rooting from the below-ground portions of its stems, and in being less hardy.

Lilium michauxii

The wood or orange cup lily (**L. philadelphicum**) is native, usually in dry, rather infertile, sandy soils in light shade or in pastures from Maine to North Carolina and Missouri. This, often balky to establish in gardens, does not root from the bases of its stems. It has white bulbs about 1 inch in diameter that send out stolons and have fragile scales. The slender, hairless, green stems 1 foot to 3 feet tall bear mostly in whorls pointed-lanceolate leaves 1 inch to 4 inches long by ¼ to ½ inch wide. The five or fewer flowers in a terminal umbel face upward, are broadly-cup-shaped, have lanceolate, bright orange-red-spotted-with-purple petals 1½ to 2½ inches long. The yellow-stalked stamens with bright red anthers are equaled in length by the red style. The western orange cup lily *L. p. andinum*, except for an uppermost whorl, has chiefly scattered leaves, often narrower than those of the typical species. It ranges in the wild from Quebec to Kentucky, British Columbia, Nebraska, and New Mexico.

The American Turk's cap lily (**L. superbum**), which as treated here includes the midwestern variant sometimes segregated as *L. michiganense,* occupies acid, moist soils and wet meadows from New Brunswick to Minnesota, Florida, Tennessee, and Missouri. The bulbs of this robust sort are large, round, white, and rhizomatous. Its stems are from 4 to 8 feet in height. Except for a few upper ones the lanceolate leaves, 3 to 4½ inches long by up to ¾ inch broad, are in whorls. Rarely solitary, the blooms are more commonly several to as many as forty in umbels or partly in umbels and partly in racemes. They nod from the ends of ascending or erect individual stalks and have strongly-recurved, orange to orange-red petals, bright green at their bases on the inside and spotted with purple. The stamens are much protruded. This lily is not stem-rooting.

Lilium superbum

The lilies of western North America, with the notable exceptions of the Humboldt lily and panther lily, tend to be sulky about settling down and prospering away from home. Nevertheless they are well worth attempting and sometimes persist and flower satisfactorily even though they fail to multiply. Most have stoloniferous or sub-stoloniferous bulbs, often fragile and difficult to ship or even handle without damage, or they have small bulbs that deteriorate rapidly out of the ground. In addition to species found only in the West, the orange cup lily of eastern North America is represented there by its variety *L. philadelphicum andinum* and *L. p. montanum.* The lilies now to be described include the great majority that occur natively west of the Rocky Mountains.

The thimble lily (**L. bolanderi**) inhabits a comparatively small mountain region in southern Oregon and northern California. It grows in dryish soils and has ovate

bulbs up to 2 inches long. The stems, not rooting from their bases, are 1 foot to 3 feet tall or sometimes taller. Oblanceolate to obovate, 2½ to 4 inches long, and glaucous on both surfaces, the leaves are in three to six whorls with one to three solitary leaves beneath each whorl. The two to nine slightly nodding to horizontal blooms are bell-shaped with the upper one-third of each approximately 1½-inch-long petal, out-turned. Inside they are light crimson spotted with reddish-purple. Their outsides are brick- to wine-red overlaid with a bluish tone.

The Columbia or Oregon lily (**L. columbianum**) is wild from British Columbia to Idaho and northern California. It has ovoid, whitish bulbs 1½ to 2 inches in diameter and slender, nonrooting stems 2 to 4 feet tall or occasionally taller on which the lower leaves are usually in whorls of five to nine, those above scattered. They are lanceolate to oblanceolate, 2 to 4 inches long by from a little under to somewhat over ½ inch wide. The few to many nodding flowers have usually purple-speckled, red to yellow, lanceolate-ovate, recurved petals up to 2¼ inches long. In aspect this lily is a smaller edition of *L. humboldtii.*

The Humboldt lily (**L. humboldtii**) is sometimes quite misleadingly called tiger lily, a name better reserved for Asian *L. tigrinum.* A variable Californian endemic, this species differs from the Columbia lily in its more robust growth and larger blooms. Its creamy-white, lopsided-egg-shaped bulbs, 2 to 6 inches tall, have bitter-tasting scales. The stout, purplish stems attain heights of 3 to 7 or occasionally 10 feet. In four to eight whorls of ten to twenty, the oblanceolate leaves are 3 to 5 inches long by ½ to slightly over 1 inch broad. The few to many nodding flowers are orange-yellow to orange-red spotted with purple or maroon. Their reflexed petals are 3 to 4 inches long by ½ to over 1 inch wide.

Of the *L. martagon* relationship, **L. kelloggii** is endemic to dryish soils in northwestern California. Its egg-shaped, white bulbs are about 2 inches in length. The slender 2- to 4-foot-tall, purplish-brown stem, which does not root from the base, is furnished with four to eight whorls of up to twelve lanceolate to oblanceolate leaves 2 to 4 inches long by ½ to ¾ inch broad. Nodding and fragrant, the ten to twenty pink to pinkish-mauve blooms have petals spotted toward their bases with dark purple and with a center band of yellow. They are 1½ to a little over 2 inches long by ⅜ inch wide, and recurved from their bases. Much shorter than the petals, the anthers are pinkish-yellow.

The Western lily (**L. occidentale**) occurs as a rare wildling from southern Oregon to northern California, mostly among ferns and in moist sandy loam, peat, or

sphagnum. A sort without roots from its stems, this has rhizome-type bulbs 1½ to 2 inches long and slender stems 2 to 6 feet in height. The narrowly-oblanceolate leaves, 2½ to 6 inches long by ¼ to 1 inch wide, are usually scattered near the bottoms and tops of the stems and are in whorls of five to twelve in between. The nodding flowers, usually ten or fewer, rarely more than twice that number, have lanceolate petals 1½ to 2½ inches long, their outer halves recurved. Orange to red, spotted with purple or dark maroon, they have green centers.

The leopard or panther lily (**L. pardalinum**) is a very variable native of watersides and springy soils in California. Its white bulbs, 2½ to 4 inches long, branch to form mats. The green nonrooting stems are 3 to 7 feet high. In three or four whorls of nine to fifteen or fewer or scattered near the tops of the stems, the leaves are linear-lanceolate to oblanceolate, 4 to 6 inches long or somewhat longer by ¼ to 1 inch wide. The one to twenty scentless or fragrant, 2- to 4-inch-wide blooms nod from the ends of long, upward-spreading individual stalks. The petals, recurved from their middles or lower, are lanceolate, 2 to 3 inches long by ½ to ¾ inch wide, orange-scarlet with yellow bases, spotted with maroon-purple. A sort known in gardens as *L. p. giganteum* (syn. *L. harrisianum*) possibly represents a hybrid between *L. pardalinum* and *L. humboldtii.* It attains heights of up to 8 feet and has especially brilliant purple-spotted, orange blooms with yellow centers.

The lemon lily (**L. parryi**), an endemic of Arizona and southern California, has rhizome-like, white bulbs 1 inch long or a little longer. Not rooting from their bases, the slender stems 2 to 5 feet tall have, except for the lowermost, which sometimes are in whorls, scattered leaves, linear-lanceolate to lanceolate, 3½ to 6 inches long by up to a little over ½ inch wide. The one to rarely as many as twenty-five trumpet-shaped blooms are held horizontally. Clear lemon-yellow, sometimes dotted with maroon or purple, they are fragrant. The upper one-third of their 2½- to 4-inch-long petals spread widely or are recurved. Not very amenable to cultivation, in the wild the lemon lily inhabits stream banks and springy soils at elevations above 4,000 feet.

The chaparral, redwood, or chamise lily (**L. rubescens**), native of dryish soils from San Francisco to Oregon, is one of the most delightfully fragrant of the lily clan. It does not root from its stems, and has decidedly lop-sided, egg-shaped, thick-scaled, white bulbs 1½ to 2 inches long. Slender, the stems are 2 to 6 feet tall. The pointed-oblanceolate leaves, glaucous on their undersides, are scattered on the lower part of the stem; above they are in three to seven whorls of five to ten, successively decreasing in size upward. The leaves are 1½ to

3½ inches long by ½ to 1 inch wide. The flowers are in loose racemes of five to thirty or less commonly as many as 100. Up-facing and trumpet-shaped, they have the upper one-third of their petals strongly recurved. The lanceolate petals, 1½ to 2 inches long by nearly ½ inch wide, are at first white finely spotted with purple. They change to pink and finally to wine-red.

An inhabitant of hillside bogs in California and Oregon, *L. vollmeri,* also known as *L. roezlii,* which name has been applied to another species. It has branchless, yellow rhizomes and stems up to 3 feet tall with linear-lanceolate leaves 4 to 6 inches long by ¼ to nearly ½ inch wide, those toward the centers of the stems whorled, the uppermost and lowermost scattered. Few to many, the nodding, yellow to orange blooms are flecked with dark spots at the bases of the petals. The latter are reflexed, 2¼ to 3½ inches long by ¼ to nearly ½ inch wide.

The Washington lily (*L. washingtonianum*), named not for the state of Washington, but in honor of the wife of the first president of the United States, is endemic to dryish soils in California and Oregon. It has lop-sided bulbs 6 to 8 inches in length, and to some extent, stolons. The only roots come from the bases of the bulbs, not from the underground parts of its 2- to 5-foot-tall stems. These last have five or six whorls of six to twelve pointed-lanceolate leaves 2 to 5 inches long by ½ inch to 1½ inches wide. The racemes are of up to twenty sweetly fragrant, trumpet-shaped blooms held horizontally. The fragrant flowers have lanceolate petals 3 to 4 inches long, their upper one-third recurved. They are white at first, later becoming blush-pink and finally deeper purplish-pink. The stamens are much shorter than the petals, have yellow anthers, and are shorter than the green style and its club-shaped stigma.

The lilies of Europe and western Asia include the kinds longest cultivated there and the first exotic sorts brought to America. Among those sorts only the orange lily has up-facing blooms. Those of the Madonna lily face outward. All others have drooping flowers. Most notable is the Madonna lily, so ready to make itself at home in gardens and the only white-flowered species native to Europe. Scarcely less familiar, at least to Europeans, and as adaptable to domestication, is the orange lily, that handsome pawn of politics symbolic of the Dutch royal House of Orange. Because of the color of its blooms and season of their flaunting the Orangemen of Northern Ireland employ them in their July 12 celebration of the battle of the Boyne, which in 1690 resulted in the defeat of deposed Roman Catholic James II of Great Britain and Ireland by Prince William of Orange, who by then was William III of England. In Holland, for political reasons, it was at one time forbidden to grow orange lilies.

Notable characteristics of the lilies of Europe and western Asia are that all tolerate and most thrive better in soils containing lime than in acid ones, that they are slow to recover from transplanting, and that they come slowly from seeds, usually taking a few years from sowing to first blooming. Among them only the orange lily and *L. carniolicum* develop stem roots.

The scarlet Turk's cap lily (*L. chalcedonicum*), native in limestone soils in southern Greece and nearby islands, is remarkable for its up to about ten brilliant orange-red, usually spotless, blooms. One of the oldest cultivated lilies, this has ovoid, whitish or yellowish bulbs about 3 inches in diameter. Its 2- to 4-foot-tall, purple-tinged stems, which do not root from their bases, are clothed with numerous scattered leaves 1½ to 4 inches long by ¼ to ½ inch wide, the central ones linear, the lower ones oblanceolate. They have fine glandular hairs along their margins. The few to several disagreeably-scented, nodding blooms, with strongly reflexed thick, waxy petals about 2½ inches long are 2 to 3 inches in diameter, have long-protruded stamens with scarlet anthers.

Lilium chalcedonicum

The Caucasian lily (*L. monadelphum*) is a lovely kind with 3- to 5-inch-wide, bright yellow blooms with a few red to blackish dots. The flowers have a rather unpleasant odor. They are produced somewhat later in the season than those of closely related *L. szovitsianum.* Native to the northern Caucasus and Black Sea, where it grows in soils rich with leaf mold in light woodlands at high altitudes, the Caucasian lily has large, whitish ovoid bulbs and stems not rooting from their bases that are 3 to 5 feet high and clothed with scattered lanceolate to oblanceolate leaves up to 5 inches long by 1 inch wide.

The yellow Turk's cap lily (*L. pyrenaicum*) inhabits the Pyrenees. It has spherical bulbs, whitish and about 2¾ inches in diameter, and green to purplish stems not

Lilium monadelphum

rooting from their bases, 1 foot to 3 feet tall, clothed throughout their lengths with numerous scattered, linear-lanceolate leaves 3 to 5 inches long by up to ⅔ inch wide and fringed with glandular hairs. In loose, leafy clusters of three to eight or rarely up to twelve, the greenish-yellow to brighter yellow, nodding, ill-scented blooms marked with purplish-black dots, have strongly-reflexed petals 1½ to 2 inches long. More beautiful *L. p. rubrum* has maroon-spotted, orange-red flowers with a thick style.

The European red lily or lesser Turk's cap (*L. pomponium*) much resembles the yellow Turk's cap, but differs in having a portion of stem below the blooms leafless except for a few small samples, in its silvery-edged leaves not being over ⅛ inch wide and channeled above and keeled beneath, and in the blooms, which like those of the other are unpleasantly scented, being scarlet or less commonly bright orange-red dotted with purplish-black and having a slender style. This native of the Maritime Alps of France and Italy, where it occupies open, sunny, southern slopes and limestone cliffs, is 1½ to 2½ feet tall and has spherical-ovoid bulbs and stems that do not root from their bases. The blooms, with very much rolled-back petals, are up to ten on a stem.

The martagon or Turk's cap lily (*L. martagon*), which ranges from southern Europe to Siberia and Mongolia, is the most widely naturally distributed of all lilies. Its egg-shaped bulbs yellow and 1 inch long or longer, this does not root from the sometimes purple-spotted stems, which are 3 to 6 feet in height. The oblanceolate to spatula-shaped leaves 2 to 3 inches long by 1 inch to 1½ inches wide, on the upper portions of the stem or occasionally throughout their lengths, are scattered, but more usually for the greater parts of their lengths are in closely-set whorls of six to nine. The mostly twenty to fifty ill-scented, nodding blooms are in long terminal panicled racemes. They are 2 to 3 inches wide by up to 2 inches in depth and have strongly-reflexed, lanceolate petals of

Lilium martagon

Lilium candidum

Lilium martagon album

Lilium szovitsianum

terminal umbel, have bright orange-yellow 2-inch-long petals slightly spotted with red-orange. Far more commonly cultivated than the typical sort, which is rare even in the wild, *L. b. croceum* (syn. *L. aurantiacum*), which attains heights of 3 to 6 feet, has umbels of up to twenty usually reddish-brown-spotted, yellow-orange flowers. This sort rarely has bulbs in the axils of its upper leaves and then only few. A low variety, *L. b. chaixii*, occurs natively in the French Maritime Alps.

Beautiful **L. szovitsianum** closely resembles *L. monadelphum* and was once considered a variety of that species. It differs in its stamens not being united at their bases and in their pollen being reddish-brown instead of yellow. As a wildling this inhabits regions to the south of the range of *L. monadelphum*.

ceolate leaves up to 10 inches in length that remain through the winter. The only other lily with green foliage evident through that season is *L. catesbaei*, of eastern North America. The stems of the Madonna lily produce no roots from their bases. Stiffly erect, they are 2½ to 5 feet tall. Their leaves are many and scattered, the lower oblanceolate and 6 to 8 inches long, those higher gradually diminishing until the uppermost leaves are not over 1 inch in length, are narrow and pointed, and hug the stem. Carried horizontally or angled slightly downward, the sweetly fragrant flowers, from few to fifteen or twenty in a close raceme, are broadly-funnel- to bell-shaped with somewhat recurved, obovate petals, 2 to 3 inches long, and a style much longer than the stamens. Except for the bright yellow pollen that coats the ripe anthers, they are pure waxy-white.

Much like the martagon lily in habit and form of flowers, **L. carniolicum** is less frequently seen in gardens. Native of central Europe, in the wild this favors well-drained, limestone soils that contain fair amounts of humus. Chiefly an inhabitant of mountain meadows, the Carnolian lily, 1 foot to 3 feet tall, has stems that root from their bases and carry up to six exceedingly fragrant, bright red blooms. Variety *L. c. albanicum* is a dwarfer sort with glossy foliage and amber-yellow flowers. The blooms of *L. c. jankae* are bright yellow with black markings and yellow anthers.

The orange or fire lily (**L. bulbiferum**) and its varieties are among the notable glories of the native floras of central and southern Europe. Long cultivated and well illustrated in sixteenth-century herbals, this stem-rooting species has spherical, white bulbs 2 to 3 inches in diameter that proliferate rapidly. From 2 to 4 feet tall and with hair toward their tops and in the leaf axils, the green stems bear scattered, pointed-lanceolate leaves 1½ to 2 inches long by ¼ to ⅝ inch wide. In the typical species bulbils usually form in the axils of the upper leaves. The goblet-shaped, up-facing blooms, in the typical species one to few in a compact

a dull purplish-lilac, purple, or purple-red hue densely spotted toward their bases with black-purple. The stamens are much shorter than the petals. Their anthers are red. Several varieties exist including one with double flowers and *L. m. album* with white blooms. Especially fine is *L. m. dalmaticum*, a tall grower with wine-red flowers.

The Madonna lily (**L. candidum**) is the only white-flowered lily native to Europe. Because of this until a little more than a century ago when from the Orient other sorts with white blooms came to the attention of Europeans, what we now know as the Madonna lily was called simply the white lily. Its provenance is not surely known, but eastern Europe and adjacent western Asia are believed to be its native region. Cultivated as a medicinal and food plant for at least 1,500 years and quite probably for twice that time, it has undoubtedly been carried by man to some parts of Europe where it now is apparently native.

The bulbs of the Madonna lily are ovoid, white to yellowish, and 2 to 3 inches in diameter. From their tops in early fall come a rosette of spreading shiny, narrow-oblan-

The lilies of eastern Asia and offshore islands are most numerous as to species and include nearly all with trumpet- or funnel-shaped flowers. Many are well known in gardens, none more so perhaps than the Easter lily and regal lily. Some are easy or relatively easy to grow, some are less responsive, a few are well-nigh impossible, perhaps chiefly because of virus disease infection. In addition to the many trumpet-flowered sorts, there come from this region also a very considerable number with nodding, Turk's cap, or martagon-type blooms, a very few with up-facing flowers, and the glorious gold-banded lily, which carries its more or less bowl-shaped flowers horizontally.

The goldband lily (**L. auratum**), of Japan, has greenish-yellow bulbs up to 4 inches across. It roots from the below-ground parts of its 3- to 7-foot-tall purple stems. The scattered leaves are lanceolate, 4 to 6 inches long by ½ inch to 1½ inches wide. In racemes of ten to thirty, on good specimens averaging about twenty, the strongly fragrant, short, trumpet-shaped blooms, up to 10 inches or even 1 foot across, have widely-flaring petals 1 inch to 1½ inches wide. They are white spotted

Lilium auratum platyphyllum

with red or yellow and with a bold central band of yellow. There are several varieties, among them *L. a. platyphyllum*, distinguished by its leaves being 1½ to 2½ inches wide, the blooms with the spots mostly in their throats, and the petals broader than those of the typical kind.

The star lily (*L. concolor*) owes its colloquial designation to the petals of its vividly red blooms spreading widely to form six-pointed stars. One of the very best species for garden adornment and cut flowers, including its varieties, this is a variable native of China, Korea, and Japan. Barely 1 inch in diameter, its solid, creamy-white bulbs egg-shaped, consist of few scales. The stems, which root from their below-ground parts and are to some degree purple-tinged, rise to heights of 1 foot to 3 feet. The leaves are scattered, pointed-narrow-lanceolate, from 1 inch to 2 inches in length by up to ¼ inch wide. The flowers face upward and are one to ten on each stem, with petals 1 inch to 2 inches long. Petals, stamens, and style are of the same vermilion color. The petals are without spots. Varieties of note are *L. c. coridion*, with lemon-yellow flowers with fine brown spots; *L. c. pulchellum*, with green stems and black spotted vermilion to orange-red blooms; and *L. c. 'Okihime'*,

Lilium concolor coridion

with spotless, clear yellow blooms bigger than those of the typical sort.

The Japanese Turk's cap lily (*L. hansonii*) is a highly satisfactory garden plant that belies its popular name in being a native of Korea rather than Japan, although much cultivated and even naturalized there. A close relative of *L. martagon*, this has pink-tinged, white, egg-shaped to nearly spherical bulbs 2 inches long or longer and hollow stems that root from their bases and are 2½ to 4 feet tall. The leaves are oblanceolate to lanceolate, 4 to 7 inches long by ordinarily 1 inch to 1½ inches wide, and in whorls of eight to twelve. In open racemes of few to several, the nodding, somewhat fragrant, purplish-brown-spotted, bright orange-yellow, waxy blooms are 1 inch to 2½ inches across. They have recurved petals and stamens, much shorter than the petals, with green stalks and purple anthers. When grown in full sun the flowers are paler than in partial shade.

Lilium hansonii

Lilium hansonii (flowers)

Henry's lily (*L. henryi*) of China, is a very dependable sort that, because its blooms bleach unattractively in sun, should be located in part-shade. In the wild it inhabits such places among thickets of shrubs and grasses on limestone cliffs. The nearly spherical mahogany-red bulbs

are 3 to 7 inches in diameter. From 4 to 8 feet tall, the stems, which root underground, have numerous, scattered elliptic-lanceolate to ovate-lanceolate leaves 2 to 6 inches in length by up to 1¼ inches wide, and shortening above until the uppermost are scarcely more than bracts. The individually long-stalked, more or less nodding, scentless blooms are orange-yellow, greenish toward the bases of petals, spotted with brown. The widely spreading to recurved, prominently-warted petals are 2½ to 3 inches long. Stamens and style are of similar lengths. The anthers are orange.

The Easter lily is probably more familiar to more Americans than any other true lily. The name is applied to varieties of the white trumpet lily (*L. longiflorum*), a native of Japan. The white trumpet lily has white, subspherical bulbs about 2 inches long and stems up to 3 feet tall that root from their bases. Its leaves are scattered, pointed-lanceolate, and 4 to 7 inches long by ⅜ to ⅝ inch wide. The fragrant, pure white, waxy blooms, green-tinged toward their bases, almost 7 inches in length and trumpet-shaped with flaring mouths, are carried nearly horizontally in racemes of few to several. The species is not nearly as frequently grown as are its varieties com-

Lilium longiflorum, part of a conservatory display

Lilium longiflorum variety

monly grouped as Easter lilies. These have larger bulbs, usually longer flowers, and typically are more vigorous and often taller than typical *L. longiflorum*. Of the Easter lilies *L. l. eximium* (syn. *L. l. harrisii*), for long called the Bermuda lily after the island where the commercial production of its bulbs was once a major industry, is taller, has longer blooms, and if disease-free is more vigorous than its species. Characterized by its flowers being carried horizontally and their individual stalks being erect, *L. l. insulare* is popular. This, in gardens sometimes called *L. l. formosum*, is distinct from the species *L. formosanum*. The horticultural variety 'Erabu' belongs here. Purple-brown stems and flowers in the bud stage flushed with purple are characteristics of *L. l.* 'Takeshima' (syn. *L. l. giganteum*). This last must not be confused with the plant previously named *L. giganteum*, now identified as *Cardiocrinum giganteum*.

A cause of much nomenclatural confusion, **L. maculatum** (syns. *L. elegans*, *L. thunbergianum*), of Japan, now accepted by Japanese botanists as a variable species native to their land, and the producer of numerous horticultural variants, has by other authors been considered a hybrid between *L. pensylvanicum* and *L. concolor*. Be that as it may, it occurs as a wildling among rocks along seashores and is cultivated in many varieties. It has stoloniferous bulbs with more or less jointed scales. Its stems, mostly 8 inches to 2½ feet tall, are more or less white-woolly when young. The scattered, lanceolate to linear-lanceolate leaves are 1½ to 4 inches long by up to ¾ inch wide. Usually orange-red, but varying in cultivated selections to yellow or scarlet and with darker spottings, the upward-facing flowers have petals 3 to 4 inches long. Variety *L. m. bukosanense*, its stems with only one or rarely two blooms, is a native of rock cliffs in the mountains.

The candlestick lily (**L. pensylvanicum** syns. *L. maculatum dahuricum*, *L. dahuricum*) grows natively in rocky and sandy meadows along seashores and elsewhere in Japan, Korea, China, and Manchuria. The first eastern Asian lily introduced to Europe, it was grown in England as early as 1745. This has white bulbs 1 inch to 1½ inches in diameter. Its ribbed, slightly cobwebby stems, up to 3 feet tall, have alternate, linear to oblong-lanceolate, sometimes hairy leaves 2 to 6 inches long. The up-facing flowers, up to about six in an umbel or raceme open widely, are 4 to 5 inches wide and have yellow-based, red to scarlet petals spotted with purplish-black. The flowers of *L. p. luteum* are yellow spotted with black-purple or black.

The coral lily (**L. pumilum** syn. *L. tenuifolium*) is one of the most charming and dainty lilies and one of the easiest to grow. A slender-stemmed native of northeastern Asia, where it grows in grassy places and full sun in loamy soils, this sort rarely exceeds 1½ feet in height, although occasional robust specimens may be twice as tall. Its bulbs are small, white, and conical. The grassy, extremely slender to narrowly-linear leaves, scattered along the stems except toward their bases and tops, are 2 to 4 inches long. Brilliant, glossy scarlet, rarely with a few darker dots, the pendulous, Turk's-cap-type blooms 1½ to 2 inches wide are on widely spaced slender individual stalks. They have strongly-recurved petals 1½ to 2 inches long. The red-anthered stamens are one-half as long as the style. Differing only in its flowers being pure yellow, *L. p.* 'Golden Gleam', although reported to be a hybrid raised in New York about 1892 between *L. pumilum* and *L. martagon album*, almost surely represents an albino form of the former that reproduces true from seeds.

The regal lily (**L. regale**), deservedly a great favorite, is one of the easiest to satisfy. Native to western China, this magnificent hardy, stem-rooting sort has reddish-purple bulbs up to 6 inches in diameter. Rising to heights of 3 to 5 feet, its purple stems are clothed with numerous scattered, linear leaves 2 to 5 inches long by up to ¼ inch wide. The pleasantly scented blooms in racemes of few to several are trumpet-shaped, 6 to 9 inches long, and displayed horizontally. Their outsides are purplish-pink, their interiors pure white with sulfur-yellow bases. A beautiful variety named 'Royal Gold', which has golden-yellow blooms is either a mutation or a hybrid development of *L. regale*.

Speciosum lily is the only approximately common name that seems to be used for beautiful **L. speciosum** and its varieties. Native of Japan, this fine species adapts to a variety of soils and is easy to grow. Its bulbs are white and 3 to 4 inches tall. Its stems, from 2- to 3-foot-high, root from their bases and above produce bulblets in the leaf axils. The scattered, not crowded, short-stalked leaves are broadly-lanceolate, 3 to 4 inches long by 1 inch to 2 inches wide. The very fragrant flowers are declined or down-facing from the ends of long, nearly horizontal stalks. From 3 to 6 inches in diameter, they have strongly-recurved, wavy-edged petals 3 to 4 inches long by 1 inch to 2 inches wide, white suffused with pink and with rosy-purple warts. Stamens and style, of nearly equal lengths, are long-projected. There are several varieties of this lily. Native to Taiwan and China, *L. s. gloriosoides*, so named because its flowers suggest in form those of

Lilium regale in a cut flower garden

Lilium speciosum in a cut flower garden

Lilium regale (flowers)

Lilium speciosum variety (flowers)

gloriosas, has blooms with much-reflexed petals that are white at their bases and apexes, and pink with scarlet spots between. The blooms of excellent *L. s. magnificum* are flushed with pink and spotted with crimson. Another splendid variety, *L. s.* 'Melpomene', is not the original of that name raised in Boston, Massachusetts about the middle of the nineteenth century, but propagations from a very similar seedling raised in Japan much later. It has richly colored, deep carmine flowers with white edges to the petals. Vigorous *L. s. punctatum*, which blooms earlier than other varieties, has white blooms spotted with rose-pink. A natural variety, *L. s. rubrum* (syn. *L. rubrum* of florists) has rich carmine-pink flowers not quite as handsome as those of *L. s.* 'Melpomene'. Pure white-flowered *L. s. album* is usually a weak grower, perhaps because it is so commonly infected with virus. From it very beautiful *L. s. kraetzeri* differs in its otherwise virginal white blooms having a green stripe down the middle of each petal.

The tiger lily (**L. lancifolium** syn. *L. tigrinum*), an easy-to-grow native of Japan, China, and Korea, naturalizes to some extent in North America. In China it has been cultivated for over 1,000 years for its edible bulbs. These are broadly-egg-shaped, white, 2 to 3 inches wide, with very thick scales. The dark brown stems, rooting from their bases, are 2 to 6 feet tall. They carry numerous scattered, narrowly-lanceolate leaves 4 to 6 inches long by ½ to ¾ inch wide, in the axils of which develop small black bulbils. The few to many nodding flowers, their individual stalks black, have much-reflexed, conspicuously-black-spotted, bright orange- to brick-red petals 3 to 4 inches long by ½ to 1 inch wide. Its purple-anthered stamens are only slightly shorter than the petals. The style is longer and tipped with a little purple stigma. Especially attractive, *L. l. splendens* has unusually large and numerous black-spotted, salmon-pink blooms, with sharply-pointed

Lilium lancifolium splendens

petals. A particularly vigorous variety with stems more densely covered with spiderweb-like hairs than those of the typical species is *L. l. fortunei*. A double-flowered variety, more attractive than might be expected, is *L. l. flore-pleno*.

Attractive **L. lankongense**, of western China, has much the habit of *L. duchartrei*. It is similar in that it produces wandering underground rhizomes but differs in that its 2- to 4-foot-tall stems are usually furnished with foliage to their bases. The many leaves are oblong to oblong-lanceolate and up to 4 inches long. In racemes of up to fifteen, the nodding, delicately-fragrant, 2½-inch-long flowers have strongly-reflexed, white petals toned with rosy-purple and spotted with purple. The anthers are rusty-brown.

Lilium lankongense

Other Asian lilies in cultivation include these: **L. amabile**, of Korea, has small, ovoid bulbs, stems 1 foot to 4 feet high that root from their bases and have short, stiff hairs and scattered, lanceolate leaves up to 3½ inches long by ½ inch wide. The up to six nodding, unpleasantly-scented blooms have 2-inch-long, black-spotted, brick- to grenadine-red, strongly-recurved petals. In *L. a. luteum* the flowers are glossy orange-

yellow. **L. brownii** is a very beautiful, vigorous sort with 2-inch-wide bulbs and stems that root from their bases, and above produce bulblets in the leaf axils. From 2 to 3 feet tall, this native of southern China has purple stems and sharply-pointed, lanceolate to elliptic-lanceolate, scattered leaves 4 inches to 1 foot long by up to ¾ inch wide. The up to four horizontally-held, scarcely fragrant, trumpet-shaped blooms from 6 to 9 inches long are creamy-white to white inside, purplish-red and green outside. They have very long styles. Variety *L. b. colchesteri* (syn. *L. b. viridulum*) has very fragrant blooms that at first are light yellow, but soon change to white with the inner petals marked with a central stripe of rose-purple. This variety has not proved hardy in southern New England. **L. callosum**, native from Japan and Taiwan to China, Korea, and Manchuria, is a stem-rooter much like the coral lily, but is generally considered inferior. It differs in its broader leaves having three or more instead of only one vein, and in the flowers having styles shorter instead of twice as long as the ovaries. **L. cernuum**, another close relative of the coral lily, a native of Korea, Manchuria, and adjacent parts to the west, is readily distinguished by its pleasantly-scented, purple-spotted, lilac flowers. A stem-rooter, this has small white bulbs and stems 1 foot to 2 feet tall with scattered, narrowly-linear leaves up to 7 inches long by about ⅛ inch wide. The up to six pendulous blooms have strongly-recurved petals 1½ to 2 inches long. **L. davidii**, of western China, has small white bulbs and more or less brown-purple stems 3 to 6 feet tall that root from their bases and are cobwebby-hairy in their upper parts. The scattered leaves are crowded, linear, and 4 to 5 inches long by under ⅛ inch wide. Each stem carries up to twenty nodding, black-spotted, scarlet to orange-red flowers with reflexed petals about 3 inches in length, hairy at their tips. From the tiger lily, which it much resembles, more elegant and refined *L. davidii* is distinguishable by its leaves having

Lilium lancifolium showing bulbils in leaf axils

Lilium davidii

one instead of five to seven veins and in not producing bulbils in its leaf axils. Varieties are *L. d. macranthum*, with larger blooms, *L. d.* 'Oriole', with pale apricot-orange flowers, and *L. d. willmottiae* (syn. *L. willmottiae*), a vigorous sort that produces an abundance of black-spotted, orange-red flowers but because of its weak stems needs staking. **L. duchartrei**, of China, inhabits wet soils and bogs at high altitudes. It has small, white, ovoid bulbs up to 1½ inches in diameter on underground rhizomes that wander widely. The stems, which root from their bases, are 1½ to 5 feet tall. The lanceolate scattered leaves are up to 4 inches long by ½ inch wide. The up to twelve nodding, fragrant blooms on erect individual stalks are in umbels. They are creamy-white spotted with wine-purple. **L. formosanum** (syn. *L. philippinense formosanum*), of Taiwan, is an especially lovely trumpet lily. In the wild found from sea level to altitudes of over 11,500 feet, it has roundish, whitish bulbs and purplish-brown stems up to 6 feet in height. Linear-lanceolate and 3 to 8 inches long by up to ⅜ inch wide, the leaves, crowded on the lower parts of the stem, are few and small for some distance beneath the flowers. Carried horizontally and slender-funnel-shaped, the delicately fragrant blooms are one to several on a stem. They are white, commonly suffused on their outsides with wine-purple. Their 5- to 6-inch-long petals are gracefully recurved at their apexes. *L. f. pricei* (syn. *L. f.* 'Price's variety'), an excellent dwarf variety that attains a maximum height of about 1½ feet, has fewer, smaller, more slender flowers, deeper purple on their outsides. **L. japonicum**, notoriously poorly adapted to cultivation, inhabits thickets in low mountains in Japan. It has small, ovoid bulbs and slender stems 2 to 3½ feet tall that root from their bases and have scattered, broadly-lanceolate to narrowly-oblong leaves up to 4 inches long by up to 1½ inches wide. The fragrant, rose-pink, nodding or horizontal flowers have petals 4½ to 6 inches long. *L. leichtlinii maximowiczii* is much better as a garden plant than difficult-to-grow Japanese *L. leichtlinii*. The variety is indigenous to Japan, China, and Korea. Much resembling the tiger lily in habit, form of flower, and coloring, it differs in lacking stem bulbils. This sort has rhizomatous bulbs and basal-rooting stems, 2 to 4 feet tall with many scattered, linear leaves 3 to 6 inches long by about ⅓ inch wide. The up to twelve reddish-orange flowers heavily spotted with black-purple are essentially like those of the tiger lily. **L. leucanthum**, of China, is represented in cultivation by two slightly tender, closely similar varieties. *L. l. centifolium* has spherical bulbs 2¾ inches in diameter and basal-rooting stems up to 9 feet tall with many scattered, linear leaves up to 4 inches long by about ¾ inch wide. The white, horizon-

tally-held, funnel-shaped, fragrant blooms are in racemes of up to about seventeen. Light yellow inside, on their outsides they are marked with pinkish-purple to reddish-brown. The other variety *L. l. chloraster*, about 3 feet tall, has similar flowers that are white with a green keel to each petal. **L. mackliniae**, native at high altitudes in Burma, is not hardy. It has bulbs 1 inch to 2 inches in diameter and stems 1 foot to 3 feet tall that bear usually one or two or sometimes as many as seven nodding, bowl-shaped, pink-toned, white flowers about 2 inches wide. The leaves are scattered, narrowly-lanceolate, up to 2½ inches long by ¼ to nearly ½ inch wide. **L. medeoloides**, native to Japan and nearby islands, China, and Korea, is a martagon-type with apricot to scarlet, scentless flowers marked with few to many dark spots. It has white bulbs up to 1 inch in diameter and stems 1 foot to 3 feet tall. Most of the lanceolate to narrowly-ovate leaves, 2 to 4½ inches long by up to 2 inches wide, are in whorls of four to ten, but the smaller upper ones are scattered. The up to ten, but usually fewer ill-scented blooms have petals 1½ to 2 inches long. This has proven rather difficult to grow. **L. neilgherrense** as a wildling reaches farther south than any other lily, to within ten degrees north of the equator. Native to India and not hardy, this has spherical, rhizomatous bulbs some 4 inches wide. About 3 feet tall, its stems, which root from their bases, are furnished with lanceolate leaves up to 5 inches long by 1 inch wide. They bear in a horizontal position one, two, or rarely up to four richly scented, trumpet-shaped blooms 7 to 10 inches in length, their insides pure white with yellow throats, their outsides creamy-white. **L. nepalense** is a beautiful nonhardy native of damp, well-drained soils in the Himalayan region. This has bulbs that produce long stolons. Its basal-rooting stems, about 3 feet tall, have rather few, scattered, lanceolate to oblong-lanceolate leaves up to 5½ inches long by 1¼ inches wide. The one to few flowers are funnel-shaped, yellow to greenish-yellow, and stained toward their bases with wine-purple. *L. n. concolor* has flowers without purple staining. Those of *L. n. robustum*, a sort hardier than the others, are pendulous, emerald-green with purple centers. **L. philippinense**, of the Philippine Islands, is closely related to the Easter lily, but has much narrower leaves and longer blooms. It has purple-tinged, white, subspherical bulbs about 1½ inches in diameter and slender brown-purple-suffused stems 1 inch to 1½ inches in height. Its scattered leaves are about ⅛ inch wide. The trumpet-shaped blooms, 7 to 10 inches in length, are in racemes or sometimes solitary. **L. primulinum**, of China and Burma, is not reliably hardy. Related to *L. nepalense*, it is a stem-rooting sort with scattered leaves. It has drooping, primrose-yellow,

Lilium nepalense robustum

martagon-type flowers. There are two varieties, *L. p. burmanicum* and *L. p. ochraceum* (syn. *L. ochraceum*). The first, 4 to 8 feet tall, has a few bell-shaped, drooping blooms with the scent of orange peel. They have greenish-yellow petals flecked with purple on their insides. The other, about 4 feet in height, has flowers with strongly-reflexed, wine-red petals with greenish-ochre-yellow tips. **L. rubellum**, of Japan, closely similar to *L. japonicum*, but more amenable to cultivation, 1 foot to 2 feet tall, has small, whitish bulbs and stems that root from their bases and that have rather few, scattered, lanceolate-ovate leaves 3 to 4 inches long by 1 inch to 1½ inches wide. The few fra-

Lilium rubellum

grant blooms have rose-pink petals that recurve slightly at only their tips and are 2 to 3½ inches in length. *L. r. album* has white flowers. **L. sargentiae** in habit of growth and aspect resembles *L. regale*, from which it differs chiefly in its leaves being wider and having three to five instead of only one vein, in producing bulbils in the leaf axils, and in blooming about two weeks later. Native to China, this splendid sort has spherical bulbs 6 inches in diameter, stems 4 to 5 feet tall, and large trumpet-shaped blooms, pure white within except for their yellow throats and sometimes suggestions of purplish-pink, shaded outside with purplish-pink, brown, or green. **L. sulphureum** (syn. *L. myriophyllum*) is a nonhardy native of China and Burma. A stem-rooter, this has bulbs about 4 inches across and stems 4 to 8 feet tall abundantly clothed with scattered, linear-lanceolate leaves, the lower ones 3 to 5 inches long, the upper ones smaller and with bulbils in their axils. The up to fifteen but usually fewer narrow-trumpet-shaped flowers, more or less drooping, have flaring mouths. They are fragrant, 6 to 8 inches long, and inside are delicate sulfur-yellow with yellow throats and outside suffused with claret-pink. *L. taliense*, of China, is a stem-rooting sort similar to *L. duchartrei*, from which it differs chiefly in its strongly-fragrant, nodding blooms being in racemes and in having in the center of each petal a dark purple nectary furrow. *L. wallichianum* is not hardy in the north. Native to limestone regions in Nepal, this trumpet-flowered species has stoloniferous, ovoid bulbs and stems that root from their bases 3 to 6 feet tall. The many scattered leaves are linear to narrow-lanceolate. Carried horizontally, the creamy-white flowers, 7 to 8½ inches long, have slender tubes and flaring mouths 6 to 8 inches across. *L. wardii* is a Tibetan mountain species that occurs in dryish, acid soils. The flattened-spherical, stoloniferous bulbs are about 2 inches wide. The stems, which root from their bases, attain heights of about 5 feet and bear many scattered, lanceolate to oblong-elliptic leaves about 2¾ inches long. The racemes are of nodding, carmine-dotted, deep pink, martagon-type blooms.

Hybrid lilies chiefly developed since the end of the first quarter of the twentieth century are far more satisfactory and easier to grow than most natural species. Indeed, with their coming, lily growing in quantity by home gardeners became as practical as growing tulips in the garden. The development of modern hybrid lilies must be accounted as one of the tremendous horticultural achievements of the twentieth century. A look through dealers' catalogs will reveal the great array of such sorts, together with a very few older hybrids, that are available. It is an encouraging exercise.

Classification of hybrid lilies is based on the predominant parental stocks from which they have been derived. Eight groups are commonly recognized.

Asian hybrids, of which many hundreds have been named, have as ancestors two or more of the group of lilies with saucer-shaped or Turk's-cap-type blooms that, except for *L. bulbiferum*, of Europe, and *L. philadelphicum*, of America, are all of Asian origin. The Asians involved include *L. amabile, L. callosum, L. cernuum, L. concolor, L. dauricum, L. davidii, L. leichtlinii maximowiczii, L. pumilum, L. tigrinum,* and *L. wilsonii,* as well as *L. maculatum* and *L. hollandicum,* the first of the last two possibly, the second surely of hybrid origin.

A selection of modern hybrid lilies

From 1½ to 2 feet tall with some varieties taller, *L. maculatum* (syn. *L. elegans*) has sparingly-hairy to hairless stems well furnished with alternate, lanceolate to elliptic, five- to nine-veined leaves up to 4 inches long. Its up-facing, cup-shaped flowers, 4 to 5½ inches wide, are in a terminal umbel or are occasionally solitary. Called the candlestick lily, *L. hollandicum* is up to 2½ feet tall or sometimes taller. It has stems with many, usually three-veined, alternate leaves. The stems terminate in an umbel or short raceme of up-facing, red, orange, or yellow, cup-shaped flowers, sometimes with darker spots, and up to 4 inches long.

Lilium hollandicum

Prominent among the Asian hybrids are named varieties of *L. maculatum* and *L. hollandicum*, which may be had in a fine range of flower colors from lemon-yellow through apricot and orange to deep red and spotted or not with darker hues. Other sorts that belong here are the 'Golden Chalice', 'Fiesta', 'Harlequin', 'Mid-Century', and 'Rainbow' hybrids, and the 'Stenographer' and 'Preston' hybrids. There are many others raised by breeders in the United States, Canada, England, New Zealand, and elsewhere.

Turk's cap or Martagon hybrids, derived from *L. martagon* and its varieties, *L. hansonii*, and *L. medeoloides*, include old *L. dalhansonii* (the first of the group, raised in 1890) and the Marhan and the Backhouse hybrids as well as much more recent sorts, such as 'Painted Lady', 'Paisley', and 'Terrace City' hybrids. These Turk's cap or Martagon hybrids are remarkable for the rich range of their flower colors, which encompasses pearly-whites, lemon-yellows, various shades of orange, variously spotted and marked with lilac, brown, or red, to deep reds.

Candidum hybrids include the first known lily hybrid, the Nankeen lily (*L. testaceum*), which resulted from a chance crossing of the Madonna lily (*L. candidum*) and *L. chalcedonicum* in Germany in 1836. This ancient sort, which displays such lovely soft, Nankeen-yellow blooms, prospers especially well in limy soils. Since the original cross the parents have been crossed again in both directions and have been backcrossed in America and England to give rise to other Candidum hybrids.

The American hybrids derive from species native to North America. Sorts native to the eastern part of the continent that have been used are *L. canadense*, *L. catesbaei*, *L. grayi*, *L. michauxii*, *L. michiganense*, and *L. philadelphicum*. Western species used include *L. bolanderi*, *L. columbianum*, *L. humboldtii*, *L. kelloggii*, *L. maritimum*, *L. occidentale*, *L. pardalinum*, *L. parryi*, *L. rubescens*, *L. vollmeri*, and *L. washingtonianum*. Although Luther Burbank as early as 1901 had raised a cross between *L. parryi* and *L. pardalinum* named *L. burbankii*, it was not until the Bellingham hybrids were introduced in 1924 that significant results were obtained in hybridizing American lilies. The parents of the Bellingham hybrids were *L. humboldtii ocellatum*, *L. pardalinum*, and *L. parryi*. Of the original Bellingham hybrids only 'Shuksan' seems still to be in cultivation, but modern varieties raised from them are vigorous sorts with Turk's-cap-type blooms that are yellow to orange, lemon-yellow spotted with brown. Other hybrid strains of American lilies are the Monterey hybrids, which include strong-growing magenta-flowered varieties with as parents *L. kelloggii* and *L. pitkinense* and the scarlet-bloomed hybrid *L. burbankii*. There are also hybrids between *L. pardalinum* and *L. bolanderi*, and *L. rubescens* and *L. columbianum*. In addition to crosses involving only American lilies as parents, *L. philadelphicum* has been hybridized with Asian *L. dauricum* and *L. canadense* with *L. dauricum willmottiae*.

The Longiflorum hybrids represent crosses between the Asian species *L. formosanum*, *L. longiflorum*, *L. neilgherrense*, and *L. wallichianum*. All have white, trumpet-shaped blooms.

Trumpet hybrids is the name given a large group of varieties that have resulted from crossing the Chinese species *L. brownii*, *L. henryi*, *L. leucanthum centifolium*, *L. regale*, *L. sargentiae*, and *L. sulphureum*. With the exception of *L. henryi*, which has Turk's-cap-type blooms, all these have trumpet flowers. The Trumpet hybrids are further divided into (a) Chinese trumpets, which include all hybrids with decidedly trumpet-shaped blooms except those classified as Longiflorum hybrids; (b) bowl-shaped varieties with wide open blooms that face outward or upward; (c) pendant varieties with nodding, generally wide-open blooms; and (d) sunburst varieties with starry, nearly flat, wide-open blooms. Among the most interesting and outstanding trumpet hybrids are *L. sulphurgale*, the result of a cross made in Germany in 1913 between *L. sulphureum* and *L. regale*, and *L. imperiale*, produced three

years later in America, its parents *L. regale* and *L. sargentiae*. Later, *L. leucanthum centifolium* was crossed with the early hybrids. In France in 1928 and shortly after in Germany, *L. sargentiae* was successfully hybridized. The results, named *L. aurelianense*, provided the materials from which by further breeding the splendid aurelian hybrids we have today were derived. Pink-flowered trumpet hybrids have resulted from crossing and selection from a hybrid of *L. leucanthum centifolium* and *L. regale*. A yellow-flowered variety was developed by crossing and selecting from hybrids between *L. leucanthum*, *L. regale*, *L. sargentiae*, and *L. sulphureum*.

Oriental or Japanese hybrids are sorts the parentage of which includes varieties based on *L. auratum*, *L. japonicum*, *L. rubellum*, and *L. speciosum*, and one or more of these and *L. henryi*. There are many sorts, many of extraordinary beauty, but they are generally accounted among the more difficult hybrid lily groups to raise and successfully maintain. They seem to be particularly susceptible to virus infection.

Other hybrid lilies are derived from species native of the Caucasus region, including *L. monadelphum* and *L. szovitsianum*.

Garden and Landscape Uses. Placing lilies to advantage in the landscape is deserving of a little thought. In the main, unlike bulb plants such as hyacinths and tulips, they do not lend themselves to formal arrangements, although under some circumstances it is not impossible to employ such low sorts as *L. hollandicum* and *L. maculatum* varieties in that fashion. And the stately deportment of Madonna lilies planted somewhat irregularly as the chief feature in season on either side of a straight path or allee may be used with emphatic dignity. It is even possible to employ Turk's cap lilies, tiger lilies, and orange lilies similarly.

Groups of strong-growing lilies, such as regals, Madonnas, speciosums, and their varieties and hybrids, as well as many other hybrid sorts make fine accents in mixed flower beds, but may not be very permanent there and may need replacing from time to time. It is even possible with good taste to plant *L. pumilum* with good effect in rock gardens. Most lilies are too bold and big for such sites.

But chiefly lilies are at their best in informal or at most semiformal surroundings. They are for the fringes of woodlands and the interiors of thinned woodlands, where the canopy is light, and for planting informally among and in front of low shrubs, particularly those of slow growth and not too vigorous rooting propensities. Evergreen shrubs, which supply rich backgrounds that complement the chalices, trumpets, or bells of the lilies, are splendid.

Lilies delight in cool and rather humid atmospheres. True, most like their heads in the sun, but for their lower parts and the ground in which they grow they crave shade. Where these plants grow natively this invariably is supplied by tall grasses, low shrubs, or the like, and the wise gardener when locating lilies takes a leaf from nature's book and seeks or supplies similar protection. Among plants that can fill this need are tall ferns, heathers, lavender, azaleas and other low rhododendrons, vacciniums, and leucothoes. Exposed sites are not for lilies. Shelter from strong winds is a must, which is another reason for taking advantage of suitably placed trees and shrubs.

As cut flowers, lilies of many kinds lend themselves well, chiefly for large arrangements. But the heavy fragrances of some sorts, such as *L. auratum* and *L. formosanum*, are likely to prove much too overpowering to encourage their use in confined spaces.

A point to bear in mind when cutting lilies is that, for them to be effective in arrangements, it is usually necessary to take them with long stems and thus to remove from the bulb a large proportion of stem tissue and foliage that if left to complete the season's growth would contribute to nourishing the bulb and fattening it in preparation for the following year's effort. When this is thwarted instead of increasing or even maintaining its size the bulb is likely to split into several smaller ones that either will not bloom or if they will, give fewer or smaller flowers.

All in all if you want lilies for cutting it is best to grow them apart from display garden areas in a plot reserved for cut flowers or perhaps in a section of a vegetable garden and to plant them in such numbers that flowers need be harvested from not more than one-half the bulbs each year.

As container plants the most commonly grown is undoubtedly the Easter lily. But other kinds can be bloomed in pots and tubs and are very useful for the summer embellishment of sheltered terraces, patios, and similar places.

Cultivation. If a start is made with bulbs free of virus diseases (healthy ones of many kinds are much more readily available than formerly) and the climate is reasonably agreeable, the great majority of lilies are easy to grow. This is especially true of modern hybrid sorts. There are, however, aspects of their cultivation that need special consideration.

Soil is important, although not to the finicky degree sometimes thought. Many failures of the past blamed on unsuitable soil were doubtless caused by virus infections. Naturally, neither semiparched, nutrient-poor, very sandy soil nor dense, compacted clay soils contribute to the well-being of lilies and unless properly modified are likely to make their cultivation impracticable. The most agreeable

earth for most lilies is one that affords a minimum of 9 inches of friable, fertile topsoil overlying a porous substratum. It should contain a generous proportion of decayed organic matter (humus) and not be dry for long periods. But long spells of saturation occasioned by poor subsurface drainage are fatal to practically all lilies including those that in the wild favor swampy soils. Generally ground capable of producing good crops of vegetables, especially such heavy feeders as corn, onions, and potatoes, or fine chrysanthemums, dahlias, delphiniums, and peonies will satisfy lilies. Its precise acidity or alkalinity is of minor importance. Most lilies exhibit considerable tolerance about this and good examples of most can be had in soil from somewhat acid to mildly alkaline. As a generalization it may be said native American and Asian lilies usually do best in somewhat acid soils, Europeans in alkaline ones. Both are likely to adapt well to neutral earths.

Prior to planting lily bulbs, prepare the soil thoroughly by spading or otherwise turning it to a minimum depth of 1 foot, more is better. Mix in liberal amounts of suitable organic additives. These may be good compost, leaf mold, peat moss, partially decayed sawdust, or the like. Cow or horse manure if well decayed is excellent, and half-decayed material may be spaded under at depths where the bulbs do not come into immediate contact with it, but their roots later may reach it. It is very harmful to have fresh or even half-decayed manure against lily bulbs. The incorporation of a liberal dressing of bonemeal or superphosphate before planting is strongly advisable, but it is better to delay application of nitrogen fertilizers until the plants are established and growing.

When to plant purchased bulbs is often determined by their availability. As a rule it is well to accept delivery at the very beginning of the period in which they are for sale and to plant immediately. Certainly August or at latest early September is the best time to plant Madonna lilies. It is important that these be set before they develop their fall rosettes of foliage. Other sorts are available later in fall or in early spring. Many growers prefer early fall planting, but some maintain they obtain better results from planting in early spring, especially when transplanting in their own gardens as contrasted with setting out bulbs obtained from commercial sources. Of course home-transplanted specimens have the great advantage of not having their roots reduced or dried to nearly the extent that purchased bulbs normally have, hence shock of moving and difficulty of reestablishment are greatly reduced.

Spacing and depth to plant should be regulated by a number of factors. Small lilies get along well and are effective if the bulbs are 6 to 8 inches apart, tall, vigorous

Many lilies like this *Lilium henryi* root from the bottom of the stem above the bulb as well as the base of the bulb

growers need 9 inches to 1 foot or somewhat more between individuals. Usually stressed and certainly of considerable importance is whether the lilies to be set develop roots from the bases of the bulbs only or from there and also from the annual stems that grow from their tops. Plant the first, of which Madonna, martagon, and American Turk's cap lilies are prime examples, with the tips of the bulbs not more than 2 inches below the surface. Set stem-rooters considerably deeper, so that their tops are covered two or three times the depth of the bulb from tip to base, the greater depths in fairly loose ground the lesser in more compact, heavier soils. Some lily enthusiasts recommend planting even more deeply. Whatever depth is selected be sure there are several inches of soil encouraging to roots beneath the bulb. It is useless to dig holes into unkindly subsoil, plant in them, and then cover with even the best garden earth. It is also usually of no avail to try to correct poor drainage by digging deep holes and filling under the bulbs with stones. This can only work if the bottoms of the holes reach a porous stratum. Such a hole in compact clay becomes a basin filled with stones and water. Make holes for lily bulb planting big enough to spread the roots in an outward and downward direction without crowding. By hand work fine soil under the bulb and among the roots. It is extremely harmful to thrust the bulbs into holes barely big enough to hold them and thus cause the roots to be forced into an up-pointing position.

Routine care involves weed control and keeping the soil uniformly moist and cool. A mulch positioned in late spring or early summer and maintained at a depth of 2 to 3 inches from then on serves both purposes admirably. Any organic material usually employed for such purpose is satisfactory, compost, leaf mold, and peat moss come to mind as among the most commonly employed. Even with a mulch periodic deep watering may be needed in hot, dry weather.

Fertilizing is very beneficial if carefully done. Like most bulb plants lilies are easily harmed by strong applications of quickly available nitrogen. Apply this nutrient only in mild, slowly available forms, such as the organics dried blood, tankage, cottonseed meal, or well-rotted manure, or the slow-release synthetic fertilizers now available. A spring application is desirable.

Other cultural routines may include staking to afford support and anticipate storm damage. Be careful when this is done to keep the bottom of the stake far enough away from the bulb that it does not pierce it. Unless seed is required, and then only two or three capsules should be permitted to develop on each plant, remove faded blooms promptly, but do not cut the stems back until fall frosts have killed the foliage.

In cold regions, covering the ground in winter with a thick layer of loose material, such as salt hay, straw, strawy manure, corn stalks, or branches of evergreens prevents excessively deep penetration by frost and more importantly checks alternate freezing and thawing so likely to tear roots. Do not put winter covering on until the ground is frozen to a depth of an inch or two, otherwise mice or other rodents may be encouraged to burrow beneath it.

Transplanting established lilies that are prospering should not be done unless quite necessary. A hands-off policy is best with thrifty lilies. However, the bulbs of some sorts increase so rapidly that every four or five years it is necessary to separate them and replant. This necessity is signaled by the production of an excessive number of crowded thin stems bearing few blooms. With some kinds need for transplanting can be delayed by annual removal of the bulbils that develop in considerable numbers at the bases of the stems.

Propagation can be by various vegetative methods or by seed. The last results in stock free from virus diseases, but it can of course become infected later. Vegetative

Bulblets: (a) On the lower part of the stem immediately above the mother bulb

(b) Planting the bulblets in a flat

propagation if done with virus-infected stock gives virus-infected offspring. The chief means of vegetative increase is by offset bulbs or bulblets, naturally produced, and by bulbils, scales, and stems.

Offset bulbs are simply separated from their parents and replanted. Bulbils, pea-sized small bulbs developed in the leaf axils of the tiger lily, orange lily, and a few others, can be taken off and sown much like seeds in a cold frame or outdoors. At the end of the first year's growth they are transplanted to nursery beds to grow to flowering size.

Bulbils on the stem of a tiger lily

Multiplication by scales is the most widely used method of vegetative propagation. The best time to do this is when flowering has just about finished. Then, dig the bulbs, remove some of the thick outer scales, and, without letting them dry, plant them in a bed of sandy peaty soil in a cold frame or outdoors. Set them vertically, tips up, 1 inch apart in rows of 6 to 9 inches apart. Outdoors protect from excessive rain by setting over them two boards slanted to meet at their tops in an inverted V or with polyethylene plastic stretched over a framework of wood laths or wire. Alternatively, scales can be started in flats or boxes of sandy soil kept barely damp in a shed or similar covered place and two to three months later, when they have formed tiny bulblets, planted in outdoor nursery beds. The last method can also be done in fall to

Scales for propagation: (a) Separated from a lily bulb

(b) Planting the scales in a flat

give bulblets to set out in early spring and in spring to have bulblets to set in nursery beds in July.

Stem propagation is designed to stimulate the production of bulbils, which many lilies develop naturally from the bases of their stems. The procedure is to, just as flowering finishes, disengage the stem from the bulb. Do this with a twist and quick upward jerk. Plant the stems fairly close together at an angle of about 45 degrees so that 1 foot of their bases are covered with sandy soil. In fall after the foliage has died lift the stems, remove the little bulblets, and plant them in nursery rows.

Raising lilies from seed, although with some sorts a rather slow procedure, is not difficult. Eighty percent of fresh, well-ripened seeds are likly to germinate. Some kinds, including the seeds of *L. amabile, L. concolor, L. davidii, L. pumilum, L. regale, L. tigrinum,* and certain hybrids, sprout in three to six weeks from the time of sowing and soon develop their first leaves; others may take a year to a year and one-half. Among these last are the seeds of *L. auratum, L. canadense, L. hansonii, L. martagon, L. speciosum, L. superbum,* and some hybrid lilies. With some sorts, *L. speciosum* for example, the seeds germinate and grow in the soil for several weeks or months before the first leaf breaks ground.

A pot of lily seedlings

In greenhouses most lilies can be forced to bloom earlier than their natural seasons and some few are especially well adapted for this. Most familiar is the Easter lily of which literally millions are brought into bloom by florists each year at Easter. Others that lend themselves to growing indoors in pots and tubs are *L. auratum*, *L. bulbiferum*, *L. candidum*, *L. hollandicum*, *L. maculatum*, *L. pumilum*, *L. regale*, *L. speciosum*, and most of the splendid modern hybrids.

Easter lilies (varieties of *L. longiflorum*) are forced almost exclusively to bloom as pot plants at Easter. For this, bulbs propagated and grown to forcing size by specialists, chiefly in the western and southern United States and Japan, are shipped to growers in November. Usually before shipment they are treated to a minimum of six weeks of controlled low temperature. This facilitates later forcing, but some growers prefer to pot the bulbs as soon as they are dug from the fields in the first week in October on the West Coast or earlier in the south, and put them directly in a cold frame or cool greenhouse where they can be held at 40 to 50°F for five or six weeks before being subjected to higher temperatures. Easter lily bulbs are graded according to size from 6½ to 7 inches to 10 to 11 inches in circumference. The larger ones produce stronger, taller stems and more blooms than the smaller.

Pot precooled bulbs in late November or December depending upon the date of Easter. In a greenhouse where the night temperature is 60°F, and daytime temperatures average ten degrees higher, the time needed from potting to blooming by the popular 'Croft' variety is approximately 120 days. Some sorts require less time. At slightly lower temperatures a longer period, at somewhat higher temperatures less time, is needed. It is quite practicable to keep the bulbs for their first two or three weeks after potting in a temperature ranging between 50 and 60°F, and this may prove a convenience if poinsettias or other soon-to-be-moved plants are occupying all available warm greenhouse space. This starting in lower temperatures does not materially affect the time needed for forcing.

Use coarse, well-aerated soil of medium fertility and organic content and of neutral or slightly alkaline pH. The inclusion in the mix of up to one-quarter part by bulk of peat moss, compost, or very well-rotted manure is allowable, but excessive amounts of organic material increase water retention to the extent that the roots may rot. Do not add nitrogenous chemical fertilizers. Dried blood or bonemeal may be used to supply nitrogen, but are rarely necessary. The addition of a little superphosphate to some soils may be beneficial. Make sure the pots are well drained and set the bulbs low in them so that their tips will be well below the surface when soil is filled in to within ½ or 1 inch of the rim of the pot. The advantage of setting the bulbs low is that it assures soil for roots that develop from the lower parts of the new shoots. Sometimes bulbs sprout before they are dug from the fields and are shipped with the sprouts on. Do not remove such sprouts. If they are not damaged they are no serious detriment. When planting sprouted bulbs set them so that the sprout is buried in the soil. Commercial growers usually fill soil into the pots to the final level at potting time, but many gardeners prefer to fill only to within an inch or two of the final soil level when the bulbs are potted and to add more as a top dressing later.

Full exposure to sun is essential. Too close crowding after the leaves begin to spread causes shade and may result in yellowing and drying of the lower foliage. Keep the soil evenly moist, but avoid constant saturation. After the pots are well filled with healthy roots, water more generously and give regular weekly or biweekly applications of dilute liquid fertilizer. Maintain a humid atmosphere. Spraying the foliage lightly on sunny days is beneficial, but not if the water does not dry within about an hour or if the foliage remains wet at nightfall.

Timing flowering so that Easter lilies are in prime condition for the holiday calls for good judgment. Seasons vary in the number and disposition of sunny days, a factor of great importance. Also, growing conditions in the fields the previous summer and fall, as well as the precooling treatment the bulbs received, can have an effect. Plants behind schedule can be hastened into bloom by increasing the night temperature to 70°F beginning in January or early February. Increasing day length by use of artificial lights may also be used to hasten blooming. Lowering the temperature to about 40 to 50°F after the flower buds are well developed and bloated, but have not yet begun to open is employed to hold back blooming of plants too far advanced.

Other lilies satisfactory as greenhouse pot or tub plants can be brought into bloom at their natural seasons, or by gentle forcing, earlier. Most are hardy kinds that do better at lower temperatures than those recommended for Easter lilies and in the main bloom from May to August or later depending upon the treatment accorded them. For the best results pot bulbs of these as early in fall as they are obtainable from dealers or, if they are to be dug from the garden, about the time of the first frost. Exceptions are *L. candidum*, which should be potted in August, and bulbs of *L. speciosum* or other sorts that have been held in cold storage and can be potted in spring or at other seasons.

Soil and potting procedures are the same as for Easter lilies, except that bulbs of *L. candidum* are not set deeply in the pots but with their tips just peeping out of what is the final level of the soil. This sort makes no stem roots and so has no need for soil above the bulbs. Plant one bulb in a pot just big enough to hold it comfortably or three or more in a larger container. Tubs holding several bulbs make handsome decorations for patios, terraces, porches, and similar locations.

After potting, water well and stand the containers in a cold frame, cool greenhouse, or other place where temperatures so far as outdoor conditions permit will be in the 40 to 50°F range and where they will not be subjected to frost. Take care that the soil does not become dry, but avoid excessive watering or the earth will become sodden and rooting will be discouraged. In from five to eight weeks, depending upon the kind of lily, the time of potting, and the temperatures maintained, new shoots will sprout from the bulbs. It is then time to stand the containers on a sunny bench in a greenhouse where the night temperature is 45 to 55°F, that by day about ten degrees higher.

After flowering is through, the bulbs of Easter lilies are not suitable for forcing the next year and are usually discarded, but if

If properly cared for after flowering, you may, in climates to their liking (a) Plant potted Easter lilies outdoors

(b) Use well-drained, fertile soil

(c) They will recuperate and bloom bountifully in succeeding years

the foliaged parts of their stems are not cut off and the plants are kept in a sunny, fairly cool place and watered regularly, and then, after danger of frost is over, are planted in a sheltered place outdoors they will, even in climates as harsh as that of the vicinity of New York City recover, settle down as permanent perennials, and bloom freely in late summer for many years.

Some lilies, including *L. hollandicum, L. regale, L. speciosum,* and *L. tigrinum,* can be successfully maintained in pots and bloomed regularly for several years. To achieve this, after the plants have finished blooming give them good care. If neglected they are unlikely to bloom satisfactorily the following year. Remove faded blooms, but do not cut the stems down. Keep the soil watered and give weekly or biweekly applications of dilute liquid fertilizer until the foliage begins to turn yellow and die. Then cease fertilizing and gradually lengthen the periods between waterings and finally discontinue. Store in a cool, frost-proof place, well away from heating pipes or other sources of dry heat. In January turn them out of the pots, remove any offsets or small bulbs, and repot and start into growth the old large bulbs

in the manner recommended for newly purchased ones.

Diseases and Pests. Unfortunately lilies are subject to diseases and pests that unless controlled can work havoc. The most serious and prevalent by far results from infection by any of a group of related viruses that cause the diseases identified as lily mosaic, mottle disease, streak, and by other names. Debilitating and completely incurable, these sicknesses cause various symptoms or may be symptomless. Common indications of infection are a light and darker green mottling, spotting, or streaking of the foliage, with in some cases a reduction in the size or distortion of the leaves and in others dying and browning of their tissues in spots. Dwarfing of the plant, premature dying of foliage from the base of the stem upward, and distortion and poor color of the flowers are other frequent indications of infection with these abhorrent viruses.

Transmission of lily viruses from lily plant to lily plant and from a great many other common plants that harbor the cucumber-mosaic group of viruses to lilies is by aphids. Therefore control of this pest is a first must in preventing the spread of lily mosaic. Other control measures consist of the prompt elimination and destruction of suspected infected plants. Do this as far as possible in spring before aphids become active. Try to avoid introducing infected stock to the garden, a counsel not always practicable to achieve if one has commendable liking for hybrid lilies. Species if raised from seeds are initially free of virus diseases although they may of course later become infected.

Another serious disease is fusarium rot, the cause of which is a fungus that causes the bulbs and roots to blacken and soon destroys them. Prevention, if the bulbs are not too heavily infected, is had by disinfecting the soil before planting with any one of several fungicides sold for the purpose and by treating the bulbs with a fungicide before planting.

Botrytis or gray-mold disease, which damages stems, foliage, and blooms, is especially troublesome in hot, humid weather. Affected parts become covered with a gray fuzz of fungus. Regular applications of bordeaux mixture or other fungicide at weekly or ten-day intervals through the growing season are effective.

Animal life that harms lilies includes aphids, bulb mites, mice and other rodents, slugs, snails, thrips, and some others, all of which must be watched for and appropriate early action taken at the first sign of infestation.

LILLYPILLY is *Acmena smithii.*

LILY. Without modification lily refers to species of the genus *Lilium,* may be extended to include those now segregated as

Cardiocrinum. Other plants with colloquial names that include the word lily are adobe-lily (*Fritillaria pluriflora*), Amazon-lily (*Eucharis grandiflora*), atamasco-lily (*Zephyranthes*), Australian climbing-lily (*Eustrephus*), avalanche-lily (*Erythronium*), Aztec-lily (*Sprekelia*), belladonna-lily (*Amaryllis belladonna*), blackberry-lily (*Belamcanda chinensis*), blood-lily (*Haemanthus*), blue-African-lily or blue-lily-of-the-Nile (*Agapanthus*), Brisbane-lily (*Eurycles cunninghamii*), calla-lily (*Zantedeschia*), checkered-lily (*Fritillaria meleagris*), Chinese-sacred-lily (*Narcissus tazetta orientalis*), climbing-lily (*Gloriosa*), corn-lily (*Ixia* and *Veratrum californicum*), cow-lily (*Nuphar*), crinum-lily (*Crinum*), Cuban-lily (*Scilla peruviana*), day-lily (*Hemerocallis*), desert-lily (*Hesperocallis*), Easter-lily (*Erythronium,* the true lily called Easter lily is *Lilium longiflorum*), fairy-lily (*Zephyranthes*), false-lily-of-the-valley (*Maianthemum*), fawn-lily (*Erythronium*), fire-lily (*Cyrtanthus* and *Zephyranthes tubiflora*), flax-lily (*Dianella*), foxtail-lily (*Eremurus*), fringed-lily (*Thysanotus*), ginger-lily (*Hedychium*), glory-lily (*Gloriosa*), Guernsey-lily (*Nerine sarniensis*), Ifafa-lily (*Cyrtanthus mackenii*), Impala-lily (*Adenium obesum multiflorum*), Jacobean-lily (*Sprekelia*), Josephine's-lily (*Brunsvigia josephinae*), Kafir-lily (*Clivia* and *Schizostylis*), lily-of-the-Incas (*Alstroemeria*), lily-of-the-palace (*Hippeastrum aulicum*), lily-of-the-valley (*Convallaria majalis*), lily-of-the-valley-vine (*Salphichroa rhomboidea*), Malagas-lily (*Cybistetes longifolia*), mariposa-lily (*Calochortus* and *Erythronium*), milk-and-wine-lily (*Crinum latifolium zeylanicum*), mountain-lily (*Ranunculus lyallii*), pine-woods-lily (*Eustylis*), plantain-lily (*Hosta*), pond-lily (*Nymphaea,* yellow pond-lily is *Nuphar*), prairie-lily (*Zephyranthes*), queen-lily (*Phaedranassa*), rain-lily (*Zephyranthes*), renga-lily or rock-lily (*Arthropodium cirrhatum*), St.-Bernard's-lily (*Anthericum liliago*), St.-Bruno's-lily (*Paradisea liliastrum*), St.-James-lily (*Sprekelia formosissima*), St.-John's-lily (*Crinum asiaticum sinicum*), St.-Joseph's-lily (*Cybistetes longifolia* and *Hippeastrum johnsonii*), sand-lily (*Leucocrinum montanum*), Scarborough-lily (*Vallota speciosa*), sego-lily (*Calochortus nuttallii*), Siskiyou-lily (*Fritillaria glauca*), snake-lily (*Dichelostemma volubilis*), spear-lily (*Doryanthes*), spider-lily (*Hymenocallis*), star-lily (*Erythronium, Leucocrinum montanum,* and *Zigadenus fremontii*), thorn-lily (*Catesbaea spinosa*), toad-lily (*Tricyrtis hirta*), torch-lily (*Kniphofia*), triplet-lily (*Triteleia laxa*), trout-lily (*Erythronium*), voodoo-lily (*Sauromatum guttatum*), water-lily (*Nymphaea* and *Victoria*), and zephyr-lily (*Zephyranthes*).

LILY-OF-THE-VALLEY. This charming, old-fashioned flower (*Convallaria majalis*) and its varieties are elegant for massing and using as deciduous groundcovers in shaded and partially shaded places where the soil is never excessively dry, but is not poorly drained and wet. The sweetly fragrant

Lily-of-the-valley: (a) As a groundcover in partial shade

(b) Flowers

flowers, delightful for posies and small arrangements last well when cut. Lily-of-the-valleys can be forced into out-of-season bloom with great ease, and by employing roots from cold storage can be had in bloom at any time of the year.

For the best results prepare the soil for planting by spading it deeply and incorporating very generous amounts of partially decayed organic matter, such as compost, leaf mold, peat moss, or well-decayed manure. Early fall is perhaps the best time for planting, but it can also be done satisfactorily in late winter or early spring and if necessary after flowering is through. If planting after the plants are in leaf is practiced by sure to keep them well watered afterward.

You may plant single crowns with roots attached, called pips, or divisions of old clumps each consisting of about three pips. Either is better than larger divisions. Set single pips 3 to 4 inches apart, small divisions a little farther apart. Spread the roots in as natural positions as possible after, if necessary, shortening excessively long ones to facilitate planting. Finish with the tips of the growth buds an inch beneath the surface. Firm the soil about the roots, make its surface level, and mulch

with an inch or two of leaf mold, peat moss, or other suitable material.

Routine care makes little demands on the gardener's time. The maintenance of an organic mulch is very beneficial, as, during long dry spells, are periodic deep waterings. An application of a complete fertilizer each spring promotes vigor. As long as the plants flower freely it is better not to disturb them, but if, as is likely to happen after a period of several years, they become crowded to the extent that the quality and amount of bloom deteriorates it is time to dig them up, spade and improve the soil as recommended for a first planting, divide the old clumps and replant the strongest pips or small divisions.

For forcing into out-of-season bloom in pots or flats, plant strong single pips about an inch apart in sandy soil, peat moss, a mixture of peat moss and sand, perlite, or vermiculite. You may do this with cold storage (retarded) pips at any time of the year, and these, if set as soon as planted where the temperature of 60 to 75°F and kept well watered, will bloom in three to four weeks. To ensure long stems, keep them in the dark for the first week or two, then gradually accustom them to full light.

Pot pips dug from the outdoors in September in a sandy soil mix, then put the pots in a cold frame or sheltered place outdoors and cover them with a few inches of peat moss, sawdust, or something similar. From January on bring them indoors in successive batches to ensure a long season of bloom and treat them as advised for retarded pips.

Forced lily-of-the-valley in decorative containers

After forcing, lily-of-the-valley pips are not useful for forcing the following year, but if kept watered and growing until danger of frost has passed and then planted outdoors they will recover and flower in the future. For descriptions of the lily-of-the-valley and its varieties see Convallaria.

LILYTURF. See Liriope and Ophiopogon.

LIMA BEAN. See Beans. The Chickasaw-lima-bean is *Canavalia ensiformis.*

LIME. Besides its use for the citrus fruit treated in the next entry, the word lime forms part of the names of these: Australian desert-lime (*Eremocitrus*), Australian finger-lime (*Microcitrus australasica*), lime-berry (*Triphasia trifolia*), Ogeechee-lime (*Nyssa ogeche*), Spanish-lime (*Melicoccus bijugatus*), and wild-lime (*Zanthoxylum fagara*). In the British Isles lindens (*Tilia*) are called limes or lime trees.

LIME. The fruits called limes, botanically *Citrus aurantifolia*, in cultivation for many centuries, were brought to Florida from the Old World in about 1565. They have become naturalized in the southern part of the peninsula and on the Keys, hence the name Key lime, and in parts of the West Indies and Caribbean region.

Limes are of two types, those with exceedingly acid fruits and those with sweet limes. The fruits of the latter, because of their insipid flavor, have little acceptance in the United States. There are small- and

Lime (*Citrus aurantifolia*), young plant

Lime (fruits)

larger-fruited acid sorts. Of all commercial citrus fruits, they are most tender to frost.

The West Indian, Mexican, or Key lime is a bushy, spreading, evergreen tree of medium size and vigor, with many slender stems thickly furnished with small, slender spines. Small flowers followed by fruits are produced almost continuously, but chiefly in winter. The fruits, about 1½ inches long and short-elliptic, obovoid, or nearly spherical, have thin, smooth, tight skins, greenish-yellow when ripe, and pale greenish flesh. At maturity they drop to the ground.

The Tahiti or Persian lime, a larger, more robust tree, nearly spineless and with wide-spreading, somewhat drooping branches, is slightly less cold-sensitive than the West Indian. Its flowers are a little bigger and are succeeded by ovoid, short-ellipsoid, or oblongish fruits the size of small lemons. These larger limes, with thin, smooth, tight rinds and light greenish-yellow, juicy flesh, are borne more or less throughout the year, but chiefly in summer. Very similar, variety 'Bearss' is distinguished by having usually seedless fruits. This originated in California, presumably as a seedling of the Tahiti lime, about 1895. Hybrids between limes and lemons, called *lemonimes*, are not much grown; those between limes and kumquats, called *limequats*, have had more acceptance.

Garden and Landscape Uses. Besides supplying fruits esteemed for ades and other beverages, for making Key lime pie, and as a source of lime juice, limes are planted to some extent as ornamentals. They thrive only in regions of high summer heat, are more intolerant of cold than oranges and lemons, and do better in regions of high humidity than the latter. Exposure to strong winds is detrimental to the production of unmarred fruits. In the continental United States their cultivation is pretty much restricted to Arizona, California, and Florida. Care calls for little or no pruning, but generous fertilization and in arid regions irrigation.

Cultivation. Except for their higher heat requirements and greater intolerance of low temperatures, limes respond to conditions that favor lemons and oranges. They succeed in various soils, but are intolerant of those containing alkali and of poorly drained ones. Container specimens or those dug with a ball of earth are preferred for planting, the best time to do this is when the soil is warm enough to stimulate root growth. West Indian limes may be spaced 15 feet apart, Tahiti types about 20 feet. The West Indian lime is usually raised from seeds, sometimes by budding superior sorts on seedlings. 'Tahiti' and 'Bearss' limes are generally budded onto understocks of 'Rough' lemon or bitter orange. Pests and diseases are those of oranges and other citrus fruits.

LIME and LIMING. Liming is an ancient agricultural and horticultural practice, of immense benefit when rightly done, harmful if abused. It consists of applying to or mixing with the soil calcium carbonate in any of several forms. Calcium is a nutrient needed by all plants, except perhaps those of the heath family ERICACEAE. But because most earths contain enough for the needs of plants, lime is not usually used as a fertilizer. Its chief practical merits are that it reduces acidity and flocculates clay fractions of soils so that sticky, clayey ground is made more granular, crumbly, porous to water and air, and sandy ones more compact and moisture-retentive. By reducing acidity, lime stimulates the proliferation and activity of microorganisms that decompose organic matter into humus, and humus into simpler compounds and elements and in so doing releases nutrients needed by plants. It also acts to release for plant use various nutrients, notably phosphorus and potassium, held in the soil in unavailable forms.

Do not lime indiscriminately. Unless you are well acquainted with your soil and its needs do so only after a test shows these is no danger of making the ground too alkaline for the plants you want to grow. Such tests can be arranged through your Cooperative Extension Agent, or they can be made with one of the testing kits sold by dealers in garden supplies.

Kinds of lime commonly available are ground limestone (agricultural lime) and hydrated or slaked lime (builders' lime). The first, by far the best for gardens, may consist chiefly of calcium carbonate or be a mixture of that and magnesium carbonate. The mixture, called dolomitic limestone, contains magnesium. It is of special benefit if that element is deficient, as it is in many garden soils, especially acid ones, in the eastern and southern United States.

Ground limestone should be of such fineness that all will pass a screen with 10 meshes, and one-half through one with 100 meshes, to the inch. The finer it is the faster its action in the soil. Hydrated lime, made by burning limestone, then slaking it with water, works even faster than the most finely ground limestone.

Amounts to apply vary considerably according to the region and the type and acidity of the soil. In the warm south somewhat lighter applications than those appropriate for northern soils are in order. In the north from 3 to 12 pounds of ground limestone to 100 square feet are satisfactory, the smaller amount for quite sandy soils, the larger for decidedly clayey ones. Intermediate quantities may be used on loamy lands neither decidedly sandy nor clayey. Hydrated lime is used at about three-quarters the rate of ground limestone. Do not ordinarily apply more lime in one year than is enough to change the pH more than one point, from pH 5.5 to

pH 6.5 for instance. Excessive liming, easily done on sandy soils in humid regions, can tie up, in forms unavailable to plants, the meager supplies of certain nutrients. These include iron, the lack of which causes foliage to become chlorotic (unhealthily yellow with the veins usually green). It is important to spread lime evenly and mix it thoroughly with the upper few inches of soil. Indifferent attention to these matters can bring spotty results.

The time of year to apply lime is not of great importance, except that it should not be spread at the same time as manure. If these come in contact on the soil surface ammonia gas, containing the valuable fertilizing element nitrogen, is released into the atmosphere. If manure is used, turn it under two weeks to a month or more before applying the lime, then fork or harrow the lime into the upper 3 or 4 inches. It tends to sink in the soil by leaching. Often it is convenient to manure in fall and to lime in spring.

Substitutes for lime include oyster shells and marl (a soft, earthy form of calcium carbonate available as natural deposits in some localities). Limestone chips, pieces of limestone that will pass through a ½- or ¾-inch mesh, with all fine and dustlike particles removed, are used in soils for selected alpine and rock garden plants. Wood ashes and basic slag (a fertilizer) contain, in addition to phosphorus and potassium, respectively, appreciable amounts of lime.

LIMEQUAT. These are hybrids between kumquats and limes. For more information see Fortunella and Citrofortunella.

LIMNANTHACEAE—Limnanthes Family. Two genera, *Floerkea* and *Limnanthes*, totaling eleven species of annuals compose this family of dicotyledons endemic to North America. They have alternate, pinnately-cleft or pinnate leaves and long-stalked, symmerical flowers solitary from the leaf axils. The blooms have three to five each sepals and petals with small glands alternating with the latter, twice as many stamens as petals, and one style carrying three to five stigmas. The fruits consist of three to five seedlike nutlets. Only *Limnanthes* is cultivated.

LIMNANTHES (Lim-nánthes) — Meadow Foam. The limanthes family LIMNANTHACEAE is wholly American. It contains two genera, *Floerkea* of which there is only one species, of no horticultural importance, and *Limnanthes*, with ten species. From the latter *Floerkea* differs in having blooms with three sepals and the same number of shorter petals. The name *Limnanthes* comes from the Greek *limne*, a marsh, and *anthos*, a flower, in allusion to preferred habitats.

Low, branched annuals, members of this genus favor moist soils. They have alternate, pinnately-dissected or -lobed leaves and solitary, axillary flowers with usually five, but sometimes four or six, sepals and five, or less commonly four or six, petals. The petals are longer than the sepals. Their claws (narrow basal portions) have a u-shaped band of hairs. The fruits consist of five erect nutlets.

The species ordinarily cultivated, the meadow foam (**L. douglasii** syn. *Floerkea douglasii*) is a variable native from California to Oregon. Up to 1¼ feet tall, it is hairless and has pinnate and pinnately-lobed leaves up to 4½ inches long, with five to eleven divisions that are again lobed or toothed. Its saucer-shaped, fragrant flowers, ¾ inch to 1¼ inches in diameter, on stalks 2 to 4 inches long, have hairless, pointed sepals and obovate, white-tipped, yellow petals. In *L. d. sulphurea* the petals are all yellow, in *L. d. nivea* they are all white, in *L. d. rosea* they are white with pink veins.

Limnanthes douglasii

Garden and Landscape Uses. The meadow foam is charming as an edging to paths, for the fronts of flower borders, and for rock gardens. One of the most free-flowering of annuals where summers are cool, it makes a lovely display for an extended period. Unfortunately, like most Western annuals, it fades or dies in torrid weather. As a greenhouse pot plant for spring display it is charming and easy to grow.

Cultivation. For its best accommodation, meadow foam needs an open, sunny location and moist, moderately fertile soil. Where winters are not excessively severe seeds may be sown in fall where the plants are to bloom, or they may be sown in spring. They germinate in about three weeks and the seedlings are thinned to 4 inches apart. No special care is needed. It is not unusual for seedlings from self-sown seeds to develop in undisturbed ground where the plant was grown the previous year. To have plants blooming in late winter and spring in greenhouses, seeds are sown in six-inch pots or pans (shallow pots) in

September or October in porous, fertile earth. The seedlings are thinned so that five remain in each container. Alternatively, the seedlings may be potted individually in 2½-inch pots and the young plants later be potted several together in larger receptacles. They are grown in full sun in a night temperature of 45 to 50°F, and five or ten degrees more by day. The greenhouse must, on all favorable occasions, be ventilated freely. Especially in their early stages care must be taken not to keep the soil too wet; on the other hand, it must not become excessively dry. At later stages, when the pots are well filled with roots and the days are longer and the sun is stronger, more generous watering will be needed. Then weekly applications of dilute liquid fertilizer are helpful.

LIMNOBIUM (Lim-nòbium)—Frog's Bit. In addition to this genus, the related *Hydrocharis morsus-ranae* is called frog's bit. Consisting of one species in temperate North America and two in tropical America, *Limnobium* belongs in the frog's bit family HYDROCHARITACEAE. Its name is from the Greek *limnos*, a lake, and *bios*, life, and alludes to the habitat.

Limnobiums are aquatic or wet-soil perennial herbaceous plants that root in mud and form tufts of basal leaves on long stems. When the roots are under water the rosettes of foliage and flowers, usually attached to them by the stems, float; in deep water they sometimes separate from the roots and float free. The flowers are unisexual, the males two or three together on long stalks from a one-bracted spathe, the females solitary from a two-bracted spathe. Sepals and petals are similar in both sexes, which usually occur on the same plant; there are three of each. The filaments (stalks) of the stamens are joined to a central column. There are six to nine styles, forked nearly to their bases into two branches. The leaves are much longer than the flower stalks and have swollen, spongy undersurfaces to the blades. The fruits are many-seeded dry berries.

From Lake Ontario to Illinois, Florida, and Texas, **L. spongia** is found in ponds, bayous, and other quiet waters. Its leaves have slightly convex, ovate or heart-shaped blades 1½ to 3 inches in diameter, more or less purplish beneath and spotted with brownish-red above. The white flowers are ¾ inch wide. The males have nine to twelve stamens, some of which are sterile. The sepals and petals of the female blooms are almost hidden by the six forked styles.

Ranging in the wild from Mexico to Brazil and the West Indies, **L. stoloniferum** is of similar habit. It has broad, slightly heart-shaped leaves with convex blades glossy on their upper sides and spongy beneath. They are without trace of purple. Usually, but not always, individual plants produce flowers of only one sex. The se-

pals and petals are greenish-white, the former slender, the latter reduced to small scales. The deeply-forked, yellowish stigmas spread horizontally.

Garden Uses and Cultivation. These New World frog's bits are interesting plants for aquariums, pools, and ponds. The North American *L. spongia* is hardy and suitable for unheated aquariums and outdoor pools. *L. stoloniferum* needs tropical conditions. As aquarium plants these are superior to the European frog's bit (*Hydrocharis morsus-ranae*). They must have full sun to bloom. For *L. stoloniferum* it is important that the atmosphere be very humid; it succeeds best in aquariums that are covered with glass or transparent plastic. Strong winter light is important. Although these plants can be grown as free-floaters much better results are had when they are rooted in soil. They are easily propagated by runners and offsets.

LIMNOCHARIS (Lim-nócharis). Tropical American and West Indian in its natural distribution, the only species of *Limnocharis* is quite variable as to size and leaf shape. It belongs in the butomus family BUTOMACEAE or, according to some authorities, in the limnocharis family LIMNOCHARITACEAE. The name is from the Greek *limne*, a marsh, and *chairo*, to delight in, and refers to the habitat. From nearly related *Hydrocleys* it differs in having flowers with fifteen to twenty instead of six or fewer stamens and in its stigmas being without styles (stalkless). The plant sometimes called *Limnocharis humboldtii* is *Hydrocleys nymphoides*.

A milky-juiced, tender, evergreen perennial aquatic, **L. flava** thrusts to a height of 1 foot to 2 feet above the water its velvety green, long-stalked leaves with egg-shaped to lanceolate blades up to 6 inches long that have usually rounded, but sometimes heart-shaped bases. The bisexual flowers, about 1 inch in diameter, are in umbels of two to twelve atop erect, triangular stalks. They are borne in summer and have three green persistent sepals and the same number of spreading, quickly deciduous, pale yellow petals that are whitish at their margins. When the fruit capsules form, their stalks bend to the water to shed the seeds. At the point of contact a new plant arises and as this process is repeated the plants spread. A dwarf variety, *L. f. minor*, is known.

Garden and Landscape Uses and Cultivation. Although not the most showy aquatic, *L. flava* is worth planting in a modest way for the sake of variety and to give height to pool plantings. It is not hardy, but where winters are not to its liking, it may be accommodated in containers and grown outdoors in summer and indoors in winter. It responds to a fertile soil and, neutral or slightly acid water, and prefers full sun. It grows best when the roots are covered with 6 to 9 inches of water. Water temperatures of 68°F or higher are most favorable to growth; indoors in winter a temperature of 50 to 55°F is sufficient. Propagation is by division, by plantlets that develop among the seed heads, and by seed (which must be kept constantly moist if stored). Seeds are sown in containers of soil and covered with one-half an inch of sand. After sowing, the receptacles are submerged so that the sand surface is an inch or two beneath the water.

LIMONIA. See Feronia.

LIMONIUM (Limòn-ium)—Sea Lavender, Statice. A member of the leadwort family PLUMBAGINACEAE, this genus consists of 300 species of mostly herbaceous perennials, some low shrubs, and annuals, natives chiefly of salt marshes, sea cliffs, and semidesert and desert regions. Its name is a modified form of *leimonion*, an ancient Greek one for some unidentified plant that grew in salt marshes. Of wide natural distribution, *Limonium* was for long wrongly named *Statice*, which name is still the vernacular one for some species.

Limoniums have undivided, lobeless, or pinnately-lobed leaves, all basal, or in shrubby kinds alternate. The flowers, from the axils of bracts, are in clusters, racemes, or often airy panicles of small clusters. They have tubular, cylindrical to funnel-shaped, shallowly-five- or ten-lobed, papery, often colored calyxes, five petals joined for a short distance at their bases, five stamens, and five styles ending in cylindrical stigmas. The fruits are enclosed in the persistent calyxes. Some species previously in *Limonium* are separated as *Goniolimon* and *Psylliostachys*.

Best known of hardy herbaceous perennial kinds, **L. latifolium** (syn. *Statice latifolia*) is a native of dry grasslands from southeast Europe to southeast Russia. Usually with stellate (star-shaped) hairs, its blunt, lobeless, elliptic to spatulate, evergreen leaves narrow to long stalks. Their blades are up to about 10 inches long.

Limonium latifolium

Limonium latifolium (flowers)

Erect and 1 foot to 2½ feet tall, the flowering stalks end in wide-branched, airy, wiry-stalked panicles of one- or two-flowered spikelets in brief, one-sided spikes. The blooms have white calyxes, mauve, purplish, or pink, ¼-inch-wide corollas, and slender, cylindrical stigmas.

Common European sea-lavender (**L. vulgare** syn. *Statice limonium*) is a salt marsh hardy perennial of western and southern Europe. Up to about 1 foot in height, it has long-stalked, lanceolate, all basal leaves up to about 5 inches long, and erect, wiry, flat-topped panicles of ⅓-inch-wide reddish-violet flowers in two rows of two-flowered spikelets along the upper sides of the branches. An inhabitant of alkaline soils, **L. gmelinii** (syn. *Statice gmelinii*) is endemic to southcentral and eastcentral Europe. A hardy herbaceous perennial, it has short-stalked or nearly stalkless, hairless, blunt, ovate to spatula-shaped, blue-glaucous leaves 9 inches to 1 foot long. The blooms, about ¼ inch wide, in one- or rarely two-flowered spikelets that form short, one-sided spikes arranged in panicles 1 foot to 2 feet tall, have purple-blue calyxes and rose-pink to reddish or purple corollas ¼ inch wide.

Native from New York to Mexico, **L. carolinianum** inhabits salt marshes. A hardy perennial, this has elliptic to oblanceolate, stalked leaves with blades up to 6 inches long. Up to about 2 feet tall, its widely-branched panicles are of tiny lavender flowers with hairless calyxes, in stalkless, one-sided clusters. Similar except that the calyxes of its blooms are bristly-hairy in their lower parts, **L. nashii** occurs in similar habitats from Labrador to Mexico. A coastal plant of California, **L. californicum** has a woody stem, and long-stalked, mostly blunt, oblong to oblong-obovate leaves with blades up to 8 inches in length. The loose, densely-flowered panicles are of pale violet blooms. They are up to 1½ feet tall.

Other herbaceous perennials sometimes cultivated include the following. **L. auriculae-ursifolium** (syns. *L. lychnidifolium*, *Statice lychnidifolia*), native to marshes and sea cliffs of Europe, is variable. It has tufts of gray-green, oblanceolate leaves 1 inch to 4 inches long, and panicles of soft blue-lavender to violet-blue flowers 9 inches to over 1 foot high. **L. bellidifolium** (syn. *Statice bellidifolia*), hairless and up to 9 inches tall, has obovate to lanceolate leaves up to 1½ inches long. Its blooms, in one-sided spikes at the ends of the panicle branches, are under ¼ inch wide. They have white calyxes and lilac corollas. This sort inhabits coastal salt marshes and saline soils inland, in Europe and the Baltic region. **L. binervosum** is a variable inhabitant of sea cliffs in Europe. Up to 1 foot tall and hairless, it has lanceolate-spatula-shaped leaves up to ½ inch long, and muted-lavender flowers in pyramidal panicles. **L. emarginatum,** an endemic of Spain and Gibralter, occurs on sea cliffs. Hairless, and 1 foot to 1½ feet tall, this has blue-gray, linear-spatula-shaped leaves and cylindrical spikes of purple and white flowers. It has been confused with North African **L. spathulatum** (syn. *Statice spathulata*), which has longer, pointed leaves. **L. gougetianum** (syn. *Statice gougetiana*), a native of salt marshes in the Balearic Islands and North Africa, is 4 inches to 1 foot tall. It has dense rosettes of obovate-spatula-shaped, one-veined leaves up to a little over 1 inch long and pale violet flowers with reddish calyxes. **L. minutum** (syn. *Statice minuta*), 2 to 6 inches tall and usually hairless, forms cushion-like rosettes of spatula-shaped, hoary-gray leaves scarcely over ⅓ inch long. It has sprays of tiny lavender-blue flowers. This is native on limestone cliffs along the Mediterranean coast. **L. oleifolium** (syn. *Statice oleifolia*), from 2 inches to 1½ feet tall, is a very variable native of the Mediterranean region. It has linear-spatula-shaped, one-veined leaves on long basal branches. The flowers are violet. **L. ramosissimum** (syns. *L. globulariifolium*, *Statice globulariifolia*), of the Mediterranean region, inhabits salt marshes. From 9 inches to 1¼ feet in height, it has obovate to oblanceolate or spatula-shaped leaves and ¼-inch-wide pinkish blooms. **L. sieberi** (syns. *L. graceum*, *Statice sieberi*) is a native of the Mediterranean region where it inhabits rocks and sandy soils. From 4 inches to about 1 foot tall, it has linear-lanceolate to ovate-spatula-shaped leaves up to 1½ inches long. The violet blooms are along one side of the branches of the panicles. **L. thouinii**, of the Mediterranean region and the Canary Islands, is 4 to 8 inches tall. Its obovate leaves are pinnately-round-lobed. The winged-branched panicles have white to pale lilac calyxes and yellow corollas.

Subshrubby kinds with woody, more or less branched stems include several natives of the Canary Islands. About 2 feet in height, **L. arborescens** (syn. *Statice arborescens*) has broad, blunt, ovate-oblong, stalked leaves up to 6 inches long and narrowly-winged branches to its panicles. The flowers have blue calyxes and yellow corollas. Very similar to *L. arborescens* is *L. fruticans* (syns. *L. arborea*, *Statice fruticans*, *S. arborea*). The chief differences are that the flower stalks are not winged, and the leaves are smaller, up to 2 inches long. *L. brassicaefolium* (syn. *Statice brassicaefolia*) has the branches of its panicles with broad, wavy wings that broaden to leafy ears below the forks. Its leaves, up to 1 foot long, are fiddle-shaped. They have three or four lobes on each side. The flowers have bluish-violet calyxes and yellowish-white corollas. From it *L. imbricatum* differs in the entire plant being clothed with short, soft, down and its fiddle-shaped leaves having eight or nine small side lobes on each side. The branches of its panicles have broad, wavy wings. The white flowers have blue calyxes. Up to 3 feet tall, *L. macrophyllum* has very large, slightly hairy, obovate-spatula-shaped leaves, broad-winged branches to its much-branched panicles, and flowers with blue to purple calyxes and yellow to white corollas. Leaves deeply-pinnately-lobed are characteristic of *L. macropterum*. This, up to 2 feet in height, has the branches of its panicles winged. Its flowers are purple. Long-stalked, broad-triangular leaves, narrowed to their bases and up to 6 inches long, are characteristic of 3-foot-tall *L. perezii* (syn. *Statice perezii*). Its flowers have lavender-blue calyxes, and light yellow corollas. This is naturalized in California. About 2 feet in height and hairless, *L. preauxii* (syn. *Statice preauxii*) has very leathery, rounded-triangular leaves 2½ to 4 inches across. The flattened branches of the panicles bear distantly spaced spikelets of blooms. The flowers have lavender-blue calyxes, and pale blue corollas. White-hairy foliage is characteristic of 9-inch-tall *L. puberulum.* Its leaves are ovoid-lozenge-shaped, about ¾ inch long. The flowers have violet calyxes, and yellowish-white corollas.

Annuals or biennials commonly grown as annuals are *L. bonduellii*, of Algeria, and *L. sinuatum*, from the Mediterranean region and somewhat naturalized in California. These are excellent garden plants. Attaining a height of about 2 feet, *L. bonduellii* has deeply-pinnately-lobed, fiddle-shaped leaves up to about 6 inches long. Its panicles of soft, clear yellow flowers have winged branches. Approximately as tall, with similarly shaped leaves up to about 8 inches long, *L. sinuatum* has panicles with winged branches. The flowers typically have blue calyxes and yellowish-white corollas, but various color forms in which white, purple, pink, or red predominate are cultivated.

Garden and Landscape Uses. The hardiness of limoniums must be gauged by their geographical origins. None of the shrubby kinds survive winters outdoors in

Limonium sinuatum

the north. They are suited only to dryish, frost-free or nearly frost-free climates, such as that of California, and for cool greenhouses. Most of the herbaceous perennials are hardy and satisfactory outdoors in the north. The taller ones are suitable for flower beds, the lower ones for rock gardens. The annuals are good in flower gardens and greenhouses. They and the taller herbaceous perennials are excellent for cutting for use fresh or dried in arrangements. They are especially useful for mixing with other flowers to give grace and lightness. Among the best for cut flowers are *L. bonduellii*, *L. latifolium*, and *L. sinuatum*. Limoniums stand dry conditions well, and most of them, saline soils. They need full sun and are well suited for planting near the sea. Deep, well-drained soils are most suitable and are satisfactory even for most of those that in the wild live in salt marshes.

Cultivation. No special difficulties attend the cultivation of limoniums. All are easily raised from seed, the herbaceous perennials also by careful division in spring, the shrubby kinds by cuttings in a greenhouse propagating bench. Popular *L. latifolium*, and undoubtedly others, can be increased by root cuttings. The annuals may be raised by sowing outdoors in spring where the plants are to remain, and thinning out the seedlings sufficiently to prevent excessive crowding, or seeds can be sown about eight weeks earlier indoors in a temperature of 60 to 65°F, and the seedlings grown in flats or small pots until freedom from danger of frost makes it possible to plant them outdoors. The annuals can be had in bloom in sunny greenhouses in late winter and spring from seeds sown in September. They may be grown in pots or in beds or benches of soil. A night temperature of 50°F suits *L. bonduellii* and *L. sinuatum*. Daytime temperatures five to fifteen degrees above night levels are appropriate. As greenhouse plants the shrubby kinds do well in well-drained pots of fertile, porous soil. Winter temperatures of 45 to 50°F by night and up to fifteen degrees

warmer by day are needed, as is exposure to full sun. Benefit results from summering the plants outdoors with their pots buried to their rims in peat moss, sawdust, sand, or similar material. Moderate watering from spring to fall and occasional applications of dilute liquid fertilizer are in order. In winter the soil is kept dryish, but not dry.

LINACEAE—Flax Family. Of cosmopolitan distribution in the wild, this family of dicotyledons consists of 290 species arranged in a dozen genera. It includes herbaceous sorts and shrubs with alternate or rarely opposite, undivided leaves. Its symmetrical, red, blue, yellow, or white flowers, in raceme-like or spraylike arrangements, and often short-lived, have five or rarely four each sepals and petals, the former sometimes united at their bases, as many stamens as petals, often accompanied by staminodes (nonfertile stamens), and generally three to five styles. The fruits are usually capsules, less often drupes. Genera cultivated are *Linum* and *Reinwardtia*.

LINANTHUS (Linán-thus). At one time included in nearly related *Gilia*, this genus, of the phlox family POLEMONIACEAE, is now accepted as a separate entity of some forty or more species mostly of western North America and Chile. The name, from the Greek *linon*, flax, and *anthos*, a flower, alludes to the blooms having the general aspect of those of *Linum*.

The genus *Linanthus* includes annuals and herbaceous perennials with alternate or opposite usually more or less dissected leaves. The flowers, bell- to funnel-shaped or with spreading petals, have five each sepals, petals, and stamens, and one style. The fruits are capsules.

Annual *L. liniflorus* (syn. *Gilia liniflora*), of California, 1 foot to 1½ feet in height, has erect or spreading stems. Nearly hairless, its lower leaves are opposite, its upper alternate. They are palmately-divided into three to nine needle-like segments up to ½ inch long. The slender-stalked flowers, in clusters, are shortly-funnel-shaped and from under ½ inch to almost 1 inch long. They are white, pink, or pale lilac. Another attractive Californian annual, usually represented in cultivation by its subspecies *L. a. luteus* (syn. *Gilia lutea*), is *L. androsaceus* (syns. *Gilia androsacea*, *Leptosiphon androsaceus*). A slender, somewhat hairy, erect annual, 1 foot tall, the species has opposite leaves palmately-divided into five to nine linear to oblanceolate lobes up to ½ inch long. The stalkless flowers are in dense, leafy-bracted clusters. They are white, yellowish, lilac, rose-pink, or violet and have long slender tubes that lift the spreading, blunt petals that are much shorter than the tube well above the foliage. The variety *L. a. luteus* is shorter and has yellow, brown-throated blooms. From

Linanthus androsaceus

Linanthus androsaceus luteus

the last species and its variety, **L. grandiflorus** (syns. *Gilia grandiflora, Leptosiphon grandiflorus*) differs in that the corolla tubes and the petals are equal in length. This somewhat hairy annual native to California, 1 foot to 2 feet tall, has opposite, rather distantly-spaced leaves palmately-cleft into five to eleven linear lobes up to 1¼ inches long. The flower heads are of few to several blooms and many leafy bracts. The flowers have densely-white-hairy calyxes and funnel-shaped, white to pale lilac corollas with tubes about ½ inch long and spreading petals of about the same length.

Other sorts cultivated include these: **L. aureus** (syn. *Gilia aurea*), of southern California and Baja California, is a hairy or glandular annual, branched from the base and up to 9 inches tall. It has alternate, three- to seven-cleft leaves and flowers that are yellow, often spotted with orange to brownish-purple in the throat, or are whitish. **L. dianthiflorus,** of southern California and Baja California, is an annual, tufted, and up to 6 inches tall. It has mostly opposite, undivided, threadlike leaves and, solitary or few together, lilac, pink, or white flowers ¾ to 1 inch long and with toothed petals. **L. dichotomus,** of Nevada, Arizona, and California, approx-

imately 1 foot in height, has branchless or forked stems. Generally hairless and more or less glaucous, it has opposite leaves usually cleft into three to seven slender-linear lobes. Opening in the evening, the white, sometimes brown- or purple-throated flowers are about 1¼ inches long. This species is called evening snow. **L. nuttallii,** from Colorado to California and Mexico, is a subshrubby perennial with erect, much-branched stems up to 1 foot tall or a little taller. Its leaves are opposite and cut into five to nine linear-oblanceolate lobes. From the upper leaf axils, and stalkless or nearly so, the white to creamy-yellow flowers are in headlike clusters. In *L. n. floribundus* the leaves have three to five lobes and the flowers may have longer stalks than those of the typical species.

Garden Uses and Cultivation. In gardens linanthuses serve the same purpose and need the conditions and care that suit gilias.

LINARIA (Linàr-ia) — Butter-and-eggs, Toadflax. Linarias number 150 species of annuals, herbaceous perennials, and a few subshrubs of temperate parts of the northern hemisphere. They are most abundant in the Mediterranean region. From related snapdragons (*Antirrhinum*) they differ in their flowers having definite spurs instead of being merely pouched at their bases. From *Cymbalaria* they are distinguished by their pinnately-veined leaves. As with snapdragons, the throats of the blooms of *Linaria* are closed with a prominent palate, a prominence or projection of the lower lip that prevents insects other than bees heavy enough to depress the lip and thus open the throat of the flower from entering. The flowers depend upon bees for pollination. The insects enter to obtain the abundant nectar produced by a nectary at the base of the ovary, which collects in the spur. Toadflaxes belong in the figwort family SCROPHULARIACEAE. The generic name is derived from the Greek *linon*, flax. Some species resemble flax plants. For other plants sometimes included see *Chaenorhinum, Cymbalaria,* and *Kickxia.*

The leaves of toadflaxes are opposite or whorled on the lower parts of the plants, but above are often alternate. They may be smooth-margined, toothed, or lobed. The flowers, of various colors, have long tubes, spurred at their bases, and asymmetrical, snapdragon-like blooms, each with four stamens, in terminal racemes or spikes. The fruits are capsules.

One of the best-known kinds, common throughout most of temperate North America as a naturalized immigrant from Europe and Asia, and usually considered to be just a little too weedy to be generally admitted to gardens, although it may serve well in semiwild areas, is the butter-and-eggs (**L. vulgaris**). Perennial and 1 foot to 3 feet tall, this cheerful plant colonizes roadsides,

Linaria vulgaris

fields, and waste places and blooms for a long period in summer. Its flowers, lemon-yellow with a bearded, orange palate, are about 1¼ inches long. They have spurs about as long as the corollas and are in erect spikes. The stalkless, lobeless, and toothless, linear, glaucous green leaves are up to 1½ inches in length. Butter-and-eggs occasionally produces variants in which the blooms are symmetrical and the flowers have more than one spur or none. These constitute the variety *L. v. peloria*, which usually does not produce fertile seeds. A double-flowered kind also exists. Closely resembling butter-and-eggs and also naturalized to some extent in North America is the European **L. genistifolia.** It differs from butter-and-eggs in that its wider leaves broaden rather than narrow at their bases and the flower spurs are shorter than the corollas. This kind grows up to 2 feet in height and has flowers up to ¾ inch long. Handsomer is *L. g. dalmatica* (syn. *L. dalmatica*), a similar yellow-flowered kind with blooms 1 inch to 2 inches in length that have orange palates and curved spurs shorter than the corollas. Its nearly stalkless, grayish-green leaves are ovate-lanceolate. This variety is indigenous to southeastern Europe. Macedonian **L. macedonica** resembles *L. genistifolia dalmatica.* Over 1 foot tall and a native of the Mediterranean region, it has brown or yellow blooms with orange, hairy palates and curved spurs shorter than the corollas. Variety *L. m.* 'Nymph' has cream flowers. A low-growing perennial of considerable virtue is **L. alpina,** of the European Alps. This is compact and tufted and has erect stems 2 to 6 inches in height and thickish linear or lanceolate, glaucous leaves in whorls of four. Its bluish-violet flowers have yellow or orange palates and more or less straight spurs as long as the corollas. They are ½ to ¾ inch long. Variety *L. a. alba* has white flowers with yellow centers. The blooms of *L. a. rosea* have yellow centers and are pink. Another low perennial is **L. supina,** a native of Europe sparingly naturalized in the

United States. It has decumbent stems up to 9 inches long, linear leaves, and pale yellow blooms about 1 inch long.

Two perennial toadflaxes that in gardens are usually grown as annuals are *L. tristis* (syn. *L. melanantha*) and *L. triornithophora*. The formidable specific designation of *L. triornithophora* translates as "three birds" and alludes fancifully to the appearance of the blooms, which are violet, striped with purple, and have yellow or orange palates. They are 1½ inches long with spurs exceeding the corollas in length. This species, native to Spain and Portugal, attains a height of 3 or 4 feet. About 1 foot tall, *L. tristis* has linear leaves, the lower in whorls, the upper opposite, and brown or yellow blooms with dark brown or purple throats and thick, curved spurs as long as or shorter than the corollas. This species is a native of the Mediterranean region.

Annual linarias of horticultural interest include several rather pretty ones. The most common is *L. maroccana*, which, as its botanical name indicates, is a native of Morocco. It is 1 foot to 1½ feet tall, erect and branched, with narrow-linear, pointed leaves and long, slender, dense spikes of violet-purple flowers with small yellow or white palates and pointed spurs one-half as long again as the corollas. This is the kind, in its variety *L. m.* 'Excelsior', most frequently listed in seedsmen's catalogs.

Linaria maroccana

The seedsmen's variety includes plants with purple, blue, lilac, pink, yellow, and white flowers and is offered under such 'fancy' names as 'Fairy Bouquet', 'Northern Lights', and 'Diadem'. The purple-net toadflax (*L. reticulata*), of North Africa and Portugal, another attractive annual, is 3 to 4 feet tall, with glaucous, linear leaves. It has purple, conspicuously net-veined flowers with proportionately shorter spurs than those of *L. maroccana* that equal the corolla tubes in length. Variety *L. r. aureopurpurea* has deeper-colored blooms than those of the typical species. Sometimes called cloven-lip toadflax, *L. bipartita*, of North

Africa and Portugal, is one of the more attractive annual toadflaxes. Usually not over 1 foot in height, it has linear leaves and violet-purple flowers with orange palates, deeply-cleft upper lips, and curved spurs slightly shorter than the corollas. Varieties are *L. b. alba*, with white flowers, and *L. b. splendida*, with dark purple blooms. Native to Morocco, *L. gharbensis*, about 1¼ feet tall, has linear leaves and yellowish-white, violet-spurred flowers about 1 inch in length in nearly 1-foot-long spikes. It is an annual. From Morocco also comes *L. sapphirina*. This has narrow-linear leaves and dark blue, long-spurred flowers about ¾ inch long. The spurs are much longer than its corolla tubes.

Lower-growing annual toadflaxes of merit include *L. amethystea* (syn. *L. broussonnetii*) and *L. flava*, both 6 inches to 1 foot tall or a little taller and endemics of the Mediterranean region. With linear to lanceolate leaves up to ¾ inch long, *L. amethystea* has flowers that are lilac with pale yellow lower lips dotted with violet or are yellow, cream, or white, spotted with purple. Its lower leaves are in whorls. Yellow- or pale orange-flowered *L. flava* has lanceolate to ovate, stalkless leaves under ½ inch in length, and blooms, solitary or in clusters of up to five, about ½ inch long. Another interesting low annual is the Spanish *L. faucicola*, rarely over 6 inches tall, which has linear leaves and slender few-flowered racemes of straight-spurred deep violet blooms with paler throats.

Garden Uses. Although not among the most splendid of herbaceous perennials and annuals, toadflaxes have sufficient merit for them to warrant a respectable place in gardens, but their worth is underestimated and they are too rarely cultivated. Only the horticultural variety of the annual *L. maroccana* and, by rock gardeners, the alpine toadflax (*L. alpina*) are much grown. There are others as worthy. Even the ubiquitous butter-and-eggs (*L. vulgaris*) can be charming as a well-grown clump or colony adjacent to a large outcropping rock or boulder, springing from a chink in a dry wall, or as a restrained, tidy patch at the front of a flower border. Provided with fertile soil and freed of the competition of other plants, with which in the wild it must usually contend, it takes on something of a new look and blooms freely throughout late summer and fall. The taller growing perennial kinds, such as *L. genistifolia* and *L. g. dalmatica*, are appropriate for flower borders. The alpine toadflax (*L. alpina*) is a choice item for rock gardens and dry walls.

Annual toadflaxes are suitable for flower borders and beds and, the shorter ones, for rock gardens. The flowers of the taller ones, especially *L. maroccana* and *L. reticulata*, are useful for cutting. The florists' variety of the former, *L. m.* 'Excelsior', is to some extent grown in greenhouses for

late winter and spring bloom and is pretty as a pot plant for conservatory decoration.

Cultivation. Toadflaxes are easy to grow. All they need is full sun and soil porous enough to carry water away from their roots to the extent that they do not suffer from constantly "wet feet." This is an especially insistent need in the case of the alpine toadflax. They are moderate in their requirements as to the richness of the soil, an earth of rather low fertility is to be preferred to one that contains more abundant available nitrogen; the latter is likely to result in gross growth and flower displays less attractive than those in leaner soils.

All kinds are easily raised from seeds, and this is the method of necessity followed with the annuals, with such perennials as *L. triornithophora* and *L. tristis* that are grown as annuals, and with kinds cultivated as perennials, when stock for dividing is not available in sufficient quantities. Seeds of perennial toadflaxes give good results when sown in cold frames or outdoor seed beds in May or started earlier in containers indoors. The seedlings are transplanted to nursery beds and are big enough to be transferred to their permanent locations the following spring.

Seeds of the annuals are sown in early spring where the plants are to bloom and are covered with soil to a depth of about ¼ inch. For ornamental plantings they are broadcast, for cut flower production scattered in rows 1 foot to 1½ feet apart. The seedlings are thinned out, those of the taller growers, such as *L. maroccana*, to about 6 inches apart if in patches, 3 or 4 inches apart if grown in rows; the low kinds suitable for rock gardens are thinned to stand 3 to 4 inches apart. No special care during the growing season is needed; the taller kinds may need a little support from twiggy brushwood inserted between the plants or from strings strung between stakes set alongside the rows.

For early bloom in greenhouses, seeds are sown from late August to January. A good method is to scatter a few seeds in 3- or 4-inch pots filled with ordinary fertile, porous potting soil, to cover them with soil to a depth of ⅛ inch and later, when the pots are filled with roots, to repot into containers of 5 or 6 inches diameter. Other methods are to sow directly in 5- or 6-inch pots and grow the seedlings on without repotting or to sow in pots or flats and transplant the seedlings as soon as they are big enough to handle comfortably the 5- or 6-inch pots in which they are to bloom. If the latter method is followed the seedlings are set three to a 5-inch or five to a 6-inch pot. If the seedlings are grown on without transplanting, they are thinned out while small to the same spacing. Annual linarias must be grown under cool conditions and in full sun. At night through the winter the temperature should be held at 45 to 50°F, and as soon as the day temperature exceeds the night minimum by five to ten degrees the green-house ventilators must be opened to admit as much air as weather conditions permit. The atmosphere should never be dank or oppressively humid. The plants need staking unobtrusively before they begin to topple. Watering should be done with caution, especially during the early stages of the growth of the plants and during dull weather. Let the soil dry appreciably between waterings, but not of course to the extent that the plants wilt. As spring approaches and the final pots are filled with active roots, but not until then, weekly applications of dilute liquid fertilizer may be supplied with benefit.

For flowers for cutting seeds may be sown in early fall in greenhouse ground beds or in benches in rows about 6 inches apart and the seedlings thinned to 3 or 4 inches apart. Quite good results can be had by sowing in 3- to 4-inch-deep flats, thinning the young plants to about 4 inches apart, and allowing them to bloom in the flats.

Diseases and Pests. Linarias are subject to root and stem rots and may be harmed by aphids, flea beetles, and nematodes.

LINDELOFIA (Lin-delòfia). Differing from *Cynoglossum* in having stamens that protrude from the throats of the flowers, *Lindelofia* consists of ten species of temperate Asia. It belongs in the borage family BORAGINACEAE and was named to honor Friedrich von Lindelof, a mid-nineteenth-century German patron of botany.

Lindelofias are hardy herbaceous perennials with undivided leaves and small blue to purple flowers in long racemes that curve in the fashion of those of forget-me-nots, hounds' tongues, and others of the borage relationship. The blooms have five-lobed calyxes and cylindrical corolla tubes with five blunt, spreading lobes (petals) and cone-shaped scales in their throats. There are five stamens. The ovary is four-lobed and the fruits consist of four nutlets, often thought of as seeds, with hooked bristles.

Native to the Himalayas, *L. longiflora* (syn. *L. spectabilis*) is a worthwhile, easy-to-grow plant that in bloom suggests an anchusa or a hound's tongue (*Cynoglossum*). It is 1 foot to 2 feet tall and hairy throughout. Its leaves have prominent mid-veins. The basal ones are stalked, and ovate-elliptic to pointed-oblong and 3 to 4 inches in length. Its many stem leaves are oblong to oblong-lanceolate, stalkless, and are somewhat smaller than the basal ones.

There is considerable variation in flower size and color. Ordinarily the blooms are rather more than ¼ inch across. The best forms are glorious gentian blue without suspicion of less desirable hues, but often they are in the rosy-purple range and then are less exciting, although still pleasing, especially if planted near pale yellow or white flowers. This species blooms in May at The New York Botanical Garden.

Garden Uses and Cultivation. Rock gardens and the fronts of flower borders are suitable locations for lindelofias. Unlike so many Himalayan plants, the kind described can be grown in eastern North America with little trouble. In climates as cold as that of southern New York it is grateful for a place sheltered a little from the full severity of winter, and sharp soil drainage is a must. It adapts to ordinary garden earths and is readily propagated by division (the sensible way of increasing stocks of particularly good forms) and by seed. Seedlings bloom in their second year.

LINDEN. See Tilia.

LINDERA (Lindèr-a) — Spice Bush. Although there are 100 species of trees and shrubs in *Lindera*, of the laurel family LAURACEAE, only one is well known in gardens. A very few others are cultivated in special collections. The name of the group honors Johann Linder, a Swedish botanist and physician, who died in 1723.

Linderas, deciduous and evergreen aromatic trees and shrubs chiefly indigenous to Asia, are represented by two species in the native flora of North America. Linderas have lobeless or lobed leaves and small flowers in clusters in the leaf axils. Each cluster has a collar of four scales or bracts. The flowers are unisexual, without petals, and usually have six sepals, the males nine stamens, the females a spherical ovary and nine to fifteen abortive stamens called staminodes. The fruits are berry-like. The North American native kinds have been used medicinally and their leaves as a substitute for tea. Other plants sometimes included belong in *Parabenzoin*.

The spice bush (**L. benzoin** syn. *Benzoin aestivale*) is a common native of moist woods and lowlands from Maine to Ontario, Kansas, Florida, and Texas, where it lights the fall landscape with its brilliant

Lindera benzoin (flowers)

yellow foliage and delights in late winter and early spring with branches modestly wreathed with its clusters of slightly greenish, yellow blooms that appear before the leaves. It is easily identified by the spicy odor its twigs emit when bruised or broken, one reminiscent of that of its close relative, the sassafras. The spice bush is a dense shrub up to 15 feet in height with shoots with little or no pubescence, and alternate, hairless or nearly hairless oblong-obovate, short-stalked, pinnate-veined leaves up to 5 inches long and paler beneath than on their upper sides. The scarlet fruits are about ⅓ inch long. A variety, *L. b. xanthocarpa*, has yellow fruits, another, *L. b. pubescens*, has leaves with hairs on the veins beneath and fringing their margins. The only other native American species is **L. melissaefolia**, a shrub native to swamps and watersides from North Carolina to Illinois, Missouri, and Florida. Up to 10 feet tall, it has pubescent shoots and elliptic-ovate leaves up to 5 inches long that are narrower than those of *L. benzoin*.

A native of Japan, China, and Korea, **L. obtusiloba** is a deciduous, tall shrub or small tree up to 30 feet in height. It has broadly-ovate leaves, usually three-lobed at their ends, prominently three-veined, and dark glossy green above and softly-hairy on the veins beneath. The flowers are yellow, the fruits black. This species is hardy in sheltered locations in southern New England. Another deciduous sort, a native of Japan and China, is **L. umbellata**, which blooms when in leaf rather than on leafless shoots. Its flowers are yellow and in 1-inch-wide, silky-hairy clusters. Its leaves are elliptic-obovate to obovate-oblong and are slightly glaucous on their undersides. Their veins are pinnately-arranged. The black fruits are about ⅓ inch long. This is probably hardy as far north as Long Island, New York.

Evergreen **L. megaphylla**, native to China, is a shrub or tree sometimes 65 feet in height. It has purplish-brown shoots and oblong to lanceolate leaves 4 to 9 inches long and 1 inch to 2¼ inches broad, lustrous green with paler undersurfaces. The yellow flowers are in silky-hairy clusters about 1 inch across. The black fruits are nearly ¾ inch long. This is not hardy in the north.

Garden and Landscape Uses. Linderas are essentially plants for informal landscapes and can be used to good purpose in open woods and at the fringes of woodlands where the soil is damp and they receive a little shade. The only kind likely to be at all commonly cultivated is the native spice bush (*L. benzoin*).

Cultivation. Linderas can be raised from seeds sown as soon as ripe or shortly afterward in sandy peaty soil kept uniformly moist. The seeds do not retain their germinating power for long, especially if they are permitted to dry. They can also be increased by summer cuttings, preferably placed under mist, and by layering. They thrive in any ordinary neutral or somewhat acid soil that is at least moderately moist, and transplant without undue difficulty. If plants are dug from the wild they should be pruned so that the top of the plant is reduced to one-half its original size. This is usually best accomplished by removing some branches completely and shortening others. Established specimens need little or no care. If they become ungainly they may be pruned back fairly severely at intervals of a few years. They need no regular, systematic pruning.

LINDERNIA (Lind-èrnia)—False-Pimpernel, Carpet-Pimpernel. Chiefly tropical and subtropical, but with a few sorts native of temperate regions, *Lindernia*, accepted here as including plants by some botanists segregated as *Ilysanthes*, is little known horticulturally. It consists of about eighty species of the figwort family SCROPHULARIACEAE. The name commemorates Franz B. Lindern, German botanist and physician, who died in 1755.

Lindernias include annuals, biennials, and herbaceous perennials, mostly low and with opposite, toothed or toothless leaves. The flowers, solitary from the leaf axils, have five sepals, a tubular or funnel-shaped, two-lipped corolla, two stamens or two stamens and two staminodes (infertile stamens), a long style, and two stigmas. The fruits are capsules.

The carpet-pimpernel (*L. grandiflora* syn. *Ilysanthes grandiflora*) is native to Florida and Georgia. In moist sandy places and at roadsides it forms solid carpets of greenery sprinkled in season with blooms that at a casual glance suggest those of *Veronica* or *Mazus*. The leaves are opposite, stalkless, from nearly round to somewhat kidney-shaped, ¼ to ½ inch long, with sometimes a few shallow teeth. The slender-stalked blooms, solitary from the leaf axils, are attractive and ⅜ inch or a little more in diameter. They have a lower lip of

Lindernia grandiflora

three large, lilac or white lobes (petals), each with a pair of violet spots. The upper lip, very much smaller and notched at its apex, is white or whitish. There are two fertile stamens and two staminodes (infertile stamens).

Garden Uses and Cultivation. Not hardy in the north, in mild climates this can be used in rock gardens and similar places. It also is quite charming in pots and hanging baskets in greenhouses and windows. It propagates readily by division and from cuttings and seed and thrives in any porous soil kept moderately moist.

LINDHEIMERA (Lindheìm-era). One species constitutes *Lindheimera*, of the daisy family COMPOSITAE. Its name commemorates Ferdinand Jacob Lindheimer, discoverer of the genus, who died in 1879.

A native of Texas, *L. texana* is 2 to 3 feet tall and rough-hairy. It has reddish stems usually branched in their upper parts, furnished with generally opposite, or stalkless, spatula-shaped to ovate-lanceolate leaves up to 1½ inches long and often somewhat toothed. The daisy-like flower heads, about 1 inch in diameter, have five, broad-ovate, golden-yellow to cream ray florets and a yellow central eye. There are a number of leafy bracts beneath the flower heads. The flowers are produced in profusion.

Lindheimera texana

Garden Uses and Cultivation. The chief value of this annual is to add variety and color to summer beds and borders. Its blooms are not suitable for cut flowers. It needs full sun and porous, well-drained garden soil of moderate fertility.

Cultivation. Seeds sown outdoors in spring give satisfactory results if the seedlings are thinned so the plants stand about 6 inches apart. Or seeds may be sown earlier indoors and the young plants grown in flats or individually in 3-inch pots for transplanting to the garden after all danger from frost is passed. When the latter plan is followed the seeds are sown about

eight weeks before planting out time. To induce branching it is advisable to pinch out the tips of the young plants when they are about 4 inches high. Flowering begins about twelve weeks from seed sowing and continues for a long season. Ordinarily this plant stands without staking and no particular care is needed beyond that necessary to keep down weeds and remove faded flower heads.

LINDMANIA. See Fosterella.

LINEAR. Long and narrow with parallel or nearly parallel sides. The leaves of many grasses are linear.

LINGARO is *Elaeagnus philippensis*.

LIGONBERRY is *Vaccinium vitis-idaea*.

LINK VINE is *Vanilla barbellata*.

LINNAEA (Linn-aèa)—Twin-Flower. The smallest member of the very considerable honeysuckle family CAPRIFOLIACEAE, which contains such well-known garden plants as elderberries, snowberries, viburnums, and honeysuckles, and the only species of *Linnaea*, the twin-flower is a native of cool moist woods and bogs throughout the temperate regions of the northern hemisphere. The common American representative of the species differs slightly from the European and Asian populations in having slightly longer and more tubular flowers. Because of this it is named *L. borealis americana*. In Alaska both the typical species and the variety occur. The botanical name honors the father of modern botany, the great Karl von Linnè, known to the world by the latinized form of his name Linnaeus. It is said that Linnaeus loved this little flower above others, and portraits of him invariably depict a sprig in his buttonhole or hand.

The twin-flower (*L. procumbens*) is an exquisite low plant with slender, prostrate, warm-brown, branching stems that trail over mossy rocks and rotting logs on shaded woodland floors. Its tiny, opposite, stalked, nearly round, evergreen leaves, ¼ to 1 inch long, are few-toothed and medium green. The bell-shaped, nodding, delightfully fragrant blooms are held aloft on slender, erect stems 2 to 3 inches long. Each carries two five-petaled flowers, those of *L. borealis* less than ⅓ inch long, but those of *L. b. americana* up to ½ inch. They are deep pink to white, hairy on the inside, and have four stamens, two long and two short, and a solitary pistil. The flowers are pollinated by a particular beetle and a tiny gnat. The fruits of the twin-flower are yellow, round, and about ⅛ inch in diameter; each has a single seed.

Garden Uses and Cultivation. Notoriously difficult to establish in gardens, this little plant can test the patience and

Linnaea borealis americana

Linum perenne

the skill as a cultivator of even the most accomplished gardener. Obviously, the fortunate possessor of a cold, humid, acid woodland that favors the growth of mosses and such plants as partridge berry, gold thread, and creeping snowberry, stands the best chance of success, but even then persuading the twin-flower to become a permanent resident is likely to prove futile. One can only try. An obvious place to attempt this is in choice locations in woodland gardens and rock gardens. This plant must have a strongly acid soil and plenty of moisture, but with good drainage. Shade is needed. Except in the mountains the twin-flower cannot be expected to prosper south of New England. It may be propagated by careful division in early summer, by cuttings taken with a heel (sliver of the stem from which the shoot used as the cutting arises) at their bases, and seed sown in acid peaty soil under cold frame conditions.

LINOSPADIX (Linospà-dix). A dozen species, natives of Australia and New Guinea, are included in *Linospadix*, of the palm family PALMAE. The name is derived from the Greek *linon*, flax or thread, and *spadix*, a spike of small flowers attended by a spathe or bract. It alludes to the stalks of the inflorescences (flower clusters). The group is little known in American horticulture, but one species has been recently introduced.

The Australian walking stick palm (*L. monostachya*) has an erect stem up to 10 feet in height and 1½ inches in diameter with the dark green leaves in a tuft at its termination. The leaves are 8 inches to 1 foot long, and the basal parts of their stalks sheath the stem. The ends of the leaflets are ragged. From among the leaves the long, slender, branchless, tail-like flower spikes, bearing flowers of both sexes, arch downward. The flowers, like the fruits, are green.

Garden and Landscape Uses and Cultivation. This miniature palm promises to be very suitable for cultivation in partial shade

in any ordinary garden soil not excessively dry. It may be expected to prosper outdoors in southern Florida, the warmest parts of California, and Hawaii. It probably will not stand frost. It is likely to be very satisfactory in greenhouses and perhaps as a houseplant. The most suitable greenhouse environment is one that assures a humid atmosphere, shade from strong sun, a minimum winter night temperature of 60 to 65°F, with higher temperatures by day and at other times of the year, and a fertile porous soil kept always evenly moist. Its seeds, about the size of wheat grains, germinate in four or five months if sown in sandy, peaty soil in a temperature of 75 to 90°F. For further information see Palms.

LINOSYRIS VULGARIS is *Aster linosyris*.

LINSEED. Seeds of common flax (*Linum usitatissimum*), used medicinally and as the source of linseed oil are known as linseed.

LINUM (Lìn-um)—Flax. The genus *Linum* is the type of the flax family LINACEAE. It contains 230 species, natives of many parts of the world, but chiefly temperate regions. Most sorts are herbaceous, a few are subshrubs. They include annuals, biennials, and perennials. The name is the Latin one for the common flax.

Flaxes characteristically have fine foliage. Their leaves are usually alternate and mostly narrow. They are stalkless and without lobing or toothing. The blue, white, yellow, or red flowers, in mostly loose, terminal clusters have five sepals and five petals that are shed after the blooms have been open a few hours in the morning. There are five stamens and five styles. The fruits are capsules.

Common flax (*L. usitatissimum*) is of considerable commercial importance as the source of the fiber from which linen is made and of the seeds from which linseed oil is expressed. This, the most important of the drying oils, is used chiefly in paints and varnishes and for making printer's ink and linoleum. Flax seed is used medicinally for poultices. Flax fibers are exceedingly strong and have been used by man since prehistoric times, certainly as far back as the Swiss Lake Dwellers, who are the earliest Europeans of which remains exist. The cloths in which the Egyptians wrapped their mummies were of linen and so were some of the clothes they wore. The respect the Egyptians had for the flax plant is indicated by the carvings of it that decorate their tombs.

Ornamental flaxes are numerous and include many delightful plants. Among perennial kinds, European *L. perenne* is one of the most popular. Of light and almost frail appearance, this grows up to 2 feet in height and has several to many erect, slender stems usually bare of leaves in their lower parts, but abundantly clothed with

Linum perenne (flowers)

bluish-green, narrowly-linear leaves above. The leaves are up to 1 inch long. The blue flowers, about 1 inch in diameter, have petals that do not overlap. A white-flowered variety is *L. p. album*. Differing but slightly except that it is somewhat more robust and may attain a height of 3 feet is the prairie flax (*L. p. lewisii* syn. *L. lewisii*), of western North America north to Alaska. The leaves of this are up to 1¼ inches long. Rarely exceeding 1 foot, but occasionally up to 1½ feet tall, *L. p. alpinum* (syn. *L. alpinum*) of Europe differs from typical *L. perenne* in having smaller, narrower leaves up to ¾ inch long, less loosely branched flower clusters, and blooms with petals that overlap all along their margins. Another not dissimilar flax is *L. narbonense*, which is about 2 feet tall and has stoutish stems furnished with ¾-inch-long leaves. Its white-eyed, blue flowers are up to 1¾ inches in diameter. It has longer stigmas and longer sepals and is a sturdier plant than *L. perenne*. Variety *L. n. album* has white flowers. This species has its home in the Mediterranean region. Entirely different is the golden flax (*L. flavum*). This native of southern and central Europe has broader leaves than any of the above. Its lower ones are bluntly-obovate, those above narrower and more pointed. At each side of the base of the leaf there is a gland. The flowers,

Linum flavum

rich golden-yellow, and 1 inch in diameter, are numerous in the clusters. The golden flax attains a height of about 2 feet and has stems that become slightly woody at their bases. Variety *L. f. compactum* is shorter.

Hardy only in climates not markedly more severe than that of New York City, partially evergreen, more or less prostrate, *L. suffruticosum salsoloides* (syn. *L. salsoloides*), of southern Europe, has needle-like to linear-lanceolate leaves up to 1¾ inches long, but often much shorter, and usually mostly near the ends of the stems, and purple- or violet-veined, white flowers up to 1 inch in diameter. The sepals are somewhat fringed with glandular hairs. A dwarf form not exceeding 3 or 4 inches in height, *L. s. nanum* is prostrate and usually has longer leaves. It forms patches up to 1½ feet across. The typical species *L. suffruticosum* does not seem to be cultivated.

A red-flowered species is the finest annual flax. This showy native of North Africa, *L. grandiflorum*, is 2 to 3 feet tall and has slender, branched stems with narrow, pointed leaves and broad-petaled flowers 1½ inches across of a good clear red to a purplish-red hue. It has become naturalized in some parts of North America. Variety *L. g. caeruleum* unfortunately does not

live up to the expectations of its varietal name. Its blooms are violet to bluish-purple. Variety *L. g. coccineum* has nearly scarlet blooms. The flowers of *L. g. roseum* are pink, those of *L. g. rubrum* bright red.

Blue-flowered annual flaxes worth cultivating are only two, the common flax (*L. usitatissimum*) and quite charming *L. bienne* (syn. *L. augustifolium*). The origin of the common flax is unknown but is certainly Old World. Most likely it hails from southwestern Asia. This species is naturalized in most of the United States and southern Canada and inhabits roadsides and fields. Up to 4 feet tall, *L. usitatissimum* has slender stems, linear-lanceolate leaves, and bright blue flowers ½ inch in diameter. Differing from common flax in the inner sepals of its flowers being longer (one-half as long as the petals) and fringed with hairs, *L. angustifolium*, of the Mediterranean region, about 2 feet tall, has linear to needle-form leaves and blue flowers up to ½ inch across. It sometimes behaves as a short-lived perennial.

Yellow is the predominant flower color among cultivated annual flaxes, and one rather pretty kind native to North America with blooms of this hue is *L. sulcatum*, a species widespread east of the Rocky Mountains, especially favoring dry, sandy soils. It has erect stems, branched above, and narrowly-lanceolate leaves almost 1 inch long. The flowers are ½ inch across. With blooms one-half the size of those of *L. sulcatum*, the European yellow-flowered natives *L. gallicum* and *L. strictum* are sometimes cultivated. Both inhabit the Mediterranean region and central Europe and are 1¼ to 1½ feet tall. Its more or less lanceolate, pointed leaves almost ¾ inch long, with their margins only slightly rolled back, *L. gallicum* has blooms in lax, open clusters. The sepals are not longer than the seed pods. The flowers of *L. strictum* are in tight, compact clusters or heads, a characteristic responsible for its very distinctive appearance. Its linear-lanceolate leaves are 1 inch long and have margins markedly rolled under. The sepals are much longer than the seed pods. A biennial, *L. corymbiferum* is a native of southern Europe. It has hairy stems and is 1½ feet tall or slightly taller. The linear-lanceolate leaves have edges fringed with hairs, midribs that are downy. They are up to ¾ inch long. The bright yellow blooms of this species, ½ inch in diameter, have sepals fringed with glandular hairs.

Additional kinds, all perennials, include these: *L. africanum*, of tropical Africa, is nonhardy, shrubby, and 3 feet tall, with mostly opposite, linear to ovate leaves and small yellow flowers. *L. arboreum* is a shrubby, not hardy native of the eastern Mediterranean region. About 2 feet in height, it has glaucous, obovate leaves and clear yellow blooms up to 1½ inches across. They are in few-flowered clusters.

L. aretioides differs from all other species here discussed. It forms a tight cushion of branched, woody stems about 2 inches in height. The leaves are tiny and the golden flowers nearly stemless. This choice alpine comes from the mountains of Europe. *L. campanulatum*, of southern Europe, about 1¼ feet in height and woody at the base, has lanceolate or spatula-shaped leaves with a tiny gland at each side of their bases. The flowers, pale yellow with orange veins, are up to 2 inches across. *L. hirsutum*, which inhabits central Europe and the Mediterranean region, and is 1 foot to 2 feet tall, has broadly-lanceolate leaves a little over ½ inch long and lavender to white flowers up to 2 inches wide. As its name indicates, this is usually a hairy species, but an almost hairless form is in cultivation. *L. hologynum*, from the central European mountains, up to 2 feet in height, has linear-lanceolate leaves and blue flowers 1 inch in diameter that have their stamens twisted or joined for about one-half their lengths. *L. monogynum* is a not-too-hardy, somewhat shrubby, New Zealander with narrow, linear-lanceolate leaves and clusters of 1-inch-wide, white flowers. It is 2 feet tall. *L. nervosum* comes from eastern Europe and has stems usually pubescent on their lower parts. It is 1½ feet tall and has lanceolate leaves and blue flowers about 1½ inches in diameter. *L. rigidum*, of western North America, attains a height of about 1½ feet and has linear, erect leaves and yellow flowers 1¼ inches in diameter. Their sepals are glandular along their margins. *L. suffruticosum* is a tender, shrubby, much-branched perennial densely covered with short hairs and about 8 inches in height. It has densely-clustered linear to awl-shaped leaves, ⅜ inch long, and few-flowered clusters of 1-inch-wide blue blooms. This is native to southern Europe. *L. tenuifolium* is somewhat like *L. salsoloides*, but taller, coarser, and looser. It is European. It has linear-lanceolate to awl-shaped leaves and lilac-pink or purple-veined or purple-centered white flowers about 1-inch across. The sepals are glandular-margined. *L. viscosum*, up to 2 feet tall, has oblong-lanceolate leaves with margins fringed with glandular hairs and violet-veined, pink flowers 1¼ inches in diameter. Its sepals also have glandular-hairy edges. This is a native of southern Europe.

Garden Uses. Flaxes are for many locations and best suited for light, well-drained soils. They bloom profusely and make colorful summer displays for quite long periods. As cut flowers they have little merit because their petals drop a few hours after the blooms open. Chiefly, these are plants for flower beds and borders and the lower ones, such as *L. alpinum*, the dwarf form of *L. suffruticosum salsoloides* (often grown as *L. salsoloides nanum*), and that marvelous alpine gem *L. aretioides*, for rock gardens.

Linum grandiflorum

For the latter use the dwarf form of *L. suffruticosum salsoloides* is especially recommended. The annuals are also delightful when grown in pots for late winter and spring embellishment of display greenhouses and conservatories.

Cultivation. The flaxes give little trouble to gardeners. All are raised from seeds with the greatest ease. Those of perennial kinds are sown in May or June in an outdoor seed bed or a cold frame. The seedlings are transplanted to nursery beds where they complete their summer growth and are set out in their permanent locations in fall or the following spring. Seeds of annual flaxes are sown either in early spring or in late fall where the plants are to bloom, and the seedlings are thinned to about 4 inches apart. The biennial *L. corymbiferum* is treated in the same way as the annual kinds, except that its seeds are sown early in fall or in late summer so that the plants have time to make appreciable growth before winter. It is possible to increase perennial flaxes from cuttings, but because seeds grow so readily and are usually available they generally provide the preferred method of propagation. A kind that is increased by cuttings, made in early summer and rooted in a humid cold frame or under mist, is the dwarf form of *L. suffruticosum salsoloides*.

When annual flaxes are to be grown in pots in greenhouses the seeds are sown, in porous soil, in the containers in which the plants remain. This is done in September. The seedlings are thinned so that six or seven are left in each pot and are grown in full sun in a night temperature of 50°F. By day the temperature may rise five to ten degrees. Considerable care must be exercised in watering, especially during the early stages of growth and during the period when days are short and light intensity is comparatively low. With the coming of spring generous watering is in order, but at any time a constantly wet condition of the soil is detrimental. It should always be permitted to become dryish between waterings. Little in the way of fertilizing is necessary or even desirable, but it may be helpful to give occasional applications of dilute liquid fertilizer after the plants have filled the pots with roots and before they open their flowers.

LION'S EAR or LION'S TAIL. See Leonotis.

LIPARIS (Líp-aris)—Twayblade. Ground orchids closely related to *Malaxis* constitute this nearly cosmopolitan genus of 250 species. They belong to the orchid family ORCHIDACEAE. The name, alluding to the shining leaves, is from the Greek *liparos*, fat or greasy. One of the only three representatives of the orchid family native to the Hawaiian Islands is *Liparis hawaiiensis*. The vernacular name twayblade is also applied to *Listera*.

Twayblades have small, usually subterranean pseudobulbs or swollen bases to their stems and few leaves. The small flowers are in terminal racemes, the stalks of which are leafless. They have three sepals, two petals much like them, but often rolled so that they appear threadlike, a three-lobed or lobeless lip, and a short column. There is one anther. In addition to the species described below, *L. nervosa* (syn. *L. elata*), a species of pantropical natural distribution, occurs in the United States in Florida where it grows in swamps and drier habitats.

Found in rich woodlands from Maine to Minnesota, Missouri, Georgia, and Alabama, *L. liliifolia* has usually two elliptic to broad-elliptic leaves 2 to 7 inches long by one-third to one-half as wide, and some scale leaves below them. The fairly showy flowers are in loose racemes of five to thirty, carried to heights of 4 to 9 inches. About 1 inch across, they have slender, linear-oblong, greenish-white, spreading sepals and greenish or light purple, threadlike petals. The broadly-ovate to lozenge-shaped lip is pale purple. The column is very short. From the last, *L. loeselii* differs in having flowers about one-half as large. They have yellowish-green lips with turned-up margins. This inhabits humid and wet woodlands from Nova Scotia to Manitoba, New Jersey, and Ohio and occurs also in Europe and temperate Asia.

Liparis liliifolia

Garden Uses and Cultivation. These North American twayblades are best suited for woodlands, native plant gardens, and rock gardens. As with most native orchids, they are best accommodated under conditions that approximate as closely as possible those of their native woodlands. They need soil with an appreciable organic content and shade from direct sun. For *L. lilifolia* a well-drained location is essential; *L. loeselii* thrives best at shaded watersides. They should be planted fairly shallowly, and the ground mulched with leaf mold or peat moss. For further information see Orchids.

LIPPIA. See *Aloysia* and *Phyla*.

LIPSTICK PLANT is *Aeschynanthus radicans*, lipstick tree *Bixa orellana*.

LIQUID FERTILIZER. Plant nutrients applied in water solutions are called liquid fertilizers. Chiefly they supply nitrogen, phosphorus, and potassium, sometimes lesser amounts of trace elements. They are a convenient means of supplementing soil fertility and especially of keeping plants in pots, tubs, and other containers growing satisfactorily after they have filled their available soil with roots. For foliar feeding they are used exclusively.

Commercially prepared liquid fertilizers, usually containing all three of the major nutrient elements just mentioned, are available under many brand names. Mostly they are sold as concentrated solutions needing only the addition of water before application, sometimes they come in powders, cartridges, or other solid forms for dissolving in water. Always use these in strict accordance with the manufacturers' directions, erring if at all in the direction of overdilution rather than using them in too strong concentrations.

Dissolvable fertilizers, such as nitrate of soda, sulfate of ammonia, and urea can be mixed in small amounts with water and used as liquid fertilizers. See also Liquid Manure.

LIQUID MANURE. An old-fashioned and highly effective stimulant to plant growth, liquid manure is made by steeping manure, usually cow, horse, or chicken, for a week or more in water, straining out the solid portions, and diluting the resulting liquid to the appropriate strength before applying it to the soil.

The advise is often given to use old, rotted manure for this purpose, but fresh or partly rotted material is to be preferred. The procedure is to tie one-half a bushel of cow or horse manure or one-half that amount of chicken manure in a burlap sack and steep it in about fifteen gallons of water. At time of use the resulting liquid is diluted in the proportion of about one to three of water. Because of variances in the nutrient qualities of manures, the amounts suggested here are only approximations. Some little experience is needed to gauge the strengths to use. The advice given by British gardeners to dilute liquid manure to the color of weak tea is scarcely definitive enough. As with all fertilizers it is better to use liquid manure at less than the maximum strength the plants will accept without damage and to make more frequent applications than would be wise if maximum acceptable-strength dilutions were given.

LIQUIDAMBAR (Liquid-ámbar)—Sweet Gum. The sweet gum of eastern North

America, like many another native plant of the region, has its only close relatives in eastern Asia, a circumstance that argues strongly for the one-time existence of a land bridge between Asia and America. Abundant fossils indicate that the genus to which it belongs formerly inhabited Europe, but disappeared from that continent during the ice age. There are six species of *Liquidambar*, all but one Asian. They are deciduous trees of the witch hazel family HAMAMELIDACEAE. The generic name is from the Latin *liquidus*, liquid, and the Arabic *ambar*, amber. It alludes to a fragrant resin produced by these trees.

Sweet gums are stately. They have abundant foliage that in fall assumes astonishingly brilliant hues. The leaves are maple-like or starlike, with three to seven pointed, toothed lobes. Mostly unisexual, the minute flowers, without sepals or petals, are densely packed in spherical clusters, those of female blooms solitary, those of males in short racemes. The male flowers consist of numerous stamens, the females of an ovary with two long styles. They are interspersed with small scales or bristles. The fruits, small, beaked, woody capsules with persistent protruding styles, are in compact, spherical, pendent heads.

Sweet gums are important commercially as sources of lumber and of balsamic resins called styrax or storax. The wood is extensively employed for interior trim, furniture, veneers, boxes, and barrels. The resins are used in incense and perfumes, to scent soaps, cosmetics, and medicines, and to flavor tobacco. That known as Levant styrax is a product of *L. orientalis*. American styrax comes from *L. styraciflua*. Its commercial source is Central America.

The American sweet gum (**L. styraciflua**) occurs natively from Connecticut to Illinois, Florida, Mexico, and Central America and is abundant through much of its range. Characteristically, it has a tall, straight trunk, often buttressed at its base, and is of comely habit. In its youth and middle years pyramidal, with age it is likely to develop an oval or rounded crown. It attains heights of 125 to 150 feet. The branchlets of the sweet gum usually have corky wings. Its glossy, long-stalked leaves, 4 to 7 inches across, at maturity hairless except for tufts in the leaf axils beneath, have usually five or seven pointed lobes. Their margins are finely-toothed. When crushed, the leaves are pleasantly fragrant. The terminal racemes of male flowers are 2 to 3 inches long. The clusters of females, after pollination, develop into long-stalked globular spiny seed heads, about 1¼ inches in diameter, that remain throughout the winter.

There are several varieties of the American sweet gum. In *L. s. aurea* the foliage is irregularly variegated with yellow. Variety *L. s.* 'Palo Alto' colors very uniformly brilliant orange-red in fall. Pendulous

Liquidambar styraciflua

Liquidambar styraciflua (trunk)

Liquidambar styraciflua (male and female flowers)

Liquidambar styraciflua (fruits)

branches and an arching leading shoot are characteristics of *L. s. pendula*. Variety *L. s. rotundiloba* has lobes that are short and rounded with less distinct teeth than those of the typical species.

Native to Taiwan and southern China, **L. formosana** is distinct from its American relative in that its branchlets are without corky ridges or wings and its leaves, which are 3½ to 6 inches across, have only three lobes. They are often hairy on the veins beneath and sometimes over the entire under surface. This species is not hardy north of Virginia, but its variety *L. f. monticola* is more cold-tolerant and may succeed as far north as New Jersey. The variety differs from the typical species in its leaves having wedge-shaped, or rounded, rather than heart-shaped bases and in being always hairless.

Rare in cultivation in North America, slow-growing **L. orientalis** is reported to attain a height of 100 feet in its natural range, but often is not over 60 feet, and may be smaller in cultivation. Native to western Asia, it has leaves 2½ to 3½ inches in diameter, usually five-lobed, and with each of the lobes again lobed and toothed in such a way that the leaves resemble those of certain Japanese maples.

Garden and Landscape Uses. Except in arboretums and other special collections, the only sweet gums likely to be much cultivated in America are the native species and its varieties. A magnificent, shapely shade and ornamental tree, it is well adapted for parks, parkways, and home grounds. Beautiful at all seasons, in fall it presents a superb display of foliage color in tones of orange, flame, scarlet, and mauve. The sweet gum is a sun-lover. It will not tolerate shade. Always it should be allowed ample room for development and display, never should it be crowded among other trees. It succeeds in a variety of soils, but prefers those that are fertile, moist, but well drained, and deep.

Cultivation. Once established, sweet gums give little or no trouble. In some places, however, their fallen seed heads, which are abundant, persistent, and uncomfortable to step on, may be something of a nuisance unless kept raked or brushed up. They are rather difficult to transplant, especially in large sizes, and special care to preserve intact as many roots as possible must be taken. Root pruning, performed a year before transplanting is done, is sound preparation for the operation. Propagation is usually by seed. These may be sown in fall in a cold frame or outdoor bed protected from rodents or be stored dry and then stratified prior to being sown in a greenhouse, cold frame, or outdoors in spring. Stratification is accomplished by placing them in a mixture of slightly moist sand and peat moss in a tightly closed polyethylene bag in a refrigerator where the temperature is about 40°F and leaving them for ten or twelve weeks. The seeds, which must be sown promptly on removal from the refrigerator, usually germinate within about three weeks.

LIRIODENDRON (Liriodén-dron)—Tulip Tree. For long it was supposed that there was only one species of *Liriodendron,* the well-known tulip tree of North America. This attracted the attention of early colonists and was introduced to cultivation in Europe as early as 1663. In 1875 a second species was discovered in central China. Tulip trees belong in the magnolia family MAGNOLIACEAE. Their name is from the Greek *leirion,* lily, and *dendron,* a tree, and refers to the form of the flowers. Fossil records clearly indicate that the genus once had a much wider natural distribution than at present. In preglacial times it was present in Alaska, Greenland, and Europe, areas where it is not now indigenous.

Tulip trees are deciduous and readily distinguished by their alternate, few-lobed, saddle-shaped leaves, about as broad as they are long, and by their large and very handsome, solitary, greenish-yellow, up-facing, tulip-like flowers. The flowers are marked on their insides with bright orange blotches, are delicately fragrant, and have three reflexed sepals, six petals, many stamens, and many pistils. The fruits are also distinctive. They are technically samaras, flattened and winged like those of the tree of heaven (*Ailanthus*), but attached to a central axis to form a conelike structure that remains attached well into the winter. In addition to being a handsome ornamental, the American tulip tree is of great commercial importance as a source of lumber, which is marketed as yellow poplar, poplar, and whitewood. It is used for building, interior trim, fixtures, moldings, framing, furniture, and for boxes and crates.

The American tulip tree (**L. tulipifera**) is one of the noblest denizens of the forests of North America. Its natural range extends from Vermont to Michigan, Florida, and Louisiana. Exceptionally, it attains a height of 200 feet. It has a straight trunk,

(b) In winter

under forest conditions free of branches for two-thirds or more of the height of the tree. Its leaves, up to 5 inches long and wide, are paler on their undersides than above. The cup-shaped flowers have petals 1½ to 2 inches long. The fruit cones are up to 3 inches long. Standing in a grove of these stately giants, one cannot help but compare their towering trunks to the interior columns of some vast cathedral. They typify Longfellow's forest primeval.

Liriodendron tulipifera (trunk)

Liriodendron tulipifera (branching system)

Liriodendron tulipifera (leaves and flowers)

Liriodendron tulipifera (fruits)

When grown in the open, tulip trees retain their lower branches and form handsome irregularly-pyramidal, open-crowned specimens. Varieties of *L. tulipifera* are *L. t. aureo-marginatum,* which has yellow-edged leaves, *L. t. fastigiatum,* an attractive kind that forms a narrow head of upright branches, *L. t. integrifolium,* which has leaves rounded, but lobeless at their bases, and *L. t. obtusilobum,* distinguished by its leaves having one rounded lobe at the base at each side. The Chinese tulip tree (**L. chinense**) differs from the American in having much more deeply-lobed leaves that are somewhat glaucous beneath, and somewhat smaller flowers with their filaments one-half as long as those of *L. tulipifera.* This species, rare in cultivation, attains a height of about 60 feet.

Garden and Landscape Uses. Tulip trees are too big for small gardens, but can be used with advantage in larger landscapes either as single specimens or in groups. They are best adapted to deep, fertile, reasonably moist soils, but not for dry locations. Even where the earth is fairly moist, well-branched specimens in the open that produce abundant foliage early in the year are likely to start dropping leaves shortly after mid-summer and to keep this up with exasperating monotony until fall frosts de-

Liriodendron tulipifera: (a) In summer

nude them. On lawns and other areas where neat garden housekeeping is practiced, this unhappy habit adds considerably to maintenance. Infestations of aphids and scale insects not only intensify the leaf dropping but such beasts excrete a sticky honey-dew that drips from the trees and is most unpleasant on clothing, garden furniture, and automobiles. Because of their muted colors the flowers of the tulip tree make no great display. One must look rather carefully to see them, but when cut they can be used charmingly in arrangements and then, when they are examined at close range, their extraordinary beauty can be fully appreciated. The foliage turns bright yellow in fall.

Cultivation. Tulip trees recover rather slowly from transplanting and large specimens are decidedly difficult to move. With all but quite small nursery-grown individuals it is wise to root-prune specimens to be transplanted at least a year in advance. Once established in a favorable location they need no special care, but as young trees attention should be given to restricting their growth to a single leader. Specimens with two or more leaders are likely to suffer storm damage. Propagation is best by seed, but varieties of *L. tulipifera* and the Chinese tulip tree, of which seeds are likely to be unavailable, may be increased by grafting onto seedlings of *L. tulipifera*.

LIRIOPE (Lirìo-pe)—Lilyturf. Lilyturf as a common name is applied not only to this group of plants, but also to the allied genus of similar aspect, *Ophiopogon*. Both belong in the lily family LILIACEAE. From *Liriope* the latter differs in that its flowers have the lower parts of their perianths joined to the ovaries and the perianth lobes (petals) originating at or near the top of the ovary, with the result that the latter is apparently inferior. In *Liriope* the perianth is separate from and arises from beneath the ovary, which therefore is distinctly superior. There are six species of *Liriope*, all natives of eastern Asia and all evergreen, tufted or sod-forming, low herbaceous perennials with grasslike foliage and small whitish, blue, or violet flowers in spikes or racemes. The name is that of the nymph Liriope.

Liriopes have short, thick rhizomes, often tuberous roots, and, the sod-forming kinds, stolons that spread just beneath the ground surface. The flowers have six petals, six stamens with stalks longer than the blunt anthers, and a solitary style ending in a small stigma. The berry-like, usually single-seeded fruits are purple to black.

A popular species is big blue lilyturf *L. muscari* (syn. *L. m. densiflora*), an attractive native to Japan, Taiwan, and China. This sturdy kind roots deeply and has few tubers. It is not sod-forming, but develops dense tufts of stiffish, erect or arching, dark green, glossy leaves about ½ inch wide and

Liriope muscari

Liriope muscari (fruits)

1 foot long or longer. Its lilac-purple flowers are clustered in dense, freely-produced spikes that in length approximate the leaves. The fruits are black. Horticultural varieties of this lilyturf are popular and numerous. An early-flowering one, *L. m.* 'Blue Spire', has compact masses of foliage and carries its tapering flower spikes, often forked in somewhat cockscomb-like manner at their apexes, well above them. A tall grower, *L. m.* 'Lilac Beauty' has brownish-violet flower stalks with dark lilac flowers lifted well above the foliage. Its foliage, more spreading than that of most kinds, *L. m.* 'Purple Bouquet' has narrow leaves under 1 foot long, and pinkish-lavender blooms. Curious *L. m.* 'Curly Twist' has yellowish-green, contorted leaves and rather scarce flower spikes, shorter than them. This is a strong grower. Variety *L. m.* 'Monroe White' (syn. *L. m.* 'Monroe No. 1') is delightful. It has narrow, arching leaves up to about 1 foot tall, and over-topped by spikes of pure white flowers. Variegated-leaved varieties of *L. muscari* are fairly numerous. A good one, *L. m. variegata*, has young leaves margined with yellow, but becoming green as they mature. Its dark violet blooms are in spikes shorter than the foliage. Compact and slow growing, *L. m.* 'Silver Banded' has strongly

Liriope muscari 'Monroe White'

Liriope muscari variegata in a rock garden in New York City

Variegated *Liriope*, as a pot plant

arched leaves edged with yellow that changes to white and finally becomes green. The compact spikes of deep violet flowers are hidden among the foliage. Variety *L. p.* 'Silvery Midget' has comparatively broad, spreading leaves usually not over 8 inches high and dark green with white margins. The spikes of light lavender flowers are scarcely lifted above the foliage. Good varieties of *L. muscari*, both plain-foliaged and variegated, are to be sought in dealers' catalogs. A kind usually designated as a variety of this species but possibly a derivative of another species is *L.* 'Christmas Tree' (syn. *L.* 'Monroe No. 2'). This forms compact clumps of upright, narrow, yellowish leaves about 6 inches long, above which rise broadly-conical or club-shaped flower spikes usually branched at their bases and consisting of masses of light violet buds that never open, but make a good show of color.

Other species cultivated include these: *L. exiliflora,* of Japan and China, forms a dense tuft of dark green leaves up to 1 foot long or a little longer. Its flower spikes have violet-brown stalks up to 1¼ feet tall, violet blooms, and black fruits. *L. graminifolia,* of China and Indochina, has leaves 1 foot long or longer and about ¼ inch wide. Its spikes of nearly white flowers are 9 or 10 inches tall. *L. spicata* is a turfing kind with spreading rhizomes, a native of China and Japan. Its leaves are up to 2 feet long by ½ inch wide. The flowers, in 10-inch or shorter spikes scarcely taller than the foliage, are whitish. The fruits are glossy-black.

Garden and Landscape Uses. These are identical with those of *Ophiopogon.* Tufted liriopes, such as *L. muscari* and its varieties, serve the same purposes as the white lilyturf (*Ophiopogon jaburan*), and the turfing kinds have the same uses as the dwarf lilyturf (*O. japonicus*). Although the hardiness limits of cultivated liriopes are not definitely established, as a group they can be regarded as safely hardy as in the climate of Washington, D.C., and some certainly survive severer winters. There are reports of *L. spicata* proving satisfactory at Cleveland, Ohio, and both green-leaved and variegated varieties of *L. muscari* are perfectly hardy in sheltered locations near New York City. They are also good pot plants for cool greenhouses and sunny windows.

Cultivation. This is the same as for *Ophiopogon.*

LISIANTHUS (Lisi-ánthus). The plant most commonly known to gardeners as *Lisianthus* is *Eustoma russellianum.* Like it, *Lisianthus* belongs to the gentian family GENTIANACEAE. It consists of fifty species, natives from Mexico to tropical South America and the West Indies. The name derives from the Greek *lysis,* dissolution, and *anthos,* a flower, in allusion to a bitter principle of some species having been used medicinally. The one species of *Lisianthus* occasionally cultivated is remarkable because its flowers are almost black (they are actually very deep violet-black).

Native to southern Mexico, *L. nigrescens* is known locally as *flor de muerto* (flower of the dead), and its blooms are used to decorate wayside shrines. In its native land it grows about 2 feet tall, but in cultivation is often two or three times that height and has quite luxuriant foliage. Its stems are erect. Its slender, trumpet-shaped flowers

Lisianthus nigrescens

are 1½ to 3 inches long and have five sepals, five pointed, spreading corolla lobes (petals) about one-half as long as the corolla tube, five stamens, and one style. The fruits are capsules. The blooms are in terminal clusters and are displayed in great profusion.

Garden Uses and Cultivation. This is a handsome plant in full bloom and of exceptional interest because of the unusual color of its flowers. It is suitable for flower beds in frost-free and nearly frost-free climates and possibly for greenhouse cultivation. Its blooms last well in water and suggest themselves as being useful to flower arrangers. Little experience is recorded about the cultivation of *Lisianthus nigrescens,* but it has proved hardy and successful in southern Florida in limestone soil in both sun and shade. It needs very well-drained soil. Seeds apparently germinate without difficulty, and the seedlings, transplanted to suitable locations, bloom within a year.

LISSOCHILUS (Lisso-chìlus). The approximately fifty species of the orchid family ORCHIDACEAE that constitute *Lissochilus* are natives of southern Africa. From closely related *Eulophia,* in which genus by some authorities they are included, they differ most conspicuously in having flowers with petals much broader than the sepals and differently colored. Alluding to a feature of the flowers, the name derives from the Greek *lissos,* smooth, and *cheilos,* a lip.

Terrestrial rather than tree-perching orchids, the sorts of this genus have creeping rhizomes, short leafy pseudobulbs, and generally narrow leaves. On tall, leafless stalks from the axils of the leaves the medium-sized to large flowers are displayed in loose racemes. The lip of the bloom is spurred or pouched at its base.

Native to Natal, *L. krebsii* (syn. *Eulophia krebsii*) has 2- to 3-inch-long pseudobulbs each with up to six elliptic-lanceolate leaves 1½ to 2 feet in length by about 2½ inches wide. Its 1½-inch-wide flowers are in racemes of from ten to twenty or more

that attain heights of 3 to 5 feet. They have brown-blotched, green, reflexed sepals, bright yellow petals, and a golden-yellow lip with a short spur.

Garden Uses and Cultivation. These are as for *Eulophia.* For more information see Orchids.

LISTERA (Lis-tèra) — Twayblade. Possibly thirty species of terrestrial orchids, natives mostly of colder parts of the north temperate zone, constitute *Listera,* of the orchid family ORCHIDACEAE. The name commemorates the English naturalist Martin Lister, who died in 1711. The vernacular name twayblade is applied also to *Liparis.*

Listeras are fibrous- or more rarely fleshy-rooted herbaceous perennials that have erect stems with, near their middles, a pair of opposite, stalkless, broad-ovate leaves. The small, green, purplish or red flowers have spreading or backward-turned sepals and similar or nearly similar petals. The cleft lip, in many kinds much longer than the sepals and petals, projects horizontally or downward.

Native from Greenland to Alaska, New York, Michigan, and Minnesota, and in the mountains to North Carolina and California, *L. cordata* is 4 to 10 inches tall. Its

Listera cordata

Listera australis

leaves, ¾ inch to 2¼ inches long, are usually below the middles of the stems. About ⅓ inch long, the purplish to yellowish-green flowers have deeply-lobed lips about twice as long as the sepals and petals. Native from Vermont to Ontario, Florida, and Louisiana, *L. australis* is 6 inches to 1 foot tall. It has pointed-ovate leaves up to about 1 inch long. Its flowers, up to about ½ inch long, have a dull red lip about four times as long as the sepals and petals and cleft for at least one-half its length into two narrow lobes. Unlike those of *L. cordata*, the stems and flower stalks of *L. australis* are finely-glandular.

Garden Uses and Cultivation. Of interest only to fanciers of rare natives, the species described are sometimes grown in native plant gardens and rock gardens where the conditions under which they grow in the wild can be closely approximated. The conditions are those of wet woodlands and sphagnum bogs where summers are fairly cool. For more see Orchids.

LITCHI (Lìt-chi)—Lychee or Leechee or Litchi. There are one or perhaps two species of the southern Chinese and Philippine Island genus *Litchii*, of the soapberry family SAPINDACEAE. The name is the Chinese one for the lychee, which has been extensively cultivated for centuries in warm parts of the Orient and is still much cultivated for its edible fruits. To a lesser extent it is grown elsewhere, including Florida, California, and Hawaii, for its fruits and as an ornamental. Dried, the fruits are dark brown, wrinkled, and sticky, and look somewhat like raisins. They are marketed as lychee nuts, although they are not technically nuts. Lychees are also eaten fresh. Frequently canned, lychees so preserved retain many of the characteristics of the fresh fruits.

The lychee (*L. chinensis* syn. *Nephelium litchi*) is a freely-branched, evergreen tree that attains heights of 40 feet or more and is as broad as it is tall. It has lustrous, leathery, pinnate leaves, with two to four pairs of oblong-lanceolate to pointed-ovate, opposite or alternate leaflets 2½ to 8 inches long by 1 inch to 2½ inches wide. The greenish-white or yellowish flowers are in terminal panicles up to 1 foot long. They are up to ⅛ inch wide, have four or five sepals, but are without petals. There are three types of blooms, males with six to ten stamens but not pistils, females with a pistil with a two-lobed stigma, but no stamens, and bisexual blooms with both stamens and a pistil. Following flowering, the panicles develop up to several dozen fruits. These, spherical to somewhat egg-shaped, and up to 1½ inches in diameter, have a thin, finely-warted, red shell containing a single large and fertile seed or a small abortive one surrounded by pearly white, translucent, grapelike flesh, which is the edible part. Several varieties are cultivated in the Orient. The most popular in the United States is known as Brewster or Royal Chen and seems to be identical with the Chinese variety Chen-tze.

Garden and Landscape Uses and Cultivation. As an ornamental the lychee is handsome, densely-foliaged, and suitable for displaying singly or in mixed plantings. It will not grow satisfactorily where heavy frosts are experienced. Even the lightest visitation damages tender young growth, but mature foliage successfully withstands 28°F. Hot summers and winters with temperatures above freezing but that do not exceed 40°F at night are required for satisfactory fruiting. Where winters are warmer the trees grow well, but fruit is rarely produced. Deep, well-drained, fertile soil, preferably somewhat acid and with ample moisture during the growing and fruiting seasons gives the best results. Good growth is made on limestone soils, but then applications of chelated iron to correct a deficiency are often needed. High humidity is desirable. Lychees do not do well in exposed, windy locations, and in such places windbreak plantings should be installed.

Propagation of lychees for fruit is nearly always done by air layering, less commonly by grafting or inarching onto seedlings, and by cuttings under mist. Lychees raised from seeds are satisfactory as ornamentals, but because they do not fruit until they are ten to fifteen or more years old, and because the quality of the fruit of seedlings varies, they are not practicable for orchard planting. For fruit production, spacing of 30 to 50 feet is recommended, the greater distances being advisable on fertile soils. If planted closer to other trees than suggested above for orchards, lychees may serve decorative purposes in mixed landscapes, but they tend to develop narrower heads and to fruit only at their tops where the branches are exposed to full sun.

In preparation for planting lychees, improve soils deficient in organic matter by plowing or spading in considerable well-rotted manure, compost, or humus, or at least treat the planting holes and immediate surroundings in that way, mixing the additive very thoroughly with the soil. For preference, plant at the beginning of a new season of growth. Water or irrigate during dry weather; drought severely limits the growth of lychees. A heavy organic mulch maintained around the trees is decidedly advantageous. Protect young trees in open areas from wind by fixing around them on suitable frames burlap, Saran cloth, or some similar material over a base of chicken wire. Only the sides, not the tops, of the plants need this protection. The screens also provide the partial shade desirable for young lychees.

Maintenance of established trees is not demanding. Do not cultivate the soil, but instead maintain a mulch, or in the case of trees planted for ornament, a groundcover around the trees. Cultivating damages the shallow roots. Regular, systematic pruning is not needed, but do any necessary to encourage young trees to develop well-placed and well-spaced branches. Old, deteriorating trees can be rejuvenated by heavy pruning accompanied by fertilizing. Younger specimens also need fertilizing regularly to maintain a fairly high level of nutriton. Harvest the fruits when they are fully ripe, and free of dew, by breaking off the entire panicle rather than picking individual fruits. Take care to avoid bruising or crushing. Alternatively, harvesting may be done as soon as the fruits are fully grown, have reddened on one side, and are beginning to change color on the other side. Such early harvested samples will keep for up to a month in cold, dry storage. Ripe lychee fruits, quick frozen, retain their qualities well and are delicious. Drying and canning, as done in the Orient, is not usually done in the United States.

LITHOCARPUS (Litho-cárpus)—Tanbark-Oak. One species of *Lithocarpus* is native in western North America, about 300 in Asia and Europe. None is hardy. Belonging to the beech family FAGACEAE, these are evergreen trees related to oaks, chestnuts, and chinquapins. The name, alluding to the hard-shelled fruit of one kind, is derived from the Greek *lithos*, stone, and *karpos*, a fruit.

Lithocarpuses have alternate, undivided, toothed or toothless leaves not in two ranks. Their unisexual flowers, without petals, have four- to six-lobed calyxes. The males have usually ten to twelve stamens considerably longer than the calyx. Female flowers, at the bottoms of erect spikes of mostly males or in separate spikes, have three styles. The fruits are solitary nuts usually partially, rarely completely, enclosed in a spineless, cuplike involucre of separate, overlapping scales or of scales more or less joined in concentric rings. From oaks (*Quercus*) lithocarpuses differ in having erect rather than pendulous flower spikes, in the styles of their female flowers being cylindrical instead of flattened, and in having terminal stigmas.

Tanbark-oak (*L. densiflorus*) occasionally but rarely exceeds 75 feet in height, and often is lower. When grown in the open it makes a more squatty specimen, often with branches and foliage nearly to the ground. Native from Oregon to California, it has toothed, oblong to oblong-obovate, prominently-veined leaves 3 to 4½ inches long, with stout, hairy stalks. The undersides of the blades, at first rusty-hairy, later lose most of the hairs and assume a leaden hue. Male flowers, whitish, tiny, and in large, branching clusters, emit a peculiar odor, which is disagreeable to many people. The egg-shaped nuts, ¾ to 1 inch long, are seated in shallow cups with

Lithocarpus densiflorus at Rancho Santa Ana Botanic Garden, Claremont, California: (a) Young specimen

(b) Older specimen

spreading or reflexed scales. They are single or in twos on thick stalks up to 1 inch long. Shrubby *L. d. montanus* has toothless, usually blunt leaves up to 2 inches long.

Garden and Landscape Uses and Cultivation. The tanbark-oak makes a good specimen where conditions are to its liking. It is used as a street tree and lawn tree. For best success it requires fertile, moist, but well-drained soil, but when established it will stand some dryness. Propagation is by seed.

LITHODORA (Litho-dóra). Seven species of low shrubs and subshrubs long familiar to gardeners as *Lithospermum* constitute the genus *Lithodora*. They belong in the borage family BORAGINACEAE and differ from *Lithospermum* in that the nutlets of their fruits when mature break off just above their bases leaving a small cup- or saucer-shaped portion. No other plant in the borage family does this. The name is derived from the Greek *lithos*, rock, and *dora*, hide or skin.

Lithodoras inhabit open, rocky places in southern and western Europe, North Africa, and Asia Minor. They have alternate, undivided leaves and solitary or in clusters

of up to ten, that unlike those of many of the borage family are not coiled, blue, purple, or white flowers. Each bloom has a five-lobed calyx, a corolla with five spreading lobes (petals), five stamens, and one branched or branchless style. The fruits consist of one, rarely two, small nutlets.

From other cultivated kinds **L. fruticosa** (syn. *Lithospermum fruticosum*) differs in having flowers with their outsides hairless. An erect shrublet up to 1 foot tall, this has narrow leaves, green and hairy above, white-hairy on their undersides and with strongly rolled-under margins. They are up to ¾ inch long. Its deep blue flowers faintly streaked with reddish-violet are about ½ inch across and are in terminal leafy spikes. This grows in limestone regions of southern Spain and Algeria. The plant commonly cultivated under its name is **L. diffusa** (syns. *Lithospermum diffusum*, *L. prostratum*), a lovely native of Spain, Portugal, and Morocco, that in its native habitats seems indifferent to whether or not the soil is alkaline and under happy circumstances forms broad mats of prostrate stems and foliage up to 1 foot high. Its linear-oblong to lanceolate leaves, up to ¾ inch long and with slightly rolled-under margins, are rough-hairy on both sides. The flowers resemble those of *L. fruticosa*, but are hairy

Lithodora diffusa

Lithodora diffusa (flowers)

on their outsides. The stamens join the corolla tube at unequal levels. A splendid garden variety is *L. d.* 'Heavenly Blue', which has flowers of an especially glorious blue. Variety *L. d. alba* has white flowers.

Two other cultivated species, *L. oleifolia* and *L. rosmarinifolia* are characterized by having stamens arising from one level in the corolla tube, either from near its base or from close to its top. A native of the Pyrenees, **L. oleifolia** (syn. *Lithospermum oleifolium*) is a prostrate subshrub not exceeding 1 foot in height and usually lower. Its elliptic-oblong leaves, about ½ inch long, are green above and white-hairy beneath; they are clustered toward the ends of the branches and are not rolled under at their margins. The flowers, violet, or more rarely blue or pink, are few, comparatively large, and in terminal clusters. A native of Italy, Sicily, and North Africa, **L. rosmarinifolia** (syn. *Lithospermum rosmarinifolium*) is an erect subshrub up to 2 feet in height with linear leaves 1 inch or more long, with margins that are rolled under, and terminal clusters of bright blue flowers lined with white, each about ¾ inch across.

Garden Uses and Cultivation. These beautiful and not always easy-to-grow plants are splendid additions to rock gardens when they can be persuaded to flourish. Some are challenging subjects for the connoisseur of choice alpines who has at command an alpine greenhouse or who cultivates his treasures in cold pits or frames. The last two species discussed are more likely to be comfortable under such conditions than in the open. Despite reports of the places it grows in the wild, *L. diffusa* in cultivation usually resents alkalinity of the soil and should be given an acid root run. The others appreciate limestone. A deep soil, well-drained, but never parched is needed, as is full sun. Climates not excessively cold in winter nor burning hot in summer are most to the liking of lithodoras. They are not reliably hardy outdoors at New York City, but *L. diffusa* and probably some of the others winter there satisfactorily in cold frames.

LITHOFRAGMA. See Lithophragma.

LITHOPHRAGMA (Litho-phrágma)—Woodland Star or Prairie Star. Western North America is home to the eight or nine species of *Lithophragma*, of the saxifrage family SAXIFRAGACEAE. The name, from the Greek *lithos*, stone, and *phragma*, a wall, presumably alludes to the habitats of some species. The genus is allied to *Tellima* and *Mitella*. Its name has also been spelled *Lithofragma*.

Lithophragmas are usually glandular, herbaceous perennials with numerous tiny bulblets on their roots, often in the axils of the stem leaves, and sometimes in those of the bracts of the flower clusters. In some species the blooms are replaced partially or entirely by bulblets. The branchless stems terminate in sometimes branched racemes of flowers. The blooms have shallowly-five-lobed calyxes, five white, pink, or purple-tinged, toothed or more deeply-cleft petals, ten stamens, and three styles. The slender-stalked leaves are chiefly basal. They have round to kidney-shaped blades, divided palmately (in handlike fashion) to their bases, less deeply-lobed, or merely round-toothed. The stem leaves, smaller than the basal ones, are reduced in size upward. The fruits are capsules.

One of the prettiest woodland stars, *L. affine* (syn. *Tellima affinis*) grows chiefly on moist, mossy banks from California to Oregon. From 8 inches to 2 feet tall, it has roundish, shallowly- to fairly deeply-three-lobed, round-toothed basal leaves, ½ inch to 1½ inches wide, with hairy stalks. There are three or fewer stem leaves. The flowers, up to a dozen, are ½ inch wide or a little wider, and have white petals with usually three-lobed apexes.

Variable *L. tenellum* (syn. *Tellima tenella*) has basal leaves usually hairy on both surfaces. They are up to slightly over ½ inch broad and are three-lobed or divided into three parts, with the lobes or segments toothed. The flower stems, 4 inches to 1 foot tall, have usually two or three shorter-stalked or stalkless, more finely-dissected leaves. There are five to ten white or pinkish blooms, ¼ inch wide or slightly wider. Their petals mostly have three main lobes and two smaller basal ones. This is found from Montana to Colorado, Washington, and California.

Another variable species, *L. parviflorum* (syn. *Tellima parviflora*) is 8 inches to 1½ feet tall, and has stems often purplish in their upper parts. Its basal leaves are from a little under ½ to slightly over 1 inch broad and are split nearly to their bases into usually five deeply-cleft or lobed segments. The ten or fewer flowers have petals with mostly five to seven, but sometimes as few as three, deep lobes. They are up to ½ inch wide. This is indigenous from the Rocky Mountains to California and British Columbia.

Garden and Landscape Uses and Cultivation. These are dainty plants for rock and woodland gardens and, within their natural ranges, native plant gardens. They are in evidence for only a short season, the entire tops dying to the ground by midsummer. When the plants are dormant, the soil should be kept as dry as possible. At other times moistish conditions are desirable. Propagation is by seed, bulblets, and division. Little information is available regarding the hardiness of these plants outside their natural ranges. They are for trial elsewhere.

LITHOPS (Lí-thops)—Stone Plant or Pebble Plant or Stoneface. The fascinating genus *Lithops,* of the *Mesembryanthemum* relationship of the carpetweed family AIZOACEAE, consists of about fifty species endemic to South Africa and southwest Africa. Its name, from the Greek *lithos,* stone, and *ops,* appearance, alludes to the marvelous exactness with which its members mimic pebbles and small stones. Despite their lack of high visibility, except when in bloom, these plants in the wild are subject to a number of disturbing and destroying influences. These include such hazards as harmful insects, browsing animals, certain birds and rodents and, most importantly, humans who destroy the plants in the relentless construction of highways, airfields, and other facilities, and who strip areas to obtain gravel and other surface materials to further the work. Less justifiable is the harm done by unauthorized collectors who gather plants for their gardens and for sale in such quantities that the eradication of species from the wild is a serious possibility. Throughout South Africa rigid laws forbid the taking of lithops without a permit from the regional governmental authority and written assent of the landowner, but unfortunately these conservation measures are often flouted.

Because of the great variability in the wild as well as in cultivation, lithops are often difficult to identify as to species. One complication is that the flowers and fruits of all are so remarkably similar that classification is largely based upon the forms, colors, and markings of the plant bodies, which are difficult to describe satisfactorily and are regarded as being of secondary importance in the classification of most other kinds of plants.

Lithops are small, nonhardy, perennial succulent plants splendidly adapted to withstand the brilliant sun, high temperatures, and searing winds of their desert habitats. As further protection against dehydration, as wildlings they commonly grow with the greater portions of their plant bodies buried in often stony soil and only small parts of their tops exposed. So hidden are they, and so beautifully do their exposed parts blend with their surroundings that, except when they are in bloom, experienced botanists easily pass them by unnoticed. Mostly they are up to 1 inch tall; some attain heights of 2 inches. Their flowers approximate 1 inch in diameter.

These plants are constructed simply. Each plant body consists of a pair of inverted, subconical, very fleshy, water-storing leaves joined for much of their lengths, and at their bases attached to a scarcely differentiated short stem from which extends ramifying roots. The upper surfaces or apexes of the leaves often have windows of translucent tissue through which light enters and is filtered and reduced in intensity before it reaches the chlorophyll-containing cells that use light energy in photosynthesis. The windows may cover the entire top of the plant body or be variously branched, with opaque areas between the branches. Islands of opaque tissue are often surrounded by the translucent areas. Between each pair of mature leaves in the rainy season is produced a white or yellow flower that upon casual inspection looks daisy-like. But it is structured very differently from daisies. It is a solitary bloom, not a head composed of numerous florets. Ordinarily each lithops plant produces two new leaves each year. As these develop the old pair shrivels and dies, but sometimes two new pairs of leaves are formed and if this occurs more than once a multi-headed plant results. Some species are more likely to do this than others. The fruits are five- to seven-chambered capsules that discharge their seeds only after moisture triggers a hygroscopic action. After this has happened, if water continues to be available, germination takes place in a few days, otherwise the seeds may remain dormant for up to several years, until rains come to awaken them to growth. This capability is ideal for plants that grow where long droughts are prevalent.

Species discussed here are representative of the genus. Others cultivated by specialists are described in the quite abundant and often well-illustrated specialized literature devoted to these curious plants. Lithops are divided into two groups, those in which the tops of the young seedlings tend to be convex and the cleft between the leaves extends for more than one-half their length, and have white flowers, and those with nearly flat-topped young seedlings the two leaves of which are joined completely except for a comparatively shallow groove at the top, and have straw-colored to yellow or pale orange flowers.

The white-flowered group includes *L. bella,* a kind about 1 inch high with a convex pearl-gray to yellowish-gray top with sometimes indistinct brownish markings, and an irregular and slightly depressed, branched, darker window without a whitish border.

Lithops bella

Variety *L. b. eberlanzii* (syn. *L. eberlanzii*) has less sunken, more opaque windows, and the opaque central portion is gray, bluish-gray, brown, or purplish. In *L. b. lericheana* (syn. *L. lericheana*) the markings are darker than in typical *L. bella,* and the flowers are fragrant. Predominantly leaden-gray **L. salicola** is a native of saline soils. Its top has an olive-gray window usually plentifully studded with pale gray-green to grayish-pink islands. The flowers have five sepals and five styles. Variety *L. s. reticulata* has its top netted with brown and the window bordered with white. Its blooms have six each petals and styles.

Highly variable white-flowered *L. karasmontana* typically has a pale grayish-yellow to light reddish-brown, wrinkled

Lithops karasmontana opalina

Lithops olivacea

Lithops karasmontana

Lithops karasmontana summitata

top with rather broad, sometimes gray-edged markings. Variety *L. k. summitata* (syn. *L. summitata*) has a much deeper reddish-brown top. In *L. k. mickbergensis* (syns. *L. mickbergensis, L. jacobseniana*), a network of finer lines marks the yellowish-red top. An opaque opal to pale amethyst-hued top with indistinct or no markings is characteristic of *L. k. opalina* (syn. *L. opalina*).

Grayish-green or greenish, sometimes tinged with amethyst, is the characteristic

coloring of **L. marmorata,** which includes the population previously distinguished as *L. framesii*. This species has gray islands in the windows of its rounded tops and white flowers mostly with six each petals and styles. Having rounded tops with large windows with few or no islands, **L. optica** has flowers with mostly five sepals and five styles. Its rare variety *L. o. rubra* is purplish-red. Both grow near the sea and are subject to frequent misty rains. Small brown marks that appear like stitching around the edgings of the large windows are a distinguishing characteristic of typical **L. fulleri.** A white-flowered, flat-topped, dove-gray to tan-colored species often over 1 inch tall, its green windows have few to many small islands. Variety *L. f. brunnea* has brownish windows with fewer islands and less conspicuous stitching. In *L. f. ochracea* the windows are deep ochre-yellow and the islands paler.

Considerable variation is shown by **L. julii,** a white-flowered species with gently rounded, light-colored top surfaces with an impressed network of the same color or darker, and an ochre-brown line margining the cleft. In *L. j. reticulata* the network is very much darker. Larger size and the absence of a brown line along the cleft give to *L. j. littlewoodii* much the appearance of *L. karasmontana opalina*. With a flat ochre-yellow to brownish top with a fine network of markings that sometimes merge to form windows, **L. hallii** also has white blooms.

Yellow-flowered *Lithops* are more numerous than those with white blooms. One of the most distinct and most lovely, **L. olivacea,** is light gray to olive-green, sometimes tinged pink. It is flat-topped or slightly convex and has a large window darker than the surrounding tissue, generally with a few islands. Viewed from above, its plant body is oval with a narrow cleft. Very different is variable, yellow-flowered **L. turbiniformis.** Its top is flat, ochre-yellow to reddish, usually without windows, and very warted. Smooth-topped, yellow-flowered, **L. insularis** has

Lithops turbiniformis

greenish-gray, translucent windows with yellowish-brown islands. It is much like **L. bromfieldii,** which, however, is more yellowish-brown than bluish-green in general appearance. The solitary or sometimes clumped plant bodies of **L. divergens** have leaves, at first of unequal lengths but later equal, that spread outward as they age. Their apexes are rounded or oblique. The large, gray-green, transparent windows often have a cobwebby aspect. The flowers are yellow.

A variably marked, yellow-flowered kind is **L. pseudotruncatella.** In its typical form this has a flat or slightly rounded grayish to brownish top with more or less distinct branched markings. Variety *L. p. dendritica* has grayish-brown tops with conspicuous, branched, dark markings. Variety *L. p. edithae* (syn. *L. edithae*) has bluish-gray tops with indistinct markings. In *L. p. elizabethae* (syn. *L. elizabethae*), the top is mostly copper-tinged, grayish-blue.

Another species comprising several varieties is yellow-flowered, flat-topped, **L. lesliei,** which has slender apertures between the lobes and often irregularly-shaped windows. Typically, its plant body is brownish-yellow to greenish. In *L. l. venteri*, the plant body is grayer and the windows form a branching pattern. In *L. l. maraisii*, the windows sometimes occupy the whole top, or they may be branched.

It is greenish-brown to reddish with ochre-colored islands. Kinds previously named *L. peersii* and *L. terricolor* are varieties of *L. localis*. All have yellow blooms. In the typical species the tops are fawn-gray with numerous translucent dots, but are generally without windows. Variety *L. l. peersii* may or may not have a window in its bluish-purple top. It is somewhat larger than *L. localis*. Also larger, *L. l. terricolor* has a grayish or yellowish-green top with a large or small window.

Lithops localis terricolor

Another kind with several yellow-flowered variants previously treated as separate species, *L. schwantesii* (syn. *L. kuibisensis*) typically has slightly rounded, grayish, yellowish-red, generally grooved tops with reddish-brown markings mostly in interrupted lines and usually a yellowish or pinkish border. Very similar, but more pronounced grooves are characteristic of *L. s. kunjasensis*. Variety *L. s. rugosa* is almost without a pinkish border to its rather amethyst-colored tops, which are very distinctly grooved. In *L. s. triebneri* the pinkish-bordered tops are gray to light brown and have distinct blue points. Light gray coloration and absence of a pinkish border are typical of the tops of *L. s. urikosensis*.

Other yellow-flowered *Lithops* likely to be cultivated include flat-topped *L. aucampiae*, which has dark olive-green to reddish-brown windows branched in antler-like fashion, and *L. a. koelemanii*, in which the windows are absent, but which has many translucent dots usually joined by small, sunken red lines. Also belonging here are *L. comptonii*, a smallish, reddish species with round tops with small islands in its windows, and *L. franciscii*, in which the branched windows in the rounded, gray tops are very indistinct, and the translucent dots are small and often inconspicuous. Lack of windows in the flat or slightly rounded bluish or reddish-brown tops is typical of *L. fulviceps*. Large, raised, translucent, bluish-green dots, often with red-

dish lines between, besprinkle the tops and stand out prominently. Rather similar to white-flowered *L. marmorata*, but with fragrant, yellow blooms, *L. helmutii* is grayish-green, with large pale green windows spotted light gray, and irregular islands. Somewhat rounded, grayish-green tops with indistinct islands in the windows are characteristics of *L. herrei*. Variety *L. h. hillii* has more prominent islands and is commonly suffused with pink. Another variant, *L. h. geyeri*, is distinguished by its yellowish-gray-green hue and distinct islands. Without windows, the flat to slightly rounded, somewhat rough-surfaced, pinkish-brown tops of *L. mennellii* are marked with dark brown interrupted, scriptlike lines. The blooms are yellow. Having brownish to greenish-blue, flat, smooth tops edged with yellow, and with vague brownish-red spots or lines, but no blue dots, *L. marthae* grows in clusters. Also forming clumps, *L. meyeri* has bluish-gray, deeply-fissured, more or less crescent-shaped plant bodies with poorly defined windows, sometimes with indistinct markings.

Garden Uses and Cultivation. Although lithops are of chief interest to specialist collectors of choice succulents, the cultivation of most offers no insuperable difficulties, and it is quite practicable to grow them in an ordinary greenhouse or sunny window. They are so intriguing that they can with confidence be recommended to all who find pleasure in growing other than commonplace plants and who are prepared to take a little trouble to provide agreeable environments for them. Some advantages over many plants gardeners treasure are possessed by lithops. They are very easily raised from seeds and need little routine attention. They are relatively free of pests and diseases, and they take little space.

Important matters to bear in mind are that these stone plants are extremely succulent and are well able to withstand arid atmosphere and dry soil, but are completely intolerant of imperfect soil drainage, and of air or earth excessively humid. They require maximum sun at all times. Winter temperatures should not be excessively high. At night 50°F is adequate, and five or ten degrees more by day is sufficient. Their season of dormancy must be respected by keeping them dry during the winter. From spring to fall watering should be done moderately.

Lithops are not deep-rooting. They usually prosper best and are displayed to most advantage when accommodated in pans (shallow pots) rather than regular pots. It is better that several be in each container. If they are spaced irregularly, but because of their small size generally fairly closely, and if the soil is surfaced with pebbles or small pieces of rock chosen to match the plants as closely as possible, very attractive and convincing effects can be had. People

unfamiliar with them, except when they are in bloom, may have difficulty in distinguishing the plants from the stones. This mimicry is, of course, one of the most fascinating features of *Lithops* and a source of much pleasure.

Transplanting lithops is best done just as new growth begins. The chemical composition of the soil is of less importance than its physical state. It must be so porous and well aerated that water drains through it quickly. With this in mind it should be decidedly sandy. It seems, too, that the addition of crushed limestone is helpful, although by no means necessary. Seeds sprout readily and are an easy source of new plants. Propagation can also be by offsets. For more information see Succulents.

LITHOSPERMUM (Litho-spérmum)—Puccoon. Many species formerly known by this name now are placed in other genera; this is true of all cultivated kinds with blue or purple flowers. The genera to which they have been assigned are *Buglossoides*, *Lithodora*, and *Moltkia*. Remaining in *Lithospermum* are over forty species, all except one uncultivated kind with yellow, orange, or sometimes white flowers. The exception, *L. hancockiana*, a native of China, has purplish blooms. The genus is represented in the native floras of all continents, except Australia. It belongs in the borage family BORAGINACEAE and its name derives from the Greek *lithos*, stone, and *sperma*, a seed, and refers to the shining, usually white and porcelain-like nutlets of the fruits that resemble small stones. The name is an ancient one used by Dioscorides.

As now interpreted *Lithospermum* comprises mostly herbaceous perennials with a few annuals and a few subshrubby kinds. The flowers, in fiddle-head clusters, are tubular, or funnel-shaped and usually have spreading corolla lobes; if entirely white their throats are conspicuously crested.

The only kinds seemingly in cultivation in North America are native perennials. Best known are those to which the common name puccoon is applied, *L. canescens* and *L. incisum* (syn. *L. angustifolium*). The former ranges from Pennsylvania to Saskatchewan and Alabama, the latter from Ontario to Illinois, British Columbia, and Mexico. From 6 inches to 1½ feet tall, *L. canescens* is an erect, branched, softly-hoary-hairy plant with oblong or linear-oblong scarcely stalked leaves up to 1½ inches long and about one-third as wide. The brilliant and profuse orange-yellow flowers, each from slightly under to slightly over ½ inch wide, have smooth-edged corolla lobes and are not hairy inside at their bases, but are crested in their throats. The nutlets are white and glossy. From this kind *L. incisum* differs in having stalkless, linear leaves up to 2 inches long and leafy spikes of two kinds of flowers, the earlier, sterile ones bright yellow, about 1 inch long and with spreading, fringed or irregularly-toothed corolla lobes, and those produced later, paler and smaller, fertile, and not opening. The throats of the flowers have well-developed crests. This species is 6 inches or 2 feet tall.

From *L. canescens* short hairs inside the flowers at the base of the corolla serve to differentiate *L. carolinense,* which despite the limiting implications of its name, occurs as a native from New York to Montana, Florida, and New Mexico. Its linear to lanceolate leaves are rough-hairy. Its flowers, up to 1 inch wide, are orange-yellow with toothless corolla lobes. It attains heights up to 2½ feet. The Mexican *L. distichum* is an erect, silky-hairy plant with oblong-lanceolate leaves and flowers that are white or white with the crests in the throat yellow.

Distinguished from the kinds already discussed by their flowers being without crests in their throats are *L. ruderale* and *L. multiflorum.* A native of the region between the Rocky Mountains and the Sierra Nevadas, *L. ruderale* has greenish-yellow flowers with corolla tubes about as long as the calyxes. Up to 2 feet in height, with linear to linear-lanceolate leaves, *L. multiflorum* is native from Wyoming to Mexico. Its yellow to orange blooms have corolla tubes twice as long as the calyx.

Garden Uses and Cultivation. These quite lovely American natives can be grown in flower borders, rock gardens, and native plant gardens and are reliably hardy in climates as severe and perhaps more severe than those of their natural ranges. They need full sun and sharply drained, not excessively fertile soil. Too rich a rooting medium results in taller, more vigorous growth and probably tends to shorten the lives of the plants. In rock gardens especially, a compact habit is desirable. Lithospermums are raised from seeds sown in sandy, peaty soil in a cold frame or in a likely spot outdoors where the seeds will not be disturbed and the young plants can be kept free of weeds. The seedlings should be transplanted individually to pots and be grown in them, with the pots buried to their rims in a bed of sand or ashes, until they are ready for transferring to their permanent locations. Final spacing of 6 or 9 inches apart is appropriate. Because of their usually deep, woody roots transplanting sizable plants from the open ground or from the wild threatens the survival of these plants.

LITHRAEA (Lith-raèa). Close relatives of the California and Brazilian pepper trees (*Schinus*), the three species of *Lithraea* are evergreen shrubs or small trees of South America. They belong to the cashew family ANACARDIACEAE. Their name is an adaptation of a Chilean vernacular one of

one species. Some kinds and possibly all contain sap that affects some people in the same way as poison-ivy.

Lithraeas have alternate leaves, undivided, or of pinnately-arranged leaflets with one terminal. The small, greenish or whitish, unisexual flowers are in panicles. Their calyxes are usually five-lobed, and there are generally five petals. The males have twice as many fertile stamens as petals and an aborted stamen. The females have one style and staminodes (nonfertile stamens). The fruits are dryish, spherical, berry-like drupes. In its native regions the bark of *L. molleoides* is used for tanning and dyeing, its wood for a variety of purposes.

Sometimes planted for ornament, *L. molleoides* is hairless, 10 to 15 feet tall, and has pinnate leaves up to about 6 inches in length, usually with five, less frequently three, pointed-lanceolate to narrow-elliptic leaflets 1½ to 3 inches long. The leafstalks and the midribs between the leaflets are narrowly winged. In panicles up to 3 inches long, the little whitish or greenish flowers are succeeded by quite decorative, lustrous, whitish, spherical berries under ¼ inch in diameter. This is native to Brazil, Argentina, and Bolivia. Very different in appearance, Chilean *L. caustica* is a shrub or tree up to 12 feet tall, with short-stalked, undivided, broad-elliptic to ovate-oblong leaves 1½ to 2½ inches in length. Its flowers, in short, axillary racemes, are succeeded by whitish, lustrous berries approximately ¼ inch in diameter.

Garden and Landscape Uses and Cultivation. These plants have much the same landscape uses as evergreen species of sumac (*Rhus*). They have attractive foliage and make fair displays with their fruits. In mild climates they succeed in well-drained soil in sun. Propagation is by seed and perhaps root cuttings.

LITSEA (Lít-sea)—Pond Spice. Its name a latinized form of its Japanese one, *Litsea* consists of 400 species of nonhardy, evergreen and deciduous, aromatic trees and shrubs, natives of Australia, New Zealand, eastern Asia, and one kind of the southeastern United States. It belongs in the laurel family LAURACEAE. Some sorts have been used medicinally. Certain species previously included are segregated as *Neolitsea.*

Litseas have alternate, undivided, very rarely opposite, toothless, generally pinnately-veined, evergreen leaves. Their unisexual flowers, in small umbels, have four- to six-lobed, usually white or yellow calyxes, but are without petals. The males commonly have six to twelve stamens, and an aborted ovary, the females, staminodes (sterile stamens), and a style ending in a dilated, lobed stigma. The fruits are drupes (fruits of plumlike structure) with

the perianth tube, usually enlarged, retained at their bases.

The American species *L. aestivalis* (syns. *L. geniculata, Glabraria geniculata*) is a rare, deciduous shrub that inhabits swampy soils and shallow ponds from Tennessee to Florida and Louisiana. Early records indicate that it formerly occurred in Virginia, but it perhaps does not now. From 5 to 10 feet tall and wide-spreading, this has zigzag, forked branches, and elliptic leaves with blades ¾ inch to 2¼ inches long, hairless except for a little down on the veins of their undersides. The ¼-inch-wide yellow flowers, in umbels of up to four, come before the leaves. The fruits, about ¼ inch in diameter, are subglobular and red.

New Zealand *L. calicaris* is a tree up to 40 feet in height. Its alternate, somewhat leathery, rather short-stalked leaves have ovate to ovate-elliptic blades 2 to 4½ inches long by 1 inch to 2 inches wide. Their undersides are glaucous. The little, cream flowers, in umbels of four or five, have five to eight calyx lobes, the males about twelve stamens. The reddish, ovoid-spherical fruits are ½ to ¾ inch long. A tree up to 80 feet in height, *L. ferruginea,* of Java and Singapore, may be cultivated. This has elliptic to lanceolate-oblong leaves up to 7 inches long with reddish hairs on the veins of their undersides. Its fruits are small and spherical.

Garden and Landscape Uses and Cultivation. The American species, because of its rarity and interest, is worth including in collections of native plants and arboretum plantings. It requires an environment similar to that in which it grows natively. The New Zealand kind described flourishes in ordinary fairly well-drained soils in sun or part-day shade. It may be used in mild climates to add variety to landscape plantings. Propagation is by seed and by cuttings.

LITTLE PICKLES is *Othonna capensis.*

LITTLE RED ELEPHANTS is *Pedicularis groenlandica.*

LITTONIA (Lit-tònia). Natives of Africa and Arabia, eight tuberous-rooted, tender herbaceous perennials, of the lily family LILIACEAE, constitute *Littonia.* They are related to *Gloriosa,* differing in their petals (more correctly, tepals) being neither reflexed nor narrowed markedly toward their bases into claws. Their slender stems climb or sprawl. Their flowers are bell-shaped, nodding, usually 1 inch long or longer, and yellow or orange. They have six stamens and are succeeded by capsules containing brown or scarlet seeds as big as small peas. The name of this genus honors Dr. S. Litton, one-time Professor of Botany in Dublin, Ireland.

The only cultivated species *L. modesta*

Littonia modesta

Livistona chinensis, Hong Kong

Livistona australis, Huntington Botanical Gardens, San Marino, California:
(a) Fairly young specimen

Livistona chinensis, Huntington Botanical Garden, San Marino, California

(b) Older tree

Livistona rotundifolia, young plant

is a native of South Africa. Its stems 4 to 6 feet long bear ovate to linear leaves with tendrils at their ends. The upper leaves are alternate or opposite, those lower on the stems are in whorls (circles of three or more). The solitary blooms are on slender, 2-inch-long stalks from the axils of the upper leaves. They are 1¼ inches long and bright orange.

Garden Uses and Cultivation. Although less showy than the cultivated gloriosas, *L. modesta* has the quiet charm its specific name suggests. Its uses and cultural needs are the same as for *Gloriosa*.

LIVE FENCE POST. See Gliricidia.

LIVE-FOR-EVER is *Sedum telephium*.

LIVERLEAF. See Hepatica.

LIVING FENCE is *Rosa multiflora*.

LIVING ROCK is the common name of *Roseocactus fissuratus* and *Pleiospilos bolusii*.

LIVISTONA (Livistò-na). Thirty tall, single-trunked, bisexual, fan-leaved palms, of Australia and Indomalasia, comprise *Livistona*, of the palm family PALMAE. The name commemorates Patrick Murray, Baron of Livingston, near Edinburgh, Scotland, whose fine plant collection became the basis of the Royal Botanic Garden, Edinburgh. He lived in the seventeenth century. The group includes several species much esteemed for planting outdoors and for cultivating in pots and tubs.

Livistonas have rough or smoothish trunks ringed with old leaf scars and up to 1 foot or more in diameter. Their upper parts are usually clothed with the basal portions of leaves that have died and fallen. The huge, nearly circular leaves are variously divided into segments with single mid-veins and cleft tips. Their stalks are often furnished with strong, curved teeth. The flowers, in long, branched clusters with several spathes, originate among the foliage. They are greenish to yellowish, solitary or grouped. The berry-like fruits are usually blue or blue-green, sometimes yellow or brown.

The most popular kinds are the Chinese fan or fountain palm (*L. chinensis*), of China, the Australian cabbage palm (*L. australis*), of Australia, and *L. rotundifolia*, of Java. Attaining a height of 20 to 30 feet, **L. chinensis** has a stout trunk. Its bright green leaves form a dense, rounded crown, with the lowermost leaves drooping, the uppermost erect. They are 3 to 6 feet in diameter and round to kidney-shaped. The leaf divisions are cut to one-half or less the depth of the blade and at their tips are again divided, with the ultimate divisions or the leaves of mature trees drooping. The leafstalks, 2 to 6 feet in length, may be furnished with small spines on their undersides. The olive-shaped fruits are dull blue and about ½ inch long. Rather slender-trunked, *L. australis* attains a height of 60 feet or sometimes more and has a massive globular head of orbicular leaves, 4 to 8 feet in diameter, divided to their middles or beyond into numerous segments, and with conspicuously spiny stalks. Its small flowers in immense numbers are in clusters up to 4 feet long, with spathes 6 inches to 1 foot in length. The seeds, slightly larger than peas, are brownish-black. Javanese **L. rotundifolia**, up to 80 feet in height, has a rather slender, obscurely-ringed trunk and round leaves up to 6 feet across that have stalks about as long armed with long, recurved spines. The leaf blade is divided beyond its middle into sixty to ninety segments.

Other kinds cultivated include these: *L. humilis*, native of Australia, is 6 to 15 feet in height and has leaves up to 3 feet across with stalks with short prickles. *L. jenkinsiana*, the only kind native to India, is about 30 feet tall and has leaves up to 6 feet in diameter. They are used for thatching and other purposes. Its fruits are blue. *L. mariae*, of central Australia, is similar to *L. australis*, but is more slender and taller and has slightly smaller leaves, which, when young, are distinctly reddish. This kind occurs naturally only in a very limited area in a sunken river bed surrounded by arid desert, as contrasted with *L. australis*, which inhabits a much larger rain forest region of eastern Australia. *L. saribus* (syns. *L. cochinchinensis, L. hoogendorpii*), of Malaya, has a comparatively slender trunk and is up to 50 feet tall. Its leaves, with deeply-cleft segments, are up to 6 feet in diameter and have stout spines on their stalks.

Garden and Landscape Uses. Among fan-leaved palms these are great favorites. Of easy culture, they are impressive as single specimens, in groups, or planted formally in avenues or along driveways. They associate effectively with such architectural features as steps and terraces and are of good appearance when grown in containers. They are suitable for full sun or light part-shade.

Cultivation. Among the easiest of palms to grow, these prosper in most ordinary garden soils, although some kinds do not respond well to alkaline ones. This is particularly true of *L. australis* and *L. mariae*. Propagation is by fresh seed sown in sandy peaty soil in a temperature of 70 to 75°F. Indoors, livistonas thrive in well-drained pots or tubs in coarse, fertile, porous soil or planted in ground beds in large conservatories. They need a fairly moist atmosphere and some shade from strong summer sun. Watering should be adequate to prevent the soil from ever really drying, and with well-rooted specimens should be supplemented by regular applications of dilute liquid fertilizer from spring through fall. For more tropical species, such as *L. rotundifolia* and *L. humilis*, the minimum winter night temperature should be 65 to 70°F. Those from more temperate climates, such as *L. chinensis* and *L. australis*, succeed where the winter minimum is 55 to 60°F. For further information see Palms.

LIZARD'S TAIL. See Saururus.

LLOYDIA (Llóyd-ia). Related to tulips and to dog's-tooth-violets (*Erythronium*), the genus *Lloydia* inhabits mountains in Europe and Asia and the Rocky Mountains. It consists of twenty bulbous herbaceous plants of the lily family LILIACEAE. The name commemorates Edward Lloyd, who discovered *L. serotina* in Wales. He died in 1709.

Lloydias have small, slender bulbs, several narrowly-linear basal leaves, and stems with few leaves and usually one or two blooms. The latter are small, white or yellowish, with six spreading petals (correctly, tepals) and six stamens. The fruits are capsules containing flattish seeds.

The only kind likely to be cultivated is *L. serotina*, a native of the Rocky Mountains, European mountains, and arctic regions. This, the most widely naturally distributed member of the lily family, has somewhat rhizomatous bulbs that give rise to four or five slender leaves. The flowers are usually solitary, but may be in clusters of up to five, on stems 3 to 6 inches tall. They are whitish with yellowish-purple bases.

Garden Uses and Cultivation. The most appropriate use for these plants is in rock gardens. Perfectly hardy to cold, *L. serotina* is less patient of hot dry summers and in many gardens is not easy to grow. It should be tried in gritty, damp, but well-drained, peaty soil, in sun with perhaps a little shade during the hottest part of the day. Propagation is by offsets and seed.

LOAM. In old literature, especially that of Great Britain, the term loam generally meant any freely-workable, mellow, fertile soil that contained generous amounts of organic matter. A more technical and restricted modern usage of the word is as the name of a particular textural type of soil, one that contains 7 to 27 percent clay, 28 to 50 percent silt, and less than 52 percent sand. Such soil may or may not contain organic matter, be mellow or be fertile. Loam soils are further distinguished as sandy loam, silt loam, and clay loam according to the relative proportions they contain of the critical mineral fractions their names imply.

LOASA (Lo-àsa). From closely related *Cajophora*, the sorts of *Loasa* differ in their seed capsules not being spirally twisted. They belong in the loasa family LOASACEAE and are natives from Mexico to temperate South America. There are about 100 species. The name comes from a native South American one.

Loasas are usually bushy, rarely vining, subshrubby perennials and annuals with stinging hairs. Their leaves are opposite or alternate and may be lobeless, lobed, or divided into leaflets. The flowers, from the leaf axils, are solitary, in clusters, or racemes. They face downward and are curiously shaped. They have usually five, but sometimes up to seven, sepals, and the same number of spreading or sometimes almost erect, boat-shaped petals. There are usually five nectar scales each with two or three bristle-like sterile filaments at the back and with two staminodes (sterile stamens) opposite each. The fertile stamens are in groups concealed in the petals.

Native to northern South America, *L. triphylla* is an annual up to 2 feet tall with opposite, coarsely-toothed, mostly deeply-three-lobed leaves, or the upper ones lobeless. Its nearly 1-inch-wide flowers are white with the nectar scales yellow crossbanded with red and white. A more attractive ornamental more frequently culti-

Loasa triphylla vulcanica

vated than the species, *L. t. vulcanica* (syn. *L. vulcanica*) is a bushy annual 2 to 3 feet in height, with leaves three- to five-lobed in handlike fashion, and 3 to 6 inches across. The flowers, in leafy racemes of six to eight, are about 1½ inches across. They have white, spreading petals, and red nectar scales crossbanded with red and white. The seed capsules are about ¾ inch long. This kind is sometimes wrongly identified in gardens as *Blumenbachia hieronymii*.

Among other loasas sometimes cultivated is *L. acanthifolia*, of Chile, which is 3 to 4 feet tall and has pinnately-lobed leaves 3 to 4 inches long. Its solitary yellow flowers are about ¾ inch in diameter and have sepals longer than the petals. Another Chilean, *L. tricolor*, attains a height of 2 feet and has opposite, twice-pinnate leaves. The sepals of its yellow-petaled flowers are about as long as the petals. The crown of the bloom is red, the stamens, white. The plant previously known as *L. lateritia* is *Cajophora lateritia*.

Garden Uses and Cultivation. Although by no means among the showiest of annuals, loasas have a charm and quaintness that wins for them a modest place in gardens, at the fronts of flower borders, and in rock gardens, for example. Because they, when handled, sting like nettles, it is well to locate them where they will not attract children.

Cultivation. Seed sown thinly in early spring where the plants are to bloom is the best method of raising loasas. The seedlings are thinned to stand 6 inches apart. (Gloves should be worn when this is done.) Full sun and fertile garden soil, not too sandy and one that does not dry excessively, provide suitable growing conditions. No staking is needed, and the plants bloom for a long summer season.

LOASACEAE—Loasa Family. Mostly natives of tropical, subtropical, and warm-temperate parts of the Americas, but represented as well in southwest Africa and Arabia, the fifteen dicotyledonous genera of the *Loasaceae* comprise 250 species of chiefly herbaceous plants. Often with twining stems, they have opposite or alternate leaves, and stems, leaves, and other parts are usually furnished with bristly, sometimes stinging hairs. In spraylike clusters, the yellow, white, or occasionally red flowers commonly have five sepals, rarely fewer or more, the same number of petals as sepals, usually numerous stamens, but sometimes only ten, five, or two, and often staminodes (aborted stamens), which may be stamen- or petal-like. The style may be two- or three-branched or branchless. The fruits are capsules. Cultivated genera are *Blumenbachia*, *Cajophora*, *Eucnide*, *Loasa*, and *Mentzelia*.

LOBE. In its botanical sense this refers to a partial division of an organ. Thus a leaf the margin of which is more deeply incised than it would be if merely toothed, but not incised to the extent that the clefts extend to the midrib or base as they do in a leaf with separate leaflets, is said to be lobed. In like manner a calyx or corolla of a flower may consist of separate sepals or petals, respectively, or be merely slashed partway to its base to produce calyx or corolla lobes that extend above the lower tubular part of the calyx or corolla. Or a single sepal or petal may be lobed, as is often true of the lips of orchids. Other organs, including styles, can be lobed. The use of the word lobe is sometimes restricted to divisions not extending appreciably more than halfway from the margins or apexes to the bases of the parts.

LOBELIA (Lo-bèlia)—Cardinal Flower or Indian-Pink, Indian-Tobacco. Fantastic is scarcely too strong a word to use in describing the immense diversity of forms of *Lobelia*. Its species range from a partially submerged aquatic that inhabits North America and Europe, to the giant tree lobelias of mountains of East Africa. These attain heights of 10 to nearly 30 feet and live for twenty years or more. In addition, there are the brilliant cardinal flower and other attractive, herbaceous perennials of North and South America, as well as lower, frailer perennials, usually grown as annuals, of South Africa and Australia. A truly remarkable genus, this contains between 200 and 300 species. By some authorities it is segregated, together with related genera, as the lobelia family LOBELIACEAE, but more often it is accommodated in the bellflower family CAMPANULACEAE. Those who accept the split do so largely on the basis of the blooms of the species they include in *Lobeliaceae* being asymmetrical and having the anthers united around the style, in contrast to those of *Campanula* and other genera they accept in the bellflower family, which have symmetrical blooms with anthers not cohering. The name *Lobelia* honors the Flemish botanist Matthias de Lobel, or L'Obel, who died in 1616. Some, perhaps most lobelias, including the Indian-tobacco and

L. tupa, are poisonous if eaten. Indian-tobacco is used medicinally.

Lobelias are mostly annuals and herbaceous perennials. A few develop somewhat woody stems. They have alternate leaves, the larger sometimes all basal, and those of the stems represented by bracts. The blue, red, yellowish, or white flowers are solitary or in terminal racemes, spikes, or panicles. They have calyxes with five unequal lobes and a tubular, two-lipped corolla slit along one side almost or quite to its base. The lower lip of the corolla is three-lobed, the upper one two-lobed. The anthers of the five stamens are united around the style. Two or all of them are hairy at their tips. The fruits are capsules.

Lobelia cardinalis

Cardinal flower or Indian-pink (*L. cardinalis*) is a beautiful native of moist soils from New Brunswick to Michigan, Florida, and Texas. A hairless or essentially hairless perennial 2 to 4 feet tall, it has erect, mostly branchless, leafy stems, and bracted, raceme-like spikes of brilliant cardinal-red blooms 1 inch to 1½ inches long. The lower lips of the flowers are cleft into three narrow lobes. The pointed, lanceolate to oblong leaves, up to 6 inches long by 2 inches wide, have toothed margins. Much like the cardinal flower, but with slightly larger blooms, **L. splendens** (syn. *L. fulgens*) has linear to linear-lanceolate leaves 2 to 7 inches long. A native of Mexico, in Great Britain this is frequently confused with *L. cardinalis*. Unlike the latter, it is not hardy in the north. In cultivated varieties the foliage is often rich bronze or purplish-crimson.

Lobelia siphilitica

Lobelia siphilitica (flowers)

Bright blue-flowered **L. siphilitica** is a handsome, stiffly erect, herbaceous perennial. Its name indicates a medical virtue it was at one time mistakenly supposed to possess. This sort occurs wild in moist and wet soils from Maine to Manitoba, Louisiana, and Texas. Hairless, or with scattered hairs, it has rarely branched, leafy stems 2 to 3 feet tall. The stalkless or winged-stalked, toothed leaves are lanceolate to oblong-elliptic or oblanceolate and 3½ to 6 inches long. The rich blue to purplish blooms, interspersed with narrow bracts, are in slender, erect spikes. About 1 inch long, they have very small upper lips and much larger, down-pointing, lower ones. Variety *L. s. alba* has white flowers. A dwarf variety is *L. s. nana*. Blue-flowered **L. glandulosa** inhabits wet soils from Virginia to North Carolina and Florida. Probably less hardy than the last, it has a branchless stem, 1 foot to 3 feet tall. Its

Lobelia vedrariensis

leaves are linear and toothed, the upper ones much smaller than those below, 2 to 4 inches long by up to ⅓ inch wide. The rather distantly spaced blue flowers, ¾ to 1 inch long, are in one-sided spikes.

Beautiful hybrids between *L. cardinalis* and *L. siphilitica* have been raised. Intermediate between their parents, these usually have lovely rosy-purple blooms. Many such hybrids were developed about the mid-twentieth century by Dr. A. B. Stout of The New York Botanical Garden, others reportedly in England. Hybrids stated to be of the same parentage had been raised earlier in England. However, in view of the long-standing and persistent confusion that has existed in Great Britain regarding the identities of *L. cardinalis* and *L. splendens,* it is possible hybrids developed there resulted from mating the last-named species and *L. siphilitica,* rather than *L. cardinalis* and *L. siphilitica.* The hybrids are usually grouped as *L. vedrariensis,* although *L. milleri* is probably the older and therefore more correct name for them. As an illustration of confusion in British literature on this subject, a hybrid reported to be between *L. cardinalis* 'Queen Victoria' and *L. siphilitica* was named *L. gerardii.* But well-known *L.* 'Queen Victoria' is not a variety of *L. cardinalis,* but of *L. splendens.*

Indian-tobacco (*L. inflata*) is more interesting, because of its medicinal properties, than beautiful. Native from Labrador to Georgia and Arkansas, it is a hairy annual 1 foot to 3 feet in height, with slender, usually branched stems, and toothed, ovate to ovate-lanceolate leaves up to 3½ inches long by 2 inches wide. The lower leaves are blunt, the upper ones sometimes pointed. The pale blue or white blooms, about ¼ inch long, are arranged loosely in terminal spikelike racemes. The corolla tube exceeds the lower lip in length. This species is the source of the alkaloid lobeline.

Aquatic *L. dortmanna,* a hairless perennial that grows partly submerged near the shores of ponds and lakes from Newfoundland to Minnesota and New Jersey, and in Europe, has basal rosettes of hollow, linear, fleshy leaves, curved toward their apexes, and ¾ inch to 4 inches long. Its erect, branchless stem, depending upon the depth of the water, is up to 3 feet long and furnished with tiny bracts. The few ½-inch-long, nodding, pale blue or white flowers make little show. This plant also is more botanically interesting than beautiful.

A subshrub or evergreen herbaceous perennial, freely-branched, and 2 to 5 feet in height, *L. laxiflora* is a native of Mexico. It has toothed, narrowly-lanceolate to ovate-lanceolate, nearly stalkless leaves. The red and yellow, 1½-inch-long, slender, cylindrical, pubescent flowers come from the axils of the upper leaves. They termi-

nate long, slender stalks. The stamens protrude to one side of the bloom. Variety *L. l. angustifolia* has narrower leaves and smaller blooms than the typical species.

Native to Baja California *L. dunnii* (syn. *Palmerella debilis*) is less well known than its variety *L. d. serrata* (syn. *P. debilis serrata*), of southern California. This last differs from the species in having broader, toothed leaves and in other details. A sprawling to erect herbaceous perennial 1 foot to 2 feet tall, it has hairless, lanceolate to oblanceolate, toothed leaves up to 3 inches long and in terminal racemes often compact and rather headlike, two-lipped flowers ¾ to 1 inch long, with corollas with whitish tubes and blue lobes (petals).

Very distinctive *L. tupa,* of Chile, is not hardy in the north. A beautiful herbaceous perennial or subshrub, this sort is 4 to 7 feet tall. It has pointed, finely-toothed, finely-hairy, oblong-elliptic leaves that have somewhat the appearance of those of flowering tobacco (*Nicotiana*). In long, terminal, loose, spirelike racemes, its long-stalked, muted-crimson flowers are about 2 inches long and swollen at their bases. The three lobes of the long, down-curled corolla lip are joined at their apexes. The stamens arch upward.

Lobelia tupa

Lobelias commonly grown as annuals, but really nonhardy herbaceous perennials, include many garden varieties of South African *L. erinus.* This is a slender-stemmed semitrailing, hairless or slightly hairy kind with leafy stems. The leaves are small, the lower round-toothed and obovate to spatula-shaped, the upper oblanceolate to linear and angled. The slender-stalked flowers are ½ to ¾ inch wide. Only two of the anthers are bearded. This popular, variable species is represented in cultivation by numerous varieties with such fancy horticultural names as 'Crystal Palace', 'Sapphire', and 'Waverly Blue'. Some of these kinds are low and very compact. Some are taller and looser. Others have trailing stems. In some varieties the foliage is yellowish or bronzy-red. Varieties vary in flower color from palest to deepest blue and purple-blue often with a white eye, to pink and

Lobelia erinus 'Waverly Blue'

crimson, as well as pure white. Some varieties are double-flowered.

Australian *L. tenuior* (syn. *L. ramosa*) and *L. gracilis* are not unlike some varieties of *L. erinus,* and serve much the same purposes. Pubescent *L. tenuior* has slender, erect stems up to 1 foot tall or taller, and rather widely spaced, usually thrice-divided or three-lobed lower leaves, and practically lobeless, linear or lanceolate upper ones. On slender stalks, the rather distantly spaced bright blue flowers are 1 inch long. The middle lobe of the lip is much longer than the others. All the anthers are hairy. From the last, *L. gracilis* differs in its stems and foliage being hairless. It is under 1 foot tall, and has deeply-pinnately-cleft leaves, the lower ovate, those above linear, the very uppermost neither cleft nor lobed. In loose, usually one-sided clusters, the white-eyed, blue flowers are ½ to ¾ inch in diameter. The small upper pair of corolla lobes is curved and usually hairy.

Garden and Landscape Uses. The native North American perennials discussed above, among which the cardinal flower and *L. siphilitica* are outstandingly beautiful, and their hybrids, are best adapted for naturalizing at watersides and in other moist soil areas where there is a little shade such as may come from nearby trees or buildings. They seem to do better when left to accommodate without too much human interference than they do in the tended, tidier surroundings of well-maintained flower beds, although it is by no means impossible to have them prosper in such places. The keys to success are to give them, as immediate neighbors, plants that do not root too aggressively, and to make sure that the soil from spring to fall is never dry.

Much less hardy, perennial *L. splendens,* popular in Great Britain and other parts of Europe, and there available in several fine varieties such as 'Huntsman', is little known in North America. It does not prosper where summers are excessively hot and will not stand much winter cold. Areas such as the Pacific Northwest afford conditions most nearly to its liking. Where

Lobelia laxiflora

hardy, it may be used in the same ways as the cardinal flower. It is also satisfactory for forcing into early bloom in greenhouses. In Europe it is usual to dig the plants up in fall and to winter them in cold frames or cool greenhouses, then in late winter or early spring to divide them into single-shoot pieces, and pot these separately to give plants ready to set in the outdoor beds at the time begonias, geraniums, fuchsias, and other temporary summer display plants are planted. In parts of California and the Pacific Northwest, splendid *L. tupa* succeeds. Tender to more than very light frost, this grows in ordinary, preferably deep soil, in sheltered locations in sun or part-day shade. It resents root disturbance. Once established, it should be permitted to develop without interference. Aquatic *L. dortmanna* is likely to appeal only to collectors of aquatic plants. It is suitable for growing in ponds and other still waters.

Annual lobelias, or to be more precise, kinds commonly grown as annuals, especially varieties of *L. erinus*, are much esteemed as edging plants and for window and porch boxes, garden vases, and other containers. They are often used effectively with sweet alyssum. The trailing kinds are fine in hanging baskets. Annual lobelias can also be grown in pots to decorate cool greenhouses. They do better where summers are fairly cool than under more torrid conditions. Indian-tobacco is likely to be cultivated only in collections of medicinal plants.

Cultivation. If suitably located, hardy perennial lobelias need no special care. Only when they begin to show signs of deterioration should they be dug up, divided, and transplanted. This is best done in early spring. It is helpful to keep them mulched with peat moss, compost, or similar material, and in cold regions to afford them the winter protection of a covering of branches of evergreens, salt or marsh hay, or straw. Propagation is easy by seed sown in moist soil in fall or, after storing overwinter in a refrigerator at 40°F, in early spring. Careful division in spring is a means of increase. The cardinal flower can be multiplied by pinning stems in summer onto beds of moist sand. This results in young plants developing along their lengths. When rooted these can be separated and potted or planted individually. Of perennials not hardy in the north, *L. tupa* is growable only in particularly favored regions. It may be increased by seed and by cuttings. Where well located it calls for no special attention, but benefits from being kept mulched. In climates suitable for its permanent growth outdoors, the same is true of *L. splendens*. In other areas of cool summers it may be managed as is done in Europe, explained under Garden and Landscape Uses, above. Varieties of *L. splendens* are easily forced for spring bloom. In late summer or early fall, pot strong plants in

fertile soil in containers 6 or 7 inches in diameter. Plunge (bury) the pots to their rims in peat moss, sand, cinders, or sawdust in a cold frame and keep them well watered. Do not cover the cold frame with sash until the weather turns decidedly cold at night, and even then ventilate the frame on all mild days. On very cold nights mats spread over the sash may be needed for additional protection. In January or February transfer the plants to a sunny greenhouse where the night temperature is 45 to 50°F and water to keep the soil evenly moist. After growth is well started apply dilute liquid fertilizer at seven- to ten-day intervals. After blooming is through remove the plants from their pots and divide and plant them in a fertile, moist soil in part shade outdoors to provide plants for forcing the following year.

Lobelias of the *L. erinus*, *L. tenuior*, and *L. gracilis* types are easily grown as annuals. In their early stages they develop more slowly than many popular annuals. To have plants for setting in the garden in late May, sow the seeds in a greenhouse or under equivalent conditions indoors in February or early March. The seed is fine. Cover it very lightly with soil. Keep the seed pots where the temperature is 60 to 65°F at night, a few degrees warmer by day. Shade until germination begins, then after a few days with only light shade from strong sun, expose them to full sun and lower the temperature to 55°F at night and proportionately by day. Too little light and excessively high temperatures result in the seedlings becoming weak, spindly, and targets for damping off fungus that soon kills them. Before the seedlings become too crowded, and as soon as they are large enough to handle, transplant them to flats or trays. Let these be shallower than for many annuals. An interior depth of 2½ inches is sufficient. Set the plants in tiny clumps or tufts, not singly as is done with most annuals, about 2 inches apart. Return the flats to conditions similar to those in which the seedlings were growing for about a week and then transfer them to where the night temperature is 50°F and by day up to fifteen degrees warmer. A couple of weeks before the plants are to be planted outside, move them to a cold frame or sheltered place outdoors to harden.

LOBIVIA (Lo-bívia). The name of this genus, of the cactus family CACTACEAE, is an anagram of *Bolivia* where many of its sorts are native. Comprising seventy-five species, *Lobivia* is endemic to the southern Andean region of South America. Species of *Pseudolobivia* are by some botanists accommodated in *Lobivia*.

Lobivias are small to medium-sized cactuses, often with big taproots. Their plant bodies or stems are spherical to nearly cylindrical, solitary or clustered, distinctly ribbed, and more or less spiny. The comparatively large, short-tubed, funnel- to

Lobivia, undetermined species

bell-shaped, usually red to violet-pink, but sometimes white or yellow flowers remain open during the day and generally close at night. They have scaly and hairy perianth tubes and ovaries. The fruits also are scaly and hairy.

A considerable number of kinds are cultivated; among them are these: *L. allegraiana*, of Peru, has usually solitary, slightly glaucous, green stems with spiraled, lumpy ribs. Each cluster of spines consists of about a dozen, curved and yellowish-brown. The red flowers are about 2 inches long. *L. arachnacantha* is a Bolivian with small, flattish-spherical plant bodies with about fourteen rounded ribs. Its spine clusters are of nine to fifteen white, thin radials and one black, upward-bent central. The slender-tubed, yellow blooms are 1½ inches across. *L. backebergii* is a small to medium-sized native of Bolivia. It has spherical to egg-shaped plant bodies, solitary or clustered, about 2 inches in diameter. They have about fifteen low ribs and clusters of three to seven gray, pliable radial spines ¼ inch to 2 inches in length. There are no centrals. The crimson blooms are 1 inch wide. *L. binghamiana*, of Peru, has solitary or clustered, flattened-spherical, white-dotted, light green stems about 3½ inches wide and with twenty-two shallow, wavy ribs. The spines are in clusters of nine to twelve uneven, sharp, orange-yellow radials and three to six centrals up to a little over ½ inch in length. The 2-inch-long blooms are purplish-red. *L. boliviensis* is a native of Bolivia. It has clusters of spherical to longish-cylindrical plant bodies with about twenty notched ribs. The spines, in clusters of six to eight, are 2 to 4 inches long. Pale lilac-red with yellow throats, the blooms are 1½ inches across. *L. caespitosa*, of Bolivia, has cylindrical plant bodies up to 4 or 5 inches high by 1¾ inches thick. They have ten to twelve straight, lumpy ribs and spine clusters of twelve ½-inch-long, brown radials and one 2-inch-long central similarly colored. The blooms, which do not open fully, are 2 to 3 inches long by 1 inch wide. They are yellowish-red. *L. chrysantha*, a variable native of Argentina, has solitary, cylindrical plant bodies with ten to thirteen low, rounded ribs and clusters of five to seven or in some varieties up to fourteen dark-tipped radial spines ¾ inch long, and few or no centrals. The 2-inch-wide, funnel-shaped flowers are yellow, sometimes with a red throat. *L. cinnabarina*, of Bolivia, has solitary plant bodies broader than tall with about twenty lumpy ribs. The spine clusters are of eight to ten backward-bent radials and two or three centrals. The scarlet blooms are 1¾ inches wide. *L. famatimensis* is a variable species native of Argentina. It has clustered or solitary stems 1 inch to 1½ inches tall by up to 1 inch wide. They have clusters of fifteen to twenty whitish radial spines and sometimes one or two brown centrals. In the typical species the 2-inch-wide flowers are yellow with a green throat. Those of varieties may be white, orange, or red. *L. haageana,* a native of Argentina, is a highly variable clustering species with cylindrical stems with about twenty-two notched ribs. The spine clusters are of approximately ten straw-yellow, 1-inch-long radials and two to four darker centrals 2 to 3 inches long. The light yellow flowers, 2½ inches across, have red throats. In varieties of this species the blooms vary from beige-yellow to crimson. The red blooms of *L. h. grandiflora-stellata* are 3½ inches in diameter. *L. mistiensis* is a Peruvian, usually solitary-stemmed species with spherical or subspherical plant bodies with twenty-five to thirty notched ribs. In clusters of seven to nine or more the all radial, whitish-gray, needle-like spines are about 2 inches long. The 2-inch-wide blooms are yellowish-red. *L. pentlandii* is a variable native of Bolivia and Peru. It has clustering, egg-shaped, often somewhat glaucous plant bodies about 6 inches wide. They have about twelve notched ribs with clusters of seven to fifteen needle-like spines 1 inch to 1½ inches long. The orange, pink, or white blooms about 1½ inches in diameter have incurved petals. *L. pseudocachensis,* of Argentina, has solitary or clustered, flattened-spherical plant bodies about 2½ inches in diameter with about fourteen ribs. The spine clusters are of about ten brownish-yellow radials up to ½ inch long and one slightly longer almost black central. The dark red flowers are 2½ inches wide. Variety *L. p. cinnabarina* has cinnabar-red blooms. Those of *L. p. san-*

guinea are fiery-red. *L. raphidacantha,* of Bolivia, is a clustering sort with flattened-spherical plant bodies with about sixteen ribs. The clusters of spines usually are of about six radials and one longer central up to 3 inches in length. The blooms are dark red. *L. rebutioides,* of Argentina, forms dense cushions of dull bluish-green, flattened-spherical plant bodies a little over ½ inch wide. Each has twelve to fourteen lumpy ribs and clusters of eight or nine translucent, glossy-white, radial spines about ¾ inch long and one longer one. The bright red blooms are 1½ inches wide. Those of *L. r. citriniflora* are 2½ inches wide and yellow, those of *L. r. chlorogona* as wide and deep golden-yellow, those of *L. r. sublimiflora* as broad and salmon-pink. *L. rubescens,* of Argentina, resembles *L. haageana,* but has spine clusters of twelve radials and four centrals, the latter up to 1¾ inches long. The flowers are reddish and about 2½ inches wide. *L. sanguiniflora,* native to Argentina, has plant bodies with eighteen low, notched ribs and spine clusters of about ten short, thin, twisted, white radials and several centrals one of which is up to 3 inches long and hooked. The blood-red blooms are 2 inches in diameter. *L. schieliana* is Bolivian. Small and daintily-spined, this has nearly spherical plant bodies about 1½ inches across with about fourteen ribs. The clusters are of approximately fourteen yellowish spines with or without one central 2 inches long or slightly longer. The red flowers are 1 inch or somewhat more across. *L. schreiteri* is a clump-forming species from Argentina. Its spherical, grayish-green plant bodies, barely up to 1½ inches in diameter, have nine to fourteen notched, low ribs. The spine clusters are of seven to nine grayish radials and one brown-tipped, slightly hooked central about ¾ inch long. The bright red blooms with blackish throats are about 1¼ inches wide. *L. shaferi* is Argentinian. It has clusters of cylindrical, very spiny stems 3 to 6 inches tall and 1 inch to 1½ inches in diameter. They have about ten ribs. Its clusters of all white, brown-mottled spines are of ten to fifteen needle-like, ½-inch-long radials and one to three stouter centrals 1½ inches in length. The yellow blooms are 1½ to 2½ inches long. *L. tiegeliana,* of Bolivia, has glossy-green plant bodies nearly 2½ inches thick. Each has about eighteen notched ribs and spine clusters of eight to twelve brown-tipped, pale yellow radials about ⅜ inch long and one to three much longer, glistening, dark brown centrals, paler toward their bases. The flowers, glowing violet-pink, just exceed 1½ inches in diameter. *L. varians* is a Bolivian species with clusters of flattened-spherical stems about 3½ inches tall by 5 inches across and with about twenty notched ribs. Each spine cluster consists of ten stiff, grayish-pink, slender spines some 4 inches long. The funnel-shaped flowers

are orange-red and approximately 1½ inches wide. In *L. v. croceantha* the blooms are deep yellow. Those of *L. v. rubro-alba* are red and white. *L. westii* is a Peruvian species with clusters of plant bodies with sixteen to eighteen notched ribs and in clusters of about nine dark-tipped, straw-colored, needle-like spines that become gray with age. They are ½ to 1 inch long. The golden-yellow flowers, with long, slender perianth tubes, are 1½ inches in diameter. *L. wegheiana,* of Bolivia, has subglobose to cylindrical, branching stems with fourteen to twenty notched ribs. The spines are in clusters of seven or eight radials ½ to 1 inch long and one central spine up to 1½ inches long. The violet-rose flowers are about 1½ inches across.

Garden Uses and Cultivation. Lobivias are among the most attractive cactuses for including in collections, outdoors in warm desert and semidesert regions, and in greenhouses. They respond readily to the conditions and care that suit the majority of small to medium-sized desert cactuses and are propagated by offsets and seed. For more information see Cactuses.

LOBLOLLY-BAY is *Gordonia lasianthus.*

LOBOSTEMON (Lobo-stémon). Confined in the wild to Africa, and with most of its perhaps fifty species South African, *Lobostemon,* of the borage family BORAGINACEAE, is closely related to *Echium.* From that genus it differs in its flowers having styles not distinctly cleft, but only minutely two-lobed at their apexes, and in the stalks of the stamens having a tuft of hairs or a hairy scale at their bases. The name, from the Greek *lobos,* a lobe, and *stemon,* a thread or stamen, alludes to the stamens being opposite the petals.

Lobostemons are shrubs, subshrubs, and perennial herbaceous plants with alternate, usually rough-hairy, stalkless leaves. Their flowers, blue, violet, red, pink, or white, are in terminal heads, panicles, or spikes, or less commonly are solitary or in pairs from the leaf axils. They have a five-lobed calyx and a tubular or funnel-shaped, five-lobed corolla. The stamens, protruding or enclosed by the corolla, number five. The style ends in a small headlike stigma. The fruits consist of four distinct, erect nutlets.

Lobivia pentlandii with, grafted upon it, *Mammillaria microhelia*

Lobostemon fruticosus

Lobostemon trichotomus

Lobularia maritima

A beautiful shrub or subshrub up to 3 feet tall, *L. fruticosus* bears multitudes of blue, pink, or nearly white, asymmetrical, funnel-shaped flowers up to 1 inch long, with corollas hairy on their outsides. Its lanceolate to ovate-lanceolate or oblanceolate leaves are silky-hairy and ¾ inch to 2¼ inches in length. From it *L. trichotomus* differs in the corollas being hairless or essentially hairless on their outsides and in having well-developed scales instead of hairy ridges representing them at the bases of the stalks of the stamens. The plant is much branched, up to 3 feet tall, with linear to linear-lanceolate leaves up to 2 inches long, with scattered hairs. The blue or more rarely pink flowers are ¾ inch long.

Garden and Landscape Uses and Cultivation. Lobostemons are suitable for outdoors in a warm, dryish, Mediterranean-type climate, such as that of California. They are handsome ornamentals for flower beds and rock gardens and succeed in ordinary well-drained soil in sun. Propagation is by seed and cuttings.

LOBSTER CLAW. This is a colloquial name for *Heliconia humilis* and *H. jacquinii*.

LOBSTER CLAWS is *Vriesia carinata*.

LOBULARIA (Lobulàr-ia) — Sweet-Alyssum. Its name derived from *lobulus*, a small pod, in allusion to the fruits, *Lobularia* is a genus of five species of the Mediterranean region, the Near East, and the Canary Islands. It belongs in the mustard family CRUCIFERAE. One species is commonly cultivated as an annual, although, like the others of the genus, it is truly perennial. This, the sweet-alyssum, is almost always cataloged by seedsmen under its older name *Alyssum maritimum*. The more correct *Lobularia* is not much used in seed catalogs or by gardeners. From true *Alyssum* the genus *Lobularia* differs in having predominantly white or purple blooms and in technical details of the flowers. The blooms of *Alyssum* are yellow.

In its wild form, sweet-alyssum (*L. maritima*) is spreading or sprawling and up to 1 foot tall. It has slender, much-branched stems and alternate, toothless, linear to narrowly-lanceolate leaves up to 3 inches long. Its small flowers are borne in such profusion that they almost hide the plant. Delightfully fragrant, they occur in racemes that lengthen as the lower blooms fade and those above develop. There are many garden varieties of sweet-alyssum, most of which are dwarfer and more compact than the wild sort. They include such popular kinds as *L. m. benthamii*, *L. m. compacta*, and *L. m. minima*, as well as varieties with double flowers and with variegated leaves. Their flower colors range from purest white through pink to violet.

Garden Uses. No plant cultivated as a garden annual is easier to grow or more

A path edging of *Lobularia maritima*

A small bed of *Lobularia maritima*

useful for certain purposes than this. As an edging for paths and flower beds and borders, as a low temporary summer groundcover, as a subject to furnish quickly bare spots in the garden with blooming plants, it is nearly unrivaled. It is useful in rock gardens and for setting in crevices in planted dry walls and flagged paths. As its specific designation *maritima* suggests, it is thoroughly at home near the sea. It revels in brilliant sunshine and responds to salt air. Any passingly good garden soil suits this popular plant. If any plant be foolproof it is this. In addition to its employment in outdoor gardens sweet-alyssum is attractive when grown in pots in greenhouses. For this purpose the double-flowered and variegated-leaved kinds are especially suitable.

Cultivation. Except for double-flowered sorts and those with variegated foliage, which are easily increased from cuttings made from young non-flowering shoots, sweet-alyssums are invariably grown from seeds. These germinate surely and quickly, and the plants begin to bloom when not over six or seven weeks old, and often sooner. The seeds are sown outdoors in early spring or later to fill spaces left by the fading of other flowers. Sowing consists of scattering the seed thinly and raking it into the surface of the ground. A common mistake is to sow too thickly. If the seedlings are too crowded they should be thinned to stand 5 or 6 inches apart. If plants almost in bloom are needed to set out as soon as spring flowers, such as pansies, forget-me-nots, primroses, tulips, and hyacinths, are through and are lifted from the beds, they may be had by sowing sweet-alyssum indoors about six weeks before planting out time and growing the seedlings, spaced about 2 inches apart, in flats of porous soil in a cool, sunny greenhouse or under approximately similar conditions. Good soil drainage is essential, and overwatering, especially when the plants are small must be avoided. A night temperature of 50 to 55°F with a few degrees rise during the day is satisfactory. Similar environmental conditions are suitable for sweet-alyssums cultivated in pots or pans for indoor display. For these pots or pans 4 or 5 inches in diameter are appropriate.

Diseases and Pests. Sweet-alyssums are usually not seriously bothered by diseases and pests, but they are subject to a number. Club-root disease infects them (liming the soil sufficiently to keep it alkaline avoids this) and they may be whitened by downy mildew. White rust causes yellowish patches on the undersides of the leaves and deforms the stems and blooms. If the soil is poorly aerated or kept constantly too wet seedlings are likely to damp off and older plants to die from wilt disease. The virus disease aster yellows also infects sweet-alyssum. The most common insect pests are caterpillars.

LOCKHARTIA (Lock-hártia). Named to honor David Lockhart, first superintendent of the botanic garden of Trinidad, who died in 1846, *Lockhartia* belongs to the orchid family ORCHIDACEAE. Its thirty species range in the wild from Mexico to northern South America and Trinidad.

Distinctive in appearance, lockhartias are tufted epiphytes (tree-perchers that take no nourishment from their hosts). They have erect, ascending or pendulous, remarkably flattened stems with along their lengths two neat ranks of small, overlapping leaves that produce a distinctly braided effect. The small flowers, from the upper leaf axils, are solitary or in short racemes or loose panicles. They have three sepals, two nearly similar petals, and a longer, usually three-lobed lip, the lateral lobes linear, incurved or upcurved, the center lobe obovate to oblong, two- to four-lobed, and with a hairy or warty disk. The column is short.

Its erect stems 4 to 6 inches or rarely up to 1 foot tall, **L. elegans,** of tropical South America and Trinidad, has narrow-triangular, blunt leaves ½ to ¾ inch long and solitary or paired yellow or yellowish-green flowers with purple-spotted lips, about ½ inch across. Native from Panama to northern South America and Trinidad, **L. acuta** (syn. *L. pallida*) differs from the last in having pointed leaves up to 1 inch long and flowers several to many together in loose panicles 2 to 3 inches long. The arching or pendulous stems are 8 inches to nearly 2 feet long. The blooms, under ⅝ inch across, are white or whitish with a yellowish or yellow lip, the center lobe of which is four-lobed. Brazilian **L. lunifera** has erect to pendulous stems 4 to 8 inches long. Its pointed-triangular leaves are nearly ¾ inch in length. Solitary or in two or threes, the golden-yellow blooms, about ¾ inch wide, have brownish-red-veined lips with two-lobed center lobes.

Lockhartia acuta

Garden Uses and Cultivation. Lockhartias are delightful in orchid collections, being neat of foliage and pleasing in bloom. They are easy to grow in warm, humid greenhouses, and in the humid tropics and subtropics outdoors. They may be grown in smallish pots, pans (shallow pots), or baskets, in osmunda or tree fern fiber or fir bark, or attached to slabs of tree fern trunk. Water is needed throughout the year, in lesser amounts in winter than other seasons. Moderate fertilizing is helpful. Sufficient shade from strong sun to prevent yellowing or scorching of the foliage is necessary. Because these orchids resent interference with their roots, repotting must not be done oftener than quite necessary but the rooting compost must be changed before it becomes stagnant and sour. Old worn-out stems no longer capable of producing satisfactory bloom should be removed by cutting them out cleanly at their bases without damaging adjoining stems. For more information see Orchids.

LOCOWEED is the common name of certain species of *Astragalus* and *Oxytropis.*

LOCUST. See Robinia. Honey-, swamp-, sweet-, and water-locusts are species of *Gleditsia.* The West-Indian-locust is *Hymenaea courbaril.*

LODOICEA (Lodoìc-ea)—Double-Coconut or Coco-De-Mer. The only species of *Lodoicea* is a fan-leaved member of the palm family PALMAE. One of the most remarkable plants in the world, it has the biggest of all seeds and occurs wild on only two small islands of the Seychelles group in the Indian Ocean. Its name honors Louis XV of France, whose name may be latinized as Lodoicus. He died in 1774.

The double-coconut or coco-de-mer is not closely related to the common coconut (*Cocos nucifera*), but received its name because its immense fruits resemble pairs of coconuts joined in Siamese-twin fashion. Because these great fruits, which when fresh, are heavier than water, sometimes roll into the sea, become partially rotted and then float, on occasion for long distances, to be washed up on distant shores, notably those of the Maldive Islands, India, and Indonesia, they were familiar to man long before their origin was known.

Their scarcity, peculiar shape, and mysterious origin inspired a variety of tales. Some thought them fruits of a giant submarine plant. Others, detecting in the form of the fruits a likeness to the human female pelvis, attributed aphrodisiac properties to them and the stranded nuts were prized and sought by kings and emperors. It is recorded that Rudolph II, of the Hapsburgs, offered, unsuccessfully, four thousand gold florins for one.

Not until 1768 was the plant that bore them discovered. Then a French engineer surveying the island of Praslin recognized the fruits and tree and gathered specimens. Soon collected nuts were dumped on the Indian market in such great quantities that prices paid for them dropped precipitously. The double-coconut still flourishes in the Seychelles as a native on Praslin and on Curieuse Island, but it has been exterminated on Round Island where it also once grew wild. Fortunately small original forests of these palms on Praslin Island are now public preserves, the largest and best being the Vallee de Mai reservation. An interesting question is raised by the fact that lodoiceas grow at various altitudes on valley hillsides. The heavy nuts after falling cannot roll uphill so progeny must always develop below or at the same altitude as the parents. From where, then, did the palms at the highest elevations come?

The double-coconut (**L. maldivica**) at home attains a height in excess of 100 feet and has a crown of heavy fan-shaped leaves with stalks 10, 20, or even 30 feet long and blades 10 to 16 feet long by 6 to 8 feet wide. The blades are cleft but not very deeply into numerous segments that tend to droop. Male and female flowers are on separate trees, the former, which are yellow and quite attractive, in massive sausage-like spikes 3 to 6 feet long and the females in less crowded spikes of similar lengths. The flower clusters of both sexes originate in the leaf axils and are pendulous. On low trees they may touch the ground. The fruits are truly remarkable. From the time the female flower is fertilized by male pollen to maturity of the fruit, six years or more elapse. Typically the heart-shaped fruits are two-lobed, about 1½ feet long, and weigh twenty to forty pounds. They usually contain a single seed. Occasional specimens contain two or three seeds and may weigh a hundred pounds or more. Lodoiceas mature slowly, begin fruiting when about twenty-five years old and attain maturity at about the century mark. The oldest specimens in the Vallee de Mai are estimated to be about eight hundred years. In the Seychelles the leaves are employed for thatching and making hats, mats, and baskets, and the shells of the nuts are used for bowls, plates, and other utensils. The sweetish, white, jelly-like contents of young nuts is eaten as a delicacy.

Garden and Landscape Uses and Cultivation. Fresh seeds of this amazing palm are rarely available, and its cultivation is almost entirely confined to a very few botanical gardens and other special plant collections. Outdoors it needs an intensely tropical and humid climate. So far as is known there are no large specimens in Hawaii, and the plant does not really thrive in Florida, although young plants have been grown there. In the greenhouses of botanical gardens young specimens are sometimes displayed. Fresh seeds, planted horizontally in sandy peaty soil with their tops showing above the surface and placed in strong bottom heat in a tropical greenhouse take a year or sometimes considerably more before top growth begins. The temperature of the soil should be maintained at 80 to 90°F and the atmospheric temperature at a minimum of 70°F, rising to 90°F or above in summer. Root growth begins well before shoot growth and, as the primary root descends vertically to a depth of 3 feet or more before shoot activity shows, it is of the utmost importance that the seed be planted where this growth can be made without interruption, such as in a deep bed or atop a drainpipe filled with suitable soil. At all times both soil and atmosphere must be kept moist. Once past the seedling stage, this palm may be grown in greenhouses under the conditions recommended for *Verschaffeltia*. For further information see Palms.

LOESELIA (Loes-èlia). Comprising ten or more species, *Loeselia*, of the phlox family, POLEMONIACEAE, is indigenous from the southwestern United States to South America. Its name commemorates Johann Loesel, a European botanist, who died in 1657.

Loeselias are pubescent annuals, herbaceous perennials, and subshrubs with lower leaves opposite, and those above nearly so or alternate. The leaves are undivided, ovate to oblong or lanceolate, and toothed. The purple, red, pink, or white blooms are solitary or in clusters. They have usually papery, five-lobed calyxes associated with veiny bracts with membranous areas between the veins, and two-lipped, funnel- to salver-shaped, tubular corollas with five spreading lobes (petals), five protruding stamens, and a single style. The fruits are capsules with seeds that when wet are sticky.

Native to Mexico and southwestern Texas, *L. mexicana* is an attractive, branched, herbaceous perennial or subshrub up to 3 feet tall. Its sharp-toothed, elliptic to lanceolate leaves are up to 1½ inches long or sometimes longer. The solitary, brilliant rose-red to scarlet blooms, about ¾ inch across and with corolla tubes ¾ to 1 inch long, are displayed in long, spirelike, crowded, leafy panicles with elliptic bracts. Differing in having leaves up to 1 inch long, and white-centered, pink or blue flowers about ⅓ inch wide, with corolla tubes about ½ inch long, *L. scariosa* also is native of southwest Texas and Mexico. Its blooms are solitary or in twos or threes, associated with broad-ovate bracts, and less crowded on the stems than those of *L. mexicana*.

Garden and Landscape Uses and Cultivation. Not hardy in the north, loeselias are best suited for warm, dryish regions. They are appropriate for naturalistic plantings and flower beds, and succeed in sunny locations in well-drained earth. Propagation is by seed and cuttings planted in a cold frame or greenhouse propagating bench or under mist.

LOGANBERRY. See Blackberry.

LOGANIA (Lo-gània). The Irish-born botanist James Logan, who became Governor of Pennsylvania and died in 1751, is commemorated in the name of this genus, which typifies the logania family LOGANIACEAE. It comprises approximately twenty-five species, one endemic to New Zealand, the others Australian.

Loganias are shrubs and herbaceous plants with opposite, undivided leaves and small, white or pink, bisexual or unisexual flowers, most often in axillary and terminal clusters or sometimes assembled in leafy panicles. More rarely they are solitary. The blooms have five-lobed calyxes, five- or sometimes four-lobed corollas, five or four stamens, and one style topped with a rounded or an oblong stigma. The fruits are leathery, egg-shaped to globose capsules.

Cultivated in California, *Logania vaginalis* (syn. *L. longifolia*) is an Australian hairless shrub 3 to 6 feet tall. It has short-stalked, conspicuously-veined, pointed ovate to obovate lower leaves, and often broad-lanceolate upper ones. They have glossy upper sides and are ½ inch to 3½ inches long by ⅓ inch to nearly 1½ inches broad. The flowers, in long, narrow, leafy, terminal panicles, have blackish-green calyxes, and corollas approximately ¼ inch across, with spreading, white lobes (petals) and hairy throats.

Garden and Landscape Uses and Cultivation. Loganias are not hardy in the north. The species described is an interesting flowering shrub for mild, dryish climates. It needs well-drained ordinary soil, and a sunny location. It is increased by seed and by summer cuttings.

LOGANIACEAE—Logania Family. In the broad sense accepted here, this family of dicotyledons comprises 550 or more species contained in more than thirty genera. By some authorities certain of these are split away to form other families including *Buddleiaceae* and *Strychnaceae*. Species of the last are the source of the important poisonous drug strychnine.

The logania family consists of herbaceous plants, shrubs, and trees, mostly natives of warm-temperate, subtropical, and tropical regions of many parts of the world. Commonly they have opposite, undivided, toothed or toothless leaves. The symmetrical flowers are usually in clusters or in spikes or panicles. They have a four- or five-lobed calyx, a four- or five-cleft corolla, as many stamens as corolla lobes or very rarely only one, and a two- or seldom a four-cleft style. The fruits are capsules, berries, or drupes. Genera cultivated include *Buddleia*, *Desfontainea*, *Gelsemium*, *Geniostoma*, *Logania*, *Spigelia*, and *Strychnos*.

LOGWOOD is *Haematoxylum campechianum*.

LOISELEURIA (Loisel-eùria)—Alpine-Azalea. The French botanist and physician Jean Louis Auguste Loiseleur-Deslong-champs, who died in 1849, is commemorated in the name of this genus of the heath family ERICACEAE. It consists of a single species, an inhabitant of subarctic and high mountain regions of the northern hemisphere. In North America it ranges from high mountain tops in New York and New England to Alaska.

The alpine-azalea (*Loiseleuria procumbens*) is a prostrate, evergreen shrub of rare charm. Rarely exceeding 4 inches in height, it has very short-stalked, opposite, narrowly-elliptic, leathery leaves that have strongly rolled-under margins. They are up to ⅓ inch long and shortly-hairy on the mid-vein beneath. The short-stalked flowers, from the upper leaf axils, are in umbel-like clusters. White or pink, they have deeply-five-lobed, persistent calyxes and bell-shaped corollas cleft to about their middles into five lobes (petals). The five stamens and the pistil, about as long, do not protrude. The fruits are egg-shaped capsules containing many seeds.

Garden Uses and Cultivation. This is a challenging plant to grow away from its native haunts, yet, inevitably, any who have enjoyed its loveliness in the wild will wish to possess it. Although extremely hardy to cold, and when happy an entrancing addition to rock gardens and collections of alpine plants, few gardeners report success. It is most likely to persist where summers are cool and humid, and winters long and cold, but even so, in cultivation it rarely blooms with the freedom it does at home. A gritty, acid, peaty soil that never lacks for moisture, but is not boglike, and a location in the sun or part-day shade (this last is important where summers are hot) is recommended. A north-facing slope is likely to afford the best site. There the heat of the sun is tempered, but light is good, and this is essential for flowering. Increase may be had by seed, layering, and cuttings under mist or in a propagating bed in a cool greenhouse or cold frame. Specimens transplanted from the wild are unlikely to reestablish themselves.

LOLIUM (Lòl-ium)—Rye Grass. The chief horticultural use of this genus of the grass family GRAMINEAE is as inexpensive, temporary lawn grasses. They must not be confused with the cereal rye (*Secale cereale*), one form of which is employed horticulturally as a cover crop under the name winter rye. There are about eight species of *Lolium*, natives of Europe, North Africa, and temperate Asia. The name is an ancient Latin one for some weedy plant.

Loliums include annual and perennial tufted plants with usually erect stems and leaves with flat, narrow-linear blades. Their erect or nodding flower spikes are composed of solitary, stalkless, one- to many-flowered spikelets arranged edgewise and alternately on opposite sides of a zigzagged stalk and so spaced that the top of each spikelet does not reach to the bottom of the next above it on the same side of the stalk. Because of this arrangement the flower spikes have a plaited appearance. The darnel (*L. temulentum*) is a weed grass, believed to be the tares referred to in the Bible. Supposedly because of a parasitic fungus that invades it, it is poisonous to cattle. This species as well as the others discussed are naturalized in North America.

Italian rye grass (*L. multiflorum*) is an annual or a biennial 1 foot to 3 feet tall, with hairless leaf blades, shining on their undersides and up to almost ½ inch in width, that when young are rolled. The compressed flower spikes, 6 inches to 1 foot long, are composed of spikelets with awns (bristles) at their tips. Perennial or English rye grass (*L. perenne*) is a short-lived perennial with erect or spreading stems 6 inches to 3 feet long, and hairless leaves with blades up to ¼ inch broad that when young are folded along the midribs. They are glossy on their undersides. The flattened flower spikes, 2 inches to 1 foot long, are composed of spikelets without awns. Variety *L. p. paceyi*, which has smaller seeds, is used in lawn seed mixtures. Also used in lawn seed mixtures, domestic rye grass, Oregon rye grass, or Western rye grass, a hybrid of *L. multiflorum* and *L. perenne* more resembles the former than the latter. For more information see Lawns, Their Making and Renovation.

LOMARIA. See Blechnum.

LOMATIA (Lo-màtia). A few genera of woody plants are natives of Australia and South America and nowhere else, among them *Lomatia*, of the protea family PROTEACEAE. About six or so species inhabit each continent. They are much like grevilleas, but differ in having fruits that contain more than two seeds. Their name, alluding to the winged seeds, comes from the Greek *loma*, an edge.

Evergreen shrubs or trees, lomatias have alternate, toothless, toothed, or pinnately-divided leaves, often very variable even on the same plant. The flowers, generally creamy-white, but sometimes becoming pinkish, are bisexual. In pairs, they are grouped in terminal or axillary heads, loose racemes, or few-branched panicles. Their perianths are tubular, oblique at their apexes, and have four, usually considerably curled or twisted, linear lobes (petals) and four stamens. The slender style ends in an oblique, flat stigma. The fruits are small, leathery, podlike follicles, each containing several winged seeds.

The holly-lomatia (*L. ilicifolia*), of Australia, is a shrub up to 6 feet tall or taller, or sometimes a small tree. It has stalked, ovate-lanceolate, holly-like leaves 2 to 3 or occasionally 6 inches long. They have prickly or sometimes lobed margins; silky-hairy on their undersides, they have upper surfaces decorated with a network of paler, raised veins. The cream-colored flowers are in long, sometimes branched racemes. The mostly pinnate leaves of *L. fraxinifolia* are lustrous and leathery, and have three to seven coarsely-toothed leaflets 2 to 4 inches long. The flowers are in racemes or panicles 6 to 8 inches long. This native of Australia is a tall shrub or small tree. From 2 to 4 feet tall, shrubby *L. silaifolia*, of Australia, has mostly twice- or thrice- or less often once-pinnate leaves 4 to 8 inches in length and almost as broad as long. Pointed, the ultimate divisions are up to ¼ inch wide. The creamy-white flowers, about ⅓ inch long, are in erect, terminal, loose racemes or panicles 4 to 6 inches long. Chilean *L. hirsuta* (syn. *L. obliqua*) is a shrub or tree up to 20 feet high or sometimes higher. This has ovate, coarsely-blunt-toothed leaves, downy at first, later hairless, and 1½ to 4 inches long by ¾ inch to 2½ inches broad. The ½-inch-long, white flowers are in racemes from the leaf axils, their stalks at first are covered with rusty hairs. Also Chilean, graceful *L. ferruginea* has twice-pinnate leaves of ferny aspect, with dark green upper surfaces and hairy undersides. Their segments are three-toothed at their apexes. About ½ inch long, the yellow and scarlet blooms are hairy on their outsides.

Lomatia ferruginea

Garden and Landscape Uses and Cultivation. Lomatias are good flowering evergreens for outdoors in mild, dryish, almost or quite frostless climates, and can be grown in cool greenhouses. They prefer sunny locations, and well-drained soil of ordinary quality, peaty rather than of limestone derivation. In general they respond to the conditions and care that suit grevilleas. They can be increased by seed, and by cuttings made from firm, but not hard and woody, shoots planted in a mixture of peat moss and sand or perlite in a greenhouse propagating bench.

LOMATIUM (Lomàt-ium) — Desert-Parsley, Spring Gold. The approximately seventy-five species of *Lomatium* belong to the carrot family UMBELLIFERAE. They are natives of western and central North America, chiefly of dry soils. Their name, from the Greek *loma*, a border, alludes to the winged edges of the fruits.

Lomatiums are little known to gardeners, yet several are sufficiently decorative to warrant planting in regions where climates are suitable. They are hardy herbaceous perennials with woody, thick or tuberous, deep roots. Most kinds have all basal foliage or at most only a few leaves low on the stems. A few develop foliage higher on the stems. The leaves are divided, sometimes finely, into small segments or sometimes into larger leaflets. The tiny flowers, usually yellow or white, more rarely purplish, are in umbels composed of smaller, more crowded umbels. They have calyxes without teeth or with five minute ones, five each petals and stamens, and two styles. The seedlike fruits, linear, obovate, or circular, are usually encircled by a prominent corky wing that is clearly of a paler color than the central portion.

Low masses of all-basal, attractive ferny foliage are characteristic of variable *L. foeniculaceum* (syns. *L. villosum, Cogswellia villosa*) and *L. martindalei*. Gray-hairy *L. foeniculaceum* has leaves 2 to 7 inches long, thrice-divided into numerous narrow segments under ¼ inch long. The flower stalks, 3 inches to 1 foot long, carry umbels 1 inch to 2 inches across of yellow blooms. This favors limestone soils. Having rather coarser foliage than *L. foeniculaceum* and hairless or essentially so, *L. martindalei* has leaves 2 to 4 inches in length, once- or twice-divided into comparatively few, strongly-toothed or cleft segments, broader than those of *L. foeniculaceum*. The flower stalks are 4 inches to 1 foot long or longer. The blooms are white, yellowish, or rarely yellow.

Finely-hairy throughout or nearly hairless, and 1 foot to 2½ feet tall, *L. triternatum* has most of its foliage basal and on the lower parts of the stems, with a few leaves higher. The leaves of this very variable kind are up to 7 inches long, and are two or three times divided into slender segments mostly ¾ inch to 4 inches long, and toothless or with shallow teeth. In *L. t. anomalum*, the ultimate leaf segments are very much broader.

Blue-glaucous, hairless stems and foliage are characteristic of *L. nudicaule* and *L. columbianum* (syn. *Leptotaenia purpurea*). Both have stems, leafless except at their bases. Branchless or sparsely-branched, *L. nudicaule* is 1 foot to 3 feet tall, and has leaves one- to three-times-divided into up to thirty broad, paddle-shaped leaflets 2 to 4 inches long and often toothed at their apexes. Its yellow flowers are in loose umbels. From it *L. columbianum*, which most frequently is 1 foot to 2 feet tall, differs in having leaves twice- or thrice-divided into ultimate segments generally under ½ inch long and so slender they are almost hair-like. The purple or much more rarely yellow flowers begin to open before the foliage is fully expanded.

Kinds with leaves higher up the stems as well as lower and basal ones include *L. ambiguum* and *L. utriculatum*. From 6 inches to 2½ feet tall and hairless, **L. ambiguum** has usually much-branched stems and leaves two- or more times divided into narrow segments ½ inch to 3½ inches long. Its flowers are yellow. Hairless or short-hairy, and commonly called spring gold, **L. utriculatum**, 6 inches to 2 feet tall, has very soft, finely-dissected, ferny leaves three-times-divided into crowded, threadlike segments rarely exceeding ⅜ inch long. The flowers are yellow.

Garden and Landscape Uses and Cultivation. Within the native range of the genus, lomatiums are occasionally grown, less often elsewhere. They are best adapted to dryish soils and climates and open, sunny locations in wild gardens and other informal areas. The dwarfer ones are suitable for rock gardens. They are unlikely to transplant well. New plants raised from seeds should be set in their permanent locations while quite small.

LOMATOPHYLLUM (Lomato-phýllum). The genus *Lomatophyllum*, of the lily family LILIACEAE, contains fourteen species. An endemic of Malagasy (Madagascar) and the Mascarine Islands, it bears a name alluding to a character of the foliage, derived from the Greek *loma*, a border, and *phyllon*, a leaf. This genus differs from related *Aloe*, which it otherwise resembles, in its fruits being berries instead of capsules and in its leaves having red or purplish, horny-toothed borders.

A native of Mauritius, thick-stemmed **L. borbonicum** (syn. *L. aloiflorum*), up to 8 feet tall, has leaves up to 3 feet long. Its ¾-inch-long flowers are red-brown on their outsides, yellow within. Endemic to Malagasy, **L. occidentale** has a stem up to 3 feet tall or may be stemless. Its mostly recurved leaves have channeled upper surfaces and are from 2 to 3 feet long. The branched stalks that carry the dense racemes of flowers are shorter than the leaves. The flowers are purple or purplish and 1 inch to 1¼ inches long.

Garden and Landscape Uses and Cultivation. These are as for *Aloe*.

LONAS (Lòn-as)—African-Daisy. One species, native to Italy, Sicily, and northwestern Africa, is the only member of the genus *Lonas*. It belongs in the daisy family COMPOSITAE and has a name of uncertain derivation. With much more daisy-like flowers than *Arctotis stoechadifolia*, it shares with that the common name African-daisy.

Botanically **L. annua** (syn. *L. inodora*) is a bright yellow-flowered annual, attaining a height of about 1 foot. It has branching stems and alternate leaves, pinnately-divided into narrow, linear segments. Its flower heads, ⅜ inch across, are without rays. Borne in dense 3- to 5-inch-wide

Lonas annua

clusters, they consist of all disk florets, and remain attractive on the plant for a very long period. The fruits are achenes.

Garden Uses and Cultivation. An interesting annual for flower garden display and supplying cut flowers that can be used fresh or dried as everlastings, this species is easy to grow in ordinary well-drained garden soil in full sun. Seeds may be sown outdoors in early spring and the seedlings thinned to 5 or 6 inches apart, but earlier and often better results are had by starting the seeds indoors in a temperature of 60 to 65°F some eight weeks prior to setting the plants in the garden. This may be done after danger of frost has passed and the weather is fairly warm and settled. A planting distance of 6 inches is satisfactory. Until planting out time the young plants are grown, spaced about 2 inches apart, in flats to which the seedlings are transplanted as soon as they are large enough to handle comfortably, in a sunny greenhouse with a night temperature of 60°F and day temperature a few degrees higher. They are hardened by standing the flats in a cold frame or sheltered place outdoors for a week or two before planting out. From seeding to the commencement of flowering takes fifteen or sixteen weeks. Routine garden care consists of suppressing weeds and watering if necessary. Staking is rarely needed. To prepare the flowers as everlastings they are cut as soon as they are well open, tied into bundles, and hung upside down in a dry, airy place in shade until they are thoroughly dry.

LONCHOCARPUS (Loncho-cárpus)—Lancepod. The name of this genus, of the pea family LEGUMINOSAE, derives from the Greek *lonche*, a lance, and *karpos*, a fruit. It alludes to the form of the seed pods. Chiefly native of tropical America including the West Indies, but represented also in Africa and Australia, *Lonchocarpus* comprises about 150 species of trees and vines some of which, except for their fruits, much resemble *Robinia*.

Lonchocarpuses have alternate, pinnate

leaves, with an uneven number of fairly large leaflets, and pea-shaped flowers each with a roundish standard or banner petal, in racemes or panicles. The blooms are white, pink, or purple. The fruits are flat, non-splitting pods with usually one to four seeds. Some species are used in regions where they are native as dyes and some as fish poisons. Some are sources of the insecticide rotenone, and some, including *L. domingensis*, are esteemed for their lumber. For the plant sometimes called *L. speciosus* see Bolusanthus.

In Florida **L. punctatus** does very well. A tree up to 20 feet tall, it begins blooming when only shrub size and from then on makes a lavish display each year. Its fragrant, ½-inch-long or longer, pinkish-mauve to purple blooms are in erect racemes 5 to 8 inches long. The leaves are hairless, and mostly have seven leaflets, sometimes five or nine, densely sprinkled with tiny black dots, ovate-oblong, and 2 to 3 inches long. The seed pods are 3 to 4 inches in length. This species is a native of dryish soils in northern South America and Trinidad.

From Central and South America and the West Indies comes **L. latifolius**, less free-flowering than some kinds and attaining a height of 75 feet or more. This has hairless leaves with five or nine elliptic to lanceolate-oblong, short-stalked leaflets, 5 to 9 inches long, and with paler under than upper sides. The pale purple to dull crimson blooms are in short panicles.

A small tree of tropical America, **L. domingensis** (syn. *L. sericeus*) has leaves densely-finely-hairy on their undersides. They have seven to thirteen short-stalked, prominently veined, oblong to elliptic leaflets 2 to 5 inches long and pinkish to bright rose-purple blooms ½ to ¾ inch long in dense racemes or in slender, raceme-like panicles about 4 inches long. The seed pods are approximately 4 inches long.

Garden and Landscape Uses and Cultivation. In tropical and warm subtropical places the species described above are planted for ornament. They succeed in dryish soils, and need full sun. Propagation is by seed.

LONDON PLANE is *Platanus acerifolia* (syn. *P. hybrida*).

LONDON PRIDE is a common name applied to *Saxifraga umbrosa* and *S. urbana*.

LONGAN. See Euphoria.

LONG JOHN ANT TREE is *Triplaris surinamensis*.

LONICERA (Lon-ícera)—Honeysuckle. The word honeysuckle excites thoughts of twining vines with sweetly fragrant flowers, flourishing in hedgerows, favorites in old-fashioned gardens. There are such, but many honeysuckles are not vines, do not twine, are without fragrance, and never graced grandmother's garden. Among these, as well as among vining kinds, are good ones. Named to commemorate the German physician and naturalist Adam Lonicer or Lonitzer, who died in 1586, *Lonicera* consists of 200 species as well as many hybrids and garden varieties. It belongs in the honeysuckle family CAPRIFOLIACEAE and is widely distributed as a native chiefly in the northern hemisphere, extending as far south as Mexico and Java. Most honeysuckles are deciduous.

The genus *Lonicera* has opposite, rarely slightly-lobed, usually short-stalked leaves and tubular flowers either in pairs in the leaf axils or in clusters at the branch ends. If from the leaf axils, the twin blooms share a stalk with two bracts and usually four bractlets, if in terminal clusters, the flowers are stalkless. Honeysuckle blooms have five-toothed calyxes. Their corollas have slender tubes, often swollen at their bases. There are five corolla lobes (petals), which may be very asymmetrically arranged into distinct lips or may spread more regularly with nearly equal spaces between them. There are five stamens and a slender style. The fruits are juicy berries with few to many seeds.

The first honeysuckles to bloom are the bush kinds, **L. fragrantissima** and **L. standishii,** natives of China. These flower in March or April. They differ in that the branchlets of the former are hairless and its leaves abruptly pointed instead of tapering gradually to long points. Because the blooms of *L. fragrantissima* are slightly larger and are often in clusters of more than one or two pairs, it is the more showy. Both kinds are shrubs up to 8 feet tall, with spreading branches. In mild climates they retain some of their foliage throughout the winter, but under harsher conditions are fully deciduous. The leaves of *L. fragrantissima* are elliptic to broad-ovate or obovate and 1 inch to 3 inches long. Its distinctly two-lipped, very fragrant, creamy-white flowers ⅝ inch long,

Lonicera standishii

are on hairless stalks. The blooms of *L. standishii* are similar, but not over ½ inch long. Its leaves are oblong-ovate to ovate-lanceolate and up to 4 inches long. In early summer both kinds produce red fruits, joined in pairs. These are much relished by birds.

The hardiest shrub honeysuckles are *L. chrysantha, L. maackii,* and *L. tatarica.* Up to 12 feet in height and of upright habit, *L. chrysantha* usually has pubescent branchlets. Its somewhat lozenge-shaped, ovate to lanceolate, pointed leaves are more or less hairy and 2 to 5 inches long. In pairs on hairy stalks, the decidedly two-lipped, creamy-yellow flowers deepen in color as they age. About ¾ inch long, they have corolla tubes markedly swollen at their bases, and stamens hairy on their lower halves. The berries are coral-red.

One of the tallest and hardiest bush honeysuckles, *L. maackii,* a native of Korea and Manchuria, attains 15 feet in height. It survives winters well north into Canada and in June has a profusion of white flowers that become yellowish as they age. The blooms, in pairs from the leaf axils and distinctly two-lipped, are on stalks shorter than those of the leaves. They have short tubes not markedly swollen at their bases and usually not hairy on their outsides. The

stamens are twice as long as the ¾-inch-long corolla and downy in their lower parts. The style is hairy. The fruits are red, and like the dark green leaves, remain until very late in the season. The young shoots of this spreading shrub are pubescent, its short-stalked leaves elliptic-ovate to ovate-lanceolate and 1½ to 3 inches long. They are pubescent on the veins. Variety *L. m. podocarpa,* somewhat less hardy than the typical species, has smaller blooms pubescent on their outsides and is a wider-spreading shrub.

The tatarian honeysuckle (**L. tatarica**) is one of the most satisfactory hardy, deciduous shrubs. Vigorous, up to 10 feet in height, and with attractive foliage, flowers, and fruits, it forms a tidy, billowy, dense bush. Its branchlets are pubescent.

Lonicera tatarica (foliage and fruits)

Its leaves ovate to oblong-ovate, 1 inch to 2½ inches long, are paler on their undersides than above. The paired blooms on slender stalks from the leaf axils come in late spring and are succeeded by bright red or sometimes yellow fruits. From ¾ to 1 inch long, the white, pink, or red, two-lipped flowers have corolla tubes much shorter than the petals and pouched at their bases. They are hairy on their insides only. This species is native from Russia to Turkestan. Variable it includes varieties *L. t. alba,* with pure white flowers; *L. t. 'Arnold Red',* with dark red blooms; *L. t. grandiflora,* with large white flowers; *L. t. leroyana,* 3 feet in height and with only a few pink-and-white striped flowers; *L. t. lutea,* with white flowers with a pink center stripe to each petal and yellow fruits; *L. t. nana,* a 3-foot-tall kind with pink flowers; *L. t. parvifolia,* a very good white-flowered variety; *L. t. rosea,* with flowers deep pink on their outsides, paler inside; *L. t. sibirica,* with larger leaves than other varieties and flowers with white, pink-striped petals; and *L. t. virginalis,* with bigger, rosy-pink flowers than any other variety of *L. tatarica.*

Lonicera fragrantissima

Lonicera maackii (foliage and fruits)

Lonicera amoena

Lonicera morrowii: (a) Flowers

(b) Fruits

Hybrids of *L. tatarica* are *L. amoena* and *L. bella*. The first has for its other parent *L. korolkowii*, the other has in this relationship *L. morrowii*. Both are somewhat variable. Both have ovate leaves up to 2 inches long. A profuse bloomer, **L. amoena** has ¾-inch-long, two-lipped flowers, typically pinkish, aging to yellow. The fruits are red. The blooms of **L. bella** are two-lipped, ½ inch long, and white or pink changing to yellow as they age. Its fruits are red. Pure white flowers are borne by *L. bella candida*, which is probably the plant grown in gardens as *L. b. albida*. In *L. b. rosea* the flowers are pale pink, those of *L. b. atrorosea* deep pink. Differing from *L. bella*, which it otherwise much resembles, in having darker green, more decidedly pointed leaves, **L. muendeniensis** is a hybrid between *L. bella* and *L. ruprechtiana*. Variety *L. m. xanthocarpa* has orange fruits.

Good looking, gray-green to bluish foliage and attractive growth habits are the chief attractions of **L. korolkowii** and its varieties. The best-known variant is *L. k. floribunda*, which is supposed to bloom more freely than the typical species, but the two are so mixed in cultivation and are so similar that it is difficult to distinguish between them. Another variety, *L. k. 'Aurora'*, produces slightly larger, purplish-

Lonicera muendeniensis xanthocarpa

pink flowers in abundance and is considered superior. These plants, once established, are vigorous growers, but following transplanting are often reluctant to "take hold" and are given to dying without obvious cause. About 12 feet tall, *L. korolkowii* and its varieties form broad, rounded bushes hardy in southern New England. Their ovate to broad-elliptic leaves, up to 1 inch long, except those of *L. k. zabelii*, which are hairless, are pubescent on their undersides and slightly so above. The two-lipped blooms, usually pink or purplish-pink, rarely white, are ½ inch long and in pairs. Those of *L. k. zabelii* are red. The fruits of all are bright red. Japanese **L. morrowii**, a deciduous shrub 6 to 8 feet tall and with wide-spreading branches, has elliptic to oblongish leaves, softly pubescent on their undersides and 1¼ inch to 2 inches long. Its two-lipped, ½-inch-long flowers are in pairs. At first white, changing to yellow, they are succeeded by dark red or rarely yellow fruits.

An especially charming bush honeysuckle hardy throughout most of New England is Chinese **L. syringantha.** Its variety, *L. s. wolfii*, distinguished by its partly prostrate branches, narrower, longer leaves, and carmine blooms, is also quite lovely. Unfortunately, these are sometimes rather shy bloomers. From 6 to 10 feet tall, of rounded outline, and slender-branched, they have ovate to oblongish leaves, hairless on their undersides and often in circles of three. The flowers are fragrant, about ½ inch long, and in pairs. They are not hairy on their outsides. They are symmetrical rather than obviously two-lipped. Those of the species are pinkish to lilac. The fruits are red. Differing from the last species and its variety in having leaves white-pubescent on their undersides and flowers hairy on their outsides, **L. thibetica** is 4 to 5 feet tall and has partly prostrate, sprawling branches and young shoots that are hairy. Often in circles of three, its leaves are elliptic to oblong and up to 1 inch long or slightly longer. Their upper sides are glossy. The strongly fragrant, nearly symmetrical flowers are light purple and in pairs. The fruits are red.

Mistletoe honeysuckle (**L. quinquelocularis**) is worth planting for its interesting, freely-produced, mistletoe-like fruits. These are creamy-white and so wonderfully translucent that the black seeds are clearly visible. Without other particular merit, this deciduous shrub is hardy in southern New England. Native to the Himalayan region, it attains heights of 10 feet or more and has broad-elliptic to nearly round leaves 1 inch to 2½ inches long. In short-stalked pairs from the leaf axils, the flowers change from creamy-white to yellow as they age. They are about ¾ inch across. Variety *L. q. translucens* (syn. *L. translucens*) has longer-pointed, more obviously hair-fringed leaves.

Lonicera quinquelocularis (fruits)

Other deciduous bush honeysuckles worth considering include **L. alpigena nana,** a variety not over 3 feet high of a much taller European species. Of interest chiefly because of its low stature, this has oblong-ovate leaves hairy on their undersides. Its red flowers make no worthwhile show. The fruits are bright red. Upright and some 10 feet tall, Chinese and Tibetan **L. deflexicalyx,** hardy in southern New England, has spreading or arching branches with branchlets in opposite rows. Its short-stalked, oblong-lanceolate to lanceolate leaves are 1½ to 3 inches long by scarcely one-half as wide, pubescent on the veins beneath, sparingly so on the upper surfaces. In pairs from the leaf axils, the up-pointing flowers, a little over ½ inch long and with the lower lip strongly down-turned, are yellow. The fruits are orange-red.

Hardy in southern New England, upright and about 4½ feet tall, Chinese **L. saccata** has hairless shoots and blunt, oblong-elliptic to oblong leaves up to 2 inches in length, at first pubescent, later hairless except along the veins. The pinkish flowers, pouched at their bases, nod on slender stalks from the leaf axils. They are succeeded by scarlet fruits. Its often lobed leaves, those of strong non-flowering shoots usually deeply-cleft, aid in identifying **L. tatsienensis,** of China. Hardy in southern New England and up to about 8 feet tall, this has ovate to elliptic-ovate or oblong-lanceolate, pointed leaves 1½ to 3 inches long, hairy to nearly hairless. The ½-inch-long dark purple blooms are succeeded by red fruits. The fly honeysuckle, **L. xylosteum,** of Europe and temperate Asia, is 10 feet tall and wider than high. It has short-stalked, broad-elliptic to obovate leaves up to 2½ inches long, downy on both surfaces. The sometimes red-tinted, yellowish-white, downy flowers, a little over ½ inch across, are in pairs on downy stalks from the leaf axils. They have pouched corolla tubes and are succeeded by red fruits. The fruits of L. x. lutea are yellow. Compact L. x. claveyi, 3 to 6 feet tall, makes a good hedge that needs little shearing. This species and its variety are hardy through much of New England.

Evergreen or partially evergreen shrubs are the box honeysuckle (L. nitida) and L. pileata, both natives of China and both hardy in sheltered places in southern New England, but more satisfactory in milder climates. Earning its vernacular name from its evergreen foliage having much the aspect of that of boxwood, **L. nitida** attains a height of about 6 feet. Its slender stems are erect, much-branched, and downy when young. The closely-set, very short-stalked, blunt, glossy leaves, ovate to roundish with heart-shaped bases and up to ⅜ inch long, are smooth except for a few tiny bristles, which eventually are shed. The fragrant, creamy-white flowers, in very short-stalked pairs from the leaf axils, are succeeded by ¼-inch-wide, blue-purple berries. Variety L. n. 'Baggesen's Gold' has yellow leaves that become greener toward fall. More erect and more robust than the commonly grown form of L. nitida sometimes identified as 'E. H. Wilson', is L. n. fertilis (syn. L. pileata yunnanensis). Related **L. pileata** is of quite different habit. A low shrub, evergreen in mild climates, only partially so or sometimes deciduous in colder ones, this sort has stiff, more or less

Lonicera pileata

horizontally-spreading branches and very downy, purplish shoots. Rarely exceeding 3 feet in height, it usually is lower. It has closely-set, practically stalkless, hairless, lustrous leaves suggestive of those of a small-leaved privet and ½ inch to 1¼ inches long by from under ¼ inch to ½ inch wide, ovate-oblong to somewhat lozenge-shaped. The little yellowish-white flowers are in very short-stalked pairs from the leaf axils. The fruits are violet-purple.

Vining honeysuckles include a number of splendid kinds some familiar, others less well known. With them belongs the classical honeysuckle of Europe, known to Shakespeare and called woodbine, the well-known immigrant from Asia, called Japanese honeysuckle, and the handsome native American trumpet honeysuckle. There are many other species and hybrids of garden worth.

Woodbine (**L. periclymenum**) is one of the most fragrant kinds. Native to Europe, North Africa, western Asia, and hardy through most of New England, this has stems sometimes 20 feet in length. Deciduous, its ovate to ovate-oblong or obovate, mostly pointed, sometimes somewhat downy leaves up to 2½ inches long and 1½ inches wide, are green above and slightly bluish-glaucous on their undersides. Those of each pair are always separate, never joined at their bases. The more or less red-tinged, yellowish-white, slender-tubed, two-lipped blooms, 1½ to 2 inches long, are displayed in stalked spikes of three to five whorls (circles) at the shoot ends. They are succeeded by red berries. Less rampant Dutch honeysuckle (L. p. belgica) is more bushy. It has purplish stems and blooms with purplish-red exteriors. The oak-leaved woodbine (L. p. quercina) has lobed leaves. In L. p. aurea the foliage is variegated with yellow. Late-blooming L. p. serotina has flowers at first dark purple on their outsides, becoming paler later, and yellow on their insides. It is one of the most attractive vining honeysuckles.

Much like the woodbine, European and western Asian **L. caprifolium,** naturalized in eastern North America, may be distinguished by the uppermost two or three pairs of leaves of the shoots being joined at their bases to form distinct cups in the axils of which the flowers are borne. The latter are fragrant, slender-tubed, 1½- to 2-inch-long, two-lipped, yellowish-white blooms tinged with pink. They are succeeded by orange-red fruits. Except sometimes its young foliage, this is essentially hairless. Its short-stalked, blunt leaves, elliptic to broad-elliptic, dark green above and bluish-green beneath, are 1½ to 4 inches long. This honeysuckle is hardy in southern New England. A hybrid between L. caprifolium and European L. etrusca that has the somewhat misleading name of **L. americana** is even more ornamental than L. caprifolium. It has hairless, broad-elliptic to obovate leaves and terminal, compact spikes consisting of several whorls of flowers, the lower arising from cups formed by the uniting of the bases of the uppermost pairs of leaves. The yellowish fragrant blooms, 1½ to 2 inches long, usually have purplish exteriors. In L. a. rubella the flowers are pale purple. Those of L. a. atrosanguinea are dark purple.

A splendid deciduous hybrid, presumably between L. americana and L. sempervirens, but its origin unrecorded, is the gold flame honeysuckle (**L. heckrottii**). This

Lonicera periclymenum

Lonicera heckrottii

bushy twiner may reach heights of 12 to 15 feet. Its nearly stalkless, pointed, elliptic to elliptic-oblong leaves, dark green above and glaucous on their undersides, are up to 2¼ inches long. In longish-stalked spikes of several rather distantly spaced whorls, its two-lipped flowers are in the axils of short bracts. From 1½ to 2 inches long, in bud they are coral-pink, when expanded coral-pink to reddish-purple outside, yellow within. The names 'Gold Flame' and 'Pine Gold Flame' have been applied to *L. heckrottii*, a sort remarkable for its long blooming season. It is hardy in southern New England.

Highly ornamental and variable *L. etrusca*, of the Mediterranean region, is deciduous or in mild climates more or less evergreen. A vigorous vine, it has round-ended, broad-elliptic to obovate leaves, glaucous and usually somewhat downy beneath, 1 inch to 3 inches long or sometimes a little longer. The uppermost pairs of leaves have united bases. Fragrant, the strongly two-lipped, slender-tubed flowers, yellowish suffused with red, darken as they age. They are 1½ to 2 inches long. Variety *L. e. superba* has larger leaves and creamy-yellow blooms that become almost orange-yellow as they age.

Lonicera etrusca

The handsomest North American vining honeysuckle *L. flava*, native from southern Missouri and Kentucky to North Carolina, Georgia, and Arkansas, has fragrant, orange-yellow, trumpet-shaped flowers 1 inch to 1¼ inches long, not swollen at their bases. They are in terminal clusters of one to three whorls. Rather glaucous on their undersides, but not above, the elliptic leaves are up to 3 inches long. Those of each of the one to three uppermost pairs are fused at their bases to form collars encircling the stems. This fine species is hardy in southern New England.

Trumpet or coral honeysuckle (*L. sempervirens*) is the hardiest vining kind. Native from Connecticut to Nebraska, Florida, and Texas, it is evergreen in mild climates, deciduous elsewhere. Its short-

Lonicera sempervirens

Lonicera sempervirens (flowers)

stalked to nearly stalkless leaves, elliptic to ovate, are up to abut 3 inches long. They have dark green upper surfaces, undersides more or less glaucous and sometimes with hairs. The uppermost pairs of leaves below the blooms have their bases united into rounded or oblong disks. The slender-tubed flowers, up to about 2 inches long and bright orange-yellow to scarlet, are in rather distantly spaced whorls forming slender-stalked spikes. Unlike those of most vining honeysuckles, they are not fragrant. Variety *L. s. superba* has scarlet blooms. Those of *L. s. sulphurea* are yellow. Usually partially evergreen *L. s. minor* has elliptic to oblong-lanceolate leaves and flowers not over 1½ inches long. Hybrids between *L. sempervirens* and *L. hirsuta* are grouped as *L. brownii*. These are grown under various horticultural names such as 'Dropmore Scarlet', 'Dreer's Everblooming', and 'Red Trumpet'.

Chinese *L. tragophylla* is a showy-flowered species that attains heights of up to 50 feet. Hardy in southern New England, it has oblong or sometimes elliptic leaves 2 to 4½ inches long by ¾ inch to 2 inches wide, and glaucous and hairy beneath, at least on the midribs. The uppermost pair of leaves of each shoot are united by their bases, the next lower pair are partly joined. In heads of ten to twenty usually in two

Lonicera tragophylla

whorls, the bright yellow blooms are 2½ to 3½ inches long. The fruits are red.

One of the best hybrid honeysuckles, *L. tellmanniana* is an offspring of *L. tragophylla* and *L. sempervirens superba*. A vigorous, deciduous vine, this has stems that twine only slightly and elliptic-ovate leaves 2 to 3½ inches long. The bases of the upper pair on each stem are united so that the leaves form a collar below the blooms. In terminal heads of usually two whorls (circles) of six to twelve, the slender blooms are about 2 inches long. In the bud stage they are suffused with bronzy-pink or red and associate pleasingly with the deep yellow of the fully open flowers, which are bronzy-red only at the tips of the petals.

Japanese honeysuckle (*L. japonica*) is extremely rampant. If allowed to grow without restraint it can in many places become a weedy nuisance, clambering over shrubs and other plants and choking out less vigorous neighbors. Native to Japan, Korea, China, and Manchuria, in mildish climates this is partially evergreen, in more severe ones deciduous. Its ovate to ovate-oblong leaves are 1½ to 3 inches long or sometimes longer, when young hairy on both sides, later nearly or quite hairless above. The very fragrant flowers, in stalked clusters from the leaf axils, are

Lonicera japonica

white tinged with purple, becoming yellowish with age. They are up to 2 inches long. The fruits are black. This honeysuckle is naturalized, often to the extent of being pestiferous, from New England to Florida, Missouri, and Texas. Hall's honeysuckle (*L. j. halliana*) differs but little from the typical species. Its white flowers, which change to yellow as they age, have the upper lip divided almost to its middle into two lobes. Variety *L. j. repens* is neater, less vigorous than the typical species or than Hall's honeysuckle. Its lower leaves are sometimes lobed. Especially attractive because of its foliage, *L. j. aureoreticulata* has considerably smaller leaves than the others, and the younger ones especially, are netted with yellow veins.

Lonicera japonica halliana

A semievergreen or in cold regions nearly deciduous vine with bristly-hairy shoots, *L. henryi,* native to western China, is hardy in southern New England. It has lanceolate to broadly-ovate leaves 1½ to 4 inches long by up to about 1½ inches wide. They have pointed apexes and are usually downy on the midribs beneath and at their margins. Purplish-red to sometimes yellowish-red, the flowers come in short spikes or clusters 2 to 3 inches across at the ends of current season's shoots. About ¾ inch across, they have corollas with tubes ½ to ¾ inch long and lips strongly reflexed. The hairy style protrudes. The fruits are purplish-black.

Extraordinarily large leaves, flowers, and fruits are outstanding features of *L. hildebrandtiana,* a nonhardy evergreen vine of China, Thailand, and Burma. Under optimum conditions this remarkable honeysuckle attains heights of 50 to 80 feet. No other sort equals it in size of leaves, flowers, or fruits. The leaves are short-stalked, broad-ovate to roundish-oval, and end in a brief point. They are 3 to 6 inches long by one-half or more as wide. Creamy-white changing to bright orange, the 3½- to 6-inch-long flowers have two-lobed corollas. One of the lobes is shortly-four-lobed, the other narrow,

lobeless, and strongly recurved. The egg-shaped fruits are 1 inch to 1¼ iches long.

Garden and Landscape Uses. Honeysuckles are less appreciated by gardeners than their merits deserve. Most are adaptable to garden and landscape uses, the vines for growing on trellises, fences, and other supports around which their stems can twine, the shrubs as general-purpose furnishings for beds, borders, foundation plantings, and other places where bushes can be used. A few of the latter, notably *L. nitida* and *L. xylosteum,* are useful as hedges. The trumpet or coral honeysuckle makes a delightful vine for a cool greenhouse, and *L. japonica aureo-reticulata* is attractive as a pot or hanging basket plant for growing under similar conditions. As a group they thrive in sun or part-day shade and flourish in ordinary soils.

A bank of *Lonicera japonica halliana*

Cultivation. The care of honeysuckles makes small demands on the time of gardeners. As young specimens, pruning to shorten stems and encourage branching so that a good basic framework is established may be desirable. Later, pruning to keep climbers within bounds and to prevent excessive crowding of their stems or those of the bush kinds may be needed from time to time, but not on any regular annual basis. The best time to prune is as soon as the blooms fade or with those that bloom in late summer in early spring. When used as hedges bush sorts need shearing at fairly frequent intervals. Propagation is easily achieved by seed and by leafy cuttings taken in July or August and planted in a cold frame, greenhouse propagating bench, or under mist. Bush honeysuckles can also be increased by leafless hardwood cuttings. Some honeysuckles lend themselves to increase by division. Aphids are pestiferous insects fond of some kinds of honeysuckles. They are likely to congregate in great numbers on the young shoots and foliage.

LOOFAH. See Luffa.

LOOSESTRIFE. This common name is used for species of *Lysimachia*. Purple-loosestrife is *Lythrum salicaria*, swamp-loosestrife *Decodon verticillatus*.

LOPEZIA (Lo-pèzia)—Mosquito Plant. Belonging to the evening-primrose family ONAGRACEAE and endemic to Mexico and Central America, *Lopezia* consists of seventeen species of annuals, herbaceous perennials, and subshrubs. One or two are fairly commonly cultivated as window plants, in greenhouses, and in mild climates outdoors. The name commemorates the Spanish botanist Tomas Lopez, who, in the mid-sixteenth century, wrote about the plants of South America.

Lopezias have ovate to lanceolate, toothed to nearly toothless, stalked leaves, alternate or the lower ones opposite. The flowers, usually small and on longish, slender stalks are in leafy racemes. They have four sepals, four dissimilar petals, the upper two angled upward, the others bigger and more widely spreading. There is one stamen and one staminode joined by their bases and united there with the slender style. The staminode (nonfertile stamen) is petal-like. The fruits are capsules.

Mosquito plant (**L. hirsuta** syn. *L. lineata*) is a sometimes somewhat sprawling or trailing, much-branched subshrub 1 foot to 3 feet in height. It has slender

Lopezia hirsuta

stems, like the leafstalks hairy, and often rooting when in contact with the ground. Usually hairy on both surfaces, the lanceolate-ovate to round-ovate leaves, from ½ inch to 1½ inches long, become smaller and narrower in the upper parts of the plant. The peculiarly shaped flowers, about ⅝ inch wide and on stalks longer than the leaves in the axils from which they arise, are fancifully likened to mosquitoes. In short racemes of few, they are deep coral-pink to salmon-pink with purplish-red sepals. The two narrow petals are usually paler than the others. From the last, *L. coronata* differs in being usually an annual and in having nearly hairless to hairy, definitely angled stems. Also, the flower stalks are usually shorter than the leaves in the axils from which they come. Woody-stemmed *L. grandiflora*, up to 6 feet tall, has finely-toothed, ovate to elliptic leaves 3 to 6 inches in length, and blooms about 1½ inches across with rose-red sepals and petals plentifully produced from near the branch ends.

Garden and Landscape Uses and Cultivation. Although not spectacular, lopezias are interesting because of their dainty, curiously mosquito-like flowers produced almost continuously and in considerable abundance. They are among the easiest of plants to grow, doing well in almost any well-drained soil in sunny locations or even where they get a little part-day shade. As pot plants and hanging basket plants they are satisfied indoors with a winter night temperature of about 50°F, rising by day from five to fifteen degrees. Water them moderately, to maintain the soil just moist, not saturated. By pinching the tips out of the shoots occasionally, desirable bushiness is achieved. Lopezias come very readily from seed and are easy to propagate from cuttings.

LOPHANTHERA (Loph-ánthera). The Brazilian genus *Lophanthera* of the malpighia family MALPIGHIACEAE consists of three species. Its name, from the Greek *lophos*, a crest, and *anthera*, an anther, alludes to a feature of the flowers.

The sorts of this genus are evergreen trees and shrubs with opposite, undivided leaves and, in terminal panicles or racemes, small yellow blooms. The flowers have a five-parted calyx with ten glands on the outside at its base. There are five petals, their lower parts narrowed to a claw, and ten stamens. The fruits are capsules.

Up to 45 feet tall, *L. lactescens* contains in its younger parts a bitter, white latex. Its short-stalked, leathery, broad-elliptic to obovate leaves are toothless, 8 inches to 1 foot long, and approximately half as wide. The flowers are in drooping cylindrical panicles or racemes up to 1½ feet long,

Lophanthera lactescens

each consisting of as many as 500 blooms. On individual stalks about ¾ inch long, the golden-yellow flowers are ¼ inch long and have spreading petals.

Garden and Landscape Uses and Cultivation. An attractive tree for the humid tropics and occasionally cultivated in tropical greenhouses, the species described prospers in any well drained, reasonably fertile soil that never becomes excessively dry. In greenhouses a winter night temperature of 60 to 65°F is satisfactory, and the daytime temperature may increase from five to fifteen degrees depending upon the brightness of the weather. Propagation may be effected by seed, cuttings, and air layering.

LOPHIOLA (Lophì-ola)—Gold Crest. The one species of *Lophiola* inhabits acid swamps and bogs from Nova Scotia to Florida and Mississippi. It belongs in the bloodwort family HAEMODORACEAE and has a name from the Greek *lophia*, a crest, in allusion to the tufts of hairs at the bottoms of the perianth segments.

Gold crest (*L. americana*) has linear, mostly basal, erect leaves, the lower ones up to 1 foot long, the others diminishing in size upward. They are much exceeded by the slender flowering stems, which are up to 2 feet in height and are tomentose, especially in their upper parts. The flowers, in loose, rounded, or squatly pyramidal, densely-white-woolly-branched clusters, up to 3½ inches wide, are a little under ½ inch in diameter, golden-yellow, and densely-woolly on their outsides and at the bases of their perianth lobes (petals) inside. They have six spreading petals, six erect stamens, and a persistent style. The fruits are capsules containing straw-colored seeds.

Garden Uses and Cultivation. For bog gardens and, in its home territory, native plant gardens, this little-cultivated plant is suitable. Conditions as nearly as possible like those under which it grows naturally should be provided. Propagation is by seed and by division.

LOPHOCEREUS (Lopho-cèreus). Some authorities recognize four species in *Lophocereus*, of the cactus family CACTACEAE. Others regard them as variants of one, and more conservative botanists include that in *Cereus*. Whatever the disposition, the plants so classified are endemic to Mexico except for about fifty individuals that exist in Arizona. The American authority Dr. Lyman Benson believes that probably never more than twice that number lived as wildlings in the United States. The name is from the Greek *lophos*, a crest, and the name of the genus *Cereus*. It alludes to the long beards of hair on the stems.

Attractive and conspicuous elements in their native regions, lophocereuses have numerous columnar branches, their up-

permost parts usually clothed with dense, comblike brushes of long bristle-like spines. The branches are ribbed and in their lower parts have short, thick-based, needle-like spines. Usually in groups, the funnel-shaped, white or pink flowers open only at night. The stamens do not protrude. The fruits are fleshy.

By far the best known is variable *L. schottii* (syn. *Cereus schottii*), of Baja California, the Sonoran Desert, and Arizona. This forms broad clumps of sometimes fifty to exceptionally several hundred erect and ascending stems. It branches freely from the base, rarely above. The stems, 3 to 21 feet tall and 4½ to 5 inches in diameter, have six or seven, seldom five or up to nine ribs. The spine clusters on their lower parts are of seven to nine awl-shaped gray radials, ⅜ inch long and with swollen bases, and one slightly stouter and longer central. The upper parts of the stems are decorated with vertical brushlike bands of gray or pinkish, more or less downswept, flattened, bristle-like spines up to 3 inches in length and thirty to forty from each areole. The ill-scented blooms, which open at night, have pink inner petals and greenish outer ones. They are 1 inch to 1½ inches in diameter. The nearly spherical to ovoid, fleshy, red fruits are 1 inch long or a little longer. The totem pole cactus, *L. s. monstrosus*, is a remarkable and handsome variety with curious, irregular lumps on the stems in place of the more orderly ribs of the typical species and is generally almost or quite without spines.

Lophocereus schottii

Other species include *L. gatesii* and *L. sargentianus*. Up to 30 feet tall, *L. gatesii* has stems with ten to fifteen ribs and clusters of eleven to fifteen or from flowering areoles as many as twenty awl-shaped spines ½ inch long. Its dark coral-red blooms are 1 inch in diameter. Up to 4 to 5 feet high, *L. sargentianus* has stems with five or six ribs and from the flowering areoles clusters of up to fifty spines, fewer from other areoles. The pink blooms are ¾ inch across.

Garden and Landscape Uses and Cultivation. The sorts of this genus, distinctive because of the unusual effect produced by the upper portions of their stems having conspicuous, horse-hair-like beards, while their lower parts are naked of such decorations, are excellent for outdoor cultivation in warm, desert and semidesert regions and in small sizes for including in greenhouse collections of cactuses. They revel in well-drained, even stony soil, but are reported to be averse to limestone. A warm, sunny location is to their liking. For more information see Cactuses.

LOPHOMYRTUS (Lopho-myrtus). The two species of this New Zealand genus of the myrtle family MYRTACEAE were formerly included in *Myrtus*. The name *Lophomyrtus* is derived from that of the genus *Myrtus* and the Greek *lophos*, a crest.

Lophomyrtuses are evergreen shrubs or small trees with short-stalked, undivided, smooth-edged leaves and solitary white flowers from the leaf axils. The blooms have four-lobed calyxes, four petals, numerous stamens, and one style. The fruits are many-seeded berries. A natural hybrid between the two species, named *L. ralphii*, has characteristics intermediate between those of its parents.

Up to twenty-five feet tall, *L. bullata* (syn. *Myrtus bullata*) has somewhat leathery, broad-ovate to nearly round, strongly puckered, blunt or pointed leaves 1 inch to 2 inches long, and often reddish or purplish-tinged. The approximately ½-inch-wide flowers are on hairy stalks ¾ inch long. Broadly egg-shaped, the berries are dark red to nearly black and ¼ inch or a little more in diameter. From the last, *L. obcordata* (syn. *Myrtus obcordata*) differs in its maximum height being rather less and in having reverse-heart-shaped, unwrinkled leaves under ¼ inch long. The berries, broadly-egg-shaped and about ⅓ inch long, are bright to dark red or sometimes violet.

Garden and Landscape Uses and Cultivation. Lophomyrtuses have much the same horticultural uses as the common myrtle (*Myrtus communis*). In North America they are most likely to succeed in mild climate areas of the Pacific Northwest. Increase is by seed and by cuttings.

LOPHOPHORA (Lophóph-ora)—Peyote or Mescal Button. Variously interpreted as being of one variable or three separate species, *Lophophora*, of the cactus family CACTACEAE, is restricted in the wild to Mexico and southern Texas. Its name, alluding to the tufts of hairs from the areoles (spine-bearing or potentially spine-bearing regions on cactuses), comes from the Greek *lophos*, a crest, and *phoreo*, I bear. Great interest has surrounded peyote because of its use as a hallucinogen in Indian religious rituals. Among other powerful

substances, it contains mescaline and LSD. In 1938 the United States Food and Drug Administration prohibited, except for its employment as a sacramental by members of a small, chiefly Indian church, the collection, sale, and use of peyote.

The peyote or mescal button (*L. williamsii*) is low, fleshy, and dull blue-green or gray-green. It tapers from a blunt top to a thick taproot. The plant body consists of one or a cluster of depressed-globose stems with low, flat or hollow-topped tubercles (bulges) united into five to thirteen broad, shallow ribs. Except for minute spines on young seedlings, the plants are

Lophophora williamsii

Lophophora diffusa

spineless. From each areole comes a pencil-like brush of fairly long, erect hairs. The flowers originate from near the centers of the plants. They are pale pink to cream or white, shortly-bell-shaped, ¾ to 1 inch in diameter, and have many spreading perianth segments (petals). The stamens are few. The oblong or club-shaped, red fruits, similar to those of *Mammillaria*, are approximately ½ inch long. Endemic to central Mexico and differing but little from the last, *L. diffusa* has yellowish-green plant bodies and whitish or yellowish-white flowers.

Garden Uses. Lophophoras are prized by collectors of succulents. They succeed in soil containing limestone under conditions that suit *Ariocarpus*. For further information see Cactuses.

LOQUAT is *Eriobotrya japonica*.

LORANTHACEAE—Mistletoe Family. The most familiar sorts of this very rarely cultivated assemblage of thirty-six genera and 1,300 species are the American and European mistletoes *Phoradendron flavescens* and *Viscum album* respectively. Inhabiting many temperate to tropical parts, this family of dicotyledons consists mostly of semiparasitic shrubs that invade the tissues of their hosts with haustoria (modified roots). Some few are shrubs or trees that root into the ground. Notable among such is the Australian Christmas tree (*Nuytsia floribunda*) a beautiful flowering tree 20 to 40 feet tall, parasitic on the roots of other plants.

Species of the *Loranthaceae* generally have jointed, forking stems and evergreen leaves, the latter usually opposite or in whorls (circles of more than two), much more rarely alternate. The flowers, in spikes, racemes, or panicles, or less often solitary, are bisexual or unisexual with the sexes then generally on separate plants. They have perianths each of two or three similar sepals and petals, those of some tropical sorts large and brilliantly colored, but often small and greenish. There are as many stamens as perianth lobes and one pistil (rudimentary in male flowers). The berry- or drupe-like fruits generally have very sticky flesh.

LORD ANSON'S BLUE-PEA is *Lathyrus magellanicus*.

LORD'S CANDLESTICK is *Yucca gloriosa*.

LORDS-AND-LADIES is *Arum maculatum*.

LORINSERIA. See Woodwardia.

LOROPETALUM (Loro-pétalum). Of the three species of *Loropetalum*, of the witch-hazel family HAMAMELIDACEAE, only one appears to be cultivated. The group consists of evergreen shrubs closely related to witch-hazel (*Hamamelis*). Native to China and the Himalayas, its name derived from the Greek *loron*, a strap, and *petalon*, a leaf or petal, alludes to the form of the petals.

Loropetalums have alternate, undivided leaves and flowers much like those of witch-hazels, with four-lobed calyxes, four narrow, strap-shaped petals, the same number of short stamens, and two styles. The fruits are woody, two-seeded capsules.

A much-branched, twiggy shrub 6 to 15 feet tall, *H. chinense* is not hardy in the north. Its shoots are densely clothed with reddish down. Its toothless or sometimes

Loropetalum chinense

Lotus corniculatus

finely-toothed, dull green, ovate leaves, with markedly asymmetrical bases, 1 inch to 2½ inches long, have scattered hairs on their upper surfaces. The white, creamy-yellow, or light greenish flowers come in late winter or early spring. They have petals ¾ to 1 inch long, that in the mass give a feathery effect to the clusters of blooms.

Garden and Landscape Uses. From Virginia southward and in other regions of relatively mild winters, *L. chinense* is attractive for beds and foundation plantings and as single specimens. It has neat foliage and associates pleasingly with azaleas and many other shrubs. For its best health it needs a slightly acid, peaty soil, moistish, but not wet. Full sun or part-day shade are satisfactory. This is also a good species for pots or tubs in cool greenhouses, where it produces a most welcome display of bloom in late winter.

Cultivation. Out-of-doors loropetalums need no special care. Little or no pruning is required. Any necessary cutting is best done after the flowers fade. A mulch of peat moss, bagasse, compost, or other organic material maintained over the roots is beneficial. Propagation is easy by summer cuttings of firm, but not hard, shoots planted under mist or in a greenhouse or cold frame propagating bed. Seed may also be used.

As greenhouse specimens loropetalums must not be subjected to high temperatures. In winter the thermometer at night should hold between 40 and 50°F, and only five to ten degrees higher by day. Even at New York City this shrub can be brought safely through the winter in a well-protected, unheated cold frame. As spring approaches slightly higher temperatures are in order. In summer the plants are best in a sunny location outdoors, with their pots or tubs buried to their rims in

sand, ashes, peat moss, or soil. Watering is done to keep the earth moderately moist at all times, and from spring through fall well-rooted specimens are given dilute liquid fertilizer regularly. Repot as soon as flowering is through, and at that time attend to any pruning needed to shape or restrict the plants to size. The potting soil should contain a generous admixture of peat moss as well as coarse sand and some dried cow manure and bonemeal. It should be sufficiently porous to admit air and the free passage of water. The pots or tubs must be well drained.

LOTE BUSH is *Ziziphus obtusifolia*.

LOTUS (Lò-tus)—Asparagus-Pea or Winged-Pea, Bird's-Foot-Trefoil, St.-James'-Trefoil. A few only of the 100 or more species of *Lotus,* of the pea family LEGUMINOSAE, are cultivated, some for forage. The genus consists of annuals, herbaceous perennials, and subshrubs, natives of the Old World, particularly the Mediterranean region, and western North America. Some kinds are naturalized in other parts of North America and elsewhere. American plants previously named *Hosackia* are included in *Lotus.* The name is from the Greek *lotos,* used for various plants. As a common name lotus is applied to the aquatic genera *Nelumbo* and *Nymphaea.*

Species of *Lotus* are erect or trailing. Their leaves are alternate, and have three to several leaflets, sometimes with the middle three set on a stalk away from two, which then look like stipules (appendages at the bases of leafstalks of some kinds of plants). Sometimes the leaflets are stalkless and may be mistaken for separate small leaves directly sprouting from the stems. The white, pink, red, purple, or yellow blooms, usually in stalked umbels from the leaf axils, but sometimes solitary

or in pairs, and sometimes without stalks, are pea-shaped. They have calyxes with five equal or approximately equal lobes, five petals, one of which is a broad standard or banner, and two of which form a pointed keel. The stamens are ten, nine united and one free, some or all with stalks thickened at their tops. Usually several-seeded, the fruits are cylindrical pods.

The asparagus-pea or winged-pea (*L. tetragonolobus* syn. *Tetragonolobus purpureus*) is cultivated for its edible pods. Native from southern Europe to the Ukraine, this is a vigorous, softly-hairy, spreading annual with stems up to 1¼ feet long. The obovate to more or less lozenge-shaped leaflets are up to 1½ inches long. Solitary or in pairs on stalks not longer than the leaves, the crimson blooms are ½ to 1 inch long. From 1¼ to 3½ inches in length, the pods have four broad, wavy wings. Another plant, *Psophocarpus tetragonolobus,* is used in the tropics in the same way and is also known as asparagus-pea and sometimes as winged-bean.

Bird's-foot-trefoil (*L. corniculatus*), a native of temperate Europe and Asia, is freely naturalized in North America. A low, hairy or nearly hairless, hardy herbaceous perennial, it has prostrate or procumbent stems. In poor soils the plants often are flat mats of slender stems and leaves with the flowers lifted just above the foliage. The leaves have three chief, ovate to oblanceolate leaflets ¼ to ½ inch long, and two smaller, stipule-like basal ones. The flowers, ½ to ¾ inch long, are in flattish umbels of up to ten. They are golden-yellow, sometimes stained with red. The slender pods are 1 inch long. Variety *L. c. flore-plena* has double flowers. Similar to *L. corniculatus,* but considerably taller and coarser, *L. pedunculatus,* native to wet soils in Europe and North Africa, can be distinguished by the teeth of its ca-

Lotus berthelotii

lyxes spreading in the bud stage instead of being erect. This is a hardy perennial.

St.-James-trefoil (*L. jacobaeus*) is a nonhardy, slightly hairy subshrub native of the Cape Verde Islands. From 1 foot to 3 feet tall, it has leaves of three to five essentially stalkless, linear leaflets ½ inch to 1¼ inches long. In umbels of up to six, its ½-inch-long flowers vary on the same plant from blackish-purple to yellow, or may combine these hues in the same bloom. The pods are hairless. Native to the Canary Islands, nonhardy *L. mascaensis* is a broad, spreading, silvery-hairy shrublet, 1 foot to 1½ feet tall, that partially cascades if planted atop a wall or in a hanging basket. In season it fairly covers itself with umbels of golden-yellow blooms ½ to ¾ inch long. Its pinnate leaves are of very narrow leaflets. This sort is very beautiful.

A silvery-hairy, freely-branched, shrubby, evergreen trailer with, where opportunity affords, pendulous stems, or a semitrailer, *L. berthelotii*, of the Canary Islands and Cape Verde Islands, is delightful, but not hardy. It may attain a height of 1 foot to 2 feet, but often is considerably lower. Its grayish-green leaves consist of stalkless clusters of three to seven slender, linear leaflets up to 1 inch long. Few together, the scarlet-crimson blooms, varying to darker crimson, lighten to orange-red as they age. Up to 1¼ inches long, they have pointed keels longer than the wing petals and a narrow, recurved, hood-shaped or banner petal. In *L. b. atrococcineus*, flowers are darker red with a conspicuous spot or band of black.

Annual, occasionally longer-lived *L. angustissimus*, of southern Europe, is more or less clothed with white hairs. Its stems are long and prostrate or erect and up to 3 inches long. The leaves have obovate to ovate-lanceolate leaflets, the biggest up to ½ inch long, the others much smaller. Golden-yellow with the ends of the petals often reddish, the flowers are up to three together on stalks longer than the leaves. Also annual, *L. ornithopioides*, of the Mediterranean region, is hairy and 4 inches to a little over 1 foot tall. Its leaves

have elliptic-lozenge-shaped leaflets. The clusters of five or fewer small yellow blooms have at their bases three spreading bracts as long or longer than the clusters. These stay green. Later from below them hang the slender, curved seed pods.

Western American natives, all discussed here perennials, but probably not hardy in the north, include a few sometimes cultivated. Quite beautiful *L. formosissimus* (syn. *Hosackia gracilis*) is hairless and has more or less prostrate stems. Its leaves are of five to eleven broad-elliptic to ovate leaflets up to 1 inch in length. The flower stalks, longer than the leaves, carry umbels of three to seven ½-inch-long blooms with yellow banners and keels and wing petals at first rose-red, but fading as the blooms age. At the bases of the umbels is a three- or five-cleft leafy bract. This prefers damp soil. Much like the last, but more erect and usually without leafy bracts at the bases of the umbels, *L. pinnatus* (syn. *Hosackia bicolor*) has flowers with yellow banners and keels and white wing petals. This, too, grows in moist places. It attains heights of 1 foot or somewhat more. Favoring dry slopes, *L. scoparius* (syn. *Hosackia glabra*) is bushy, subshrubby, and up to 4 feet tall. Its wandlike stems have leaves with three to five oblong to oblanceolate leaflets up to ½ inch long. The stalkless flowers, yellow sometimes tinged red and approximately ⅓ inch long, are in stalkless umbels in the leaf axils.

Garden and Landscape Uses. Bird's-foot-trefoil, especially the double-flowered variety, is attractive in rock gardens and similar places, and so is *L. angustissimus*. Taller *L. pedunculatus* may be located at watersides in naturalistic surroundings. Nonhardy, subshrubby kinds are useful in warm, dry Mediterranean-type climates for planting outdoors, and for decorating cool greenhouses. Of these, *L. berthelotii* is especially pleasing in hanging baskets. It is a nice window plant. The asparagus-pea is grown as a vegetable.

Cultivation. With the exception of *L. pedunculatus*, *L. formosissimus*, and *L. pinnatus*, which favor moist soils, the kinds discussed above need well-drained soil kept slightly dryish rather than wet. Except for the need for sharp porosity, the type of soil is not very important. It may be sandy, peaty, loamy, or limy. Sunny locations are needed. In greenhouses night temperatures in winter of about 50°F are appropriate, with daytime increases of five to fifteen degrees permitted. On all favorable occasions the greenhouse must be ventilated freely. A dank, stagnant atmosphere is very much resented by these plants. The subshrubby and shrubby kinds need shearing or pruning to shape as soon as flowering is through. Sometimes they tend to deteriorate with age, and then it is best to discard them and start again with young plants. The annuals

are raised from seeds sown in early spring where the plants are to stay, with the seedlings thinned out to prevent undue crowding. Seed, and with some kinds division and cuttings, afford ready means of increasing perennial kinds. For cultivation of the asparagus-pea see Asparagus-pea.

LOUSEWORT. See Pedicularis.

LOVAGE is *Levisticum officinale*. Alpine-, Scotch-, and small-alpine-lovage belong in *Ligusticum*.

LOVE. The word love occurs as part of the common names of these plants: Australian love creeper (*Comesperma volubile*), lad's love (*Artemisia abrotanum*), love-apple [an old name for the tomato and the mandrake (*Mandragora*)], love-in-a-mist (*Nigella damascena*), love-lies-bleeding (*Amaranthus caudatus*), love vine (*Cuscuta*), and Mexican love grass (*Eragrostis mexicana*).

LOVE-APPLE. This name, in times past applied to tomatoes, is sometimes used for the mandrake (*Mandragora officinarum*).

LOWIA. See Orchidantha.

LOXANTHOCEREUS (Loxantho-cèreus). Those who interpret the cactus family CACTACEAE as consisting of comparatively few, broadly inclusive genera rather than more numerous smaller ones include this group in *Borzicactus*. Others recognize approximately thirty species of *Loxanthocereus*, natives of Peru, some previously named *Maritimocereus*. The name *Loxanthocereus* from the Greek *loxos*, oblique or slanting, *anthos*, a flower, and the name of allied *Cereus*, alludes to the form of the blooms.

These cactuses range according to species from erect and bushy to prostrate or creeping. Sometimes they develop big woody roots. Their thick, cylindrical, tubercled, ribbed stems are armed, often fiercely, with clusters of fairly short to long, strong spines. The funnel-shaped blooms, which open by day, have tubular perianth tubes that, like the ovaries and fruits, are woolly on their outsides. The petals spread to form a markedly oblique face to the bloom.

Among sorts cultivated are these: *L. acanthurus* (syns. *Borzicactus acanthurus*, *Cereus acanthurus*) has usually prostrate stems upturned near their ends, about 1 foot long by 1½ inches in diameter, with fifteen to twenty ribs. The very woolly areoles bear clusters of fifteen to twenty-two ¼-inch-long, yellowish, bristly radial spines and a few centrals up to slightly over ½ inch long. The scarlet flowers are about 1 inch wide. *L. jajoianus* (syn. *Borzicactus jajoianus*), up to 2 feet tall, has clusters of erect to procumbent stems some 2½ inches in diameter with about twelve low, blunt ribs. The spines are yellowish, thickened at their bases. The radials in each cluster number about twenty and are ¼ inch long. The one to four centrals are 1½ to 2 inches or a little more in length. The flowers are orange. *L. nanus* (syn. *Maritimocereus nana*) has stems only about 4 inches long with about eleven ribs and yellow spines in groups of about eight radials and three or fewer centrals. The flowers are orange-scarlet. *L. piscoensis* (syn. *Borzicactus piscoensis*) has formidably-armed stems up to about 3 feet long by approximately 3½ inches thick. They have ten to twelve ribs and spine clusters of about fifteen radials from somewhat less to a little over ½ inch long and one stout central some 2 inches long. The flowers have orange petals cinnabarred at their apexes. *L. splendens* has stems 1¼ inches thick or thicker with twelve to fourteen ribs. The spine clusters are of about fourteen slender radials and one to four stronger, reedlike, 1-inch-long, brown centrals. The flowers are red. *L. sulcifer* has 3- to 6-foot-long stems that creep along the ground like giant caterpillars with their front ends raised and pointing upward and forward. Approximately 3½ inches in diameter, they have about eight ribs nearly separated into more or less hexagonal tubercles. The spine clusters consist of nine to ten short radials and four 1½-inch-long, yellowish centrals.

Garden and Landscape Uses and Cultivation. These are as for *Borzicactus*. For further information see Cactuses.

LOXOSTIGMA (Loxo-stígma). Comprising three species, *Loxostigma*, of the gesneria family GESNERIACEAE, inhabits the Himalayan region of India. Its name, derived from the Greek *loxos*, slanting, and *stigma*, alludes to the stigma.

Loxostigmas are nonhardy, stemmed herbaceous plants with opposite leaves, those of each pair of unequal size. The flowers, borne on stalks from the leaf axils, have a five-lobed calyx, a somewhat two-lipped, tubular corolla, four stamens the anthers of which are joined in pairs, and a style terminating in a two-lobed stigma. The fruits are slender capsules.

Occasionally cultivated, *L. griffithii* has slender stems and short- to long-stalked, rather distantly-spaced, short-hairy, toothed ovate leaves 3 to 7 inches long by approximately one-half as broad. Stalks about 3 inches long terminate in a few 1½-inch-long, brown-flecked, yellow flowers.

Garden Uses and Cultivation. These are as for *Nematanthus*.

LUCERNE. See Alfalfa.

LUCKHOFFIA (Luck-hóffia). Named in honor of the South African botanists Dr. J. Luckhoff and his son Carl, *Luckhoffia*, of the milkweed family ASCLEPIADACEAE, consists of one species, an endemic of South Africa.

From closely allied *Stapelia* this differs in having many-angled stems with the angles consisting of conspicuous, compressed tubercles, each when young tipped with a short spine. In addition there are technical differences between the flowers of the two genera. The fruits are similar.

Erect and clustered, the knobby stems of *L. beukmanii* (syn. *Stapelia beukmanii*) are cylindrical, gray-green, and a little over 1 inch in diameter. Branched from its base, this species attains a height of 2 to 2½ feet. Its short-stalked flowers, which develop from near the apexes of the stems, are flat, five-pointed stars, approximately 2½ inches in diameter and with a central depression housing a dark purple-brown crown or corona. The triangular lobes (petals) of the corolla extend halfway to the center of the bloom. Their basal halves, like the middle part of the flower, is brown spotted with yellow. The outer halves are uniformly brown. The face of the bloom is covered with tiny pustules, each tipped with a short, horizontal, black hair. The margins of the petals are recurved and sparingly-fringed with hairs.

Garden Uses and Cultivation. These are as for *Stapelia*.

LUCKY NUT is *Thevetia peruviana*.

LUCULIA (Lucù-lia). The madder family RUBIACEAE contains many worthwhile ornamentals, from lowly, hardy, sweet woodruff to familiar gardenias and bouvardias and brilliant tropical ixoras and warszewiczias. To it also belong the plants to which we are indebted for coffee, quinine, and ipecac. Among the decorative genera of the relationship, *Luculia* rates highly. It consists of five species of nonhardy, deciduous shrubs and trees, natives from China to India. The name is an adaptation of a native one.

Luculias are shrubs and trees with opposite, undivided leaves and flowers in terminal, often handsome clusters. The blooms have five-lobed calyxes, slender-tubed corollas with five spreading lobes (petals), five short-stalked stamens, and a two-branched style. The fruits are capsules containing winged seeds.

The best-known species *L. gratissima* is a variable shrub or tree up to 18 feet tall. It has reddish-hairy shoots and pointed-ovate-oblong leaves 4 to 8 inches long by approximately one-half as wide, with the veins on their undersides downy. The slender-tubed, light rosy-pink blooms, 1 inch to 1½ inches across, are in rounded clusters up to 9 inches in diameter. From the last, 6-foot-tall *L. pinceana* differs in having pink-tinged, creamy-white blooms 1¼ to 2 inches wide and about as long, with a pair of wartlike processes at the bases of the clefts between the corolla lobes. The leaves of this kind are pointed-broad-lanceolate and 4 to 6 inches in length. From 10 to 25 feet in height, *L. intermedia* has

rough-surfaced shoots, slender-pointed, oblong-lanceolate to obovate leaves up to 6 inches long by 2½ inches wide, and fragrant, reddish blooms 1¼ inches in diameter in clusters up to 7 inches wide. A distinguishing characteristic is the flaplike development between the corolla lobes.

The largest-leaved of the genus, *L. grandifolia* is a native at high elevations in Bhutan. A shrub or tree up to 20 feet in height, this has broadly-elliptic to ovate leaves 10 inches to considerably over 1 foot long and up to 10 inches wide, with magenta-crimson stalks and midribs, and the margins often brownish-red. The trusses of sixteen to twenty very fragrant, greenish-white to snow-white flowers are 6 to 8 inches in diameter. The individual blooms are 3 inches long and 1 inch wide.

Luculia grandifolia

Garden and Landscape Uses and Cultivation. Luculias are choice for regions of no or little frost and moderate summer temperatures, and for cool greenhouses. They succeed splendidly in parts of California. They are suitable for planting as single specimens and in association with other shrubs and trees. They succeed in ordinary, fertile, well-drained soil, moderately moist, but not wet, that contains ample humus. Usually they are planted in light shade, but if they receive sufficient water they seem to do as well in full sun in many places. They may be increased with fair ease from cuttings made, after flowering is through, from firm shoots, and are easy to raise from seed. Although technically deciduous, the new foliage usually appears at about the time the old leaves are dropping. There is no long period of leaflessness.

In greenhouses, luculias can be grown in pots, tubs, and ground beds. They prefer fertile, peaty, well-drained soil and succeed where the winter night temperature is 50°F and that by day five to ten degrees higher. Specimens in containers may be stood outdoors in summer. Light shade in summer and full sun at other times are needed. From spring to fall luculias need plenty of water. From December until new growth begins in spring, plants in greenhouses are kept nearly dry, water is only given if there is danger of the shoots shriveling. Pruning is done as soon as flowering is through. It consists of cutting back old flowering shoots close to their bases and of removing any branches that seem likely to crowd. In spring, new shoots that will flower the same year start from below pruning cuts. Well-rooted specimens benefit from regular dilute liquid fertilizer applied at weekly or two-weekly intervals from spring to fall.

LUCUMA. See Pouteria.

LUDISIA. See Haemaria.

LUDWIGIA (Lud-wígia) — False-Loosestrife, Water-Purslane, Rattle-Box or Seed-Box, Primrose-Willow. As accepted here, *Ludwigia* includes plants treated separately by some authorities as *Jussiaea*. Under the broader concept, it includes about seventy-five species, members of the evening-primrose family ONAGRACEAE. The name commemorates the German botanist C. G. Ludwig, who died in 1773.

Chiefly inhabiting warm regions, but some sorts native of more temperate climates, this genus consists of aquatic and wet-soil perennials, many floating or creeping, some erect. Their leaves are generally alternate, less often opposite. The flowers, solitary in the leaf axils or in terminal clusters, are yellow or white. They have four to seven persistent sepals and either no corolla or one of four to seven petals, as many stamens as petals or sepals, and one style. The fruits are many-seeded capsules.

Water-purslane (*L. palustris*), widely distributed in North America, Central America, the West Indies, Europe, and Asia, has weak stems that float in shallow water or creep on mud. Its lanceolate to elliptic-ovate leaves, with blades ¼ to 1 inch long or slightly longer, have stalks about the same length. They are opposite and have red or red-purple undersides, especially when grown in sun. The minute, solitary, stalkless flowers, in the leaf axils, are without petals. Similar *L. natans*, of the southern United States, Mexico, and the West Indies, differs in having leaves usually smaller, narrower, and shorter-stalked than those of *L. palustris*. The plant grown in aquariums as *L. mulerttii*, more robust and larger-leaved than *L. palustris* and said to have originated in South America, may be a form of *L. natans*.

The rattle-box or seed-box (*L. alternifolia*), as its name indicates, has alternate leaves. Native of bogs and wet woodlands from Ontario to Iowa, Kansas, Florida, and Texas, it has erect, branched stems 1½ to 3½ feet in height and linear to linear-lanceolate, stalkless or very short-stalked leaves 1½ to 4 inches long. Its

flowers, solitary from the upper leaf axils and stalked, have four each sepals and minute yellow petals. Differing in being a creeper with quite showy, yellow-petaled flowers ½ to ¾ inch in diameter, *L. arcuata* is a native of the southeastern United States. It has opposite, practically stalkless, elliptic-linear to oblanceolate leaves up to ¾ inch long.

Primrose-willow is a common name of several sorts of *Ludwigia* previously segregated as *Jussiaea*, among them those now to be discussed. Floating *L. helminthorrhiza* (syn. *Jussiaea helminthorrhiza*), a native from Mexico to South America, has leaves with roundish blades ½ inch to 2 inches long. From the leaf axils are produced solitary, white flowers, mostly with five each sepals and petals, the latter ⅓ to ½ inch long and with a yellow spot at the bottom of each. Erect, from 1½ to 6 feet tall, and with narrowly-winged stems that usually branch only near their summits, *L. longifolia* (syn. *Jussiaea longifolia*) is generally hairless. Its stalkless or nearly stalkless leaves are lanceolate to lanceolate-linear, the lower ones 4 to 6 inches long,

Ludwigia longifolia

those above smaller. The conspicuous light yellow to cream blooms, from the upper leaf axils, have broad-ovate, slightly notched petals ¾ to 1 inch long. This native of Brazil to Argentina may in gardens have been misidentified as *L. decurrens*, a much less worthy annual species of North and South America. Also with four-petaled flowers, *L. octovalvis*, frequently identified as *Jussiaea suffruticosa*, is a native of the Old World and New World tropics. A leafy, well-branched herbaceous perennial or shrub 2 to 8 feet in height, it is hairy to nearly hairless and has short-stalked to nearly stalkless, pointed, lanceolate-ovate to lanceolate-linear leaves up to 4 inches long and 1 inch wide. The deep yellow flowers have ovate-wedge-shaped petals ⅓ to ¾ inch long. Creeping or floating stems, generally upturned at their ends, and glossy, stalked, oblong leaves with blades ½ inch to 2 inches long are

characteristic of *L. peploides* (syns. *Jussiaea peploides*, *J. repens peploides*, *J. californica*), which occurs natively from Oregon to South America and the West Indies. The yellow solitary flowers, from the leaf axils, have five each sepals and petals, the latter notched at their apexes and ¼ to 1 inch long. Native of the eastern and southeastern United States, *L. p. glabrescens* (syn. *Jussiaea repens glabrescens*) has leaves with longer stalks and blades up to 4 inches in length. A subshrubby or shrubby perennial 2 to 6 feet tall or sometimes taller, *L. peruviana* (syn. *Jussiaea peruviana*) is loosely-branched and more or less hairy. Its ovate to lanceolate-elliptic leaves are 2 to 6 inches long by one-quarter to one-third as broad. The flowers, solitary from the axils of the upper leaves, have typically four petals that are pale to deep yellow, round-ovate, toothed at their apexes, and ½ to over 1 inch long. This kind is wild from Florida to Argentina and Peru. Native in wet places from southern New York to Argentina, *L. uruguayensis* (syn. *Jussiaea grandiflora*) has creeping rhizomes and floating or erect stems, conspicuously hairy in their upper parts, that bear rather short-stalked, lanceolate to oblanceolate, hairy leaves. The bright yellow flowers are 1¼ to 2 inches across.

Garden and Landscape Uses. Kinds with floating stems may be grown in outdoor pools and aquariums, terrestrial sorts, in bog gardens and at watersides.

Cultivation. In suitable environments these plants grow with little care. Needing moist, fertile soil and sunny locations, they are easily propagated by seed and by division. Not all are hardy in the north. Those that are not (their range in the wild gives indication of this) can be managed by taking them into a greenhouse in fall and planting them out in spring or by treating them as tender annuals and sowing seeds in pots of soil in a greenhouse in spring. Cover the seeds with a sifting of fine sand and submerge the pots so the sand surface is an inch or two beneath water kept at a temperature of 60 to 70°F. As soon as the seedlings are big enough to handle comfortably, pot them individually in small pots and keep them growing in congenial warmth in full sun indoors until the soil and weather outdoors are warm enough to encourage growth. Then plant them outside.

As aquarium plants ludwigias succeed with minimal care. Within reasonable limits the degree of hardness of the water seems not to be important. A winter water temperature of about 55°F is satisfactory. In summer it may be five to fifteen degrees higher. Good light is needed. Even in aquariums these plants lose their lower leaves at the approach of winter, and so it is usually advisable to propagate them anew each spring either by using the leafy tops of the stems as cuttings (they root very readily) or by sowing seeds.

LUEHEA (Lue-hèa). A member of the linden family TILIACEAE, the genus *Luehea* has a name commemorating Karl Emil von der Luhe, who wrote about plants of South Africa. He died in 1801.

Lueheas are handsome tropical and subtropical American trees allied to *Sparmannia*. They have alternate, short-stalked, often toothed leaves, clothed on their undersides with stellate (star-shaped) hairs. In showy, branched clusters from the leaf axils or in terminal panicles, their usually pink or white flowers have five each sepals and petals, many stamens, and one style. The fruits are capsules.

Native to Argentina, southern Brazil, Uruguay, and Paraguay, **L. divaricata** is a tree 20 to 75 feet tall. It has irregularly-toothed, pointed-oblong to elliptic leaves, grayish-white to light tan on their undersides, and 2 to 6 inches long. The pinkish-white to purplish-pink flowers, in leafy panicles of considerable size from the ends of the branches, are 1½ to 2 inches wide. The capsules, ovoid and about 1 inch long, are clothed with a fuzz of hairs.

Luehea divaricata

Garden and Landscape Uses and Cultivation. Attractive ornamentals for the tropics and warm subtropics, lueheas prosper in ordinary fertile soil. They may be propagated by seed and by cuttings of firm, but not hard shoots planted in a propagating bed with bottom heat.

LUETKEA (Luét-kea). The only species of this genus of the rose family ROSACEAE inhabits damp rocky places at high altitudes in the mountains from California to Alaska. Its name commemorates a Russian sea captain, Count F. P. Luetke, who led an expedition that circumnavigated the earth.

Allied to *Spiraea*, and a low, mat-forming subshrub, **Luetkea pectinata** has prostrate or creeping woody stems and alternate leaves one-, two-, or three-times-divided, the final divisions being linear. Its whitish, bisexual flowers are ⅓ inch to 2 inches long. They have five sepals, five

petals, about twenty stamens, and usually five separate pistils. The filaments (stalks) of the stamens are joined at their bases into a short tube.

Garden Uses and Cultivation. The general aspect of this quite charming plant is that of certain mossy saxifrages. Like them, it is best suited for rock gardens and similar locations. It needs gritty, porous, non-alkaline, fairly moist soil, and full sun. Propagation is by division, cuttings in summer, and seed.

LUFFA (Lúf-fa)—Luffa Gourd or Dishcloth Gourd or Rag Gourd or Vegetable Sponge. Six species constitute *Luffa*, of the gourd family CUCURBITACEAE. The name is a modification of *luff*, an Arabic name for these plants. The common name is sometimes spelled loofah. The remarkable interior fibrous skeletons of the fruits of luffas, divested of their surrounding flesh, are used as sponges. Because of this, such names as dishcloth gourd, rag gourd, and vegetable sponge are applied to cultivated kinds. In the Orient young fruits of *L. acutangula* are cooked and eaten like squash.

Natives of the Old World tropics, luffas are vigorous, nonwoody vines that are annuals or at least are cultivated as annuals. Nearly or quite hairless, they have alternate leaves with five or seven lobes or angles. They have branched tendrils and showy yellow or yellowish, unisexual flowers, the males in racemes, the females solitary. Each has a deeply-five-lobed calyx and five petals, and the males usually have three or five stamens. Technically pepos, the fruits are long and gourd-like. At maturity their skins become dry and papery.

The dishcloth gourd, rag gourd, or vegetable sponge (**L. aegyptiaca** syn. *L. cylindrica*), probably a native of the Old World now widely naturalized in the tropics, has stems up to 15 feet long. Its large, rough-hairy leaves of more or less rounded outline, are decidedly three- to seven-lobed and toothed. The flowers are 2 to 2½ inches across, the males with five stamens. The straight or curved cylindrical

Luffa aegyptiaca

Luffa aegyptiaca (leaves and flowers)

Luffa aegyptiaca (fruit)

Luffa aegyptiaca (fruits), the near fruit with shell removed to show interior fibrous skeleton

fruits are up to 2 feet long. From the dishcloth gourd **L. acutangula** differs in having leaves that are angled, but not lobed, and male flowers with three stamens. The fruits are club-shaped, have ten strongly evident longitudinal ridges, and are not over 1 foot long. Hybrids between this species and *L. aegyptiaca* have been raised.

Garden Uses and Cultivation. In gardens luffa gourds are cultivated chiefly as curiosities. They may be trained on fences and other supports and be used as temporary screens. Their cultivation is similar to that of cucumbers and squashes and the same as for *Lagenaria*. For additional information see Gourds, Ornamental.

LUFFA GOURD is *Luffa acutangula*.

LUINA (Lu-ìna). Four species, including the plant previously named *Rainiera*, belong in *Luina*. Natives of western North America, they belong in the daisy family COMPOSITAE. The name is an anagram of the name of the related genus *Inula*.

Luinas are herbaceous perennials, the species remarkably different in appearance. They have alternate leaves, lobed palmately (in hand-fashion) or lobeless and sometimes slightly toothed. The flower heads are without ray florets (those that look like petals in daisy-type flower heads). They consist of all disk florets (the kind that form the centers of daisies). They are yellow or yellowish, and all are fertile, producing seedlike fruits called achenes.

The first two species described here have lobeless leaves. Of very local occurrence in the wild, **L. hypoleuca** is tufted and up to 1 foot tall. It has white-hairy stems and foliage. Its stalkless, broadly-elliptic to ovate leaves are 1 inch to 2 inches long and more than one-half as wide. The ⅓-inch-long, cream flower heads form flattish-topped clusters. Quite different **L. stricta** (syn. *Rainiera stricta*) is plentiful on and near Mount Rainier and is found at other places in Washington and Oregon. Thick-rooted, 1½ to 3 feet tall, and essentially hairless, this sort has broadly-oblanceolate lower leaves, which, including their tapered, stalklike bases, are from 6 inches to rather more than 1 foot long and up to 3 inches wide. From the base of the plant upward, the leaves are progressively reduced in size, until the uppermost are stalkless and linear. The little, yellowish flower heads are clustered in erect, terminal, spikelike racemes from 4 inches to over 1 foot long.

Conspicuously palmately-lobed, kidney-shaped to roundish leaves are typical of 2- to 3-foot-tall **L. nardosmia** (syn. *Cacaliopsis nardosmia*), of the Cascade Mountains in Washington and to California. Long-stalked and hairy on their undersides, the most numerous leaves are basal and have blades 4 to 8 inches wide. The upper leaves are fewer and much smaller. The about 1-inch-wide heads of yellow flowers are in loose, flattish-topped or raceme-like arrangements.

Garden Uses and Cultivation. Likely only to be attempted by gardeners interested in alpines, and accommodated in rock gardens or other places that seem likely to suit high mountain plants, luinas are little known in cultivation. They may be expected to be hardy and to need cool, humid summers and porous, moist soil. Seed and division are means of propagation.

LULO is *Solanum quitoense*.

LUMA (Lù-ma). This South American genus of four species of the myrtle family MYRTACEAE is very closely related to *Myrtus*, differing chiefly in technical details of its seeds. The name *Luma* is a Chilean vernacular one. In gardens *L. apiculata* is sometimes confused with *Amomyrtus luma*.

Lumas are evergreen shrubs or trees with opposite, undivided leaves and small flowers from the leaf axils, solitary or in groups of three. The blooms have a four-lobed calyx, four petals, numerous protruding stamens, and one style. The fruits are berries.

An attractive evergreen shrub or tree, **L. apiculata** (syns. *Myrceugenia apiculata*, *Eugenia apiculata*) is a native of temperate Argentina and Chile. From 4 to 50 feet tall or taller, it has very short-stalked, pointed-broad-elliptic, evergreen leaves ½ to 1 inch long. Its mostly solitary, long-stalked flowers are white, sometimes becoming pink as they age. They have almost round, concave petals nearly ½ inch long and stamens tipped with yellow anthers. The nearly spherical, purple-black fruits are approximately ⅜ inch in diameter. Magnificent stands of picturesque old specimens are in reservations under state supervision near Bariloche, Argentina. From the last, **L. chequen** (syn. *Myrceugenia chequen*) differs most noticeably in its lighter green leaves being more crowded and having clearly visible tiny dots.

Garden and Landscape Uses and Cultivation. The sorts described are suitable for outdoor cultivation in mild climates only. They are effective as single specimens and in groups. They respond to conditions and care that suit the common myrtle (*Myrtus communis*) and many eugenias.

LUMBANG NUT is *Aleurites trisperma*.

LUNARIA (Lun-ària) — Honesty, Moonwort, Satin Flower. The European genus *Lunaria*, of the mustard family CRUCIFERAE, consists of two or three species, one of which, *L. annua*, is sparingly naturalized in parts of North America. The name, from the Latin *luna*, moon, alludes to the more or less circular center partitions of the big seed pods of honesty, which remain, silvery-white, decorative, and set in their thin surrounding rims like spectacle lenses in frames after the outer parts of the pods and the seeds are shed. Branches of these are used for dried flower arrangements.

Lunarias are erect, branched, sparsely-hairy, hardy biennials and herbaceous perennials. They have alternate and opposite, lobeless, coarsely-toothed, ovate to triangular-ovate leaves that diminish in size upward. The showy purple or sometimes white flowers are in terminal racemes. They have four sepals and four spreading petals narrowed conspicuously toward their bases and arranged as a cross. There are six stamens, two shorter than the others, and a short, slightly-lobed style. The seed pods are disklike, with a short, but prominent beak at the apex.

Honesty, moonwort, or satin flower (**L.**

annua syn. *L. biennis*) is the most decorative and popular kind. A biennial, it is 1½ to 3 feet tall and has usually pinkish-purple, fragrant flowers ¾ to 1 inch across. In variety *L. a. alba* the blooms are white. The oblongish, nearly circular seed pods, 1 inch long or longer, contain nearly round seeds.

Lunaria annua, in bloom

Lunaria annua, center partitions of seed pods

Perennial honesty (**L. rediviva**) differs from the above in having its upper leaves distinctly stalked and its seed pods unequal-sided, about twice as long as broad,

Lunaria rediviva

and tapering rather than rounded at their ends. They are 2 to 3 inches long. The seeds are kidney-shaped.

Garden and Landscape Uses. These plants are attractive for beds and borders, fringes of shrub plantings and woodlands, and semiwild places where the soil is fertile and moist and a little shade is available. The cultivated perennial species is persistent, and the biennial usually self-sows its seeds so satisfactorily that it maintains itself from year to year. The latter is the more attractive, particularly its seed pods. If these are to be cut for indoor decoration this should be done as soon as they begin to change from green to brown. If the outer walls of the pods separate outdoors, the papery moons that are the attractive decorative features are likely to become discolored. Very pleasing results are had by growing a few of the white-flowered variety of honesty along with the more common purple kind.

Cultivation. These are quite hardy plants and no difficulty attends their cultivation in soils and locations recommended above. The perennial kind can be increased by division in spring and early fall and, as is the biennial, by seed. These are sown in May in a shaded seed bed kept evenly moist. The seedlings are transplanted to nursery beds, in rows 1 foot to 1½ feet apart, with about 9 inches between individuals. There they make their summer growth. They are transferred to their flowering quarters preferably in fall, or in early spring, spacing them about 1 foot apart. If the plants self-sow, the seedlings should be thinned early to allow adequate room for their development, and, of course, weeds must be kept from smothering them.

LUNGAN. See Euphoria.

LUNGWORT. See Pulmonaria.

LUPINE. See Lupinus.

LUPINUS (Lupìn-us)—Lupine, Texas Bluebonnet. This notable genus, of the pea family LEGUMINOSAE, contains about 200 species, a few esteemed as fodder or for food, a considerable number decidedly ornamental. In addition there are many improved horticultural varieties. As wildlings the sorts of *Lupinus* are chiefly North American, but others occur in South America and in Europe and Africa particularly in the lands around the Mediterranean basin. Supposedly applied because of an old-time belief that these plants preyed on (robbed) the soil, the name is derived from the Latin *lupus*, a wolf.

Lupines include annual, herbaceous perennial, and shrubby sorts, the last sometimes called tree lupines. Nearly all have stalked leaves with from five to sixteen narrow leaflets that spread from the top of the leafstalk like the rays of an umbrella or the fingers of a hand. A very few have leaves of one or three leaflets. Generally showy, and in terminal, spikelike panicles, more rarely in whorls (tiers), the characteristically pea-shaped flowers are white, yellow, pink, red, purple, lavender, or blue. They have a two-lipped, five-lobed calyx and a corolla consisting of a broad, erect standard or banner petal, two wing petals, and an incurved keel. There are ten stamens united in one group and an incurved style. The fruits are pea-like pods.

The chief herbaceous perennial lupines cultivated are horticultural varieties and hybrids of **L. polyphyllus.** This native of moist soils from California to British Columbia exhibits considerable variation in the wild. Robust, erect, and from 3 to 5 feet tall, sparsely-hairy to nearly hairless, it has very long-stalked leaves of nine to sixteen pointed, lanceolate to oblanceolate leaflets 2 to 6 inches long and hairless on their upper sides. The flowers, in crowded, erect, terminal racemes 6 inches to 2 feet in length, are about ½ inch long. They have a purplish standard petal, blue wing petals, and a dark-tipped spur. The about six-seeded pods, woolly-hairy, are 1 inch to 1½ inches long. The seeds are variously mottled.

Lupinus polyphyllus

A handsome group of hybrids involving *L. polyphyllus* and other species and including Russell lupines and other perennial sorts of garden origin is classified as **L. regalis** (syn. *L. hybridus* of gardeners, not of botanists). These have much the appearance of *L. polyphyllus* and occur in a wonderful range of flower colors from pure white through pinks to rich reds, from palest to deepest blues and purples, from white and creamy-white to bright yellows. Many have two-colored blooms. Especially notable are the lovely peach and apricot-pinks, bronzes, smoky hues, and other art shades. The flower spikes are freely produced and are often massive. Unfortunately these magnificent examples of the hybridizers' art are often not as reliably long-lived as older varieties of *L. polyphyllus.*

Lupinus regalis, Russell strain

Lupinus regalis, Russell strain (flowers)

Another West Coast herbaceous perennial lupine is very variable *L. latifolius,* which as a native ranges from Washington to southern California. From 1 foot to 6 feet tall and minutely-hairy, this favors moist soils. It has leaves of mostly seven to nine, less often fewer or more, broadly-oblanceolate, usually pointed leaflets 1½ to 4 inches long. The rather loosely arranged blooms are scattered or in whorls in spires 6 inches to 1½ feet long. They are blue, purplish, or pinkish. The hairy pods, about 1¼ inches long, contain seven

Lupinus latifolius parishii in California

to ten seeds mottled with dark brown. From 1½ to 6 feet tall, *L. l. parishii* has denser racemes up to 1 foot long of rose-pink to lavender flowers.

Herbaceous perennials of eastern North America occasionally cultivated are the sundial lupine or quaker bonnets (*L. perennis*) and the deer-cabbage (*L. diffusus*). Inhabiting sandy soils from Maine to Ontario, Florida, and Louisiana, and from 8 inches to 2 feet tall, *L. perennis* has erect stems and short-stalked leaves of seven to eleven oblanceolate leaflets up to 2 inches long. The blue, pink, or white, ½-inch-long blooms are in spikes 4 to 10 inches in length. The hairy seed pods contain four to six seeds. Native from North Carolina to Florida, *L. diffusus* has decumbent stems and leaves hairless on their upper surfaces with seven to nine ¾-inch-long leaflets. In spikes up to 1 foot long, the flowers are light blue with a yellow spot in the middle of the standard petal.

The tree lupine most usually cultivated is *L. arboreus,* of California. A bushy shrub, sometimes low, more often 3 to 8 feet tall, occasionally higher, this has many short branches. Its more or less silky-hairy, short-stalked leaves have five to twelve oblanceolate leaflets ¾ inch to 2 inches in length. The sulfur-yellow or more rarely lilac to blue blooms are in loose racemes up to 10 inches long. The flowers of *L. a. eximius* have a yellow standard and blue wing petals. There are also white-flowered varieties. The pods, hairy and 1¼ to 3 inches long, contain eight to twelve dark seeds.

A broad, much-branched, leafy shrub 3 to 5 feet tall, *L. albifrons,* of California, has silky-hairy leaves of seven to ten spatula-shaped to obovate leaflets up to 1¼ inches in length. Blue to reddish-purple or lavender, with white or yellow centers, the ⅓- to ½-inch-long flowers are in erect spikes up to 1 foot long. The pods, 1½ to 2 inches long, contain five to nine mottled or spotted seeds. Variety *L. a. douglasii* has larger leaves.

North American annuals, of the West

Coast region, likely to be cultivated include those now to be described and others may from time to time be grown locally in wild gardens and similar places. A highly variable endemic of California, of which twenty-four botanical varieties have been recognized is **L. densiflorus.** Characteristically this is stout, hairy, 1 foot to 2 feet tall, and has leaves with seven to nine oblanceolate leaflets hairy on their under surfaces. The flowers, ½ inch long or somewhat longer, are white or white tinted or veined with rose-pink or violet or, in *L. d. aureus,* yellow. They are in long-stalked racemes of crowded whorls up to 10 inches in length. The hairy two-seeded pods are about ¾ inch long.

Another endemic of California, the sky lupine (*L. nanus*) is a slender, more or less minutely-hairy annual 6 inches to 1¼ feet in height. It has leaves of five to seven linear to spatula-shaped leaflets up to 1¼ inches long and fragrant flowers in well-separated whorls forming spikes up to 6 inches long. Usually they are rich blue with a white or yellowish spot on the standard petal, but this is a variable sort and white- and pink-flowered forms occur. The 1-inch-long, hairy pods have five to eleven white seeds.

The Texas bluebonnet (**L. subcarnosus**), famed endemic of its native state, is a silky-hairy annual rarely over 1 foot tall. Its leaves, almost or quite hairless above and sparsely-hairy on their undersides, have five oblanceolate to narrow-oblong-obovate leaflets ¾ inch to 1½ inches long. In short terminal racemes the ½-inch-long blue flowers are marked in the middle of the standard petal with a white or yellowish spot. Mottled seeds are contained in the 1½-inch-long, hairy pods.

Lupinus subcarnosus

A showy annual from South America, robust *L. mutabilis* is 3 to 5 feet tall. Except for the seed pods hairless, this has leaves of seven to eleven gray-green, lanceolate to broad-oblanceolate leaflets 2 to 3 inches long. In long terminal spires, the conspicuously stalked, ¾-inch-long flow-

Lupinus mutabilis

ers are white with yellow or violet markings on the standard petal. On the lower parts of the spike the flowers are in whorls. The hairy pods are 2 to 3 inches long. Their seeds are white, sometimes mottled with brown.

Native to Mexico, *L. hartwegii* is an annual 2 to 3 feet tall and shaggy-hairy. Sparsely-branched, this has very hairy, long-stalked leaves of seven to ten narrowly-oblong to oblong-oblanceolate leaflets 2 to 3 inches long. In long terminal racemes, the mostly alternate flowers are chiefly blue, with the ½-inch-long standard petal rose-pink toward its middle. The pods are hairy, 1 inch long or a little longer. They contain shiny, white seeds.

The yellow lupine (*L. luteus*), of southern Europe, an annual grown for fodder, is of sufficient decorative merit to be admitted to gardens. It has erect, hairy stems up to 2 feet tall and leaves of seven to eleven linear-lanceolate to narrowly-obovate, hairy leaflets up to 1½ inches long. The yellow, nearly stalkless, fragrant blooms, about ¾ inch in length, are in whorls in long terminal spikes. The 2-inch-long pods contain four to seven seeds marked with brown.

The blue lupine (**L. hirsutus**), of Europe, is a large-seeded annual esteemed as an

Lupinus albifrons in California

Lupinus luteus

agricultural crop as well as for garden ornament. Up to 2 feet tall, but often considerably lower, and brown-hairy, it has leaves with five to seven oblanceolate to oblong-obovate leaflets up to 1½ inches in length. From ½ to ¾ inch long and blue, with their keels mostly tipped with white, the flowers are arranged alternately or those toward the top of the spikes in whorls. The very hairy pods contain gray to brownish, ½-inch-long seeds.

Garden and Landscape Uses. In regions where they thrive lupines are excellent for embellishing flower gardens and supplying cut flowers. Where summers are very hot the annuals are short-lived and must be sown early to bloom before the arrival of torrid weather. They are also satisfactory for blooming in winter and spring in greenhouses.

Modern herbaceous perennial sorts, such as the Russell lupines, tend not to be very permanent in regions of hot summers and cold winters. Under such conditions a fairly high percentage of individuals in a planting are likely to die each winter after the first. Tree lupines are not winter hardy in the north, but in milder regions they are excellent for garden decoration. They do splendidly near the sea, even when planted on shores only a short distance above high tide. They lend themselves well to espaliering against walls.

Cultivation. These are easy plants to manage. All need well-drained, reasonably fertile soil, mildly acid to neutral in reaction. Full sun is required for the best results. As a group lupines respond badly to root disturbance. Sow the annuals where they are to remain. Do the same with perennials or sow them in small pots, and set the young plants in their blooming quarters while yet quite small.

Seeds afford the best means of increase for all kinds. They have hard coats and unless helped are likely to germinate erratically. This tendency can be overcome by cutting a small nick with a knife or file in the coat of each seed before sowing, or somewhat less certainly by soaking them for twenty-four hours in lukewarm water.

Sow annual lupines outdoors as early in spring as the ground can be had in nice friable condition. Later thin the seedlings to stand 4 to 6 inches apart. July or August is a good time to sow herbaceous perennial sorts. In cold climates these benefit from being given the protection of a winter covering of salt hay, branches of evergreens, or some similar loose material. Tree lupines are also usually raised from seeds sown in July or August.

For winter and spring blooming in greenhouses, sow annual lupines in small pots, two or three seeds in each from August to October and again in January. Thin out from each pot all but the strongest seedling. When the roots begin to crowd plant in soil beds or benches or pot into larger pots.

Grow in full sun where the night temperature is 45 to 50°F, that by day five to ten degrees, or on very sunny days fifteen degrees, higher. Airy, rather than dank, humid atmospheric conditions must be maintained. Water with nice discretion. Constantly wet soil soon results in rotting.

LUVUNGA (Luv-únga). The name of this member of the rue family RUTACEAE, sometimes spelled *Lavanga*, is adapted from a native one of Bengal. The genus consists of a dozen species of horticulturally little known, spiny, sometimes climbing shrubs of tropical Asia, related but not very closely, to the orange.

Luvungas have alternate leaves with long, wingless stalks, three leaflets, and in the leaf axil a strong spine. The orange-blossom-like flowers, in axillary clusters, have tubular four- or five-toothed calyxes, four or five petals, twice as many stamens, and one style. The fruits are ovoid to oblong-ovoid. They have a thick, lemon-like rind and resinous insides.

A straggling, scarcely climbing, evergreen, hairless shrub, **Luvunga scandens** has distantly-spaced leaves with stalks 2 to 3 inches long. The short-stalked, toothless leaflets are lanceolate to narrowly-elliptic, 2½ to 6 inches long by 1 inch to 1½ inches wide. The spines are sharp, straight or strongly curved, and up to 1½ inches long. Very fragrant, the fleshy, white blooms are crowded in short racemes. Egg-shaped or oblongish, the yellowish fruits are approximately 1 inch long.

Garden and Landscape Uses and Cultivation. Planted to some extent as an ornamental, the species described here succeeds in climates favorable to oranges and other citrus fruits and is satisfied with the same general conditions. It is propagated by seed and by cuttings.

LUZULA (Lùz-ula)—Wood-Rush. An unimportant group horticulturally, *Luzula* belongs in the rush family JUNCACEAE. Its name is derived from the ancient one for one kind, *Gramen luzulae*. The wood-rushes number about sixty-five species and are almost worldwide in their natural distribution. They are distinguishable from true rushes (*Juncus*) by having leaves with hairs on them; there are other, more difficult to assess, technical differences. The identification of the species often depends upon careful examination of the seeds.

Wood-rushes are rather grasslike, herbaceous plants of dryish or sometimes moistish soils in open woodlands. The common wood-rush (**Luzula campestris**), which is indigenous throughout much of the northern and southern hemispheres, including North America, is the one most likely to be cultivated. It is a highly variable species that grows up to 1½ feet tall and has soft, flat leaves up to ¼ inch wide. Its small brown flowers are in grace-

ful, loosely-branched clusters. The fruits are capsules containing three seeds.

Garden Uses and Cultivation. Wood-rushes are suitable for wild gardens and for naturalizing in lightly shaded places in well-drained soils. They are easily propagated by seed.

LUZURIAGA. See Eustrephus.

LYCASTE (Lycás-te). Restricted in the wild to tropical America including the West Indies, *Lycaste*, of the orchid family ORCHIDACEAE, comprises forty-five species. Its name, assumed from Greek mythology, is that of Lycaste one of the daughters of Priam, King of Troy.

Lycastes, prevailingly handsome in bloom, are often difficult to identify with certainty as to species. Mostly they grow perched on trees, but take no nourishment from them, in other words they are epiphytes. Rarely they grow in the ground. They have egg-shaped to oblong-ovate pseudobulbs with, from their tops, one to several leaves and other sheathing ones from their bases. The leaves are pleated lengthwise. Generally solitary, but sometimes in twos or threes, and mostly large, the flowers have three nearly similar spreading sepals, the lateral ones joined to the foot of the column, and two smaller, commonly forward-pointing petals often recurved at their apexes that arch above the column. The three-lobed lip has a disk with a lengthwise, tongue-like callus. The side lobes are erect. There are four pollinia. Some orchids once called *Lycaste* belong in *Bifrenaria*.

Most frequently cultivated and the national flower of Guatemala, *L. virginalis* (syn. *L. skinneri*) is indigenous from Mexico to Honduras. This is a variable sort with oblong-ovate, sometimes angular and furrowed pseudobulbs 3 to 5 inches tall, each with one to several oblong-lanceolate leaves 9 inches to 2¼ feet long by up to 6 inches wide. Much shorter than the foliage, the flowering stalks carry a solitary, fragrant, waxy bloom 5 to 6 inches wide and ranging in color from pure white to more often having pale purplish-pink se-

Lycaste virginalis

pals, deeper purplish-pink or violet petals, and a crimson lip marked and spotted with lighter tones or white. Many horticultural variants have been given names.

Central American **L. cruenta** has flattened, long-ovoid pseudobulbs 3 to 4 inches high by one-half as thick, with two or three elliptic to elliptic-lanceolate, pointed leaves up to 1½ feet in length. The very fragrant, waxy, long-lasting flowers, usually solitary, are 2 to 2½ inches across. They have brownish- to yellowish-green, ovate sepals and smaller, orange-yellow to bright yellow petals. The three-lobed lip, except for its blood-red base, is orange-yellow flecked with maroon. About one-half as long as the sepals, it has a broad-ovate to nearly round middle lobe. Similar, but with narrower leaves and flowers 1 inch to 1½ inches wide, **L. aromatica,** also of Central America, has two- or three-leaved pseudobulbs approximately 3 inches tall. The leaves are about 1½ feet long. Very fragrant, the yellow to orange-yellow blooms have richer colored petals than sepals and a usually spatula-shaped, wavy-edged middle lobe often spotted with red.

Lycaste cruenta, showing pseudobulbs

Lycaste cruenta (flower)

Mexican and Guatemalan **L. deppei** has compressed, ovate pseudobulbs about 3½ inches long by approximately 2 inches

Lycaste deppei

wide. Each has three or four broad-elliptic-lanceolate leaves 1½ inches to nearly 2 feet in length by approximately 4 inches wide. Often exceeding 4 inches in diameter, the flowers, one or two on a stalk, and waxy and fragrant, have pointed-oblong, purplish- or brownish-spotted, greenish sepals and considerably smaller, hooded, white or creamy-white petals, red-spotted toward their bases. The lip is bright yellow with a few purple-red spots. Its center lobe is pointed-ovate.

Native to Ecuador and Peru, **L. gigantea** has flattened pseudobulbs 4 to 5 inches long by 1½ inches wide. Its pointed, elliptic-lanceolate leaves are 1½ to 2 inches long by under 2 inches wide. Up to 7 inches across, the waxy, fragrant blooms have pointed, olive-brown sepals, the two laterals sickle-shaped, similarly-colored petals, and the yellow-brown lip marked with violet-purple. The column is whitish. In habit **L. schillerana,** of Colombia, has much in common with the last. Its long-lanceolate leaves, two to each pseudobulb, are 1 foot to 2 feet long. The solitary flowers, up to 5 inches across, have olive-green sepals sometimes over 4 inches in length and long-lanceolate. The petals, about 1½ inches long, are white speckled on their backs with brown. At their apexes they are recurved. Equaling the petals in length, the downturned, three-lobed lip has a

Lycaste schillerana

white, fringed, ovate center lobe tinted and speckled with rose-pink. Another exhibiting a strong resemblance to *L. gigantea,* but with shorter foliage, Costa Rican and Ecuadorean **L. xytriophora** has very fragrant, short-stalked, waxy blooms 3 to 4 inches in diameter. Their greenish sepals are mottled with brown. The shorter, broader petals are white above their middles, greenish-yellow below. They curve outward at their ends. The lip, three-lobed with the center lobe crisped at its edges and down-turned, is white suffused with rose-pink.

Lycaste xytriophora

A robust native from Central America to Brazil and Peru, **L. macrophylla** has ovoid pseudobulbs up to 4 inches long and

Lycaste macrophylla

Lycaste macrophylla (flowers)

slightly wider than long. Each has two or three pointed-oblanceolate leaves up to 2 feet long by 5 inches wide. Waxy, fragrant, and tending to droop slightly, the blooms are up to 4½ inches wide. Mostly they have olive-green to light brownish sepals, shaded or not with reddish-brown. Petals and lip are white or creamy-white, the former frequently spotted with rose-red, the latter blotched or spotted with the same color or with lavender-pink.

Native to the West Indies, **L. barringtoniae** has ovate pseudobulbs 3 to 5 inches tall. Each produces two or three oblong-ovate to oblong-elliptic leaves 9 inches to nearly 2 feet long by 4 to 5 inches wide. The somewhat nodding, fragrant blooms, solitary or two on a stalk and 2½ to 3½ inches or sometimes more across, have pointed oblong-ovate olive-green to tawny-yellow sepals and petals, the latter smaller than the former. The lip is similarly colored and three-lobed, the center lobe ovate-oblong and frilled at its edges.

Garden Uses and Cultivation. Lycastes are valued as components of orchid collections. Given a little understanding of the somewhat varied temperature needs of different kinds at different seasons of the year, they are not difficult to grow and bloom. In general a winter night temperature of 50 to 55°F, with a rise of five to ten degrees by day at that season, suits. Summer temperatures considerably higher are in order.

Lycastes need shade from strong sun and a humid, but never stagnant atmosphere. When growing actively generous supplies of water are needed. Established specimens benefit from fertilizing. When the ripening and falling of the leaves signals the completion of the development of the season's pseudobulbs, withhold water for two to three weeks to encourage them to harden.

The best rooting medium appears to be tree fern fiber, but success is also had with osmunda fiber, bark chips, and mixtures of one or more of these with chopped oak leaves, sphagnum moss, and crushed charcoal. For more information see Orchids.

LYCHEE. See Litchi.

LYCHNIS (Lých-nis). Rose-of-Heaven, Mullein-Pink, Flower-of-Jove, Cuckoo Flower, Maltese Cross, German Catchfly. There are several good garden plants in this group of perhaps fifty species of the pink family CARYOPHYLLACEAE. The genus, which includes plants sometimes named *Agrostemma, Coronaria, Melandrium, Silene,* and *Viscaria,* is related to and not infrequently confused with *Silene.* An easily observable distinction, in the vast majority of cases holding, is that the flowers of *Lychnis* have usually five, rarely four styles, those of silenes usually three, or rarely in some flowers of an individual plant, four. In other features these genera often closely resemble each other. The name *Lychnis,* in allusion to the flame-colored blooms of some species, is derived from the Greek *lychnos,* a lamp.

Lychnises include annuals, biennials, and hardy herbaceous perennials, commonly with undivided, lobeless and toothless, opposite leaves and solitary or clustered, often showy blooms. They are inhabitants of temperate parts of the northern hemisphere, including North America. The flowers have ten-veined, five-toothed, sometimes inflated calyxes, five petals narrowing at their bases into slender claws, often notched and sometimes fringed at their apexes, ten stamens, and five or rarely four styles. The fruits are capsules. The plant sometimes grown as *L. lagascae* is *Petrocoptis glaucifolia.*

Rose-of-heaven (**L. coeli-rosa** syns. *Silene coeli-rosa, Agrostemma coeli-rosa*) is an attractive annual, native to southcentral and southwestern Europe and the Canary Islands. From 9 inches to 1½ feet tall and hairless, it has slender, erect stems and linear-lanceolate leaves approximately 1 inch long. Its loosely-arranged, rose-pink flowers, about 1 inch wide, have petals notched at the apex and with a lobed scale near the base. The blooms of *L. c. candida* are white, those of *L. c. kermesina,* red, and those of *L. c. oculata* have a center "eye" of purple. Variety *L. c. nana* is dwarf.

The mullein-pink, rose-campion, or dusty miller (**L. coronaria** syn. *Agrostemma coronaria*), of southeast Europe, is an old-fashioned garden biennial or perennial that generally self-sows with enthusiasm so that volunteer seedlings spring up around established plants and in more unexpected places. This is naturalized in parts of North America. Densely-white-

Lychnis coronaria: (a) Basal foliage

Lychnis coeli-rosa

(b) In bloom

Lychnis coeli-rosa (flowers)

Lychnis coronaria (flowers)

woolly and 1 foot to 3 feet tall, the mullein-pink has broad-elliptic to ovate-lanceolate or ovate leaves up to 4 inches long, those above stalkless, the lower ones narrowed into stalks. Each stem bears comparatively few, loosely-spaced, long-stalked, up-turned blooms, 1 inch or more across. They have more or less bell-shaped calyxes with slender, twisted teeth and bright magenta-pink, notched petals, with appendages in the throats of the blooms. Horticultural varieties include some with double flowers; *L. c. alba*, with white, and *L. c. atrosanguinea*, with red, blooms.

Lychnis coronaria alba

Flower-of-Jove (*L. flos-jovis* syn. *Agrostemma flos-jovis*), also white-woolly, but less so than the last, differs from the mullein-pink in having 1-inch-wide, pink, red, or purple flowers in dense clusters of up to about ten. From 1 foot to 1½ feet tall, and perennial, flower-of-Jove has elliptic-lanceolate leaves in basal rosettes and on the stems, the latter stalkless and somewhat clasping. The petals are two-lobed with the lobes often again lobed. This perennial, is a native of the European Alps and eastward.

Cuckoo flower (*L. flos-cuculi* syn. *Agrostemma flos-cuculi*) is native throughout most of Europe and naturalized in North

Lychnis flos-jovis

Lychnis flos-jovis (flowers)

America. From 9 inches to 3 feet tall and sparsely-branched, this perennial has bristly-hairy, oblong-spoon-shaped basal leaves and those higher on the stems linear-lanceolate. The 1-inch-wide red or pink flowers, in loose panicles, have petals cleft into two or four lobes. Double-flowered varieties are cultivated.

Lychnis flos-cuculi

Maltese cross or scarlet lightning (*L. chalcedonica*) is a native of Russia, including Siberia, that is naturalized in eastern North America. It is a sturdy, usually loosely-hairy but not white-woolly perennial 1 foot to 2 feet tall with mostly stem-clasping, ovate to lanceolate leaves 2 to 4 inches long. The brilliant scarlet blooms, in terminal heads of ten to fifty, are about ¾-inch-wide and have strongly-notched petals, each with, in the throat, two appendages. There are varieties, *L. c. rosea* and *L. c. salmonea*, with pink, *L. c. alba*, with white, and others with double blooms.

Differing from the maltese cross in its fewer flowers being larger, *L. fulgens* is a native of Siberia. Approximately 1 foot tall, this sort has stalkless, ovate-lanceolate leaves 1½ to 2 inches long. In crowded terminal heads, its brilliant red blooms are 1½ to 2½ inches wide. The petals are deeply-

Lychnis chalcedonica

two-lobed and at the throat of the flower have appendages that form a central corona (crown). This is a perennial.

Its petals rather deeply- and irregularly-toothed, *L. coronata*, of China and Japan, is a nearly hairless perennial or biennial about 1½ feet tall, with stalkless, ovate to elliptic leaves 2 to 3 inches long edged with short hairs. It has loosely-disposed, yellowish-red, salmon-red, or cinnabar-red blooms 2 inches or more in diameter. Variety *L. c. sieboldii* (syn. *L. sieboldii*) has hairy stems and leaves and deep red or rarely pure white flowers. Similar to *L. coronata*, Japanese *L. miqueliana* differs in having salmon-red or rarely white flowers 1½ to 2½ inches wide with petals scarcely or not toothed and not notched. They have ¼-inch-long stalks.

The arctic campion (*L. alpina* syn. *Viscaria alpina*), native to northern North America, Europe and Asia, forms tufts of thickish, oblong to lanceolate leaves. From 2 to 10 inches tall, it has many white or pink, short-stalked flowers in dense clusters.

Popular hybrid perennials are *L. haageana*, *L. arkwrightii*, and *L. walkeri* (syn. *L. media*). The result of a cross between *L. fulgens* and *L. coronata*, somewhat hairy *L. haageana* has characteristics intermediate

Lychnis haageana

between those of its parents. It has scarlet to crimson blooms about 2 inches in diameter, with hairy calyxes. The petals are toothed, but not deeply-lobed. Of more complicated ancestry, **L. arkwrightii** is a hybrid between L. haageana and L. chalcedonica. Like the latter, from which it is distinguished by its blooms being from ⅓ to scarcely over ½ inch in diameter, and in clusters of fifteen or fewer, its petals are cleft into two lobes. The parents of **L. walkeri** are L. coronaria and L. flos-jovis. The hybrid resembles the former, but has more numerous, slightly shorter-stalked, rather dull carmine-red to crimson blooms in dense heads.

German catchfly (**L. viscaria**) is a perennial easily recognized by the prominent sticky patches on the stems beneath the blooms. This native of Europe and temperate Asia is 1 foot to 2 feet tall. It has erect, sometimes branched stems and linear to ovate-lanceolate, mostly basal leaves, hairless except near their bases along the margins, where they are usually hair-fringed. The magenta-red to purplered or rarely white flowers are in clusters of three to six in raceme-like spikes. Varieties are L. v. alba, with white flowers, L. v. nana, of dwarf stature, L. v. rosea, with pink blooms, and L. v. splendens, with rose-pink flowers.

Lychnis viscaria

Garden and Landscape Uses. The taller, showy-flowered lychnises are admirable flower garden plants that thrive with minimal attention and make good displays of bloom. Their flowers are quite delightful in cut arrangements and last fairly well. Low lychnises are suitable for rock gardens and similar places. Most are sun-lovers that do very well in ordinary soils of average moisture content. Dampish earth is to the liking of L. chalcedonica, whereas L. coronaria thrives even in quite dry places.

Cultivation. Perennial sorts are multiplied by division in early fall or spring and the species by seeds sown in a cold frame or sheltered place outdoors in May or June,

or earlier indoors. Routine care of established plants makes few demands on gardeners' time or skill. A scattering about the plants in spring of a complete fertilizer helps growth. Unless seeds are needed, faded flower spikes should be promptly removed. Rose-of-heaven is raised from seeds sown outdoors where the plants are to bloom as soon in spring as the ground can be easily worked. Thin out the seedlings so that they stand 4 to 5 inches apart.

LYCIUM (Lý-cium) — Boxthorn, Matrimony Vine. Deciduous and evergreen shrubs numbering about ninety species compose *Lycium*, of the nightshade family SOLANACEAE. Originally *lykion*, the name used by the Greeks for a thorny shrub, probably a *Rhamnus*, that grew in Lycia, a country of Asia Minor, the name was modified and transferred by the Swedish botanist Linnaeus to the quite different plants we shall now consider. As natives they inhabit temperate, subtropical, and tropical regions, approximately one-half the species indigenous to the Old World and one-half to the New World.

Boxthorns have erect or spreading, often clambering, or more or less vining stems, thorny or not. They have alternate, often clustered, short-stalked, undivided, lobeless and toothless, usually grayish-green leaves. The little whitish, greenish, purplish, or dull purple blooms are in the leaf axils. They make no very conspicuous display, but are often plentiful and wreathe the long branches. They have three- to five-toothed, bell-shaped calyxes and a funnel-shaped corolla usually with five lobes (petals). The stamens, generally protruding, and often with a circle of hairs around their bases, are most commonly five. There is one style. The fruits are berries, usually bright red, and often quite showy.

Common matrimony vine (**L. halimifolium**) is an upright or spreading shrub, but not a vine, up to 10 feet tall, and hardy throughout most of New England. Deciduous, it has arching or recurved, usually

Lycium halimifolium

spiny branches and oblong-lanceolate to lanceolate or occasionally elliptic-lanceolate, bluntish or pointed, thickish, gray-green leaves ¾ inch to 2½ inches long. The dull, lilac-purple blooms, with corolla tubes longer than the petals, in groups of up to four or solitary, are succeeded by ovoid or oblongish, scarlet to orange-scarlet berries up to ¾ inch long. This species is native to southern Europe and adjacent Asia. Its leaves are used in the Orient for flavoring foods. Variety L. h. lanceolatum has lanceolate leaves and ellipsoid berries. A dwarfer variety, with lanceolate leaves and nearly spherical fruits, is L. h. subglobosum.

Chinese matrimony vine (**L. chinense**) is very similar to L. halimifolium and is as hardy. It tends to be a little bigger, less thorny, or without spines, and often has somewhat larger fruits. More definitive, but not always constant differences are that its leaves are lozenge-shaped-ovate to ovate-lanceolate, and the corolla tubes of its blooms are slightly shorter than the petals. This is a native of eastern Asia. Variety L. c. ovatum has lozenge-shaped-ovate leaves up to 4 inches long and fruits with dented apexes.

Most pleasing in bloom, **L. pallidum**, native from Utah to Mexico, is hardy in southern New England. Deciduous, erect,

Lycium chinense (fruits)

Lycium chinense ovatum (fruits)

and up to about 6 feet tall, this has spreading, often tortuous, spiny branches. Its thick, glaucous, narrowly-wedge-shaped leaves are ½ inch to 2 inches long. Solitary or in pairs, the nodding blooms have five-lobed calyxes and purplish-tinged, greenish-yellow corollas ¾ inch long, with tubes three times the length of the rounded petals. Stamens and style conspicuously protrude. The subspherical, scarlet berries are ½ inch long. This species rarely has sucker shoots, and is considered much more difficult to propagate by cuttings than other kinds.

Not hardy in the north, *L. carolinianum,* sometimes called Christmas-berry, inhabits coastal areas, including sand dunes and salt marshes, from South Carolina to Florida and Texas. From 1 foot to 3 feet tall, it has recurving branches and fleshy, club-shaped leaves ¼ to ¾ inch long. The blue, lilac, or rarely white flowers have corollas with petals longer than their tubes. Another species that will not survive outdoors in the north, *L. barbarum* is native from North Africa to Iraq. From common matrimony vine it is distinguished by its smaller, narrower, linear to linear-lanceolate leaves and its stamens not being hairy at their bases. This is probably somewhat more tender to cold than the matrimony vine. Native to Hawaii, Juan Fernandez, and the Pacific island Rapa, *L. sandwicense* is hardy only in the tropics and subtropics. A spreading shrub 3 feet tall to much lower, it grows near the sea and salt marshes. Its 1-inch-long, fleshy leaves, broadest toward their blunt apexes, are solitary or clustered. The solitary, white, lavender or bluish flowers have four-lobed corollas. They are about ½ inch long and are succeeded by glossy, red, spherical berries ⅓ inch in diameter.

Garden and Landscape Uses. Boxthorns are easy to satisfy. They succeed in ordinary, even rather poor, well-drained soils and are well suited for exposed, sunny locations. The common and Chinese kinds are especially adapted to seaside planting, succeeding even where they are wetted to some extent by salt spray. They are useful for stabilizing banks, for clambering over rocks, tree stumps, and suchlike objects, and for planting on the tops of walls supporting banks of soil, so that the branches drape their faces. They may be espaliered against walls and sheared as hedges. Because most kinds sucker freely they should not be planted where they are likely to invade nearby flower beds. The berries, usually produced in great abundance, make colorful displays and remain attractive for long periods.

Cultivation. This is of the simplest. Pruning to keep the plants shapely and not too dense is done in winter or early spring. It involves cutting out weak branches and shortening excessively long ones, in such a way that the plants retain grace. Formal hedges are likely to need shearing two or three times each season. Espaliered specimens may be pruned after fruiting, in winter or spring. Propagation is very easy by seed, and most kinds can be readily increased by cuttings, layering, and transplanting rooted suckers.

LYCOPERSICON (Lyco-pérsicon)—Tomato. Closely related to *Solanum,* the six or seven species of *Lycopersicon* include annuals and evergreen herbaceous perennials of the nightshade family SOLANACEAE. The name, sometimes spelled *Lycopersicum,* is from the Greek *lykos,* a wolf, and Latin *persica,* a peach. It probably alludes to a former belief that the fruits were poisonous. As is true of many plants grown for food and other economic uses, it is difficult to be definite about the original homeland of the ancestors of our cultivated tomatoes, but all evidence points to northwestern South America. To that region are restricted as natives all species of the genus not commonly grown as food. The more familiar kinds are abundant there, but they also occur spontaneously in other parts of the Americas and in warm parts of the Old World. Quite certainly they were transplanted to the Old World by man after the discovery of America, and their occurrence in other parts of the Americas is almost surely due to the activities of Indians before and after the arrival of Europeans.

Lycopersicons have alternate, pinnate, or pinnately-lobed leaves and small, starry, wheel-shaped, bisexual, yellow flowers in clusters. The blooms have five-lobed calyxes, corollas with five lobes (petals), and five stamens joined in a column around the single style. From *Solanum* the genus differs in never being thorny, in the stamens being joined, and in technical details of the anthers. The fruits are berries, although those of the common tomato are too large to be commonly thought of as such. The genus is divided into two sections, species that normally have red or in some cultivated varieties yellow fruits, and those with green, greenish-white, or purplish-green, unpalatable fruits. All cultivated tomatoes belong to the first group, which comprises only two species.

The common tomato (*L. lycopersicum* syn. *L. esculenta*) is a more or less hairy perennial, ordinarily cultivated as an annual, and is so well known as to not require detailed description. It is a vigorous grower, available in numerous varieties. They range in size from kinds not more than a foot or two tall to those with stems several feet in length and have foliage that smells strongly when bruised. The fruits are red, yellow, or whitish, large or small, spherical, plum-shaped or pear-shaped, and smooth or, in a very few kinds, covered with a fine, velvety fuzz of hairs. There is considerable variation in the appearance of the foliage. The cherry tomato (*L. l. cerasiforme*) and the pear tomato (*L. l. pyriforme*) are distinctive variants. The first has longer clusters of more numerous flowers than the common tomato and smoothly spherical, red or yellow fruits ¾ to 1 inch in diameter. The 1- to 1½-inch-long, red or orange-yellow fruits of the pear tomato are the shape that their name indicates.

The currant tomato (*L. pimpinellifolium*) lacks the odor characteristic of varieties of *L. lycopersicum.* This species has slender, weak, finely-pubescent stems and pinnate leaves up to 9 inches long each with five or seven long-stalked leaflets. Currant-like and about ½ inch in diameter, the edible red fruits are in clusters longer than the leaves.

Garden Uses and Cultivation. For these see Tomato.

LYCOPODIACEAE—Clubmoss Family. Belonging to the group of cryptogams popularly called fern allies, the clubmoss family LYCOPODIACEAE totals some 450 species all except one in the genus *Lycopodium.* The exception is *Phylloglossum drummondii,* a rare endemic of Australia and New Zealand not known in cultivation. From *Lycopodium* this tiny species differs in its leaves being all basal instead of spiraled along the lengths of the stems and branches. For further details see Lycopodium.

LYCOPODIUM (Lyco-pòdium) — Clubmoss, Running-Pine, Ground-Cedar, Ground-Pine. These fern allies are more closely related to *Selaginella* than to ferns. They number 450 species, in the wild distributed throughout most of the world except in arid regions. They are especially numerous on mountains in the tropics. The name, from the Greek *lykos,* a wolf, and *podion,* a foot, alludes to the appearance of the ends of the leafy stems. Clubmosses have neither flowers nor seeds. Like ferns and selaginellas they reproduce by spores. They belong to the clubmoss family LYCOPODIACEAE, which has, besides *Lycopodium,* only one other genus, and that containing only one species, *Phyloglossum* of Australia and New Zealand, not known to be cultivated. In aspect clubmosses resemble giant mosses, mosses looked at under strong magnification.

The present world population of clubmosses is but a remnant of a mighty group of extinct ancestors that inhabited the earth and formed great forests during the Carboniferous Period when the coal measures were being laid down, and long before the coming of flowering plants. Several extant species are extensively collected from the wild for use as Christmas greens, an exploitive practice to be deplored. The spores, extremely small and powderlike, contain about fifty percent fixed oils. They are used by druggists to coat pills and for other purposes, and by manufacturers of fireworks, flares, and tracer bullets. Formerly lycopodium spores were ignited to produce flash lighting for photography.

Clubmosses are evergreen herbaceous plants, those of tropical regions often epiphytes (plants that perch on trees without taking nourishment from them), those of temperate regions ground plants. They have forked stems clothed, usually thickly, with small to minute needle-like or scale-like leaves arranged in four to sixteen ranks, those of some species overlapping like tiles on a roof. In many kinds, because one prong of each fork of the stem is shorter than the other and is erect while its companion remains prostrate and running, the erect stems appear to be branches. They are here referred to as such. Their true nature is most clearly evident in some tropical epiphytic species. Spores are borne by leaves (called sporophylls) only on certain parts of the stems, most commonly at their apexes. Generally, but not in all species, the sporophylls are smaller than normal leaves and are combined into distinctive, more or less conelike spikes called strobili (singular, strobolus), and those of some species branched. The strobili may be separated or not by stalks from the normal leafy portions of the stems. Each sporophyll has associated with it, on its upper surface, at its base, or on the stem immediately above it a single spore case or capsule.

Running-pine (**L. clavatum**), of North America, Europe, and temperate Asia, has prostrate, arching stems up to several feet in length that root into the ground at intervals. Their erect branches are apparently pinnately-branched with each of the branches often once-forked. The leaves, awl-shaped-linear, more or less toothed, and with long, hairlike apexes, point upward or spread, and are commonly in ten ranks. The slender, cylindrical strobili are on stalks 1½ to 6 inches long. From the last, ground-pine (**L. obscurum**), native to North America and temperate Asia, differs in having deep underground running stems from which at intervals arise erect

Lycopodium obscurum

branches up to 1 foot long. The branches, freely-branched above, have six or eight ranks of glossy-green, closely-spaced, toothless, sharp-pointed, linear-awl-shaped leaves. The stalkless strobili are ½ inch to 1½ inches long.

Ground-cedar (**L. complanatum**), indigenous to North America, Europe, and temperate Asia, has slender, creeping, mostly underground stems up to 3 feet long from which arise erect branches up to 1 foot tall, with flattened branchlets. The branchlets continue to grow for more than one season and have constrictions marking the ends of each year's growth. The cylindrical strobili, up to 1 inch long, are at the ends of forked stalks 1½ to 4 inches long. The tiny lanceolate-awl-shaped, bright green leaves are quite widely separated and are in four ranks. From the typical species *L. c. flabelliforme* differs in its stems creeping above ground. Their erect branches are regularly fan-shaped, and their branchlets without constrictions. This variety is identified by some botanists as **L. digitatum.**

Lycopodium complanatum flabelliforme

Other species native to North America, and the second-mentioned to Europe and temperate Asia, include *L. lucidulum, L. selago,* and *L. tristachyum.* With spreading, loosely ascending stems, up to 1½ feet long and one- to three-times-forked, **L. lucidulum** has glossy, mostly six-ranked, scarcely-toothed, lanceolate-awl-shaped leaves in alternating zones of longer and shorter ones that give a shaggy appearance to the shoots. The spore capsules are borne in the axils of the shorter leaves instead of in strobili. Its horizontal stems short and their branches erect and 3 to 10 inches tall, **L. selago** has erect or ascending lanceolate-awl-shaped leaves, usually in eight ranks. Like *L. lucidum,* this is without strobili. Its spore capsules are in the axils of the leaves of the ends of the current season's growth. The leaves of *L. s. patens* are spreading. Wide-creeping underground stems are characteristic of **L. tristachyum.** Their erect, more or less flattened branches have constrictions indicating the completion of each

Lycopodium selago

year's growth. The lanceolate-awl-shaped, bluish-green leaves are in two ranks of larger, and two of much smaller leaves. The cylindrical up to 1-inch-long strobili are arranged in candelabra fashion at the tops of stalks 1½ to 3½ inches long.

Native of Hawaii and there employed as Christmas greens, **L. cernuum** occurs also in many other parts of the tropics. It has widely creeping stems that root at intervals, and repeatedly forked branches 1 foot to 5 feet tall, clothed with curved, awl-shaped leaves. The stalkless, cylindrical strobili, ¼ to 1 inch long, terminate the branchlets.

Lycopodium cernuum, sterile frond, left; fertile frond, right

Tropical **L. phlegmaria** is an epiphyte with pendulous, branched stems, glossy, dark green leaves nearly 1 inch long, and numerous strobili in loose, tassel-like clusters. Other tropical kinds include *L. gnidioides, L. squarrosum,* and *L. tetrastichum.* Native to southern Africa, Malagasy (Madagascar), Reunion, and Mauritius, **L. gnidioides** (syn. *Urostachys gnidioides*) has pendulous, forked stems up to 2 feet long. Bright to dark green, the broad-lanceolate leaves are up to a little more than ½ inch long. Tropical Asian **L. squarrosum** (syn.

Lycopodium phlegmaria

Lycopodium gnidioides

Lycopodium squarrosum

Lycopodium tetrastichum

Urostachys squarrosus) has forked stems, at first erect, later drooping, 3 to 8 feet long and, with the leaves, ¾ to 1 inch thick. The leaves are lanceolate, bright green, and a little less to a little more than ½ inch long. Native to New Guinea and Australia, **L. tetrastichum** (syn. *Urostachys tetrastichus*) has forked stems up to 1½ feet long that, including the leaves, are about ¼ inch thick. The slender, pointed-linear, bright green to yellowish-green leaves are ⅓ inch or less long.

Garden and Landscape Uses and Cultivation. The North American clubmosses described above are hardy. They are charming additions to native plant and woodland gardens, but are often difficult to establish in places where they are not growing natively. They need somewhat acid, usually moist soil containing an abundance of organic matter, and shade. Propagation is by division, cuttings, and spores. Tropical epiphytic sorts require conditions appropriate for epiphytic orchids, ferns, and nepenthes from the tropics. They need a minimum night temperature of 60°F rising to from 65 to 70°F by day and higher in summer as well as high humidity and shade from strong sun. A loose, very well-drained rooting mix of a type that suits the other plants just mentioned is required, and this should be kept always moist. Propagation is by division, cuttings, and spores.

LYCOPUS (Lýco-pus)—Water-Hoarhound. A few sorts of *Lycopus* have rather limited use for planting in wet soils. There are about fifteen species, all natives of north temperate regions, including North America. They belong in the mint family LABIATAE and are puzzling to identify as to species. To do this with certainty fully developed nutlets (commonly called seeds) must be carefully examined under a hand lens. The name is derived from the Greek *lykos*, a wolf, and *pous*, a foot.

This genus consists of hardy herbaceous perennials, mostly of wet soils and mostly spreading by underground stolons. They have square, usually branchless stems, and opposite leaves. The small, nearly symmetrical tubular flowers have four corolla lobes and two stamens that barely protrude or are included in the corolla tube. In addition, there are sometimes a pair of small staminodes (aborted, nonfunctional stamens). The flowers are in dense, stalkless clusters in the axils of the leaves.

Kinds sometimes cultivated are **L. americanus**, native throughout most of the United States and southern Canada, and the very similar **L. europaeus**, a native of Europe naturalized in North America from Massachusetts to Mississippi. Up to 2½ feet tall, these have erect stems and lanceolate to oblong-lanceolate, coarsely-toothed to pinnately-lobed, short-stalked

Lycopus europaeus

leaves up to 4 inches long. The flowers are whitish with crimson spots. The leaves of *L. americanus* are usually narrower and more deeply-lobed than those of *L. europaeus*.

Garden Uses and Cultivation. Of distinctly minor horticultural importance, water-hoarhounds are best located by watersides and in bog gardens and wild gardens. They need sun, but are not showy enough to warrant places in ordinary flower gardens. Propagation is simply accomplished by division in spring or fall and by seed sown in spring in damp or wet soil.

LYCORIS (Lýcor-is). Eleven species of bulb plants, of the amaryllis family AMARYLLIDACEAE, belong here. The group is native from Japan to the Himalayas. The name commemorates a Roman actress, a mistress of Marc Antony. The botanical separation of *Lycoris* and closely similar *Amaryllis* is based on the number of ovules in each compartment of the ovary, two or three in *Lycoris*, many in *Amaryllis*. A more easily observed distinction is that the flowers of the latter are 4 to 5 inches long, those of *Lycoris* 1½ to 3 inches.

Lycorises have strap-shaped, often narrow leaves and somewhat asymmetrical, funnel-shaped flowers usually displayed while the plants are leafless, the foliage either dying before the blooms appear or not developing until later. The flower stalks are solid and bear at their tops a cluster of few to many blooms with short tubes that have scales in their throats. Each bloom has six petals (more correctly, tepals) and six stamens joined to the upper part of the throat of the corolla. The long style terminates in a knoblike stigma. The fruits are capsules.

Hardy **L. squamigera** (syn. *Amaryllis hallii*) is endemic to Japan, where it usually inhabits wet soils. It has the largest bulb, up to 8 inches long, of all cultivated kinds and in summer displays fragrant, pale lilac-pink flowers in clusters of four to seven. The strap-shaped leaves come in spring and die before the blooms appear.

Lycoris squamigera

Lycoris squamigera (flowers)

leaves and white flowers, **L. albiflora** (syn. *L. radiata albiflora*) is thought to be a hybrid between *L. radiata* and *L. aurea*. It occurs spontaneously in Japan.

A kind with bright golden-yellow flowers 3 inches long in clusters of five to eight, **L. africana** (syns. *L. aurea*, *Amaryllis aurea*) is very beautiful. It has a wider natural distribution than other cultivated kinds, being found in Japan, China, Taiwan, and Viet Nam. Its nearly round bulbs are about 2 inches in diameter. Each produces several glaucous leaves 1½ to 2 feet long and flower stalks about as long. The blooms, which appear in summer or early fall, have reflexed, wavy corolla segments, very long stamens with white filaments (stalks) and

Lycoris africana

Lycoris africana (flowers)

pale yellow anthers, and a longer red style. Leaf growth follows flowering. Summer-blooming **L. sanguinea**, native to Japan and China, differs from *L. radiata* in having smaller bulbs and whitish-green leaves lacking any central stripe of white. Variety *L. s. kiushiana* (syn. *L. kiushiana*) has larger blooms and longer, protruding stamens. In *L. s. koreana* (syn. *L. koreana*) the flowers are the same size as those of *L. sanguinea*, but the stamens are longer. Rarer in cultivation than the species discussed above are two

The latter are 3 inches long with corolla segments ½ inch wide or wider. The stamens are about twice as long as the segments. The style protrudes.

One of the most common kinds in Japan is **L. radiata**, but since it genetically is a triploid it does not produce seeds. The same species is found along the Yangtze Valley in China. It seems certain that this triploid population developed from the Chinese *L. r. pumilla*, a smaller plant with fewer blooms than *L. radiata*. If this be so it could hardly be an original native of Japan, but must have been brought there from China unrecorded centuries ago. The bright red flowers of this species appear in fall with new foliage developing at the same time or immediately afterward. They have corolla segments about 1½ inches long, crisped at their margins, and strongly reflexed. The stamens are twice as long as the corolla segments, and the style protrudes. The bulbs of *L. radiata* are 1 inch to 2 inches in diameter. Its blunt-ended, linear-strap-shaped leaves, about ½ inch wide, are glaucous and have a whitish center stripe. Because Japanese tradition holds that this species is possessed of the soul of a dead person, it is not cultivated in Japan. Differing from *L. radiata* in being bigger and having broader

Chinese natives, *L. sprengeri* and *L. straminea*. Rosy-pink to purplish flowers in clusters of several to many and with stamens and style about as long as the corolla segments are characteristic of Chinese **L. sprengeri**, a species with much the aspect of *L. squamigera*. Pale-straw-yellow blooms with a few red dots and with the keels of the corolla segments pink are borne by **L. straminea**, a close ally of *L. africana*.

Garden Uses. Hardier than most lycorises, *L. squamigera* flourishes outdoors in southern New England and is an admirable garden plant. It is especially lovely when interplanted with *Artemisia albula*, the gray foliage of which forms a delightful foil for the delicately colored flowers of the lycoris. About as resistant to cold, but much rarer in cultivation, is *L. sprengeri*. The others are not hardy in the north and can be cultivated there only in greenhouses. In the south, *L. africana* and *L. radiata* are favorite garden plants. Like *L. squamigera* they are effective in beds and borders and provide useful flowers for cutting.

Cultivation. An important detail in the cultivation of these plants is to leave them undisturbed as long as possible if they are doing well. Digging up the bulbs, separating and transplanting them is often followed by their refusal to bloom for one, two, or more years. They need deep, fertile, well-drained soil and full sun or the slightest shade. While in foliage they must not suffer from lack of moisture. An annual application of a complete slow-acting fertilizer given shortly before new leaf growth begins helps to maintain vigor.

Indoors lycorises may be grown in sunny greenhouses in a winter night temperature of 50°F. By day the thermometer may register five to ten degrees higher before ventilation is necessary. From the time new leaves begin to peep until they begin to die naturally, abundant moisture must be supplied; when the leaves begin to fade intervals between applications are gradually increased and finally water is withheld completely for the duration of the dormant season. Plants that have been in their pots more than a year should be fed dilute liquid fertilizer from the appearance of leaf growth until the foliage begins to die. So long as the plants flourish, repotting is unnecessary and ordinarily will be needed only at intervals of a few years. It is done just before new leaf growth begins. The pots must be well drained, the soil fertile and porous.

Propagation is by offsets, bulb cuttings, and seed. The latter germinate readily in pots of sandy, peaty soil in a temperature of 60 to 70°F, but since seedlings usually take three years or more to attain flowering size, vegetative propagation is more often employed. It is the only means of securing increase of *L. radiata*, which does not produce seeds.

LYGODIUM (Ly-gòdium)—Climbing Fern. Climbing, often rampant, deciduous and evergreen ferns compose *Lygodium*, of the schizea fern family SCHIZAEACEAE. The name, from the Greek *lygodes*, flexuous, alludes to the stemlike climbing parts. In the broad sense accepted here the genus comprises about forty species, mostly tropical and subtropical, but represented in the native floras of northeastern North America, Japan, New Zealand, and South Africa.

The true stems of lygodiums are their forking, hairy, horizontal rhizomes. The more or less vining above-ground parts are leaves. What are commonly thought of as stems are the stalks and midribs of the leaves, and what are usually called leaves are leaflets or pinnae, the primary divisions of which are pinnules, and the secondary divisions segments. In *Lygodium* the leaflets are one- or more-times-divided-palmately (in hand-fashion) or are pinnately-divided or lobed. Each leaflet has a brief stalk or petiolule (for convenience referred to in this discussion as the footstalk). In some species this is so short that it is virtually unobservable. There are both barren and fertile (spore-bearing) leaflets. The parts of the latter are very much narrowed, sometimes to such an extent that they no longer resemble portions of leaves, and are displayed in feathery panicles. Often they are toothed or pinnately-cleft. The spore capsules are solitary, beneath overlapping, scale-like covers (indusia).

The only North American species, the Hartford fern (**L. palmatum**) occurs in acid soils in woodlands and thickets from New Hampshire to Ohio, Florida, and Tennessee. Its rhizomes are black, its slender-stalked, above-ground parts 1 foot to 5 feet long. The barren leaflets are of two similar pinnules joined by their long stalks to a short, common footstalk. The pinnules are roundish to kidney-shaped and 1 inch to 3 inches in diameter. They are deeply-fingered into usually six, but sometimes fewer or more segments one-third to one-

Lygodium palmatum

half as wide as their lengths. The fertile leaflets, confined to the upper parts of the plant, are 1 inch to 3 inches long and are repeatedly divided into many slender, spore-bearing segments, the ultimate ones about ¼ inch long. From the last, **L. circinatum,** of tropical Asia, differs in its barren leaflets having very brief footstalks and their pair of long-stalked pinnules being cleft into lobes at least four times as long as their widths, and 2½ inches to 1 foot long. The fertile leaflets bear spore capsules in short spikes along the margins of their narrower segments.

Native to Japan, the Ryukyu Islands, Taiwan, China, and Korea, **L. japonicum** is a graceful species with lacy foliage that attains heights of 6 to 8 feet. Its leaflets have short footstalks and a pair of pinnules divided into five to eleven alternate segments that are pinnate or conspicuously-pinnately-lobed, particularly toward their bases, and with toothed edges. Smaller than the barren leaflets, the much-divided fertile ones have along the margins of their narrow segments slender, short spikes with spores underneath overlapping scales.

Lygodium japonicum: (a) Sterile fronds

(b) Fertile fronds

The bluish-green leaflets of **L. microphyllum** (syn. *L. scandens*) consist of a pair of fairly long-stalked pinnules pinnately-divided and attached to short common footstalks. The pinnules are up to 6 inches

long or longer and have ovate to ovate-lanceolate segments, lobeless or more or less lobed toward their bases. The fertile leaflets bear spores in brief spikes around the margins of their short, broad segments. This is a native of eastern Asia. Much-larger-leaved **L. volubile**, of tropical America and the West Indies, differs from *L. microphyllum* in the pinnules of its leaflets being long-lanceolate and 4 inches to 1 foot in length. Not much smaller than those of the barren leaflets, the segments of the fertile ones have spore capsules in short spikes that fringe their edges.

Lygodium volubile

Garden and Landscape Uses. The Hartford fern is choice for including in specialists' collections of hardy ferns and for native plant gardens. Unfortunately, it does not adapt as easily as some ferns to domestication. The others described here above are suitable for outdoors in warm-temperate to tropical climates only. They can also be grown in greenhouses in ground beds, pots, or large hanging baskets, and *L. microphyllum* as a window plant.

Cultivation. With the exception of the Hartford fern, lygodiums are not difficult to grow. They need porous, well-drained, somewhat acid, spongy soil that contains an abundance of leaf mold, peat moss, compost, or other semidecayed organic material, which is kept damp, but not stagnant at all times when foliage is present. Abundant moisture at the roots is especially necessary from spring to fall. Then, too, applications of dilute liquid fertilizer benefit specimens that have filled their containers with roots. The soil of deciduous kinds is best kept dry during their dormant season. High humidity and sufficient shade to prevent the foliage from yellowing or scorching are essential to success. Lygodiums need abundant root room, and realize their largest dimensions only when planted in ground beds. Even so, very respectable specimens can be had in fairly large pots. In greenhouses winter night temperatures of 55 to 60°F are suitable for tropical species, ten degrees lower for those from temperate climates. Repotting is best done in early spring. Supports for the vining leafstalks are needed. These may be canes, stakes, trellises, wires, or strings. The leaves of some kinds are deciduous. After they die in fall they should be cut off close to the ground. Propagation is by spores and by careful division in spring. For more information see Ferns.

LYGOS. See Genista.

LYMANARA. This is the name of orchid hybrids the parents of which include *Aerides*, *Arachnis*, and *Renanthera*.

LYON-BEAN is *Mucuna cochinchinensis*.

LYONIA (Lyòn-ia) — Staggerbush, He-Huckleberry or Male Berry. The name *Lyonia* commemorates the American botanist John Lyon, who died about 1818. It identifies a genus of forty to fifty species of North American, West Indian, and Asian evergreen and deciduous shrubs or sometimes small trees of the heath family ERICACEAE. At one time *Lyonia* was included in *Andromeda*. From that genus and from nearly related *Leucothoe* and *Pieris* it differs in its seed pods having vertical, raised, thickened ribs (sutures), which split to release the minute seeds.

Lyonias have alternate, lobeless leaves and clusters of small globose or cylindrical, white or pink flowers that develop from old shoots. The flowers have a usually five-lobed calyx, an urn-shaped to cylindrical corolla, generally ten stamens, and one style. The fruits are capsules.

Two deciduous kinds are cultivated, the staggerbush (*L. mariana*), native from southern New England to Florida and Texas, and the he-huckleberry or male berry (*L. ligustrina*), which ranges from Maine to Florida and Texas. Up to about 6 feet tall, *L. mariana* has elliptic to oblong, short-stalked, smooth-edged leaves up to 2½ inches long. Its ½-inch-long, white or pinkish, nodding, cylindrical flowers are in axillary clusters on leafless terminal shoots, forming in effect racemes or panicles of small flower clusters. The shoots of the current season arise from below the flowering portion of the stem. This quite handsome shrub inhabits moist, sandy, acid soil, mostly near the coast. A plant of wet soils and swamps, *L. ligustrina* is up to 12 feet tall. It differs from the staggerbush in its flowers being nearly globular and not over ⅕ inch long, and its seed capsules being almost globular and not drawn out to pointed tips as are those of the staggerbush. The elliptic to oblong-lanceolate leaves of the male berry are up to 3 inches long and very finely-toothed; they have the aspect of privet leaves, but unlike those are not in pairs.

Evergreen kinds include two distinguished by their leaves, flower stalks, and flowers being covered with scales, tiny, but visible to the naked eye. A shrub or small tree of coastal regions from South Carolina to Florida and also in Mexico, *L. ferruginea* is not hardy in the north. It has obovate to oblong leaves 1 inch to 2 inches long with wedge-shaped bases and rolled margins. They do not diminish in size toward the ends of the branches. The nodding, globular flowers, in clusters in the upper leaf axils, are white. From the above, *L. fruticosa* (syn. *L. ferruginea fruticosa*) differs in its leaves not being revolute at their margins and gradually becoming smaller toward the branch ends. It has a natural range from South Carolina to Florida and is not hardy in the north.

The fetterbush (*L. lucida*), evergreen and easily distinguished from others by its three-angled shoots and branchlets and its glossy, leathery foliage, is indigenous in wet woods from Virginia to Florida and Louisiana. About 6 feet in height, it has elliptic to narrowly-obovate leaves up to 3 inches long, with a prominent vein close to and paralleling the in-rolled margins, and white to pink flowers, up to ⅓ inch long, in the axils of leafy shoots. The fetterbush is not hardy in the north.

Lyonia lucida (foliage)

Native to western China and the Himalayas, *L. ovalifolia* is the only cultivated species with flowers in distinctly one-sided, axillary racemes. Evergreen or partially so, it sometimes becomes a small tree. It has ovate to elliptic leaves up to 5 inches in length. The flowers, in pubescent axillary and terminal racemes, are whitish, about ⅜ inch long, and downy. Variety *L. o. elliptica* occurs in Japan, Taiwan, and China. A large shrub or small tree, it has deciduous leaves thinner than those of the typical species. Its flower clusters are shorter. The limits of hardiness of this species and its variety are not well understood. The latter is the hardier and may survive as far north as Philadelphia. Rare *L. folioisa* of Thailand is an attractive evergreen shrub with broad,

Lyonia foliosa (flowers and foliage)

oblong-elliptic to ovate leaves up to about 2 inches long. Its flowers, in somewhat drooping racemes, are pure white with narrow tan margins to the petals.

Garden and Landscape Uses. Lyonias are handsome for landscaping and are less used than they deserve to be. The staggerbush, one of the best in bloom, is useful as far north as southern New England, being especially well suited for acid, moist and boggy soils. The hardiest, the male berry, succeeds in cultivation in southern Ontario. It, too, is a wet-acid-soil plant. The others are suited only for milder climates where they succeed in similar soils. They are good shrubs for massing and for creating naturalistic effects, yet are not out of place in tidier, more groomed landscapes. They are much-branched and generally well-foliaged so that they provide good low screening.

Cultivation. The most essential requirements are acid soil and ample moisture. Given these, lyonias grow in full sun or part-day shade without special care. No regular pruning is needed, but any necessary to keep the plants shapely or to size may be done with impunity in late winter or spring. Propagation is achieved by seeds sown on the finely sifted surface of sandy peaty soil or milled sphagnum moss kept evenly moist with non-alkaline water and shaded until germination and by cuttings taken in summer and inserted in a propagating bed in a humid cold frame or greenhouse, preferably under mist.

LYONOTHAMNUS (Lyon-othámnus) — Catalina Ironwood, Santa Cruz Island Ironwood. One species of evergreen tree and a variety of it, natives of islands off the coast of California, are the only members of this genus. They belong in the rose family ROSACEAE. The name is derived from that of an early resident of Los Angeles, W. S. Lyon, and the Greek *thamnos*, a shrub.

Lopezia hirsuta

Blue *Lobelia siphilitica* **and red** *Lobelia cardinalis*

Lloydia serotina

Lunaria annua

Luffa aegyptiaca

Lobelia siphilitica

Lychnis haageana

Lupinus polyphyllus

Lonicera heckrottii

Lythrum virgatum variety

Lupinus albifrons

The Catalina ironwood (*Lyonothamnus floribundus*) is 15 to 50 feet in height. It has stalked, opposite, thickish, lanceolate-oblong leaves 4 to 7 inches long, glossy dark green above, and to a greater or lesser extent pubescent beneath. They may be more or less lobed toward their bases, and toothed or toothless. The small white flowers are in dense terminal panicles. They have five persistent sepals, five petals, about fifteen stamens, and two pistils. The styles are stout. The fruits are paired, woody, glandular-pubescent follicles (pods), containing, usually, four seeds. The Santa Cruz Island ironwood (*L. f. asplenifolius*) occurs on Santa Cruz, Santa Catalina, and nearby islands, and intergrades with the typical species. Characteristically its leaves, broadly-ovate in outline, are pinnately-divided into two to seven leaflets pinnately-cleft into many lobes. The Santa Cruz Island ironwood is particularly beautiful. It may be 50 feet tall or taller. Usually it is single-trunked, but sometimes it has more than one trunk and then is usually lower than 50 feet. Multi-stemmed individuals commonly result from the tree having been burned or cut back. New sprouts come freely from the base of such injured trees. Because several-stemmed specimens are often preferred for landscaping it is well to remember that they are easily produced by cutting back young trees.

Garden and Landscape Uses. Both the species and its variety are fine for general landscaping in warm-temperate and sub-tropical climates where dry summers prevail.

Cultivation. Propagation by seed is an easy way of raising *Lyonothamnus*. Vegetative propagation is very much more uncertain. The seeds are freed of chaff by working them through a screen and are sown in flats and covered with a shallow layer of sand. They are then watered and put in a greenhouse or cold frame. Germination takes place in two to three weeks. The seedlings are transferred to small pots and later to gallon cans from which they are transplanted to their final locations.

LYSICHITON (Lysichìt-on)—Yellow-Skunk-Cabbage. The designation yellow-skunk-cabbage is applied to the one North American species of *Lysichiton*. It is scarcely appropriate for the only other species, a native from eastern Siberia to Japan that has white showy parts to its floral structures. The generic name, which is sometimes spelled *Lysichitum*, derives from the Greek *lysis*, loose, and *chiton*, a cloak or covering, and alludes to the spathe breaking off and falling after flowering. This genus belongs in the arum family ARACEAE, and so is kin to the skunk-cabbage (*Symplocarpus*), the calla-lily (*Zantedeschia*), anthuriums, and philodendrons.

Lysichitons are stemless, hardy, herbaceous perennials with thick horizontal rootstocks and large elliptic to oblong leaves. The flower stalks are not as high as the mature foliage, but, because they appear early in the year before the leaves have made appreciable growth they are displayed effectively. As is characteristic of the family, the flowers are tiny and crowded on spikes called spadices (singular, spadix). In the calla-lily, the spadix is the yellow central column. A bract called a spathe (in the calla-lily this is the petal-like white envelope that surrounds the yellow column) arises from just beneath the spadix. Unlike many aroids, the individual flowers are bisexual in *Lysichiton*.

The American species (*L. americanum*) is indigenous from California to Alaska, favoring wet soils in woods and in the open. Its leaves are 1 foot to 3 feet long or sometimes longer at maturity. The expanded part of the showy yellow or greenish-yellow spathe is up to 8 inches long. The stem that supports the spadix is 1 foot to 1½ feet and the spadix 2 to 5 inches long. All parts of this plant emit a disagreeable odor when they are bruised. The Asian species *L. camtschatcense* is generally like its American relative, but is odorless or sweet-scented and has pure white spathes. Its blooms appear three or four weeks later than those of *L. americanum*.

Lysichiton americanum

Lysichiton camtschatcense

Garden Uses. These are handsome subjects for bog gardens, stream sides, and other wet places either in full sun or light shade. Their showy floral displays attract attention and interest in spring and their bold leaves provide a touch of lushness entirely appropriate for such locations. They provide a strong design element.

Cultivation. These plants are easy to grow provided they do not lack for moisture. They prefer a deep soil well enriched with organic matter, such as compost or leaf mold. Planting may be done in late summer or early fall or in earliest spring. They are easily propagated by dividing the rhizomes, and fresh seeds, especially those of *L. americanum*, germinate readily if sown in pots of peaty soil kept always moist. To be sure the soil in the seed containers does not dry, it is well to set them in saucers kept filled with water so that it reaches the soil through the drainage hole and can rise by capillarity.

LYSIDICE (Lysídi-ce). The only species of *Lysidice*, of the pea family LEGUMINOSAE, is a beautiful flowering evergreen shrub or tree, in the wild sometimes 70 feet tall. Native to southern China, it succeeds in southern Florida and perhaps somewhat further north, and displays its sweet-scented blooms from spring to fall. The name is that of *Lysidice*, in Greek mythology the daughter of Pelops.

The leaves of *L. rhodostegia* are leathery and pinnate. They have three or four pairs of finely-red-margined, narrow- to broad-elliptic leaflets, the largest from 2 to 6 inches long by ¾ inch to 2 inches wide. The flowers, of the *Cassia* type rather than pea-like, are in large, loose, axillary and terminal panicles and are accompanied by showy, pink bracts that remain and are decorative long after the flowers fade. The blooms have red, funnel-shaped, four-parted calyxes with strongly reflexed lobes. The three spoon-shaped petals are shorter than the calyx. There are six protruding, white stamens, joined at their bases, and a long, slender style. The fruits are flat, straight, beaked pods up to 8 inches long by 1½ inches wide.

Garden and Landscape Uses and Cultivation. For decorating lawns and other areas this spectacular species is highly desirable. It is at its best in moistish, but not wet, fertile soil in sun. Propagation is by seed and probably can be achieved by cuttings under mist or in a greenhouse propagating bench.

LYSILOMA (Lysil-òma) — Sabicú, Wild-Tamarind. Of the many tropical trees of the pea family LEGUMINOSAE, the genus *Lysiloma* of the mimosa group accounts for thirty-five species. It occurs indigenously from the southern United States to South America and the West Indies, but is chiefly Mexican.

Lysilomas have twice-pinnate leaves and white to greenish-white flowers in globular heads or cylindrical spikes. The lower parts of their stamens are joined into a tube. The fruits are flat pods with margins that at maturity separate from the remainder of the pod. The name is derived from the Greek and probably means "free border," in allusion to the manner in which the seed pods disintegrate.

The sabicú (**L. latisiliqua** syn. *L. sabicu*) has a common name sometimes applied to other trees including *Pithecellobium dulce*. It is the only species of *Lysiloma* much cultivated and supplies one of the best native woods of Cuba. Native of Cuba, the Bahamas, and Hispaniola, its maximum height is 65 feet, but often it is lower. It has a pyramidal crown and branches that droop slightly at their ends. The leaves, deciduous and 4 to 8 inches long, have an even number (four to eight) of primary divisions in opposite pairs. Each consists of usually three to five pairs of asymmetrical, elliptic, obovate or nearly round, short-stalked leaflets up to 1¼ inches long. In spring the not very showy, long-stalked, rounded heads of greenish-white flowers appear. An inch or somewhat more in diameter, they are succeeded by brown or black and brown pods up to 6 inches long by up to 2 inches broad, which contain flat, brown seeds. The individual leaflets of the sabicú much resemble those of the horseradish tree (*Moringa oleifera*), but the leaves of that species have an uneven number of primary divisions each with an uneven number of leaflets.

The wild-tamarind (**L. bahamensis**), native to southern Florida, Cuba, and the Bahamas, is sometimes confused with *L. latisiliqua*. This species is 50 to 65 feet tall and has spreading branches. Its leaves have linear-oblong, more numerous, and decidedly smaller leaflets than those of *L. latisiliqua*, and its globular heads of greenish-white flowers are not over ½ inch in diameter. Native of the southwestern United States, **L. microphylla** is a deciduous feathery-foliaged shrub up to about 9 feet in height. Its flowers are white.

Garden and Landscape Uses and Cultivation. In southern Florida and other warm regions, *L. latisiliqua* is appreciated as a shade tree and is used for street planting. It is adaptable to various soils and sites and is propagated by seed.

LYSIMACHIA (Lysim-àchia)—Loosestrife, Creeping Charlie. Although the structure of its flowers clearly indicates that *Lysimachia* belongs in the primrose family PRIMULACEAE, in appearance its members do not greatly resemble certain other familiar genera of that family, such as *Primula*, *Cyclamen*, and *Dodecatheon*. The genus *Lysimachia* probably numbers 200 species and is of cosmopolitan distribution in temperate and subtropical regions, being especially abundant in North America and eastern Asia. Its name is derived from *Lysimacheios*, the ancient Greek name for some member of the group and probably applied in honor of Lysimachys, King of Thracia. Plants by some botanists segregated as *Steironema* are here included in *Lysimachia*. The purple-loosestrife is *Lythrum salicaria*, the swamp loosestrife *Decodon verticillatus*.

The lysimachias are summer-blooming annual and perennial herbaceous plants with flowers usually yellow or white, more rarely purple or blue-purple. The cultivated kinds are all perennials. They have alternate, opposite, or whorled (with three or more forming a circle around the stem) leaves, which very commonly are dotted with minute glands. The blooms may be solitary from the leaf axils or in clusters. They are nearly flat to bell-shaped and have five or six sepals, petals, and stamens, and one style. The fruits are dry capsules containing few to many seeds.

Commonly cultivated species are only three or four, but several others are occasionally grown. One of the best known is one of the most distinct, the plant known variously as creeping Charlie, creeping Jennie, and moneywort (**L. nummularia**). This rampant trailer often forms considerable mats of slender stems. Its opposite, short-stalked, more or less round leaves are about 1 inch in diameter. The red-spotted, golden-yellow flowers, ¾ to 1 inch wide, are solitary in the leaf axils. This species, native of Europe, has established itself in woods in parts of North America and sometimes invades lawns. It is partial to moist and wet soils. Variety *L. n. aurea* has rather sickly-yellow foliage. Trailing **L. henryi** of western China has stems upturned at their ends, and almost opposite, thick, slender-stalked, ovate-lanceolate leaves. Clustered at the ends of the branches, the flowers are yellow and about 1 inch wide.

A native of Japan, **L. japonica** is a pubescent perennial with creeping stems and opposite, short-stalked, ovate leaves ½ to 1 inch long or a little longer. Solitary from the leaf axils, the yellow flowers are about ¼ inch wide. Variety *L. j. minuta* is a delightful miniature.

The principal tall-growing, yellow-flowered kinds are **L. punctata** and **L. vulgaris**. Both are natives of Europe and Asia, now naturalized and adventive in parts of North America. They attain heights up to 3 feet and form bushy plants with many erect stems. Their leaves are in whorls or are opposite and up to about 4 inches long. Those of *L. punctata* are lanceolate, those of *L. vulgaris*, lanceolate to ovate-lanceolate. Despite a general similarity in

Lysimachia henryi

Lysimachia punctata

Lysimachia japonica minuta

Lysimachia punctata (flowers)

Lysimachia vulgaris

Lysimachia ephemerum

Lysimachia ciliata

their appearance these species are easily told apart. The flowers of *L. punctata* arise from the axils of the upper leaves and form leafy flower clusters, whereas those of *L. vulgaris* are in clusters above the uppermost stem leaves. Other differences are that the sepals of the first-named are uniformly green and fringed with glandular hairs, those of the latter are very dark-margined and not lined with hairs. The flowers of *L. punctata* may exceed 1 inch in diameter, those of *L. vulgaris* are usually under 1 inch across.

White-flowered loosestrifes of garden merit include *L. clethroides*, *L. ephemerum*, and *L. barystachys*. The first two attain heights of 3 feet, the latter is about 2 feet tall. All have erect stems and flowers in terminal racemes. The first-named is the commonest. Native of China and Japan, **L. clethroides** has many erect stems and alternate, ovate-lanceolate leaves, tapered at both ends, and 3 to 6 inches long; their margins are rolled under. Almost ½ inch in diameter, the numerous flowers are in slender racemes very markedly and gracefully arched or curved at flowering time, but straightening later. From this species, **L. ephemerum,** native to southwestern Europe, differs in having opposite leaves and upright racemes of bloom. The stalkless,

linear-lanceolate leaves, joined at their bases and 4 to 6 inches long, distinguish this from all other cultivated kinds. Quite charming is the eastern Asian **L. barystachys.** It has erect stems and alternate, thick, linear to lanceolate leaves, glaucous beneath and covered with hairs that lie flat on the surface. The terminal racemes of white flowers, each under ½ inch wide, are at first drooping.

Lysimachia barystachys

Other kinds include these: **L. ciliata** (syn. *Steironema ciliatum*) is common in wet soils, usually in sunny locations, over much of North America from Florida to the Yukon. About 3 feet tall, its flowers are yellow. The leaves are ovate to ovate-lanceolate with their bases rounded and fringed with hairs as are the leafstalks. **L. decurrens,** indigenous from India to southern China, the Philippine Islands, New Caledonia, and other Pacific islands, and not hardy in the north, has opposite or alternate leaves and white flowers with long-protruding anthers. **L. fortunei,** of China and Japan, is very like *L. clethroides,* but the plant is more slender, its spikes of bloom do not curve, and the flowers are not over ⅙ inch long. **L. lanceolata** (syn. *Steironema lanceolatum*) is a native of moist

woods and prairies in eastern North America from Pennsylvania to Michigan, Florida, and Louisiana. It is similar to *L. ciliata,* but it has linear to linear-lanceolate leaves that taper to their bases. **L. leschenaultii,** from the Himalayas, erect, sparsely-branched, and about 1 foot tall, is not hardy in the north. Its bluish or purple flowers with prominently protruding anthers are in dense racemes. Its leaves are alternate, opposite, or in whorls (circles) of three or more. **L. lichiangensis,** Chinese and 1½ feet tall, has alternate leaves and terminal racemes of pinkish-white broad-bell-shaped flowers veined with pink, with exerted stamens. **L. lobelioides** is hairless, slender-stemmed, about 1½ feet tall, and native to northern India and western China. It has ovate to roundish leaves and white, wide-bell-shaped flowers in slender, loose racemes. **L. mauritiana,** native to seashores from Japan and China to the Philippine Islands, New Caledonia, and Mauritius, has blunt, spoon-shaped leaves and racemes of white flowers. **L. ramosa,** native from the Himalayas to Ceylon, Java, and the Philippine Islands, the only cultivated yellow-flowered species with alternate leaves, resembles *L. thyrsiflora* in its manner of blooming. **L. thyrsiflora** (syn. *Naumbergia thyrsiflora*) occurs in North America, northern Europe, and northern Asia. Its stamens are quite separate to their bases, and its pale yellow flowers are in stalked, dense racemes. The leaves are stalkless and opposite. The plant is 1 foot to 1½ feet tall.

Garden Uses. The loosestrifes are primarily plants for moist soils in sun or light shade. They accommodate readily to watersides and look at home there. The soil for most should be some inches above the water, but at least one, *L. thyrsiflora,* will grow even in shallow water. Another, *L. punctata,* stands drier conditions than most. In addition to their usefulness near pools, ponds, and streams, the erect-growing loosestrifes are good border plants provided the soil is not arid. The trailing *L. nummularia* forms a good

Lysimachia clethroides

groundcover in likely places, but beware of introducing it to rock gardens and other places that necessitate curbing its growth, for although it is not difficult to up-root, it is such a persistent and comparatively rapid spreader that the gardener is likely to have to restrain its exploring shoots more frequently than he cares to. The flowers of *L. clethroides* and *L. barystachys* are fine for cutting and those of other kinds can be used for this purpose also.

Cultivation. The cultural needs of lysimachias are simple indeed. In the main they take care of themselves with very little effort on the part of the gardener. From time to time, when they become obviously too big or too crowded, or when they begin to deteriorate from having exhausted the soil to the extent that surface applications of fertilizer do not remedy the condition, they should be dug up, divided, and replanted in soil made agreeable by mixing with it to a depth of several inches rotted manure or compost and a slow-acting fertilizer such as bonemeal. This work may be done in early spring or early fall. In dry weather the plants need watering copiously if the place they occupy tends to dryness. Staking is rarely necessary, but in exposed locations simple supports may be desirable. Established plants benefit from an annual fertilizing in early spring. In fall their stems are cut to the ground after killing frost and, in severe climates, after the ground has frozen to a depth of a couple of inches, a light winter covering of salt hay, cut branches of evergreens, or other protective material may be provided. Propagation is easily and rapidly achieved by seeds sown in spring or early summer in cold frames or well-cared-for outdoor beds where the soil is always fairly moist, by cuttings of leafy shoots taken in late spring (early enough to give the new plants a chance to build up considerable root systems and top growth before winter), and, most simple of all methods, by division in early spring or fall.

LYSIONOTUS (Lysion-òtus). Like closely related and better-known *Aeschynanthus*, most species of *Lysionotus*, of the gesneria family GESNERIACEAE, grow naturally on trees, fallen logs, and rocks, accepting root holds, but not nourishment from their hosts. They are epiphytes. The about twenty species of this genus are Asian, occurring natively from Japan to the Himalayas, and represented in the warmer parts of China, southeast Asia, and Borneo. The name comes from the Greek *lysis*, loosening, and *notos*, the back, and alludes to the way in which the fruits split.

Lysionotuses are shrubs and subshrubs, as known in cultivation not exceeding 1 foot in height. They have spindle-shaped, smooth rhizomes and rigid stems with pairs or whorls (circles of more than two) of smooth, thick, leathery, undivided,

toothed or toothless leaves. Either solitary or in clusters from the upper leaf axils, the trumpet-shaped flowers are white, lavender, or purple, a circumstance that conveniently distinguishes this genus from *Aeschynanthus*. They have five-parted calyxes with the two upper segments joined, and straight, tubular corollas with two-lobed upper lips and lower ones with three lobes. There are two fertile stamens with flattened stalks and a prominent tooth longer than the anthers at their apexes, and two abortive ones (staminodes). The ovary is surrounded by a fleshy, cuplike disk. There is a long style and two stigmas. Slender and rigid, the seed capsules contain seeds with hairs at each end as long as themselves.

Native to India and adjacent China, *L. serratus*, a bushy plant 9 inches to 1 foot in height, has elliptic, dark green leaves up to 6 inches long in pairs or in whorls of three or four. They have pale veins and, on their under surfaces, splashes of red. The pendulous blooms, 1½ inches long, pale lilac veined with purple, and with a yellow blotch in the throat, are in clusters from the axils of the upper leaves. They have small red calyxes.

Much hardier than the last, *L. pauciflorus*, 2 to 8 inches tall, is an evergreen shrub that grows as an epiphyte on trees in the mountains of Japan and the Ryukyu Islands. It has oblong-lanceolate to oblanceolate leaves up to 3 inches long, with prominent indented midribs, and a few coarse teeth. The solitary short-stalked blooms are 1½ inches long with lavender-pink corollas.

Garden Uses and Cultivation. Chiefly plants for gesneriad fans and others who enjoy growing choice and unusual species, lysionotuses are ordinarily best accommodated in greenhouses, but success may be had with them in terrariums and under artificial light in houses. Those from warm regions grow more or less continuously with no period of complete dormancy. They thrive in loose soil or substitute mixes of kinds that suit orchids, bromeliads, and other epiphytes. These and other pertinent matters are discussed under Gesneriads. Night temperatures in the 60 to 70°F range suit *L. serratus*, with daytime increases of five to fifteen degrees allowed; *L. pauciflorus* is suited with, and indeed for its comfort needs, considerably less warmth, especially in winter. For it night temperatures at that season of 40 to 50°F are likely to prove satisfactory. It is quite likely that this species will prove hardy in mild parts of the Pacific Northwest and there be of interest to rock gardeners. Fairly high humidity is appreciated, but stagnant wetness of the soil is to be avoided. These plants stand considerable shade. They are propagated by seed, rhizomes, division, cuttings, and leaf cuttings.

LYTHRACEAE—Loosestrife Family. This assemblage of 25 genera and 550 species of dicotyledons is represented in the native floras of most parts of the world except the most frigid. It includes annuals, herbaceous perennials, shrubs, and trees, with usually opposite, undivided, lobeless, toothless leaves. The flowers are symmetrical or rarely asymmetrical. The leaves opposite, less frequently in whorls (circles of more than two), rarely are alternate. The blooms, most commonly from the leaf axils, are solitary, clustered, or in panicles. They have a tubular to bell-shaped, persistent calyx of generally four or six, sometimes fewer or more sepals. There are as many petals as sepals, or sometimes none, and few to many stamens, although most often twice as many as the sepals. There is one style. The fruits are usually capsules. Genera cultivated include *Cuphea*, *Decodon*, *Ginoria*, *Heimia*, *Lagerstroemia*, *Lawsonia*, *Lythrum*, *Rotala*, and *Woodfordia*.

LYTHRUM (Lý-thrum) — Purple-Loosestrife. Usually inhabiting moist and frequently brackish soils, this genus of the loosestrife family LYTHRACEAE is in number of species most abundant in North America. It occurs also in Europe, Asia, Africa, and Australia. The name, believed to allude to the color of the flowers, although if so not very aptly, derives from the Greek *lythron*, blood.

Lythrums include annuals, herbaceous perennials, and shrubs. There are thirty-five species. Their short-stalked or stalkless leaves are opposite, with alternate pairs set at right angles to each other, or are occasionally alternate. They are ovate, obovate, or linear. In terminal spikes or racemes, solitary, or in pairs in the leaf axils, the flowers are predominantly rose-purple or rarely white. Their calyx lobes, corolla lobes (petals), and stamens are mostly in sixes, but sometimes fives or fours. Rarely the stamens are as many as twelve. Occasionally petals are wanting. The style is slender. In some kinds flowers of two or three forms occur, the differences being in the relative lengths of the stamens and style. The fruits are capsules.

Purple-loosestrife (*L. salicaria*), a native of Europe and temperate Asia, is naturalized along lake sides and river banks and in marshes from Quebec to Michigan and Maryland. Robust, erect, and 2½ to 5 feet tall, it is hairless or pubescent and has squarish, four-angled or four-winged stems. The stalkless, lanceolate to narrowly-oblong or linear leaves are opposite or in whorls (circles of more than two). Their bases are more or less heart-shaped. The purple-red blooms are in clusters forming erect, terminal racemes 6 inches to well over 1 foot long and furnished with lanceolate to ovate, leafy bracts. The narrow-oblong petals, ⅓ inch long or slightly longer, are crumpled or wrinkled. Variety

A natural stand of *Lythrum salicaria*

Lythrum salicaria

L. s. *roseum superbum*, of gardens, has bright rose-pink blooms larger than those of the typical species. Much like the purple loosestrife, but with its leaves narrowing to their bases and the appendages between the sepals not appreciably longer than the sepals, **L. virgatum** is quite hair-less. Native to Europe, it is naturalized to some extent in Massachusetts. Improved garden varieties of *L. virgatum* or perhaps hybrids between it and *L. salicaria* are popular. Such kinds have fancy horticultural names, such as 'Robert', 'Morden Gleam', and 'Morden Pink'.

Endemic to the United States, **L. alatum** occupies moist soils throughout the central and southcentral states and in New England, and in its variety, *L. a. lanceolatum* (syn. *L. lanceolatum*), to Florida. This is hairless, and has erect, wandlike stems, and linear-oblong to ovate-lanceolate leaves. The lower ones are up to 2 inches long, those higher on the stems considerably smaller, narrower, and more crowded. The flowers, solitary in the axils of the upper leaves, are rosy-purple. They are of two types, one with the stamens, the other with the styles protruding.

Trailing to somewhat erect **L. flexuosum** (syn. *L. graefferi*), of the Mediterranean region, has stems up to 2½ feet long and

Lythrum 'Morden Pink' with, at left front, *Monarda*

Lythrum 'Morden Pink' (flowers)

oblong to linear-oblong leaves, the lower ones sometimes opposite, the others alternate, ¼ inch to 1¼ inches long. Bright pink to purple, the flowers, from the upper leaf axils, are about ½ inch wide.

Garden and Landscape Uses and Cultivation. The species described above and their varieties are vigorous herbaceous perennials best adapted for moist soils and especially well suited for pool and stream sides. Trailing *L. flexuosum* is sometimes accommodated in hanging baskets as a greenhouse or porch plant. The last is probably less cold-resistant than the other species, which are very hardy. Rich soil and sunny places are preferred by lythrums. Few plants are easier to manage. They need no special attention and are multiplied with greatest ease by seeds, division, and cuttings. Because lythrums are rather slow to become established after transplanting it is better not to do this any oftener than necessary. Spring or early fall are the most favorable seasons for planting and transplanting. Distances of 2 to 3 feet between individuals are satisfactory.

M

MAACKIA (Maàck-ia). Of the ten species of eastern Asian deciduous trees, or sometimes shrubs, that compose *Maackia* only *M. amurensis* seems to be at all well known in cultivation. The group belongs in the pea family LEGUMINOSAE and is related to *Cladrastis*. Its name honors the Russian naturalist Richard Maack, who died in 1886.

Maackias have pinnate leaves with an uneven number of nearly stalkless leaflets, all except the terminal one in opposite or almost opposite pairs. In this, they differ from *Cladrastis*, in which the leaflets are decidedly alternate. They also differ from that genus in their dense racemes of pea-like flowers being more or less erect instead of pendulous. The racemes are often several together in somewhat panicle-like arrangements. The blooms are white. They have bell-shaped, five-toothed calyxes, five petals, ten stamens united at their bases, and one style. The fruits are linear-oblong, few-seeded, flattened pods.

Native to Manchuria, *M. amurensis* is up to about 45 feet tall. Its leaves, 8 inches to 1 foot long, have seven to eleven hairless, short-pointed, oblong-ovate leaflets 2 to 3¼ inches long. In panicled racemes 4 to 6 inches long or occasionally longer, the

Maackia amurensis (flowers and foliage)

dull white flowers are nearly ½ inch long. They are succeeded by 1½- to 2-inch-long seed pods. Variety *M. a. buergeri,* of Japan, differs in having blunter leaflets, hairy on their under surfaces. The leaves of closely related *M. chinensis,* a tree in the wild up to 70 feet high, have eleven to thirteen bluntish leaflets ¾ inch to 2¼ inches long, with hairy undersides. Its flowers a little under ½ inch long, this kind is native to China. Indigenous to Korea, *M. fauriei,* about 25 feet tall, has leaves with nine to seventeen elliptic-ovate to oblong leaflets from 1¼ to a little over 2 inches in length, and when mature hairless. The flowers are somewhat under ½ inch long. The pods are 1¼ to 1¾ inches in length.

Garden and Landscape Uses and Cultivation. Except that they bloom in summer, later than most trees, maackias have no exceptional merits as ornamentals. They are more likely to be found in arboretums than in general landscape plantings. The kinds discussed above are hardy in southern New England, and *M. amurensis* through most of New England. They need sunny locations and ordinary well-drained soil. No more pruning should be done than is essential to shape the trees, and this is best attended to when they are young and the branches small. Cuts and wounds on older trees do not heal readily. Propagation is easy by seed, which should be soaked overnight in water at about 190°F before sowing. Root cuttings also afford an easy means of increase, and varieties may be grafted onto understocks of the species.

MABA (Mà-ba)—Lama. The botanical name of this genus of the ebony family EBENACEAE is an adaptation of a native one in the Tonga Islands. The group comprises sixty or seventy species of mostly hard-wooded trees and shrubs nearly related to the persimmon and ebony (*Diospyros*) and by some authorities included in that genus. A chief difference is that the parts of the flowers of *Maba* are generally in threes instead of fours or fives.

Mabas are natives of tropical and subtropical regions. They have alternate, undivided, toothless leaves. The bell-shaped to tubular flowers are in short clusters or are solitary from the leaf axils. Nearly always individual plants have blooms of one sex only. The flowers have usually a three-lobed calyx, a three-lobed corolla, and the male flowers three to many, but most commonly nine, stamens. In female blooms the stamens are represented by staminodes (nonfunctional stamens) or are absent, and there is a three-branched style or three separate styles. The fruits are few-seeded, ovate to spherical berries.

Native of all the Hawaiian Islands and Fiji, the lama (*M. sandwicensis* syn. *Ebenus sandwicensis*), a tree of pleasing aspect, is 20 to 40 feet high. Its dull, leathery, two-ranked leaves are ovate-oblong and 1 inch to 5 inches long. Usually solitary, but the males, which have twelve to eighteen stamens, sometimes in clusters, the small blooms have corollas densely-hairy in their upper parts. The dryish, but somewhat fleshy, edible fruits, about ⅔ inch long, are bright reddish-yellow.

The only South African species *M. natalensis* (syn. *Ebenus natalensis*) is an evergreen, much-branched shrub or small tree up to 20 feet tall. It has blunt, broad, ovate, oblong or elliptic, hairless leaves ¾ to 1 inch long, and paler beneath than on their upper surfaces. The fruits are clustered black berries.

Garden and Landscape Uses and Cultivation. In warm, frost-free and almost frost-free climates the kinds discussed above are useful general-purpose evergreens. They grow without special attention in ordinary fertile soil in sun or part-shade. Propagation is by seed and by cuttings.

MABOLO is *Diospyros discolor.*

MACADAMIA (Macad-àmia)—Queensland Nut, Macadamia Nut. The only native plants of Australia that have attained any importance as sources of food are two species of *Macadamia,* of the protea family

PROTEACEAE. They are the Queensland nut, or smooth-shelled macadamia nut, and the rough-shelled macadamia nut. Of the other eight species of the genus, three are Australian, three are natives of New Caledonia, and one is endemic to the Celebes Islands and one to Malagasy (Madagascar). The name commemorates John Macadam, a physician, who died in 1865.

In Hawaii, where the first trees were planted in 1890, macadamias are grown commercially for their nuts and are planted for reforestation. Their fine-grained, reddish wood is used for cabinetwork. Because they are so extremely hard, the fruits cannot be opened by hand nutcrackers, but can be cracked by powerful vise-grip pliers. Power machinery is used by commercial growers to break the shells and extract the kernels, which have a pleasant, sweetish flavor and are eaten raw or roasted and salted. They are used to a considerable extent in confectionary.

Macadamias are trees and shrubs with toothed or toothless leaves mostly in whorls (circles of three or more) and small, bisexual flowers in groups of two to four forming terminal or axillary racemes. The dry fruits split to release one or two seeds usually called nuts, but differing from true nuts, which are fruits that do not split and have the seed attached to the inside of the shell.

The Queensland nut or smooth-shelled macadamia nut (**M. integrifolia**) is the sort most commonly cultivated. It is a handsome, irregularly-topped, dense, evergreen tree that under the most favorable circumstances is about 60 feet tall, but when grown in the continental United States is lower. It has blunt, oblong-lanceolate, shining, dark green leaves, usually toothed and somewhat prickly at their margins, and mostly in threes (occasionally in twos or fours). They are 3 inches to 1 foot long. The numerous flowers, ivory-white or pinkish and about ¼ inch across, are in pendulous racemes about as long as the leaves. Only a small proportion of

Macadamia integrifolia (foliage and flowers)

them set fruits, which are nearly hairless. The rough-shelled macadamia nut (**M. tetraphylla**) differs from the Queensland nut in having longer, pointed, nearly stalkless leaves ordinarily four to a whorl and in its fruits being distinctly hairy. Their meats are less highly esteemed than those of the Queensland macadamia nut. Trees sometimes grown as *M. ternifolia* are usually one of the two species already described. True **M. ternifolia,** called gympie nut, is a small tree with practically inedible fruits.

Garden Uses. Macadamias are good ornamentals as well as nut producers and are adaptable to a variety of soils, but on shallow ones are apt to be uprooted by storms. Seedling trees exhibit considerable variation. For nut production it is better to plant selected strains or varieties propagated by grafting. In addition to their value for planting outdoors in the tropics and subtropics, these trees may be grown in greenhouses as foliage ornamentals, but are not known to fruit then.

Macadamia ternifolia

Cultivation. Under suitable conditions macadamias are easy to grow. They need a frost-free climate and may be propagated by seeds or side grafting. In greenhouses they succeed in well-drained containers in porous, fertile soil kept moderately moist at all times. Any needed pruning, potting, or top dressing is done in spring. In summer the plants benefit from being stood outdoors. Winter night temperatures of 50 to 55°F are adequate, with a rise of a few degrees by day allowed.

MACE is a product of *Myristica fragrans.*

MACFADYENA (Macfády-ena)—Cat's Claw. Only one of the four or five species of *Macfadyena,* of the bignonia family BIGNONIACEAE, seems to be cultivated. Native from Mexico to South America, and in Trinidad and Tobago, the genus is very closely allied to *Bignonia.* Its name commemorates Dr. James Macfadyen, author of *Flora of Jamaica.* He died in 1850.

Macfadyenas are hairless or hairy perennial vines with woody stems and opposite, stalked leaves, the lower ones sometimes of one or three leaflets, but most with a pair of lateral leaflets and between them a tendril with three branches ending in hooked claws representing a third. Usually thinnish in texture, the leaflets may be toothed or not. The rather large yellow blooms are solitary or in short few-flowered panicles. They have a tubular calyx with an irregular or a lobed edge, a tubular corolla becoming bell-shaped above and with five lobes or petals of often unequal size, four non-protruding stamens in pairs, one style, and a two-lobed stigma. The fruits are slender-linear, podlike capsules.

The cat's claw (**M. unguis-cati** syn. *Doxantha unguis-cati*) is an evergreen vine with leaves each consisting of two oblong, sometimes toothed, leaflets, heart-shaped at their bases, up to 3 inches long and between them a three-branched tendril. The showy flowers resemble those of *Allamanda.* They have a bell- to trumpet-

Macfadyena unguis-cati

shaped, bright yellow corolla 2½ to 4 inches across with flaring, unequal lobes (petals) and orange lines in its throat. The blooms, solitary or in few-flowered panicles, appear in spring or early summer. The capsules, 1 foot long or longer, are about ½ inch wide. In gardens the name *Bignonia chamberlaynii,* which is a synonym of *Anemopaegma chamberlaynii,* is sometimes wrongly applied to this vine. The plant that has been known as *M. cynanchoides* is *Dolichandra cynanchoides.*

Garden and Landscape Uses. The cat's claw is a handsome vine for outdoors in warm climates. A tall grower, often sparse of foliage and bloom below, it is at its best where it can climb high walls, pillars, pergolas, and similar supports. It is also suitable for large conservatories and greenhouses. In California it withstands considerable frost and is probably the only bignonia-like vine that will grow in the Imperial Valley.

Cultivation. This vine succeeds in any ordinary, well-drained garden soil and needs full sun. Young specimens newly planted should be pruned in spring to within 2 or 3 feet of the ground. Resulting branches should have their tips pinched out when they are 4 or 5 feet long, and this may be repeated as often as new branches attain that length until the space the vine is to occupy is filled. By following this procedure the young shoots are encouraged to attach themselves firmly to the support and a good framework of permanent branches is developed. Pruning in later years is done as soon as flowering is through. It consists of shortening severely all shoots that stand out from the support and of removing any that are crowded. In greenhouses a winter night temperature of 50°F with a five or ten degree increase in the day agrees with this plant. Higher temperatures are in order at other seasons. Watering should be done generously from spring through fall, more sparingly in winter. Container-grown specimens benefit from regular applications of liquid fertilizer from spring through fall.

MACHAERANTHERA (Machaer-anthèra)— Tahoka-Daisy. Very closely related to *Aster* and by some authorities included there, *Machaeranthera*, of the daisy family COMPOSITAE, comprises twenty-five to thirty species, natives of western North America. The name, alluding to the anthers, comes from the Latin *machaera*, a dagger, and *anthera*, an anther.

From asters, machaerantheras differ most obviously in having spine-tipped leaves. They are annuals, biennials, herbaceous perennials, or shrubs with alternate, often pinnately-cleft, lobed or toothed leaves. The flower heads are in clusters. Each has a central eye of bisexual disk florets and usually a surrounding circle of petal-like, female ray florets. When both types of florets are present the heads are daisy-like. The flower heads of some species lack ray florets. The involucres (collars at the backs of the flower heads) consist of several rows of bracts, whitish and often papery in their lower halves and greenish above. Flower color ranges from blue-violet to purple for the ray florets, and yellow, red, or brown for the disk flowers. Yellow-rayed species sometimes included in *Machaeranthera* are more commonly referred to *Haplopappus*. The seedlike fruits are achenes.

The Tahoka-daisy (*M. tanacetifolia*), native from Texas and Arizona to Canada, a biennial or annual, is bushy and 1 foot to 2 feet tall. It has leaves, some 3 inches long, divided two or three times into narrow, sharp-pointed or bristle-tipped segments. Freely produced and up to 2 inches wide, the long-stalked flower heads have yellow eyes and light blue-purple rays.

Garden Uses and Cultivation. An attractive summer-bloomer for flower gardens and cutting, the Tahoka-daisy thrives in ordinary, fertile garden soil in full sun. It may be treated as an annual by sowing seeds outdoors where the plants are to remain, or earlier indoors to produce plants to be set in the garden after there is no danger of frost. Indoor sowings are made about eight weeks before it is safe to set the plants in the open ground. In the interim the seedlings are grown, spaced about 2 inches apart, in flats in a sunny greenhouse with a night temperature of about 50°F and daytime temperatures five to fifteen degrees higher. For a week or two before planting in the garden, the flats are stood in a cold frame or sheltered, sunny place outdoors to permit the plants to become accustomed to outdoor conditions to harden them. Another plan is to sow seeds in fall, outdoors where the plants are to bloom. Plants from such sowings bloom the following year. Spacing of 6 to 9 inches between individuals is satisfactory. Routine care is minimal. Staking is rarely needed.

MACHAERIUM. See Tipuana.

MACHAEROCEREUS (Machaero-cèreus)— Creeping Devil. Baja California is the home of the two species of the cactus family CACTACEAE that compose this genus. The name comes from the Greek *machaira*, a dagger, and the name of the genus *Cereus* and alludes to the dagger-like spines. From *Lemaireocereus*, to which it is most closely related and in which some authorities include it, *Machaerocereus* differs in the shape of its spines and its more elongated, longer-lasting flowers.

The creeping devil (*M. eruca*) has prostrate stems 3 to 9 feet long and 1½ to 3 inches in diameter that suggest huge caterpillars crawling over the ground. Their tips are erect and they root along their undersides. As they grow forward the stems die from the rear. They have about a dozen ribs and large areoles (points of origin of spines) with about twenty very unequal-sized, whitish spines from each. The inner spines are flattish, the outer ones cylindrical. The largest exceed 1 inch in length. The yellow

Machaerocereus eruca

flowers are 4 to 4½ inches long and across their faces 1¾ to 2¼ inches wide. The spiny fruits, 1⅓ inches long, contain black seeds.

Usually under 3 feet tall, *M. gummosus* is chiefly an erect plant with sometimes prostrate branches. It forms broad clumps of stems 1¾ to 2¼ inches in diameter. The largish areoles give rise to twelve to eighteen stout spines of which the central three to six are flattened and one of which, 1½ to 1¾ inches in length, is markedly longer than the others. The slender, funnel-shaped flowers are 4 to 5½ inches long and about 2 inches in diameter. They are purple. The spiny, bright red, subspherical fruits are 1 inch to 3 inches in diameter and contain purple pulp. They are much esteemed for eating in Baja California and provided one of the most important foods of the aboriginal Indians. A fish poison is prepared from the stems of this species.

Machaerocereus gummosus in Baja California

Garden and Landscape Uses and Cultivation. These are the same as for most other desert cactuses. See Cactuses.

MACHAIROPHYLLUM (Machairo-phýllum). There are nine species of *Machairophyllum*, all natives of South Africa. They belong to the carpetweed family AIZOACEAE and are similar to *Bergeranthus*. Their name, from the Greek *machaira*, a dagger, and *phyllon*, a leaf, alludes to the shape of the leaves.

Machairophyllums are low, perennial succulents, stemless or with short, thick, branched stems. They have long, pointed, bluish-gray to green fleshy leaves, triangular in section, with flat upper surfaces and usually asymmetrical keels. The comparatively large, solitary flowers, mostly in threes, and with seven to fifteen stigmas, are straw-yellow to orange, sometimes with the outsides of the petals red.

Without evident stems, clump-forming *M. albidum* (syns. *Bergeranthus albidus*, *Mesembryanthemum albidum*) has crowded, incurved leaves 3 to 4 inches long and at their bases about ¾ inch wide. Those of each pair are united at their bases and are set at right angles to the pairs below and above them. With red undersides to the petals, the long-stalked, yellow flowers are 2½ inches in diameter. Another stemless kind, *M. bijlii* (syn. *Perissolobus bijlii*) forms dense mats or clumps of foliage. The light green leaves, often reddish or purplish along their edges and joined briefly at their bases, are ½ to 1 inch long and at their bases up to ½ inch wide. On very short stalks, the golden-yellow to orange solitary flowers, with red undersides to the petals, are 2 to 2¼ inches in diameter.

Garden and Landscape Uses and Cultivation. Machairophyllums are cultivated by fanciers of succulent plants in rock gardens and similar locations, in warm desert and semidesert regions, and in greenhouses and sunny windows. They are easy to manage and are not fussy about soil so long as it is porous and drains rapidly. In earth too compact and wet, the fleshy roots are likely to rot. From spring to fall machairophyllums need watering moderately, allowing the soil to become nearly dry between applications. In winter they are kept drier, if indoors in a place where the night temperature is 50 to 55°F, and by day a few degrees warmer. Full sun is needed. Pans (shallow pots) are better suited than pots for these low succulents. Increase is easy by division, by uprooting small pieces and treating them as cuttings, and by seed.

MACKAYA (Mack-àya). Differing from closely related *Asystasia* in its flowers having two instead of four fertile stamens and two staminodes (nonfunctional stamens) without even rudimentary anthers, the only species of *Mackaya*, of the acanthus family ACANTHACEAE, is a native of South Africa. It is an erect, hairless, evergreen subshrub of considerable beauty in bloom. The name commemorates James T. Mackay, an Irish botanist, who died about 1862.

Attaining a height up to 6 feet, *M. bella* (syn. *Asystasia bella*) has opposite, short-stalked, slender-pointed, ovate-oblong, sinuously-toothed leaves 3 to 5 inches long. Its 2-inch-long, lilac-blue, bell-shaped blooms, in loose, terminal racemes, have a five-parted calyx, a corolla with a tube narrow below and widening above, and five spreading, broad lobes (petals). The fruits are capsules.

Garden and Landscape Uses and Cultivation. The outdoor cultivation of this beautiful plant is practicable only in the south and other subtropical places where the climate approximates that of its homeland. In greenhouses *Mackaya* is considered rather difficult to grow well, a circumstance probably related to keeping it too warm in winter. At that season a night temperature 45 to 50°F is adequate, with an increase during the day of five to ten degrees. From spring to fall considerably higher temperatures are appropriate, but excessively humid, oppressively dank at-

mospheric conditions are to be avoided. Throughout the summer the greenhouse must be ventilated freely. Propagation is by seed or more usually by cuttings taken as soon as flowering is through or in spring. They root readily in a greenhouse propagating bench in a temperature of about 70°F and are then potted individually in small pots in sandy peaty soil and grown under conditions suitable for begonias. As soon as the young plants are well established in their first pots, the tips of the stems are pinched out. This induces branching. Repotting into 4-inch and later to 6-inch containers is done as growth makes necessary. Shade, just enough to prevent the foliage from being scorched is given. Throughout the winter the soil is kept drier than before, only enough water being given to prevent the leaves from wilting. In spring the plants are transferred to pots or tubs 9 or 10 inches in diameter, the night temperature is increased to 55°F, and day temperatures to 60 to 65°F, and more generous watering is resumed. During summer well-rooted specimens are encouraged by weekly applications of dilute liquid fertilizer. As soon as blooming is over the shoots are pruned back moderately, and the plants are then repotted or top dressed with rich soil.

MACLEANIA (Mac-leània). The native territory of *Macleania*, of the heath family ERICACEAE, extends from Mexico to Peru. There are about thirty-two species. The name commemorates John Maclean, a Scottish merchant who, between 1832 and 1834, sent many plants from Peru to Britain.

Macleanias are evergreen often semivining shrubs that in the wild frequently, but not always perch on trees as epiphytes. They have alternate, undivided, toothless, short-stalked leaves. The flowers have a five-lobed calyx, a cylindrical to long-urn-shaped, tubular corolla with five small lobes, ten separate or united stamens, and a slender style. The fruits are berries.

Native to Costa Rica to Panama, *M. glabra* is a low, more or less vining shrub, in the wild often an epiphyte. It has hairless

Macleania glabra

Macleania insignis

stems and thick, leathery elliptic to ovate or oblong leaves 1½ to 4½ inches long, by ¾ inch to 2¼ inches wide. The flowers, approximately 1 inch long, in short racemes of up to twenty from the leaf axils, have old-rose-colored to coral-red corollas with a white apex. Native from Mexico to Guatemala, *M. insignis* is a shrub 3 to 12 feet tall with ovate, leathery leaves 1 inch to 3 inches long. Solitary or in sprays of two or three from the leaf axils, the flowers are scarlet and about 1½ inches long.

Garden and Landscape Uses and Cultivation. These are attractive for outdoor landscaping in warm-temperate and subtropical regions and for inclusion in collections of greenhouse plants. They thrive in well-drained soil of a sandy, peaty nature, kept moderately moist. In greenhouses a winter night temperature of 55°F is appropriate. Propagation is by cuttings, layering, and seed.

MACLEAYA (Mac-leàya)—Plume-Poppy or Tree-Celandine. In gardens these plants are often called bocconias although they are distinct from the genus *Bocconia*. Both macleayas and bocconias belong in the poppy family PAPAVERACEAE. There are two species of *Macleaya*, the name of which commemorates a Colonial Secretary of New South Wales, who died in 1848, Alexander Macleay.

Macleayas, known as plume-poppies and tree-celandines, are stout, erect, deciduous, hardy herbaceous, more or less glaucous perennials, which contain yellow sap. They have hollow stems furnished along their lengths with alternate, stalked, pinnately-lobed, large leaves with heart-shaped bases. The small flowers, with two creamy-white, quickly-deciduous sepals, no petals, numerous stamens, and a short style tipped with a two-lobed stigma, are in large panicles, but because of their lack of color make no great show. The fruits are pendulous flat capsules containing few seeds.

The common plume-poppy (*M. cordata* syns. *Bocconia cordata*, *B. japonica*), a native

Macleaya cordata

of Japan, China, and Taiwan, is a suckering plant 5 to 8 feet tall with stems branched only in their upper parts, and leaves heart-shaped in outline with blades 6 inches to 1 foot long. Their undersides are densely covered with short white hairs. The flowers have twenty-four to thirty stamens, and the fruits four to six seeds. In *M. c. thunbergii* the leaves are hairless beneath. From *M. cordata* the central Asian **M. microcarpa** (syn. *Bocconia microcarpa*) differs in its blooms having not over a dozen stamens and its fruits being one-seeded. Believed to be a hybrid between *M. cordata* and *M. microcarpa*, the plant named **M. kewensis** attains a height of about 7 feet and has leaves with five to nine primary lobes. The stamens number twelve to eighteen to each flower. Its fruits, rarely produced, contain no fertile seeds.

Garden and Landscape Uses. Plume-poppies are distinctive. Of bold appearance, they attract attention by their handsome foliage and, in high summer, their large, creamy or slightly pinkish, feathery panicles of bloom. They have one bad habit, that of spreading quite rapidly by suckers. Because of this they should not be located near plants they can infiltrate and overwhelm. In large perennial borders they may be allotted places at the rear provided they are watched so that they do not take the space of other plants. A little deft work with a spade each spring around their perimeters successfully limits their spread. It is rarely advisable to include them in small flower borders. Satisfactory locations can often be found at the fronts of shrub borders, and plume-poppies show to special advantage against evergreen backgrounds. As plants for setting by themselves in lawn beds they are also useful. So located the mowing of the surrounding grass prevents suckering. The panicles of bloom are useful, both fresh and dried, for flower arrangements.

Cultivation. For their well-being, plume-poppies need deep, fertile soil and full sun. Throughout the growing season the earth should be uniformly moist, but standing water in winter is harmful and may kill the roots. Replanting is needed every four or five years; early spring is the best time to attend to it. Propagation is by suckers, transplanted in early spring, and by seed.

MACLUDRANIA. This is the name of a bigeneric hybrid between *Maclura* and *Cudrania*. See *Cudrania*.

MACLURA (Mac-lùra)—Osage-Orange or Bow Wood. Its most familiar common name stemming from the appearance of its fruits, which outwardly somewhat resemble oranges, the osage-orange is not botanically related to *Citrus*, the genus to which oranges belong. It is a kin of mulberries and a member of the mulberry family MORACEAE. Its name commemorates the American geologist William Maclure, who died in 1840. There is only one species, native of Arkansas and Texas, but now naturalized more widely. Its wood is strong, hard, and durable. By the Indians it was esteemed for making bows, and bow wood is sometimes used as an alternative vernacular name. Its roots were the source of a yellow dye.

The osage-orange (**Maclura pomifera** syn. *M. aurantiaca*) is a deciduous tree up to 60 feet tall, but in cultivation often not more than one-half that height, with a rounded, irregular, open head. It has rugged, orange-brown bark and branches, when young green, with stout thorns up to 1 inch long. Its slender-stalked leaves are alternate, pointed-ovate, bright green, and have lustrous upper sides. They are 2 to 6 inches in length, and in fall turn clear yellow. Male and female flowers are on separate trees. The former are in racemes 1 inch to 1½ inches long from short, spurlike branchlets on shoots of the previous year. The females are in dense, spherical heads up to 1 inch in diameter. Individual blooms are tiny and without petals. They have four-lobed calyxes, the males four stamens, the females a long, slender stigma. Each female flower after pollination matures into a little

Maclura pomifera, in winter

Maclura pomifera (trunk)

Maclura pomifera (fruits)

fruit, with the numerous ones of each flower cluster joined to form the familiar large compound fruits called osage-oranges. These are roughly spherical, 3½ to 5 inches in diameter, and have coarse pebbly surfaces. At first green, they become orange when ripe. Variety *M. p. inermis* is without thorns. The sap of the osage-orange is milky and can cause a contact dermatitis in sensitive individuals.

Garden and Landscape Uses. Formerly extensively used, especially in the Midwest, for field hedges, the osage-orange has been practically superseded as a boundary marker and restrainer of livestock by wire fencing. It is still planted for windbreaks and can be sheared to form impenetrable barriers. As a shade and specimen tree it is not without merit, but except as a curiosity is scarcely worth planting in regions where better ornamentals are plentiful. It flourishes where summers are hot and dry and withstands winters as cold as those of southern New England. The strange-looking fruits invariably occasion the interest of those unfamiliar with them. They are borne only by female trees and then only if a male is nearby.

Cultivation. Seeds, sown outdoors in fall or stored for up to a year and then stratified for two months at 40°F before sowing, germinate satisfactorily. The sexes of the resulting seedlings are not determinable until they flower, and if plants of known sex are required it is better to raise them from root cuttings, or from summer cuttings under mist, in a greenhouse or cold frame propagating bed. The management of established specimens calls for no particular care other than any shearing or pruning deemed desirable. Do this in winter or spring.

MACODES (Macò-des)—Jewel Orchid. Native to Malaysia, Indonesia, the Solomon Islands, and the Philippine Islands, the ten species of *Macodes*, of the orchid family ORCHIDACEAE, are colloquially known as jewel orchids, a name they share with *Anoectochilus*, *Dossinia*, and *Haemaria*. The botanical name, alluding to the long lips of the flowers, is derived from the Greek *mekos*, length.

The sorts of *Macodes* are terrestrial (ground-inhabiting) orchids admired chiefly for their beautiful foliage. They have a few handsomely variegated, stalked basal leaves and long, erect racemes of small flowers that differ from those of nearly related *Haemaria* in that the lip is at the top of the bloom. The sepals and the somewhat narrower petals spread. The lip is three-lobed and like the column is twisted. Native from Virginia to Florida and from the Bahamas and West Indies, *M. spicata* (syns. *M. floridana*, *Microstylis floridana*) has a few small, fleshy pseudobulbs and, in pairs, ovate to nearly circular, glossy leaves 1 inch to 4 inches long and with midribs noticeably keeled on their undersides. From 3 inches to rather more than 1 foot tall, the flowering stalks terminate in loose racemes of few to many ¼-inch-long flowers with green sepals and petals and a pale yellow to orange-red lip.

Native from Sumatra to the Philippine Islands, *M. petola* has broad-ovate to almost circular, dark green leaves decorated with a netting of golden-yellow veins. The racemes, with their stalks, 4 to 6 inches tall and furnished with small bracts, are of about fifteen flowers with reddish-brown sepals and petals and a white lip.

Garden Uses and Cultivation. These are as for *Anoectochilus*.

MACRADENIA (Macra-dènia). Mostly small, the eight species of *Macradenia* belong to the orchid family ORCHIDACEAE. They are natives of warm parts of the Americas. The name, alluding to the stalks of the pollen masses, is from the Greek *makros*, long, and *aden*, a gland.

Epiphytic (tree-perching without taking nourishment from the host), these orchids have pseudobulbs with a solitary, generally somewhat leathery leaf. The flower stalks arise from the bases of the pseudobulbs. The flowers have sepals and petals that are similar, except that the latter are generally a little smaller than the former,

and a three-lobed lip with the side lobes enveloping the column.

Slender and slightly flattened, the nearly cylindrical, clustered pseudobulbs of *M. lutescens* are up to 2 inches long. The pointed, oblong-lanceolate leaves are up to 7 inches in length. Not opening widely, the flowers, about ¾ inch across, in arching or pendulous racemes, have whitish to pink sepals and petals, often marked with reddish-brown or purple, and a usually whitish lip with three raised ridges or keels. This is a rare native of southern Florida and of the West Indies, northern South America, and Trinidad. Similar *M. paraensis*, of Brazil, has dark red-brown sepals and petals and a lip with pointed side lobes. The linear, white center lobe of the lip is marked with purple.

Macradenia, undetermined species:
(a) Plant

(b) Flowers

Native from Guatemala to northern South America, *M. brassavolae* forms dense clumps of 1½- to 1¾-inch-long pseudobulbs. Its leaves are up to 6 inches long. The pendulous racemes, up to 10 inches long, are of chestnut-brown flowers with 1-inch-long, lanceolate sepals and petals with translucent-green margins. The lip is about ¾ inch long. Native of Colombia, *M. modesta* has pseudobulbs about 2 inches tall, leaves up to 9 inches long by about 2 inches wide, and flowers 1¼ inches across in arching, crowded ra-

cemes up to 10 inches long. The sepals and petals are reddish, edged with yellow. The whitish to yellowish lip is sometimes streaked with purple.

Garden Uses and Cultivation. Of interest for orchid collections, macradenias respond to conditions and care that suit most epiphytic orchids from the humid tropics and warm subtropics. They succeed in pots or attached to pieces of tree fern trunk. For more information see Orchids.

MACRADESA. This is the name of orchid hybrids the parents of which are *Gomesa* and *Macradenia*.

MACRANGRAECUM (Macran-gràecum). This is the name of orchid hybrids the parents of which are *Macroplectrum* and *Angraecum*. The hybrids are intermediate in appearance between the parent genera. The best known, *M. veitchii* (syn. *Angraecum veitchii*), has as parents *Angraecum superbum* and *Macroplectrum sesquipedale*. Its flowers resemble those of the last named, but are only about one-half as big.

MACROCATALPA. The evergreen trees formerly named *Macrocatalpa* are included in Catalpa.

MACROPIPER (Macro-pìper)—Pepper Tree. Shrubs and small trees, frequently with shoots swollen at the nodes (joints), constitute *Macropiper*, a group sometimes included in *Piper*, that inhabits New Zealand and islands of the South Seas to New Guinea. There are about half a dozen species, belonging in the pepper family PIPERACEAE. The name comes from the Greek *makros*, long or large, and *Piper*, the name of a related genus.

Macropipers have alternate, undivided leaves and minute, unisexual flowers, the males and females in separate spikes, opposite the leaves. The flowers are without perianths, the males consisting of two or three stamens, the females with a few stigmas. The fruits are small, berry-like drupes.

Native of lowland forests in New Zealand and the Chatham Islands, *M. excelsum* is an evergreen, aromatic shrub or

Macropiper excelsum

tree, in New Zealand called pepper tree, up to about 20 feet tall. Its zigzagged shoots have swollen joints and short-stalked, somewhat leathery, broad-ovate to nearly round, wavy-edged leaves, up to 5 inches long, and with heart-shaped bases. They are olive-green with distinctly lighter veins, and paler undersides. Short-stalked, the solitary or paired flower spikes are ¾ inch to 3½ inches long. The tiny yellow to orange fruits are in crowded spikes. Variety *M. e. majus* (syn. *M. psittacorum*) has leaves up to 8 inches long, and flower spikes up to 6 inches long.

Garden and Landscape Uses and Cultivation. Only in frostless regions are macropipers hardy. The pepper tree of New Zealand is cultivated in containers as an indoor decorative. It thrives in ordinary, fertile soil and does well in part-shade. In greenhouses it prospers where the night temperature in winter is about 50°F, and by day five to fifteen degrees higher. At other seasons higher temperatures are in order. Repotting is done in spring, and at that time any pruning needed to keep the specimen shapely or restrain it to size is given attention. At all times the soil is kept moderately moist, and from spring to fall dilute liquid fertilizer is supplied to well-rooted specimens every week or two. Increase is by seed, cuttings rooted in a greenhouse propagating bench preferably with a little bottom heat, and layering.

MACROPLECTRUM (Macro-pléctrum). Formerly accommodated in *Angraecum*, the four species of *Macroplectrum*, of the orchid family ORCHIDACEAE, are natives of Madagascar and the Comoro Islands. The name, alluding to a feature of the flowers, derives from the Greek *macros*, long, and *plectron*, a spur.

Macroplectrums are robust, tree-perching (epiphytic) orchids with fleshy leaves in two ranks that completely envelop the stems. The flowers, solitary or several on each stalk and arising from the axils of the leaves, have similar spreading sepals and petals, a short, fleshy column, and a lip with a long tubular spur.

Native to the hot lowlands of Madagascar, *M. sesquipedale* (syn. *Angraecum sesquipedale*) typically has a single erect stem up to about 3 feet tall. Its strap-shaped, fleshy leaves, densely arranged and up to 1 foot long by 1 inch wide, fold inward toward their bases. Their tips are notched. The racemes of five or fewer flowers are generally horizontal or somewhat drooping and up to 1 foot long. Long-lasting, fragrant, ivory-white, and waxy-textured, the blooms, 5 to 7 inches in diameter, are the largest of the genus. Starry in aspect, they have a slender, greenish-white spur up to almost 1 foot long. Observing this remarkable development, which has a nectar gland at its base, naturalist Charles Darwin predicted that there must exist a moth with a 1-foot-long tongue capable of

Macroplectrum sesquipedale

Macroplectrum sesquipedale (flower)

pollinating such a curious flower. Contemporary entomologists and others scoffed at this suggestion, and it was not until after Darwin's death that such a moth was discovered in Madagascar.

Short-stalked *M. leonis* (syn. *Angraecum leonis*), a native of the Comoro Islands, has lanceolate, sickle-shaped leaves with closely overlapped bases and down-pointed tips. From 5 to 10 inches long by about ¾ inch wide, they are fleshy, rigid, and unusual in that the upper surface, by reason of the cohesion of the two sides of the leaf, has a knife-edge form. Carried erect to horizontally, the racemes are of three to seven long-lasting, fragrant blooms approximately 3 inches wide. Their white to yellowish sepals and petals are lanceolate and recurved, the petals slightly shorter and somewhat wider than the sepals. The white or ivory-white lip is heart-shaped and concave. Its spur, white with a green tip, is slender, curved, twisted and 4 to 6 inches long.

Garden Uses and Cultivation. These handsome orchids, which respond to humid, tropical environments, are interesting for including in collections. Winter night temperatures of 60 to 65°F are appropriate with increases of five to fifteen degrees, depending upon the brightness of the weather, permitted by day. Some

growers find macroplectrums succeed better in osmunda fiber than planted in bark chips, others advocate a mixture of osmunda fiber and shredded tree fern fiber. Good dainage is necessary. Provide shade from strong sun and water generously when the plants are in active growth, moderately at other times. For more information see Orchids.

MACROZAMIA (Macro-zàmia) — Burrawang. A dozen species of *Macrozamia* inhabit eastern Australia. The only other species are one from central Australia and one from western Australia. Two other species formerly included constitute *Lepidozamia*. Macrozamias belong in the cycad family CYCADACEAE, or according to those who favor splitting that into three, to the zamia family ZAMIACEAE. The name, from the Greek *makros*, large, and *Zamia*, the name of another genus of cycads, was perhaps more descriptive of the group when the tall kinds now segregated as *Lepidozamia* were included. Some species of *Macrozamia* contain poison that causes animals that feed on the foliage to develop a paralysis called the wobblies. This prevents the creatures from seeking food and results in death by starvation.

Macrozamias are more or less palmlike evergreens with massive, unusually branchless stems, entirely subterranean or extending as stocky trunks for several feet above ground, crowned with few to many pinnate fronds (leaves) interspersed with rudimentary leaves called cataphylls. The bases of the leafstalks, at least at first, are silky- or woolly-hairy. Borne along the twisted or twistless midrib, the many, straight or sickle-shaped leaflets are sometimes one to three times forked. As is characteristic of cycads, there are no flowers. The reproductive cells are in large, very evidently-stalked, male and female cones. After being fertilized by pollen from males, female cones produce large seeds. The fronds of young macrozamias often differ markedly from those of older specimens. Their stalks are often proportionately longer, and the leaflets are usually toothed at their apexes.

Native to central Australian deserts, *M. macdonnellii* has a trunk 3 to 6, rarely up to 10 feet tall, and often more or less procumbent. Its markedly glaucous, palmlike fronds, when young erect, later spreading or pendulous, attain lengths up to 7 feet. They have many straight, rigid, sharp-pointed, linear leaflets, the biggest 8 inches to 1 foot long by up to ½ inch wide, that angle sharply toward the leaf apex. Toward the base they become progressively smaller and eventually spinelike. Male cones, cylindrical and often somewhat curved, are 6 inches to 1¼ feet long. Females, ovoid-cylindrical and sometimes over 1½ feet long by nearly 1 foot in diameter, have orange-red seeds from 2¼ to more than 3 inches in length by up to about 2 inches thick. Western Australian *M. riedlei* differs chiefly in its fronds being not or very slightly glaucous and its seeds being 1½ to 2 inches long by ¾ inch to 1½ inches in diameter. Also, it is sometimes without a trunk, but more often has one 3 to 15 feet tall or procumbent.

The tallest species, eastern Australian *M. moorei*, when very old may attain 20 feet or somewhat more, but more usually is 6 to 12 feet high. Specimens in the botanic garden at Sydney attained 6 feet in a little less than a century. This kind has numerous fronds, at first erect, later spreading, then drooping. Their linear, undivided leaflets spread horizontally and point sharply toward the leaf apex. They are straight, the longest 8 inches to 1¼ feet long, tapering, and spine-tipped. Below they are gradually reduced in size and finally become spinelike. They extend to very close to the base of the leaf. Female cones are 1¼ to 2½ feet long, males approximately one-half that. In Australia called burrawang, *M. communis* has commonly been misnamed *M. spiralis*. It may or may not have an above-ground trunk up to 6 feet tall. The dullish fronds, at first erect, then spreading, have a much longer spine-free stalk than those of *M. moorei*. The spreading, sharp-pointed, undivided leaflets point at an acute angle toward the leaf apex. They are up to about 1 foot long. Both male and female cones are cylindrical and 8 inches to 1¼ feet long. The females are decidedly thicker than the males.

Several small species with usually up to a dozen fronds are natives of eastern Australia. Here belong *M. fawcettii* and variable *M. pauli-guilielmii*, both with stems mostly underground and fronds 2- to 4-feet-long with strongly-spiraled midribs. The leaflets of *M. fawcettii* are considerably broader than the ¼-inch-wide ones of *M. pauli-guilielmii* and at their apexes are two- to seven-toothed; those of *M. pauli-guilielmii* have two-toothed or toothless apexes. The male cones of *M. fawcettii* are 5 to 10 inches long and cylindrical; those of *M. pauli-guilielmii* are about as long and cylindrical to cylindrical-ellipsoid. The female cones of *M. fawcettii* are ovoid and 4 to 7 inches long; those of *M. pauli-guilielmii* are ovoid and 4 to 10 inches long. A native of New South Wales, *M. heteromera* has a usually subterranean stem and 1½- to 2-foot-long leaves with numerous leaflets 4 to 8 inches long that spread in several directions and are mostly once- or twice-divided nearly to their bases. Its male cones are cylindrical and 5 to 8 inches long. The female cones are up to 11 inches long and are wider than the males. Another native to New South Wales, *M. stenomera* differs from *M. heteromera* chiefly in its leaves having more twisted midribs and in its leaflets being divided into more and slenderer segments. Its stem mostly subterranean, *M. spiralis* (syn. *M. corallipes*) of New South Wales has fronds 2 to 3 feet long with the bases of

their stalks pinkish to red or orange. The fronds of young plants have midribs more conspicuously spiraled than those of older specimens. The numerous 4- to 8-inch-long leaflets spread, but not in the same plane. The male cones are cylindrical to cylindrical-ellipsoid and 6 to 8 inches long. About as long, female cones are proportionately wider.

Macrozamia stenomera

Garden and Landscape Uses and Cultivation. Macrozamias are interesting for inclusion in collections of rare plants and in warm climates for general landscaping. The lower kinds are satisfactory for the fronts of shrub borders and in similar locations, the taller ones as featured specimens and accents. They stand dry conditions well and are among the easiest of the cycads to grow. They may be located in full sun, but prefer perhaps a little shade. The soil must be sharply porous. In greenhouses a temperature on winter nights of 50 to 60°F, with a daytime increase of up to fifteen degrees depending upon the brightness of the weather, is satisfactory. At other seasons considerably higher temperatures are in order. Because growth is very slow repotting is needed at long intervals only. From spring to fall keep the soil medium-moist, drier in winter.

MADAGASCAR and MADAGASCAN. These words form part of the common names of these plants: Madagascar-jasmine (*Stephanotis floribunda*), Madagascar-olive (*Noronhia emarginata*), Madagascar-periwinkle (*Catharanthus roseus*), and Madagascan raffia palm (*Raphia farinifera*).

MADDEN-CHERRY is *Maddenia hypoleuca*.

MADDENIA (Mad-dènia)—Madden-Cherry. Named to commemorate Colonel E. Madden, who collected plants in India and died in 1856, *Maddenia*, of the rose family ROSACEAE, consists of four or five species of deciduous, alternate-leaved trees or shrubs and is native from China to the Himalayas. Closely related to *Prunus*, it differs in its blooms being without petals or having minute ones and in their having ten instead of five sepals. There are ten to twenty stamens. The style is long. Male

and female flowers are on separate plants. The one-seeded fruits are drupes (fruits constructed like plums).

Hardy in southern New England, the Madden-cherry (*M. hypoleuca*) has little claim to merit as an ornamental. Except to collectors of unusual trees and shrubs, this native of China and adjacent territory is unlikely to be of interest. A shrub or tree up to 20 feet in height, it has short-stalked, oblong to ovate-oblong, hairless leaves 1½ to 3 inches long. They have fourteen to sixteen pairs of parallel lateral veins, glaucous undersides, and double-toothed margins. The lower teeth are conspicuously gland-tipped. On vigorous young shoots the leaves are often longer. The crowded racemes of yellow flowers, which appear in spring, terminate short leafy shoots. They are up to 2 inches long. The stamens, tipped with yellow anthers, are conspicuous. The ellipsoid fruits are ⅓ inch long and black. Very similar, but with the undersides of its leaves yellowish instead of whitish and with hairs on the veins beneath, *M. hypoxantha* is Chinese.

Garden and Landscape Uses and Cultivation. Only in arboretums and similar special collections are the species described likely to be cultivated. They are satisfied with ordinary soil and a sunny location. Propagation is by seed and by cuttings under mist.

MADDER is *Rubia tinctorum*.

MADEIRA VINE is *Anredera cordifolia*.

MADIA (Màd-ia)—Tarweed. Tarweeds, as members of the genus *Madia* are called, number eighteen species of Pacific North America and South America. They belong to the daisy family COMPOSITAE, and among garden plants are most closely related to *Layia*. Their name is a modification of a Chilean native one, *madi*, applied to the first known kind.

Madias include annuals and perennials, most without horticultural importance. Many have the curious habit of closing their flowers in sunshine, opening them only in the mornings and evenings. They are usually strongly-scented, glandular natives of deserts and semideserts and have linear to oblong leaves, the lower ones sometimes toothed. The flower heads have disk and ray florets. The latter, few to many, are the outer, spreading, strap-shaped ones that nonbotanists are likely to call petals, the disk florets form the eyes of the daisy-like flower heads.

Common tarweed (*M. elegans*) is most likely to be cultivated. A variable annual, it and its varieties, ranging from Oregon to Baja California, have usually branching stems 8 inches to 2½ feet in height. It is hairy in its lower parts. Variety *M. e. densifolia* is sometimes 8 feet tall. The leaves, linear to broadly-lanceolate, are crowded below, on the upper parts of the stems more

Madia elegans

distantly spaced. The flower heads have eight to sixteen ray florets that are yellow or yellow with maroon bases and are ½ to ¾ inch long. The disk florets are yellow or maroon and have yellow, purple-black, or black anthers.

Garden Uses and Cultivation. The common tarweed is a loose-growing attractive plant useful for flower borders and, in its native area, as a component of wild gardens. It is easily raised from seeds sown outdoors in early spring where the plants are to bloom. The seedlings are thinned to about a foot apart. A well-drained moderately fertile soil and shade from strong sun are conducive to the best results. An alternative method of cultivation is to sow the seeds indoors early, grow the young seedlings, spaced about 2 inches apart, in flats in a greenhouse in a night temperature of 50°F and day temperatures a few degrees higher until all danger of frost is passed. Then they are transplanted to the open ground. The seeds should be sown eight to ten weeks before planting out time.

MADRE DE CACAO is *Gliricidia sepium*.

MADRONE or MADRONO is *Arbutus menziesii*.

MADWORT. See Alyssum.

MAESA (Maè-sa). Two hundred species of the tropics and subtropics of the Old World are the components of *Maesa*, of the myrsine family MYRSINACEAE. The name is from the Arabian *maas*, applied to one kind.

Maesas are shrubs, trees, or vines that differ from other members of the family in technical details of their ovaries and in the fruits having many seeds. They have alternate, undivided, toothed or toothless leaves and racemes or panicles of small, white, commonly bisexual flowers, usually from the leaf axils. The calyxes, with tubes united with the ovaries, have five lobes (sepals). The shortly-bell-shaped corollas have five lobes (petals). There are five stamens and a short style. The fruits are berries with, at their apexes, the persistent calyxes and styles.

Native of India, *M. indica* is a much-branched shrub or tree up to 30 feet tall. It has broad-elliptic to lanceolate, toothed, leathery leaves 3 to 6 inches long and one-half as broad. Its axillary racemes, 3 to 4 inches long, of tiny, faintly fragrant flowers are succeeded by creamy-white, edible berries about ⅛ inch in diameter. A shrub about 3 feet tall, less often higher or sometimes prostrate, *M. japonica* is a native of Japan, Taiwan, China, and Indochina. It has elliptic-lanceolate to oblong-ovate or ovate, toothed or toothless leaves up to 6 inches long, with glossy upper sides and paler lower ones. The flowers are in short racemes or panicles from the leaf axils. Himalayan *M. argentea* is a shrub with prominently-veined, toothed, elliptic leaves 4 to 8 inches long and about one-half as wide. In crowded clusters in the leaf axils,

Maesa argentea (fruits)

its flowers are small, white, and bell-shaped. They are succeeded by ornamental whitish to pale pink berries.

Garden and Landscape Uses and Cultivation. Not well known in North America, the species just described are adaptable only in warm, frostless or nearly frostless regions, where they may be used to give variety and interest to plantings. They are propagated by seed and cuttings and respond to ordinary soils and locations.

MAGA is *Montezuma speciosissima*.

MAGGOTS. The larvae of flies are maggots. Somewhat wormlike, they live on or within the tissues upon which they feed. Of flies that are pests of plants some are known to gardeners as flies, for instance the cattleya fly and the lesser bulb fly, others are called leaf miners, as are the boxwood leaf miner and chrysanthemum leaf miner, and some few are referred to as maggots.

Among the last are the apple maggot or apple fruit fly, also known as railroad worm, which attacks apples and a number of other fruits causing them to become wormy and often unacceptable for use. Other species include the cabbage maggot, which feeds on the roots of cabbages and closely related vegetables as well as some other kinds. The onion maggot bores into the bulbs, often causing serious harm.

Other maggots are responsible for damaging corn, gladioluses, sunflowers, and other crops. Consult a Cooperative Extension Agent or State Agricultural Experiment Station about the best methods of control.

MAGNOLIA (Mag-nòlia). Most American gardeners are familiar with magnolias. Several sorts are natives of the United States. Others are indigenous in Mexico, Central America, the West Indies, and Asia. There are eighty species belonging to the magnolia family MAGNOLIACEAE. The name commemorates the French botanist Pierre Magnol, who died in 1715.

Magnolias are trees and tall shrubs, some evergreen, many deciduous, some hardy, others not. They have alternate, undivided, toothless leaves. Their large and mostly showy blooms are at the shoot ends. White, yellowish, pink, or purple, each has three sepals (often petal-like), six to eighteen petals, many stamens, and many pistils (female elements) clustered around a stalkless axis called a receptacle and eventually developing into a more or less conelike compound fruit. At maturity the seeds drop from the receptacle and remain suspended from it on threads for some considerable time. Sometimes botanists group the sepals and petals and refer to them as tepals, but since most gardeners call petal-like parts petals irrespective of their strict botanical classification, we do so here.

For horticultural purposes the kinds of *Magnolia* can be sorted into those that bloom in early spring before or while the new foliage is developing and those that flower when in full foliage in late spring or summer. A few of the first sometimes have a second sparser crop of blooms in summer.

These basic separations are further divided in the case of early spring-bloomers into sorts in which all of the flower segments are petal-like, and essentially similar, and kinds in which the three outer segments are much smaller, green or greenish-brown, and sepal-like. All early spring-blooming magnolias are Asian; all are deciduous. Here belong some of the most prized and spectacular flowering trees and one that is usually a shrub.

Late spring- and summer-bloomers, in full leaf at flowering time, may be sorted into those that are definitely deciduous and those that are evergreen at least in mild climates. The former in turn can be grouped as sorts with moderate-sized leaves not crowded near the tips of the shoots and sorts with large to very large leaves clustered near the shoot ends. The presentation that follows is in the order of this useful horticultural classification.

The yulan (**M. denudata** syns. *M. heptapeta*, *M. conspicua*) is typical of early spring-blooming sorts with sepals and pet-

Magnolia denudata

Magnolia soulangiana

Magnolia soulangiana (flowers)

als essentially alike. The only hardy species in its group, the yulan is satisfactory in southern New England. Its common name is a Chinese one meaning lily tree. Native to China, this handsome deciduous species was introduced to Japan sometime before the year 900 and to Europe in 1780. In the wild sometimes 50 feet in height, but often lower in cultivation, the yulan is somewhat variable. It has spreading branches and short-pointed, obovate to obovate-oblong leaves, tapered to their bases, 4 to 6 inches long, sparingly-hairy above, minutely so, especially on the veins, on their undersides. The fragrant flowers, when fully open bell-shaped and 4½ to 6 inches in diameter, have nine similar oblong-obovate, white petals. Sometimes a few summer blooms are produced when the plants are in foliage, and these are purplish. The spindle-shaped, brownish fruits are up to 5 inches long. Variety *M. d. purpurascens* has pink flowers with rose-red outsides to their petals.

Saucer magnolia (**M. soulangiana**) is undoubtedly the most widely planted magnolia in the northern United States. A hybrid between *M. denudata* and *M. liliflora*, first recorded in France in the second decade of the nineteenth century, this very variable sort is a tree 15 feet or so tall and usually as wide as high, or it is sometimes a tall, broad shrub. Blooming immediately after *M. kobus*, *M. stellata*, *M. salicifolia*, and the yulan, and before its leaves appear, like the star magnolia the saucer magnolia flowers when very young and regularly thereafter. Some varieties not uncommonly produce second, much sparser crops of smaller flowers in summer. Borne in great profusion and shaped like cups or inverted vases, the 5- to 10-inch-wide flowers, with similar sepals and petals, are white on their insides, stained on their outsides with light to deep red-purple or purple. The leaves, downy on their undersides, pointed-elliptic to pointed-obovate, are 4 to 8 inches long. Seedlings vary considerably in flower color, and many have been selected and named as horticultural varieties. Unfortunately the naming of some is confused and it is not always easy to determine which variety a particular individual represents.

Varieties of saucer magnolia include these: *M. s. alba-superba* (syn. *M. s. alba*) is compact, with white flowers lightly suffused with purple on the outsides. *M. s. alexandrina* flowers early, with blooms flushed with rosy-purple to purple on their outsides. More than one variant appears to pass under this name. *M. s.* 'Andre LeRoy' has cup-shaped blooms colored dark purplish-pink on their outsides. *M. s. brozzonii*, one of the latest saucer magnolias to bloom and one of the handsomest, has white flowers up to 10 inches across when expanded, and flushed with purple at their bases on the outside. *M. s.* 'Burgundy' has blooms burgundy-wine in the lower halves of their petals, paler above. It flowers earlier than most sorts. *M. s.* 'Grace McDade' has exceptionally big blooms, with pink-based, white petals. *M. s. lennei* is a broad tree with larger leaves than most varieties and darker-colored flowers than any other saucer magnolia. The blooms have very fleshy petals with concave upper sides. *M. s.* 'Lilliputian' is a slow-growing, smallish sort, with smaller blooms than most other saucer magnolias. *M. s.* 'Lombardy Rose' has flowers deep rose-pink on their outsides, white inside. They are produced over an especially long period. *M. s. rustica-rubra* (syn. *M. s. rubra*) much resembles *M. s. lennei*,

but has more rosy-red flowers with shorter, broader petals. *M. s.* 'San Jose' is an early-bloomer, with large white blooms delicately flushed with pink. *M. s. speciosa* is late-flowering, with nearly white blooms. *M. s. verbanica* is a slow-growing late bloomer, with flowers rose-pink on their outsides.

Other sorts that flower before new leaves appear and have all segments of the flowers essentially petal-like are *M. campbellii*, *M. veitchii*, *M. dawsoniana*, *M. sargentiana*, and *M. sprengeri*. In that order we shall consider them. None is hardy in the north.

Himalayan *M. campbellii* in its home territory is sometimes more than 100 feet tall, but in cultivation rarely achieves one-half that height. One of the loveliest of magnolias, this has broad-elliptic to somewhat narrower leaves with pointed apexes. They are 6 to 10 inches long by 4 to 5 inches wide, hairless above, beneath clothed at least when young with hairs lying parallel with the surface. Appearing in spring before the foliage, the 10-inch-wide flowers have twelve to sixteen petals that are pink or crimson on their outsides, white or paler pink on their insides. The four inner petals are erect, the other spread. In *M. c. alba* the blooms are white. Sometimes accepted as a separate species under the name *M. mollicomata*, but too similar to warrant such distinction, *M. c. mollicomata*, a native of western China and adjacent regions to the west, can most conveniently be separated from *M. campbellii* by the stalks of its flowers being downy instead of hairless as are those of the last. The variety has the great advantage of beginning to bloom when seven or eight years old. The species takes much longer to achieve first flowering. Neither is hardy in the north. Hybrids between *M. campbellii* and *M. c. mollicomata* recognized in the British Isles are 'Charles Raffill', with flowers with petals on their insides white bordered with pinkish-purple, on the outsides deep purple, and 'Kew's Surprise', with deeper-colored blooms than the last; 'Lanarth', which has leaves with hairless undersides and deep lilac-purple blooms; and 'Mary Williams', the flowers of which are rosy-purple.

A hybrid between *M. campbellii* and the yulan magnolia, handsome **M. veitchii** is a robust tree that in England, where it was raised from a cross made in 1907, exceeds 80 feet in height. Unfortunately it is not hardy in the north. This has obovate to oblong leaves 6 inches to 1 foot long by approximately one-half as wide, purplish especially on their undersides when young. The approximately 6-inch-wide flowers, borne before the new leaves come, have nine blush-pink or white sepals and petals. The white-flowered variant is named *M. v.* 'Isca', the pink-flowered one *M. v.* 'Peter Veitch'.

Chinese **M. dawsoniana,** is a beautiful broad tree up to 40 feet high or a tall shrub. It has obovate to elliptic, blunt to pointed leaves 3½ to 6 inches long with prominent networks of veins, slightly glaucous on their undersides. The nodding, short-stalked blooms 8 to 10 inches across have usually nine to eleven white petals suffused and streaked with pale rosy-purple. Rather similar **M. sargentiana,** also Chinese, differs in having less leathery leaves, flowers with twelve to fourteen petals, and in minor botanical details. Superior *M. s. robusta* begins bearing blooms up to 1 foot in diameter while comparatively young and displays more of them nearer eye level than the species.

Closely related to the yulan magnolia and at one time treated as a variety of it, **M. sprengeri,** a Chinese species pyramidal in outline, is about 65 feet tall. It has oblanceolate to obovate leaves 3 to 7 inches long by up to nearly 5 inches wide, more or less hairy on their under surfaces. Coming before the foliage, the usually twelve-petaled, 8-inch-wide flowers have white petals suffused at their bases with purple or pink. Variety *M. s. elongata* has white flowers. The leaves of *M. s.* 'Diva' are broadly-ovate. Its white blooms, streaked with pink on their insides, deep rose-pink on their outsides, have stamens with rose-red stalks. Those of *M. s.* 'Claret Cup' are rosy-purple on their outsides, lighter colored fading to white inside. Although *M. sprengeri* is probably not hardy as far north as Philadelphia, Pennsylvania, a specimen of its variety *M. s.* 'Diva' at the nearby Arboretum of the Barnes Foundation has survived for many years and has flowered.

Spring-flowering magnolias that bloom before their leaves appear and have flowers with the outermost segments small, sepal-like, and forming an apparent calyx are *M. stellata, M. kobus, M. salicifolia, M. cylindrica,* and their varieties and hybrids.

Earliest to bloom, the star magnolia (**M. stellata** syn. *M. kobus stellata*) has flowers with eleven to twenty-one petal-like sepals and petals (more than those of any other Asian magnolia). Generally a tall shrub, but sometimes a tree up to more than 20 feet tall, this native of Japan is often broader than high. Its obovate-oblong to oblanceolate leaves are 3 to 4 inches long by about 1½ inches wide. When fully open the flowers, which are one to three at the shoot ends, are about 3½ inches across. White and strap-shaped, most of the petals become reflexed as the blooms age. There are one to three very small sepal-like outer segments. Variety *M. s. rosea* scarcely lives up to the expectations its name may suggest. It blooms open a delicate pink, but soon fade to white. Those of *M. s. rubra* have the outsides of the petals fuchsia-purple, the insides paler. The white flowers of *M. s.* 'Waterlily' have wider petals than those of typical *M. stellata*. A few other varieties are cultivated.

The species **M. kobus** differs from *M. stel-*

Magnolia stellata

Magnolia stellata (flowers)

Magnolia stellata (fruits)

lata, to which it is very closely related, and its varieties in having white flowers with only six to nine petals and three much smaller sepals. Native to Japan and Korea, this, unlike the star magnolia, does not bloom until it has attained considerable age. It is a tree 30 to 75 feet in height with broad-obovate to obovate, short-pointed leaves, narrowed to their bases, 4 to 6 inches long. The blooms are 4 to 4½ inches wide. Specimens with leaves and flowers approximating the largest dimensions given and that at maturity approach the maximum

Magnolia kobus

height for the species are distinguished as *M. k. borealis.* Hardiest of Asian magnolias, this variety endures throughout New England and is believed to be of more northerly origin than the more typical species, which is hardy only in southern New England. Generally considered to be a variety of *M. kobus* but thought by some to be a hybrid between that species and *M. salicifolia* or possibly a variety of *M. salicifolia, M.* 'Wada's Memory' is an especially fine magnolia. Raised in Seattle, Washington, from seed received from Japan, it bears a profusion of white flowers larger than those of *M. kobus.*

Hybrids between *M. kobus* and *M. stellata* are grouped as **M. loebneri.** Belonging here and resembling *M. stellata* in habit of growth, but generally having larger, more obovate leaves and bigger blooms, are several fine sorts. One such, *M. l.* 'Merrill', was raised at the Arnold Arboretum near Boston, Massachusetts. This is a shapely tree 25 feet tall or taller that bears in spring, before its foliage develops, white flowers much like those of *M. kobus,* but with twelve to eighteen petals that are broader than those of *M. stellata.* It blooms when very young. Other varieties of *M. loebneri* are 'Ballerina', 'Leonard Messel', 'Spring Snow', and 'Willowwood'.

A hybrid between *M. kobus* and *M. salicifolia* discovered as a chance seedling at the Royal Botanic Gardens, Kew, England, in 1938, **M. kewensis** first bloomed in 1957. It has leaves 4 to 5 inches long. Its orange-blossom-scented flowers have pure white petals and at the center a lime-green stigmatic column.

Differing from *M. kobus* in having generally hairless leaf buds and narrower oblong-lanceolate to narrowly-elliptic leaves broader below rather than at their middles, closely related, variable **M. salicifolia** is a narrow-headed tree up to about 30 feet tall. When bruised the leaves and bark are usually pleasantly fragrant of anise, although this may not be true of all specimens. The pointed leaves 3 to 4½ inches long are slightly glaucous and sparingly-hairy on their undersides. The flowers, white or white tinged with purple at the bases of the petals on their outsides, have six narrow, oblong-obovate petals 2 inches long or a little longer and three lanceolate, greenish-white sepals one-half as long. The cylindrical fruits are 1½ to 3 inches in length. Native to Japan and hardy in southern New England, this magnolia begins to bloom when quite young. A hybrid between M. salicifolia and M. kobus, the flowers of which have sometimes nine petals, is **M. proctoriana.** Pyramidal and bearing a plentitude of pure white blooms, this comparatively fast grower has leaves that when crushed have a faint fragrance of anise, a characteristic inherited from its parent M. salicifolia. Variety M. p. 'Slavin's Snowy' (syn. M. slavinii) has white blooms tinged pink at the bases of the petals.

Rare **M. cylindrica,** a spring-bloomer discovered in 1925 in shaded ravines in China, is reported to attain in the wild a height of about 30 feet. Not hardy in the north, this deciduous species has narrow- to broad-ovate or elliptic-obovate leaves 4 to 6½ inches long by approximately one-half as wide, hairless except for a few hairs on the veins beneath. The blooms have six white petals blushed with pink along their mid-veins, the inner three approximately 4 inches long by 1½ inches wide, the others slightly shorter and narrower, and three very different smaller sepals.

Its flowers appearing in late spring with or after the leaves have developed and having three distinct, small sepals that fall early, **M. liliflora** (syn. M. quinquepeta) is a variable shrub 12 feet tall. Long a favorite of Japanese gardeners and a parent of the popular saucer magnolia, this is native of China. Often somewhat ungainly in habit, M. liliflora has pubescent winter buds and obovate to elliptic-ovate, pointed leaves, tapered to their bases and up to 7 inches in length, paler beneath than on their sparingly-hairy upper sides, and hairy on the veins beneath. The blooms, which open over a long period from early to late spring, have six or sometimes seven erect, obovate to spatula-shaped petals 3 to 4 inches long, white on their insides, on their outsides vinous-purple or a combination of that hue and white. The blooms of M. l. gracilis, a narrower tree with more slender branches than the typical species, are uniformly deep purple on their outsides. The deep reddish-purple flowers of M. l. nigra have petals 4 to 5 inches long, paler on their insides than on their outsides.

Asian deciduous magnolias that bloom in summer when in full foliage and have moderate-sized leaves not clustered at the branch ends include a number of choice sorts some, unfortunately, not hardy in the north. The kinds next to be described belong in this Asian group.

Three somewhat similar species are M.

wilsonii, M. sinensis, and M. sieboldii. A Chinese shrub or tree up to 25 feet tall, **M. wilsonii** is hardy in sheltered places in southern New England and has ovate-lanceolate to narrowly-ovate, pointed leaves 3 to 6 inches long by almost one-half as broad, woolly-hairy on their undersides. The white pendulous, fragrant, cupped flowers 3½ to 4 inches wide have a conspicuous center of crimson stamens. Also Chinese, but not hardy in the north, **M. sinensis** is about 20 feet tall and broader than the last. It has obovate to obovate-oblong or elliptic leaves 3 to 7 inches in length by 2 to 5½ inches wide, slightly glaucous on their undersides, velvety there when young, and hairless above. The nodding, saucer-shaped, fragrant blooms, 4 to 5 inches in diameter, have usually nine white petals and a central

Viewed from below, the flowers of Magnolia sinensis are displayed to advantage

Magnolia sinensis (flower)

cluster of bright crimson stamens. The third species of this group, **M. sieboldii** is a native of Japan and Korea. A tall shrub or small tree hardy in sheltered places in southern New England, this has oblong-obovate leaves about 3½ to 6 inches long, downy and glaucous on their under surfaces, hairless above. The white-petaled flowers, on stalks 1½ to 2½ inches long, face outward rather than downward. Their stamens are pink to crimson. A hy-

Magnolia sieboldii: (a) Characteristic long flower stalk

(b) Fully open flower

Magnolia 'Charles Coates'

brid between this and M. tripetala is named M. 'Charles Coates'.

Originally from Japan, summer-blooming **M. watsonii** (syn. M. weiseneri) is probably a hybrid between M. sieboldii and M. hypoleuca. A shrub or small tree of rigid habit and much resembling M. sieboldii, but with larger blooms, this has short-stalked, obovate leaves 4 to 8 inches long and saucer-shaped, fragrant flowers 5 to 6 inches in diameter with outer petals blushed with rose-pink, the inner ones ivory-white. A central bunch of crimson stamens provides striking contrast. This sort, probably hardier than generally supposed, has for several years proved hardy at Philadelphia, Pennsylvania, and is reported to have survived a temperature of twenty-five degrees below zero in Michigan.

Summer-blooming, deciduous Asian magnolias with large to immense leaves clustered near the branch ends include *M. hypoleuca, M. officinalis,* and *M. rostrata.*

Japanese **M. hypoleuca** (syn. *M. obovata*), one of the outstanding forest trees of its native land, where its lumber is esteemed for various purposes, is very beautiful.

Magnolia hypoleuca

From 50 to 80 feet or in the wild sometimes 100 feet tall, this has purplish young shoots and obovate, leathery leaves grouped near the branch ends. They are 9 inches to 1½ feet long by approximately one-half as broad, with slightly glaucous upper surfaces and bluish-white, somewhat downy undersides. The very fragrant, 8-inch-wide blooms, produced in early summer, are creamy-white with a bold central cluster of bright purple-red stamens tipped with yellow anthers. Easily confused with the last and similar to it, Chinese **M. officinalis** is 20 to 50 feet tall. From *M. hypoleuca* this smaller tree differs in its young shoots being yellowish and its fruits being flat-topped. Some of the leaves of *M. officinalis* are sometimes notched at the apexes. All those of *M. o. biloba* are conspicuously cleft in this fashion. Because of the comparatively small size of its blooms disappointing as a flowering tree, Chinese **M. rostrata** has leaves rivaled in size only by those of American *M. macrophylla, M. tripetala,* and *M. fraseri.* Not hardy in the north, this sort, 40 to 80 feet tall, has obovate leaves sometimes more than 1½ feet in length by 1 foot wide, purplish and downy when young. The white or pink blooms are hidden from below by the immense foliage.

Native American deciduous magnolias that bloom in summer when in full foliage and that have large to immense leaves are now to be considered. They include several sorts called cucumber trees and include the umbrella tree, which must not be confused with the entirely different and quite unrelated Texas umbrella tree (*Melia azedarach umbraculiformis*).

The umbrella tree (**M. tripetala**) attains heights of 30 to 40 feet. It has a rather open, irregular crown with the foliage radiating in clusters from the ends of the branches. Oblong-obovate to obovate, when young pubescent on their undersides, the short-pointed, 1- to 2-foot-long leaves have wedge-shaped bases narrowed to short stalks. Ill-scented, the purple-stamened, cupped blooms, 6 to 10 inches in diameter, have pale green, reflexed sepals and six or nine oblong-obovate white petals. The ovoid to long-ovoid fruits, 2½ to 4 inches long, are rose-pink when mature. This is native from Pennsylvania to Alabama, Arkansas, and Mississippi. From Japanese *M. hypoleuca,* this species differs in its leaves tapering more obviously to their bases and having less glaucous undersides.

Magnolia tripetala

The cucumber tree (**M. acuminata**), native from New York to Illinois, Georgia, and Arkansas, is the northernmost and hardiest native American magnolia. Under forest conditions attaining a maximum height of nearly 100 feet, it has a straight, columnar trunk with furrowed bark. In the open it is lower and develops a rounded-pyramidal head. Rounded or slightly heart-shaped at their bases, the short-pointed, ovate to almost obovate leaves, scattered along the shoots, are 6 to 10 inches long, paler on their undersides than above and somewhat pubescent there. The light yellowish-green flowers without display value, are 2 to 3 inches long. They have reflexed sepals and six ovate to obovate petals. The fruits are 3 to 4 inches long. The yellow cucumber tree (*M. a. cordata* syn. *M. cordata*) is a rare native of the coastal plain from North Carolina to Georgia. It differs from typical *M. acuminata* in rarely exceeding 35 feet in height and in having proportionately wider leaves, clothed with matted hairs on their undersides and 4 to 6 inches long. Also, its blooms are much more attractive. About 4 inches in diameter, they have petals with greenish-yellow or yellow on their outsides and canary-yellow on their faces. Variety 'Miss Honeybee' has larger, pale yellow blooms. The yellow cucumber tree and its variety must be accounted as among the finest of American magnolias. They are hardy at least as far north as Philadelphia, Pennsylvania.

The large-leaved cucumber tree (**M. macrophylla**) is very different from its generally more northern namesake, *M. acuminata.* Native from Kentucky to Florida, Arkansas, and Louisiana, it is a tall shrub or broad-headed tree up to 50 feet in height. This sort has the largest leaves and blooms of any hardy native North American tree. The leaves, 1 foot to 3 feet long, are oblong-obovate and blunt-pointed. Their heart-shaped bases form two short earlike lobes; their undersides are white-pubescent. Cup-shaped and fragrant, the flowers, 10 inches to 1 foot in diameter, have six white petals broader than the sepals, the three inner ones usually with a rose-red blotch at their bases. The fruits, 2½ to 3 inches long, egg-shaped to nearly spherical, are deep rose-red when mature. This is hardy in southern New England. Very closely allied to the last, *M. ashei,* native from Florida to Texas, does not exceed 25 feet in height, and is often lower. It has smaller blooms than the large-leaved cucumber tree, commonly without red blotches at the bases of the inner petals. Hardy as far north as southern New England, it is remarkable for beginning to bloom when very young and small and so is better adapted for compact landscapes than its more robust relative.

Magnolia ashei

The ear-leaved cucumber tree (**M. fraseri**) ranges in the wild from Virginia to Georgia and Alabama. Up to 45 feet tall, it has hairless shoots and buds. Its spatula-shaped to obovate, hairless leaves 8 inches to more than 1½ feet long have heart-shaped bases with a pair of prominent ears. The fragrant

Magnolia fraseri

Magnolia grandiflora at Colonial Williamsburg, Virginia

Magnolia grandiflora (foliage)

blooms, 8 to 10 inches in diameter, have early-deciduous sepals and six to nine narrowly-clawed petals. The egg-shaped to cylindrical fruits, rose-colored at maturity, are 3 to 5 inches long. Closely allied to *M. fraseri* but smaller, and with smaller, notably rhomboid leaves with basal ears, **M. pyramidata** blooms slightly later. Its fragrant, 3- to 4-inchwide flowers have narrow-strap-shaped, creamy-white petals. Native from Georgia to northern Florida and along the Gulf Coast of Texas, and probably less hardy than *M. fraseri*, this species has survived for several years and bloomed at the Arboretum of the Barnes Foundation, near Philadelphia, Pennsylvania.

Evergreen magnolias in cultivation are extremely few. By far the most important is the Southern evergreen magnolia or bull-bay. In mild climates the sweet-bay is partially evergreen, but where winters are cold is deciduous. Little-known *M. nitida* also retains its foliage throughout the year. We shall now consider these and one hybrid of the sweet bay.

The Southern evergreen magnolia or bull-bay (**M. grandiflora**) is one of the handsomest evergreen flowering trees. A native of coastal regions from North Carolina to Florida and Texas, this imposing species at its finest is 100 feet tall or even taller. It has handsome foliage and astonishingly beautiful, fragrant flowers. The leaves are oblong-elliptic to oblong-ovate and short-stalked and have leathery blades 4 to 10 inches long, less than onehalf as wide as long, glossy-green above, and generally generously clothed with rusty hairs on their undersides, but sometimes only sparsely so. From 7 to 10 inches in diameter, the great waxy-white to creamy-white flowers have six to twelve obovate petals. The stamens are purple. Varieties are *M. g.* 'Goliath', which has broad, blunt leaves and flowers up to 1 foot in diameter; *M. g.* 'Exmouth' (syn. *M. g. lanceolata*), a rather narrow tree, has leaves not as wide as those of the typical species; and *M. g.* 'St. Mary', is notable for the rich brown surfaces of its leaves.

Magnolia grandiflora in a sheltered courtyard at The New York Botanical Garden

Magnolia grandiflora in southern California

An espaliered specimen of *Magnolia grandiflora* in England

Magnolia grandiflora (flower)

Magnolia grandiflora 'Exmouth'

Less hardy than the bull-bay, **M. delavayi**, of southern China, is a broad evergreen tree up to about 35 feet tall with 9- to 10-inch-long, oblong to ovate, graygreen leaves somewhat glaucous on their undersides. The white flowers are 6 to 8 inches in diameter.

Semievergreen in the south, deciduous in the north, the sweet-bay (**M. virginiana** syn. *M. glauca*) is a native in coastal regions from Massachusetts to Florida and Texas. This is a large shrub or a tree up to 60 feet

Magnolia delavayi at the Royal Botanic Gardens, Kew, England

tall. It has blunt, oblong to elliptic leaves 3 to 6 inches long and displays over a long summer period of succession of deliciously fragrant, globose, white blooms 2 to 3 inches across and with nine to twelve broad, obovate petals. Varieties in cultivation include *M. v. australis*, with densely-silky-hairy branchlets, and *M. v.* 'Henry Hicks', which has evergreen foliage.

Magnolia virginiana

Much like the sweet-bay, but with leaves 4 to 10 inches long, and larger, less spherical blooms, **M. thompsoniana** was discovered in 1808 among a batch of seedlings raised by a nurseryman in England. Accepted as a hybrid between *M. virginiana* and *M. tripetala*, except for its greater vigor and larger parts, it much more resembles the former than the latter. Of loose, rather awkward habit, it is a tall shrub with leaves very glaucous on their undersides and creamy-white, fragrant flowers 4½ to 6 inches in diameter. Rather surprisingly, at the Arboretum of the Barnes Foundation near Philadelphia, Pennsylvania, this has proved tenderer than its parent species.

Chinese **M. nitida** is an evergreen hardy only in regions where little or no frost is experienced. A tall shrub or tree sometimes 40 feet in height, this has lustrous,

leathery, broad-elliptic, oblong, or somewhat ovate, hairless, short-stalked leaves 2½ to 4½ inches long by 1 inch to 2 inches broad, when young coppery-bronze. Its 2- to 3-inch-wide, creamy-white blooms with crimson outsides have nine or twelve oblanceolate to obovate petals that appear early in the year.

Garden and Landscape Uses. The genus *Magnolia* supplies deciduous trees hardy in temperate regions equaled by few and surpassed by none in the magnificence of their floral displays. There are hardy sorts with leaves of such impressive size they suggest the tropics rather than New England or New York. A few are beautiful flowering shrubs. Nonhardy magnolias are equally as splendid. Most are deciduous. A few are evergreen, among them that marvelous and gracious symbol of the south, the Southern magnolia or bull-bay. But floral merit and foliage size are not the only features that commend magnolias to planters of gardens and other landscapes. The trunks, branching patterns, and barks of many have much character, and the fruits of all are attractive. Noticeably missing from the list of assets is any striking fall foliage color. For that the landscaper must look elsewhere.

In locating magnolias in the landscape keep these points in mind. Most have large rather coarse leaves easily torn or otherwise damaged and made unsightly by strong winds. Therefore select sheltered sites where bold foliage fits satisfactorily and advantageously with the surroundings. Early-blooming sorts may have their flowers damaged by late frosts, which is another reason for seeking sheltered sites and for these, avoiding low frost pockets where cold air collects at night. Deciduous sorts that bloom before their foliage appears are displayed to best advantage if planted where they are viewed against a background of tall evergreens.

Other points to bear in mind are that magnolias do best in deep, fertile soil not excessively dry, but with good subsurface drainage. Sunny locations are to their liking, but they will stand part-day shade.

For landscape effects they are admirable as single specimens and in groups, but are not seen to advantage crowded among other trees or shrubs. The fringes of woodlands can be decorated pleasingly with magnolias. The Southern magnolia or bull-bay lends itself splendidly for espaliering against walls.

Cultivation. Little difficulty attends the cultivation of established magnolias. If conditions are right they pretty much take care of themselves. But these trees and shrubs are not as readily transplantable as many other sorts, and so it is important to give a little special attention to moving them. The difficulty is related to their thick, fleshy, wide-ranging roots. If transplanting is done when these are not ready

to immediately start into growth cut ends are likely to die back to an extent that the newly moved specimen is harmed, its life perhaps endangered. To avoid this, delay transplanting until the new leaf buds begin to open in spring. With largish specimens it is very advisable to root prune them a full year in advance of moving. After transplanting mulch the soil and take care that it is kept reasonably moist throughout the first summer.

Pruning on a regular scheduled basis is quite unnecessary except in the case of espaliered specimens. However, magnolias are not adversely affected by cutting and one should not hesitate to attend to any deemed necessary. Wounds usually heal quickly. Paint cuts more than 1 inch in diameter with tree wound paint. Need for pruning may result from storm damage or a desire to shape specimens or to limit them to size. Shaping is of special importance during their early years. The best time to prune is in spring after danger of severe freezing is over.

Dryness at the roots is inimicable to best success with magnolias. To counteract any tendency toward this it is helpful to keep the ground around them mulched. Deep soakings with water at intervals during dry spells are highly beneficial.

Propagation of species magnolias is best accomplished by seed. These do not retain vitality for long and must not be allowed to dry out before sowing. The recommended procedure is to free them of surrounding pulp, mix them with slightly damp sand, peat moss, or similar material and stratify them for four months at 40°F before sowing. Even then some may not germinate for several months. Hybrid sorts and selected varieties, and species when seeds are not available, are multiplied by grafting or budding deciduous sorts commonly on *M. kobus* and *M. acuminata*. Some kinds, notably varieties of *M. kobus*, *M. stellata*, and *M. loebneri*, come readily from summer cuttings planted under mist or in a propagating bed in a greenhouse or cold frame.

Pests and Diseases. The most prevalent of these is a large scale insect called magnolia scale and some leaf spot diseases. The first is controlled by dormant spraying with a scalecide (insecticide of a type effective against scales), the diseases by using a fungicide that controls leaf spot diseases.

MAGOLIACEAE — Magnolia Family. The dozen genera of deciduous and evergreen shrubs, trees, and woody vines of this family of dicotyledons include 230 species, natives of temperate and warmer parts of North America and eastern Asia. Included are many splendid ornamentals and some sources of good lumber. Among the best known are magnolias and tulip trees (*Liriodendron*). The genera *Schisandra* and *Kad-*

sura included here are by some segregated as the family SCHISANDRACEAE. Members of MAGNOLIACEAE have alternate, often large, lobeless or lobed, usually toothless leaves. Their usually solitary, terminal flowers, considered by botanists to be of a primitive type, have perianth parts without usually sharp distinction between sepals and petals in circles of three or more. There are generally six to many petals, commonly many stamens. The pistils, usually numerous and nearly or quite separate, are arranged on an elongated axis. The fruits are follicles or samaras frequently clustered as conelike structures. Genera cultivated are *Drimys, Kadsura, Liriodendron, Magnolia, Michelia, Pseudowintera, Schisandra, Talauma,* and *Tetracentron.*

MAHALA MAT is *Ceanothus prostratus.*

MAHALEB is *Prunus mahaleb.*

MAHERNIA. See Hermannia.

MAHOBERBERIS (Maho-bérberis). Although more interesting to the botanically curious than to seekers of first-rate decoratives, this hybrid shrub genus is not without ornamental appeal. It includes all results of the mating of *Mahonia* with *Berberis* and has a name composed from those of its parents. It belongs in the barberry family BERBERIDACEAE.

Originating as a seedling in a French nursery about 1850, *Mahoberberis neubertii* (syn. *Berberis neubertii*) developed from a seed borne by a plant of *Mahonia aquifolium* pollinated by *Berberis vulgaris.* Of rather loose habit, it has erect, spineless stems 4 to 6 feet tall. Its leaves are alternate and mostly undivided, but mixed with the undivided ones are some with three or sometimes five leaflets. Usually the foliage is thinner in texture than that of its *Mahonia* parent, but the leaves of younger shoots are stiffer and more definitely spined than the finely-toothed ones on older shoots. The undivided leaves and the leaflets are obovate-oblong and 1½ to 3 inches long.

Mahoberberis neubertii

These partially evergreen plants lose some of their foliage before winter. This probably reflects inner conflict between the genes received from the parents, evergreen (*Mahonia aquifolium*) and deciduous (*Berberis vulgaris*). Most authorities make no mention of *M. neubertii* flowering, but A. Osborn, late Assistant Curator of the Arboretum at the Royal Botanic Gardens, Kew, England, reports that it "bears yellow flowers in April and May." It has never produced fertile seeds. A century after *M. neubertii* appeared two other kinds were raised in Sweden, *M. aquicandidula,* with *Mahonia aquifolium* and *Berberis candidula* as parents, and *M. aquisargentii,* the parents of which are *Mahonia aquifolium* and *Berberis sargentiana.* In 1958 a kind similar to *M. aquisargentii* was raised in the United States and named *M. miethkeana.*

Garden Uses and Cultivation. As features of scientific interest and to give variety, mahoberberises may be planted in shrub collections. Hardy in southern New England, *M. neubertii* succeeds in part-shade or sun in well-drained, not excessively dry soil. Propagation is by summer cuttings in a greenhouse propagating bench provided with mild bottom heat and by layering. Pruning consists of cutting out old, worn-out branches in winter. Insufficient data are available about the other kinds. They probably are less hardy than *M. neubertii,* but otherwise may be expected to respond to the same conditions. Because *M. neubertii* is an alternate host of wheat rust fungus disease its planting is prohibited in wheat-growing areas. Information as to where it and other kinds may not be planted may be obtained from the Bureau of Entomology and Plant Quarantine, United States Department of Agriculture, Washington, D.C.

MAHOE. This is the common name of *Hibiscus tiliaceus* and *Melicytus ramiflorus.* Mountain mahoe is *Hibiscus elatus.*

MAHOGANY. See Swietenia. African-mahogany is *Detarium senegalense,* bastard-mahogany *Eucalyptus botryoides,* Hawaiian-mahogany *Acacia koa,* mountain-mahogany *Cercocarpus,* red-mahogany *Eucalyptus resinifera,* and swamp-mahogany *Eucalyptus robusta.*

MAHONIA (Ma-hònia)—Oregon-Grape. Mahonias were once included in closely related *Berberis,* and under that name they are rather commonly grown in gardens. The only constant difference is that the leaves of *Mahonia* are composed of three or more leaflets, whereas those of *Berberis* are undivided. In addition, mahonias never have spines on their stems whereas most berberises do. Both genera belong in the barberry family BERBERIDACEAE. The name commemorates one of America's distinguished early horticulturists, Bernard

M'Mahon of Philadelphia, who died in 1816.

Mahonias are evergreen shrubs or rarely small trees indigenous in North America, Central America, Cuba, and eastern and southeastern Asia. Numbering more than 100 species, they have alternate, leathery leaves with an uneven number of three or more, usually toothed leaflets arranged pinnately. The attractive, small yellow flowers are commonly in clusters of racemes, more rarely in solitary racemes, umbel-like clusters, or panicles of often considerable size. The flowers have nine sepals, six petals, six stamens, and one style. The stamens, like those of *Berberis,* are irritable and move inward when touched. The mostly black fruits generally appear bluish because of a waxy coating. Unfortunately, many mahonias are hosts to wheat rust fungus disease and planting them is prohibited in wheat-growing areas. They are under quarantine regulations of the United States Department of Agriculture. Fortunately some kinds are immune or highly resistant. These include *M. aquifolium* and *M. bealii.*

The Oregon-grape or holly mahonia (*M. aquifolium*) is very beautiful. From 3 to 6 feet tall or rarely taller, it has handsome foliage and dense, showy clusters of racemes, 1¼ to 3 inches long, of bright yellow flowers succeeded by nearly spherical,

Mahonia aquifolium

Mahonia aquifolium (flowers and foliage)

Mahonia aquifolium (fruits)

glaucous-blue berries up to ⅓ inch long. Its leaves, 4 to 10 inches long, have five to nine, rarely eleven, oblong-lanceolate to oblong-ovate leaflets 1¼ to 3 inches long and one-half as broad, shallowly-toothed and with slender spines along the margins. Their upper surfaces are very glossy. The undersides are paler and less lustrous. The leaflets are usually not crowded or overlapping, and the basal ones are ¾ inch or more from the bottom of the leafstalk. In fall the rich green of the foliage

Mahonia 'Golden Abundance'

Mahonia 'Golden Abundance' (flowers)

turns a pleasing purplish hue. Compact horticultural varieties have been distributed as *M. a. compacta* and *M. a.* 'Mayhan Strain', the latter said to come true from seeds. Native from California to Idaho and British Columbia, *M. aquifolium* and its variants are hardy in New England. Probably much of the stock grown in gardens as *M. aquifolium* represents hybrids between that species and *M. repens*. A handsome mahonia, presumably a variety or hybrid of *M. aquifolium*, deservedly popular in California, *M.* 'Golden Abundance' is a densely-foliaged shrub 5 to 6 feet tall. It has glossy green leaves with red midribs. Its plentiful large clusters of golden flowers are succeeded by attractive fruits.

Similar to *M. aquifolium*, but not hardy in the north, is **M. pinnata**, a native from Oregon to Baja California. An important distinction between this and *M. aquifolium* is that the flower stalks of *M. pinnata* have little bracts near their middles. It also differs in having duller leaves, 2 to 4½ inches long, with leaflets so crowded that they often overlap, and in its bottom leaflets being closer to the leafstalk than those of *M. aquifolium*. Occasionally the leaves have as many as seventeen leaflets, more rarely five to nine. They are lustrous on both surfaces and paler beneath than on

Mahonia pinnata

their tops. The racemes of yellow flowers, 1¼ to 2½ inches long, are clustered. The glaucous-blue berries are ¼ inch long. This species is 1 foot to 3½ feet tall. Variety *M. p. insularis* in the wild is 6 to 18 feet tall and supports itself by leaning on trees. Its leaves are more shallowly-toothed than those of the species. A hybrid between *M. pinnata* and *M. aquifolium*, **M. wagneri** is described as resembling the first-named, but hardier.

A creeping, suckering kind 6 to 9 inches tall that spreads by underground runners, **M. repens** is about as hardy as *M. aquifolium*. Its dull leaves, up to 10 inches long, have usually five leaflets, but sometimes three or seven. The leaflets are broad-ovate to oblong-ovate and up to 3½ inches

Mahonia repens

long by 1¾ inches broad. They have usually twelve or more bristle-tipped teeth on each side. The dense racemes of flowers, in clusters, are up to 3 inches in length. The glaucous-blue-black berries are ¼ to ⅓ inch long. This species ranges from California to New Mexico and British Columbia. It is somewhat variable and a few varieties have been named. Some may be hybrids between *M. repens* and *M. aquifolium*.

Another low, suckering kind, **M. nervosa**, from California to Idaho and British Columbia, is 1 foot to 2 or rarely 3 feet tall. A distinguishing feature is that it has persistent bud scales. Its leaves, in tufts at the ends of the stems, are 1 foot to 2 feet long or sometimes longer. They have seven to twenty-one ovate to ovate-lanceolate leaflets up to 3 inches long by one-half as wide, with six to twelve spiny teeth on each side. Lustrous gray-green on their upper sides, they are yellowish beneath. The erect, clustered racemes of bright yellow flowers are 3 to 9 inches long. The dark glaucous-blue berries are about ⅓ inch wide.

From the kinds discussed above *M. fremontii* and *M. nevinii* differ, among other ways, in having their flowers three to nine together in loose racemes rather than many together and densely crowded. Also, their leaflets are mostly up to ⅔ inch wide rather than larger. A very beautiful-foliaged plant, *M. fremontii* is 3 to 6 feet or sometimes taller, with rigid, erect branches. Its leaves are stiff, glaucous-blue-green, paler beneath than above, and dull on both surfaces. There are three to seven leaflets with usually three to five spines on each side that spread at diverse angles instead of approximately in one plane. The terminal leaflet, more or less ovate, and up to 1 inch long by about two-thirds as wide, is larger than the lateral ones. The small flowers are borne in racemes ¾ inch to 1½ inches long. They are succeeded by dry, spongy berries ½ inch or slightly more or less in diameter, and yellow to red when ripe. This desert and

Mahonia fremontii

Mahonia lomariifolia

semidesert species is indigenous from Arizona to Colorado, Utah, and California.

The dull blue-green leaves of *M. nevinii,* paler on their lower than their upper surfaces, differ from those of *M. fremontii* in being thinner, almost flat, and with their five to fifteen bristly spines on each side spreading in the plane of the leaf surface. The leaves, up to 3 inches long, mostly have three to five lanceolate or lanceolate-ovate leaflets ¾ inch to 1½ inches long. The racemes of small flowers are 1 inch to 2 inches long. The blooms are succeeded by juicy, yellowish-red to red berries up to ⅓ inch in diameter. This is an attractive sort.

Mahonia lomariifolia (trunks and leaves)

Mahonia nevinii

A few handsome Asian mahonias are cultivated. Most splendid of the entire genus is *M. lomariifolia,* native to western China and Burma. This is reported to attain on occasion heights of 30 or 40 feet in damp forest habitats, but to be no more than a shrub 4 to 8 feet tall in more exposed locations. In cultivation it commonly assumes the latter dimensions. It is beautiful in foliage, flower, and fruit. Unfortunately it is too tender to survive outdoors in the north. Its leaves are up to 2 feet long and have twelve to twenty pairs of rigid leaflets, with

the lowermost close to the bottom of the leafstalk. The leaflets, 2½ to 3½ inches long, and not over ¾ inch broad, have two to six sharp teeth on each margin. Developing late in the year, the flower spikes, 3 to 7 inches long, are in clusters of four to eight. The fruits are black with a waxy-blue coating. An intermediate hybrid between *M. lomariifolia* and *M. japonica* has been named *M.* 'Charity'.

Much older in cultivation than the last species discussed, *M. napaulensis* was brought from its native Nepal to Europe in the middle of the nineteenth century. It, too, is too tender to be grown outdoors in the north. From 8 to 20 feet tall, it has nearly stalkless leaves with five to eleven pairs of lustrous leaflets, the lowermost of which are very small and near the bottoms of the leafstalks. The larger ones, 2 to 4 inches long by 1 inch to 1½ inches broad, have four to ten teeth along each margin. In clusters of five to seven, the spikes, 5 inches to 1 foot in length, develop in fall and expand their blooms in early spring. The slightly egg-shaped fruits, ⅓ inch long, are bluish.

Two Asians that have been much confused are *M. japonica* and *M. bealei.* The latter is often grown under the name of the former, and vice versa. Although long cul-

tivated in Japan, *M. japonica* is not native there. It may be identical with the Taiwan *M. tikushiensis* and if so was probably brought to Japan from Taiwan centuries ago. It differs from *M. bealei* in having its flowers in pendulous, clustered racemes, 4 to 10 inches long, and in its much narrower terminal leaflets. Its leaves are up to 1½ feet long and have thirteen to nineteen narrowly-oblong-ovate to lanceolate leaflets with usually two to five spiny teeth on each side. The fruits are waxy-bluish-black.

The hardiest Asian mahonia in cultivation (it lives outdoors in sheltered locations in southern New England) is *M. bealei* (syn. *M. japonica bealei*). This native of China attains a height of up to 12 feet and has stout, erect stems. Its dull, rigid, bluish-green leaves, 1 foot to 1½ feet long, have nine to fifteen roundish ovate to ovate-oblong leaflets 2 to 4½ inches in length, usually with three to six big spiny teeth on each side. The lowermost leaflets are much smaller than those above. The largest, the terminal, conspicuously broad one, is stalked. The erect, crowded racemes of small, lemon-yellow, fragrant flowers are clustered and 3 to 6 inches long. The fruits are waxy-bluish-black.

Mahonia bealei

Mahonia bealei (fruits)

Garden and Landscape Uses. In regions where they luxuriate, mahonias are among the most beautiful and useful of evergreens, splendid for shrub beds, foundation plantings, backgrounds, and many other purposes. Low-growing *M. repens* is excellent as a groundcover. Unfortunately, few are hardy in the north and those that are must be afforded shelter with protection from wind and sun. In less harsh climates, such as that of California, all thrive in sun or part-shade. The most cold-resistant are *M. aquifolium, M. repens,* and *M. bealei.* At The New York Botanical Garden *M. fremontii* has lived outdoors for many years in a very sheltered courtyard. The beauty of these shrubs lies particularly in their handsome and durable foliage, but they also make good displays of blooms and fruits. The foliage of some species is very beautiful when cut for use in flower arrangements and other decorations. This is especially true of that of *M. aquifolium* when in fall it assumes its gorgeous shades of bronze and vinous-red.

Cultivation. Mahonias are not demanding shrubs. They succeed in a wide variety of soils provided they are fairly well drained and neither excessively wet nor dry. They are grateful for a reasonable organic content in their root run, and so, when preparing ground for their reception, it helps to spade in compost, peat moss, decayed manure, or other humus-forming additive with some generosity. Planting may be done in spring or early fall. In cold climates the former is preferable. Like most shrubs these respond to being kept mulched with compost, peat moss, or other suitable material. Pruning consists of cutting out old, worn-out branches and shortening any that become too long and straggly, after flowering. In most cases very little cutting is required. It is, however, practicable to keep *M. aquifolium* to a height of 2 to 3 feet by following a program of annual pruning. Propagation is by seeds sown in sandy peaty soil in a cold frame or cool greenhouse as soon as the seeds are ripe. Before sowing they are freed from their surrounding pulp. Cuttings of most kinds root fairly easily if taken in late summer or early fall and planted in a greenhouse propagating bench with a little bottom heat, or under mist. Suckering kinds are also easily increased by division in spring.

MAIANTHEMUM (Maí-anthemum)—Wild-Lily-of-the-Valley or False-Lily-of-the-Valley. This genus is unusual in the lily family LILIACEAE in that its flowers are not six- or three-parted, but have four separate, spreading, petal-like segments, a pattern found also in *Aspidistra,* of the same family. The name *Maianthemum* comes from the Latin *maius,* May, and the Greek *anthemon,* a flower. It refers to the time of blooming.

Maianthemums are deciduous, low, herbaceous perennials with slender roots and rhizomes and erect, branchless, few-leaved stems bearing alternate, more or less heart-shaped to ovate leaves and terminal racemes of small white flowers with four slender-stalked stamens. The fruits are berries containing one or two seeds. There are three species.

Common in moist woods in Canada and over much of the eastern and central United States, **M. canadense** is a carpeting plant that attains a maximum height when in bloom of 4 to 8 inches. Its leaves, the basal ones with stalks up to 4 inches in length, the stem ones stalkless or the lowermost very short-stalked, have blades with a comparatively narrow opening between the basal lobes, less than one-eighth

Maianthemum canadense

Maianthemum canadense (flowers)

Maianthemum canadense (fruits)

as long as the leaf blades. The other cultivated kinds have broader leaf sinuses, one-eighth to one-half as long as the leaf blade. The fragrant flowers of *M. canadense* are in clusters about 2 inches long and are succeeded by light red fruits. Variety *M. c. interius* has larger leaves fringed with hairs and hairy on their undersides and stalks; it is reported to bloom two weeks later than the typical species.

Attractive **M. bifolium** is a wide-ranging native of Europe and northern Asia including Japan. In bloom it may be 9 inches tall. The upper portions of its stems and the main axis of the flower cluster are usually clothed with stiff, white hairs. The triangular-ovate basal leaves, up to 2½ inches in length, have stalks 2 inches long or longer. The stem leaves are sometimes almost or quite stalkless. The fruits are red. The other cultivated kind, **M. kamtschaticum** (syns. *M. bifolia kamtschatica, M. dilatatum*) occurs as a native from California and Idaho to Alaska, Japan, and continental northeast Asia. From *M. bifolium* it differs in being hairless, having leaf blades up to 5 inches long, and attaining a height, when in bloom, of 1¼ feet.

Garden Uses. These hardy, spring-blooming plants are excellent for colonizing in woodlands and other shaded places where they have room to spread and form considerable mats. They are suitable for use beneath trees and shrubbery, in rock gardens and other informal areas, and, in regions where they are native, in wild flower gardens. They possess a delicacy of appearance and refinement that is appealing.

Cultivation. Somewhat acid, humus-rich soil on the moistish side is most agreeable to these plants. They thrive even in heavy shade and can be transplanted without difficulty if fairly large sods or mats are moved. Propagation is by division in early fall or early spring or by sowing seeds in sandy peaty soil in fall or spring. Seeding may be done in a shaded cold frame, cool greenhouse, or in an outdoor bed protected from disturbance by animals or from other causes. Practically no routine attention is needed if the plants are happily located. Occasional weeds or volunteer seedlings of other plants must be removed, and a light mulch of sifted leaf mold, peat moss, or compost applied in fall or early spring is beneficial.

MAIDEN. Also known as a whip, a maiden is a one-year-old, single-stemmed tree or shrub raised as an understock upon which to graft or bud another species or variety.

MAIDENHAIR. As part of their common names, the word maidenhair applies to these plants: maidenhair fern (*Adiantum*), maidenhair spleenwort (*Asplenium trichomanes*), maidenhair tree (*Ginkgo biloba*), and maidenhair vine (*Muehlenbeckia complexa*).

MAIDS, MAIDEN, and MAIDEN'S. These words appear in the common names of these plants: red maids (*Calandrinia ciliata menziesii*), maiden pink (*Dianthus deltoides*), and maiden's wreath (*Francoa ramosa*).

MAIHUENIA (Mai-huènia). The five species of *Maihuenia*, of the cactus family CACTACEAE, all natives of Argentina and Chile, are rather poorly defined. The name is an adaptation of a native one.

These are low, clumping, or densely mounded plants with fleshy stems composed of spherical or short-cylindrical joints furnished with tiny, cylindrical or awl-shaped, persistent leaves. The areoles (spine-bearing cushions) have three or fewer spines and woolly hairs. Unlike those of *Opuntia*, they are without glochids (minute, barbed, bristle-like spines). The yellow or red flowers are solitary and stalkless and are at or close to the apexes of the stems. They have scaly calyx tubes. The petals, spreading to upright, are longer than the stamens and style. The more or less fleshy fruits have scattered scales.

In aspect much like a cylindrical-stemmed *Opuntia*, slow-growing *M. poeppigii* forms wide mats of white-spined, green stems about 2½ inches long, by ½ inch thick or a little thicker. Three spines ½ to ¾ inch long sprout from each areole. Its flowers are yellow. The thin-skinned, usually juicy fruits, about 2 inches long, bear small, scattered, persistent leaves.

Garden Uses and Cultivation. Suitable for inclusion in collections of succulents, maihuenias respond to conditions and care that suit nonhardy opuntias. For more information see Cactuses.

MAILE. See Alyxia.

MAJORANA. Plants previously named *Majorana* are included in Origanum.

MAKAMAKA is *Ackama rosaefolia.*

MALABAR NIGHTSHADE. See Basella.

MALACOCARPUS. See Wigginsia.

MALACOTHAMNUS (Malaco-thámnus). Shrubs and subshrubs with usually long, flexuous stems comprise *Malacothamnus*, a genus of about twenty species of the southwestern United States and Mexico and one native in Chile. They belong to the mallow family MALVACEAE. The name comes from the Greek *malakos*, soft or pliant, and *thamnos*, a shrub, and alludes to the characteristic growth.

Malacothamnuses have stems more or less furnished with stellate (starry) hairs, and leaves to a greater or lesser extent palmately- (in hand-fashion) lobed. Their pink to lavender blooms are solitary or several together in spikes or panicles from the leaf axils. Below the calyx is a collar of small bracts. The blooms have five sepals, five petals, numerous stamens, the stalks of which are joined into a tube, and fruits of several to many sections (carpels) that when mature split into halves. This does not happen in woody species of closely related *Malvastrum*, but does in one yellow-flowered annual kind.

Native to California, *M. davidsonii* (syn. *Malvastrum davidsonii*) is a coarse, stout-branched shrub 6 to 15 feet tall. It has thick, broadly-heart-shaped, shallowly-three- to five-lobed or five-angled, densely-hairy leaves 1 inch to 4 inches wide. The very many pink flowers are in panicles of short racemes. The blooms have petals ¼ to ½ inch long. This is native in dry sandy and stony washes. An inhabitant of California and Baja California, *M. fasciculatus* (syn. *Malvastrum fasciculatum*) is an erect shrub up to 6 feet tall or sometimes taller. It has slender, mostly pubescent branches and generally three- to seven-lobed, but sometimes lobeless, thin to leathery leaves rarely over 2 inches long and wide. They have paler under than upper surfaces. The light to deep mauve flowers, many together in interrupted spikes or loose panicles, are up to 1½ inches in diameter.

Garden and Landscape Uses and Cultivation. In warm, dry climates the species described are planted for ornament. They succeed in well-drained soil in sunny locations and may be increased by seed and by cuttings.

MALACOTHRIX (Mala-cóthrix) — Desert-Dandelion. Fifteen to twenty species of annuals, herbaceous perennials, and sub-shrubby plants of the daisy family COMPOSITAE constitute *Malacothrix*. All are natives of western North America. The name comes from the Greek *malakos*, soft, and *thrix*, hair.

In most kinds the foliage is basal and the stalks of the flower heads are leafless, but some have leafy flower stalks. The leaves are toothed, or pinnately-lobed or -dissected. Solitary or in panicles, the yellow, white, or pink flower heads are of small to medium size and, like dandelions, are composed of all strap-shaped florets. They have no central eye of disk florets as do daisies. Usually in the bud stage the flower heads are nodding. The seedlike fruits are achenes.

An annual 6 inches to 1 foot or a little more in height, *M. californica* has dense basal rosettes of foliage, markedly woolly-hairy when young. The leaves, 2½ to 4½ inches long, are pinnately-lobed into almost threadlike linear segments. The pale yellow, fragrant flower heads, solitary on leafless, branchless stalks, are about 1¾ inches in diameter. They open only in sun. This species occupies dry, sandy soils from California to Idaho and Arizona.

Desert-dandelion (*M. glabrata*) is much like the last, but has flower stalks that are few-branched and bear two or more heads as well as a few leaves. The stems and foliage are without hairs. From 4 inches to 1¼ feet tall, this inhabits deserts from California to Idaho and Arizona.

Perennial *M. saxatilis* has several variants of which the Carmel variety *M. s. arachnoidea* is the most attractive. Up to 2 feet tall, the entire plant is densely-woolly-hairy. It has several leafy stems, woody toward their bases, and leaves broadly- to linear-lanceolate and up to 4 inches long. The lower leaves are often pinnately-lobed. The white to pink flower heads, 1½ inches across, are few together. From *M. s. arachnoidea* typical *M. saxatilis* and other varieties of it differ in being less conspicuously hairy or hairless.

Garden Uses. Annual species of this genus are attractive in flower gardens where they may be used effectively at the fronts of borders, as edgings, and for furnishing sunny slopes. The perennial described is reliably hardy only in mild, dryish climates. It is appropriate for flower beds and naturalistic plantings.

Cultivation. These plants need full sun and thoroughly drained soil. They are raised from seeds. Those of the annuals are sown in early spring, or in regions of mild winters in fall, where the plants are to remain, and the seedlings are thinned sufficiently to prevent harmful overcrowding. Seeds of perennials may be sown in spring or early summer, and the seedlings, while small, transplanted to nursery beds, to be transferred in fall or spring to permanent locations.

MALAGAS-LILY is *Cybistetes longifolia.*

MALANGA. See Xanthosoma.

MALATHION. This contact insecticide is considered the safest of the sorts called organic phosphates, some of which, parathion for example, are so toxic that their general use is forbidden by law. Malathion is effective against many insects, but somewhat less so against mites. It has low toxicity for humans and other mammals, but kills bees and certain other beneficial insects. It is available in sprays, aerosols, and dusts, always to be used in strict accordance with the manufacturer's directions.

MALAXIS (Mal-áxis)—Adder's Mouth. Of nearly cosmopolitan distribution in the wild, but not occurring in Australia or New Zealand, *Malaxis*, of the orchid family ORCHIDACEAE, includes kinds previously segregated as *Microstylis*. It comprises possibly 300 species. Its name, from the Greek *malakos*, weak or delicate, alludes to the appearance of some species.

Of minor horticultural significance, the genus consists of ground orchids, mostly with tubers, with branchless stems that bear one to few leaves and terminate in a raceme of tiny blooms. The flowers have three spreading sepals, two spreading petals, and a lip, cleft or not, with earlike appendages at its base.

Green adder's mouth (*M. unifolia* syn. *Microstylis unifolia*) occurs in bogs and damp woodlands from eastern North America to Mexico and the West Indies. Its stems, up to about 1 foot tall, have near their middles one or sometimes two ovate-orbicular to ovate-lanceolate leaves up to 3½ inches long. The crowded, cylindrical racemes, up to about 4 inches long, of tiny greenish blooms, have threadlike, reflexed petals and a three-lobed lip. A native of damp, calcareous soil from Virginia to Florida and in the Bahamas and West Indies, **M. spicata** (syns. *M. floridana*, *Microstylis floridana*) has a few small, fleshy pseudobulbs and, in pairs, ovate to nearly circular, glossy leaves 1 inch to 4 inches long and with midribs noticeably keeled on their undersides. From 3 inches to rather more than 1 foot tall, the erect flowering stalks terminate in loose racemes of few to many ¼-inch-long flowers with green sepals and petals and a pale yellow to orange-red lip.

Malaxis calophylla

Malaxis lowii

Malaxis latifolia

Malaxis soulei, left; *M. ocreata*, right

Malaxis spicata

Native to the Malay Peninsula and Thailand, **M. calophylla** (syn. *Microstylis calophylla*) has short, conical pseudobulbs each with two or three pointed-broad-elliptic leaves up to 6 inches long and 2 inches broad and waved or crisped along their margins. Their upper surfaces are yellowish-green to light bronze striped down their centers with brown, their undersides are reddish. The ¼-inch-long flowers, in dense, cylindrical spikes lifted on stalks to a height of almost 1 foot, have greenish, cream-colored, light pink, or pale violet sepals and petals and usually a yellow-green lip. Native to tropical Asia and Polynesia, **M. latifolia** has clustered pseudobulbs 3 to 4 inches long, each with usually five pointed-elliptic, wavy-margined leaves with blades 5 to 9 inches long by approximately one-third as broad. The dense, cylindrical spikes of yellowish-green to pur-

plish-chocolate flowers top slender, erect stalks up to 9 inches long. Delightful **M. lowii** (syn. *Microstylis lowii*), of Borneo, has a short, erect stem furnished with spreading, essentially stalkless, ovate leaves 3 to 4 inches long. They are light brown to dark-coppery-brown with a broad, grayish center stripe and have crisped margins. The flowers are golden-yellow or purple with the earlike appendages of the lip yellowish. Mexican **M. ocreata** (syn. *Microstylis ocreata*) has two erect, stalkless, elliptic leaves, 2 to 3 inches long, and with their bases clasped by a short bract. The pencil-thin, erect flower spike overtops the leaves to attain a height of 6 to 9 inches. Its numerous minute blooms are green or are yellow with a purple lip. A native of the Seychelles **M. seychellarum**, in bloom 8 to 9 inches tall, has three or four pointed-elliptic, thinnish leaves about 4 inches long by 1¾ inches wide, longitudinally pleated, and with sheathing bases. The stalk of the erect, slender spike of tiny flowers is wine-purple. The flowers, at first pale green, gradually become wine-purple. Native to the southwestern United States and Mexico, **M. soulei** (syn. *Microstylis montana*) has a tuber about 1 inch in diameter and one or two blunt, broad-elliptic to ovate leaves with sheathing bases and blades about 2¾

Malaxis seychellarum

inches long by 1½ inches wide. The many little, stalkless flowers are in an erect, slender, tail-like spike 7 to 8 inches tall.

Garden Uses and Cultivation. The North American species described above is appropriate for native plant gardens and similar places where conditions approximating those under which it grows in the wild can be afforded. The others discussed here are suitable for humid, warm greenhouses. They respond to the care suggested for *Phaius*. For more information see Orchids.

MALAY. The word Malay occurs as part of the common names of the following plants: Malay-apple (*Syzygium malaccensis*), Malay-ginger (*Costus speciosus*), and Malay jewel vine (*Derris scandens*).

MALCOLM-STOCK. See Malcomia.

MALCOLMIA (Malcòlm-ia) — Malcolm-Stock. Virginia-Stock. Despite its popular name, Virginia-stock is not a native of America nor is it nearly as popular a garden plant in North America as in the British Isles and other parts of northern Europe. Belonging in the genus *Malcolmia*, it hails from the Mediterranean region and is one of a genus of thirty-five species that belong in the mustard family CRUCIFERAE. Its name honors William Malcolm, an English horticulturist of the eighteenth century. Virginia-stock was extremely popular in Europe in Victorian times and in the early years of the present century.

Malcolmias are low annuals and herbaceous perennials, usually branched and hairy or sometimes hairless. They have alternate, undivided, lobeless or pinnately-lobed leaves. The flowers, in terminal racemes, have four erect sepals, four spreading petals, and six stamens, four of which are longer than the others. There is no style. The stigma is deeply-two-lobed. The fruits are podlike.

The Virginia-stock (*M. maritima*) has slender, branched stems, attains a height of about 6 inches, and blooms profusely. Its leaves are pubescent, blunt-elliptic or blunt-oblong, and lobeless. The flowers are white, pale yellow, pink, lavender, or red. About ¾ inch in diameter, they are borne in great abundance. Other less common species are *M. flexuosa,* of the Mediterranean region, which is similar to the Virginia-stock in general appearance, but has curved seed pods and differs in other minor characteristics; *M. bicolor,* from Greece, a bushy perennial, 6 inches tall, with softly-hairy, lanceolate to ovate leaves and pink or yellow flowers; and *M. littorea,* also perennial, of the Mediterranean region, 1 foot tall, with pointed, narrow, white-hairy leaves and showy purple-pink blooms. Both perennial kinds bloom freely the first year from seeds and are usually treated as annuals.

Garden Uses and Cultivation. As easy to grow as sweet-alyssum, these pretty annuals and plants grown as annuals are especially well suited for edgings to paths, for patches at the fronts of flower borders, and for rock gardens. The Virginia-stock in particular makes a gay, colorful carpet of bloom; the others are not quite as showy. They bloom best under fairly cool conditions. They do not prosper in hot, humid weather, especially when high temperatures prevail at night. Because of this in many parts of North America the seeds should be sown outdoors as early as possible in spring or even in late fall to remain dormant in the ground all winter and germinate in earliest spring. Where summers are comparatively cool, successful sowings can be made to assure bloom from late spring to frost. Malcolm-stocks grow well in any ordinary garden soil that is well drained and not excessively wet. They are at their best in one that is not too fertile and nearly neutral or slightly alkaline; the addition of lime to acid soils is beneficial for these plants. Sowing consists of scattering the seed thinly and raking it into the soil surface. The young plants are thinned to stand 3 inches apart. No other care is needed. If the ground where malcolm-stocks have grown is left undisturbed, volunteer seedlings are likely to appear abundantly the following year.

MALE. This word is used in the colloquial names of these plants: male bamboo (*Dendrocalamus strictus*), male berry (*Lyonia ligustrina*), and male fern (*Dryopteris filix-mas*).

MALEPHORA (Maléph-ora). The plants of the *Mesembryanthemum* relationship formerly identified as *Hymenocyclus* are now *Malephora*. There are nine species, natives of southern Africa and belonging to the carpetweed family AIZOACEAE. They much resemble *Lampranthus,* but have more pliable leaves, often with a bluish, waxy coating. The name from the Greek *male*, armhole, and *pherein*, to bear, presumably refers to the fruits.

Malephoras are succulent, nonhardy subshrubs, erect or procumbent, with freely-branching, often rooting, woody stems and opposite, soft, fleshy leaves, the pairs united at their bases. Long in comparison to their thickness, the leaves are semicylindrical to triangular in section. They are not speckled with dots. The stalked flowers, terminal or from the leaf axils, are usually yellow, less often pink. Usually they have only four sepals and up to eight feathery stigmas. Of somewhat daisy-like aspect, unlike daisies they are single blooms rather than heads of florets, and are from under 1 inch to 2 inches in diameter. The fruits are capsules.

Admired for its handsome displays of terminal, solitary 1¼-inch-wide blooms, yellow-faced, and reddened on their outsides to give an over-all coppery-saffron effect, *M. crocea* (syn. *Hymenocyclus croceus*) has 1-foot-long, lumpy stems closely strung with short, erect shoots that have bluntish, waxy-mealy, light green, slightly three-angled leaves 1 inch to nearly 2 inches long and ¼ inch wide. Bright red reverses to the petals and redder foliage than the species distinguish even more vigorous *M. c. purpureo-crocea* (syn. *Hymenocyclus purpureocroceus*). Less robust than *M. crocea* and its variety, *M. lutea* is erect and up to 1 foot tall. It has stems with many short shoots

Malephora crocea

with spreading, three-angled, tapering, curved leaves 1 inch to 1¾ inches long by about ⅙ inch wide. They are yellowish-green and have a white-waxy coating. The orange-yellow flowers are solitary, terminal, and 1 inch in diameter. Much like the last, and perhaps only a variety of it, *M. luteola* (syn. *Hymenocyclus luteolus*) has smaller, yellow flowers.

Also in cultivation, *M. herrei* (syn. *Hymenocyclus herrei*) has mostly prostrate branches and erect shoots, with the alternate pairs of opposite leaves set at right angles to each other. The leaves are green, up to 2 inches long by one-tenth as wide, and triangular in section. The 2-inch-wide flowers, golden-yellow with the undersides of their petals stained orange, come from the leaf axils. Its somewhat lumpy stems rigid, prostrate, and 1 foot to 1½ feet long, *M. thunbergii* (syn. *Hymenocyclus thunbergii*) has bluntly-three angled, rough-surfaced leaves, narrowed to their apexes, up to over 2 inches in length and ⅓ inch wide. They are green, with reddish bases. The solitary, terminal, yellow flowers, approximately 1½ inches wide, open around noon. At first erect, later spreading, the 5- to 10-inch-long branches of *M. latipetala* bear sharp-edged, purplish leaves 1 inch or so long by under ¼ inch wide. Not opening until evening, its yellow or purplish blooms are 1¼ to 1½ inches across. Up to 1 foot tall, *M. englerana* has waxy-coated, bluntly-three-angled, green leaves up to approximately 1½ inches long that are arched upward. Its flowers, solitary at the shoot ends and ¾ inch wide, are orange-yellow with orange-red undersides to the petals.

Garden and Landscape Uses and Cultivation. Malephoras are among the best of the *Mesembryanthemum* clan for creating colorful displays on sunny slopes, banks, rock gardens, and at other well-drained sites in warm semidesert and desert climates. They make effective ribbon borders or edgings. In southern California they are used as roadside groundcovers. These plants are also suitable for greenhouses, where they flourish under conditions that suit cactuses and other succulents. Trailing kinds, such as *M. herrei*, are effective in hanging baskets. Most kinds grow with great rapidity. Cuttings, transplanting rooted portions from established plants, and seed afford sure means of increase. For more information see the Encyclopedia entry Succulents.

MALESHERBIA (Malesh-èrbia). Thirty-five species of *Malesherbia* constitute the only genus of the malesherbia family MALESH-ERBIACEAE, a group related to the passion flower family PASSIFLORACEAE from which it differs in the styles of its flowers being more deeply inserted and widely separated. Its name commemorates the French statesman Chretien de Malesherbes, who died in 1794.

The sorts of *Malesherbia* are subshrubs with alternate, often deeply-lobed leaves and often showy yellow or blue flowers in panicles or clusters. The blooms have a five-lobed, bell- to top-shaped calyx, five petals, a slightly-toothed corona (crown), five stamens, and three or four styles. The fruits are capsules.

A native of Chile *M. linearifolia* (syn. *Gynopleura linearifolia*) is 1 foot to 1½ feet tall. It has stalkless, linear to narrow-elliptic leaves 1½ to 3 inches long. The 1-inch-wide flowers, in terminal panicles, have a green-striped perianth tube, pale rosy-lavender, petal-like sepals, and pale blue petals.

Malesherbia linearifolia

Garden Uses and Cultivation. The species described here is for outdoor gardens in places, such as California, with mild, dryish climates. It may also be grown in pots in a cool greenhouse. Although perennial, it gives good results when treated as an annual. It prospers in well-drained, sandy peaty soil.

MALESHERBIACEAE. The characteristics of the malesherbia family MALESHERBIACEAE are those of its only genus, *Malesherbia*.

MALLEE. In Australia several low species of *Eucalyptus* are called mallees.

MALLING STOCKS, EAST. See Dwarfing Stocks.

MALLOTUS (Mal-lòtus). Related to *Ricinus* and chiefly native of the tropics of the Old World, *Mallotus*, of the spurge family EU-PHORBIACEAE, contains nearly 150 species. Its name, alluding to the white-spiny fruits of some kinds, comes from the Greek *mallotos*, woolly.

Mallotuses are trees and shrubs with alternate or opposite, undivided, sometimes three-lobed, stalked leaves. Their small flowers, in spikes or panicles, are unisexual and without petals. The males have numerous stamens, the females three styles. The fruits are capsules.

Native to Australia, the Philippine Islands, and islands of the Pacific, *M. ricinoides* is a tall shrub or tree with broadly-ovate leaves up to 10 inches across, which when young are felted beneath with brown hairs. Its flowers are in spikelike or broader panicles 2 to 6 inches long. Native to China, Korea, Japan, the Ryukyu Islands, and Taiwan, *M. japonicus* is a tree with pointed-broad-ovate leaves, their blades up to about 8 inches long. Its flowers are in panicles up to 8 inches in length.

Garden and Landscape Uses and Cultivation. The sorts described are occasionally planted in warm countries as ornamentals and succeed in sun or part-shade in ordinary soils. Propagation is by seed and by cuttings.

MALLOW. See Malva. Plants not of the genus *Malva* that have common names of which the word mallow is a part include these: desert-mallow, globe-mallow, prairie-mallow (*Sphaeralcea*), jews'-mallow (*Corchorus olitorius*), marsh-mallow (*Althaea officinalis* and *Hibiscus moscheutos palustris*), musk-mallow (*Abelmoschus moschatus*), poppy-mallow (*Callirhoe*), rose-mallow (*Hibiscus moscheutos*, *H. m. palustris*, and *Lavatera trimestris*), Texas- or wax-mallow (*Malvaviscus arboreus drummondii*), tree-mallow (*Lavatera arborea*), and Virginia-mallow (*Sida hermaphrodita*). The common name musk mallow is applied to a true mallow (*Malva moschata*).

MALOPE (Málop-e). The four species of Mediterranean region, mallow-like annuals that constitute *Malope* belong to the mallow family MALVACEAE. The name was used by Pliny for a kind of mallow.

Malopes are hairy or hairless and have alternate, three-lobed or lobeless leaves and usually showy, shallow, saucer-shaped flowers, white, pink, or rosy-purple. Solitary from the leaf axils and long-stalked, the blooms have three large, heart-shaped, leafy bracts and five separate petals. Like those of other members of the family, their

many stamens are united in a tube around the pistil. At its top the tube frays into many anther-bearing filaments. The style is branched. The fruits at maturity separate into many dry carpels.

Most commonly cultivated are *M. trifida* and its varieties. These are 2 to 3 feet tall, and have erect, branching stems and three-lobed, toothed, rounded, hairless leaves 2 to 3 inches across. The blooms are 2½ to 3 inches in diameter. The species grows wild in sandy soils in Spain and North Africa. About 1 foot tall, *M. malacoides* has toothed or pinnately-cleft, oblong-lanceolate to ovate leaves, the upper sometimes three-lobed, and purple-tinged, and rose-pink flowers 1½ to 2 inches wide.

Malope trifida

Malope malacoides

Garden Uses. Malopes are excellent flower garden annuals, succeeding best under comparatively cool conditions and usually failing with the onset of hot, humid weather. The cut flowers last well in water. In addition to their usefulness outdoors, when grown in cool greenhouses they make attractive pot plants for late winter and early spring display. They succeed in any ordinary, well-drained garden soil in full sun.

Cultivation. Seeds are sown outdoors in earliest spring where the plants are to bloom, and the seedlings are thinned to about 9 inches apart. In regions of fairly cool summers, later sowings can be made to provide a succession of flowering plants. This is especially desirable when malopes are grown for cut flowers. Little care is needed other than that necessary to keep down weeds and to provide water in very dry weather. Ordinarily, staking is not required. The blooming season is extended if faded flowers are removed promptly, before seed heads form.

For greenhouse cultivation seeds are sown in light soil in a temperature of about 60°F from late August to October and in January. Plants from the earliest sowings may be finished in 8-inch pots, those from January sowings in containers 5 or 6 inches in diameter. For cut flowers they may be planted about 6 inches apart in beds or benches. The soil must be porous, well drained, and moderately rather than very fertile. A little lime added to soils that are acid is helpful. The seedlings, as soon as they are large enough to handle comfortably, are transplanted individually to small pots. When they are big enough and well rooted, they are transferred to beds or benches or are potted into successively larger pots until those in which they are to bloom are attained. No pinching is needed, but as their stems lengthen staking becomes necessary. Water moderately through the winter; constantly wet soil is harmful. As spring advances more generous watering is needed and plants that have filled their available soil with roots benefit from weekly applications of dilute liquid fertilizer. At all times malopes must be grown in full sun. A winter night temperature in the greenhouse of 50°F is adequate, with a rise of five degrees on dull days and ten degrees on sunny days permitted. The atmosphere should be dryish, never excessively humid.

Diseases and Pests. Malopes are sometimes affected by rust disease. The most likely insect pests to prove troublesome are aphids.

MALPIGHIA (Mal-píghia) — Barbados-Cherry, Acerola. The genus *Malpighia* occurs in the wild from the southern United States to the West Indies and tropical America. It belongs in the malpighia family MALPIGHIACEAE, a group chiefly confined to the tropics. There are thirty-five species. The name commemorates Marcello Malpighi, Italian naturalist, who died in 1693.

Malpighias are trees and shrubs with opposite, undivided, short-stalked, spiny-toothed or toothless leaves and, usually in axillary clusters but sometimes solitary, red, purple, or white blooms succeeded by berry-like fruits, technically drupes. The flowers are bisexual. Each has a calyx of five sepals with up to ten large glands, and five petals that narrow to slender claws at their bases. There are ten stamens and three styles. Some malpighias, but not those here described, have stinging hairs.

Barbados-cherry (*M. glabra*) is a variable, slender-branched hairless shrub up to 10 feet high and bushy. Its toothless, ovate to elliptic-lanceolate leaves 1 inch to 3 inches long are lustrous dark green above, paler on their undersides, and without teeth. The ½-inch-wide flowers are produced in clusters of three to eight. They are pink and have petals with more or less fringed margins. About the size of small cherries, the acid-flavored, thin-skinned, pulpy fruits, which are used in jams, pre-

Malpighia glabra

Malpighia glabra (flowers)

Malpighia glabra (fruits)

serves, beverages, and ices, contain three four-angled seeds. The Barbados-cherry is native from southern Texas to northern South America and the West Indies.

Acerola (*M. punicifolia*) is a South American and West Indian shrub or small tree with elliptic to oblongish toothless leaves, 1 inch to 3 inches in length, and small clusters of ½-inch-wide, pink, lilac, or white flowers. This species is cultivated for the high vitamin C content of its nearly spherical, cherry-like, bright red fruits, about ½ inch in diameter. At one time it was grown commercially in Hawaii, but the introduction of synthetic vitamins led to the abandonment of the project.

A popular ornamental, *M. coccigera*, a native of the West Indies, is an evergreen, hairless shrub commonly not over 1 foot to 3 feet, but sometimes 6 feet tall. Rather loose to compact, it has spiny-toothed, holly-like leaves with which are sometimes intermingled a few toothless ones, up to ¾ inch long, and broad-elliptic to obovate. Their upper surfaces are rich shining-green, beneath they are dull. Solitary, or two or sometimes more together, the fringe-petaled flowers are pink and ½ inch in diameter. Almost spherical, the red fruits are ⅓ inch in diameter.

Garden and Landscape Uses. In addition to the usefulness of the Barbados-cherry and acerola as edible fruits, they and *M. coccigera* are attractive ornamentals in tropical and essentially frostless subtropical climates. The last-mentioned is excellent for foundation plantings and fronting shrub borders and, because it stands shearing well, is a good low hedge plant. Malpighias are grown to some extent in greenhouses, and *M. coccigera*, as a window plant.

Cultivation. Malpighias are not fussy. They prosper in almost any reasonably fertile, well-drained, and not excessively dry soil. Full sun or part-day shade suit them. They are readily multiplied by cuttings and seed. Except to shape the plants, limit their size, or grow them as hedges, no pruning is needed. Regular shearing of formal hedges is a necessary routine.

In greenhouses and window gardens these plants respond to fertile, porous, well-drained soil kept moderately moist, a fairly humid atmosphere, and shade from strong summer sun. Well-rooted specimens benefit from regular applications of dilute liquid fertilizer. On winter nights a temperature of 55 to 60°F is satisfactory, with five to fifteen degrees increase by day allowed. At other seasons higher temperatures are in order. Pruning to limit size and to shape the specimens is done in late winter, and at that time needed repotting should be given attention.

MALPIGHIACEAE—Malpighia Family. Sixty genera accounting for 800 species of dicotyledons belong here. Shrubs, small trees, and many woody vines of the tropics, subtropics, and warm-temperate regions, their kinds are most numerous in South America. They are frequently clothed with branched, sometimes stinging hairs and most usually have opposite, undivided leaves often with glands, more rarely leaves that are alternate or in whorls (circles) of three.

The symmetrical or asymmetrical, frequently showy flowers are variously arranged, often in raceme-like inflorescences. Each has a five-parted calyx sometimes with large glands on its outside, five unequal, toothed or fringed petals generally narrowed toward their bases into stemlike claws, ten or fewer stamens or stamens and staminodes (nonfunctioning stamens), and two to five but most commonly three styles. The fruits, generally of three nutlike parts, less often are samaras, berries, or drupes. Genera cultivated are *Acridocarpus*, *Galphimia*, *Heteropterys*, *Lagunaria*, *Malpighia*, and *Stigmaphyllon*.

MALTESE CROSS is *Lychnis chalcedonica*.

MALUS (Mà-lus)—Apple, Crab Apple. Apples and crab apples are among the most important and most beautiful ornamental flowering and fruiting trees of temperate climates. The genus *Malus* they constitute belongs to the rose family ROSACEAE. It comprises thirty-five species, natives of the northern hemisphere, extending in the United States as far south as Florida and Texas. The name is an ancient Latin one for the apple. In addition to the natural species, there are numerous pomological varieties (orchard apples and crab apples) and great numbers of varieties and hybrids admired for their splendid ornamental qualities. Apples are closely related to pears (*Pyrus*), the two being by some botanists united. The chief differences, not completely exclusive, are that the styles of the flowers of *Malus* are joined at their bases and the fruits, usually apple- rather than pear-shaped, contain few or no grit cells such as are plentiful in pears.

Apples and crab apples, the last name usually restricted to kinds with fruits under about 2 inches in diameter, are deciduous or rarely semievergreen trees or occasionally shrubs. They have alternate, toothed or lobed leaves and white, pink, or carmine-red flowers in umbel-like racemes. The blooms, according to kind, come before or with the foliage. They have a five-lobed calyx, five usually obovate to nearly round petals, fifteen to fifty stamens with generally yellow anthers, and two to five styles, their bases joined. The fleshy fruits, technically pomes, are typified by the familiar orchard apples and crab apples. Those of all kinds are edible but unless cooked and sweetened not all are palatable. In practice, only the fruits of orchard apples and or-

chard crab apples are used for food and for making cider. Those of the numerous kinds of *Malus* grown primarily for ornament are not commonly eaten. Apple wood is splendid firewood.

The common orchard apple is derived from *M. pumila* or hybrids of it and *M. sylvestris*. There are numerous pomological varieties distinguished by such names as 'Winesap', 'Cortland', and 'Delicious'. Seedlings, generally inferior to named va-

The common orchard apple: (a) Trunk and branching pattern

(b) In bloom

(c) In fruit

rieties, occur spontaneously in North America. Orchard apples are round-headed trees 20 to 40 feet tall, often picturesque, especially when old. Of sturdy appearance, they are beautiful in blossom and fruit. They have thickish, short-pointed, round-toothed, veiny leaves, 2 to 4 inches long, downy on their undersides. Appearing about the time the new foliage expands, the white to pink, downy-stalked blooms are 1½ to 2 inches across. The fruits, indented at both ends, are nearly spherical to more or less ovoid.

Native to southeastern Europe and adjacent Asia, **M. pumila** (syn. *M. domestica*), a sturdy tree 15 to 40 feet high, in the wild has pointed, ovate to elliptic leaves, mostly downy on their undersides, and pink, pinkish, or white flowers in clusters of up to seven. Typically this has large, usually sweet fruits. Variety *M. p. apetala* has flowers lacking showy petals and fertile stamens. Twigs with reddish bark and wood, red-veined leaves, deep red flowers, and fruits with purple-red skins and flesh are typical of *M. p. niedzwetzkyana*, which is bushy and rarely over 12 feet in height. Notable because selections of it are much employed as dwarfing understocks for orchard apples, *M. p. paradisiaca* is dwarf and compact. Differing from *M. pumila* in being usually decidedly thorny and in its 1-inch-wide fruits being sour, **M. sylvestris** is endemic to Europe and southwestern Asia.

The Siberian crab apple (**M. baccata**), itself or hybridized with the common apple or other species, is the source of most orchard crab apples. Grown for their edible fruits, these are conveniently grouped as **M. adstringens**. Included are such varieties as 'Dolgo', 'Hopa', 'Hyslop', 'Martha', and 'Transcendent'. They mostly have pinkish flowers and fruits with calyxes usually persistent. In its typical wild form the Siberian crab apple, native from Siberia to northern China, is a broad tree 30 to 40 feet tall, with hairless shoots, and thinnish, long-stalked, sharp-toothed, broad-elliptic to ovate leaves up to 3¼ inches long. About 1½

Malus adstringens 'Dolgo' (fruits)

inches across, its slender-stalked, white flowers are succeeded by waxy-looking, red or yellow fruits ¾ inch in diameter, with calyxes that fall away rather than remaining attached to the ends of the fruits.

A few native North American maluses are cultivated for ornament. The most popular are the garland crab apple, the Southern crab apple, and Bechtel's crab apple, a double-flowered variety of the prairie crab apple. Native from New York to Alberta, Alabama, and Missouri, the garland crab apple (**M. coronaria**) is 20 to 30 feet tall. It has thornlike short branchlets or spurs and ovate to broad-elliptic, sharp-toothed, pointed leaves 2 to 4 inches long. The fragrant blooms change as they age from pink to white. They have downy stalks and calyxes. Approximately 1 inch across, they are succeeded by sour, greenish-yellow fruits 1 inch long or a little longer, with persistent calyxes. Variety *M. c. nieuwlandiana* has double pink flowers 1¼ to over 2 inches wide. Similar *M. c. charlottae* has smaller blooms. Indigenous in coastal regions from Virginia to Florida and Mississippi, the Southern crab apple (**M. angustifolia**) is semievergreen, up to about 25 feet tall, and has narrow-lanceolate to narrow-oblong-ovate leaves up to 3 inches long, with markedly or slightly toothed margins. The fragrant, rose-pink flowers are 1 inch wide. The yellow-green spherical to slightly pear-shaped fruits are ¾ to 1 inch long. The prairie crab apple (**M. ioensis**) is wild from Indiana to Minnesota and Kansas. From 20 to 30 feet tall, it has pointed, ovate to slightly obovate, irregularly-toothed, sometimes shallowly-lobed leaves 2 to 4 inches long. The usually downy-stalked, white or pink flowers, 1 inch to 2 inches across, have downy calyxes. The pale-dotted, dull green fruits, about 1 inch long, have persistent calyxes. Bechtel's crab apple (**M. ioensis plena**) is the usual variety cultivated. It has beautiful double pink blooms.

Oriental crab apples, admired for their magnificent displays of flowers and abundant small fruits, are among the most lovely hardy flowering trees. In addition to hybrids and garden varieties, to be discussed later, a number of species deserve attention, for instance **M. spectabilis**, unknown in the wild but of Chinese origin. This, about 25 feet tall, has short-pointed, round-toothed leaves 2 to 4 inches long, lustrous on their upper sides and becoming hairless or nearly so beneath. The red flower buds open to pink blooms 1½ to 2 inches across that pale as they age. They mostly have four or five styles. The yellow-green fruits, from ¾ to 1 inch across, without basal hollows, have persistent calyxes. They have little decorative appeal. Excellent varieties are *M. s. riversii*, the mostly double flowers of which have five to twenty petals, and double-flowered *M. s. albiplena*, with thirteen to twenty petals

Malus ioensis plena

Malus ioensis plena (flowers)

to each bloom. Another fine ornamental, **M. floribunda** is round-headed, densely-branched, and 25 feet tall or sometimes taller. A profuse, reliable bloomer, it has pointed, oblong to oblong-ovate, sharp-toothed leaves 1½ to 3 inches long, downy beneath at first, nearly hairless later. In the bud stage their two halves are folded face to face. The flower buds are red. The deliciously fragrant blooms, 1 inch to 1½ inches wide, are white on their insides, pink and white outside. The bases of the stamens are pink, the styles green. The spherical to somewhat conical, golden-brown to dull red fruits are ⅓ to ½ inch or slightly more in diameter. The calyxes are deciduous. Introduced to Western gardens from Japan about 1862, but not native to Japan, **M. floribunda** may be of hybrid origin. From it, smaller **M. halliana** is distinguishable by its leaves in the bud stage being rolled instead of folded face to face, and its shoots, flower stalks, and usually the midribs of the leaves being decidedly purplish. This sort, not known in the wild, was introduced from China to Japan and from there to the United States about 1863. Under 20 feet tall and more or less vase-shaped, *M. halliana* has long-ovate to oblong, finely-toothed or sometimes toothless, firm leaves 1½ to 3 inches long. Its rose-pink flowers are 1 inch to 1½ inches wide. The purplish fruits, ⅓ to ½

inch or slightly more in diameter, do not at maturity retain the calyxes. Double-flowered *M. h. parkmanii* has flowers with about fifteen petals.

Other fine Orientals include the tea crab apple (**M. hupehensis**), native from China to the Himalayas. This sort develops into a picturesque, stiff-branched specimen up to 25 feet tall. Its pointed, finely-toothed,

Malus hupehensis

broad-ovate to ovate-oblong leaves are 2 to 4 inches long, downy on the veins beneath. The delightfully fragrant white to pink blooms, about 1½ inches across, are in clusters of few. They have three or rarely four pinkish styles. Red-tinged, the greenish fruits are about ⅜ inch in diameter. The toringo crab apple (**M. sieboldii**), up to 15 feet tall, blooms later than most kinds, as does its variety *M. s. arborescens*, which may attain 30 feet in height. The species has downy young shoots, short-pointed, ovate to oblong leaves 1 inch to 2½ inches long, in the bud stage folded along their midribs rather than rolled, at first downy on both surfaces, later becoming nearly hairless below. The variety has larger, less downy leaves. The flowers of both, pink in bud, and about ¾ inch wide, open white. About ⅓ inch in diameter, their calyxes deciduous, the fruits are yellow or red. The species is Japanese, the variety native to Japan and Korea. Another late bloomer, **M. toringoides**, of China, unfortunately tends to bloom well only in alternate years. Pyramidal and up to 25 feet tall, it has ovate to

Malus toringoides (fruits)

oblong, often lobed, toothed leaves 2 to 4 inches in length, hairless except on the veins beneath. About ¾ inch in diameter, the creamy-white blooms, in clusters of few, and with four or five styles, are succeeded by somewhat pear-shaped, glaucous fruits ½ inch long, yellow, with the side exposed to the sun red. Variety *M. t. macrocarpa* has larger flowers and fruits. Probably native to northeast Asia, but possibly of hybrid origin, **M. prunifolia** is a small tree with downy shoots that has not been found in the wild. Its ovate to broad-elliptic, sharp-toothed, short-pointed leaves are 2 to 4 inches long, when young hairy on their undersides. The white flowers, 1½ inches wide or a little wider, have usually four styles. The yellow or red fruits, hollowed at their bases and about 1 inch in diameter, have persistent calyxes. Variety *M. p. rinkii* has pinkish blooms and leaves clothed with a persistent down on their undersides.

A broad shrub, **M. sargentii** of Japan attains a maximum height of 6 to 7 feet. By some authorities this is regarded as only a variant of *M. sieboldii*. Its branches have short, thornlike spurs. The short-pointed, iregularly-toothed, ovate to oblong, sometimes lobed leaves, 2 to 3 inches long, are hairless above at maturity. The fragrant, 1-inch-wide flowers, white to pinkish in bud and pure white when open, are in clusters of up to six. The nearly spherical, sometimes somewhat glaucous fruits, about ½ inch in diameter, are green and red. In *M. s. rosea* the flowers are red in bud, white tinged with pink when expanded.

Hybrid crab apples of known ancestry include a number of popular ones. Here belongs **M. arnoldiana.** It is a hybrid between *M. baccata* and *M. floribunda*. This is an outstanding tall shrub or small tree with somewhat pendulous branches, 2-inch-wide flowers, red in bud, white when open, and yellow fruits blushed on one side with red. Beautiful **M. atrosanguinea,** its parents *M. halliana* and *M. sieboldii*, has rich carmine flowers, 1½ inches in diameter, that become paler as they age. A reliable bloomer up to about 20 feet tall, this favorite has dark red fruits. The hybrid between *M. halliana* and *M. baccata*, named **M. hartwigii,** is an attractive intermediate between its parents. Its 2-inch-wide, semidouble blooms are white when open, pink in bud. A small tree with upright branches, **M. micromalus** is a hybrid of *M. baccata* and *M. spectabilis*. Esteemed for its showy, deep pink blossoms, 1¾ inches across, this sort, about 15 feet tall, usually bears well only in alternate years. Its small red fruits are not very ornamental.

Crab apples, the parents of which are *M. niedzwetzkyana* and *M. atrosanguinea*, are grouped under **M. purpurea.** They have as inheritances from *M. niedzwetzkyana* purplish shoots and foliage, rosy-red to wine-red flowers, and purplish fruits.

Malus atrosanguinea

Malus purpurea eleyi (foliage and fruits)

Typical *M. purpurea* is lovely and up to 25 feet tall. Its flowers are rosy-crimson, its fruits crimson. Excellent varieties are *M. p. aldenhamensis*, a small tree with single or semidouble wine-red flowers and red-purple fruits; *M. p. eleyi*, dark-flowered, and with purple-red fruits; and erect-growing *M. p. lemoinei*, with wine-red blooms. Sometimes incorrectly called Siberian crab apples, varieties of **M. robusta,** a hybrid of *M. baccata* and *M. prunifolia*, attain a height of up to 40 feet and have red or yellow, cherry-like fruits ¾ inch to 1½ inches in diameter, without persistent calyxes. Their nearly globular, white or pinkish blooms, 1¾ inches across, are fragrant. A mating of *M. floribunda* and *M. prunifolia* produced free-flowering, rather upright **M. scheideckeri,** which is up to 20 feet tall or sometimes taller. This excellent free-bloomer has semidouble, light pink blooms 1½ inches across. Its yellow to orange-yellow fruits are of no great display value. Large pink flowers and yellow fruits flushed with red are characteristic of **M. soulardii,** an intermediate hybrid of *M. pumila* and *M. ioensis*. Pale pink flowers and yellow fruits are borne by **M. sublobata,** a small, pyramidal hybrid between *M. prunifolia* and *M. sieboldii*. A pyramidal tree about 20 feet tall **M. zumi** (syn. *M. sieboldii zumi*)

Malus scheideckeri

much resembles *M. sieboldii*, but has bigger blooms and fruits. The flowers, pink in bud, open white. The fruits are bright red. Some authorities accept this as a variety of *M. sieboldii*, others believe it to be a hybrid between *M. baccata mandshurica* and *M. sieboldii*. Variety *M. z. calocarpa* has more widely spreading branches, smaller foliage and flowers, and very long-lasting bright red fruits. This usually bears well only in alternate years.

Splendid horticultural varieties of ornamental crab apples are plentiful. The following is a selection of the best. 'Adams', flower buds pink, flowers single, white becoming pink with age, 1½ inches across, fruits yellow and reddish; 'Barbara Ann', flowers double, rich purple-pink; 'Baskalong', flowers carmine-pink in bud dullish pink when open, 1¼ inches wide, fruits red, foliage reddish-bronze; 'Bob White', 1-inch-wide white blooms fading to pink, long-lasting yellow fruits; 'Cashmere', flowers pale pink, 1¼ to 1¾ inches across, fruits yellow; 'Dorothea', exceptionally fine, flowers semidouble, deep pink, 1½ to 2 inches wide, fruits bright yellow; 'Flame', white flowers, pink in bud, fruits red; 'Henry F. DuPont', a low, spreading tree, single or semidouble pink flowers that hold

At the right, an old ornamental crab apple in bloom adds charm to this garden

Magnolia tripetala

Macleaya cordata

Maianthemum canadense

Magnolia stellata

Mahonia 'Golden Abundance' with blue-flowered *Ceanothus*

Malus, ornamental crab apple variety

Mammillaria winterae

Mammillaria melanocentra

Mammillaria albicoma

Mahonia aquifolium

Ornamental crab apples: (a) Flowers of an unidentified horticultural variety

(b) Flowers of an unidentified horticultural variety

(c) Fruits of an unidentified horticultural variety

their color well, red fruits; 'Katherine', one of the best in bloom, less interesting in fruit, flowers double, 2¼ inches across, pink to white, fruits dull red; 'Makamik', a tall tree, flowers rose-purple, 1½ inches across, fruits purple-red; 'Oekonomierat Echtermeyer', a low, graceful tree with semipendulous branches, purplish-red blooms 1½ inches wide, and reddish-pur-

Malus 'Red Jade' (fruits)

ple fruits; 'Radiant', flowers red in bud, deep pink when open, fruits bright red, foliage reddish when young; 'Red Jade', outstandingly fine, branches pendulous, white flowers, long-lasting bright red fruits; 'Rosseau', a tall tree much like 'Makamik', but with brighter pink blooms, fruits rosy-red; 'Sissipuk', a tall tree, flowers purplish-red, 1 inch across, long-lasting, purplish-red fruits; 'Van Eseltine', a tree of upright growth, pink, double blooms 1¾ inches wide; and 'Winter Gold', vase-shaped tree, white flowers, beautiful yellow fruits borne heavily in alternate years, becoming brown after hard freezing.

Garden and Landscape Uses. Orchard apples and orchard crab apples serve obvious utilitarian uses. In addition, they are highly decorative, especially, when old, knarled, and picturesque, even though they have ceased to be as productive of usable fruits as younger, more vigorous trees. But old or young, orchard varieties of apples and crab apples, singly, in informal groups, or in orchards, can bring to home landscapes the kind of rustic charm one associates with lilacs. Among ornamental flowering crab apples is found a wide variety of tree sizes and forms, flower and fruit colors. Also, the fruits of these are less likely to attract boys (or girls) and are less troublesome when they drop than those of orchard kinds, which unless the trees are sprayed regularly are likely to be malformed and diseased.

The great majority of crab apples are reliably hardy in all but the coldest parts of New England. Some few are satisfactory throughout New England and in southern Canada. Here belong the common orchard apple, *M. prunifolia*, *M. robusta*, and the varieties 'Evelyn' and 'Flame'. Even more cold-resistant than these, surviving nearly as far north as trees will grow, are the Siberian crab apple and Bechtel's crab apple. Kinds slightly more tender to cold than the majority, generally reliable only in southern New England, are *M. angustifolia*, *M. sieboldii*, *M. toringoides*, and *M. zumi* and its variety.

Cultivation. Planting is done in early fall or spring. It is advantageous to keep the soil mulched around newly set trees for the first summer. Once established in reasonably good earth and locations crab apples are not demanding. They are long-lived and not susceptible to storm damage. The only pruning is any required to contain the trees to size and to shape them, plus the removal of shoots or young branches heading in directions likely to cause them to cross other branches or congest the head of the tree. In addition, watersprouts (vigorous, erect shoots that may develop in the interior from older branches) should be cut out, as well as sucker shoots that sometimes sprout low down on the trunk, most particularly any from below the graft. Pruning is best done in late winter or spring before growth begins or immediately after the flowers have faded. Old, neglected specimens can be rejuvenated, and reduced in size if desirable, by heading back older branches fairly severely, and perhaps judiciously removing some so that a good framework for a new head is left. Drastic pruning of this kind should be accompanied by fertilizing the ground occupied by the roots, an area extending from the trunk to 3 feet or more beyond the original spread of the branches, with a complete fertilizer, lightly forking this into the surface. Following this treatment it is helpful if, during dry weather the first summer, the ground is watered very thoroughly at ten-day or two-week intervals. Species crab apples are raised from seed, hybrids and garden varieties most commonly by grafting onto seedling understocks. For cultivation of orchard apples see Apples.

Diseases and Pests. Crab apples are generally susceptible to the same diseases and pests as orchard apples, but because edible fruits are not the objective it is less necessary to follow regular spray schedules, and this is not ordinarily done. Apple scab disease affects crab apples. Kinds differ markedly as to susceptibility. Of those we have discussed the following are reported to be resistant. 'Adams', *M. atrosanguinea*, *M. coronaria*, *M. c. nieuwlandiana*, *M. c. charlottae*, 'Dorothea', 'Evelyn', 'Flame', 'Henry F. DuPont', *M. purpurea lemoinei*, and *M. scheideckeri*. Native American crab apples, such as Bechtel's crab apple, if grown near the red-cedar (*Juniperus virginiana*) are likely to be affected by cedar-apple rust. Fire blight is also occasionally troublesome, *M. toringoides* being more susceptible to this than most.

MALVA (Mál-va)—Mallow. The forty species of mallows (*Malva*) include some of garden value. The group is native of temperate and warm temperate parts of the Old World. Some species are naturalized in North America. Malvas belong in the mallow family MALVACEAE. The name is an ancient Latin one. Care must be taken to distinguish these true mallows from rose-mallows, which are species and varieties of *Hibiscus,* and from the marsh-mallow, which is an *Althaea.*

Mallows are erect or prostrate annuals, biennials, and hardy herbaceous perennials. They have alternate leaves, variously lobed or cleft, and toothed. Their white, pink, or purplish flowers, solitary or clustered, and axillary, have a false calyx of three, or rarely two, bracts, just beneath the true calyx, which is five-lobed. There are five reverse-heart-shaped petals that at their apexes are squarish, and bayed or two-lobed. The numerous stamens are fused into a tube that surrounds the pistil, which is composed of many styles united below and free above. The fruits cohere like the pieces of a pie to form circular bodies with depressed centers that in shape are remindful of doughnuts with closed centers or certain disk-shaped cheeses, and by country children sometimes called cheeses.

Hardy perennial kinds cultivated are the musk mallow (*M. moschata*) and *M. alcea,* both natives of Europe and naturalized in North America. Roughly hairy and 1 foot to 3 feet tall, *M. moschata* has five- to

Malva moschata

Malva moschata (flowers)

Malva alcea

seven-lobed leaves, roundish in general outline, with the lobes of the upper ones deeply-pinnately-cleft. The satiny flowers, partly crowded in terminal clusters, but also solitary and long-stalked from the axils of the upper leaves, are about 2 inches across. The parts of their false calyxes are linear to narrowly-ovate, three or more times as long as wide and conspicuously hairy only at their margins. They range from rose-pink to white. The fruits are densely-downy. Variety *M. m. rosea* has pleasing pink flowers, those of *M. m. alba* are white. From the musk mallow *M. alcea* differs in having the parts of the false calyx ovate or ovate-triangular, not more than three times as long as wide, and densely-pubescent on their backs. Its fruits are nearly or quite without hairs. Variety *M. a. fastigiata* is narrower and less spreading.

Annual mallows and kinds cultivated as annuals include *M. sylvestris.* In the wild this is usually biennial or perhaps sometimes perennial. Native to Europe and naturalized in North America, it is up to 4 feet tall and has roundish to more or less kidney-shaped leaves, with three to seven semicircular to oblong, round-toothed lobes. The purple-pink flowers, often with darker veins, on stalks up to 2 inches long, are 1½ to 2 inches across. They are in clusters from the upper leaf axils. Their sepals have stellate (starry) hairs. Similar, but never perennial, not over 2½ feet tall, and with somewhat smaller blooms, *M. nicaeensis,* has leaves semicircular in outline and only slightly heart-shaped at their bases. Its sepals are usually hairless and its petals without deeper veinings. This is a native of southern Europe.

The curled mallow, previously distinguished as *M. crispa,* is now considered to be a variety of *M. verticillata.* It occurs spontaneously from central and southern Europe to China and is naturalized in North America. Annuals up to 6 or 7 feet tall, *M. verticillata* and its variety have long-stalked, kidney-shaped leaves with five to seven rounded, round-toothed

lobes or angles. In *M. v. crispa* the leaves are beautifully crisped and decidedly decorative. The blooms have little or no decorative appeal. They are white or bluish-white, under ½ inch in diameter, and clustered in the leaf axils. The curled mallow is cultivated for its stately appearance and ornamental foliage.

Garden and Landscape Uses. Mallows are easily grown summer-bloomers appropriate for flower borders and of some value as cut flowers. The curled mallow is suitable for background planting and can be used effectively as a temporary screen. All thrive in sun or part-day shade.

Cultivation. Well-drained soil of moderate fertility suits mallows. The perennials are propagated by seed or by division, in early spring or early fall. Established plants benefit from a spring application of a complete fertilizer. They are winter-hardy. The annuals and kinds grown as such are raised from seeds sown in early spring where the plants are to remain. The seedlings of the lower-growing kinds are thinned to about 9 inches apart; 1 foot is allowed between curled mallow seedlings.

MALVACEAE—Mallow Family. Of considerable ornamental and economic importance, this distinctive family of 1,000 or more species of dicotyledons distributed among seventy-five genera is of nearly worldwide natural occurrence. Among it more familiar sorts are abutilons, cotton, hibiscuses, hollyhocks, mallows, and okra. Included are annuals, herbaceous perennials, shrubs, and trees, with alternate, undivided, generally palmately-veined, often palmately-lobed leaves.

The white, yellow, pink, red, or purplish flowers, with rare exceptions symmetrical, may be solitary from the leaf axils or in clusters, racemes, or spikes. They have a calyx of five sepals, separate or joined at their bases, and often with just below it an involucre or epicalyx of sepal-like bracts. There are five petals, many stamens with their stalks united for most of their lengths into a tube and only their apexes free, and generally one style much branched at its apex. The fruits may be capsules or may separate into individual carpels that botanically are achenes or follicles or may be samaras or berries. Cultivated genera include *Abelmoschus, Abutilon, Alcea, Althaea, Alyogyne, Anisodontea, Anoda, Callirhoe, Corynabutilon, Cristaria, Goethea, Gossypium, Hibiscadelphus, Hibiscus, Hoheria, Iliamna, Ingenhouzia, Kitaibelia, Kokia, Kosteletzkya, Lagunaria, Lavatera, Malacothamnus, Malope, Malva, Malvastrum, Malvaviscus, Montezuma, Pavonia, Phymosia, Plagianthus, Robinsonella, Sida, Sidalcea, Sphaeralcea, Thespesia, Triplochlamys,* and *Wercklea.*

MALVASTRUM (Malv-ástrum). As now understood, *Malvastrum,* of the mallow family MALVACEAE, consists of twelve species, native to tropical, subtropical, and temperate South America. Species of *Anisodontea*, *Malacothamnus*, and *Sphaeralcea* are sometimes grown in gardens as *Malvastrum*. The name, from the Latin *malva*, mallow, and *aster*, meaning an incomplete resemblance, alludes to similarities between *Malvastrum* and *Malva*.

The plant cultivated as **M. lateritium,** and said to be a native of Argentina and Uraguay, is a more or less prostrate, hairy, herbaceous perennial about 6 inches tall. It has leaves with three or five toothed, wedge-shaped to broad-oblong lobes and solitary, long-stalked, cupped, pale pink flowers with the bases of the petals red and the anthers yellow.

Malvastrum lateritium

Garden and Landscape Uses and Cultivation. In temperate regions where winters are not notably severe, **M. lateritium** is satisfactory for the fronts of flower beds and similar places. It thrives in sunny locations in ordinary well-drained soil and is readily propagated by seed and by cuttings.

MALVAVISCUS (Malva-víscus) — Texas-Mallow or Wax-Mallow, Turk's-Cap-Hibiscus. Gay-flowered examples of this American genus of the mallow family MALVACEAE are frequent in landscape plantings in the warmer parts of the south. Their cheerful, usually bright red flowers show to advantage against the lively green of the foliage and present attractive displays over an extended season. Botanically, *Malvaviscus* is a complicated group with the species merging and often exhibiting much variation within themselves. Because of this botanists differ in estimating the number of species from as few as three to as many as twenty. Its name comes from that of the related genus *Malva*, and the Latin *viscum*, sticky, and alludes to the fruits.

Shrubs, sometimes clambering and vinelike, malvaviscuses are deep-rooted, And have freely-branching stems. Their leaves are alternate, stalked, broadly-ovate-heart-shaped to linear-lanceolate, and prominently net-veined. They may be palmately (in handlike fashion) strongly lobed, deeply-toothed, or without lobes and nearly toothless. They exhibit various degrees of hairiness, the hairs being branchless, stellate (star-shaped), or a mixture of both. The rather short-stalked flowers are in small clusters at the branch ends or singly or in groups in the leaf axils. They vary much in size, according to species or variety, and never open fully, but remain tubular or bell-shaped, which is reason for the colloquial designation Turk's-cap-hibiscus. The blooms have an involucre (collar of bracts) that forms a false calyx and more or less encloses the true calyx, which is bell-shaped and has generally five lobes. There are five overlapping, obovate petals, usually notched at their apexes, narrowing to their clawed bases, and with earlike appendages there. The stamens are joined in a slender column that protrudes conspicuously from the mouth of the flower. From its end protrude the ten branches of the style. The flattened-globose fruits consist of five one-seeded carpels enclosed in a soon-drying, fleshy coat.

Most frequently cultivated are variants of **M. arboreus** (syn. *M. mollis*), which in one or more of its many varieties occurs in the wild from the southern United States to South America, and the West Indies.

Malvaviscus arboreus mexicanus

This has variously shaped and lobed, or lobeless, toothed leaves 2 to 4½ inches long and wide. The involucres are of six or more linear to spatula-shaped bracts. The column of stamens, not over 3 inches long, is exerted for one-quarter to one-third of its length. The free parts of the stamen stalks are about ⅛ inch in length. Called Texas-mallow and wax-mallow, *M. a. drummondii*, native of often limestone areas from Florida to Texas, Mexico, and Cuba, procumbent, clambering or erect, has leaves as broad as long, with three short lobes and blunt teeth and with many stellate hairs on their under surfaces, and mostly straight hairs on the upper sides. The red flowers scarcely exceed 1 inch in length. Even more attractive as an ornamental, *M. a. mexicanus* (syns. *M. conzattii*, *M. penduliflorus*), a native from Mexico to Colombia and naturalized in the southern United States, is bushy or somewhat vinelike. The lobeless or slightly-lobed, variously-hairy leaves are lanceolate to broad-ovate-lanceolate. The nodding flowers are 1 inch to 2 inches long.

Very different from *M. arboreus* and its varieties is Mexican **M. candidus.** This has five-lobed leaves up to 7½ inches across, and hairy on both surfaces. The showy flowers are terminal or subterminal in clusters or occasionally solitary. Their corollas exceed 3 inches in length, and the column of stamens is 4½ to 6 inches long. The involucres are of usually a dozen narrow bracts. The long-protruding column of stamens, with the anthers terminating a much longer free portion of the stamen than is true of *M. arboreus* and its varieties, curves upward.

A hedge of *Malvaviscus arboreus mexicanus*

Garden and Landscape Uses and Cultivation. The better varieties of *M. arboreus*, especially *M. a. mexicanus*, are highly attractive and easily grown general-purpose shrubs for warm countries. They prosper in any ordinary soil, including those of a limestone character and revel in full sun. Propagation is easy by cuttings and by seed.

MAMANE is *Sophora chrysophylla*.

MAMEY is *Mammea americana*.

MAMEYUELO is *Ardisia obovata*.

MAMILLOPSIS (Mamil-lópsis). There are only two species of *Mamillopsis*, of the cactus family CACTACEAE, and these by some authorities are included in closely related *Mammillaria*. They are small, spherical or low-cylindrical, and thickly covered with soft white bristles. They resemble *Mammillaria* and their name, composed of a modification of that generic name and the Greek *opsis*, like, reflects this. From *Mammillaria* these plants differ in their flowers having long, scaly perianth tubes and in their stamens projecting. They are natives of Mexico.

Most common in cultivation, *M. senilis* grows in large clusters. Its stems, about 6 inches tall and 3 inches in diameter, are not ribbed, but have surfaces of projecting cones tipped with areoles (cushions from which spines develop). From each areole sprout thirty to forty soft, white hairlike spines almost 1 inch long. The handsome, orange-yellow to red flowers are about 2½ inches long and wide. They are tubular and have spreading perianth lobes (petals).

Garden Uses and Cultivation. These are plants for collectors of cactuses and succulents. They need the conditions and care appropriate for mammillarias. General information about cactus culture is given under Cactuses.

MAMMEA (Mám-mea)—Mammee-Apple. As now understood, this genus consists of about fifty species, mostly of tropical Asia and Malagasy (Madagascar), and one species in tropical Africa and one in tropical America. The last is cultivated. The group belongs in the garcinia family GUTTIFERAE. Its name is a modification of *mamey*, an aboriginal West Indian name for *M. americana*.

The mammee-apple or mamey (**Mammea americana**) is a fine-looking evergreen tree of northern South America and the West Indies. It forms a short-trunked, heavy-branched, somewhat cylindrical and compact head up to 70 feet in height and has an abundance of opposite, glossy, dark green, leathery leaves, oblong-obovate to elliptic, with blunt or rounded ends. They are 4 to 8 inches long, have bold midribs and numerous fine, parallel lateral veins, and are speckled with tiny semitransparent dots that can be seen if the leaf is held to the light and viewed through a hand lens. The flowers are of three kinds, male, female, and bisexual. All are borne on the same tree, but some trees are predominantly female and fruit heavily, whereas others have mostly male blooms and bear few or no fruits. The flowers are white, fragrant, and 1 inch or more in diameter. Solitary or few together in the leaf axils, they have two sepals and four to six petals and numerous stamens. The fruits, nearly spherical with a slight nipple or beak at the end, have slightly rough, russetted exteriors and are 4 to 8 inches in diameter. Their bright yellow to reddish flesh contains one to four ellipsoid seeds.

Garden and Landscape Uses and Cultivation. This excellent tropical tree, well adapted for cultivation in tropical and frost-free subtropical climates, is occasionally grown in southern Florida and Hawaii. It is an attractive ornamental as well as a useful producer of delicious fruits. These have much the flavor of apricots, but their skins and seeds are bitter. The flavor varies in the fruits from different trees from sweet

to mildly acid. The sweeter ones may be eaten out of hand, the others served with sugar and cream, stewed with sugar, or made into preserves. In South America the fruits, flowers, and sap are used to prepare refreshing drinks. The liqueur eau de Créole is prepared from the flowers. The mammee-apple grows in soil of ordinary fertility and is propagated by seeds, which require about two months to germinate.

MAMMEE-APPLE is *Mammea americana*.

MAMMILLARIA (Mammil-lària). This important genus of the cactus family CACTACEAE is most abundant as to native species in Mexico, but is represented also in natural floras from the southwestern United States to Colombia and Venezuela and the West Indies. The number of its species is a matter of some dispute, but probably is between 200 and 300. Although there is yet no agreement, the trend, undoubtedly a wise one, among modern botanists is to return to *Mammillaria* sorts that have been segregated as *Coryphantha, Dolichothele, Escobaria, Krainzia, Neobesseya, Phellosperma*, and some other genera. However, this cannot yet be done conveniently or uniformly for horticultural collections partly because not all that have been named in the segregate genera have been officially transferred to *Mammillaria* and partly because

Mammillarias at Huntington Botanical Gardens, San Marino, California

growers of cactuses nearly always recognize the segregates and dealers list their offerings under their names. In any case, as has so often been necessary in dealing with the cactus family in this Encyclopedia, the smaller genera are treated separately, although without conviction that that is the most satisfactory botanical procedure. The name *Mammillaria*, sometimes wrongly spelled *Mamillaria*, is derived from the Latin *mammilla*, a teat. It alludes to the tubercles on the stems.

Mammillarias are mostly small, sometimes tiny plants with solitary or clustered, flattish to spherical or sometimes cylindrical plant bodies (stems) that in only a few sorts branch appreciably above their bases. Unlike those of most cactuses, the stems of mammillarias are not ribbed, but are completely covered with nipple-like protrusions called tubercles, usually disposed in rows that spiral around the stem, sometimes less orderly placed. The tubercles frequently differ from those of *Coryphantha* in not having grooves along their upper sides.

In classifying the numerous species of this genus, the German botanist Curt Backeberg made a primary separation into three sections each of which he divided in a rather complicated manner into series and subseries. His Section 1 (*Galactochylus*) consists of kinds with white, milky sap in the plant bodies including the tubercles that exudes if the tubercles are scratched. Section 2 (*Subhydrochylus*) includes sorts in which the sap in the tubercles is milky, but not as decidedly so as the kinds in Section 1 when the plants are in active growth, but when they are dormant is watery, although even then a small amount of the sap of the main plant body may be milky. Section 3 (*Hydrochylus*) comprises all mammillarias in which the sap is watery and clear to amber throughout. Other botanists unite Backeberg's Sections 2 and 3 as Section 2 (*Subhydrochylus*). In the treatment that follows the numbers given in parentheses after each species allude to Backeberg's classification.

The sorts of mammillarias in cultivation are very numerous. Here is a substantial and representative, but by no means complete listing of them. Unless otherwise indicated all are natives of Mexico: *M. alamensis* (3) has solitary, grayish-green plant bodies up to 2 inches tall and wide, the axils of their tubercles hairless. The spine clusters are of nine ¼-inch-long, dark-tipped, white radials that lie against the stem and one longer, hooked, central, purplish-brown to black when young. The flowers are not described. *M. albicoma* (3) has clusters of nearly spherical plant bodies up to about 2 inches in diameter and completely covered with white hairs. The small tubercles have flattened tips. The spines are in clusters of thirty or more soft, white, hairlike radials up to ½ inch long and sometimes one to four brown-tipped centrals about ¼ inch in length. Approximately ½ inch wide, the flowers are creamy- to greenish-white. *M. albilantha* (1) has mostly solitary, convex-topped, spherical to short-cylindrical plant bodies up to 6 inches tall by a little more than 2 inches in diameter with white, short, curly hairs in the axils of the tubercles. The spine clusters are of twenty or somewhat fewer very short, pure white radials and two or less commonly three or four short, brown-tipped, white or creamy-white centrals. The flowers are small and carmine. *M. applanata* (1), of Texas, has solitary, spherical plant bodies conspicuously flattened or slightly depressed at their apexes and up to 4 inches wide. The spine clusters are of eight to eighteen spreading radials and one ¼-inch-long darker central. The cream-colored to greenish-white flowers are about 1¼ inches across. *M. armillata* (3) has solitary or clustered, cylindrical plant bodies up to 1 foot tall by almost 2 inches thick with a few woolly hairs and two or three bristles in their axils. The spine clusters are of nine to fifteen slender, rigid, dark-tipped, yellowish or gray radials up to nearly ½ inch long and up to four dark-tipped or dark-banded centrals, up to ¾ inch long, the lower ones hooked. The flowers, about ¾ inch wide, are greenish-white to pinkish. *M. aureilanata* (syn. *M. cephalophora*) (3) has usually solitary, spherical to subcylindrical plant bodies about 3 inches in diameter with rather distant tubercles without hairs in their axils. The spine clusters, which lack centrals, have twenty-five to thirty white to golden-yellow, silky, wavy, bristle-like radials that darken as they age and are up to a little over ½ inch long. The ½-inch-wide flowers are rose-pink to white. *M. barbata* (3) has nearly spherical, clustered plant bodies up to 2 inches in diameter with small, cylindrical tubercles without hair in their axils. The spine clusters are of forty to sixty ¼-inch-long, needle-like, white to brownish-yellow radials, the inner ones tipped with brown, and one or less often two or more, longer, brown, hooked centrals. The flowers, about ¾ inch across, have green or bronzy-green outer petals and pink inner ones with a darker center stripe. *M. baxterana* (1) has flattened-spherical plant bodies up to 6 inches tall and wide, usually solitary, but when old branching from their bases. The axils of the tubercles are furnished with short woolly hairs. The spine clusters are of seven to thirteen white radials and one or occasionally two centrals. The lower radials are up to slightly over ½ inch long, the young ones often tipped with brown. The flowers, ¾ inch in diameter, have purple-brown outer petals, greenish-yellow inner ones with a rose-purple mid-line. *M. blossfeldiana* (3) has mostly solitary plant bodies 4 to 5 inches thick, depressed at their apexes, and spherical when young, but later cylindrical. They have tubercles with, when young, a few white, woolly hairs in their axils. The spines are in clusters of fifteen to twenty stiff, dark-tipped, gray radials approximately ¼ inch long and four black-tipped, gray and purplish, stiff centrals, the largest under ½ inch long and hooked. From ¾ inch to 1¼ inches across, the flowers are white with greenish-white outer petals and pink-striped inner ones. Variety *M. b. shurliana* has spine clusters with only three centrals and stamens with reddish-purple instead of white stalks. *M.*

Mammillaria bocasana with young fruits

bocasana (3) is variable, several varieties are recognized. Typically it forms mounds of many approximately spherical plant bodies 1½ to 2 inches in diameter. The slender tubercles may have a few hairs or bristles in their axils. The spines are in clusters of twenty-five to thirty or more silky, white, hairlike, interlacing radials that form a haze or cloud around the plant bodies and one to four yellow to brown centrals, up to ¾ inch long, one or more hooked. The flowers, nearly ½ inch in diameter, are creamy-white with a reddish center line and reddish undersides to the petals. *M. bocensis* (1) has plant bodies that when young are flattened-spherical; at maturity they are up to 4 inches tall and wide with depressed apexes. They have rigid, pyramidal tubercles, with sparse grayish hairs in their axils. The spines are in clusters of six to eight white radials ¼ to ½ inch long and one dark-tipped, reddish-brown central. About ¾-inch wide, the flowers are creamy-white with the inner petals edged pink and the outer ones pink to brownish margined with green. *M. bombycina* (3) has solitary or clustered plant bodies, at first spherical, and later more elongated, and up to 8 inches tall and 2½ inches wide. From the axils of their tubercles sprouts an abundance of white, woolly hairs. The spines are in clusters of thirty to forty stiff, slender, shining white, ⅜-inch-long radials and one to four yellowish and reddish-brown centrals, the largest ¾ inch long and hooked, that protrude from the plant bodies like pins from a pincushion. About 1½ inches across, the flowers are light carmine-red. *M. boolii* (3) has spherical or nearly spherical plant bodies up to 1½ inches tall with starry spine clusters of about twenty white radials approximately ½ inch long and one strongly-hooked, dark-tipped, amber-yellow central up to ¾ inch long. The 1-inch-wide flowers are rose- or purple-pink. *M. brandegeei* (1) has plant bodies solitary when young, branching when older. Flattened-spherical to cylindrical and up to 3½ inches across, they have tubercles with white wool and occasional white bristles in their axils. From woolly areoles, the spines are in clusters of eight to fourteen yellowish- to brown-tipped, stiff, white to gray radials up to

about ½ inch long and three to seven or less often one or two needle-like reddish-brown centrals, which are twice as long. The flowers are yellowish-green with tan outer petals and inner ones with a central pink stripe. *M. brauneana* (1) has usually solitary, spherical plant bodies up to about 3 inches across. Rarely they branch from their bases; they tend to elongate and become club-shaped as they age and have bristles in the axils of the tubercles. The spines are sparkling white, in clusters of twenty-five to thirty hairlike radials under ¼ inch long and two to four centrals about as long and reddish changing to light brown or buff as they age. The reddish-violet flowers are about ½ inch across. *M. bravoae* (1) has mostly solitary, glossy-green, spherical plant bodies with markedly depressed tops and an abundance of white woolly hairs and longer bristles in the axils of the younger tubercles. The spine clusters are of thirty or slightly fewer white, interlaced radials up to a little more than ¼ inch in length and two longer, black-tipped, cream-colored to tannish centrals. The flowers, about ⅜ inch wide, have pink outer petals, deeper pink inner ones with darker mid-stripes, and the inner ones with nearly black apexes. *M. caerulea* (1) has seldom-branched ovoid to cylindrical plant bodies up to 5 inches tall by one-half as wide. The axils of young tubercles sprout white woolly hairs and sometimes a few bristles. The spine clusters are of eighteen to twenty-five white, bristly radials not quite ¼ inch long and three or four longer, needle-like centrals at first dark brown, later paler. The flowers are not described. *M. calacantha* (3) has solitary, spherical to subcylindrical plant bodies up to 4½ inches high by 2½ to 3 inches in diameter, the older ones depressed at their apexes. The spine clusters are of twenty-five to thirty-five yellowish or grayish, ¼-inch-long radials and two to four dark-tipped, purplish- to reddish-brown centrals up to ½ inch long, one of which points upward. The axils of the tubercles are slightly hairy only when young. The flowers, ½ inch wide and shallow, are bright carmine with greenish-cream bases to the outer petals. *M. candida* (3) has plant bodies solitary when young, clustered later, spherical to somewhat longer. Up to 3½ inches high, they are crowded with rather slender tubercles mostly hidden by snowy-white spines. White hairs and bristles sprout from the axils of the tubercles. The starry spine clusters are of about fifty radials shorter than the centrals and of uneven length and a dozen or fewer ¼-inch-long centrals. Not usually freely produced, the flowers are rose-pink. Variety *M. c. rosea* has longer central spines that are pink. *M. capensis* (3) has cylindrical plant bodies up to 1 foot long by 1½ to 2 inches in diameter. Branched from below, they sometimes have up to three bristles in the axils of the tubercles. The spine clusters are of approximately a dozen dark-apexed, stiff, white radials about ½ inch long and one longer, similarly colored, rigid, hooked central. The flowers are pink. *M. carnea* (1) has light to dark green, usually solitary, spherical to cylindrical plant bodies up to 4 inches high with tubercles with white or cream-colored wool in the axils of only the young ones. The spine clusters, without radials but sometimes with one or two bristles, have four or sometimes five centrals, the lower 1 inch long or longer, the others one-half that size. They are pink and dark-tipped when young, later becoming gray. The flowers, flesh- to purple-pink with inner petals green toward their bases, are nearly or quite 1 inch long. *M. celsiana* (2) with age has clustered plant bodies, but those of young specimens are solitary. They are subspherical to cylindrical and up to 5 inches tall by 3½ inches wide. The tubercles when young are woolly-hairy in the axils. The clusters of spines are of from twenty-five to thirty translucent white radials about ¼ inch long and from four to seven about ½-inch-long, brown-tipped, yellow centrals. The flowers are bright carmine to rose-red with reddish-brown outer petals. *M. chionocephala* (1) has spherical, bluish-green plant bodies 3 to 4½ inches across that sometimes branch as they age. They have clusters of mostly about twenty-three ⅓-inch-long white radial spines, perhaps sometimes more, and two to four or on occasion more, shorter, thicker, dark-tipped, gray to brownish centrals. The outer petals of the white to pink flowers are striped with reddish-brown. *M. collinsii* (1) forms large clumps of clustered, often reddish, spherical plant bodies about 1½ inches in diameter, with tubercles that have hairs in their axils only when young. The spine clusters are of seven dark-tipped, light yellow radials and one slightly longer dark brown or black central up to ⅓ inch in length. The flowers, about ½ inch long, have yellow outer petals with reddish mid-stripes and inner ones of pinkish-yellow with mid-stripes of rose-red. *M. columbiana* (3), of Colombia and Venezuela, has spherical to club-shaped plant bodies up to 10 inches tall by 4 inches thick, slightly depressed at their apexes, and with woolly hairs in the axils of the tubercles. The spine clusters are of twenty to thirty glassy, white radials about ¼ inch long, with usually three to six dark-tipped, reddish-brown to yellowish, somewhat longer centrals. The flowers are pink to carmine, the inner ones with darker mid-stripes on their petals. *M. compressa* (1) eventually forms large hemispherical clumps, but when young has usually solitary plant bodies. Spherical to cylindrical, they are up to 8 inches tall by one-half as wide. In the axils of their tu-

Mammillaria compressa

bercles, at least the younger ones, is dense white, woolly hair. The spines are in clusters of usually four to six, but sometimes fewer flexuous radials from ¾ inch to 2½ inches long, the lower ones down-curved. When young reddish, they later become gray or whitish. There are no centrals. The flowers, pinkish to purple with the inner petals darker than the outer ones, are from a little under to a little over ½ inch wide. Their petals have a mid-stripe of deeper color than its borders. *M. confusa* (syn. *M. karwinskiana*) (1) has flattened-spherical to cylindrical plant bodies branched from their bases, up to 6 inches tall by two-thirds as wide, with white wool and bristles in the axils of the widely spaced tubercles. The spine clusters are of four to six radials at first black, later white with dark tips. In the typical species centrals are lacking, but *M. c. longiseta* (syn. *M. longiseta*) has one up to 1½ inches long in each cluster. The flowers, under ½ inch wide, are creamy-white to greenish-yellow. *M. conspicua* (3) has solitary, spherical to subcylindrical plant bodies up to 6 inches tall by two-thirds as wide and with slightly depressed tops, and white, woolly hairs and bristles in the axils of the tubercles. The spines are in clusters of fourteen to twenty-five, white, bristle-like radials up to ¼ inch long and two or sometimes three or four ½-inch-long, reddish-brown to brown centrals, with a whitish or grayish band at their middles. The flowers have carmine petals with darker mid-stripes. They are ¾ inch long. *M. crinita* (3), closely related to *M. glochidiata*, has clustered spherical to cylindrical plant bodies up to 1½ inches in diameter, their tubercles without hairs in their axils. The spines are in clusters of fifteen to twenty, white, hairlike radials up to ¾ inch long and four or five slender centrals up to ½ inch in length, yellow to pale brown, and at least one hooked. The flowers have cream-colored to pinkish petals with pink to red mid-stripes. *M. crispiseta* (1) has flattened-spherical plant bodies 3½ inches across, woolly-hairy at their tops and with

long white bristles in the axils of the tubercles. The spines are in clusters of seven brown-tipped, white radials up to nearly ⅓ inch long and four or five rigid, curved, dark-apexed, pinkish-cream to brown or black, needle-like centrals. The flowers are not described. *M. crucigera* (2) develops large clusters of flattened-spherical to cylindrical or obovoid plant bodies up to 6 inches tall by one-half as wide. The axils of the younger tubercles have abundant white, woolly hairs. The spine clusters are of twenty or more ¹⁄₁₀-inch-long, bristle-like, white radials and usually four, less often two, three, or five yellowish to white, sometimes brown- to black-tipped slightly longer centrals. The flowers are purplish-red to crimson. *M. densispina* (3) has plant bodies usually solitary, but sometimes branching from their bases as they age. Spherical to short-cylindrical, and up to 7 inches high by 4 inches wide, they are closely covered with white and yellow spines. Each cluster is of twenty radials of unequal lengths, the longest exceeding ½ inch, and six or occasionally five needle-like centrals up to ¾ inch long and becoming brown or red at their apexes. The flowers have yellowish inner petals, deep pink or purplish-pink, shorter outer ones with yellowish bases. *M. dioica* (2), of California and Baja California, has usually clustered, spherical to cylindrical plant bodies mostly up to 1 foot tall by 2 to 3 inches in diameter, but sometimes bigger. In the axils of the tubercles there are five to fifteen bristles. The spine clusters are of ten to twenty white radials up to ⅓ inch long and one to four needle-like, brown centrals, the lowest and longest up to ¾ inch in length and hooked. From ¾ to 1 inch long, the flowers have creamy-white to yellowish petals with pink to purplish mid-veins. *M. discolor* (3) has usually solitary, spherical to ovoid plant bodies that rarely branch, are up to 4 inches tall and about 3 inches wide. There are very few or no hairs in the axils of the tubercles. The spines are in clusters of sixteen to twenty-four white radials up to ⅜ inch long, the upper shorter than the lowers. There are five to six, rarely up to eight yellow to brownish, dark-tipped centrals. Rather over ½ inch wide, the flowers have white to pinkish petals with rose-pink to rose-red mid-stripes. *M. durispina* (2) has usually solitary, spherical to short-cylindrical plant bodies up to 1 foot tall by 4½ inches in diameter and with white woolly hairs in the axils of the young tubercles only. The starry spine clusters are of six to eight stiff, grayish radials banded with reddish-brown and varying in length from ⅓ to ½ inch. Only very rarely are centrals developed. The flowers, with purple-red petals with greenish bases, are up to ¾ inch across. *M. eichlamii* (1) is a native of Guatemala. Producing offshoots freely, its spherical to cylindrical plant bodies are up to 10 inches long by 2 inches thick or a little thicker. The axils of the younger tubercles sprout whitish or yellowish woolly hairs and a few bristles. The spine clusters are of six to eight, dark-tipped, yellowish-white to gray radials and one or rarely two centrals of nearly the same coloring and ⅜ inch long. The flowers have cream-colored outer petals with yellow to brown mid-stripes and cream- to lemon-yellow inner petals. *M. elegans* (2) has plant bodies clustered on old specimens, solitary with younger ones. Spherical to more or less cylindrical, they have tubercles that when young have in their axils long, bristle-like, white, woolly hairs that extend beyond the tubercles. The spine clusters are of twenty-five to thirty ½-inch-long, chalky-white radials and usually two, but sometimes one or up to four brown- or black-tipped, longer centrals. The flowers have purple to red petals with darker mid-stripes. *M. elongata* (3), the lady finger or golden lace cactus, is extremely variable and includes many varieties that unfortunately are often tagged with only the generic and varietal parts of their trinomial designations so that to the uninitiated they appear to be the names of distinct species. An easy, quick grower, *M. elongata* has cylindrical stems up to 6 inches long that sprout freely from their bases and have very short, blunt, conical tubercles woolly in their axils when young. The starry clusters of typically yellow spines consist of up to twenty radials and up to three centrals, the latter often missing from the lower clusters. The flowers from somewhat under to rather over ½ inch long, white to light yellow sometimes striped with red, have a four-lobed white stigma. Varieties include the lace cactus (*M. e. minima*), with plant bodies scarcely more than 2 inches long and correspondingly slender; *M. e. rufida*, the spines of which are chestnut-brown for one-half their lengths; *M. e. rufispina*, which has spines dark red for one-half their lengths; *M. e. rufocrocea*, with slender, more or less prostrate plant bodies with reddish-brown-tipped yellow spines with a zone of white between the red and yellow and usually only one central to each cluster; *M. e. schmollii*, which has very slender plant bodies with rich yellow spines, the centrals sometimes with orange apexes; and *M. e. stella-aurata*, called golden stars, which has slender plant bodies up to 4 inches long that branch freely below, and have strongly recurved, sometimes orange-tipped, golden to honey-yellow spines. *M. eriacantha* (3) has solitary or clustered, cylindrical plant bodies up to 6 inches tall with eight to thirteen spiraled rows of tubercles. The spine clusters are of approximately twenty yellow to brown radials and two centrals. The flowers are yellow, about ½ inch wide. *M. erythrosperma* (3) has spherical to subcylindrical plant bodies up to 2

inches in height and rather less in diameter that produce offsets freely and soon form sizable clusters or mounds. The tubercles have a few bristles and no hairs in their axils. The spines are white, in clusters of fifteen to twenty radials up to ⅜ inch long and up to four stouter centrals about as long. The flowers have bright carmine petals with darker mid-stripes. *M. fasciculata* (syn. *M. thornberi*) (3), native from Arizona to Mexico, forms large clumps of clustered, cylindrical plant bodies up to about 3 inches in diameter, without hair in the axils of the tubercles. The spine clusters are of twelve to twenty flexible, slender, brown- or black-tipped, white radials approximately ¼ inch long and one or rarely two or three hooked centrals up to ¾ inch long. The flowers, with brownish-purple outer petals, the inner ones carmine with a purplish mid-stripe, are up to 1½ inches wide. *M. formosa* (1) has spherical to somewhat club-shaped plant bodies depressed at their apexes and without hair in the axils of the tubercles. The spine clusters are of eighteen to twenty-five irregularly spreading, chalky-white, thin, rigid radials up to ¼ inch long and two to six stouter ⅓-inch-long centrals at first light red with darker tips, but later grayish. The flowers have purplish-red inner petals with darker mid-stripes and tips and white or creamy-white outer ones with pinkish-brown mid-stripes. *M. fragilis* (syn. *M. gracilis fragilis*) (3) has cylin-

Mammillaria fragilis

drical plant bodies that branch freely above, which have small tufts of hair in the axils of the tubercles. The branches are easily detached. Each cluster of spines consists of twelve to sixteen spreading, white radials under ¼ inch long and very rarely a solitary central. The flowers are creamy-yellow to light yellow, the petals with pink to tan mid-stripes. *M. fraileana* (3) develops clusters of cylindrical plant bodies up to 6 inches tall, their tubercles with a few bristles in their axils. The spine clusters are of eleven or twelve stiff, white radials ⅓ inch long or slightly longer and three or four scarcely longer brown cen-

Mammillaria fuliginosa

trals, the lower one strongly hooked. About ¾ inch wide, the flowers are pink to creamy-pink. *M. fuliginosa* (3), believed to be a native of Venezuela, has spherical to ovoid, rarely branched plant bodies about 3 inches in diameter with twenty-one to thirty-four spiraled rows of tubercles. The spine clusters are of sixteen very short, white radials and, spreading in the form of a cross, four black-tipped, ⅓-inch-long centrals. The deep pink flowers are ⅔ inch long. *M. gasseriana* (3) has spherical to egg-shaped, grayish-green plant bodies up to about 1½ inches wide, sprouting offsets freely from their bases and with white-woolly hairs in the axils of the young tubercles. The spine clusters are of forty to fifty sometimes brownish-tipped, white radials and one or two similar, but hooked centrals about ⅓ inch long. About ⅓ inch wide, the flowers are white with a greenish throat. *M. geminispina* (1) forms broad clumps of crowded, spherical, club-shaped, or cylindrical plant bodies up to 6 inches tall and 3 inches thick and with thirteen to twenty-one spirals of tubercles. The axils of the tubercles are densely furnished with white wool and ten to twenty twisted bristles. The spine clusters are of sixteen to twenty needle-like, white, ¼-inch-long radials and two to four longer, brown-tipped cen-

Mammillaria geminispina

trals, the largest up to 1½ inches long. The carmine-pink flowers are ¾ inch in diameter. *M. glareosa* (syn. *M. dawsonii*) (1) has flattened-spherical plant bodies 2 inches or considerably less in diameter. The axils of the tubercles have sparse-woolly hairs. The spine clusters are of six to ten radials, the lower ones shorter than the upper three, which are nearly ¼ inch in length, and usually not more than one somewhat longer, dark-tipped, light brown central. The flowers are greenish-yellow with reddish-brown mid-stripes to the petals. *M. grusonii* (3) has spherical to cylindrical plant bodies up to 10 inches across. The spine clusters are of fourteen at first reddish, later snow-white radials up to ⅓ inch long and two to four shorter centrals. The 1-inch-wide flowers are bright yellow. *M. guerreronis* (2) has clustered, cylindrical plant bodies up to 2 feet in height and 2½ inches in diameter, with bristles in the axils of their tubercles and in those of young ones, white, woolly hairs. The spines are in clusters of twenty to thirty creamy-white radials ¼ to a little over ½ inch long and two to four, or rarely five tan to white, pinkish-tipped centrals approximately ½ inch in length, with one usually hooked. The flowers are red. *M. gummifera* (1) has light grayish-green, flattened-spherical plant bodies depressed at their apexes, up to 4½ inches tall and wide with scanty whitish, woolly hairs in the axils of the younger tubercles. The spine clusters are of ten to twelve brown- or black-tipped white radials from ¼ to ½ inch long or longer and one or two shorter, black-tipped light brown centrals. The 1-inch-wide flowers are creamy-white to white with brownish to purplish mid-stripes to the petals. *M. haehneliana* (3) has solitary or clustered, approximately spherical plant bodies depressed at their apexes and with cylindrical tubercles with a few bristles on their axils. The spine clusters are of about twenty-five spreading, very slender, white radials and five to seven ⅓-inch-long, amber centrals, those toward the tops of the stems hooked, the ones below straight. The flowers are straw-colored with reddish mid-stripes on the petals. They are about ½ inch long. *M. hahniana* (1), the old lady or old woman cactus, has nearly spherical plant bodies about 4 inches in diameter, flattened or depressed at their tops and, with age, forming clusters. From the axils of their tubercles sprout short white, woolly hairs and white, curly bristles up to 2 inches long that almost completely obscure the plant body. The radial spines, in clusters of twenty to thirty and interlacing, are white and hairlike, ½ inch long or a little longer. From one to seven easily detachable, reddish-brown-tipped, translucent, white centrals present in the younger spine clusters are usually absent from older ones. The flowers, about ¾ inch

across, are carmine-pink to purple-red. In *M. h. werdermanniana* the hairs and bristles are shorter, the spines black. *M. hamilton-hoytiae* (1) has usually solitary plant bodies up to 6 inches wide, spherical with depressed apexes, and with white, woolly hairs in the axils of the younger tubercles. The spines are in clusters of five to eight curved, brown- or black-tipped, white to cream-colored radials, the upper ones under ¼ inch in length, the lowers much longer, and two or three straight, pink to gray, dark-tipped centrals, the uppers up to ⅜ inch in length, the lowers up to 1¼ inches long. The flowers have purplish-pink inner petals with darker mid-stripes, olive-green outer ones, their mid-stripes brownish. *M. hemisphaerica* (1), of Texas and Mexico, has hemispherical plant bodies up to 5 inches in diameter, with widely-spaced tubercles without hairs or bristles in their axils. The spine clusters are of nine to thirteen brown- or black-tipped, cream-colored radials, the upper ones shorter than the lower, which are about ⅓ inch in length. The flowers, white to creamy-white, have grayish, brownish-purple, or pink mid-stripes on the petals. *M. herrerae* (3) has mostly solitary, small, spherical to broadly-ovoid plant bodies 1 inch to 1½ inches in diameter that in aspect suggest little balls of cotton. Their tubercles are without hairs in their axils. The spine clusters are of ninety or more spreading radials up to ¼ inch long. There are no centrals. The 1-inch-wide flowers are light pink to purplish. Variety *M. h. albiflora* has larger, white flowers. *M. heyderi* (1), native from Texas to Mexico, has small, solitary, spherical to flattened-spherical, light to dark green plant bodies. Its spine clusters are of twenty to twenty-two white to creamy-white radials from ¼ to ½ inch long and one stout, yellowish-gray to brown central tipped with reddish-brown. From ¾ to 1 inch in diameter, the flowers have cream-edged, brownish-pink petals. The fruits are red. *M. hidalgensis* (3) has rarely branched, cylindrical to club-shaped plant bodies up to a little over 1 foot tall by 4 inches thick and with widely spaced tubercles, with whitish woolly hairs in the axils of the younger ones. Usually the extremely short radial spines, of which there may be up to eight, are lacking. There are two or more often four ⅜-inch-long, yellowish-brown to gray centrals with brown apexes. The flowers are carmine. *M. humboldtii* (3) has spherical to short-cylindrical plant bodies branched from their bases and up to 3½ inches in diameter. In the axils of the tubercles are white, woolly hairs and up to eight bristles. The spine clusters, devoid of centrals, are of up to eighty slender, pure white radials ⅓ inch long, or shorter. The flowers, about ¼ inch wide, are carmine-red. *M. hutchisoniana* (syn. *M. bullardiana*) (3) has clustered stems up to 6 inches tall, cylin-

drical and 1½ to a little over 2 inches thick. Its spine clusters are of twenty or a few less slender radials up to ⅓ inch long, changing from purplish-black to whitish as they age and three centrals about as long, the lowest hooked. The bell-shaped blooms have greenish-white outer petals with center stripes of pinkish-purple and pale pink inner ones with a darker stripe down their centers. *M. inaiae* (3) has cylindrical plant bodies branched from their bases, rounded at their tops, and up to 8 inches tall and 2¼ inches wide. In the axils of the younger tubercles are white, woolly hairs and sometimes a few bristles. The spine clusters are of from seventeen to twenty-four rigid, white radials up to ¼ inch in length and two or less often three reddish- to purple-brown centrals about twice as long. The flowers, about ¾ inch across, are white to creamy-white or have pinkish outer petals, with reddish mid-stripes to the petals. *M. insularis* (3) has large clusters of flattish-spherical plant bodies about 2 inches in diameter with the axils of the tubercles practically naked of hairs or bristles. The spine clusters are of twenty to thirty slender, white, ¼-inch-long radials and a solitary hooked central ⅜ inch long, black shading to brown and yellow. The flowers, ¾ to 1 inch across, have white petals with green to pink mid-stripes. *M. jaliscana* (3) forms clusters of flattish-spherical about 2-inch-wide plant bodies with tubercles in thirteen rows. The spine clusters are of thirty or more white radials up to ⅓ inch long and four to eight dark-tipped, reddish-brown centrals ⅓ to ½ inch long, and the lowest hooked. The flowers are pinkish-purple, about ½ inch wide. *M. johnstonii* (1) has usually solitary, more or less spherical plant bodies slightly depressed at their apexes and 6 to 8 inches tall. The tubercle axils contain a few white, woolly hairs. The spine clusters are of ten to eighteen radials ¼ to ⅜ inch long, white to tan tipped with reddish-brown to black, and two or less commonly up to six dark purple to black centrals ½ to 1 inch long. The bell-shaped flowers have white to creamy-white petals with purplish mid-stripes. *M. kewensis* (3) has spherical plant bodies that as they age become cylindrical and branch from their bases. Up to 5 inches tall by 3½ inches wide, they have tubercles with curly, white, woolly hairs in their axils. The four to six radial spines (there are no centrals) in each starry cluster are ¼ to 1 inch long or longer. When young they are reddish to purplish or black, later paler. The flowers are bell-shaped, magenta to purplish-pink, and ½ inch wide or a little wider. *M. klissingiana* (1) has spherical to cylindrical plant bodies up to about 6 inches tall and 3½ inches wide that branch from their bases when about three years old. They have abundant white, woolly hairs and bristles ⅜ inch long in the axils of their tubercles. The spine clusters consist of thirty to thirty-five fine, white, sometimes slightly wavy radials under ¼ inch long, and almost completely hiding the plant bodies, and two to five shorter, needle-like, white centrals tipped with dark brown when young. The flowers are bell-shaped, ⅜ inch across, and rose-pink with darker mid-stripes to the petals. *M. knebeliana* (3) has solitary or clustered, short-cylindrical plant bodies, 2 to 2½ inches high, flattened at their spiny, not woolly apexes. The tubercles have a few bristles in their axils. The spine clusters are of twenty to twenty-five spreading, ¼-inch-long, white, hairlike radials and four to seven erect, rust-colored, hooked centrals, ⅓ to ½ inch in length. The yellow flowers are ¾ inch wide. *M. kunzeana* (3) has clusters of spherical to short-cylindrical plant bodies with cylindrical tubercles, without wool but with bristles in their axils. The spine clusters are of up to twenty-five bristle-like, snow-white, ⅜-inch-long radials and three or four rough-surfaced, brown centrals, the longest ¾ inch in length and hooked. The white to yellowish-white flowers, pink on their outsides, are almost or quite ¾ inch wide. *M. lanata* (3) has solitary or clustered, short-cylindrical plant bodies slightly depressed at their tops, up to 1¼ inches in diameter, and with copious white, woolly hairs in the axils of the tubercles, especially the younger ones. Under ¹⁄₁₀ inch long, the white to pale brown radial spines are in clusters of twelve to twenty. There are no centrals. From ¼ to ⅓ inch wide, the flowers have white to light pink petals with darker pink mid-stripes. *M. lasiacantha* (3), of Texas, has clustered, spherical to ovoid plant bodies up to 1 inch high with small, cylindrical tubercles without hairs in their axils. The spines, which almost completely hide the plants, are in clusters of forty to sixty very short, bristly, rough-surfaced, white radials; there are no centrals. The flowers are white with a purplish to brownish center stripe to each petal. *M. l. denudata* (syn. *M. denudata*) has larger plant bodies with clusters of up to eighty spines. *M. lenta* (2) forms clusters of spherical to short-cylindrical plant bodies up to 2½ inches across, almost hidden by fragile, white, all radial spines in clusters of about forty. The axils of the tubercles are woolly. The flowers, about 1 inch wide, are whitish. *M. leona* (syn. *M. pottsii*) (3), of Texas and Mexico, has somewhat clustered cylindrical plant bodies about 5 inches long and 1½ inches wide and thickly clothed with spines. Each spine cluster has about thirty interlacing white radials and six to eight stouter centrals. The flowers are light purple, with petals edged with orange-pink. *M. leucantha* (3) has usually solitary, spherical to cylindrical plant bodies up to 1½ inches in diameter. They have tubercles that when young have short, white,

woolly hairs and a few bristles in their axils. The spine clusters are of about eighteen pale-tipped, amber, slender radials, three amber, hooked centrals, and sometimes one straight central of the same hue. The flowers are white, with a green stripe down the center of each petal. *M. lloydii* (1) rarely makes offsets. Its usually solitary plant bodies are at first flattish-spherical, but later cylindrical. They are 2¼ to 3½ inches in diameter and have a few woolly hairs in the axils of the younger tubercles only. The spines, all radials ¼ inch long or shorter, are in clusters of three or four. Approximately ½ inch wide, the flowers have greenish outer petals with brownish mid-stripes, white to pink inner ones with darker mid-stripes of deeper pink. *M. longicoma* (3) has spherical to somewhat cylindrical plant bodies 1½ to 2 inches in diameter that typically form wide clumps. They have tubercles with long, white hairs in their axils. The spine clusters are of twenty-five interlaced, weak, white, hairlike radials and four pale-based, brown centrals about ½ inch long, one or two of them hooked. The flowers are rose-pink or white strongly suffused with pink. *M. magallanii* (3), which seldom branches, has spherical to club-shaped plant bodies up to about 3½ inches tall and 2 inches wide with sparse woolly hairs in the axils of the tubercles. The spine clusters are of seventy to seventy-five interlacing radials up to ¼ inch long, with tan bases, white centers, and brown apexes. There may be one central spine much like the radials, or none. The flowers are cream-colored with pink to brownish mid-stripes to the petals. *M. magnimamma* (1) is highly variable and at various times many different names have been applied to its sorts. It forms large clumps of broadly-spherical plant bodies 3 to 4 inches in diameter with long tubercles with woolly hairs in the axils of the younger ones. The spine clusters are of three to five gray to amber radials of unequal lengths, the largest, the lower ones, up to 1 inch long. Infrequently there is one central similar to the radials. About 1 inch across, the flowers are dull cream-colored with petals with brownish to reddish mid-

Mammillaria magnimamma

stripes. *M. mainiae* (3), native to Arizona and Mexico, has spherical to cylindrical plant bodies up to 4 inches tall by one-half or slightly more as wide that branch from their bases and above as they age. The axils of their tubercles are without hairs or bristles. The spine clusters are of ten to fifteen rigid, yellowish, sometimes brown- or black-tipped or all black radials and one or less often up to three strongly-hooked centrals ½ to ¾ inch long. The flowers, about 1 inch wide, have white or creamy-white petals with brownish to pink mid-stripes. *M. martinezii* has solitary, cylindrical or slightly club-shaped, bluish-green plant bodies up to about 6 inches tall and

Mammillaria martinezii

one-half as thick. The axils of its numerous small tubercles are filled with woolly hair. The starry spine clusters are of about twenty very slender, yellow-based, white, ½-inch-long radials and two similar centrals. The carmine flowers are about ½ inch in diameter. *M. matudae* (2) has clustered cylindrical stems up to 8 inches long by about 1¼ inches thick. The axils of the tubercles are without hairs. The spine clusters are of eighteen to twenty up to ⅛ inch long, needle-like, translucent white radials and one stouter, somewhat longer central, white with pink tips when young, later becoming brownish. The flowers are reddish-purple. *M. mazatlanensis* (3) has clustered, cylindrical plant bodies up to 4½ inches tall and 1½ inches wide that branch freely from their bases and have tubercles with sometimes a very few short bristles in their axils. The spine clusters are of thirteen to fifteen white radials, up to or rarely exceeding ⅜ inch in length, and three, four, or seldom more stouter, reddish- or brownish-tipped centrals, up to ½ inch long. The flowers are small and carmine-red, with reddish-tipped, white outer petals. *M. melanocentra* (1), of the southwestern United States and Mexico, has nearly always solitary plant bodies, spherical with depressed tops, up to 6 inches tall by 5 inches wide. The axils of the tubercles, especially the younger ones, have white, woolly hairs. The spine clusters are of seven to nine radials, the upper about ¼ inch long, the lower up to 1 inch long, and one stiff, black central ¾ inch to 2¼ inches long. The flowers are dark pink to red with greenish-pink outer petals. *M. mercadensis* (3) forms clusters of depressed-topped, spherical plant bodies about 2 inches in diameter, their tubercles without hairs in their axils. Each cluster of spines consists of twenty-five to thirty slim, white radials, up to ⅓ inch long, and four to seven centrals, the uppers approximately ½ inch long, the lowers up to twice that length and hooked. All are white tipped with brown or brownish-red. The flowers are light pink and up to 1 inch wide. *M. mexicensis* (1) has solitary, spherical plant bodies containing milky sap and about 2¼ inches in diameter. The axils of the tubercles have at first a small amount of woolly hairs, later they are naked. The spine clusters are of similar white-tipped-with-brown radials and centrals up to ½ inch long. There are fifteen or sixteen of the former and two or three of the latter. The flowers are not described. *M. microcarpa* (3), of the southwestern United States and Mexico, with spherical to cylindrical plant bodies branching freely from their bases, are up to 6 inches tall by 2 inches wide or slightly wider. The axils of the tubercles are without hairs. Each spine cluster consists of twenty to thirty brown-tipped, white to yellow radials, the upper ones up to ¼ inch long, the lowers up to twice that length, and one to three, one of which is strongly hooked, tan to black centrals up to 1¼ inches long. The flowers have pale

Mammillaria microhelia

greenish outer petals with a brownish stripe down their centers and inner ones light pink with a deeper center stripe. *M. microhelia* (3) has sometimes clustered, cylindrical plant bodies up to 6 inches long by 2 inches thick with short, blunt tubercles and rounded apexes. The axils of young tubercles sprout a few woolly hairs. The spine clusters, which almost completely cover the plant bodies, are of about fifty bristly, recurved, white-tipped, golden-yellow to reddish-brown radials up to ¼ inch long and, except on young plants, four or fewer somewhat longer reddish to brown centrals. The cream-colored to greenish-white, sometimes slightly pink-tinged flowers are approximately ½ inch wide. Variety *M. m. microheliopsis* is similar to *M. microhelia*, but has spine clusters of thirty to forty radials and always six to eight centrals. Its flowers are purplish-red. *M. microthele* (1) has spherical plant bodies up to 3½ inches wide, often clustered, and usually with some woolly hairs in the axils of the tubercles. The spine clusters are of twenty-two to twenty-four fine, white radials up to ⅕ inch long and two smaller white centrals. The tiny flowers are white with pink outsides. *M. moellerana* (3) has spherical to club-shaped, rarely branched plant bodies, rounded at their apexes and without hairs in the axils of their tubercles. The spine clusters are of thirty-five to forty white-tipped yellowish, stiff radials and eight to ten yellow-tipped reddish-brown centrals, the lower ones up to ¾ inch long, and strongly hooked, the uppers shorter and straight. The flowers, a little more than ½ inch wide, are pinkish to pink with brownish to pink center stripes to the petals. *M. muehlenpfordtii* (syn. *M. neopotosina*) (1) has usually solitary plant bodies, spherical to cylindrical, and markedly depressed at their apexes. They are up to 4 inches tall by 3½ inches wide. The axils of the younger tubercles have white, woolly hairs and bristles up to ⅜ inch long. The spines are in clusters of forty to fifty white radials, the upper ⅒ inch in length, the lowers up to three times as long, bent and flexible, and four yellow, brown-tipped, stiff centrals of different lengths, the largest 1 inch to nearly 1½ inches long. The flowers, about ⅜ inch wide, are purple-red with pinkish-brownish outer petals with brown center stripes. *M. multiceps* (3), of Texas and Mexico, which resembles *M. prolifera*, forms large clumps of numerous spherical or cylindrical plant bodies up to 4 inches long and ¾ inch in diameter, with in the axils of their tubercles, fine white bristles. The spines, the radials hairlike, white, and up to ¼ inch long, the centrals slender, needle-like, and white with reddish or orange-colored apexes, are in clusters of thirty to fifty of the former and usually six to eight, occasionally a few more centrals. The flowers ½ to ¾ inch wide are greenish-

Mammillaria multiceps

yellow with brownish center stripes to the petals. *M. multiseta* (3) has spherical to cylindrical plant bodies up to 5 inches tall by 3 inches wide, with white, woolly hairs and twenty or more white bristles ½ inch long or longer in the axils of the tubercles. The spine clusters are of four to six brown-tipped white radials and one brownish central ⅓ inch long or slightly longer. The flowers are not described. *M. mundtii* (3) has spherical to cylindrical plant bodies with depressed apexes. Approximately 3 inches in diameter, they have tubercles devoid of hairs in their axils and clusters of ten to twelve about ¼-inch-long, dark-tipped, white radial spines and two or rarely four dark-tipped, brown centrals ⅜ inch long or longer. Approximately ½ inch wide, the bell-shaped flowers are red. *M. mystax* (1) has plant bodies solitary when young, later branching from their bases. Spherical to shortly-cylindrical and with depressed apexes and 3 to 4 inches in diameter, they have in the axils of their tubercles white hairs and long, white bristles. The spine clusters are often almost without radials, but may have up to ten in addition to two, three, or rarely four centrals. The radials are wavy, white tipped with brown, and up to ⅓ inch long. The centrals are twisted or curved, purplish or red fading to gray and tipped with brown. One is up to 3 inches long, the others about ¾ inch long. The carmine to purplish-red flowers are bell-shaped with paler outer petals. *M. napina* (3), of Texas and Mexico, has flattish spherical plant bodies 1½ to 2½ inches wide with a few woolly hairs in the axils of the tubercles. The spine clusters are of ten to twelve sometimes white-tipped, light yellow, somewhat curved radials and no centrals. The bell-shaped flowers, about 1¼ inches across, are rose- to violet-pink with paler outer petals with darker center stripes. Variety *M. n. centrispina* has spine clusters with one central spine up to ⅓ inch long in addition to the radials. *M. neopalmeri* (3) has somewhat elongated plant bodies up to 4 inches tall by 2 inches wide and depressed at their tops, with white, woolly hairs and some short white bristles in the axils of the tubercles. The spine clusters consist of twenty-five to thirty very slender, stiff, white, about ¼-inch-long radials and usually four, sometimes three or five, dark-tipped, brownish centrals up to ⅓ inch in length. The flowers, about ⅜ inch wide, have white to cream-colored inner petals with olive-green stripes and light brown outer petals with darker mid-stripes. *M. nivosa* (1), of the West Indies, develops clusters of spherical to cylindrical, very spiny plant bodies from 3½ to 7 inches in diameter, with abundant persistent, white, woolly hairs in the axils of their tubercles. The spine clusters are of six to eight radials, the longest up to 1¼ inches long, the other about ⅜ inch long, and one ¾-inch-long central. All are stiff, bright yellow when young later becoming dark brown. The flowers are cream to lemon-yellow. *M. nunezii* (3) has spherical to cylindrical plant bodies, sometimes branched from their bases, up to 6 inches tall and 3½ inches wide. There are eight to ten white bristles in the axils of the tubercles. The spine clusters are of twenty-five to thirty needle-like, white radials and two to four or less commonly up to six stout, brown- or black-tipped, creamy-yellow centrals up to about ½ inch in length. The flowers are deep rose- to magenta-pink with tannish outer petals with darker center stripes. *M. n. solisii* (syn. *M. solisii*) has plant bodies solitary at first, which eventually branch, up to 8 inches tall by one-half as wide. In the axils of their tubercles are several wavy bristles, no woolly hairs. The spine clusters are of twenty to twenty-five stiff, white radials up to ⅓ inch long and three to six, most commonly four, stouter, yellowish-brown centrals up to ¾ inch long, one hooked, and dark-tipped. The flowers are dark rose-pink to magenta with darker center stripes to the petals. *M. occidentalis* (3) has freely-clustering, cylindrical plant bodies up to 6 inches in height and 1¼ inches in diameter, without hairs but sometimes with a few white bristles in the axils of the tubercles. The spine clusters are of twelve to eighteen stiff, brown-tipped, white to cream-colored radials and four or five rigid, reddish-brown centrals, ¼ to ½ inch long, one usually hooked. The flowers are rose-pink with darker center stripes to the petals. *M. ocotillensis* (1) has flattish-spherical plant bodies up to 3 inches tall and wide, naked of hairs in the axils of the tubercles. Each spine cluster has usually three, sometimes two or four chalky-white radials and one to three, but commonly two purple-brown to black centrals, the lower one up to 1½ inches long, the others considerably shorter. The flowers have cream-colored petals with reddish center stripes. *M. oliviae* (3) has spherical to sub-cylindrical plant bodies up to 4 inches tall by 2½ inches wide, solitary at first, those of old specimens clustered. There are

small tufts of woolly hairs in the axils of the tubercles and a little wool on young areoles. The spines, the lower of the four or fewer centrals of each cluster tipped with brown, are otherwise pure white. Each cluster has ¼-inch-long twenty-five to thirty-five radials, somewhat shorter than the centrals. The flowers, pink to purplish-red and about 1¼ inches across, have seven-lobed, green stigmas. The 1-inch-long, club-shaped fruits are scarlet. *M. orcuttii* (1) has solitary, spherical to short-cylindrical plant bodies depressed at their apexes and 2 to 3 inches in diameter, with white persistent woolly hairs in the axils of the tubercles. The spine clusters are of all black to gray centrals of which there are four or rarely five, the lower ones ¾ inch long, the upper ones to 4 inches long. About ½ inch in diameter, the flowers are bright carmine with brownish outer petals with darker mid-stripes. *M. painteri* (3) has solitary, spherical to short-cylindrical plant bodies, ¾ inch across, with sometimes in the axils of the tubercles a few woolly hairs. The spine clusters are of twenty or more bristle-like, white radials up to ¼ inch long and four or five black-tipped, dark brown centrals up to ⅜ inch long, one or more hooked. The flowers, ½ inch or rather less wide, are greenish-white, the petals with yellowish mid-stripes. *M. parkinsonii* (1) forms great clumps of spherical to club-shaped plant bodies about 6 inches tall and 2½ to 3½ inches wide, with abundant white, woolly hairs and wavy bristles in the axils of the tubercles. The spine clusters are of twenty to thirty-five snow-white, bristly radials and two or less frequently three, four, or five brown-tipped white centrals, the upper ones up to ⅓ inch long, the lowers up to 1¼ inches long and curved backward. The flowers are small, pinkish to yellowish-cream with darker mid-stripes to the petals. *M. peninsularis* (1) is a clustering sort, its plant bodies flattened-spherical and about 1½ inches across. The axils of the tubercles, later bare, are at first furnished with white, woolly hairs. The spine clusters are of all radials, although occasionally one has the appearance of a central. Light yellow tipped with brown, they are about ¼ inch long. The flowers are yellowish-green, sometimes with brown mid-stripes. *M. perbella* (2) has spherical to short-cylindrical plant bodies about 2¼ inches in diameter, sometimes grouped, but often solitary. The tubercles have in their axils white, woolly hairs. The spine clusters are of fourteen to eighteen radials not over ⅛ inch long and bristle-like and one or two similarly colored centrals up to ¼ inch in length, or the centrals may be absent. The flowers, ⅜ inch wide, are predominantly carmine but may be suffused with pink or white. *M. petrophila* (1) forms clusters of flattened to spherical to slightly cylindrical plant bodies up to 6

inches in diameter with in the axils of their tubercles considerable white or brownish, woolly hairs that become fewer with age, and a few bristles. Each spine cluster has eight to ten rigid, brown-tipped, whitish radials up to ¾ inch long and one or two dark brown centrals, up to 1¼ inches long, that become paler as they age. The flowers are greenish-yellow, about ¾ inch wide. *M. picta* (3) has occasionally branching, more often solitary, spherical to club-shaped plant bodies up to about 1½ inches in diameter with a few wavy, white bristles but without hairs in the axils of their tubercles. The spine clusters are of twelve to fourteen fine, brown-tipped white to yellowish radials, up to ⅓ inch in length, and one or sometimes two brown-tipped, yellow centrals that become paler as they age. The flowers are creamy-white to white, with olive-green center bands to the petals. *M. plumosa* (3), the feather ball cactus, is one of the loveliest of its genus. It forms considerable mounds of spherical plant bodies 2 to 3 inches in diameter, with soft, slender-cylindrical tubercles up to ½ inch long in the axils of which is long, white wool. The spine clusters are of as many as forty pure white, feathery radials. About ¾ inch wide, the flowers are white with greenish-white inner petals and a three- to five-lobed greenish-yellow stigma. *M. polythele* (1) has usually solitary spherical to cylindrical plant bodies up to about 1¾ feet tall and 4 inches wide, with many soon deciduous white hairs in the axils of younger tubercles. The spine clusters, without radials, consist of one to five needle-like brownish-yellow to dark brown centrals up to 1 inch long. The flowers are rose-pink to carmine. *M. pringlei* (3) has spherical to short-cylindrical plant bodies with flattish tops up to 7 inches tall by two-thirds as wide. In their early years usually solitary, eventually they form clusters. The axils of the tubercles are furnished with white, woolly hairs and some bristles. Each spine cluster has fifteen to twenty fine, bright yellow to white radials up to ⅜ inch long and usually six but from five to ten rigid reddish-based yellow centrals ½ to 1 inch in length, red-tipped when young. The red flowers are about ⅜ inch wide. *M. prolifera* (3), of the West Indies, is sometimes confused with *M. multiceps*, which it much resembles. Variable, it characteristically forms large clumps of easily detachable conical to ovoid plant bodies up to 2¼ inches long and one-half as thick. In the axils of the tubercles are a few white, woolly hairs and long white bristles. The spine clusters are of forty or fewer fine, white radials, up to ⅜ inch long, and five to twelve stouter yellow centrals, up to ⅓ inch long, that fade as they age. The flowers are small, yellowish to greenish-white. *M. pseudocrucigera* (1) has solitary, flattened-spherical plant bodies about 2

Mammillaria prolifera

Mammillaria prolifera (flowers)

Mammillaria prolifera, in fruit

inches wide depressed at their apexes and with, in the axils of their tubercles, some white, woolly hairs. The spine clusters are of twelve or thirteen fine, white radials, up to ⅛ inch long, and four slightly larger centrals with brown or black tips and orange-brown bases. About ½ inch in diameter, the bell-shaped flowers have white petals with pink stripes down their centers. ***M. pseudoperbella*** (3) has clustered, very spiny plant bodies up to 6 inches in diameter, flattened-spherical when young, and later short-cylindrical, with in the axils of their tubercles a few white, woolly hairs. The spine clusters are of twenty to thirty bristle-like, white radials up to ⅛ inch in length and two brown centrals up to twice as long, one recurved. The flowers are purple-red to carmine. ***M. pubispina*** (3) has solitary plant bodies up to 1½ inches across, spherical with slightly-flattened tops. In the axils of the tubercles are a few white, woolly hairs and a few long hairlike bristles. The spine clusters are of about fifteen spreading, hairlike radials up to ½ inch long and three or four red to dark brown centrals, up to ⅜ inch long, the lower ones hooked, that pale with age. The ½-inch-wide flowers have white to cream-colored petals with reddish mid-bands. ***M. pygmaea*** (3) has freely-clustering, spherical to cylindrical plant bodies up to about 1½ inches long and nearly as wide. The axils of their tubercles, without hairs, have a few fine, white bristles. The spine clusters are of about fifteen very fine white radials up to ⅜ inch long and four golden-yellow to reddish centrals, the uppers up to ¼ inch long the lowers up to ⅓ inch long, and hooked. The flowers have cream-colored petals with tannish mid-stripes. ***M. pyrrhocephala*** (1) has clustered, short-cylindrical plant bodies, up to 3½ inches tall, with depressed tops. The axils of their tubercles sprout white to tan woolly hairs and long, white, wavy bristles. Each spine cluster is composed of four to eight dark-tipped, reddish-brown radials ⅒ to ⅕ inch long. Generally centrals are lacking, but sometimes there is one black central, becoming gray tipped with black. The flowers have pink inner petals with red mid-stripes and reddish outer petals, olive-green toward their bases. ***M. rekoi*** (2) has spherical to short-cylindrical plant bodies up to 5 inches tall and about one-half as wide with tubercles in the axils of which are short white hairs and up to eight long white bristles. The spine clusters are of about twenty needle-like white radials, up to ¼ inch long, and four centrals, up to a little more than ½ inch long, the lowest hooked. The flowers are dark purple, the outer petals with brownish center stripes. ***M. rhodantha*** (3), which varies considerably, has plant bodies at first spherical, later cylindrical to club-shaped and branching from their bases. Up to 1 foot long by 4 inches wide, they have white, woolly hairs and a few bristles in the axils of their tubercles. The spine clusters are of sixteen to twenty pale yellow to white, needle-like radials up to ⅓ inch long and commonly four, but sometimes up to seven centrals that vary much in color in different varietal forms: light brown, in *M. r. callaena;* rich brown, in *M. r. chrysacantha;* yellow to reddish-brown, in *M. r. crassispina;* deep red, in *M. r. ruberrima;* lighter red, in *M. r. rubra;* and so on. The ½-inch-wide or slightly larger flowers are rose-pink with the outer petals yellowish-green, all with darker mid-stripes. ***M. ritterana*** (1) has usually solitary spherical plant bodies slightly depressed at their tops. Their tubercles have in their axils short white, woolly hairs and long white bristles. The spine clusters are of eighteen to twenty hairlike pure white radials, approximately ¼ inch long, and one or two ⅜-inch-long white, yellow, or brown central. About ½ inch wide, the flowers have white petals with rose-red mid-stripes. ***M. roseocentra*** (3) has clusters of plant bodies with short tubercles naked of hairs in their axils. The spine clusters are of two circles of radials, the outer white, the inner ones longer and rose-red. The flowers are undescribed. ***M. ruestii*** (3), native to Honduras and Guatemala, develops clusters of spherical to cylindrical plant bodies with flattened apexes. Up to 3 inches tall and 2 inches in diameter, they have white woolly hairs and bristles in the axils of their tubercles. The spines are in clusters of sixteen to twenty-four fine, white radials, up to ¼ inch long, and four or rarely five strong, needle-like, chestnut-brown centrals, up to ⅓ inch long. The bell-shaped flowers, up to ¾ inch across, have white to pinkish petals with carmine tips and mid-stripes. *M. sartorii* (1) has spherical to short-cylindrical plant bodies, at first solitary, later clustered, up to about 5 inches in diameter, and with the axils of their younger tubercles filled with white, woolly hairs. The spine clusters are generally of four, sometimes of up to six brown-tipped, off-white radials, up to ⅓ inch long, and usually no centrals, but occasionally one or more similar to the radials. The flowers are bell-shaped, up to ¾ inch wide, and yellowish to bright carmine with petals with darker mid-stripes. *M. schiedeana* (3) forms crowded clusters of softish, spherical plant bodies up to 4

Mammillaria schiedeana

inches high and 1½ inches wide, their tubercles with long, white bristles in their axils. The spine clusters are of about seventy-five interlacing, yellow-tipped, white, rough-pubescent radials and no centrals. The flowers, white and about ½ inch wide, have four-lobed stigmas. *M. scrippsiana* (1) has clustered spherical to short-cylindrical plant bodies, depressed at their tops and up to 2½ inches tall. The axils of their tubercles are thickly furnished with woolly hairs. The spine clusters are of eight to ten or perhaps sometimes fewer reddish-tipped, needle-like white radials, up to ⅓ inch long, and two stout, brown centrals, up to ⅜ inch long. The delicate pink flowers, with pink center stripes to their petals, are about ½ inch in diameter. *M. seideliana* (3) develops clusters of spherical to short-cylindrical plant bodies 3 inches long by two-thirds as thick with the axils of the tubercles naked except for an occasional bristle. The spines are in clusters of eighteen to twenty-five white radials, up to ⅓ inch long, and three or four brown-tipped, white centrals about as long, the lowermost hooked. A little over

½ inch wide, the flowers are yellow to cream-colored, with pink stripes on the outsides of the outer ones. *M. sempervivi* (1) has solitary, or as they become older or more or less clustered, flattened-spherical to short-cylindrical plant bodies, up to 4 inches in diameter, with an abundance of woolly hairs in the axils of their tubercles, especially the younger ones. The spine clusters have usually three or four, sometimes up to seven white radials, up to ⅛ inch long, that are shed after one or two years and two stouter centrals as long as the radials or a little longer and reddish-brown fading to yellowish or whitish. The flowers are dull white with petals with a reddish mid-stripe on their undersides. *M. sheldonii* (3) has clustered, cylindrical stems up to 10 inches long and nearly 2½ inches thick without hairs in the axils of their tubercles. The spines are in clusters of ten to fifteen needle-like reddish-brown radials darkening toward their tips, up to about ⅓ inch in length, and one to three reddish-brown centrals, up to about 1¼ inches wide, ½ inch long, the lower one hooked. The flowers are pink to light purple with darker mid-stripes to the petals. *M. simplex* (syn. *M. mammillaris*) (1), of northern Venezuela and offshore islands, has clusters of spherical to short-cylindrical plant bodies, sometimes up to 8 inches tall but, more often less than one-half that. There are a few hairs in the axils of the tubercles. The spine clusters are of ten to sixteen reddish-brown to gray, needle-like radials, up to ⅓ inch long, and three to five centrals, similar except for sometimes darker tips. The flowers are small, white to yellowish with greenish to brownish outer petals. *M. sinistrohamata* (3) has solitary or clustered spherical plant bodies, 1½ to 2 inches in diameter, with depressed apexes, their axils naked of hairs. The spine clusters are of about twenty slender, white to pale yellow radials, up to ½ inch long, and four stouter, amber-yellow centrals, about ⅝ inch in length, and one hooked. The flowers are ½ inch wide, greenish-cream. *M. sphacelata* (3) has cylindrical plant bodies up to 8 inches long and 1½ inches in diameter that branch freely from their bases and upper parts; the tubercles have at first a few woolly hairs and some bristles. The spine clusters are of nine to twenty white radials ⅜ inch long, the younger ones tipped with red, the older with brown, and one to four, mostly only one, central, similar to, but shorter than the radials. About ⅓ inch across, the flowers are dark red with greenish outer petals, with brownish to reddish center stripes. *M. spinosissima* (3) is highly variable and individuals are cultivated under many varietal names. Their plant bodies are cylindrical or when young spherical, up to 1 foot tall by 4 inches thick, and very spiny. Solitary or branched from their bases to form small clumps,

they have woolly hairs and bristles in the axils of the tubercles. The spine clusters are of twenty to thirty white, hairlike radials, ⅒ to ⅓ inch long, and the seven to fifteen needle-like centrals that vary greatly in color in different varieties are up to ¾ inch long. The flowers are red to purple-red with brownish outer petals, about ¾ inch across. *M. standleyi* (1) forms clumps of spherical plant bodies, depressed at their tops, 4 to 6 inches in diameter, with dense growths of white woolly hairs and bristles in the axils of the tubercles. The spine clusters are of sixteen to nineteen dark-tipped white radials, up to ⅓ inch long, the upper ones considerably shorter, and four stouter reddish-brown centrals, the lower ones ⅓ inch long, the others shorter. The flowers, about ½ inch wide, are purple-pink with deeper colored outer petals. *M. swinglei* (3) has clustered stems. Up to 8 inches tall and 2 inches thick, they have in the axils of their tubercles woolly hairs at first yellow that become white, and finally shed, and some persistent bristles. The spine clusters are of eight to ten scarcely noticeable radials and four to six brown-tipped, paler brown centrals. The flowers, ⅓ inch in diameter, have purple-red inner petals bordered with white or cream and brownish outer petals. *M. tesopacensis* (1) has spherical to cylindrical plant bodies up to 7 inches tall by 5 inches wide, sometimes with a few white, woolly hairs in the axils of the younger tubercles. The spine clusters are of four to seven slender radials, approximately ¼ inch long, at first tan with dark tips, later gray, and one or two similarly colored, stout centrals, up to twice as long. The flowers are cream, their outer petals tinged green, and all petals have a pink to reddish center band. *M. tetracantha* (1) forms clusters of spherical to cylindrical plant bodies, up to 1 foot tall by 4½ inches wide; the axils of the tubercles contain white, woolly hairs. The spine clusters are without or have only vestigial radials and four to six centrals, at first reddish, fading to grayish or whitish, up to little over 1 inch long. The flowers, with pink or purplish petals with carmine center stripes, are a little over ½ inch across. *M. trichacantha* (3) has usually solitary 2-inch-wide plant bodies, spherical to short-cylindrical, with depressed tops. They have a few hairlike bristles in the axils of their tubercles. The spine clusters are of fifteen to eighteen white to pale yellow radials, up to ⅓ inch long, and two or rarely three centrals, the lower one, strongly hooked, at first warm brown, later fading to brown or gray with a brown tip, the others white to gray, tipped with brown. The flowers, a little over ½ inch wide, have yellowish to greenish-cream petals with darker center bands. *M. uncinata* (3) has mostly solitary spherical plant bodies 3½ to 4 inches across, occasionally with

Mammillaria trichacantha

offsets from their bases and with depressed apexes. In the axils of the younger tubercles only are a few white, woolly hairs. The spine clusters are of four to seven up to ¼-inch-long, black-tipped, white radials, the upper ones curved, and usually one, but up to three stout, strongly-hooked, dark-tipped, brown centrals, up to ½ inch long. The flowers are pink with brownish mid-stripes to the petals and the outer petals brownish-green. *M. vaupelii* (2) has solitary, flattened-spherical plant bodies 1½ to 2 inches high and somewhat broader than tall with in the axils of the tubercles curly, white, woolly hairs and grayish-white bristles. The spines are in clusters of sixteen to twenty-one ¼-inch-long, yellow-based, white-ended radials that fade to gray as they age and two centrals the larger over ½ inch long, the other somewhat shorter; when young the centrals are orange, later they become cream-colored to pinkish with brown tips and eventually gray. The ⅜-inch-wide flowers have purplish-pink petals with white bases. *M. verhaertiana* (3) has plant bodies rarely branched, long-cylindrical, and up to 1 foot tall by one-half as wide. The axils of the tubercles contain white, woolly hairs and as many as twenty pure white bristles. The spine clusters are of fifteen to twenty or more yellowish-brown to paler radials, the longest, the lowers, over ½ inch long, and four to six stout, spreading, brown-tipped, yellowish-white, spreading centrals, up to ½ inch long, the lower one hooked. The

flowers are creamy-white to yellowish, the petals with pink to greenish mid-stripes. *M. vetula* (3) has freely-clustering cylindrical to club-shaped plant bodies up to 8 inches long by 1½ inches wide, flattened at their tops, and with the axils of the tubercles usually naked, sometimes with a few white, woolly hairs. The spine clusters are of twenty-five to fifty slender, white radials, ⅛ to ⅓ inch long, and one or two or perhaps sometimes up to six stout centrals, up to ⅜ inch long, at first reddish-brown to red, later gray. From slightly under to somewhat over ½ inch wide, the flowers are yellow, their inner petals with reddish-orange center stripes, their outer ones so striped on their undersides. *M. viereckii* (3) has nearly always solitary, sometimes clustered, spherical plant bodies, about 1½ inches in diameter, that have white woolly hairs and up to ten white bristles in the axils of their tubercles. The spine clusters are of up to ten sometimes slightly wavy, white or light yellow radials, not quite ½ inch long, and about the same number of similar centrals disposed with the radials. The flowers, cream- to yellowish-cream with greenish throats, are about ⅜ inch wide. *M. wiesingeri* (3) has solitary, decidedly flattened-spherical plant bodies, up to 1½ inches high and more than twice as wide, with the axils of their tubercles bare of woolly hairs, but sometimes with one or two white bristles. The spine clusters are of eighteen to twenty-five, white ¼-inch-long radials and four to six stouter, red-

dish-brown centrals of about the same length. The bell-shaped flowers are carmine-pink with deeper mid-stripes to the petals. *M. wildii* (3) has broad clumps of many cylindrical plant bodies, up to 6 inches tall and 2 inches in diameter, and with in the axils of the tubercles several long, whitish to pinkish, wavy hairs or bristles. The spines are in clusters of eight to ten bristle-like, white radials, up to ⅓ inch long, and three or four slender, needle-like centrals, at first light yellow, but darkening later, the lower one hooked. The dullish flowers, ½ inch in diameter, are whitish to bronzy-white with brownish mid-stripes to the outer petals. *M. winterae* (1), of Mexico, has solitary, broad-spherical, light green to bluish-green plant bodies with four-angled tubercles. Its spine clusters are of four radials up to 1¼ inches long. About 1 inch in diameter, the flowers are yellowish-white edged with white and with a reddish center line. The fruits are pink. *M. woburnensis* (syn. *M. chapinensis*) (1), of Guatemala, has clusters of spherical to cylindrical plant bodies with rounded tops and tubercles with persistent white, woolly hairs and wavy bristles in their axils. The spines are in clusters of five to nine yellowish-white radials, up to ¼ inch long, and one to sometimes three ⅜-inch-long centrals at first dark brown, later ivory-white tipped with reddish-brown. The up to ¾-inch-wide flowers have yellowish to yellow petals with reddish center stripes. *M. woodsii* (1) has solitary, flattened-spherical plant bodies about 2 inches high by 3 inches wide with a dense growth of white, woolly hairs and many hairlike bristles up to 1 inch long of the same color in the axils of the tubercles. The spine clusters are of twenty-five to thirty wavy, hairlike radials, up to ⅓ inch long, and mostly two, sometimes four black-tipped, purplish-pink centrals, the uppers under ¼ inch, the lowers over ½ inch, long. The flowers are pink with deeper pink to brownish mid-stripes to the petals. *M. wrightii* (3), of Texas and Mexico, has usually solitary flattened-spherical plant bodies, 1½ to 3½ inches in diameter, with depressed tops and tubercles with axils bare of spines or bristles. The spine clusters are of ten to fourteen fine, white radials, ½ inch or somewhat less long, some of which are tipped with dark brown or black and usually two, but from one to four dark brown to black radials, up to ½ inch long, one or more hooked. The 1-inch-wide flowers are purplish with purplish-green outer petals. *M. yaquensis* (3) forms large mounds of numerous cylindrical plant bodies, up to 3 inches long by almost ¾ inch wide, with a very few short woolly hairs in the axils of the tubercles. The spine clusters are of about eighteen fine cream-colored, ¼-inch-long radials with light brown tips and one strongly hooked, slightly longer, dark-tipped, reddish-brown central. The flowers are bell-shaped, whitish-pink, and about ¾ inch long. *M. yucatanensis* (3) has clusters of cylindrical plant bodies 4 to 6 inches tall by 1¼ to 2½ inches thick. White, woolly hairs are present in varying amounts in the axils of the tubercles. The spines are in clusters of twenty to thirty white, needle-like radials, under ¼ inch long, and three to six centrals, up to ⅓ inch long, and when young yellowish-red to crimson, becoming brownish later. The flowers, ½ inch or rather less wide, have pink petals the inner ones with darker center stripes. *M. zeilmanniana* (3) has solitary or somewhat branched cylindrical plant bodies, somewhat depressed at their apexes,

Mammillaria zeilmanniana

about 2½ inches high and nearly as wide. The axils of the tubercles are without hairs. The spines are in clusters of fifteen to eighteen about ⅓-inch-long, stiff, white radials and four reddish-tipped, yellowish-brown centrals, the lower ones hooked. The flowers, about ¾ inch wide, are purple to reddish-violet with paler throats, or rarely are white. *M. zeyerana* (1) has solitary spherical to conical plant bodies depressed at their apexes, with a diameter of about 4 inches. There are no hairs in the axils of the tubercles. The spine clusters are of about ten spreading, fine, white radials the upper one up to ¼ inch long, the lowers up to ⅓ inch long, and three or four stouter centrals when young red, later chestnut-brown. The flowers have yellow inner petals, tan outer ones, all with orange-red to reddish-brown center stripes. *M. zuccariniana* (1) has solitary spherical to cylindrical plant bodies, up to 10 inches high by 6 inches wide, flattened or depressed at their apexes. The spine clusters are frequently without radials or may have three or four brown-tipped white ones, up to ¼ inch long, in addition to two to four centrals, at first white with purplish tips aging to gray or amber. The

uppers are up to ½ inch, the lowers 1 inch, long. About 1 inch in diameter, the flowers have purplish to magenta petals, the outer ones edged with pink.

Garden and Landscape Uses. Among the most attractive and popular of cactuses, mammillarias enchant by their great diversity of forms and colorings and because of the comfortable ease with which most submit to domestication. True, a few demand rather special attention, but the majority respond generously to ordinary, reasonably understanding care.

They are splendid outdoors in warm, dry climates as is so well demonstrated by the magnificent plantings at the Huntington Botanical Gardens, San Marino, California, and at other places in the west and southwest. At San Marino specimens well over one-half a century old display their fulsome beauty decorating long rocky banks. Locations of this sort, which assure perfect drainage and abundant sunlight, are much liked by mammillarias. But their usefulness is by no means confined to outdoors. They are among the "backbone" genera of most greenhouse collections of cactuses and many sorts succeed surprisingly well as window plants.

As a group mammillarias are notable for reliability of blooming. Their flowers are mostly smallish, but their abundance and in many cases bright colors are likely to compensate for that.

Cultivation. As may be easily imagined, the cultural requirements of a group as vast as this differs somewhat according to species. Because of this a certain amount of intelligent observation combined with a readiness to modify environments and cultural practices based on the responses of the plants is needed for the most complete success. Still some ground rules can be established.

Soils must permit free percolation of water and access of air. Like the majority of cactuses, mammillarias are intolerant of stagnant moisture about the roots. In general a fertile rooting medium containing enough limestone or lime to bring the pH to 6.5 to 8.0 is appreciated by the sorts with watery sap, but those with milky sap for the most part prefer soils on the slightly acid side of neutral, say from pH 5 to 6.5.

Although good light is needed, and many sorts revel in exposure to full sunshine, others are grateful for a slight amelioration of the full intensity of summer sun. They do best with a little shade. Excessive watering is to be avoided. Allow the soil to become noticeably dry before drenching it. Indoors winter night temperatures ranging from 50 to 60°F are acceptable, with increases of ten to fifteen degrees by day and considerably warmer conditions at other seasons.

Propagation is easy by seed and by offsets. Weaker-growing sorts succeed when grafted onto strong species of the same or

other genera. For more information see Cactuses.

MAMONCILLO is *Melicoccus bijugatus.*

MAN-EATING TREE. See Carnivorous or Insectivorous Plants.

MAN ROOT is *Marah oreganus.*

MANCO CABALLO is *Homalocephala texensis.*

MANDARIN is *Citrus reticulata.*

MANDEVILLA (Mandevíl-la). The genus *Mandevilla* consists of more than 100 species of nonhardy, woody, twining vines and shrubs. Native from Mexico to Argentina, it belongs in the dogbane family APOCYNACEAE. Quite often it is grown in gardens as *Dipladenia.* Its name honors Henry John Mandeville a nineteenth-century British Minister in Buenos Aires.

Mandevillas have opposite or whorled leaves and funnel-shaped flowers in axillary or terminal racemes. The blooms have a five-parted calyx and five spreading corolla lobes (petals) that in the bud stage are twisted. There are five short-stalked stamens with united anthers adherent to the two-lobed stigma. The fruits are paired follicles containing seeds with tufts of hair at their tips.

Chilean-jasmine (*M. laxa* syn. *M. suaveolens*), native to Argentina and Bolivia, grows rapidly to about 20 feet tall. It has warty stems and stalked, oblong-ovate leaves up to 6 inches long, with heart-shaped bases. They are hairless above,

Mandevilla laxa

glaucous on their undersides. The white or blush-pink, deliciously fragrant blooms are in racemes of up to nine. Each is 2 to 2¼ inches long by 2 to 3 inches wide. The fruits, about 1 foot long, are in pairs joined at their tips. This is the most frequently cultivated kind. Native to Bolivia and Ecuador, hairless *M. boliviensis* (syn. *Dipla-*

Mandevilla boliviensis

denia boliviensis) has opposite, short-pointed, elliptic to obovate-elliptic, stalked leaves with blades 2½ to 4 inches long by ¾ inch to 1¾ inches wide. Its showy, freely-produced, funnel-shaped blooms, white with yellow throats, are in racemes of three to seven from the leaf axils. They are 1¾ to 2 inches long by up to 3 inches wide. Discovered toward the close of the nineteenth century in Brazil and not found in the wild since, *M. sanderi* (syn. *Dipladenia sanderi*)

Mandevilla sanderi

is a vigorous vine with opposite, short-stalked, broadly-oblong-elliptic leaves 1½ to 2 inches long. It has lateral racemes of three to five showy, rose-pink flowers

nearly 2 inches long by 2½ to 3 inches across their faces. Another Brazilian, *M. splendens* has stems, hairy when young, becoming hairless later. Its opposite, short-stalked or almost stalkless, broad-el-

Mandevilla splendens

liptic, thinnish leaves, up to 8 inches long, are minutely-hairy. The rose-pink, funnel-shaped flowers, 3 to 4 inches across, have wide-spreading corolla lobes (petals).

Hybrid mandevillas, often difficult to identify with certainty as to kind, include *M. amabilis* (syns. *M. amoena, Dipladenia amabilis*), a hybrid with one parent *M. splendens* and the other unidentified. A woody, twining vine this free-flowering hybrid has pointed, ovate-oblong to elliptic-oblong leaves and beautiful funnel-shaped blooms up to 3½ inches long and wide, with rounded corolla lobes (petals). At first pale pink, the flowers soon deepen to a richer rose-pink. Another *M. splendens* hybrid, *M.* 'Alice du Pont' first flowered at Longwood Gardens, Kennett Square, Pennsylvania, in 1960. A seedling of a plant labeled *M. amoena* (a synonym of *M. amabilis*), but perhaps wrongly identified, this is believed by some authorities to have an ancestry that reflects *M. splendens, M. superba*, and *M. glabra*, the last a native of Guiana and not known to be in cultivation. Be that as it may, *M.* 'Alice du Pont' is a vigorous vine with opposite, lustrous, oblong-ovate leaves 4 to 8 inches long by 2 to 4 inches wide. The axillary racemes carry up to twenty beautiful pink, funnel-shaped blooms with deeper pink

throats. They are 2¼ to 2½ inches in diameter and darken in color as they age.

Garden and Landscape Uses. Mandevillas are handsome free-flowering ornamentals for outdoors in warm climates and for greenhouses. They bloom over a long season and are useful for arbors, pergolas, pillars, other supports, and for covering walls fitted with wires or other devices about which the stems can twine. As pot or tub plants they can be trained over spherical wire frameworks, or other shapes. Chilean-jasmine is deciduous in California, evergreen under warmer conditions.

Cultivation. Mandevillas are not particular as to soil so long as it is well-drained and reasonably fertile. They succeed in sun or part-shade. Pruning, done in late winter or early spring, may involve severe cutting back to limit the plants to allotted space. Even if pruned almost to the ground they bloom the same summer on new shoots that develop from the base of the plants.

In greenhouses Chilean-jasmine succeeds in a winter minimum night temperature of 55°F rising by day five to fifteen degrees relative to the brightness of the weather. From spring through fall minimum night temperatures of 60 to 65°F are appropriate, with day temperatures proportionately higher. Most other mandevillas prefer winter temperatures five to ten degrees higher than those suggested for Chilean-jasmine. Good light with only a little shade from strong summer sun is needed. Water moderately in winter, freely at other seasons. Specimens that have filled their containers with healthy roots benefit from regular applications of dilute liquid fertilizer from spring through fall. In late winter or spring, just before new growth begins, prune by removing old, crowded stems and shortening others and repot or top-dress as required by the condition of the roots. Use porous, fertile, coarse, loamy soil and be sure that the pots or tubs are well drained. Take particular care not to water excessively following potting, but on all bright days spray the foliage occasionally with water. Propagation is easy by cuttings set in a propagating bed, preferably with bottom heat, in a humid greenhouse. Plants can also be raised from seed. The most common pests are mealybugs, scales, and red spider-mites.